KEY TO MAPS

By reference to this Key to Maps, and its continuation on the back endpaper, the most suitable map of a required area can be found.

The map pages of the core World Atlas section are keyed according to their continental subsections and scale category. There are three scale categories, as indicated below. All scales are quoted as representative ratios expressed in millions (as denoted by the abbreviation M).

 Large scale: between 1:1M and 2½M

 Medium scale: between 1:2½M and 1:7½M

 Small scale: smaller than 1:7½M

ASIA
MAPS 46 - 67

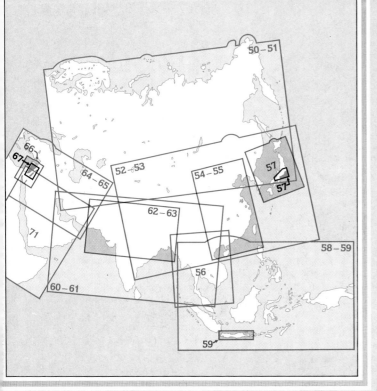

AFRICA
MAPS 68 – 81

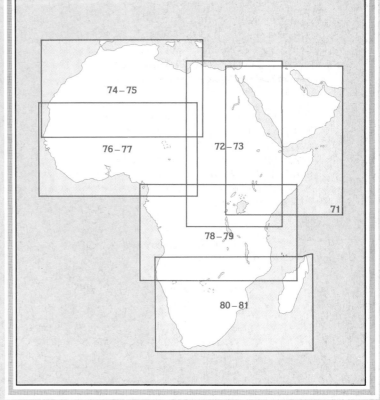

Continued on Back Endpaper

COLLINS
ATLAS OF THE
WORLD

COLLINS

Atlas OF THE WORLD

HarperCollins*Publishers*

Collins Atlas of the World
First published 1983 by William Collins Sons & Co Ltd
Reprinted 1983, 1985, 1986, 1987
2nd Edition 1988 Reprinted 1989, 1990
3rd Edition 1991
4th Edition 1993

Maps © HarperCollins*Publishers* and Collins-Longman Atlases
Geographical Encyclopaedia and statistics © HarperCollins*Publishers*
Collins is an imprint of Bartholomew/Times
A Division of HarperCollins*Publishers*
77-85 Fulham Palace Road
Hammersmith
London W6 8JB

Printed in Italy

The contents of this edition of the Collins Atlas of the World are believed to be correct at the time of printing.
Nevertheless, the publishers can accept no responsibility for errors, or for omissions, or for changes in detail given.

ISBN 0 00 448038 4

Photograph credits

XII-XIII David Parker/Science Photo Library; Peter Menzell/Science Photo Library; Professor Stewart Lowther/Science
Photo Library

XX-XXI David Campione/Science Photo Library; Dr L. Wright

XXII-XXIII Dr Morley Read/Science Photo Library

XXVI-XXVII D. R. Austen/Telegraph Colour Library; Martin Bond/Science Photo Library

XXVIII-XXIX Marcelo Brodsky/Science Photo Library

XXX-XXXI Simon Fraser/Science Photo Library

XXXII-XXXIII Oxfam; Jeremy Hartley/Oxfam; Hugh Goyder/Oxfam; Malcolm McClean/Oxfam

XXXIV-XXXV Bibliothèque Nationale, Paris; National Maritime Museum, London; Österreichische Nationalbibliothek,
Vienna; New York Public Library, New York; British Library, London

XXXVI-XXXVII Sefton Photo Library

XXXVIII-XXXIX USGS; The Times Atlas and Encyclopaedia of the Sea

XL © Nicholson, produced from the Bartholomew London Digital Database

The Publishers would like to thank the following:

Dr J. Allen, Dr B. Alloway, Professor B. Atkinson, Dr R. Hall and Dr L. Wright
from Queen Mary and Westfield College, University of London

H. A. G. Lewis OBE

Illustrations: Contour Publishing and Swanston Graphics

FOREWORD

MAPS, as essential aids in the understanding of the world around us, would appear to have been made ever since man first moved about the Earth. To begin with they were relatively primitive plans of very limited areas, carved in wood or painted on rock, bark or skins. Later, the highly organized peoples of the ancient civilizations, in conducting their everyday life, made many functional maps on such materials as clay tablets, papyrus and eventually paper.

However, the first attempt to map the whole of the known world, as opposed to producing local plans of small areas, is attributed to the famous Greek cosmographer, Ptolemy (AD 87-150). The many maps of the classical world that accompanied his celebrated manuscript Geographia – itself to be regarded as the standard geographical reference work for many centuries – represent the forerunner of the atlas as we know it today.

ATLASES, in the modern sense of systematic collections of maps of uniform size, were born, much later still, in the Netherlands of the 16th century, during the world's great age of exploration. Indeed, it was the eminent Flemish cartographer Mercator (1512-1594) who first used the word Atlas: taking the name of the ancient Greek mythological titan who symbolically supported the world on his shoulders.

Since the time of these early atlases our knowledge of the world has been greatly increased through continued exploration and scientific discovery. Today, the fast developing space age technology allows man to survey our planet, and beyond, in the most precise detail. The resulting mass of geographical and astronomical data is such that the non-specialist atlas user could easily be overwhelmed. This current information explosion, combined with a new awareness of our world brought about by the views of our planet from space, improved communications, greater opportunity for leisure and travel, and increased media exposure, we believe, calls for a new type of atlas that presents to the general reader, not only an up-to-date collection of well-documented maps, but also an illuminating and readily accessible record of the latest findings and essential facts about our world.

COLLINS ATLAS OF THE WORLD is published with the explicit aim of meeting this need for a convenient and moderately priced reference atlas, that places at our fingertips an accurate, authoritative, comprehensive and clearly presented picture of the world as it is known today. To achieve this objective, Collins, building on its traditions and experience of over one hundred years' innovative atlas publishing, assembled a talented team of geographers, cartographers, designers, editors and writers. Working to a carefully devised plan, this team has brought together in a single volume a complete set of maps, a compendium of contemporary geographical data, and an informative and in-depth geographical encyclopaedia.

As a result of the detailed process of research, compilation and design, together with the latest cartographic techniques, which have gone into the production of Collins Atlas of the World, we believe that our readers will have the best and most up-to-date atlas available in its class. In terms of cartographic presentation, geographical knowledge and visual elegance, the publication of Collins Atlas of the World represents a major step forward, which we hope will contribute to a better awareness and understanding of our fascinating and fast changing world as we approach the 21st century.

CONTENTS

WORLD ATLAS

VII

GUIDE TO THE ATLAS

COLLINS ATLAS OF THE WORLD consists of three self-contained but interrelated sections. First, in the GEOGRAPHICAL ENCYCLOPAEDIA there is a complete and informative guide to contemporary geographical issues. Next, the WORLD ATLAS section, comprising 128 pages of maps, using the most modern cartographic techniques and up-to-date sources. Finally, a detailed compendium of GEOGRAPHICAL DATA.

GEOGRAPHICAL ENCYCLOPAEDIA

This illustrated section covers essential topics such as the structure of the Earth, earthquakes and volcanoes, atmosphere and climate, vegetation, population, food, minerals, energy and environmental problems. There is a special feature on the history of cartography and the use of maps.

WORLD ATLAS

The main section of 128 pages of maps has been carefully planned and designed to meet the contemporary needs of the atlas user. Full recognition has been given to the many different purposes that currently call for map reference.

Map coverage extends to every part of the world in a balanced scheme that avoids any individual country or regional bias. Map areas are chosen to reflect the social, economic, cultural or historical importance of a particular region. Each double spread or single page map has been planned deliberately to cover an entire physical or political unit. Generous map overlaps are included to maintain continuity. Following two world maps, giving separate coverage of the main political and physical features, each of the continents is treated systematically in a subsection of its own. Apart from being listed in the contents, full coverage of all regional maps of each continent is also clearly depicted in the Key to Maps to be found on the front and back endpapers. Also at the beginning of each continental subsection, alongside a special Global View political map, all map coverage, country by country, is identified in an additional handy page index. Finally, as a further aid to the reader in locating the required area, a postage stamp key map is incorporated into the title margin of each map page.

Map projections have been chosen to reflect the different requirements of particular areas. No map can be absolutely true on account of the impossibility of representing a spheroid accurately on a flat surface without some distortion in either area, distance, direction or shape. In a general world atlas it is the equal area property that is most important to retain for comparative map studies and feature size evaluation and this principle has been followed wherever possible in this map section. As a special feature of this atlas, the Global View projections used for each continental political map have been specially devised to allow for a realistic area comparison between the land areas of each continent.

Map scales, as expressions of the relationship which the distance between any two points of the map bears to the corresponding distance on the ground, are in the context of this atlas grouped into three distinct categories.

Large scales, of between 1:1 000 000 (1 centimetre to 10 kilometres or 1 inch to 16 miles) and 1:2 500 000 (1 centimetre to 25 kilometres or 1 inch to 40 miles), are used to cover particularly densely populated areas of Western Europe, United States, Canada and Japan, as well as a special detailed map of the Holy Land.

Medium scales, of between 1:2 500 000 and 1:7 500 000 are used for maps of parts of Europe, North America, Australasia, India, China, etc.

Small scales, those of less than 1:7 500 00 (e.g. 1:10 000 000, 1:15 000 000, 1:25 000 000 etc.) are selected for maps of the complete world, continents, oceans, polar regions and many of the larger countries.

The actual scale at which a particular area is mapped therefore reflects its shape, size and density of detail, and as a basic principle the more detail required to be shown of an area, the greater its scale. However, throughout this atlas, map scales have been limited in number, as far as possible, in order to facilitate comparison between maps.

Map measurements give preference to the metric system which is now used in nearly every country throughout the world. All spot heights and ocean depths are shown in metres and the relief and submarine layer delineation is based on metric contour levels. However, all linear scalebar and height reference column figures are given metric and imperial equivalents to facilitate conversion of measurements for the non-metric reader.

Map symbols used are fully explained in the legend to be found on the first page of the World Atlas section. Careful study and frequent reference to this legend will aid in the reader's ability to extract maximum information.

Topography is shown by the combined means of precise spot heights, contouring, layer tinting and three-dimensional hill shading. Similar techniques are also used to depict the sea bed on the World Physical map and those of the oceans and polar regions.

Hydrographic features such as coastlines, rivers, lakes, swamps and canals are clearly differentiated.

Communications are particularly well represented with the contemporary importance of airports and road networks duly emphasized.

International boundaries and national capitals are fully documented and internal administrative divisions are shown with the maximum detail that the scale will allow. Boundary delineation reflects the 'de facto' rather than the 'de jure' political interpretation and where relevant an undefined or disputed boundary is distinguished. However there is no intended implication that the publishers necessarily endorse or accept the status of any political entity recorded on the maps.

Settlements are shown by a series of graded town stamps from major cities to tiny villages.

Other features, such as notable ancient monuments, oases, national parks, oil and gas fields, are selectively included on particular maps that merit their identification.

Lettering styles used in the maps have been chosen with great care to ensure maximum legibility and clear distinction of named feature categories. The size and weight of the various typefaces reflect the relative importance of the features. Town names are graded to correspond with the appropriate town stamp.

Map place names have been selected in accordance with maintaining legibility at a given scale and at the same time striking an appropriate balance between natural and man-made features

worthy of note. Name forms have been standardized according to the widely accepted principle, now well established in international reference atlases, of including place names and geographical terms in the local language of the country in question. In the case of non-Roman scripts (e.g. Arabic), transliteration and transcription have either been based on the rules recommended by the Permanent Committee on Geographical Names and the United States Board of Geographical Names, or as in the case of the adopted Pinyin transcription of Chinese names, a system officially proposed by the country concerned. The diacritical signs used in each language or transliteration have been retained on all the maps and throughout the index. However the english language reader's requirements have also been recognised in that the names of all countries, oceans, major seas and land features as well as familiar alternative name versions of important towns are presented in English.

Map sources used in the compilation of this atlas were many and varied, but always of the latest available information. At each stage of their preparation the maps were submitted to a thorough process of research and continual revision to ensure that on publication all data would be as accurate as practicable. A well-documented data bank was created to ensure consistency and validity of all information represented on the maps.

GEOGRAPHICAL DATA

This detailed data section forms an appropriate complement to the preceding maps and illustrated texts. There are three parts, each providing a different type of geographical information.

World Facts and Figures Drawn from the latest available official sources, these tables present an easy reference profile of significant world physical, political and demographic as well as national data.

Glossary of Geographical Terms This explains most of the foreign language and geographical terms which are to be found incorporated in the place names on the maps and the index.

World Index This concluding part of the atlas lists in alphabetical order all individual place names to be found on the maps, which total about 40,000. Each entry in the index is referenced to the appropriate map page number, the country or region in which the name is located and the position of the name on the map, given by its co-ordinates of latitude and longitude. A full explanation of how to use the index is to be found on page 140.

EARTH STRUCTURE

The major three-fold division of the solid Earth into an inner core, a mantle and an outer crust is based largely on the physical properties of these layers as revealed by the passage of seismic waves generated by both earthquakes and man-made explosions.

THE Earth's crust is a thin shell covering the whole surface of the planet, but only accounts for 0.2% of the total mass of the Earth. There is a fundamental difference between the crust of the continents and that beneath the ocean basins. The oceanic crust is very thin (average 7km), and is composed of relatively dense material. By contrast, the continental crust is thicker and less dense. The crust as a whole is split into a number of distinct plates, which float on the chemically distinct and denser second layer, the mantle. The boundary between the crust and the underlying mantle is known as the Mohorovičić Discontinuity (Moho). At the centre of the Earth lies the core itself, which forms 33% of the planet's mass, and is divided into two zones: the outer layer, thought to be liquid, probably metallic iron with sulphur, silicon, oxygen, potassium or hydrogen; and the inner core, which evidence suggests consists of nickel-iron alloy.

The measurement by a world-wide network of seismographic stations of the vibrational waves generated by earthquakes has provided a relatively accurate picture of where the boundaries between the layers of the Earth lie. The velocity of seismic waves depends on the composition and physical state of the transmitting medium. At the point where the physical or chemical properties of the Earth change, the velocity and path of the waves are changed, too.

The outer layer, the crust in conjuction with that part of the upper mantle immediately below, is in a constant state of movement. Plate tectonics is the name given to the study of the processes which produce faults, joints or folds or cause magma (hot molten rock) to rise to the surface in response to forces deep within the Earth. At the mid-ocean ridges, new crust is created by the rise of magma. This intrusion of new material forces the plates apart. Where two plates meet, pushing from different directions, one plate is forced under the other. Where plates slide past each other, along fault lines, crust is neither created or destroyed.

By studying the way in which new crust has been formed in the ocean beds, a fairly authoritative account can be given of the way the continents have drifted over the past 200 million years. Only a very incomplete picture can be inferred of the preceding 400 million years, and only a sketchy picture before that.

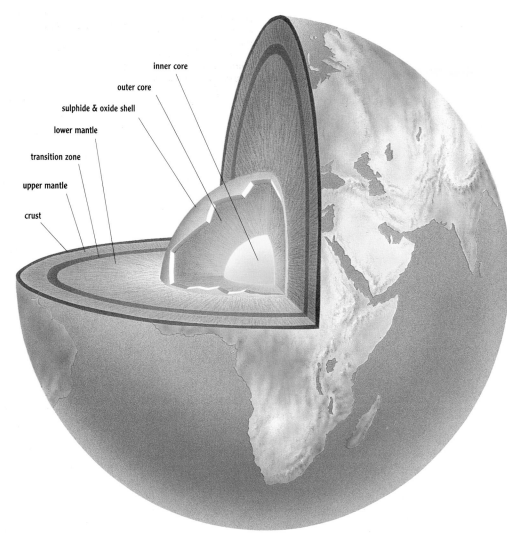

inner core
outer core
sulphide & oxide shell
lower mantle
transition zone
upper mantle
crust

(above) *A section through the Earth's crust. Internally, the Earth is divided into three main areas: crust, mantle and core. The mantle is divided into two parts separated by a transition zone. The core, likewise, is divided into two parts. The solid inner core is surrounded by a liquid outer layer.*

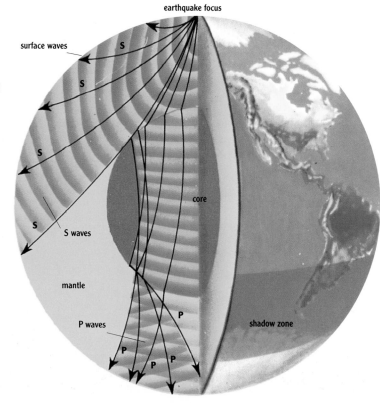

earthquake focus
surface waves
S
S
S
S
S waves
core
mantle
P waves
P
P
P
P
shadow zone

(right) *In an earthquake, the shock generates vibrations, or seismic waves, which radiate from the focus. Surface waves cause most motion at ground level. The body waves, both primary (P) and secondary (S), reveal by the way they travel, the internal layers of the Earth.*

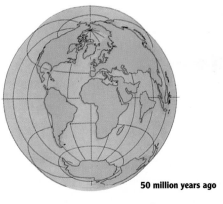

50 million years ago

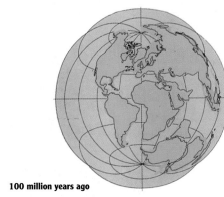

100 million years ago

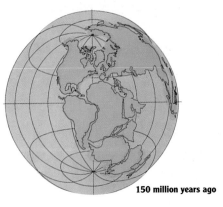

150 million years ago

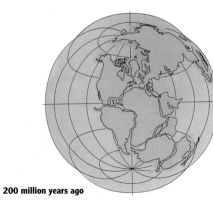

200 million years ago

(left) *From around 200 million years ago, when the Earth's landmasses formed one giant super-continent known as Pangaea, the continents have drifted, divided and collided to produce the present disposition of land and sea.*

(right) *Plate tectonic cycle from continental rifting to continental collision. (1) Rifting following old faults. (2) Continental break-up with the formation of new oceanic crust. Transform faults follow continental fractures. (3) A large Atlantic-type ocean has now formed on the site of the former continent. A mountain belt is formed where the subduction zone dips beneath the continent. (4) Where continental collision occurs a Himalayan-type mountain belt is formed.*

(right) *Faults occur when the Earth's surface breaks. When tension stretches the crust, normal faulting occurs and the rocks on one side of the fault-plane override those on the other. A horst is a block of the crust thrust up between faults; the reverse is a graben or rift valley.*

(below) *Particular features are associated with different types of mineral deposits: continental rifts with tin and fluorine, mid-ocean ridges with marine metallic sulphides, island arcs and cordilleran-type mountains with a variety of metallic deposits.*

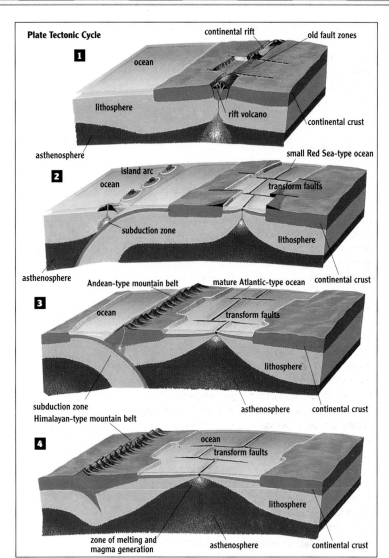

Plate Tectonic Cycle

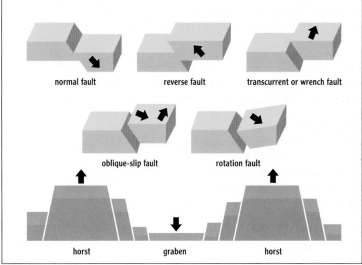

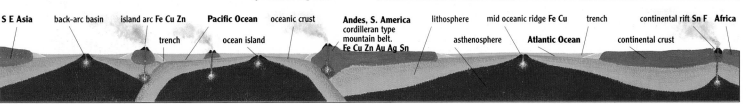

EARTHQUAKES AND VOLCANOES

Violent earthquakes and spectacular volcanic eruptions, the most destructive natural events, are controlled by processes occurring deep below the Earth's surface. Although we understand broadly why and where they happen, we are still some way from being able to predict the exact time and place of the next catastrophic event.

MAJOR zones of seismic and volcanic activity follow the boundaries of the tectonic plates into which the Earth's rigid surface layers are divided (see map right). Where these are moving apart from each other (in the deep oceans), the lithosphere is relatively thin and pliant, earthquakes are shallow and weak, and volcanic lava flows out of long fissures, solidifying to make new ocean floor (see diagram bottom right). If the flow of lava is copious and sustained, a giant shield volcano may build up on the ocean floor and project above the surface as a island. Hawaii is part of a chain of shield volcanoes that have grown over a sustained source of lava, called a hot spot, which is unrelated to plate boundaries and has remained active while the Pacific ocean plate has moved slowly over it.

The most powerful earthquakes and most violent volcanic eruptions occur at boundaries where two plates are in collision. When a thick continental plate meets a thin oceanic plate then the latter is overridden by the former, a process known as subduction. The oceanic plate remains rigid to depths of a few hundred kilometres, causing earthquakes along an inclined surface (referred to as the Wadati-Benioff zone). The frictional heat developed along this zone encourages local partial melting of the rocks; the rather sticky lava ascends slowly to the surface, where highly explosive eruptions send vast clouds of ash and larger fragments into the atmosphere. While the lightest particles may reach the stratosphere and be carried all round the world, most of the material falls back to earth where, in combination with intermittent flows of lava, a massive stratovolcano builds up. Some volcanic eruptions produce searingly hot dense clouds of gas and ash (known as *nuées ardentes*) that descend from the crater at very high speeds, hugging the ground and destroying everything in their path.

Where the colliding plates are both oceanic, subduction of one of the plates results in a similar descending zone of violent earthquakes, and the accompanying volcanic activity builds up an arc of islands on the overriding plate. However, if both plates carry thick continental crust, subduction is no longer possible and volcanic activity ceases, but, as in the Himalayas, the compressive forces continue to generate powerful earthquakes along the collision zone.

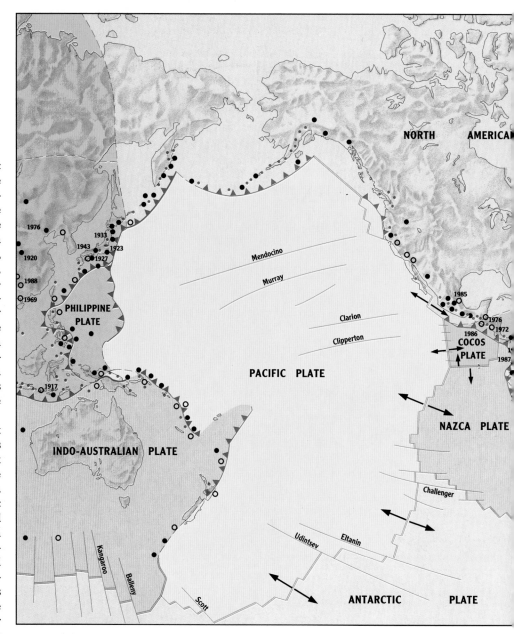

(left) *The San Andreas Fault in California marks the boundary between the Pacific plate and the American plate.*
(top right) *Mauna Loa on the Island of Hawaii, a shield volcano.*
(centre right) *Mount St. Helens, a stratovolcano, in the Cascade Range. The violent eruption of 18 May* 1980 killed 57 people.
(below) *The place at which an earthquake originates within the Earth's crust is known as the focus, while the point on the surface directly above is called the epicentre. The strain energy released by the earthquake spreads out in all directions as shock waves from the focus.*

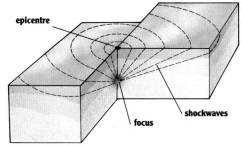

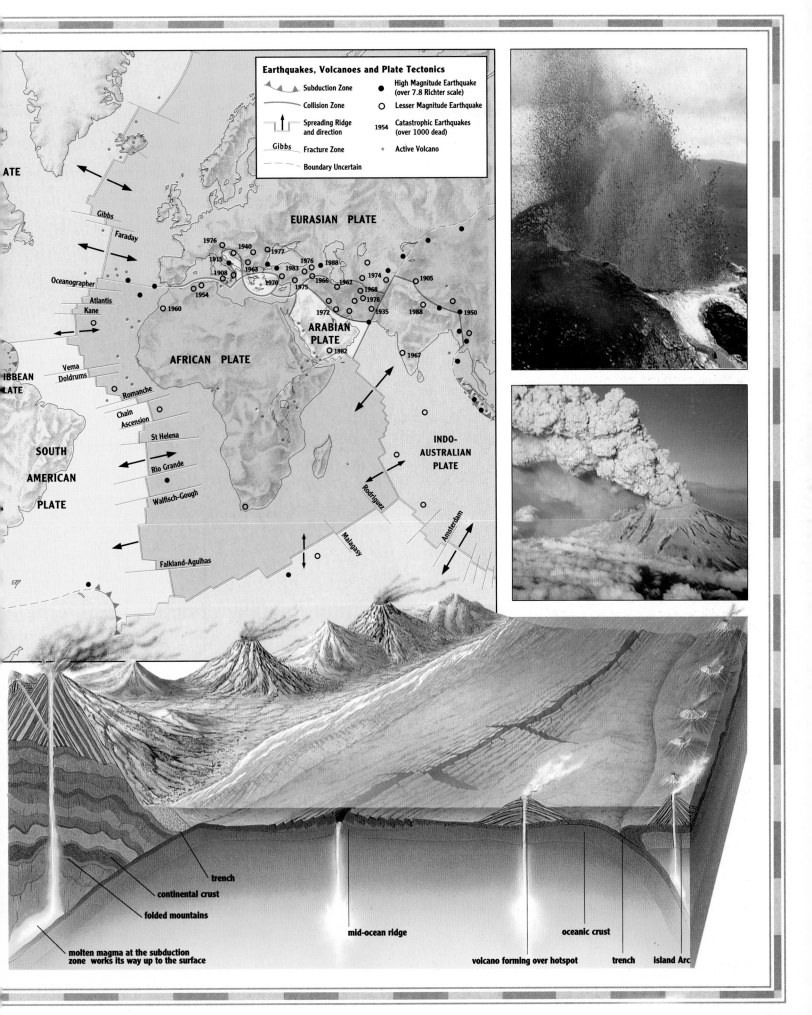

Earthquakes, Volcanoes and Plate Tectonics

Subduction Zone	● High Magnitude Earthquake (over 7.8 Richter scale)
Collision Zone	○ Lesser Magnitude Earthquake
Spreading Ridge and direction	1954 Catastrophic Earthquakes (over 1000 dead)
Gibbs Fracture Zone	• Active Volcano
Boundary Uncertain	

EURASIAN PLATE

ARABIAN PLATE

AFRICAN PLATE

INDO-AUSTRALIAN PLATE

SOUTH AMERICAN PLATE

Gibbs
Faraday
Oceanographer
Atlantis
Kane
Vema
Doldrums
Romanche
Chain
Ascension
St Helena
Rio Grande
Walfisch-Gough
Falkland-Agulhas
Malagasy
Rodriguez
Amsterdam

1976 1940 1977
1915 1976 1988
1908 1963 1983 1974 1905
1954 1970 1975 1966 1962 1968 1978
1960 1972 1935 1988 1950
1982 1967

trench
continental crust
folded mountains
molten magma at the subduction zone works its way up to the surface
mid-ocean ridge
volcano forming over hotspot
oceanic crust
trench   island Arc

OCEANS

Covering some 70% of the Earth's surface, oceans have long been vital for navigation, and they are becoming increasingly important for their resources of food, minerals and energy, and also as a final depository for waste. They affect our daily weather and influence long-term changes of climate, but their relative inaccessibility means our knowledge of them is fragmentary.

THE dramatic topography of the ocean floors has been fully revealed only within the last 40 years (see map below right). Its most striking feature, the world's longest mountain chain, is the system of mid-oceanic ridges that extends from the Arctic southwards through the Atlantic, then passes eastwards through the Indian Ocean and northwards into the Pacific. It marks the boundary where adjacent tectonic plates are moving apart from each other as new ocean floor is created from solidifying lava flows. This junction is typically marked by a deep rift valley along the crest of the ridge, and the rugged topography of the ridge flanks is dissected by the cliff-like features of innumerable fracture zones.

Away from the ridges, the level of topography of the deep ocean floors, or abyssal plains, is disturbed by extinct submarine volcanoes.

Some project above sea level as isolated islands, while others, whose tops have been planed off by the erosive power of the waves, may provide a foundation for coral atolls. In the Pacific Ocean, they often occur in long chains where a deep source of lava, or hot spot, has remained active while the Pacific plate has moved slowly over it. The Hawaiian-Emperor chain formed over a period of 75 million years, the sharp bend west of Midway Island signifying a change in the direction of plate movement about 45 million years ago. Elsewhere, sustained volcanic activity combined with plate motion has produced linear features, such as the Walvis Ridge in the eastern South Atlantic. Iceland has formed on the North Atlantic ridge over an unusually active and relatively immobile source of lava.

Deep narrow trenches are a feature of the margins of the Pacific Ocean. The margins of other oceans, especially the North Atlantic, are characterized by wide continental shelves; geologically these are part of the continents, not the oceans, and their width has varied over time in response to changing sea levels. Significant fragments of largely submerged continental lithosphere have been identified in the deep oceans; for example, the Faeroe-Rockall Plateau in the North Atlantic.

The surface waters of the oceans are driven by the prevailing wind systems in the large-scale circulatory patterns, or gyres, which are broadly symmetrical north and south of the equator (see map below). Along the western boundaries of the major ocean basins, intense warm currents, such as the Gulf Stream, travel polewards; these are counterbalanced by less intense cool currents flowing towards the equator along the eastern margins. Close to the equator an eastwards flowing countercurrent separates the circulations of the two hemispheres. The pattern of currents in the northern Indian Ocean reverses seasonally with the monsoon. In the North Atlantic and Pacific Oceans, weaker anticlockwise circulations complement the main gyres, while in the Southern Ocean the vigorous Antarctic Circumpolar current is unimpeded by the presence of any land masses.

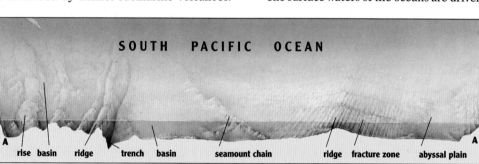

SOUTH PACIFIC OCEAN

rise   basin   ridge   trench   basin   seamount chain   ridge   fracture zone   abyssal plain

(above and right) The relative proportions of the topographic features in the three ocean basins relate to their tectonic geological histories. An extensive mid-oceanic ridge dominates the relatively narrow Atlantic; its margins are tectonically passive with wide continental shelves. The much larger Pacific Ocean, in contrast, has a less extensive ridge system, with active trenches around most of its margins and generally narrow continental shelves. Like the Pacific, the Indian Ocean is dominated by deep ocean floor and has poorly developed continental margins, but it shares with the Atlantic its relative lack of island arcs and trenches.

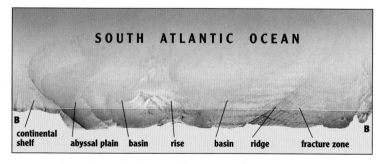

SOUTH ATLANTIC OCEAN

continental shelf   abyssal plain   basin   rise   basin   ridge   fracture zone

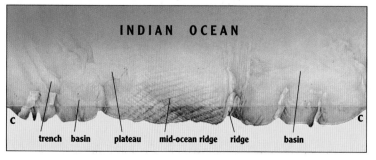

INDIAN OCEAN

trench   basin   plateau   mid-ocean ridge   ridge   basin

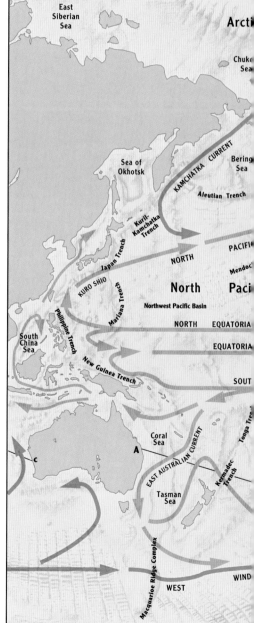

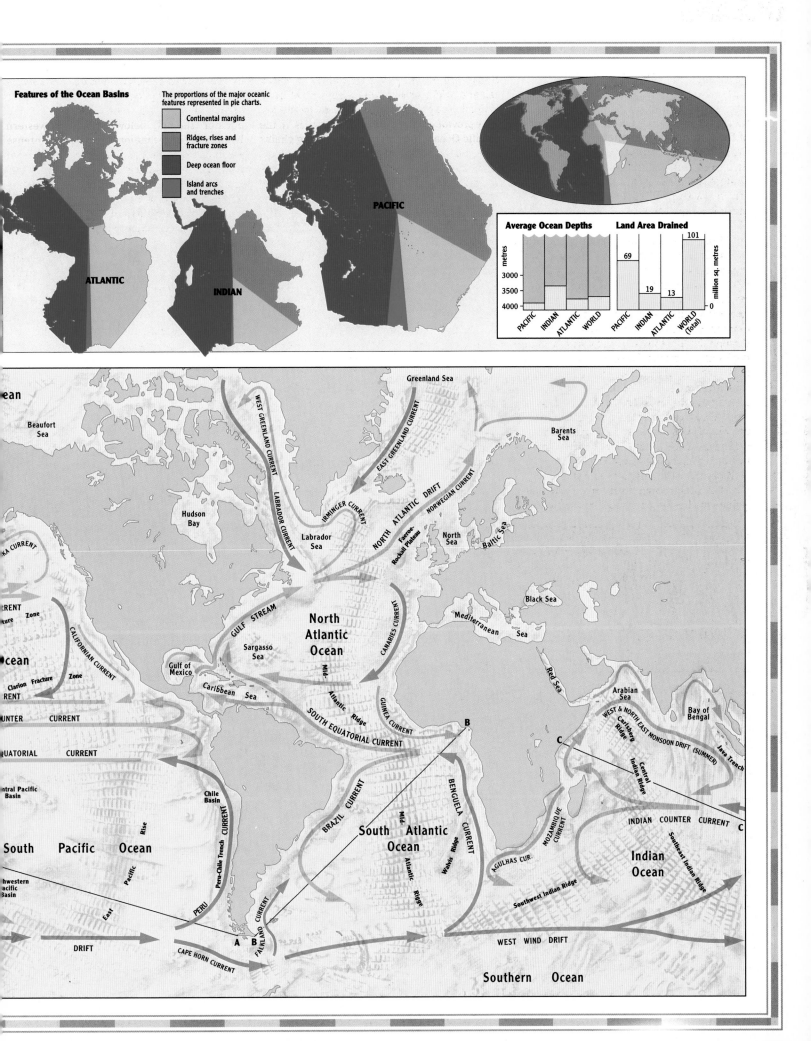

ATMOSPHERE

The atmosphere is a mixture of gases with constant proportions up to a height of 80km. The main constituents are: nitrogen (78%); oxygen (21%); and argon; (less than 1%). Other minor constituents include carbon dioxide, ozone and water vapour. All three have important effects on the energy budget of the atmosphere.

OZONE, lying largely in the stratosphere, absorbs ultraviolet solar radiation which would otherwise damage lifeforms. A reduction in ozone, the ozone hole, is therefore cause for concern. Carbon dioxide, being an effective absorber of terrestrial long-wave radiation, is an important 'greenhouse' gas. If it increases, it may lead to an increase in temperature – global warming. Water vapour is also an important greenhouse gas and varies in quantity from 1-4% by volume.

As air is compressible, its lower layers are much more dense than those above. Half of the total mass of air is found below 5km, with the average surface pressure being 1013.25 millibars.

The atmosphere receives heat from the sun by solar radiation, and loses heat by terrestrial radiation. In general the input and output balance and the Earth's climate changes relatively little. Nevertheless, such changes as do occur create the glacial and inter-glacial periods such as experienced in the past million years. The mean temperature structure of the atmosphere reveals five layers: troposphere; stratosphere; mesosphere; thermosphere and exosphere. About 80% of the atmosphere lies in the troposphere, where all weather occurs.

The input and output of radiation vary in different ways with latitude. There is a net input between latitudes 38°, and a net output in other latitudes. This inequality leads to pressure gradients that drive the winds. In turn, these broadly transfer heat down the thermal gradient produced by the radiation distribution. Such a transfer could be achieved by a single large cell comprising air rising at low latitudes, moving polewards at high levels, sinking over the poles, and returning equatorwards at low levels. The rotation of the earth prevents such an occurrence, leading instead to two regimes: the Hadley cell in the tropics; and the Rossby waves in the extra-tropics. The former is associated with the Trade Winds, the latter with the Westerlies. Within these large wind regimes, frontal cyclones, hurricanes and anticyclones form in preferred locations, and within these systems, smaller circulations (for example, sea breezes) and individual clouds bring our day-to-day weather.

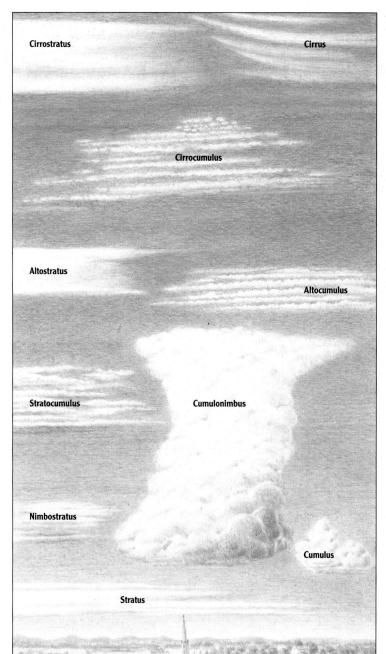

(left) Ten major cloud types are recognized in the International Cloud Classification.

At high levels: cirrus; cirrocumulus; cirrostratus.

At middle levels: alto-cumulus; altostratus.

At low and middle levels: cumulus

At low levels: nimbostratus; stratus; stratocumulus.

At all levels: cumulonimbus.

The high-level clouds comprise ice; the middle and low-level clouds usually comprise a mixture of ice and water, the latter frequently supercooled with temperatures between 0° C and -15° C. Cumuliform clouds are heaped; stratiform clouds are layered. The cumulonimbus frequently has an anvil-shaped top and may cause thunder and lightning.

(right) The vertical distribution of mean temperature highlights five layers in the atmosphere. The troposphere has a mean lapse rate of 6.5° C/km. Temperature increases in the stratosphere to values a little less than those at the surface. At the top of the mesosphere, temperatures fall to about -90° C and then increase into the thermosphere. The exosphere starts at heights of 500 - 750km where the atmosphere is very tenuous indeed.

(left) Over three-quarters of the atmosphere is nitrogen. Water vapour, carbon dioxide (greenhouse gases) and ozone are very small in quantity but critical in their effects on the planetary energy balance.

(right) The atmospheric circulation is three-dimensional, and comprises two main regimes: vertical over-turning in the Hadley cell, and waves in the Rossby regime. These are manifest as the Trade Winds (which meet in the Inter-Tropical Convergence Zone) and the Westerlies.

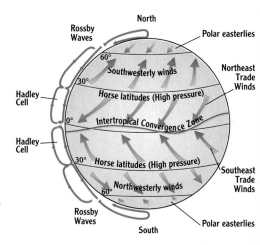

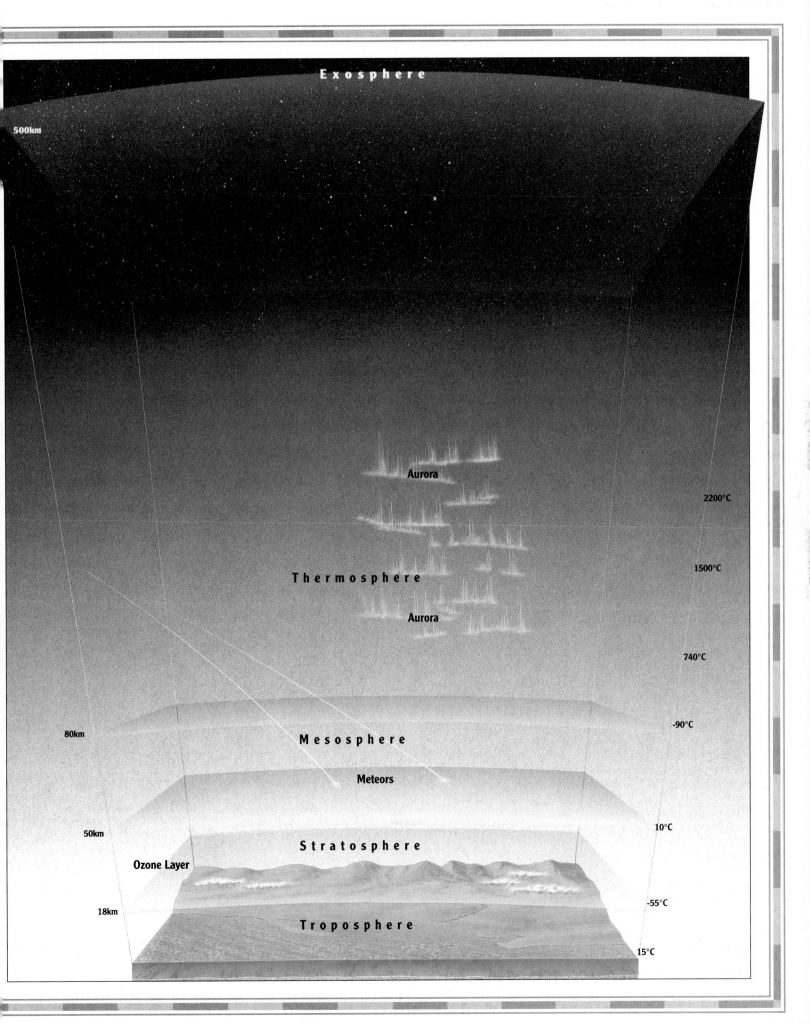

Exosphere

500km

Aurora

2200°C

Thermosphere

1500°C

Aurora

740°C

-90°C

80km

Mesosphere

Meteors

50km

10°C

Stratosphere

Ozone Layer

18km

-55°C

Troposphere

15°C

CLIMATE

The climate of an area is represented by the statistical description of its weather conditions during a specified time. Weather consists of short-term atmospheric variations, most particularly temperature, humidity, precipitation, cloudiness and wind. Earth's climate results from the general circulation of its atmosphere, which produces different regimes of atmospheric variables in different parts of the globe. This allows us to identify different climatic types.

THE mean conditions so frequently used to describe climate result from transfers and transformations of energy, water and momentum between the atmosphere and the Earth. The main source of energy is the Sun, which radiates energy at a virtually constant rate. The Earth's daily rotation and annual precession around the Sun mean that more solar radiation is received near the surface in lower than in higher latitudes. As the Earth's long-wave radiation out to space is distributed more evenly with latitude, the net radiation (input minus output) is positive between latitudes 38 degrees and negative in other latitudes. This energy imbalance leads to pressure gradients that drive the general circulation, which in turn transports heat polewards and upwards. These transports mean that climatic gradients of temperature are smaller than they would be in the absence of the transports.

Nevertheless, it is clear that surface temperatures in January (map top right) range from about -40°C to +40°C, the lowest values being in the continental areas of the northern hemisphere. Land areas gain and lose heat far more rapidly than water areas. As the Sun is in the southern hemisphere in January, the hottest areas are in the Australian desert and parts of South America. In July (map centre right) the desert stretching from the west coast of North Africa to Iran has the highest temperatures. The more maritime southern hemisphere does not reveal very low land temperatures in its winter season, with the notable exception of Antarctica.

The annual precipitation distribution (map below right) also reflects the general circulation. The large amounts in the tropics result from the frequent occurrence of deep cloud systems capable of producing heavy downpours. In the sub-tropics, subsiding air leads to the classic, hot deserts such as the Sahara and Central Australia. Further polewards eastward-moving cyclones produce wet west-coast regimes such as in the UK. In the continental interiors precipitation amounts are less. Further polewards again, precipitation amounts are low, but the water remains on the surface as ice, which gives the impression of a high precipitation area.

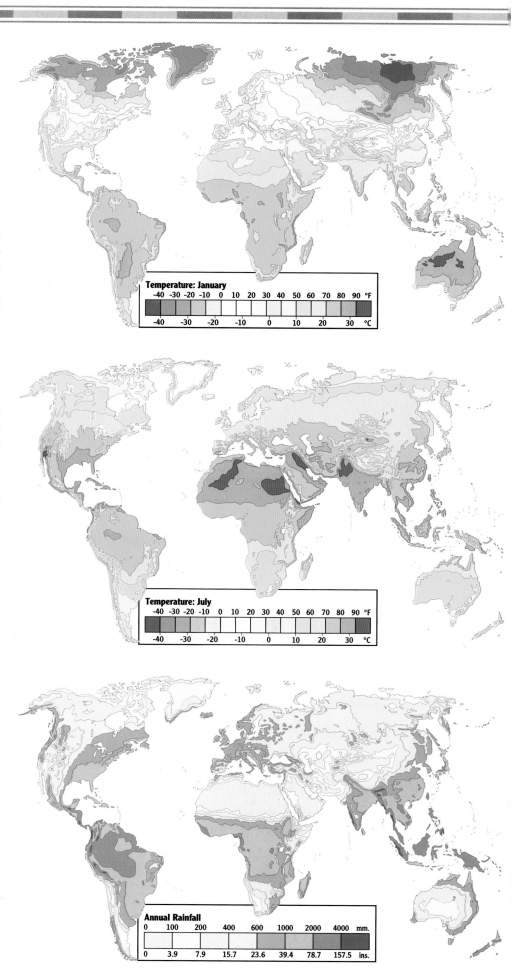

Temperature: January
-40 -30 -20 -10 0 10 20 30 40 50 60 70 80 90 °F
-40 -30 -20 -10 0 10 20 30 °C

Temperature: July
-40 -30 -20 -10 0 10 20 30 40 50 60 70 80 90 °F
-40 -30 -20 -10 0 10 20 30 °C

Annual Rainfall
0 100 200 400 600 1000 2000 4000 mm.
0 3.9 7.9 15.7 23.6 39.4 78.7 157.5 ins.

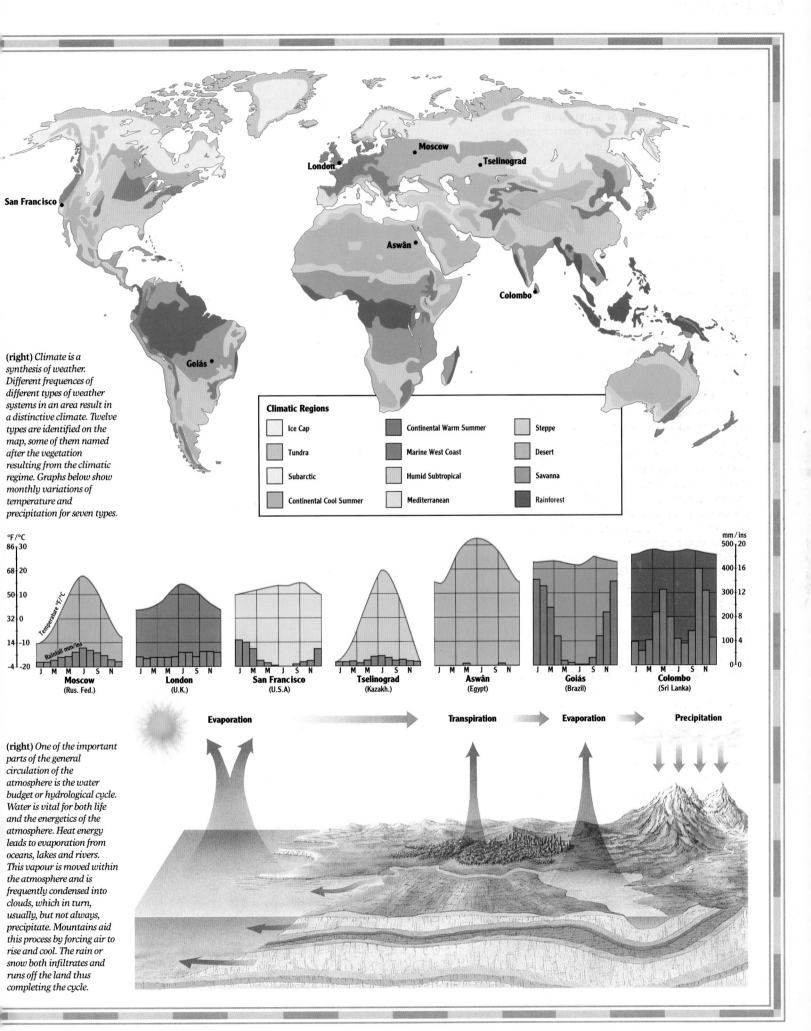

Climatic Regions

Ice Cap	Continental Warm Summer	Steppe
Tundra	Marine West Coast	Desert
Subarctic	Humid Subtropical	Savanna
Continental Cool Summer	Mediterranean	Rainforest

(right) *Climate is a synthesis of weather. Different frequences of different types of weather systems in an area result in a distinctive climate. Twelve types are identified on the map, some of them named after the vegetation resulting from the climatic regime. Graphs below show monthly variations of temperature and precipitation for seven types.*

Moscow (Rus. Fed.)
London (U.K.)
San Francisco (U.S.A)
Tselinograd (Kazakh.)
Aswân (Egypt)
Goiás (Brazil)
Colombo (Sri Lanka)

Evaporation → Transpiration → Evaporation → Precipitation

(right) *One of the important parts of the general circulation of the atmosphere is the water budget or hydrological cycle. Water is vital for both life and the energetics of the atmosphere. Heat energy leads to evaporation from oceans, lakes and rivers. This vapour is moved within the atmosphere and is frequently condensed into clouds, which in turn, usually, but not always, precipitate. Mountains aid this process by forcing air to rise and cool. The rain or snow both infiltrates and runs off the land thus completing the cycle.*

LANDSCAPES

The shape of the Earth's surface has been produced through a combination of internal and external forces. The former tend to produce the major landforms of structural origin, notably the great mountain ranges and oceanic rises (underwater mountains) but also volcanic cones, lava fields and faulted (crevassed) landscapes. The externally driven forces of running water, ice, waves and wind produce a greater variety of features, though on a smaller scale. To both of these must be added the landforms produced by weathering processes, notably the erosional and depositional features of limestone (karst) areas.

JUST a few areas of the Earth's surface appear to have been exposed to the external processes continually for tens and even hundreds of millions of years. The area around the Macdonnell Range in Central Australia is one such example. However, most of the landforms we see today are geologically quite young. Most date in large part from the Quaternary Era, which began 2 million years ago, and many have been created in the past 25,000 years as the ice sheets in the northern hemisphere began their final retreat, and the sea level started to rise from its low point.

Our planet's surface today is probably more dynamic and varied than at almost any time in its history. Tertiary (occurring from 65 million years ago) and Quaternary mountain building coupled with the effects of the Ice Age have combined to produce great relief and an intricately varied land surface. This contrasts with the extensive plains and more uniform climate that seem to have been the norm through most of geological time.

The ever-changing nature of the land surface is illustrated by the occurrence of landslip seas and the huge amounts of sediments that are moved annually by the world's rivers and by coastal waves and currents. Sometimes erosion and deposition are so rapid that the surface form can be seen to be changing. More often the full extent of the changes going on can only be determined by careful field measurements. The development of instruments and techniques to record these data has been a major advance over the past few years.

(right) *Stalactites are icicle-like growths of calcium carbonate formed by moisture percolating through calcareous substance, usually the roof of a limestone cave. The mineral is deposited from solution and over time increases in length and width.*

(far right) *Landslips usually require a trigger action. In this case it was a small earthquake but, more often, it is a heavy rainstorm. The basic movement is initially in the form of a fall, slide or flow, but as movement proceeds, clear distinction disappears.*

1 *Solution in limestone areas produces karst landforms: swallow holes, polje and caves. There is often little surface drainage.*

2 *Fluvial (stream) action creates distinctive river patterns, meanders, oxbow lakes, gorges, flood plains and river terraces. In rivers with shingle beds, braiding occurs.*

3 *Glacial erosion in mountain areas may create cirques (deep semicircular basins) and glacial troughs which may later become lakes.*

4 *Deltas form where large river sediment loads enter the sea (or lake), where wave and current action is weak. The classic delta shape (e.g. the Nile) is just one of the many forms.*

5 Desert landforms
include both windblown
sand deposits (seif dunes,
barchans) and eroded
areas littered with stones
or bare rock.

6 Glaciers help create
pyramidal peaks and
sharp ridges (aretes).
They also carry rock
debris (moraine).

7 Landslides occur on
steep slopes and under
favourable geological
conditions, notably on
clays and especially in
areas of heavy rainfall.

8 Hard-rock coasts have
steep cliffs and often off-
shore rocks and natural
arches. The slope of the
cliff is variable and
depends on the interac-
tion between geology,
climate and the energy of
the waves at the base.

9 U-shaped valleys may
result from glacial
erosion. Beyond the ice
limit fluvio-glacial deposition and erosion occurs,
often creating terraces.

10 Soft-rock coasts are
characterized by deposi-
tion. Beaches abound.
Spits may dominate
river mouths, and salt
marsh accumulates in
sheltered localities.

NATURAL VEGETATION

Our natural vegetation has evolved in conjunction with the other elements of the environment to produce clear-cut patterns. Climate is an especially important control, but many other factors are influential. Vegetation is a resource for human-kind, and as such has been subject to modification and destruction at an ever-increasing rate.

THE natural vegetation has increased in diversity and complexity over the past 400 million years. Trees are the dominant plant form. Gymnosperms (conifers) evolved first, but have been out-stripped by the angiosperms (flowering plants) and now only dominate in harsher, often cooler, environments. Exceptions include the famous redwood forests on the Pacific coast of North America, and the Podocarp forests of New Zealand.

Most plants require warmth, moisture and sunlight for growth, and a soil to act as an anchor and provide nutrients. Equatorial regions provide the optimum conditions for growth, and support the greatest diversity of tree species. A 10 x 1000m sample area of vegetation through the Amazon forest might contain over 150 species. A similar area in an ancient woodland in Britain might reveal only 15-20 tree types. Species diversity is even lower in northern coniferous forests.

Plants are adapted to the prevailing climate. In equatorial regions there are few limits to growth, and trees are tall, rarely deciduous, and often large leaved. In the absence of strong winds, pollination is mainly by insects, bats and birds. Brightly coloured, highly scented flowers are characteristic. Competition for light is important, and many plants (lianes) scramble and climb up existing trunks or grow directly on the branches (epiphytes).

In drier areas, conservation of moisture is necessary. Leaf loss, small leaves, sunken stomata (similar to skin pores), and aromatic oils within leaves are some of the many survival strategies adopted. Eventually moisture availability is insufficient to support trees, which are replaced by scrub and grass communities.

The impact of human action has been more dramatic and speedy than the gradual evolution of the pattern of natural vegetation over the past 2 million years. The effects have been especially marked in the last 50 years on both forests and rangelands. The speed and scale of tropical forest destruction for timber, settlements, shifting agriculture and large-scale ranching have raised fears about soil erosion and climatic change both locally and globally. Destruction of rangeland vegetation through fire, over-grazing and ploughing has prompted fears of desertification. One resolution is to establish conservation areas but their successful implementation is very difficult.

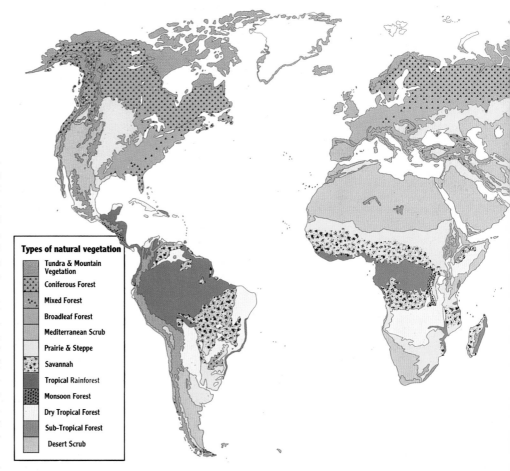

Types of natural vegetation

- Tundra & Mountain Vegetation
- Coniferous Forest
- Mixed Forest
- Broadleaf Forest
- Mediterranean Scrub
- Prairie & Steppe
- Savannah
- Tropical Rainforest
- Monsoon Forest
- Dry Tropical Forest
- Sub-Tropical Forest
- Desert Scrub

The Amazon rainforest is the largest area of natural tropical forest remaining, but it too, is now being exploited by human activities, particularly since a road network has been pushed through the area. Much of the forest is being burnt to provide pasture land or land for peasant farms, or is cleared for the timber industry. Mineral extraction and oil exploration (right) are other causes of deforestation. It is expected that forest destruction will cause climatic changes to Amazonia, and there may also be globally felt effects.

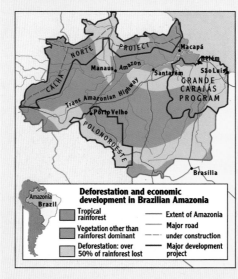

Deforestation and economic development in Brazilian Amazonia

- Tropical rainforest
- Vegetation other than rainforest dominant
- Deforestation: over 50% of rainforest lost
- Extent of Amazonia
- Major road
- --- under construction
- Major development project

CALHA NORTE PROJECT
Macapá
Belém
Manaus
Amazon
Santarém
São Luís
GRANDE CARAJÁS PROGRAM
Trans Amazonian Highway
Porto Velho
POLONOROESTE
Brasília

Amazonia
Brazil

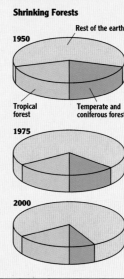

Shrinking Forests

1950
Rest of the earth

Tropical forest
Temperate and coniferous forest

1975

2000

In 1950 the forests of the temperate and tropical areas covered about 40% of the Earth's land surface. European forests had almost been depleted. Since 1950 there has been a dramatic increase in forest destruction. By 1975 forests occupied 30% of the land surface; by 1985 this had declined towards 20%. Destruction is taking place in both temperate and tropical areas although most publicity has focused on the tropical rain forests.

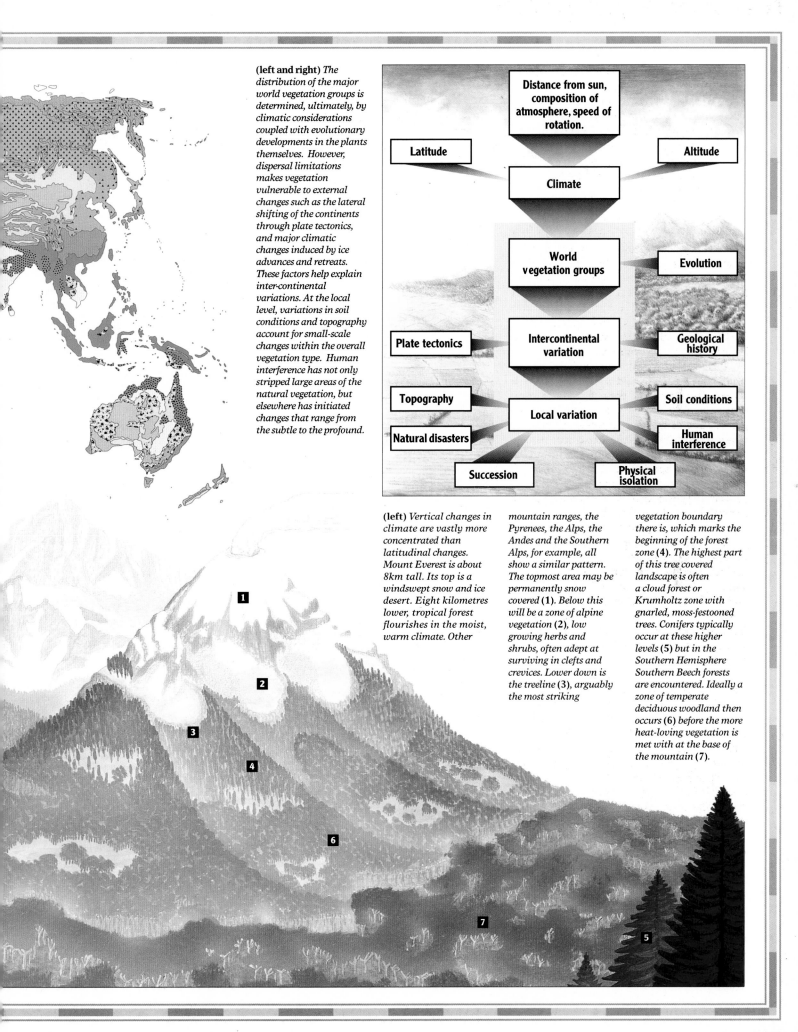

(left and right) *The distribution of the major world vegetation groups is determined, ultimately, by climatic considerations coupled with evolutionary developments in the plants themselves. However, dispersal limitations makes vegetation vulnerable to external changes such as the lateral shifting of the continents through plate tectonics, and major climatic changes induced by ice advances and retreats. These factors help explain inter-continental variations. At the local level, variations in soil conditions and topography account for small-scale changes within the overall vegetation type. Human interference has not only stripped large areas of the natural vegetation, but elsewhere has initiated changes that range from the subtle to the profound.*

Distance from sun, composition of atmosphere, speed of rotation.

Latitude

Altitude

Climate

World vegetation groups

Evolution

Intercontinental variation

Geological history

Plate tectonics

Topography

Local variation

Soil conditions

Natural disasters

Human interference

Succession

Physical isolation

(left) *Vertical changes in climate are vastly more concentrated than latitudinal changes. Mount Everest is about 8km tall. Its top is a windswept snow and ice desert. Eight kilometres lower, tropical forest flourishes in the moist, warm climate. Other mountain ranges, the Pyrenees, the Alps, the Andes and the Southern Alps, for example, all show a similar pattern. The topmost area may be permanently snow covered (1). Below this will be a zone of alpine vegetation (2), low growing herbs and shrubs, often adept at surviving in clefts and crevices. Lower down is the treeline (3), arguably the most striking vegetation boundary there is, which marks the beginning of the forest zone (4). The highest part of this tree covered landscape is often a cloud forest or Krumholtz zone with gnarled, moss-festooned trees. Conifers typically occur at these higher levels (5) but in the Southern Hemisphere Southern Beech forests are encountered. Ideally a zone of temperate deciduous woodland then occurs (6) before the more heat-loving vegetation is met with at the base of the mountain (7).*

POPULATION

The growth of world population is among the most important features of this century, and has sparked debate about its economic, social and environmental implications. Growth may not cease until numbers reach over 12 billion, more than double present figures. The most rapidly growing populations are in poorer regions, and the pressures on resources are enormous.

WORLD population reached 5.5 billion in mid-1992, and is projected to grow to 6.2 billion by the year 2000. Numbers have increased rapidly in the second half of the 20th century, with growth rates reaching 2.1% per annum in the 1960s. The present growth rate is 1.7% per annum (an extra 93 million people each year), and is projected to decline to about 1.0% per annum by 2025 when population is projected to be 8.5 billion.

The exceptional nature of this growth is apparent when placed in the context of world population history. In the past, population growth was exceedingly slow, with birth and death rates generally in balance. Growth rates began to increase around the beginning of the 18th century, and the first thousand million was reached in the early 19th century. In 1900 the world total was less than 1.7 billion.

The major impetus behind growth has been the lowering of mortality and improvements in life expectancy. These have been especially important in the period after the Second World War for the populations of the less developed regions of the world. Meanwhile, declines in birth rates have been much less rapid; parts of Africa have even seen increases in fertility. The result has been explosive rates of growth, particularly in the less developed world, where between 1950 and 1990 the population increased by 143% compared with 45% elsewhere.

Today, growth is most rapid in Africa, parts of Asia and Latin America. Growth is projected to remain high in Africa well into the next century, so that by 2025 Africa will account for 35% of world population growth (20% in 1990) and make up 19% of total world population (12% in 1990). Kenya has one of the highest rates of growth of any country, and population here is expected to increase 13 times from the 1950 total.

How rapidly world population growth decelerates depends on the speed with which birth rates are reduced in those countries where they are still high. Fertility reduction depends on many factors, including the education levels and status of women. For many poor people, children remain their greatest security. The success of government efforts to lower birth rates will depend to a great extent on how successfully they also improve economic and social conditions for their people.

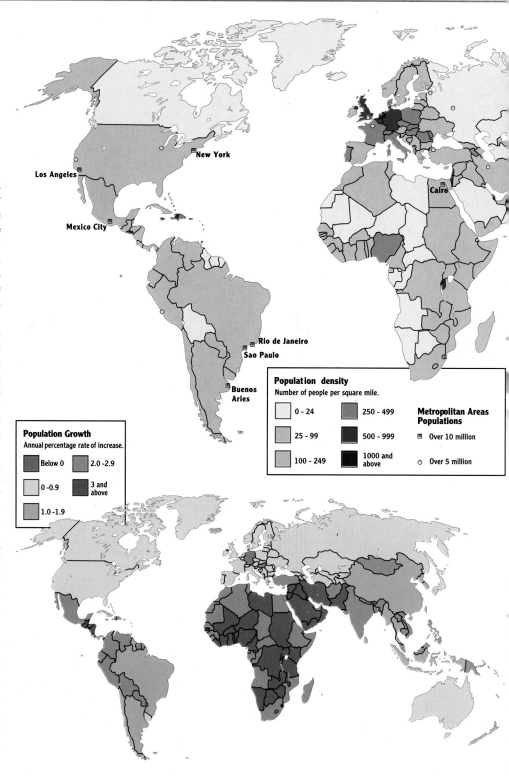

Population density
Number of people per square mile.

0 - 24	250 - 499
25 - 99	500 - 999
100 - 249	1000 and above

Metropolitan Areas Populations

Over 10 million

Over 5 million

Population Growth
Annual percentage rate of increase.

Below 0	2.0 -2.9
0 -0.9	3 and above
1.0 -1.9	

(above) *World population growth rates show a clear north-south division with dramatic growth gradients evident where the less developed world impinges on the more developed world. This is particularly evident in the countries surrounding the Mediterranean Sea where some of the faster growing* populations of the world in north Africa are adjacent to the slowest growing in Europe.
(above right) *World population grew at a steady rate until the 18th century when the rate of growth accelerated dramatically.*
(right) *Demographic transition model showing* the four broad stages of development as undeveloped societies with high birth and death rates and low rates of growth progress through periods of rapidly growing population before reaching stage 4 where birth and death rates are very low and growth rates stable or even declining.

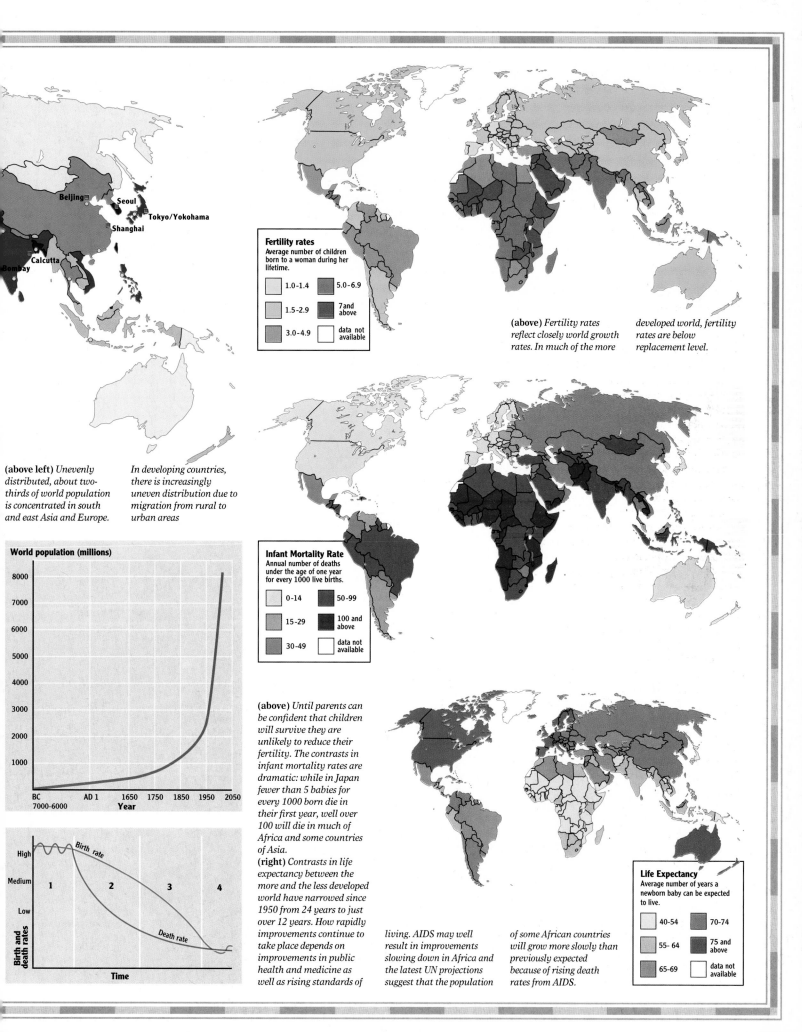

Fertility rates
Average number of children born to a woman during her lifetime.

- 1.0-1.4
- 1.5-2.9
- 3.0-4.9
- 5.0-6.9
- 7 and above
- data not available

(above) *Fertility rates reflect closely world growth rates. In much of the more* *developed world, fertility rates are below replacement level.*

(above left) *Unevenly distributed, about two-thirds of world population is concentrated in south and east Asia and Europe.*

In developing countries, there is increasingly uneven distribution due to migration from rural to urban areas

World population (millions)

Infant Mortality Rate
Annual number of deaths under the age of one year for every 1000 live births.

- 0-14
- 15-29
- 30-49
- 50-99
- 100 and above
- data not available

(above) *Until parents can be confident that children will survive they are unlikely to reduce their fertility. The contrasts in infant mortality rates are dramatic: while in Japan fewer than 5 babies for every 1000 born die in their first year, well over 100 will die in much of Africa and some countries of Asia.*

(right) *Contrasts in life expectancy between the more and the less developed world have narrowed since 1950 from 24 years to just over 12 years. How rapidly improvements continue to take place depends on improvements in public health and medicine as well as rising standards of* *living. AIDS may well result in improvements slowing down in Africa and the latest UN projections suggest that the population* *of some African countries will grow more slowly than previously expected because of rising death rates from AIDS.*

Life Expectancy
Average number of years a newborn baby can be expected to live.

- 40-54
- 55-64
- 65-69
- 70-74
- 75 and above
- data not available

FOOD

Enough food is produced in the world to satisfy the basic needs of all its 5.5 billion inhabitants, yet malnutrition and famine are commonplace. While food production has increased steadily in nearly all countries over the last 50 years, the UN nevertheless estimates that under-nourishment still afflicts one person out of every five.

ABOUT one third of the world's land area is too cold, dry or mountainous for food production. Of the rest, about 10% is under intensive cultivation and 25% used for extensive grazing, with some of the remaining land, mostly semi-arid or forested, potentially available for agricultural use (see map right). The most productive regions of the oceans are nearly all located in relatively shallow waters.

Since 1950, world food production has been increasing at an annual rate of between 2 and 3%. Today the more developed countries produce half the world's food with less than 10% of its agricultural workforce through the intense application of chemicals and widespread use of machinery, giving very high yields per hectare of land. In many developing countries, especially in Africa, farming is labour intensive and yields are low; over much of the Far East and Latin America, on the other hand, the development of high-yielding varieties of cereals, together with increased use of irrigation, fertilizers and pesticides (often referred to as the green revolution), has achieved much greater yields.

The sea is an important source of food for many coastal and island peoples, particularly in the Far East, but opportunities for further expansion of the marine harvest appear limited. Food production in many developing countries has generally kept pace with population growth, and a few, such as Thailand, have become net exporters of food. Most countries in Africa, on the other hand, have experienced a decline in food availability as their population has grown faster than the food supply; technological innovations there have often been in respect of high-value crops intended for export (so-called cash crops), rather than staple foods such as cereals.

Over much of Africa, together with parts of Asia and Latin America, average daily food consumption is below optimum levels both in quantity, or energy content, as well as quality, or nutritional make-up. In contrast, a similar proportion of the population in nearly all developed countries suffers from over-nutrition, with its attendant problems of obesity and dietary-related diseases. This inequality is apparent not only in the average daily intake of food energy (see diagram top right), but more especially in the proportion of the diet derived from animal sources (see map bottom right).

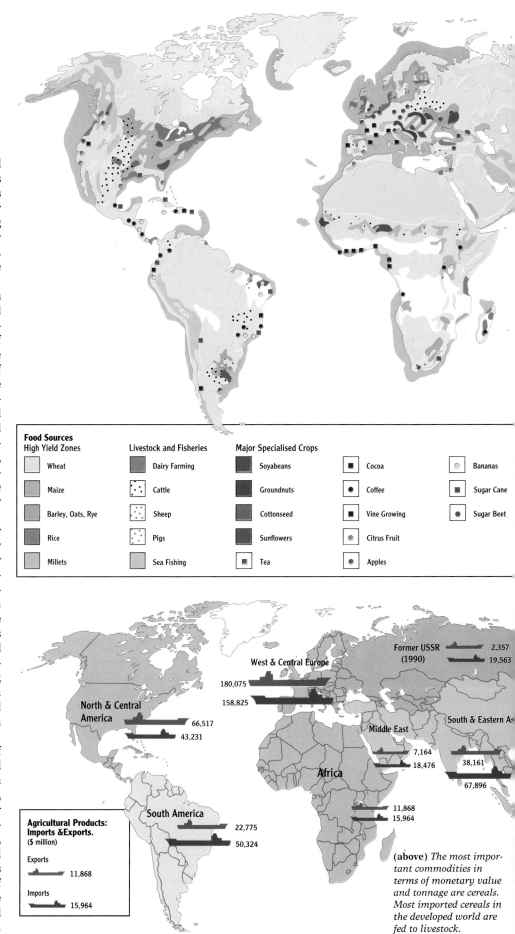

Food Sources

High Yield Zones
- Wheat
- Maize
- Barley, Oats, Rye
- Rice
- Millets

Livestock and Fisheries
- Dairy Farming
- Cattle
- Sheep
- Pigs
- Sea Fishing

Major Specialised Crops
- Soyabeans
- Groundnuts
- Cottonseed
- Sunflowers
- Tea
- Cocoa
- Coffee
- Vine Growing
- Citrus Fruit
- Apples
- Bananas
- Sugar Cane
- Sugar Beet

Agricultural Products: Imports &Exports.
($ million)

Exports — 11,868
Imports — 15,964

North & Central America
66,517
43,231

South America
22,775
50,324

West & Central Europe
180,075
158,825

Former USSR (1990)
2,357
19,563

Middle East
7,164
18,476

South & Eastern Asia
38,161
67,896

Africa
11,868
15,964

(above) *The most important commodities in terms of monetary value and tonnage are cereals. Most imported cereals in the developed world are fed to livestock.*

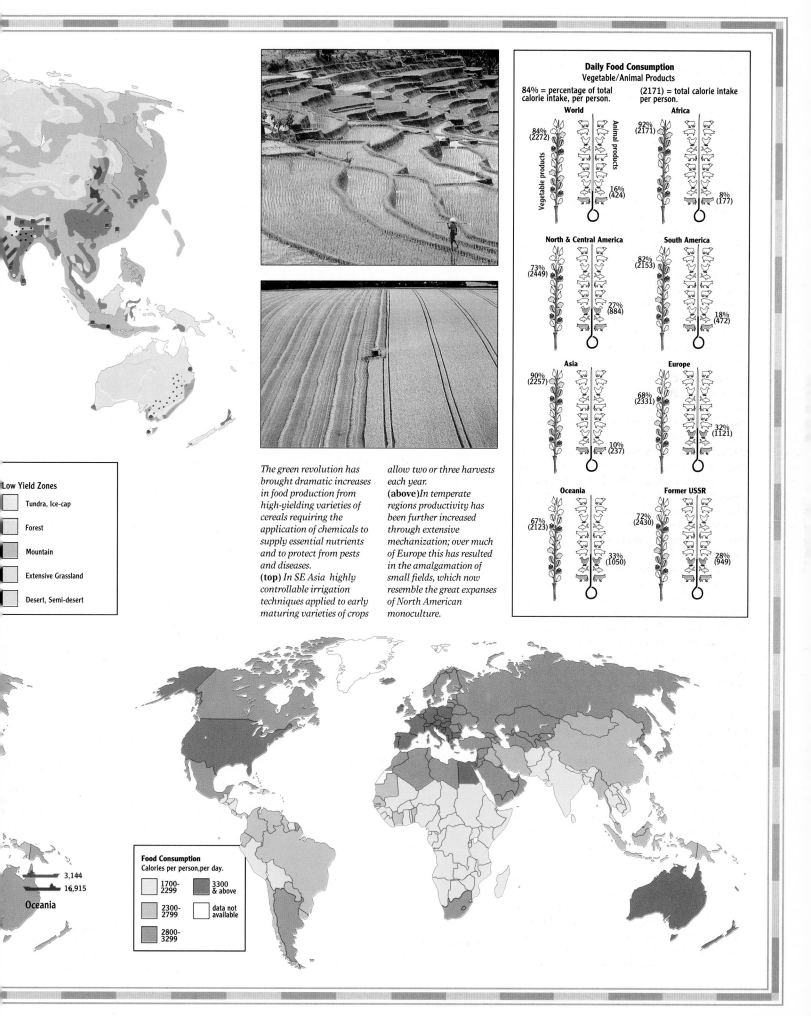

Daily Food Consumption
Vegetable/Animal Products

84% = percentage of total calorie intake, per person.

(2171) = total calorie intake per person.

World

Vegetable products — 84% (2272)

Animal products — 16% (424)

Africa

92% (2171)

8% (177)

North & Central America

73% (2449)

27% (884)

South America

82% (2153)

18% (472)

Asia

90% (2257)

10% (237)

Europe

68% (2331)

32% (1121)

Oceania

67% (2123)

33% (1050)

Former USSR

72% (2430)

28% (949)

The green revolution has brought dramatic increases in food production from high-yielding varieties of cereals requiring the application of chemicals to supply essential nutrients and to protect from pests and diseases.

(top) *In SE Asia highly controllable irrigation techniques applied to early maturing varieties of crops* allow two or three harvests each year.

(above) *In temperate regions productivity has been further increased through extensive mechanization; over much of Europe this has resulted in the amalgamation of small fields, which now resemble the great expanses of North American monoculture.*

Low Yield Zones

- Tundra, Ice-cap
- Forest
- Mountain
- Extensive Grassland
- Desert, Semi-desert

3,144
16,915

Oceania

Food Consumption
Calories per person, per day.

- 1700-2299
- 2300-2799
- 2800-3299
- 3300 & above
- data not available

MINERALS AND ENERGY

Life for most people in the world today is sustained by the consumption of both minerals and energy, often in quite considerable quantities. Knowledge of their location and availability is therefore of great importance, and in many cases the search for new or alternative sources has very high priority.

WHILE metal-yielding minerals are widely distributed in the Earth's crust, it is usually only where they have been concentrated into an ore body that exploitation is possible. The quantity of ore that can be extracted at sufficient profit is known as the reserve of that mineral; its size will change in response to variations in demand and technological advances, as well as to findings of new deposits.

Although no metal is destroyed by use, the proportion that can be recycled seldom exceeds 50%, so there is a continuing need for new sources of supply or the introduction of substitutes. While metals such as aluminium and iron are widely distributed and relatively plentiful, the supply of others, such as copper, has only been maintained with recourse to increasingly less concentrated ore deposits. A few important metals are intrinsically rare and deposits are limited to very few countries; for example, metals of the platinum group occur mainly in South Africa. The economy of many developing countries is largely dependent upon the export of one particular metal (Guinea and Jamaica rely extensively on their reserves of aluminium).

Compared with metals, non-metalliferous minerals (those that do not yield or contain metals) generally have lower intrinsic value but a wider distribution; they are, however, rarely capable of being recycled. The most important sources of energy, fossil hydrocarbon fuels, are totally consumed by use. Whereas coal and lignite are widely distributed and relatively abundant, reserves of gas and oil are more localized. World dependence on oil and gas has increased dramatically since 1945, and supplies are predicted to approach exhaustion during the next century. Nuclear and hydro-power each account for about 20% of world electricity supply, but the uranium fuel on which the former depends has few rich deposits and is non-renewable. Hydro-power, however, constitutes an inexhaustible resource in principle, though most of its potential contribution resides in developing countries.

The amount of energy obtained from fuel-wood is estimated to be comparable with that supplied by nuclear and hydro-power. It is the dominant fuel in much of Africa and parts of Latin America and southeast Asia. Although it is a renewable resource, many developing countries are already experiencing an acute shortage of this source of energy.

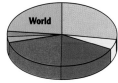

World Energy Consumption

- North America
- Latin America
- Western Europe
- Eastern Europe plus former USSR (1990)
- Middle East
- Africa
- Asia and Australia

Colours also refer to World Energy Reserves.

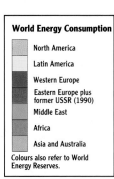

World

(above) *The industrialized world's high standard of living requires the consumption of huge quantities of energy.*

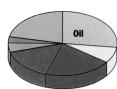

Oil

(left) *Because it supplies essential fuels for transport, and despite political uncertainties, oil remains the world's most important source of energy.*

(right) *Widely available, coal is a significant source of energy, and is especially prominent in the (former) communist states and in many developing countries.*

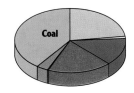

Coal

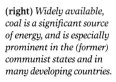

Natural Gas

(left) *Consumption of natural gas has doubled over the last 20 years, and is now the principal energy source for many industrialized countries.*

Renewable sources are making an increasing contribution to world energy needs. One of the most promising is wind power (see diagram and photograph below), which already supplies some 2% of electricity demand in both California and Denmark and also has a realistic potential contribution of up to 20% in many countries. The cost of solar cells is still falling, encouraging an expansion of applications mainly within tropical latitudes. In favoured locations electricity from the sea (from both tidal energy and wave power), and geothermal heat can be significant. As valuable replacements for fossil hydrocarbons, similar fuels can be derived from organic material (biomass) of many kinds, including crops such as sugar cane or timber which is grown specifically for the purpose, as well as agricultural or domestic wastes.

European Wind Energy Resources
The potential for wind energy development based upon mean speeds greater than 5m/s.

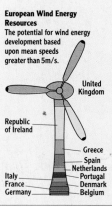

United Kingdom
Republic of Ireland
Greece
Spain
Netherlands
Italy
France
Portugal
Germany
Denmark
Belgium

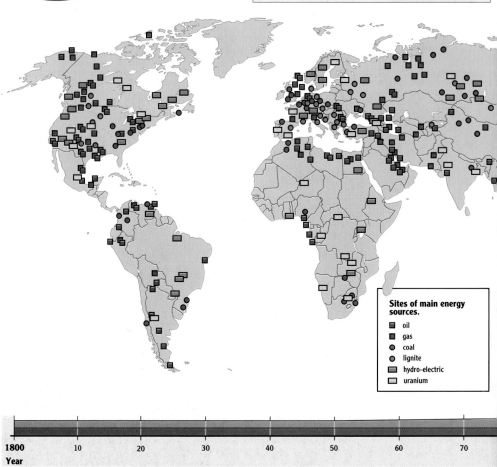

Sites of main energy sources.
- oil
- gas
- coal
- lignite
- hydro-electric
- uranium

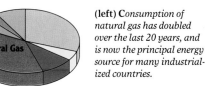

1800 10 20 30 40 50 60 70
Year

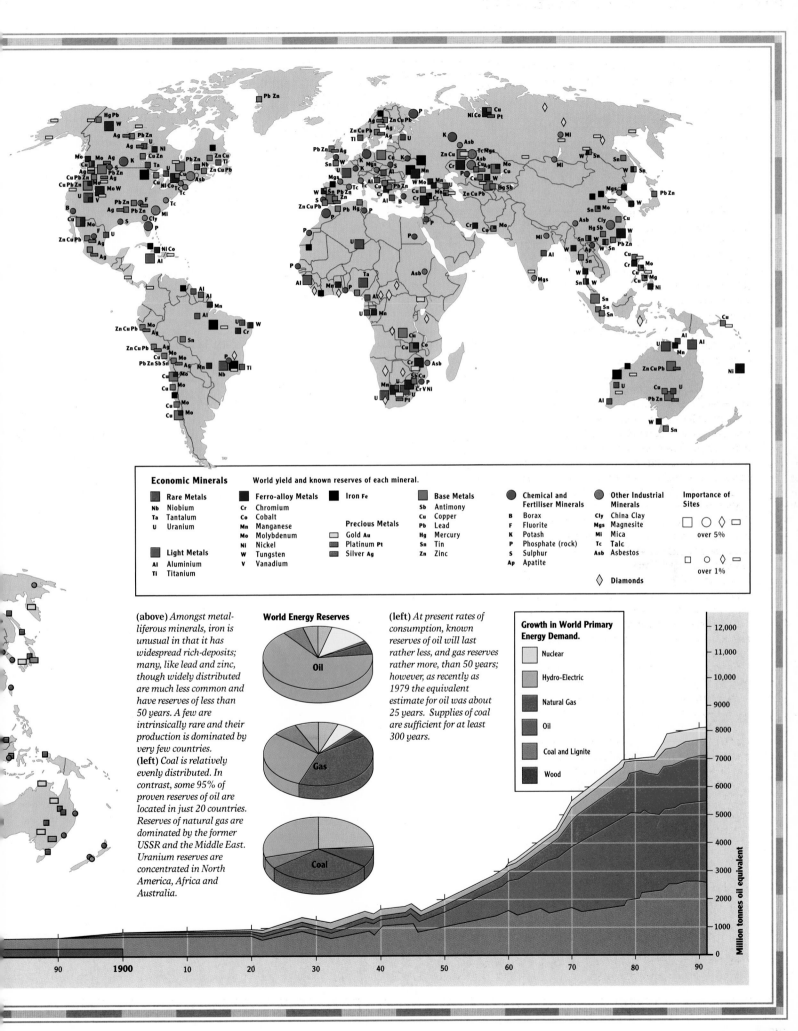

Economic Minerals   World yield and known reserves of each mineral.

Rare Metals		Ferro-alloy Metals		Iron Fe	Base Metals		● Chemical and Fertiliser Minerals		● Other Industrial Minerals		Importance of Sites
Nb	Niobium	Cr	Chromium		Sb	Antimony	B	Borax	Cly	China Clay	
Ta	Tantalum	Co	Cobalt		Cu	Copper	F	Fluorite	Mgs	Magnesite	over 5%
U	Uranium	Mn	Manganese	**Precious Metals**	Pb	Lead	K	Potash	Mi	Mica	
		Mo	Molybdenum	Gold Au	Hg	Mercury	P	Phosphate (rock)	Tc	Talc	
		Ni	Nickel	Platinum Pt	Sn	Tin	S	Sulphur	Asb	Asbestos	
Light Metals		W	Tungsten	Silver Ag	Zn	Zinc	Ap	Apatite			over 1%
Al	Aluminium	V	Vanadium								
Ti	Titanium								◇	Diamonds	

(above) *Amongst metal-liferous minerals, iron is unusual in that it has widespread rich-deposits; many, like lead and zinc, though widely distributed are much less common and have reserves of less than 50 years. A few are intrinsically rare and their production is dominated by very few countries.*
(left) *Coal is relatively evenly distributed. In contrast, some 95% of proven reserves of oil are located in just 20 countries. Reserves of natural gas are dominated by the former USSR and the Middle East. Uranium reserves are concentrated in North America, Africa and Australia.*

World Energy Reserves

Oil

Gas

Coal

(left) *At present rates of consumption, known reserves of oil will last rather less, and gas reserves rather more, than 50 years; however, as recently as 1979 the equivalent estimate for oil was about 25 years. Supplies of coal are sufficient for at least 300 years.*

Growth in World Primary Energy Demand.

- Nuclear
- Hydro-Electric
- Natural Gas
- Oil
- Coal and Lignite
- Wood

Million tonnes oil equivalent

ENVIRONMENTAL PROBLEMS

People have always suffered from the results of too little or too much water but, as world population has grown and people have been obliged to live in more marginal areas, so pressure on the environment has intensified. As a result droughts, floods and other related problems are increasing in severity and frequency.

DROUGHTS are a natural part of climatic variability, but in temperate latitudes such as Britain they are seldom long-lived or give rise to more than local inconvenience. Nearer to the equator, where rainfall is both seasonal and highly variable from year to year, drought is much more likely to occur, and it is quite common for unusually dry (or wet) years to follow each other in sequence. Much of Africa experiences low rainfall regimes of this type.

Gradual erosion of the land surface by wind and water is an ongoing natural process, but removal of vegetation cover and short-sighted farming practices can result in accelerated loss of topsoil. Preventative measures involve direct protection from the erosive effects of wind and water (using windbreaks or terracing, for example) and modifying cultivation practices to maximize the extent and persistence of vegetation cover.

Floods are the most frequent natural disasters and cause the most damage in terms of loss of life and livelihood. River floods, which occur when the volume of water exceeds the capacity of the channel, are the most common , but incursions by the sea can be equally disastrous. Low lying coasts and the flood plains of large rivers are most at risk, regions which typically support dense populations and intensive agricultural activity. The risk of flooding is often further increased by human activities such as urbanization and deforestation. Although considerable protection to life and property is provided by engineering works, regulation of land use together with warning systems is usually more cost effective.

The borders of desert regions are slowly changing all the time, but human activity can greatly accelerate their advance. The semi-arid margins of subtropical deserts are at risk where rising numbers of poor people struggle to survive. The sparse vegetation cover is rapidly lost through increased collection of fuelwood and grazing of more livestock, and the soil is impoverished through expansion of cultivated land and reductions in the fallow period. Erosion and drought hasten the degradation of the land. An important additional factor in regions where irrigation is common is an excessive concentration of salts in the soil, resulting from high evaporation rates coupled with insufficient drainage.

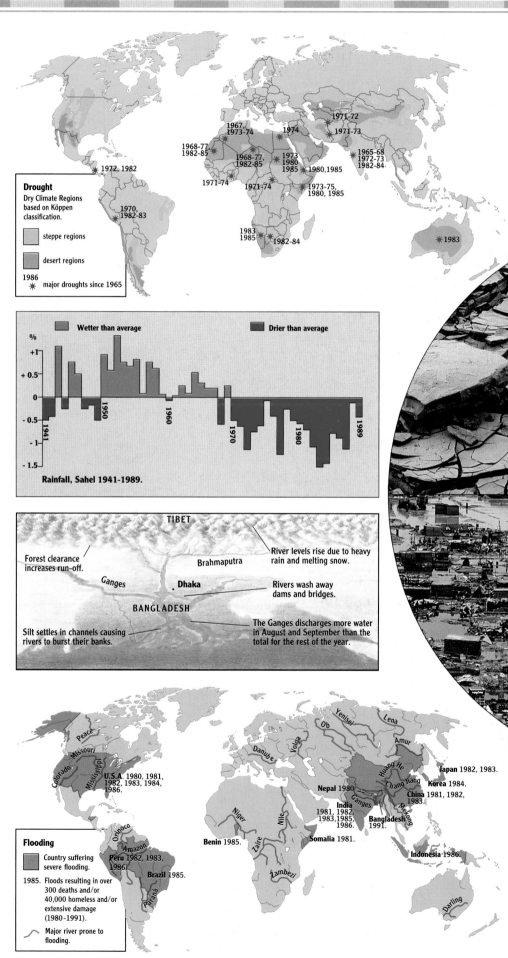

Drought
Dry Climate Regions based on Köppen classification.

steppe regions

desert regions

1986
✳ major droughts since 1965

Wetter than average ■   Drier than average ■

%
+1
+ 0.5
0
- 0.5
- 1
- 1.5

Rainfall, Sahel 1941-1989.

TIBET

Forest clearance increases run-off.

Ganges

Brahmaputra

. Dhaka

River levels rise due to heavy rain and melting snow.

Rivers wash away dams and bridges.

BANGLADESH

Silt settles in channels causing rivers to burst their banks.

The Ganges discharges more water in August and September than the total for the rest of the year.

Flooding

Country suffering severe flooding.

1985. Floods resulting in over 300 deaths and/or 40,000 homeless and/or extensive damage (1980-1991).

Major river prone to flooding.

U.S.A. 1980, 1981, 1982, 1983, 1984, 1986.

Peru 1982, 1983, 1986.

Brazil 1985.

Benin 1985.

Nepal 1980

India 1981, 1982, 1983, 1985, 1986.

Somalia 1981.

Bangladesh 1991.

Japan 1982, 1983.

Korea 1984.

China 1981, 1982, 1983.

Indonesia 1986.

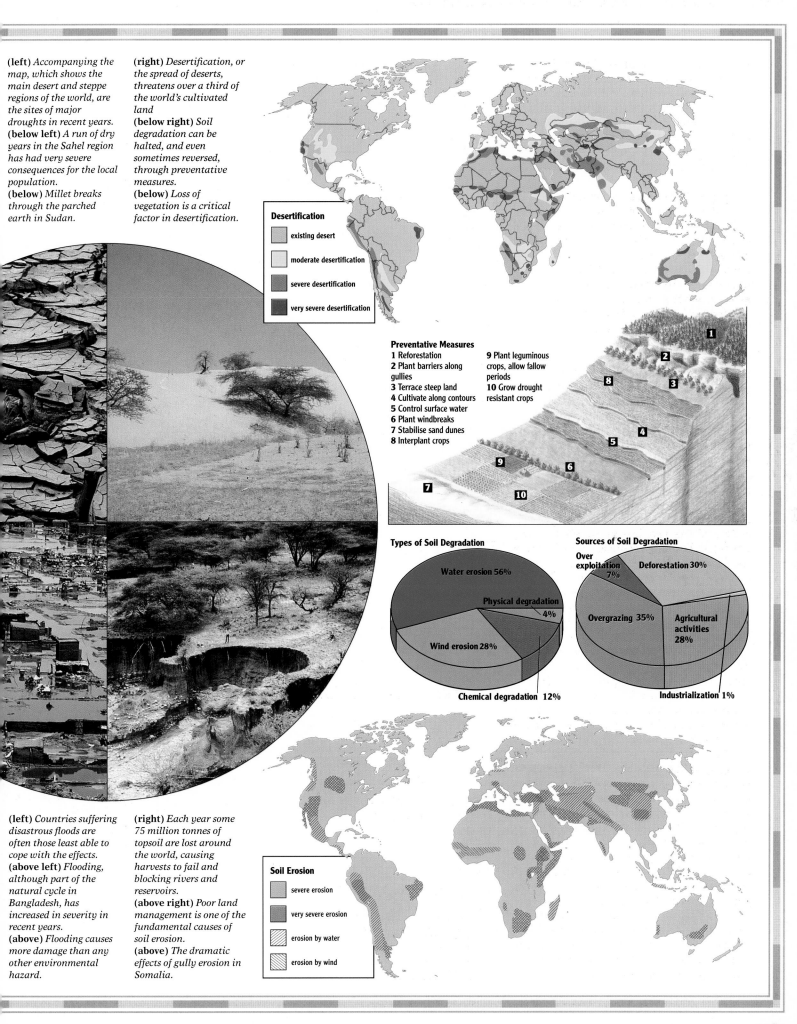

(left) *Accompanying the map, which shows the main desert and steppe regions of the world, are the sites of major droughts in recent years.*
(below left) *A run of dry years in the Sahel region has had very severe consequences for the local population.*
(below) *Millet breaks through the parched earth in Sudan.*

(right) *Desertification, or the spread of deserts, threatens over a third of the world's cultivated land*
(below right) *Soil degradation can be halted, and even sometimes reversed, through preventative measures.*
(below) *Loss of vegetation is a critical factor in desertification.*

Desertification

existing desert

moderate desertification

severe desertification

very severe desertification

Preventative Measures
1 Reforestation
2 Plant barriers along gullies
3 Terrace steep land
4 Cultivate along contours
5 Control surface water
6 Plant windbreaks
7 Stabilise sand dunes
8 Interplant crops
9 Plant leguminous crops, allow fallow periods
10 Grow drought resistant crops

Types of Soil Degradation

Water erosion 56%

Physical degradation 4%

Wind erosion 28%

Chemical degradation 12%

Sources of Soil Degradation

Over exploitation 7%

Deforestation 30%

Overgrazing 35%

Agricultural activities 28%

Industrialization 1%

(left) *Countries suffering disastrous floods are often those least able to cope with the effects.*
(above left) *Flooding, although part of the natural cycle in Bangladesh, has increased in severity in recent years.*
(above) *Flooding causes more damage than any other environmental hazard.*

(right) *Each year some 75 million tonnes of topsoil are lost around the world, causing harvests to fail and blocking rivers and reservoirs.*
(above right) *Poor land management is one of the fundamental causes of soil erosion.*
(above) *The dramatic effects of gully erosion in Somalia.*

Soil Erosion

severe erosion

very severe erosion

erosion by water

erosion by wind

POLLUTION

Over the last two centuries, advances in science and technology and a rising standard of living have led to increasing volumes of waste materials, which are beginning to have a world-wide impact on the environment.

IT is easy to suppose that the atmosphere has an unlimited capacity for our waste products. Its local capacity is often exceeded in large cities, however, and while the demise of the open coal fire has eliminated dense smogs from cities such as London, other cities, where high traffic densities coincide with intense sunlight, (Los Angeles, Mexico City and Tokyo, for example), increasingly suffer from smogs of a different kind. Increasing road traffic is one reason for a steadily rising consumption of fossil fuels; when burnt these produce carbon dioxide which will in time lead to a significant warming of the climate.

Most fossil fuels, particularly coal, contain sulphur as an impurity. When burnt, both sulphur dioxide and oxides of nitrogen are produced, which may escape into the atmosphere and give rise to acid rain and snowfall. In susceptible regions this has the effect of killing fish and other aquatic life, as well as forest trees.

Chlorofluorocarbons, or CFCs, are a group of highly inert, non-toxic, volatile chemicals with widespread applications as aerosol propellants, refrigerants, foam-blowing agents and industrial solvents. Their extreme stability in the lower atmosphere means they disperse over the globe and only decompose when exposed to ultra-violet sunlight high in the stratosphere. Chlorine atoms are set free and act to decrease the concentration of the protective ozone layer. Although losses have been detected in northern latitudes, at present they are most severe above the Antarctic.

Four million tonnes of waste are produced every day. While household and municipal waste is adequately dealt with via recycling, reclamation, incineration, composting, landfilling or, less desirably, dumping at sea, about a quarter is industrial waste for which there is no safe disposal method other than total isolation from the environment.

The accidental discharge of toxic industrial effluent into rivers and lakes results in the large-scale loss of fish stocks. More widespread is an increase of nutrient levels from agricultural drainage or sewage effluent, which initiates an explosive growth of aquatic plants, followed by depressed levels of oxygen when they die and decompose; this, too, leads to the death of fish. Pollutants released into lakes and rivers find their way to the sea, where sewage contaminated beaches pose less of an environmental threat than does oil, large quantities of which are discharged every day.

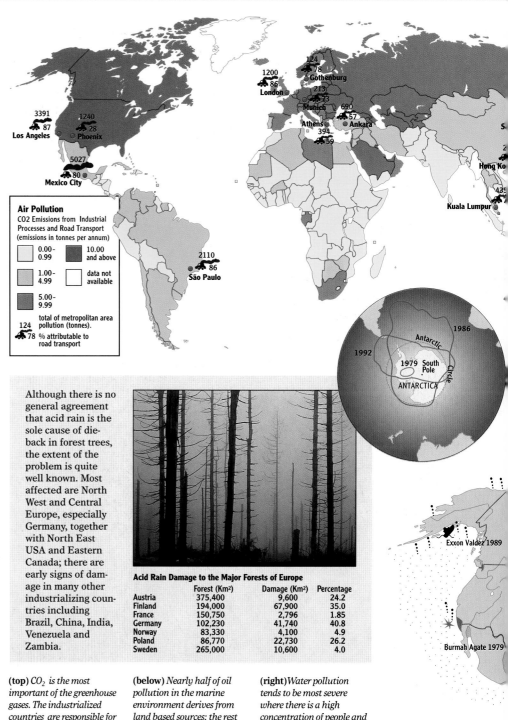

Air Pollution
CO2 Emissions from Industrial Processes and Road Transport (emissions in tonnes per annum)

- 0.00-0.99
- 1.00-4.99
- 5.00-9.99
- 10.00 and above
- data not available

124 total of metropolitan area pollution (tonnes).
78 % attributable to road transport

Although there is no general agreement that acid rain is the sole cause of die-back in forest trees, the extent of the problem is quite well known. Most affected are North West and Central Europe, especially Germany, together with North East USA and Eastern Canada; there are early signs of damage in many other industrializing countries including Brazil, China, India, Venezuela and Zambia.

Acid Rain Damage to the Major Forests of Europe

	Forest (Km²)	Damage (Km²)	Percentage
Austria	375,400	9,600	24.2
Finland	194,000	67,900	35.0
France	150,750	2,796	1.85
Germany	102,230	41,740	40.8
Norway	83,330	4,100	4.9
Poland	86,770	22,730	26.2
Sweden	265,000	10,600	4.0

(top) CO_2 is the most important of the greenhouse gases. The industrialized countries are responsible for 75% of global emissions.

(below) Nearly half of oil pollution in the marine environment derives from land based sources; the rest from shipping activities.

(right)Water pollution tends to be most severe where there is a high concentration of people and industrial activities.

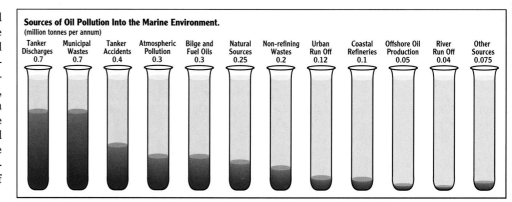

Sources of Oil Pollution Into the Marine Environment.
(million tonnes per annum)

Tanker Discharges	Municipal Wastes	Tanker Accidents	Atmospheric Pollution	Bilge and Fuel Oils	Natural Sources	Non-refining Wastes	Urban Run Off	Coastal Refineries	Offshore Oil Production	River Run Off	Other Sources
0.7	0.7	0.4	0.3	0.3	0.25	0.2	0.12	0.1	0.05	0.04	0.075

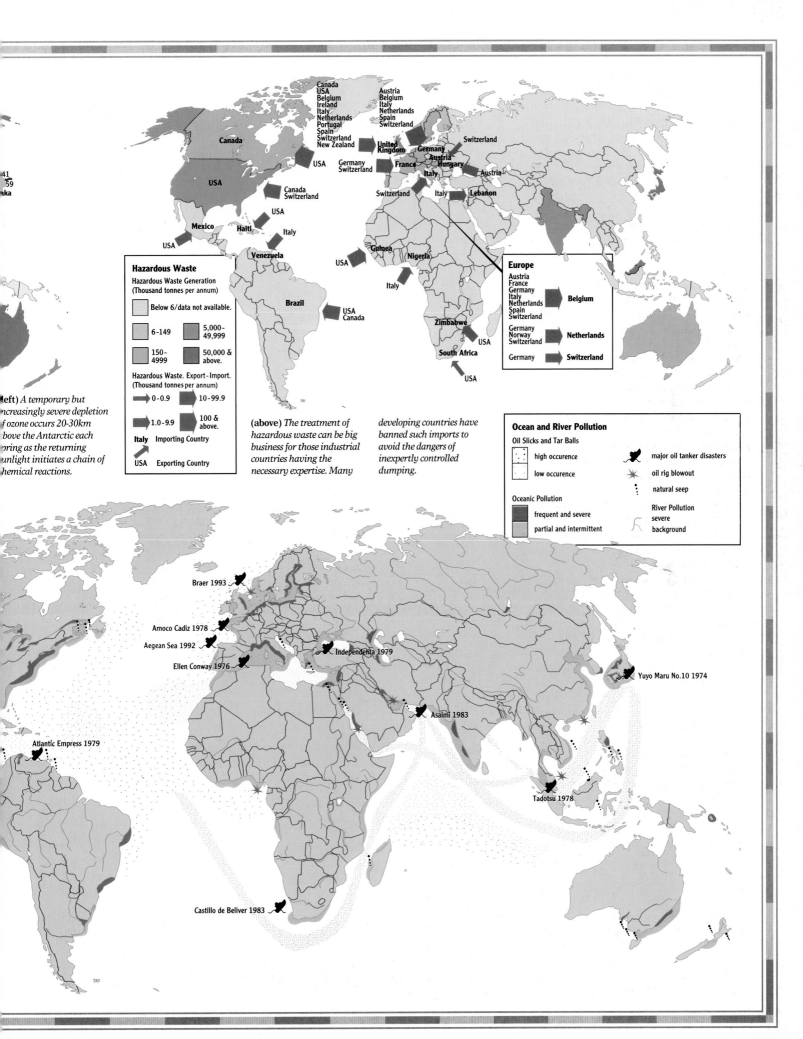

Hazardous Waste

Hazardous Waste Generation
(Thousand tonnes per annum)

- Below 6/data not available.
- 6-149
- 150-4999
- 5,000-49,999
- 50,000 & above.

Hazardous Waste. Export-Import.
(Thousand tonnes per annum)

- 0-0.9
- 1.0-9.9
- 10-99.9
- 100 & above.

Italy — Importing Country
USA — Exporting Country

Europe

Austria
France
Germany
Italy
Netherlands
Spain
Switzerland — Belgium

Germany
Norway
Switzerland — Netherlands

Germany — Switzerland

(left) *A temporary but increasingly severe depletion of ozone occurs 20-30km above the Antarctic each spring as the returning sunlight initiates a chain of chemical reactions.*

(above) *The treatment of hazardous waste can be big business for those industrial countries having the necessary expertise. Many developing countries have banned such imports to avoid the dangers of inexpertly controlled dumping.*

Ocean and River Pollution

Oil Slicks and Tar Balls
- high occurence
- low occurence

Oceanic Pollution
- frequent and severe
- partial and intermittent

- major oil tanker disasters
- oil rig blowout
- natural seep

River Pollution
- severe
- background

Braer 1993
Amoco Cadiz 1978
Aegean Sea 1992
Ellen Conway 1976
Independenta 1979
Yuyo Maru No.10 1974
Asaimi 1983
Atlantic Empress 1979
Tadotsu 1978
Castillo de Beliver 1983

HISTORY OF MAPS

Maps were drawn long before words were written, which was some time before 3200 BC. In the third millennium BC, maps were given an orientation. Finally, land-division in Mesopotamia, Egypt and China brought into use the concept of scale and the accurate spatial relationship required in the true map.

GEOGRAPHY developed in Greece from the 7th century BC, leading to the first world maps. The world was known to be a sphere from the 4th century BC. Eratosthenes, in the 3rd century BC, measured the circumference as 252,000 stades.(The Greek stade had many values. It was the length of the short foot-race , 125 double paces). In the following century, Hipparchus devised our system of 360 degrees, with 60 minutes of 60 seconds. Claud Ptolemy (c AD 150) wrote his *Geography* based on the work of a Phoenician predecessor, Marinus of Tyre, the culmination of Greek geography. By Ptolemy's reckoning, the world's circumference was only 180,000 stades. The Romans abandoned Greek concepts of mapping in favour of road maps and itineraries.

With the eclipse of Rome, the ancient world's geographical knowledge was lost to the West, and passed into the hands of Arab geographers. It was painfully rediscovered only in the late Middle Ages. New types of ocean-going ships, the compass, and, from the mid-13th century, a new type of chart, known as the portolan, revolutionized navigation.

The introduction into Europe of paper and the invention of printing led to widespread dissemination of the rediscovered maps of Ptolemy in the Age of Discovery. The supposedly small size of Ptolemy's world misled Columbus and others into believing China could be reached across the western ocean.

The theodolite, invented in 1570, the plane-table 20 years later and the telescope another 20 years on, followed by the invention of triangulation in 1617, established foundations of modern surveying and mapping. Satellites now provide the ultimate precision in surveying.

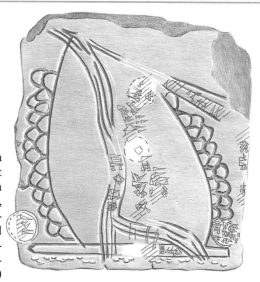

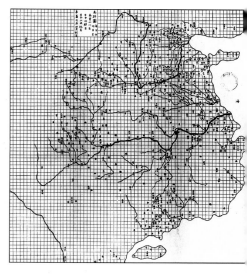

(above) *This map of 2500 BC in cuneiform script, on a clay tablet, is the earliest known map with true orientation. It contains the words north, west and east. A private estate is shown near a river with mountains on either side, east and west.*
(above right) *Chinese cartography developed in* isolation from the rest of the world. This map drawn on silk in the 2nd century BC is typical of the period. After the invention of paper, maps were widely distributed in China.*
(below) *A reconstruction of a map by Hecataeus of Miletus in c 500 BC. (It shows the world known to the Greeks at the time).*

(bottom left) *Muslim geographers made only a small contribution to cartography. Their main interests were astronomy, mathematics and the calculation of distances and the size of the Earth.*
(bottom centre) *Portolans were made from the mid-13th century by which time the magnetic compass* was in widespread use. Coastlines were accurately drawn on sheepskin. One o two central wind-roses wer joined by lines of various colours to 16 peripheral roses. All the lines were, therefore, compass bearing but their use is not known. Portolans continued to be made up to the end of the 16th century.*

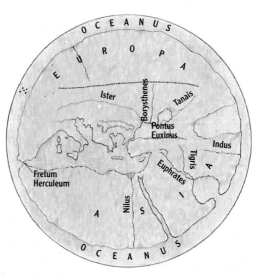

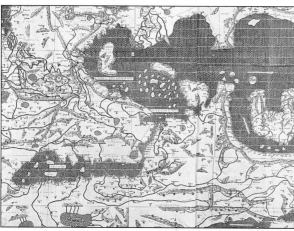

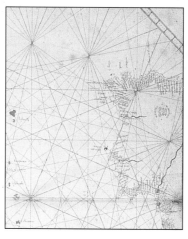

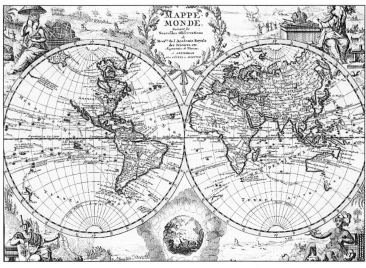

(**above left**) *A 10th century Anglo-Saxon map reflects Roman cartography, a decline from Greek cartography of the 2nd century.*

(**below left**) *In about AD 150, Claud Ptolemy of Alexandria described how to make maps and gave the latitude and longitude of 8000 places. His world map showed seven climatic zones (climes). He made the length of the Mediterranean 62° instead of 42°. This error, and others, were not finally corrected until 1700. Translated into Latin in 1405, Ptolemy dominated European geography for most of three centuries.*

(**above**) *Delisle's map of 1700 marked a turning point. He restored the Mediterranean to its true length. Lower California became once more a*

peninsula. It had been shown as an island.

(**below**) *In Tasman's map of New Holland (Australia), New Guinea is connected to Queensland. From the time of the Greeks Terra Australis had been an imaginary southern continent which proved to be the lands we now call Australia and Antarctica.*

(**bottom**) *This satellite map of Las Vegas and environs was prepared from Landsat imagery. The map is in false colour. Crops and grass are bright red; trees a duller red. The yellow patch at the eastern edge is red rock. This map is best used together with a normal map, preferably one of the same scale.*

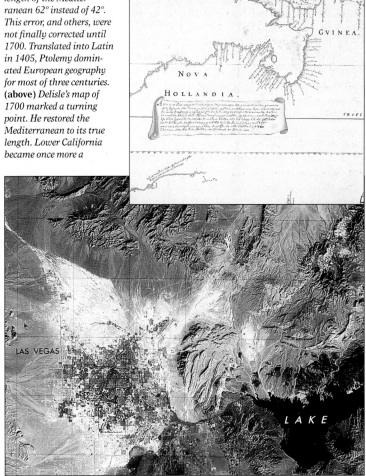

THE KEY TO MAPS

A map is a representation of the whole Earth or some part of it. It, therefore, reduces the Earth to a size convenient for a given purpose. In order to relate the map to the real world a knowledge of that reduction in size (the scale) is required as well as a means of defining orientation and position relative to other places on the surface of the Earth.

MAP scale defines the relationship of distances on the ground to corresponding distances on the Earth. It can be expressed as 1 cm represents 50 km or as a representative fraction 1:5,000,000. The content of a map depends on the map scale. Orientation determines the way directions are defined. It ought to mean finding the direction of east, but the Pole Star and the magnetic compass have led to the north supplanting the east as the primary reference. It is customary to put north at the top of a map, but that has not always been the case. Muslim geographers placed south at the top and at various times, and in various places, east or west have been put there. The direction of north should be indicated when north is not at the top of a map.

Our system of geographical co-ordinates (latitude and longitude) dates back to the 2nd century BC. It is based on 360° in a circle with degrees sub-divided into minutes, seconds and fractions of a second. Co-ordinates can be given to any desired degree of accuracy e.g. 48°40'51" N, 35°51'35" E (latitude is normally given first).

Because such coordinates are unwieldy, rectangular grids are used. A simple system of letters and numerals will show that a point lies within the quadrangle A3, for example. A kilometric grid is a system of squares formed by lines spaced at 1 km or 10 km intervals. In grid references the eastings co-ordinate is given before the northings co-ordinate, the reverse of latitude and longitude.

Map projection is the means by which the graticule (the lines of latitude and longitude) are transferred from the round Earth to flat paper. That transfer cannot be made without introducing distortion. Each map projection is designed to meet certain limited criteria only. In no projection can all distances and all bearings be preserved as true.

Spot heights and contour lines show the elevation of the land with respect to mean sea-level. Contour lines join points with the same elevation. Hypsometric (layer) tints indicate the major character of the relief. Hill-shading simulates the shadows cast by an imaginary sun placed in the north-west so that the shadows falling to the south and east reveal the varying slopes of the terrain. Tonal relief produces an effect similar to the combination of hill-shading and hypsometric tints.

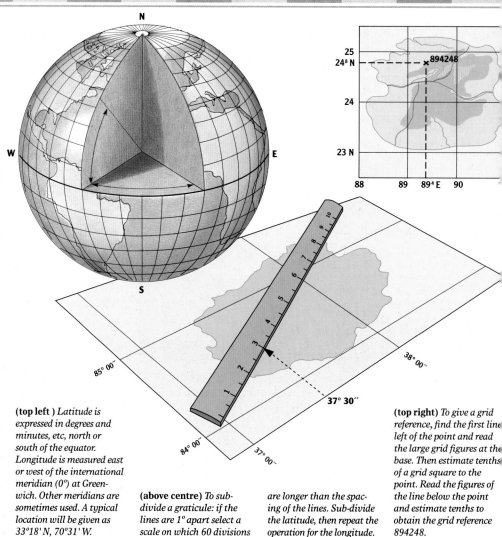

(top left) Latitude is expressed in degrees and minutes, etc, north or south of the equator. Longitude is measured east or west of the international meridian (0°) at Greenwich. Other meridians are sometimes used. A typical location will be given as 33°18' N, 70°31' W.

(above centre) To subdivide a graticule: if the lines are 1° apart select a scale on which 60 divisions are longer than the spacing of the lines. Sub-divide the latitude, then repeat the operation for the longitude.

(top right) To give a grid reference, find the first line left of the point and read the large grid figures at the base. Then estimate tenths of a grid square to the point. Read the figures of the line below the point and estimate tenths to obtain the grid reference 894248.

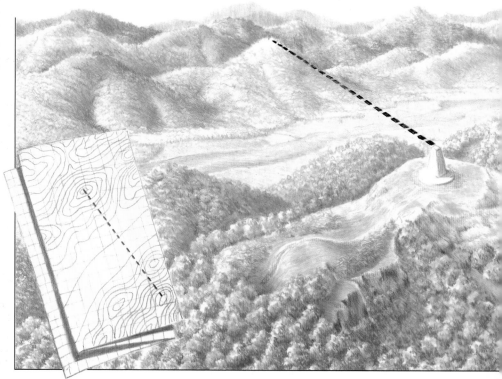

(right) *Map projection is the means by which the lines of latitude and longitude on the globe are transferred to a flat sheet of paper. This is conveniently performed by way of an encircling cylinder or by a cone or plane which rests on the globe. The projection can be made to preserve scale at any point or areas or else distances and bearings from a selected point. No single projection can preserve any two of these three properties - conformality, equal-area, equidistance. Scale errors may be reduced by making* the cylinder, cone or plane intersect the globe. The projection is then said to be secant conic, etc. The darker the colour on the map examples shown, the greater the level of distortion
(below) *Polar Azimuthal projection allows comparison of the various projections. Parallels are equally spaced in the equidistant projection. They become more widely spaced as they near the equator in the stereographic and gnomonic, and more closely spaced in the equal-area and orthographic.*

tangent cylinder

cylindrical projection

tangent cone

conic projection

tangent plane

azimuthal projection

secant cone

conic projection

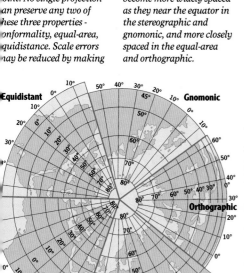

Equidistant

Gnomonic

Orthographic

Stereographic

Lambert Azimuthal Equal Area

(left) *Scale is the relationship of distances on a map compared to the corresponding distances on the surface of the Earth. Scale is indicated either by a 'bar scale' showing the length of kilometres, miles or nautical miles as represented on the map. Scale is also expressed as a 'representative fraction' e.g. 1/25,000 which means 1 cm on the map represents 250m on the ground (1 mm represents 25 m). A map at 1/6,000,000 is, compared with a map at 1/25,000 a small-scale map, the larger the number in the denominator, the smaller the scale. A degree of latitude is approximately equal to 111 km (about 69 miles or 60 nautical miles). Each meridian is therefore a kind of barscale which can be used to measure distances on a map or chart. Navigators in ships and aircraft make use of meridians in this way to plot distances.*

(right) *Relief representation. From the earliest times mountains have been shown on maps. For many centuries they were drawn in profile as seen from one direction, usually the south. Later viewed from above they were drawn as so-called 'hairy caterpillars'. By the end of the 18th century hachures were employed to give an accurate representation of slopes but they gave no indication of the elevation above sea-level. Spot heights provide such information for selected points. Contour lines also show elevations above sea-level. They replaced hachures from the mid-19th century onwards. Adding hypsometric (layer) tints aided the reading of relief. Hill-shading brings out the form of the land. A realistic depiction is obtained when contours, hypsometric tints and hill shading are used together on a map.*

Field Sketch

Hill Drawing

Hachures

Hachured Map

Contours

Contours with layer tints

Contours with layer tints and hill shading

Tonal Relief

THE USE OF MAPS

The scale and content of a map are determined by the purpose for which it was designed. Thematic maps are a valuable aid in the presentation of complex statistical data. Computers aid their production and increase their scope. Modern databases offer access to map data in digital form to an ever-widening range of users as well as providing new types of maps and related products.

MORE than 1000 years ago the Greeks distinguished geography from chorography. Geography was concerned with the whole world and chorography with only a local area. The word chorography has passed from our vocabulary but the word topography (to do with places) is used in its place. A topographic map contains details of the land surface appropriate for its scale. It is usually part of a map series whose sheets cover all or part of a country. It is typically the standard map of a national map series. Cadastral maps are maps of very large scale which serve the purposes of land ownership, valuation and taxation.

Scale is the dominant factor in determining the contents of maps. A compromise has to be made between what is desired and what can be achieved in the quantity of information included. Choice of scale and type of map is critical in the use of maps. Small scale maps are used for general planning but the need for larger scales becomes evident when more detailed information is needed of a specific area.

The English language, unlike other languages, makes a distinction between a chart and a map. In its original use, the word chart implied a nautical chart but aviators took over the word for their own navigational charts. Nautical charts pay little attention to the land. Aeronautical charts require much less topographical information than maps used on the ground. Elevations are in feet to conform with aircraft instrumentation. Originally aeronautical charts were of the same size as land maps but increases in the speed of aircraft necessitated a change in size. Many charts are four times their previous size to reduce the number handled by the navigator. Both at sea and in the air the nautical mile (1852m) is used for measuring distance.

Maps play an important part in recording and disseminating statistical information. Those maps which are specifically designed for a particular topic are known as thematic maps (maps with a theme). They range from simple diagrams to complex forms of the conventional map. Numerous special symbols have been invented in the presentation of statistics. Among the commonest terms are isopleths (lines of equal area), choropleths

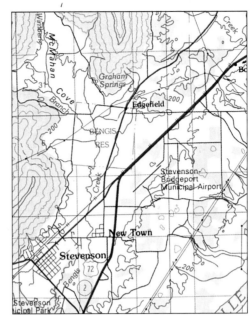

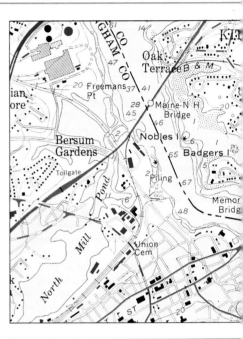

(above) *A topographic map at 1:100 000 scale has a wide range of uses, including study of terrain, land use, environmental planning, transportation and hydrological studies. Road widths and individual buildings are exaggerated. Other map detail is displaced.*
(above right) *A topographic map at a scale of 1:24 000 contains much more detail and has less exaggeration in the size of features than the map at 1:100 000. One mm represents 24m and more than 16 maps*

are required to cover the same area of ground as a map at 1:100 000 scale.
(right) *In a cadastral map at 1:1000 scale, map detail is drawn to scale without generalization. Maps of this type are used for recording land ownership, taxation and urban planning. Unless such maps are contoured, they are of limited use in engineering works.*
(below) *Isopleths, or isorithms, are lines which join points of the same numerical value. The maps use isopleths to show heat flow from the interior of the Earth.*

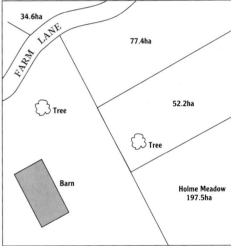

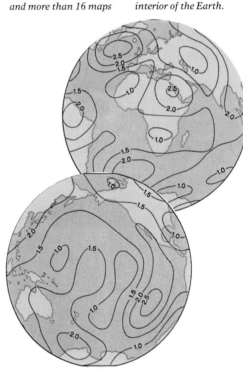

(top right) *Nautical charts show depths of water by soundings and bathymetric contours. Attention is paid to under-sea features, rocks, wrecks and other hazards and to lights, beacons and aids to navigation, including magnetic variation. The Mercator projection is used for sea charts.*
(right) *Relief, including man-made vertical obstructions, is of great importance in aeronautical charts. Navigation aids, aerodromes and other air information are shown at the expense of map detail not essential to air use. Elevations are in feet.*
(top far right) *Maps which show relief, like the one on the right, must, of necessity, be highly coloured and this*

makes political information difficult to extract when it is included in the same map. For this reason a separate political map, like the one on the left, is required.
(centre right) *Choropleth (measure per area) maps show statistical data by use of line patterns, or colour, applied to areas. Choropleth maps can be used to show density of population by country, state or province using data from a census.*
(below right) *Dot maps belong to the family of distribution maps. In a population map the dot represents a certain number of people. On the example shown, the density of dots gives an immediate impression of the distribution of world population.*

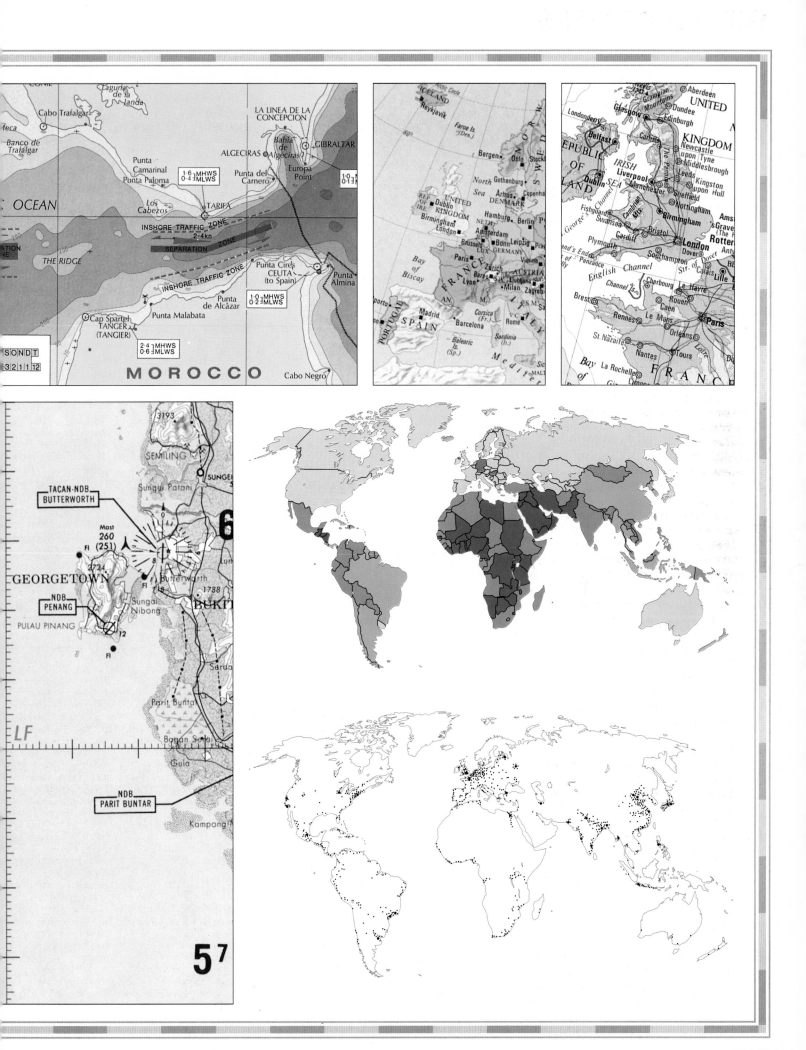

(areas of equal measure) and isorithms (lines of equal number).

Dots, circles, squares, cubes and spheres, as well as an untold number of pictorial symbols, graphs and bar charts are among the items used for thematic maps.

Cartograms are widely used in conveying statistical information. As its name implies, a cartogram is neither a true map nor a diagram. Roman road maps were an early type of cartogram. Road distances were given, but true road alignments were ignored. Determining relative areas of countries by visual comparison on a map is extremely difficult. The areas can be readily compared when they are converted to rectangular form in a cartogram. Some ingenuity is required in arranging the rectangular figures to preserve their geographical position in relation to other countries similarly portrayed.

A popular form of symbol is the pie-chart or pie-graph. It can be used like any other circular symbol, the value of the quantity being in proportion to the area of the circle. Giving the pie-graph thickness can add another set of values.

The computer processing of economic and other types of statistical data led to a requirement for systems capable of handling geographic information by computer. Geographic information systems (GIS) were developed as a tool for handling vast amounts of geographical information and associated data to supply an infinite range of outputs which include graphs, diagrams, cartograms, tabular summaries and maps. Applying the same computer techniques to the production of the ordinary topographic map was not feasible until computers of sufficient power and capacity were available at low cost. A major obstacle was the unavoidable requirement for a very large database whose

creation demanded a colossal amount of time and manpower. The benefits which flow from its creation are undeniable. Maps can be designed, produced and stored without going through the conventional processes of manual drafting and printing. Maps held in the computer can be displayed on a screen or can be transmitted from computer to computer. An infinite variety of data can be superimposed. The output can be a map or part of a map or a combination of parts of several maps extracted from the individual source maps which are stored in the database. Perspective views can be generated and construction and engineering problems solved on the computer screen. Such is the ultimate goal in the management of geographic information. That does not mean the end of the paper map. On the contrary, it promises a future in which an endless variety of paper maps can be produced to suit any purpose.

(far left) *A cartogram showing countries by area. In cartograms geographic shape is lost but the rectangular outline which replaces it allows areas to be readily compared. Economic and other statistical data are conveniently presented in this way.*
(below right) *Pie-charts or pie-graphs are used to present statistical data. When used on a map, the diameter of the circle can be made proportion-* *ate to the quantity involved.*
(below left) *Map data stored in a database can be viewed on a graphics screen in whole, or in part, in a range of scales. Any element can be selected for display. Information can be superimposed. Aerial photography or satellite imagery can be combined with the map data. Output can be in plotted form or as digital data.*

WORLD ATLAS

SYMBOLS

Relief

		Feet	Relief	Metres
⬭	Land contour	16404		5000
▲ 8848	Spot height (metres)	9843		3000
⩊	Pass	6562		2000
		3281		1000
▭	Permanent ice cap	1640		500
		656		200
		0	Land Dep.	Sea Level
		656		200
		13123		4000
		22966		7000

Hydrography

⬭	Submarine contour
▼ 11034	Ocean depth (metres)
(217)	Lake level
⌁	Reef
∿	River
⌁	Intermittent river
⌢	Falls
⌢	Dam
⌇	Gorge
⊔⊔⊔	Canal
⬭	Lake/Reservoir
⬭	Intermittent lake
⬭	Marsh/Swamp

Communications

Tunnel ══	Main railway
⊕	Main airport
- - - -	Track

Road representation varies with the scale category.

═══	Principal road	} 1:1M-1:2½M
───	Other main road	
───	Principal road	} 1:2½M-1:7½M
───	Other main road	
───	Principal road	1:7½M or smaller

Administration

───────	International boundary
─ ─ ─	Undefined/Disputed international boundary
·········	Cease-fire line
─·─·─	Internal division : First order
─··─··─	Internal division : Second order
▨ ◉ ⊙ / ◎ ▢ ▪	National capitals

Settlement

Each settlement is given a town stamp according to its relative importance and scale category.

		1:1M-1:2½M	1:2½M-1:7½M	1:7½M or smaller
▨		Major City	Major City	Major City
◉		City	City	City
◎		Large Town	Large Town	Large Town
⊙		Town	Town	Town
○		Small Town	Small Town	—
•		Village	—	—
⬭		Urban area (1:1M-1:2½M only)		

The size of type used for each settlement is graded to correspond with the appropriate town stamp.

Other features

∴	Ancient monument
⌣	Oasis
⬭	National Park
▲	Oil field
△	Gas field
─▪─▪─	Oil/Gas pipeline

Lettering

Various styles of lettering are used-each one representing a different type of feature.

ALPS	Physical feature	KENYA	Country name
Red Sea	Hydrographic feature	IOWA	Internal division
Paris	Settlement name	*(Fr.)*	Territorial administration

THE WORLD : Political

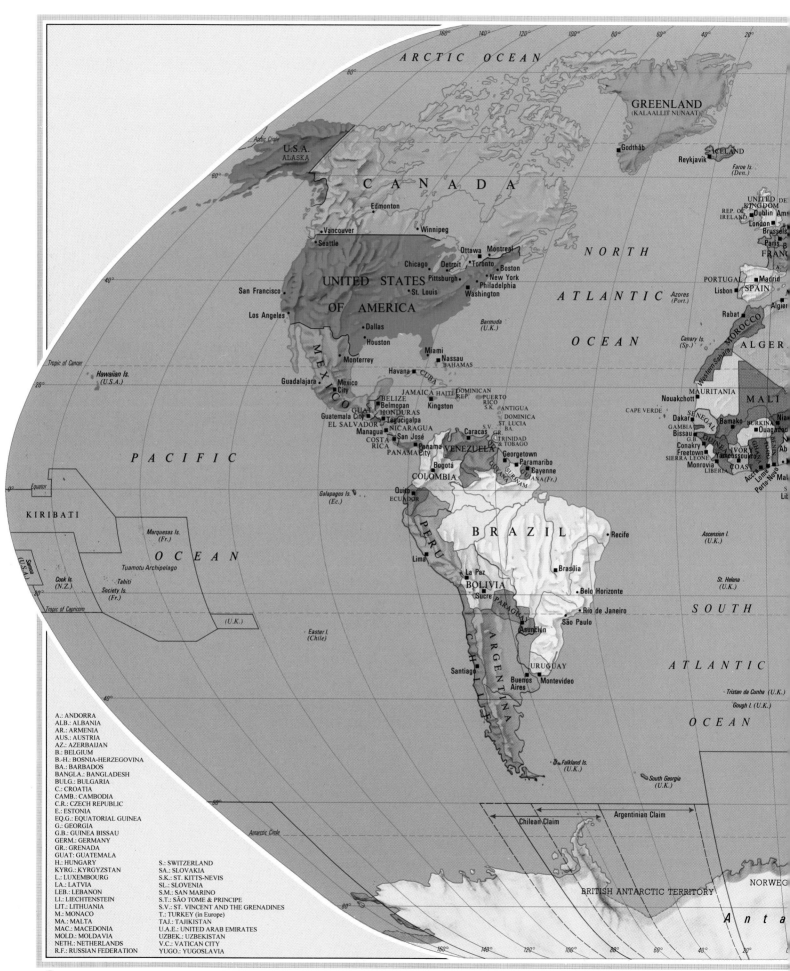

ARCTIC OCEAN

GREENLAND
(KALAALLIT NUNAAT)

Arctic Circle

U.S.A.
ALASKA

CANADA

Godthåb

Reykjavík   ICELAND

Faroe Is.
(Den.)

Edmonton

UNITED DE
KINGDOM
REP. OF   Dublin Ams
IRELAND   London
Brussels
Paris B
FRANC

Vancouver   Winnipeg

Seattle

Ottawa   Montreal

Chicago   Detroit   Toronto

NORTH

San Francisco

UNITED STATES   Pittsburgh   Boston
New York
Philadelphia

OF AMERICA   St. Louis   Washington

PORTUGAL   Madrid
Lisbon   SPAIN

ATLANTIC

Los Angeles

Azores
(Port.)

Algier

Dallas

Bermuda
(U.K.)

Rabat   MOROCCO

Houston

OCEAN

Canary Is.
(Sp.)   ALGER

Tropic of Cancer

Miami   Nassau

Monterrey   BAHAMAS

Havana   CUBA

MAURITANIA   MALI

Hawaiian Is.
(U.S.A.)

Nouakchott

CAPE VERDE

Guadalajara   Mexico
City

JAMAICA HAITI   DOMINICAN
REP.

BELIZE   PUERTO
RICO

Dakar   SENEGAL   Bamako   BURKINA   Nia
GAMBIA   Ouagadou
Bissau   G.B   GUINE

BELIZE
GUAT.   Belmopan   S.K.   ANTIGUA
HONDURAS   DOMINICA
Guatemala City   Tegucigalpa   ST. LUCIA
EL SALVADOR   BA.
Managua   NICARAGUA   S.V.
COSTA   San José   GR.
RICA   Caracas   TRINIDAD
PANAMA   Panama   & TOBAGO
City   VENEZUELA
Georgetown
Bogotá   Paramaribo
COLOMBIA   Cayenne
GUIANA (Fr.)

Conakry
Freetown
SIERRA LEONE
Monrovia   IVORY   Yamoussoukro
LIBERIA   COAST   Acce
Lome   Mal
Porto-Nov
Li

PACIFIC

Quito
ECUADOR

Galapagos Is.
(Ec.)

Equator

KIRIBATI

Marquesas Is.
(Fr.)

PERU

BRAZIL   Recife

Ascension I.
(U.K.)

OCEAN

Tuamotu Archipelago

Lima

La Paz   Brasília

Cook Is.
(N.Z.)

Samoa (U.S.A.)

Tahiti   BOLIVIA   Belo Horizonte
Society Is.   Sucre
(Fr.)

St. Helena
(U.K.)

Tropic of Capricorn

PARAGUAY   Rio de Janeiro

SOUTH

(U.K.)

Easter I.
(Chile)

São Paulo

Asunción

ATLANTIC

CHILE   ARGENTINA   URUGUAY

Santiago   Buenos   Montevideo
Aires

Tristan da Cunha (U.K.)

Gough I. (U.K.)

OCEAN

40°

Falkland Is.
(U.K.)

South Georgia
(U.K.)

Argentinian Claim

Chilean Claim

Antarctic Circle

BRITISH ANTARCTIC TERRITORY   NORWEG

Anta

160°   140°   120°   100°   80°   60°   40°   20°

A.: ANDORRA
ALB.: ALBANIA
AR.: ARMENIA
AUS.: AUSTRIA
AZ.: AZERBAIJAN
B.: BELGIUM
B.-H.: BOSNIA-HERZEGOVINA
BA.: BARBADOS
BANGLA.: BANGLADESH
BULG.: BULGARIA
C.: CROATIA
CAMB.: CAMBODIA
C.R.: CZECH REPUBLIC
E.: ESTONIA
EQ.G.: EQUATORIAL GUINEA
G.: GEORGIA
G.B.: GUINEA BISSAU
GERM.: GERMANY
GR.: GRENADA
GUAT.: GUATEMALA
H.: HUNGARY   S.: SWITZERLAND
KYRG.: KYRGYZSTAN   SA.: SLOVAKIA
L.: LUXEMBOURG   S.K.: ST. KITTS-NEVIS
LA.: LATVIA   SL.: SLOVENIA
LEB.: LEBANON   S.M.: SAN MARINO
LI.: LIECHTENSTEIN   S.T.: SÃO TOME & PRINCIPE
LIT.: LITHUANIA   S.V.: ST. VINCENT AND THE GRENADINES
M.: MONACO   T.: TURKEY (in Europe)
MA.: MALTA   TAJ.: TAJIKISTAN
MAC.: MACEDONIA   U.A.E.: UNITED ARAB EMIRATES
MOLD.: MOLDAVIA   UZBEK.: UZBEKISTAN
NETH.: NETHERLANDS   V.C.: VATICAN CITY
R.F.: RUSSIAN FEDERATION   YUGO.: YUGOSLAVIA

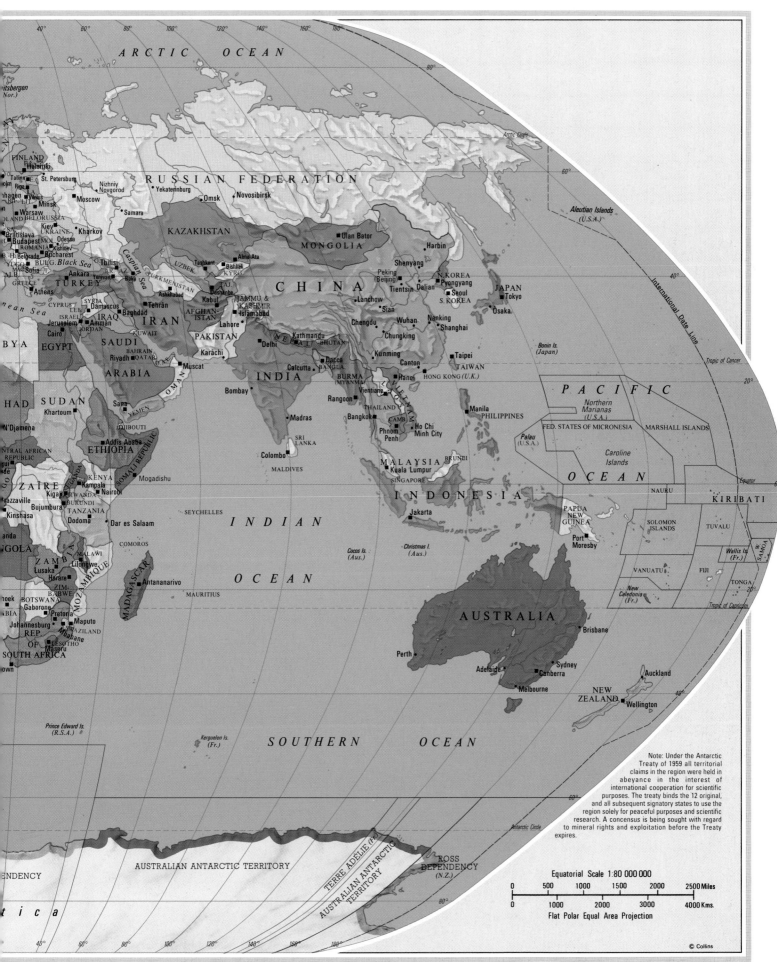

ARCTIC OCEAN

Arctic Circle

Spitsbergen (Nor.)

FINLAND
Helsinki
Tallinn
oln Riga
hagen Vilnius
Minsk
Warsaw
OLAND BELORUSSIA
Kiev UKRAINE
Budapest MOL
Bratislava ROMANIA
B-H Belgrade Bucharest
YUGO Sofia
MAC.E BULG. *Black Sea*
GREECE
Athens TURKEY Ankara

St. Petersburg

Nizhniy Novgorod
Moscow

Samara

Kharkov

Odessa
Kishinev

Tbilisi
Yerevan
Baku
ARAZ

Caspian Sea

R U S S I A N   F E D E R A T I O N

Yekaterinburg

Omsk   Novosibirsk

KAZAKHSTAN

Tashkent
UZBEK
Ashkhabad
TURKMENISTAN
Dushanbe
TAJ.

Alma-Ata
Bishkek
KYRG

Arctic Circle

60°

M O N G O L I A

Ulan Bator

Harbin

Shenyang

N. KOREA
Peking (Beijing)   Pyongyang
Tientsin   Dalian   Seoul
S. KOREA

40°

Aleutian Islands (U.S.A.)

International Date Line

C H I N A

Lanchow

Sian

JAPAN
Tokyo

Osaka

CYPRUS LEB.
Damascus
ISRAEL SYRIA
Jerusalem Amman
JORDAN
Cairo
EGYPT

IRAQ
Baghdad
KUWAIT

Tehran

IRAN

Kabul
AFGHAN-
ISTAN

JAMMU &
KASHMIR
Islamabad

Lahore

PAKISTAN

Kathmandu
N E P A L   BHUTAN

Chengdu

Wuhan

Chungking

Nanking
Shanghai

nean Sea

BAHRAIN
Riyadh QATAR
SAUDI
ARABIA
U.A.E.
Muscat
OMAN

Delhi

Karachi

Kunming

Canton

Taipei
TAIWAN

Bonin Is. (Japan)

Tropic of Cancer

20°

P A C I F I C

BYA

HAD SUDAN
Khartoum
N'Djamena

Sana
YEMEN

DJIBOUTI

Calcutta
BANGLA.
Dacca
BURMA
(MYANMAR)
Hanoi
HONG KONG (U.K.)

Bombay

I N D I A

Madras

Rangoon

Vientiane

L A O S   V I E T N A M

THAILAND

Manila
PHILIPPINES

Northern
Marianas
(U.S.A.)

FED. STATES OF MICRONESIA   MARSHALL ISLANDS

ETHIOPIA
Addis Ababa

CENTRAL AFRICAN
REPUBLIC

SRI
LANKA

Colombo

MALDIVES

Bangkok
CAMB.
Phnom
Penh

Ho Chi
Minh City

Palau
(U.S.A.)

Caroline
Islands

O C E A N

Equator

0°

ZAIRE
KENYA
Kampala
Kigali Nairobi
RWANDA
BURUNDI
Bujumbura
TANZANIA
Kinshasa Dodoma

UGANDA

SOMALI REPUBLIC

Mogadishu

MALAYSIA
Kuala Lumpur

SINGAPORE

BRUNEI

I N D O N E S I A

NAURU

KIRIBATI

azzaville

Dar es Salaam

SEYCHELLES

PAPUA
NEW
GUINEA

SOLOMON
ISLANDS

TUVALU

anda
GOLA

COMOROS

I N D I A N

Cocos Is.
(Aus.)

Christmas I.
(Aus.)

Port
Moresby

VANUATU

New
Caledonia
(Fr.)

FIJI

Wallis Is.
(Fr.)

W.
SAMOA

ZAMBIA
Lusaka
MALAWI
Lilongwe
MOZAMBIQUE

Harare
ZIM-
BABWE

Antananarivo

MADAGASCAR

O C E A N

MAURITIUS

A U S T R A L I A

Brisbane

TONGA

Tropic of Capricorn

noek BOTSWANA
Gaborone
BIA
Pretoria
Johannesburg Maputo
SWAZILAND
REP. Mbabane
OF LESOTHO
SOUTH AFRICA Maseru

Perth

Adelaide

Sydney
Canberra

Melbourne

Auckland

NEW
ZEALAND
Wellington

40°

Prince Edward Is.
(R.S.A.)

Kerguelen Is.
(Fr.)

S O U T H E R N   O C E A N

Note: Under the Antarctic
Treaty of 1959 all territorial
claims in the region were held in
abeyance in the interest of
international cooperation for scientific
purposes. The treaty binds the 12 original,
and all subsequent signatory states to use the
region solely for peaceful purposes and scientific
research. A concensus is being sought with regard
to mineral rights and exploitation before the Treaty
expires.

Antarctic Circle

60°

ENDENCY

AUSTRALIAN ANTARCTIC TERRITORY

TERRE ADÉLIE (Fr.)

AUSTRALIAN ANTARCTIC
TERRITORY

ROSS
DEPENDENCY
(N.Z.)

ctica

80°

Equatorial Scale 1:80 000 000

0	500	1000	1500	2000	2500 Miles
0	1000	2000	3000	4000 Kms.

Flat Polar Equal Area Projection

© Collins

3

THE WORLD : Physical

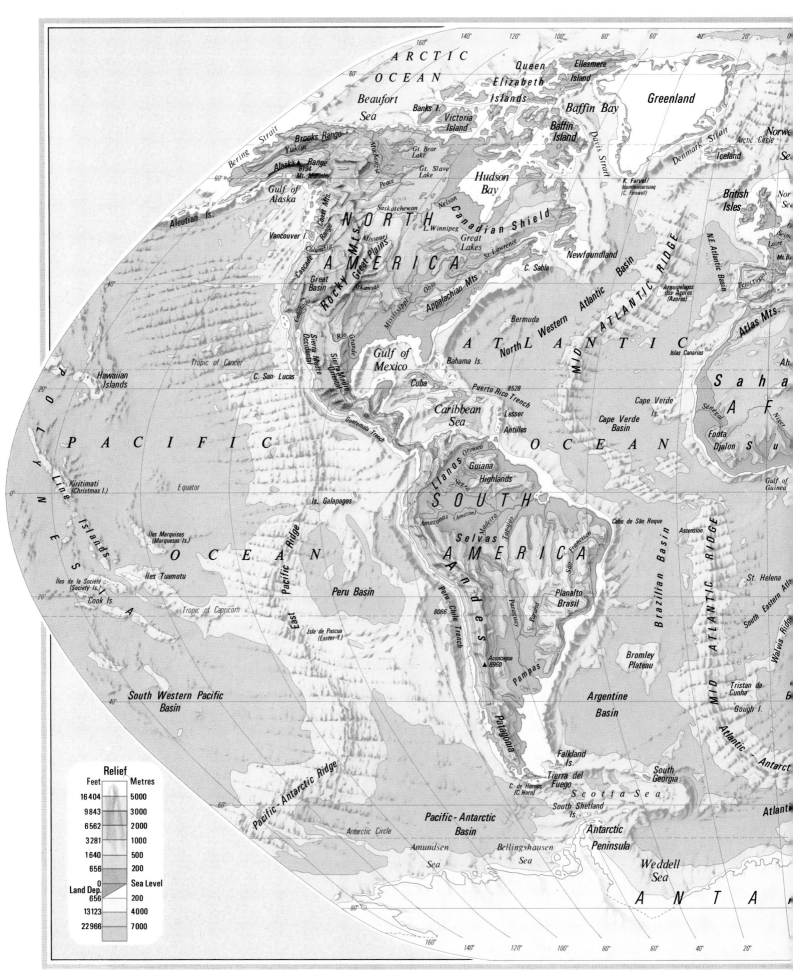

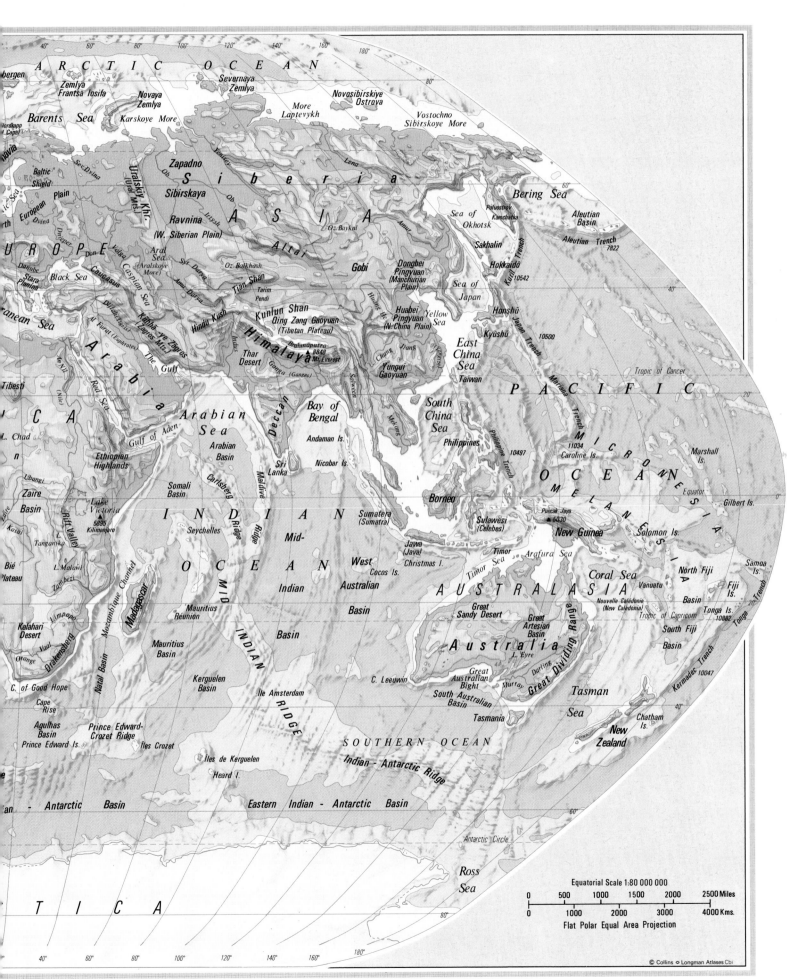

ARCTIC OCEAN

bergen
Zemlya
Frantsa Iosifa
Severnaya
Zemlya
Novosibirskiye
Ostrova
Novaya
Zemlya
More
Laptevykh
Vostochno
Sibirskoye More
Barents Sea
Karskoye More
Nordkapp
(Cape)

Baltic
Shield
Sev. Dvina
Zapadno
Sibirskaya
Yenisey
Lena
Bering Sea
Poluostrov
Kamchatka
Aleutian
Basin

European
Plain
Uralskiy Khr.
(Ural Mts.)
Sibirskaya
Ob
Ob
Irtysh
Sea of
Okhotsk
Aleutian Trench
7822

Don
Volga
Ravnina
(W. Siberian Plain)
Altai
Oz. Baykal
Amur
Sakhalin
Kuril Trench
10542
Hokkaidō

Dnieper
Aral
Sea
(Aralskoye
More)
Oz. Balkhash
Gobi
Dongbei
Pingyuan
(Manchurian
Plain)
Sea of
Japan
Honshū
Japan Trench
10500

EUROPE
Danube
Stara
Planina
Black Sea
Caucasus
Caspian Sea
Syr Darya
Amu Darya
Tian Shan
Tarim
Pendi
Hindu Kush
Kunlun Shan
Huang He
Chang Jiang
Huabei
Pingyuan
(N. China Plain)
Yellow
Sea
East
China
Sea
Kyūshū
Mariana Trench
10500

Stara
Planina
Kūhhā-ye Zagros
(Zagros Mts.)
Dzhambajtau
Qing Zang Gaoyuan
(Tibetan Plateau)
Himalaya
8848
Mt. Everest
Yungui
Gaoyuan
Taiwan
Tropic of Cancer

anean
Sea
Al Furāt (Euphrates)
The Gulf
Arabia
Indus
Thar
Desert
Brahmaputra
Ganga (Ganges)
Chang Jiang
Salween
South
China
Sea
PACIFIC
20°

Tibesti
Red Sea
Nile
Arabian
Sea
Deccan
Bay of
Bengal
Andaman Is.
Mekong
Philippines
Mariana Trench
11034
10497
Caroline Is.
MICRONESIA
Marshall
Is.

L. Chad
Gulf of Aden
Arabian
Basin
Sri
Lanka
Nicobar Is.
Philippine Trench
OCEAN

CA
n
Ethiopian
Highlands
Somali
Basin
Carlsberg
Maldive
Sumatera
(Sumatra)
Borneo
Sulawesi
(Celebes)
Puncak Jaya
6030
New Guinea
MELANESIA
Solomon Is.
Gilbert Is.
Equator
0°

Ubangi
Zaire
Basin
Lake
Victoria
5895
Kilimanjaro
Seychelles
INDIAN
Ridge
Ridge
Mid-
Indian
West
Australian
Jawa
(Java)
Christmas I.
Cocos Is.
Timor
Arafura Sea
North Fiji
Basin
Samoa
Is.

Kasai
L. Tanganyika
L. Malawi
Tanzezi
OCEAN
MID
Basin
Basin
Timor
Sea
Coral Sea
Vanuatu
Fiji
Is.

Bié
Plateau
Mozambique Channel
Madagascar
Mauritius
Réunion
Mauritius
Basin
AUSTRALASIA
Nouvelle Calédonie
(New Caledonia)
Tonga Is.
10882
South Fiji
Basin
Tropic of Capricorn

Kalahari
Desert
Drakensberg
Limpopo
Natal Basin
INDIAN
Kerguelen
Basin
Great
Sandy Desert
Great
Artesian
Basin
Great Dividing Range
Tonga Trench

Orange
Vaal
Ile Amsterdam
Australia
L. Eyre
Darling
Kermadec Trench
10047

C. of Good Hope
Cape
Rise
Prince Edward-
Crozet Ridge
Iles Crozet
RIDGE
C. Leeuwin
Great
Australian
Bight
Murray
Tasman

Agulhas
Basin
Prince Edward Is.
Iles de Kerguelen
South Australian
Basin
Tasmania
Sea
Chatham
Is.

Heard I.
SOUTHERN OCEAN
New
Zealand

Indian - Antarctic Ridge

an - Antarctic Basin
Eastern Indian - Antarctic Basin
60°

Antarctic Circle

Ross
Sea

TICA
80°

Equatorial Scale 1:80 000 000

0   500   1000 1500 2000   2500 Miles

0   1000   2000   3000   4000 Kms.

Flat Polar Equal Area Projection

© Collins ◇ Longman Atlases Cbi

5

ARCTIC OCEAN

North America

Spitsbergen
(Nor.)

Barents
Sea

Novaya
Zemlya
(Rus. Fed.)

Denmark Strait

70°

Arctic Circle

ICELAND

Reykjavik

Faroe Is.
(Den.)

60°

Bergen

Oslo

NORWAY

Stockholm

SWEDEN

FINLAND

Helsinki

St. Petersburg
(Leningrad)

RUSSIAN

Nizhniy
Novgorod

North
Sea

Gothenburg

Tallinn

ESTONIA

Moscow

FEDERATION

Árhus

Copenhagen

Riga

LATVIA

Samara

NORTH

REP.
OF
IRE.

Dublin

UNITED
KINGDOM

DENMARK

LITHUANIA

Vilnius

R.F.

ATLANTIC

50°

Birmingham

Hamburg

Berlin

POLAND

Minsk

BELORUSSIA

Kharkov

London

NETH.

Amsterdam

Warsaw

Łódź

Kiev

ATLANTIC

B.

Bonn

Leipzig

Brussels

LUX.

GERMANY

CZ.R.

Prague

Brno

UKRAINE

Azores
(Port.)

40°

Paris

Zurich

Vienna

SLOVAKIA

MOLDAVIA

OCEAN

FRANCE

SW.

Bratislava

Kishinev

Berne

AUSTRIA

Budapest

Odessa

Caspian Sea

Lyon

L.

SLOV.

HUNGARY

Oporto

Bay
of
Biscay

Milan

Ljubljana

Zagreb

CRO.

ROMANIA

Bucharest

Tbilisi

Lisbon

PORTUGAL

Madrid

AN.

ITALY

S.M.

B.-H.

Sarajevo

YUG.

Belgrade

Black Sea

GEORGIA

ARM.

AZER.

Baku

Corsica
(Fr.)

Rome

Sofia

BULGARIA

Istanbul

Yerevan

BAIJAN

SPAIN

Barcelona

Skopje

T.

OCEAN

Balearic
Is.
(Sp.)

Sardinia
(It.)

MAC.

Tirane

ALB.

Salonika

GREECE

30°

Madeira
(Port.)

Canary Islands
(Sp.)

Sicily

MALTA

Crete

Athens

Mediterranean Sea

Tropic of Cancer

20°

10°

0°

Equator

Africa

10°

SOUTH

20°

ATLANTIC

Tropic of Capricorn

30°

OCEAN

60°

South America

ALB.: ALBANIA
AN.: ANDORRA
B.: BELGIUM
B.-H.: BOSNIA-
          HERZEGOVINA
CRO.: CROATIA
CZ.R.: CZECH REPUBLIC
L.: LIECHTENSTEIN
LUX.: LUXEMBOURG
M.: MONACO
MAC.: MACEDONIA
NETH. NETHERLANDS
REP. OF IRE.: REPUBLIC OF IRELAND
SLOV.: SLOVENIA
S.M.: SAN MARINO
SW.: SWITZERLAND
T.: TURKEY (in Europe)
V.C.: VATICAN CITY

6

EUROPE

© Collins

EUROPE

Relief

Feet		Metres
16 404		5000
9843		3000
6562		2000
3281		1000
1640		500
656		200
0		Sea Level
Land Dep.		
656		200
13123		4000
22966		7000

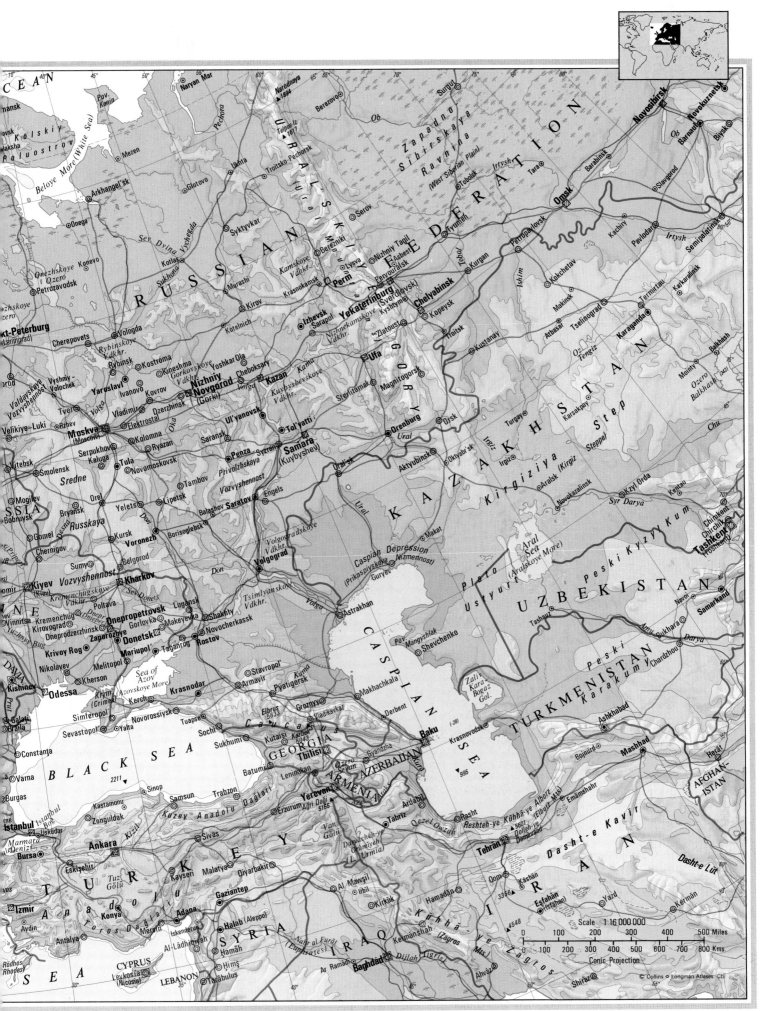

CEAN

Mezen

Kólskiy
Poluostrov

Beloye More (White Sea)

Naryan Mar

Pov.
Kanin

Narodnaya
▲1894

Berezovo

Ob

Surgut

Novosibirsk

Novokuznetsk

Bisyk

Onega

Arkhangel'sk

Pechora

Troitsko-Pechorsk

Ukhta

Zapadno
Sibirskaya
Ravnina
(West Siberian Plain)

Irtysh

Tara

Barabinsk

Ob

Barnaul

Onezhskoye
Ozero

Petrozavodsk

Konevo

Sukhona

Syktyvkar

Talpos Iz
▼1617

URAL'SKIYE

Serov

Tobol'sk

Tyumen'

Omsk

Petropavlovsk

Kachiry

Pavlodar

Irtysh

Semipalatinsk

zhskoye
zero

Vologda

Kotlas

Ser Dvina

Vychegda

Murashi

Kamskoye
Vdkhr.

Berezniki

Nizhniy Tagil

Asbest

Pervoural'sk

Tobol

Kurgan

Ishim

Makinsk

Kokchetav

Tselinograd

Atbasar

Karakalinsk

RUSSIAN

FEDERATION

kt-Peterburg
(Leningrad)

Cherepovets

Kirov

Kotel'nich

Krasnokamsk

Perm

Sarapul

Sverdlovsk)

Yekaterinburg

Chelyabinsk

Kopeysk

Zlatoust

Troitsk

Kustanay

GORY

Turgay

Karsakpay

Oz.
Tengiz

Karaganda

Mointy

Ozero
Balkhash

Balkhash

Rybinskoye
Vdkhr.

Rybinsk

Yaroslavl'

Ivanovo

Kovrov

Yoshkar Ola

Izhevsk

Kama

Nizhnekamskoye
Vdkhr.

Ufa

Sterlitamak

Magnitogorsk

Irgiz

Irgiz

KAZAKHSTAN

Kirgiziya Step

Steppei

Chu

rod

Vyshniy-
Volochek

Tver'

Vladimir

Dzerzhinsk

Nizhniy
Novgorod
(Gorki)

Cheboksary

Kazan

Volga

Kuybyshevskoye
Vdkhr.

Orsk

Ural

Valdayskaya
Vozvyshennost'

Moskva
(Moscow)

Elektrostal

Kolomna

Ryazan

Ul'yanovsk

Saransk

Tol'yatti

Orenburg

Aktyubinsk

Okyabr'sk

Aralsk (Kirgiz)

Novokazalinsk

Kzyl Orda

Kentau

Chimkent

Velikiye-Luki

Serpukhov

Kaluga

Tula

Novomoskovsk

Penza

Syzran

Samara
(Kuybyshev)

Privolzhskaya

Ural'sk

Makat

Tashkent

Chirchik

SSA

Vitebsk

Smolensk

Sredne

Orel

Yelets

Lipetsk

Tambov

Balashov

Saratov

Engels

Vozvyshennost'

Syr Darya

PESKI
Kyzyl Kum

Mogilev

Bryansk

Russkaya

Kursk

Borisoglebsk

Volgogradskoye
Vdkhr.

Caspian Depression

Makat

Aral
Sea
(Aralskoye More)

Bobruysk

Gomel'

Chernigov

Belgorod

Voronezh

Don

Volgograd

(Prikaspiyskaya Nizmennost')

Guryev

Plato
Ustyurt
(Aralskoye More)

UZBEKISTAN

Samarkand

Navoi

omir

Kiyev
(Kiev)

Kharkov

Kremenchugskoye
Vdkhr.

Poltava

Lugansk

Shakhty

Tsimlyanskoye
Vdkhr.

Volga

Astrakhan

Pov.
Mangyshlak

Shevchenko

Tashauz

Sukhara

Amu

Chardzhou

Darya

NE

Vinnitsa

Kremenchug

Kirovograd

Dneprodzerzhinsk

Dnepropetrovsk

Zaporozhye

Makeyevka

Gorlovka

Donetsk

Novocherkassk

Rostov

Taganrog

CASPIAN

Zaliv
Kara
Bogaz
Gol

Peski

Karakumy

TURKMENISTAN

Ashkhabad

Yuzhnyy Bug

Krivoy Rog

Nikolayev

Melitopol'

Mariupol'

Sea of
Azov
(Azovskoye More)

Kerch

Kherson

Kuma

Stavropol'

Armavir

Pyatigorsk

Makhachkala

SEA

(-28)

Krasnovodsk

Bojnurd

Mashhad

Herat

AFGHAN-
ISTAN

DAVIA

Kishinev

Odessa

Simferopol

Krym
(Crimea)

Novorossiysk

Krasnodar

Groznyy

Vladikavkaz

Derbent

Galaţi

Brăila

Sevastopol

Yalta

Tuapse

Sochi

Elbrus
5633

Caucasus

5043

Kazbek

Kutaisi

Sukhumi

Batumi

Leninakan

Gyandzha

Baku

(-28)

Kúhhá-ye Alborz
(Elburz Mts)

5601

Emamshahr

Reshteh-ye

Dolfeh-ye
Damavand

Constanta

Varna

Burgas

BLACK SEA

2211 ▼

Sinop

Samsun

Trabzon

GEORGIA

Tbilisi

Ozero
Sevan

AZERBAIJAN

Kura

995 ▲

Rasht

Qezel Owzan

Qom

Tehrān

Dasht-e Kavir

Dasht-e Lūt

Istanbul
İstanbul
Boğ.

Kastamonu

Zonguldak

Kuzey Anadolu Dağları

Erzurum

ARMENIA

Yerevan

Agri Daği
5165

Ararat

Tabriz

Marmara
Denizi

Bursa

Ankara

Eskişehir

Sivas

Van
Gölü

Darvácheh-ye
Orumiyeh
(L. Urmia)

3356

Hamadān

Esfahan
(Isfahan)

Kashan

Kerman

Yazd

İzmir

Konya

Anadolu

Kayseri

Malatya

Diyarbakir

TURKEY

Al Mawşil

İrbil

Kirkūk

Kermanshah

Kúhhá-ye Zagros
(Zagros Mts)

4548

Tuz
Gölü

Toros Dağları

Aydın

Antalya

Adana

Mersin

Gaziantep

İskenderun

Halab (Aleppo)

Ḥamāh

Nahr al Furāt
(Euphrates)

SYRIA

Ar Ramadi

IRAQ

Baghdād

Dijlah (Tigris)

Ahvāz

Shiraz

Rhodes

Ródhos

SEA

CYPRUS
Leukosia
(Nicosia)

LEBANON

Al-Ládhiqiyah

Ḥimş

Tarābulus

Scale 1 : 16 000 000

0   100   200   300   400   500 Miles

0   100   200   300   400   500   600   700   800 Kms

Conic Projection

© Collins ○ Longman Atlases Cbi

9

BRITISH ISLES

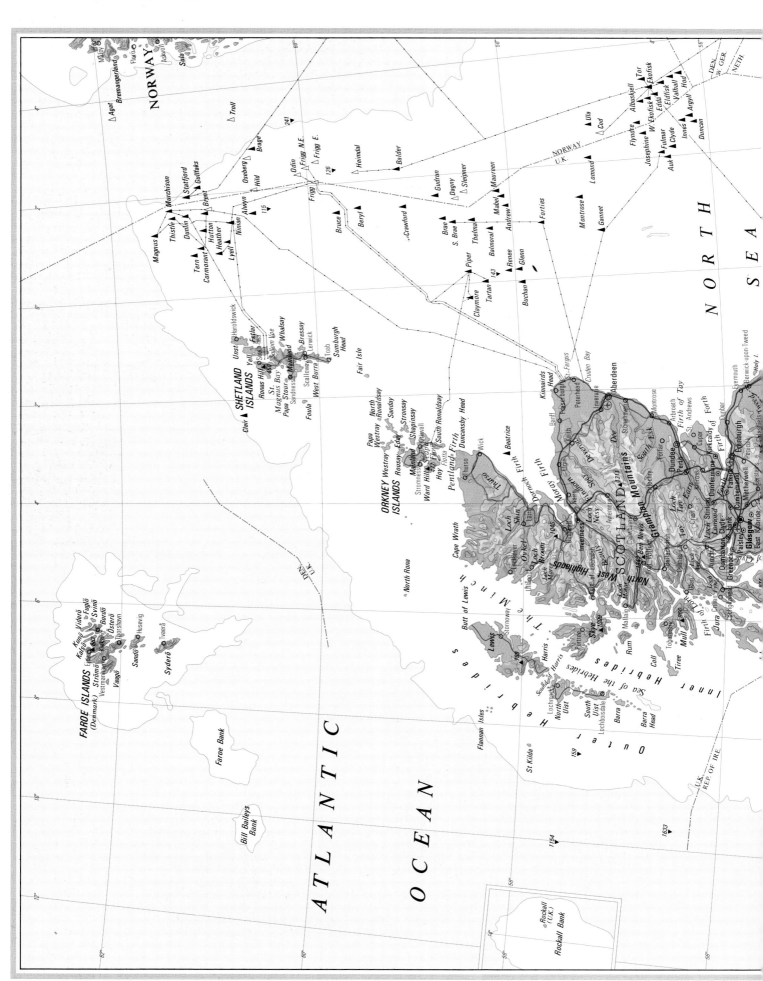

NORWAY

Måløy
Askvøll
Sula
Bremangerland
Florø

△ Agat

△ Troll

241

Murchison ▲
Statfjord ▲
Gullfaks ▲
Brent ▲
△ Oseberg
Hild △
Odin □
Frigg N.E. □
Frigg △
Frigg E. □
126

Magnus ▲
Thistle ▲
Dunlin ▲
Hutton ▲
Heather ▲
Tern ▲
Cormorant ▲
Lyell ▲
Ninian ▲
Alwyn △
115

Frigg

△ Heimdal

△ Balder

Bruce ▲
Beryl ▲

△ Gudrun
Dagny □
□ Sleipner

Maureen ▲
Mabel ▲
Andrew ▲

Forties ▲

NORWAY
U.K.

Ula △
△ Cod
Lomond △

Flyndre ▲
Josephine ▲
Auk ▲

W. Ekofisk ▲
Edda ▲
Fulmar ▲

Albuskjell ▲
Tor ▲
Ekofisk ▲
Eldfisk ▲
Valhall ▲
Hod ▲
Argyll ▼
Innes ▼
Duncan ▼

DEN.
W. GER.
NETH.

.Crawford

Brae ▲
S. Brae ▲
Thelma ▲

Balmoral ▲
Renee ▲
Glenn ▲

Montrose ▲
Gannet ▲

Piper ▲
Claymore ▲
Tartan 43

Buchan ▲

N   O   R   T   H

S   E   A

Hardlswick
Unst
Fetlar
Yell
South Yell
Sullom Voe
Whalsay
Bressay
Lerwick
SHETLAND
ISLANDS
Ronas Hill
St.
Magnus Bay
Mainland
Papa Stour
Sandness
Scalloway
West Burra
Clair ▲
Foula
Toab
Sumburgh
Head

Fair Isle

Aberdeen
Cruden Bay
Peterhead
Fraserburgh
Kinnairds
Head
St.-Fergus
Inverurie
Banff
Keith
Elgin
Strathdon
Inverness
Nairn
Grantown
Forres
Elgin
Montrose
Arbroath
Firth of Tay
St. Andrews
Dundee
Forfar
Perth
Cupar
Kirkcaldy
Firth of Forth
Dunfermline
Dunbar

Beatrice ▲

Wick

Thurso
Dunnet Head
Duncansby Head
Pentland Firth
Hoy
Flotta
South Ronaldsay

ORKNEY
ISLANDS
Westray
Rousay
Eday
Shapinsay
Mainland
Stromness
Kirkwall
Scapa
Flow
Ward Hill
Papa
Westray
North
Ronaldsay
Sanday
Stronsay

Cape Wrath

Loch
Shin

• North Rona

Kinlochbervie
Scourie
Loch
Broom
Ullapool

Dornoch Firth
Moray Firth
Cromarty Firth
Loch
Ness
Ben Nevis
1346
Loch
Ericht
Loch
Tay

Grampian Mountains
SCOTLAND
4431

Dee
Devon
Spey
South Esk

Loch
Lomond
Loch
Long
Stirling

Dalwhinnie
Aviemore

North
West
Highlands
Cairngorm
Mountains

Butt of Lewis
Stornoway
Lewis

The Minch

Harris
998

Skye
Uig

Rum

Mallaig
Loch
Linnhe
Oban

Ben More
966

Coll
Tiree
Mull

Jura
Islay

Firth of
Lorn

Inner

Hebrides

Sea of the Hebrides

Flannan Isles

St Kilda

Lochmaddy
North
Uist
South
Uist
Lochboisdale
Barra
Barra
Head

Sollas
Harris

Inner
Hebrides

159

Glasgow
Paisley
Greenock
Dumbarton
Clyde
East Kilbride
Motherwell
Cumbernauld
Hamilton
Edinburgh

Eyemouth
Berwick-upon-Tweed
Holy I.
Peebles

U.K.
REP. OF IRE.

A   T   L   A   N   T   I   C

O   C   E   A   N

FAROE ISLANDS
(Denmark)
Kunø
Kalsø
Østerø
Vestmanhavn
Vaagø
Strømø
Bordø
Svinø
Fuglø
Viderø
Thorshavn
Hvalsvig
Nolsø
Sandø
Syderø
Vaerø

Faroe Bank

Faroe Bank

DEN.
U.K.

Bill Baileys
Bank

1154

1633

58°
58°

Rockall
(U.K.)
Rockall
Bank

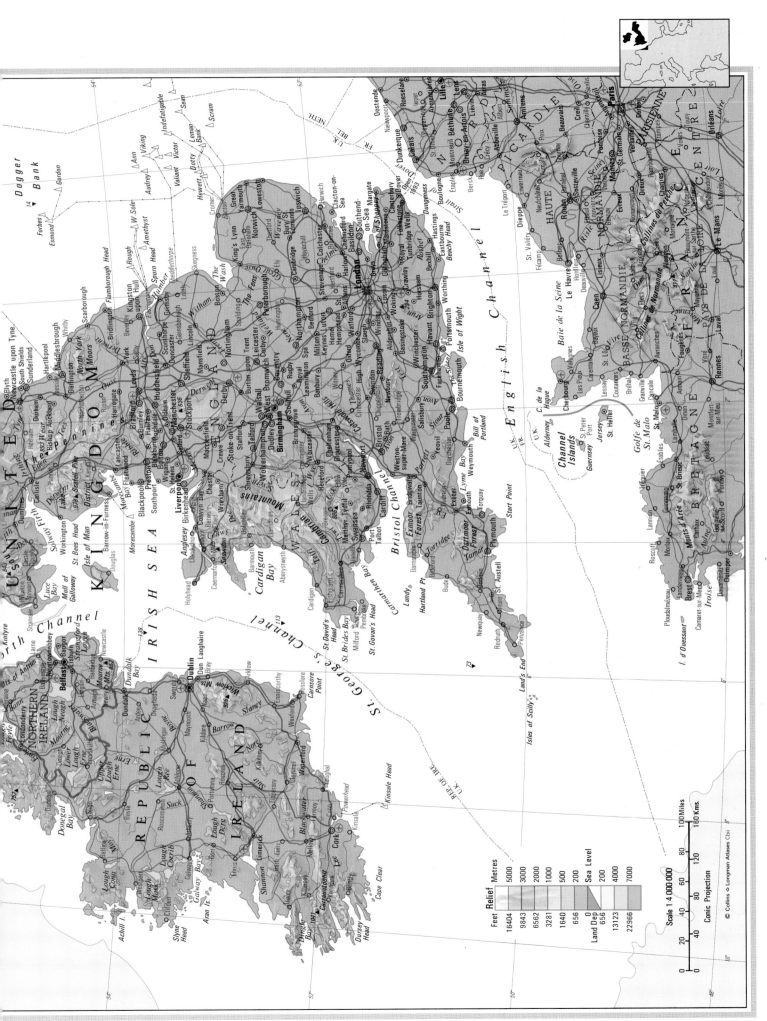

ENGLAND AND WALES

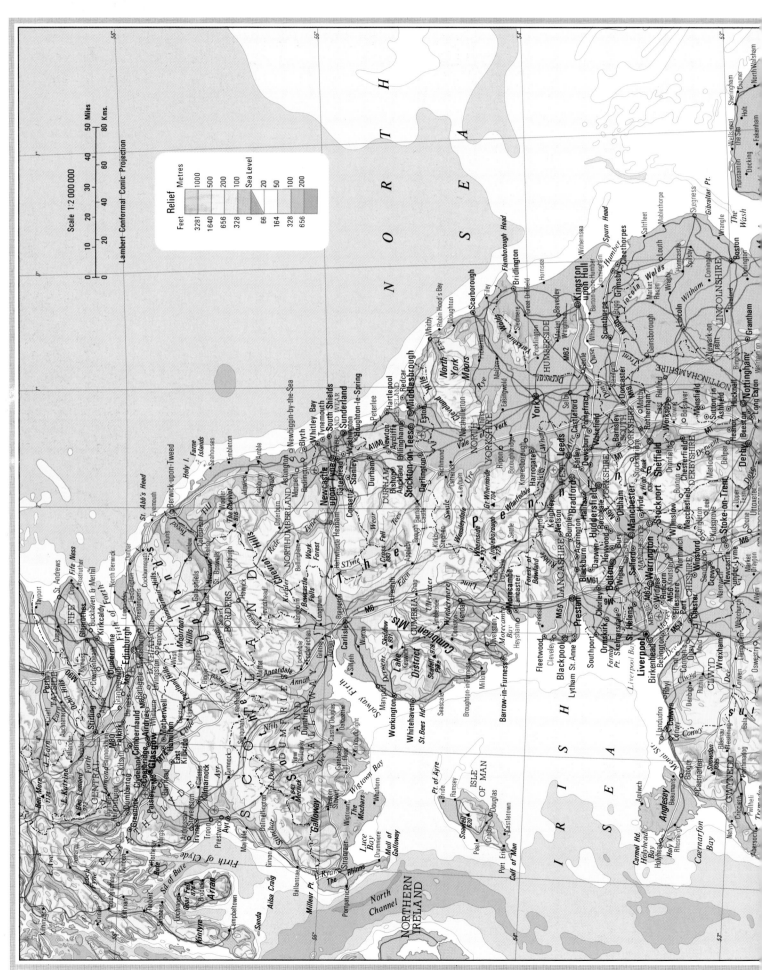

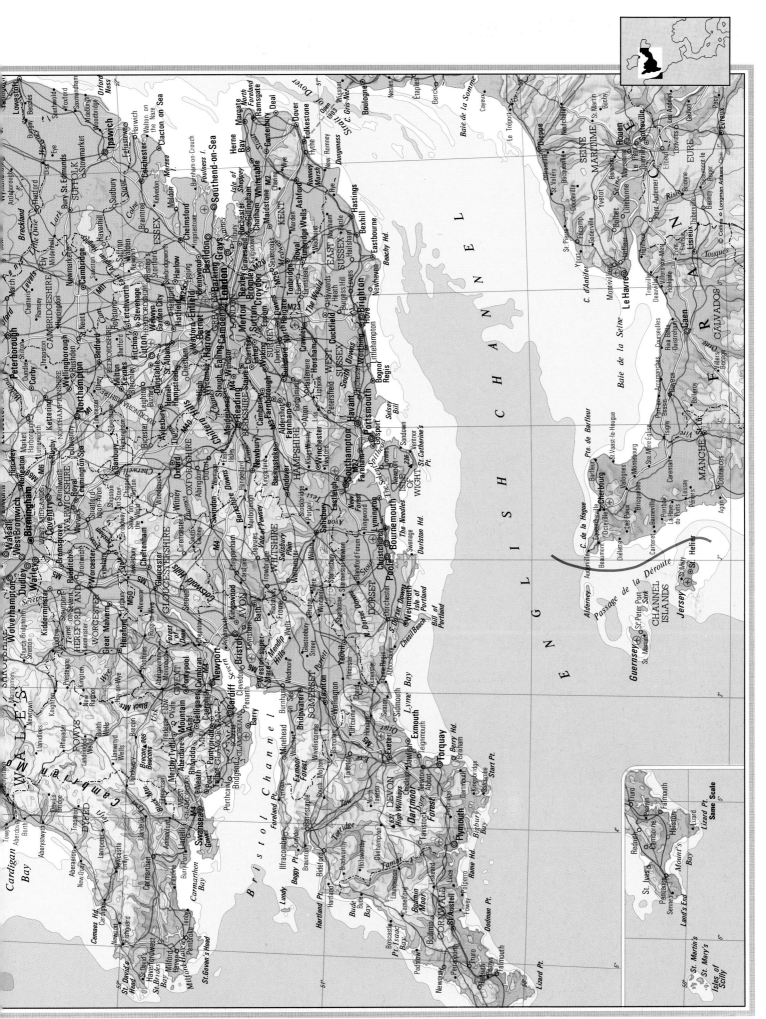

SCOTLAND

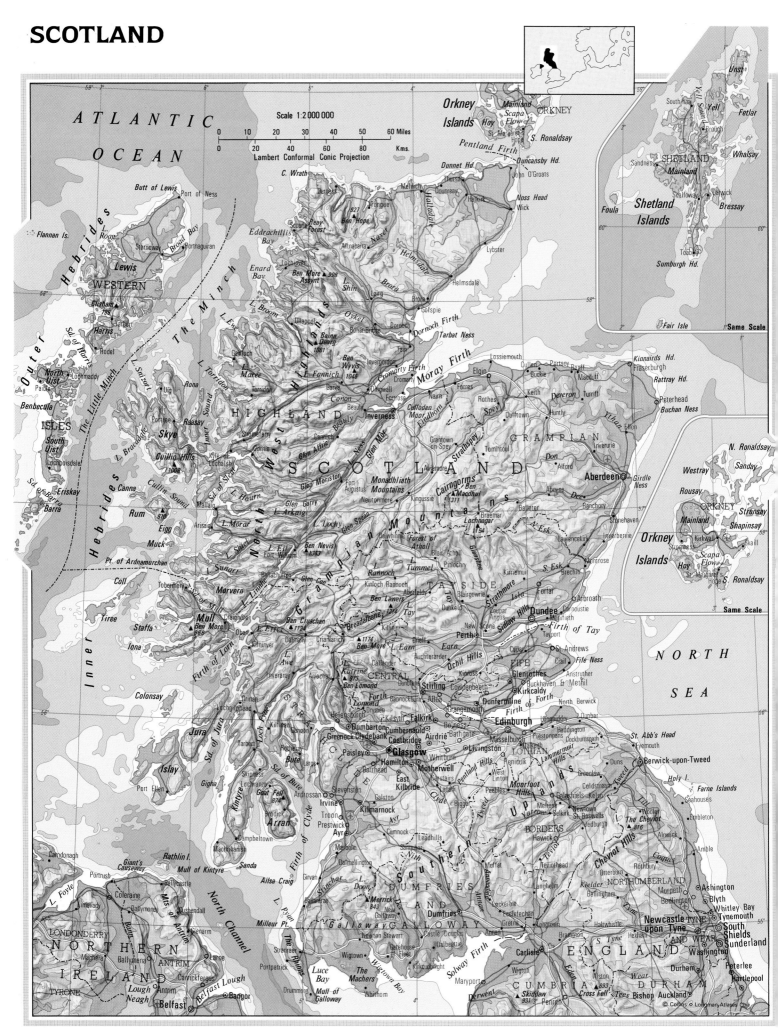

Scale 1:2 000 000

0 10 20 30 40 50 60 Miles

0 20 40 60 80 Kms.

Lambert Conformal Conic Projection

ATLANTIC
OCEAN

Orkney
Islands

Shetland
Islands

NORTH
SEA

ENGLAND

NORTHERN
IRELAND

14

IRELAND

Relief

Feet	Metres
3281	1000
1640	500
656	200
328	100
0	Sea Level
66	20
164	50
328	100
656	200

Scale 1: 2 000 000

0 10 20 30 40 Miles

0 20 40 60 Kms.

Lambert Conformal Conic Projection

© Collins ◇ Longman Atlases Cbiii

THE LOW COUNTRIES

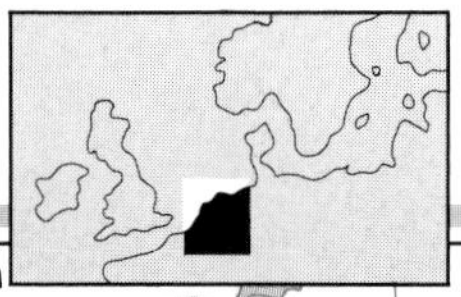

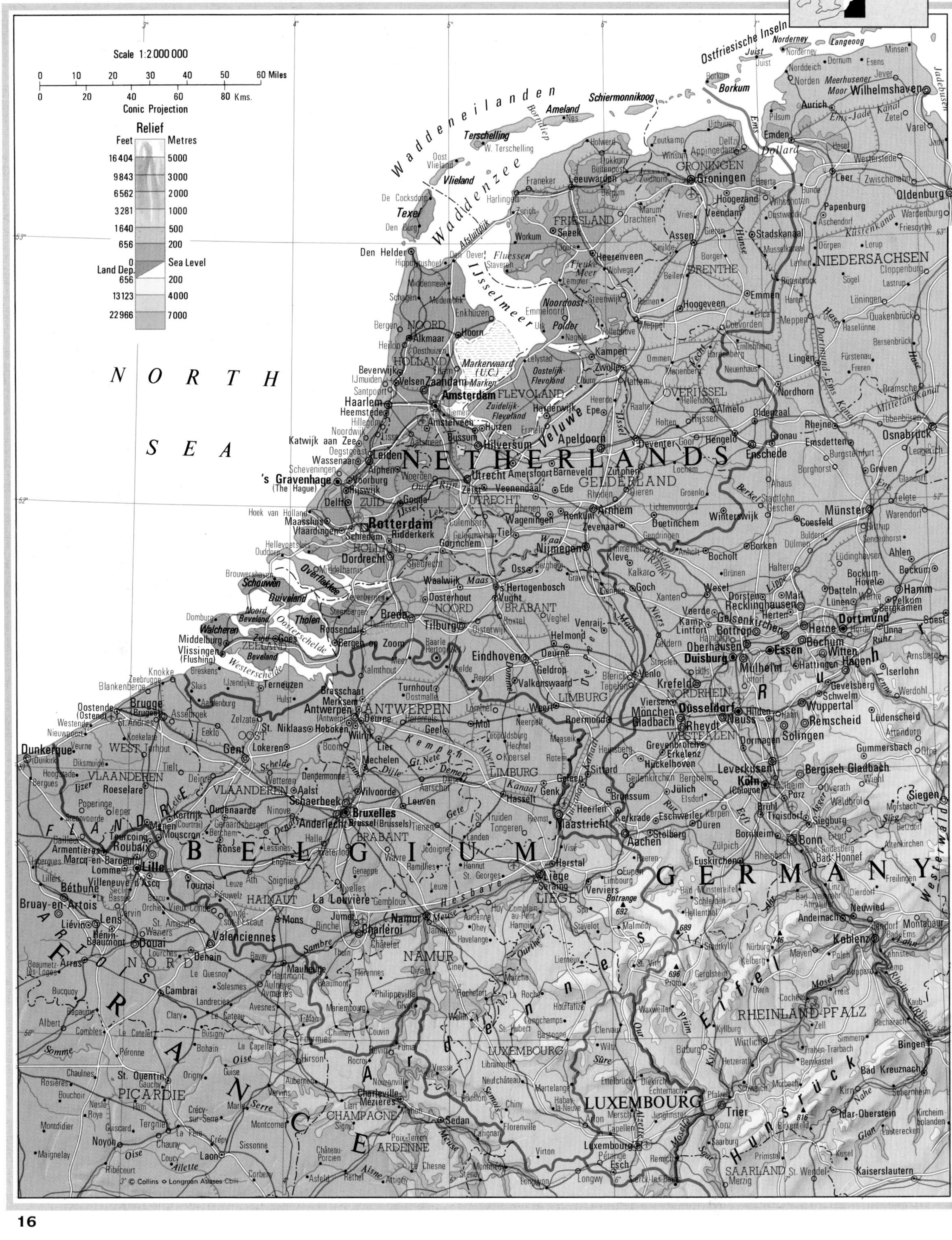

Scale 1:2 000 000
0 10 20 30 40 50 60 Miles
0 20 40 60 80 Kms.
Conic Projection
Relief
Feet Metres
16404 5000
9843 3000
6562 2000
3281 1000
1640 500
656 200
0 Sea Level
Land Dep.
656 200
13123 4000
22966 7000
NORTH SEA
NETHERLANDS
BELGIUM
GERMANY
FRANCE
LUXEMBOURG
Waddeneilanden
Waddenzee
IJsselmeer
Ostfriesische Inseln
Texel
Vlieland
Terschelling
Ameland
Schiermonnikoog
Borkum
Juist
Norderney
Langeoog
Den Helder
Alkmaar
Haarlem
Amsterdam
Zaandam
Leiden
's Gravenhage (The Hague)
Rotterdam
Dordrecht
Utrecht
Hilversum
Amersfoort
Apeldoorn
Arnhem
Nijmegen
Groningen
Leeuwarden
Zwolle
Enschede
Hengelo
Eindhoven
Tilburg
Breda
's Hertogenbosch
Maastricht
Vlissingen (Flushing)
Middelburg
FRIESLAND
GRONINGEN
DRENTHE
OVERIJSSEL
FLEVOLAND
GELDERLAND
UTRECHT
NOORD HOLLAND
ZUID HOLLAND
ZEELAND
NOORD BRABANT
LIMBURG
Noordoost-Polder
Oostelijk-Flevoland
Zuidelijk-Flevoland
Markerwaard (U.C.)
Afsluitdijk
Veluwe
Oosterschelde
Westerschelde
Walcheren
Schouwen
Duiveland
Tholen
Brugge
Oostende (Ostend)
Gent
Antwerpen (Antwerp)
ANTWERPEN
Bruxelles Brussel (Brussels)
BRABANT
Mechelen
Leuven
Liège
LIÈGE
Namur
NAMUR
Charleroi
Mons
HAINAUT
LUXEMBOURG
VLAANDEREN
WEST VLAANDEREN
OOST VLAANDEREN
Kempen
Hesbaye
Ardennes
Luxembourg
Dunkerque
Lille
Roubaix
Tourcoing
Valenciennes
Douai
Lens
Arras
Cambrai
St. Quentin
Laon
Sedan
Charleville-Mézières
NORD
PICARDIE
CHAMPAGNE-ARDENNE
ARTOIS
FLANDRE
Köln (Cologne)
Düsseldorf
Duisburg
Essen
Dortmund
Bochum
Wuppertal
Aachen
Bonn
Koblenz
Trier
Münster
Osnabrück
Oldenburg
Wilhelmshaven
Emden
NIEDERSACHSEN
NORDRHEIN WESTFALEN
RHEINLAND-PFALZ
SAARLAND
Ruhr
Eifel
Hunsrück
Westerwald
Rhein
Maas
Meuse
Schelde
Moselle
Sambre
Somme
Oise
Ems
3° © Collins Longman Atlases Cbiii

FRANCE

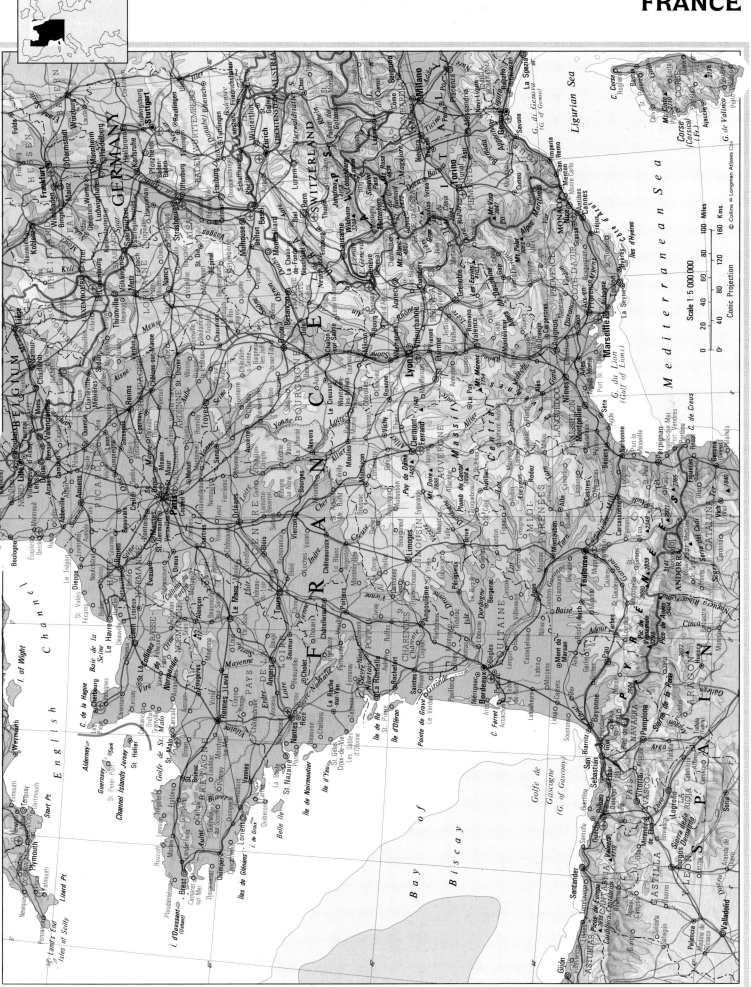

Scale 1 : 5 000 000

Conic Projection

© Collins · Longman Atlases Cbu

NORTHERN FRANCE

Scale 1 : 2 500 000

Feet	Relief	Metres
16404		5000
9843		3000
6562		2000
3281		1000
1640		500
656		200
0		Sea Level
Land Dep.		
656		200
13123		4000
22966		7000

Scale 1 : 2 500 000

0   25   50   75   100 Miles
0   50   100   150 Kms
Conic Equidistant Projection
© Collins

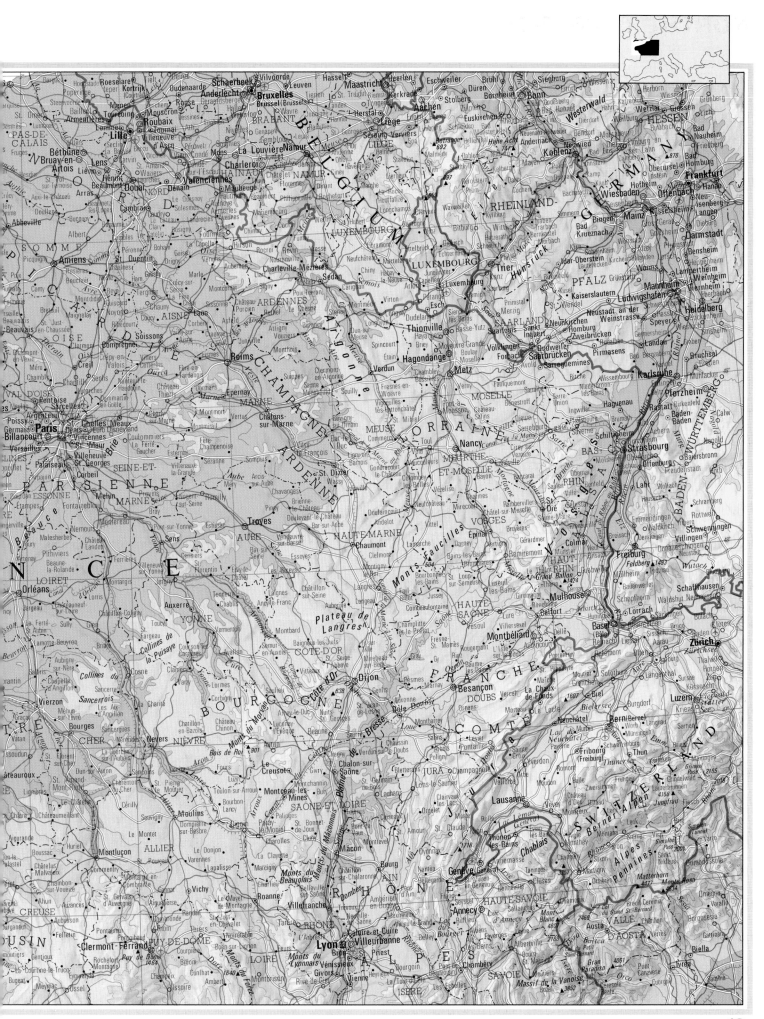

SOUTHERN FRANCE

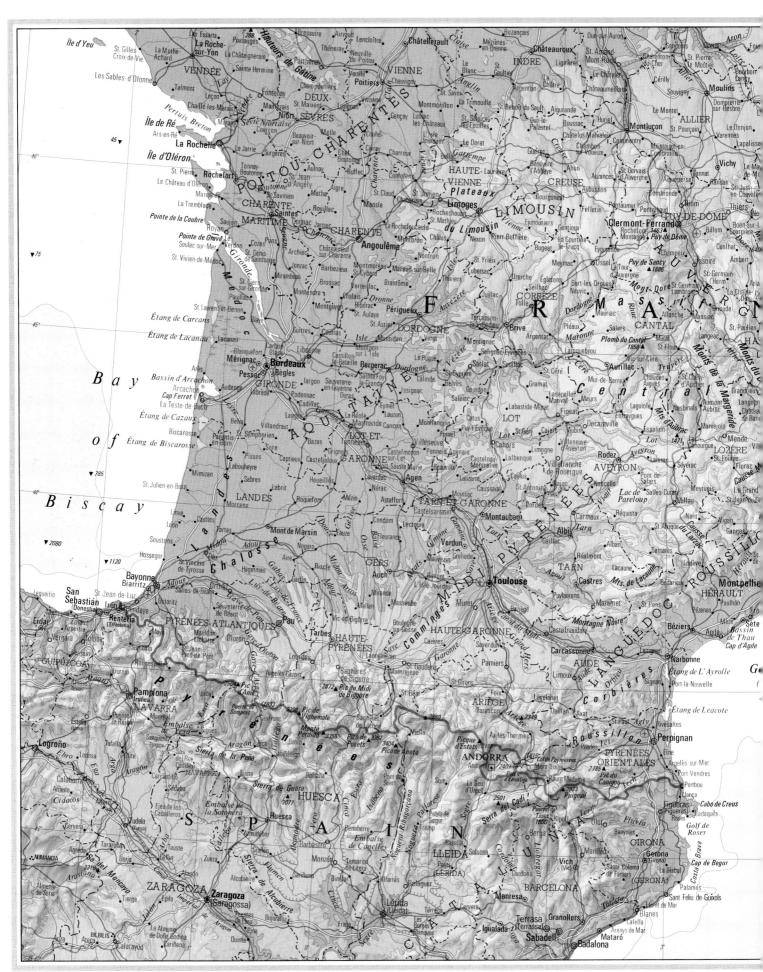

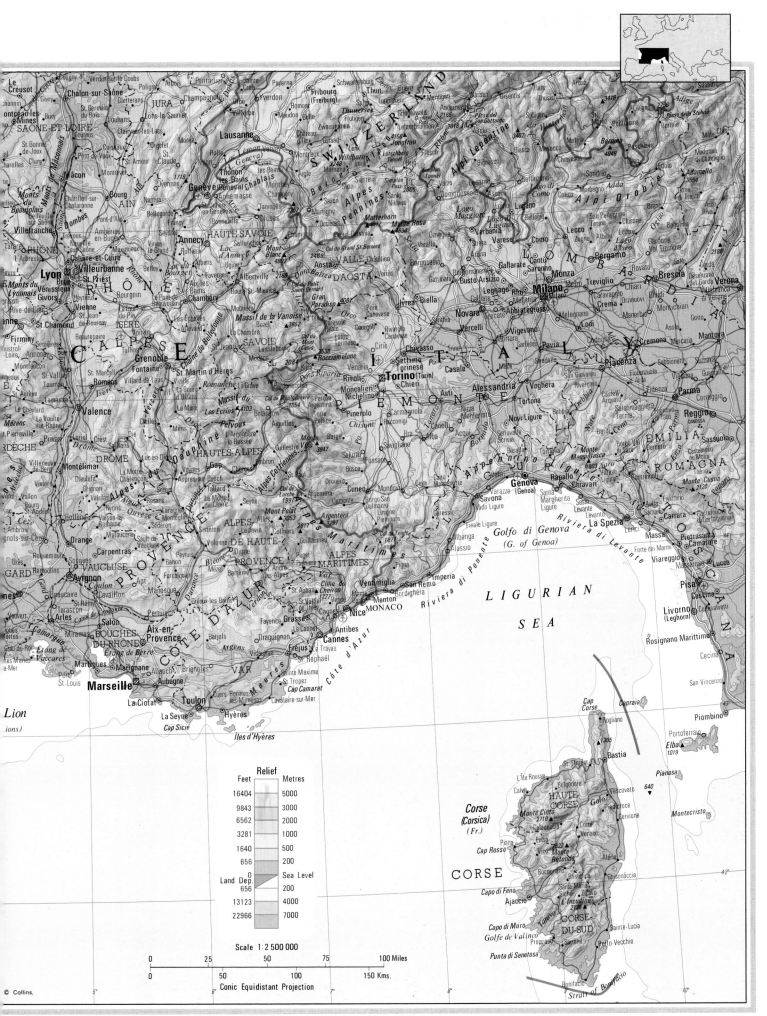

Le Creusot
Givry
ontceau-les-Mines
SAÔNE-ET-LOIRE
St. Bonnet-de-Joux
Cluny
harolles
Mâcon
Monts du Beaujolais
Villefranche
Tarare
L'Arbresle
RHÔNE
Lyon
Villeurbanne
St. Priest
Bron
Vénissieux
Givors
Monts du Lyonnais
St. Jean-de-Bournay
Vienne
St. Chamond
Firminy
 nistrol-Loire
St. Vallier
St. Marcellin
Annonay
Romans
L'Argève
Lamastre
RDÈCHE
Tournon
Mézenc
Valence
La Voulte-sur-Rhône
Privas
Le Cheylard
Crest
Die
Loriol
Montélimar
Viviers
Bourg-St-Andéol
gnols-sur-Cèze
Vallon
Orange
Carpentras
VAUCLUSE
GARD
Avignon
Beaucaire
St. Rémy
Tarascon
Arles
Camargue
ïles Maires
a-Mer
Grau-du-Roi
Port St. Louis
Marignane
Martigues
Étang de Berre
BOUCHES-DU-RHÔNE
Marseille
La Ciotat
Aubagne

Lion
ions)

JURA
Lons-le-Saunier
Clairvaux-les-Lacs
Orgelet
St. Claude
Nantua
AIN
Bellegarde
Seyssel
Belley
Lac du Bourget
Aix-les-Bains
Chambéry
ISÈRE
Grenoble
Fontaine
St. Martin-d'Hères
DAUPHINÉ
HAUTES-ALPES
Gap
DRÔME
Nyons
PROVENCE
Apt
Cavaillon
Salon
Aix-en-Provence
CÔTE D'AZUR
VAR

SWITZERLAND
Lausanne
Genève (Geneva)
Thonon-les-Bains
Évian-les-Bains
Annemasse
HAUTE-SAVOIE
Annecy
Mont Blanc 4807
Aosta
VALLE D'AOSTA
Gran Paradiso 4061
Massif de la Vanoise
SAVOIE
Modane
Romanche
Briançon
Les Écrins 4103
Pelvoux
Monte Viso 3847
Argentera 3297
Alpes Maritimes
ALPES DE HAUTE-PROVENCE
Digne
Draguignan
Fréjus
St. Raphaël
Ste. Maxime
St. Tropez
Cap Camarat
Cavalaire-sur-Mer
Toulon
La Seyne
Hyères
Cap Sicié
Îles d'Hyères

ITALY
Torino (Turin)
PIEMONTE
Cuneo
Mondovì
LIGURIA
Genova (Genoa)
Savona
Imperia
San Remo
Ventimiglia
Menton
MONACO
Nice
Cannes
Antibes

LOMBARDIA
Milano
Novara
Vercelli
Pavia
Piacenza
EMILIA ROMAGNA
Parma
Reggio

Golfo di Genova
(G. of Genoa)

Riviera di Levante
La Spezia
Massa
TOSCANA
Viareggio
Lucca
Pisa
Livorno
(Leghorn)
Rosignano Marittimo
Cecina
San Vincenzo

LIGURIAN SEA

Cap Corse
Capraia
Piombino
Portoferraio
Elba 1019
Pianosa
Bastia
St. Florent
L'Île Rousse
Calvi
HAUTE-CORSE
Monte Cinto 2710
Corse (Corsica) (Fr.)
Cap Rosso
CORSE
Montecristo
Monte Rotondo 2622
Capo di Feno
Ajaccio
Capo di Muro
Golfe de Valinco
Punta di Senetosa
CORSE-DU-SUD
L'Incudine 2136
Porto-Vecchio
Bonifacio
Strait of Bonifacio

Relief

Feet	Metres
16404	5000
9843	3000
6562	2000
3281	1000
1640	500
656	200
0	Sea Level
Land Dep.	
656	200
13123	4000
22966	7000

Scale 1:2 500 000

0   25   50   75   100 Miles
0   50   100   150 Kms.
Conic Equidistant Projection

© Collins

MEDITERRANEAN LANDS

POLAND

Gniezno • Kobrin • Pinsk • Yelsk • Chernigov • Borzna • Konotop • Sumy • Belgorod • Rossosh • Pavlovsk • Don • Kalach na-Donu • Hovla

Warszawa • Siedlce • Łuków • Brest • Polesye (Pripet Marshes) • BELORUSSIA • Nezhin • Priluki • Akhtyrka

Łódź • Lublin • Kovel • Sarny • Korosten • Kiyev (Krev) • Brovary • Piryatin • Poltava • Kharkov • Kupyansk • Valuyki • Chertkovo • Tsimlyanskoye Vdkhr.

Wrocław • Radom • Lutsk • Rovno • Novograd Volynskiy • Zhitomir • Fastov • Vasilkov • Pereyaslav • Lubny • Izyum • Krasnograd • Millerovo • Kamensk-Shakhtinskiy

UKRAINE

Kraków • Lvov • Ternopol • Volochisk • Khmelnitskiy • Vinnitsa • Cherkassy • Kremenchug • Slavyansk • Kramatorsk • Stakhanov • Kommunarsk • Shakhty • Tsimlyansk

SLOVAKIA • Uzhgorod • Ivano-Frankovsk • Kamenets Podolskiy • Mogilev • Uman • Kirovograd • Dneprodzerzhinsk • Dnepropetrovsk • Pavlograd • Donetsk • Novoshakhtinsk • Rostov • RUS. FED.

HUNGARY • Budapest • ROMANIA • Kishinev • MOLDAVIA • Odessa • Krivoy Rog • Zaporozhye • Volnovakha • Mariupol • Taganrog • Krasnodar

BOSNIA-HERZEGOVINA • YUGOSLAVIA • Beograd • Bucureşti (Bucharest) • BULGARIA • Sea of Azov (Azovskoye More) • Kerch • Novorossiysk

CROATIA • Sofiya • BLACK SEA • Krym (Crimea) • Sevastopol • Yalta • GEO.

ALBANIA • MACED • Thessaloniki • Istanbul • TURKEY • Ankara • Anadolu (Anatolia)

GREECE • Aegean Sea • İzmir • Konya • Adana • Halab (Aleppo) • SYRIA • Dimashq (Damascus)

Athínai (Athens) • Dhodhekánisos (Dodecanese) • Ródhos (Rhodes) • Antalya • CYPRUS • Levkosía (Nicosia) • LEBANON • Bayrūt

Kríti (Crete) • ISRAEL • Tel Aviv-Yafo • Yerushalayim • JORDAN • 'Ammān

MEDITERRANEAN SEA

Banghāzī (Benghazi) • Khalīj Surt (Gulf of Sidra) • Al Iskandarīyah (Alexandria) • Al Qāhirah (Cairo) • EGYPT • Port Sa'īd

Barqah (Cyrenaica) • Ad Diffah (Libyan Plateau) • Munkhafaḍ al Qaṭṭārah (Qattara Depression) • Sīnā' (Sinai)

IBERIAN PENINSULA

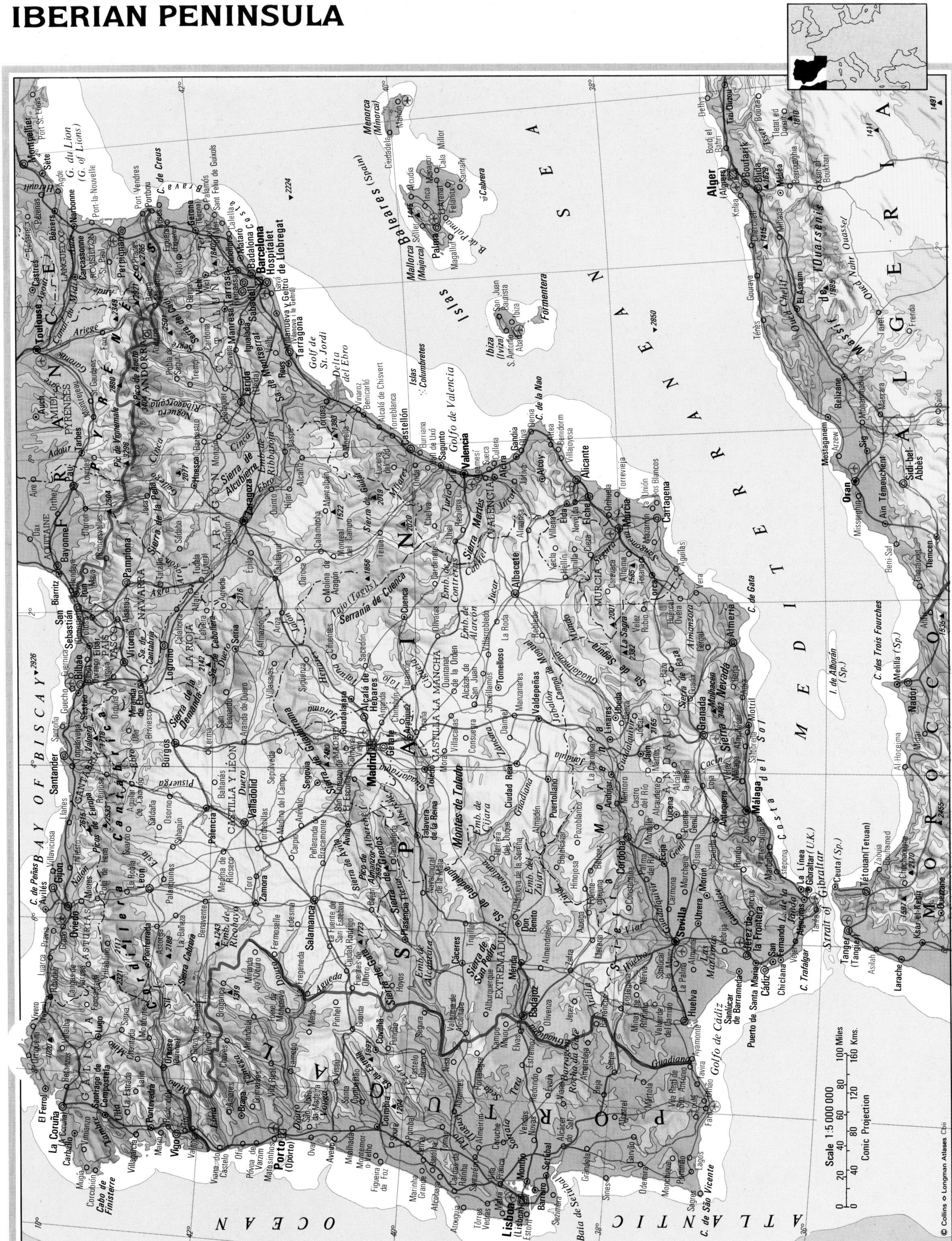

Scale 1:5 000 000
Conic Projection

© Collins ◇ Longman Atlases Ltd

BAY OF BISCAY

ATLANTIC OCEAN

MEDITERRANEAN SEA

Islas Baleares (Spain)

FRANCE

PYRENEES

ANDORRA

PORTUGAL

ESPAÑA

MOROCCO

ALGERIA

EASTERN SPAIN

GUIPÚZCOA
Vergara
Cizúrquil
Sumbilla
Vera
St Jean
Pied-de-Port
Roncesvalles
Isaba
2504 Pic d'Anie
1832
3298 Pic de Vignemale
Monte Perdido
Pico de Aneto
2880
FRANCE
Tarascon
Ariège
2349
Axat-les-Thermes
Prades
PYRENÉES ORIENTALES
Perpignan
Ille-sur-Têt
Elne
Argelès-sur-Mer

Pamplona
Iruñea
Aoiz
NAVARRA
Monreal
Puerto de Somport
Canfranc
Pico de Posets 3367
Pic d'Estats 3115
Prats
Col de Puymorens
1915
St-Louis
Pic du Canigou 2785
Céret
Port-Vendres

Logroño
Estella
Lizarra
Puente la Reina
Tafalla
Olite
Sangüesa
Yesa
Sigüés
Jaca
Broto
Sabiñánigo
Bielsa
ANDORRA
Andorra
2407
Pont de Suert
Sort
La Seu d'Urgell
2501
Puigcerdà
2923
Puigmal
Olot
Fluvià
Ripoll
Llança
Portbou
Cabo de Creus
Cadaqués
Roses
Golf de Roses

Calahorra
Arnedo
Cidacos
Embalse de Yesa
Aragón
Triste
Sierra de la Peña
Boltaña
Sierra de Guara
2077
Benabarre
Tremp
Pobla de Segur
Berga
Sierra del Cadí
1800
Manlleu
Banyoles
GIRONA
Gerona
(Girona)
Costa Brava
Cap de Begur

NAVARRA
Ejea de los Caballeros
Sádaba
Embalse de la Sotonera
HUESCA
Huesca
Almudévar
Barbastro
Monzón
Embalse de Canelles
LLEIDA
(LÉRIDA)
Basella
Cardona
Vich
(Vic)
Santa Coloma de Farners
La Bisbal
(GERONA)
Palamós
Sant Feliu de Guíxols

Tudela
Agreda
Tarazona
Tauste
Gurrea
Zuera
Sariñena
Alcubierre
Sierra de Alcubierre
Balaguer
Solsona
Ponts
Cervera
Manresa
BARCELONA
Granollers
Sabadell
Tordera
Blanes
Lloret de Mar
Calella
Arenys de Mar

SORIA
NUMANCIA
Almenar de Soria
Araviana
2316
Sa. del Moncayo
Borja
Gallur
Alagón
ZARAGOZA
Zaragoza
(Saragossa)
Fuentes de Ebro
Pina
Lérida
(Lleida)
Tàrrega
Igualada
Tarrasa
(Terrassa)
Molins
Badalona
Barcelona
Hospitalet de Llobregat

SORIA
Morón de Almazán
Ariza
Ateca
BILBILIS
Calatayud
Cariñena
La Almunia de Doña Godina
Quinto
Belchite
Azaila
Caspe
Les Borges Blanques
Montblanch
Valls
El Vendrell
Sant Boi de Llobregat
Gavà
El Prat de Llobregat
Vilanova y Geltrú
(Vilanova i la Geltrú)

GUADALAJARA
1518
Embid
Maranchón
Molina de Aragón
Calamocha
Montalbán
1522
Castellote
Embalse de Santolea
Alcañiz
Calanda
Valderrobres
1393
La Granadella
Embalse de Ribarroja
Sa. de Montsant
Falset
Reus
Cambrils de Mar
Tarragona
Golf de St. Jordi
181

Traid
Guadiela
Sa. de Albarracín
1856
Perales de Alfambra
Santa Eulalia
Albarracín
TERUEL
Alfambra
Tragacete
Montes Universales
Teruel
Peñarroya
2019
Sierra de Gúdar
Mora de Rubielos
Morella
Alcañiz
San Mateo
Tortosa
Amposta
Delta del Ebro
146
Cabo de Tortosa
Sant Carles de la Ràpita
Punta de la Baña
1870

Cuenca
Cañete
1220
Puerto de Escandón
1814
Peñagolosa
Mosqueruela
Lucena del Cid
Alcalá de Chisvert
Torreblanca
Benicarló
Peñíscola
Vinaroz

Serranía de Cuenca
Javalambre
2020
Torre Baja
VALENCIA
Viver
CASTELLÓN
Peñagolosa 1814
Onda
Villarreal
Almazora
Castellón
Burriana
Islas Columbretes
1630

CUENCA
Motilla del Palancar
Carbonera de Guadazaón
Cardenete
Chelva
Villar del Arzobispo
Liria
Bétera
Náquera
Sagunto
Vall de Uxó
Nules

Cuenca
Minglanilla
Iniesta
Requena
Utiel
Chiva
Buñol
Paterna
Burjasot
Valencia
Mislata
Catarroja
Torrente
Golfo de Valencia

Casasimarro
Tarazona de la Mancha
Casas Ibáñez
Mahora
Júcar
VALENCIA
Carlet
Alberique
Algemesí
Alcira
Sueca
Cullera
La Albufera
Cabo de Formentor
Puerto de Pollensa
Alcudia

La Roda
Barrax
ALBACETE
Albacete
1242
Chinchilla de Monte Aragón
Ayora
Enguera
Játiva
Carcagente
Tabernes de Valldigna
Gandía
Oliva
Mallorca
(Majorca)
Puig Major 1445
Sóller
Inca
La Puebla
Artá
Bahía de Alcudia
Cabo del Freu

Pozo Cañada
Almansa
Albaida
Onteniente
Cocentaina
Serpis
Pego
Denia
Jávea
Cabo de la Nao
Palma
Manacor
Lluchmayor
Felanitx
Cala Millor
Santañy

Mundo
Elche de la Sierra
Embalse de El Cenajo
Hellín
Tobarra
Yecla
Villena
Alcoy
Aitana 1558
Callosa de Ensarriá
Benisa
710
Islas Baleares
(Balearic Islands)
Magalluf
Bahía de Palma
El Arenal
Isla Dragonera
Isla Cabrera
420
Cabo de Salinas
Cabrera

Jumilla
Monóvar
Novelda
ALICANTE
Elda
Aspe
Dijona
Benidorm
Villajoyosa
Altea
Costa Blanca
90
Punta de Gal
San Juan Bautista
Ibiza
(Iviza)
San Antonio Abad
Santa Eulalia del Río
Ibiza
476
Cabo Llentrisca
BALEARES

Moratalla
Cehegín
Caravaca
Bullas
Crevillente
Alicante
Elche
Cabo de Santa Pola
Isla Plana
Cabo Berbería
Formentera

Quípar
Mula
Segura
MURCIA
Alcantarilla
Murcia
Dolores
Orihuela
Torrevieja
MEDITERRANEAN

Vélez Rubio
Lorca
Sa. de Espuña
Alhama
1585
Totana
Sangonera
Mar Menor
Cabo de Palos
Los Blancos
La Unión
Cartagena
SEA

Huércal-Overa
Sierra de Almenara
Mazarrón
Golfo de Mazarrón
Aguilas

Menorca (Minorca)

Menorca
(Minorca)
Cabo de Caballería
Ciudadela
Alayor
Mahón
Cabo d'Artuch

Relief

Feet		Metres
16404		5000
9843		3000
6562		2000
3281		1000
1640		500
656		200
0		Sea Level
Land Dep.		
656		200
13123		4000
22966		7000

Scale 1 : 2 500 000

0   25   50   75   100 Miles
0   50   100   150 Kms.

Conic Equidistant Projection

© Collins

25

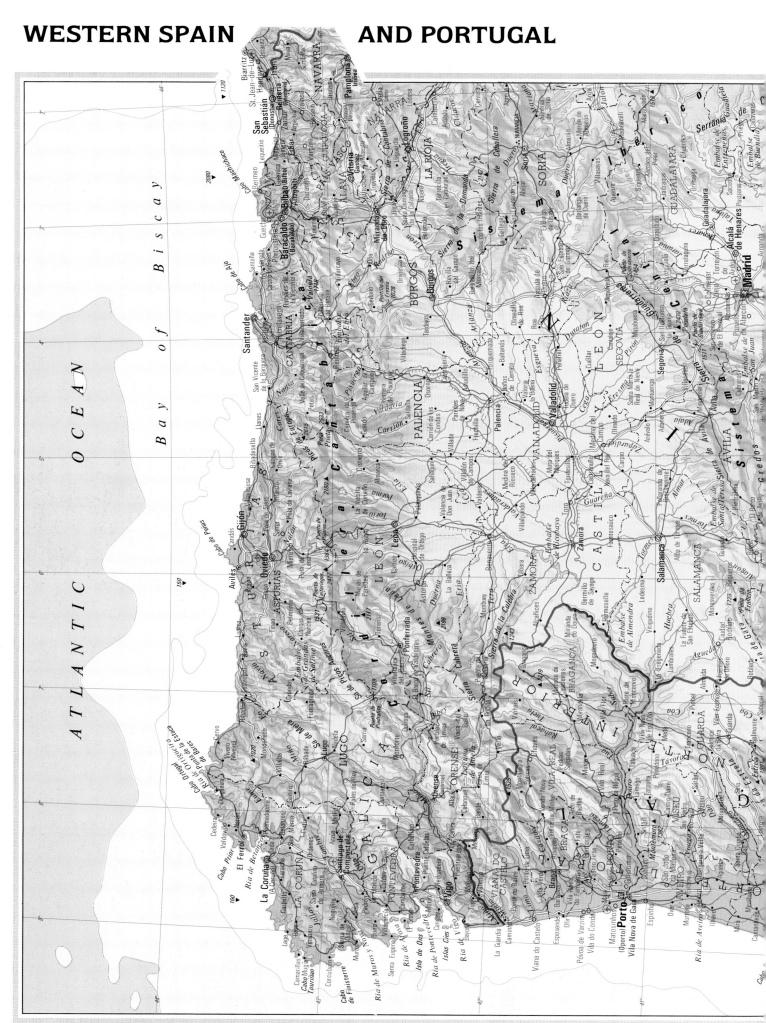

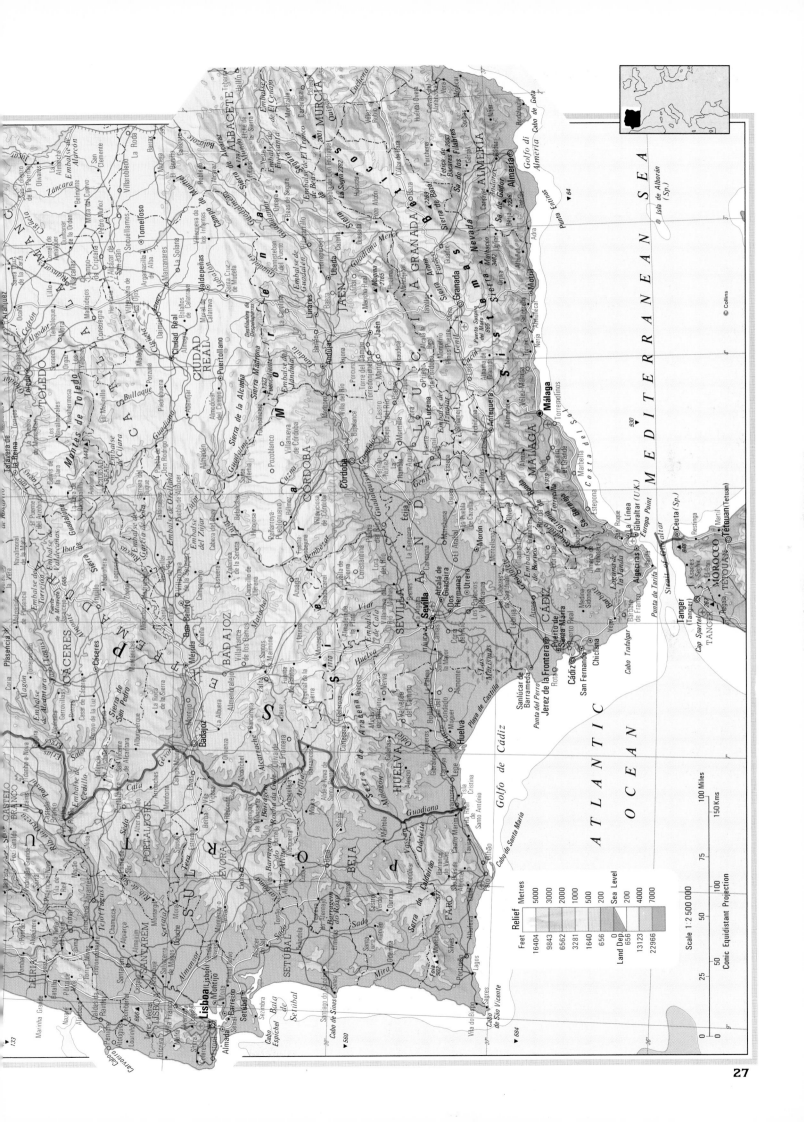

ITALY AND THE BALKANS

Scale 1:5 250 000

0   50   100   150   200 Miles

0   50   100   150   200   250   300 Kms.

Conic Projection

© Collins ○ Longman Atlases Cbii

29

LIGURIAN SEA

Riviera di Ponente

Golfo di Genova
(G. of Genoa)

Riviera di Levante

Relief

Feet		Metres
16404		5000
9843		3000
6562		2000
3281		1000
1640		500
656		200
	0	Sea Level
	Land Dep.	
656		200
13123		4000
22966		7000

Corse
(Corsica)
(Fr.)

CORSE

HAUTE CORSE

CORSE DU-SUD

Côte d'Azur

Gulf of Venice

EMILIA ROMAGNA

TOSCANA

Scale 1: 2 500 000

0	25	50	75	100 Miles
0	50	100	150 Kms	

Conic Equidistant Projection

Civitavecchia
Santa Marinella
Bracciano
ROMA
(Rome)
VATICAN CITY
VILLA ADRIANA
Tivoli
Avezzano

Ladispoli
Fiumicino
L A Z I O
Frascati
Palestrina
Subiaco
Anagni
Alatri

Ostia
Albano Laziale
Velletri
Ferentino
Frosinone
Ceccano

Nettuno
Anzio
Cisterna di Latina
Sezze
Priverno
PARCO
NAZIONALE DEL CIRCEO
Sabauda
Terracina
Fondi
Gaeta
Golfo di Gaeta

Capo di Feno
Santa-Maria
Ghisonaccia
Ajaccio
Bastelica
L'Incudine
2136
CORSE-DU-SUD
Sainte-Lucie
Capo di Muro
Golfe de Valinco
Propriano
Solenzara
Punta di Senetosa
Porto-Vecchio

Bonifacio
Strait of Bonifacio
Maddalena
Capo Testa
Santa Teresa Gallura
Maddalena
Caprera

Asinara
Punta di Scorno
Golfo dell'Asinara
Palau
Cannigione
Arzachena

Capo del Falcone
Castelsardo
Calangianus
Tempio
Olbia
Golfo degli Aranci

Porto Torres
Sennori
Sedini
1362
Monte Limbara
Posada
Posada

Sassari
Ozieri
Bitti
Siniscola
Capo Comino

Alghero
Thiesi
Lago di Coghinas
Nuoro
Orosei

Villanova Monteleone
Coghinas
Monte Rasu
1259
Monte Albo

Bosa
Bonorva
Dorgali

SARDEGNA
Abbasanta
Oliena
Golfo di Orosei

Sardegna
(Sardinia)
(Italy)
Macomer
Monte Santu

Oristano
Tirso
Sorgono
Monti del
1834
Capo di Monte Santu

Golfo di
Oristano
Arborea
Gennargentu
Seui
Tortoli
Arbatax

Terralba
NuraNao
Lanusei
Tertenia

Mogoro
Serri
Mandas

Fluminimaggiore
San Gavino Monreale
Serramanna
Flumendosa
Muravera

1236
Sanluri
Nuxis
San Vito
Punta Serpeddi
Capo Ferrato

Iglesias
Decimomannu
Simaxi
1069
Villasimius

Gonnesa
Quartu Sant'Elena
San Pietro
Carbonia
1116
Cagliari
Carloforte
Sant'Antioco
Golfo di Cagliari
Isola di
Sant'Antioco
Teulada
Capo Carbonara

Golfo di
Palmas
Capo Spartivento
Capo Teulada

Isole Ponziane
Ischia

2615

T Y R R H E N I A N

S E A

3550

1330

Ustica

M E D I T E R R A N E A N

720

Capo
San Vito
Golfo di
Castellammare
Capo
Gallo
PALERMO
Golfo di Palermo
Bagheria

Isole Egadi
Castellammare del Golfo
Monreale
Misilmeri
Termini

Trapani
Isola di Levanzo
686
Alcamo
Rocca Busambra
1613
Caccamo

Marettimo
Segesta
Calatafimi
Corleone
Lercara
Prizzi

Favignana
Salemi
Val di Mazara
Partanna
Castelvetrano
Petralia

Marsala
Capo Boeo
Mazara del Vallo
Castelvetrano
Menfi
Ribera
Pian
1578

Strait of Sicily
Campobello di Mazara
SELINUNTE
Sciacca
Raffadali
Agrigento

88
Porto Empedocle
Palma di Montechiaro

La Galite
Canal de la Galite

Cap Blanc
Binzert
(Bizerte)

Bechater
Cap Serrat
Menzel
Djemil
Ras Djebel
Porto Farina

Menzel Bourguiba
Lac de Bizerte
Île Zembra

BIZERTE
Mateur
Golfe de Tunis
El Haouaria
Cap Bon

510

Cap Rosa
El Kala
Tabarka
Djebel
Aïn Draham
Protville
Sidi Daoud
Zaouiet el Mgaiz
Zaouiet Azmour
Kelibia

ALGERIA
Bou Salem
Béja
BÉJA
Oued
Zarga
El Bab
CARTHAGE
Carthage
La Goulette
TUNIS
Tunis
La Marsa
Menzel Bou Zelfa
Menzel Temime

Monts JENDOUBA
BULLA REGIA
TUNISIA
Testour
Grombalia

Pantelleria
(Italy)
Pantelleria

ADRIATIC SEA

IONIAN SEA

SEA

PUGLIA

BASILICATA

CALABRIA

MOLISE

ALBANIA

VLORË

Strait of Otranto

Golfo di Manfredonia

Golfo di Taranto

Golfo di Policastro

Golfo di Salerno

Golfo di Sant' Eufemia

Golfo di Squillace

Golfo di Patti

Golfo di Catania

Golfo di Augusta

Golfo di Noto

Stretto di Messina

Isole Eolie

Kérkira (Corfu)

Relief		
Feet		Metres
16404		5000
9843		3000
6562		2000
3281		1000
1640		500
656		200
0		Sea Level
Land Dep.		
656		200
13123		4000
22966		7000

Scale 1 : 2 500 000

0   25   50   75   100 Miles

0   50   100   150 Kms

Conic Equidistant Projection

© Collins

GREECE AND ALBANIA

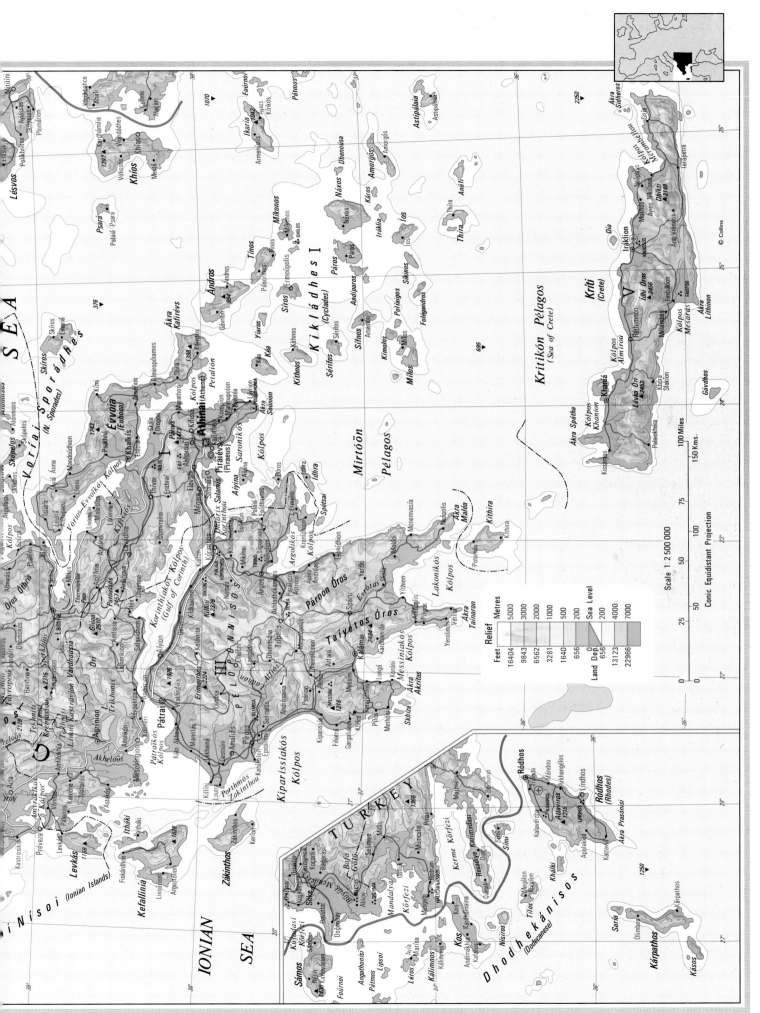

CENTRAL EUROPE

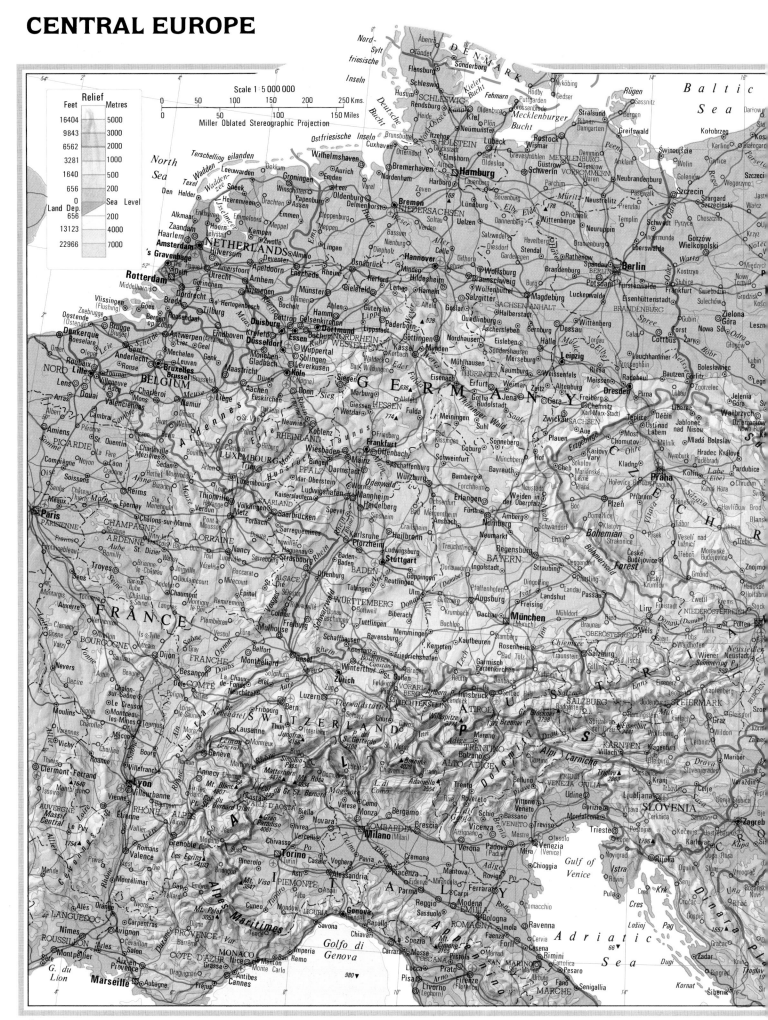

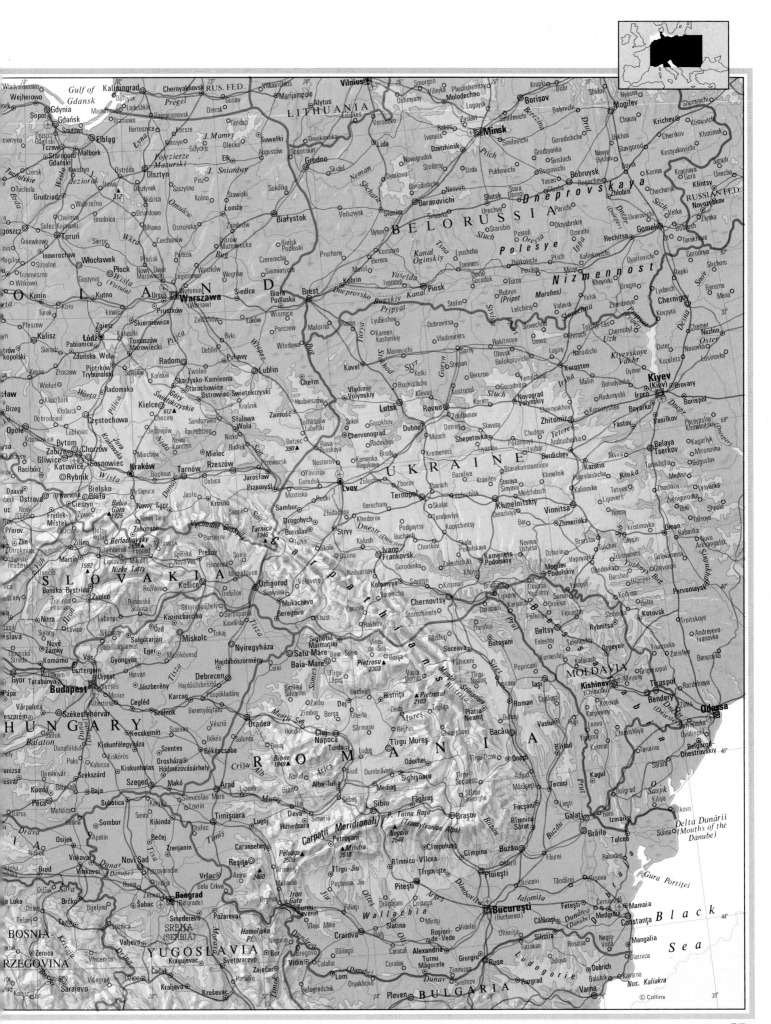

GERMANY AND SWITZERLAND

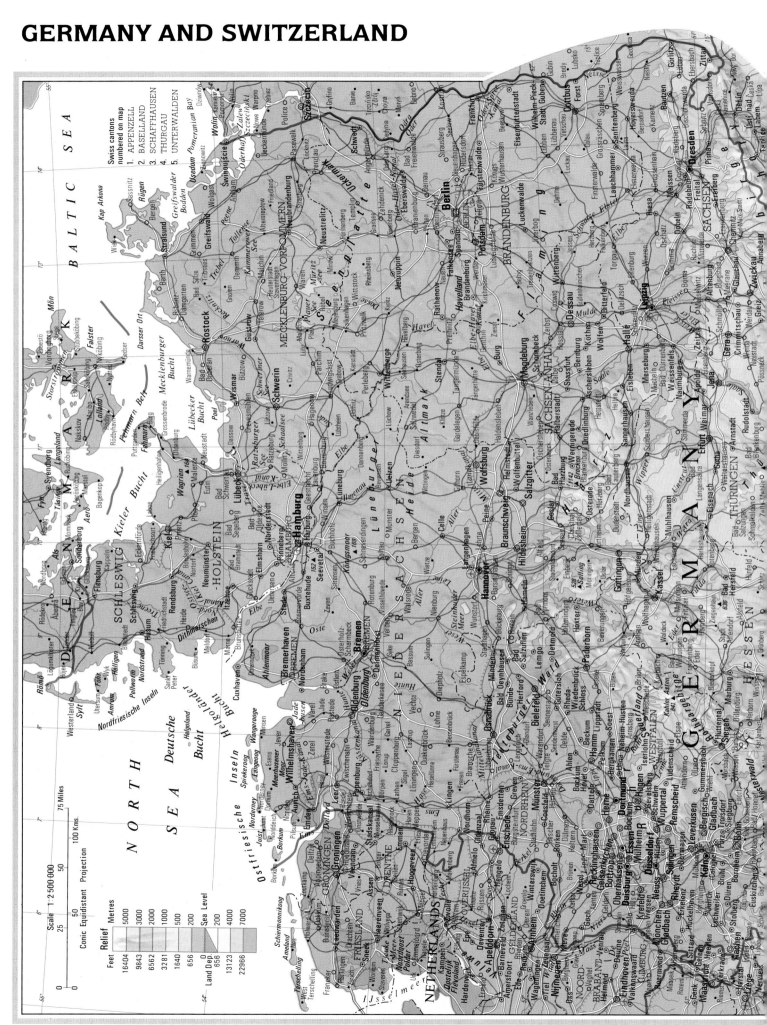

Swiss cantons
numbered on map
1. APPENZELL
2. BASELLAND
3. SCHAFFHAUSEN
4. THURGAU
5. UNTERWALDEN

Conic Equidistant Projection

Scale 1:2 500 000

Relief

Feet	Metres
16404	5000
9843	3000
6562	2000
3281	1000
1640	500
656	200
	Sea Level
656	Land Dep. 0
13123	4000
22966	7000

39

SCANDINAVIA AND BALTIC LANDS

Relief

Feet	Metres
16404	5000
9843	3000
6562	2000
3281	1000
1640	500
656	200
0	Sea Level
Land Dep.	200
656	
13123	4000
22966	7000

Scale 1 : 5 000 000
Conic Projection

100 Miles
160 Kms.

ICELAND
on the same scale

© Collins

FAROE IS.
(Denmark)
on the same scale

ATLANTIC OCEAN

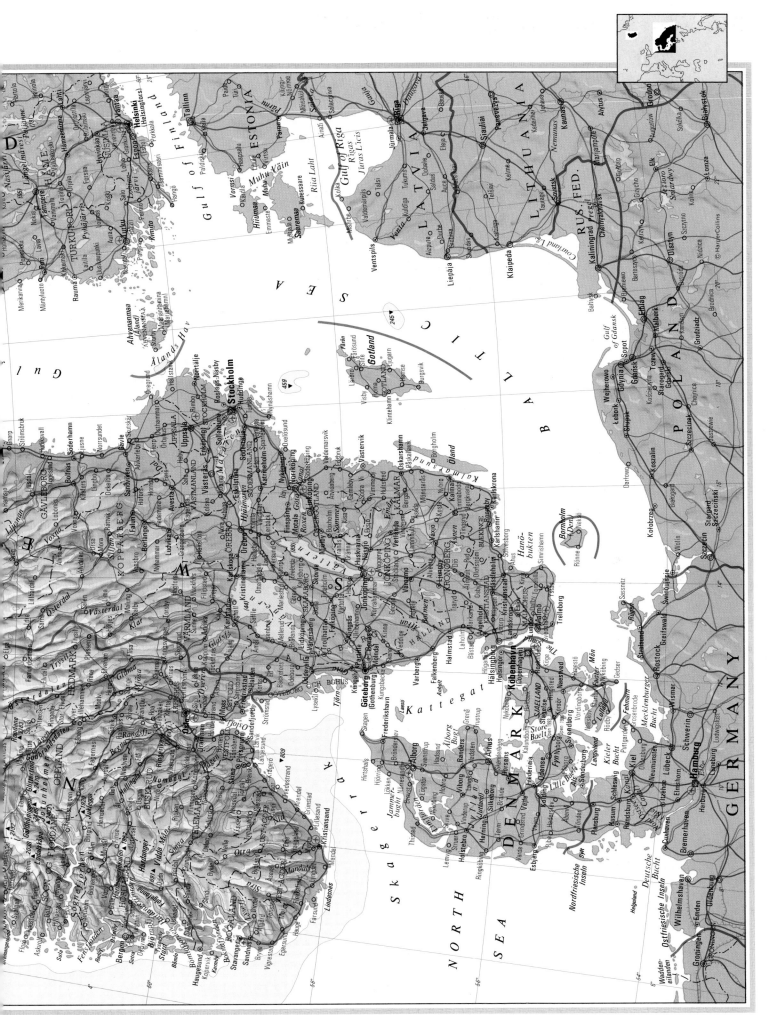

SOUTHERN SCANDINAVIA

Östmark 13° Klar 14° Nyhammar Vikmanshyttan Horndal Österbybruk Gimo Grisslehamn Maarianhamina (Mariehamn) 60°
Kyrkheden Grangärde Nyhammar Hedemora Fors Tärnsjö Österväla Österbybruk Alunda Grisslehamn Lemland AHVENANMAA Kökar
Torsby Grangärde Fredriksberg Dal Tärnsjö Östervåla Hallstavik Elmsta Degerby
Väsman Ludvika Norberg Krylbo Tämnaren Uppland Hallstavik Elmsta Ålands Lemland Degerby
Värmland Uddeholm Hagfors Grängesberg Avesta Heby Morgongåva Storvreta Elmsta Hav AHVENANMAA Kökar
VÄRMLAND Munkfors Lesjöfors Ställdalen Sala Sunnerstal Rimbo Uppsala STOCKHOLM
Charlottenberg Sunne Ransäter Filipstad Grythyttan Fråssa Hallstahammar Sigtuna Bålsta Vallentuna Roslags-Näsby Blidö
Arvika Deje Molkom Nykroppa Lindesberg Kolsva Köping Enköping Upplands-Väsby Ljusterö
Värmeln Forshaga Storfors Nora Frövi Västerås Enköping Sollentuna Roslags-Näsby Stora Möja
Glafsfjorden Vålberg Karlstad Karlskoga ÖREBRO Arboga Kunsör Mälaren Sundbyberg Solna Lidingö
Grums Skoghall Kristinehamn Bofors Örebro Hjälmaren Eskilstuna Marfjärd Stockholm Nacka
Säffle Degerfors Hallsberg Kumla SÖDERMANLAND Södertälje Tumba Huddinge Handen
Svanskog (44) Svartå Pålsboda Vingåker Flen Gnesta Järna Västerhaninge Ornö
Åmål Värmlandsnäs Otterbäcken Skagern Laxå Lerbäck Katrineholm Båven Sparreholm Östmo Muskö
Billingsfors Gullspång Näcke Askersund Zinkgruvan Reimyra Vrena Stigtomta Nynäshamn Utö
Dalbosjön Djurö Sjötorp Hova Unden Tylöskog Finspång Glan Norrköping Bråviken 459
Torsö Källandsö Mariestad Viken Medevi Borensberg Ljungsbro Göta kanal Arkösund
Läckö Kinnekulle 306 Götene Karlsborg Motala Vadstena Söderköping Stegeborg
Lidköping Skara 299 Skövde Hjo Tåkern Malmslätt Linköping
Vara Billingen Stenstorp ÖSTERGÖTLAND
SKARABORG Tidaholm 263 Mjölby Östergötland Gusum Valdemarsvik
Falköping Floby 325 Alleberg Ödeshög Boxholm Atvidaberg
Västergötland Herrljunga Vartofta 364 Tranås Sommen Kisa Åsunden Gamleby
Alingsås Habo Mullsjö Bränna Bankeryd Överum Edsbruk
ÄLVSBORG Jönköping Huskvarna Södra Gunnebo Västervik
Borås Norrahammar Forserum Eksjö Mariannelund Vimmerby Ankarsrum
Fritsla 343 Malmbäck Nässjö Silverdalen Hultsfred Fårön
Kinna JÖNKÖPING 377 Vetlanda Emån Målilla Kristdala Kappelshamn Fårösund
Svenljunga Vaggeryd Lammhult Sävsjö Viserum Mörlunda Gotland Lärbro Slite
Gislaved Anderstorp Rusken Stockaryd Fågelhem Byxelkrok Lickershamn Tingstäde
Gnosjö Värnamo KALMAR Oskarshamn Böda Visby Roma Gothem
Varberg Reftele Lammhult Aseda Högsby Böda Klintehamn GOTLAND 83 Hemse
Viskafors Småland Braås Monsterås Hemse Ronehamn
Varberg Halland Hyltebruk Moheda Lenhovda Alsterbro Timmernabben Hoburgen Burgsvik
Torup Vidöstern Ryssby Växjö Orrefors Nybro Kalmar
HALLAND Ljungby Gemla Lessebo Boda Glasbruk Färjestaden
Halmstad Oskarström KRONOBERG Emmaboda Ljungbyholm Mörbylånga
Laholmsbukten Knäred Åsnen Tingsryd Visseljarda Borgholm
Tylösand Markaryd Mien Ryd Torsås
Båstad 226 Glimåkra Blekinge Bergkvara
Torekov Vittsjö Bjärnum Lönsboda BLEKINGE Degerhamn
Skälderviken Ängelholm Klippan KRISTIANSTAD Olofström Arsarum Ronneby Karlskrona Ottenby
Höganäs Åstorp Tyringe Hässleholm Bromölla Kallinge Lyckeby Torhamn
Halsingborg Bjuv Höör Kristianstad Sölvesborg Karlshamn
Ven Landskrona Eslöv Hörby Tollarp Åhus Hanöbukten
MALMÖHUS Lund Skåne Everöd Degeberga Kivik
Malmö Dalby Sjöbo Linderödsåsen Simrishamn BALTIC
Svedala Romeleåsen Tomelilla Borrby
Trelleborg Skurup Ystad Köseberga Sandhammaren Allinge Bornholm (Den.) B
Falsterbo Smygehuk Hasle Gudhjem Svaneke
Mön Rönne Åkirkeby Neksö Primor 20°
Krokowa Primors
13° 14° 15° 16° 17° 18° 19°

S E A

B A L T I C

S W E D E N

59°

58°

57°

56°

55°

60°

RUSSIAN FEDERATION, WEST & UKRAINE

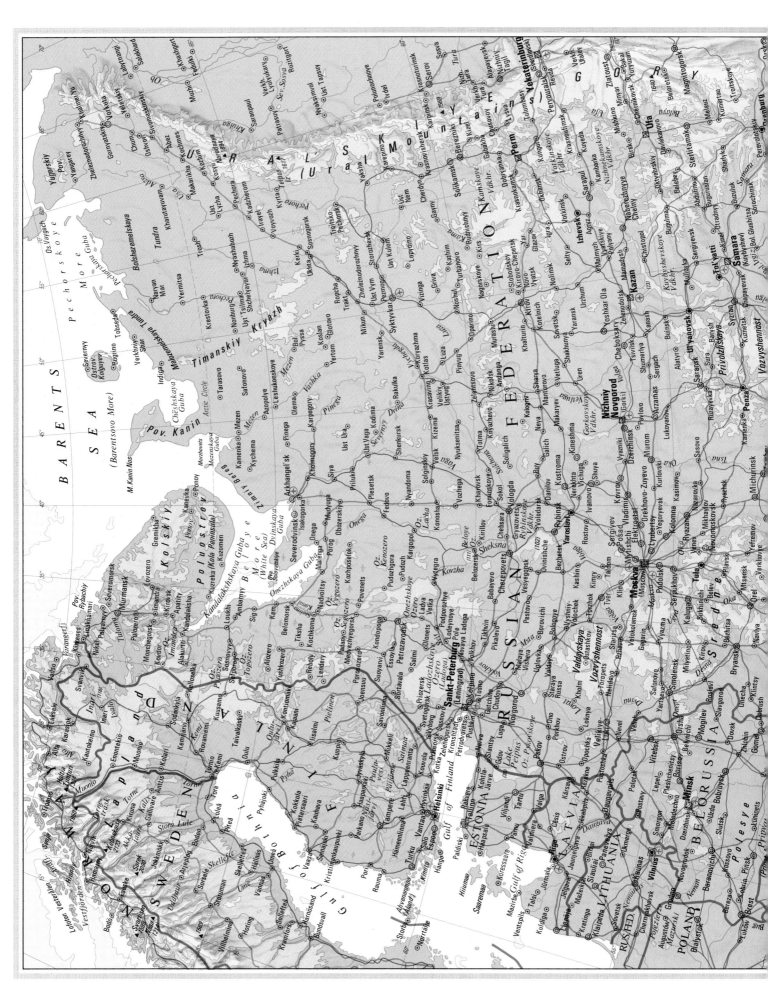

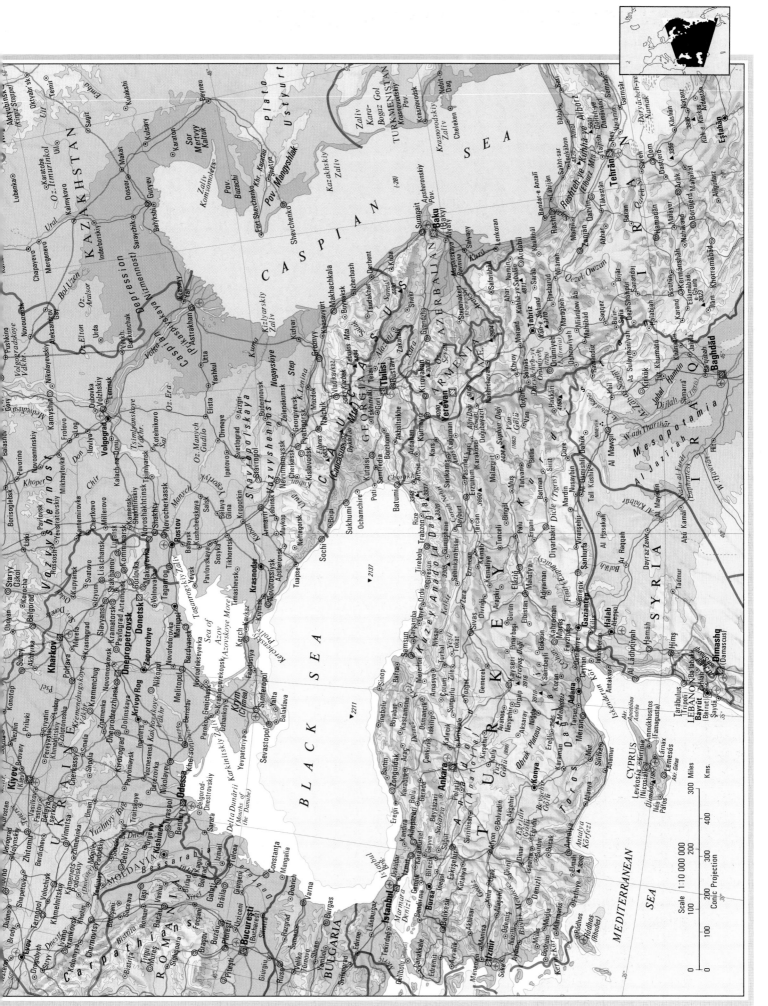

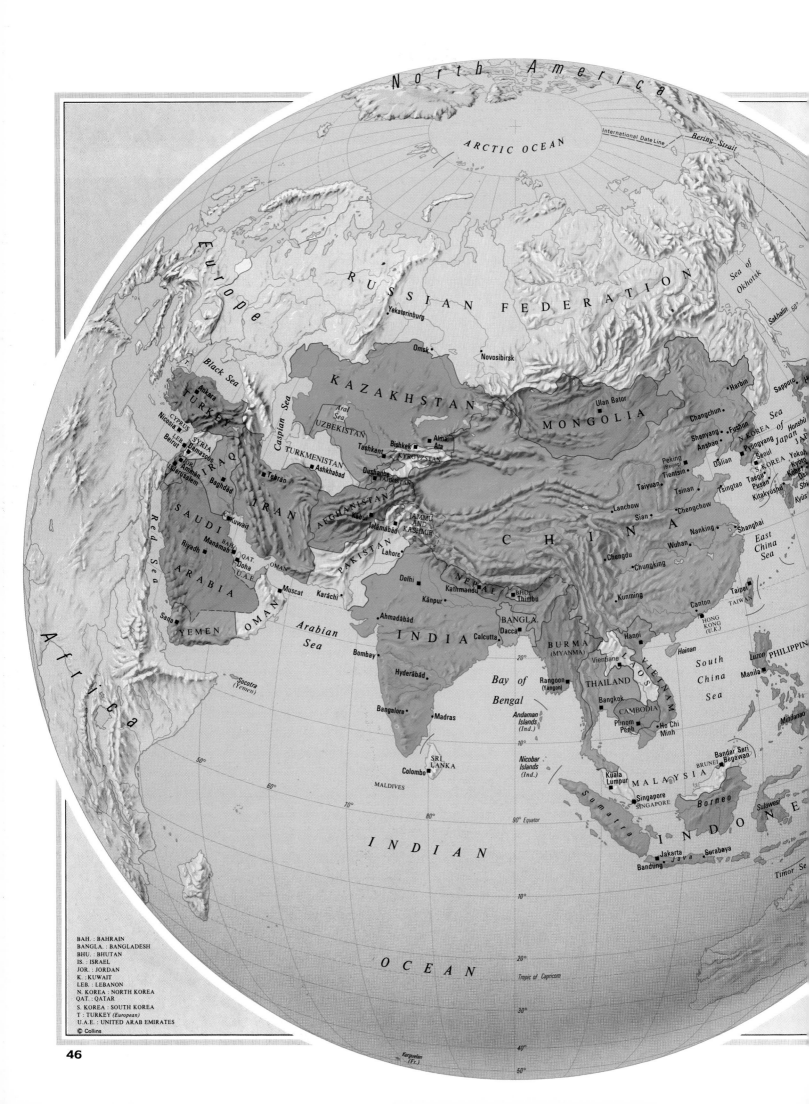

North America

ARCTIC OCEAN

International Date Line

Bering Strait

Europe

RUSSIAN FEDERATION

Sea of Okhotsk

Sakhalin

Yekaterinburg

Omsk

Novosibirsk

Black Sea

KAZAKHSTAN

Harbin

Sapporo

Sea

Ankara

Aral Sea

MONGOLIA

Ulan Bator

Changchun

of

Honshū

TURKEY

CYPRUS

Nicosia

UZBEKISTAN

Shenyang

Fushun

N.KOREA

Japan

Caspian Sea

Tashkent

Bishkek

Alma Ata

Anshan

Pyŏngyang

Seoul

S.KOREA

Kyoto

Yokol

SYRIA

LEB.

Beirut

Damascus

TURKMENISTAN

KYRGYZSTAN

Peking

(Beijing)

Dalian

Tientsin

Tsingtao

Taegu

Pusan

Kitakyūshū

Osal

Kyūs

JAF

Baghdâd

Ashkhabad

Dushanbe

TAJIKISTAN

IRAQ

Amman

JOR.

Jerusalem

Tehrān

Taiyuan

Tsinan

IS.

IRAN

AFGHANISTAN

Lanchow

Chengchow

SAUDI

Kuwait

Kabul

JAMMU

AND

KASHMIR

Sian

Nanking

Shanghai

Riyadh

Manāmah

BAH.

QAT.

Doha

Islāmābād

Wuhan

East

China

Sea

ARABIA

OMAN

U.A.E

Lahore

Chengdu

Chungking

PAKISTAN

Delhi

Muscat

Karāchi

Kānpur

NEPAL

Kathmandu

BHU.

Thimbu

Kunming

Canton

Taipei

Sana

OMAN

Red Sea

YEMEN

Arabian

Sea

Ahmadābād

INDIA

BANGLA.

Dacca

HONG

KONG

(U.K.)

TAIWAN

Socotra

(Yemen)

BURMA

(MYANMA)

Hanoi

Hainan

Luzon

PHILIPPIN

Africa

Bombay

Calcutta

20°

Vientiane

LAOS

South

China

Sea

Manila

Hyderābād

Bay of

Bengal

Rangoon

(Yangon)

THAILAND

Bangalore

Madras

Andaman

Islands

(Ind.)

10°

Bangkok

CAMBODIA

Phnom

Penh

Ho Chi

Minh

VIETNAM

Mindanao

Bandar Seri

Begawan

SRI

LANKA

Nicobar

Islands

(Ind.)

Colombo

MALDIVES

50°

60°

70°

80°

90°

Equator

Kuala

Lumpur

MALAYSIA

Singapore

SINGAPORE

Borneo

Sulawesi

BRUNEI

INDONE

Sumatra

10°

INDIAN

Jakarta

Java

Surabaya

Bandung

Timor Se

OCEAN

20°

Tropic of Capricorn

30°

40°

Kerguelen

(Fr.)

50°

ASIA

NORTH PACIFIC OCEAN

Tropic of Cancer

ASIA AND INDIAN OCEAN

SINGAPORE
Kuala Lumpur

Medan

Sumatra

Padang

Palembang

Jakarta
Bandung

Tanjungkarang
Jawa

Semarang Surabaya
Malang

Jambi

Banjarmasin

Balikpapan

Kuching

Borneo
Kalimantan

Buru

Ujung
Pandang

Sumba

Flores

Kupang

Timor

Melville I.
Darwin

Wyndham

Derby

Port Hedland

Geraldton

Perth

Albany

Mount
Magnet

Kalgoorlie

AUSTRALIA

Alice
Springs

Macdonnell Res.

Great Australian
Bight

Nth. Harbor
Plain

Port Augusta
Port Lincoln

Adelaide

Kangaroo I.

Bass Str.

Tasmania

SOUTHERN OCEAN

Timor Sea

Java Trench 7460

Christmas I.
(Aus.)

6459

Cocos Is.
(Aus.)

1011

2719

1787

West Australian Basin

INDIAN OCEAN

Mid-

INDIAN OCEAN

Indian Basin

Ninety-East Ridge

South-East Indian Ridge

S.E. Indian
Basin

6857

SW Australian
Ridge

South Australian
Basin

Indian-Antarctic Ridge

6465

Eastern Indian-Antarctic Basin

Antarctic Circle

Antarctica

MID-INDIAN RIDGE

Chagos
Archipelago
(U.K.)

dive Ridge

2352

Ridge

Madingley Rise

SEYCHELLES

Mascarene
Ridge

Mascarene
Basin

Antananarivo
(Tananarive)

Mascarene

Tromelin

Réunion
(Fr.)

MAURITIUS
Mascarene Is.

Rodrigues

16

Nazareth Trough

Mauritius
Basin

6400

2152

South-West Indian Ridge

I. Amsterdam
(Fr.)

i. St. Paul
(Fr.)

5605

Kerguelen
Basin

Is. de
Kerguelen
(Fr.)

Heard I.
(Aus.)

188

Kerguelen-Gaussberg Ridge

5441

Kerguelen

MADAGASCAR

Mahajanga

Mozambique Channel

Bassas
da India

Europa

COMOROS

Tropic of Capricorn

Durban

Natal Basin

1503

Agulhas
Basin

5116

Cape
Rise

Prince Edward
Ridge

Prince Edward Is.
(R.S.A.)

Is. Crozet
(Fr.)

Atlantic-Indian-Antarctic Basin

Scale 1 : 45 000 000

0   400   800   1200   Miles
0   400 800 1200 1600 2000 Kms.

Lambert Azimuthal Equal Area Projection

© Collins ◇ Longman Atlases

NORTH ASIA

Scale 1 : 20 000 000

0   100   200   300   400   500 Miles

0   200   400   600   800 Kms.

Conic Projection

© Collins ○ Longman Atlases Cbt

50

Relief

Feet	Metres
16 404	5000
9843	3000
6562	2000
3281	1000
1640	500
656	200
0	Sea Level

Land Dep.

656	200
13123	4000
22 966	7000

EAST ASIA

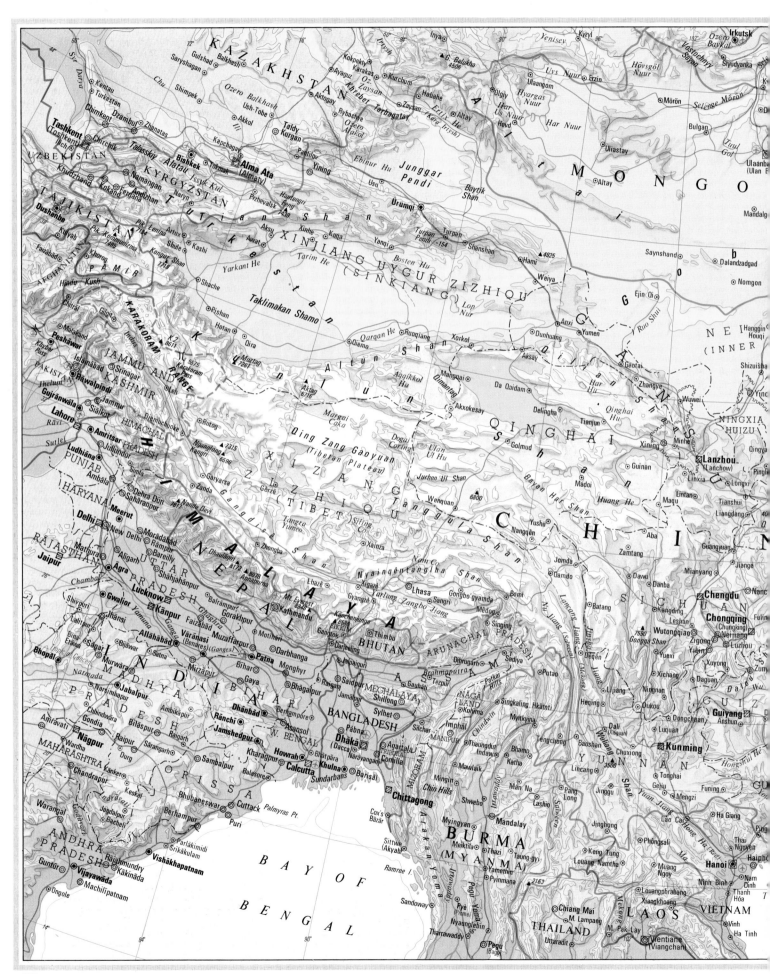

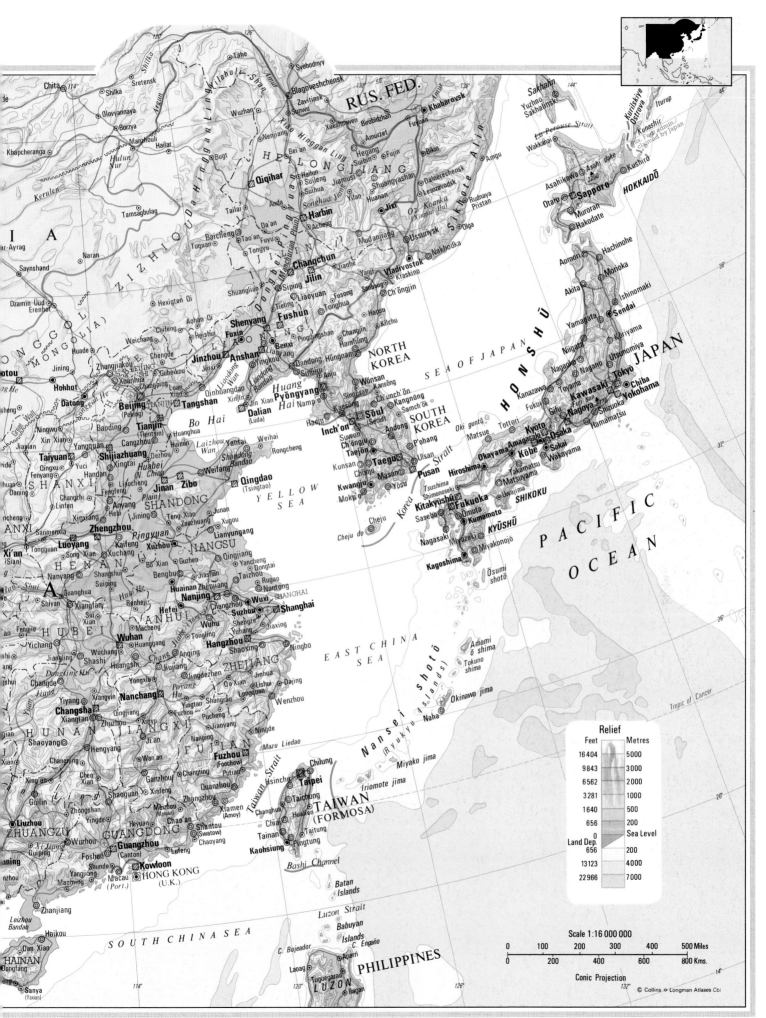

RUS. FED.

Chita
Shilka
Sretensk
Olovyannaya
Borzya
Khapcheranga
Manzhouli
Hailar
Hulun Nur
Tamsagbulag
Dzamin Üüd
Erenhot
Saynshand
MONGOLIA
Naran
Jining
Zhangjiakou
Hohhot
otou
Datong
BEIJING
SHI
Beijing
(Peking)
TIANJIN
Tianjin
(Tientsin)
Tangshan
Baoding
Huanghua
Bo Hai
SHANXI
Taiyuan
Qingxu
Shijiazhuang
Xingtai
Dezhou
Yuci
Fenyang
Yangquan
Handan
Huabei
Plain
SHANDONG
Jinan
Zibo
Qingdao
(Tsingtao)
Linfen
Anyang
Heze
Jining
Zaozhuang
Junan
ANXI
Sanmenxia
Zhengzhou
Pingyuan
Lianyungang
Xi'an
(Sian)
Luoyang
HENAN
JIANGSU
A
Nanyang
Shangshui
Guzhen
Qingjiang
Yancheng
Shiyan
Xiangfan
Suiping
Jiashan
Huainan
Zhenjiang
Nantong
HUBEI
Renheji
Bengbu
Rugao
SHANGHAI
Wuhan
Huanggang
ANHUI
Changzhou
Wuxi
Suzhou
Shanghai
Hangzhou
Jiaxing
Yichang
Wuchang
Tongling
Yuhang
Jianling
Shashi
Huangshi
Anqing
ZHEJIANG
Shaoxing
Dongting Hu
Changde
Jiujiang
Jingdezhen
Qu Xian
Lishui
Dajing
Ningbo
Yiyang
Xiangyin
Yingtan
Shangrao
Longquan
Wenzhou
Changsha
Nanchang
HUNAN
Xiangtan
Qingjiang
Xinyu
JIANGXI
Ji'an
Shaoyang
Hengyang
Nanping
Ningde
Xian
Changning
Wan'an
FUJIAN
Fuzhou
(Foochow)
Guilin
Ganzhou
Changting
Putian
ZHUANGZU
Zhongshan
Chen
Xian
Shaoguan
Xinfeng
Zhangzhou
Quanzhou
Liuzhou
Yingde
Meizhou
(Meixian)
Xiamen
(Amoy)
Heyuan
Chao'an
Shantou
(Swatow)
Wuzhou
Guiping
GUANGDONG
Guangzhou
(Canton)
Chaoyang
Foshan
Lufeng
Kowloon
Shunde
HONG KONG
Yangjiang
Macau
(Port.)
(U.K.)
Maoming
Zhanjiang
Leizhou
Bandao
Haikou
HAINAN
Dongfang
Dan Xian
Sanya
(Yaxian)

Qiqihar
HEILONGJIANG
Hailun
Suileng
Anda
Harbin
Acheng
Da'an
Tailai
Tuquan
Tongyu
Baicheng
Tao'an
Fuyu
JILIN
Changchun
Jilin
Jiaohe
Siping
Shuangliao
Liaoyuan
Fusong
Tonghua
Tieling
LIAONING
Shenyang
Fushun
Benxi
Fuxin
Liaoyang
Pingdingshan
Jinzhou
Anshan
Jinxi
Yingkou
Liaodong
Wan
Qinhuangdao
Jin Xian
Bandao
Dandong
Dalian
(Lüda)

Heishui
Chengde
Chifeng
Aohan Qi
Hexigten Qi
Weichang
Huade
ZIZHIQU
DAHINGANLING
Dong bei Ping yuan
Manchurian Plain
Songhua Jiang
Nen Jiang
Xiao Hinggan Ling
Blagoveshchensk
Zavitinsk
Sunwu
Svobodnyy
Amur
Tahe
Shilka
Argun
Amur
Wuzhan
Nenjiang
Hegang
Fuyu
Fujin
Jixi
Jiamusi
Shuangyashan
Huanan
Yichun
Hailin
Mudanjiang
Suifenhe
Yanji
Ussuriysk
Nakhodka
Olga
Rudnaya Pristan
SIKHOTE ALIN
Pristan
Khabarovsk
Fuyuan
Khanka
Oz. Khanka
(Xingkai Hu)
Vladivostok
Kraskino
Ch'ôngjin
Hamhûng
Hûngnam
NORTH KOREA
Sinûiju
Anju
P'yôngyang
Namp'o
Wônsan
Kaesông
Sariwôn
Haeju
Inch'ôn
Sôul
Seoul
SOUTH KOREA
Suwôn
Ch'ôngju
Taejôn
Kunsan
Chônju
Kwangju
Mokp'o
Cheju
Cheju do
Andong
P'ohang
Taegu
Ulsan
Masan
Pusan
Yôsu
Huang
Hai
Huimin
Weifang
Yantai
Weihai
Laizhou
Wan
Rongcheng
Shandong
Bandao
YELLOW SEA
Korea
Strait
Tsushima
Shimonoseki

SEA OF JAPAN
Sakhalin
Yuzhno
Sakhalinsk
Wakkanai
La Perouse Strait
Kurilskiye
Ostrova
Kunashir
Iturup
Claimed by Japan
Asahikawa
Asahi dake
Otaru
Sapporo
HOKKAIDŌ
Kushiro
Muroran
Hakodate
Aomori
Hachinohe
Morioka
HONSHŪ
Akita
Ishinomaki
Yamagata
Sendai
Niigata
Fukushima
Kōriyama
Nagaoka
Utsunomiya
Nagano
JAPAN
Kanazawa
Toyama
Tōkyō
Fukui
Gifu
Kawasaki
Chiba
Nagoya
Yokohama
Kyōto
Shizuoka
Tottori
Matsue
Amagasaki
Ōsaka
Kōbe
Sakai
Okayama
Hamamatsu
Wakayama
Oki guntō
Hiroshima
Takamatsu
SHIKOKU
Kitakyūshū
Fukuoka
Matsuyama
Uwajima
Saseho
Ōmuta
Kumamoto
KYŪSHŪ
Nagasaki
Miyazaki
Miyakonojō
Kagoshima
Ōsumi
shotō
Amami
ō shima
Nansei shotō
(Ryukyu Islands)
Tokuno
shima
Okinawa jima
Naha
Miyako jima
Iriomote jima
PACIFIC OCEAN
EAST CHINA SEA
Mazu Liedao
Chilung
Hsinchu
Taipei
Taichung
Changhua
Chiai
Hualien
TAIWAN
(FORMOSA)
Tainan
Kaohsiung
Pingtung
Taitung
Bashi Channel
Batan
Islands
Luzon Strait
Babuyan
Islands
C. Bojeador
C. Engaño
Laoag
Tuguegarao
Aparri
PHILIPPINES
LUZON
SOUTH CHINA SEA

Tropic of Cancer

Relief		
Feet		Metres
16 404		5000
9843		3000
6562		2000
3281		1000
1640		500
656		200
0		Sea Level
Land Dep.		
656		200
13 123		4000
22 966		7000

Scale 1:16 000 000

0   100   200   300   400   500 Miles

0   200   400   600   800 Kms.

Conic Projection

© Collins ◇ Longman Atlases Cbi

53

EAST CHINA

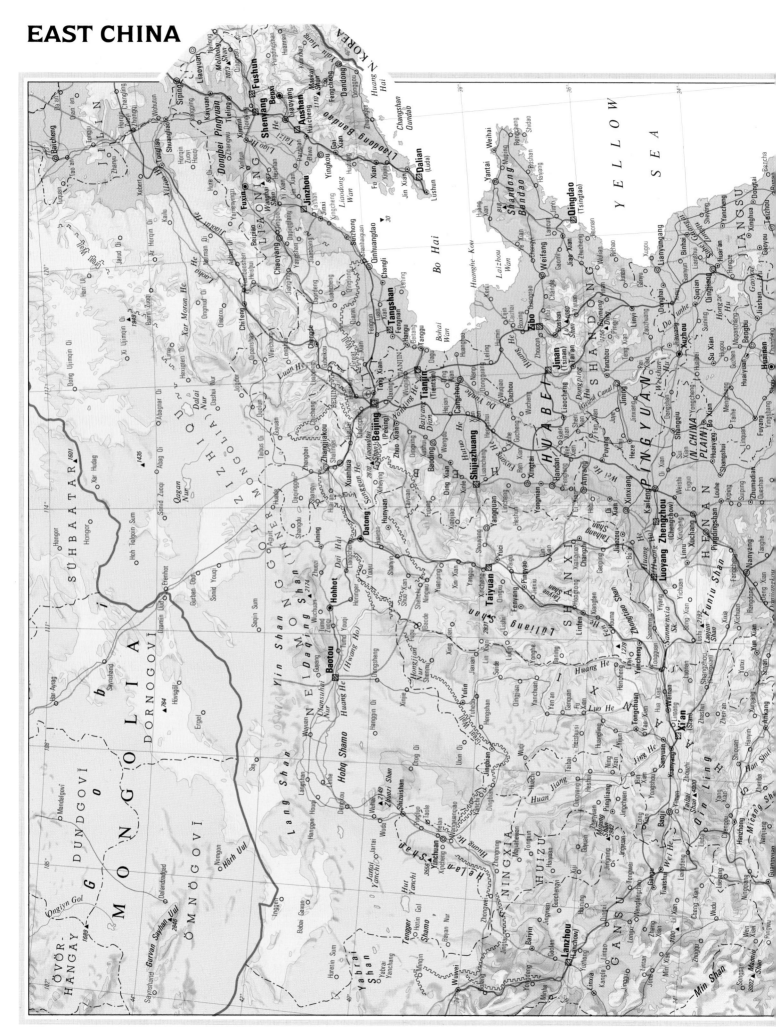

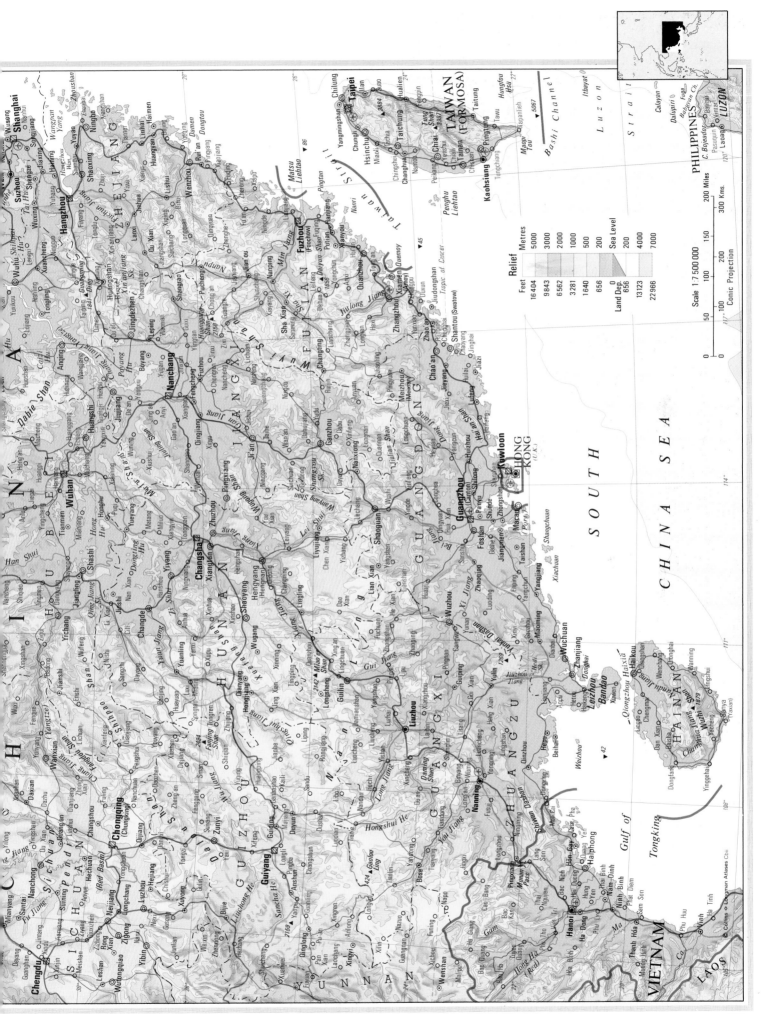

INDO-CHINA

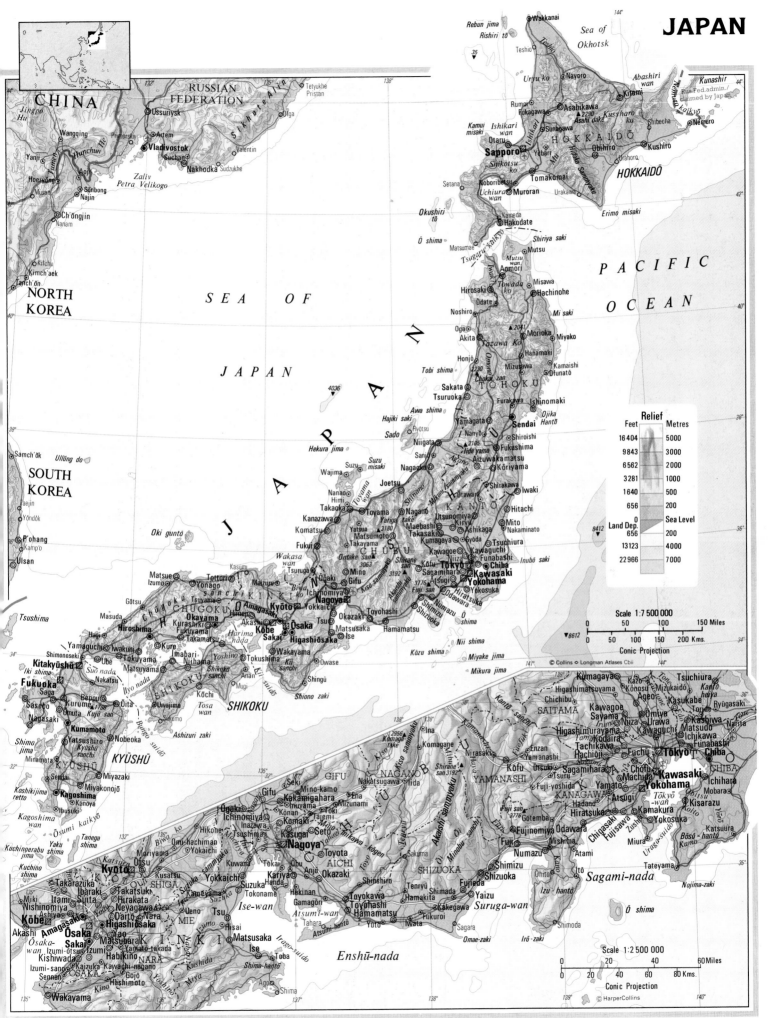

JAPAN

CHINA

RUSSIAN FEDERATION

Rebun jima
Rishiri tō
Wakkanai
Sea of Okhotsk

Teshio

Ussuriysk

Tesiho

Nayoro
Abashiri wan
Kunashir
Rus.Fed.admin.
claimed by Japan

Olga

Tetyukhé
Pristan

Uryu ko
Rumoi
Asahikawa
Kitami
Nemuro kaikyō

Nakhodka

Wangqing

Asahi dake
Kussharo ko
Shibecha
Nemuro

Artem
Suchan
Sudzukhe

Fukagawi
Kamui misaki
Sunagawa
Urahoro

Yanji

Otaru
HOKKAIDŌ

Vladivostok

Ishikari wan
Yūbari

Kushiro

Primorsky
Valentin

Sapporo
Obihiro

Shikotsu ko

HOKKAIDŌ

Hunchun

Zaliv Petra Velikogo
Najin

Noboribetsu
Tomakomai

Hoeryong

Uchiura wan
Muroran
Urakawa

Aoji
Nakhodka

Setana
Erimo misaki

Musan

Okushiri tō
Kameda

CHINA

Ōshima
Hakodate

Ch'ŏngjin
Nanam

Matsumae
Shiriya saki

Tsugaru kaikyō
Mutsu

P A C I F I C

Kitchu

Aomori
Mutsu wan

Kimch'aek
Iwaki
Hirosaki

Misawa
Hachinohe

Tanch'ŏn

Towada ko

O C E A N

NORTH KOREA

Ōdate

Mi saki

Noshiro

Oga

Morioka
Miyako

Akita

▲2041

SEA OF

Tazawa ko

Chōkai zan

Honjō
Omono
Hanamaki

Kamaishi

Tobi shima
Mizusawa
Ōfunato

JAPAN

Sakata
T O H O K U

Tsuruoka
Ishinomaki

Awa shima
Furakawa

4036▼

Yamagata
Ojika Hantō

JAPAN

Hajiki saki
Sendai

Shiroishi

Hekura jima
Sado
Niigata
Fukushima

Ryōtsu
Nan'yō

▲2105

Suzu

Iide yama

Samch'ŏk

Wajima

Suzu misaki
Sanjō

Aizuwakamatsu
Iwaki

Nanao

SOUTH KOREA

Ullŭng do

Himi
Nagaoka
Kōriyama

Toyama

Shirakawa

P'ohang

Toyama wan
Takaoka
Nagano
H
Ōtawara

Kamp'o

Joetsu
Mikuni sammyaku
Hitachi

Kanazawa
Utsunomiya
K A N T Ō

Ulsan

Komatsu
▲3192
Maebashi
Ashikaga
Mito

Oki guntō
Matsumoto
Takasaki
Nakaminato

Fukui
Takayama
C H Ū B U
Kumagaya
Gyōda
Tsuchiura

Ōgaki
▲3180
Kawagoe

Yatsuo
Kōfu
Kawaguchi
Funabashi

Wakasa wan
Ontake san
Gifu
Shirane san
Tōkyō
Chiba

Kasumi
3063
Mino
▲3776
Sagamihara
Kawasaki
Inubō saki

Matsue
Tsuruga
Fuji san
Atsugi
Yokohama

Izumo
Maizuru
Ichinomiya
Akaishi sammyaku
Yokosuka

Tottori
Biwa
Kyōto
Yokkaichi
Hiratsuka

Yonago
N
Ōkazaki
Numazu
Ō shima

Gōtsu
Chūgoku sanchi
Ōtsu
Akashi sammyaku
Odawara

K I N K I
Tsu
Shimizu

Masuda
C H Ū G O K U
Toyohashi
Shizuoka

Okayama
Ōsaka

Hamamatsu

Hagi
Kurashiki
Amagasaki
Tsu
Nii shima

Kōzu shima

Hiroshima
Himeji
Kōbe
Matsusaka

Yamaguchi
Akashi
Sakai
Ise

Iwakuni
Takatsuki
Higashiōsaka
Miyake jima

Shimonoseki
Kure
Imabari
Harima nada

8612▼

Ube
Takamatsu
Wakayama

Kitakyūshū
Nihama
Yoshino

Suō nada
Nakatsu
Shikoku sanchi

Matsuyama
Tokushima

Fukuoka

Iki shima
Iyo nada
Anan
Kil sanchi

Saga

S H I K O K U

Mikura jima

Beppu

Kōchi

Kurume

Ōita
Owase

Sasebo
Ōmuta
Kuju san

Shingū

Nagasaki

Kumamoto

Yatsushiro
Bungo suidō
Tosa wan

Nobeoka
Ashizuri zaki
Shiono zaki

Shimo jima
Kyūshū sanchi

Minamata
K Y Ū S H Ū

Sendai

Miyazaki

Kagoshima
Miyakonojō

Kōshikijima rettō
Kanoya

Ibusuki

Kagoshima wan
Ōsumi kaikyō

Tanega shima

Kuchinoerabu jima
Yaku shima

Kuchino shima

Relief

Feet		Metres
16 404		5000
9843		3000
6562		2000
3281		1000
1640		500
656		200
0		Sea Level
Land Dep.		
656		200
13123		4000
22 966		7000

8412▼

Scale 1:7 500 000

| 0 | 50 | 100 | 150 Miles |
| 0 | 50 | 100 | 150 | 200 Kms. |

Conic Projection

Inset map (lower right)

Kumagaya
Tsuchiura

Kazo
Mizukaido

Higashimatsuyama
Ageo
Kasukabe

Chichibu
SAITAMA
Kawagoe
Sayama
Iruma
Niza
Urawa
Kashiwa

Komaga-take
Higashimurayama
Kodaira
Kawaguchi
Matsudo
Ichikawa

Ina
Komagane
Tachikawa
Hachiōji
Fuchū
Tōkyō
Chiba

Nirasaki
Enzan
Yamanashi
Tama
Chōfu
Machida
Kawasaki

GIFU
Kōfu
Tsuru
Sagamihara
Yamato
Yokohama

NAGANO
YAMANASHI
KANAGAWA
Ichihara

Seki
Shirane san 3192
Fuji-yoshida
Hadano
Atsugi
Yokosuka
Mobara

Gifu
Nakatsugawa
Fuji san 3776
Gotemba
Hiratsuka
Bōsō hantō

Kakamigahara
Mino-kamo
Ena
Fujinomiya
Odawara
Chigasaki
Fujisawa
Zushi
Kisarazu

Ōgaki
Mizunami
Fuji
Mishima
Kamakura
Uraga-suidō

Ichinomiya
Toki
SHIZUOKA
Numazu
Miura

Komaki
Kasugai
Seto
Shinshiro
Atami
Sagami-nada

Nagoya
Toyota
Ōi
Shimizu
Izu hantō

AICHI
Ōbu
Kariya
Anjō
Okazaki
Shizuoka
Ō shima

Tokai
Toyokawa
Tenryū
Shimada
Yaizu
Fujieda

Handa
Hekinan
Toyohashi
Hamakita
Kakegawa
Suruga-wan
Ōhito

Atsumi-wan
Hamamatsu
Iwata
Fukuroi
Shimoda

Atsumi-hantō
Yūto
Sagara

Kyōto
SHIGA
Kusatsu
Ōtsu
MIE
Tsu
Hisai
Matsusaka
Omae-zaki
Irō-zaki

Takarazuka
Ibaraki
Takatsuki
Suita
Nara
Ise
Enshū-nada
Shimoda

Miki
Nishinomiya
Ashiya
Hirakata
Neyagawa
Ueno
Iga
MIE

Kōbe
Amagasaki
Higashiōsaka
Yao
Kushida

Akashi
Ōsaka
Daitō
NARA
Matsubara

Ōsaka-wan
Sakai
Izumi
Yamato-takada
Toba
Agos
Shima-hantō

Kishiwada
Kawachi nagano
Gojō

Izumi-ōtsu
Izumi-sano
Habikino
Hashimoto

Sennan
Kino
Yoshino
Miya

Wakayama

Scale 1:2 500 000

| 0 | 20 | 40 | 60 Miles |
| 0 | 20 | 40 | 60 | 80 Kms. |

Conic Projection

© HarperCollins

SOUTHEAST ASIA

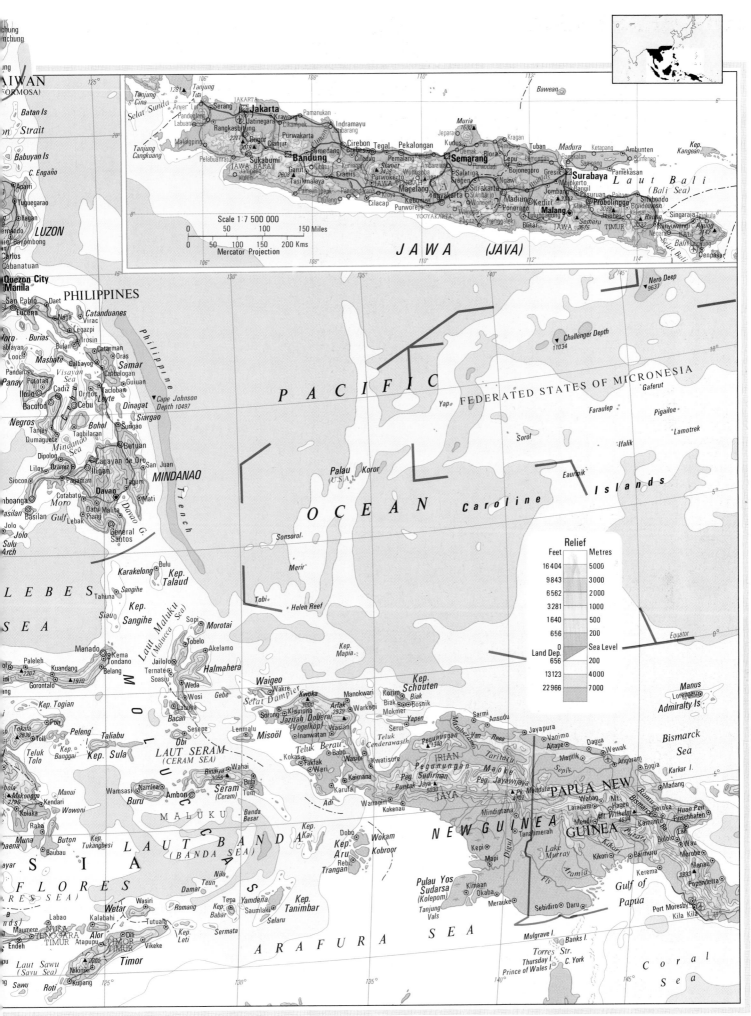

SOUTH ASIA

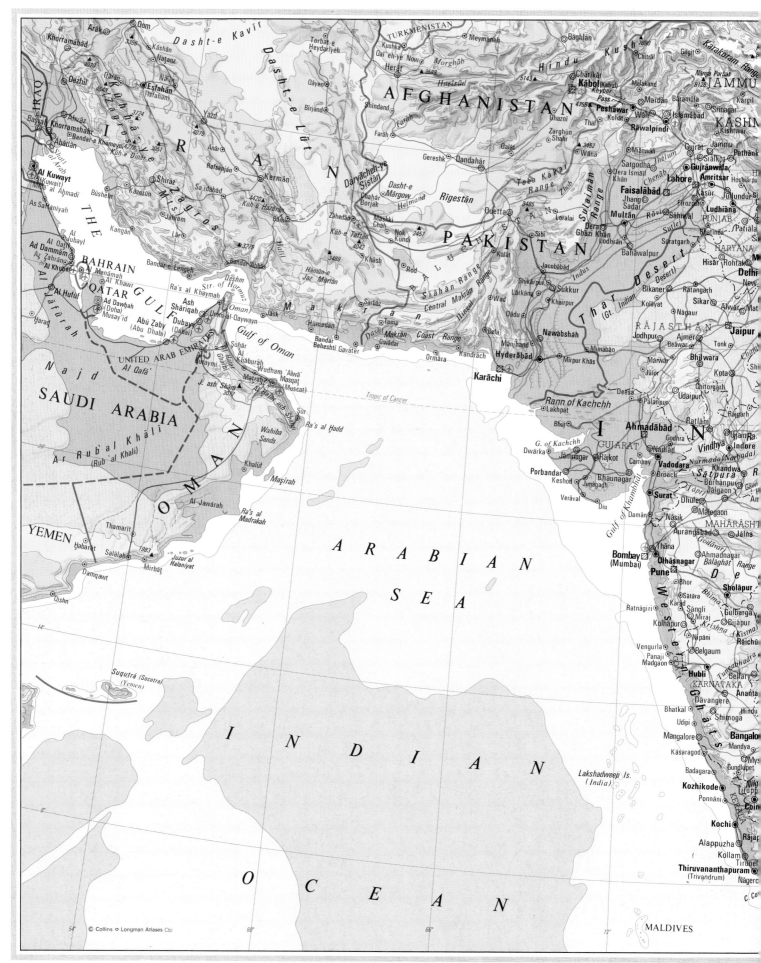

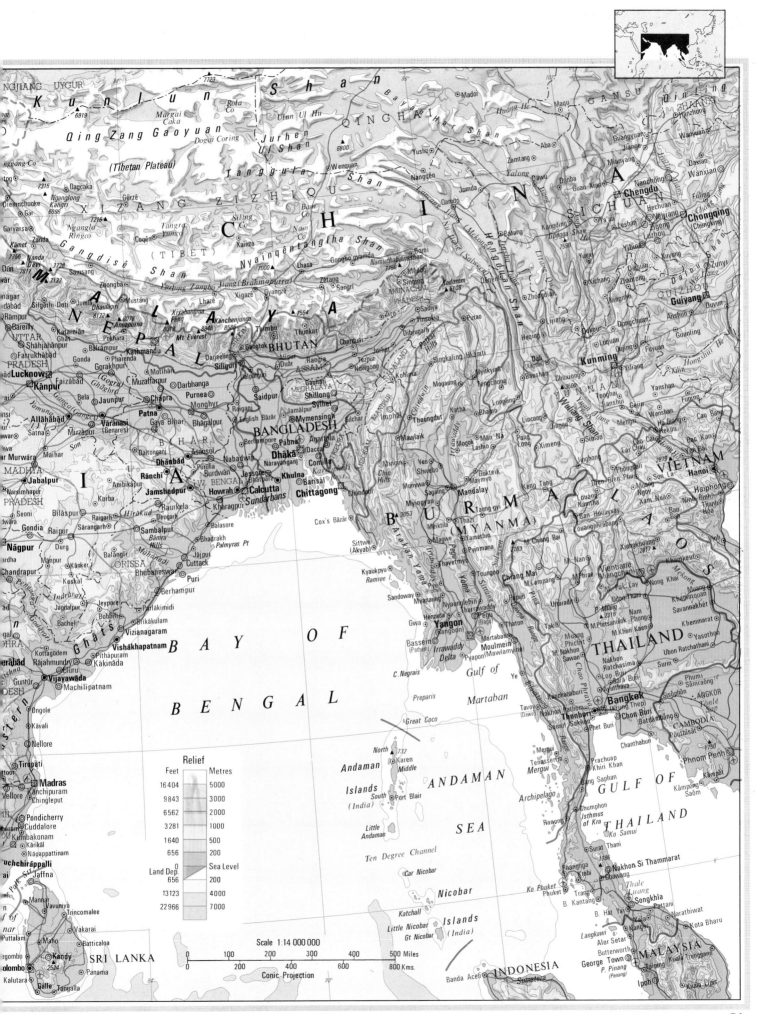

NORTHERN INDIA, PAKISTAN AND BANGLADESH

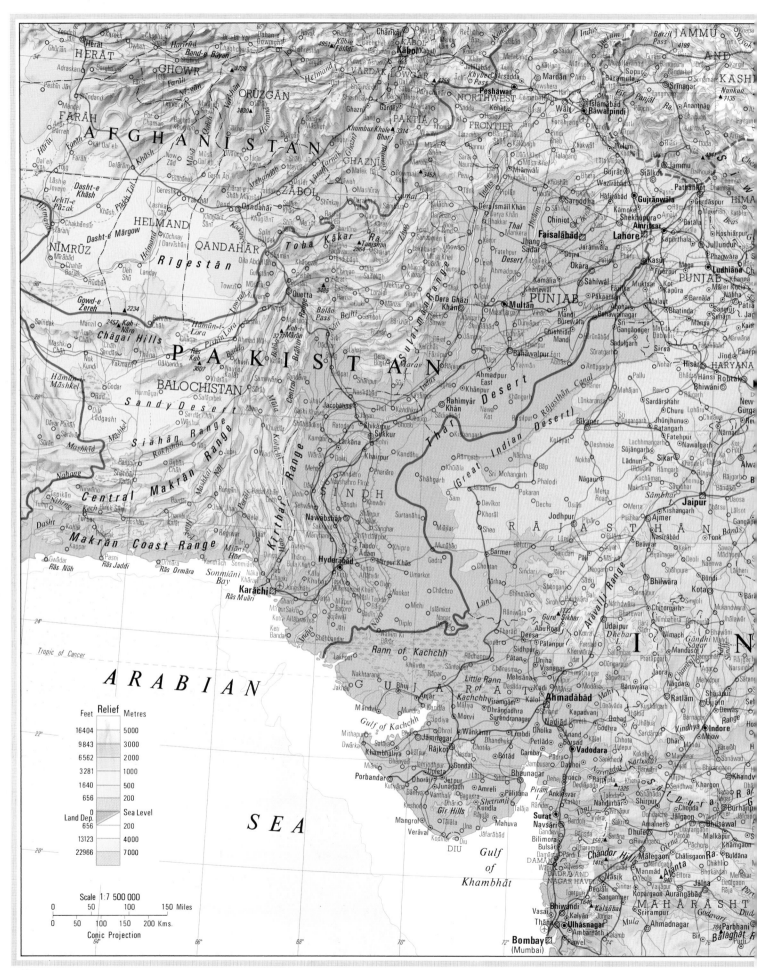

ARABIAN

SEA

Relief		
Feet		Metres
16404		5000
9843		3000
6562		2000
3281		1000
1640		500
656		200
0		Sea Level
Land Dep.		
656		200
13123		4000
22966		7000

Scale 1:7 500 000

0   50   100   150 Miles

0   50   100   150   200 Kms.

Conic Projection

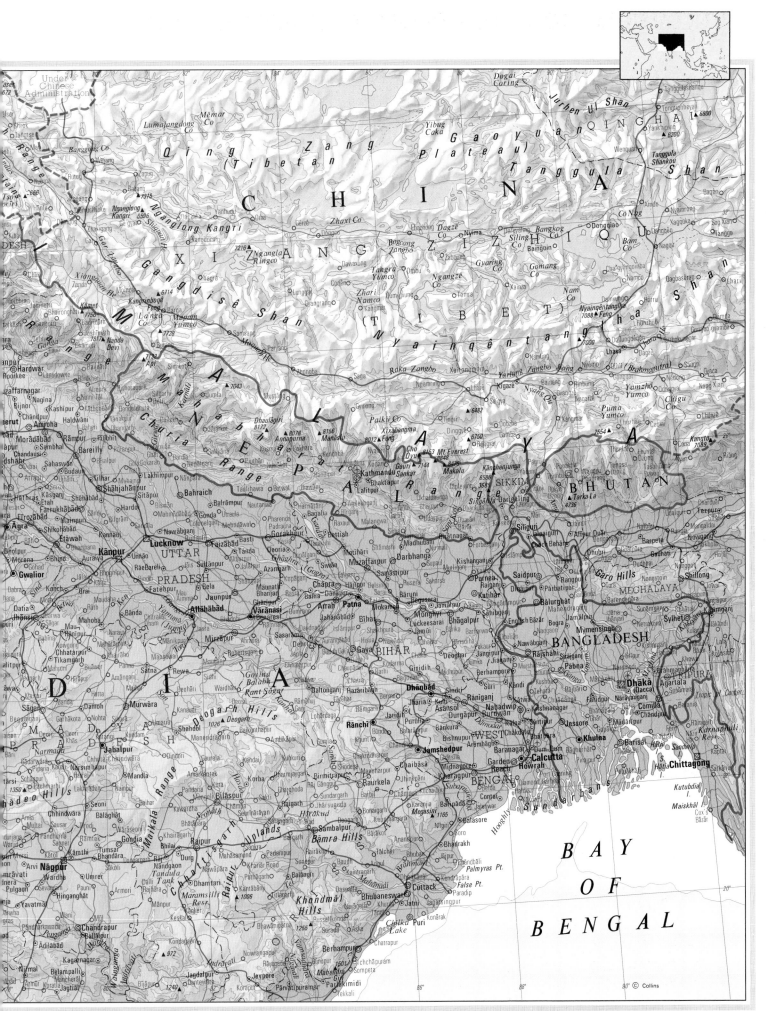

SOUTHWEST ASIA

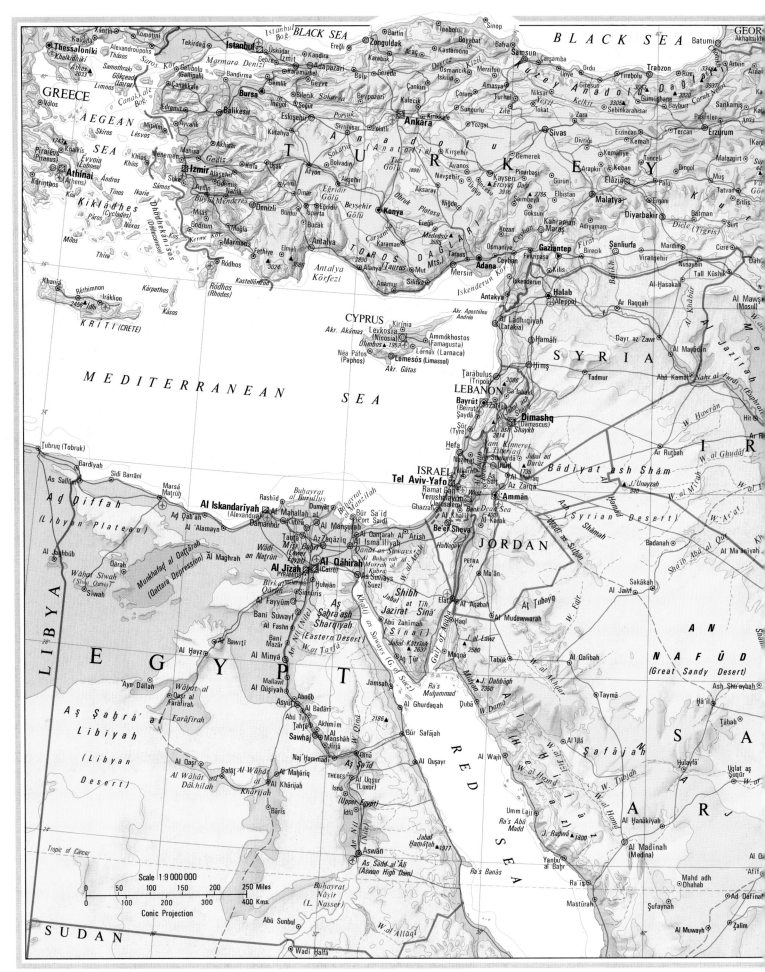

GREECE

Thessaloníki

Athínai (Athens)

AEGEAN SEA

KIKLÁDHES (Cyclades)

KRITI (CRETE)

MEDITERRANEAN SEA

BLACK SEA

Istanbul

Bursa

İzmir

Konya

Ankara

T U R K E Y

TOROS DAĞLARI / TAURUS MTS.

Adana

Gaziantep

Şanlıurfa

Malatya

Diyarbakir

Samsun

Trabzon

CYPRUS

Levkosía (Nicosia)

Lemesós (Limassol)

Halab (Aleppo)

Hamāh

Ḥimṣ

LEBANON

Bayrūt (Beirut)

Dimashq (Damascus)

S Y R I A

Ar Raqqah

Dayr az Zawr

Tadmur

Bādiyat ash Shām (Syrian Desert)

ISRAEL

Tel Aviv-Yafo

Yerushalayim (Jerusalem)

Be'er Sheva

Dead Sea

'Ammān

JORDAN

PETRA

Ma'ān

Al 'Aqabah

Al Iskandarīyah (Alexandria)

Al Qāhirah (Cairo)

Al Jīzah

E G Y P T

LIBYA

Aş Şaḥrā' al Lībīyah (Libyan Desert)

Munkhafaḍ al Qaṭṭārah (Qattara Depression)

An Nīl (Nile)

Aswān

As Sadd al 'Ālī (Aswan High Dam)

Buḥayrat Nāṣir (L. Nasser)

RED SEA

Sinai

Gulf of Suez

Gulf of Aqaba

AN NAFŪD (Great Sandy Desert)

S A U D I A R A B I A

Tabūk

Al Madīnah (Medina)

SUDAN

Wadi Halfa

Tropic of Cancer

Scale 1:9 000 000

| | 50 | 100 | 150 | 200 | 250 Miles |

| | 100 | 200 | 300 | 400 Kms. |

Conic Projection

THE LEVANT

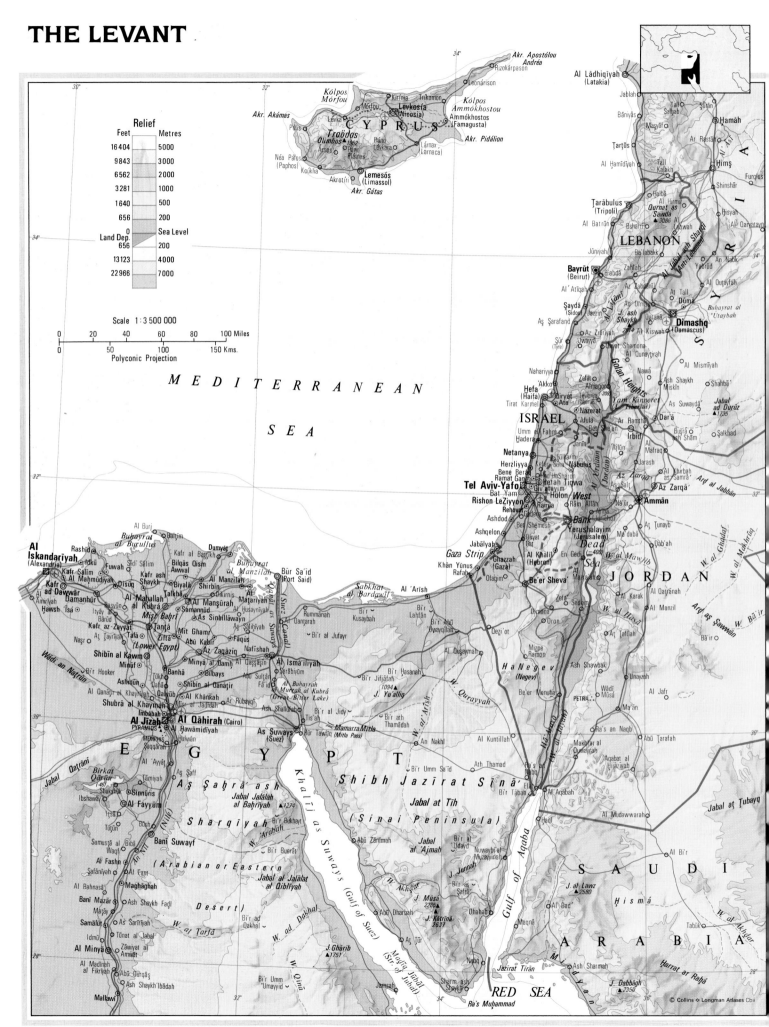

Relief

Feet	Metres
16 404	5000
9843	3000
6562	2000
3281	1000
1640	500
656	200
0	Sea Level
Land Dep.	
656	200
13123	4000
22966	7000

Scale 1 : 3 500 000

0   20   40   60   80   100 Miles
0   50   100   150 Kms.

Polyconic Projection

CYPRUS

Kólpos Mórfou
Akr. Akámas
Akr. Apostólou Andréa
Rizokárpason
Leonárison
Kirínia
Trikomon
Morfou
Levkosía (Nicosia)
Kólpos Ammókhostou
Ammókhostos (Famagusta)
Akr. Pidálion
Levka
Páno Léfkara
Troödos Olimbos ▲1952
Arsos
Néa Páfos (Paphos)
Koúklia
Páno Plátres
Lárnax (Larnaca)
Akrotíri
Lemesós (Limassol)
Akr. Gátas

MEDITERRANEAN

SEA

SYRIA
Al Ládhiqiyah (Latakia)
Jablah
Bāniyās
Şāfītā
Şūrān
Hamāh
Maşyāf
Ar Rastān
Al Ḥmīdīyah
Ţarţūs
Shinshār
Furqluş
Ḥimş
Al Hirmil
Tall Kalakh
Halbā
Bsharri
Qurnat as Sawdā ▲3086
Al Labwah
Al Qaryatayn
At Batrūn
LEBANON
Ba'labakk
An Nabk
Jūnīyah
Zahlah
Yabrūd
Al Qutayfah
BAYRŪT (Beirut)
B'abdā
Al 'Atīqah
Az Zabdānī
At Tall
Dūmā
DIMASHQ (Damascus)
Şaydā (Sidon)
Jazzīn
J. ash Shaykh
Qaţanā
Buhayrat al 'Utaybah
Aş Şarafand
Az Zrārīyah
'Ayn al Kiswah
Şūr (Tyre)
Jwayyā
Qiryat Shemona
Al Qunayţirah
As Suwaydā'
Jabal ad Durūz ▲1735
Nahariyya
Zefat
Almagor
Golan Heights
Yam Kinneret (Tiberias)
Nawá
Ash Shaykh Miskīn
Shahbā
Ḥefa (Haifa)
Qiryat Ata
Tirat Karmel
Ţeverya (Tiberias) ▲209
Nazerat
Ar Ramtha
Dar'ā
ISRAEL
Afula
Bet She'an
Irbid
Busrá ash Shām
Şalkhad
Umm el Fahm
Hadera
Jenin
'Ajlūn
Mafraq
Netanya
Tulkarm
Nābulus
Az Zarqā'
Al Khirbah as Samrā'
Herzliyya
Kefar Sava
Ramat Hasharon
Jarash
Bene Beraq
Ramat Gan
Petah Tiqwa
Az Zarqā'
TEL AVIV-YAFO
Giv'atayim
W. al Yābīs
Ard al Jabbān
Bat Yam
Holon
West
Rishon LeZiyyon
Ramla
Rām Allāh
Nā'ūr
AMMĀN
Rehovot
Gedera
Bank
Arīhā (Jericho)
Ma'daba
Ashdod
Bet Shemesh
YERUSHALAYIM (Jerusalem)
Dead
At Tunayb
Ashqelon
Qiryat Gat
Jabālyah
Al Khalīl (Hebron)
En Gedi
▲–400
Sea
Dhāb'ah
Gaza Strip
Ghazzah (Gaza)
W. al Mawjib
Khān Yūnus
Rafah
Be'er Sheva'
JORDAN
Oţaqim
Zefa
Al Karak
At Qaţrānah
Sedom
Al Manzil
Dimona
Oron
W. al Hasā
W. al Mōjib
Ard aş Şawwān
Qezī'ot
Mizpe Ramon
Tafīlah
Ba'ir
HaNegev (Negev)
Ash Shawbak
Be'er Menuha
Unayzah
Wādī Mūsá
PETRA
Ma'ān
Ra's an Naqb
Al Jafr

EGYPT

Al Burj
Baltīm
Buhayrat al Burullus
ALEXANDRIA
Al Iskandarīyah (Alexandria)
Rashīd
Idkū
Kafr Salīm
Fuwah
Kafr ash Shaykh
Disūq
Dumyāţ
Bilqās Qism Awwal
Biyala
Al Manzilah
Būr Sa'īd (Port Said)
Sidi Sālim
Kafr ad Dawwār
Al Maḥmūdīyah
Shirbīn
Al Manşūrah
Al Maţarīyah
Sabkhat al Bardawīl
Al 'Arīsh
Damanhūr
'Amrīyah
Ḥawsh 'Īsá
Kafr az Zayyāt
Disyūţ
Iţyay al Bārūd
Al Maḥallah al Kubrá
Samannūd
Mīt Ghamr
Ţalkhā
As Sinbillāwayn
Al Ḥusaynīyah
Aş Şāliḩīyah
Rummānah
Bi'r Kusaybah
Bi'r Abū 'Uwayqīlah
Bi'r Lahfān
Naşr
Ţanţā
Zittā
Aţ Ţawīlah
Abū Kabīr
Fāqūs
Al Qanţarah
Bi'r al Jufayr
Al Qaşşāşīn
Bi'r al Mazār
Al Qusaymah
Shibīn al Kawm
Minūf
Minya al Qamḥ
Az Zaqāzīq
Nafīshah
Al Ismā'īlīyah
Banhā
Bilbays
Abū Sulţān
Sarābiyūm
Bi'r Jifjāfah
1094 ▲
W. al 'Arīsh
Ashmūn
Qaha
Shibīn al Qanāţir
Fā'id
Al Buhayrah al Murrah al Kubrá (Great Bitter Lake)
J. Yu'alliq
Bi'r Ḥasanah
Bi'r Hooker
Qalyūb
Al Khānkah
Ar Rubayqī
Ash Shallūfah
Bi'r al Jidy
Al Qanāţir al Khayrīyah
Shubrā al Khaymah
Tis'ah
Bi'r ath Thamādah
Mamarra Mitla
Jabal Qaţrāni
Imbābah
AL QĀHIRAH (Cairo)
As Suways (Suez)
Mitla Pass
Bi'r Umm Sa'īd
AL JĪZAH
Al Hawāmidīyah
Būr Tawfīq
PYRAMIDS
Ḥulwān
Saqqārah
MEMPHIS
Ras Sudr
An Nakhl
Al Kuntillah
Abū Ţarafah
Aţ Ţāmiyah
Al 'Ayyāţ
Aş Şaff
Ath Thamad
Makhfar al Quwayrah
'Aqabat al Hijāzīyah
Jabal aţ Ţubayq
Birkat Qārūn
E G Y P T
Ra's en Naqb
Al 'Aqabah
Al Fayyūm
Aş Şaff
Ibshawāy
J. al 'Ajmah
Al Mudawwarah
Aţ Ţūr
Aţ Ţ
Tūnis
Aş Şahrā' ash Sharqīyah (Arabian or Eastern Desert)
Jabal Jalālah al Bahrīyah ▲1274
Bi'r Bukhayt
Sharm el Sheikh
Abū Zanīmah
S A U D I
Sinnūris
Al Fayyūm
Shibh Jazīrat Sīnā' (Sinai Peninsula)
Jabal at Tīh
Nuwayba' al Muzayyinah
Ḥaql
A R A B I A
Bani Suwayf
W. 'Arabah
Bi'r Bu'erāt
Abū Dharbah
J. Junnah
Bi'r 'Udayd
Al Bad'
Ḥismá
Al Fashn
Jabal al Jalālat al Qiblīyah
W. Akhḍar
Dhahab
Al Bi'r
Şafānīyah
Al Fant
W. al Ţarfā
J. Mūsá ▲2285
Magnā
Ţābūk
Samālūţ
Aş Şarīrīyah
J. Katrīnā ▲2637
J. al Lawz ▲2580
W. al Akhḍar
Idmū
Tūnat al Jabal
Bi'r ad Dakhal
W. ad Dakhal
Abū Dharbah
Nabq
Jazīrat Tīrān
Midyan
Ash Sharmah
J. Dabbāgh ▲2350
Al Minyā
Zāwiyat al Amwāt
W. al Ţarfā
An Nīl (Nile)
Magiq Jubal (Str. of Jubal)
Khalīj as Suways (Gulf of Suez)
Gulf of Aqaba
RED SEA
Al Madīnah al Fikrīyah
Abū Qurqāş
J. Gharib ▲1751
Bi'r Umm 'Umayyid
Bi'r Qinā
Jamsah
Sharm ash Shaykh
Ra's Muhammad
Mallawi
© Collins ◇ Longman Atlases Cbii

Feet Relief Metres

16404   5000
9843   3000
6562   2000
3281   1000
1640   500
656   200
0   Sea Level
Land Dep.
656   200
13123   4000
22966   7000

M E D I T E R R A N E A N   S E A

LEBANON

AL JANUB

S Y R I A

AL QUNAYTIRAH

Golan Heights
Under Israeli Occupation

Cease Fire Lines 1967

D A R ' A

I R B I D

⊚Irbid

J O R D A N

AL BALQA

⊚Amman

AL 'ASIMAH

Hefa (Haifa)
HAZAFON
Nazerat (Nazareth)
HAGALIL (Galilee)
Yam Kinneret (L. Tiberias)
(Sea of Galilee)
Teverya (Tiberias) (-209)

HEFA
Netanya

Tel Aviv-Yafo
(Jaffa)
Ramat Gan
Givatayim
Bat Yam
Holon
Rishon LeZiyyon
Rehovot
TEL AVIV-HAMERKAZ
Petah Tiqwa

NABULUS
Nabulus
Samiriah
Samaria
West Bank

Ashdod
Ashqelon
Jabalyah
Ghazzah (Gaza)
Khan Yunus
Rafah

Yerushalayim (Jerusalem)
AL QUDS
YERUSHALAYIM
Bayt Lahm (Bethlehem)

Al Khalil (Hebron)
AL KHALIL

(Yam HaMelah) (Al Bahr al Mayyit)
D e a d S e a

H A D A R O M

Be'er Sheva

AL KARAK

Scale 1:1 000 000

0   10   20   30 Miles
0   10   20   30   40   50 Kms.
Conic Projection

© Collins

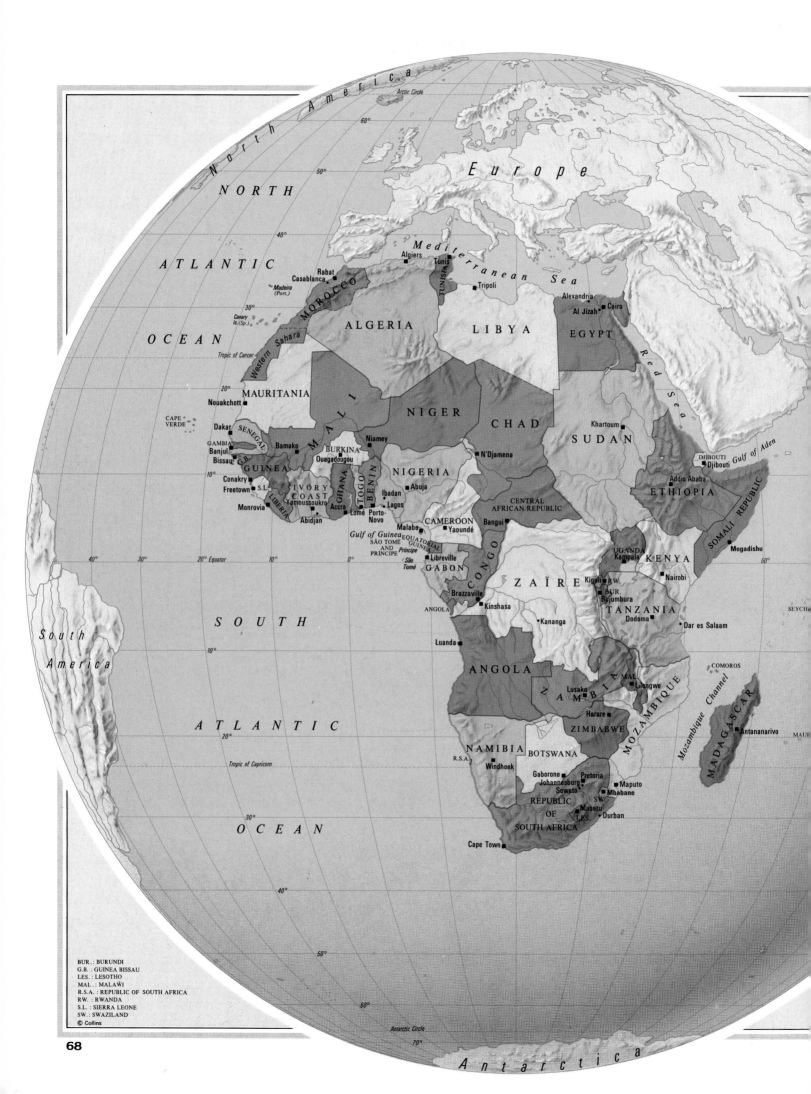

North America

Arctic Circle

60°

Europe

North Atlantic Ocean

NORTH

50°

ATLANTIC

40°

OCEAN

30°

Mediterranean Sea

Algiers
Tunis
Tripoli

Rabat
Casablanca
Madeira (Port.)
MOROCCO

Alexandria
Al Jizah • Cairo

Canary Is.(Sp.)

ALGERIA

LIBYA

EGYPT

Sahara

Tropic of Cancer

Western Sahara

20°

MAURITANIA

MALI

NIGER

CHAD

Khartoum

Red Sea

Nouakchott

SUDAN

Dakar
SENEGAL
GAMBIA Banjul
Bamako
Bissau G.B.
GUINEA
10°
Conakry
Freetown S.L.
LIBERIA
Monrovia

Niamey

BURKINA
Ouagadougou

NIGERIA

N'Djamena

DJIBOUTI *Gulf of Aden*
Djibouti

Addis Ababa

GHANA
TOGO
BENIN
IVORY COAST
Yamoussoukro
Accra Lomé Porto-Novo
Abidjan

Ibadan
Abuja
Lagos

CENTRAL AFRICAN REPUBLIC

ETHIOPIA

SOMALI REPUBLIC

CAMEROON
Malabo Yaoundé
Bangui

Gulf of Guinea EQUATORIAL GUINEA
SÃO TOMÉ AND PRÍNCIPE Príncipe
São Tomé
Libreville
GABON

UGANDA
Kampala
KENYA
Mogadishu

Equator 0°

CONGO

ZAÏRE

Kigali RW.
BUR.
Bujumbura

Nairobi

40°
30°
20° Equator
10°
0°
50°

Brazzaville
ANGOLA
Kinshasa

• Kananga

TANZANIA
Dodoma

Dar es Salaam

SEYCH

SOUTH

Luanda

10°

ATLANTIC

ANGOLA

ZAMBIA
Lusaka

MAL.
Lilongwe

COMOROS

Mozambique Channel

South America

20°

Harare
ZIMBABWE

MOZAMBIQUE

MADAGASCAR
Antananarivo

Tropic of Capricorn

OCEAN

NAMIBIA
BOTSWANA
R.S.A.
Windhoek

MAUR

30°

Gaborone
Johannesburg Pretoria
Soweto
Maputo
SW. Mbabane

REPUBLIC OF SOUTH AFRICA
Maseru LES. Durban

40°

OCEAN

Cape Town

50°

60°

Antarctic Circle

70°

Antarctica

BUR. : BURUNDI
G.B. : GUINEA BISSAU
LES. : LESOTHO
MAL. : MALAWI
R.S.A. : REPUBLIC OF SOUTH AFRICA
RW. : RWANDA
S.L. : SIERRA LEONE
SW. : SWAZILAND

© Collins

AFRICA

an

an

INDIAN

OCEAN

70°   80°   90°

AFRICA

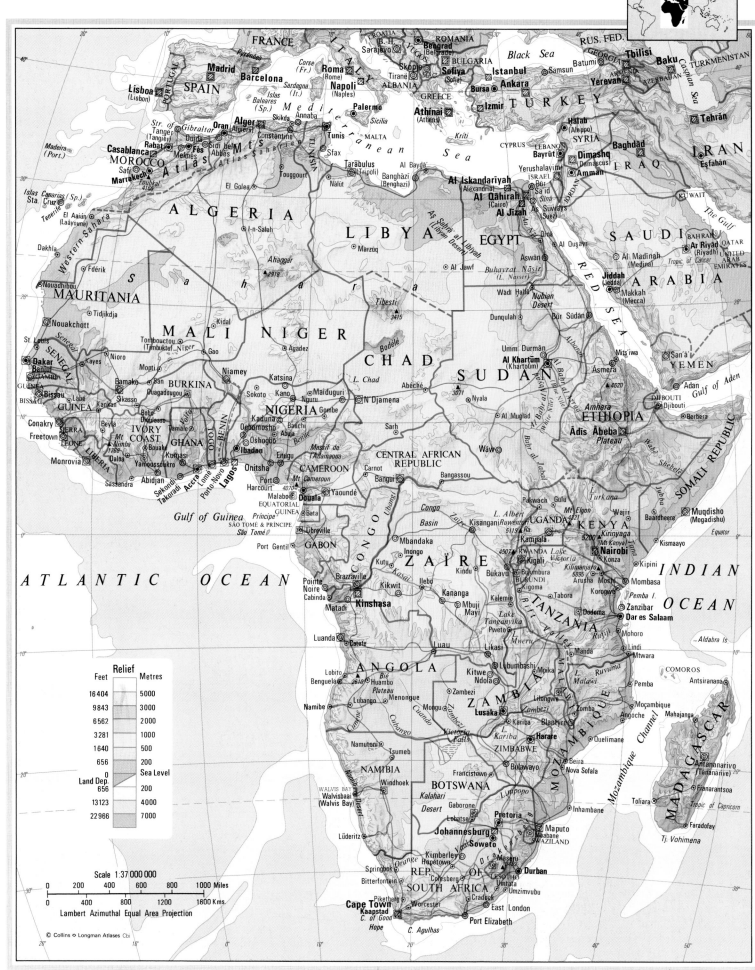

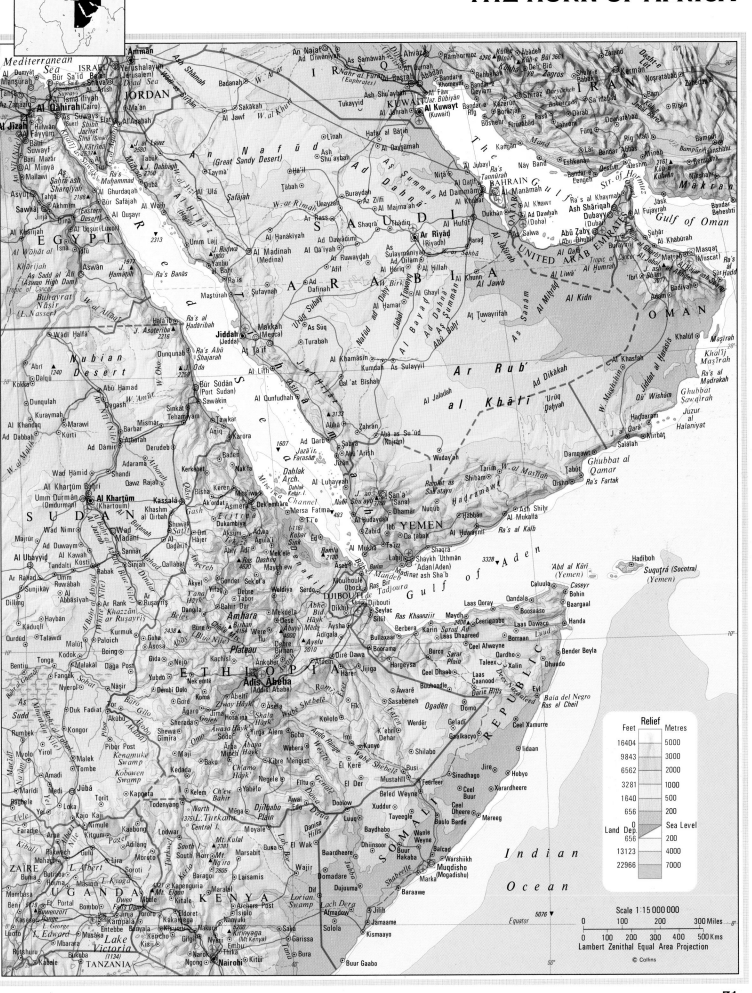

Relief

Feet		Metres
16404		5000
9843		3000
6562		2000
3281		1000
1640		500
656		200
0		Sea Level
Land Dep.		
656		200
13123		4000
22966		7000

Scale 1:15 000 000

0   100   200   300 Miles

0   100   200   300   400   500 Kms

Lambert Zenithal Equal Area Projection

© Collins

NILE VALLEY

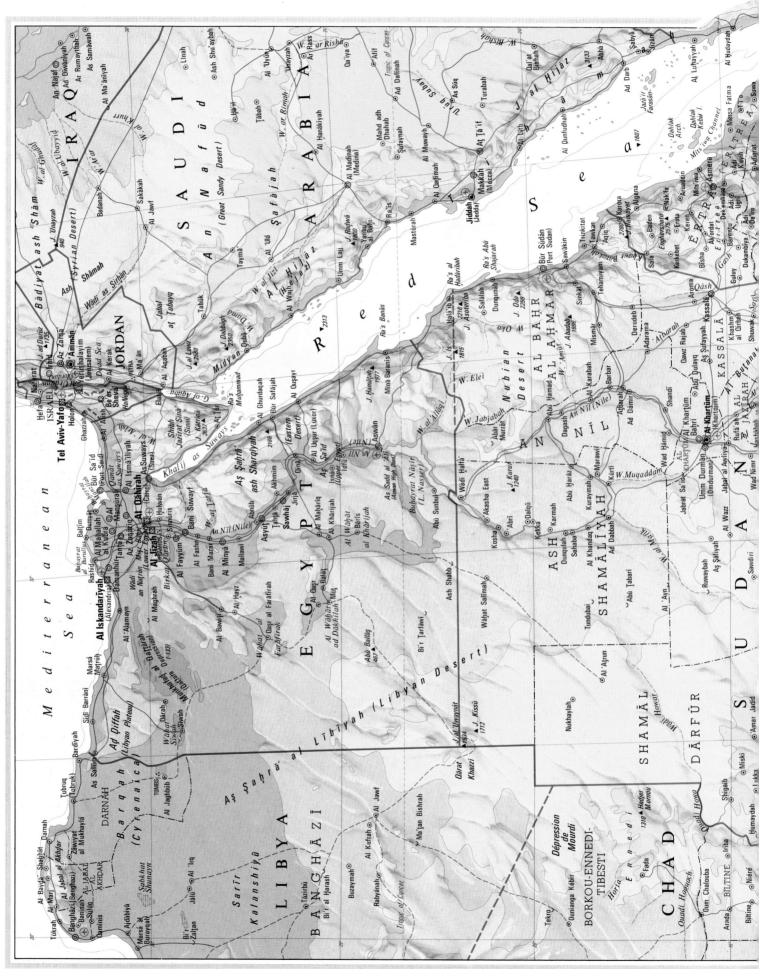

NORTHWEST AFRICA

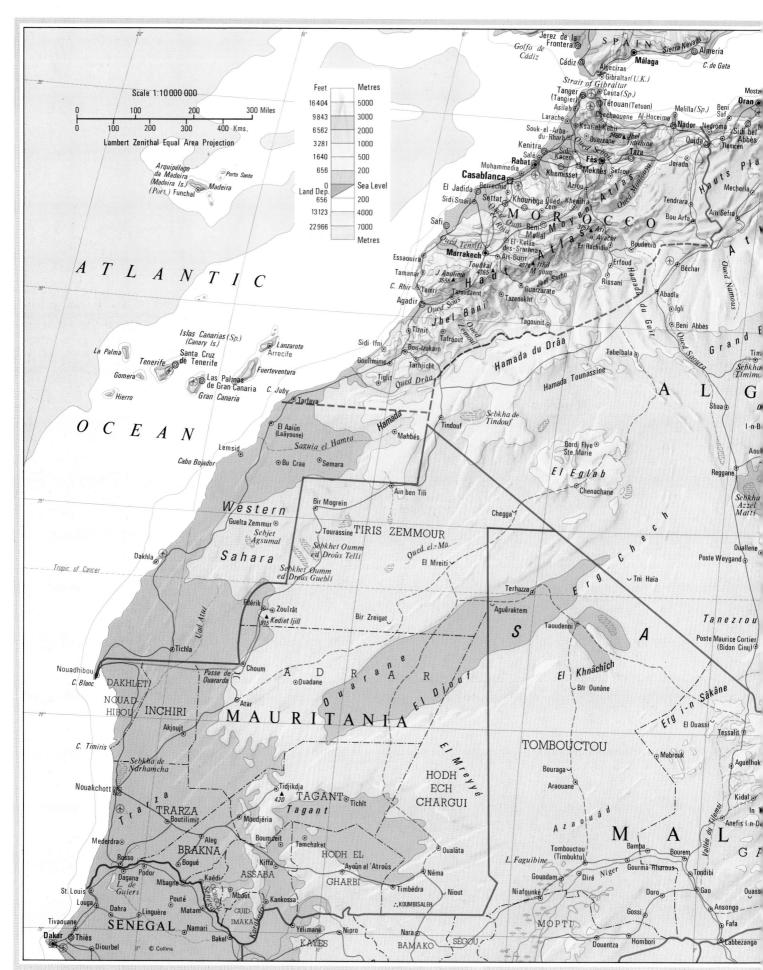

Scale 1:10 000 000

| 0 | 100 | 200 | 300 Miles |
| 0 | 100 | 200 | 300 | 400 Kms. |

Lambert Zenithal Equal Area Projection

Feet	Metres
16 404	5000
9843	3000
6562	2000
3281	1000
1640	500
656	200
0	Sea Level
Land Dep.	
656	200
13123	4000
22966	7000
Metres	Metres

ATLANTIC

OCEAN

Arquipélago da Madeira (Madeira Is.) (Port.) Funchal

Porto Santo

Madeira

Islas Canarias (Sp.) (Canary Is.)

La Palma

Tenerife

Gomera

Hierro

Santa Cruz de Tenerife

Lanzarote

Arrecife

Las Palmas de Gran Canaria

Gran Canaria

Fuerteventura

C. Juby

Tarfaya

Cabo Bojador

Dakhla

Tropic of Cancer

Nouadhibou

C. Blanc

C. Timiris

Sebkha de Ndrhamcha

Nouakchott

DAKHLET

NOUAD HIBOU INCHIRI

Akjoujt

Trarza

TRARZA

Boutilimit

Mederdra

Rosso

BRAKNA

Aleg

Bogué

Dagana

Podor

Mbagne

St. Louis

L. de Guiers

Louga

Dahra

Pouté

Linguère

Matam

Kaédi

Mbout

GUID IMAKA

Kankossa

SENEGAL

Tivaouane

Dakar

Thiès

Diourbel

KAYES

© Collins

Bakel

Yélimané

Namari

Nioro

Nara

BAMAKO

SÉGOU

MOPTI

El Aaiún (Laâyoune)

Lemsid

Western

Sahara

Bu Craa

Semara

Saguia el Hamra

Hamada

Mahbés

Bir Mogrein

Guelta Zemmur

Sebjet Agsumal

Tourassine

TIRIS ZEMMOUR

Sebkhet Oumm ed Droûs Telli

Sebkhet Oumm ed Droûs Guebli

Oued el-Ma

El Mreiti

Fdérik

Zouîrât

Kediet Ijill

915

Tichla

Uad Atui

Choum

Passe de Ouararda

Ouadane

ADRAR

Atar

Ouarane

El Djouf

Bir Zreigat

Aguêraktem

Taoudenni

El Khnâchîch

Bîr Ounâne

Erg en-Sâkâne

Erg Chech

Tni Haïa

Terhazza

S

A

A

Tni Haïa

Tanezrou

Poste Maurice Cortier (Bidon Cinq)

El Ouassi

Tessalit

Aguelhok

Kidal

In

Anefis I-n-Da

MALI

GA

Bamba

Bourem

Gourma-Rharous

Tondibi

Gao

Ansongo

Fafa

Labbezanga

Douentza

Hombori

Gossi

Doro

MAURITANIA

Tidjikdja

420

TAGANT

Tichît

Tagant

Moudjéria

Boumdeit

Tamchaket

HODH EL GHARBI

Kiffa

Ayoûn el 'Atroûs

ASSABA

Timbédra

Niout

∴ KOUMBISALEH

HODH ECH CHARGUI

Oualâta

Néma

El M'reyyé

TOMBOUCTOU

Bouraga

Araouane

Azaouâd

Tombouctou (Timbuktu)

L. Faguibine

Goundam

Diré

Niger

Mabrouk

Niafounké

Nara

Moudjéria

Tamchaket

SPAIN

Jerez de la Frontera

Golfo de Cádiz

Málaga

Sierra Nevada

Almería

C. de Gata

Cádiz

Algeciras

Ceuta (Sp.)

Strait of Gibraltar

Gibraltar (U.K.)

Tanger (Tangier)

Asilah

Larache

Tétouan (Tetuan)

Chechaouene

Al-Hoceima

Melilla (Sp.)

Nador

Nedroma

Beni Saf

Oran

Mosta

Sidi bel Abbès

Tlemcen

Ksar el-Kebir

Souk-el-Arba-du-Rharb

Ouezzane

Jbel Tidirhine 2460

Taza

Jerada

Oujda

Kenitra

Salé

Rabat

Mohammedia

Casablanca

El Jadida

Berrechid

Sidi Smaïl

Settat

Safi

Mazagan

Sidi Kacem

Meknès

Sefrou

Fès

Azrou

Khemisset

Khouribga

Oued-Zem

Khenifra

MOROCCO

Moyen Atlas

Oued Moulouya

Boudenib

Béchar

Abadla

Igli

Beni Abbès

Oued Namous

Oued Guir

Oued Saoura

Hamada du Guir

Er Rachidia

Erfoud

Rissani

Jbel Sarho

Hamada du Drâa

Tabelbala

Hamada Tounassine

Sbaa

ALGERIA

Sebkha Timimo

Reggane

Sebkha Azzel Matti

Ouallene

Poste Weygand

Chenachane

El Eglab

Bordj Flye Ste. Marie

Chegga

Tindouf

Sebkha de Tindouf

Ain ben Tili

Khemisset

Beni Mellal

El-Kelâa-des-Srarhna

Aït-Ourir

Marrakech

Ouarzazate

Tazenakht

Tagounit

Jbel Bani

Tanami

Tamri

C. Rhir

Agadir

Oued Sous

Taroudannt

J. Aoulime 4165

3555

Ifni

M'goun 407

Jbel Toubkal

Haut Atlas

Afri 3251

n' Ayachi

Tiznit

Tafraout

Oued Zemoul

Bou-Izakarn

Goulimime

Tarhjicht

Tiglit

Sidi Ifni

Oued Drâa

Essaouira

Tamanar

Oum er Rbia

Oued Tensift

Hauts Pla

Ain Sefra

Mecheria

Tendrara

Bou Arfa

74

Alger (Algiers)
Boufarik Blida Tizi-Ouzou
El Asnam Bouira
Chélif Boufarik Médéa Bordj Bou Arreridj Sétif Jijel Skikda Annaba
El Asnam Bou Saâda Barika Batna Constantine Guelma Tabarka Béja
Ksar el Boukhari Aïn Beïda Khenchela Tébessa El Kef Souk-Ahras
Tiaret Barika 1378 Djebel M'hila El Kairouan
Djelfa Biskra El Kasserine
Aflou Laghouat Oued Ittel Chott Melrhir Gafsa
Hassi er Rmel Oued el Attar El Metlaoui Tozeur Nefta
Ghardaïa El Oued Touggourt Chott Djerid Kebíli
Ouargla Hassi Messaoud Ksar Rhilane Médenine
El Golea Fort Lallemand TUNISIA Dehibat Zuwārah
Fort Miribel Grand Erg Oriental Fort Saint Nālūt Jādū
Miliana I-n-Salah Hassi bel Guebbour Ohanet Ghadāmis Dirj GHARYĀN Bani Walid
Tadjmout Amguid Bordj Omar Driss GHARYĀN (Tripolitania) Mizdah
Arak Illizi W. Irauen Al 'Uwaynāt Awbārī Ghaddūwah
Tassili-n-Ajjer Ḥamādat Marzūq W. Barjūj Marzūq
Garet el Djenoun 2327 Azao 2158 Zaouatallaz Ghāt Ṣaḥrā' Marzūq Al Qaṭrūn
I-n-Eker Ideles Tajarhī
I-n-Amguel Ahaggar Djebel 2306 Serkout I-n-Ezzane
Tit 2918 Tahat 2132 Toummo
Abalessa Tamanrasset Plateau du Djado
Silet Amsel A Djado
Admer R A
Anou Ti-n- Elhaoua Tassili oua-n-Ahaggar 1994 Mt.Gréboun Séguédine
1795 AGADEZ Aney
Iferouâne Aïr (Azbine)
Sidaouet Bilma Grand Erg de Bilma
In Abbangarit Teguidda I-n-Tessoum NIGER DIFFA
I-n-Gall Agadez ZINDER KANEM
TAHOUA Tegouma 508
Tanout Nokou Zigey BATHA

Menzel Bourguiba Binzert (Bizerte) C. Bon
Tunis La Goulette
Hammam Lif Nabeul
Béja G. de Hammamet
Enfida Sousse
Msaken Monastir
El Mahdia
Ra's Kaboudia
Sfax
Îles Kerkenna
Gabès Île de Djerba
G. de Gabès

Sicilia (Sicily) Catania
Ragusa Siracusa
C. Passero
MALTA Valletta
Lampedusa (Italy)

Mediterranean Sea

Ṭarābulus (Tripoli) Qaṣr al Qarābullī Al Khums
AZ ZĀWIYAH TARĀBULUS Zlīṭan
Gharyān Al Qaṣabāt Miṣrātah
Sīnāwin Tarābulus Sabkhat Tawurghā'
Abyār ash Shuwayrif Qaryat al Qaddāḥīyah Surt As Sulṭān
AL KHUMS An Nawfalīyah Ra's al Unūf Ajdābiyā
Hūn Waddān Marādah Bi'r Zaltan
Jabal as Sawdā' Zillah
Ṣaḥrā' Awbārī SABHĀ Birāk Samnū
LIBYA Sabhā Al Harūj al Aswad
Tmassah Zillah BANGHĀZĪ Bi'r al Harash
Zawīlah Waw al Kabīr Buzaymah
Sarīr Tibesti Ṣaḥrā' Rabyānah (Rebiana Sand Sea) Rabyānah
Tropic of Cancer
Bette 2286
Aozou Tarso Ouri 3150 Ouri
Bardai
3265 Wour Tibesti Tarso Ahon 3325
Zouar 3415 Emi Koussi
Tekro
Gouro Ounianga Kébir
BORKOU-ENNEDI-TIBESTI Horta
Aïn Galakka Largeau Fada
CHAD
Bodélé Ouadi Haouach
Bahr el Ghazal Oum Chalouba
Koro Toro Arada BILTINE
Biltine

Al Bayḍā' Shaḥḥāt
Tūkrah Al Marj Al Jabal al Akhḍar
Banghāzī (Benghazi) Banīnah AL JABAL AL AKHDAR
Qamīnis Sulūq
Khalīj Surt (Gulf of Sidra)
Marsá al Burayqah Al 'Uqaylah Sabkhat Shunayn
Jālū Al 'Irq
Tāzirbū
Sarir Kalanshiyū

Kalamái GREECE
Akr. Akrítas
Akr. Taínaron

WEST AFRICA

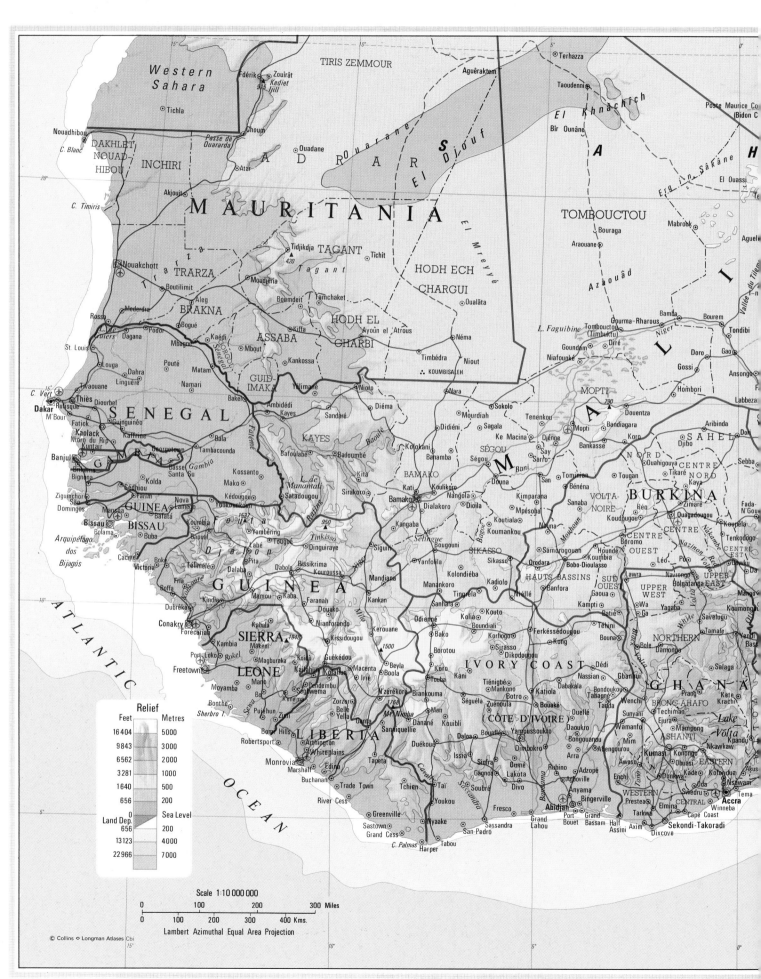

Western Sahara

TIRIS ZEMMOUR

Nouadhibou
C. Blanc
DAKHLET NOUAD-HIBOU
INCHIRI

Fdérik
Zouîrât
Kediet Ijill 915
Choum
Passe de Ouararda

Ouadane
Atar

Aguêraktem
Taoudenni
El Khnâchich
Poste Maurice Co (Bidon C

A
Bîr Ounâne
El Ouassi
Erg In Sâkâne
El Ouassi

A
Aguel

MAURITANIA

C. Timiris
Akjoujt
Nouakchott
TRARZA
Boutilimit
Tidjikdja 420 TAGANT
Tichît
Tich*T
Tagant

TOMBOUCTOU
Bouraga
Araouane
Mabrouk
Azaouâd
Aguel

Rosso
Mederdra
Aleg
BRAKNA
Boumdeit
Bogué
Moudjéria
Tamchaket
Kiffa
HODH EL GHARBI
ASSABA
Mbout
Kankossa
Ayoûn el Atrous
Néma
Timbédra
Niout
KOUMBISALEH

HODH ECH CHARGUI
Oualâta

L. Faguibine
Goundam
Niafounké
Tombouctou (Timbuktu)
Diré
Gourma-Rharous
Bamba
Bourem
Niger
Tondibi
Gao
Ansongo
Doro
Gossi

St Louis
Podor
Dagana
Louga
Dahra
Linguère
Matam
Namari
Bakel
Ambidédi
Kayes

Mbagne
Kaédi
Senegal
Pouté
GUID-IMAKA
Yilimane
Nioto
Diéma
Nara
Sandaré
Sokolo
Mourdiah
Sagala
Didiéni
Ke Macina
Diénné
Douentza
Djibo
SAHEL
Aribinda
Bandiagara
Koro
MOPTI 790
Mopti
Bankass
Hombori
Labbeza
Douentza

Dakar
Thiès
Diourbel
Rufisque
M'Bour
Fatick
Kaolack
Kaffrine
SENEGAL
Bala
Tambacounda
KAYES
Bafoulabé
Badoumbé
Banamba
Kolokani
Koulikoro
BAMAKO
Kati
Nangola
Dialakoro
Dioila
Mpésoba
Koutiala
VOLTA-NOIRE
Réo
Koudougou
Ouahigouya
Tikaré
Kaya
CENTRE NORD
Tougan
Bénéna
San
NORD
CENTRE
BURKINA
Fada-N'Gourma
Koupela
Tenkodogo
UPPER EAST
Mamo

C. Vert
Ntoro du Rip
Kuntair
Banjul
GAMBIA
Georgetown
Brikama
Bignona
Ziguinchor
São Domingos
GUINEA BISSAU
Bissau
Bolama
Arquipélago dos Bijagós
Buba
Cacine
Victoria

Kaolack
Gambia
Kossanto
Mako
Kédougou
Satadougou
Kita
Sirakoro
Bamako
Kangaba
L. de Manantali
1537
950
Youkounkoun
Labé
Tougé
Dinguiraye
Siguiri
Yanfolila
Kimparana
Sanaba
Nouna
Moutiala
HAUTS BASSINS
Bobo-Dioulasso
Houndé
Orodara
Banfora
SUD OUEST
Gaoua
Kampti
Batié
UPPER WEST
Wa
Yagaba
Lawra
Bolgatanga
Navrongo
Ga
Saveluku
Koumong

Mansoa
Bafatá
Nova Lamego
Bambadinca
Boké
Télimélé
Fria
Boffa
Dubréka
GUINEA
Mamou
Kindia
Conakry
Forécariah
Kambia
Port Loko
Rokel
Freetown
Moyamba
Bonthe
Sherbro I.

Koundara
Mali
Fouta Djalon
Pita
Dabola
Bissikrima
Kouroussa
Mandiana
L. de Sélingue
Bougouni
SIKASSO
Sikasso
Kolondiéba
Kadiolo
Tingréla
Mananankoro
Sanhala
Kouto
Odiemé
Kolia
Boundiali
Korhogo
Sirasso
Dikodougou
Ferkéssédougou
Kong
Bouna
NORTHERN
Bole
Damongo
Tamale
Salaga
GHANA
BRONG-AHAFO

Kindia
Dalaba
Dabola
Labé
Mamou
Kaba
Faranah
Kissidougou
Kerouane
Beyla
Boola
Touba
Séguéla
ASHANTI

SIERRA LEONE 1948
Makeni
Magburaka
Kabala
Koidu
Kailahun
Koindu
Guékédou
Macenta
Irié
Nzérékoré
Biankouma
Man
Duékoué
IVORY COAST
CÔTE D'IVOIRE
Bouaflé
Daloa
Issia
Gagnoa
Oumé
Lakota
Divo
Soubré
Sassandra
Fresco
Abidjan
Bingerville
Grand Bassam

Kambia
Rokel
Mano
Pendembu
Segbwema
Kenema
Zorzor
Belle Yella
Ganta
Sanniquellie
Mt Nimba 1768
Danané
Kouibli
Kouibli
Tapeta
Tchien
Taï
Youkou
Tabou
C. Palmas
Harper

Freetown
Moyamba
Bonthe
Pujehun
Zimi
Bomi Hills
LIBERIA
Arthington
Whiteplains
Robertsport
Monrovia
Marshall
Edina
Buchanan
Trade Town
River Cess
Greenville
Sastown
Grand Cess
Nyaake

ATLANTIC OCEAN

Arra
Sinfra
Gagnoa
Rubino
Agboville
Anyama
Adzopé
Aboisso
WESTERN
CENTRAL
Kumasi
Obuasi
Dunkwa
Bibiani
Enchi
Swedru
Oda
Winneba
Cape Coast
Elmina
Tarkwa
Half Assini
Axim
Dixcove
Sekondi-Takoradi
EASTERN
Koforidua
Nsawam
Accra
Tema

Relief

Feet	Metres
16 404	5000
9843	3000
6562	2000
3281	1000
1640	500
656	200
0	Sea Level
Land Dep.	
656	200
13 123	4000
22 966	7000

Scale 1:10 000 000

0   100   200   300 Miles

0   100   200   300   400 Kms.

Lambert Azimuthal Equal Area Projection

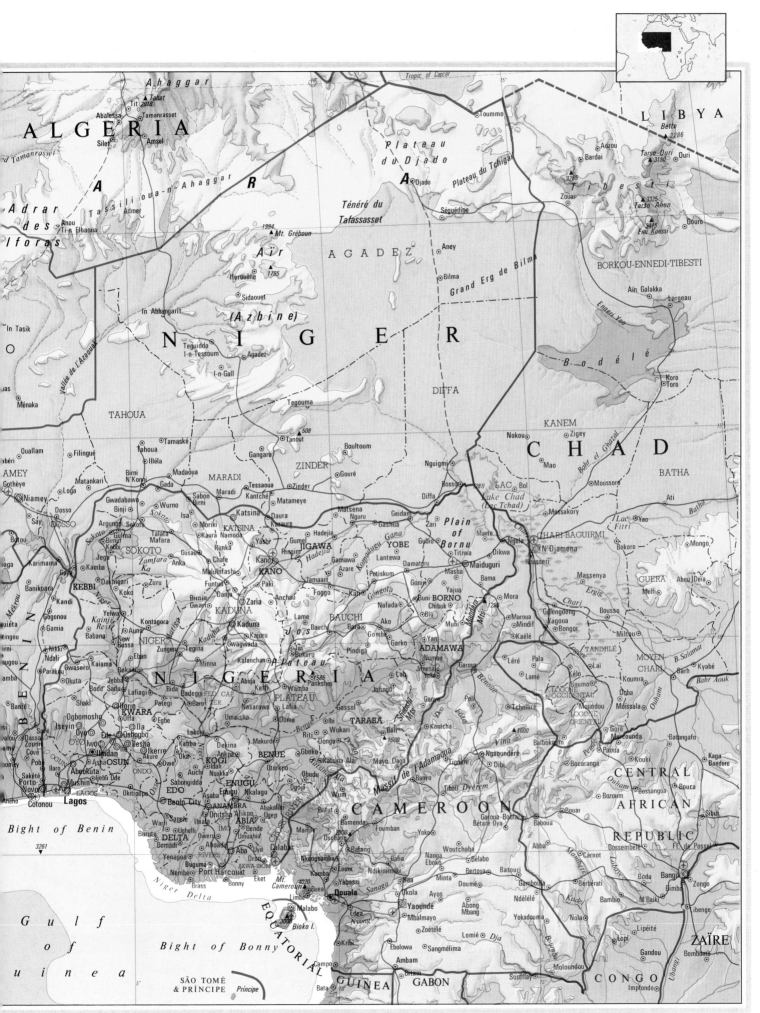

ALGERIA

Ahaggar

▲Tehat
2918
Tit
Abalessa ◦Tamanrasset
◦Silet   ◦Amsel

Wad Tamanrasset

Adrar des Ifloras

◦Anou Ti-n Elhaoua
◦Admer

◦In Tasik

◦Ménaka

Tassili oua-n-Ahaggar

A H A G G A R

Plateau du Djado

◦Toummo

LIBYA

▲Bette
2286

◦Aozou
◦Bardai

Tibesti

▲3285
▲3325

Tarso-Ouri
▲3155 Ouri

Plateau du Tchiga

◦Zouar   ▲Tarso Ahon

◦Djado

▲3445
Emi Koussi

◦Séguédine

◦Gouro

Ténéré du Tafassasset

▲1994 Mt. Gréboun

Aïr (Azbine)

▲1795

◦Iferouâne

◦Sidaouet

◦In Abbangarit

◦Teguidda I-n-Tessoum
◦Agadez

◦I-n-Gall

A G A D E Z

◦Aney

◦Bilma

Grand Erg de Bilma

BORKOU-ENNEDI-TIBESTI

◦Aïn Galakka
◦Largeau

Ennezi Yoo

◦Koro Toro

B o d é l é

N I G E R

DIFFA

TAHOUA

◦Tegouma

◦508

◦Tanout

KANEM

◦Nokou   ◦Zigey
◦Ziguey
◦Mao

C H A D

BATHA

◦Ati

Batho

◦Gangara

◦Boultoum

◦Tessaoua

◦Gouré

◦Nguigmi

ZINDER

◦Tamaské

◦Tahoua
◦Illéla

◦Birni N'Konni
◦Madaoua

MARADI

◦Gada
◦Maradi
◦Kantché
◦Matameye

◦Bosso   LAC. Bol
Diffa ◦   (281) ◦Bol
◦Massakory
◦Moussoro

Lac Fitri
◦Yao

◦Mongo

GUERA

◦Melfi

◦Matankari
◦Loga
◦Niamey

◦Gwadabawa
◦Binji   ◦Wurno
◦Sabon Birni

◦Isa   ◦Moriki
◦Kaura Namoda

◦Daura ◦Katsina
◦Karaure

◦Matsena
◦Nguru
◦Gashua

◦Geidam

◦Zari

Plain of Borno

◦Gubio

◦Marte

◦Dikwa

◦Ngala ◦N'Djamena

CHARI-BAGUIRMI

◦Kousseri
◦Bokoro

Chari

◦Massenya

◦Bousso

Ergig

◦Abou Deia

◦Mongo

◦Gulma ◦Argungu ◦Sokoto
◦Talata Mafara

SOKOTO

◦Gusau

◦Yabo

JIGAWA

◦Hadejia

◦Gumel

◦Kano

KANO

◦Gamawa

◦Azare

◦Potiskum

◦Damaturu

◦Lantewa

YOBE

◦Titiwa

◦Maiduguri

◦Masba

◦Bama

◦Mora

◦Maroua
◦Mindif

◦Gelengdeng
◦Yagoua

◦Bongor

MOYEN-CHARI

◦Sarh

◦Koumra

Bahr Aouk

◦Kaélé

TANDJILÉ

Bibliography note — (map content)

B. Salamar
◦Kyabé

◦Kebbi

KEBBI

◦Dakingari
◦Koko

◦Zuru

◦Birnin Gwari

◦Zaria

KADUNA

◦Kaduna

◦Kajuru

◦Anchau

◦Funtua
◦Malumfashi

◦Kari

◦Nafada

◦Chibuk

◦Biu

BORNO

◦Buni

◦Gonini

◦Yajua

◦Mubi

Mandara Mts.
▲1286

◦Gombi

◦Yan

ADAMAWA

◦Numan

◦Jimeta/Yola

◦Garoua

Benoue

◦Léré

◦Pala

◦Lamé

◦Kélo   ◦Laï

◦Tchollire

LOGONE OCCIDENTAL

◦Moundou

LOGONE ORIENTAL

◦Doba

◦Goré

◦Moissala
◦Mbaiki

◦Baibokoum

◦Gore Maroundou

◦Batangafo

C E N T R A L

A F R I C A N

R E P U B L I C

◦Kabba
◦Dekina

BENUE

◦Makurdi

◦Gboko

◦Katsina Ala

◦Wukari

TARABA

◦Beli
◦1508

◦Bali

◦Donga

◦Serti

◦Kontcha

◦Mayo-Daga

◦Tignère

◦Dibi

◦Ngaoundéré

◦Tibati *Dyérem*

◦Banyo

◦Bétaré Oya

◦Garoua-Boulaï

◦Abba

◦Bocaranga

◦Bozoum

◦Bouar

◦Baboua

◦Bossembélé

◦Bouca

◦Kouki
◦Bando

◦Bossangoa

◦Sibut

◦Fl. de Possel

N I G E R I A

◦Abuja

◦Keffi

FED. CAP. TER.

PLATEAU

◦Nasarawa
◦Lafia
◦Doma

◦Wamba

◦Pankshin

◦Panshin
◦1585

◦Jos

◦Bukuru

◦Pindiga

◦Garko

◦Bauchi

BAUCHI

◦Bara
◦Gombe

◦Ako

◦Foggo

◦Jamaari

◦Paki

◦Danja

Jos Plateau

◦Lafiagi

◦Bida

◦Badeggi

◦Baro

◦Patigi

KWARA

◦Ilorin
◦Offa
◦Egbe

◦Ila

◦Lokoja

◦Umaisha

KOGI

◦Ankpa

◦Oturkpo

◦Idah

◦Obubra

◦Obudu

◦Ogoja

◦Bamenda

◦Foumban

◦Yoko

◦Bafia

◦Bélabo

◦Bertoua

◦Batouri

◦Doumé

◦Carnot

◦Berbérati

◦Bambio

◦Nola

◦M'Baiki

◦Zongo

◦Bimbo

BENIN

◦Kandi

◦Banikoara

◦Gogounou

◦Gamia

◦Nikki

◦Ndali

◦Parakou

◦Gwasero

◦Kaiama

◦Save

◦Zoume

◦Pobé

◦Iseyin

◦Ogbomosho

OYO

◦Oyo
◦Iwo
◦Ede   ◦Oshogbo
◦Ila

◦Ibadan

◦Ife

OSUN

◦Ilesha

◦Ikerre

◦Akure

◦Owo

◦Ikare

ONDO

◦Ondo

◦Ode

◦Okitipupo

◦Auchi

◦Nsukka

◦Abakaliki

◦Ugep

◦Ikom

◦Mamfe

◦Bafut

◦Bamenda

◦Dschang

◦Bafang

◦Nkongsamba

◦Loum

◦Kumba

◦Yabassi

◦Edea

C A M E R O O N

◦Nanga Eboko

◦Yaoundé

◦Mbalmayo

◦Zoétélé

◦Ayos

◦Abong Mbang

◦Yokadouma

◦Lomié ◦Dja

◦Sangmélima

◦Ebolowa

◦Lipéité

◦Lopi

◦Gandou

ZAÏRE

◦Bombom

◦Ibenge

Ubangi

◦Impfondo

C O N G O

◦Saketé
◦Porto-Novo

◦Ilaro

◦Abeokuta

◦Mushin

Lagos

◦Cotonou

◦Ijebu Ode

OGUN

◦Benin City

EDO

◦Sapele

◦Warri

◦Ughelli

DELTA

◦Bomadi

◦Burutu

◦Yenagoa

◦Nembe

RIVERS

◦Buguma

◦Port Harcourt

◦Brass

◦Bonny

Onitsha

◦Awka

ANAMBRA

◦Enugu

ENUGU

◦Nkalagu

◦Abakaliki

◦Afikpo

◦Bende

◦Umuahia

ABIA

◦Aba

IMO

◦Owerri

◦Uyo

◦Oron

AKWA-IBOM

◦Eket

◦Calabar

◦Mbe

◦Kumba

◦Buea

▲Mt. Cameroun
4070

◦Limbe

◦Malabo

◦3008

Bioko I.

EQUATORIAL

GUINEA

◦Douala

◦Edea

Nyong

◦Kribi

◦Campo

◦Ambam

◦Bitam

◦Moloundou

◦Souffla

◦Bata

GABON

Bight of Benin

◦3261

Niger Delta

Gulf of Guinea

Bight of Bonny

CENTRAL AND EAST AFRICA

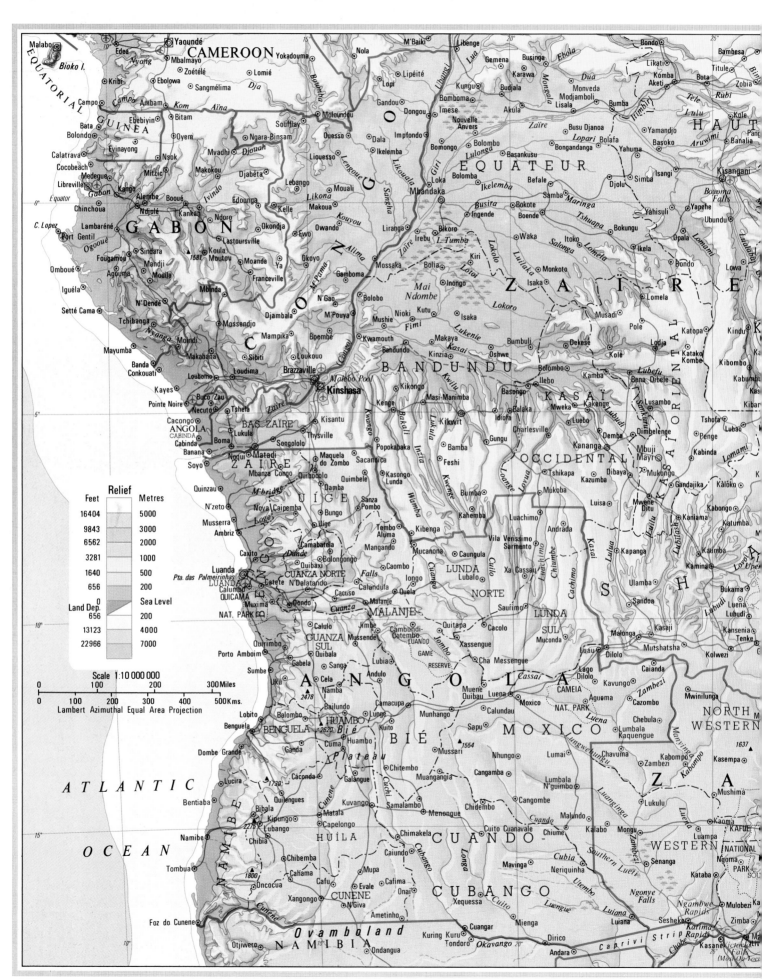

Relief

Feet		Metres
16404		5000
9843		3000
6562		2000
3281		1000
1640		500
656		200
0		Sea Level

Land Dep.
656		200
13123		4000
22966		7000

Scale 1:10 000 000

0   100   200   300 Miles

0   100   200   300   400   500 Kms.

Lambert Azimuthal Equal Area Projection

SOUTHERN AFRICA AND MADAGASCAR

Tj. Bobaomby
Antsiranana
▲7475
Nosy Be
Ambilobe
Andoany
Vohimarina
Anorotsangana
Ambanja
Massif de
Analalava
Tsaratanana ▲7876
Sambava
Antsohihy
Bealanana
Befandriana
Antalaha
Mahajanga
Port-Bergé
Maroantsetra
Mitsinjo
Tj. Masoala
Soalala
Matovoay
Mampikony
Mandritsara
Ambato-Boeni
Tsaratanana
Maevatanana
Mananara
Tanjona
Vilanandro
Besalampy
Kandreho
Soanierana
Ivongo
Nosy
Boraha
Tamboharano
Morafenobe
Andriba
Ankazobe
Ambatondrazaka
Fenoarivo
Atsinanana
Maintirano
Fenoarivo
Anjozorobe
L. Alaotra
Antsalova
Tsiroanomandidy
Toamasina
Arivonimamo
Anivorano
Ambohidratrimo
Manjakandriana
Vohibinany
Miarinarivo
Antananarivo
Moramanga
Andevoranto
Soavinandriana
(Tananarive) ▲2643
Miandrivazo
Faratsiho
Vatomandry
Belo-sur-Tsiribihina
Ambatolampy
Mandoto
Antsirabé
Betafo
Mahanoro
Berevo
Fandriana
Marolambo
Morondava
Malaimbandy
Ambositra
Nosy-Varika
Mahabo
Ambatofinandrahana
Ambohimanga du Sud
Mandabe
Ambohimahasoa
Mananjary
Manja
Massif du Makay
Fianarantsoa
Ifanadiana
Morombe
Beroroha
Ambalavao
Ikalamavony
Fort Carnot
Tanjona
Ankaboa
Befandriana
Ankaramena
▲1761
Manakara
Ankazoabo
Ihosy
Ivohibe
Vohipeno
Manombo
Ranohira
Vondrozo
Toliara
Tongobory
Iakora
Farafangana
Betioky
Benenitra
Betroka
Vangaindrano
Bekily
Tsivory
Midongy-Sud
Tropic of Capricorn
Manantenina
▲1956
Ampanihy
Tranopa
Behara
Androka
Tsihombe
Tôlanaro
Ambovombe
Tj. Vohimena

Mozambique Channel

Metangula
Maniamba
Namecala
Ancuabe
Guerra
Lichinga
Marrupa
Pemba
Nkhotakota
Montepuez
Mecufi
CABO
Mponela
Balama
DELGADO
Lurio
Ft.Maguire
NIASSA
Nungo
Ocua
Chaonde
Dowa
Belem
Maua
Namapa
Simuco
Salima
Massangulo
Intute
Memba
Lilongwe
Vatiua
Lalaua
Nacala
Dedza
Mandimba
Cuamba
Malema
Ribaué
NAMPULA
Mossuril
Ulongwé
Ncheu
Balaka
Chinga
Nampula
Moçambique
Mangochi
Alto
Meconta
Matope
Molocue
Zomba
Namarroi
Mutala
Mogincual
Blantyre
Erregoa
Gilé
Namaponda
Chikwawa
Milange ▲3000
Moma
ZAMBEZIA
Lugela
Mocuba
Angoche
Chiromo
Mopêia Velha
Nsanje
Marromeu
Moebase
Namacurra
Vila da
Chinda
Maganja
Pebane
Quelimane
Conceição

INDIAN
OCEAN

Relief		
Feet		Metres
16 404		5000
9 843		3000
6 562		2000
3 281		1000
1 640		500
656		200
0		Sea Level
Land Dep.		
656		200
13 123		4000
22 966		7000

Scale 1:10 000 000

0   100   200   300 Miles

0   100   200   300   400   500 Kms.

Lambert Azimuthal Equal Area Projection

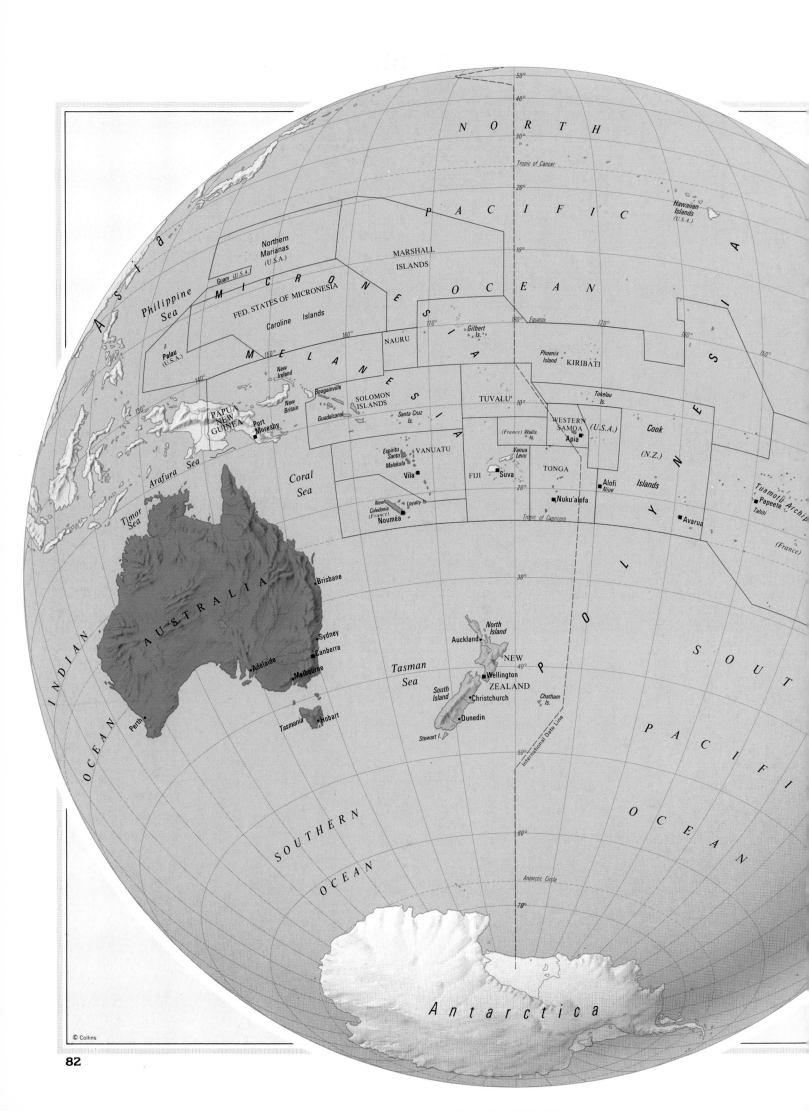

NORTH

Tropic of Cancer

PACIFIC

Hawaiian
Islands
(U.S.A.)

ASIA

OCEAN

MICRONESIA

Northern
Marianas
(U.S.A.)

Guam (U.S.A.)

MARSHALL
ISLANDS

Philippine
Sea

FED. STATES OF MICRONESIA

Caroline   Islands

Palau
(U.S.A.)

MELANESIA

NAURU

Equator

Gilbert
Is.

Phoenix
Island

KIRIBATI

New
Ireland

New
Britain

Bougainville

SOLOMON
ISLANDS

Santa Cruz
Is.

TUVALU

Tokelau
Is.

PAPUA
NEW
GUINEA

Guadalcanal

Port
Moresby

WESTERN
SAMOA

(U.S.A.)

Cook

Apia

Arafura
Sea

Espiritu
Santo

Malekula

VANUATU

(France) Wallis
Is.

Vanua
Levu

(N.Z.)

Tuamotu Archip

Timor
Sea

Coral
Sea

Vila

FIJI

Suva

TONGA

Islands

Papeete

Alofi
Niue

Avarua

Tahiti

New
Caledonia
(France)

Loyalty Is.

Nouméa

Nuku'alofa

Tropic of Capricorn

(France)

Brisbane

POLYNESIA

SOUT

AUSTRALIA

Sydney

Adelaide

Canberra

Auckland

North
Island

NEW

PACIFI

Melbourne

Tasman
Sea

ZEALAND

Wellington

INDIAN

Perth

South
Island

Christchurch

Chatham
Is.

Dunedin

OCEAN

OCEAN

Tasmania

Hobart

Stewart I.

International Date Line

SOUTHERN

Antarctic Circle

OCEAN

Antarctica

© Collins

82

OCEANIA

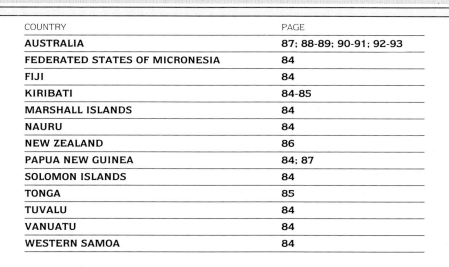

Oceania as a continental name is used for the area extending from Australia in the west, to the most easterly island of Polynesia and from New Zealand in the south, to the Hawaiian Islands in the north. Australasia is that portion of Oceania which lies between the equator and 47°S but in general the term is not often used because of confusion with Australia the country name.

PACIFIC OCEAN

SAMOA ISLANDS
Scale 1:7 500 000

Falealupo Aopo Fagamalo
Salailua Matautu Puapua
Salelologa
Savai'i Matautu Upolu
Tana Apia Tiavea
Salani
WESTERN Manua Is.
SAMOA Samoa (U.S.A.)
Ofu Olosega
Tau
Pago Pago
Tutuila C. Matatula
Steps Pt.

FIJI
Gt. Sea Reef
Undu C.
Lambasa Mbutha Vanua Levu
Mbua Taveuni
Koro Yathata
Lautoka Ngau Koro
Nandi Viti Sea
Levu Lau
Singatoka Suva Group
Kandavu Passage
Kandavu
Scale 1:15 000 000

RAROTONGA
(N.Z.)
Pokoinu Avatiu Avarua
438
Arorangi Matavera
Te 653 Ngatangiia
Manga
Muri
Titikaveka
Scale 1:500 000

NIUE
(N.Z.)
Hikutavake Mutalau
Makefu Tuapa Tui Lakepa
Alofi Liku
Bay Alofi Motutapu
Avatele 66
Bay Avatele
Tepa Pt. Vaiea Hakupu
Scale 1:1 000 000

GUAM
(U.S.A.)
Ritidian
Pt.
Philippine Pati Pt.
Sea Mt Santa Rosa
262 Catalina
Agana Pt.
Orote Yona
Pen. Talofofo
Merizo Malofos
Inarajan
Scale 1:2 000 000

VANUATU AND NEW CALEDONIA
Banks Is.
C. Cumberland
C. Quiros
Espiritu Maewo
Santo I. 1880 Oba
Luganville Pentecost I.
Coral
Sea Malekula Ambrim
Epi Shepherd
Islands
Emae Tongoa
VANUATU
Vila Efate
Récifs
d'Entrecasteaux Eromanga
Grand Passage Tana
Grand Lenakel
Récif Aneityum
de
Cook
Koumac Ile
Uvéa Îles Loyauté
Vah 1624 Lifou (Loyalty Is.)
Koné Houailou
Bourail Ile
Maré
Nouvelle Yaté
Calédonie Ile des
(New Caledonia) Pins
(Fr.) Nouméa
© Collins
Scale 1:15 000 000

BERING SEA
Aleutian Basin
Komandorskiye
Ostrova
Poluostrov
Kamchatka 8100 7429
Aleutian Islands

Sea of
Okhotsk
Amur
Sakhalin
Vladivostok Sapporo
Beijing Pyongyang
(Peking) NORTH
Xi'an KOREA Sea of
Sian Qingdao Japan
Tsingtao Seoul Sapporo
CHINA SOUTH
Chengdu Nanjing KOREA Kobe
(Nanking) Osaka Tokyo
Chongqing Wuhan JAPAN
(Chungking) Shanghai Shikoku
Nanchang East China Kyushu
Taipei Sea
Guangzhou Nansei Shotō
(Canton)
Nanning TAIWAN Nansei Shotō
HONG KONG
Beibu (U.K.)
Wan Hainan
South China Luzon
Sea Quezon PHILIPPINE
City Manila SEA
PHILIPPINES 7559
Ho Chí Minh Mindanao
(Saigon) Palawan 10497
Sulu Philippine
Sea Trench
BRUNEI Sulu
Archipelago Celebes
Sea Sea
5520 Halmahera
Borneo Celebes
(Kalimantan) Sulawesi
(Celebes) Buru
INDONESIA Laut Maluku
Kep Sula Seram
Laut Jawa (Java Sea) Laut
Banda Puncak Jaya
Jakarta 4530
Jawa Kep. PAPUA
(Java) Surabaya Flores Tanimbar NEW
Sumba Arafura GUINEA
Java Trench Timor Sea Port
7450 6218 Sea Torres Strait Moresby
Wyndham Thursday I.
Darwin Gulf
of Cairns
Broome Carpentaria
Tennant
Creek
AUSTRALIA
Geraldton Great Dividing Range
Brisbane
Kalgoorlie Darling Middleton
Perth Newcastle Reef
Port Sydney
Augusta Canberra 126
Adelaide Murray
Great Melbourne
Australian King I. Flinders
Bight Furneaux
Albany South Australian Group
Basin Tasmania
Hobart
Bruny I.
S. Tasmania Ridge
SOUTHERN OCEAN
INDIAN OCEAN

P A C I F I C
1962 1634
Midway Is.
(U.S.A.) Hawaiian
Lisianski Laysan Islands
(U.S.A.)
1477
6148 Wake I. 1440
(U.S.A.)
Marcus I. Johnston I.
(Jap.) (U.S.A.)
10542 Bonin Is.
(Jap.)
Volcano Is.
(Jap.)
Northern
Marianas International Date Line
(U.S.A.)
Guam (U.S.A.)
1034
Mariana Trench Enewetak Bikini
Yap Caroline Namonuito MARSHALL
Woleai Hall Is. ISLANDS
Palau Eauripik Truk Is. Pohnpei
(U.S.A.) West Caroline Pingelap Ralik Chain
Caroline Basin East Islands Ebon Jaluit
Caroline Basin
FED. STATES OF MICRONESIA
Butaritari
Admiralty Is. NAURU Tarawa
Manus Banaba Gilbert
Bismarck (Ocean I.) Is.
New Sea New
Ireland
Bougainville Britain SOLOMON TUVALU Kingsmill
New Hebrides Basin ISLANDS Nui Vaitupu Group
Guadalcanal Malaita Nanumea Phoenix
Santa Cruz Funafuti Islands
Is. Nukunonu
Coral Sea Basin Espiritu Wallis WESTERN
4710 Santo North (Fr.) SAMOA
Iles Chesterfield Malekula VANUATU Vanua Levu
(Fr.) Vila Fiji FIJI Apia
Nouvelle Viti Suva Tutuila
Calédonie Levu Lau TONGA Alofi
(New Caledonia) Iles Group Niue
(Fr.) Loyauté Hunter I. Ridge Nuku'alofa
Nouméa (Loyalty Is.) Tongatapu 10882
CORAL 5303 South Group
SEA Fiji
Basin
Norfolk I. Kermadec
Lord Howe I. (Aus.) Is. Raoul
Ball's Pyramid Norfolk I. (N.Z.)
TASMAN 126 Three Kings Is. 10047
Auckland NEW
ZEALAND
SEA Wellington
North Island
NEW
ZEALAND Christchurch
Chatham Rise Chatham Is.
South Island
Bluff Dunedin
The Snares Stewart I.
New Zealand Antipodes Is.
Auckland Is. Bounty Is.
Plateau
Campbell I.
6098
Macquarie I.
(Aus.)
Indian-Antarctic Ridge
Macquarie Balleny
Ridge Ridge
Eastern Indian-
Antarctic Basin Balleny Is.
(N.Z.)

NEW ZEALAND

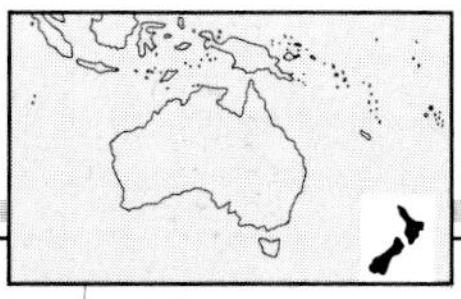

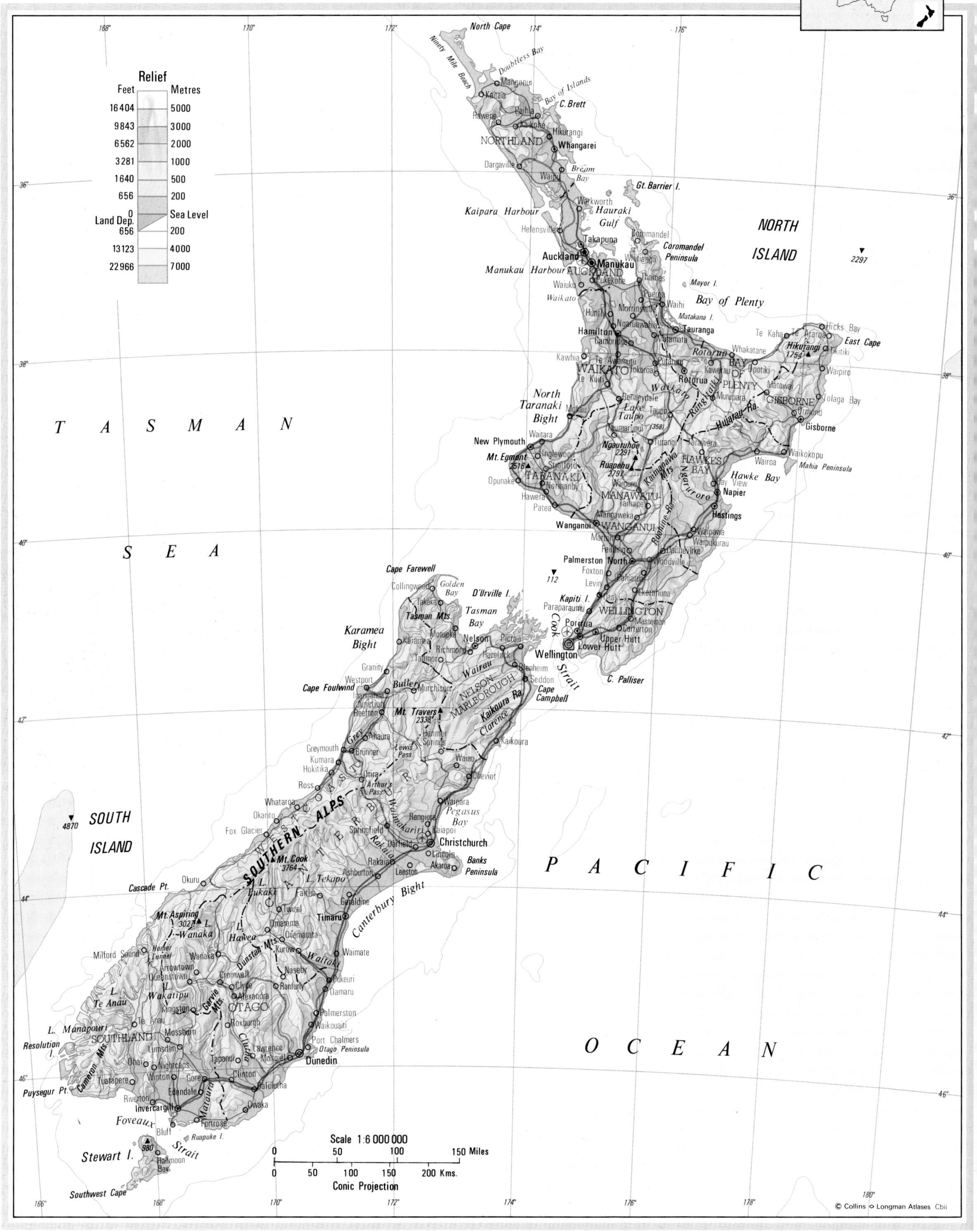

Relief

Feet	Metres
16 404	5000
9843	3000
6562	2000
3281	1000
1640	500
656	200
0	Sea Level
Land Dep.	
656	200
13123	4000
22966	7000

North Cape
Ninety Mile Beach
Doubtless Bay
Mangonui
Kaitaia
Rawene
Paihia
Kaikohe
Bay of Islands
C. Brett
Hikurangi
NORTHLAND
Whangarei
Dargaville
Waipu
Bream Bay
Gt. Barrier I.
Kaipara Harbour
Helensville
Warkworth
Hauraki Gulf
Coromandel
Takapuna
Coromandel Peninsula
NORTH ISLAND
▼ 2297
Auckland
Whitianga
● **Manukau**
AUCKLAND
Manukau Harbour
Pukekohe
Thames
Mayor I.
Waiuku
Waihi
Waikato
Huntly
Ngaruawahia
Morrinsville
Tauranga
Bay of Plenty
Te Aroha
Matakana I.
Whakatane
Te Kaha
Hicks Bay
Te Araroa
East Cape
Hamilton
Cambridge
Matamata
Rotorua
Kawerau
Opotiki
Hikurangi ▲ 1754
Kuratau
Te Awamutu
Putaruru
Waipiro
WAIKATO
Tokoroa
Rotorua
Kawhia
Te Kuiti
Whakatane
Te Puke
Ruatahuna
Matawai
Tolaga Bay
GISBORNE
Ormond
Rangitaiki
BAY OF PLENTY
Wairoa
Hawke Bay
Gisborne
North Taranaki Bight
Benneydale
Lake Taupo
Waiotapu
Mokau
Waitara
Huiarau Ra.
HAWKE'S BAY
Waikokopu
New Plymouth
Inglewood
Ngauruhoe ▲ 2291
Kaimanawa Mts
Mahia Peninsula
Mt. Egmont ▲ 2518
Stratford
Ruapehu ▲ 2797
Ngaruroro
Bay View
Opunake
TARANAKI
Normanby
Waiouru
Napier
Hawera
MANAWATU
Mangaweka
Hastings
Patea
Waipawa
WANGANUI
Marton
Waipukurau
Wanganui
Feilding
Dannevirke
Woodville
Palmerston North
Foxton
Levin
▼ 112
Eketahuna
Kapiti I.
Paraparaumu
WELLINGTON
Masterton
Porirua
Carterton
Cape Farewell
Collingwood
Golden Bay
D'Urville I.
Upper Hutt
Takaka
Tasman Mts.
Tasman Bay
Wellington
Lower Hutt
Cook Strait
Karamea Bight
Karamea
Motueka
Nelson
Picton
C. Palliser
Granity
Richmond
Wairau
Blenheim
Westport
Tadmor
Havelock
Seddon
NELSON
Cape Foulwind
Inangahua
Buller
Murchison
MARLBOROUGH
Cape Campbell
Reefton
Mt. Travers ▲ 2338
Clarence
Kaikoura Ra.
Greymouth
Gre.
Ahaura
Hanmer Springs
Kaikoura
Brunner
Lewis Pass
Kumara
Hokitika
Waiau
Ross
Otira
Arthur's Pass
Cheviot
Whataroa
Okarito
Waipara
Waimakariri
Pegasus Bay
Rangiora
Kaiapoi
Fox Glacier
SOUTHERN ALPS
Springfield
Darfield
Christchurch
Cascade Pt.
Oku
Lincoln
SOUTH ISLAND
▼ 4870
Mt. Cook ▲ 3764
Rakaia
Akaroa
Banks Peninsula
L. Pukaki
Ashburton
Leeston
Mt. Aspiring ▲ 3027
L. Tekapo
Canterbury Bight
Milford Sound
Homer Tunnel
L. Wanaka
L. Hawea
Fairlie
Geraldine
Arrowtown
Wanaka
Dunstan Mts.
Twizel
Timaru
Queenstown
Cromwell
Omarama
Kingston
Clyde
Otematata
Waitaki
L. Wakatipu
Garvie Mts.
Alexandra
Kurow
Waimate
L. Te Anau
Naseby
OTAGO
Ranfurly
Pukeuri
Oamaru
Te Anau
Roxburgh
Palmerston
L. Manapouri
Mossburn
Waikouaiti
Resolution I.
SOUTHLAND
Lawrence
Port Chalmers
Lumsden
Milton
Otago Peninsula
Ohai
Tapanui
Mosgiel
Dunedin
Nightcaps
Clutha
Clinton
Winton
Gore
Invercargill
Edendale
Owaka
Mataura
Puysegur Pt.
Riverton
Foveaux
Bluff
Ruapuke I.
Stewart I. ▲ 980
Halfmoon Bay
Southwest Cape
Strait

T A S M A N

S E A

P A C I F I C

O C E A N

Scale 1:6 000 000

| 0 | 50 | 100 | 150 Miles |

| 0 | 50 | 100 | 150 | 200 Kms. |

Conic Projection

Scale 1:20 000 000

| 0 | 100 | 200 | 300 | 400 | 500 Miles |

| 0 | 200 | 400 | 600 | 800 Kms. |

Lambert Azimuthal Equal Area Projection

© Collins ◇ Longman Atlases Cbi

WESTERN AUSTRALIA

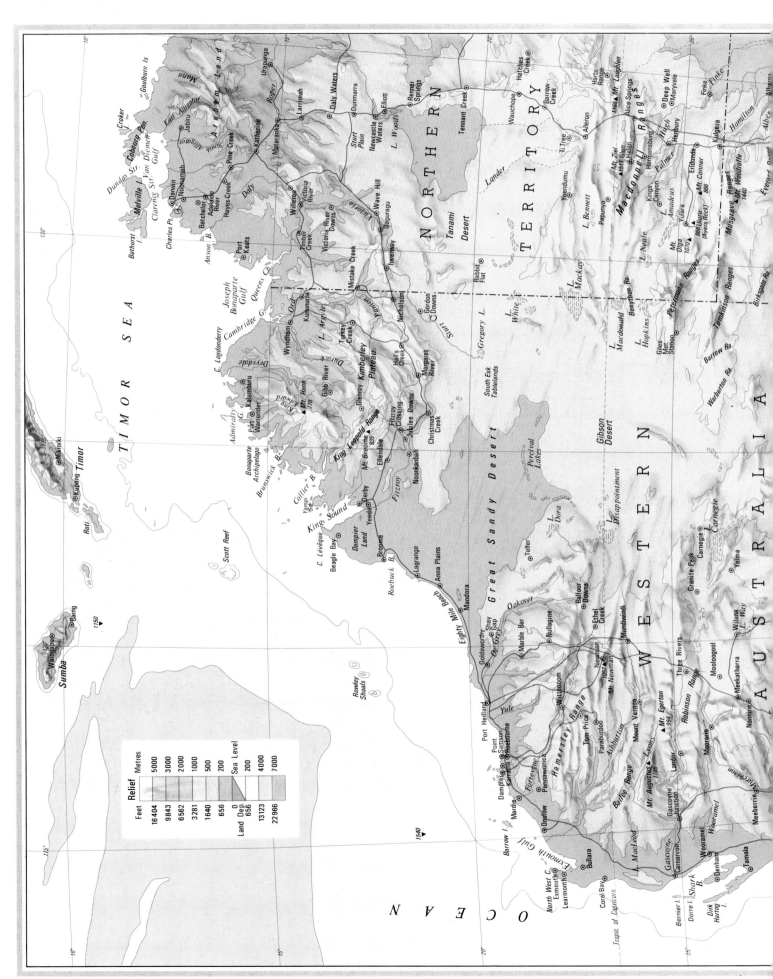

TIMOR SEA

INDIAN OCEAN

NORTHERN TERRITORY

WESTERN AUSTRALIA

Arnhem Land

Goulburn Is
Croker I.
Cobourg Pen.
Van Diemen Gulf
Melville I.
Bathurst I.
Dundas Str.
Clarence Str.
Charles Pt.
Darwin
Noonamah
Batchelor
Adelaide River
Hayes Creek
Pine Creek
Anson B.
Port Keats
Daly Waters
Larrimah
Dunmarra
Elliott
Renner Springs
Newcastle Waters
L. Woods
Sturt Plain
Katherine
Mataranka
Ddy
Willeroo
Victoria River Downs
Wave Hill
Daguragu
Inverway
Nicholson
Gordon Downs
Hatches Creek
Wauchope
Barrow Creek
Tennant Creek
Ti Tree
Harts Range
Mt. Ziel 1468
Alice Springs
Aileron
Deep Well
Marvale
Maryvale
Finke
Finke
Hamilton
Albert
Frewena
Birtragate Ra
Ti Tree
Yuendumu
Papunya
Mt. Liebig
L. Bennett
L. Neale
Hermannsburg
Henbury
Kings Canyon
L. Amadeus
Yulara
886 Uluru (Ayers Rock)
Mt. Olga 1070
Mt. Conner 866
Erldunda
Kulgera
Musgrave Ranges
Mt. Woodroffe 1440
Tomkinson Ranges
Petermann Ranges
Giles Met. Station
L. Hopkins
Bonython Ra.
Barrow Ra.
Warburton Ra.
Macdonnell Ranges
L. Macdonald
L. White
L. Mackay
Rabbit Flat
Tanami Desert
Lander
Sturt
Gibson Desert
Gregory L.
South Esk Tablelands
Percival Lakes
L. Disappointment
L. Dora
Telfer
Carnegie
L. Carnegie
Granite Peak
Yelma
Wiluna
L. Way

TIMOR SEA
Timor
Kupang
Roti
Kikinki
Sumba
Waingapu
Bang
1150
1135

Timor Sea
C. Londonderry
Joseph Bonaparte Gulf
Cambridge G.
Queens Ch.
Ord
Kununurra
L. Argyle
Wyndham
Turkey Creek
Halls Creek
Margaret River
Christmas Creek
Hall's Creek
Jubilee Downs
Noonkanbah
Fitzroy Crossing
Ellendale
Fitzroy
Derby
Yeeda
Broome
Lagrange
Anna Plains
Mandora
Eighty Mile Beach
Roebuck B.
Dampier Land
King Sound
Beagle Bay
C. Lévêque
Yampi Sd.
Collier B.
Brunswick B.
Bonaparte Archipelago
Admiralty G.
Port Warrender
Kalumburu
Drysdale
King Edward
Mt. Hann 776
Gibb River
Glenroy
Kimberley Plateau
King Leopold Range
Mt. Broome 935
Duncan
Victoria River
Timber Creek
Mistake Creek

Great Sandy Desert
Oakover
Goldsworthy
Shay Gap
De Grey
Marble Bar
Nullagine
Balfour Downs
Ethel Creek
Mundiwindi
Port Hedland
Yule
Point Samson
Roebourne
Dampier
Karratha
Mardie
Onslow
Barrow I.
North West C.
Exmouth
Learmonth
Exmouth Gulf
Coral Bay
Bernier I.
Dorre I.
Dirk Hartog I.
Shark B.
Denham
Tamala
Carnarvon
Gascoyne Junction
Woorantel
Wooramel
Meeberrie
Nanutarra
Mooarie
Landor
Murchison
Meekatharra
Mooloogool
Robinson Range
Mt. Egerton 994
Ashburton
Lyons
Mt. Augustus 1105
Barlee Range
Paraburdoo
Tom Price
Mount Vernon
Newman
Mt. Newman 1057
Wittenoom
Hamersley Range
Pannawonica
Fortescue
Three Rivers
Namurrie
L. Macleod

Tropic of Capricorn

Relief

Feet	Metres		
16404	5000		
9843	3000		
6562	2000		
3281	1000		
1640	500		
656	200		
	Sea Level		
	0 Land Dep.		
656	200		
13123	4000		
22966	7000		

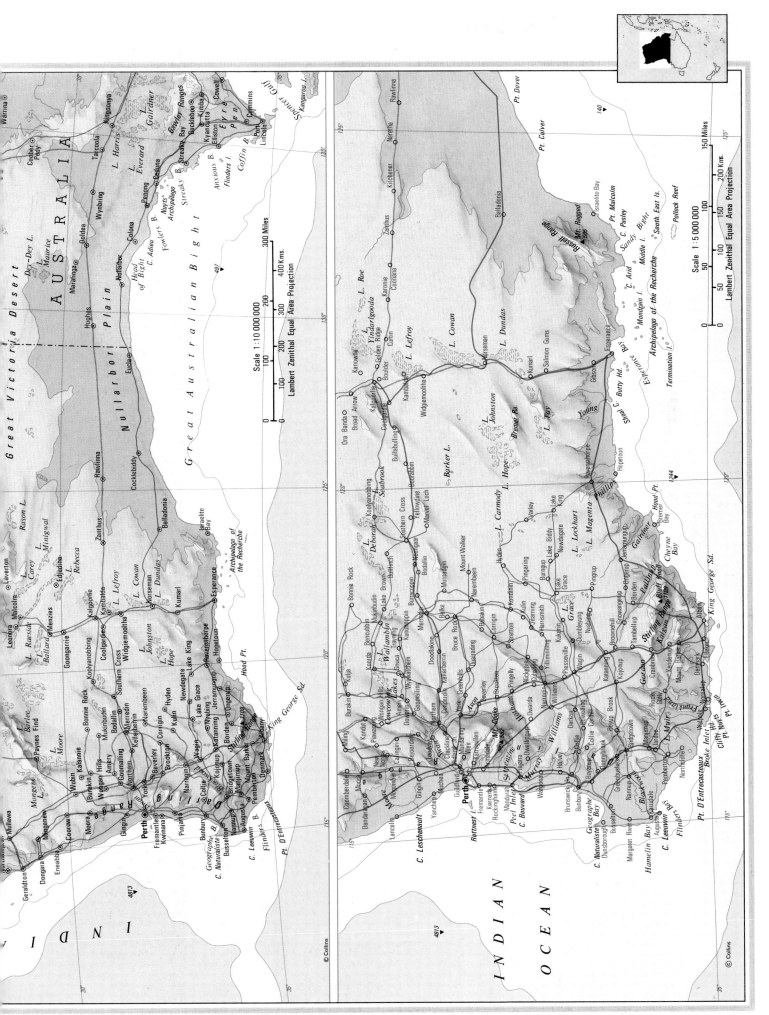

EASTERN AUSTRALIA

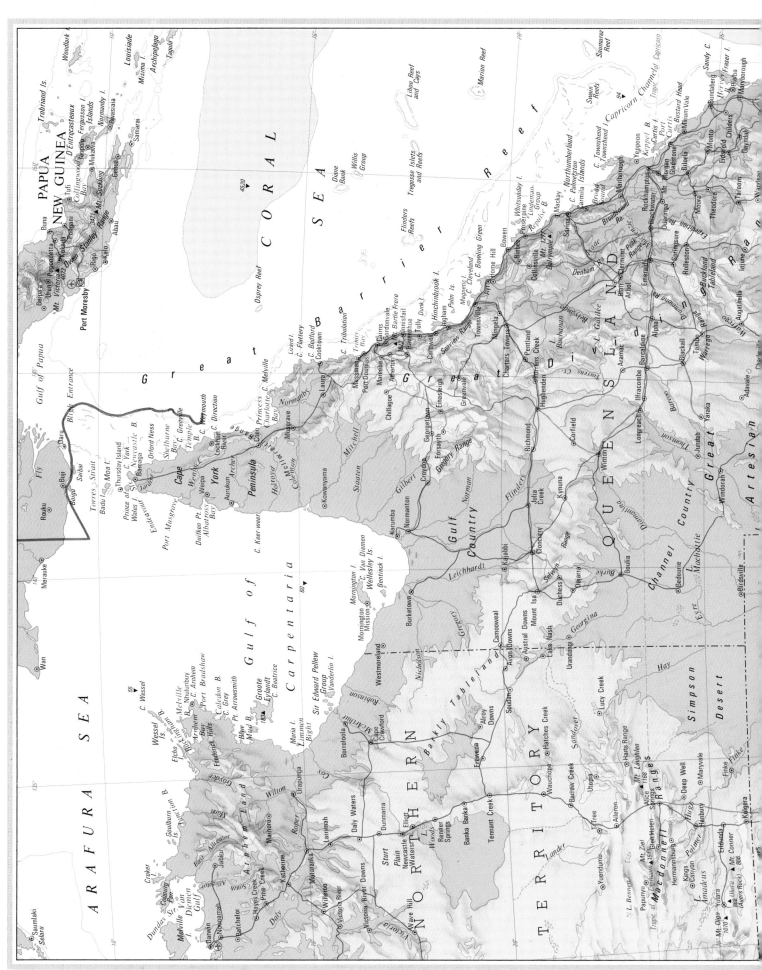

Woodlark I.
Louisiade Archipelago
Misima I.
Tagula
Trobriand Is.
D'Entrecasteaux
Fergusson I.
Normanby I.
Kiriwina
Kwasiaia
Samarai
Tufi
Collingwood Bay
Mukawa
Getua
Abau

PAPUA
NEW GUINEA
Buna
Popondetta
Uruti
Mt. Victoria
3827
Kokoda
Popondai
Owen Stanley Range
Rigo
Berpa
Port Moresby

Gulf of Papua
Bligh Entrance
Daru
Fly
Rouku
Wan
Buji
Saibai
Bogu
Badu I.
Moa I.
Torres Strait
Merauke
Saumlaki
Selaru

CORAL SEA
4520
Osprey Reef
Diane Bank
Willis Group
Lihou Reef and Cays
Marion Reef
Saumarez Reef
Squin Reefs
84
Tregosse Islets and Reefs
Flinders Reefs

Great Barrier Reef

Capricorn Channel
Tropic of Capricorn

Prince of Wales I.
Thursday Island
C. York
Newcastle B.
Banaga
Endeavour Str.
Jardine
Cape York
Wenlock
Weipa
Aurukun
Duifken Pt.
Albatross Bay
C. Keer-weer
Port Musgrave

Orford Ness
Shelburne B.
C. Grenville
Temple B.
C. Direction
Weymouth
Lockhart River
Coen
Archer
Holroyd
Coleman
Peninsula

York
Kowanyama

Mitchell
Staaten
Gilbert
Normanton
Karumba
Gulf Country

C. Melville
Princess Charlotte Bay
Laura
Normanby
Lizard I.
C. Flattery
Cooktown
C. Bedford
C. Tribulation
Trinity Bay
Cairns
Port Douglas
Mossman
Mareeba
Atherton
Chillagoe
Georgetown
Einasleigh
Greenvale
Forsayth
Croydon

Bartle Frere
Innisfail
Tully
Cardwell
Dunk I.
Hinchinbrook I.
Ingham
Palm Is.
Townsville
Ayr
Ravenswood
Charters Towers
Pentland
Torrens Cr.
Hughenden
Richmond

Magnetic I.
C. Cleveland
C. Bowling Green
Bowen
Proserpine
Repulse B.
Lindeman Group
Whitsunday I.
Mackay
Sarina
Broadsound
Northumberland Is.
C. Palmerston
Carmila

Bowen
Collinsville
Mt. Dryander
Mt. Dalrymple
Nebo
Clermont
Peak Downs
Capella
Emerald
Blackwater
Dingo
Duaringa

Mt. Townshend
C. Townshend
Broad Sound
Yeppoon
Rockhampton
Keppel B.
Curtis
Gladstone
Bustard Head
Monto
Biloela
Theodore
Moura

Port Curtis
Miriam Vale
Bundaberg
Childers
Pialba
Fraser I.
Sandy C.
Hervey B.
Maryborough
Wanbah
Gayndah
Eidsvold

QUEENSLAND

Great Dividing Range
Belyando
Clermont
Alpha
Barcaldine
Aramac
Muttaburra
Longreach
Ilfracombe
Isisford
Blackall
Tambo
Jundah
Winton
Stonehenge
Windorah
Birdsville
Bedourie
Boulia
Diamantina
Channel Country
Machattie
Eyre
Simpson Desert

Gulf of Carpentaria

Mornington I.
Mornington Mission
C. Van Diemen
Wellesley Is.
Bentinck I.
60
Sweers I.
Burketown
Westmoreland
Nicholson
Doomadgee
Gregory
Camooweal
Mount Isa
Cloncurry
Duchess
Dajarra
Selwyn
Mary Kathleen
Kajabbi
Julia Creek
Kynuna
McKinlay
Flinders
Leichhardt

Sir Edward Pellew Group
Vanderlin I.
Maria I.
Limmen Bight
Borroloola
Cape Crawford
McArthur
Robinson
Calvert Hills
Wollogorang

NORTHERN
TERRITORY

Barkly Tableland
Brunette Downs
Avon Downs
Austral Downs
Lake Nash
Urandangi
Harts Range
Alroy Downs
Soudan
Frewena
Tarlton Downs
Hatches Creek
Sandover
Lucy Creek
Hay
Georgina

ARAFURA SEA
55
C. Wessel
Wessel Is.
Marchinbar I.
Elcho I.
Goulburn Is.
C. Stewart
Nhulunbuy
C. Arnhem
Port Bradshaw
Caledon B.
C. Grey
Blue Mud B.
Groote Eylandt
C. Beatrice
Pt. Arrowsmith

Melville B.
Arnhem B.
18
Blyth
Liverpool

Croker I.
Cobourg Pen.
Van Diemen Gulf
Melville I.
Bathurst I.
Dundas Str.
Darwin
NGukurr
Batchelor
Hayes Creek
Pine Creek
Katherine
Willeroo
Victoria River Downs
Victoria River
Daly
Daly Waters
Larrimah
Mataranka
Elliott
Newcastle Waters
Renner Springs
Banka Banka
Tennant Creek
Barrow Creek
Ti Tree
Aileron
Yuendumu
Papunya
Hermannsburg
Kings Canyon
Yulara
Mt. Olga
Uluru (Ayers Rock)
866
1070
Mt. Conner
Curtin Springs
Erldunda
Finke
Kulgera
Alice Springs
Glen Helen
MacDonnell Ranges
Mt. Zeil
1510
Mt. Liebig
168
Harts Range
Deep Well
Hanbury
Palmer
Finke
Lander
Wauchope
Utopia
L. Bennett
Amadeus
L. Neale

Arnhem Land
Roper
Wilton
Urapunga
Mainoru
Main
Goyder
East Alligator
South Alligator
Jabiru
Nourlangie

Arafura Sea

Gulf of Carpentaria

Sturt Plain
Lander

N O R T H E R N T E R R I T O R Y

Q U E E N S L A N D

Great Artesian Basin
Warrego
Adavale
Yaraka
Augathella
Tambo
Taroom

90

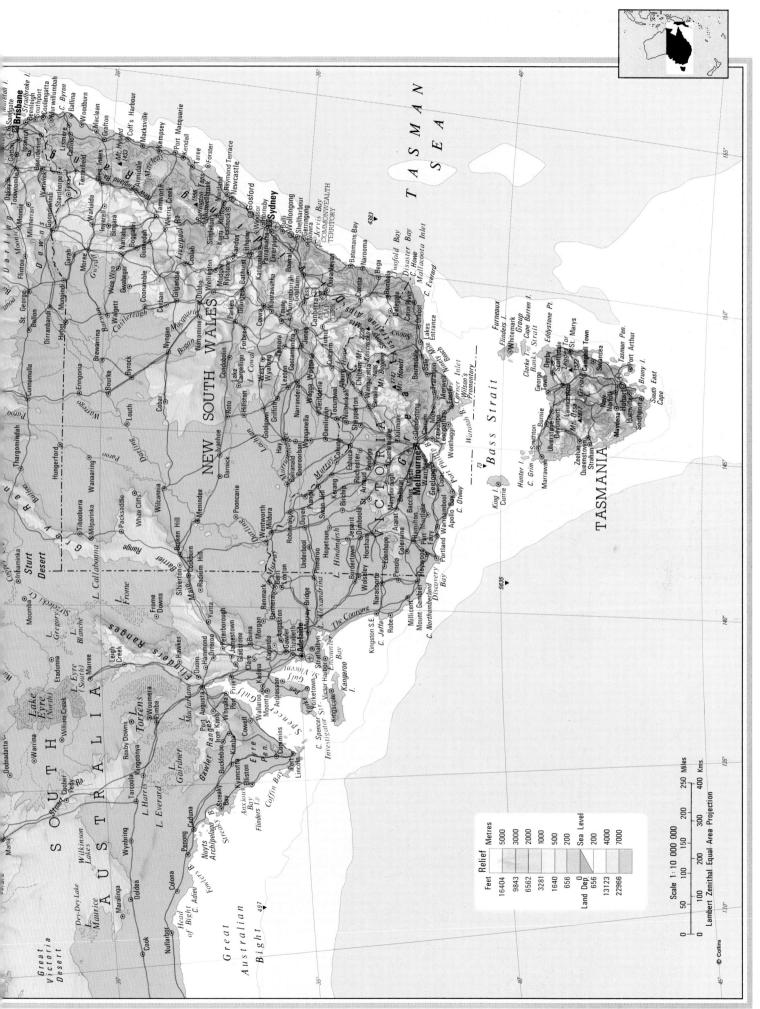

TASMAN SEA

NEW SOUTH WALES

QUEENSLAND

Brisbane

Sydney

VICTORIA

Melbourne

SOUTH AUSTRALIA

Adelaide

Great Australian Bight

Great Victoria Desert

Sturt Desert

TASMANIA

Bass Strait

Relief

Feet	Metres
16404	5000
9843	3000
6562	2000
3281	1000
1640	500
656	200
	Sea Level
Land Dep. 656	200
13123	4000
22966	7000

Scale 1:10 000 000

0   50   100   150   200   250 Miles

0   100   200   300   400 Kms.

Lambert Zenithal Equal Area Projection

© Collins

91

SOUTHEAST AUSTRALIA

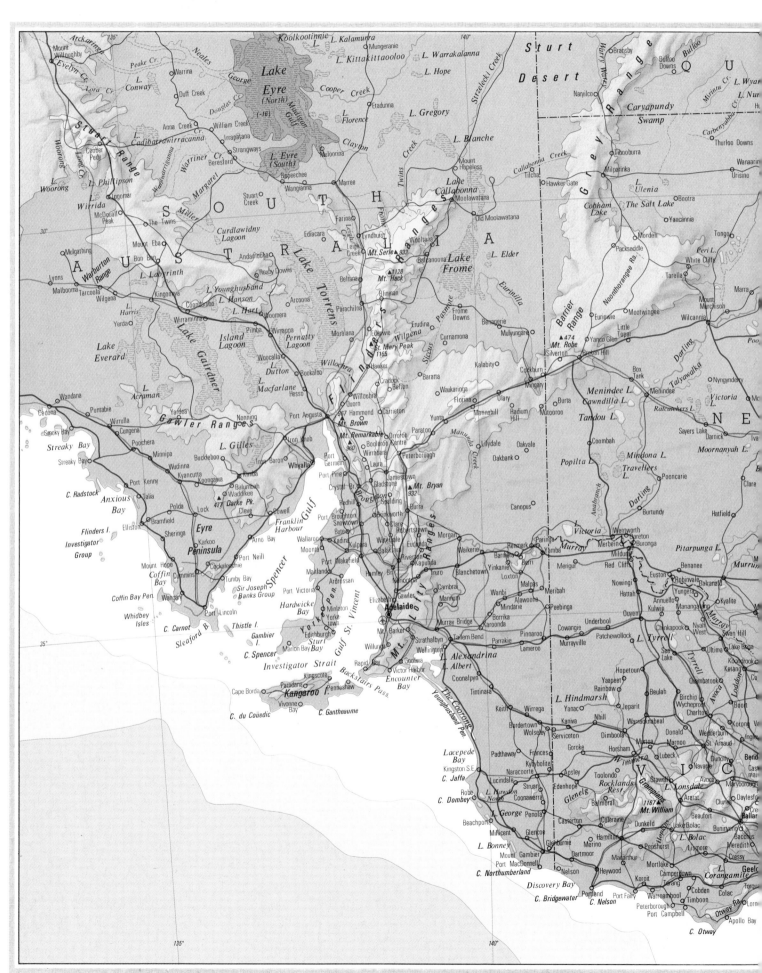

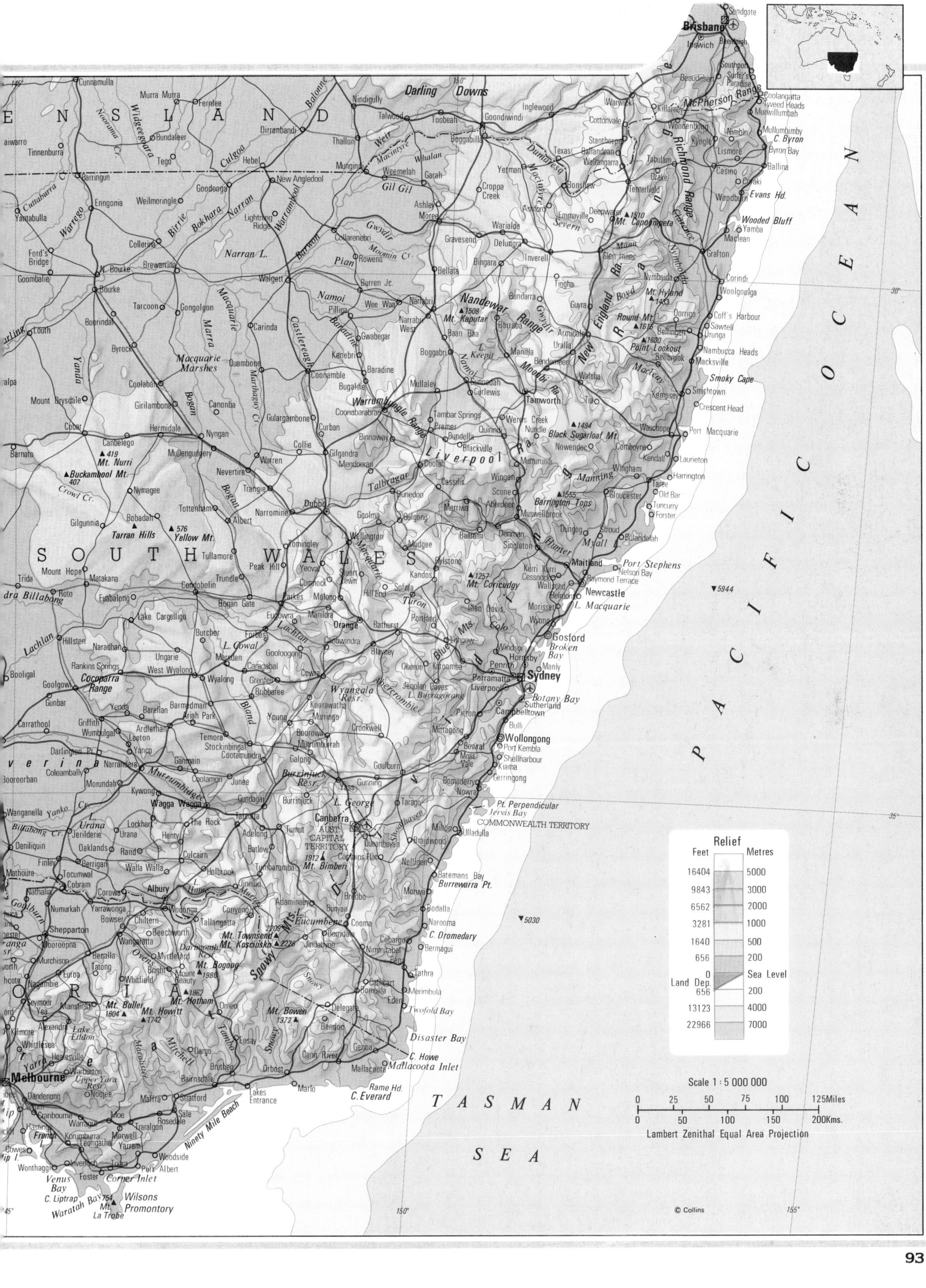

QUEENSLAND

Brisbane
Ipswich
Beenleigh
Beaudesert
Southport
Surfers Paradise
Coolangatta
Tweed Heads
Murwillumbah
Nimbin
C. Byron
Byron Bay
Ballina
Evans Hd.
Wooded Bluff
Yamba
Maclean

Darling Downs
Nindigully
Talwood
Toobeah
Goondiwindi
Inglewood
Warwick
Killarney
McPherson Range
Woodenbong
Kyogle
Casino
Lismore
Richmond Range

Cunnamulla
Murra Murra
Fernlee
Widgeegoara Cr.
Tinnenburra
Tego
Bundaleer
Dirranbandi
Thallon
Weir
Boggabilla
Texas
Stanthorpe
Ballandean
Wallangarra
Tenterfield
Tabulam
Drake
Grafton
Corindi
Woolgoolga

Barringun
Enngonia
Weilmoringle
Goodooga
New Angledool
Lightning Ridge
Ashley
Moree
Croppa Creek
Ashford
Yetman
Bonshaw
Emmaville
Deepwater
Mt. Capoompeta 1510
Glen Innes
Nymboida
Coff's Harbour
Sawtell
Urunga

Cuttaburra
Yantabulla
Ford's Bridge
Goombalie
Warrego
Collerina
Brewarrina
Narran L.
Barwon
Pian
Rowena
Collarenebri
Moomin Cr.
Gwydir
Bellata
Bingara
Inverell
Delungra
Gravesend
Tingha
Bundarra
Guyra
Armidale
Uralla
Point Lookout 1600
Round Mt. 1615
Dorrigo
Bellingen
Nambucca Heads
Macksville

M. Bourke
Bourke
Tarcoon
Gongolgon
Byrock
Walgett
Namoi
Pilliga
Wee Waa
Narrabri
Nandewar Range
Mt. Kaputar 1508
Baan Baa
Barraba
Manilla
Moonbi Ra.
Bendemeer
Walcha
Maclean
Smoky Cape
Kempsey
Smithtown
Crescent Head

Louth
Boorindal
Gilgandra
Macquarie Marshes
Coolabah
Girilambone
Quambone
Coonamble
Baradine
Coonabarabran
Warrumbungle Range
Gwabegar
Kenebri
Baradine
Bugaldie
Mullaley
Boggabri
Gunnedah
Curlewis
Carroll
Tamworth
Nundle
Black Sugarloaf Mt. 1494
Nowendoc
Comboyne
Wauchope
Port Macquarie
Kendall
Laurieton

Cobar
Canbelego
Hermidale
Nyngan
Warren
Nevertire
Trangie
Narromine
Dubbo
Talbragar
Gilgandra
Mendooran
Coolah
Cassilis
Wingen
Scone
Aberdeen
Barrington Tops 1555
Gloucester
Taree
Harrington
Old Bar
Tuncurry
Forster

Mt. Nurri 419
Buckambool Mt. 407
Crowl Cr.
Nymagee
Tottenham
Albert
Narromine
Goolma
Gulgong
Merriwa
Denman
Muswellbrook
Dungog
Stroud
Bulahdelah
Myall L.

Barnato
Barnard
Gilgunnia
Bobadah
Tarran Hills
Yellow Mt. 576
SOUTH WALES
Tullamore
Peak Hill
Yeoval
Stuart Town
Wellington
Baerami
Kerri Kerri
Maitland
Port Stephens
Nelson Bay
Raymond Terrace
Newcastle
Belmont
L. Macquarie

Mount Hope
Matakana
Condobolin
Trundle
Parkes
Molong
Cumnock
Hill End
Kandos
Rylstone
Mt. Coricudgy 1257
Wallsend
Cessnock
Morisset
Wyong

Roto
Evalebong
Lake Cargelligo
Bogan Gate
Forbes
Manildra
Orange
Bathurst
Portland
Sofala
Turon
Glen Davis
Colo
Gosford
Broken Bay

Ungarie
L. Cowal
Marsden
Eugowra
Canowindra
Blayney
Oberon
Jenolan Caves
L. Burragorang
Blue Mts.
Katoomba
Windsor
Hornsby
Manly

Naradhan
Rankins Springs
West Wyalong
Wyalong
Grenfell
Cowra
Lithgow
Penrith
Parramatta
Sydney
Liverpool

Hillston
Goolgowi
Cocoparra Range
Barmedman
Ariah Park
Quandialla
Young
Koorawatha
Murringo
Bowral
Botany Bay
Sutherland
Campbelltown

Gunbar
Griffith
Yenda
Barellan
Leeton
Temora
Stockinbingal
Cootamundra
Boorowa
Crookwell
Mittagong
Wollongong
Port Kembla
Shellharbour
Kiama

Carrathool
Darlington Pt.
Wumbulgal
Ardlethan
Ganmain
Narrandera
Junee
Galong
Goulburn
Bomaderry
Gerringong

Coleambally
Morundah
Coolamon
Wagga Wagga
Gundagai
Burrinjuck Resr.
Yass
Gunning
Taralga
Nowra
Pt. Perpendicular
Jervis Bay

Booligal
Wanganella
Yanco
The Rock
Tarcutta
Tumut
L. George
Canberra
AUST. CAPITAL TERRITORY
Queanbeyan
Braidwood
COMMONWEALTH TERRITORY
Ulladulla

Deniliquin
Urana
Lockhart
Henty
Adelong
Batlow
Captains Flat
Nelligen
Batemans Bay
Burrewarra Pt.

Mathoura
Jerilderie
Oaklands
Rand
Culcairn
Tumbarumba
Mt. Bimberi 1912
Braidwood
Moruya
Bodalla

Finley
Berrigan
Walla Walla
Holbrook
Jindabyne
Cooma
Narooma
C. Dromedary

Tocumwal
Cobram
Corowa
Albury
Wodonga
Corryong
L. Eucumbene
Berridale
Nimmitabel
Bega
Bermagui

Numurkah
Yarrawonga
Bowser
Chiltern
Beechworth
Tallangatta
Mt. Townsend 2205
Mt. Kosciusko 2228
Dalgety
Cobargo
Merimbula
Pambula
Eden

Shepparton
Mooroopna
Murchison
Euroa
Benalla
Wangaratta
Myrtleford
Bright
Mt. Bogong 1986
Mount Beauty
Snowy Mts.
Jindabyne
Cathcart
Bombala
Twofold Bay

Nagambie
Whitfield
Owens
Mt. Feathertop 1922
Mt. Hotham 1862
Delegate
Merimbula
Disaster Bay

Seymour
Yea
Mt. Buller 1804
Mt. Hewitt 1742
Omeo
Mt. Bowen 1372
Bendoc
Genoa
C. Howe

Alexandra
Lake Eildon
Mansfield
Tambo
Swifts Creek
Buchan
Orbost
Mallacoota
Mallacoota Inlet

Kilmore
Healesville
Warburton
Upper Yarra Resr.
Noojee
Maffra
Stratford
Lakes Entrance
Marlo
Rame Hd.
C. Everard

Melbourne
Dandenong
Cranbourne
Warragul
Moe
Morwell
Traralgon
Rosedale
Sale
Ninety Mile Beach

French I.
Korumburra
Leongatha
Yarram
Woodside
Port Albert
Wonthaggi
Foster
Toora
Venus Bay
C. Liptrap
Waratah Bay
Mt. La Trobe 754
Wilsons Promontory
Corner Inlet

PACIFIC OCEAN

TASMAN SEA

Relief
Feet / Metres
16404 / 5000
9843 / 3000
6562 / 2000
3281 / 1000
1640 / 500
656 / 200
0 / Sea Level
Land Dep.
656 / 200
13123 / 4000
22966 / 7000

Scale 1 : 5 000 000
0 25 50 75 100 125 Miles
0 50 100 150 200 Kms.
Lambert Zenithal Equal Area Projection

© Collins

93

A s i a

E u r o p

DOM. REP. : DOMINICAN REPUBLIC
EL SAL. : EL SALVADOR
GUA. : GUATEMALA
ST. V. AND G. : ST. VINCENT AND THE GRENADINES
© Collins

A R C T I C
OCEAN

Ellesmere I.

G R E E N L A N D
(KALAALLIT NUNAAT)

Denmark
Arctic Circle
Strait

Bering Strait

Parry Islands

Baffin
Bay

Baffin Island

ALASKA
U.S.A.
Anchorage

Victoria
Island

Godthåb
Nuuk

International Date Line

Hudson
Bay

C A N A D A

Newfoundland

Edmonton

50°

Vancouver
Seattle

Winnipeg

Québec
Montreal
Ottawa
Toronto
Boston
Buffalo
Paterson
Newark
New York

N O R T H

Portland UNITED STATES

Hamilton
Milwaukee Detroit
Chicago Cleveland
Pittsburgh Baltimore Philadelphia
Indianapolis Washington
Cincinnati

40°

P A C I F I C

San Francisco

OF

San Jose

Denver

Honolulu

Hawaiian
Islands
(U.S.A.)

Los Angeles San Bernardino
San Diego
Tijuana

A M E R I C A

Kansas City
St. Louis

Bermuda
(U.K.)

30°

Dallas

Atlanta

180°

I. de
Guadalupe
(Mex.)

Ciudad
Juárez

Houston

New Orleans

170°

O C E A N

Tropic of Cancer

Miami

BAHAMAS

160°

20°

Monterrey

Gulf of
Mexico Havana

CUBA

Santiago
de Cuba

PUERTO
RICO San
Juan

150°

Is. de
Revilla Gigedo
(Mex.)

León
Guadalajara

M E X I C O

HAITI DOM.
REP.
Port-
au-
Santo
JAMAICA Prince Domingo
Kingston

Guadelou
DOMINIC
Martin
ST. V. AN
GRENA

140°

Mexico
City

Belmopan
BELIZE

Caribbean Sea

(Neth.)

10°

Guatemala GUA.
City
San Salvador
EL SAL.

HONDURAS
Tegucigalpa
NICARAGUA

130° Equator

120°

Managua

COSTA RICA

Panama
City
PANAMA

S a

110°

San José

A m

100°

90°

10°

S O U T H

20°

P A C I F I C

Tropic of Capricorn

30°

O C E A N

NORTH AMERICA

NORTH AMERICA

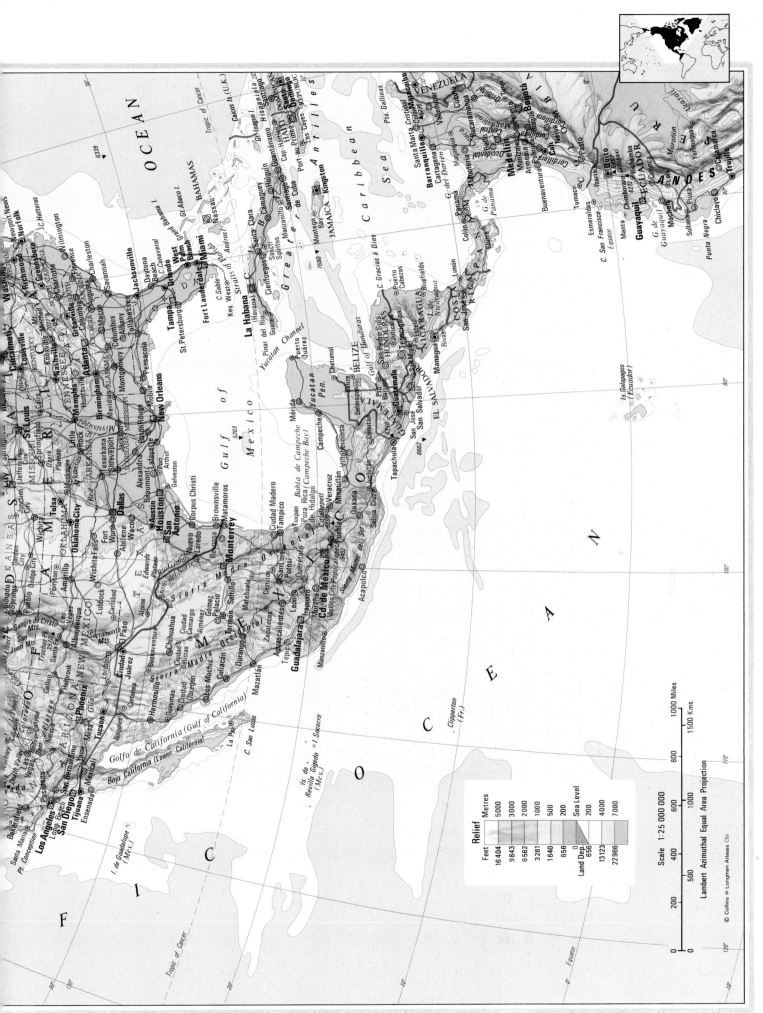

OCEAN

Tropic of Cancer

BAHAMAS

Caicos Is. (U.K.)

Key West of Florida

Straits of Florida

La Habana
(Havana)

Pinar del Río

Santa Clara
Cienfuegos
Sancti
Spíritus

Cuba

Manzanillo
Santiago
de Cuba

Greater

Antilles

HISPANIOLA
HAITI
DOMINICAN REPUBLIC
Santo
Domingo

JAMAICA
Kingston
Montego
Bay

Caribbean

Sea

VENEZUELA
Maracaibo
Barranquilla
Cartagena
COLOMBIA
Medellín
Bogotá
Cali
PERU

ANDES
ECUADOR
Quito
Guayaquil

Gulf

of

Mexico

M e x i c o

Mérida
Campeche
Bahía de Campeche
(Campeche Bay)

Yucatán Channel

Yucatán
Pen.

BELIZE
Belize

GUATEMALA
Guatemala
San Salvador
EL SALVADOR

HONDURAS
Tegucigalpa

NICARAGUA
Managua

COSTA RICA
San José

PANAMA
Panamá
Colón

Gulf of Honduras

OCEAN

PACIFIC

I. de Guadalupe
(Mex.)

Golfo de California (Gulf of California)
Baja California (Lower California)

Is. de
Revilla Gigedo
(Mex.)

I. Socorro

Clipperton
(Fr.)

Is. Galapagos
(Ecuador)

Relief

Feet	Metres
16404	5000
9843	3000
6562	2000
3281	1000
1640	500
656	200
0	Sea Level
656	200
Land Dep.	
13123	4000
22966	7000

Scale 1:25 000 000

Lambert Azimuthal Equal Area Projection

© Collins © Longman Atlases Cbi

1000 Miles
1500 Kms.

CANADA AND ALASKA

Relief

Feet	Metres
16 404	5000
9843	3000
6562	2000
3281	1000
1640	500
656	200
0	Sea Level
Land Dep.	200
656	4000
13 123	7000
22 966	

Scale 1 : 17 000 000

0 100 200 300 400 500 Miles

0 100 200 300 400 500 600 700 800 Kms.

Bonne Projection

GREENLAND
(KALAALLIT NUNAAT)

Kong Christian den IX. Land
Mt. Forel ▲3360
K. Gustav Holm
Arctic Circle
Ammassalik
Tasiilaq
Kong Frederik den VI. Kyst
Kösel Bugt
K. Møsting
Sukkertoppen/ Maniitsoq
Kangerlussuaq/
Søndre Strømfjord
Holsteinsborg/
Sisimiut
Godthåb
Nuuk
Fiskenæsset/
Qeqertarsuatsiaat
Paamiut
Frederikshåb/
Paamiut
Ivigtut/
Ittut
Julianehåb/
Qaqortoq
Narsarssuaq/
Narsarsuaq
K. Farvel/
Uummannarsuaq
(C. Farewell)

ATLANTIC OCEAN

Labrador
Sea

NEWFOUNDLAND
LABRADOR

Hebron
Nutak
Nain
Hopedale
Indian Harbour
C. Harrison
Cartwright
Rigolet
Smallwood Resr
North West River
Churchill
Battle Harbour
C. Bauld
St. Anthony

Bonavista
Gander
Carbonear
St. John's
Grand Falls
Buchans
Placentia
Trepassey
C. Race

Cape Breton I.
St. Pierre and Miquelon (Fr.)

Gaspé
Gulf of St. Lawrence
Île d'Anticosti

NOVA SCOTIA
Halifax
Dartmouth
Bridgewater
Liverpool
Shelburne
C. Sable
Yarmouth

NEW BRUNSWICK
Fredericton
Saint John
Moncton
Truro
Sydney
Port Hawkesbury
Mulgrave

MAINE
Bangor
Portland
Bay of Fundy

NEW HAMPSHIRE
Concord
Manchester

VERMONT
Montpelier

Boston
Worcester
Providence
Hartford
New Haven
Long Island

NEW YORK
Albany
Syracuse
Rochester
Buffalo
Utica
Scranton
Newark
NEW YORK
Paterson
Reading

PENNSYLVANIA
Harrisburg
Williamsport
Philadelphia
Baltimore
MARYLAND
Pittsburgh
NEW JERSEY

Québec
Montréal
Ottawa
Hull
Trois Rivières
Sherbrooke
Chicoutimi
Jonquière
Roberval

ONTARIO
Toronto
Hamilton
Kitchener
London
Windsor
Sudbury
North Bay
Thunder Bay
Sault Sainte Marie

QUÉBEC

Winnipeg
MANITOBA

UNITED STATES

MINNESOTA
Minneapolis
St. Paul
St. Cloud

WISCONSIN
Milwaukee
Madison
Green Bay

MICHIGAN
Detroit
Grand Rapids

Chicago
ILLINOIS
INDIANA
Toledo
Cleveland
OHIO
Fort Wayne
Lima
Youngstown

© Collins ◇ Longman Atlases Cbi

99

WESTERN CANADA

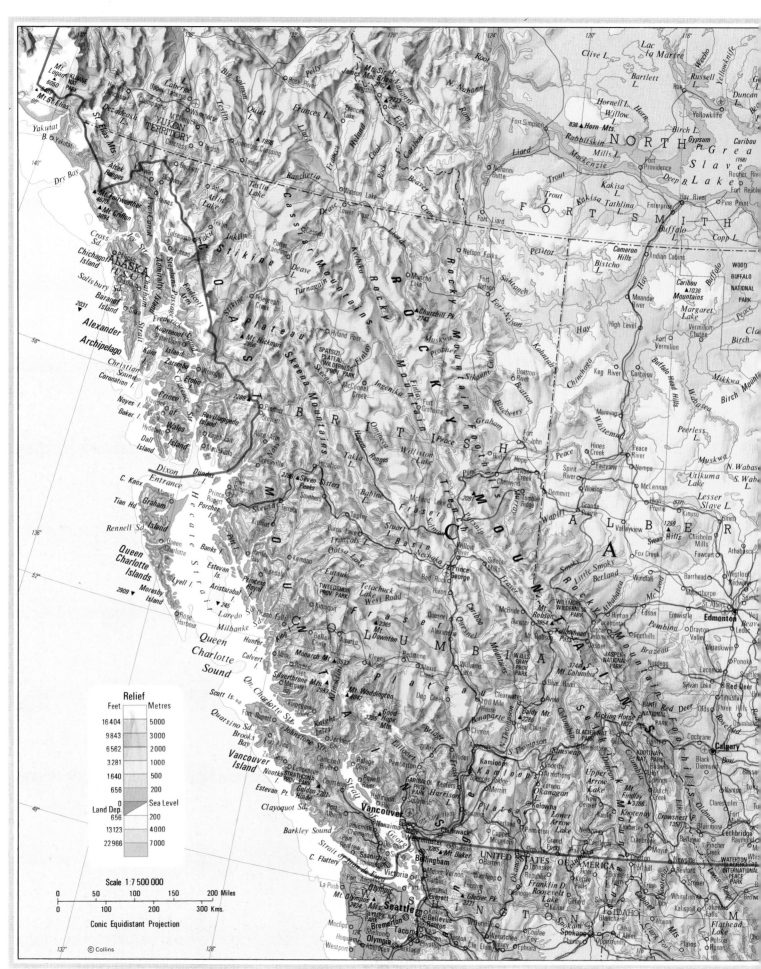

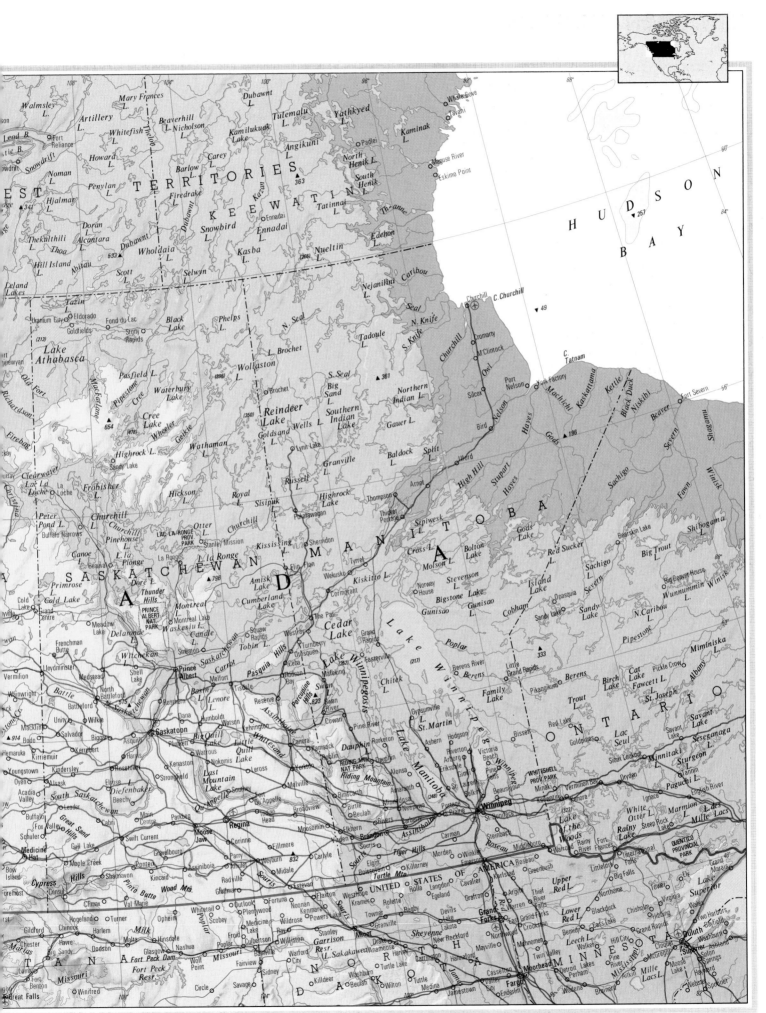

EASTERN CANADA

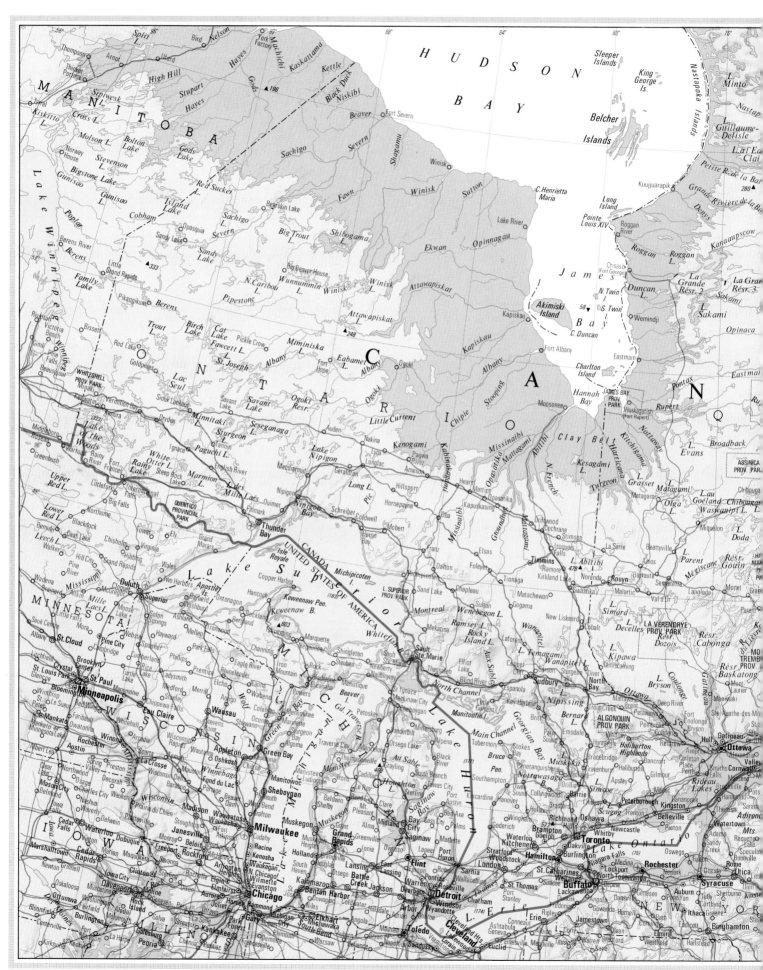

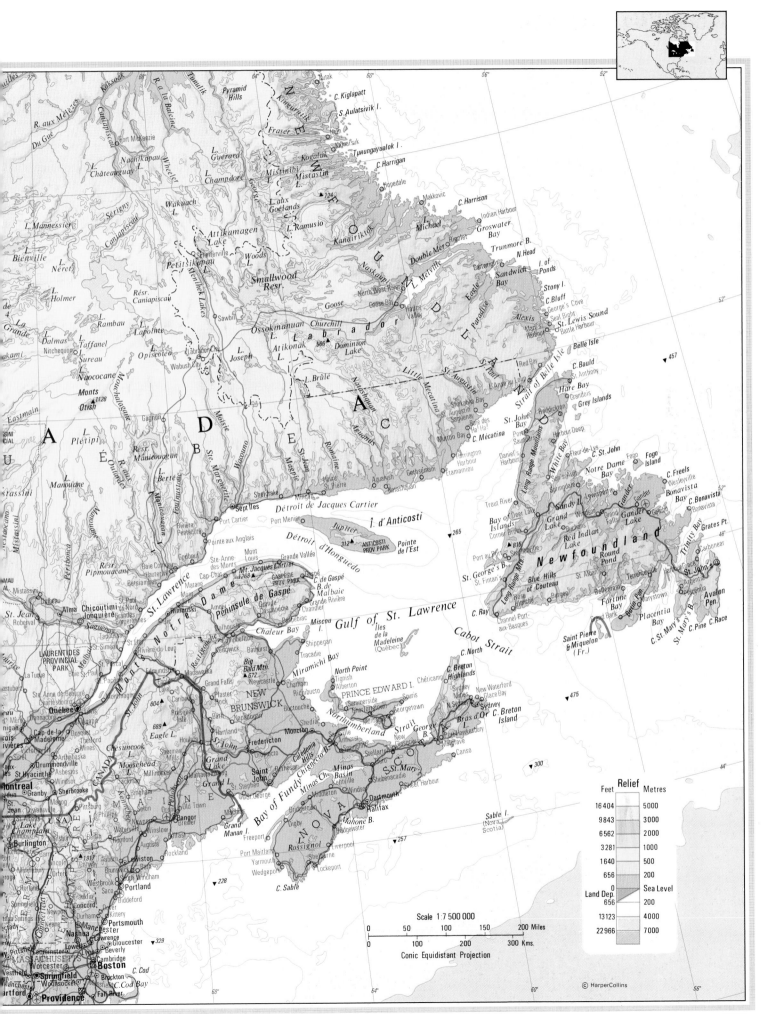

SOUTH CENTRAL CANADA

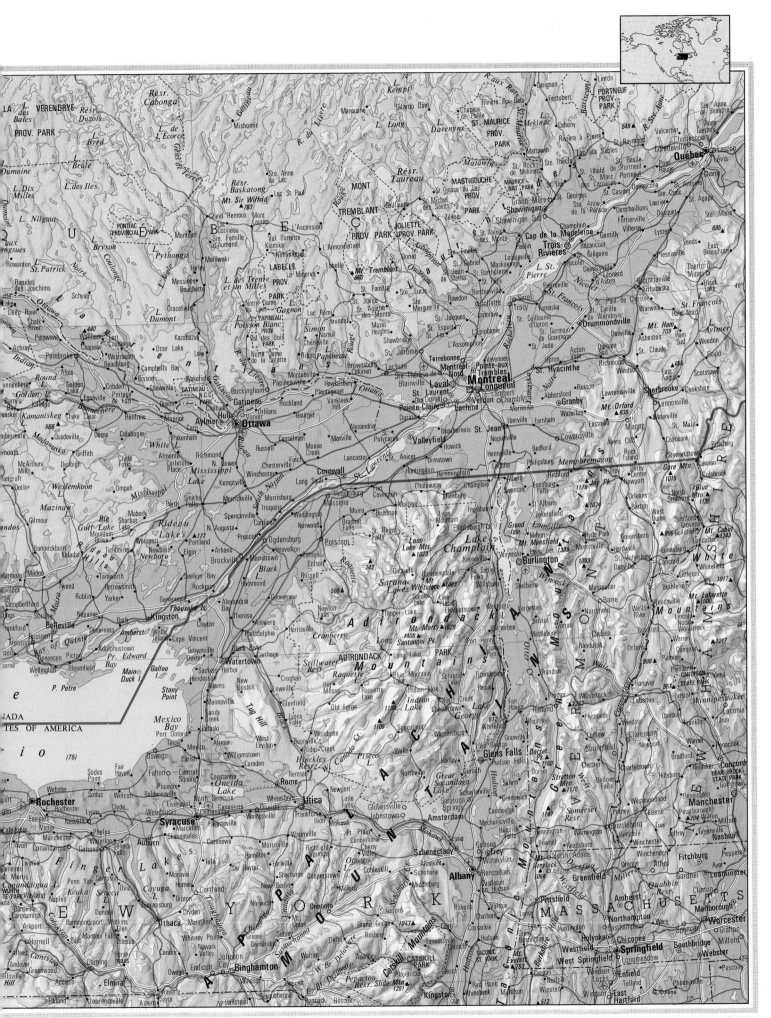

UNITED STATES

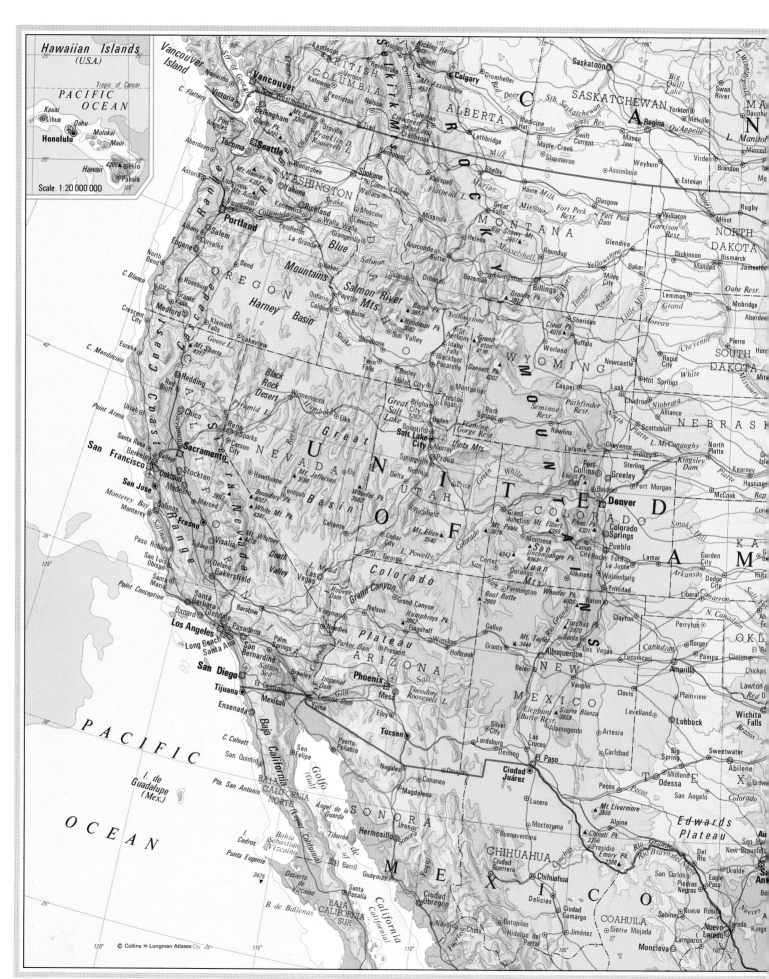

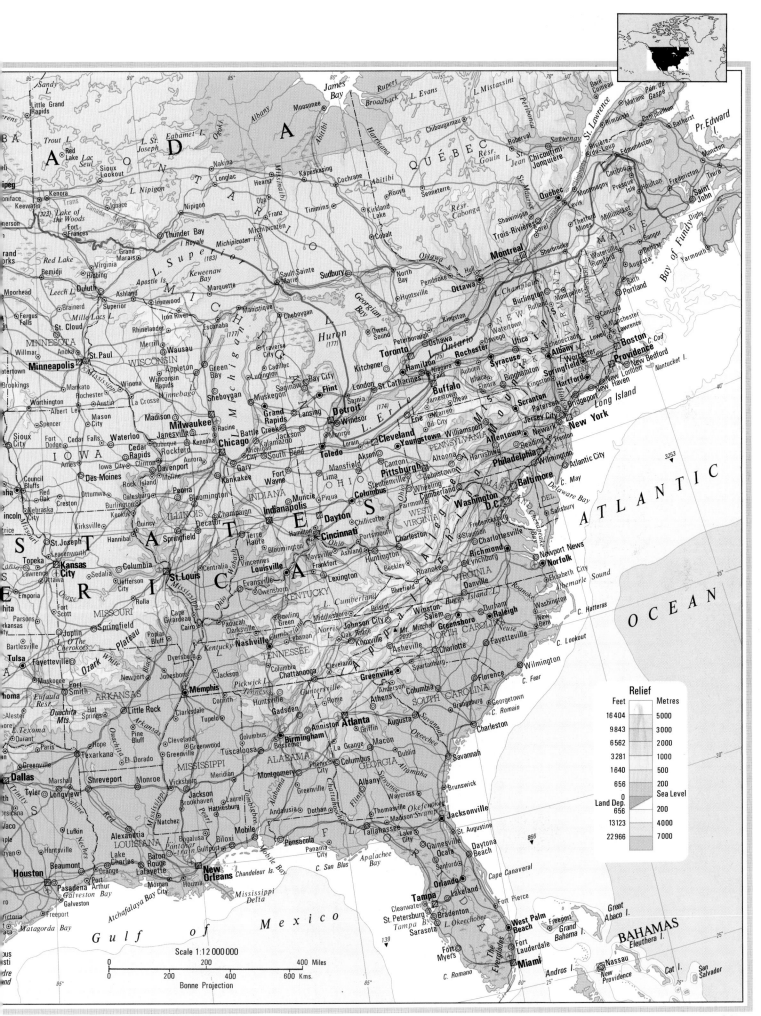

WESTERN UNITED STATES

CENTRAL UNITED STATES

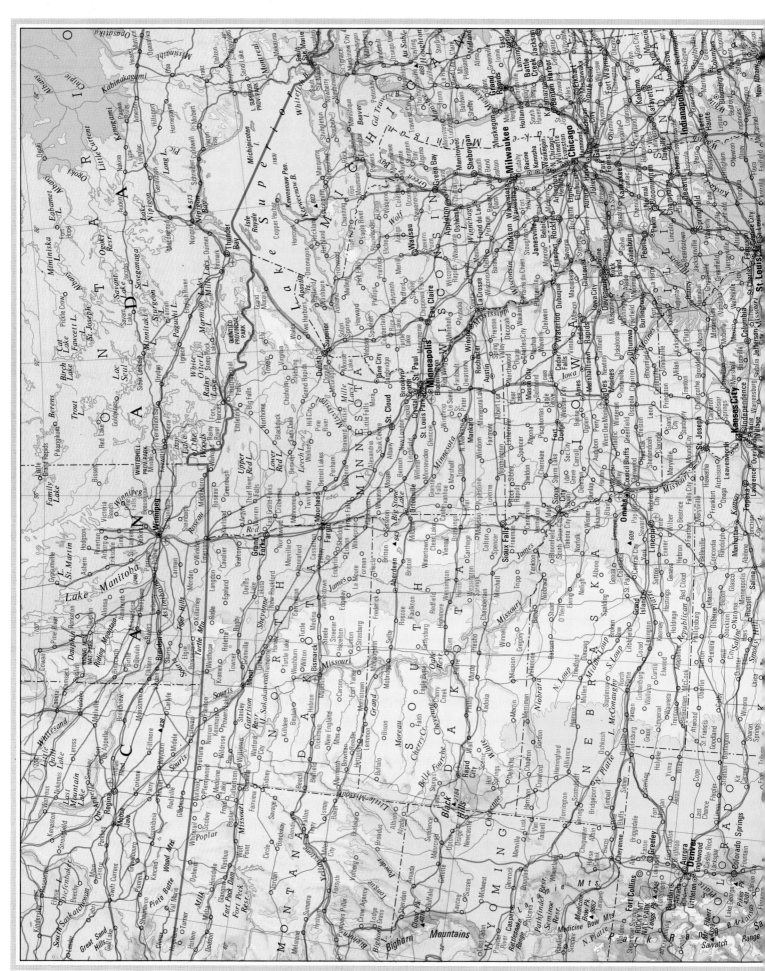

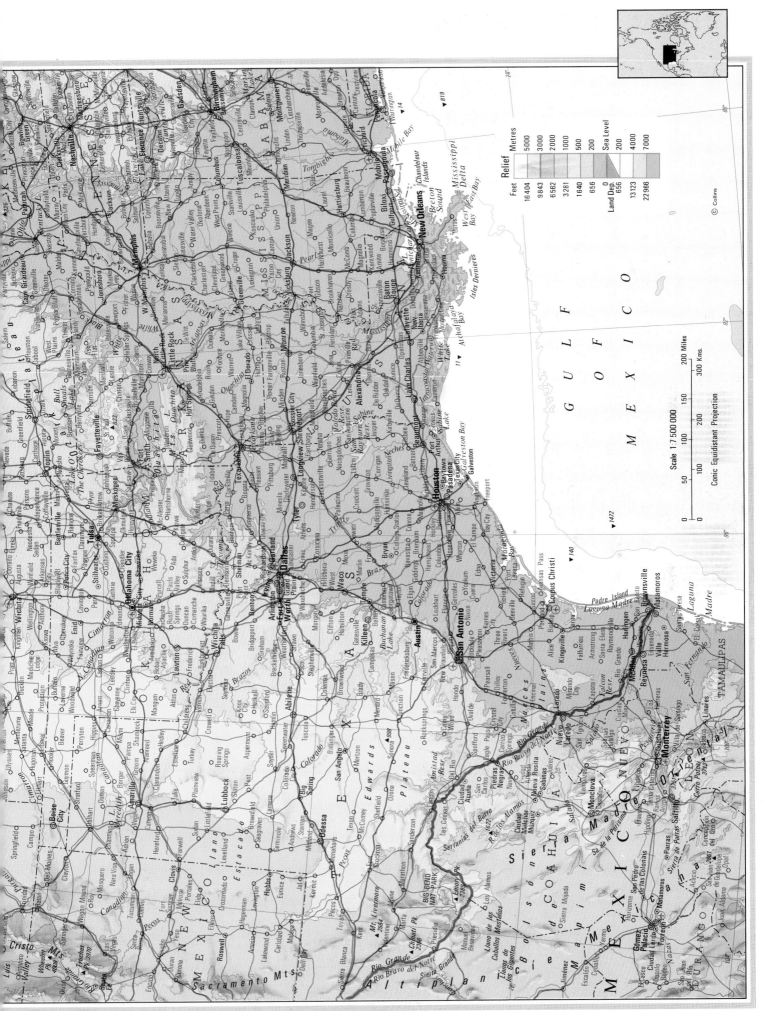

GULF OF MEXICO

MEXICO

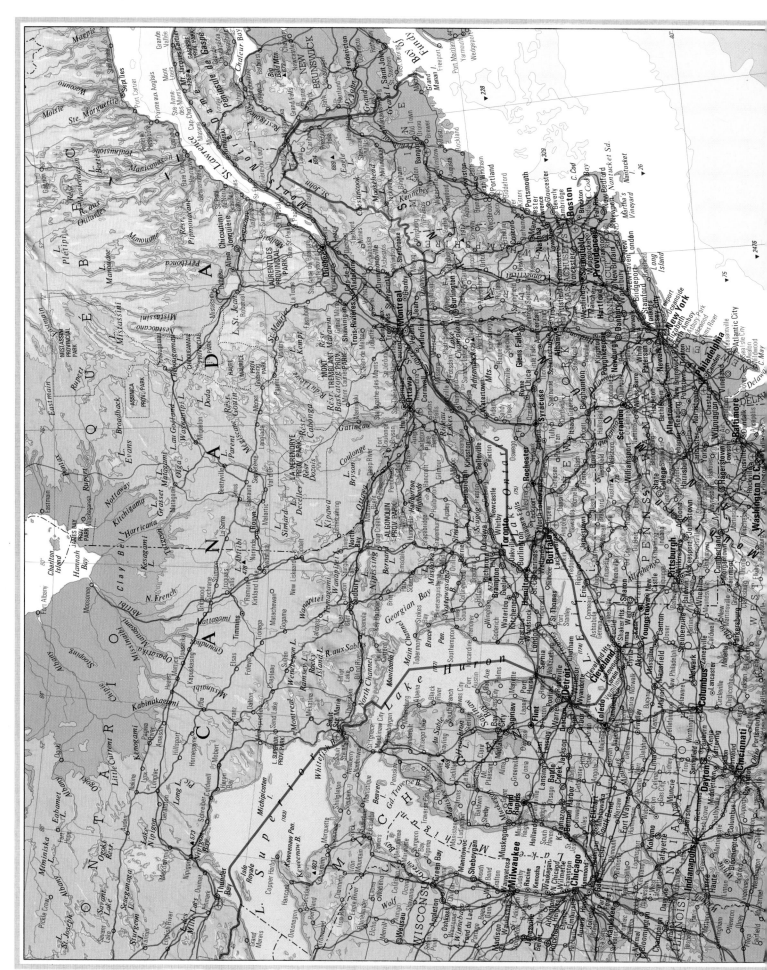

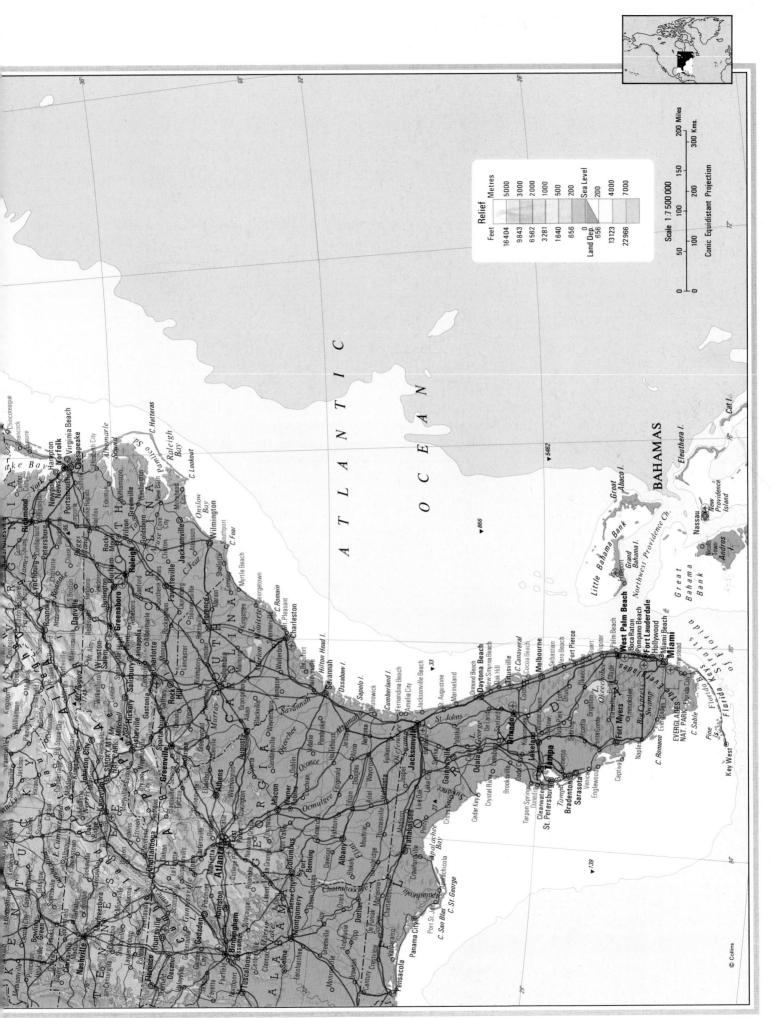

ATLANTIC

OCEAN

BAHAMAS

Relief

Feet	Metres
16404	5000
9843	3000
6562	2000
3281	1000
1640	500
656	200
	Sea Level
	Land Dep.
656	0
13123	200
22966	4000
	7000

Scale 1:7 500 000

Conic Equidistant Projection

0   50   100   150   200 Miles
0   100   200   300 Kms.

© Collins

NORTHEASTERN UNITED STATES

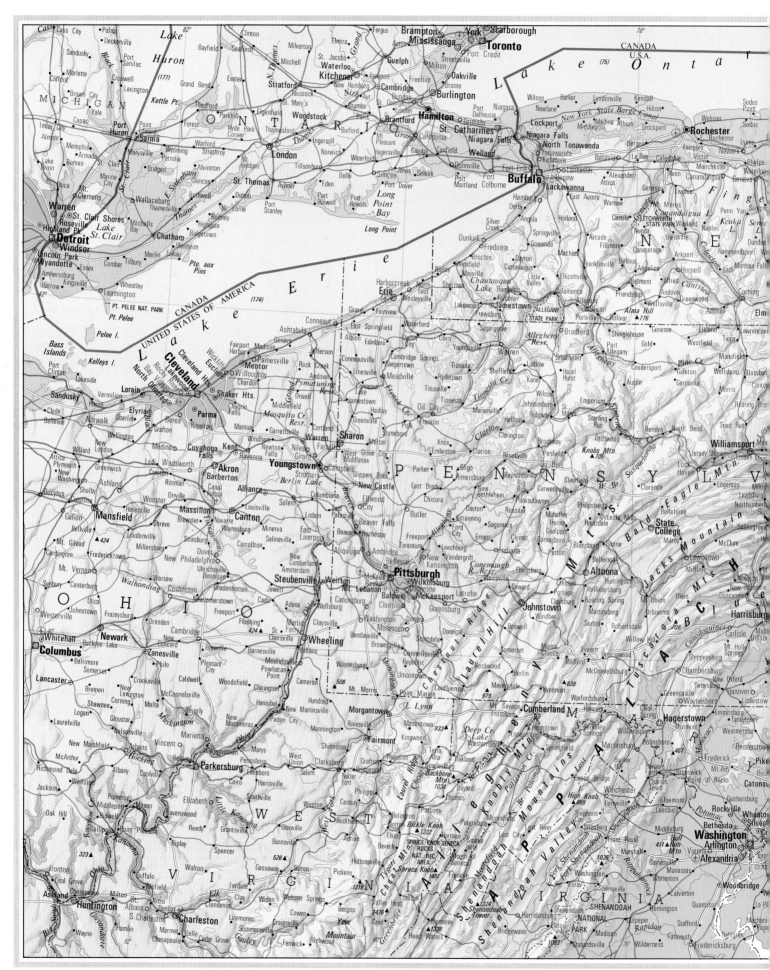

CENTRAL AMERICA AND THE CARIBBEAN

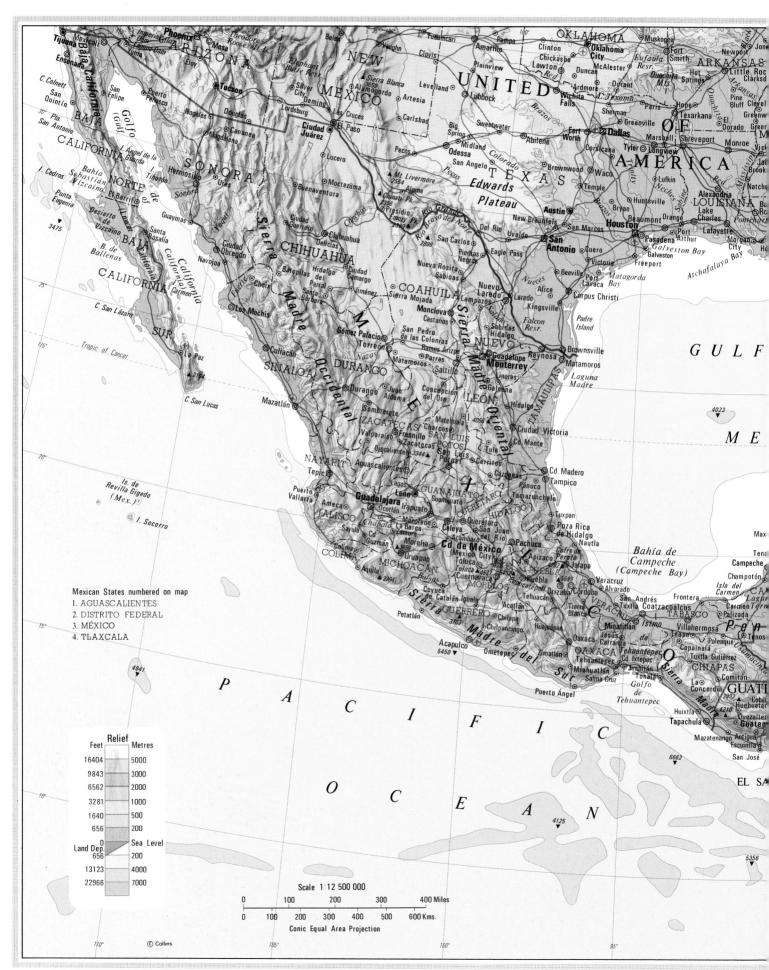

Mexican States numbered on map
1. AGUASCALIENTES
2. DISTRITO FEDERAL
3. MÉXICO
4. TLAXCALA

Feet | Relief | Metres
16404 | | 5000
9843 | | 3000
6562 | | 2000
3281 | | 1000
1640 | | 500
656 | | 200
0 | | Sea Level
Land Dep.
656 | | 200
13123 | | 4000
22966 | | 7000

Scale 1:12 500 000

0   100   200   300   400 Miles

0   100   200   300   400   500   600 Kms.

Conic Equal Area Projection

© Collins

TENNESSEE
Asheville • NORTH • Charlotte • Fayetteville • New Bern
Chattanooga • Cleveland • CAROLINA • C. Lookout
Pickwick L. • Cleveland • Spartanburg • SOUTH • Wilmington
Huntsville • Gadsden • Greenville • CAROLINA • Florence • C. Fear
Corinth • Rome • Anderson • Columbia • Georgetown
Tennessee • Gadsden • Athens • CAROLINA • C. Romain
TATES • Anniston • Atlanta • Augusta • Orangeburg • Charleston
Birmingham • Griffin • Macon • Savannah
Tuscaloosa • Bessemer • Columbus • GEORGIA • Dublin • Ogeechee
IPPI • Montgomery • Phenix • La Grange • Altamaha • Savannah
ALABAMA • City • Albany • Waycross
Greenville • Andalusia • Dothan • Brunswick
Mobile • Pensacola • Thomasville • Madison • ATLANTIC
Chandeleur • Panama • Tallahassee • Lake City • Jacksonville
Is • City • C. San Blas • Gainesville • St. Augustine • OCEAN
Mississippi • Apalachee • Ocala • Sanford • 866
Delta • Bay • Orlando • Cape Canaveral
Clearwater • Lakeland • Fort Pierce • 1137 • Tropic of Cancer
St. Petersburg • Tampa • West • Freeport • Great
Tampa B. • Bradenton • Palm • Grand • Abaco I.
Sarasota • Lake • Beach • Bahama I.
Fort Myers • Okeechobee • Fort • Eleuthera I.
C. Romano • Lauderdale • New • Rock Sound
OF • Miami • Providence • Cat I.
C. Sable • Nicolls • Nassau • San
Key West • Florida Keys • Town • Andros • Salvador
Straits • Rolleville
CO • of Florida • Andros I. • The Bight • Rum Cay
Gt. • Long I. • Samana Cay
Exuma • Mayaguana I.
Crooked I. • Plana Cays • Turks and Caicos Is.
Acklin's I. • Caicos Is. • (U.K.)
Yucatan • La Habana • Matanzas • Cárdenas • Little • Turks Is.
C. San • (Havana) • Sagua • Archo. de Sabana • Inagua
Channel • Marianao • la Grande • Archo. de Camagüey • Great
Tizimín • Pinar del Río • Guines • Santa Clara • Moron • Inagua I. • Matthew
Puerto • Guane • Golfo de Batabanó • Cienfuegos • Sancti • Ciego de Avila • Nuevitas • Town • Île de
Juárez • Nueva • Trinidad • Spiritus • Camagüey • Holguín • la Tortue • Puerto Plata • San Francisco
YUCATAN • Gerona • Archo. de los • CUBA • Banes • Baracoa • Port-de-Paix • de Macorís
Valladolid • Isla de Pinos • Canarreos • Jardines de la • Victoria • Bayamo • S. Luis • Cap-Haïtien • Valverde • Santiago • DOMINICAN • 8528 • Puerto Rico Trench
Tekax • Reina • de las Tunas • Guantánamo • G. de la • La Vega • REP • La Romana • San Juan
QUINTANA • Isla de Cozumel • Little • Manzanillo • Sa. Maestra • Gonâve • San Juan • Santo • S. Pedro • Mayagüez
ROO • Cayman • Cayman Brac • Turquino • Santiago de Cuba • HAITI • Azua • Domingo • Saona • PUERTO
Chetumal • 4647 • Grand Cayman • C. Cruz • Île de la • Jérémie • Port-au-• 2680 • Barahona • RICO
Corozal • Georgetown • Cayman Is. • Montego Bay • St. Ann's Bay • Gonâve • Prince • Hispaniola • (U.S.A.)
Belize • (U.K.) • Black River • Port • 2414 • Les • 4297 • Antilles
BELIZE • Turneffe Is. • May Pen • Antonio • Cayes
Dangriga • Kingston • Greater • Windward Passage
Punta • JAMAICA
Gorda • Gulf of Honduras • CARIBBEAN SEA
Pto. • Ambergris
Barrios • Balfate • C. Camarón
Pto. Cortés • Trujillo • Laguna de • Netherlands
La Ceiba • Caratasca • Antilles
S. Pedro Sula • Yoro • Mosquitia • Curaçao (Neth.)
Sta. • HONDURAS • Patuca • C. Gracias á Dios • Aruba • Bonaire
Rosa • Juticalpa • (Neth.) • Willemstad
Comayagua • Tegucigalpa • Coco • Pta. Gallinas • Pen. de
San Salvador • Danlí • Pto. Cabezas • Pen. de la • Golfo de
S. Vicente • Ocotal • I. de • Guajira • Paraguaná
Chinandega • NICARAGUA • Providencia • Castilletes • Punto Fijo • La Vela
León • (Col.) • Riohacha • Uribia • La Concepción • Coro
Corinto • Lago de • Prinzapolca • Río Grande • Santa • Maracaibo • Tucacas • Puerto
Managua • Managua • I. de • Marta • Cabimas • San Felipe • Cabello
Granada • Rama • San Andrés • Sa. Nevada de • Ciudad Ojeda • Barquisimeto • Valencia
Jinotepe • L. de • Bluefields • (Col.) • Barranquilla • Sta. Marta • VENEZUELA • Yaritagua • Maracay
Rivas • Nicaragua • Cartagena • Baranoa • L. de • Cabudare
San Carlos • Sabanalarga • Maracaibo • Valera
COSTA • San Juan del Norte • Turbaco • Calamar • Agustín • San Carlos • Acarigua • El Baúl
Liberia • Pen. de • San • Carmen • Plato • del Zulia • Trujillo • Guanare
Nicoya • Juan • Golfo del • Sincelejo • Magangué • Ocaña • Bocono • Mérida • Guanarito
Puntarenas • Limón • Darién • Monteria • S. Jorge Mompós • Cúcuta • COLOMBIA • Cordillera • Guanare
San • RICA • Golfo • Colón • Puerto Rey • Barrancabermeja • de Mérida • Apure
José • de los • Gatun • Turbo • 4200 • San Cristóbal • Barinas
Irazú • Mosquitos • Lake • Cerete • Magdalena • Arauca • Arauca
Cartago • Chirripó • PANAMA • Panamá • El Real • Rubio • Pamplona • Meta
C. Blanco • 3477 • City • G. de Uraba • Riosucio • Bucaramanga
Golfito • Balboa • Jurado • Santa Fe • Yarumal • Socorro
David • Penonomé • Archo. de • COLOMBIA
Pta. S. Pedro • las Perlas • Santiago • Pen. de
Pen. de Osa • Golfo • de • Azuero
Pto. Armuelles • Isla • de Panamá
Pta. Burica • de Coiba

PUERTO
RICO • San Juan • Virgin Is.(U.K.)
(U.S.A.) • Bayamón • Anegada
Arecibo • St. Thomas • Virgin • Anguilla (U.K.)
Mayagüez • Ponce • Caguas • Tortola • Virgin • BARBUDA
Vieques • St. John • Gorda • St. Martin • St. Barthélemy
Sint Maarten (Fr.Neth.) • ANTIGUA
St. Croix (U.S.A.) • Saba (Neth.) • ST. KITTS • Montserrat • St. John's
Sint Eustatius (Neth.) • NEVIS • Guadeloupe • Pointe-à-Pitre
Lesser • (Fr.) Basse-Terre • Marie-Galante
• DOMINICA • Roseau
Antilles • Martinique • (Fr.)
Fort-de-France
5630 • Castries • ST. LUCIA • Windward Islands • BARBADOS
St. Kingstown • Bridgetown
Lesser Antilles • ST. • VINCENT • AND THE • GRENADINES • St. George's • GRENADA
Bonaire • La Blanquilla • TOBAGO
Los • La Orchila • Dragon's Mouth • Port of Spain
Roques • Isla de • Pen. de Paria • San Fernando
Margarita • Porlamar • Carupano • G. of • TRINIDAD
La Tortuga • Pen. de Araya • Cumaná • Paria • Serpent's Mouth
Pto. La Cruz • Delta
La Guaira • Barcelona • Maturin • del Orinoco
Same Scale

GULF OF MEXICO
CUBA

117

North America

NORTH

ATLANTIC

OCEAN

40°

30°

Tropic of Cancer

20°

Caribbean Sea

Barranquilla

Maracaibo · Caracas

TRINIDAD
AND TOBAGO

VENEZUELA

Georgetown

Paramaribo

GUYANA

SURINAM

Cayenne

GUIANA
(Fr.)

10°

Medellin

Bogotá

Cali

COLOMBIA

Quito

ECUADOR

Guayaquil

Galapagos
Is. (Ec.)

90°

100°

110°

120°

130°

140°

PERU

Lima

P E R U

B R A Z I L

Belém

40°

30° Equator

Fortaleza

Recife

10°

La Paz

BOLIVIA

Sucre

Brasília

Salvador

Belo
Horizonte

SOUTH

PARAGUAY

Rio de
Janeiro

São Paulo

Santo André

Asunción

Curitiba

Tropic of Capricorn

San Félix (Chile)

San Ambrosio

CHILE

ARGENTINA

Córdoba

Rosario

URUGUAY

Pôrto
Alegre

S

A T L A

20°

Islas
Juan
Fernández

(Chile)

Valparaíso

Santiago

Buenos
Aires

La
Plata

Montevideo

30°

O C E

PACIFIC

40°

OCEAN

Falkland
Is. (U.K.)

50°

South
Georgia
(U.K.)

Tierra del
Fuego

60°

Antarctic Circle

70°

International Date Line

Antarctica

© Collins

118

SOUTH AMERICA

South America as a continental name is used for the land area extending south from the Isthmus of Panama to Cape Horn and lying between 34°W and 82°W. Latin America is a term widely used to cover those parts of the Americas where Spanish, or Portuguese as in Brazil, are the adopted national languages, and thus refers to an area that includes all of South America, Central America, Mexico and the Caribbean, except for the few English, French and Dutch speaking countries and dependencies.

SOUTH AMERICA

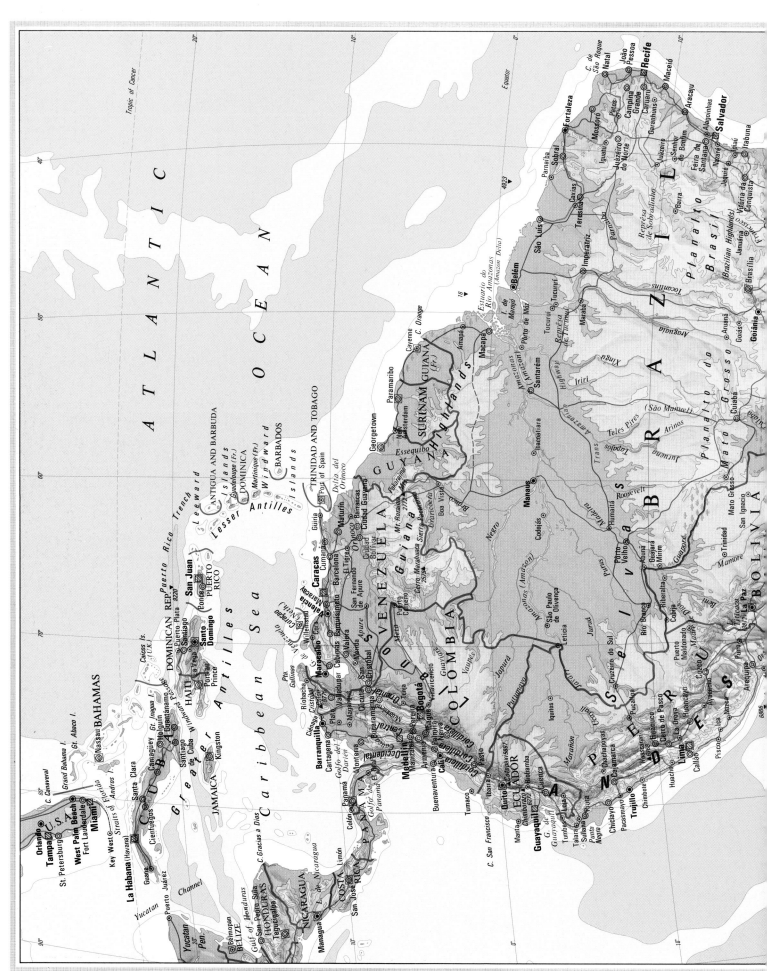

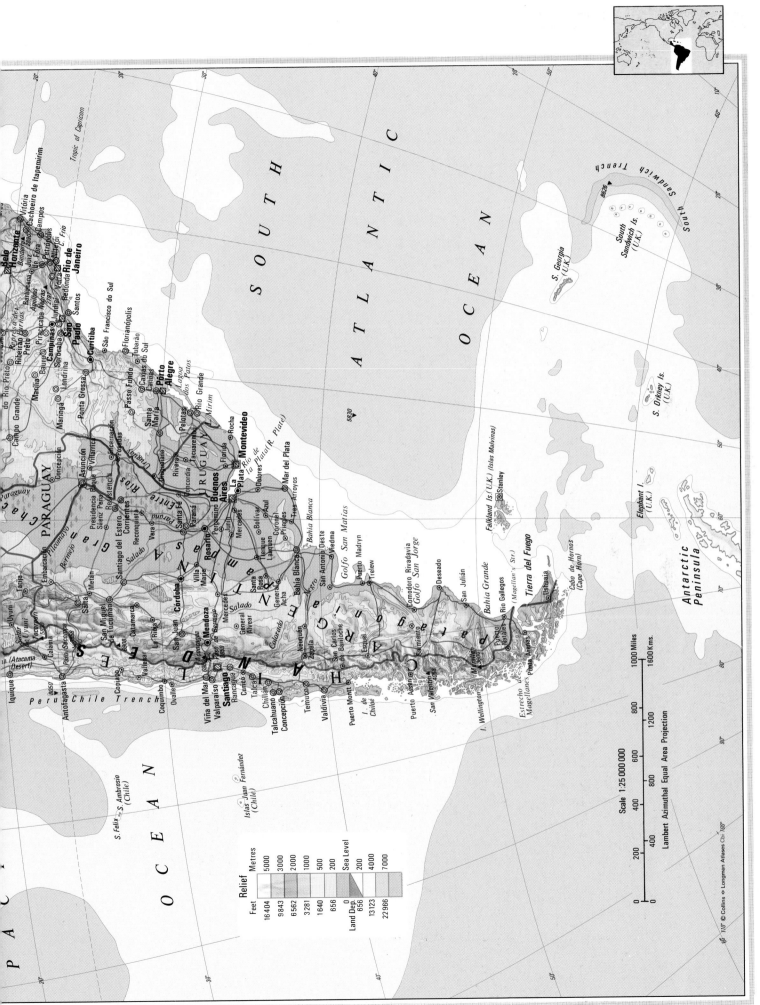

P A C I F I C   O C E A N

PACIFIC OCEAN

S O U T H   A T L A N T I C   O C E A N

South Sandwich Trench

8626

South Sandwich Is. (U.K.)

S. Georgia (U.K.)

S. Orkney Is. (U.K.)

Elephant I. (U.K.)

Falkland Is (U.K.) (Islas Malvinas)

Stanley

Antarctic Peninsula

Tropic of Capricorn

5820

BRAZIL / countries not labelled

Belo Horizonte
Vitória
Bandeira 2890
Cachoeiro de Itapemirim
Juíz de Fora
Campos
C. de São Tomé
Petrópolis
Niterói
C. Frio
Rio de Janeiro
Volta Redonda
Campinas
São Paulo
Sorocaba
Santos
Curitiba
São Francisco do Sul
Florianópolis
Tubarão
Caxias do Sul
Canoas
Porto Alegre
Lagoa dos Patos
Rio Grande
Pelotas
Lagoa Mirim

Campo Grande
Ribeirão Prêto
Rio Prêto
Bauru
Marília
Londrina
Maringá
Ponta Grossa
Passo Fundo
Santa Maria

PARAGUAY
Paraguay
Gran Chaco
Asunción
Concepción
Pilcomayo
Encarnación
Posadas
Villarrica
Corrientes
Resistencia
Presidencia R. Sáenz Peña
Embarcación
Tarija
Salta
Metán
Santiago del Estero

URUGUAY
Montevideo
Rivera
Tacuarembó
Paysandú
Salto
Concordia
Florida
Rocha
Río de la Plata (R. Plate)
Dolores
Mar del Plata

Buenos Aires
La Plata
Rosario
Santa Fe
Paraná
Córdoba
Villa María
Mercedes
San Juan
Mendoza
San Luis
Río Cuarto
Bahía Blanca
Azul
Olavarría
Bolívar
Tandil
Necochea
Tres Arroyos
Pringles
Lincoln
Junín
Pergamino
Reconquista

A N D E S

Iquique
Antofagasta
Copiapó
Coquimbo
Ovalle
Valparaíso
Viña del Mar
Santiago
Rancagua
Curicó
Talca
Chillán
Talcahuano
Concepción
Temuco
Valdivia
Puerto Montt
I. de Chiloé
I. Wellington
I. Valentín

Peru-Chile Trench

(Atacama Desert)
S. Felix — S. Ambrosio (Chile)
Islas Juan Fernández (Chile)

A R G E N T I N A

General Acha
General Alvear
Santa Rosa
Colorado
Neuquén
Zapala
San Carlos de Bariloche
Viedma
San Antonio Oeste
Golfo San Matías
Puerto Madryn
Trelew
Río Negro
Golfo San Jorge
Comodoro Rivadavia
Deseado
San Julián
Bahía Grande
Río Gallegos
Puerto Natales
Punta Arenas
Estrecho de Magallanes (Magellan's Str.)
Tierra del Fuego
Ushuaia
Cabo de Hornos (Cape Horn)

P A T A G O N I A

Relief

Metres	Feet
5000	16404
3000	9843
2000	6562
1000	3281
500	1640
200	656
Sea Level 0	
Land Dep. 200	656
4000	13123
7000	22966

Scale 1:25 000 000

Lambert Azimuthal Equal Area Projection

1000 Miles
1600 Kms.

© Collins © Longman Atlases Cbi

121

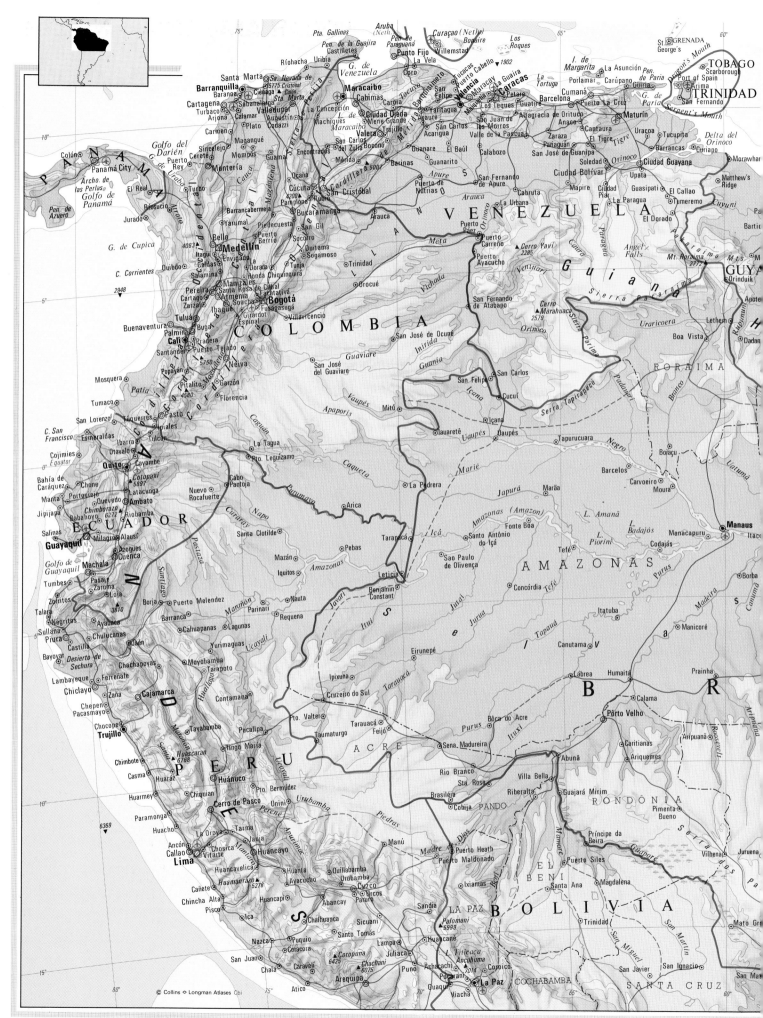

122

Relief

Feet		Metres
16 404		5000
9843		3000
6562		2000
3281		1000
1640		500
656		200
0		Sea Level
Land Dep.		
656		200
13123		4000

Scale 1:12 500 000

0 100 200 300 400 500 Miles
0 100 200 300 400 500 600 700 800 Kms.

Lambert Azimuthal Equal Area Projection

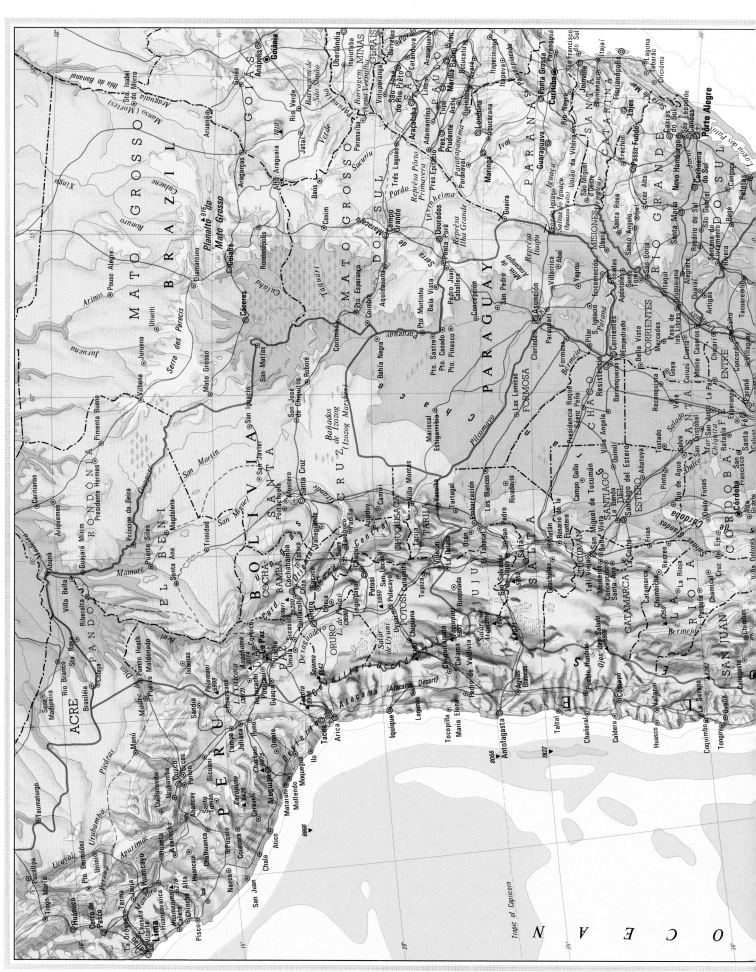

SOUTH

ATLANTIC

OCEAN

444▲

5530▼

283▼

BRAZIL

RIO GRANDE DO SUL

URUGUAY

Montevideo

CORRIENTES

SANTA FÉ

ENTRE RIOS

Paraná

Rosario

BUENOS AIRES

Buenos Aires

La Plata

Montevideo

A R G E N T I N A

Río de la Plata (R. Plate)

Bahía Samborombón

Punta Norte

Punta Sur

Cabo San Antonio

Stanley
East
Falkland
West
Falkland
Falkland Sound
Falkland Is.
(U.K.)
(Islas Malvinas)

Scale 1:7 500 000

40 80 120 Kms.
0 40 80 Miles

© Collins

Buenos Aires
Montevideo
Río de la Plata (R. Plate)
Bahía Samborombón
Punta Norte
General Madariaga
Mar del Plata
Necochea

B U E N O S   A I R E S

Bahía Blanca
Punta Alta
Carmen de Patagones

Golfo San Matías

Pen. Valdés
Punta Delgada
Golfo Nuevo
Puerto Madryn
Rawson
Trelew

C. Dos Bahías

Golfo San Jorge

Comodoro Rivadavia

C. Blanco

Deseado
Mazarredo

Bahía Laura

Pto. Santa Cruz
Río Gallegos
C. Vírgenes

C. San Juan
(Staten I.)
I. de los Estados

TIERRA DEL FUEGO
Río Grande
Ushuaia

Cabo de Hornos
(Cape Horn)

S A N T A   C R U Z

C H U B U T

R I O   N E G R O

N E U Q U E N

L A   P A M P A

M E N D O Z A

S A N   L U I S

C O R D O B A

C H I L E

Santiago
Valparaíso
Concepción
Temuco
Valdivia
Puerto Montt
I. de Chiloé

PACIFIC

OCEAN

Relief
Metres Feet
5000 16404
3000 9843
2000 6562
1000 3281
500 1640
200 656
Sea Level 0
Land Dep. 656
200 13123
4000 22966
7000

Scale 1:12 500 000

0 100 200 300 400 Miles
0 200 400 600 Kms.

Lambert Azimuthal Equal Area Projection

© Collins © Longman Atlases Cbi-95°

125

SOUTH AMERICA – EAST

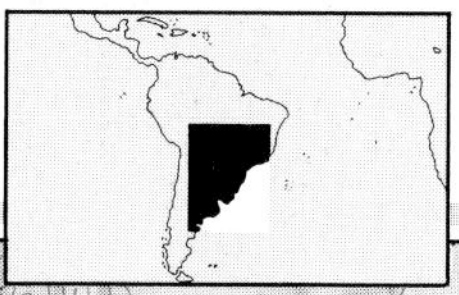

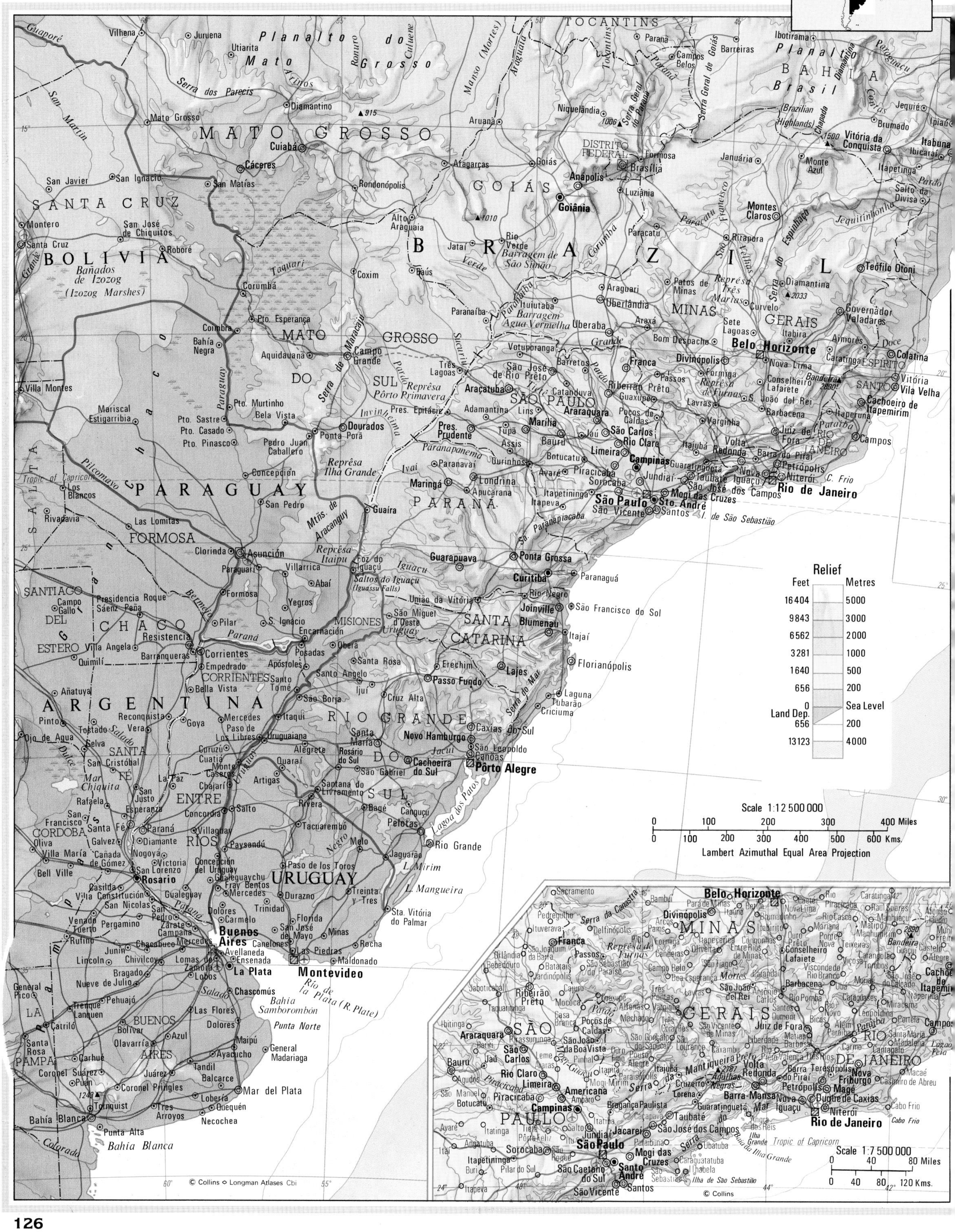

Relief

Feet	Metres
16 404	5000
9843	3000
6562	2000
3281	1000
1640	500
656	200
0	Sea Level
Land Dep.	
656	200
13123	4000

Scale 1:12 500 000

0   100   200   300   400 Miles
0   100   200   300   400   500   600 Kms.

Lambert Azimuthal Equal Area Projection

Scale 1:7 500 000

0   40   80 Miles
0   40   80   120 Kms.

© Collins

© Collins ○ Longman Atlases Cbi

Countries and regions: BOLIVIA, SANTA CRUZ, PARAGUAY, BRAZIL, MATO GROSSO, MATO GROSSO DO SUL, GOIÁS, MINAS GERAIS, DISTRITO FEDERAL, TOCANTINS, BAHIA, ESPÍRITO SANTO, SÃO PAULO, PARANÁ, SANTA CATARINA, RIO GRANDE DO SUL, ARGENTINA, FORMOSA, CHACO, CORRIENTES, MISIONES, ENTRE RIOS, SANTA FE, CORDOBA, BUENOS AIRES, LA PAMPA, URUGUAY, SALTA

Selected places: Cuiabá, Cáceres, Corumbá, Campo Grande, Goiânia, Brasília, Anápolis, Uberlândia, Uberaba, Belo Horizonte, Vitória da Conquista, Vitória, São Paulo, Santos, Campinas, Curitiba, Rio de Janeiro, Niterói, Florianópolis, Pôrto Alegre, Montevideo, Buenos Aires, La Plata, Rosario, Santa Fe, Asunción, Santa Cruz

Tropic of Capricorn

Bahía Blanca

Rio de la Plata (R. Plate)

126

ATLANTIC OCEAN

BERMUDA (U.K.)
Scale 1:1 000 000

CANARY ISLANDS (Spain)
Scale 1:10 000 000

MADEIRA ISLANDS
Scale 1:4 000 000 (Portugal)

ASCENSION (U.K.)
Scale 1:1 000 000

ST. HELENA (U.K.)
Scale 1:1 000 000

TRISTAN DA CUNHA (U.K.)
Scale 1:1 000 000

Scale 1:60 000 000

Zenithal Equal-Area Projection

© Collins

GEOGRAPHICAL DATA
Part 1

WORLD
FACTS
AND
FIGURES

WORLD PHYSICAL DATA

Earth's Dimensions

Superficial area	196 936 679 miles^2	510 066 000 km^2
Land surface	57 268 725 miles^2	148 326 000 km^2
Water surface	139 667 953 miles^2	361 740 000 km^2
Equatorial circumference	24 902 miles	40 075 km
Meridional circumference	24 859 miles	40 007 km
Volume	259 902x10^6 miles^3	1 083 230x10^6 km^3
Mass	5.882x10^{21} tons	5.976x10^{21} tonnes

The Continents

Asia	16 837 065 miles^2	43 608 000 km^2
Africa	11 720 077 miles^2	30 355 000 km^2
North America	9 787 258 miles^2	25 349 000 km^2
South America	6 799 613 miles^2	17 611 000 km^2
Antarctica	5 150 000 miles^2	13 338 500 km^2
Europe	4 053 281 miles^2	10 498 000 km^2
Oceania	3 300 000 miles^2	8 547 000 km^2

Oceans and Sea Areas

Pacific Ocean	63 854 826 miles^2	165 384 000 km^2
Atlantic Ocean	31 744 015 miles^2	82 217 000 km^2
Indian Ocean	28 371 042 miles^2	73 481 000 km^2
Arctic Ocean	5 427 027 miles^2	14 056 000 km^2
Mediterranean Sea	967 181 miles^2	2 505 000 km^2
South China Sea	894 980 miles^2	2 318 000 km^2
Bering Sea	876 061 miles^2	2 269 000 km^2
Caribbean Sea	750 193 miles^2	1 943 000 km^2
Gulf of Mexico	596 138 miles^2	1 544 000 km^2
Okhotskoye More	589 961 miles^2	1 528 000 km^2
East China Sea	481 853 miles^2	1 248 000 km^2
Hudson Bay	476 061 miles^2	1 233 000 km^2
Sea of Japan	389 189 miles^2	1 008 000 km^2
North Sea	222 007 miles^2	575 000 km^2
Black Sea	177 992 miles^2	461 000 km^2

Island Areas

Greenland; Arctic / Atlantic Ocean	839 998 miles^2	2 175 597 km^2
New Guinea; Indonesia / P. N. G.	312 166 miles^2	808 510 km^2
Borneo; Malaysia / Indonesia / Brunei	292 297 miles^2	757 050 km^2
Madagascar; Indian Ocean	229 413 miles^2	594 180 km^2
Sumatera (Sumatra) ; Indonesia	202 355 miles^2	524 100 km^2
Baffin Island; Canada	183 810 miles^2	476 068 km^2
Honshū; Japan	88 978 miles^2	230 455 km^2
Great Britain; United Kingdom	88 751 miles^2	229 867 km^2
Ellesmere Island; Canada	82 118 miles^2	212 688 km^2
Victoria Island; Canada	81 930 miles^2	212 199 km^2
Sulawesi (Celebes) ; Indonesia	72 988 miles^2	189 040 km^2
South Island; New Zealand	58 093 miles^2	150 461 km^2
Jawa (Java) ; Indonesia	51 754 miles^2	134 045 km^2
North Island; New Zealand	44 281 miles^2	114 688 km^2
Cuba; Caribbean Sea	44 218 miles^2	114 525 km^2

River Lengths

An Nīl (Nile) ; Africa	4160 miles	6695 km
Amazonas (Amazon) ; South America	4048 miles	6516 km
Chang Jiang (Yangtze) ; Asia	3964 miles	6380 km
Mississippi - Missouri; North America	3740 miles	6020 km
Ob-Irtysh; Asia	3461 miles	5570 km
Huang He (Hwang Ho) ; Asia	3395 miles	5464 km
Zaïre; Africa	2900 miles	4667 km
Mekong; Asia	2749 miles	4425 km
Amur; Asia	2744 miles	4416 km
Lena; Asia	2734 miles	4400 km
Mackenzie; North America	2640 miles	4250 km
Yenisey; Asia	2541 miles	4090 km
Niger; Africa	2504 miles	4030 km
Murray - Darling; Oceania	2330 miles	3750 km
Volga; Europe	2291 miles	3688 km

Mountain Heights (Selected)

Everest; Nepal / China	29 028 feet	8848 m
K2; Jammu & Kashmir / China	28 251 feet	8611 m
Kānchenjunga; Nepal / India	28 169 feet	8586 m
Dhaulāgiri; Nepal	26 794 feet	8167 m
Annapurna; Nepal	26 545 feet	8091 m
Aconcagua; Argentina	22 834 feet	6960 m
Ojos del Salado; Argentina / Chile	22 664 feet	6908 m
McKinley; Alaska, U.S.A.	20 321 feet	6194 m
Logan; Canada	19 524 feet	5951 m
Kilimanjaro; Tanzania	19 340 feet	5895 m
Elbrus; Russian Federation	18 510 feet	5642 m
Kirinyaga; Kenya	17 060 feet	5200 m
Vinson Massif; Antarctica	16 860 feet	5139 m
Puncak Jaya; Indonesia	16 502 feet	5030 m
Blanc; France / Italy	15 774 feet	4808 m

Lake and Inland Sea Areas

Some areas are subject to seasonal variations.

Caspian Sea; Central Asia	143 550 miles^2	371 795 km^2
Lake Superior; U.S.A. / Canada	32 150 miles^2	83 270 km^2
Lake Victoria; East Africa	26 828 miles^2	69 485 km^2
Lake Huron; U.S.A. / Canada	23 436 miles^2	60 700 km^2
Lake Michigan; U.S.A.	22 400 miles^2	58 016 km^2
Aral Sea; Central Asia	14 092 miles^2	36 500 km^2
Lake Tanganyika; East Africa	12 700 miles^2	32 893 km^2
Great Bear Lake; Canada	12 274 miles^2	31 792 km^2
Ozero Baikal (Lake Baykal) ; Rus. Fed.	11 779 miles^2	30 510 km^2
Great Slave Lake; Canada	11 169 miles^2	28 930 km^2
Lake Erie; U.S.A. / Canada	9910 miles^2	25 667 km^2
Lake Winnipeg; Canada	9464 miles^2	24 514 km^2
Lake Malaŵi; Malaŵi / Mozambique	8683 miles^2	22 490 km^2
Lake Ontario; U.S.A. / Canada	7540 miles^2	19 529 km^2
Ladozhskoye Ozero (Lake Ladoga) ; Rus. Fed.	7100 miles^2	18 390 km^2

Volcanoes (Selected)

	Last Eruption	Height	Height
Cameroun; Cameroon	1922	13 353 feet	4070 m
Cotopaxi; Ecuador	1975	19 347 feet	5897 m
Elbrus; Russian Federation	extinct	18 510 feet	5642 m
Erebus; Antarctica	1979	12 447 feet	3794 m
Etna; Sicilia, Italy	1983	10 958 feet	3340 m
Fuji san (Fujiyama) ; Japan	extinct	12 388 feet	3776 m
Hekla; Iceland	1981	4891 feet	1491 m
Kilimanjaro; Tanzania	extinct	19 340 feet	5895 m
Mauna Loa; Hawaii	1978	13 684 feet	4171 m
Ngauruhoe; New Zealand	1975	7516 feet	2291 m
Popocatépetl; Mexico	1920	17 887 feet	5452 m
St. Helens; U.S.A.	1981	9675 feet	2949 m
Stromboli; Italy	1975	3038 feet	926 m
Tristan da Cunha; Atlantic Ocean	1962	7086 feet	2160 m
Vesuvio (Vesuvius) ; Italy	1944	4189 feet	1277 m

WORLD POLITICAL DATA

National Areas

Russian Federation; Asia / Europe	6 593 822 miles^2	17 078 000 km^2
Canada; North America	3 831 036 miles^2	9 922 385 km^2
China; Asia	3 698 455 miles^2	9 579 000 km^2
United States; North America	3 615 108 miles^2	9 363 130 km^2
Brazil; South America	3 286 472 miles^2	8 511 965 km^2
Australia; Oceania	2 966 138 miles^2	7 682 300 km^2
India; Asia	1 222 714 miles^2	3 166 830 km^2
Argentina; South America	1 072 515 miles^2	2 777 815 km^2
Sudan; Africa	967 496 miles^2	2 505 815 km^2
Saudi Arabia; Asia	926 988 miles^2	2 400 900 km^2
Algeria; Africa	919 592 miles^2	2 381 745 km^2
Zaïre; Africa	905 563 miles^2	2 345 410 km^2
Greenland; North America	840 000 miles^2	2 175 600 km^2
Mexico; North America	761 600 miles^2	1 972 545 km^2
Indonesia; Asia	741 098 miles^2	1 919 445 km^2
Libya; Africa	679 359 miles^2	1 759 540 km^2
Iran; Asia	636 293 miles^2	1 648 000 km^2
Mongolia; Asia	604 247 miles^2	1 565 000 km^2
Peru; South America	496 222 miles^2	1 285 215 km^2
Chad; Africa	495 752 miles^2	1 284 000 km^2

National Populations

China; Asia	1 139 060 000
India; Asia	843 931 000
United States; North America	249 975 000
Indonesia; Asia	179 300 000
Brazil; South America	150 368 000
Russian Federation; Asia / Europe	148 263 000
Japan; Asia	123 537 000
Bangladesh; Asia	115 594 000
Pakistan; Asia	112 049 000
Nigeria; Africa	88 500 000
Mexico; North America	86 154 000
Germany; Europe	79 479 000
Vietnam; Asia	66 200 000
Philippines; Asia	61 480 000
Italy; Europe	57 662 000
United Kingdom; Europe	57 411 000
Thailand; Asia	57 196 000
France; Europe	56 440 000
Turkey; Asia / Europe	56 098 000
Iran; Asia	54 608 000

World Cities

Ciudad de México (Mexico City) ; Mexico	20 200 000
Tōkyō; Japan	18 100 000
São Paulo; Brazil	17 400 000
New York; United States	16 200 000
Shanghai; China	13 400 000
Chicago; United States	11 900 000
Calcutta; India	11 800 000
Buenos Aires; Argentina	11 500 000
Bombay; India	11 200 000
Sŏul (Seoul) ; South Korea	11 000 000
Beijing (Peking) ; China	10 800 000
Rio de Janeiro; Brazil	10 700 000
Tianjin; China	9 400 000
Jakarta; Indonesia	9 300 000
Al Qāhirah (Cairo) ; Egypt	9 000 000

Major International Organisations

United Nations - On December 1990 the United Nations had 160 members. Independent States not represented include Liechtenstein, Monaco, Nauru, North Korea, San Marino, South Korea, Switzerland, Taiwan, Tonga.

Commonwealth

Antigua	Australia	Bahamas	Bangladesh
Barbados	Belize	Botswana	Brunei
Canada	Cyprus	Dominica	Fiji
Gambia	Ghana	Grenada	Guyana
Hong Kong	India	Jamaica	Kenya
Kiribati	Lesotho	Malaŵi	Malaysia
Maldives	Malta	Mauritius	Nauru
New Zealand	Nigeria	Pakistan	Papua New Guinea
St. Kitts & Nevis	St. Lucia	St. Vincent	Seychelles
Sierra Leone	Singapore	Solomon Islands	Sri Lanka
Swaziland	Tanzania	Tonga	Trinidad & Tobago
Tuvalu	Uganda	United Kingdom	Vanuatu
Western Samoa	Zambia	Zimbabwe	

OAU - Organisation of African Unity

Algeria	Angola	Benin	Botswana
Burkina	Burundi	Cameroon	Cape Verde
Central African Rep.	Chad	Comoros	Congo
Djibouti	Egypt	Equatorial Guinea	Ethiopia
Gabon	Gambia	Ghana	Guinea
Guinea Bissau	Ivory Coast	Kenya	Lesotho
Liberia	Libya	Madagascar	Malaŵi
Mali	Mauritania	Mauritius	Mozambique
Namibia	Niger	Nigeria	Rwanda
São Tomé & Príncipe	Senegal	Seychelles	Sierra Leone
Somali Rep.	Sudan	Swaziland	Tanzania
Togo	Tunisia	Uganda	Western Sahara
Zaïre	Zambia	Zimbabwe	

OAS - Organisation of American States

Antigua	Argentina	Bahamas	Barbados
Bolivia	Brazil	Chile	Colombia
Costa Rica	Dominica	Dominican Rep.	Ecuador
El Salvador	Grenada	Guatemala	Haiti
Honduras	Jamaica	Mexico	Nicaragua
Panama	Paraguay	Peru	St. Kitts & Nevis
St. Lucia	St. Vincent	Surinam	Trinidad & Tobago
United States	Uruguay	Venezuela	

EEC - European Economic Community

Belgium	Denmark	France	Germany
Greece	Ireland	Italy	Luxembourg
Netherlands	Portugal	Spain	United Kingdom

EFTA - European Free Trade Association

Austria	Finland (assoc.)	Iceland	Norway
Sweden	Switzerland		

ASEAN - Association of Southeast Asian Nations

Brunei	Indonesia	Malaysia	Philippines
Singapore	Thailand		

ECOWAS - Economic Community of West African States

Benin	Burkina	Cape Verde	Gambia
Ghana	Guinea	Guinea Bissau	Ivory Coast
Liberia	Mali	Mauritania	Niger
Nigeria	Senegal	Sierra Leone	Togo

CARICOM - Caribbean Community and Common Market

Antigua	Bahamas	Barbados	Belize
Dominica	Grenada	Guyana	Jamaica
Montserrat	St. Kitts & Nevis	St. Lucia	St. Vincent
Trinidad & Tobago			

NATIONS OF THE WORLD

COUNTRY	AREA		POPULATION			FORM OF GOVERNMENT	CAPITAL CITY	MAIN LANGUAGES	CURRENCY
	miles²	km²	total	density per mile²	km²				
AFGHANISTAN	251,824	652,225	16,120,000	64	25	republic	Kābol	Pushtu,Dari	afghani
ALBANIA	11,100	28,750	3,250,000	293	113	republic	Tiranë	Albanian	lek
ALGERIA	919,593	2,381,745	25,012,000	27	11	republic	Alger (Algiers)	Arabic	dinar
ANDORRA	180	465	52,000	290	112	principality	Andorra	Catalan	French franc,Spanish peseta
ANGOLA	481,351	1,246,700	10,020,000	21	8	republic	Luanda	Portuguese	kwanza
ANTIGUA & BARBUDA	171	442	77,000	451	174	constitutional monarchy	St John's	English	East Caribbean dollar
ARGENTINA	1,072,515	2,777,815	32,322,000	30	12	federal republic	Buenos Aires	Spanish	austral
ARMENIA	11,506	29,800	3,324,000	289	112	republic	Yerevan	Armenian,Russian	rouble
AUSTRALIA	2,966,139	7,682,300	17,086,000	6	2	monarchy (federal)	Canberra	English	dollar
AUSTRIA	32,376	83,855	7,712,000	238	92	federal republic	Wien (Vienna)	German	schilling
AZERBAIJAN	33,436	86,600	7,153,000	214	83	republic	Baku	Azerbaijani,Russian	rouble
BAHAMAS	5353	13,865	253,000	47	18	constitutional monarchy	Nassau	English	dollar
BAHRAIN	255	661	503,000	1971	761	emirate	Al Manāmah	Arabic	dinar
BANGLADESH	55,598	144,000	115,594,000	2079	803	republic	Dhaka	Bengali	taka
BARBADOS	166	430	255,000	1536	593	constitutional monarchy	Bridgetown	English	dollar
BELGIUM	11,784	30,520	9,845,000	835	323	constitutional monarchy	Bruxelles (Brussels) Brussel	French,Dutch, German	franc
BELIZE	8867	22,965	188,000	21	8	constitutional monarchy	Belmopan	English	dollar
BELORUSSIA (BELARUS)	80,309	208,000	10,278,000	128	49	republic	Minsk	Belorussian	rouble
BENIN	43,483	112,620	4,736,000	109	42	republic	Porto-Novo	French	CFA franc
BHUTAN	18,000	46,620	1,517,000	84	33	constitutional monarchy	Thimbu	Dzongkha	Indian rupee,ngultrum
BOLIVIA	424,160	1,098,575	7,400,000	17	7	republic	La Paz / Sucre	Spanish,Aymara	boliviano
BOSNIA-HERZEGOVINA	19,741	51,130	4,200,000	213	82	republic	Sarajevo	Serbo-Croat	dinar
BOTSWANA	231,804	600,372	1,291,000	6	2	republic	Gaborone	English,Tswana	pula
BRAZIL	3,286,473	8,511,965	150,368,000	46	18	federal republic	Brasília	Portuguese	cruzeiro
BRUNEI	2226	5,765	266,000	120	46	sultanate	Bandar Seri Begawan	Malay	dollar
BULGARIA	42,822	110,910	8,980,000	210	81	people's republic	Sofiya (Sofia)	Bulgarian	lev
BURKINA	105,869	274,200	9,001,000	85	33	republic	Ouagadougou	French	CFA franc
BURMA (MYANMA)	261,788	678,030	41,675,000	159	61	military regime	Yangon (Rangoon)	Burmese	kyat
BURUNDI	10,747	27,834	5,458,000	508	196	republic	Bujumbura	French,Kirundi	franc
CAMBODIA	69,884	181,000	8,246,000	118	46	republic	Phnom Penh	Cambodian,Khmer	riel
CAMEROON	183,591	475,500	11,834,000	64	25	republic	Yaoundé	French,English	CFA franc
CANADA	3,831,037	9,922,385	26,603,000	7	3	monarchy (federal)	Ottawa	English,French	dollar
CAPE VERDE	1558	4,035	370,000	237	92	republic	Praia	Portuguese,Creole	escudo
CENTRAL AFRICAN REPUBLIC	241,303	624,975	3,039,000	13	5	republic	Bangui	French,Sango	CFA franc
CHAD	495,753	1,284,000	5,679,000	11	4	republic	N'Djamena	French,Arabic	CFA franc
CHILE	290,203	751,625	13,173,000	45	18	republic	Santiago	Spanish	peso
CHINA	3,698,456	9,579,000	1,139,060,000	308	119	people's republic	Beijing (Peking)	Mandarin	yuan
COLOMBIA	439,736	1,138,915	32,987,000	75	29	republic	Bogotá	Spanish	peso
COMOROS	718	1,860	551,000	767	296	federal republic	Moroni	Comoran,Arabic,French	CFA franc
CONGO	132,046	342,000	2,271,000	17	7	republic	Brazzaville	French	CFA franc
COSTA RICA	19,653	50,900	2,994,000	152	59	republic	San José	Spanish	colon
CROATIA	21,830	56,540	4,600,000	211	81	republic	Zagreb	Serbo-Croat	Dinar
CUBA	44,218	114,525	10,609,000	240	93	people's republic	La Habana (Havana)	Spanish	peso
CYPRUS	3571	9,250	702,000	197	76	republic	Levkosía (Nicosia)	Greek	pound
CZECH REPUBLIC	30,448	78,864	10,300,000	340	131	federal republic	Praha (Prague)	Czech	koruna
DENMARK	16,631	43,075	5,140,000	309	119	constitutional monarchy	Köbenhavn (Copenhagen)	Danish	krone
DJIBOUTI	8880	23,000	409,000	46	18	republic	Djibouti	French,Somali,Afar	franc
DOMINICA	290	751	83,000	286	111	republic	Roseau	English,French	East Caribbean dollar
DOMINICAN REPUBLIC	18,703	48,440	7,170,000	383	148	republic	Santo Domingo	Spanish	peso
ECUADOR	178,176	461,475	10,782,000	61	23	republic	Quito	Spanish	sucre
EGYPT	386,197	1,000,250	53,153,000	138	53	republic	Al Qāhirah (Cairo)	Arabic	pound
EL SALVADOR	8261	21,395	5,252,000	636	245	republic	San Salvador	Spanish	colón
EQUATORIAL GUINEA	10,830	28,050	348,000	32	12	republic	Malabo	Spanish	CFA franc
ESTONIA	17,413	45,100	1,583,000	91	35	republic	Tallinn	Estonian,Russian	kroon
ETHIOPIA	471,776	1,221,900	50,974,000	108	42	people's republic	Ādīs Ābeba (Addis Ababa)	Amharic	birr
FEDERATED STATES OF MICRONESIA	271	702	99,000	365	141	federal republic	Palikir on Pohnpei	English,Kosrean,Yapese, Pohnpeian,Trukese	US dollar
FIJI	7077	18,330	765,000	108	42	republic	Suva	English,Fiji,Hindustani	dollar
FINLAND	130,127	337,030	4,986,000	38	15	republic	Helsinki	Finnish,Swedish	markka
FRANCE	210,025	543,965	56,440,000	269	104	republic	Paris	French	franc
GABON	103,346	267,665	1,172,000	11	4	republic	Libreville	French	CFA franc
GAMBIA	4127	10,690	861,000	209	81	republic	Banjul	English	dalasi
GEORGIA	26,911	69,700	5,464,000	203	78	republic	Tbilisi	Georgian,Russian	rouble
GERMANY	138,173	357,868	79,479,000	575	222	federal republic	Berlin,Bonn	German	mark
GHANA	92,010	238,305	15,028,000	163	63	military regime	Accra	English	cedi

COUNTRY	AREA		POPULATION			FORM OF GOVERNMENT	CAPITAL CITY	MAIN LANGUAGES	CURRENCY
	miles²	km²	total	density per mile²	km²				
GREECE	50,959	131,985	10,123,000	199	77	republic	Athinai (Athens)	Greek	drachma
GRENADA	133	345	85,000	638	246	constitutional monarchy	St George's	English	East Caribbean dollar
GUATEMALA	42,042	108,890	9,197,000	219	84	republic	Guatemala	Spanish	quetzal
GUINEA	98,400	254,855	5,756,000	58	23	military regime	Conakry	French	franc
GUINEA-BISSAU	13,948	36,125	965,000	69	27	republic	Bissau	Portuguese	peso
GUYANA	83,000	214,970	796,000	10	4	republic	Georgetown	English	dollar
HAITI	10,714	27,750	6,486,000	605	234	republic	Port-au-Prince	French, Creole	gourde
HONDURAS	43,276	112,085	5,105,000	118	46	republic	Tegucigalpa	Spanish	lempira
HUNGARY	35,919	93,030	10,553,000	294	113	republic	Budapest	Magyar	forint
ICELAND	39,699	102,820	255,000	6	2	republic	Reykjavík	Icelandic	króna
INDIA	1,222,714	3,166,830	843,931,000	676	266	republic	New Delhi	Hindi, English	rupee
INDONESIA	741,098	1,919,445	179,300,000	242	93	republic	Jakarta	Bahasa Indonesia	rupiah
IRAN	636,293	1,648,000	54,608,000	86	33	Islamic republic	Tehrān	Persian	rial
IRAQ	169,284	438,445	18,920,000	112	43	republic	Baghdād	Arabic, Kurdish	dinar
IRELAND, REPUBLIC OF	26,600	68,895	3,503,000	132	51	republic	Dublin	English, Irish	punt
ISRAEL	8019	20,770	4,659,000	581	224	republic	Yerushalayim (Jerusalem)	Hebrew	shekel
ITALY	116,311	301,245	57,662,000	496	191	republic	Roma (Rome)	Italian	lira
IVORY COAST (CÔTE D'IVOIRE)	124,504	322,465	11,998,000	96	37	republic	Yamoussoukro	French	CFA franc
JAMAICA	4411	11,425	2,420,000	549	212	constitutional monarchy	Kingston	English	dollar
JAPAN	142,741	369,700	123,537,000	865	334	monarchy	Tōkyō	Japanese	yen
JORDAN	37,066	96,000	4,010,000	108	42	monarchy	Ammān	Arabic	dinar
KAZAKHSTAN	1,049,151	2,717,300	16,742,000	16	6	republic	Alma-Ata	Kazakh, Russian	rouble
KENYA	224,959	582,645	24,032,000	107	41	republic	Nairobi	Kiswahili, English	shilling
KIRGHIZIA (KYRGYZSTAN)	76,641	198,500	4,394,000	57	22	republic	Bishkek	Kirghiz, Russian	rouble
KIRIBATI	264	684	66,000	250	96	republic	Bairiki on Tarawa Atoll	English, Gilbertese, I-Kiribati	Australian dollar
KUWAIT	9375	24,280	2,143,000	229	88	emirate	Al Kuwayt (Kuwait)	Arabic	dinar
LAOS	91,400	236,725	4,139,000	45	17	people's republic	Vientiane (Viangchan)	Lao	new kip
LATVIA	24,595	63,700	2,686,000	109	42	republic	Rīga	Latvian, Russian	Latvian rouble
LEBANON	4015	10,400	2,701,000	673	260	republic	Bayrūt (Beirut)	Arabic	pound
LESOTHO	11,716	30,345	1,774,000	151	58	monarchy	Maseru	English, Sesotho	maluti
LIBERIA	43,000	111,370	2,607,000	61	23	republic	Monrovia	English	dollar
LIBYA	679,359	1,759,540	4,545,000	7	3	socialist state	Tarābulus (Tripoli)	Arabic	dinar
LIECHTENSTEIN	62	160	29,000	469	181	constitutional monarchy	Vaduz	German	Swiss franc
LITHUANIA	25,174	65,200	3,731,000	148	57	republic	Vilnius	Lithuanian	rouble, Litas prop.
LUXEMBOURG	998	2,585	381,000	382	147	constitutional monarchy	Luxembourg	Letzeburgish, French, German	franc
MADAGASCAR	229,413	594,180	11,197,000	49	19	republic	Antananarivo	Malagasy, French	Malagasy franc
MALAŴI	36,324	94,080	8,289,000	228	88	republic	Lilongwe	English, Chichewa	Kwacha
MALAYSIA	128,558	332,965	17,861,000	139	54	constitutional monarchy	Kuala Lumpur	Bahasa Maláy	ringgit
MALDIVES	115	298	215,000	1869	721	republic	Malé	Divehi	rufiyaa
MALI	478,819	1,240,140	8,156,000	17	7	republic	Bamako	French, Bambara	CFA franc
MALTA	122	316	354,000	2901	1120	republic	Valletta	Maltese, English	pound
MARSHALL ISLANDS	70	181	40,000	572	221	republic	Dalap-Uliga-Darrit	Marshallese, English	US dollar
MAURITANIA	397,954	1,030,700	2,025,000	5	2	republic	Nouakchott	Arabic, French	ouguiya
MAURITIUS	720	1,865	1,075,000	1493	576	constitutional monarchy	Port Louis	English, Creole	rupee
MEXICO	761,600	1,972,545	86,154,000	113	44	federal republic	Ciudad de México (Mexico City)	Spanish	peso
MOLDAVIA (MOLDOVA)	13,012	33,700	4,368,000	336	130	republic	Kishinev	Romanian, Russian	rouble
MONACO	1	2	29,000	29,000	14500	constitutional monarchy	Monaco	French	French franc
MONGOLIA	604,247	1,565,000	2,190,000	4	1	republic	Ulaanbaatar (Ulan Bator)	Khalka Mongol	tugrik
MOROCCO	172,413	446,550	25,061,000	145	56	monarchy	Rabat	Arabic	dirham
MOZAMBIQUE	302,994	784,755	15,656,000	52	20	republic	Maputo	Portuguese	metical
NAMIBIA	318,261	824,295	1,781,000	6	2	republic	Windhoek	Afrikaans, English	Namibian dollar
NAURU	8	21	10,000	1233	476	republic	Yaren	Nauruan, English	Australian dollar
NEPAL	54,600	141,415	18,916,000	346	134	monarchy	Kathmandu	Nepali	rupee
NETHERLANDS	15,892	41,160	14,935,000	940	363	constitutional monarchy	Amsterdam	Dutch	guilder
NEW ZEALAND	102,375	265,150	3,346,000	33	13	constitutional monarchy	Wellington	English, Maori	dollar
NICARAGUA	57,143	148,000	3,871,000	68	26	republic	Managua	Spanish	córdoba
NIGER	458,073	1,186,410	7,732,000	17	7	republic	Niamey	French	CFA Franc
NIGERIA	356,699	923,850	88,500,000	248	96	federal republic	Abuja	English	naira
NORTH KOREA	47,224	122,310	21,773,000	461	178	people's republic	Pyŏngyang	Korean	won
NORWAY	125,056	323,895	4,242,000	34	13	constitutional monarchy	Oslo	Norwegian	krone
OMAN	105,000	271,950	1,502,000	14	6	sultanate	Masqaṭ (Muscat)	Arabic	rial
PAKISTAN	310,402	803,940	112,049,000	361	139	federal Islamic republic	Islāmābād	Urdu, Punjabi, English	rupee
PANAMA	30,315	78,515	2,418,000	80	31	republic	Panamá City	Spanish	balboa

NATIONS OF THE WORLD

COUNTRY	AREA		POPULATION			FORM OF GOVERNMENT	CAPITAL CITY	MAIN LANGUAGES	CURRENCY
	miles²	km²	total	density per mile²	km²				
PAPUA NEW GUINEA	178,703	462,840	3,699,000	21	8	constitutional monarchy	Port Moresby	English,Pidgin,Motu	kina
PARAGUAY	157,046	406,750	4,277,000	27	11	republic	Asunción	Spanish,Guarani	guarani
PERU	496,222	1,285,215	21,550,000	43	17	republic	Lima	Spanish,Quechua	sol
PHILIPPINES	115,830	300,000	61,480,000	531	205	republic	Manila	Pilipino,English	peso
POLAND	120,728	312,685	38,180,000	316	122	republic	Warszawa (Warsaw)	Polish	zloty
PORTUGAL	34,340	88,940	10,525,000	306	118	republic	Lisboa (Lisbon)	Portuguese	escudo
QATAR	4415	11,435	486,000	110	43	emirate	Ad Dawḥah (Doha)	Arabic	riyal
ROMANIA	91,699	237,500	23,200,000	253	98	republic	Bucureşti (Bucharest)	Romanian	leu
RUSSIAN FEDERATION	6,593,822	17,078,000	148,263,000	22	9	republic	Moskva (Moscow)	Russian	rouble
RWANDA	10,166	26,330	7,181,000	706	273	republic	Kigali	Kinyarwanda,French	franc
ST KITTS-NEVIS	101	261	44,000	437	169	constitutional monarchy	Basseterre	English	East Caribbean dollar
ST LUCIA	238	616	151,000	635	245	constitutional monarchy	Castries	English,French	East Caribbean dollar
ST VINCENT & THE GRENADINES	150	389	116,000	772	298	constitutional monarchy	Kingstown	English	East Caribbean dollar
SAN MARINO	24	61	24,000	1019	393	republic	San Marino	Italian	Italian lira
SÃO TOMÉ & PRÍNCIPE	372	964	121,000	325	126	republic	São Tomé	Portuguese,Creole	dobra
SAUDI ARABIA	926,988	2,400,900	14,870,000	16	6	monarchy	Ar Riyāḍ (Riyadh)	Arabic	riyal
SENEGAL	75,954	196,720	7,327,000	96	37	republic	Dakar	French	CFA franc
SEYCHELLES	156	404	67,000	430	166	republic	Victoria	English,French,Creole	rupee
SIERRA LEONE	27,925	72,325	4,151,000	149	57	republic	Freetown	English	leone
SINGAPORE	238	616	3,003,000	12,626	4875	republic	Singapore	Bahasa Malay,English,Chinese,Tamil	dollar
SLOVAKIA	18,933	49,035	5,300,000	278	108	republic	Bratislava	Slovak	koruna
SLOVENIA	7819	20,250	1,900,000	243	94	republic	Ljubljana	Slovene	dinar
SOLOMON ISLANDS	11,502	29,790	321,000	28	11	constitutional monarchy	Honiara	English	dollar
SOMALI REPUBLIC	243,243	630,000	7,497,000	31	12	republic	Muqdisho (Mogadishu)	Arabic,Somali,Italian,English	shilling
SOUTH AFRICA,REPUBLIC OF	457,461	1,184,825	35,282,000	77	30	republic	Cape Town (Kaapstad) / Pretoria	Afrikaans,English	rand
SOUTH KOREA	38,010	98,445	42,793,000	1126	435	republic	Sŏul (Seoul)	Korean	won
SPAIN	194,934	504,880	38,959,000	200	77	constitutional monarchy	Madrid	Spanish	peseta
SRI LANKA	25,332	65,610	16,993,000	671	259	republic	Colombo	Sinhala,Tamil	Rupee
SUDAN	967,496	2,505,815	25,204,000	26	10	military regime	Al Kharṭūm (Khartoum)	Arabic	pound
SURINAM	53,251	163,820	422,000	7	3	republic	Paramaribo	Dutch,English	guilder
SWAZILAND	6705	17,365	768,000	115	44	monarchy	Mbabane	English,Siswati	lilangeni
SWEDEN	173,664	449,790	8,559,000	49	19	constitutional monarchy	Stockholm	Swedish	krona
SWITZERLAND	15,940	41,285	6,712,000	421	163	federal republic	Bern (Berne)	German,French,Italian,Romansh	franc
SYRIA	71,691	185,680	12,116,000	169	65	republic	Dimashq (Damascus)	Arabic	pound
TAIWAN	13,896	35,990	20,300,000	1461	564	republic	Taipei	Mandarin	dollar
TAJIKISTAN	55,251	143,100	5,303,000	96	37	republic	Dushanbe	Tajik,Russian	rouble
TANZANIA	362,842	939,760	25,635,000	71	27	republic	Dodoma	Kiswahili,English	shilling
THAILAND	198,456	514,000	57,196,000	288	111	monarchy	Bangkok (Krung Thep)	Thai	baht
TOGO	21,925	56,785	3,531,000	161	62	republic	Lomé	French	CFA franc
TONGA	270	699	95,000	352	136	constitutional monarchy	Nuku'alofa	English,Tongan	pa'anga
TRINIDAD AND TOBAGO	1981	5,130	1,227,000	619	239	republic	Port of Spain	English	dollar
TUNISIA	63,378	164,150	8,180,000	129	50	republic	Tunis	Arabic	dinar
TURKEY	300,946	779,450	56,098,000	186	72	republic	Ankara	Turkish	lira
TURKMENISTAN	188,456	488,100	3,670,000	19	8	republic	Ashkhabad	Turkmenian	rouble
TUVALU	10	25	10,000	1036	400	constitutional monarchy	Funafuti	English,Tuvaluan	Australian dollar
UGANDA	91,344	236,580	18,795,000	206	79	republic	Kampala	Kiswahili,English	shilling
UKRAINE	233,089	603,700	51,857,000	222	86	republic	Kiev	Ukrainian,Russian	rouble
UNITED ARAB EMIRATES	29,015	75,150	1,589,000	55	21	federation of emirates	Abū Ẓaby (Abu Dhabi)	Arabic	dirham
UNITED KINGDOM	94,500	244,755	57,411,000	608	235	constitutional monarchy	London	English	pound
UNITED STATES OF AMERICA	3,615,108	9,363,130	249,975,000	69	27	federal republic	Washington	English	dollar
URUGUAY	72,172	186,925	3,096,000	43	17	republic	Montevideo	Spanish	peso
UZBEKISTAN	172,741	447,400	20,531,000	119	46	republic	Tashkent	Uzbek,Russian	rouble
VANUATU	5701	14,765	147,000	26	10	republic	Vila	English,French,Bislama	vatu
VATICAN CITY	0.5	1	1000	2000	1000	ecclesiastical state	Vatican City	Italian	lira
VENEZUELA	352,141	912,045	19,735,000	56	22	federal republic	Caracas	Spanish	bolívar
VIETNAM	127,245	329,565	66,200,000	520	201	people's socialist republic	Hanoi	Vietnamese	dong
WESTERN SAMOA	1097	2,840	164,000	150	58	constitutional monarchy	Apia	Samoan,English	tala
YEMEN	203,850	527,969	11,282,000	55	21	republic	San'a	Arabic	rial,dinar
YUGOSLAVIA	49,376	127,885	10,000,000	203	78	federal republic	Beograd (Belgrade)	Serbo-Croat,Macedonian,Albanian	dinar
ZAÏRE	905,564	2,345,410	35,562,000	39	15	republic	Kinshasa	French,Lingala	zaïre
ZAMBIA	290,585	752,615	7,818,000	27	10	republic	Lusaka	English	kwacha
ZIMBABWE	150,699	390,310	9,369,000	62	24	republic	Harare	English	dollar

GEOGRAPHICAL DATA
Part 2

GLOSSARY
OF
GEOGRAPHICAL
TERMS

GLOSSARY

Introduction to Glossary

The Glossary of Geographical Terms lists in alphabetical order a selection of foreign language names and geographical terms, inclusive of any abbreviations, which are found in the names on the maps and in the index. The terms occur either as separate words (e.g. côte which means coast) or as parts of compound words (e.g. - oog in Langeoog which means island). A term preceded by a hyphen usually appears as an ending of a name on the map (e.g. -vesi in Puulavesi; -holm in Bornholm). Each term is followed by its language which is identified by abbreviations in brackets. A complete list of the language abbreviations used in the glossary is found below.

Language Abbreviations

Afr.	Afrikaans	Fin.	Finnish	Man.	Manchurian
Alb.	Albanian	Fr.	French	Mon.	Mongolian
Ar.	Arabic	Gae.	Gaelic	Nor.	Norwegian
Ba.	Baluchi	Ger.	German	Per.	Persian
Ber.	Berber	Gr.	Greek	Pol.	Polish
Blg.	Bulgarian	Heb.	Hebrew	Port.	Portugese
Bur.	Burmese	Hin.	Hindi	Rom.	Romanian
Cat.	Catalan	I.-C.	Indo-Chinese	Rus.	Russian
Cbd.	Cambodian	Ice.	Icelandic	S.-C.	Serbo-Croat
Ch.	Chinese	It.	Italian	Sp.	Spanish
Cz.	Czech	Jap.	Japanese	Swe.	Swedish
Dan.	Danish	Kor.	Korean	Th.	Thai (Siamese)
Dut.	Dutch	Lao.	Laotian	Tur.	Turkish
Est.	Estonian	Lat.	Latvian	Ur.	Urdu
Eth.	Ethiopian	Ma.	Malagasy	Viet.	Vietnamese
Fae.	Faeroese	Mal.	Malay		

Glossary of Geographical Terms

A

āb *(Per.)*	water
ada *(Tur.)*	island
adrar *(Ber., Ar.)*	mountain region
ákra, akrotírion *(Gr.)*	cape
alb *(Rom.)*	white
alin *(Man., Mon.)*	mountain range
alpes *(Fr.)*	alps
alpi *(It.)*	alps
alt/a/o *(It., Sp., Port.)*	high
-an *(Swe.)*	river
ao *(Ch., Th.)*	bay, gulf
arquipélago *(Port.)*	archipelago
-ås, -åsen *(Swe.)*	hills

B

bāb *(Ar.)*	gate
backe *(Swe.)*	hill
bādiya/t *(Ar.)*	desert
baelt *(Dan.)*	strait
b., bahía *(Sp.)*	bay
baḥr *(Ar.)*	great river/lake
baía *(Port.)*	bay
b., baie *(Fr.)*	bay
ban *(Hin., Ur.)*	forest
ban *(I.-C.)*	village
bañados *(Sp.)*	marshes
bandao *(Ch.)*	peninsula
bassin *(Fr.)*	basin
baṭḥa *(Ar.)*	plain
beloyy *(Rus.)*	white
ben, beinn *(Gae.)*	mountain
bereg *(Rus.)*	shore

berg/en *(Ger., Swe.)*	mountain/s
biq'at *(Heb.)*	valley
birkat *(Ar.)*	lake
bog., bogazi *(Tur.)*	strait
bois *(Fr.)*	woods
bol., bol'shaya *(Rus.)*	big
bory *(Pol.)*	forest
bredning *(Dan.)*	bay
brú *(Ice.)*	bridge
bucht *(Ger.)*	bay
bugt *(Dan.)*	bay
buḥayrat *(Ar.)*	lake
bukt/en *(Nor., Swe.)*	bay
burnu *(Tur.)*	cape
busen *(Ger.)*	bay
büyük *(Tur.)*	big

C

c., cabo *(Sp., Port.)*	cape
campo *(Sp.)*	field
c., cap *(Fr.)*	cape
capo *(It.)*	cape
causse *(Fr.)*	upland
cerro *(Sp.)*	mountain
chaco *(Sp.)*	jungle region
chaîne *(Fr.)*	chain
chapada *(Port.)*	hills
chott *(Ar.)*	salt lake
cime *(Fr.)*	summit
co *(Ch.)*	lake
co *(Viet.)*	mountain
col *(Fr.)*	pass

colline/s *(Fr.)*	hill/s
con *(Viet.)*	islands
cordillera *(Sp.)*	mountain range
costa *(Sp.)*	coast
côte *(Fr.)*	coast

D

d., daği, daǧlari *(Tur.)*	mountain, mountain range
dake *(Jap.)*	peak
dal/en *(Nor., Swe.)*	valley
danau *(Mal.)*	lake
daqq *(Per.)*	salt flat
darya *(Rus.)*	river
daryācheh *(Per.)*	lake
dasht *(Per.)*	desert
denizi *(Tur.)*	sea
desierto *(Sp.)*	desert
détroit *(Fr.)*	strait
dhiórix *(Gr.)*	canal
dian *(Ch.)*	lake
-dijk *(Dut.)*	dyke
ding *(Ch.)*	mountain
do *(Kor.)*	island

E

eiland/en *(Afr., Dut.)*	island/s
embalse *(Sp.)*	reservoir
'emeq *(Heb.)*	valley
erg *(Ar.)*	sand desert
estrecho *(Sp.)*	strait
estuario *(Sp.)*	estuary

étang *(Fr.)*	pond	i., is., isla/s *(Sp.)*	island/s	lule *(Swe.)*	eastern

F

feng *(Ch.)*	peak
firth *(Gae.)*	strait
fjället *(Swe.)*	mountain
fjell *(Nor.)*	mountain
fj., fjorden *(Dan., Nor., Swe.)*	fjord
fjördhur *(Fae., Ice.)*	fjord
flói *(Ice.)*	bay
fonn *(Nor.)*	glacier

G

gau *(Ger.)*	district
gave *(Fr.)*	torrent
gebirge *(Ger.)*	mountains
ghubbat *(Ar.)*	bay
gji *(Alb.)*	bay
gobi *(Mon.)*	desert
gol *(Mon.)*	river
g., golfe *(Fr.)*	gulf
g., golfo *(Sp., It.)*	gulf
gölö *(Tur.)*	lake
golyam *(Blg.)*	great
g., gora/y *(Rus.)*	mountain/s
gorje *(S.C.)*	mountain range
gross *(Ger.)*	great
guba *(Rus.)*	bay
guntō *(Jap.)*	island group
guoyuan *(Ch.)*	plateau
gura *(Rom.)*	mouth

H

hai *(Ch.)*	sea
haixia *(Ch.)*	strait
ḥajar *(Ar.)*	mountain range
halvö *(Dan.)*	peninsula
halvöya *(Nor.)*	peninsula
hāmūn *(Per.)*	plain
hantō *(Jap.)*	peninsula
har *(Heb.)*	mountain range
hauteurs *(Fr.)*	hills
hav *(Dan., Nor., Swe.)*	sea
hawr *(Ar.)*	lake
hāyk' *(Eth.)*	lake
he *(Ch.)*	river
heiya *(Jap.)*	plain
hoch *(Ger.)*	high
hohe *(Ger.)*	height
höj *(Dan.)*	high, height
-holm *(Dan.)*	island
holt *(Nor.)*	wood
hory *(Cz.)*	mountain
hu *(Ch.)*	lake
-huk *(Swe.)*	cape

I

Î., Îs., Île/s *(Fr.)*	island/s
ilha/s *(Port.)*	island/s
insel/n *(Ger.)*	island/s

i., is., isla/s *(Sp.)*	island/s
isola/e *(It.)*	island/s
istmo *(Sp.)*	isthmus
iztochni *(Blg.)*	eastern

J

j., jabal *(Ar., Per.)*	mountain
jarvi *(Fin.)*	lake
jaure *(Swe.)*	lake
jawb *(Ar.)*	basin, waterhole
jazā'ir *(Ar.)*	island
jezero *(S.-C., Cz.)*	lake
jezioro *(Pol.)*	lake
jiang *(Ch.)*	river
jima *(Jap.)*	island
jökulen *(Nor.)*	glacier
jökull *(Ice.)*	glacier
jūras līcis *(Lat.)*	gulf, bay

K

kaikyō *(Jap.)*	strait
kaise *(Swe.)*	mountain range
kamm *(Ger.)*	ridge
k., kanal *(Ger., Pol., Rus., S.-C., Swe.)*	canal
kap *(Ger.)*	cape
kapp *(Nor.)*	cape
kep *(Alb.)*	cape
kep., kepulauan *(Mal.)*	archipelago
khalīj *(Ar., Per.)*	gulf, bay
khazzān *(Ar.)*	dam
khr., khrebet *(Rus.)*	mountain range
kladenets *(Blg.)*	well
klong *(Th.)*	canal, creek
ko *(Jap.)*	lake, bay
ko *(Th.)*	island
-kogen *(Jap.)*	plateau
koh *(Per.)*	mountains
kílpos *(Gr.)*	gulf
kör., körfezi *(Tur.)*	gulf, bay
kou *(Ch.)*	estuary
kryazh *(Rus.)*	ridge
kūh/ha *(Per.)*	mountain/s
kul *(Rus.)*	lake
kuppe *(Ger.)*	hilltop
kyst *(Dan.)*	coast

L

lac *(Fr.)*	lake
lacul *(Rom.)*	lake
l., lago *(It. Sp.)*	lake
lagoa *(Port.)*	lagoon
laguna *(Sp.)*	lagoon, lake
laut *(Mal.)*	north, sea
liedao *(Ch.)*	islands
liehtao *(Ch.)*	islands
l., límni *(Gr.)*	lake
ling *(Ch.)*	mountain range
llanos *(Sp.)*	plains
l., loch *(Gae.)*	lake
lora *(Ba.)*	stream
l., lough *(Gae.)*	lake

M

maa *(Est., Fin.)*	land
mae *(Th.)*	river
mar/e *(It., Port., Sp.)*	sea
marsch *(Ger.)*	marsh
meer *(Afr., Dut.)*	lake, sea
mer *(Fr.)*	sea
mifraz *(Heb.)*	bay
misaki *(Jap.)*	cape
mont *(Fr.)*	mountain
montagne *(Fr.)*	mountain
mont/e/i *(It., Port., Sp.)*	mountain/s
moor *(Ger.)*	swamp, moor
more *(Rus.)*	sea
mörön *(Mon.)*	river
mui *(Viet.)*	point
mull *(Gae.)*	headland
munkhafaḍ *(Ar.)*	depression
munti/i *(Rom.)*	mountain/s
m., mys *(Rus.)*	cape

N

nada *(Jap.)*	sea, bay
nafūd *(Ar.)*	sandy desert
najd *(Ar.)*	pass
nam *(I.-C., Kor.)*	southern
nes *(Ice., Nor.)*	promontory
ness *(Gae.)*	promontory
nevada *(Sp.)*	snow-capped mountains
ngoc *(Viet)*	mountain
nísoi *(Gr.)*	islands
nizh., nizhne, nizhniy *(Rus.)*	lower
nizmennost' *(Rus.)*	depression
nord *(Dan., Fr., Ger., Nor., Swe.)*	northern
nur *(Ch.)*	lake, salt lake
nusa *(mal.)*	island
nuur *(Mon.)*	lake

O

occidental *(Sp.)*	western
odde *(Dan., Nor.)*	headland
ojo/s *(Sp.)*	spring/s
oki *(Jap.)*	bay
-oog *(Ger.)*	island
óros, óri *(Gr.)*	mountain, mountains
oriental/e *(Sp.)*	eastern
ort *(Ger.)*	settlement
o., os., ostrov/a *(Rus.)*	island/s
ost *(Ger.)*	east
oued *(Ar.)*	dry river bed
öy, öya *(Nor.)*	island
oz., ozero *(Rus.)*	lake

P

pampa/s *(Sp.)*	plain/s
parbat *(Ur.)*	mountain
passo *(It.)*	pass
peg., pegunungan *(Mal.)*	mountain range

GLOSSARY

pélagos (Gr.)	sea			träsk (Swe.)	marsh		
pelleg (Alb.)	bay			tunturi (Fin.)	treeless mountain		

pélagos *(Gr.)* — sea
pelleg *(Alb.)* — bay
peña *(Sp.)* — cliff
pendi *(Ch.)* — depression
péninsule *(Fr.)* — peninsula
pertuis *(Fr.)* — strait
peski *(Rus.)* — sand
phanom *(I.-C., Th.)* — mountain
phou *(Lao.)* — mountain
phu *(Th.)* — mountain
pic *(Fr.)* — peak
pico *(Sp.)* — peak
pik *(Rus.)* — peak
pingyuan *(Ch.)* — plain
plaine *(Fr.)* — plain
plana *(Sp.)* — plain
planalto *(Port.)* — plateau
pl., planina *(Blg., S.-C.)* — mountain range
plato *(Afr., Blg., Rus.)* — plateau
platosu *(Tur.)* — plateau
platte *(Ger.)* — plateau, plain
playa *(Sp.)* — beach
ploskogor'ye *(Rus.)* — plateau
pohorie *(Cz.)* — mountain range
pointe *(Fr.)* — promontory
pojezierze *(Pol.)* — lakeland
poleseye *(Rus.)* — area of marsh
polje *(S.-C.)* — plain, basin
pov., poluostrov *(Rus.)* — peninsula
porthmós *(Gr.)* — strait
porţi *(Rom.)* — entrance
portillo *(Sp.)* — gap
prliv *(Rus.)* — strait
puig *(Cat.)* — peak
pulau *(Mal.)* — island
pta., punta *(It., Sp.)* — point
puy *(Fr.)* — peak

Q

qā' *(Ar.)* — salt flat
qanāt *(Ar., Per.)* — canal
qolleh *(Per.)* — mountain
qu *(Ch.)* — canal, stream
qūr *(Ar.)* — buttes, ridge

R

ramlat *(Ar.)* — dunes
rann *(Hin.)* — swampy region
ras, ra's, rās *(Per., Ar.)* — cape
ravnina *(Rus.)* — plain
reprêsa *(Port.)* — reservoir
reshteh *(Per.)* — mountain range
retto *(Jap.)* — island group
ria, ría *(Port., Sp.)* — mouth of river
rijeka *(S.-C.)* — river
r., rio, río *(Port., Sp.)* — river
riviera *(It.)* — coast, river
r., rivière *(Fr.)* — river
rocca *(It.)* — rock
rücken *(Ger.)* — ridge
rūd *(Per.)* — river

S

sable/s *(Fr.)* — sand/s
sadd *(Ar.)* — dam
sāgar *(Hin., Ur.)* — lake
şaḥrā *(Ar.)* — desert
şa'īd *(Ar.)* — highland
saki *(Jap.)* — cape
salar *(Sp.)* — salt flat
salina/s *(Sp.)* — salt marsh
sammyaku *(Jap.)* — mountain range
san *(Jap., Kor.)* — mountain
-sanchi *(Jap.)* — mountains
see *(Ger.)* — lake
seenplatte *(Ger.)* — lakeland
selat *(Mal.)* — strait
selatan *(Mal.)* — southern
selkä *(Fin.)* — ridge
selseleh *(Per.)* — mountain range
selva *(Sp.)* — forest
serra *(Port.)* — mountain range
serranía *(Sp.)* — ridge
sev., severo, severnyy *(Rus.)* — north
sha'īb *(Ar.)* — ravine, wadi
shamo *(Ch.)* — desert
shan *(Ch.)* — mountain
shankou *(Ch.)* — mountain pass
shaṭṭ *(Ar.)* — large river
shibh jazīrat *(Ar.)* — peninsula
shima *(Jap.)* — island
shotō *(Jap.)* — island group
shui *(Ch.)* — river
sa., sierra *(Sp.)* — mountain range
-sjon *(Swe.)* — lake
skog *(Nor., Swe.)* — forest
skov *(Dan.)* — forest
slieve *(Gae.)* — mountain
sor *(Rus.)* — salt flat
sör *(Nor.)* — southern
spitze *(Ger.)* — peak
sredne *(Rus.)* — central
step *(Rus.)* — steppe
stora *(Fae.)* — large
strath *(Gae.)* — valley
stretto *(It.)* — strait
suidō *(Jap.)* — strait
īummān *(Ar.)* — escarpment
sund *(Dan., Ger., Ice., Nor., Swe.)* — sound
svart *(Nor., Swe.)* — black

T

take *(Jap.)* — peak
tall *(Ar.)* — mountain
tanjona *(Ma.)* — cape
tanjung *(Mal.)* — cape
tau *(Rus.)* — mountain
teluk *(Mal.)* — bay
testa *(It.)* — head
thale *(Th.)* — lagoon, sea
tierra *(Sp.)* — land, territory
tind *(Nor.)* — sharp peak
tō *(Jap.)* — island, eastern
tônlé *(Cbd.)* — lake

träsk *(Swe.)* — marsh
tunturi *(Fin.)* — treeless mountain

U

'urūq *(Ar.)* — dunes
utara *(Mal.)* — northern
uul *(mon., Rus.)* — mountain range

V

väïn *(Est.)* — strait
val *(Fr., It.)* — valley
vand *(Dan.)* — water
vatn *(Ice., Nor.)* — lake
vatnet *(Nor.)* — lake
vatten *(Swe.)* — lake
veld *(Afr.)* — field
veliki *(S.-C.)* — large
verkh., verkhne, verkhniy *(Rus.)* — upper
-vesi *(Fin.)* — lake
vest, vester *(Dan., Nor.)* — west
vidda *(Nor.)* — plateau
-viken *(Nor., Swe.)* — gulf, bay
vdkhr., vodokhranilishche *(Rus.)* — reservoir
volcán *(Sp.)* — volcano
vostochno, vostochnyy *(Rus.)* — eastern
vozvyshennost *(Rus.)* — uplands
vrata *(Blg.)* — gate
vrh *(S.-C.)* — peak

W

wāhāt *(Ar.)* — oasis
wald *(Ger.)* — forest
wan *(Ch., Jap.)* — bay

Y

yam *(Heb.)* — sea
yama *(Jap.)* — mountain
yanchi *(Ch.)* — salt lake
yarimadasi *(Tur.)* — peninsula
yazovir *(Blg.)* — dam
yoma *(Bur.)* — mountain range
yumco *(Ch.)* — lake
yunhe *(Ch.)* — canal
yuzhnyy *(Rus.)* — south

Z

zaki *(Jap.)* — cape, peninsula
zaliv *(Rus.)* — bay
zan *(Jap.)* — mountain range
zangbo *(Ch.)* — stream, river
zapadno, zapadnyy *(Rus.)* — western
zatoka *(Pol.)* — bay
zemlya *(Rus.)* — land
zhou *(Ch.)* — island
zuid *(Dut.)* — south

GEOGRAPHICAL DATA
Part 3

WORLD INDEX

WORLD INDEX

Introduction to World Index

The index includes an alphabetical list of all names appearing on the maps in the World Atlas section. Each entry indicates the country or region of the world in which the name is located. This is followed by a page reference and finally the name's location on the map, given by latitude and longitude co-ordinates. Most features are indexed to the largest scale map on which they appear, however when the name applies to countries or other extensive features it is generally indexed to the map on which it appears in its entirety. Areal features are generally indexed using co-ordinates which indicate the centre of the feature. The latitude and longitude indicated for a point feature gives the location of the point on the map. In the case of rivers the mouth or confluence is always taken as the point of reference.

Names in the index are generally in the local language and where a conventional English version exists, this is cross referenced to the entry in the local language. Names of features which extend across the boundaries of more than one country are usually named in English if no single official name exists. Names in languages not written in the Roman alphabet have been transliterated using the official system of the country if one exists, e.g. Pinyin system for China, otherwise the systems recognised by the United States Board on Geographical Names have been used.

Names abbreviated on the maps are given in full in the Index. Abbreviations are used for both geographical terms and administrative names in the Index. All abbreviations used in the Index are listed below.

Abbreviations of Geographical Terms

b., B.	bay, Bay
c., C.	cape, Cape
d.	internal division e.g county, region, state
des.	desert
est.	estuary
f.	physical feature e.g. valley, plain, geographic district or region
g., G.	gulf, Gulf
i., I., is., Is.	island, Island, islands, Islands
I., L.	lake, Lake
mtn., Mtn.	mountain, Mountain
mts., Mts.	mountains, Mountains
pen., Pen.	peninsula, Peninsula
Pt.	Point
r.	river
resr., Resr.	reservoir, Reservoir
Sd.	Sound
str., Str.	strait, Strait

Abbreviations of Country / Administrative Names

Afghan.	Afghanistan	Man.	Manitoba	Raj.	Rājasthān
A.H. Prov.	Alpes de Haut Provence	Mass.	Massachusetts	Rep. of Ire.	Republic of Ireland
Ala.	Alabama	Md.	Maryland	Rhein.-Pfalz	Rheinland-Pfalz
Alas.	Alaska	Mich.	Michigan	R.I.	Rhode Island
Alta.	Alberta	Minn.	Minnesota	R.S.A.	Republic of South Africa
Ariz.	Arizona	Miss.	Mississippi	Russian Fed.	Russian Federation
Ark.	Arkansas	Mo.	Missouri	S.A.	South Australia
Baja Calif.	Baja California	Mont.	Montana	Sask.	Saskatchewan
Baja Calif. Sur	Baja California Sur	M.-Pyr.	Midi-Pyrénées	S.C.	South Carolina
Bangla.	Bangladesh	N.B.	New Brunswick	Sch.-Hol.	Schleswig-Holstein
B.C.	British Columbia	N.C.	North Carolina	S. Dak.	South Dakota
Bos.-Her.	Bosnia-Herzegovina	N. Dak.	North Dakota	S. Korea	South Korea
B.-Würt	Baden-Württemberg	Nebr.	Nebraska	S. Mar.	Seine Maritime
Calif.	California	Neth.	Netherlands	Sogn og Fj.	Sogn og Fjordane
C.A.R.	Central African Republic	Nev.	Nevada	Somali Rep.	Somali Republic
Char. Mar.	Charente Maritime	Nfld.	Newfoundland	Switz.	Switzerland
Colo.	Colorado	N.H.	New Hampshire	Tas.	Tasmania
Conn.	Connecticut	N. Ireland	Northern Ireland	Tenn.	Tennessee
C.P.	Cape Province	N.J.	New Jersey	Tex.	Texas
D.C.	District of Columbia	N. Korea	North Korea	T.G.	Tarn-et-Garonne
Del.	Delaware	N. Mex	New Mexico	Trans.	Transvaal
Dom. Rep.	Dominican Republic	Nschn.	Niedersachsen	U.A.E.	United Arab Emirates
Equat. Guinea	Equatorial Guinea	N.S.W.	New South Wales	U.K.	United Kingdom
Eth.	Ethiopia	N. Trönd.	North Tröndelag	U.S.A.	United States of America
Fla.	Florida	N.T.	Northern Territory	Uttar P.	Uttar Pradesh
Ga.	Georgia	N.-Westfalen	Nordrhein-Westfalen	Va.	Virginia
Guang. Zhuang	Guangxi Zhuangzu	N.W.T.	Northwest Territories	Vic.	Victoria
H.-Gar.	Haute Garonne	N.Y.	New York State	Vt.	Vermont
Himachal P.	Himachal Pradesh	O.F.S.	Orange Free State	W.A.	Western Australia
H. Zaïre	Haut Zaïre	Okla.	Oklahoma	Wash.	Washington
Ill.	Illinois	Ont.	Ontario	W. Bengal	West Bengal
Ind.	Indiana	Oreg.	Oregon	Wisc.	Wisconsin
Kans.	Kansas	P.E.I.	Prince Edward Island	W. Sahara	Western Sahara
K. Occidental	Kasai Occidental	Penn.	Pennsylvania	W. Va.	West Virginia
K. Oriental	Kasai Oriental	Phil.	Philippines	Wyo.	Wyoming
Ky.	Kentucky	P.N.G.	Papua New Guinea	Xin. Uygur	Xinjiang Uygur Zizhiqu
La.	Louisiana	Poit.-Char.	Poitou-Charente	Yugo.	Yugoslavia
Liech.	Liechtenstein	Pyr. Or.	Pyrénées Orientales		
Lux.	Luxembourg	Qld.	Queensland		
Madhya P.	Madhya Pradesh	Que.	Québec		

Aa to **Akhelóös**

A

Aa *r.* France **19** 51.01N 2.06E
Aachen Germany **38** 50.47N 6.05E
Aalen Germany **39** 48.50N 10.05E
A 'âlî an Nîl *d.* Sudan **73** 9.35N 31.05E
Aalsmeer Neth. **16** 52.17N 4.46E
Aalst Belgium **16** 50.57N 4.03E
Äänekoski Finland **40** 62.36N 25.44E
Aarau Switz. **39** 47.23N 8.03E
Aarburg Switz. **39** 47.19N 7.54E
Aardenburg Neth. **16** 51.16N 3.26E
Aare *r.* Switz. **39** 47.37N 8.13E
Aargau *d.* Switz. **39** 47.25N 8.10E
Aarschot Belgium **16** 50.59N 4.50E
Aba China **61** 32.55N101.42E
Aba Nigeria **77** 5.06N 7.21E
Aba Zaïre **73** 3.52N 30.14E
Abâ as Su'ûd Saudi Arabia **71** 17.28N 44.06E
Abadab, Jabal *mtn.* Sudan **72** 18.53N 35.59E
Âbâdân Iran **65** 30.21N 48.15E
Abadan, Jazîreh-ye *i.* Iran **65** 30.10N 48.30E
Âbâdeh Iran **65** 31.10N 52.40E
Abadla Algeria **74** 31.01N 2.44W
Abaetetuba Brazil **123** 1.45S 48.54W
Abagnar Qi China **54** 43.58N116.02E
Abag Qi China **54** 43.53N114.33E
Abaí Paraguay **124** 26.01S 55.57W
Abajo Peak *mtn.* U.S.A. **108** 37.51N109.28W
Abakaliki Nigeria **77** 6.17N 8.04E
Abakan Russian Fed. **51** 53.43N 91.25E
Abalessa Algeria **75** 22.54N 4.50E
Abancay Peru **124** 13.35S 72.55W
Abariringa *i.* Kiribati **84** 2.50S171.40W
Âbâr Murrât *wells* Sudan **72** 21.03N 32.55E
'Abasân Egypt **67** 31.19N 34.21E
Abashiri wan *b.* Japan **57** 44.02N144.17E
Abasolo Mexico **111** 25.18N104.40W
Abau P.N.G. **90** 10.10S148.40E
Abay Kazakhstan **50** 49.40N 72.47E
Abây *r.* Ethiopia *see* Azraq, Al Bahr al *r.* Sudan **72**
Âbaya Hâyk' Ethiopia **73** 6.20N 37.55E
Abba C.A.R. **77** 5.20N 15.11E
Abbadia San Salvatore Italy **30** 42.53N 11.41E
Abbasanta Italy **32** 40.08N 8.50E
Abbekås Sweden **43** 55.24N 13.36E
Abbeville France **19** 50.06N 1.50E
Abbeville La. U.S.A. **111** 29.58N 92.08W
Abbeville S.C. U.S.A. **113** 34.10N 82.23W
Abbiategrasso Italy **30** 45.24N 8.54E
Abbotsbury U.K. **13** 50.40N 2.36W
Abbotsford Canada **105** 45.27N 72.55W
Abbottâbâd Pakistan **62** 34.09N 73.13E
'Abd al Kûrî *i.* Yemen **71** 12.12N 52.13E
Abdêra *site* Greece **34** 40.59N 24.58E
Abdulino Russian Fed. **44** 53.42N 53.40E
Abéché Chad **72** 13.49N 20.49E
Abéjar Spain **26** 41.48N 2.47W
Âbeltî Ethiopia **73** 8.10N 37.37E
Abengourou Ivory Coast **76** 6.42N 3.27W
Abenójar Spain **26** 38.53N 4.21W
Åbenrå Denmark **42** 55.02N 9.26E
Abensberg Germany **39** 48.49N 11.51E
Abeokuta Nigeria **77** 7.10N 3.26E
Aberayron U.K. **13** 52.15N 4.16W
Abercrombie *r.* Australia **93** 33.50S149.10E
Aberdare U.K. **13** 51.43N 3.27W
Aberdare Range *mts.* Kenya **79** 0.20S 36.40E
Aberdeen Australia **93** 32.10S150.54E
Aberdeen R.S.A. **80** 32.28S 24.03E
Aberdeen U.K. **14** 57.08N 2.07W
Aberdeen Md. U.S.A. **115** 39.30N 76.14W
Aberdeen Miss. U.S.A. **111** 33.49N 88.33W
Aberdeen Ohio U.S.A. **112** 38.39N 83.46W
Aberdeen S. Dak. U.S.A. **110** 45.28N 98.29W
Aberdeen Wash. U.S.A. **108** 46.59N123.50W
Aberdovey U.K. **13** 52.33N 4.03W
Aberfeldy U.K. **14** 56.37N 3.54W
Abergavenny U.K. **13** 51.49N 3.01W
Abersoch U.K. **12** 52.50N 4.31W
Aberystwyth U.K. **13** 52.25N 4.06W
Abetone Italy **30** 44.08N 10.40E
Abez Russian Fed. **44** 66.33N 61.51E
Abhâ Saudi Arabia **72** 18.13N 42.30E
Abhar Iran **65** 36.09N 49.13E
Âbhê bid Hâyk' *l.* Ethiopia **73** 11.06N 41.50E
Abia *d.* Nigeria **77** 5.45N 7.40E
Abidjan Ivory Coast **76** 5.19N 4.01W
Abilene Kans. U.S.A. **110** 38.55N 97.13W
Abilene Tex. U.S.A. **111** 32.27N 99.44W
Abingdon U.K. **13** 51.40N 1.17W
Abisko Sweden **40** 68.20N 18.51E
Abitau *r.* Canada **101** 59.53N109.03W
Abitibi *r.* Canada **102** 51.03N 80.55W
Abitibi, L. Canada **102** 48.42N 79.45W
Âbîy Âdî Ethiopia **73** 13.36N 39.00E
Abnûb Egypt **64** 27.16N 31.09E
Åbo *see* Turku Finland **41**
Abohar India **62** 30.08N 74.12E
Abomey Benin **77** 7.14N 2.00E
Abong Mbang Cameroon **77** 3.59N 13.12E
Abou Deïa Chad **77** 11.20N 19.20E
Aboyne U.K. **14** 57.05N 2.48W
Abrantes Portugal **27** 39.28N 8.12W
'Abrî Sudan **72** 20.48N 30.20E
Abring Jammu & Kashmir **62** 33.42N 76.35E
Abrud Romania **37** 46.17N 23.04E
Abruzzi *d.* Italy **31** 42.35N 13.38E
Abruzzo, Parco Nazionale d' *Nat. Park* Italy **31** 41.45N 13.45E
Absaroka Range *mts.* U.S.A. **108** 44.45N109.50W
Absecon U.S.A. **115** 39.26N 74.30W
Abtenau Austria **39** 47.33N 13.21E
Abû 'Arîsh Saudi Arabia **71** 16.58N 42.50E
Abû Bahr *f.* Saudi Arabia **71** 21.30N 48.15E
Abû Ballâș *hill* Egypt **72** 24.26N 27.39E
Abu Dhabi *see* Abû Zaby U.A.E. **65**
Abû Dharbah Egypt **66** 28.29N 33.20E
Abû Dulayq Sudan **72** 15.54N 33.49E
Abû Hamad Sudan **72** 19.32N 33.19E
Abû Harâz Sudan **72** 19.04N 32.07E
Abuja Nigeria **77** 9.12N 7.11E
Abû Jâbirah Sudan **73** 11.04N 26.51E
Abû Kabîr Egypt **66** 30.44N 31.40E
Abû Kamâl Syria **64** 34.27N 40.55E
Abû Madd, Ra's *c.* Saudi Arabia **64** 24.50N 37.07E
Abû Matâriq Sudan **73** 10.58N 26.17E
Abunâ Brazil **122** 9.41S 65.20W
Abû Qashsh Jordan **67** 31.57N 35.11E
Abû Qurqâș Egypt **66** 27.56N 30.50E
Abu Road *town* India **62** 24.29N 72.47E
Abû Shajarah, Ra's *c.* Sudan **72** 21.04N 37.14E
Abû Shanab Sudan **73** 10.47N 29.32E
Abû Sultân Egypt **66** 30.25N 32.19E
Abû Sunbul Egypt **64** 22.18N 31.40E
Abû Tabarî *well* Sudan **72** 17.35N 28.31E
Abû Tarafah Jordan **66** 30.00N 35.56E
Abû Tîj Egypt **64** 27.06N 31.17E
Abuya Mexico **109** 24.16N107.01W
Âbuyê Mêda *mtn.* Ethiopia **73** 10.28N 39.44E
Abû Zabad Sudan **73** 12.21N 29.15E
Abû Zaby U.A.E. **65** 24.27N 54.23E
Abû Zanîmah Egypt **66** 29.03N 33.06E
Abwong Sudan **73** 9.07N 32.12E
Åby Sweden **43** 58.40N 16.11E
Abyad Sudan **72** 13.46N 26.28E
Abyad, Al Bahr al *r.* Sudan **72** 15.38N 32.31E
Abyâr ash Shuwayrif *wells* Libya **75** 29.59N 14.16E
Åbybro Denmark **42** 57.09N 9.45E
Abyei Sudan **73** 9.36N 28.26E
Acacio Mexico **111** 24.50N102.44W
Acadia Valley *town* Canada **101** 51.08N110.13W
Acámbaro Mexico **116** 20.01N101.42W
Acapulco Mexico **116** 16.51N 99.56W
Acará Brazil **123** 1.57S 48.11W
Acarigua Venezuela **122** 9.35N 69.12W
Acatlán Mexico **116** 18.12N 98.02W
Accra Ghana **76** 5.33N 0.15W
Accrington U.K. **12** 53.46N 2.22W
Aceh *d.* Indonesia **58** 4.00N 97.30E
Acerra Italy **33** 40.57N 14.22E
Acevedo Argentina **125** 33.46S 60.27W
Achacachi Bolivia **124** 16.03S 68.43W
Achalpur India **63** 21.16N 77.31E
Achar Uruguay **125** 32.25S 56.10W
Acheng China **53** 45.32N126.59E
Achern Germany **39** 48.37N 8.04E
Achill I. Rep. of Ire. **15** 53.57N 10.00W
Âchîn Afghan. **62** 34.08N 70.42E
Achinsk Russian Fed. **50** 56.10N 90.10E
Achray Canada **105** 45.52N 77.45W
Acireale Italy **33** 37.37N 15.10E
Acklin's I. Bahamas **117** 22.30N 74.10W
Aconcagua *mtn.* Argentina **124** 32.39S 70.00W
Açores, Arquipélago dos *is.* Atlantic Oc. **127** 38.30N 28.00W
A Coruña *see* La Coruña Spain **26**
Acquapendente Italy **30** 42.44N 11.52E
Acqui Italy **30** 44.41N 8.28E
Acraman, L. Australia **92** 32.02S135.26E
Acre *d.* Brazil **122** 8.50S 71.30W
Acri Italy **33** 39.29N 16.23E
Acton Canada **104** 43.37N 80.02W
Acton Vale Canada **105** 45.39N 72.34W
Açu Brazil **123** 5.35S 36.57W
Acuña Argentina **125** 29.54S 57.57W
Ada U.S.A. **111** 34.46N 96.41W
Ada Yugo. **31** 45.48N 20.08E
Âdaba Ethiopia **73** 7.07N 39.20E
Adair, Bahía de *b.* Mexico **109** 31.30N113.50W
Adair, C. Canada **99** 71.24N 71.13W
Adaja *r.* Spain **26** 41.32N 4.52W
Adam Oman **71** 22.23N 57.32E
Adamantina Brazil **126** 21.42S 51.04W
Adamaoua, Massif de l' *mts.* Cameroon / Nigeria **77** 7.05N 12.00E
Adamawa *d.* Nigeria **77** 9.55N 12.30E
Adamello *mtn.* Italy **30** 46.09N 10.30E
Adaminaby Australia **93** 36.04S148.42E
Adamintina Brazil **124** 21.42S 51.04W
Adams Mass. U.S.A. **115** 42.37N 73.07W
Adams N.Y. U.S.A. **112** 43.49N 76.01W
Adams, Mt. U.S.A. **108** 46.12N121.28W
'Adan Yemen **71** 12.50N 45.00E
Adana Turkey **64** 37.00N 35.19E
Adanero Spain **26** 40.56N 4.36W
Adapazari Turkey **64** 40.45N 30.23E
Adarama Sudan **72** 17.05N 34.54E
Adare, C. Antarctica **128** 71.30S171.00E
Adavale Australia **90** 25.55S144.36E
Adda *r.* Italy **30** 45.08N 9.53E
Ad Dab'ah Egypt **64** 31.02N 28.26E
Ad Dabbah Sudan **72** 18.03N 30.57E
Ad Dafinah Saudi Arabia **64** 23.18N 41.58E
Ad Dahnâ' *des.* Saudi Arabia **65** 26.00N 47.00E
Ad Dâmir Sudan **72** 17.35N 33.58E
Ad Dammâm Saudi Arabia **65** 26.23N 50.08E
Ad Darb Saudi Arabia **72** 17.44N 42.15E
Ad Dawâdimî Saudi Arabia **65** 24.29N 44.23E
Ad Dawhah Qatar **65** 25.15N 51.34E
Ad Diffah *f.* Africa **64** 30.45N 26.00E
Ad Dikâkah *f.* Saudi Arabia **71** 19.25N 51.30E
Ad Dilam Saudi Arabia **65** 23.59N 47.10E
Ad Dîmâs Syria **66** 33.35N 36.05E
Addis Ababa *see* Âdîs Âbeba Ethiopia **73**
Addison U.S.A. **114** 42.06N 77.14W
Ad Dîwânîyah Iraq **65** 31.59N 44.57E
Ad Du'ayn Sudan **73** 11.26N 26.09E
Ad Duwaym Sudan **72** 14.00N 32.19E
Adel U.S.A. **113** 31.07N 83.27W
Adelaide Australia **92** 34.56S138.36E
Adelaide Pen. Canada **99** 68.09N 97.45W
Adelaide River *town* Australia **88** 13.14S131.06E
Adelong Australia **93** 35.21S148.04E
Aden *see* 'Adan Yemen **71**
Aden, G. of Indian Oc. **71** 13.00N 50.00E
Adena U.S.A. **114** 40.13N 80.53W
Adendorp R.S.A. **80** 32.18S 24.31E
Adi *i.* Indonesia **59** 4.10S133.10E
Âdî Da'iro Ethiopia **72** 14.27N 38.16E
Adieu, C. Australia **89** 31.59S132.09E
Âdîgala Ethiopia **73** 10.25N 42.17E
Adige *r.* Italy **30** 45.10N 12.20E
Âdîgrat Ethiopia **72** 14.18N 39.31E
Âdî K'eyih Ethiopia **72** 14.49N 39.23E
Âdilâbâd India **63** 19.40N 78.32E
Adilang Uganda **79** 2.44N 33.28E
Adin U.S.A. **108** 41.12N120.57W
Adirondack Mts. U.S.A. **115** 44.00N 74.00W
Adirondack Park U.S.A. **115** 43.28N 74.23W
Âdîs Âbeba Ethiopia **73** 9.03N 38.42E
Âdî Ugrî Ethiopia **72** 14.55N 38.53E
Adiyaman Turkey **64** 37.46N 38.15E
Adjud Romania **37** 46.04N 27.11E
Admer *well* Algeria **75** 20.23N 5.27E
Admiralty G. Australia **88** 14.20S125.50E
Admiralty I. U.S.A. **100** 57.50N134.30W
Admiralty Is. P.N.G. **59** 2.30S147.20E
Admiralty Range *mts.* Antarctica **128** 72.00S164.00E
Adolphustown Canada **105** 44.04N 77.00W
Adour *r.* France **20** 43.32N 1.32W
Adra Spain **27** 36.44N 3.01W
Adrano Italy **33** 37.40N 14.50E
Adrar *d.* Mauritania **74** 21.00N 10.00W
Adrar des Iforas *mts.* Mali / Algeria **75** 20.00N 2.30E
Adraskan Afghan. **62** 33.39N 62.16E
Adria Italy **30** 45.03N 12.03E
Adrian Mich. U.S.A. **104** 41.54N 84.02W
Adrian Mo. U.S.A. **110** 38.24N 94.21W
Adrian Tex. U.S.A. **111** 35.16N102.40W
Adrian W.Va. U.S.A. **114** 38.54N 80.17W
Adriatic Sea Med. Sea **31** 43.30N 14.30E
Âdwa Ethiopia **72** 14.12N 38.56E
Adzopé Ivory Coast **76** 6.07N 3.49W
Adzva *r.* Russian Fed. **44** 66.30N 59.30E
Aegean Sea Med. Sea **34** 37.00N 25.00E
Aerö *i.* Denmark **42** 54.53N 10.20E
Aëtos Greece **35** 37.15N 21.50E
Afándou Greece **35** 36.18N 28.12E
Âfdem Ethiopia **73** 9.26N 41.02E
Afghanistan Asia **62** 32.45N 65.00E
'Afîf Saudi Arabia **64** 23.53N 42.59E
Afikpo Nigeria **77** 5.53N 7.55E
Afjord Norway **40** 63.57N 10.12E
Aflou Algeria **75** 34.07N 2.06E
Afmadow Somali Rep. **79** 0.27N 42.05E
Afobaka Surinam **123** 5.00N 55.05W
Afognak I. U.S.A. **98** 58.15N152.30W
Afonso Cláudio Brazil **126** 20.05S 41.06W
Africa 70
Afsluitdijk *f.* Neth. **16** 53.04N 5.11E
'Afula Israel **67** 32.36N 35.17E
Afyon Turkey **64** 38.46N 30.32E
Agadez Niger **77** 17.00N 7.56E
Agadez *d.* Niger **77** 19.25N 11.00E
Agadir Morocco **74** 30.26N 9.36W
Agalak Sudan **73** 11.01N 32.42E
Agana Guam **84** 13.28N144.45E
Agano *r.* Japan **57** 37.58N139.02E
Agapa Russian Fed. **51** 71.29N 86.16E
Agar India **62** 23.42N 76.01E
Âgaro Ethiopia **73** 7.50N 36.40E
Agartala India **63** 23.49N 91.16E
Agaru Sudan **73** 10.59N 34.44E
Agboville Ivory Coast **76** 5.55N 4.15W
Agde France **20** 43.19N 3.28E
Agde, Cap d' *c.* France **20** 43.16N 3.30E
Agen France **20** 44.12N 0.37E
Ageo Japan **57** 35.58N139.36E
Agger *r.* Germany **16** 50.45N 7.06E
Aghada Rep. of Ire. **15** 51.50N 8.13W
Agia India **63** 26.05N 90.32E
Aginskoye Russian Fed. **51** 51.10N114.32E
Agira Italy **33** 37.39N 14.32E
Agly *r.* France **20** 42.47N 3.02E
Agnew Australia **89** 28.01S120.30E
Agnone Italy **31** 41.48N 14.22E
Ago Japan **57** 34.17N136.48E
Agordo Italy **30** 46.17N 12.02E
Agouma Gabon **78** 1.33S 10.08E
Agout *r.* France **20** 43.47N 1.41E
Agra India **63** 27.11N 78.01E
Agra *r.* Spain **24** 42.12N 1.43W
Agraciada Uruguay **125** 33.48S 58.15W
Agreda Spain **25** 41.51N 1.56W
Agri *r.* Italy **33** 40.13N 16.44E
Agri Turkey **64** 39.44N 43.04E
Agri Bavnehöj *hill* Denmark **42** 56.14N 10.33E
Agri Daği *mtn.* Turkey **65** 39.45N 44.15E
Agrigento Italy **32** 37.18N 13.35E
Agrínion Greece **35** 38.37N 21.24E
Agropoli Italy **33** 40.21N 15.00E
Agryz Russian Fed. **44** 56.30N 53.00E
Agsumal, Sebjet *f.* W. Sahara **74** 24.21N 12.52W
Agua Caliente, Cerro *mtn.* Mexico **109** 26.27N106.12W
Aguanish Canada **103** 50.16N 62.10W
Aguanus *r.* Canada **103** 50.12N 62.10W
Agua Prieta Mexico **109** 31.18N109.34W
Aguas *r.* Spain **27** 37.09N 1.49W
Aguas Blancas Chile **124** 24.13S 69.50W
Aguascalientes Mexico **116** 21.51N102.18W
Aguascalientes *d.* Mexico **116** 22.00N102.00W
Aguasvivas *r.* Spain **25** 41.20N 0.25W
Agudos Brazil **126** 22.27S 49.03W
Águeda Portugal **26** 40.34N 8.27W
Águeda *r.* Spain **26** 41.02N 6.56W
Aguelhok Mali **74** 19.28N 0.52E
Aguema Angola **78** 12.03S 21.52E
Aguêraktem *well* Mali **74** 23.07N 6.12W
Aguilar Spain **27** 37.31N 4.39W
Aguilar de Campóo Spain **26** 42.47N 4.15W
Aguilas Spain **25** 37.24N 1.35W
Aguit China **54** 41.42N113.20E
Âgula'i Ethiopia **72** 13.42N 39.35E
Agulhas, C. R.S.A. **80** 34.50S 20.00E
Agulhas Basin *f.* Indian Oc. **49** 45.00S 28.00E
Agulhas Negras *mtn.* Brazil **126** 22.20S 44.43W
Agung, Gunung *mtn.* Indonesia **59** 8.20S115.28E
'Agur Israel **67** 31.41N 34.54E
Ahaggar *f.* Algeria **75** 23.36N 5.50E
Ahar Iran **65** 38.25N 47.07E
Ahaura New Zealand **86** 42.21S171.33E
Ahaus Germany **16** 52.04N 7.01E
Ahirli Turkey **35** 38.37N 26.31E
Ahklun Mts. U.S.A. **98** 59.15N161.00W
Ahlen Germany **38** 51.46N 7.53E
Ahlenmoor *f.* Germany **38** 53.40N 8.45E
Ahmadâbâd India **62** 23.02N 72.37E
Ahmadî Iran **65** 27.56N 56.42E
Ahmadnagar India **62** 19.05N 74.44E
Ahmadpur East Pakistan **62** 29.09N 71.16E
Ahmadpur Siâl Pakistan **62** 30.41N 71.46E
Ahmad Wâl Pakistan **62** 29.25N 65.56E
Ahmar Mts. Ethiopia **73** 9.15N 41.00E
Ahmic Harbour Canada **104** 45.39N 79.42W
Ahmic L. Canada **104** 45.37N 79.42W
Ahoada Nigeria **77** 5.06N 6.39E
Ahr *r.* Germany **16** 50.34N 7.16E
Ahram Iran **65** 28.52N 51.16E
Ahraura India **63** 25.01N 83.01E
Ahsâ', Wâhat al *oasis* Saudi Arabia **65** 25.37N 49.40E
Ähtäri Finland **40** 62.34N 24.06E
Ahun France **20** 46.05N 2.05E
Åhus Sweden **43** 55.55N 14.17E
Ahvâz Iran **65** 31.17N 48.44E
Ahvenanmaa *d.* Finland **43** 60.15N 20.00E
Ahvenanmaa *is.* Finland **41** 60.15N 20.00E
Aichach Germany **39** 48.28N 11.08E
Aichi *d.* Japan **57** 35.02N137.15E
Aigle Switz. **39** 46.19N 6.58E
Aigre France **20** 45.54N 0.01E
Aigueperse France **20** 46.01N 3.12E
Aigues *r.* France **21** 44.07N 4.43E
Aigues-Mortes France **21** 43.34N 4.11E
Aiguilles France **21** 44.47N 6.52E
Aigurande France **19** 46.26N 1.50E
Aiken U.S.A. **113** 33.34N 81.44W
Aileron Australia **90** 22.38S133.20E
Ailette *r.* France **16** 49.35N 3.09E
Ailsa Craig *i.* U.K. **14** 55.15N 5.07W
Aim Russian Fed. **51** 58.50N134.15E
Aimorés Brazil **126** 19.30S 41.04W
Ain *d.* France **21** 46.05N 5.20E
Ain *r.* France **21** 45.48N 5.10E
Aïna *r.* Gabon **78** 0.38N 12.47E
Ainaži Estonia **41** 57.52N 24.21E
Aïn Beïda Algeria **75** 35.50N 7.27E
Aïn ben Tili Mauritania **74** 26.00N 9.32W
Aïn Draham Tunisia **32** 36.47N 8.42E
Aïn Galakka Chad **75** 18.04N 18.24E
Aïn Sefra Algeria **74** 32.45N 0.35W
Aïr *mts.* Niger **77** 18.30N 8.30E
Aird I. Canada **104** 46.08N 82.25W
Airdrie U.K. **14** 55.52N 3.59W
Aire France **20** 43.42N 0.16W
Aire *r.* France **19** 49.19N 4.49E
Aire *r.* U.K. **12** 53.42N 0.54W
Airolo Switz. **39** 46.32N 8.37E
Airvault France **18** 46.50N 0.08W
Aisch *r.* Germany **39** 49.46N 11.01E
Aisne *d.* France **19** 49.30N 3.30E
Aisne *r.* France **19** 49.26N 2.50E
Aitana *mtn.* Spain **25** 38.40N 0.16W
Aitape P.N.G. **59** 3.10S142.17E
Aitkin U.S.A. **110** 46.32N 93.43W
Aitolikón Greece **35** 38.27N 21.22E
Aït Ourir Morocco **74** 31.38N 7.42W
Aitutaki Atoll Cook Is. **85** 18.52S159.46W
Aiud Romania **37** 46.19N 23.44E
Aix-en-Provence France **21** 43.32N 5.26E
Aix-les-Bains France **21** 45.42N 5.55E
Aíyina Greece **35** 37.44N 23.27E
Aíyina *i.* Greece **35** 37.46N 23.26E
Aiyínion Greece **34** 40.30N 22.33E
Aíyion Greece **35** 38.15N 22.05E
Aizpute Latvia **41** 56.43N 21.38E
Aizuwakamatsu Japan **57** 37.30N139.58E
Ajaccio France **21** 41.55N 8.44E
Ajanta Range *mts.* India **62** 20.15N 75.30E
Ajax Canada **104** 43.51N 79.02W
Ajdâbiyâ Libya **72** 30.46N 20.14E
Ajdovščina Slovenia **31** 45.53N 13.53E
Ajibar Ethiopia **73** 10.41N 38.37E
'Ajlûn Jordan **67** 32.20N 35.45E
'Ajmah, Jabal al *f.* Egypt **66** 29.12N 33.58E
'Ajmân U.A.E. **65** 25.23N 55.26E
Ajmer India **62** 26.27N 74.38E
Ajnâla India **62** 31.51N 74.47E
Ajo U.S.A. **109** 32.22N112.52W
Ajo, Cabo de *c.* Spain **26** 43.31N 3.35W
Akaishi sammyaku *mts.* Japan **57** 35.20N138.10E
Akâmas, Akrotírion *c.* Cyprus **66** 35.06N 32.17E
Akaroa New Zealand **86** 43.50S172.59E
'Akasha East Sudan **72** 21.05N 30.43E
Akashi Japan **57** 34.38N134.59E
Akbarpur India **63** 26.25N 82.33E
Akbulak Russian Fed. **45** 51.00N 55.40E
Akelamo Indonesia **59** 1.35N129.40E
Akershus *d.* Norway **42** 60.05N 11.25E
Aketi Zaïre **78** 2.46N 23.51E
Akhaltsikhe Georgia **64** 41.37N 42.59E
Akharnaí Greece **35** 38.05N 23.44E
Akhdar, Al Jabal al *mts.* Libya **72** 32.30N 21.30E
Akhdar, Al Jabal al *mts.* Oman **65** 23.10N 57.25E
Akhdar, Wâdî *r.* Egypt **66** 28.42N 33.41E
Akhdar, Wâdî al *r.* Saudi Arabia **66** 28.30N 36.48E
Akhelóös Greece **29** 38.20N 21.04E

Akhelóös *r.* Greece **35** 38.36N 21.14E
Akhisar Turkey **29** 38.54N 27.49E
Akhladhókambos Greece **35** 37.31N 22.35E
Akhmīm Egypt **64** 26.34N 31.44E
Akhtyrka Ukraine **45** 50.19N 34.54E
Akimiski I. Canada **102** 53.00N 81.20W
Åkirkeby Denmark **43** 55.04N 14.56E
Akita Japan **57** 39.44N140.05E
Akjoujt Mauritania **74** 19.44N 14.26W
Akkajaure *l.* Sweden **40** 67.40N 17.30E
'Akko Israel **67** 32.55N 35.05E
Akkol Kazakhstan **52** 45.04N 75.39E
Akkoy Turkey **35** 37.29N 27.15E
Aklavik Canada **98** 68.12N135.00W
Ako Nigeria **77** 10.19N 10.48E
Ākobo *r.* Ethiopia **73** 8.30N 33.15E
Akola India **62** 20.44N 77.00E
Āk'ordat Ethiopia **72** 15.35N 37.55E
Akot India **62** 21.11N 77.04E
Akpatok I. Canada **99** 60.30N 68.30W
Åkrafjorden *est.* Norway **42** 59.46N 6.06E
Akranes Iceland **40** 64.19N 22.05W
Åkrehamn Norway **42** 59.16N 5.11E
Akrítas, Ákra *c.* Greece **35** 36.43N 21.54E
Akron Colo. U.S.A. **110** 40.10N103.13W
Akron Ohio U.S.A. **114** 41.05N 81.31W
Akrotíri Cyprus **66** 34.36N 32.57E
Aksaray Turkey **64** 38.22N 34.02E
Aksarka Russian Fed. **50** 66.31N 67.50E
Aksay China **52** 39.28N 94.15E
Aksay Kazakhstan **45** 51.24N 52.11E
Akşehir Turkey **64** 38.22N 31.24E
Aksu China **52** 42.10N 80.00E
Āksum Ethiopia **72** 14.08N 38.48E
Aktag *mtn.* China **52** 36.45N 84.40E
Aktogay Kazakhstan **52** 46.59N 79.42E
Aktyubinsk Kazakhstan **45** 50.16N 57.13E
Akūbū Sudan **73** 7.47N 33.01E
Akūbū *r. see* Ākobo *r.* Sudan **73**
Akula Zaïre **78** 2.22N 20.11E
Akure Nigeria **77** 7.14N 5.08E
Akureyri Iceland **40** 65.41N 18.04W
Akuse Ghana **76** 6.04N 0.12E
Akwa-Ibom *d.* Nigeria **77** 4.45N 7.50E
Akxokesay China **52** 36.48N 91.06E
Akyab *see* Sittwe Burma **56**
Akyel Ethiopia **73** 12.30N 37.04E
Ål Norway **41** 60.38N 8.34E
Alabama *d.* U.S.A. **113** 32.50N 87.00W
Alabama *r.* U.S.A. **111** 31.08N 87.57W
Al 'Abbāsīyah Sudan **73** 14.27N 33.31E
Alaçati Turkey **35** 38.16N 26.23E
Ālādāgh, Kūh-e *mts.* Iran **65** 37.15N 57.30E
Alagoas *d.* Brazil **123** 9.30S 37.00W
Alagoinhas Brazil **123** 12.09S 38.21W
Alagón Spain **24** 41.46N 1.12W
Alakol, Ozero *l.* Kazakhstan **52** 46.00N 81.40E
Alakurtti Russian Fed. **44** 67.00N 30.23E
Al'Āl Syria **67** 32.48N 35.44E
Al 'Alamayn Egypt **64** 30.49N 28.57E
Al 'Amārah Iraq **65** 31.52N 47.50E
Al Āmirīyah Egypt **66** 31.01N 29.48E
Alamogordo U.S.A. **109** 32.54N105.57W
Alamos, Rio de los *r.* Mexico **111** 27.53N101.12W
Alamosa U.S.A. **108** 37.28N105.52W
Åland *is. see* Ahvenanmaa *is.* Finland **41**
Ålands Hav *sea* Finland **43** 59.50N 19.25E
Alanreed U.S.A. **111** 35.14N100.45W
Alanson U.S.A. **104** 45.27N 84.47W
Alanya Turkey **64** 36.32N 32.02E
Alaotra, Lac *l.* Madagascar **81** 17.30S 48.30E
Alapayevsk Russian Fed. **44** 57.55N 61.42E
Alappuzha India **60** 9.30N 76.22E
Al 'Aqabah Jordan **66** 29.32N 35.00E
Al 'Aramah *f.* Saudi Arabia **65** 25.30N 46.30E
Alarcón, Embalse de *resr.* Spain **27** 39.36N 2.10W
Al 'Arīsh Egypt **66** 31.08N 33.48E
Alaşehir Turkey **29** 38.22N 28.29E
Al 'Āṣimah *d.* Jordan **67** 31.45N 36.05E
Alaska *d.* U.S.A. **98** 65.00N153.00W
Alaska, G. of U.S.A. **98** 58.45N145.00W
Alaska Pen. U.S.A. **98** 56.00N160.00W
Alaska Range *mts.* U.S.A. **98** 62.10N152.00W
Alassio Italy **30** 44.00N 8.10E
Al 'Atīqah Lebanon **66** 33.42N 35.27E
Alatri Italy **30** 41.43N 13.21E
Al 'Aṭrun Sudan **72** 18.11N 26.36E
Alatyr Russian Fed. **44** 54.51N 46.35E
Alausí Ecuador **122** 2.00S 78.50W
Álava *d.* Spain **26** 42.55N 2.50W
Alavus Finland **40** 62.35N 23.37E
Alawoona Australia **92** 34.44S140.33E
Al 'Ayn *wells* Sudan **72** 16.36N 29.19E
Alayor Spain **25** 39.56N 4.08E
Al 'Ayyāṭ Egypt **66** 29.37N 31.15E
Alazani *r.* Georgia **65** 41.06N 46.40E
Alba Italy **30** 44.42N 8.02E
Albacete Spain **25** 38.59N 1.51W
Albacete *d.* Spain **25** 39.05N 1.45W
Al Bad' Saudi Arabia **66** 28.29N 35.02E
Al Badārī Egypt **64** 26.59N 31.25E
Alba de Tormes Spain **26** 40.49N 5.31W
Ålbaek Denmark **42** 57.36N 10.25E
Al Bahnasā Egypt **66** 28.32N 30.39E
Al Baḥr al Aḥmar *d.* Sudan **72** 19.30N 35.30E
Al Baḥr al Mayyit *see* Dead Sea Jordan **67**
Albaida Spain **25** 38.51N 0.31W
Alba-Iulia Romania **37** 46.04N 23.33E
Al Balqā' *d.* Jordan **67** 32.00N 35.40E
Alban France **20** 43.54N 2.28E
Albania Europe **34** 41.00N 20.00E
Albano Laziale Italy **30** 41.44N 12.39E
Albany Australia **89** 34.57S117.54E
Albany *r.* Canada **102** 52.10N 82.00W
Albany Ga. U.S.A. **113** 31.37N 84.10W
Albany Ky. U.S.A. **113** 36.42N 85.08W
Albany Minn. U.S.A. **110** 45.38N 94.34W
Albany N.Y. U.S.A. **115** 42.39N 73.45W
Albany Ohio U.S.A. **114** 39.14N 82.12W
Albany Oreg. U.S.A. **108** 44.38N123.06W
Al Bāriḥah Jordan **67** 32.34N 35.50E
Albarracín Spain **25** 40.25N 1.26W
Albarracín, Sierra de *mts.* Spain **25** 40.30N 1.40W
Al Başrah Iraq **65** 30.33N 47.50E
Al Bāṭinah *f.* Oman **65** 24.25N 56.50E
Albatross B. Australia **90** 12.45S141.43E
Al Batrūn Lebanon **66** 34.16N 35.40E
Al Bawīṭī Egypt **64** 28.21N 25.52E
Al Bayāḍ *f.* Saudi Arabia **71** 22.00N 47.00E
Al Bayḍā' Libya **75** 32.46N 21.43E
Albegna *r.* Italy **30** 42.30N 11.11E
Albemarle Sd. U.S.A. **107** 36.10N 76.00W
Albenga Italy **30** 44.03N 8.13E
Albens France **21** 45.47N 5.57E
Alberche *r.* Spain **27** 39.58N 4.46W
Alberga Australia **91** 27.12S135.28E
Alberga *r.* Australia **91** 27.12S135.28E
Albergaria-a-Velha Portugal **26** 40.42N 8.29W
Alberique Spain **25** 39.07N 0.31W
Albermarle U.S.A. **113** 35.21N 80.12W
Albermarle Sd. U.S.A. **113** 36.03N 76.12W
Alberobello Italy **33** 40.47N 17.15E
Albert Australia **93** 32.21S147.33E
Albert France **19** 50.00N 2.39E
Albert, L. Australia **92** 35.38S139.17E
Albert, L. Uganda / Zaïre **79** 1.45N 31.00E
Alberta *d.* Canada **100** 54.00N115.00W
Alberti Argentina **125** 35.01S 60.16W
Albertirsa Hungary **37** 47.15N 19.38E
Albert Kanaal *canal* Belgium **16** 51.00N 5.15E
Albert Lea U.S.A. **110** 43.39N 93.22W
Albert Nile *r.* Uganda **79** 3.30N 32.00E
Alberton Canada **103** 46.49N 64.04W
Albertville France **21** 45.41N 6.23E
Albi France **20** 43.56N 2.08E
Al Bidia Chad **73** 10.33N 20.13E
Albin U.S.A. **108** 41.26N104.08W
Albina Surinam **123** 5.30N 54.03W
Albino Italy **30** 45.46N 9.47E
Albion Mich. U.S.A. **112** 42.14N 84.45W
Albion Mont. U.S.A. **108** 45.11N104.15W
Albion Nebr. U.S.A. **110** 41.42N 98.00W
Albion N.Y. U.S.A. **114** 43.15N 78.12W
Albion Penn. U.S.A. **114** 41.53N 80.22W
Al Bi'r Saudi Arabia **66** 28.52N 36.15E
Al Bīrah Jordan **67** 31.54N 35.13E
Albo, Monte *mtn.* Italy **32** 40.29N 9.33E
Albocácer Spain **25** 40.21N 0.02E
Alborán, Isla de *i.* Spain **27** 35.58N 3.02W
Ålborg Denmark **42** 57.03N 9.56E
Ålborg Bugt *b.* Denmark **42** 56.55N 10.30E
Alborz, Reshteh-ye Kūhhā-ye *mts.* Iran **65** 36.00N 52.30E
Albufeira Portugal **27** 37.05N 8.15W
Al Buḥayrāt *d.* Sudan **73** 6.50N 29.40E
Albuñol Spain **27** 36.47N 3.12W
Albuquerque U.S.A. **109** 35.05N106.40W
Al Buraymī U.A.E. **65** 24.15N 55.45E
Alburg U.S.A. **105** 44.59N 73.18W
Al Burj Egypt **66** 31.35N 30.59E
Alburquerque Spain **27** 39.13N 7.00W
Albury Australia **93** 36.03S146.53E
Al Buṭanah *f.* Sudan **72** 14.50N 34.30E
Al Buwayḍah Jordan **67** 32.21N 36.03E
Alby Sweden **40** 62.30N 15.25E
Alcácer do Sal Portugal **27** 38.22N 8.30W
Alcains Portugal **27** 39.55N 7.27W
Alcalá de Chisvert Spain **25** 40.19N 0.13E
Alcalá de Guadaira Spain **27** 37.20N 5.50W
Alcalá de Henares Spain **26** 40.29N 3.22W
Alcalá la Real Spain **27** 37.28N 3.56W
Alcamo Italy **32** 37.59N 12.58E
Alcanadre *r.* Spain **25** 41.37N 0.12W
Alcanar Spain **25** 40.33N 0.29E
Alcañices Spain **26** 41.42N 6.21W
Alcañiz Spain **25** 41.03N 0.08W
Alcántara Spain **27** 39.43N 6.53W
Alcántara, Embalse de *resr.* Spain **27** 39.45N 6.25W
Alcantara L. Canada **101** 60.57N108.09W
Alcantarilla Spain **25** 37.58N 1.13W
Alcaraz Spain **26** 38.40N 2.29W
Alcaraz, Sierra de *mts.* Spain **27** 38.40N 2.30W
Alcarrache *r.* Portugal **27** 38.16N 7.24W
Alcaudete Spain **27** 37.36N 4.05W
Alcázar de San Juan Spain **27** 39.24N 3.12W
Alcira Spain **25** 39.09N 0.26W
Alcobaça Portugal **27** 39.33N 8.59W
Alcobendas Spain **26** 40.32N 3.38W
Alcolea del Pinar Spain **26** 41.02N 2.28W
Alconchel Portugal **27** 38.31N 7.04W
Alcova U.S.A. **108** 42.35N106.34W
Alcoy Spain **25** 38.42N 0.28W
Alcubierre Spain **25** 41.48N 0.27W
Alcubierre, Sierra de *mts.* Spain **25** 41.45N 0.21W
Alcudia Spain **25** 39.52N 3.07E
Alcudia, Bahía de *b.* Spain **25** 39.48N 3.13E
Alcudia, Sierra de la *mts.* Spain **27** 38.34N 4.30W
Aldabra Is. Seychelles **70** 9.00S 46.30E
Aldan Russian Fed. **51** 58.44N125.22E
Aldan *r.* Russian Fed. **51** 63.30N130.00E
Aldeburgh U.K. **13** 52.09N 1.35E
Aldeia Nova de Santo Bento Portugal **27** 37.55N 7.25W
Alder Creek *town* U.S.A. **115** 43.27N 75.17W
Alderney *i.* Channel Is. Europe **13** 49.42N 2.11W
Aldershot U.K. **13** 51.15N 0.47W
Alderson Canada **101** 50.20N111.25W
Aldridge U.K. **13** 52.36N 1.55W
Aledo U.S.A. **110** 41.12N 90.45W
Aleg Mauritania **74** 17.03N 13.55W
Alegre Brazil **126** 20.44S 41.30W
Alegrete Brazil **125** 29.46S 55.46W
Aleksandrov Gay Russian Fed. **45** 50.08N 48.34E
Aleksandrovsk Sakhalinskiy Russian Fed. **51** 50.55N142.12E
Aleksinac Yugo. **34** 43.31N 21.42E
Alembe Gabon **78** 0.03N 10.57E
Além Paraíba Brazil **126** 21.49S 42.36W
Alençon France **18** 48.26N 0.05E
Alenuihaha Channel Hawaiian Is. **85** 20.26N156.00W
Aleppo *see* Ḥalab Syria **64**
Aléria France **21** 42.05N 9.30E
Alès France **21** 44.08N 4.05E
Alessandria Italy **30** 44.54N 8.37E
Alessano Italy **33** 39.53N 18.20E
Ålestrup Denmark **42** 56.42N 9.31E
Ålesund Norway **40** 62.28N 6.11E
Aleutian Basin Bering Sea **84** 57.00N179.00E
Aleutian Is. U.S.A. **48** 57.00N180.00
Aleutian Range *mts.* U.S.A. **98** 58.00N156.00W
Aleutian Trench Pacific Oc. **84** 50.00N176.00W
Alexander *r.* Israel **67** 32.24N 34.52E
Alexander U.S.A. **114** 42.54N 78.16W
Alexander Archipelago *is.* U.S.A. **100** 56.30N134.30W
Alexander Bay *town* R.S.A. **80** 28.36S 16.26E
Alexander I. Antarctica **128** 72.00S 70.00W
Alexandra Australia **93** 37.12S145.14E
Alexandra New Zealand **86** 45.14S169.26E
Alexandria B.C. Canada **100** 52.35N122.27W
Alexandria Ont. Canada **105** 45.19N 74.38W
Alexandria *see* Al Iskandarīyah Egypt **66**
Alexandria Romania **34** 43.58N 25.20E
Alexandria R.S.A. **80** 33.39S 26.24E
Alexandria La. U.S.A. **111** 31.18N 92.27W
Alexandria Minn. U.S.A. **110** 45.53N 95.22W
Alexandria Va. U.S.A. **114** 38.48N 77.03W
Alexandria Bay *town* U.S.A. **105** 44.20N 75.55W
Alexandrina, L. Australia **92** 35.26S139.10E
Alexandroúpolis Greece **34** 40.50N 25.52E
Alexis *r.* Canada **103** 52.32N 56.08W
Alexis Creek *town* Canada **100** 52.05N123.20W
Aleysk Russian Fed. **50** 52.32N 82.45E
Alfambra Spain **25** 40.33N 1.02W
Al Fant Egypt **66** 28.46N 30.53E
Alfaro Spain **25** 42.11N 1.45W
Alfarrás Spain **25** 41.49N 0.35E
Al Fāshir Sudan **73** 13.38N 25.21E
Al Fashn Egypt **66** 28.49N 30.54E
Al Fāw Iraq **65** 29.57N 48.30E
Al Fayyūm Egypt **66** 29.19N 30.50E
Alfeld Germany **38** 51.59N 9.50E
Alfenas Brazil **126** 21.28S 45.48W
Al Fifi Sudan **73** 10.03N 25.01E
Alfiós *r.* Greece **35** 37.40N 21.33E
Alfonsine Italy **30** 44.30N 12.03E
Alford U.K. **14** 57.14N 2.42W
Alfred U.S.A. **114** 42.15N 77.47W
Al Fujayrah U.A.E. **65** 25.10N 56.20E
Alga Kazakhstan **50** 49.49N 57.16E
Ålgård Norway **42** 58.46N 5.51E
Al Gebir Sudan **73** 13.43N 29.49E
Algeciras Spain **27** 36.08N 5.30W
Algemesí Spain **25** 39.11N 0.26W
Algena Ethiopia **72** 16.20N 38.34E
Alger Algeria **75** 36.50N 3.00E
Alger U.S.A. **104** 44.08N 84.08W
Algeria Africa **74** 28.00N 2.00E
Al Ghawr *f.* Jordan **67** 32.00N 35.30E
Al Ghayl Saudi Arabia **65** 22.36N 46.19E
Alghero Italy **32** 40.34N 8.19E
Al Ghurdaqah Egypt **64** 27.14N 33.50E
Algiers *see* Alger Algeria **75**
Alginet Spain **25** 39.16N 0.28W
Algoa B. R.S.A. **80** 33.50S 26.00E
Algodor *r.* Spain **27** 39.55N 3.53W
Algoma U.S.A. **110** 44.36N 87.27W
Algoma Mills Canada **104** 46.10N 82.50W
Algoma Uplands Canada **104** 47.00N 83.35W
Algona U.S.A. **110** 43.04N 94.14W
Algonquin Park *town* Canada **104** 45.34N 78.36W
Algonquin Prov. Park Canada **104** 45.27N 78.26W
Algonquin Upland Canada **104** 45.40N 78.47W
Algorta Uruguay **125** 32.25S 57.23W
Al Ḥajar al Gharbī *mts.* Oman **65** 24.00N 56.30E
Al Ḥajar ash Sharqī *mts.* Oman **65** 22.45N 58.45E
Alhama Spain **25** 37.51N 1.25W
Al Ḥamād *des.* Saudi Arabia **64** 31.45N 39.00E
Alhama de Granada Spain **27** 37.00N 3.59W
Al Ḥamar Saudi Arabia **65** 22.26N 46.12E
Alhambra U.S.A. **109** 34.06N118.08W
Al Ḥamīdīyah Syria **66** 34.43N 35.56E
Al Ḥanākīyah Saudi Arabia **64** 24.53N 40.30E
Al Ḥarāk Syria **67** 32.44N 36.18E
Al Ḥarīq Saudi Arabia **65** 23.37N 46.31E
Al Ḥārrah Syria **67** 33.03N 36.00E
Al Harūj al Aswad *hills* Libya **75** 27.00N 17.10E
Al Ḥasakah Syria **64** 36.29N 40.45E
Alhaurín el Grande Spain **27** 36.38N 4.41W
Al Ḥawāmidīyah Egypt **66** 29.54N 31.15E
Al Ḥayz Egypt **64** 28.02N 28.39E
Al Ḥijāz *f.* Saudi Arabia **64** 26.00N 37.30E
Al Ḥillah Iraq **65** 32.28N 44.29E
Al Ḥillah Saudi Arabia **65** 23.30N 46.51E
Al Hirmil Lebanon **66** 34.25N 36.23E
Al Ḥişn Jordan **67** 32.29N 35.53E
Al-Hoceima Morocco **74** 35.15N 3.55W
Al Ḥudaydah Yemen **72** 14.50N 42.58E
Al Hufūf Saudi Arabia **65** 25.20N 49.34E
Al Ḥumrah *des.* U.A.E. **65** 22.45N 55.10E
Al Ḥusaynīyah Egypt **66** 30.52N 31.55E
Al Ḥuwaymī Yemen **71** 14.05N 47.44E
Alīābād, Kūh-e *mtn.* Iran **65** 34.09N 50.48E
Aliaga Spain **25** 40.40N 0.42W
Aliákmon *r.* Greece **34** 40.30N 22.36E
Aliákmona, Limni *resr.* Greece **34** 40.15N 22.00E
Alicante Spain **25** 38.23N 0.29W
Alicante *d.* Spain **25** 38.30N 0.40W
Alice Canada **105** 45.44N 77.19W
Alice R.S.A. **80** 32.47S 26.49E
Alice U.S.A. **111** 27.45N 98.04W
Alice, Punta *c.* Italy **33** 39.24N 17.10E
Alice Arm Canada **100** 55.29N129.31W
Alice Springs *town* Australia **90** 23.42S133.52E
Alicudi, Isola *i.* Italy **33** 38.33N 14.21E
Al Ifranj Jordan **67** 31.11N 35.41E
Alīgarh India **63** 27.53N 78.05E
Alīgūdarz Iran **65** 33.25N 49.38E
'Alījūq, Kūh-e *mtn.* Iran **65** 31.27N 51.43E
Alima *r.* Congo **78** 1.36S 16.35E
Alindao C.A.R. **73** 5.02N 21.13E
Alingsås Sweden **43** 57.56N 12.31E
Alīpur Pakistan **62** 29.23N 70.55E
Alīpur Duār India **63** 26.29N 89.44E
Alīpur Janūbi Pakistan **62** 30.13N 71.18E
Aliquippa U.S.A. **114** 40.37N 80.15W
Al 'Irq Libya **75** 29.05N 15.48E
Ali Sabieh Djibouti **73** 11.09N 42.42E
Aliseda Spain **27** 39.26N 6.41W
Al Iskandarīyah Egypt **66** 31.13N 29.55E
Al Ismā'īlīyah Egypt **66** 30.36N 32.15E
Alistráti Greece **34** 41.04N 23.57E
Alivérion Greece **35** 38.24N 24.02E
Aliwal North R.S.A. **80** 30.41S 26.41E
Al Jabal al Akhḍar *d.* Libya **75** 32.00N 21.30E
Al Jafr Jordan **66** 30.16N 36.11E
Al Jāfūrah *des.* Saudi Arabia **65** 24.40N 50.20E
Al Jaghbūb Libya **72** 29.45N 24.31E
Al Jahrah Kuwait **65** 29.20N 47.41E
Al Jaladah *f.* Saudi Arabia **71** 18.30N 46.25E
Al Janūb *d.* Lebanon **67** 33.10N 35.22E
Al Jawārah Oman **60** 18.55N 57.17E
Al Jawb *f.* Saudi Arabia **65** 23.00N 50.00E
Al Jawf Libya **72** 24.12N 23.18E
Al Jawf Saudi Arabia **64** 29.49N 39.52E
Al Jawsh Libya **75** 32.00N 11.40E
Al Jazirah *f.* Iraq **64** 35.00N 41.00E
Al Jazīrah *d.* Sudan **72** 14.35N 33.30E
Al Jazīrah *f.* Sudan **72** 14.25N 33.00E
Al Jibāb Syria **67** 33.06N 36.15E
Al Jifārah Saudi Arabia **65** 23.59N 45.11E
Al Jīzah Egypt **66** 30.01N 31.12E
Al Jīzah Jordan **67** 31.42N 35.57E
Al Jubayl Saudi Arabia **65** 27.59N 49.40E
Al Judayyidah Jordan **67** 31.15N 35.49E
Al Junaynah Sudan **73** 13.27N 22.27E
Aljustrel Portugal **27** 37.52N 8.10W
Al Karabah Sudan **72** 18.33N 33.42E
Al Karak Jordan **67** 31.11N 35.42E
Al Karak *d.* Jordan **67** 31.10N 36.00E
Al Kawah Sudan **73** 13.44N 32.30E
Al Khābūr *r.* Syria **64** 35.07N 40.30E
Al Khābūrah Oman **65** 23.58N 57.10E
Al Khalīl Jordan **67** 31.32N 35.06E
Al Khalīl *d.* Jordan **67** 31.29N 35.10E
Al Khamāsīn Saudi Arabia **71** 20.29N 44.49E
Al Khandaq Sudan **72** 18.36N 30.34E
Al Khānkah Egypt **66** 30.12N 31.21E
Al Khārijah Egypt **64** 25.26N 30.33E
Al Kharṭūm Sudan **72** 15.33N 32.35E
Al Kharṭūm *d.* Sudan **72** 15.45N 32.30E
Al Kharṭūm Baḥrī Sudan **72** 15.39N 32.34E
Al Khasfah *well* Oman **71** 19.45N 54.19E
Al Khawr Qatar **65** 25.39N 51.32E
Al Khirbah as Samrā' Jordan **67** 32.11N 36.10E
Al Khubar Saudi Arabia **65** 26.18N 50.06E
Al Khufayfīyah Saudi Arabia **65** 24.55N 44.42E
Al Khums Libya **75** 32.39N 14.16E
Al Khums *d.* Libya **75** 31.20N 14.10E
Al Khunn Saudi Arabia **65** 23.18N 49.15E
Al Khushnīyah Syria **67** 33.00N 35.48E
Al Kidn *des.* Saudi Arabia **65** 22.20N 54.20E
Al Kiswah Syria **66** 33.21N 36.14E
Alkmaar Neth. **16** 52.37N 4.44E
Al Kufrah Libya **72** 24.14N 23.15E
Al Kuntillah Egypt **66** 30.00N 34.41E
Al Kūt Iraq **65** 32.30N 45.51E
Al Kuwayt Kuwait **65** 29.20N 48.00E
Al Labwah Lebanon **66** 34.11N 36.21E
Al Lādhiqīyah Syria **66** 35.31N 35.47E
Al Lagowa Sudan **73** 11.24N 29.08E
Allāhābād India **63** 25.27N 81.51E
Allakaket U.S.A. **98** 66.30N152.45W
'Allān *r.* Syria **67** 32.45N 35.57E
Allanche France **20** 45.14N 2.56E
'Allāqī, Wādī al *r.* Egypt **64** 22.55N 33.02E
Allariz Spain **26** 42.11N 7.48W
Allauch France **21** 43.20N 5.29E
Ålleberg *hill* Sweden **43** 58.08N 13.36E
Allegany U.S.A. **114** 42.06N 78.30W
Allegany State Park U.S.A. **114** 42.04N 78.44W
Allegheny *r.* U.S.A. **114** 40.27N 80.00W
Allegheny Mts. U.S.A. **114** 38.30N 80.00W
Allegheny Resr. U.S.A. **114** 42.00N 78.56W
Allen, Lough Rep. of Ire. **15** 54.07N 8.04W
Allenby Bridge *see* Jisr al Ḥusayn Jordan **67**
Allenford Canada **104** 44.32N 81.10W
Allentown U.S.A. **115** 40.37N 75.30W
Aller *r.* Germany **38** 52.57N 9.11E
Allevard France **21** 45.24N 6.04E
Allgäu *f.* Germany **38** 47.40N 10.15E
Allgäuer Alpen *mts.* Germany **38** 47.26N 10.15E
Alliance Nebr. U.S.A. **110** 42.06N102.52W
Alliance Ohio U.S.A. **114** 40.55N 81.06W
Allier *d.* France **20** 46.25N 3.00E
Allier *r.* France **20** 46.58N 3.30E
Allinge Denmark **43** 55.16N 14.49E
Al Lisān *pen.* Jordan **67** 31.17N 35.28E
Alliston Canada **104** 44.09N 79.52W
Al Līṭānī *r.* Lebanon **66** 33.22N 35.14E
Al Līth Saudi Arabia **72** 20.09N 40.16E
Al Līwā' *f.* U.A.E. **71** 23.00N 54.00E
Alloa U.K. **14** 56.07N 3.49W
Allos France **21** 44.14N 6.38E
Al Luḥayyah Yemen **72** 15.43N 42.42E
Alluitsup-Paa *see* Sydpröven Greenland **99**
Alma Canada **103** 48.32N 71.40W
Alma Ga. U.S.A. **113** 31.33N 82.29W
Alma Mich. U.S.A. **112** 43.23N 84.40W
Al Ma'ānīyah *well* Iraq **64** 30.44N 43.00E
Alma-Ata Kazakhstan **52** 43.19N 76.55E
Almada Portugal **27** 38.41N 9.09W

Almadén to **Anefis I-n-Darane**

Almadén Spain **26** 38.46N 4.50W
Almadén de la Plata Spain **27** 37.52N 6.04W
Al Madīnah Saudi Arabia **64** 24.30N 39.35E
Al Madīnah al Fikrīyah Egypt **66** 27.56N 30.49E
Al Madwar Jordan **67** 32.17N 36.00E
Al Mafraq Jordan **67** 32.21N 36.12E
Al Maghrah *well* Egypt **64** 30.14N 28.56E
Almagor Israel **67** 32.55N 35.36E
Almagro Spain **26** 38.53N 3.43W
Al Maḩallah al Kubrá Egypt **66** 30.59N 31.12E
Al Maḩāriq Egypt **64** 25.37N 30.39E
Alma Hill U.S.A. **114** 42.03N 78.01W
Al Maḩmūdīyah Egypt **66** 31.10N 30.30E
Al Majma'ah Saudi Arabia **65** 25.52N 45.25E
Al Manāmah Bahrain **65** 26.12N 50.36E
Almanor U.S.A. **108** 40.15N121.08W
Almansa Spain **25** 38.52N 1.05W
Al Manshāh Egypt **64** 26.28N 31.48E
Almansor *r.* Portugal **27** 38.56N 8.54W
Al Manşūrah Egypt **66** 31.03N 31.23E
Almanza Spain **26** 42.39N 5.02W
Al Manzil Jordan **66** 31.03N 36.01E
Al Manzilah Egypt **66** 31.10N 31.56E
Almanzor, Pico de *mtn.* Spain **26** 40.15N 5.18W
Almanzora *r.* Spain **24** 37.16N 1.49W
Almar *r.* Spain **26** 40.54N 5.29W
Al Marj Libya **72** 32.30N 20.50E
Al Maţarīyah Egypt **66** 31.12N 32.02E
Al Matnah Sudan **72** 13.47N 35.03E
Almaty *see* Alma-Ata Kazakhstan **52**
Al Mawşil Iraq **64** 36.21N 43.08E
Al Mayādīn Syria **64** 35.01N 40.28E
Almazán Spain **26** 41.29N 2.32W
Almazora Spain **25** 39.57N 0.03W
Al Mazra'ah Jordan **67** 31.16N 35.31E
Almeida Portugal **26** 40.43N 6.54W
Almeirim Portugal **27** 39.12N 8.38W
Almelo Neth. **16** 52.21N 6.40E
Almenara, Sierra de *mts.* Spain **25** 37.30N 1.40E
Almenar de Soria Spain **25** 41.41N 2.12W
Almendra, Embalse de *resr.* Spain **26** 41.15N 6.10W
Almendralejo Spain **27** 38.41N 6.24W
Almería Spain **27** 36.50N 2.27W
Almería *d.* Spain **27** 37.05N 2.30W
Almería, Golfo di *g.* Spain **27** 36.45N 2.30W
Älmhult Sweden **43** 56.33N 14.08E
Al Midhnab Saudi Arabia **65** 25.52N 44.15E
Al Miḩrāḑ *des.* Saudi Arabia **65** 20.00N 52.30E
Al Minyā Egypt **66** 28.06N 30.45E
Almirópótamos Greece **35** 38.16N 24.11E
Almirós Greece **35** 39.11N 22.46E
Almiroú, Kólpos *g.* Greece **35** 35.23N 24.20E
Al Mismīyah Syria **66** 33.08N 36.24E
Almodôvar Portugal **27** 37.31N 8.36W
Almodóvar del Campo Spain **26** 38.43N 4.10W
Almont U.S.A. **114** 42.55N 83.03W
Almonte Canada **105** 45.14N 76.12W
Almonte Spain **27** 37.15N 6.31W
Almonte *r.* Spain **27** 39.42N 6.20W
Almora India **63** 29.37N 79.40E
Al Mudawwarah Jordan **66** 29.20N 36.00E
Almudébar Spain **25** 42.03N 0.35W
Al Muglad Sudan **73** 11.02N 27.44E
Al Muḩarraq Bahrain **65** 26.16N 50.38E
Al Mukallā Yemen **71** 14.34N 49.09E
Al Mukhā Yemen **73** 13.19N 43.15E
Almuñécar Spain **27** 36.43N 3.41W
Al Muwaqqar *site* Jordan **67** 31.39N 36.06E
Al Muwayh Saudi Arabia **64** 22.41N 41.37E
Alnwick U.K. **12** 55.25N 1.41W
Alofi Niue **84** 19.03S169.55W
Alofi B. Niue **84** 19.02S169.55W
Alónnisos Greece **35** 39.08N 23.50E
Alónnisos *i.* Greece **35** 39.08N 23.50E
Alonsa Canada **101** 50.50N 99.00W
Alor *i.* Indonesia **59** 8.20S124.30E
Álora Spain **27** 36.48N 4.42W
Alor Setar Malaysia **58** 6.06N100.23E
Alosno Spain **27** 37.33N 7.07W
Alozero Russian Fed. **44** 65.02N 31.10E
Alpena U.S.A. **104** 45.04N 83.26W
Alpes-de-Haute-Provence *d.* France **21** 44.08N 6.10E
Alpes Maritimes *d.* France **21** 44.00N 7.10E
Alpes Maritimes *mts.* France **17** 44.07N 7.08E
Alpes Pennines *mts.* Switz. **39** 46.08N 7.34E
Alpha Australia **90** 23.39S146.38E
Alphen Neth. **16** 52.08N 4.40E
Alpiarça Portugal **27** 39.15N 8.35W
Alpine U.S.A. **111** 30.22N103.40W
Alps *mts.* Europe **17** 46.00N 7.30E
Al Qaḑārif Sudan **72** 14.02N 35.24E
Al Qaḑīmah Saudi Arabia **72** 22.21N 39.09E
Al Qāfā' *des.* U.A.E. **65** 23.30N 53.30E
Al Qāhirah Egypt **66** 30.03N 31.15E
Al Qā'īyah Saudi Arabia **64** 24.18N 43.30E
Al Qā'īyah *well* Saudi Arabia **65** 26.27N 45.35E
Al Qalībah Saudi Arabia **64** 28.24N 37.42E
Al Qanāţir al Khayrīyah Egypt **66** 30.12N 31.08E
Al Qanţarah Egypt **66** 30.52N 32.20E
Al Qaryatayn Syria **66** 34.13N 37.13E
Al Qaşabāt Libya **75** 32.35N 14.03E
Al Qaşr Egypt **64** 25.43N 28.54E
Al Qaşr Jordan **67** 31.19N 35.45E
Al Qaşşāşīn Egypt **66** 30.34N 31.56E
Al Qaţīf Saudi Arabia **65** 26.31N 50.00E
Al Qaţrānah Jordan **67** 31.15N 36.03E
Al Qaţrūn Libya **75** 24.56N 14.38E
Al Qayşūmah Saudi Arabia **65** 28.20N 46.07E
Al Qişfah Jordan **67** 32.38N 35.52E
Al Quds *d.* Jordan **67** 31.46N 35.25E
Al Qunayţirah Syria **67** 33.08N 35.49E
Al Qunayţirah *d.* Syria **67** 33.07N 35.50E
Al Qunfudhah Saudi Arabia **72** 19.08N 41.05E
Al Qurnah Iraq **65** 31.00N 47.26E
Al Quşaymah Egypt **66** 30.40N 34.22E
Al Quşayr Egypt **64** 26.06N 34.17E
Al Qūşīyah Egypt **64** 27.26N 30.49E
Al Quţayfah Syria **66** 33.44N 36.36E
Alroy Downs *town* Australia **90** 19.18S136.04E
Als *i.* Denmark **42** 54.59N 9.55E
Alsace *d.* France **19** 48.25N 7.40E
Alsask Canada **101** 51.23N109.59W
Alsasua Spain **25** 42.54N 2.10W
Älsborg *d.* Sweden **41** 58.00N 12.20E
Alsek Ranges *mts.* Canada **100** 59.21N137.05W
Alsfeld Germany **38** 50.45N 9.16E
Alsten *i.* Norway **40** 65.55N 12.35E
Alsterbro Sweden **43** 56.57N 15.55E
Alston U.K. **14** 54.48N 2.26W
Alta Norway **40** 70.00N 23.15E
Alta *r.* Norway **40** 69.50N 23.30E
Altafjorden *est.* Norway **40** 70.10N 23.00E
Alta Gracia Argentina **124** 31.40S 64.26W
Altagracia de Orituco Venezuela **122** 9.54N 66.24W
Altai *mts.* Mongolia **52** 46.30N 93.30E
Altamaha *r.* U.S.A. **113** 31.19N 81.17W
Altamira Brazil **123** 3.12S 52.12W
Altamont N.Y. U.S.A. **115** 42.42N 74.02W
Altamont Oreg. U.S.A. **108** 42.12N121.44W
Altamura Italy **33** 40.50N 16.33E
Altar, Desierto de *des.* Mexico **109** 31.50N114.15W
Altavista U.S.A. **113** 37.07N 79.18W
Altay China **52** 47.48N 88.07E
Altay Mongolia **52** 46.20N 97.00E
Altdorf Switz. **39** 46.53N 8.39E
Altea Spain **25** 38.38N 0.02W
Altenburg Germany **38** 50.59N 12.27E
Altenkirchen Germany **16** 50.41N 7.40E
Altentreptow Germany **38** 53.42N 13.14E
Alter do Chão Portugal **27** 39.12N 7.40W
Althofen Austria **31** 46.54N 14.27E
Altiplanicie Mexicana *mts.* Mexico **111** 29.00N105.00W
Altkirch France **19** 47.37N 7.15E
Altmar U.S.A. **115** 43.31N 76.00W
Altmark *f.* Germany **38** 52.45N 11.15E
Altmühl *r.* Germany **39** 48.55N 11.52E
Altnaharra U.K. **14** 58.16N 4.26W
Alto Araguaia Brazil **123** 17.19S 53.10W
Alto Molocue Mozambique **79** 15.38S 37.42E
Altomünster Germany **39** 48.28N 11.58E
Alton Canada **104** 43.52N 80.04W
Alton U.K. **13** 51.08N 0.59W
Alton U.S.A. **110** 38.55N 90.10W
Altona Germany **38** 53.32N 9.56E
Altoona U.S.A. **114** 40.30N 78.24W
Altötting Germany **39** 48.13N 12.40E
Altsasu *see* Alsasua Spain **25**
Altun Shan *mts.* China **52** 38.10N 87.50E
Altus U.S.A. **111** 34.38N 99.20W
Al Ubayyiḑ Sudan **73** 13.11N 30.13E
Al Uḑayyah Sudan **73** 12.03N 28.17E
Aluk Sudan **73** 8.26N 27.32E
Al 'Ulá Saudi Arabia **64** 26.39N 37.58E
Alunda Sweden **43** 60.04N 18.05E
Al 'Uqaylah Libya **75** 30.16N 19.12E
Al Uqşur Egypt **64** 25.41N 32.24E
Al Urdunn *r.* Asia **67** 31.47N 35.31E
Al 'Uwaynah *well* Saudi Arabia **65** 26.46N 48.13E
Al 'Uwaynāt Libya **75** 25.48N 10.33E
Al 'Uyūn Saudi Arabia **65** 26.32N 43.41E
Alva U.S.A. **111** 36.48N 98.40W
Alvaiázere Portugal **27** 39.49N 8.23W
Älvängen Sweden **43** 57.58N 12.07E
Alvarado Mexico **116** 18.49N 95.46W
Älvdalen Sweden **41** 61.14N 14.02E
Alverca Portugal **27** 38.54N 9.02W
Alvesta Sweden **43** 56.54N 14.33E
Älvho Sweden **41** 61.30N 14.46E
Alvin U.S.A. **111** 29.25N 95.15W
Alvinston Canada **104** 42.49N 81.52W
Alvito Portugal **27** 38.15N 8.00W
Alvito, Barragem do *resr.* Portugal **27** 38.20N 7.50W
Älvkarleby Sweden **41** 60.34N 17.27E
Älvsborg *d.* Sweden **43** 57.50N 12.50E
Älvsbyn Sweden **40** 65.39N 20.59E
Al Wajh Saudi Arabia **64** 26.16N 36.28E
Al Wakrah Qatar **65** 25.09N 51.36E
Alwar India **62** 27.34N 76.36E
Al Wazz Sudan **72** 15.01N 30.10E
Al Yamāmah Saudi Arabia **65** 24.11N 47.21E
Al Yāmūn Jordan **67** 32.29N 35.14E
Alyaty Azerbaijan **65** 39.59N 49.20E
Alytus Lithuania **37** 54.24N 24.03E
Alzada U.S.A. **108** 45.01N104.26W
Alzette *r.* Lux. **16** 49.52N 6.07E
Alzey Germany **39** 49.45N 8.07E
Amadeus, L. Australia **88** 24.50S130.45E
Amadi Sudan **73** 5.31N 30.20E
Amadjuak Canada **99** 64.00N 72.50W
Amadjuak L. Canada **99** 65.00N 71.00W
Amagasaki Japan **57** 34.43N135.25E
Amager *i.* Denmark **43** 55.37N 12.37E
Åmål Sweden **43** 59.03N 12.42E
Amalfi Italy **33** 40.38N 14.36E
Amaliás Greece **35** 37.49N 21.23E
Amalner India **62** 21.03N 75.04E
Amami ō shima *i.* Japan **53** 28.20N129.30E
Amamula Zaïre **79** 0.17S 27.49E
Amanã, L. Brazil **122** 2.35S 64.40W
Amānganj India **63** 24.26N 80.02E
Amangeldy Kazakhstan **50** 50.12N 65.11E
Amantea Italy **33** 39.08N 16.05E
Amapá Brazil **123** 2.00N 50.50W
Amapá *d.* Brazil **123** 2.00N 52.00W
Amarante Brazil **123** 6.14S 42.51W
Amaranth Canada **101** 50.36N 98.43W
Amareleja Portugal **27** 38.12N 7.14W
Amares Portugal **26** 41.38N 8.21W
Amarillo U.S.A. **111** 35.13N101.49W
Amar Jadīd Sudan **72** 14.28N 25.14E
Amarkantak India **63** 22.40N 81.45E
Amaro, Monte *mtn.* Italy **31** 42.05N 14.05E
Amasya Turkey **64** 40.37N 35.50E
Amatrice Italy **30** 42.38N 13.17E
Amazon *r. see* Amazonas *r.* Brazil **123**
Amazonas *d.* Brazil **122** 4.50S 64.00W
Amazonas *r.* Brazil **123** 2.00S 52.00W
Amazonas, Estuario do Rio *f.* Brazil **123** 0.00 50.30W
Amazon Delta *see* Amazonas, Estuario do Rio *f.* Brazil **123**
Amazya Israel **67** 31.32N 34.55E
Amb Pakistan **62** 34.19N 72.51E
Ambāla India **62** 30.23N 76.46E
Ambalavao Madagascar **81** 21.50S 46.56E
Ambam Cameroon **77** 2.25N 11.16E
Ambarawa Indonesia **59** 7.12S110.30E
Ambarchik Russian Fed. **51** 69.39N162.27E
Ambarnāth India **62** 19.11N 73.10E
Ambarnyy Russian Fed. **44** 65.59N 33.53E
Ambato Ecuador **122** 1.18S 78.36W
Ambato-Boeni Madagascar **81** 16.28S 46.43E
Ambatofinandrahana Madagascar **81** 20.33S 46.48E
Ambatolampy Madagascar **81** 19.23S 47.25E
Ambatondrazaka Madagascar **81** 17.50S 48.25E
Ámbelos, Ákra *c.* Greece **34** 39.56N 23.55E
Amberg Germany **38** 49.27N 11.52E
Ambergris Cay *i.* Belize **117** 18.00N 87.58W
Ambérieu-en-Bugey France **21** 45.57N 5.21E
Amberley Canada **104** 44.02N 81.44W
Ambert France **20** 45.33N 3.45E
Ambidédi Mali **76** 14.35N 11.47W
Ambikāpur India **63** 23.07N 83.12E
Ambilobe Madagascar **81** 13.12S 49.04E
Amble U.K. **12** 55.20N 1.34W
Ambleside U.K. **12** 54.26N 2.58W
Ambodifototra Madagascar **81** 16.59S 49.52E
Ambohidratrimo Madagascar **81** 18.50S 47.26E
Ambohimahasoa Madagascar **81** 21.07S 47.13E
Ambohimanga du Sud Madagascar **81** 20.52S 47.36E
Amboise France **18** 47.25N 0.59E
Ambon Indonesia **59** 4.50S128.10E
Ambositra Madagascar **81** 20.31S 47.15E
Ambovombe Madagascar **81** 25.11S 46.05E
Amboy U.S.A. **109** 34.33N115.44W
Ambridge U.S.A. **114** 40.36N 80.14W
Ambrières France **18** 48.24N 0.38W
Ambrim *i.* Vanuatu **84** 16.15S168.10E
Ambriz Angola **78** 7.54S 13.12E
Ambunten Indonesia **59** 6.55S113.45E
Am Dam Chad **73** 12.46N 20.29E
Amderma Russian Fed. **50** 69.44N 61.35E
Amdo China **63** 32.22N 91.07E
Ameca Mexico **116** 20.33N104.02W
Ameland *i.* Neth. **16** 53.28N 5.48E
Amelia Italy **30** 42.33N 12.25E
Amelia City U.S.A. **113** 30.37N 81.27W
Americana Brazil **126** 22.44S 47.19W
American Falls Resr. U.S.A. **108** 43.00N113.00W
American Fork U.S.A. **108** 40.23N111.48W
Americus U.S.A. **113** 32.04N 84.14W
Amersfoort Neth. **16** 52.10N 5.23E
Amery Australia **89** 31.09S117.05E
Ames U.S.A. **110** 42.02N 93.37W
Amesbury U.S.A. **115** 42.51N 70.56W
Ameson Canada **102** 49.50N 84.35W
Ametinho Angola **78** 17.20S 17.20E
Amfíklia Greece **35** 38.38N 22.35E
Amfilokhía Greece **35** 38.51N 21.10E
Ámfissa Greece **35** 38.32N 22.22E
Amga Russian Fed. **51** 60.51N131.59E
Amga *r.* Russian Fed. **51** 62.40N135.20E
Am Guéréda Chad **73** 12.52N 21.10E
Amgu Russian Fed. **53** 45.48N137.36E
Amguid Algeria **75** 26.26N 5.22E
Amgun *r.* Russian Fed. **51** 53.10N139.47E
Amhara Plateau *f.* Ethiopia **73** 11.00N 38.00E
Amherst Canada **103** 45.49N 64.14W
Amherst Mass. U.S.A. **115** 42.23N 72.31W
Amherstburg Canada **104** 42.06N 83.06W
Amherst I. Canada **105** 44.08N 76.45W
Amiata *mtn.* Italy **30** 42.53N 11.37E
Amiens France **19** 49.54N 2.18E
Amíndaion Greece **34** 40.42N 21.42E
Amīr Chāh *well* Pakistan **62** 29.13N 62.28E
Amisk L. Canada **101** 54.35N102.13W
Amistad Resr. U.S.A. **111** 29.34N101.15W
Amite U.S.A. **111** 30.44N 90.33W
Amla India **63** 21.56N 78.07E
Amlekhganj Nepal **63** 27.17N 85.00E
Åmli Norway **42** 58.47N 8.30E
Amlwch U.K. **12** 53.24N 4.21W
'Ammān Jordan **67** 31.57N 35.56E
Ammanford U.K. **13** 51.48N 4.00W
Ammassalik Greenland **99** 65.40N 38.00W
Åmmeberg Sweden **43** 58.52N 15.00E
Ammersee *l.* Germany **39** 48.00N 11.08E
'Ammī'ad Israel **67** 32.55N 35.32E
Ammókhostos Cyprus **66** 35.07N 33.57E
Ammókhostou, Kólpos *b.* Cyprus **66** 35.12N 34.05E
Amo *r.* India **63** 25.58N 89.36E
Āmol Iran **65** 36.26N 52.24E
Amorgós *i.* Greece **35** 36.49N 25.54E
Amorgós *town* Greece **35** 36.49N 25.54E
Amory U.S.A. **111** 33.59N 88.29W
Amos Canada **102** 48.35N 78.05W
Åmot Buskerud Norway **42** 59.54N 9.54E
Åmot Telemark Norway **42** 59.35N 8.00E
Amoy *see* Xiamen China **55**
Ampala Honduras **117** 13.16N 87.39W
Ampanihy Madagascar **81** 24.42S 44.45E
Amparo Brazil **126** 22.44S 46.44W
Amper *r.* Germany **39** 48.10N 11.50E
Ampezzo Italy **30** 46.25N 12.48E
Amposta Spain **25** 40.43N 0.35E
'Amqa Israel **67** 32.58N 35.10E
Amqui Canada **103** 48.28N 67.26W
Amrāvati India **63** 20.56N 77.45E
Amreli India **62** 21.37N 71.14E
Amritsar India **62** 31.38N 74.53E
Amroha India **63** 28.55N 78.28E
Amrum *i.* Germany **38** 54.39N 8.21E
Am Saterna Chad **73** 12.26N 21.25E
Amsel Algeria **75** 22.37N 5.26E
Amstelveen Neth. **16** 52.18N 4.51E
Amsterdam Neth. **16** 52.22N 4.54E
Amsterdam N.Y. U.S.A. **115** 42.57N 74.11W
Amsterdam Ohio U.S.A. **114** 40.28N 80.55W
Amsterdam, Île *i.* Indian Oc. **49** 37.52S 77.32E
Am Timan Chad **73** 11.02N 20.17E
Amu Darya *r.* Uzbekistan **9** 43.50N 59.00E
Amulet Canada **101** 49.40N104.45W
Amundsen G. Canada **98** 70.30N122.00W
Amundsen Sea Antarctica **128** 72.00S120.00W
Amuntai Indonesia **58** 2.24S115.14E
Amur *r.* Russian Fed. **51** 53.17N140.00E
'Amūr, Wādī *r.* Sudan **72** 18.56N 33.34E
Amurrio Spain **26** 43.04N 3.00W
Amurzet Russian Fed. **53** 47.50N131.05E
Amvrakikós Kólpos *b.* Greece **35** 39.00N 21.00E
Anabar *r.* Russian Fed. **51** 72.40N113.30E
Anabranch *r.* Australia **92** 34.08S141.46E
'Anabtā Jordan **67** 32.19N 35.07E
Anaco Venezuela **122** 9.27N 64.28W
Anaconda U.S.A. **108** 46.08N112.57W
Anadarko U.S.A. **111** 35.04N 98.15W
Anadolu *f.* Turkey **64** 38.00N 35.00E
Anadyr Russian Fed. **51** 64.40N177.32E
Anadyr *r.* Russian Fed. **51** 65.00N176.00E
Anadyrskiy Zaliv *g.* Russian Fed. **51** 64.30N177.50W
Anáfi *i.* Greece **35** 36.21N 25.50E
Anagni Italy **30** 41.44N 13.09E
Anaheim U.S.A. **109** 33.51N117.57W
Analalava Madagascar **81** 14.38S 47.45E
Anambas, Kepulauan *is.* Indonesia **58** 3.00N106.10E
Anambra *d.* Nigeria **77** 6.20N 7.25E
Anamoose U.S.A. **110** 47.53N100.15W
Anamur Turkey **64** 36.06N 32.49E
Anan Japan **57** 33.55N134.39E
Ānand India **62** 22.34N 72.56E
Anandpur India **63** 21.16N 86.13E
Anantapur India **60** 14.41N 77.36E
Anantnāg Jammu & Kashmir **62** 33.44N 75.09E
Anápolis Brazil **123** 16.19S 48.58W
Anapú *r.* Brazil **123** 1.53S 50.53W
Anār Iran **65** 30.54N 55.18E
Anārak Iran **65** 33.20N 53.42E
Anār Darreh Afghan. **62** 32.46N 61.39E
'Anātā Jordan **67** 31.49N 35.16E
Anatolia *f. see* Anadolu *f.* Turkey **64**
Anatone U.S.A. **108** 46.08N117.09W
Añatuya Argentina **124** 28.26S 62.48W
Ancenis France **18** 47.22N 1.11W
Anchau Nigeria **77** 11.00N 8.23E
Anchorage U.S.A. **98** 61.10N150.00W
Anchuras Spain **27** 39.29N 4.50W
Ancien Goubéré C.A.R. **73** 5.51N 26.46E
Ancohuma *mtn.* Bolivia **124** 16.05S 68.36W
Ancón Peru **122** 11.50S 77.10W
Ancona Italy **31** 43.38N 13.30E
Ancuabe Mozambique **79** 13.00S 39.50E
Ancud Chile **125** 41.05S 73.50W
Ancy-le-Franc France **19** 47.46N 4.10E
Anda China **53** 46.25N125.20E
Andalsnes Norway **40** 62.33N 7.43E
Andalucía *d.* Spain **27** 37.30N 4.30W
Andalusia U.S.A. **113** 31.20N 86.30W
Andaman Is. India **56** 12.00N 92.45E
Andaman Sea Indian Oc. **56** 10.00N 95.00E
Andamooka Australia **92** 30.27S137.12E
Andanga Russian Fed. **44** 59.11N 45.44E
Andara Namibia **80** 18.04S 21.26E
Andelot France **19** 48.15N 5.18E
Andenes Norway **40** 69.18N 16.10E
Andenne Belgium **16** 50.29N 5.04E
Anderlecht Belgium **16** 50.51N 4.18E
Andermatt Switz. **39** 46.38N 8.36E
Andernach Germany **39** 50.26N 7.24E
Anderson *r.* Canada **98** 69.45N129.00W
Anderson Ind. U.S.A. **112** 40.05N 85.41W
Anderson S.C. U.S.A. **113** 34.30N 82.39W
Anderstorp Sweden **43** 57.17N 13.38E
Andes *mts.* S. America **125** 32.40S 70.00W
Andevoranto Madagascar **81** 18.57S 49.06E
Andfjorden *est.* Norway **40** 68.55N 16.00E
Andhra Pradesh *d.* India **61** 17.00N 79.00E
Andikíthira *i.* Greece **29** 35.52N 23.18E
Andimákhia Greece **35** 36.49N 27.04E
Andíparos *i.* Greece **35** 37.00N 25.03E
Andirrion Greece **35** 38.20N 21.46E
Andissa Greece **35** 39.15N 26.00E
Andizhan Uzbekistan **52** 40.48N 72.23E
Andoany Madagascar **81** 13.25S 48.16E
Andong S. Korea **53** 36.37N128.44E
Andorra *town* Andorra **20** 42.30N 1.31E
Andorra Europe **20** 42.30N 1.32E
Andover U.K. **13** 51.13N 1.29W
Andover N.J. U.S.A. **115** 40.59N 74.45W
Andover N.Y. U.S.A. **114** 42.09N 77.48W
Andover Ohio U.S.A. **114** 41.36N 80.34W
Andöy *i.* Norway **40** 69.05N 15.40E
Andrada Angola **78** 7.41S 21.22E
Andrews N.C. U.S.A. **113** 35.13N 83.49W
Andrews Tex. U.S.A. **111** 32.19N102.33W
Andrews Pt. U.S.A. **115** 42.42N 70.44W
Andreyevo-Ivanovka Ukraine **37** 47.28N 30.29E
Andria Italy **33** 41.13N 16.18E
Andriba Madagascar **81** 17.36S 46.55E
Andrijevica Yugo. **34** 42.45N 19.48E
Andrítsaina Greece **35** 37.29N 21.52E
Androka Madagascar **81** 25.02S 44.05E
Ándros Greece **35** 37.50N 24.57E
Ándros *i.* Greece **35** 37.45N 24.42E
Andros I. Bahamas **113** 24.25N 78.00W
Andros Town Bahamas **117** 24.43N 77.47W
Andrushevka Ukraine **37** 50.00N 28.59E
Andújar Spain **26** 38.03N 4.04W
Andulo Angola **78** 11.28S 16.43E
Anduze France **20** 44.03N 3.59E
Aneby Sweden **43** 57.50N 14.48E
Anefis I-n-Darane Mali **76** 17.57N 0.35E

Anegada to **Arlanzón**

Anegada i. B.V.Is. 117 18.46N 64.24W
Anécho Togo 77 6.17N 1.40E
Aneityum i. Vanuatu 84 20.12S169.45E
Añelo Argentina 125 38.20S 68.45W
Aneto, Pico de mtn. Spain 25 42.38N 0.40E
Aney Niger 77 19.24N 12.56E
Angara r. Russian Fed. 51 58.00N 93.00E
Angarsk Russian Fed. 51 52.31N103.55E
Angaston Australia 91 34.30S139.03E
Angathonísi i. Greece 35 37.28N 27.00E
Angatuba Brazil 126 23.27S 48.25W
Ånge Sweden 40 62.31N 15.40E
Ángel de la Guarda, Isla i. Mexico 109 29.20N113.25W
Angel Falls f. Venezuela 122 5.55N 62.30W
Ängelholm Sweden 43 56.15N 12.51E
Angelica U.S.A. 114 42.18N 78.01W
Angels Camp U.S.A. 108 38.04N120.32W
Ångereb r. Ethiopia 73 13.45N 36.40E
Ångerman r. Sweden 40 63.00N 17.43E
Angermünde Germany 38 53.01N 14.00E
Angers France 18 47.28N 0.33W
Angerville France 19 48.19N 2.00E
Ångesån r. Sweden 40 66.22N 22.58E
Angikuni L. Canada 101 62.00N100.00W
Angkor ruins Cambodia 56 13.30N103.50E
Anglesey i. U.K. 12 53.16N 4.25W
Angleton U.S.A. 111 29.10N 95.26W
Anglin r. France 18 46.42N 0.50E
Ango Zaïre 73 4.02N 25.52E
Angoche Mozambique 81 16.10S 39.57E
Angol Chile 125 37.48S 72.43W
Angola Africa 78 11.00S 18.00E
Angola Ind. U.S.A. 112 41.38N 85.01W
Angola N.Y. U.S.A. 114 42.38N 79.02W
Angoram P.N.G. 59 4.04S144.04E
Angoulême France 20 45.39N 0.09E
Angra dos Reis Brazil 126 22.59S 44.17W
Ang Thong Thailand 56 14.35N100.25E
Anguilla i. Leeward Is. 117 18.14N 63.05W
Angul India 63 20.51N 85.06E
Angumu Zaïre 79 0.10S 27.38E
Anhalt f. Germany 38 52.07N 11.15E
Anholt i. Denmark 42 56.42N 11.34E
Anholt Germany 16 51.51N 6.26E
Anh Son Vietnam 56 18.54N105.18E
Anhua China 55 28.24N111.13E
Anhui d. China 55 32.00N117.00E
Aniak U.S.A. 98 61.32N159.40W
Anie, Pic d' mtn. France 20 42.57N 0.43W
Animas U.S.A. 109 31.57N108.48W
Anin Burma 56 15.40N 97.46E
Anina Romania 37 45.05N 21.51E
Anivorano Madagascar 81 18.44S 48.58E
Anjad India 62 22.02N 75.03E
Anjangaon India 62 21.10N 77.18E
Anjār India 62 23.08N 70.01E
'Anjarah Jordan 67 32.18N 35.45E
Anjō Japan 57 34.57N137.05E
Anjouan i. Comoros 79 12.25S 44.28E
Anjozorobe Madagascar 81 18.24S 47.52E
Anju N. Korea 53 39.36N125.42E
Anka Nigeria 77 12.06N 5.56E
Ankang China 54 32.38N109.12E
Ankara Turkey 64 39.55N 32.50E
Ankaramena Madagascar 81 21.57S 46.39E
Ankarsrum Sweden 43 57.42N 16.19E
Ankazoabo Madagascar 81 22.18S 44.31E
Ankazobe Madagascar 81 18.21S 47.07E
Anklam Germany 38 53.51N 13.41E
Anklesvar India 62 21.38N 72.59E
Ānkober Ethiopia 73 9.30N 39.44E
Ankpa Nigeria 77 7.26N 7.38E
Anlong China 55 25.06N105.31E
Anlu China 55 31.15N113.40E
Anna U.S.A. 111 37.28N 89.15W
Annaba Algeria 75 36.55N 7.47E
Annaberg-Buchholz Germany 38 50.35N 13.00E
An Nabk Syria 66 34.02N 36.43E
Anna Creek town Australia 92 28.50S136.07E
An Nafūd des. Saudi Arabia 64 28.40N 41.30E
An Najaf Iraq 65 31.59N 44.19E
An Nakhl Egypt 66 29.55N 33.45E
An Nakhl Syria 67 33.01N 36.07E
Annam Highlands see Annamitique, Chaîne mts. Laos / Vietnam 56
Annamitique, Chaîne mts. Laos / Vietnam 56 17.00N106.00E
Annan U.K. 14 54.59N 3.16W
Annan r. U.K. 14 54.58N 3.16W
Annandale f. U.K. 14 55.12N 3.25W
Anna Plains Australia 88 19.18S121.34E
Annapolis U.S.A. 115 38.59N 76.30W
Annapurna mtn. Nepal 63 28.34N 83.50E
An Naqīrah well Saudi Arabia 65 27.53N 48.15E
An Nāqūrah Lebanon 67 33.07N 35.08E
Ann Arbor U.S.A. 104 42.18N 83.45W
An Nāşirīyah Iraq 65 31.04N 46.16E
An Nawfalīyah Libya 75 30.47N 17.50E
Annecy France 21 45.54N 6.07E
Annemasse France 21 46.12N 6.15E
An Nīl d. Sudan 72 18.30N 33.10E
An Nīl al Abyad d. Sudan 73 13.10N 32.00E
An Nīl al Azraq d. Sudan 73 13.00N 34.00E
Anniston U.S.A. 113 33.38N 85.50W
Annobón i. Equat. Guinea 127 1.25S 5.36E
Annonay France 21 45.14N 4.40E
Annuello Australia 92 34.52S142.54E
An Nuhūd Sudan 73 12.42N 28.26E
Anoka U.S.A. 110 45.11N 93.20W
Anorotsangana Madagascar 81 13.56S 47.55E
Anou Ti-n Elhaoua well Algeria 75 20.02N 2.55E
Anpu China 55 21.27N110.01E
Anqing China 55 30.40N117.03E
Ansager Denmark 42 55.42N 8.45E
Ansbach Germany 39 49.17N 10.34E
Anshan China 54 41.06N122.58E
Anshun China 55 26.11N105.50E
Anson B. Australia 88 13.10S130.00E
Ansongo Mali 76 15.40N 0.30E
Ansonia U.S.A. 115 41.20N 73.05W
Anstruther U.K. 14 56.14N 2.42W
Ansudu Indonesia 59 2.11S139.22E
Antakya Turkey 64 36.12N 36.10E
Antalaha Madagascar 81 14.53S 50.16E
Antalya Turkey 64 36.53N 30.42E
Antalya Körfezi g. Turkey 64 36.38N 31.00E
Antananarivo Madagascar 81 18.55S 47.31E
Antarctica 128
Antarctic Pen. Antarctica 121 65.00S 64.00W
Antas Brazil 123 10.20S 38.20W
Antela, Laguna de l. Spain 26 42.07N 7.41W
Antequera Spain 27 37.01N 4.33W
Anthony U.S.A. 111 37.09N 89.02W
Antibes France 21 43.35N 7.07E
Anticosti, Île d' i. Canada 103 49.20N 63.00W
Anticosti Prov. Park Canada 103 49.20N 63.00W
Antifer, Cap d' c. France 18 49.41N 0.10E
Antigo U.S.A. 110 45.09N 89.09W
Antigua Guatemala 116 14.33N 90.42W
Antigua i. Leeward Is. 117 17.09N 61.49W
Anti-Lebanon mts. see Sharqī, Al Jabal ash mts. mts. Lebanon 66
Antipodes Is. Pacific Oc. 84 49.42S178.50E
Antlers U.S.A. 111 34.14N 95.47W
Antofagasta Chile 124 23.39S 70.24W
Antônio Bezerra Brazil 123 3.44S 38.35W
Antônio Carlos Brazil 126 21.18S 43.48W
Antonito U.S.A. 108 37.05N106.00W
Antrain France 18 48.27N 1.29W
Antrim U.K. 15 54.43N 6.14W
Antrim d. U.K. 15 54.58N 6.20W
Antrim, Mts. of U.K. 15 55.00N 6.10W
Antrodoco Italy 30 42.25N 13.05E
Antsalova Madagascar 81 18.40S 44.37E
Antsirabé Madagascar 81 19.51S 47.02E
Antsiranana Madagascar 81 12.16S 49.17E
Antsohihy Madagascar 81 14.52S 47.59E
Anttis Sweden 40 67.16N 22.52E
Antwerp see Antwerpen Belgium 16
Antwerp U.S.A. 105 44.12N 75.37W
Antwerpen Belgium 16 51.13N 4.25E
Antwerpen d. Belgium 16 51.16N 4.45E
Anūpgarh India 62 29.11N 73.12E
Anvik U.S.A. 98 62.38N160.20W
Anxi Fujian China 55 25.03N118.13E
Anxi Gansu China 52 40.32N 95.57E
Anxious B. Australia 92 33.25S134.35E
Anyama Ivory Coast 76 5.30N 4.03W
Anyang China 54 36.05N114.20E
Anyer Lor Indonesia 59 6.02S105.57E
Anyi China 55 28.50N115.32E
Anyuan China 55 25.09N115.21E
Anyue China 55 30.09N105.18E
Anzhero-Sudzhensk Russian Fed. 50 56.10N 86.10E
Anzio Italy 32 41.27N 12.37E
Ao Ban Don b. Thailand 56 9.00N 99.20E
Aohan Qi China 54 42.23N119.59E
Aoíz Spain 25 42.47N 1.22W
Aoji N. Korea 57 42.31N130.23E
Aomori Japan 57 40.50N140.43E
Aóös r. Greece 34 40.37N 19.20E
Aopo W. Samoa 84 13.29S172.30W
Aosta Italy 30 45.44N 7.20E
Aoulef Algeria 74 26.58N 1.05E
Aoulime, Jbel mtn. Morocco 74 30.48N 8.50W
Aozou Chad 77 21.49N 17.25E
Apache U.S.A. 111 34.54N 98.22W
Apalachee B. U.S.A. 113 30.00N 84.13W
Apalachicola U.S.A. 113 29.43N 85.01W
Apalachicola r. U.S.A. 113 29.44N 84.59W
Apaporis r. Colombia 122 1.40S 69.20W
Aparri Phil. 59 18.22N121.40E
Apatin Yugo. 31 45.40N 18.59E
Apatity Russian Fed. 44 67.32N 33.21E
Apeldoorn Neth. 16 52.13N 5.57E
Api mtn. Nepal 63 30.01N 80.56E
Apia W. Samoa 84 13.48S171.45W
Apizaco Mexico 116 19.25N 98.09W
Apoka Uganda 73 3.42N 33.38E
Apolakkiá Greece 35 36.04N 27.48E
Apolda Germany 38 51.01N 11.31E
Apollo Bay town Australia 92 38.45S143.40E
Apostle Is. U.S.A. 110 46.50N 90.30W
Apóstoles Argentina 124 27.55S 55.45W
Apostólou Andréa, Akrotírion c. Cyprus 66 35.40N 34.35E
Apoteri Guyana 122 4.02N 58.32W
Appalachian Mts. U.S.A. 114 41.00N 77.00W
Appennino mts. Italy 30 44.33N 9.55E
Appennino Abruzzese mts. Italy 30 42.10N 13.25E
Appennino Ligure mts. Italy 30 44.30N 9.00E
Appennino Lucano mts. Italy 33 40.30N 15.50E
Appennino Tosco-Emiliano mts. Italy 30 44.05N 11.00E
Appennino Umbro-Marchigiano mts. Italy 30 43.05N 13.00E
Appenzell Switz. 39 47.20N 9.25E
Appenzell d. Switz. 39 47.00N 8.05E
Appiano Italy 30 46.28N 11.15E
Appingedam Neth. 16 53.18N 6.52E
Appleby U.K. 12 54.35N 2.29W
Appleton U.S.A. 110 44.16N 88.25W
Apsheronsk Russian Fed. 45 44.26N 39.45E
Apsheronskiy Poluostrov pen. Azerbaijan 65 40.28N 50.00E
Apsley Australia 92 36.58S141.08E
Apsley Canada 104 44.45N 78.06W
Apt France 21 43.53N 5.24E
Apucarana Brazil 126 23.34S 51.28W
Apure r. Venezuela 122 7.40N 66.30W
Apurimac r. Peru 122 10.43S 73.55W
Aqaba, G. of Asia 66 28.45N 34.45E
Aqabat al Ḩijāzīyah Jordan 66 29.40N 35.55E
'Aqdā Iran 65 32.25N 33.38E
'Aqīq Sudan 72 18.14N 38.12E
Aqqikkol Hu l. China 52 35.44N 81.34E
'Aqrabā Syria 67 33.28N 36.20E
'Aqrabah Jordan 67 32.08N 35.21E
Aquidauana Brazil 124 20.27S 55.45W
Aquila Mexico 116 18.30N103.50W
Aquitaine d. France 20 44.40N 0.00
'Ara Israel 67 32.30N 35.05E
'Arab, Baḩr al r. Sudan 73 9.12N 29.28E
'Arab, Wādī al Jordan 67 32.35N 35.35E
Arabādād Iran 65 33.02N 57.41E
'Arabah, Wādī r. Egypt 66 29.07N 32.40E
Arabian Basin f. Indian Oc. 48 12.00N 65.00E
Arabian Sea Asia 60 16.00N 65.00E
Araç Turkey 64 41.14N 33.20E
Aracaju Brazil 123 10.54S 37.07W
Aracanguy, Montañas de mts. Paraguay 124 24.00S 55.50W
Aracati Brazil 123 4.32S 37.45W
Araçatuba Brazil 126 21.12S 50.24W
Aracena Spain 27 37.53N 6.33W
Aracena, Sierra de mts. Spain 27 37.50N 7.00W
'Arad Israel 67 31.15N 35.13E
Arad Romania 37 46.12N 21.19E
Arada Chad 75 15.01N 20.40E
Arafura Sea Austa. 90 9.00S133.00E
Aragarças Brazil 123 15.55S 52.12W
Aragats mtn. Armenia 65 40.32N 44.11E
Aragón d. Spain 25 41.30N 0.30W
Aragón r. Spain 25 42.13N 1.44W
Aragona Italy 32 37.24N 13.37E
Araguacema Brazil 123 8.50S 49.34W
Araguaia r. Brazil 123 5.20S 48.30W
Araguari Brazil 126 18.38S 48.13W
Araguari r. Brazil 123 1.15N 50.05W
Arak Algeria 75 25.18N 3.45E
Arāk Iran 65 34.06N 49.44E
Araka Sudan 73 4.16N 30.21E
Arakan d. Burma 56 19.00N 94.15E
Arakan Yoma mts. Burma 56 19.30N 94.30E
Arákhova Greece 35 38.28N 22.35E
Arakhthros r. Greece 35 39.01N 21.03E
Araks r. Azerbaijan 65 40.00N 48.28E
Aral Sea Asia 9 45.00N 60.00E
Aralsk Kazakhstan 9 46.56N 61.43E
Aralskoye More sea see Aral Sea Asia 9
Aralsor, Ozero l. Kazakhstan 45 49.00N 48.40E
Aramac Australia 90 22.59S145.14E
Arāmbāgh India 63 22.53N 87.47E
Aramia r. P.N.G. 59 8.00S143.20E
Arana, Sierra mts. Spain 27 37.20N 3.30W
Aranda de Duero Spain 26 41.41N 3.41W
Aran I. Rep. of Ire. 15 55.00N 8.32W
Aran Is. Rep. of Ire. 15 53.07N 9.38W
Aranjuez Spain 27 40.02N 3.36W
Aranos Namibia 80 24.09S 19.09E
Aransas Pass town U.S.A. 111 27.54N 97.09W
Araouane Mali 76 18.53N 3.31W
Arapahoe U.S.A. 110 40.18N 99.54W
Arapey Uruguay 125 30.58S 57.30W
Arapey Grande r. Uruguay 125 30.55S 57.49W
Arapiraca Brazil 123 9.45S 36.40W
Arapkir Turkey 64 39.03N 38.29E
Araquil r. Spain 25 42.48N 1.45W
'Ar'ar, Wādī r. Iraq 64 32.00N 42.30E
Araraquara Brazil 126 21.46S 48.08W
Araras Brazil 126 22.20S 47.23W
Ararat Australia 92 37.20S143.00E
Ararat mtn. see Ağri Daği mtn. Turkey 65
Aras r. Turkey see Araks r. Azerbaijan 64
Arauca Colombia 122 7.04N 70.41W
Arauca r. Venezuela 122 7.05N 70.45W
Araure Venezuela 122 9.36N 69.15W
Arāvalli Range mts. India 62 25.00N 73.45E
Araviana Spain 25 41.41N 2.07W
Araviana r. Spain 26 41.35N 2.25W
Araxá Brazil 126 19.37S 46.50W
Araxes r. Iran see Araks r. Azerbaijan 65
Arba r. Spain 25 41.52N 1.18W
Ārba Minch' Ethiopia 73 6.02N 37.40E
Arbatax Italy 32 39.57N 9.42E
Arboga Sweden 43 59.24N 15.50E
Arbois France 19 46.54N 5.46E
Arbon Switz. 39 47.31N 9.26E
Arborea Italy 32 39.47N 8.34E
Arborg Canada 101 50.55N 97.15W
Arbroath U.K. 14 56.34N 2.35W
Arc r. France 21 45.34N 6.12E
Arcachon France 20 44.37N 1.12W
Arcachon, Bassin d' b. France 20 44.40N 1.10W
Arcade U.S.A. 114 42.32N 78.25W
Arcadia Fla. U.S.A. 113 27.12N 81.52W
Arcadia Wisc. U.S.A. 110 44.15N 91.30W
Arcata U.S.A. 108 40.52N124.05W
Arce Italy 32 41.35N 13.34E
Arcevia Italy 30 43.30N 12.56E
Archbald U.S.A. 115 41.30N 75.32W
Archer r. Australia 90 13.28S141.41E
Archers Post Kenya 79 0.42N 37.40E
Archiac France 20 45.31N 0.18W
Archidona Spain 27 37.05N 4.23W
Arcidosso Italy 30 42.52N 11.33E
Arcis-sur-Aube France 19 48.32N 4.08E
Arckaringa r. Australia 92 27.56S134.45E
Arco Italy 30 45.55N 10.53E
Arco U.S.A. 108 43.38N113.18W
Arco de Baúlhe Portugal 26 41.29N 7.58W
Arcoona Australia 92 31.06S137.19E
Arcos Brazil 126 20.12S 45.30W
Arcos Spain 27 36.45N 5.48W
Arcoverde Brazil 123 8.23S 37.00W
Arctic Bay town Canada 99 73.05N 85.20W
Arctic Ocean 128
Arctic Red r. Canada 98 67.26N133.48W
Arctic Red River town Canada 98 67.27N133.46W
Arda r. Greece 34 41.39N 26.29E
Ardabīl Iran 65 38.15N 48.18E
Ardahan Turkey 64 41.08N 42.41E
Årdalstangen Norway 41 61.14N 7.43E
Ardara Rep. of Ire. 15 54.46N 8.25W
Arḑ aş Şawwān f. Jordan 66 30.45N 37.15E
Ardbeg Canada 104 45.38N 80.05W
Ardèche d. France 21 44.40N 4.20E
Ardèche r. France 21 44.16N 4.39E
Ardee Rep. of Ire. 11 53.51N 6.33W
Ardennes mts. Belgium 16 50.10N 5.30E
Ardennes d. France 19 49.40N 4.40E
Ardennes, Canal des France 19 49.26N 4.02E
Ardestān Iran 65 33.22N 52.25E
Ardfert Rep. of Ire. 15 52.20N 9.48W
Ardila r. Portugal 27 38.09N 7.28W
Ardino Bulgaria 34 41.35N 25.08E
Ardlethan Australia 93 34.20S146.53E
Ardmore Rep. of Ire. 15 51.58N 7.43W
Ardmore Okla. U.S.A. 111 34.10N 97.08W
Ardmore Penn. U.S.A. 115 40.01N 75.18W
Ardnamurchan, Pt. of U.K. 14 56.44N 6.14W
Ardrossan Australia 92 34.25S137.55E
Ardrossan U.K. 14 55.38N 4.49W
Ards Pen. U.K. 15 54.30N 5.30W
Åre Sweden 40 63.25N 13.05E
Arecibo Puerto Rico 117 18.29N 66.44W
Areia Branca Brazil 123 4.56S 37.07W
Arena, Pt. U.S.A. 106 38.58N123.44W
Arena, Punta c. Mexico 109 23.32N109.30W
Arenas de San Pedro Spain 26 40.12N 5.05W
Arendal Norway 42 58.27N 8.48E
Arendsee Germany 38 52.53N 11.30E
Arenys de Mar Spain 25 41.35N 2.33E
Areópolis Greece 35 36.40N 22.22E
Arequipa Peru 122 16.25S 71.32W
Arès France 20 44.46N 1.08W
Arévalo Spain 26 41.04N 4.43W
Arezzo Italy 30 43.25N 11.53E
Arfak mtn. Indonesia 59 1.30S133.50E
Arfará Greece 35 37.10N 23.03E
Arga Spain 25 42.18N 1.47W
Argalastí Greece 35 39.13N 23.13E
Argamasilla de Alba Spain 27 39.07N 3.06W
Arganda Spain 26 40.18N 3.26W
Argelès-Gazost France 20 43.01N 0.06W
Argelès-sur-Mer France 20 42.33N 3.01E
Argens r. France 21 43.24N 6.44E
Argenta Italy 30 44.37N 11.50E
Argentan France 18 48.45N 0.01W
Argentat France 20 45.06N 1.56E
Argentera Italy 30 44.24N 6.57E
Argentera mtn. Italy 30 44.10N 7.18E
Argenteuil France 19 48.57N 2.15E
Argentia Canada 103 47.18N 53.59W
Argentina S. America 125 36.00S 63.00W
Argentine Basin f. Atlantic Oc. 127 40.00S 40.00W
Argentino, L. Argentina 125 50.15S 72.25W
Argenton France 19 46.35N 1.31E
Argenton-Château France 18 47.00N 0.27W
Argentré France 18 48.05N 0.39W
Argentré du Plessis France 18 48.03N 1.08W
Argeş r. Romania 29 44.13N 26.22E
Arghandāb r. Afghan. 62 31.27N 64.23E
Argolikós Kólpos g. Greece 35 37.33N 22.45E
Argonne d. France 19 49.30N 5.00E
Árgos Greece 35 37.38N 22.43E
Árgos Orestikón Greece 34 40.27N 21.26E
Argostólion Greece 35 38.10N 20.30E
Arguello, Pt. U.S.A. 109 34.35N120.39W
Argun r. Russian Fed. 53 53.30N121.48E
Argungu Nigeria 77 12.45N 4.35E
Argyle U.S.A. 110 48.20N 96.49W
Ar Horqin Qi China 54 43.45N120.00E
Århus Denmark 42 56.09N 10.13E
Ariah Park town Australia 93 34.20S147.10E
Ariana Tunisia 32 36.52N 10.12E
Ariano Italy 33 41.09N 15.05E
Ariano nel Polesine Italy 30 44.56N 12.07E
Aribinda Burkina 76 14.17N 0.52W
Arica Chile 124 18.29S 70.20W
Arica Colombia 122 2.07S 71.46W
Arid, C. Australia 89 33.58S123.05E
Aridhaía Greece 34 40.58N 22.03E
Ariège d. France 20 43.00N 1.30E
Ariège r. France 20 43.31N 1.25E
Arieş r. Romania 37 46.26N 23.59E
Ārifwāla Pakistan 62 30.17N 73.04E
Arīḩā Al Karak Jordan 67 31.25N 35.47E
Arīḩā Al Quds Jordan 67 31.51N 35.27E
Arima Trinidad 122 10.38N 61.17W
Arinos r. Brazil 123 10.20S 57.35W
Aripuanã Brazil 122 9.10S 60.38W
Aripuanã r. Brazil 122 5.05S 60.30W
Ariquemes Brazil 122 9.56S 63.04W
Aris Namibia 80 22.48S 17.10E
Arisaig U.K. 14 56.55N 5.51W
'Arīsh, Wādī al r. Egypt 66 31.09N 33.49E
Aristazabal I. Canada 100 52.40N129.10W
Arivonimamo Madagascar 81 19.01S 47.15E
Ariza Spain 25 41.19N 2.03W
Arizgoiti Spain 26 43.11N 2.57W
Arizona d. U.S.A. 106 34.00N112.00W
Årjäng Sweden 43 59.23N 12.08E
Arjeplog Sweden 40 66.00N 17.58E
Arjona Colombia 122 10.14N 75.22W
Arjona Spain 27 37.56N 4.03W
Arkadelphia U.S.A. 111 34.07N 93.04W
Arkaig, Loch U.K. 14 56.58N 5.08W
Arkansas d. U.S.A. 111 34.20N 92.00W
Arkansas r. U.S.A. 111 33.48N 91.04W
Arkansas City U.S.A. 111 37.04N 97.02W
Arkhangélos Greece 35 36.13N 28.07E
Arkhangel'sk Russian Fed. 44 64.32N 41.10E
Árki i. Greece 29 37.22N 26.45E
Arklow Rep. of Ire. 15 52.47N 6.10W
Arkösund Sweden 43 58.30N 16.56E
Arkport U.S.A. 114 42.24N 77.42W
Arkville U.S.A. 115 42.09N 74.37W
Arlanc France 20 45.25N 3.44E
Arlanza r. Spain 26 42.06N 4.09W
Arlanzón Spain 26 42.03N 4.17W

Arlberg Pass to **Ault**

Arlberg Pass Austria 36 47.00N 10.05E
Arles France 21 43.40N 4.38E
Arlington Colo. U.S.A. 108 38.20N103.19W
Arlington Oreg. U.S.A. 108 45.16N120.13W
Arlington Tex. U.S.A. 111 32.44N 97.07W
Arlington Va. U.S.A. 114 38.52N 77.05W
Arlington Heights *town* U.S.A. 110 42.06N 88.00W
Arlon Belgium 16 49.41N 5.49E
Armada U.S.A. 114 42.51N 82.53W
Armadale Australia 89 32.10S115.57E
Armagh U.K. 15 54.21N 6.41W
Armagh *d.* U.K. 15 54.16N 6.35W
Armançon *r.* France 19 47.57N 3.30E
Armavir Russian Fed. 45 44.59N 41.10E
Armenia Colombia 122 4.32N 75.40W
Armenia Europe 65 40.00N 45.00E
Armeniş Romania 37 45.12N 22.19E
Armenistís *i.* Greece 35 37.36N 26.08E
Armentières France 19 50.41N 2.53E
Armidale Australia 93 30.32S151.40E
Armori India 63 20.28N 79.59E
Armstrong Canada 100 50.25N119.10W
Armstrong U.S.A. 111 26.55N 97.47W
Ārmūr India 63 18.48N 78.17E
Arnaía Greece 34 40.29N 23.35E
Arnaud *r.* Canada 99 60.00N 69.45W
Arnay-le-Duc France 19 47.08N 4.29E
Arnedo Spain 26 42.13N 2.06W
Årnes Norway 42 60.09N 11.28E
Arnett U.S.A. 111 36.08N 99.46W
Arnhem Neth. 16 52.00N 5.55E
Arnhem, C. Australia 90 12.10S137.00E
Arnhem B. Australia 90 12.20S136.12E
Arnhem Land *f.* Australia 90 13.10S134.30E
Árnissa Greece 34 40.47N 21.49E
Arno *r.* Italy 30 43.41N 10.17E
Arno Bay *town* Australia 92 33.54S136.34E
Arnon *r.* France 19 47.12N 2.03E
Arnot Canada 101 55.46N 96.41W
Årnotfors Sweden 43 59.46N 12.22E
Arnprior Canada 105 45.26N 76.21W
Arnsberg Germany 38 51.24N 8.03E
Arnstadt Germany 38 50.50N 10.57E
Arolsen Germany 38 51.23N 9.01E
Aroma Sudan 72 15.49N 36.08E
Aron *r.* France 19 47.15N 2.02E
Arona Italy 30 45.46N 8.34E
Arorangi Rarotonga Cook Is. 84 21.13S159.49W
Arosa Switz. 39 46.47N 9.41E
Arosa, Ría de *est.* Spain 26 42.28N 8.57W
Arpajon France 19 48.35N 2.15E
Arpino Italy 32 41.40N 13.35E
Arra Ivory Coast 76 6.42N 3.57W
Ar Rabbah Jordan 67 31.16N 35.44E
Ar Rafīd Syria 67 32.57N 35.53E
Arrah India 63 25.34N 84.40E
Ar Rahad Sudan 73 12.43N 30.39E
Ar Ramādī Iraq 64 33.27N 43.19E
Ar Ramthā Jordan 67 32.34N 36.00E
Arran *i.* U.K. 14 55.35N 5.14W
Ar Rank Sudan 73 11.45N 32.48E
Ar Raqqah Syria 64 35.57N 39.03E
Arras France 19 50.17N 2.47E
Ar Rass Saudi Arabia 64 25.54N 43.30E
Ar Rastān Syria 66 34.55N 36.44E
Arrats *r.* France 20 44.06N 0.52E
Arrecife Canary Is. 74 28.57N 13.32W
Arrecifes Argentina 125 34.05S 60.05W
Arrée, Monts d' *mts.* France 18 48.26N 3.55W
Arrey U.S.A. 109 32.51N107.19W
Ar Riyāḍ Saudi Arabia 65 24.39N 46.44E
Arrochar U.K. 14 56.12N 4.44W
Arromanches France 18 49.20N 0.38W
Arronches Portugal 27 39.07N 7.17W
Arros *r.* France 20 43.40N 0.02W
Arroux *r.* France 19 46.29N 3.58E
Arrow, Lough Rep. of Ire. 15 54.03N 8.20W
Arrowsmith, Pt. Australia 90 13.18S136.24E
Arrowtown New Zealand 86 44.56S168.50E
Arroyo de la Luz Spain 27 39.29N 6.35W
Arroyo Feliciano *r.* Argentina 125 31.06S 59.53W
Arroyo Villimanca *r.* Argentina 125 35.36S 59.05W
Ar Ru'at Sudan 73 12.21N 32.17E
Ar Rub' al Khālī *des.* Saudi Arabia 60 20.20N 52.30E
Ar Rubayqī Egypt 66 30.10N 31.46E
Ar Rumaythah Iraq 65 31.32N 45.12E
Ar Rummān Jordan 67 32.10N 35.50E
Ar Ruşayriş Sudan 73 11.51N 34.23E
Ar Ruţbah Iraq 64 33.40N 39.59E
Ar Ruwayḍah Saudi Arabia 65 23.46N 44.46E
Års Denmark 42 56.48N 9.32E
Ars-en-Ré France 20 46.12N 1.31W
Ārsī *d.* Ethiopia 73 7.50N 39.50E
Ársos Cyprus 66 34.50N 32.46E
Árta Greece 35 39.09N 20.59E
Artá Spain 25 39.42N 3.21E
Artemón Greece 35 36.59N 24.43E
Artemovsk Ukraine 45 48.35N 38.00E
Artenay France 19 48.05N 1.53E
Artesia U.S.A. 109 32.51N104.24W
Arthabaska Canada 105 46.02N 71.55W
Arthal Jammu & Kashmir 62 33.16N 76.11E
Arthington Liberia 76 6.35N 10.45W
Arthur Canada 104 43.50N 80.32W
Arthur's Pass New Zealand 86 42.50S171.45E
Artigas Uruguay 125 30.24S 56.28W
Artillery L. Canada 101 63.09N107.52W
Artois *f.* France 16 50.16N 2.50E
Artux China 52 39.40N 75.49E
Artvin Turkey 64 41.12N 41.48E
Aru, Kepulauan *is.* Indonesia 59 6.00S134.30E
Arua Uganda 79 3.02N 30.56E
Aruaddin Ethiopia 72 16.16N 38.46E
Aruanã Brazil 123 14.54S 51.05W
Aruba *i.* South America 117 12.30N 70.00W
Arucas Canary Is. 127 28.08N 15.32W
Arun *r.* U.K. 11 50.48N 0.32W
Arunachal Pradesh *d.* India 61 28.40N 94.60E
Arundel Canada 105 45.58N 74.37W
Arusha Tanzania 79 3.21S 36.40E
Arusha *d.* Tanzania 79 4.00S 37.00E
Aruwimi *r.* Zaïre 78 1.20N 23.36E
Arvada Colo. U.S.A. 108 39.50N105.05W
Arvada Wyo. U.S.A. 108 44.39N105.05W
Arvagh Rep. of Ire. 15 53.56N 7.35W
Arve *r.* France 21 46.12N 6.08E
Arvi India 63 20.59N 78.14E
Arvidsjaur Sweden 40 65.35N 19.07E
Arvika Sweden 43 59.39N 12.35E
Arzachena Italy 32 41.05N 9.22E
Arzamas Russian Fed. 44 55.24N 43.48E
Arzgir Russian Fed. 45 45.24N 44.04E
Arzignano Italy 30 45.31N 11.20E
Arzúa Spain 26 42.56N 8.09W
Ås Norway 42 59.40N 10.48E
Asaba Nigeria 77 6.12N 6.44E
Asadābād Afghan. 62 34.52N 71.09E
Asahi dake *mtn.* Japan 57 43.42N142.54E
Asahikawa Japan 57 43.46N142.23E
Asansol India 63 23.41N 86.59E
Åsarna Sweden 40 62.40N 14.20E
Asarum Sweden 43 56.12N 14.50E
Āsayita Ethiopia 73 11.33N 41.30E
Asbest Russian Fed. 9 57.05N 61.30E
Asbestos Canada 105 45.46N 71.57W
Asbury Park U.S.A. 115 40.13N 74.01W
Ascension *i.* Atlantic Oc. 127 7.57S 14.22W
Aschaffenburg Germany 39 49.59N 9.09E
Aschendorf Germany 38 53.04N 7.22E
Aschersleben Germany 38 51.45N 11.27E
Asciano Italy 30 43.14N 11.33E
Ascoli Piceno Italy 31 42.51N 13.34E
Ascoli Satriano Italy 33 41.12N 15.34E
Ascona Switz. 39 46.09N 8.46E
Āseb Ethiopia 73 13.01N 42.47E
Åseda Sweden 43 57.10N 15.20E
Asedjrad Algeria 75 24.42N 1.40E
Āsela Ethiopia 73 7.59N 39.08E
Åsele Sweden 40 64.10N 17.20E
Åsenbruk Sweden 43 58.48N 12.25E
Asenovgrad Bulgaria 34 42.01N 24.51E
Åseral Norway 42 58.37N 7.25E
Asfeld France 19 49.27N 4.05E
Asha Nigeria 77 7.07N 3.43E
Ashanti *d.* Ghana 76 6.30N 1.30W
Ashaway U.S.A. 115 41.25N 71.47W
Ashbourne Rep. of Ire. 15 53.31N 6.25W
Ashburn U.S.A. 113 31.42N 83.41W
Ashburton *r.* Australia 88 21.15S115.00E
Ashburton New Zealand 86 43.54S171.46E
Ashby de la Zouch U.K. 13 52.45N 1.29W
Ashcroft Canada 100 50.40N121.20W
Ashdod Israel 67 31.48N 34.38E
Asheboro U.S.A. 113 35.42N 79.50W
Ashern Canada 101 51.11N 98.21W
Asheville U.S.A. 113 35.35N 82.35W
Ashewat Pakistan 62 31.22N 68.32E
Ash Flat *town* U.S.A. 111 36.12N 91.38W
Ashford Australia 93 29.19S151.07E
Ashford Kent U.K. 13 51.08N 0.53E
Ash Fork U.S.A. 109 35.13N112.29W
Ashgabat *see* Ashkhabad Turkmenistan 65
Ashikaga Japan 57 36.21N139.26E
Ashington U.K. 12 55.11N 1.34W
Ashiya Japan 57 34.43N135.17E
Ashizuri zaki *c.* Japan 57 32.45N133.05E
Ashkhabad Turkmenistan 65 37.58N 58.24E
Ashland Ky. U.S.A. 114 38.29N 82.39W
Ashland N.H. U.S.A. 105 43.42N 71.38W
Ashland Ohio U.S.A. 114 40.52N 82.19W
Ashland Oreg. U.S.A. 108 42.12N122.42W
Ashland Wisc. U.S.A. 110 46.35N 90.53W
Ashley Australia 93 29.19S149.52E
Ashley U.S.A. 110 38.20N 89.10W
Ashley Snow I. Antarctica 128 72.30S 77.00W
Ashmūn Egypt 66 30.18N 30.59E
Ashoknagar India 63 24.34N 77.43E
Ashqelon Israel 67 31.40N 34.35E
Ash Shabb *well* Egypt 72 22.19N 29.46E
Ash Shāghūr Jordan 67 31.50N 35.39E
Ash Shajarah Jordan 67 32.39N 35.56E
Ash Shallūfah Egypt 66 30.07N 32.34E
Ash Shāmah *des.* Saudi Arabia 64 31.20N 38.00E
Ash Shamālīyah *d.* Sudan 72 19.30N 29.50E
Ash Shāmīyah *des.* Iraq 65 30.30N 45.30E
Ash Shāriqah U.A.E. 65 25.20N 55.26E
Ash Sharmah Saudi Arabia 66 28.01N 35.14E
Ash Shawbak Jordan 66 30.33N 35.35E
Ash Shaykh Faḍl Egypt 66 28.29N 30.50E
Ash Shaykh 'Ibādah Egypt 66 27.48N 30.52E
Ash Shaykh Miskīn Syria 67 32.49N 36.09E
Ash Shiḥr Yemen 71 14.45N 49.36E
Ash Shu'aybah Iraq 65 30.30N 47.40E
Ash Shu'aybah Saudi Arabia 64 27.53N 42.43E
Ash Shumlūl Saudi Arabia 65 26.29N 47.20E
Ashta India 62 23.01N 76.43E
Ashtabula U.S.A. 114 41.52N 80.48W
Ashton R.S.A. 80 33.49S 20.04E
Ashton U.S.A. 108 44.04N111.27W
'Āsī *r.* Lebanon 66 34.37N 36.30E
Asiago Italy 32 45.52N 11.30E
Asilah Morocco 74 35.32N 6.00W
Asinara *i.* Italy 32 41.05N 8.18E
Asinara, Golfo dell' *g.* Italy 32 41.00N 8.30E
'Asīr *f.* Saudi Arabia 71 19.00N 42.00E
Aska India 63 19.36N 84.39E
Askeaton Rep. of Ire. 15 52.36N 9.00W
Asker Norway 42 59.50N 10.26E
Askersund Sweden 43 58.53N 14.54E
Askim Norway 42 59.35N 11.10E
Askvoll Norway 41 61.21N 5.04E
Āsmera Ethiopia 72 15.20N 38.58E
Asnaes Denmark 42 55.49N 11.31E
Åsnen *l.* Sweden 43 56.38N 14.42E
Asola Italy 32 45.13N 10.24E
Āsosa Ethiopia 73 10.03N 34.32E
Asoteriba, Jabal *mtn.* Sudan 72 21.51N 36.30E
Aspe Spain 25 38.21N 0.46W
Aspe, Gave d' *r.* France 20 43.15N 0.29W
Aspen U.S.A. 108 39.11N106.49W
Aspermont U.S.A. 111 33.08N100.14W
Aspiring, Mt. New Zealand 86 44.20S168.45E
Aspres-sur-Buëch France 21 44.31N 5.45E
Asquith Canada 101 52.08N107.13W
Assaba *d.* Mauritania 74 16.40N 11.40W
As Sadd al 'Ālī *dam* Egypt 72 23.59N 32.54E
Aş Şaff Egypt 66 29.34N 31.17E
As Saffānīyah Saudi Arabia 65 28.00N 48.48E
Aş Şāfīyah Sudan 72 15.31N 30.07E
Aş Şa'īd *f.* Egypt 64 25.30N 32.00E
Aş Şāliḥīyah Egypt 66 30.47N 31.59E
As Sallūm Egypt 64 31.31N 25.09E
As Salṭ Jordan 67 32.03N 35.44E
As Salwa Saudi Arabia 65 24.44N 50.50E
Assam *d.* India 61 26.30N 93.00E
As Samāwah Iraq 65 31.18N 45.18E
As Sāmirah *f.* Jordan 67 32.15N 35.15E
As Samū' Jordan 67 31.24N 35.04E
As Sanām *f.* Saudi Arabia 71 22.00N 51.10E
Aş Şanamayn Syria 67 33.05N 36.10E
Aş Şarafand Lebanon 66 33.27N 35.18E
Aş Şarīḥ Jordan 67 32.30N 35.54E
As Sarīrīyah Egypt 66 28.20N 30.45E
Assebroek Belgium 16 51.11N 3.16E
Assen Neth. 16 53.00N 6.34E
Assens Denmark 42 55.16N 9.55E
Asseria *site* Croatia 31 44.02N 15.39E
As Simākīyah Jordan 67 31.18N 35.48E
As Sinbillāwayn Egypt 66 30.53N 31.27E
Assiniboia Canada 101 49.38N105.59W
Assiniboine *r.* Canada 101 49.53N 97.08W
Assinica Prov. Park Canada 102 50.24N 75.00W
Assis Brazil 126 22.37S 50.25W
Assisi Italy 30 43.04N 12.37E
As Sudd Sudan 73 7.50N 30.00E
Aş Şufayyah Sudan 72 15.30N 34.42E
As Sukhnah Jordan 67 32.08N 36.04E
As Sulaymānīyah Iraq 65 35.32N 45.27E
As Sulaymānīyah Saudi Arabia 65 24.10N 47.20E
As Sulayyil Saudi Arabia 71 20.27N 45.34E
As Sulṭān Libya 75 31.07N 17.09E
As Sumayḥ Sudan 73 9.49N 27.39E
Aş Şummān *f.* Saudi Arabia 65 27.00N 47.00E
As Sūq Saudi Arabia 72 21.55N 42.02E
As Suwaydā' Syria 66 32.43N 36.33E
As Suways Egypt 66 29.59N 32.33E
Astaffort France 20 44.04N 0.40E
Astakós Greece 35 38.32N 21.05E
Asti Italy 30 44.54N 8.12E
Astillero Spain 26 43.24N 3.49W
Astipálaia Greece 35 36.32N 26.22E
Astipálaia *i.* Greece 35 36.35N 26.25E
Astorga Spain 26 42.27N 6.03W
Astoria U.S.A. 108 46.11N123.50W
Åstorp Sweden 43 56.08N 12.57E
Astrakhan Russian Fed. 45 46.22N 48.00E
Åsträsk Sweden 40 64.38N 20.00E
Astudillo Spain 26 42.12N 4.18W
Asturias *d.* Spain 26 43.20N 6.10W
Asturias *d.* Spain 26 43.30N 6.00W
Asunción Paraguay 126 25.15S 57.40W
Åsunden *l.* Sweden 43 57.58N 15.50E
'Aşūr, Tall *mtn.* Jordan 67 31.59N 35.17E
Aswān Egypt 64 24.05N 32.56E
Aswan High Dam *see* As Sadd al 'Ālī Egypt 64
Asyūţ Egypt 64 27.14N 31.07E
Atacama, Desierto *des.* S. America 124 20.00S 69.00W
Atacama, Salar de *f.* Chile 124 23.30S 68.46W
Atacama Desert *see* Atacama, Desierto *des.* S. America 124
Atafu Pacific Oc. 84 8.40S172.40W
Atakpamé Togo 77 7.34N 1.14E
Atalándi Greece 35 38.39N 22.58E
Atami Japan 57 35.05N139.04E
Atapupu Indonesia 59 9.00S124.51E
Atar Mauritania 74 20.32N 13.08W
Atara Russian Fed. 51 63.10N129.10E
'Aţārūt Jordan 67 31.52N 35.13E
Atasu Kazakhstan 50 48.42N 71.38E
'Aţbarah Sudan 72 17.42N 33.59E
'Aţbarah *r.* Sudan 72 17.40N 33.58E
Atbasar Kazakhstan 9 51.49N 68.18E
Atchafalaya B. U.S.A. 111 29.25N 91.20W
Atchison U.S.A. 110 39.34N 95.07W
Ateca Spain 25 41.20N 1.47W
Aterno *r.* Italy 31 42.11N 13.51E
Ath Belgium 16 50.38N 3.45E
Athabasca Canada 100 54.45N113.20W
Athabasca *r.* Canada 101 58.40N110.50W
Athabasca, L. Canada 101 59.07N110.00W
Athea Rep. of Ire. 15 52.28N 9.19W
Athenry Rep. of Ire. 15 53.18N 8.45W
Athens Canada 105 44.38N 75.57W
Athens *see* Athínai Greece 35
Athens Ga. U.S.A. 113 33.57N 83.24W
Athens Ohio U.S.A. 114 39.20N 82.06W
Athens Penn. U.S.A. 115 41.57N 76.31W
Athens Tenn. U.S.A. 113 35.27N 84.38W
Athens Tex. U.S.A. 111 32.12N 95.51W
Atherley Canada 104 44.36N 79.22W
Atherton Australia 90 17.15S145.29E
Athínai Greece 35 38.00N 23.44E
Athlone Rep. of Ire. 15 53.26N 7.57W
Athol U.S.A. 115 42.36N 72.14W
Atholl, Forest of U.K. 14 56.50N 3.55W
Áthos *mtn.* Greece 34 40.09N 24.19E
Ath Thamad Egypt 66 29.40N 34.18E
Ath Thanīyah Jordan 67 31.10N 35.43E
Ati Chad 77 13.11N 18.20E
Atico Peru 122 16.12S 73.37W
Atienza Spain 26 41.12N 2.52W
Atikonak L. Canada 103 52.40N 64.30W
Atimaono Tahiti 85 17.46S149.28W
Atkarsk Russian Fed. 45 51.55N 45.00E
Atkinson U.S.A. 113 34.33N 78.12W
Atlanta Ga. U.S.A. 113 33.45N 84.23W
Atlanta Mich. U.S.A. 104 45.00N 84.09W
Atlanta Tex. U.S.A. 111 33.07N 94.10W
Atlantic Iowa U.S.A. 110 41.24N 95.01W
Atlantic-Antarctic Ridge *f.* Atlantic Oc. 127 53.00S 0.00
Atlantic City U.S.A. 115 39.22N 74.26W
Atlantic-Indian-Antarctic Basin *f.* Atl.Oc./Ind.Oc. 49 59.00S 40.00E
Atlantic Ocean 127
Atlas Mts. Africa 22 33.00N 2.00W
Atlas Saharien *mts.* Algeria 75 34.00N 2.00E
Atlin Canada 100 59.31N133.41W
Atlin L. Canada 100 59.26N133.45W
'Atlit Israel 67 32.41N 34.56E
'Atlit *site* Israel 67 32.42N 34.56E
Atmore U.S.A. 111 31.02N 87.29W
Atnarko Canada 100 52.25N126.00W
Atnosen Norway 41 61.44N 10.49E
Atoka U.S.A. 111 34.23N 96.08W
Atouat *mtn.* Laos 56 16.03N107.17E
Atouguia Portugal 27 39.20N 9.20W
Atrå Norway 42 59.59N 8.45E
Atrak *r.* Iran *see* Atrek *r.* Asia 65
Ätran *r.* Sweden 43 56.53N 12.30E
Atrato *r.* Colombia 122 8.15N 76.58W
Atrauli India 63 28.02N 78.17E
Atrek *r.* Asia 65 37.23N 54.00E
Atsugi Japan 57 35.27N139.22E
Atsumi-hantō *pen.* Japan 57 34.40N137.20E
Atsumi-wan *b.* Japan 57 34.45N137.10E
Aţ Ţafīlah Jordan 66 30.52N 35.36E
Aţ Ţā'if Saudi Arabia 72 21.15N 40.21E
At Tall Syria 66 33.36N 36.18E
Attapu Laos 58 14.51N106.56E
Attar, Oued el *wadi* Algeria 75 33.23N 5.12E
Attaviros *mtn.* Greece 35 36.12N 27.52E
Attawapiskat *r.* Canada 102 53.00N 82.30W
Attawapiskat L. Canada 102 52.20N 88.00W
Aţ Ţayrīyah Egypt 66 30.39N 30.46E
Aţ Ţayyibah Jordan 67 31.57N 35.18E
Attendorn Germany 38 51.07N 7.54E
Attersee *l.* Austria 39 47.55N 13.33E
Attica N.Y. U.S.A. 114 42.52N 78.17W
Attica Ohio U.S.A. 114 41.04N 82.53W
Attigny France 19 49.29N 4.35E
Attikamagen L. Canada 103 55.00N 66.38W
'Attīl Jordan 67 32.22N 35.04E
Attleboro U.S.A. 115 41.56N 71.17W
Attleborough U.K. 13 52.31N 1.01E
Attnang Austria 39 48.01N 13.43E
Aţ Ţubayq *mts.* Saudi Arabia 64 29.30N 37.15E
Aţ Ţunayb Jordan 67 31.48N 35.56E
Aţ Ţūr Egypt 66 28.14N 33.36E
Aţ Ţūr Jordan 67 31.47N 35.15E
At Ţuwayrifah *well* Saudi Arabia 71 21.30N 49.35E
Atucha Argentina 125 33.58S 59.17W
Atuel *r.* Argentina 125 36.15S 66.55W
Atui, Uad *wadi* Mauritania 74 20.03N 15.35W
Atui I. Cook Is. 85 20.00S158.07W
Atuona Is. Marquises 85 9.48S139.02W
Åtvidaberg Sweden 43 58.12N 16.00E
Atwater U.S.A. 108 37.21N120.36W
Atwood U.S.A. 110 39.48N101.03W
Aubagne France 21 43.17N 5.34E
Aube *d.* France 19 48.15N 4.05E
Aube *r.* France 19 48.34N 3.43E
Aubenton France 19 49.50N 4.12E
Auberive France 19 47.47N 5.03E
Aubigny-sur-Nère France 19 47.29N 2.26E
Aubin France 20 44.32N 2.14E
Aubinadong *r.* Canada 104 46.51N 83.22W
Aubrac, Monts d' *mts.* France 20 44.40N 3.00E
Auburn Ala. U.S.A. 113 32.38N 85.38W
Auburn Calif. U.S.A. 108 38.54N121.04W
Auburn Ind. U.S.A. 112 41.22N 85.02W
Auburn Maine U.S.A. 112 44.06N 70.14W
Auburn N.Y. U.S.A. 115 42.56N 76.34W
Auburn Wash. U.S.A. 108 47.18N122.13W
Aubusson France 20 45.57N 2.11E
Auce Latvia 41 56.28N 22.53E
Auch France 20 43.39N 0.35E
Auchi Nigeria 77 7.05N 6.16E
Auchterarder U.K. 14 56.18N 3.43W
Auckland New Zealand 86 36.55S174.45E
Auckland *d.* New Zealand 86 36.45S174.45E
Auckland Is. Pacific Oc. 84 50.35S166.00E
Aude *d.* France 20 43.05N 2.30E
Aude *r.* France 20 43.13N 3.14E
Auden Canada 102 50.17N 87.54W
Audenge France 20 44.41N 1.31W
Audierne France 18 48.01N 4.32W
Audincourt France 19 47.29N 6.50E
Audo Range *mts.* Ethiopia 73 6.30N 41.30E
Audubon U.S.A. 110 41.43N 94.55W
Aue Germany 38 50.35N 12.42E
Augathella Australia 90 25.48S146.35E
Augrabies Falls *f.* R.S.A. 80 28.33S 20.27E
Au Gres U.S.A. 104 44.03N 83.42W
Augsburg Germany 39 48.23N 10.53E
Augusta Australia 89 34.19S115.09E
Augusta Italy 33 37.13N 15.13E
Augusta Ga. U.S.A. 113 33.29N 82.00W
Augusta Ill. U.S.A. 110 40.14N 90.56W
Augusta Kans. U.S.A. 111 37.41N 96.58W
Augusta Maine U.S.A. 112 44.19N 69.47W
Augusta, Golfo di *g.* Italy 33 37.10N 15.20E
Augustín Codazzi Colombia 122 10.01N 73.10W
Augustów Poland 37 53.51N 22.59E
Augustus, Mt. Australia 88 24.20S116.49E
Aulis *site* Greece 35 38.27N 23.35E
Aulla Italy 30 44.12N 9.58E
Aulnay France 20 46.01N 0.21W
Aulne *r.* France 18 48.17N 4.16W
Aulnoye-Aymeries France 19 50.12N 3.50E
Ault France 18 50.06N 1.27E

Ault to Bakouma

Ault U.S.A. 108 40.35N104.44W
Aumale France 19 49.46N 1.45E
Aumont-Aubrac France 20 44.43N 3.17E
Auna Nigeria 77 10.11N 4.46E
Auneau France 19 48.27N 1.46E
Auning Denmark 42 56.26N 10.23E
Aura Finland 41 60.36N 22.34E
Auraiya India 63 26.28N 79.31E
Aurangābād Bihār India 63 24.45N 84.22E
Aurangābād Mahār India 62 19.53N 75.20E
Auray France 18 47.40N 2.59W
Aurdal Norway 41 60.56N 9.24E
Aure Norway 40 63.16N 8.34E
Aurich Germany 38 53.28N 7.29E
Aurillac France 20 44.56N 2.26E
Aurora Canada 104 44.00N 79.28W
Aurora Colo. U.S.A. 108 39.44N104.52W
Aurora Ill. U.S.A. 110 41.45N 88.20W
Aurora Mo. U.S.A. 111 36.58N 93.43W
Aursunden *l.* Norway 40 62.37N 11.40E
Aurukun Australia 90 13.20S141.42E
Aus Namibia 80 26.41S 16.14E
Au Sable *r.* U.S.A. 104 44.25N 83.20W
Au Sable Forks U.S.A. 105 44.27N 73.41W
Aust-Agder *d.* Norway 42 58.50N 7.50E
Austin Minn. U.S.A. 110 43.40N 92.59W
Austin Nev. U.S.A. 108 39.30N117.04W
Austin Penn. U.S.A. 114 41.38N 78.05W
Austin Tex. U.S.A. 111 30.16N 97.45W
Austin, L. Australia 88 27.40S118.00E
Austral Downs *town* Australia 90 20.28S137.55E
Australia Austa. 87
Australian Alps *mts.* Australia 91 36.30S148.30E
Australian Antarctic Territory Antarctica 128 73.00S 90.00E
Australian Capital Territory *d.* Australia 93 35.30S149.00E
Austral Ridge Pacific Oc. 85 24.00S148.00W
Austria Europe 39 47.20N 12.30E
Austvågöy *i.* Norway 40 68.20N 14.40E
Authie *r.* France 19 50.21N 1.38E
Autun France 19 46.57N 4.18E
Auvergne *d.* France 20 45.25N 2.30E
Auvézère *r.* France 20 45.12N 0.51E
Aux Barques, Pointe *c.* U.S.A. 104 44.04N 82.58W
Auxerre France 19 47.48N 3.34E
Auxi-le-Château France 19 50.14N 2.07E
Auxonne France 19 47.12N 5.23E
Aux Sables *r.* Canada 104 46.13N 82.04W
Auzances France 20 46.02N 2.30E
Ava Burma 56 21.49N 95.57E
Avaldsnes Norway 42 59.21N 5.16E
Avallon France 19 47.29N 3.54E
Avaloirs, Les *hills* France 18 48.28N 0.07W
Avalon U.S.A. 115 39.06N 74.43W
Avalon Pen. Canada 103 47.00N 53.15W
Avanos Turkey 64 38.44N 34.51E
Avaré Brazil 126 23.06S 48.57W
Avarua Rarotonga Cook Is. 84 21.12S159.46W
Åvas Greece 34 40.57N 25.56E
Avatele Niue 84 19.06S169.55W
Avatele B. Niue 84 19.05S169.56W
Avatiu Rarotonga Cook Is. 84 21.12S159.47W
Ave *r.* Portugal 26 41.20N 8.45W
Aveiro Portugal 26 40.38N 8.39W
Aveiro *d.* Portugal 26 40.50N 8.35W
Aveiro, Ria de *est.* Portugal 26 40.38N 8.44W
Avellaneda Argentina 125 34.40S 58.20W
Avellino Italy 33 40.54N 14.47E
Aversa Italy 33 40.58N 14.12E
Avery U.S.A. 108 47.15N115.49W
Avesnes France 19 50.07N 3.56E
Avesta Sweden 43 60.09N 16.12E
Aveyron *d.* France 20 44.15N 2.40E
Aveyron *r.* France 20 44.05N 1.16E
Avezzano Italy 31 42.02N 13.25E
Aviemore U.K. 14 57.12N 3.50W
Avigliano Italy 33 40.44N 15.44E
Avignon France 21 43.57N 4.49E
Ávila Spain 26 40.39N 4.42W
Ávila *d.* Spain 26 40.35N 5.00W
Ávila, Sierra de *mts.* Spain 26 40.35N 5.00W
Avilés Spain 26 43.33N 5.55W
Avis U.S.A. 114 41.11N 77.19W
Aviz Portugal 27 39.03N 7.53W
Avlum Denmark 42 56.16N 8.48E
Avoca *r.* Australia 92 35.56S143.44E
Avoca Vic. Australia 92 37.04S143.29E
Avola Canada 100 51.45N119.19W
Avola Italy 33 36.54N 15.09E
Avon *r.* Australia 89 31.40S116.07E
Avon *d.* U.K. 13 51.35N 2.40W
Avon *r.*Avon U.K. 11 51.30N 2.43W
Avon *r.* Dorset U.K. 13 50.43N 1.45W
Avon *r.* Glos. U.K. 13 52.00N 2.10W
Avon U.S.A. 114 42.55N 77.45W
Avon Downs *town* Australia 90 20.05S137.30E
Avonmouth U.K. 13 51.30N 2.42W
Avon Park *town* U.S.A. 113 27.36N 81.30W
Avranches France 18 48.41N 1.22W
Avre *r.* France 19 49.53N 2.20E
Awal Edo Ethiopia 73 4.14N 40.39E
Awara Ethiopia 73 5.30N 40.00E
Āwarē Ethiopia 71 8.15N 44.10E
'Awartā Jordan 67 32.10N 35.17E
Āwasa Hāyk' *l.* Ethiopia 73 7.05N 38.25E
Āwash *r.* Ethiopia 73 11.45N 41.05E
Awa shima *i.* Japan 57 38.30N139.20E
Awaso Ghana 76 6.20N 2.22W
Awat China 52 40.38N 80.22E
Awbārī Libya 75 26.35N 12.46E
Awbārī *d.* Libya 75 25.10N 12.45E
Awbārī, Şaḩrā' *des.* Libya 75 27.30N 11.30E
Awdah, Hawr al *l.* Iraq 65 31.36N 46.53E
Awe, Loch U.K. 14 56.18N 5.24W
'Awjā', Wādī al Jordan 67 31.56N 35.31E
Axarfjördhur *est.* Iceland 40 66.10N 16.30W
Axat France 20 42.48N 2.14E
Axel Heiberg I. Canada 99 79.30N 90.00W
Axim Ghana 76 4.53N 2.14W
Axiós *r.* Greece 34 40.35N 22.50E
Ax-les-Thermes France 20 42.43N 1.50E
Axminster U.K. 13 50.47N 3.01W
Ayabaca Peru 122 4.40S 79.53W
Ayachi, Ari n' *mtn.* Morocco 74 32.29N 4.57W
Ayacucho Argentina 125 37.10S 58.30W
Ayacucho Peru 122 13.10S 74.15W
Ayaguz Kazakhstan 52 47.59N 80.27E
Ayamonte Spain 27 37.13N 7.24W
Ayan Russian Fed. 51 56.29N138.00E
'Aybāl, Jabal *mtn.* Jordan 67 32.14N 35.16E
Aydin Turkey 64 37.52N 27.50E
Ayelu *mtn.* Ethiopia 73 10.04N 40.46E
Ayer U.S.A. 115 42.34N 71.35W
Ayers Cliff *town* Canada 105 45.10N 72.03W
Ayers Rock *see* Uluru Australia 90
Ayiá Greece 34 39.43N 22.45E
Ayiá Ánna Greece 35 38.52N 23.24E
Ayiá Marína Greece 35 37.11N 26.48E
Ayía Paraskeví Greece 35 39.14N 26.16E
Áyion Óros *f.* Greece 34 40.15N 24.15E
Áyios Andréas Greece 35 37.21N 22.45E
Áyios Evstrátios *i.* Greece 34 39.34N 24.58E
Áyios Kírikos Greece 35 37.37N 26.14E
Áyios Matthaíos Greece 34 39.30N 19.47E
Áyios Nikólaos Greece 35 35.11N 25.42E
Aylássos Greece 35 39.05N 26.23E
Aylen L. Canada 105 45.37N 77.52W
Aylesbury U.K. 13 51.48N 0.49W
Aylmer Ont. Canada 104 42.47N 80.58W
Aylmer Que. Canada 105 45.23N 75.51W
Aylmer, L. Que. Canada 105 45.50N 71.22W
Aylmer L. Canada 98 64.05N108.30W
Aylsham U.K. 12 52.48N 1.16E
'Ayn, Wādī al *r.* Oman 65 22.18N 55.35E
'Ayn Dāllah *well* Egypt 64 27.19N 27.20E
Ayod Sudan 73 8.07N 31.26E
Ayom Sudan 73 7.52N 28.23E
Ayon, Ostrov *i.* Russian Fed. 51 70.00N169.00E
Ayora Spain 25 39.04N 1.03W
Ayos Cameroon 77 3.55N 12.30E
'Ayoûn el' Atroûs Mauritania 74 16.40N 9.37W
Ayr Australia 90 19.35S147.24E
Ayr Canada 104 43.17N 80.27W
Ayr U.K. 14 55.28N 4.37W
Ayr *r.* U.K. 14 55.28N 4.38W
Ayre, Pt. of I.o.M. Europe 12 54.25N 4.22W
Ayrolle, Etang de L' *l.* France 20 43.05N 3.03E
Āysha Ethiopia 73 10.46N 42.37E
Ayutthaya Thailand 56 14.20N100.40E
Ayvacik Turkey 34 39.36N 26.23E
Ayvalik Turkey 29 39.19N 26.42E
Azaila Spain 25 41.17N 0.29W
Azambuja Portugal 27 39.04N 8.52W
Azamgarh India 63 26.04N 83.11E
Azao *mtn.* Algeria 75 25.12N 8.08E
Azaouâd *des.* Mali 76 18.00N 3.00W
Azaouak, Vallée de l' *f.* Mali 77 16.00N 3.40E
Azare Nigeria 77 11.40N 10.08E
Azay-le-Rideau France 18 47.16N 0.28E
Azbine *mts. see* Aïr *mts.* Niger 77
Azerbaijan Europe 65 40.10N 47.50E
Azogues Ecuador 122 2.35S 78.00W
Azopolye Russian Fed. 44 65.15N 45.18E
Azor Israel 67 32.01N 34.48E
Azores *is. see* Açores, Arquipélago dos *is.* Atlantic Oc. 127
Azoum *r.* Chad 73 10.53N 20.15E
Azov, Sea of Ukraine/Russian Fed. 45 46.00N 36.30E
Azovskoye More *sea see* Azov, Sea of Ukraine/Russian Fed. 45
Azpeitia Spain 26 43.11N 2.16W
Azraq, Al Baḩr al *r.* Sudan 72 15.38N 32.31E
Azrou Morocco 74 33.27N 5.14W
Aztec U.S.A. 109 32.48N113.26W
Azua Dom. Rep. 117 18.29N 70.44W
Azuaga Spain 26 38.16N 5.41W
Azuer *r.* Spain 27 39.08N 3.36W
Azuero, Península de *pen.* Panama 117 7.30N 80.30W
Azul Argentina 125 36.46S 59.50W
'Azūm, Wādī *r.* Sudan *see* Azoum *r.* Chad 73
Azurduy Bolivia 124 19.59S 64.29W
Az Zāb al Kabīr *r.* Iraq 65 35.37N 43.20E
Az Zāb aş Şaghīr *r.* Iraq 65 35.15N 43.27E
Az Zabdānī Syria 66 33.43N 36.05E
Az Ẓāhirīyah Jordan 67 31.25N 34.58E
Az Ẓahrān Saudi Arabia 65 26.18N 50.08E
Az Zaqāzīq Egypt 66 30.36N 31.30E
Az Zarqā' Jordan 67 32.05N 36.06E
Az Zarqā' *r.* Jordan 67 32.08N 35.32E
Az Zāwiyah *d.* Libya 75 32.40N 12.10E
Azzel Matti, Sebkha *f.* Algeria 74 26.00N 0.55E
Az Zilfī Saudi Arabia 65 26.15N 44.50E
Az Zrārīyah Lebanon 66 33.21N 35.20E

B

Baan Baa Australia 93 30.28S149.58E
Baardheere Somali Rep. 79 2.18N 42.18E
Baargaal Somali Rep. 71 11.18N 51.07E
Baarle-Hertog Neth. 16 51.26N 4.56E
Baba Burnu *c.* Turkey 34 39.29N 26.02E
Babadag Romania 37 44.54N 28.43E
Babahoyo Ecuador 122 1.53S 79.31W
Babai Gaxun China 54 40.30N104.43E
Babakin Australia 89 32.11S117.58E
Babana Nigeria 77 10.26N 3.51E
Babanka Ukraine 37 48.41N 30.30E
Babanūsah Sudan 73 11.20N 27.48E
Babar, Kepulauan *is.* Indonesia 59 8.00S129.30E
Babayevo Russian Fed. 44 59.24N 35.50E
B'abdā Lebanon 66 33.50N 35.31E
Babia Gora *mtn.* Slovakia/Poland 37 49.38N 19.38E
Babīna India 63 25.15N 78.28E
Babina Greda Croatia 31 45.07N 18.33E
Babine L. Canada 100 54.48N126.00W
Babo Indonesia 59 2.33S133.25E
Bābol Iran 65 36.32N 52.42E
Baboua C.A.R. 77 5.49N 14.51E
Babuyan Channel Phil. 55 18.40N121.30E
Babuyan Is. Phil. 59 19.20N121.30E
Babylon *ruins* Iraq 65 32.33N 44.25E
Babylon U.S.A. 115 40.42N 73.20W
Bacabal Maranhão Brazil 123 4.15S 44.45W
Bacabal Para Brazil 123 5.20S 56.45W
Bacău Romania 37 46.32N 26.59E
Baccarat France 19 48.27N 6.45E
Bacchus Marsh *town* Australia 92 37.41S144.27E
Bacharach Germany 39 50.04N 7.46E
Bacheli India 61 18.40N 81.16E
Bachelina Russian Fed. 50 57.45N 67.20E
Back *r.* Canada 99 66.37N 96.00W
Bac Kan Vietnam 55 22.06N105.57E
Bačka Palanka Yugo. 31 45.15N 19.24E
Bačka Topola Yugo. 31 45.49N 19.38E
Backbone Mtn. U.S.A. 114 39.18N 79.25W
Bäckefors Sweden 43 58.48N 12.10E
Bački Petrovac Yugo. 31 45.22N 19.35E
Backnang Germany 39 48.56N 9.25E
Backstairs Passage *str.* Australia 92 35.42S138.05E
Bac Lieu Vietnam 56 9.16N105.45E
Bac Ninh Vietnam 56 21.10N106.04E
Bacolod Phil. 59 10.38N122.58E
Bac Phan *f.* Vietnam 56 22.00N105.00E
Bac Quang Vietnam 55 22.30N104.52E
Bácsalmás Hungary 31 46.08N 19.20E
Bács-Kiskun *d.* Hungary 31 46.30N 19.20E
Badagara India 60 11.36N 75.35E
Badajós, Lago *l.* Brazil 122 3.15S 62.47W
Badajoz Spain 27 38.53N 6.58W
Badajoz *d.* Spain 27 38.40N 6.10W
Badal Khān Goth Pakistan 62 26.31N 67.06E
Badalona Spain 25 41.27N 2.15E
Badanah Saudi Arabia 64 30.59N 41.02E
Bad Ausee Austria 39 47.36N 13.47E
Bad Axe U.S.A. 112 43.49N 82.59W
Bad Bergzabern Germany 39 49.07N 8.00E
Bad Blankenburg Germany 38 50.41N 11.16E
Bad Bramstedt Germany 38 53.55N 9.53E
Baddo *r.* Pakistan 62 28.15N 65.00E
Bad Doberan Germany 38 54.06N 11.53E
Bad Dürrenberg Germany 38 51.18N 12.04E
Badeggi Nigeria 77 9.04N 6.09E
Bad Ems Germany 39 50.20N 7.43E
Baden Austria 36 48.01N 16.14E
Baden Ethiopia 72 17.00N 38.00E
Baden Switz. 39 47.29N 8.18E
Baden-Baden Germany 39 48.46N 8.14E
Badenweiler Germany 39 47.48N 7.40E
Baden-Württemberg *d.* Germany 39 48.15N 9.00E
Bad Freienwalde Germany 38 52.47N 14.01E
Badgastein Austria 39 47.07N 13.08E
Bad Godesberg Germany 38 50.41N 7.09E
Bad Hall Austria 39 48.02N 14.13E
Bad Harzburg Germany 38 51.53N 10.33E
Bad Hersfeld Germany 38 50.52N 9.42E
Bad Homburg Germany 39 50.13N 8.37E
Bad Honnef Germany 38 50.39N 7.13E
Badīn Pakistan 62 24.39N 68.50E
Bad Ischl Austria 39 47.43N 13.37E
Badīyah Oman 71 22.27N 58.48E
Bādiyat ash Shām *des.* Asia 64 32.00N 39.00E
Bad Kissingen Germany 39 50.12N 10.04E
Bad Kreuznach Germany 39 49.52N 7.51E
Bad Langensalza Germany 38 51.07N 10.40E
Bad Lauterberg Germany 38 51.38N 10.28E
Bad Mergentheim Germany 39 49.30N 9.46E
Bad Münstereifel Germany 38 50.33N 6.46E
Bad Nauheim Germany 39 50.22N 8.44E
Badnera India 63 20.52N 77.44E
Bad Neuenahr-Ahrweiler Germany 38 50.33N 7.08E
Bad Neustadt an der Saale Germany 39 50.19N 10.13E
Bad Oeynhausen Germany 38 52.12N 8.48E
Bad Oldesloe Germany 38 53.48N 10.22E
Badong China 55 31.02N110.20E
Bad Orb Germany 39 50.14N 9.20E
Badou Togo 76 7.37N 0.37E
Badoumbé Mali 76 13.42N 10.09W
Bad Pyrmont Germany 38 51.59N 9.15E
Bad Ragaz Switz. 39 47.00N 9.30E
Bad Reichenhall Germany 39 47.43N 12.52E
Badrīnāth India 63 30.44N 79.29E
Bad Salzuflen Germany 38 52.05N 8.44E
Bad Salzungen Germany 38 50.48N 10.13E
Bad Sankt Leonhard im Lavanttal Austria 31 46.58N 14.48E
Bad Schwartau Germany 38 53.55N 10.40E
Bad Segeberg Germany 38 53.56N 10.17E
Bad Sülze Germany 38 54.06N 12.38E
Bad Tölz Germany 39 47.46N 11.34E
Badu I. Australia 90 10.07S142.08E
Bad Waldsee Germany 39 47.55N 9.45E
Bad Wildungen Germany 38 51.07N 9.07E
Bad Wörishofen Germany 39 48.00N 10.36E
Baena Spain 27 37.37N 4.19W
Baerami Australia 93 32.23S150.30E
Baeza Spain 27 37.59N 3.28W
Bafa Gölü *l.* Turkey 35 37.30N 27.29E
Bafang Cameroon 77 5.11N 10.12E
Bafatá Guinea Bissau 76 12.09N 14.38W
Baffin *d.* Canada 99 66.00N 72.00W
Baffin B. Canada 99 74.00N 70.00W
Baffin I. Canada 99 68.50N 70.00W
Bafia Cameroon 77 4.39N 11.14E
Bafing *r.* Mali 76 14.48N 12.10W
Bafoulabé Mali 76 13.49N 10.50W
Bāfq Iran 65 31.35N 55.21E
Bafra Turkey 64 41.34N 35.56E
Bafut Cameroon 77 6.06N 10.02E
Bafwasende Zaïre 79 1.09N 27.12E
Bagaha India 63 27.06N 84.05E
Bagamoyo Tanzania 79 6.26S 38.55E
Bagarasi Turkey 35 37.42N 27.33E
Bagasra India 62 21.29N 70.57E
Bagawi Sudan 73 12.19N 34.21E
Bagbele Zaïre 73 4.21N 29.17E
Bagdarin Russian Fed. 51 54.28N113.38E
Bagé Brazil 126 31.22S 54.06W
Baggy Pt. U.K. 13 51.08N 4.15W
Baghdād Iraq 65 33.20N 44.26E
Bāgherhāt Bangla. 63 22.40N 89.48E
Bagheria Italy 32 38.05N 13.30E
Baghlān Afghan. 60 36.11N 68.44E
Baghrān Khowleh Afghan. 62 33.01N 64.58E
Bagnara Italy 33 38.18N 15.49E
Bagnères-de-Bigorre France 20 43.04N 0.09E
Bagnères-de-Luchon France 20 42.47N 0.36E
Bagni di Lucca Italy 30 44.01N 10.35E
Bagnols-sur-Cèze France 21 44.10N 4.37E
Bago *see* Pegu Burma 56
Bagodar India 63 24.05N 85.52E
Bagoé *r.* Mali 76 12.34N 6.30W
Bagolino Italy 30 45.49N 10.28E
Bagrationovsk Russian Fed. 37 54.26N 20.38E
Baguio Phil. 59 16.25N120.37E
Bāh India 63 26.53N 78.36E
Bahamas C. America 113 24.15N 76.00W
Bahāwalnagar Pakistan 62 29.59N 73.16E
Bahāwalpur Pakistan 62 29.24N 71.41E
Baheri India 63 28.47N 79.30E
Bahi Tanzania 79 5.59S 35.15E
Bahia *d.* Brazil 123 12.30S 42.30W
Bahía, Islas de la *is.* Honduras 117 16.10N 86.30W
Bahía Blanca Argentina 126 38.45S 62.15W
Bahía de Caráquez Ecuador 122 0.40S 80.25W
Bahía Kino Mexico 109 28.50N111.55W
Bahía Laura Argentina 125 48.18S 66.30W
Bahía Negra Paraguay 126 20.15S 58.12W
Bahir Dar Ethiopia 73 11.35N 37.28E
Bahraich India 63 27.35N 81.36E
Bahrain Asia 65 26.00N 50.35E
Baḩr al Ghazāl *d.* Sudan 73 8.00N 26.30E
Baḩr al Jabal *r.* Sudan 70 9.30N 18.10E
Bahrām Chāh Afghan. 62 29.26N 64.03E
Bahr Aouk *r.* C.A.R. 77 8.50N 18.50E
Bahr el Ghazal *r.* Chad 77 12.26N 15.25E
Bahr Salamat *r.* Chad 77 9.30N 18.10E
Bāhū Kalāt Iran 65 25.42N 61.28E
Baia-Mare Romania 37 47.40N 23.35E
Baião Brazil 123 2.41S 49.41W
Baia Sprie Romania 37 47.40N 23.42E
Baïbokoum Chad 77 7.46N 15.43E
Baicheng China 54 45.40N122.52E
Baie Comeau Canada 103 49.13N 68.10W
Baie des Ha! Ha! *town* Canada 103 50.56N 58.58W
Baiersbronn Germany 39 48.30N 8.22E
Baies, Lac des *l.* Canada 105 47.18N 77.40W
Baie St. Paul *town* Canada 103 47.27N 70.30W
Baigneux-les-Juifs France 19 47.36N 4.38E
Baihar India 63 22.06N 80.33E
Baijnāth India 63 29.55N 79.37E
Baikunthapur India 63 23.15N 82.33E
Bailén Spain 26 38.06N 3.46W
Băileşti Romania 37 44.02N 23.21E
Bailleul France 19 50.44N 2.44E
Bailundo Angola 78 12.13S 15.46E
Baimuru P.N.G. 59 7.30S144.49E
Bainang China 63 29.10N 89.15E
Bainbridge Ga. U.S.A. 113 30.54N 84.33W
Bainbridge *N.Y.* U.S.A. 115 42.18N 75.29W
Bain-de-Bretagne France 18 47.50N 1.41W
Baing Indonesia 88 10.15S120.34E
Baingoin China 63 31.45N 89.50E
Bains-les-Bains France 19 48.00N 6.16E
Bāir Jordan 66 30.46N 36.41E
Bā'ir, Wādī *r.* Jordan 66 31.10N 36.55E
Baird Mts. U.S.A. 98 67.35N161.30W
Bairin Zuoqi China 54 43.59N119.11E
Bairnsdale Australia 93 37.51S147.38E
Bais France 18 48.15N 0.22W
Baïse *r.* France 20 44.07N 0.17E
Baisha China 55 19.13N109.26E
Baiyang Dian *l.* China 54 38.55N116.00E
Baiyin China 54 36.40N104.15E
Baja Hungary 31 46.11N 18.57E
Baja California *pen.* Mexico 109 28.40N114.40W
Baja California Norte *d.* Mexico 109 29.45N115.30W
Baja California Sur *d.* Mexico 109 26.00N113.00W
Bajánsenye Hungary 31 46.48N 16.22E
Bajina Bašta Yugo. 31 43.58N 19.34E
Bajmok Yugo. 31 45.58N 19.25E
Bakal Russian Fed. 44 54.58N 58.45E
Bakali *r.* Zaïre 78 3.58S 17.10E
Bakel Senegal 76 14.54N 12.26W
Baker Calif. U.S.A. 109 35.16N116.04W
Baker Mont. U.S.A. 108 46.22N104.17W
Baker Oreg. U.S.A. 108 44.47N117.50W
Baker, Mt. U.S.A. 108 48.47N121.49W
Baker I. U.S.A. 100 55.20N133.36W
Baker Lake *town* Canada 99 64.20N 96.10W
Bakersfield *Calif.* U.S.A. 109 35.23N119.01W
Bakersfield Vt. U.S.A. 105 44.48N 72.42W
Bâ Kêv Cambodia 56 13.42N107.12E
Bako Ethiopia 73 5.50N 36.40E
Bako Ivory Coast 76 9.08N 7.40W
Bakony *mts.* Hungary 31 47.00N 17.50E
Bakouma C.A.R. 73 5.42N 22.47E

Baku to **Barrow Creek**

Baku Azerbaijan **65** 40.22N 49.53E
Baky *see* Baku Azerbaijan **65**
Bala Canada **104** 45.01N 79.37W
Bal'â Jordan **67** 32.20N 35.07E
Bala Senegal **76** 14.01N 13.08W
Bala U.K. **12** 52.54N 3.36W
Balabac *i.* Phil. **58** 7.57N117.01E
Balabac Str. Malaysia / Phil. **58** 7.30N117.00E
Ba'labakk Lebanon **66** 34.00N 36.12E
Bālāghāt India **63** 21.48N 80.11E
Bālāghāt Range *mts.* India **62** 19.00N 76.30E
Balaguer Spain **24** 41.50N 0.50E
Balaka Malaŵi **79** 15.00S 34.56E
Balaka Zaïre **78** 4.51S 19.57E
Balaklava Australia **92** 34.08S138.24E
Balaklava Ukraine **45** 44.31N 33.35E
Balakovo Russian Fed. **44** 52.04N 47.46E
Bal'amā Jordan **67** 32.14N 36.05E
Balama Mozambique **79** 13.19S 38.35E
Bālā Morghāb Afghan. **65** 35.34N 63.20E
Balāngīr India **63** 20.43N 83.29E
Balaquer Spain **25** 41.47N 0.49E
Balarāmpur India **63** 23.07N 86.13E
Balashov Russian Fed. **45** 51.30N 43.10E
Balasore India **63** 21.30N 86.56E
Balassagyarmat Hungary **37** 48.05N 19.18E
Balāţ Egypt **64** 25.33N 29.16E
Balaton *l.* Hungary **31** 46.50N 17.45E
Balazote Spain **26** 38.53N 2.08W
Balboa Panama **117** 8.37N 79.33W
Balbriggan Rep. of Ire. **15** 53.36N 6.12W
Balcad Somali Rep. **71** 2.22N 45.25E
Balcarce Argentina **125** 37.52S 58.15W
Balchik Bulgaria **37** 43.24N 28.10E
Balclutha New Zealand **86** 46.16S169.46E
Bald Eagle Mtn. U.S.A. **114** 41.00N 77.45W
Baldock L. Canada **101** 56.33N 97.57W
Baldwin Fla. U.S.A. **113** 30.18N 81.59W
Baldwin Mich. U.S.A. **112** 43.54N 85.50W
Baldwin Penn. U.S.A. **114** 40.23N 79.58W
Baldwinsville U.S.A. **115** 43.09N 76.20W
Baldy Mt. Canada **100** 51.28N120.02W
Balē Ethiopia **73** 6.30N 40.45E
Bâle *see* Basel Switz. **39**
Baleanoona Australia **92** 30.33S139.22E
Baleares *d.* Spain **25** 39.00N 2.10E
Baleares, Islas *is.* Spain **25** 39.20N 2.00E
Balearic Is. *see* Baleares, Islas *is.* Spain **25**
Baleine, Grande rivière de la *r.* Canada **102** 55.20N 77.40W
Baleine, Petite rivière de la *r.* Canada **102** 56.00N 76.45W
Balfate Honduras **117** 15.48N 86.25W
Balfour Downs *town* Australia **88** 22.57S120.46E
Balfouriyya Israel **67** 32.38N 35.18E
Bali India **62** 25.50N 74.05E
Bali *d.* Indonesia **59** 8.45S114.56E
Bali *i.* Indonesia **59** 8.20S115.07E
Bali, Laut *sea* Indonesia **59** 7.30S115.15E
Bali, Selat *str.* Indonesia **59** 8.21S114.30E
Balikesir Turkey **29** 39.38N 27.51E
Balīkh *r.* Syria **64** 35.58N 39.05E
Balikpapan Indonesia **58** 1.15S116.50E
Balingen Germany **39** 48.16N 8.51E
Bali Sea *see* Bali, Laut Indonesia **59**
Balkan Mts. *see* Stara Planina *mts.* Bulgaria **34**
Balkhash Kazakhstan **52** 46.51N 75.00E
Balkhash, Ozero *l.* Kazakhstan **9** 46.40N 75.00E
Ballachulish U.K. **14** 56.40N 5.08W
Balladonia Australia **89** 32.27S123.51E
Ballālpur India **63** 19.50N 79.22E
Ballandean Australia **93** 28.39S151.50E
Ballantrae U.K. **14** 55.06N 5.01W
Ballarat Australia **92** 37.36S143.58E
Ballard, L. Australia **89** 29.27S120.55E
Ballater U.K. **14** 57.03N 3.03W
Ballenas, Bahía de *b.* Mexico **109** 26.45N113.25W
Ballenas, Canal de *str.* Mexico **109** 29.10N113.30W
Balleny Is. Antarctica **128** 66.30S163.00E
Balleroy France **18** 49.11N 0.50W
Ballia India **63** 25.45N 84.10E
Ballina Australia **93** 28.50S153.37E
Ballina Rep. of Ire. **15** 54.08N 9.10W
Ballinasloe Rep. of Ire. **15** 53.20N 8.15W
Ballingeary Rep. of Ire. **15** 51.50N 9.15W
Ballinger U.S.A. **111** 31.44N 99.57W
Ball's Pyramid *i.* Pacific Oc. **84** 31.45S159.15E
Ballybay Rep. of Ire. **15** 54.08N 6.56W
Ballycastle U.K. **15** 55.12N 6.15W
Ballyclare U.K. **15** 54.45N 6.00W
Ballyconnell Rep. of Ire. **15** 54.06N 7.37W
Ballydehob Rep. of Ire. **15** 51.34N 9.28W
Ballydonegan Rep. of Ire. **15** 51.38N 10.04W
Ballygar Rep. of Ire. **15** 53.32N 8.20W
Ballygawley U.K. **15** 54.28N 7.03W
Ballykelly U.K. **15** 55.03N 7.00W
Ballymena U.K. **15** 54.52N 6.17W
Ballymoney U.K. **15** 55.04N 6.31W
Ballyquintin Pt. U.K. **15** 54.40N 5.30W
Ballyragget Rep. of Ire. **15** 52.47N 7.21W
Ballyshannon Rep. of Ire. **15** 54.30N 8.11W
Ballyvaughan Rep. of Ire. **15** 53.06N 9.09W
Ballyvourney Rep. of Ire. **15** 51.57N 9.10W
Balmoral Australia **92** 37.17S141.50E
Balochistān *d.* Pakistan **62** 28.30N 65.00E
Balombo Angola **78** 12.20S 14.45E
Balonne *r.* Australia **93** 28.30S148.20E
Bālotra India **62** 25.50N 72.14E
Balrāmpur India **63** 27.26N 82.11E
Balranald Australia **92** 34.37S143.37E
Balş Romania **37** 44.21N 24.06E
Balsam L. Canada **104** 44.35N 78.50W
Balsas *r.* Brazil **123** 9.00S 48.10W
Balsas *r.* Mexico **116** 18.10N102.05W
Bålsta Sweden **43** 59.35N 17.30E
Balta Ukraine **37** 47.58N 29.39E
Baltanás Spain **26** 41.56N 4.15W
Baltasar Brum Uruguay **125** 30.44S 57.19W
Baltic Sea Europe **41** 57.00N 20.00E
Balţīm Egypt **66** 31.34N 31.05E
Baltimore Canada **104** 44.03N 78.08W
Baltimore Md. U.S.A. **115** 39.17N 76.37W
Baltimore Ohio U.S.A. **114** 39.51N 82.36W
Baltiysk Russian Fed. **41** 54.39N 19.55E
Baluchistan *f.* Pakistan **60** 28.00N 66.00E
Balumbah Australia **92** 33.16S136.14E
Bālurghāt India **63** 25.13N 88.46E
Balygychan Russian Fed. **51** 63.55N154.12E
Balykshi Kazakhstan **45** 47.04N 51.55E
Bām Iran **65** 29.07N 58.20E
Bama Nigeria **77** 11.35N 13.40E
Bamaga Australia **90** 10.52S142.23E
Bamako Mali **76** 12.40N 7.59W
Bamako *d.* Mali **76** 12.40N 7.55W
Bamba Kenya **79** 3.33S 39.32E
Bamba Mali **76** 17.05N 1.23W
Bamba Zaïre **78** 5.45S 18.23E
Bambari C.A.R. **73** 5.45N 20.40E
Bamberg Germany **39** 49.53N 10.53E
Bambesa Zaïre **78** 3.27N 25.43E
Bambesi Ethiopia **73** 9.45N 34.40E
Bambili Zaïre **78** 3.34N 26.07E
Bambio C.A.R. **77** 3.55N 16.57E
Bambuí Brazil **126** 20.01S 45.59W
Bam Co *l.* China **63** 31.30N 91.10E
Bamenda Cameroon **77** 5.55N 10.09E
Bāmīān Afghan. **62** 34.50N 67.50E
Bamingui C.A.R. **73** 7.34N 20.11E
Bamingui Bangoran *d.* C.A.R. **73** 8.30N 20.30E
Bampton Devon U.K. **13** 51.00N 3.29W
Bampūr Iran **65** 27.13N 60.29E
Bampūr *r.* Iran **65** 27.18N 59.02E
Bāmra Hills India **63** 21.20N 84.30E
Baña, Punta de la *c.* Spain **25** 40.34N 0.38E
Banaba *i.* Kiribati **84** 0.52S169.35E
Banagher Rep. of Ire. **15** 53.12N 8.00W
Banalia Zaïre **78** 1.33N 25.23E
Banamba Mali **76** 13.29N 7.22W
Banana Zaïre **78** 5.55S 12.27E
Bananal, Ilha do *f.* Brazil **123** 11.30S 50.15W
Ban Aranyaprathet Thailand **56** 13.43N102.31E
Banās *r.* India **62** 25.54N 76.45E
Banâs, Ra's *c.* Egypt **64** 23.54N 35.48E
Ban Ban Laos **56** 19.38N103.34E
Banbridge U.K. **15** 54.21N 6.17W
Ban Bua Chum Thailand **56** 15.15N101.15E
Banbury U.K. **13** 52.04N 1.21W
Banchory U.K. **14** 57.03N 2.30W
Bancroft Canada **105** 45.03N 77.51W
Band Afghan. **62** 33.17N 68.39E
Banda Gabon **78** 3.47S 11.04E
Banda Madhya P. India **63** 24.03N 78.57E
Bānda Uttar P. India **63** 25.29N 80.20E
Banda, Laut *sea* Indonesia **59** 5.00S128.00E
Banda Aceh Indonesia **58** 5.35N 95.20E
Banda Besar *i.* Indonesia **59** 4.30S129.55E
Bānda Dāūd Shāh Pakistan **62** 33.16N 71.11E
Bandak *l.* Norway **42** 59.24N 8.15E
Bandama *r.* Ivory Coast **76** 5.10N 4.59W
Bandar 'Abbās Iran **65** 27.10N 56.15E
Bandar Beheshtī Iran **65** 25.17N 60.41E
Bandar-e Anzalī Iran **65** 37.26N 49.29E
Bandar-e Deylam Iran **65** 30.05N 50.11E
Bandar-e Khomeynī Iran **65** 30.26N 49.03E
Bandar-e-Lengeh Iran **65** 26.34N 54.53E
Bandar-e Rīg Iran **65** 29.30N 50.40E
Bandar-e Torkeman Iran **65** 36.55N 54.05E
Bandar Seri Begawan Brunei **58** 4.56N114.58E
Banda Sea *see* Banda, Laut *sea* Indonesia **59**
Bandawe Malaŵi **79** 11.57S 34.11E
Bande Spain **26** 42.02N 7.58W
Bandeira *mtn.* Brazil **126** 20.25S 41.45W
Bāndhi Pakistan **62** 26.36N 68.18E
Bandiagara Mali **76** 14.12N 3.29W
Bāndikūi India **62** 27.03N 76.34E
Bandīpur Nepal **63** 27.56N 84.25E
Bandipura Jammu & Kashmir **62** 34.25N 74.39E
Bandirma Turkey **29** 40.22N 28.00E
Bandon Rep. of Ire. **15** 51.45N 8.45W
Bandon *r.* Rep. of Ire. **15** 51.43N 8.38W
Bandundu Zaïre **78** 3.20S 17.24E
Bandundu *d.* Zaïre **78** 4.00S 18.30E
Bandung Indonesia **59** 6.57S107.34E
Banes Cuba **117** 20.59N 75.24W
Banff Canada **100** 51.10N115.34W
Banff U.K. **14** 57.40N 2.31W
Banff Nat. Park Canada **100** 51.30N116.15W
Banfora Burkina **76** 10.36N 4.45W
Bangalore India **60** 12.58N 77.35E
Bangassou C.A.R. **73** 4.50N 23.07E
Banggai, Kepulauan *is.* Indonesia **59** 1.30S123.10E
Banggi *i.* Malaysia **58** 7.17N117.12E
Banggong Co *l.* China **63** 33.45N 79.15E
Banghāzī Libya **75** 32.07N 20.05E
Banghāzī *d.* Libya **75** 25.40N 21.00E
Bangil Indonesia **59** 7.34S112.47E
Bangka *i.* Indonesia **58** 2.20S106.10E
Bangkalan Indonesia **59** 7.05S112.44E
Bangkog Co *l.* China **63** 31.45N 89.30E
Bangkok Thailand **56** 13.44N100.30E
Bangladesh Asia **63** 24.30N 90.00E
Bangor Rep. of Ire. **15** 54.09N 9.44W
Bangor Down U.K. **15** 54.40N 5.41W
Bangor Gwynnedd U.K. **12** 53.13N 4.09W
Bangor Maine U.S.A. **112** 44.49N 68.47W
Bangor Penn. U.S.A. **115** 40.52N 75.13W
Bang Saphan Thailand **56** 11.14N 99.31E
Bangui C.A.R. **77** 4.23N 18.37E
Bangui Phil. **55** 18.33N120.45E
Banguru Zaïre **79** 0.30N 27.10E
Bangweulu, L. Zambia **79** 11.15S 29.45E
Banhā Egypt **66** 30.28N 31.11E
Ban Hat Yai Thailand **56** 7.10N100.28E
Ban Houayxay Laos **56** 20.21N100.32E
Bani *r.* Mali **76** 14.30N 4.15W
Bani, Jbel *mtn.* Morocco **74** 30.00N 8.00W
Banikoara Benin **77** 11.21N 2.25E
Banī Mazār Egypt **66** 28.29N 30.48E
Banīnah Libya **75** 32.05N 20.16E
Banī Na'īm Jordan **67** 31.31N 35.10E
Banī Suwayf Egypt **66** 29.05N 31.05E
Banī Walīd Libya **75** 31.46N 13.59E
Bāniyās Syria **66** 35.09N 35.58E
Bāniyās Syria **67** 33.15N 35.41E
Banja Luka Bosnia-Herzegovina **31** 44.46N 17.11E
Banjarmasin Indonesia **58** 3.22S114.36E
Banjul Gambia **76** 13.28N 16.39W
Bānka India **63** 24.53N 86.55E
Banka Banka Australia **90** 18.48S134.01E
Ban Kan Vietnam **56** 22.08N105.49E
Ban Kantang Thailand **56** 7.25N 99.35E
Bankasse Mali **76** 14.01N 3.29W
Bankeryd Sweden **43** 57.51N 14.07E
Banks I. B.C. Canada **100** 53.25N130.10W
Banks I. N.W.T. Canada **98** 73.00N122.00W
Banks Is. Vanuatu **84** 13.50S167.30E
Banks Pen. New Zealand **86** 43.45S173.10E
Banks Str. Australia **91** 40.37S148.07E
Bānkura India **63** 23.15N 87.04E
Ban-m'drack Vietnam **56** 12.45N108.50E
Bann *r.* U.K. **15** 55.10N 6.46W
Ban Na San Thailand **56** 8.53N 99.17E
Bannockburn Canada **105** 44.38N 77.33W
Bannockburn U.K. **14** 56.06N 3.55W
Bannockburn Zimbabwe **80** 20.16S 29.51E
Bannu Pakistan **62** 32.59N 70.36E
Banon France **21** 44.02N 5.38E
Baños de Cerrato Spain **26** 41.55N 4.28W
Ban Pak Phraek Thailand **56** 8.13N100.13E
Bānsda India **62** 20.45N 73.22E
Banská Bystrica Slovakia **37** 48.44N 19.07E
Bansko Bulgaria **34** 41.52N 23.28E
Bānswāra India **62** 23.33N 74.27E
Bantaeng Indonesia **58** 5.32S119.58E
Banté Benin **77** 8.26N 1.54E
Bantry Rep. of Ire. **15** 51.41N 9.27W
Bantry B. Rep. of Ire. **15** 51.40N 9.40W
Bāntva India **62** 21.29N 70.05E
Banyak, Kepulauan *is.* Indonesia **58** 2.15N 97.10E
Banyo Cameroon **77** 6.47N 11.50E
Banyoles Spain **25** 42.07N 2.46E
Banyuwangi Indonesia **59** 8.12S114.22E
Banzare Coast *f.* Antarctica **128** 66.30S125.00E
Baode China **54** 39.00N111.05E
Baoding China **54** 38.50N115.26E
Bao Ha Vietnam **55** 22.10N104.22E
Baoji China **54** 34.20N107.17E
Baojing China **55** 28.43N109.37E
Bao-Loc Vietnam **56** 11.30N107.54E
Baoshan China **61** 25.07N 99.08E
Baotou China **54** 40.35N109.59E
Baoulé *r.* Mali **76** 13.47N 10.45W
Bāp India **62** 27.23N 72.21E
Bapaume France **19** 50.06N 2.51E
Bāqa el Gharbiyya Israel **67** 32.25N 35.03E
Baqên China **63** 31.56N 94.02E
Ba'qūbah Iraq **65** 33.45N 44.38E
Bar Ukraine **37** 49.05N 27.40E
Bar Yugo. **31** 42.05N 19.05E
Bara Nigeria **77** 10.24N 10.43E
Baraawe Somali Rep. **79** 1.02N 44.02E
Barabinsk Russian Fed. **9** 55.20N 78.18E
Baraboo U.S.A. **110** 43.28N 89.50W
Baracaldo Spain **26** 43.18N 2.59W
Baracoa Cuba **117** 20.23N 74.31W
Baradero Argentina **125** 33.50S 59.30W
Baradine Australia **93** 30.56S149.05E
Baradine *r.* Australia **93** 30.17S148.27E
Baragoi Kenya **73** 1.47N 36.47E
Bārah Sudan **73** 13.42N 30.22E
Barahona Dom. Rep. **117** 18.13N 71.07W
Baraka Zaïre **79** 4.09S 29.05E
Barakaldo *see* Baracaldo Spain **26**
Barakī Barak Afghan. **62** 33.56N 68.55E
Bārākot India **63** 21.33N 85.01E
Bāramūla Jammu & Kashmir **62** 34.12N 74.21E
Bārān India **62** 25.06N 76.31E
Baranagar India **63** 22.38N 88.22E
Baranoa Colombia **122** 10.50N 74.55W
Baranof I. U.S.A. **100** 57.00N135.00W
Baranovichi Belorussia **37** 53.09N 26.00E
Baranya *d.* Hungary **31** 45.55N 18.20E
Baratta Australia **92** 32.01S139.10E
Barbacena Brazil **126** 21.13S 43.47W
Barbadillo del Mercado Spain **26** 42.02N 3.21W
Barbados Lesser Antilles **117** 13.20N 59.40W
Barbar Sudan **72** 18,01N 33.59E
Barbastro Spain **25** 42.02N 0.05E
Barbate *r.* Spain **27** 36.11N 5.55W
Barbate de Franco Spain **27** 36.12N 5.55W
Barberton R.S.A. **80** 25.46S 31.02E
Barberton U.S.A. **114** 41.01N 81.36W
Barbezieux France **20** 45.28N 0.09W
Barbil India **63** 22.06N 85.20E
Barbuda *i.* Leeward Is. **117** 17.41N 61.48W
Barcaldine Australia **90** 23.31S145.15E
Barcarrota Spain **27** 38.31N 6.51W
Barcellona Italy **33** 38.09N 15.13E
Barcelona Spain **25** 41.23N 2.11E
Barcelona *d.* Spain **25** 41.45N 2.00E
Barcelona Venezuela **122** 10.08N 64.43W
Barcelos Brazil **122** 0.59S 62.58W
Barcelos Portugal **26** 41.32N 8.37W
Barcoo *r.* Australia **90** 25.30S142.50E
Barcs Hungary **31** 45.58N 17.28E
Bardai Chad **77** 21.21N 16.56E
Bardejov Slovakia **37** 49.18N 21.16E
Bardi Italy **30** 44.38N 9.44E
Bardīa Nepal **63** 28.18N 81.23E
Bardīyah Libya **72** 31.46N 25.06E
Bardoli India **62** 21.07N 73.07E
Bardonecchia Italy **30** 45.05N 6.42E
Bardsey *i.* U.K. **12** 52.45N 4.48W
Bardu Norway **40** 68.54N 18.20E
Bardufoss Norway **40** 69.00N 18.30E
Bareilly India **63** 28.21N 79.25E
Barellan Australia **93** 34.17S146.34E
Barengapāra India **63** 25.14N 90.14E
Barentsovo More *see* Barents Sea Arctic Oc. **44**
Barents Sea Arctic Oc. **44** 73.00N 40.00E
Barentu Ethiopia **72** 15.04N 37.37E
Barfleur France **18** 49.40N 1.15W
Barfleur, Pointe de *c.* France **18** 49.42N 1.16W
Barga China **63** 30.51N 81.20E
Bargarh India **63** 21.20N 83.37E
Bargas Spain **27** 39.56N 4.02W
Barge Ethiopia **73** 6.15N 37.00E
Barge Italy **30** 44.43N 7.20E
Barghanak Afghan. **62** 33.56N 62.26E
Barguzin Russian Fed. **51** 53.40N109.35E
Barham Australia **92** 35.37S144.10E
Barharwa India **63** 24.52N 87.47E
Barhi India **63** 24.18N 85.25E
Bāri Madhya P. India **63** 23.03N 78.05E
Bāri Rāj. India **63** 26.39N 77.36E
Bari Italy **33** 41.07N 16.52E
Baricho Kenya **79** 3.07S 39.47E
Barika Algeria **75** 35.25N 5.19E
Barīm *i.* Yemen **71** 12.40N 43.24E
Barinas Venezuela **122** 8.36N 70.15W
Baripāda India **63** 21.56N 86.43E
Bariri Brazil **126** 22.04S 48.41W
Bārīs Egypt **64** 24.40N 30.36E
Bari Sādri India **62** 24.25N 74.28E
Barisāl Bangla. **63** 22.42N 90.22E
Barisan, Pegunungan *mts.* Indonesia **58** 3.30S102.30E
Barito *r.* Indonesia **58** 3.35S114.35E
Barjac France **21** 44.18N 4.21E
Barjols France **21** 43.33N 6.00E
Barjūj, Wādī Libya **75** 26.03N 12.50E
Barker U.S.A. **114** 43.20N 78.33W
Barker L. Australia **89** 31.45S120.05E
Bārkhān Pakistan **62** 29.54N 69.31E
Barking U.K. **13** 51.32N 0.05E
Bark L. Canada **104** 46.54N 82.28W
Barkley Sd. Canada **100** 48.53N125.20W
Barkly East R.S.A. **80** 30,58S 27.33E
Barkly Tableland *f.* Australia **90** 19.00S136.40E
Barkly West R.S.A. **80** 28.32S 24.29E
Bar-le-Duc France **19** 48.47N 5.10E
Barlee, L. Australia **89** 29.30S119.30E
Barlee Range *mts.* Australia **88** 23.40S116.00E
Barletta Italy **33** 41.19N 16.17E
Barlow L. Canada **101** 62.00N103.00W
Barmedman Australia **93** 34.08S147.25E
Barmer India **62** 25.45N 71.23E
Barmera Australia **92** 34.15S140.31E
Barm Fīrūz, Kūh-e *mtn.* Iran **65** 30.21N 52.00E
Barmouth U.K. **12** 52.44N 4.03W
Barnagar India **62** 23.03N 75.22E
Barnāla India **62** 30.22N 75.33E
Barnard Castle *town* U.K. **12** 54.33N 1.55W
Barnato Australia **93** 31.38S144.59E
Barnaul Russian Fed. **9** 53.21N 83.15E
Barnegat U.S.A. **115** 39.45N 74.13W
Barnegat B. U.S.A. **115** 39.52N 74.07W
Barnegat Light U.S.A. **115** 39.46N 74.06W
Barnesboro U.S.A. **114** 40.40N 78.47W
Barnesville U.S.A. **114** 39.59N 81.11W
Barnet U.K. **13** 51.39N 0.11W
Barneveld Neth. **16** 52.10N 5.39E
Barneville France **18** 49.23N 1.45W
Barneys L. Australia **92** 33.16S144.13E
Barnsley U.K. **12** 53.33N 1.29W
Barnstable U.S.A. **115** 41.42N 70.18W
Barnstaple U.K. **13** 51.05N 4.03W
Baro *r.* Ethiopia **73** 8.26N 33.13E
Baro Nigeria **77** 8.37N 6.19E
Barpeta India **63** 26.19N 91.00E
Barqah *f.* Libya **72** 31.00N 23.00E
Barquisimeto Venezuela **122** 10.03N 69.18W
Barra Brazil **123** 11.06S 43.15W
Barra *i.* U.K. **14** 56.59N 7.28W
Barra, Sd. of U.K. **14** 57.04N 7.20W
Barraba Australia **93** 30.24S152.36E
Barra do Corda Brazil **123** 5.30S 45.15W
Barra do Piraí Brazil **126** 22.28S 43.49W
Barrafranca Italy **33** 37.23N 14.13E
Barragem Agua Vermelha *resr.* Brazil **126** 19.50S 50.00W
Barragem de São Simão *resr.* Brazil **126** 18.35S 50.00W
Barra Head U.K. **10** 56.47N 7.36W
Barra Mansa Brazil **126** 22.35S 44.12W
Barranca Peru **122** 4.50S 76.40W
Barrancabermeja Colombia **122** 7.06N 73.54W
Barrancas Venezuela **122** 8.45N 62.13W
Barranco do Velho Portugal **27** 37.14N 7.56W
Barrancos Portugal **27** 38.08N 6.59W
Barranqueras Argentina **126** 27.30S 58.55W
Barranquilla Colombia **122** 11.10N 74.50W
Barraute Canada **102** 48.26N 77.39W
Barrax Spain **27** 39.03N 2.12W
Barre U.S.A. **105** 44.12N 72.30W
Barreiras Brazil **123** 12.09S 44.58W
Barreiro Portugal **27** 38.40N 9.04W
Barreiros Brazil **123** 8.49S 35.12W
Barrême France **21** 43.57N 6.22E
Barretos Brazil **126** 20.37S 48.38W
Barrhead Canada **100** 54.10N114.24W
Barrhead U.K. **14** 55.47N 4.24W
Barrie Canada **104** 44.24N 79.40W
Barrie I. Canada **104** 45.55N 82.40W
Barrier Range *mts.* Australia **92** 31.25S141.25E
Barrington Tops *mts.* Australia **93** 32.30S151.28E
Barringun Australia **93** 29.01S145.43E
Barron U.S.A. **108** 48.44N120.43W
Barrow *r.* Rep. of Ire. **15** 52.17N 7.00W
Barrow U.S.A. **98** 71.16N156.50W
Barrow, Pt. U.S.A. **96** 71.22N156.30W
Barrow Creek *town* Australia **90** 21.32S133.53E

Barrow I. to Beloit

Barrow I. Australia **88** 21.40S115.27E
Barrow-in-Furness U.K. **12** 54.08N 3.15W
Barrow Range *mts.* Australia **88** 26.04S127.28E
Barry U.K. **13** 51.23N 3.19W
Barry's Bay *town* Canada **105** 45.30N 77.41W
Barryville U.S.A. **115** 41.29N 74.55W
Barsinghausen Germany **38** 52.18N 9.27E
Barstow U.S.A. **109** 34.54N117.01W
Bar-sur-Aube France **19** 48.14N 4.43E
Bar-sur-Seine France **19** 48.07N 4.22E
Barth Germany **38** 54.22N 12.43E
Bartica Guyana **122** 6.24N 58.38W
Bartin Turkey **64** 41.37N 32.20E
Bartle Frere, Mt. Australia **90** 17.23S145.49E
Bartlesville U.S.A. **111** 36.45N 95.59W
Bartlett L. Canada **100** 63.05N118.20W
Bartolomeu Dias Mozambique **81** 21.10S 35.09E
Barton U.S.A. **105** 44.45N 72.11W
Barton-upon-Humber U.K. **12** 53.41N 0.27W
Bartoszyce Poland **37** 54.16N 20.49E
Bartow U.S.A. **113** 27.54N 81.51W
Bāruni India **63** 25.29N 85.59E
Barwāh India **62** 22.16N 76.03E
Barwāni India **62** 22.02N 74.54E
Barwa Sāgar India **63** 25.23N 78.44E
Barwon *r.* Australia **93** 30.00S148.05E
Barysh Russian Fed. **44** 53.40N 47.09E
Basāl Pakistan **62** 33.33N 72.15E
Basankusu Zaïre **78** 1.12N 19.50E
Basavilbaso Argentina **125** 32.20S 58.52W
Basel Switz. **39** 47.33N 7.35E
Basella Spain **25** 42.01N 1.18E
Baselland *d.* Switz. **39** 47.30N 7.50E
Basento Italy **33** 40.21N 16.50E
Bashi Channel Taiwan/Phil. **55** 21.30N121.00E
Basilan Phil. **59** 6.40N121.59E
Basilan *i.* Phil. **59** 6.40N122.10E
Basildon U.K. **13** 51.34N 0.25E
Basilicata *d.* Italy **33** 40.30N 16.10E
Basin U.S.A. **108** 44.23N108.02W
Basingstoke U.K. **13** 51.15N 1.05W
Basin L. Canada **101** 52.38N105.18W
Baška Croatia **31** 44.58N 14.46E
Baskatong, Résr. Canada **105** 46.48N 75.50W
Basmat India **62** 19.19N 77.10E
Bāsoda India **63** 23.51N 77.56E
Basoko Zaïre **73** 1.20N 23.30E
Basongo Zaïre **73** 4.23S 20.28E
Bas-Rhin *d.* France **19** 48.35N 7.40E
Bassano Canada **100** 50.48N112.20W
Bassano Italy **30** 45.46N 11.44E
Bassari Togo **76** 9.12N 0.18E
Bassein Burma **56** 16.46N 94.45E
Basse-Kotto *d.* C.A.R. **73** 5.00N 21.30E
Basse Normandie *d.* France **18** 49.00N 0.00
Basse Santa Su Gambia **76** 13.23N 14.15W
Basse-Terre Guadeloupe **117** 16.00N 61.43W
Bassett U.S.A. **110** 42.35N 99.32W
Basse-Yutz France **19** 49.21N 6.11E
Bass Is. U.S.A. **114** 41.42N 82.49W
Bass Str. Australia **91** 39.45S146.00E
Bassum Germany **38** 52.51N 8.43E
Båstad Sweden **43** 56.26N 12.51E
Bastak Iran **65** 27.15N 54.26E
Bastelica France **21** 42.00N 9.02E
Basti India **63** 26.48N 82.43E
Bastia France **21** 42.42N 9.27E
Bastogne Belgium **16** 50.00N 5.43E
Bastrop U.S.A. **111** 32.47N 91.55W
Basyūn Egypt **66** 30.57N 30.49E
Bas Zaïre *d.* Zaïre **78** 5.15S 14.00E
Bata Equat. Guinea **78** 1.51N 9.49E
Batabanó, Golfo de *g.* Cuba **117** 23.15N 82.30W
Batak Bulgaria **34** 41.57N 24.12E
Batak, Yazovir *l.* Bulgaria **34** 42.00N 24.11E
Batāla India **62** 31.48N 75.13E
Batalha Portugal **27** 39.39N 8.50W
Batang China **61** 30.02N 99.01E
Batangafo C.A.R. **77** 7.27N 18.11E
Batangas Phil. **59** 13.46N121.01E
Batan Is. Phil. **59** 20.50N121.55E
Bátaszék Hungary **31** 46.12N 18.44E
Batatais Brazil **126** 20.54S 47.37W
Batavia U.S.A. **114** 43.00N 78.11W
Bataysk Russian Fed. **45** 47.09N 39.46E
Batchawana Canada **104** 46.54N 84.34W
Batchawana *r.* Canada **104** 46.55N 84.32W
Batchawana I. Canada **104** 46.45N 84.14W
Batchawana Mtn. Canada **104** 47.04N 84.24W
Batchelor Australia **90** 13.04S131.01E
Bătdâmbâng Cambodia **56** 13.06N103.12E
Batemans Bay *town* Australia **93** 35.55S150.09E
Batesville Ark. U.S.A. **111** 35.46N 91.39W
Batesville Miss. U.S.A. **111** 34.18N 90.00W
Bath N.B. Canada **103** 46.31N 67.37W
Bath Ont. Canada **105** 44.11N 76.47W
Bath U.K. **13** 51.22N 2.22W
Bath Maine U.S.A. **112** 43.55N 69.49W
Bath N.Y. U.S.A. **114** 42.20N 77.19W
Batha *d.* Chad **77** 14.30N 18.30E
Batha *r.* Chad **77** 12.47N 17.34E
Baṭḥā, Wādī al *r.* Oman **65** 20.01N 59.39E
Bathgate U.K. **14** 55.44N 3.38W
Bathurst Australia **93** 33.27S149.35E
Bathurst Canada **103** 47.36N 65.39W
Bathurst R.S.A. **80** 33.30S 26.48E
Bathurst, C. Canada **98** 70.30N128.00W
Bathurst I. Australia **88** 11.45S130.15E
Bathurst I. Canada **99** 76.00N100.00W
Bathurst Inlet *town* Canada **98** 66.48N108.00W
Batibla C.A.R. **73** 5.56N 21.09E
Batié Burkina **76** 9.42N 2.53W
Batina Croatia **31** 45.51N 18.51E
Batīr Jordan **67** 31.16N 35.42E
Batiscan *r.* Canada **105** 46.31N 72.15W
Batley U.K. **12** 53.43N 1.38W
Batlow Australia **93** 35.32S148.10E
Batman Turkey **64** 37.52N 41.07E
Batna Algeria **75** 35.35N 6.11E
Baton Rouge U.S.A. **111** 30.23N 91.11W
Batopilas Mexico **109** 27.00N107.45W
Batouri Cameroon **77** 4.26N 14.27E
Bat Shelomo Israel **67** 32.36N 35.00E
Batson U.S.A. **111** 30.15N 94.37W
Batticaloa Sri Lanka **61** 7.43N 81.42E
Battle *r.* Canada **101** 52.43N108.15W
Battle U.K. **13** 50.55N 0.30E
Battle Creek *town* U.S.A. **112** 42.20N 85.11W
Battleford Canada **101** 52.45N108.15W
Battle Harbour Canada **103** 52.17N 55.35W
Batu *mtn.* Ethiopia **73** 6.55N 39.46E
Batu, Kepulauan *is.* Indonesia **58** 0.30S 98.20E
Batumi Georgia **64** 41.37N 41.36E
Batu Pahat Malaysia **58** 1.50N102.48E
Baturaja Indonesia **58** 4.10S104.10E
Baturité Brazil **123** 4.20S 38.53W
Bat Yam Israel **67** 32.01N 34.45E
Baubau Indonesia **59** 5.30S122.37E
Bauchi Nigeria **77** 10.16N 9.50E
Bauchi *d.* Nigeria **77** 10.40N 10.00E
Baud France **18** 47.52N 3.01W
Baudh India **63** 20.50N 84.19E
Baugé France **18** 47.33N 0.06W
Bauld, C. Canada **103** 51.38N 55.25W
Baume-les-Dames France **19** 47.21N 6.22E
Baunei Italy **32** 40.02N 9.40E
Bauru Brazil **126** 22.19S 49.07W
Baús Brazil **126** 18.19S 53.10W
Bauska Latvia **41** 56.24N 24.14E
Bautzen Germany **38** 51.11N 14.26E
Bavay France **16** 50.18N 3.48E
Båven *l.* Sweden **43** 59.01N 16.56E
Bawean *i.* Indonesia **59** 5.50S112.39E
Bawku Ghana **76** 11.05N 0.13W
Bayamo Cuba **117** 20.23N 76.39W
Bayamón Puerto Rico **117** 18.24N 66.10W
Bāyan, Band-e *mts.* Afghan. **62** 34.20N 65.00E
Bayāna India **62** 26.54N 77.17E
Bayan Har Shan *mts.* China **52** 34.00N 97.20E
Bayan Nur China **54** 38.14N103.56E
Bayard U.S.A. **114** 39.16N 79.22W
Bayburt Turkey **64** 40.15N 40.16E
Bay City Mich. U.S.A. **104** 43.36N 83.53W
Bay City Tex. U.S.A. **111** 28.59N 95.58W
Baydaratskaya Guba *b.* Russian Fed. **50** 70.00N 66.00E
Baydhabo Somali Rep. **79** 3.08N 43.34E
Bayerische Alpen *mts.* Germany **39** 47.38N 11.30E
Bayerischer Wald *mts.* Germany **39** 49.00N 12.50E
Bayern *d.* Germany **38** 49.06N 11.30E
Bayeux France **18** 49.17N 0.42W
Bayfield Canada **104** 43.33N 81.41W
Bayfield U.S.A. **110** 46.49N 90.49W
Baykal, Ozero *l.* Russian Fed. **52** 53.30N100.00E
Baykit Russian Fed. **51** 61.45N 96.22E
Baykonyr Kazakhstan **50** 47.50N 66.03E
Bayo Spain **26** 43.09N 8.58W
Bay of Plenty *d.* New Zealand **86** 38.00S177.10E
Bayombong Phil. **59** 16.27N121.10E
Bayon France **19** 48.29N 6.19E
Bayona Spain **26** 42.07N 8.51W
Bayonne France **20** 43.29N 1.29W
Bayovar Peru **122** 5.50S 81.03W
Bay Port U.S.A. **104** 43.51N 83.23W
Bayramic Greece **34** 39.48N 26.37E
Bayreuth Germany **38** 49.57N 11.35E
Bayrischzell Germany **39** 47.40N 12.00E
Bayrūt Lebanon **66** 33.52N 35.30E
Bays, L. of Canada **104** 45.15N 79.04W
Bay Shore U.S.A. **115** 40.44N 73.15W
Baysville Canada **104** 45.09N 79.10W
Baytā al Fawqā Jordan **67** 32.09N 35.17E
Bayt Awlā Jordan **67** 31.36N 35.02E
Bayt Ḥānūn Egypt **67** 31.32N 34.32E
Baytik Shan *mts.* China **52** 45.15N 90.50E
Bayt Immar Jordan **67** 31.37N 35.06E
Bayt Jālā Jordan **67** 31.43N 35.11E
Bayt Lāhiyah Egypt **67** 31.33N 34.30E
Bayt Laḥm Jordan **67** 31.43N 35.12E
Baytown U.S.A. **111** 29.44N 94.58W
Bayt Rīmā Jordan **67** 32.02N 35.06E
Baytūniyā Jordan **67** 31.53N 35.10E
Bay View New Zealand **86** 39.26S176.52E
Bay Village U.S.A. **114** 41.29N 81.55W
Baza Spain **27** 37.29N 2.46W
Baza, Sierra de *mts.* Spain **27** 37.20N 2.45W
Bazaliya Ukraine **37** 49.42N 26.29E
Bazaruto, Ilha do *i.* Mozambique **81** 21.40S 35.28E
Bazas France **20** 44.26N 0.13W
Bazdār Pakistan **62** 26.21N 65.03E
Bazhong China **55** 31.51N106.42E
Bazièae France **20** 43.27N 1.37E
Bazmān Iran **65** 27.48N 60.12E
Bazmān, Kūh-e *mtn.* Iran **65** 28.06N 60.00E
Beach U.S.A. **110** 46.55N103.52W
Beachburg Canada **105** 45.43N 76.53W
Beach Haven U.S.A. **115** 39.34N 74.14W
Beachport Australia **92** 37.29S140.01E
Beachwood U.S.A. **115** 39.56N 74.12W
Beachy Head U.K. **13** 50.43N 0.15E
Beacon U.S.A. **115** 41.30N 73.58W
Beagle Bay *town* Australia **88** 16.58S122.40E
Bealanana Madagascar **81** 14.33S 48.44E
Bear Brook State Park U.S.A. **115** 43.05N 71.26W
Beardstown U.S.A. **110** 40.01N 90.26W
Bear I. *see* Bjørnøya *i.* Arctic Oc. **128**
Bear Island *town* Canada **104** 46.59N 80.05W
Bear L. U.S.A. **108** 42.00N111.20W
Bearskin Lake *town* Canada **102** 53.58N 91.02W
Beas *r.* India **62** 31.10N 75.00E
Beasain Spain **26** 43.03N 2.11W
Beas de Segura Spain **26** 38.15N 2.53W
Beatrice U.S.A. **110** 40.16N 96.44W
Beatrice, C. Australia **90** 14.15S136.59E
Beatton *r.* Canada **100** 56.15N120.45W
Beatton River *town* Canada **100** 57.26N121.20W
Beatty U.S.A. **108** 36.54N116.46W
Beattyville Canada **102** 48.53N 77.10W
Beaucaire France **21** 43.48N 4.38E
Beauce *f.* France **19** 48.22N 1.50E
Beauchêne Canada **104** 46.39N 78.55W
Beaudesert Australia **93** 27.58S153.01E
Beaufort Australia **92** 37.28S143.28E
Beaufort U.S.A. **113** 32.26N 80.40W
Beaufort Sea N. America **98** 72.00N141.00W
Beaufort West R.S.A. **80** 32.20S 22.34E
Beaugency France **19** 47.47N 1.38E
Beauharnois Canada **105** 45.19N 73.52W
Beaujolais, Monts du *mts.* France **21** 46.00N 4.30E
Beaulieu *r.* Canada **100** 62.03N113.11W
Beauly U.K. **14** 57.29N 4.29W
Beauly *r.* U.K. **14** 57.29N 4.25W
Beaumaris U.K. **12** 53.16N 4.07W
Beaumetz-lès-Loges France **19** 50.14N 2.39E
Beaumont Belgium **16** 50.14N 4.16E
Beaumont France **18** 49.40N 1.51W
Beaumont Miss. U.S.A. **111** 31.11N 88.55W
Beaumont Tex. U.S.A. **111** 30.05N 94.06W
Beaumont-le-Roger France **18** 49.05N 0.47E
Beaumont-sur-Sarthe France **18** 48.13N 0.08E
Beaune France **19** 47.02N 4.50E
Beaune-la-Rolande France **19** 48.04N 2.26E
Beaupréau France **18** 47.12N 1.00W
Beaurepaire France **21** 45.20N 5.03E
Beauséjour Canada **101** 50.04N 96.33W
Beauvais France **19** 49.26N 2.05E
Beauval Canada **101** 55.09N107.35W
Beauville France **20** 44.17N 0.52E
Beauvoir France **18** 46.55N 2.02W
Beauvoir-sur-Niort France **18** 46.11N 0.28W
Beaver *r.* N.W.T. Canada **100** 59.43N124.16W
Beaver *r.* Ont. Canada **102** 55.55N 87.50W
Beaver Alaska U.S.A. **98** 66.22N147.24W
Beaver Okla. U.S.A. **111** 36.49N100.31W
Beaver Penn. U.S.A. **114** 40.42N 80.18W
Beaver *r.* U.S.A. **114** 40.40N 80.18W
Beaver Dam *town* U.S.A. **110** 43.28N 88.50W
Beaver Falls *town* U.S.A. **114** 40.46N 80.19W
Beaverhill L. Alta. Canada **100** 53.27N112.32W
Beaverhill L. N.W.T. Canada **101** 63.02N104.22W
Beaver I. U.S.A. **112** 45.42N 85.28W
Beaverton Canada **104** 44.26N 79.09W
Beaverton U.S.A. **104** 43.53N 84.29W
Beāwar India **62** 26.06N 74.19E
Bebedouro Brazil **126** 20.54S 48.31W
Bebington U.K. **12** 53.23N 3.01W
Bécancour Canada **105** 46.20N 72.26W
Beccles U.K. **13** 52.27N 1.33E
Bečej Yugo. **31** 45.37N 20.03E
Béchar Algeria **74** 31.37N 2.13W
Bechater Tunisia **32** 37.18N 9.45E
Bechet Romania **34** 43.46N 23.58E
Beckley U.S.A. **113** 37.46N 81.12W
Beckum Germany **38** 51.45N 8.02E
Beclean Romania **37** 47.11N 24.10E
Bédarieux France **20** 43.37N 3.09E
Bedēsa Ethiopia **73** 8.50N 40.45E
Bedford Canada **105** 45.07N 72.59W
Bedford U.K. **13** 52.08N 0.29W
Bedford U.S.A. **114** 40.01N 78.30W
Bedford, C. Australia **90** 15.14S145.21E
Bedford Levels *f.* U.K. **13** 52.35N 0.08W
Bedfordshire *d.* U.K. **13** 52.04N 0.28W
Bedi India **62** 22.30N 70.02E
Bedlington U.K. **12** 55.08N 1.34W
Bedourie Australia **90** 24.21S139.28E
Beech Grove U.S.A. **112** 39.42N 86.06W
Beechworth Australia **93** 36.23S146.42E
Beenleigh Australia **93** 27.43S153.09E
Be'eri Israel **67** 31.25N 34.29E
Be'er Menuha Israel **66** 30.19N 35.08E
Be'erotayim Israel **67** 32.19N 34.59E
Be'er Sheva' Israel **67** 31.15N 34.47E
Be'er Sheva', Nahal *wadi* Israel **67** 31.11N 34.35E
Beerta Neth. **16** 53.12N 7.07E
Be'er Toviyya Israel **67** 31.44N 34.44E
Beeskow Germany **38** 52.10N 14.14E
Beeston U.K. **12** 52.55N 1.11W
Beeville U.S.A. **111** 28.24N 97.45W
Befale Zaïre **78** 0.27N 21.01E
Befandriana Madagascar **81** 15.16S 48.32E
Befandriana Madagascar **81** 22.06S 43.54E
Beg, Lough U.K. **15** 54.47N 6.29W
Bega Australia **93** 36.41S149.50E
Begamganj India **63** 23.36N 78.20E
Bègles France **20** 44.47N 0.34W
Begna *r.* Norway **42** 60.10N 10.18E
Begur, Cap de *c.* Spain **25** 41.57N 3.14E
Begusarai India **63** 25.25N 86.08E
Behara Madagascar **81** 25.00S 46.25E
Behbehān Iran **65** 30.35N 50.17E
Bei'an China **53** 48.17N126.33E
Beihai China **55** 21.29N109.09E
Bei Jiang *r.* China **55** 23.19N112.51E
Beijing China **54** 39.55N116.25E
Beijing *d.* China **54** 40.00N140.01E
Beijing Shi *d.* China **53** 40.15N116.30E
Beilen Neth. **16** 52.51N 6.31E
Beinn Dearg *mtn.* U.K. **14** 57.47N 4.55W
Beipa'a P.N.G. **90** 8.30S146.35E
Beipiao China **54** 41.47N120.44E
Beira Mozambique **81** 19.49S 34.52E
Beirut *see* Bayrūt Lebanon **66**
Beitang China **54** 39.06N117.43E
Beitbridge Zimbabwe **80** 22.10S 30.01E
Beit Jann Israel **67** 32.58N 35.23E
Beiuş Romania **37** 46.40N 22.21E
Beja Portugal **27** 38.01N 7.52W
Beja *d.* Portugal **27** 37.50N 7.55W
Béja Tunisia **32** 36.44N 9.11E
Bejaïa Algeria **75** 36.45N 5.05E
Béjar Spain **26** 40.23N 5.46W
Bejestān Iran **65** 34.32N 58.08E
Bejhi *r.* Pakistan **62** 29.47N 67.58E
Bejoording Australia **89** 31.22S116.30E
Békés Hungary **37** 46.46N 21.08E
Békéscsaba Hungary **37** 46.41N 21.06E
Bekily Madagascar **81** 24.13S 45.19E
Bela India **63** 25.56N 81.59E
Bela Pakistan **62** 26.14N 66.19E
Bélabo Cameroon **77** 5.00N 13.20E
Bela Crkva Yugo. **37** 44.54N 21.26E
Bel Air U.S.A. **115** 39.32N 76.21W
Belalcázar Spain **26** 38.34N 5.10W
Belampalli India **63** 19.02N 79.30E
Belang Indonesia **59** 0.58N124.56E
Bela Palanka Yugo. **34** 43.13N 22.17E
Bela Vista Brazil **124** 22.05S 56.22W
Bela Vista Mozambique **81** 26.20S 32.41E
Belaya *r.* Russian Fed. **50** 55.40N 52.30E
Belaya Glina Russian Fed. **45** 46.04N 40.54E
Belaya Tserkov Ukraine **37** 49.49N 30.10E
Belcher Is. Canada **102** 56.00N 79.00W
Belchite Spain **25** 41.18N 0.45W
Belcoo U.K. **15** 54.18N 7.53W
Belda India **63** 22.05N 87.21E
Belebey Russian Fed. **44** 54.05N 54.07E
Beled Weyne Somali Rep. **71** 4.47N 45.12E
Belém Brazil **123** 1.27S 48.29W
Belem Mozambique **81** 14.11S 35.59E
Belén Uruguay **125** 30.47S 57.47W
Belen U.S.A. **109** 34.40N106.46W
Belén, Cuchilla de *mts.* Uruguay **125** 30.49S 56.28W
Belene Bulgaria **34** 43.39N 25.07E
Beles *r.* Ethiopia **71** 11.10N 35.10E
Belev Russian Fed. **44** 53.50N 36.08E
Belfast U.K. **15** 54.36N 5.57W
Belfast Maine U.S.A. **112** 44.27N 69.01W
Belfast N.Y. U.S.A. **114** 42.21N 78.07W
Belfast Lough U.K. **15** 54.42N 5.45W
Belfield U.S.A. **110** 46.53N103.12W
Belfort France **17** 47.38N 6.52E
Belfry U.S.A. **108** 45.09N109.01W
Belgaum India **60** 15.54N 74.36E
Belgium Europe **16** 51.00N 4.30E
Belgodere France **21** 42.35N 9.01E
Belgorod Russian Fed. **23** 50.38N 36.36E
Belgorod-Dnestrovskiy Ukraine **37** 46.10N 30.19E
Belgrade *see* Beograd Yugo. **37**
Beli Nigeria **77** 7.53N 10.59E
Beli Drim *r.* Yugo. **34** 42.25N 20.34E
Beli Manastir Croatia **31** 45.46N 18.36E
Belin France **20** 44.30N 0.47W
Belington U.S.A. **114** 39.01N 79.56W
Belitung *i.* Indonesia **58** 3.00S108.00E
Belize Belize **117** 17.29N 88.20W
Belize C. America **117** 17.00N 88.30W
Belka Australia **89** 31.45S118.09E
Bellac France **20** 46.07N 1.02E
Bella Coola Canada **100** 52.25N126.40W
Bellagio Italy **30** 45.59N 9.15E
Bellaire Ohio U.S.A. **114** 40.02N 80.45W
Bellaire Tex. U.S.A. **111** 29.44N 95.03W
Bellaria Italy **30** 44.09N 12.28E
Bellary India **60** 15.11N 76.54E
Bellata Australia **93** 29.55S149.50E
Bella Unión Uruguay **125** 30.15S 57.35W
Bella Vista Corrientes Argentina **124** 28.30S 59.00W
Bella Vista Tucuman Argentina **124** 27.02S 65.19W
Bellbrook Australia **93** 30.48S152.30E
Belle U.S.A. **114** 38.14N 81.32W
Belledonne, Chaîne de *mts.* France **21** 45.18N 6.08E
Bellefontaine U.S.A. **112** 40.22N 83.45W
Bellefonte U.S.A. **114** 40.55N 77.46W
Belle Fourche *r.* U.S.A. **110** 44.26N102.19W
Bellegarde France **21** 46.06N 5.49E
Belle Glade U.S.A. **113** 26.41N 80.41W
Belle Île France **17** 47.20N 3.10W
Belle Île *i.* France **18** 47.20N 3.10W
Belle Isle Canada **103** 51.55N 55.20W
Belle Isle, Str. of Canada **103** 51.35N 56.30W
Bellême France **18** 48.22N 0.34E
Belleoram Canada **103** 47.32N 55.28W
Belleterre Canada **104** 47.25N 78.41W
Belleville Canada **105** 44.10N 77.23W
Belleville Kans. U.S.A. **110** 39.49N 97.38W
Belleville-sur-Saône France **21** 46.06N 4.45E
Bellevue Canada **104** 46.42N 84.09W
Bellevue Canada **100** 49.35N114.22W
Bellevue Idaho U.S.A. **108** 43.28N114.16W
Bellevue Ohio U.S.A. **114** 41.17N 82.50W
Bellevue Penn. U.S.A. **114** 40.30N 80.03W
Bellevue Wash. U.S.A. **108** 47.37N122.12W
Bell Ewart Canada **104** 44.16N 79.33W
Belley France **21** 45.46N 5.41E
Belle Yella Liberia **76** 7.24N 10.09W
Bellingen Australia **93** 30.28S152.43E
Bellingham U.K. **12** 55.09N 2.15W
Bellingham U.S.A. **108** 48.46N122.29W
Bellingshausen Sea Antarctica **128** 70.00S 88.00W
Bellinzona Switz. **39** 46.11N 9.02E
Bello Colombia **122** 6.20N 75.41W
Bellows Falls *town* U.S.A. **115** 43.08N 72.27W
Bellpat Pakistan **62** 28.59N 68.00E
Belluno Italy **30** 46.09N 12.13E
Bell Ville Argentina **125** 32.35S 62.41W
Bellville U.S.A. **114** 40.37N 82.31W
Bellwood U.S.A. **114** 40.36N 78.20W
Belmar U.S.A. **115** 40.11N 74.01W
Bélmez Spain **26** 38.16N 5.12W
Belmond U.S.A. **110** 42.51N 93.37W
Belmont Australia **93** 33.02S151.40E
Belmont U.S.A. **114** 42.13N 78.02W
Belmonte Portugal **26** 40.21N 7.21W
Belmonte Cuenca Spain **27** 39.34N 2.42W
Belmonte Oviedo Spain **26** 43.16N 6.13W
Belmopan Belize **117** 17.25N 88.46W
Belmullet Rep. of Ire. **15** 54.14N 10.00W
Belogradchik Bulgaria **34** 43.37N 22.40E
Belo Horizonte Brazil **126** 19.45S 43.54W
Beloit Kans. U.S.A. **110** 39.28N 98.06W
Beloit Wisc. U.S.A. **110** 42.31N 89.02W

Belo Jardim to **Bilimora**

Belo Jardim Brazil **123** 8.22S 36.22W
Belokorovichi Ukraine **37** 51.04N 28.00E
Belomorsk Russian Fed. **44** 64.34N 34.45E
Belonia India **63** 23.15N 91.27E
Belorado Spain **26** 42.25N 3.11W
Beloretsk Russian Fed. **44** 53.59N 58.20E
Belorussia Europe **37** 53.30N 28.00E
Beloye More *sea* Russian Fed. **44** 65.30N 38.00E
Beloye Ozero *l.* Russian Fed. **44** 60.12N 37.45E
Belozersk Russian Fed. **44** 60.00N 37.49E
Belpasso Italy **33** 37.35N 14.59E
Belper U.K. **12** 53.02N 1.29W
Belpre U.S.A. **114** 39.17N 81.34W
Beltana Australia **92** 30.40S138.27E
Belterra Brazil **123** 2.38S 54.57W
Belton Australia **92** 32.12S138.45E
Belton U.S.A. **111** 31.04N 97.28W
Beltsy Moldavia **37** 47.45N 27.59E
Belukha, Gora *mtn.* Russian Fed. **52** 49.48N 86.40E
Belvedere Marittimo Italy **33** 39.37N 15.52E
Belvès France **20** 44.47N 1.00E
Belvidere U.S.A. **115** 40.49N 75.05W
Belvís de la Jara Spain **27** 39.45N 4.57W
Belyando *r.* Australia **90** 21.38S146.50E
Belyayevka Ukraine **37** 46.30N 30.12E
Belynichi Belorussia **37** 54.00N 29.42E
Belyy, Ostrov Russian Fed. **50** 73.10N 70.45E
Belyy Yar Russian Fed. **50** 58.28N 85.03E
Belz France **18** 47.41N 3.10W
Bełżec Poland **37** 50.24N 23.26E
Belzig Germany **38** 52.08N 12.35E
Bemaraha, Plateau du *mts.* Madagascar **81** 20.00S 45.15E
Bemarivo *r.* Madagascar **81** 15.27S 47.40E
Bembézar Spain **26** 37.45N 5.13W
Bemidji U.S.A. **110** 47.29N 94.53W
Benaberre Spain **25** 42.07N 0.29E
Bena Dibele Zaïre **78** 4.07S 22.50E
Benagerie Australia **92** 31.30S140.21E
Benalla Australia **93** 36.35S145.58E
Benamejí Spain **27** 37.16N 4.32W
Ben 'Ammi Israel **67** 33.00N 35.07E
Benanee Australia **92** 34.32S142.56E
Benares *see* Vārānasi India **63**
Benavente Spain **26** 42.01N 5.41W
Benbecula *i.* U.K. **14** 57.26N 7.18W
Bencha China **54** 32.31N120.53E
Ben Cruachan *mtn.* U.K. **14** 56.26N 5.18W
Bencubbin Australia **89** 30.48S117.52E
Bend U.S.A. **108** 44.03N121.19W
Bende Nigeria **77** 5.34N 7.37E
Bendemeer Australia **93** 30.52S151.10E
Bender Beyla Somali Rep. **71** 9.30N 50.30E
Bendery Moldavia **37** 46.50N 29.29E
Bendigo Australia **92** 36.48S144.21E
Bendoc Australia **93** 37.10S148.55E
Bendorf Germany **39** 50.25N 7.34E
Bene Beraq Israel **67** 32.06N 34.51E
Bénéna Mali **76** 13.09N 4.17W
Benenitra Madagascar **81** 23.27S 45.05E
Benešov Czech Republic **36** 49.45N 14.22E
Bénestroff France **19** 48.55N 6.45E
Bénévent-l'Abbaye France **20** 46.07N 1.38E
Benevento Italy **33** 41.08N 14.45E
Benfeld France **19** 48.22N 7.36E
Bengal, B. of Indian Oc. **63** 20.00N 90.00E
Bengal Plateau *f.* Indian Oc. **48** 15.00N 89.00E
Bengbu China **54** 32.53N117.26E
Benghazi *see* Banghāzī Libya **75**
Bengkulu Indonesia **58** 3.46S102.16E
Bengo *d.* Angola **78** 9.00S 13.40E
Bengtsfors Sweden **43** 59.02N 12.13E
Benguela Angola **78** 12.34S 13.24E
Benguela *d.* Angola **78** 12.45S 14.00E
Ben Hope *mtn.* U.K. **14** 58.24N 4.36W
Beni *r.* Bolivia **124** 10.23S 65.24W
Beni Zaïre **79** 0.29N 29.27E
Beni Abbes Algeria **74** 30.08N 2.10W
Benicarló Spain **25** 40.25N 0.26E
Benidorm Spain **25** 38.32N 0.08W
Beni-Mellal Morocco **74** 32.22N 6.29W
Benin Africa **77** 9.00N 2.30E
Benin, Bight of Africa **77** 5.30N 3.00E
Benin City Nigeria **77** 6.19N 5.41E
Benisa Spain **25** 38.43N 0.03E
Beni Saf Algeria **74** 35.19N 1.23W
Benjamin Constant Brazil **122** 4.22S 70.02W
Benkelman U.S.A. **110** 40.03N101.32W
Benkovac Croatia **31** 44.02N 15.37E
Ben Lawers *mtn.* U.K. **14** 56.33N 4.14W
Ben Lomond *mtn.* U.K. **14** 56.12N 4.38W
Ben Macdhui *mtn.* U.K. **14** 57.04N 3.40W
Ben More *mtn.* Central U.K. **14** 56.23N 4.31W
Ben More *mtn.* Strath. U.K. **14** 56.26N 6.02W
Ben More Assynt *mtn.* U.K. **14** 58.07N 4.52W
Bennett Canada **100** 59.49N135.01W
Bennett, L. Australia **90** 22.50S131.10E
Bennettsville U.S.A. **113** 34.36N 79.40W
Ben Nevis *mtn.* U.K. **14** 56.48N 5.00W
Benneydale New Zealand **86** 38.31S175.21E
Bennington N.H. U.S.A. **115** 43.01N 71.56W
Bennington Vt. U.S.A. **115** 42.53N 73.12W
Benny Canada **104** 46.47N 81.37W
Benoni R.S.A. **80** 26.12S 28.18E
Bénoué *r.* Cameroon *see* Benue *r.* Nigeria **77**
Bensheim Germany **39** 49.41N 8.37E
Benson Ariz. U.S.A. **109** 31.58N110.18W
Benson Minn. U.S.A. **110** 45.19N 95.36W
Bentiaba Angola **78** 14.19S 12.23E
Bentinck I. Australia **90** 17.04S139.30E
Bentiu Sudan **73** 9.14N 29.50E
Bentley U.S.A. **104** 43.57N 84.08W
Bentleyville U.S.A. **114** 40.07N 80.01W
Benton U.S.A. **110** 38.01N 88.54W
Benton Harbor U.S.A. **112** 42.07N 86.27W
Benue *d.* Nigeria **77** 7.20N 8.00E
Benue *r.* Nigeria **77** 7.52N 6.45E
Ben Wyvis *mtn.* U.K. **14** 57.40N 4.35W
Benxi China **54** 41.21N123.47E
Beograd Yugo. **37** 44.49N 20.28E
Beohāri India **63** 24.03N 81.23E
Beowawe U.S.A. **108** 40.35N116.29W
Beppu Japan **57** 33.18N131.30E
Berat Albania **34** 40.43N 19.59E
Berau, Teluk *b.* Indonesia **59** 2.20S133.00E
Berbera Somali Rep. **71** 10.28N 45.02E
Berbérati C.A.R. **77** 4.19N 15.51E
Berbería, Cabo *c.* Spain **25** 38.38N 1.23E
Berceto Italy **30** 44.31N 9.59E
Berchem Belgium **16** 50.48N 3.32E
Berchtesgaden Germany **39** 47.38N 13.01E
Berck France **19** 50.24N 1.36E
Bercu France **19** 50.31N 3.17E
Berdichev Ukraine **37** 49.54N 28.39E
Berdsk Russian Fed. **50** 54.51N 82.51E
Berdyansk Ukraine **45** 46.45N 36.47E
Berea U.S.A. **114** 41.22N 81.52W
Beregovo Ukraine **37** 48.13N 22.39E
Bereko Tanzania **79** 4.27S 35.43E
Berens *r.* Canada **101** 52.21N 97.02W
Berens River *town* Canada **101** 52.22N 97.02W
Beresford Australia **92** 29.14S136.40E
Berettyóújfalu Hungary **37** 47.14N 21.32E
Berevo Madagascar **81** 19.44S 44.58E
Bereza Belorussia **37** 52.32N 25.00E
Berezhany Ukraine **37** 49.27N 24.56E
Berezina *r.* Belorussia **37** 54.10N 28.10E
Berezna Ukraine **37** 51.34N 31.46E
Berezniki Russian Fed. **44** 59.26N 56.49E
Berezno Ukraine **37** 51.00N 26.41E
Berezovka Ukraine **37** 47.12N 30.56E
Berezovo Russian Fed. **9** 63.58N 65.00E
Berga Spain **25** 42.06N 1.51E
Berga Sweden **43** 57.14N 16.03E
Bergama Turkey **29** 39.08N 27.10E
Bergamo Italy **30** 45.41N 9.43E
Bergen Germany **38** 54.26N 13.27E
Bergen Nschn. Germany **38** 52.48N 9.58E
Bergen Neth. **16** 52.40N 4.41E
Bergen Norway **42** 60.23N 5.20E
Bergen U.S.A. **114** 43.05N 77.57W
Bergen op Zoom Neth. **16** 51.30N 4.17E
Bergerac France **20** 44.51N 0.29E
Bergheim Germany **38** 50.55N 6.38E
Berghem Neth. **16** 51.46N 5.32E
Bergisch Gladbach Germany **38** 50.59N 7.07E
Bergkamen Germany **38** 51.38N 7.38E
Bergkvara Sweden **43** 56.23N 16.05E
Bergland U.S.A. **112** 46.36N 89.33W
Bergoo U.S.A. **114** 38.29N 80.18W
Bergslagen *f.* Sweden **43** 59.55N 15.00E
Bergues France **19** 50.58N 2.26E
Bergum Neth. **16** 53.14N 5.59E
Berhampore India **63** 24.06N 88.15E
Berhampur India **63** 19.19N 84.47E
Bering Sea N. America / Asia **98** 65.00N170.00W
Bering Str. Russian Fed. / U.S.A. **98** 65.00N170.00W
Berislav Ukraine **45** 46.51N 33.26E
Berja Spain **27** 36.51N 2.57W
Berkåk Norway **40** 62.48N 10.03E
Berkel *r.* Neth. **16** 52.10N 6.12E
Berkeley U.S.A. **108** 37.57N122.18W
Berkeley Springs *town* U.S.A. **114** 39.38N 78.14W
Berkner I. Antarctica **128** 79.30S 50.00W
Berkovitsa Bulgaria **34** 43.16N 23.08E
Berkshire *d.* U.K. **13** 51.25N 1.03W
Berkshire Downs *hills* U.K. **13** 51.32N 1.36W
Berkshire Hills *mts.* U.S.A. **115** 42.20N 73.10W
Berland *r.* Canada **100** 54.00N116.50W
Berlanga de Duero Spain **26** 41.28N 2.51W
Berlin Germany **38** 52.31N 13.24E
Berlin *d.* Germany **38** 52.30N 13.20E
Berlin Md. U.S.A. **115** 38.20N 75.13W
Berlin N.H. U.S.A. **112** 44.29N 71.10W
Berlin Penn. U.S.A. **114** 39.55N 78.57W
Berlin L. U.S.A. **114** 41.00N 81.00W
Bermagui Australia **93** 36.28S150.03E
Bermeja, Sierra *mts.* Spain **27** 36.30N 5.10W
Bermejo *r.* San Juan Argentina **124** 31.40S 67.15W
Bermejo *r.* Tucumán Argentina **124** 26.47S 58.30W
Bermeo Spain **26** 43.26N 2.43W
Bermillo de Sayago Spain **26** 41.22N 6.06W
Bermo India **63** 23.47N 85.57E
Bermuda Atlantic Oc. **127** 32.18N 64.45W
Bermuda Rise *f.* Atlantic Oc. **127** 34.00N 60.00W
Bern Switz. **39** 46.57N 7.26E
Bern *d.* Switz. **39** 46.35N 7.50E
Bernalda Italy **33** 40.24N 16.41E
Bernard L. Canada **104** 45.44N 79.24W
Bernau Germany **38** 52.40N 13.35E
Bernay France **18** 49.06N 0.36E
Bernburg Germany **38** 51.48N 11.44E
Berne *see* Bern Switz. **39**
Berner Alpen *mts.* Switz. **39** 46.30N 7.37E
Bernier I. Australia **88** 24.51S113.09E
Bernina *mtn.* Italy / Switz. **30** 46.21N 9.51E
Bernkastel Germany **39** 49.55N 7.04E
Bernsdorf Germany **38** 51.22N 14.04E
Beror Hayil Israel **67** 31.33N 34.38E
Beroroha Madagascar **81** 21.41S 45.10E
Beroun Czech Republic **38** 49.58N 14.04E
Berounka *r.* Czech Republic **39** 50.00N 14.24E
Berovo Macedonia **34** 41.42N 22.51E
Berre, Étang de *b.* France **21** 43.28N 5.11E
Berrechid Morocco **74** 33.17N 7.35W
Berri Australia **92** 34.17S140.36E
Berridale Australia **93** 36.21S148.51E
Berrigan Australia **93** 35.41S145.48E
Berry Head U.K. **13** 50.24N 3.28W
Berryville Ark. U.S.A. **111** 36.22N 93.34W
Berryville Va. U.S.A. **114** 39.09N 77.59W
Bersenbrück Germany **38** 52.33N 7.56E
Bershad Ukraine **37** 48.20N 29.30E
Berté, Lac *l.* Canada **103** 50.47N 68.30W
Berthierville Canada **105** 46.05N 73.10W
Bertinoro Italy **30** 44.09N 12.08E
Bertoua Cameroon **77** 4.34N 13.42E
Bertraghboy B. Rep. of Ire. **15** 53.23N 9.52W
Berwick Maine U.S.A. **115** 43.16N 70.51W
Berwick Penn. U.S.A. **115** 41.03N 76.15W
Berwick-upon-Tweed U.K. **12** 55.46N 2.00W
Besalampy Madagascar **81** 16.45S 44.30E
Besançon France **19** 47.15N 6.02E
Besor, Nahal *wadi* Egypt **67** 31.28N 34.22E
Bessarabia *f.* Moldavia **37** 46.30N 28.40E
Bessemer U.S.A. **113** 33.22N 87.00W
Betafo Madagascar **81** 19.50S 46.51E
Bet Alpha Israel **67** 32.31N 35.26E
Betanzos Spain **26** 43.17N 8.12W
Betanzos, Ría de *est.* Spain **26** 43.23N 8.15W
Bétaré Oya Cameroon **77** 5.34N 14.09E
Bet Dagan Israel **67** 32.00N 34.50E
Bete Hor Ethiopia **73** 11.40N 39.00E
Bétera Spain **25** 39.35N 0.27W
Bet Guvrin *site* Israel **67** 31.36N 34.54E
Bet Ha'Emeq Israel **67** 32.58N 35.09E
Bethal R.S.A. **80** 26.26S 29.27E
Bet Hananya Israel **67** 32.32N 34.55E
Bethany Canada **104** 44.11N 78.34W
Bethany Beach *town* U.S.A. **115** 38.33N 75.00W
Bet HaShitta Israel **67** 32.33N 35.26E
Bethel Alas. U.S.A. **98** 60.48N161.46W
Bethel Penn. U.S.A. **115** 40.28N 76.18W
Bethesda U.S.A. **114** 38.59N 77.06W
Bethlehem *see* Bayt Laḥm Jordan **67**
Bethlehem R.S.A. **80** 28.13S 28.18E
Bethlehem N.H. U.S.A. **105** 44.17N 71.42W
Bethlehem Penn. U.S.A. **115** 40.37N 75.25W
Béthune France **19** 50.32N 2.38E
Béthune *r.* France **18** 49.53N 1.09E
Betim Brazil **126** 19.55S 44.07W
Betioky Madagascar **81** 23.42S 44.22E
Bet Oren Israel **67** 32.44N 35.00E
Bet Qama Israel **67** 31.27N 34.46E
Bet Qeshet Israel **67** 32.43N 35.24E
Betroka Madagascar **81** 23.16S 46.06E
Bet She'an Israel **67** 32.30N 35.30E
Bet Shemesh Israel **67** 31.45N 35.00E
Betsiamites Canada **103** 48.56N 68.38W
Betsiboka *r.* Madagascar **81** 16.03S 46.36E
Bette *mtn.* Libya **75** 22.00N 19.12E
Bettiah India **63** 26.48N 84.30E
Bettles U.S.A. **98** 66.53N151.51W
Betūl India **63** 21.55N 77.54E
Betwa *r.* India **63** 25.55N 80.12E
Betws-y-Coed U.K. **11** 53.05N 3.48W
Betzdorf Germany **16** 50.48N 7.54E
Beulah Australia **92** 35.59S142.26E
Beulah Canada **101** 50.16N101.02W
Beulah U.S.A. **110** 47.16N101.47W
Beuvron *r.* France **19** 47.29N 3.31E
Bevensen Germany **38** 53.05N 10.34E
Beverley Australia **89** 32.06S116.56E
Beverley U.K. **12** 53.52N 0.26W
Beverley Hills *town* U.S.A. **109** 34.04N118.26W
Beverly Mass. U.S.A. **115** 42.33N 70.53W
Beverly Ohio U.S.A. **114** 39.33N 81.38W
Beverly W.Va. U.S.A. **114** 38.51N 79.53W
Beverungen Germany **38** 51.39N 9.22E
Beverwijk Neth. **16** 52.29N 4.40E
Bewcastle Fells *hills* U.K. **12** 55.05N 2.50W
Bewdley Canada **104** 44.05N 78.19W
Bexhill U.K. **13** 50.51N 0.29E
Bexley U.K. **13** 51.26N 0.10E
Beyla Guinea **76** 8.42N 8.39W
Beyneu Kazakhstan **45** 45.16N 55.04E
Beypazari Turkey **64** 40.10N 31.56E
Beyşehir Gölü *l.* Turkey **64** 37.47N 31.30E
Bezau Austria **39** 47.23N 9.54E
Bezet Israel **67** 33.05N 35.08E
Bezhanovo Bulgaria **34** 43.13N 24.26E
Bezhetsk Russian Fed. **44** 57.49N 36.40E
Bezhitsa Russian Fed. **44** 53.19N 34.17E
Béziers France **20** 43.21N 3.15E
Bhadohi India **63** 25.25N 82.34E
Bhādra India **62** 29.07N 75.10E
Bhadrakh India **63** 21.04N 86.30E
Bhāg Pakistan **62** 29.02N 67.49E
Bhāgalpur India **63** 25.15N 87.00E
Bhāi Pheru Pakistan **62** 31.12N 73.57E
Bhaironghāti India **63** 31.01N 78.53E
Bhaisa India **63** 19.06N 77.58E
Bhakkar Pakistan **62** 31.38N 71.04E
Bhaktapur Nepal **63** 27.42N 85.27E
Bhalwāl Pakistan **62** 32.16N 72.54E
Bhamo Burma **56** 24.10N 97.30E
Bhandāra India **63** 21.10N 79.39E
Bhānvad India **62** 21.56N 69.47E
Bharatpur India **62** 27.13N 77.29E
Bharthana India **63** 26.45N 79.14E
Bhātāpāra India **63** 21.44N 81.56E
Bhatewar India **62** 24.40N 74.05E
Bhātiāpāra Ghāt Bangla. **63** 23.12N 89.42E
Bhatinda India **62** 30.13N 74.56E
Bhatkal India **60** 13.58N 74.34E
Bhātpāra India **63** 22.52N 88.24E
Bhaunagar India **62** 21.46N 72.09E
Bhawāni Mandi India **62** 24.25N 75.50E
Bhawānipatna India **63** 19.54N 83.10E
Bhera Pakistan **62** 32.29N 72.55E
Bhikangaon India **62** 21.52N 75.57E
Bhilai India **63** 21.13N 81.26E
Bhīlwāra India **62** 25.21N 74.38E
Bhima *r.* India **60** 16.30N 77.10E
Bhind India **63** 26.34N 78.48E
Bhīnmāl India **62** 25.00N 72.15E
Bhiwandi India **62** 19.18N 73.04E
Bhiwāni India **62** 28.47N 76.08E
Bhognīpur India **63** 26.12N 79.48E
Bhojpur Nepal **63** 27.11N 87.02E
Bhokardan India **62** 20.16N 75.46E
Bhopāl India **63** 23.16N 77.24E
Bhor India **60** 18.12N 73.53E
Bhuban India **63** 20.53N 85.50E
Bhubaneswar India **63** 20.15N 85.50E
Bhuj India **62** 23.16N 69.40E
Bhusāwal India **62** 21.03N 75.46E
Bhutan Asia **63** 27.15N 91.00E
Bia, Phou *mtn.* Laos **56** 18.59N103.11E
Biābānak Afghan. **62** 32.11N 64.11E
Biak Indonesia **59** 1.10S136.05E
Biak *i.* Indonesia **59** 0.55S136.00E
Biała Podlaska Poland **37** 52.02N 23.06E
Białogard Poland **36** 54.00N 16.00E
Białystok Poland **37** 53.09N 23.10E
Biankouma Ivory Coast **76** 7.51N 7.34W
Biaora India **62** 23.55N 76.54E
Biarritz France **20** 43.29N 1.34W
Biasca Switz. **39** 46.22N 8.58E
Bibā Egypt **66** 28.56N 30.59E
Bibala Angola **78** 14.46S 13.21E
Biberach Germany **39** 48.20N 9.30E
Bibey *r.* Spain **26** 42.24N 7.13W
Bic Canada **103** 48.22N 68.42W
Bicas Brazil **126** 21.44S 43.04W
Bicester U.K. **13** 51.53N 1.09W
Bickle Knob *mtn.* U.S.A. **114** 38.56N 79.44W
Bida Nigeria **77** 9.06N 5.59E
Bīdar India **60** 17.54N 77.33E
Biddeford U.S.A. **115** 43.30N 70.26W
Biddiyā Jordan **67** 32.07N 35.05E
Biddū Jordan **67** 31.50N 35.09E
Bideford U.K. **13** 51.01N 4.13W
Bidon Cinq *see* Poste Maurice Cortier Algeria **74**
Bi Doup *mtn.* Vietnam **56** 12.05N108.40E
Bidwell U.S.A. **114** 38.55N 82.18W
Bié *d.* Angola **78** 12.30S 17.30E
Biedenkopf Germany **38** 50.55N 8.32E
Biel Switz. **39** 47.10N 7.12E
Bielefeld Germany **38** 52.01N 8.31E
Bielersee *l.* Switz. **39** 47.05N 7.10E
Biella Italy **30** 45.34N 8.03E
Bielsko-Biała Poland **37** 49.49N 19.02E
Bielsk Podlaski Poland **37** 52.47N 23.12E
Bien Hoa Vietnam **56** 10.58N106.50E
Bienville, Lac *l.* Canada **103** 55.05N 72.40W
Bié Plateau *f.* Angola **78** 13.00S 16.00E
Bietigheim Germany **39** 48.58N 9.07E
Biferno *r.* Italy **33** 41.59N 15.02E
Big Bald Mtn. Canada **103** 47.12N 66.25W
Big Bear Lake *town* U.S.A. **109** 34.15N116.53W
Big Beaver House *town* Canada **102** 52.59N 89.50W
Big Belt Mts. U.S.A. **108** 46.40N111.25W
Big Bend Nat. Park U.S.A. **111** 29.12N103.12W
Bigbury B. U.K. **13** 50.15N 3.56W
Big Cypress Swamp *f.* U.S.A. **113** 26.10N 81.38W
Big Falls *town* U.S.A. **110** 48.12N 93.48W
Biggar Canada **101** 52.04N107.59W
Biggar U.K. **14** 55.38N 3.31W
Big Hickory *mtn.* U.S.A. **115** 41.43N 74.22W
Bighorn *r.* U.S.A. **108** 46.09N107.28W
Bighorn L. U.S.A. **108** 45.06N108.08W
Bighorn Mts. U.S.A. **108** 44.00N107.30W
Bight, Head of *b.* Australia **91** 31.29S131.16E
Big Moose U.S.A. **105** 43.49N 74.57W
Bignasco Switz. **39** 46.20N 8.36E
Bignona Senegal **76** 12.48N 16.18W
Big Pine U.S.A. **108** 37.10N118.17W
Big Piney U.S.A. **108** 42.32N110.07W
Big Quill L. Canada **101** 51.55N104.22W
Big Run U.S.A. **114** 40.58N 78.53W
Big Salmon Canada **98** 61.53N134.55W
Big Salmon *r.* Canada **100** 61.52N134.56W
Big Sand L. Canada **101** 57.45N 99.42W
Big Sandy U.S.A. **108** 48.11N110.07W
Big Smoky Valley *f.* U.S.A. **108** 38.30N117.15W
Big Snowy Mtn. U.S.A. **108** 46.50N109.30W
Big Spring *town* U.S.A. **111** 32.15N101.28W
Big Stone Gap *town* U.S.A. **113** 36.52N 82.46W
Bigstone L. Canada **101** 53.42N 95.44W
Big Stone L. U.S.A. **110** 45.25N 96.40W
Big Sur U.S.A. **109** 36.15N121.48W
Big Timber U.S.A. **108** 45.50N109.57W
Big Trout L. Canada **102** 53.40N 90.00W
Bihać Bosnia-Herzegovina **31** 44.49N 15.52E
Bihar India **63** 25.11N 85.31E
Bihar *d.* India **63** 24.30N 86.00E
Biharamulo Tanzania **79** 2.34S 31.20E
Bihor *mtn.* Romania **37** 46.26N 22.43E
Bihu China **55** 28.21N119.47E
Bijagós, Arquipélago dos *is.* Guinea Bissau **76** 11.30N 16.00W
Bijainagar India **62** 25.56N 74.38E
Bijaipura India **63** 24.46N 77.48E
Bījāpur India **60** 16.52N 75.47E
Bījāpur India **63** 18.48N 80.49E
Bījār Iran **65** 35.52N 47.39E
Bijāwar India **63** 24.38N 79.30E
Bijbān Chāh Pakistan **62** 26.54N 64.42E
Bijeljina Bosnia-Herzegovina **31** 44.45N 19.13E
Bijelo Polje Yugo. **31** 43.02N 19.44E
Bijeypur India **62** 26.03N 77.22E
Bijie China **55** 27.28N105.20E
Bijnor India **63** 29.22N 78.08E
Bīkaner India **62** 28.42N 73.25E
Bikin Russian Fed. **53** 46.52N134.15E
Bikini *i.* Pacific Oc. **84** 11.35N165.23E
Bikoro Zaïre **78** 0.45S 18.09E
Bilāra India **62** 26.10N 73.42E
Bilāspur Himachal P. India **62** 31.19N 76.45E
Bilāspur Madhya P. India **63** 22.05N 82.09E
Bilauktaung Range *mts.* Thailand **56** 13.00N 99.15E
Bilbao Spain **26** 43.15N 2.58W
Bilbays Egypt **66** 30.25N 31.34E
Bilbilis Spain **25** 41.25N 1.39W
Bilbo *see* Bilbao Spain **26**
Bileća Bosnia-Herzegovina **31** 42.53N 18.26E
Bilecik Turkey **64** 40.10N 29.59E
Bilgrām India **63** 27.11N 80.02E
Bili *r.* Zaïre **73** 4.09N 22.29E
Bilibino Russian Fed. **51** 68.02N166.15E
Bilimora India **62** 20.45N 72.57E

Bílina to **Bolombo**

Bílina Czech Republic **38** 50.35N 13.45E
Billabong Creek *r.* Australia **92** 35.04S144.06E
Bill Baileys Bank *f.* Atlantic Oc. **10** 60.45N 10.30W
Billengen *f.* Sweden **43** 58.20N 13.43E
Billingham U.K. **12** 54.36N 1.18W
Billings U.S.A. **108** 45.47N108.27W
Billingsfors Sweden **43** 58.59N 12.15E
Bill of Portland *c.* U.K. **13** 50.32N 2.28W
Billom France **20** 45.44N 3.21E
Bilma Niger **75** 18.41N 12.56E
Biloela Australia **90** 24.24S150.30E
Biloxi U.S.A. **111** 30.24N 88.53W
Bilqās Qism Awwal Egypt **66** 31.14N 31.22E
Biltine Chad **75** 14.32N 20.55E
Biltine *d.* Chad **75** 15.00N 21.00E
Bilto Norway **40** 69.26N 21.35E
Bima *r.* Zaïre **78** 3.24N 25.10E
Bimberi, Mt. Australia **93** 35.40S148.47E
Bimbo C.A.R. **77** 4.15N 18.33E
Bimidji U.S.A. **96** 47.29N 94.53W
Bīna-Etāwa India **63** 24.11N 78.11E
Binaiya *mtn.* Indonesia **59** 3.10S129.30E
Bīnālūd, Kūh-e *mts.* Iran **65** 36.15N 59.00E
Binbee Australia **90** 20.20S147.55E
Binche Belgium **16** 50.25N 4.10E
Bindki India **63** 26.02N 80.36E
Bindura Zimbabwe **81** 17.18S 31.20E
Binéfar Spain **25** 41.51N 0.18E
Binga Zimbabwe **80** 17.38S 27.19E
Binga, Mt. Zimbabwe **81** 19.47S 33.03E
Bingara Australia **93** 29.51S150.38E
Bingen Germany **39** 49.58N 7.55E
Bingerville Ivory Coast **76** 5.20N 3.53W
Bingham U.K. **12** 52.57N 0.57W
Bingham U.S.A. **112** 45.03N 69.53W
Binghamton U.S.A. **115** 42.08N 75.54W
Bingkor Malaysia **58** 5.26N116.15E
Bingöl Turkey **23** 38.54N 40.29E
Bingol Daglari *mtn.* Turkey **64** 39.21N 41.22E
Binhai China **54** 34.00N119.55E
Binh Dinh Vietnam **56** 13.53N109.07E
Binjai Indonesia **58** 3.37N 98.25E
Binji Nigeria **77** 13.12N 4.55E
Binnaway Australia **93** 31.32S149.23E
Binscarth Canada **101** 50.37N101.16W
Bintan *i.* Indonesia **58** 1.10N104.30E
Bint Jubayl Lebanon **67** 33.07N 35.26E
Bintulu Malaysia **58** 3.12N113.01E
Bin Xian China **54** 35.02N108.04E
Binyamina Israel **67** 32.31N 34.57E
Binyang China **55** 23.12N108.48E
Binzert Tunisia **32** 37.17N 9.52E
Biograd Croatia **31** 43.56N 15.27E
Bioko I. Equat. Guinea **77** 3.25N 8.45E
Biq'at Bet Netofa *f.* Israel **67** 32.49N 35.19E
Bīr India **62** 18.59N 75.46E
Bir, Ras *c.* Djibouti **71** 11.59N 43.25E
Bi'r Abū 'Uwayqīlah *well* Egypt **66** 30.50N 34.07E
Bi'r ad Dakhal *well* Egypt **66** 28.40N 32.24E
Birāk Libya **75** 27.32N 14.17E
Birak Sulaymān *site* Jordan **67** 31.41N 35.10E
Bi'r al Ḩarash *well* Libya **75** 25.30N 22.06E
Bi'r al Jidy *well* Egypt **66** 30.13N 33.03E
Bi'r al Jufayr *well* Egypt **66** 30.49N 32.40E
Bi'r al 'Udayd *well* Egypt **66** 28.59N 34.05E
Birao C.A.R. **73** 10.17N 22.47E
Bi'r aş Şafrā' *well* Egypt **66** 28.46N 34.20E
Bi'r ath Thamadah *well* Egypt **66** 30.10N 33.28E
Birātnagar Nepal **63** 26.18N 87.17E
Bi'r Buerāt *well* Egypt **66** 28.59N 32.10E
Bi'r Bukhayt *well* Egypt **66** 29.13N 32.17E
Bîrca Romania **34** 43.59N 23.36E
Birch *r.* Canada **100** 58.30N112.15W
Birchip Australia **92** 35.59S142.59E
Birch L. N.W.T. Canada **100** 62.04N116.33W
Birch L. Ont. Canada **102** 51.24N 92.20W
Birch Mts. Canada **100** 57.30N112.30W
Bird Canada **101** 56.30N 94.13W
Birdsboro U.S.A. **115** 40.16N 75.48W
Birdsville Australia **90** 25.54S139.22E
Birecik Turkey **64** 37.03N 37.59E
Bīrganj Nepal **63** 27.01N 84.54E
Birhan *mtn.* Ethiopia **73** 11.00N 37.50E
Bi'r Ḩasanah *well* Egypt **66** 30.29N 33.47E
Bi'r Hooker *well* Egypt **66** 30.23N 30.20E
Bīrjand Iran **65** 32.54N 59.10E
Bi'r Jifjafah *well* Egypt **66** 30.28N 33.11E
Birk, Wādī *r.* Saudi Arabia **65** 24.08N 47.35E
Birkeland Norway **42** 58.20N 8.14E
Birkenfeld B.-Würt. Germany **39** 48.52N 8.38E
Birkenfeld Rhein.-Pfalz Germany **39** 49.39N 7.10E
Birkenhead U.K. **12** 53.24N 3.01W
Birkeröd Denmark **43** 55.50N 12.26E
Birksgate Range *mts.* Australia **88** 27.10S129.45E
Bi'r Kusaybah *well* Egypt **66** 22.41N 29.55E
Bîrlad Romania **37** 46.14N 27.40E
Bi'r Lahfān *well* Egypt **66** 31.01N 33.52E
Birmingham U.K. **13** 52.30N 1.55W
Birmingham Ala. U.S.A. **113** 33.30N 86.55W
Birmingham Mich. U.S.A. **104** 42.33N 83.15W
Birmitrapur India **63** 22.24N 84.46E
Bir Mogreïn Mauritania **74** 25.14N 11.35W
Birni Benin **77** 9.59N 1.34E
Birnin Gwari Nigeria **77** 11.02N 6.47E
Birnin Kebbi Nigeria **77** 12.30N 4.11E
Birni N'Konni Niger **77** 13.49N 5.19E
Birobidzhan Russian Fed. **53** 48.49N132.54E
Bîr Ounâne *well* Mali **74** 21.02N 3.18W
Birr Rep. of Ire. **15** 53.06N 7.56W
Birrie *r.* Australia **93** 29.43S146.37E
Birsilpur India **62** 28.11N 72.15E
Birsk Russian Fed. **44** 55.28N 55.31E
Bi'r Tābah *well* Egypt **66** 29.30N 34.53E
Bi'r Ţarfāwī *well* Egypt **72** 22.55N 28.53E
Birtle Canada **101** 50.32N101.02W
Bi'r Umm Sa'īd *well* Egypt **66** 29.40N 33.34E
Bi'r Umm 'Umayyid *well* Egypt **66** 27.53N 32.30E
Bi'r Ya'qūb *well* Jordan **67** 32.13N 35.17E
Biržai Lithuania **44** 56.10N 24.48E
Bi'r Zalţan *well* Libya **75** 28.27N 19.46E
Bir Zreigat Mauritania **74** 22.27N 8.53W
Bisaccia Italy **33** 41.01N 15.22E
Bīsalpur India **63** 28.18N 79.48E
Bisbee U.S.A. **109** 31.27N109.55W
Biscarosse France **20** 44.24N 1.10W
Biscarosse, Étang de *b.* France **20** 44.20N 1.10W
Biscay, B. of France **20** 44.00N 4.00W
Bisceglie Italy **33** 41.14N 16.31E
Bischheim France **19** 48.37N 7.45E
Bischofswerda Germany **38** 51.07N 14.10E
Biscotasi L. Canada **104** 47.19N 82.07W
Biscotasing Canada **104** 47.18N 82.08W
Bīsha Ethiopia **72** 15.28N 37.34E
Bishkek Kyrgyzstan **52** 42.53N 74.46E
Bishnupur India **63** 23.05N 87.19E
Bishop Calif. U.S.A. **108** 37.22N118.24W
Bishop Tex. U.S.A. **111** 27.35N 97.48W
Bishop Auckland U.K. **12** 54.40N 1.40W
Bishop's Stortford U.K. **13** 51.53N 0.09E
Bisina, L. Uganda **79** 1.35N 34.08E
Biskra Algeria **75** 34.48N 5.40E
Bismarck U.S.A. **110** 46.48N100.47W
Bismarck Range *mts.* P.N.G. **59** 6.00S145.00E
Bismarck Sea Pacific Oc. **59** 4.00S146.30E
Bison U.S.A. **110** 45.31N102.28W
Bīsotūn Iran **65** 34.22N 47.29E
Bispgården Sweden **40** 63.02N 16.40E
Bissau Guinea Bissau **76** 11.52N 15.39W
Bissett Canada **101** 51.02N 95.40W
Bissikrima Guinea **76** 10.50N 10.58W
Bistcho L. Canada **100** 59.45N118.50W
Bistreţ Romania **34** 43.54N 23.23E
Bistriţa Romania **37** 47.08N 24.30E
Bistriţa *r.* Romania **37** 46.30N 26.54E
Biswān India **63** 27.30N 81.00E
Bitam Gabon **78** 2.05N 11.30E
Bitburg Germany **39** 49.58N 6.31E
Bitche France **19** 49.03N 7.26E
Bitéa, Ouadi *wadi* Chad **73** 13.11N 20.10E
Bitlis Turkey **64** 38.23N 42.04E
Bitola Macedonia **34** 41.01N 21.20E
Bitonto Italy **33** 41.06N 16.42E
Bitter Creek *town* U.S.A. **108** 41.31N109.27W
Bitterfeld Germany **38** 51.37N 12.20E
Bitterfontein R.S.A. **80** 31.02S 18.14E
Bitterroot Range *mts.* U.S.A. **108** 47.06N115.10W
Bitti Italy **32** 40.29N 9.23E
Biu Nigeria **77** 10.36N 12.11E
Biumba Rwanda **79** 1.38S 30.02E
Biwa ko *l.* Japan **57** 35.10N136.00E
Biyalā Egypt **66** 31.11N 31.13E
Biysk Russian Fed. **9** 52.35N 85.16E
Bizerte *see* Binzert Tunisia **32**
Bizerte *d.* Tunisia **32** 37.07N 9.45E
Bizerte, Lac de *l.* Tunisia **32** 37.12N 9.52E
Bjärnum Sweden **43** 56.17N 13.42E
Bjelasica *mts.* Yugo. **31** 42.50N 19.40E
Bjelovar Croatia **31** 45.54N 16.51E
Bjerringbro Denmark **42** 56.23N 9.40E
Björkelangen Norway **42** 59.53N 11.34E
Bjorli Norway **41** 62.16N 8.13E
Björna Sweden **40** 63.32N 18.36E
Björnafjorden *est.* Norway **42** 60.06N 5.22E
Bjørnøya *i.* Arctic Oc. **128** 74.30N 19.00E
Bjuv Sweden **43** 56.05N 12.54E
Blace Yugo. **34** 43.18N 21.17E
Black *r.* Canada **104** 44.20N 79.20W
Black *r.* Ark. U.S.A. **111** 35.38N 91.19W
Black *r.* Mich. U.S.A. **104** 43.00N 82.25W
Black *r.* Mich. U.S.A. **104** 45.39N 84.29W
Black *r.* N.Y. U.S.A. **105** 44.01N 75.59W
Black *r.* Ohio U.S.A. **114** 41.28N 82.11W
Black *r. see* Dà *r.* Vietnam **56**
Blackall Australia **90** 24.25S145.28E
Blackburn U.K. **12** 53.44N 2.30W
Black Diamond Canada **100** 50.45N114.14W
Black Duck *r.* Canada **101** 56.51N 89.02W
Blackduck U.S.A. **110** 47.44N 94.33W
Blackfoot U.S.A. **108** 43.11N112.20W
Black Hills U.S.A. **110** 44.00N104.00W
Black L. Canada **101** 59.10N105.20W
Black L. Mich. U.S.A. **104** 45.28N 84.15W
Black L. N.Y. U.S.A. **105** 44.31N 75.35W
Black Lake *town* Canada **105** 46.03N 71.21W
Black Mtn. U.K. **13** 51.52N 3.50W
Black Mts. U.K. **13** 51.52N 3.09W
Blackpool U.K. **12** 53.48N 3.03W
Black River *town* Jamaica **117** 18.02N 77.52W
Black River *town* Mich. U.S.A. **104** 44.47N 83.19W
Black River *town* N.Y. U.S.A. **105** 44.01N 75.48W
Black Rock *town* U.S.A. **108** 38.41N112.59W
Black Rock Desert U.S.A. **108** 41.10N119.00W
Black Sand Desert *see* Karakumy, Peski Turkmenistan **65**
Black Sea Europe **37** 44.00N 30.00E
Blacksod B. Rep. of Ire. **15** 54.04N 10.00W
Blackstone U.S.A. **113** 37.05N 78.02W
Black Sugarloaf Mt. Australia **93** 31.24S151.34E
Blackville Australia **93** 31.34S150.10E
Blackville U.S.A. **113** 33.22N 81.17W
Black Volta *r.* Ghana **76** 8.14N 2.11W
Blackwater Australia **90** 23.34S148.53E
Blackwater *r.* Waterford Rep. of Ire. **15** 51.58N 7.52W
Blackwater *r.* U.K. **11** 54.31N 6.36W
Blackwell U.S.A. **111** 36.48N 97.17W
Blackwood *r.* Australia **89** 34.15S115.10E
Blaenau Ffestiniog U.K. **12** 53.00N 3.57W
Blagaj Bosnia-Herzegovina **31** 43.15N 17.50E
Blagoevgrad Bulgaria **34** 42.02N 23.05E
Blagoveshchensk Russian Fed. **53** 50.19N127.30E
Blain France **18** 47.29N 1.46W
Blain U.S.A. **114** 40.20N 77.31W
Blair U.S.A. **110** 41.33N 96.08W
Blair Athol Australia **90** 22.42S147.33E
Blair Atholl U.K. **14** 56.46N 3.51W
Blairgowrie U.K. **14** 56.36N 3.21W
Blairmore Canada **100** 49.40N114.25W
Blairsville Ga. U.S.A. **113** 34.52N 83.52W
Blairsville Penn. U.S.A. **114** 40.26N 79.16W
Blakely U.S.A. **113** 31.22N 84.58W
Blakeslee U.S.A. **115** 41.06N 75.36W
Blanc, Cap *c.* Mauritania **76** 20.44N 17.05W
Blanc, Cap *c.* Tunisia **32** 37.20N 9.50E
Blanc, Mont *mtn.* France **21** 45.50N 6.52E
Blanca, Bahía *b.* Argentina **125** 39.20S 62.00W
Blanca, Sierra *mtn.* U.S.A. **109** 33.23N105.48W
Blanchard U.S.A. **108** 48.01N116.59W
Blanche, L. Australia **92** 29.15S139.40E
Blanchetown Australia **92** 34.21S139.38E
Blanco, C. Argentina **125** 47.12S 65.20W
Blanco, C. Costa Rica **117** 9.36N 85.06W
Blanco, C. U.S.A. **108** 42.50N124.34W
Bland *r.* Australia **93** 33.42S147.30E
Blandburg U.S.A. **114** 40.41N 78.25W
Blandford Forum U.K. **13** 50.52N 2.10W
Blanes Spain **25** 41.41N 2.48E
Blangy-sur-Bresle France **19** 49.56N 1.38E
Blankenberge Belgium **16** 51.18N 3.08E
Blankenburg Germany **38** 51.48N 10.58E
Blanquefort France **20** 44.53N 0.39W
Blansko Czech Republic **36** 49.22N 16.39E
Blantyre Malaŵi **79** 15.46S 35.00E
Blarney Rep. of Ire. **15** 51.56N 8.34W
Blatná Czech Republic **38** 49.26N 13.53E
Blatnica Bulgaria **37** 43.42N 28.31E
Blaubeuren Germany **39** 48.24N 9.47E
Blaufelden Germany **39** 49.18N 9.58E
Blavet *r.* France **18** 47.43N 3.18W
Blaye France **20** 45.08N 0.39W
Blayney Australia **93** 33.32S149.19E
Bled Slovenia **31** 46.22N 14.06E
Blednaya, Gora *mtn.* Russian Fed. **50** 76.23N 65.08E
Bleiburg Austria **31** 46.35N 14.48E
Blekinge *d.* Sweden **43** 56.15N 15.15E
Blekinge *f.* Sweden **43** 56.20N 15.20E
Blenheim Canada **104** 42.20N 82.00W
Blenheim New Zealand **86** 41.32S173.58E
Bléone *r.* France **21** 44.03N 6.00E
Bléré France **18** 47.20N 1.00E
Blerick Neth. **16** 51.22N 6.08E
Bletchley U.K. **13** 51.59N 0.45W
Bletterans France **19** 46.45N 5.27E
Bleu, Lac *l.* Canada **104** 46.35N 78.20W
Blida Algeria **75** 36.30N 2.50E
Blidö *i.* Sweden **43** 59.37N 18.54E
Bligh Entrance Australia **90** 9.18S144.10E
Blind River *town* Canada **104** 46.10N 82.58W
Blinman Australia **92** 31.05S138.11E
Blitar Indonesia **59** 8.06S112.12E
Blitta Togo **77** 8.23N 1.06E
Block I. U.S.A. **115** 41.11N 71.35W
Bloemfontein R.S.A. **80** 29.07S 26.14E
Bloemhof R.S.A. **80** 27.37S 25.34E
Blois France **18** 47.35N 1.20E
Blönduós Iceland **40** 65.39N 20.18W
Bloody Foreland *c.* Rep. of Ire. **15** 55.09N 8.17W
Bloomfield Canada **105** 43.59N 77.14W
Bloomfield Iowa U.S.A. **110** 40.45N 92.25W
Bloomfield Nebr. U.S.A. **110** 42.36N 97.39W
Bloomfield N.J. U.S.A. **115** 40.48N 74.12W
Bloomingdale U.S.A. **105** 44.25N 74.06W
Bloomington Ill. U.S.A. **110** 40.29N 89.00W
Bloomington Ind. U.S.A. **112** 39.10N 86.31W
Bloomington Minn. U.S.A. **110** 44.50N 93.17W
Bloomsburg U.S.A. **115** 41.00N 76.27W
Blora Indonesia **59** 6.55S111.29E
Blossburg U.S.A. **114** 41.41N 77.04W
Blovice Czech Republic **38** 49.35N 13.33E
Bludenz Austria **39** 47.09N 9.49E
Blueberry *r.* Canada **100** 56.45N120.49W
Bluefield U.S.A. **113** 37.14N 81.17W
Bluefields Nicaragua **117** 12.00N 83.49W
Blue Hills of Couteau Canada **103** 47.59N 57.43W
Bluemont U.S.A. **114** 39.06N 77.51W
Blue Mountain Lake *town* U.S.A. **105** 43.53N 74.26W
Blue Mtn. N.H. U.S.A. **105** 44.47N 71.28W
Blue Mts. Australia **93** 33.16S150.19E
Blue Mts. U.S.A. **108** 45.30N118.15W
Blue Mud B. Australia **90** 13.26S135.56E
Blue Nile *r. see* Azraq, Al Baḩr al *r.* Sudan **72**
Bluenose L. Canada **98** 68.30N119.35W
Blue River *town* Canada **100** 52.05N119.09W
Blue Stack Mts. Rep. of Ire. **15** 54.44N 8.09W
Bluff New Zealand **86** 46.38S168.21E
Bluff U.S.A. **108** 37.17N109.33W
Bluff, C. Canada **103** 52.48N 55.53W
Bluff Knoll *mtn.* Australia **89** 34.25S118.15E
Blumberg Germany **39** 47.50N 8.31E
Blumenau Brazil **126** 26.55S 49.07W
Blunt U.S.A. **110** 44.31N 99.59W
Blyth Canada **104** 43.44N 81.26W
Blyth Northum. U.K. **12** 55.07N 1.29W
Blythe U.S.A. **109** 33.37N114.36W
Bö Nordland Norway **40** 68.38N 14.35E
Bö Telemark Norway **42** 59.25N 9.04E
Bo Sierra Leone **76** 7.58N 11.45W
Boa Esperança Brazil **126** 21.03S 45.37W
Boa Esperança, Represa da *resr.* Brazil **123** 6.45S 44.15W
Bo'ai Henan China **54** 35.10N113.04E
Boane Mozambique **81** 26.02S 32.19E
Boa Vista Brazil **122** 2.51N 60.43W
Bobadah Australia **93** 32.18S146.42E
Bobadilla Spain **27** 37.02N 4.44W
Bobbili India **61** 18.34N 83.22E
Bobbio Italy **30** 44.46N 9.23E
Bobcaygeon Canada **104** 44.33N 78.33W
Böblingen Germany **39** 48.41N 9.01E
Bobo-Dioulasso Burkina **76** 11.11N 4.18W
Bobonong Botswana **80** 21.59S 28.29E
Bobr Belorussia **37** 54.19N 29.18E
Bóbr *r.* Poland **36** 52.04N 15.04E
Bobruysk Belorussia **37** 53.08N 29.10E
Bôca do Acre Brazil **122** 8.45S 67.23W
Bocaranga C.A.R. **77** 7.01N 15.35E
Boca Raton U.S.A. **113** 26.22N 80.05W
Bochnia Poland **37** 49.58N 20.26E
Bocholt Germany **38** 51.50N 6.36E
Bochum Germany **38** 51.28N 7.13E
Bochum R.S.A. **80** 23.12S 29.12E
Bockum-Hövel Germany **38** 51.42N 7.46E
Bocognano France **21** 42.05N 9.03E
Boconó Venezuela **122** 9.17N 70.17W
Boda C.A.R. **77** 4.19N 17.26E
Böda Sweden **43** 57.15N 17.03E
Boda Glasbruk Sweden **43** 56.44N 15.40E
Bodalla Australia **93** 36.05S150.03E
Bodallin Australia **89** 31.22S118.52E
Bodélé *f.* Chad **77** 16.50N 17.10E
Boden Sweden **40** 65.50N 21.42E
Bodensee *l.* Europe **39** 47.35N 9.25E
Bode Sadu Nigeria **77** 8.57N 4.49E
Bodfish U.S.A. **109** 35.36N118.30W
Bodmin U.K. **13** 50.28N 4.44W
Bodmin Moor U.K. **13** 50.53N 4.35W
Bodo Canada **101** 52.11N110.04W
Bodö Norway **40** 67.18N 14.26E
Bodrum Turkey **35** 37.02N 27.26E
Boembé Congo **78** 2.59S 15.34E
Boende Zaïre **78** 0.15S 20.49E
Boën-sur-Lignon France **20** 45.44N 3.59E
Boeo, Capo *c.* Italy **32** 37.48N 12.26E
Boffa Guinea **76** 10.12N 14.02W
Bofors Sweden **43** 59.20N 14.32E
Bogale Burma **56** 16.17N 95.24E
Bogalusa U.S.A. **111** 30.47N 89.52W
Bogan *r.* Australia **93** 30.00S146.20E
Bogan Gate *town* Australia **93** 33.08S147.50E
Bogata U.S.A. **111** 33.28N 95.13W
Bogcang Zangbo *r.* China **63** 31.50N 87.25E
Bogen Germany **39** 48.55N 12.43E
Bogenfels Namibia **80** 27.26S 15.22E
Bogense Denmark **42** 55.34N 10.06E
Boggabilla Australia **93** 28.36S150.21E
Boggabri Australia **93** 30.42S150.02E
Boggeragh Mts. Rep. of Ire. **15** 52.03N 8.53W
Bogia P.N.G. **59** 4.16S145.00E
Bognes Norway **40** 68.15N 16.00E
Bognor Regis U.K. **13** 50.47N 0.40W
Bog of Allen *f.* Rep. of Ire. **15** 53.17N 7.00W
Bogol Manyo Ethiopia **73** 4.32N 41.32E
Bogong, Mt. Australia **93** 36.45S147.21E
Bogor Indonesia **58** 6.34S106.45E
Bogotá Colombia **122** 4.38N 74.05W
Bogra Bangla. **63** 24.51N 89.22E
Bogué Mauritania **74** 16.35N 14.16W
Boguslav Ukraine **37** 49.32N 30.52E
Bo Hai *b.* China **54** 38.30N119.30E
Bohain France **19** 49.59N 3.27E
Bohai Wan *b.* China **54** 38.30N117.55E
Bohemian Forest *see* Böhmerwald *mts.* Germany **39**
Bohin Somali Rep. **71** 11.42N 51.17E
Bohinjska Bistrica Slovenia **31** 46.17N 13.57E
Böhmerwald *mts.* Germany **39** 49.12N 12.55E
Bohol *i.* Phil. **59** 9.45N124.10E
Bohuslän *f.* Sweden **42** 58.15N 11.50E
Boiaçu Brazil **122** 0.27S 61.46W
Boiano Italy **33** 41.29N 14.29E
Boigu *i.* Australia **90** 9.16S142.12E
Boing Sudan **73** 9.58N 33.44E
Boiro Spain **26** 42.39N 8.54W
Bois, Lac des *l.* Canada **98** 66.40N125.15W
Bois Blanc I. U.S.A. **104** 45.45N 84.28W
Bois du Roi *mtn.* France **19** 47.00N 4.02E
Boise U.S.A. **108** 43.37N116.13W
Boise City U.S.A. **111** 36.44N102.31W
Bois-Guillaume France **18** 49.28N 1.08E
Boissevain Canada **101** 49.15N100.00W
Boizenburg Germany **38** 53.22N 10.43E
Bojador, Cabo *c.* W. Sahara **74** 26.08N 14.30W
Bojana *r.* Albania **31** 41.50N 19.25E
Bojeador, C. Phil. **55** 18.30N120.36E
Bojnūrd Iran **65** 37.28N 57.20E
Bojonegoro Indonesia **59** 7.06S111.50E
Bokani Nigeria **77** 9.27N 5.13E
Boké Guinea **76** 10.57N 14.13W
Bokhara *r.* Australia **93** 29.55S146.42E
Boknafjorden *est.* Norway **42** 59.10N 5.35E
Bokoro Chad **77** 12.17N 17.04E
Bokote Zaïre **78** 0.05S 20.08E
Bokpyin Burma **56** 11.16N 98.46E
Bokungu Zaïre **78** 0.44S 22.28E
Bol Chad **77** 13.27N 14.40E
Bol Croatia **31** 43.16N 16.40E
Bolac Lake *town* Australia **92** 37.42S142.50E
Bolafa Zaïre **78** 1.23N 22.06E
Bolama Guinea Bissau **76** 11.35N 15.30W
Bolān *r.* Pakistan **62** 29.05N 67.45E
Bolanda, Jabal *mtn.* Sudan **73** 7.44N 25.28E
Bolaños de Calatrava Spain **26** 38.54N 3.40W
Bolān Pass Pakistan **62** 29.45N 67.35E
Bolbec France **18** 49.34N 0.29E
Bole Ghana **76** 9.03N 2.23W
Bolesławiec Poland **36** 51.16N 15.34E
Bolgatanga Ghana **76** 10.42N 0.52W
Bolgrad Ukraine **37** 45.42N 28.40E
Bolia Zaïre **78** 1.36S 18.23E
Bolívar Argentina **125** 36.14S 61.07W
Bolivar N.Y. U.S.A. **114** 42.04N 78.10W
Bolivar Tenn. U.S.A. **111** 35.16N 88.59W
Bolivia S. America **124** 17.00S 65.00W
Bollène France **21** 44.17N 4.45E
Bollnäs Sweden **41** 61.21N 16.25E
Bollon Australia **91** 28.02S147.28E
Bollstabruk Sweden **40** 62.59N 17.42E
Bollullos par del Condado Spain **27** 37.20N 6.32W
Bolmen *l.* Sweden **43** 56.55N 13.40E
Bolobo Zaïre **78** 2.10S 16.17E
Bologna Italy **30** 44.29N 11.20E
Bologoye Russian Fed. **44** 57.58N 34.00E
Bolomba Zaïre **78** 0.30N 19.13E
Bolombo Zaïre **78** 3.59S 21.22E

Bolondo to **Bregalnica**

Bolondo Equat. Guinea **78** 1.40N 9.38E
Bolongongo Angola **78** 8.28S 15.16E
Bolovens, Plateau des *f.* Laos **56** 15.10N106.30E
Bolsena Italy **30** 42.39N 11.59E
Bolsena, Lago di *l.* Italy **30** 42.36N 11.56E
Bolshaya Glushitsa Russian Fed. **44** 52.28N 50.30E
Bolshaya Pyssa Russian Fed. **44** 64.11N 48.44E
Bolsherechye Russian Fed. **50** 56.07N 74.40E
Bol'shevik, Ostrov *i.* Russian Fed. **51** 78.30N102.00E
Bolshezemelskaya Tundra *f.* Russian Fed. **44** 67.00N 56.10E
Bolshoy Atlym Russian Fed. **50** 62.17N 66.30E
Bol'shoy Balkhan, Khrebet *mts.* Turkmenistan **65** 39.38N 54.30E
Bol'shoy Irgiz *r.* Russian Fed. **44** 52.00N 47.20E
Bol'shoy Lyakhovskiy, Ostrov *i.* Russian Fed. **51** 73.30N142.00E
Bol'shoy Onguren Russian Fed. **51** 53.40N107.40E
Bolshoy Uzen *r.* Kazakhstan **45** 49.00N 49.40E
Bolsover U.K. **12** 53.14N 1.18W
Boltaña Spain **25** 42.27N 0.04E
Bolton U.K. **12** 53.35N 2.26W
Bolton L. Canada **101** 54.16N 95.47W
Bolu Turkey **64** 40.45N 31.38E
Bolus Head Rep. of Ire. **15** 51.47N 10.20W
Bolvadin Turkey **64** 38.43N 31.02E
Boly Hungary **31** 45.58N 18.32E
Bolzano Italy **30** 46.31N 11.22E
Boma Zaïre **78** 5.50S 13.03E
Bomaderry Australia **93** 34.21S150.34E
Bomadi Nigeria **77** 5.13N 6.01E
Bombala Australia **93** 36.55S149.16E
Bombarral Portugal **27** 39.16N 9.09W
Bombay India **62** 18.58N 72.50E
Bombo Uganda **71** 0.35N 32.32E
Bomboma Zaïre **78** 2.25N 18.54E
Bom Despacho Brazil **126** 19.46S 45.15W
Bomi China **52** 29.50N 95.45E
Bomi Hills Liberia **76** 7.01N 10.38W
Bömitz Germany **38** 53.08N 11.13E
Bömlafjorden *est.* Norway **42** 59.39N 5.20E
Bömlo *i.* Norway **42** 59.46N 5.12E
Bomokandi *r.* Zaïre **79** 3.37N 26.09E
Bomongo Zaïre **78** 1.30N 18.21E
Bomu *r.* Zaïre *see* Mbomou *r.* C.A.R. **73**
Bon, Cap *c.* Tunisia **32** 37.05N 11.03E
Bonaigarh India **63** 21.50N 84.57E
Bonaire *i.* Neth. Antilles **122** 12.15N 68.27W
Bonanza U.S.A. **108** 40.01N109.11W
Bonaparte *r.* Canada **100** 50.46N121.17W
Bonaparte Archipelago *is.* Australia **88** 14.17S125.18E
Bonar-Bridge *town* U.K. **14** 57.53N 4.21W
Bonarcado Italy **32** 40.04N 8.38E
Bonavista Canada **103** 48.39N 53.07W
Bonavista, C. Canada **103** 48.42N 53.05W
Bonavista B. Canada **103** 48.45N 53.20W
Bon Bon Australia **92** 30.26S135.28E
Bondeno Italy **30** 44.53N 11.25E
Bondo Equateur Zaïre **78** 1.22S 23.53E
Bondo Haut Zaïre Zaïre **78** 3.47N 23.45E
Bondoukou Ivory Coast **76** 8.03N 2.15W
Bondowoso Indonesia **59** 7.54S113.50E
Bone, Teluk *b.* Indonesia **59** 4.00S120.50E
Bo'ness U.K. **14** 56.01N 3.36W
Bonfield Canada **104** 46.14N 79.10W
Bonga Ethiopia **73** 7.17N 36.15E
Bongaigaon India **63** 26.28N 90.34E
Bongak Sudan **73** 7.27N 33.14E
Bongandanga Zaïre **78** 1.28N 21.03E
Bongor Chad **77** 10.18N 15.20E
Bongos, Massif des *mts.* C.A.R. **73** 8.20N 21.35E
Bongouanou Ivory Coast **76** 6.44N 4.10W
Bonham U.S.A. **111** 33.35N 96.11W
Bonifacio France **21** 41.23N 9.10E
Bonifacio, Str. of Italy **32** 41.20N 9.15E
Bonin Is. Japan **84** 27.00N142.10E
Bonn Germany **38** 50.44N 7.05E
Bonnechere Canada **105** 45.39N 77.35W
Bonnechère *r.* Canada **105** 45.31N 76.33W
Bonners Ferry U.S.A. **108** 48.41N116.18W
Bonnétable France **18** 48.11N 0.26E
Bonneval France **18** 48.11N 1.24E
Bonneville France **21** 46.05N 6.25E
Bonneville Salt Flats *f.* U.S.A. **108** 40.45N113.52W
Bonney, L. Australia **92** 37.47S140.23E
Bonnie Rock *town* Australia **89** 30.32S118.21E
Bonny Nigeria **77** 4.25N 7.10E
Bonny, Bight of Africa **77** 2.58N 7.00E
Bonnyville Canada **101** 54.16N110.44W
Bonorva Italy **32** 40.25N 8.45E
Bonshaw Australia **93** 29.08S150.53E
Bontang Indonesia **58** 0.05N117.31E
Bonthe Sierra Leone **76** 7.32N 12.30W
Bonyhád Hungary **31** 46.19N 18.32E
Bonython Range *mts.* Australia **88** 23.51S129.00E
Bookaloo Australia **92** 31.56S137.21E
Boola Guinea **76** 8.22N 8.41W
Booleroo Centre Australia **92** 32.53S138.21E
Booligal Australia **93** 33.54S144.54E
Boom Belgium **16** 51.07N 4.21E
Boomrivier R.S.A. **80** 29.34S 20.26E
Boone U.S.A. **110** 42.04N 93.53W
Booneville U.S.A. **111** 34.39N 88.34W
Boonsboro U.S.A. **114** 39.30N 77.39W
Boonville Mo. U.S.A. **110** 38.58N 92.44W
Boonville N.Y. U.S.A. **115** 43.29N 75.20W
Boorabbin Australia **89** 31.14S120.21E
Boorama Somali Rep. **71** 9.58N 43.07E
Boorindal Australia **93** 30.23S146.11E
Booroorban Australia **93** 34.56S144.46E
Boorowa Australia **93** 34.26S148.48E
Boort Australia **92** 36.08S143.46E
Boosaaso Somali Rep. **71** 11.13N 49.08E
Boothia, G. of Canada **99** 70.00N 90.00W
Boothia Pen. Canada **99** 70.30N 95.00W
Bootra Australia **92** 30.00S143.00E
Booué Gabon **78** 0.00 11.58E
Bopeechee Australia **92** 29.36S137.23E
Bophuthatswana Africa **80** 27.00S 23.30E
Boppard Germany **39** 50.14N 7.35E
Boquilla, Presa de la *l.* Mexico **109** 27.30N105.30W
Bor Czech Republic **38** 49.43N 12.47E
Bor Sudan **73** 6.12N 31.33E
Bor Yugo. **29** 44.05N 22.07E
Bora Bora *i.* Îs. de la Société **85** 16.30S151.45W
Borah Peak *mtn.* U.S.A. **108** 44.08N113.38W
Borås Sweden **43** 57.43N 12.55E
Borāzjān Iran **65** 29.14N 51.12E
Borba Brazil **122** 4.24S 59.35W
Borba Portugal **27** 38.48N 7.27W
Borda Cape *town* Australia **92** 35.45S136.34E
Bordeaux France **20** 44.50N 0.34W
Borden Australia **89** 34.05S118.16E
Borden I. Canada **98** 78.30N111.00W
Borden Pen. Canada **99** 73.00N 83.00W
Borders *d.* U.K. **14** 55.30N 2.53W
Bordertown Australia **92** 36.18S140.49E
Bordesholm Germany **38** 54.11N 10.01E
Bordheyri Iceland **40** 65.12N 21.06W
Bordighera Italy **30** 43.46N 7.39E
Bordj Bou Arreridj Algeria **75** 36.04N 4.46E
Bordj Flye Sainte Marie Algeria **74** 27.17N 2.59W
Bordj Omar Driss Algeria **75** 28.09N 6.49E
Bordö *i.* Faroe Is. **40** 62.10N 7.13W
Bore Ethiopia **73** 4.40N 37.40E
Boreda Ethiopia **73** 6.32N 37.48E
Borensberg Sweden **43** 58.34N 15.17E
Borgå Finland **41** 60.24N 25.40E
Borga Sweden **40** 64.49N 15.05E
Börgefjell *mtn.* Norway **40** 65.20N 13.45E
Börgefjell Nat. Park Norway **40** 65.00N 13.58E
Borger Neth. **16** 52.57N 6.46E
Borger U.S.A. **111** 35.39N101.24W
Borgholm Sweden **43** 56.53N 16.39E
Borghorst Germany **16** 52.08N 7.27E
Borgo Italy **30** 46.03N 11.27E
Borgomanero Italy **30** 45.42N 8.28E
Borgo San Dalmazzo Italy **30** 44.20N 7.30E
Borgo San Lorenzo Italy **30** 43.57N 11.23E
Borgosesia Italy **30** 45.43N 8.16E
Borgo Val di Taro Italy **30** 44.29N 9.46E
Borgund Norway **41** 61.03N 7.49E
Borislav Ukraine **37** 49.18N 23.28E
Borisoglebsk Russian Fed. **45** 51.23N 42.02E
Borisov Belorussia **37** 54.09N 28.30E
Borispol Ukraine **37** 50.21N 30.59E
Borja Peru **122** 4.20S 77.40W
Borja Spain **25** 41.50N 1.32W
Borken Germany **38** 51.51N 6.51E
Borkou-Ennedi-Tibesti *d.* Chad **75** 18.15N 20.00E
Borkum Germany **38** 53.35N 6.40E
Borkum *i.* Germany **38** 53.35N 6.41E
Borlänge Sweden **41** 60.29N 15.25E
Borley, C. Antarctica **128** 66.15S 55.00E
Bormes-les-Mimosas France **21** 43.09N 6.20E
Bormio Italy **30** 46.28N 10.22E
Borna Germany **38** 51.07N 12.30E
Borndiep *g.* Neth. **16** 53.28N 5.35E
Borneo *i.* Asia **58** 1.00N114.00E
Bornheim Germany **38** 50.46N 6.59E
Bornholm *i.* Denmark **43** 55.10N 15.00E
Borno *d.* Nigeria **77** 11.20N 12.40E
Bornos, Embalse de *resr.* Spain **27** 36.50N 5.42W
Bornu, Plain of *f.* Nigeria **77** 12.30N 13.00E
Boro *r.* Sudan **73** 8.52N 26.11E
Borodyanka Ukraine **37** 50.38N 29.59E
Boromo Burkina **76** 11.43N 2.53W
Borotou Ivory Coast **76** 8.46N 7.30W
Boroughbridge U.K. **12** 54.06N 1.23W
Borovan Bulgaria **34** 43.27N 23.45E
Borovichi Russian Fed. **44** 58.22N 34.00E
Borraan Somali Rep. **71** 10.10N 48.48E
Borrby Sweden **43** 55.27N 14.10E
Borrika Australia **92** 35.00S140.05E
Borroloola Australia **90** 16.04S136.17E
Borşa Romania **37** 47.39N 24.40E
Borşa Romania **37** 47.39N 24.40E
Borsad India **62** 22.25N 72.54E
Borth U.K. **13** 52.29N 4.03W
Bort-les-Orgues France **20** 45.24N 2.30E
Borūjerd Iran **65** 33.54N 48.47E
Bory Tucholskie *f.* Poland **37** 53.45N 17.30E
Borzhomi Georgia **45** 41.49N 43.23E
Borzna Ukraine **45** 51.15N 32.25E
Borzya Russian Fed. **51** 50.24N116.35E
Bosa Italy **32** 40.18N 8.30E
Bosanska Dubica Bosnia-Herzegovina **31** 45.11N 16.49E
Bosanska Gradiška Croatia **31** 45.09N 17.15E
Bosanska Krupa Bosnia-Herzegovina **31** 44.53N 16.10E
Bosanski Novi Bosnia-Herzegovina **31** 45.03N 16.23E
Bosanski Petrovac Bosnia-Herzegovina **31** 44.33N 16.22E
Bosanski Šamac Bosnia-Herzegovina **31** 45.03N 18.28E
Bosansko Grahovo Bosnia-Herzegovina **31** 44.11N 16.22E
Boscastle U.K. **13** 50.42N 4.42W
Bose China **55** 23.58N106.32E
Boshan China **54** 36.29N117.50E
Boshof R.S.A. **80** 28.32S 25.12E
Bosilegrad Yugo. **34** 42.29N 22.28E
Bosna *r.* Bosnia-Herzegovina **31** 45.04N 18.29E
Bosnia-Herzegovina Europe **31** 44.20N 18.00E
Bosnik Indonesia **59** 1.09S136.14E
Bosobolo Zaïre **73** 4.11N 19.54E
Bōsō-hantō *pen.* Japan **57** 35.08N140.00E
Bosporus *str. see* Istanbul Boğazi *str.* Turkey **29**
Bossangoa C.A.R. **77** 6.27N 17.21E
Bossembélé C.A.R. **77** 5.10N 17.44E
Bossier City U.S.A. **111** 32.31N 93.43W
Bosso Niger **77** 13.43N 13.19E
Bostān Pakistan **62** 30.26N 67.02E
Bosten Hu *l.* China **52** 42.00N 87.00E
Boston U.K. **12** 52.59N 0.02W
Boston U.S.A. **115** 42.21N 71.04W
Bosut *r.* Croatia / Yugo **31** 44.57N 19.22E
Boswell U.S.A. **114** 40.10N 79.02W
Botād India **62** 22.10N 71.40E
Botany B. Australia **93** 34.04S151.08E
Botev *mtn.* Bulgaria **34** 42.43N 24.55E
Botevgrad Bulgaria **34** 42.54N 23.47E
Bothnia, G. of Europe **40** 63.30N 20.30E
Bothwell Canada **104** 42.38N 81.52W
Boticas Portugal **26** 41.41N 7.40W
Botletle *r.* Botswana **80** 21.06S 24.47E
Botoşani Romania **37** 47.44N 26.41E
Botou Burkina **77** 12.47N 2.02E
Botrange *mtn.* Belgium **16** 50.30N 6.04E
Botro Ivory Coast **76** 7.51N 5.19W
Botswana Africa **80** 22.00S 24.15E
Bottrop Germany **38** 51.31N 6.55E
Botucatu Brazil **126** 22.52S 48.30W
Bouaflé Ivory Coast **76** 7.01N 5.47W
Bouaké Ivory Coast **76** 7.42N 5.00W
Bouar C.A.R. **77** 5.58N 15.35E
Bou Arfa Morocco **74** 32.30N 1.59W
Bouaye France **18** 47.09N 1.42W
Bouca C.A.R. **77** 6.30N 18.21E
Bouches-du-Rhône *d.* France **21** 43.30N 5.00E
Bouchette Canada **105** 46.11N 75.59W
Bouchoir France **19** 49.45N 2.41E
Boudenib Morocco **74** 31.57N 4.38W
Boufarik Algeria **75** 36.36N 2.54E
Bougainville *i.* Pacific Oc. **84** 6.00S155.00E
Bougouni Mali **76** 11.25N 7.28W
Bouillon Belgium **16** 49.48N 5.03E
Bouïra Algeria **75** 36.23N 3.54E
Bou-Izakarn Morocco **74** 29.09N 9.44W
Boulay-Moselle France **19** 49.11N 6.30E
Boulder Australia **89** 30.55S121.32E
Boulder U.S.A. **110** 40.01N105.17W
Boulder City U.S.A. **109** 35.59N114.50W
Boulia Australia **90** 22.54S139.54E
Boulogne France **19** 50.43N 1.37E
Boulogne *r.* France **18** 46.50N 1.25W
Boulogne-Billancourt France **19** 48.50N 2.15E
Boulogne-sur-Gesse France **20** 43.18N 0.39E
Boultoum Niger **77** 14.45N 10.25E
Boumba *r.* Cameroon **77** 2.00N 15.10E
Boumdeit Mauritania **74** 17.26N 9.50W
Boumo Chad **77** 9.01N 16.24E
Bouna Ivory Coast **76** 9.19N 2.53W
Boundary Peak *mtn.* U.S.A. **108** 37.51N118.21W
Boundiali Ivory Coast **76** 9.30N 6.31W
Bountiful U.S.A. **108** 40.53N111.53W
Bounty Is. Pacific Oc. **84** 48.00S178.30E
Bouraga *well* Mali **76** 19.00N 3.36W
Bourail N. Cal. **84** 21.34S165.30E
Bourbon-Lancy France **19** 46.38N 3.46E
Bourbonne-les-Bains France **19** 47.57N 5.45E
Bourem Mali **76** 16.59N 0.20W
Bourg France **21** 46.12N 5.13E
Bourganeuf France **20** 45.57N 1.46E
Bourges France **19** 47.05N 2.24E
Bourget Canada **105** 45.26N 75.09W
Bourget, Lac du *l.* France **21** 45.44N 5.52E
Bourg Madame France **20** 42.26N 1.55E
Bourgneuf-en-Retz France **18** 47.02N 1.57W
Bourgogne *d.* France **19** 47.10N 4.20E
Bourgogne, Canal de France **19** 47.58N 3.30E
Bourgoin France **21** 45.36N 5.17E
Bourg-St. Andéol France **21** 44.22N 4.39E
Bourg-St. Maurice France **21** 45.37N 6.46E
Bourgueil France **18** 47.17N 0.10E
Bourke Australia **93** 30.09S145.59E
Bournemouth U.K. **13** 50.43N 1.53W
Bou Saâda Algeria **75** 35.12N 4.11E
Bou Salem Tunisia **32** 36.36N 8.59E
Boussac France **20** 46.21N 2.13E
Bousso Chad **77** 10.32N 16.45E
Bouteldja Algeria **32** 36.47N 8.13E
Boutilimit Mauritania **74** 17.33N 14.42W
Boutonne *r.* France **20** 45.53N 0.50W
Bouvard, C. Australia **89** 32.40S115.34E
Bouvetöya *i.* Atlantic Oc. **127** 54.26S 3.24E
Bovalino Marino Italy **33** 38.09N 16.11E
Bovec Slovenia **31** 46.20N 13.33E
Bovill U.S.A. **108** 46.51N116.24W
Bovril Argentina **125** 31.22S 59.25W
Bow *r.* Canada **100** 51.10N115.00W
Bowelling Australia **89** 33.25S116.27E
Bowen Australia **90** 20.00S148.15E
Bowen, Mt. Australia **93** 37.11S148.34E
Bowie Ariz. U.S.A. **109** 32.19N109.29W
Bowie Tex. U.S.A. **111** 33.34N 97.51W
Bow Island *town* Canada **101** 49.52N111.22W
Bowling Green U.S.A. **113** 37.00N 86.29W
Bowling Green, C. Australia **90** 19.19S146.25E
Bowman U.S.A. **110** 46.11N103.24W
Bowman I. Antarctica **128** 65.00S104.00E
Bowmanville Canada **104** 43.55N 78.41W
Bowral Australia **93** 34.30S150.24E
Bowser Australia **93** 36.19S146.23E
Boxholm Sweden **43** 58.12N 15.03E
Bo Xian China **54** 33.50N115.46E
Boxing China **54** 37.08N118.05E
Box Tank Australia **92** 32.13S142.17E
Boxtel Neth. **16** 51.36N 5.20E
Boyabat Turkey **64** 41.27N 34.45E
Boyang China **55** 28.59N116.42E
Boyanup Australia **89** 33.29S115.40E
Boyarka Ukraine **37** 50.20N 30.26E
Boyd *r.* Australia **93** 29.51S152.25E
Boykétté C.A.R. **73** 5.28N 20.50E
Boyle Rep. of Ire. **15** 53.58N 8.19W
Boyne *r.* Rep. of Ire. **15** 53.43N 6.17W
Boyoma Falls *f.* Zaïre **78** 0.18N 25.32E
Boyup Brook Australia **89** 33.50S116.22E
Bozburun Turkey **35** 36.43N 28.08E
Bozcaada Turkey **34** 39.49N 26.03E
Bozca Ada *i.* Turkey **34** 39.49N 26.03E
Bozel France **21** 45.27N 6.39E
Bozeman U.S.A. **108** 45.41N111.02W
Bozen *see* Bolzano Italy **30**
Bozoum C.A.R. **77** 6.16N 16.22E
Bra Italy **30** 44.42N 7.51E
Braås Sweden **43** 57.04N 15.03E
Brabant *d.* Belgium **16** 50.47N 4.30E
Brač *i.* Croatia **29** 43.20N 16.38E
Bracadale, Loch U.K. **14** 57.22N 6.30W
Bracciano Italy **32** 42.06N 12.10E
Bracciano, Lago di *l.* Italy **30** 42.07N 12.14E
Bracebridge Canada **104** 45.02N 79.19W
Bracieux France **19** 47.33N 1.33E
Bräcke Sweden **40** 62.44N 15.30E
Bracki Kanal *str.* Croatia **31** 43.24N 16.40E
Brad Romania **29** 46.06N 22.48E
Bradano *r.* Italy **33** 40.23N 16.51E
Bradenton U.S.A. **113** 27.29N 82.33W
Bradford Canada **104** 44.07N 79.34W
Bradford U.K. **12** 53.47N 1.45W
Bradford N.H. U.S.A. **115** 43.17N 71.59W
Bradford Penn. U.S.A. **114** 41.58N 78.39W
Bradford Vt. U.S.A. **105** 43.59N 72.09W
Bradley U.S.A. **111** 33.06N 93.39W
Bradworthy U.K. **13** 50.54N 4.22W
Brady U.S.A. **111** 31.08N 99.20W
Braemar U.K. **14** 57.01N 3.24W
Braga Portugal **26** 41.33N 8.26W
Braga *d.* Portugal **26** 41.30N 8.05W
Bragado Argentina **125** 35.10S 60.30W
Bragança Brazil **123** 1.03S 46.46W
Bragança Portugal **26** 41.49N 6.45W
Bragança *d.* Portugal **26** 41.30N 6.50W
Bragança Paulista Brazil **126** 22.59S 46.32W
Bragin Belorussia **37** 51.49N 30.16E
Brāhmanbāria Bangla. **63** 23.59N 91.07E
Brāhmani *r.* India **63** 20.39N 86.46E
Brahmaputra *r.* Asia **63** 23.50N 89.45E
Braidwood Australia **93** 35.27S149.50E
Brăila Romania **37** 45.18N 27.58E
Brainerd U.S.A. **107** 46.20N 94.10W
Braintree U.K. **13** 51.53N 0.32E
Brake Germany **38** 53.19N 8.28E
Brakna *d.* Mauritania **74** 17.00N 13.20W
Brålanda Sweden **43** 58.34N 12.22E
Bramfield Australia **92** 33.37S134.59E
Bramming Denmark **42** 55.28N 8.42E
Brampton Canada **104** 43.41N 79.46W
Brampton U.K. **12** 54.56N 2.43W
Bramsche Germany **38** 52.24N 7.58E
Brancaleone Marina Italy **33** 37.58N 16.06E
Branco *r.* Brazil **122** 1.00S 62.00W
Brandberg *mtn.* Namibia **80** 21.08S 14.35E
Brandbu Norway **41** 60.28N 10.30E
Brande Denmark **42** 55.57N 9.07E
Brandenburg Germany **38** 52.24N 12.32E
Brandenburg *d.* Germany **38** 52.15N 13.10E
Brandenburg *f.* Germany **38** 52.40N 13.00E
Brandfort R.S.A. **80** 28.41S 26.27E
Brandon Canada **101** 49.50N 99.57W
Brandon U.S.A. **105** 43.48N 73.05W
Brandon Mtn. Rep. of Ire. **15** 52.14N 10.15W
Brandon Pt. Rep. of Ire. **15** 52.17N 10.11W
Braniewo Poland **37** 54.24N 19.50E
Bransby Australia **92** 28.40S142.00E
Branson U.S.A. **111** 36.39N 93.13W
Brantas *r.* Indonesia **59** 7.13S112.45E
Brantford Canada **104** 43.08N 80.16W
Brantôme France **20** 45.22N 0.39E
Bras d'Or L. Canada **103** 45.52N 60.50W
Brasher Falls U.S.A. **105** 44.48N 74.48W
Brasil, Planalto *mts.* Brazil **123** 17.02S 50.00W
Brasiléia Brazil **122** 11.00S 68.44W
Brasília Brazil **123** 15.45S 47.57W
Braşov Romania **37** 45.40N 25.35E
Brass Nigeria **77** 4.20N 6.15E
Brasschaat Belgium **16** 51.18N 4.28E
Bratislava Slovakia **37** 48.10N 17.10E
Bratsk Russian Fed. **51** 56.20N101.15E
Bratsk Vodokhranilishche *resr.* Russian Fed. **51** 54.40N103.00E
Bratslav Ukraine **37** 48.49N 28.51E
Brattleboro U.S.A. **115** 42.51N 72.34W
Braunau Austria **39** 48.15N 13.02E
Braunschweig Germany **38** 52.16N 10.31E
Braunton U.K. **13** 51.06N 4.09W
Bråviken *b.* Sweden **43** 58.38N 16.32E
Bravo del Norte, Rio *r.* Mexico *see* Rio Grande *r.* Mexico / U.S.A. **111**
Brawley U.S.A. **109** 32.59N115.31W
Bray France **19** 48.25N 3.14E
Bray Rep. of Ire. **15** 53.12N 6.07W
Bray Head Kerry Rep. of Ire. **15** 51.53N 10.26W
Brazeau *r.* Canada **100** 52.55N115.15W
Brazil S. America **120** 10.00S 52.00W
Brazilian Basin *f.* Atlantic Oc. **127** 15.00S 25.00W
Brazilian Highlands *see* Brasil, Planalto *mts.* Brazil **123**
Brazos *r.* U.S.A. **111** 28.53N 95.23W
Brazzaville Congo **78** 4.14S 15.10E
Brčko Bosnia-Herzegovina **31** 44.53N 18.48E
Brda *r.* Poland **37** 53.07N 18.08E
Breadalbane *f.* U.K. **14** 56.30N 4.20W
Bream B. New Zealand **86** 36.00S174.30E
Brebes Indonesia **59** 6.54S109.00E
Brécey France **18** 48.44N 1.10W
Brechin U.K. **14** 56.44N 2.40W
Breckenridge Mich. U.S.A. **104** 43.24N 84.29W
Breckenridge *Tex.* U.S.A. **111** 32.45N 98.54W
Breckland *f.* U.K. **13** 52.28N 0.40E
Břeclav Czech Republic **36** 48.46N 16.53E
Brecon U.K. **13** 51.57N 3.23W
Brecon Beacons *mts.* U.K. **13** 51.53N 3.27W
Breda Neth. **16** 51.35N 4.46E
Bredasdorp R.S.A. **80** 34.31S 20.03E
Bredbo Australia **93** 35.57S149.10E
Bredstedt Germany **38** 54.37N 8.59E
Breezewood U.S.A. **114** 40.01N 78.15W
Bregalnica *r.* Macedonia **34** 41.50N 22.20E

Bregenz to **Burgsteinfurt**

Bregenz Austria **39** 47.30N 9.46E
Bregovo Bulgaria **29** 44.08N 22.39E
Bréhal France **18** 48.54N 1.31W
Breidhafjördhur *est.* Iceland **40** 65.15N 23.00W
Breim Norway **41** 61.44N 6.25E
Breisach Germany **39** 48.01N 7.40E
Brekstad Norway **40** 63.42N 9.40E
Bremangerland *i.* Norway **41** 61.51N 5.02E
Bremen Germany **38** 53.05N 8.49E
Bremen *d.* Germany **38** 53.08N 8.46E
Bremen U.S.A. **114** 39.42N 82.26W
Bremer Bay *town* Australia **89** 34.21S119.20E
Bremerhaven Germany **38** 53.33N 8.34E
Bremer Range *mts.* Australia **89** 32.40S120.55E
Bremerton U.S.A. **108** 47.34N122.38W
Bremervörde Germany **38** 53.29N 9.08E
Brenes Spain **27** 37.33N 5.52W
Brenham U.S.A. **111** 30.10N 96.24W
Brenner Pass Austria/Italy **39** 47.00N 11.30E
Breno Italy **30** 45.57N 10.18E
Brent Canada **104** 46.02N 78.29W
Brenta *r.* Italy **30** 45.11N 12.18E
Brentwood U.K. **13** 51.38N 0.18E
Brescia Italy **30** 45.33N 10.15E
Breskens Neth. **16** 51.24N 3.34E
Bresle *r.* France **19** 50.04N 1.22E
Bressanone Italy **30** 46.43N 11.39E
Bressay *i.* U.K. **14** 60.08N 1.05W
Bresse, Plaine de *f.* France **19** 46.20N 5.10E
Bressuire France **18** 46.51N 0.30W
Brest Belorussia **37** 52.08N 23.40E
Brest Bulgaria **34** 43.38N 24.35E
Brest France **18** 48.24N 4.29W
Brestanica Slovenia **31** 45.59N 15.29E
Brest-Nantes Canal France **18** 48.13N 3.26W
Bretagne *d.* France **18** 48.15N 2.30W
Breteuil France **19** 49.38N 2.18E
Breteuil-sur-Iton France **18** 48.50N 0.55E
Breton, Pertuis *str.* France **20** 46.25N 1.20W
Breton Sd. U.S.A. **111** 29.30N 89.30W
Brett, C. New Zealand **86** 35.15S174.20E
Bretten Germany **39** 49.02N 8.42E
Breuil-Cervinia Italy **30** 45.56N 7.38E
Brevik Norway **42** 59.04N 9.42E
Brewarrina Australia **93** 29.57S147.54E
Brewer U.S.A. **112** 44.48N 68.46W
Brewster N.Y. U.S.A. **115** 41.24N 73.37W
Brewster Ohio U.S.A. **114** 40.43N 81.36W
Brewster, Kap *c.* Greenland **96** 70.00N 25.00W
Brewton U.S.A. **113** 31.07N 87.04W
Brežice Slovenia **31** 45.54N 15.36E
Březnice Czech Republic **38** 49.33N 13.57E
Breznik Bulgaria **34** 42.44N 22.50E
Brezovo Bulgaria **34** 42.20N 25.06E
Bria C.A.R. **73** 6.32N 21.59E
Briançon France **21** 44.54N 6.39E
Briare France **19** 47.38N 2.44E
Bribbaree Australia **93** 34.07S147.51E
Brichany Moldavia **37** 48.20N 27.01E
Bricquebec France **18** 49.28N 1.38W
Bride I.o.M. Europe **12** 54.23N 4.24W
Bridge *r.* Canada **100** 50.50N122.40W
Bridgen Canada **104** 42.47N 82.16W
Bridgend U.K. **13** 51.30N 3.35W
Bridgeport Calif. U.S.A. **108** 38.10N119.13W
Bridgeport Conn. U.S.A. **115** 41.11N 73.11W
Bridgeport Nebr. U.S.A. **110** 41.40N103.06W
Bridgeport Tex. U.S.A. **111** 33.13N 97.45W
Bridgeport W.Va. U.S.A. **114** 39.17N 80.15W
Bridger U.S.A. **108** 45.18N108.55W
Bridgeton U.S.A. **115** 39.26N 75.14W
Bridgetown Australia **89** 33.57S116.08E
Bridgetown Barbados **117** 13.06N 59.37W
Bridgetown Canada **103** 44.51N 65.18W
Bridgetown Rep. of Ire. **15** 52.14N 6.33W
Bridgeville U.S.A. **115** 38.45N 75.36W
Bridgewater Canada **103** 44.23N 64.31W
Bridgewater U.S.A. **114** 38.18N 78.59W
Bridgewater, C. Australia **92** 38.25S141.28E
Bridgnorth U.K. **13** 52.33N 2.25W
Bridgwater U.K. **13** 51.08N 3.00W
Bridlington U.K. **12** 54.06N 0.11W
Brie *f.* France **19** 48.40N 3.20E
Briec France **18** 48.06N 4.00W
Brienne-le-Château France **19** 48.24N 4.32E
Brienz Switz. **19** 46.46N 8.03E
Briey France **19** 49.15N 5.56E
Brig Switz. **19** 46.19N 8.00E
Brigantine U.S.A. **115** 39.24N 74.22W
Brigg U.K. **12** 53.33N 0.30W
Briggsdale U.S.A. **110** 40.38N104.20W
Brigham City U.S.A. **108** 41.31N112.01W
Bright Australia **93** 36.42S146.58E
Brighton Canada **105** 44.02N 77.44W
Brighton U.K. **13** 50.50N 0.09W
Brighton Colo. U.S.A. **108** 39.59N104.49W
Brighton Fla. U.S.A. **113** 27.13N 81.06W
Brighton Mich. U.S.A. **104** 42.32N 83.47W
Brignoles France **21** 43.24N 6.04E
Brihuega Spain **26** 40.48N 2.52W
Brikama Gambia **76** 13.15N 16.39W
Brilon Germany **38** 51.24N 8.34E
Brindisi Italy **33** 40.38N 17.56E
Brinje Croatia **31** 45.00N 15.08E
Brinkley U.S.A. **111** 34.53N 91.12W
Brinkworth Australia **92** 33.42S138.24E
Brionne France **18** 49.12N 0.43E
Brioude France **20** 45.18N 3.23E
Briouze France **18** 48.42N 0.22W
Brisbane Australia **93** 27.30S153.00E
Brisighella Italy **30** 44.13N 11.46E
Bristol U.K. **13** 51.26N 2.35W
Bristol Conn. U.S.A. **115** 41.41N 72.57W
Bristol N.H. U.S.A. **115** 43.36N 71.45W
Bristol Penn. U.S.A. **115** 40.06N 74.52W
Bristol R.I. U.S.A. **115** 41.40N 71.16W
Bristol S.Dak. U.S.A. **110** 45.21N 97.45W
Bristol Tenn. U.S.A. **113** 36.33N 82.11W
Bristol Vt. U.S.A. **105** 44.08N 73.05W
Bristol B. U.S.A. **98** 58.00N158.50W
Bristol Channel U.K. **13** 51.17N 3.20W
British Antarctic Territory Antarctica **128** 70.00S 50.00W
British Columbia *d.* Canada **100** 55.00N125.00W
British Mts. Canada **98** 69.00N140.20W
British Virgin Is. C. America **117** 18.30N 64.30W
Britstown R.S.A. **80** 30.34S 23.30E
Britt Canada **104** 45.46N 80.35W
Britton U.S.A. **110** 45.48N 97.45W
Brive France **20** 45.10N 1.32E
Briviesca Spain **26** 42.33N 3.19W
Brixham U.K. **13** 50.24N 3.31W
Brno Czech Republic **36** 49.11N 16.39E
Broach India **62** 21.42N 72.58E
Broad Arrow Australia **89** 30.32S121.20E
Broad B. U.K. **14** 58.15N 6.15W
Broadback *r.* Canada **102** 51.20N 78.50W
Broadford Australia **93** 37.16S145.03E
Broadmere Australia **90** 25.30S149.30E
Broad Sd. Australia **90** 22.20S149.50E
Broadsound Range *mts.* Australia **90** 22.30S149.30E
Broadus U.S.A. **108** 45.27N105.25W
Broadview Canada **101** 50.20N102.30W
Broadway U.K. **13** 52.02N 1.51W
Brochet Canada **101** 57.53N101.40W
Brochet, L. Canada **101** 58.36N101.35W
Brocken *mtn.* Germany **38** 51.50N 10.50E
Brockport U.S.A. **114** 43.13N 77.56W
Brockton U.S.A. **115** 42.05N 71.01W
Brockville Canada **105** 44.35N 75.41W
Brockway Mont. U.S.A. **108** 47.15N105.45W
Brockway Penn. U.S.A. **114** 41.15N 78.47W
Brocton U.S.A. **114** 42.23N 79.27W
Brod Croatia **31** 45.10N 18.01E
Brod Macedonia **34** 41.35N 21.17E
Brodeur Pen. Canada **99** 73.00N 88.00W
Brodick U.K. **14** 55.34N 5.09W
Brodnica Poland **37** 53.16N 19.23E
Brody Ukraine **37** 50.05N 25.08E
Broglie France **18** 49.01N 0.32E
Broke Inlet Australia **89** 34.55S116.25E
Broken Arrow U.S.A. **111** 36.03N 95.48W
Broken B. Australia **93** 33.34S151.18E
Broken Bow U.S.A. **110** 41.24N 99.38W
Broken Hill *town* Australia **92** 31.57S141.30E
Bromley U.K. **13** 51.24N 0.02E
Bromley Plateau *f.* Atlantic Oc. **127** 30.00S 34.00W
Bromölla Sweden **43** 56.04N 14.28E
Bromsgrove U.K. **11** 52.20N 2.03W
Bron France **21** 45.44N 4.55E
Brönderslev Denmark **42** 57.16N 9.58E
Brong-Ahafo *d.* Ghana **76** 7.45N 1.30W
Brönnöysund Norway **40** 65.30N 12.10E
Bronte Canada **104** 43.23N 79.43W
Bronte Italy **33** 37.48N 14.50E
Brooke's Point *town* Phil. **58** 8.50N117.52E
Brookfield U.S.A. **110** 39.47N 93.04W
Brookhaven U.S.A. **111** 31.35N 90.26W
Brookings Oreg. U.S.A. **108** 42.03N124.17W
Brookings S.Dak. U.S.A. **110** 44.19N 96.48W
Brooklin Canada **104** 43.57N 78.57W
Brooklyn U.S.A. **104** 42.06N 84.15W
Brooklyn Center U.S.A. **110** 45.05N 93.20W
Brooks Canada **98** 50.35N111.53W
Brooks B. Canada **100** 50.15N127.55W
Brooks Range *mts.* U.S.A. **98** 68.50N152.00W
Brooksville U.S.A. **113** 28.34N 82.24W
Brookton Australia **89** 32.22S117.01E
Brookville U.S.A. **114** 41.09N 79.05W
Broom, Loch U.K. **14** 57.52N 5.07W
Broome Australia **88** 17.58S122.15E
Broome, Mt. Australia **88** 17.21S125.23E
Broomehill *town* Australia **89** 33.50S117.35E
Broons France **18** 48.19N 2.16W
Brora U.K. **14** 58.01N 3.52W
Brora *r.* U.K. **14** 58.00N 3.51W
Brörup Denmark **42** 55.29N 9.01E
Brosna *r.* Rep. of Ire. **15** 53.13N 7.58W
Brossac France **20** 45.20N 0.03W
Brothers U.S.A. **108** 43.49N120.36W
Broto Spain **25** 42.36N 0.06W
Brou France **18** 48.13N 1.11E
Brough England U.K. **12** 54.32N 2.19W
Brough Scotland U.K. **14** 60.29N 1.12W
Broughton *r.* Australia **92** 33.21S137.46E
Broughton in Furness U.K. **12** 54.17N 3.12W
Brouwershaven Neth. **16** 51.44N 3.53E
Brovary Ukraine **37** 50.30N 30.45E
Brovst Denmark **42** 57.06N 9.32E
Brown, Mt. Australia **92** 32.33S138.02E
Brown City U.S.A. **114** 43.13N 82.59W
Brownfield U.S.A. **111** 33.11N102.16W
Browning U.S.A. **108** 48.34N113.01W
Brownsburg Canada **105** 45.41N 74.25W
Brownsville Penn. U.S.A. **114** 40.01N 79.53W
Brownsville Tenn. U.S.A. **111** 35.36N 89.15W
Brownsville Tex. U.S.A. **111** 25.54N 97.30W
Brownville U.S.A. **105** 44.01N 75.59W
Brownwood U.S.A. **111** 31.43N 98.59W
Brozas Spain **27** 39.37N 6.46W
Bruay-en-Artois France **19** 50.29N 2.33E
Bruce Mines Canada **104** 46.18N 83.48W
Bruce Pen. Canada **104** 45.00N 81.20W
Bruce Rock *town* Australia **89** 31.52S118.09E
Bruche *r.* France **19** 48.31N 7.41E
Bruchsal Germany **39** 49.07N 8.35E
Bruck Austria **39** 47.17N 12.49E
Brückenau Germany **39** 50.18N 9.47E
Bruges *see* Brugge Belgium **16**
Brugg Switz. **19** 47.29N 8.12E
Brugge Belgium **16** 51.13N 3.14E
Brühl Germany **38** 50.48N 6.54E
Brûlé, Lac *l.* Que. Canada **103** 52.17N 63.52W
Brûlé, Lac *l.* Que. Canada **105** 46.57N 77.13W
Brumadinho Brazil **126** 20.09S 44.11W
Brumado Brazil **123** 14.13S 41.40W
Brumath France **19** 48.44N 7.43E
Brunei Asia **58** 4.56N114.58E
Brünen Germany **38** 51.43N 6.39E
Brunflo Sweden **40** 63.04N 14.50E
Brunico Italy **30** 46.48N 11.56E
Brunkeberg Norway **42** 59.26N 8.29E
Brunner New Zealand **86** 42.28S171.12E
Brunsbüttel Germany **38** 53.54N 9.05E
Brunssum Neth. **16** 50.57N 5.59E
Brunswick Ga. U.S.A. **113** 31.09N 81.30W
Brunswick Maine U.S.A. **112** 43.55N 69.58W
Brunswick Md. U.S.A. **114** 39.18N 77.37W
Brunswick B. Australia **88** 15.05S125.00E
Brunswick Junction Australia **89** 33.15S115.45E
Bruny I. Australia **91** 43.15S147.16E
Brushton U.S.A. **105** 44.51N 74.30W
Brusilovka Kazakhstan **45** 50.39N 54.59E
Brussel *see* Bruxelles Belgium **16**
Brussels *see* Bruxelles Belgium **16**
Bruthen Australia **93** 37.44S147.49E
Bruton U.K. **13** 51.06N 2.28W
Bruxelles Belgium **16** 50.50N 4.23E
Bruyères France **19** 48.12N 6.43E
Bryagovo Bulgaria **34** 41.58N 25.08E
Bryan Ohio U.S.A. **112** 41.30N 84.34W
Bryan Tex. U.S.A. **111** 30.40N 96.22W
Bryan, Mt. Australia **92** 33.26S138.27E
Bryansk Russian Fed. **44** 53.15N 34.09E
Bryne Norway **42** 58.44N 5.39E
Bryson Canada **105** 45.40N 76.36W
Bryson, Lac *l.* Canada **105** 46.27N 77.00W
Bryson City U.S.A. **113** 35.26N 83.27W
Brzeg Poland **37** 50.52N 17.27E
Bsharrī Lebanon **66** 34.15N 36.00E
Bua *r.* Malaŵi **79** 12.42S 34.15E
Bua Yai Thailand **56** 15.34N102.24E
Bu'ayrāt al Ḩasūn Libya **75** 31.24N 15.44E
Buba Guinea Bissau **76** 11.36N 14.55W
Būbiyān, Jazīrat *i.* Kuwait **71** 29.45N 48.15E
Bubye *r.* Zimbabwe **80** 22.18S 31.00E
Bucak Turkey **64** 37.28N 30.36E
Bucaramanga Colombia **122** 7.08N 73.10W
Buccino Italy **33** 40.37N 15.23E
Buchach Ukraine **37** 49.09N 25.20E
Buchanan Liberia **76** 5.57N 10.02W
Buchanan, L. Australia **90** 21.28S145.52E
Buchanan L. U.S.A. **111** 30.48N 98.25W
Buchan Ness *c.* U.K. **14** 57.28N 1.47W
Buchans Canada **103** 48.49N 56.52W
Bucharest *see* Bucureşti Romania **37**
Buchen Germany **39** 49.32N 9.17E
Buchloe Germany **39** 48.02N 10.44E
Bucholz Germany **38** 53.20N 9.52E
Buchs Switz. **39** 47.10N 9.28E
Buchy France **18** 49.35N 1.22E
Buckambool Mt. Australia **93** 31.55S145.40E
Bückeburg Germany **38** 52.16N 9.02E
Buckeye Lake *town* U.S.A. **114** 39.56N 82.29W
Buckhannon U.S.A. **114** 38.59N 80.14W
Buckhaven and Methil U.K. **12** 56.11N 3.03W
Buckhorn Canada **104** 44.33N 78.20W
Buckhorn L. Canada **104** 44.28N 78.23W
Buckie U.K. **14** 57.40N 2.58W
Buckingham Canada **105** 45.35N 75.25W
Buckingham U.K. **13** 52.00N 0.59W
Buckingham B. Australia **90** 12.10S135.46E
Buckinghamshire *d.* U.K. **13** 51.50N 0.48W
Buckland Tableland *f.* Australia **90** 25.00S148.00E
Buckleboo Australia **92** 32.55S136.12E
Buckley U.S.A. **110** 40.35N 88.04W
Bucklin U.S.A. **111** 37.33N 99.38W
Buco Zau Angola **78** 4.46S 12.34E
Bucquoy France **19** 50.08N 2.42E
Bu Craa W. Sahara **74** 26.21N 12.57W
Buctouche Canada **103** 46.28N 64.43W
Bucureşti Romania **37** 44.25N 26.06E
Bucyrus U.S.A. **114** 40.48N 82.58W
Bud Norway **40** 62.54N 6.56E
Budapest Hungary **37** 47.30N 19.03E
Budaun India **63** 28.03N 79.07E
Budda Australia **92** 31.12S144.16E
Budd Coast *f.* Antarctica **128** 67.00S112.00E
Buddh Gaya India **63** 24.42N 84.59E
Buddusò Italy **32** 40.35N 9.16E
Bude U.K. **13** 50.49N 4.33W
Bude B. U.K. **13** 50.50N 4.40W
Budennovsk Russian Fed. **45** 44.50N 44.10E
Büdingen Germany **39** 50.17N 9.07E
Budjala Zaïre **78** 2.38N 19.48E
Buea Cameroon **77** 4.09N 9.13E
Buenaventura Colombia **122** 3.54N 77.02W
Buenaventura Mexico **109** 29.51N107.29W
Buena Vista U.S.A. **113** 37.44N 79.22W
Buendia, Embalse de *resr.* Spain **26** 40.25N 2.43W
Buenos Aires Argentina **125** 34.40S 58.25W
Buenos Aires *d.* Argentina **125** 36.30S 59.00W
Buenos Aires, L. Argentina/Chile **125** 46.35S 72.00W
Buffalo Canada **101** 50.49N110.42W
Buffalo *r.* Canada **100** 60.55N115.00W
Buffalo Mo. U.S.A. **111** 37.39N 93.06W
Buffalo N.Y. U.S.A. **114** 42.54N 78.53W
Buffalo Okla. U.S.A. **111** 36.50N 99.38W
Buffalo S.Dak. U.S.A. **110** 45.35N103.33W
Buffalo W.Va. U.S.A. **114** 38.39N 81.57W
Buffalo Wyo. U.S.A. **108** 44.21N106.42W
Buffalo Head Hills Canada **100** 57.25N115.55W
Buffalo L. Canada **100** 60.10N115.30W
Buffalo Narrows *town* Canada **101** 55.51N108.30W
Bug *r.* Poland **37** 52.29N 21.11E
Buga Colombia **122** 3.53N 76.17W
Bugaldie Australia **93** 31.02S149.08E
Bugeat France **20** 45.35N 1.59E
Bugembe Uganda **79** 0.26N 33.16E
Bugene Tanzania **79** 1.34S 31.07E
Buggs Island L. U.S.A. **113** 36.35N 78.28W
Bugojno Bosnia-Herzegovina **31** 44.03N 17.27E
Bugrino Russian Fed. **44** 68.45N 49.15E
Bugt China **53** 48.45N121.58E
Bugulma Russian Fed. **44** 54.32N 52.46E
Buguma Nigeria **77** 4.43N 6.53E
Buguruslan Russian Fed. **44** 53.36N 52.30E
Buhera Zimbabwe **81** 19.21S 31.25E
Bühl Germany **39** 48.42N 8.08E
Buhuşi Romania **37** 46.43N 26.41E
Builth Wells U.K. **13** 52.09N 3.24W
Buinsk Russian Fed. **44** 54.58N 48.15E
Bu'in-Sofiā Iran **65** 35.51N 46.02E
Buitenpost Neth. **16** 53.15N 6.09E
Bujalance Spain **27** 37.54N 4.22W
Bujaraloz Spain **25** 41.30N 0.09W
Buje Croatia **31** 45.24N 13.40E
Buji P.N.G. **90** 9.07S142.26E
Bujumbura Burundi **79** 3.22S 29.21E
Bukama Zaïre **78** 9.16S 25.52E
Bukavu Zaïre **79** 2.30S 28.49E
Bukene Tanzania **79** 4.13S 32.52E
Bukhara Uzbekistan **65** 39.47N 64.26E
Buki Ukraine **37** 49.02N 30.29E
Bukima Tanzania **79** 1.48S 33.25E
Bukittinggi Indonesia **58** 0.18S100.20E
Bukoba Tanzania **79** 1.20S 31.49E
Bukovica *f.* Croatia **31** 44.10N 15.40E
Bukrale Ethiopia **73** 4.30N 42.03E
Bukuru Nigeria **77** 9.48N 8.52E
Būl, Kūh-e *mtn.* Iran **65** 30.48N 52.45E
Bula Indonesia **59** 3.07S130.27E
Bülach Switz. **39** 47.31N 8.32E
Bulahdelah Australia **93** 32.25S152.13E
Bulan Phil. **59** 12.40N123.53E
Bulandshahr India **63** 28.24N 77.51E
Bulawayo Zimbabwe **80** 20.10S 28.43E
Bulbjerg *hill* Denmark **42** 57.09N 9.02E
Buldāna India **62** 20.32N 76.11E
Buldern Germany **16** 51.52N 7.21E
Bulgan Mongolia **52** 48.34N103.12E
Bulgaria Europe **34** 42.35N 25.30E
Bullabulling Australia **89** 31.05S120.52E
Bullaque *r.* Spain **27** 38.59N 4.17W
Bullara Australia **88** 22.40S114.03E
Bullas Spain **25** 38.03N 1.40W
Bullaxaar Somali Rep. **71** 10.23N 44.27E
Bulle Switz. **39** 46.37N 7.04E
Buller *r.* New Zealand **86** 41.45S171.35E
Buller, Mt. Australia **93** 37.11S146.26E
Bullfinch Australia **89** 30.59S119.06E
Bulli Australia **93** 34.20S150.55E
Bull Mts. U.S.A. **108** 46.05N109.00W
Bulloo *r.* Australia **92** 28.43S142.27E
Bulloo Downs *town* Australia **92** 28.30S142.45E
Bull Run Mtn. U.S.A. **114** 38.52N 77.53W
Bull Shoals L. U.S.A. **111** 36.30N 92.50W
Bulolo P.N.G. **59** 7.13S146.35E
Bulsār India **62** 20.38N 72.56E
Bultfontein R.S.A. **80** 28.17S 26.09E
Bulu Indonesia **59** 4.34N126.45E
Bulu, Gunung *mtn.* Indonesia **58** 3.00N116.00E
Bulun Russian Fed. **51** 70.50N127.20E
Bulunde Tanzania **79** 4.19S 32.57E
Bumba Bandundu Zaïre **78** 6.55S 19.16E
Bumba Equateur Zaïre **78** 2.15N 22.32E
Bumbuli Zaïre **78** 3.25S 20.30E
Buna Kenya **79** 2.49N 39.27E
Buna P.N.G. **90** 8.40S148.25E
Bunbury Australia **89** 33.20S115.34E
Buncrana Rep. of Ire. **15** 55.08N 7.27W
Bundaberg Australia **90** 24.50S152.21E
Bundaleer Australia **93** 28.39S146.31E
Bundarra Australia **93** 30.11S151.04E
Bünde Nschn. Germany **38** 52.12N 8.35E
Bunde Nschn. Germany **38** 53.11N 7.16E
Bundella Australia **93** 31.35S149.59E
Būndi India **62** 25.27N 75.39E
Bundoran Rep. of Ire. **15** 54.28N 8.17W
Būndu India **63** 23.11N 85.35E
Bungay U.K. **13** 52.27N 1.26E
Bungo Angola **78** 7.26S 15.23E
Bungo suidō *str.* Japan **57** 32.52N132.30E
Bungu Tanzania **79** 7.37S 39.07E
Buni Nigeria **77** 11.20N 11.59E
Bunia Zaïre **79** 1.30N 30.10E
Buninyong Australia **92** 37.41S143.58E
Bunker Hill *town* U.S.A. **114** 39.22N 78.04W
Bunkie U.S.A. **111** 30.57N 92.11W
Buñol Spain **25** 39.25N 0.47W
Bunyala Kenya **71** 0.07N 34.00E
Bunyan Australia **93** 36.11S149.09E
Buol Indonesia **59** 1.12N121.28E
Buqayq Saudi Arabia **65** 25.55N 49.40E
Bura Coast Kenya **79** 1.09S 39.55E
Bura Coast Kenya **79** 3.30S 38.19E
Burakin Australia **89** 30.30S117.08E
Burang China **63** 30.16N 81.11E
Buras U.S.A. **111** 29.21N 89.32W
Buraydah Saudi Arabia **65** 26.18N 43.58E
Burbach Germany **38** 50.45N 8.05E
Burcher Australia **93** 33.32S147.18E
Burco Somali Rep. **71** 9.30N 45.30E
Burdur Turkey **23** 37.44N 30.17E
Burdwān India **63** 23.15N 87.51E
Bure Ethiopia **73** 10.40N 37.04E
Büren Germany **38** 51.33N 8.33E
Burford Canada **104** 43.06N 80.26W
Burg Germany **38** 54.26N 11.12E
Burg Sachsen-Anhalt Germany **38** 52.16N 11.51E
Burgas Bulgaria **29** 42.30N 27.29E
Burgas *d.* Bulgaria **34** 42.30N 26.25E
Burgdorf Switz. **39** 47.04N 7.37E
Burgenland *d.* Austria **36** 47.30N 16.20E
Burgeo Canada **103** 47.36N 57.34W
Burgess Hill U.K. **13** 50.57N 0.07W
Burghausen Germany **39** 48.09N 12.49E
Burglengenfeld Germany **39** 49.13N 12.03E
Burgos Spain **26** 42.21N 3.42W
Burgos *d.* Spain **26** 42.25N 3.40W
Burgstädt Germany **38** 50.55N 12.49E
Burgsteinfurt Germany **38** 52.08N 7.20E

Burgsvik to **Campo Grande**

Burgsvik Sweden **43** 57.03N 18.16E
Burhānpur India **62** 21.18N 76.14E
Buri Brazil **126** 23.46S 48.39W
Burias *i.* Phil. **59** 12.50N123.10E
Burica, Punta *c.* Panama **117** 8.05N 82.50W
Burin Pen. Canada **103** 47.00N 55.40W
Buriram Thailand **56** 14.59N103.08E
Burjasot Spain **25** 39.31N 0.25W
Burkburnett U.S.A. **111** 34.06N 98.34W
Burke *r.* Australia **90** 23.12S139.33E
Burketown Australia **90** 17.44S139.22E
Burkina Africa **76** 12.30N 2.00W
Burk's Falls Canada **104** 45.37N 79.25W
Burleigh Falls Canada **104** 44.34N 78.11W
Burley U.S.A. **108** 42.32N113.48W
Burlington Canada **104** 43.19N 79.47W
Burlington Iowa U.S.A. **110** 40.49N 91.14W
Burlington Kans. U.S.A. **110** 38.12N 95.45W
Burlington N.C. U.S.A. **113** 36.05N 79.27W
Burlington N.J. U.S.A. **115** 40.04N 74.49W
Burlington Vt. U.S.A. **105** 44.29N 73.13W
Burlington Wisc. U.S.A. **110** 42.41N 88.17W
Burma Asia **56** 21.45N 97.00E
Burngup Australia **89** 33.00S118.39E
Burnham-on-Crouch U.K. **13** 51.37N 0.50E
Burnham-on-Sea U.K. **13** 51.15N 3.00W
Burnie Australia **91** 41.03S145.55E
Burnley U.K. **12** 53.47N 2.15W
Burns Oreg. U.S.A. **108** 43.35N119.03W
Burns Wyo. U.S.A. **108** 41.11N104.21W
Burnside *r.* Canada **98** 66.51N108.04W
Burns Lake *town* Canada **100** 54.20N125.45W
Burnsville U.S.A. **114** 38.51N 80.40W
Buronga Australia **92** 34.08S142.11E
Burqā Jordan **67** 32.18N 35.12E
Burqīn Jordan **67** 32.27N 35.16E
Burra Australia **92** 33.40S138.57E
Burracoppin Australia **89** 31.22S118.30E
Burragorang, L. Australia **93** 33.58S150.27E
Burrel Albania **34** 41.36N 20.01E
Burren Junction Australia **93** 30.08S148.59E
Burrewarra Pt. Australia **93** 35.56S150.12E
Burriana Spain **25** 39.53N 0.05W
Burrinjuck Australia **93** 35.01S148.33E
Burrinjuck Resr. Australia **93** 35.00S148.40E
Burro, Serranías del *mts.* Mexico **111** 29.20N102.00W
Burry Port U.K. **13** 51.41N 4.17W
Bursa Turkey **29** 40.11N 29.04E
Būr Safājah Egypt **64** 26.44N 33.56E
Būr Sa'īd Egypt **66** 31.17N 32.18E
Būr Sūdān Sudan **72** 19.39N 37.01E
Burta Australia **92** 32.30S141.05E
Būr Tawfīq Egypt **66** 29.57N 32.34E
Burt L. U.S.A. **104** 45.27N 84.40W
Burton upon Trent U.K. **12** 52.58N 1.39W
Burtundy Australia **92** 33.45S142.22E
Buru *i.* Indonesia **59** 3.30S126.30E
Burullus, Buḩayrat al *l.* Egypt **66** 31.30N 30.45E
Burundi Africa **79** 3.00S 30.00E
Bururi Burundi **79** 3.58S 29.35E
Burutu Nigeria **77** 5.20N 5.31E
Burwash Canada **104** 46.19N 80.48W
Bury G.M. U.K. **12** 53.36N 2.19W
Bury St. Edmunds U.K. **13** 52.15N 0.42E
Burzil Jammu & Kashmir **62** 34.52N 75.07E
Burzil Pass Jammu & Kashmir **62** 34.54N 75.06E
Busalla Italy **30** 44.34N 8.57E
Busambra, Rocca *mtn.* Italy **32** 37.51N 13.24E
Busca Italy **30** 44.31N 7.29E
Būsh Egypt **66** 29.09N 31.07E
Būshehr Iran **65** 28.57N 50.52E
Bushkill U.S.A. **115** 41.06N 75.00W
Bushmanland *f.* R.S.A. **80** 29.25S 19.40E
Busi Ethiopia **71** 5.30N 44.30E
Busigny France **19** 50.02N 3.28E
Businga Zaïre **78** 3.16N 20.55E
Busira *r.* Zaïre **78** 0.05N 18.18E
Buskerud Norway **41** 60.20N 9.00E
Buskerud *d.* Norway **42** 60.07N 9.45E
Buşrá al Ḩarīrī Syria **67** 32.50N 36.20E
Buşrá ash Shām Syria **66** 32.30N 36.29E
Busselton Australia **89** 33.43S115.15E
Bussum Neth. **16** 52.17N 5.10E
Bustard Head *c.* Australia **90** 24.02S151.48E
Busto Arsizio Italy **30** 45.37N 8.51E
Busu Djanoa Zaïre **78** 1.42N 21.23E
Büsum Germany **38** 54.08N 8.51E
Buta Zaïre **78** 2.50N 24.50E
Butan Bulgaria **34** 43.39N 23.45E
Butari Rwanda **79** 2.38S 29.43E
Butaritari *i.* Kiribati **84** 3.07N172.48E
Buţayḩah Syria **67** 32.56N 35.53E
Bute Australia **92** 33.24S138.01E
Bute *i.* U.K. **14** 55.51N 5.07W
Bute, Sd. of U.K. **14** 55.44N 5.10W
Butedale Canada **100** 53.12N128.45W
Butera Italy **33** 37.11N 14.11E
Buthroton *site* Albania **34** 39.46N 20.00E
Butiaba Uganda **79** 1.48N 31.15E
Butler Mo. U.S.A. **111** 38.16N 94.20W
Butler N.J. U.S.A. **115** 41.00N 74.21W
Butler Penn. U.S.A. **114** 40.52N 79.54W
Butman U.S.A. **104** 44.09N 84.34W
Buton *i.* Indonesia **59** 5.00S122.50E
Butte Mont. U.S.A. **108** 46.00N112.32W
Butte Nebr. U.S.A. **110** 42.58N 98.51W
Butterworth Malaysia **58** 5.24N100.22E
Buttevant Rep. of Ire. **15** 52.14N 8.41W
Butt of Lewis *c.* U.K. **14** 58.31N 6.15W
Butty Head Australia **89** 33.52S121.35E
Butuan Phil. **59** 8.56N125.31E
Butwal Nepal **63** 27.42N 83.28E
Butzbach Germany **39** 50.26N 8.40E
Butzow Germany **38** 53.50N 11.59E
Buuhoodle Somali Rep. **71** 8.16N 46.24E
Buulo Berde Somali Rep. **71** 3.52N 45.40E
Buur Gaabo Somali Rep. **73** 1.10S 41.50E
Buur Hakaba Somali Rep. **79** 2.43N 44.10E
Buxtehude Germany **38** 53.28N 9.41E
Buxton U.K. **12** 53.16N 1.54W
Buxy France **19** 46.43N 4.41E
Buy Russian Fed. **44** 58.23N 41.27E
Buyaga Russian Fed. **51** 59.42N126.59E
Buynaksk Russian Fed. **45** 42.48N 47.07E
Büyük Turkey **34** 41.02N 26.35E
Büyük Menderes *r.* Turkey **35** 37.28N 27.10E
Buzachi, Poluostrov *pen.* Kazakhstan **45** 45.00N 51.55E
Buzançais France **18** 46.53N 1.25E
Buzancy France **19** 49.25N 4.57E
Buzău Romania **37** 45.10N 26.49E
Buzău *r.* Romania **37** 45.24N 27.48E
Buzaymah Libya **75** 24.55N 22.02E
Buzi *r.* Mozambique **81** 19.52S 34.00E
Buzuluk Russian Fed. **44** 52.49N 52.19E
Buzzards B. U.S.A. **115** 41.33N 70.47W
Bwasiaia P.N.G. **90** 10.06S150.48E
Byala Bulgaria **34** 43.28N 25.44E
Byala Slatina Bulgaria **34** 43.26N 23.55E
Byam Martin I. Canada **98** 75.15N104.00W
Bydgoszcz Poland **37** 53.16N 17.33E
Byemoor Canada **100** 52.00N112.17W
Byesville U.S.A. **114** 39.58N 81.32W
Bygland Norway **42** 58.50N 7.49E
Byglandsfjord *town* Norway **42** 58.51N 7.48E
Byglandsfjorden *l.* Norway **42** 58.48N 7.50E
Byhalia U.S.A. **111** 34.52N 89.41W
Bykhov Belorussia **37** 53.30N 30.15E
Bykle Norway **42** 59.21N 7.20E
Bylot I. Canada **99** 73.00N 78.30W
Byng Inlet Canada **104** 45.46N 80.33W
Byrd, Lac *l.* Canada **105** 47.01N 76.56W
Byrd Land *f.* Antarctica **128** 79.30S125.00W
Byrock Australia **93** 30.40S146.25E
Byron, C. Australia **93** 28.37S153.40E
Byron Bay *town* Australia **93** 28.43S153.34E
Byrranga, Gory *mts.* Russian Fed. **51** 74.50N101.00E
Byske Sweden **40** 64.57N 21.12E
Byske *r.* Sweden **40** 64.57N 21.13E
Byten Belorussia **37** 52.50N 25.28E
Bytom Poland **37** 50.22N 18.54E
Byxelkrok Sweden **43** 57.20N 17.00E
Bzipi Georgia **45** 43.15N 40.24E

C

Ca *r.* Vietnam **55** 18.47N105.40E
Caballería, Cabo de *c.* Spain **25** 40.05N 4.05E
Caballos Mesteños, Llano de los *f.* Mexico **111** 28.15N104.00W
Cabanatuan Phil. **59** 15.30N120.58E
Cabeza del Buey Spain **26** 38.43N 5.13W
Cabimas Venezuela **122** 10.26N 71.27W
Cabinda Angola **78** 5.34S 12.12E
Cabinet Mts. U.S.A. **108** 48.08N115.46W
Cabo Delgado *d.* Mozambique **79** 12.30S 39.00E
Cabo Frio *town* Brazil **126** 22.51S 42.03W
Cabonga, Résr. Canada **105** 47.20N 76.35W
Cabool U.S.A. **111** 37.07N 92.06W
Caboolture Australia **91** 27.05S152.57E
Cabo Pantoja Peru **122** 1.00S 75.10W
Cabot, Mt. U.S.A. **105** 44.31N 71.24W
Cabot Head *c.* Canada **104** 45.14N 81.17W
Cabot Str. Canada **103** 47.20N 59.30W
Cabra Spain **27** 37.28N 4.27W
Cabras Italy **32** 39.56N 8.32E
Cabrera *i.* Spain **25** 39.09N 2.56E
Cabrera *r.* Spain **26** 42.25N 6.49W
Cabrera, Sierra *mts.* Spain **26** 42.10N 6.45W
Cabri Canada **101** 50.37N108.28W
Cabriel *r.* Spain **25** 39.14N 1.03W
Cabruta Venezuela **122** 7.40N 66.16W
Čačak Yugo. **34** 43.53N 20.21E
Caçapava Brazil **126** 23.05S 45.40W
Caccamo Italy **32** 37.56N 13.40E
Caccia, Capo *c.* Italy **32** 40.34N 8.09E
Cáceres Brazil **123** 16.05S 57.40W
Cáceres Spain **27** 39.29N 6.22W
Cáceres *d.* Spain **27** 39.40N 6.20W
Cacharí Argentina **125** 36.23S 59.29W
Cache Bay *town* Canada **104** 46.23N 80.00W
Cachimo *r.* Zaïre **78** 7.02S 21.13E
Cachoeira Brazil **123** 12.35S 38.59W
Cachoeira do Sul Brazil **126** 30.03S 52.52W
Cachoeiro de Itapemirim Brazil **126** 20.51S 41.07W
Cacín *r.* Spain **27** 37.13N 4.00W
Cacine Guinea **76** 11.08N 14.57W
Cacolo Angola **78** 10.09S 19.15E
Caconda Angola **78** 13.46S 15.06E
Cacongo Angola **78** 5.11S 12.10E
Cacuso Angola **78** 9.26S 15.43E
Cadaqués Spain **25** 42.17N 3.17E
Čadca Slovakia **37** 49.26N 18.48E
Cader Idris *mtn.* U.K. **13** 52.40N 3.55W
Cadí, Sierra del *mts.* Spain **25** 42.17N 1.42E
Cadibarrawirracanna, L. Australia **92** 28.52S135.27E
Cadillac France **20** 44.38N 0.19W
Cadillac U.S.A. **112** 44.15N 85.23W
Cadiz Phil. **59** 10.57N123.18E
Cádiz Spain **27** 36.32N 6.18W
Cádiz *d.* Spain **27** 36.40N 5.50W
Cadiz U.S.A. **114** 40.16N 81.00W
Cádiz, Golfo de *g.* Spain **27** 37.00N 7.00W
Cadomin Canada **100** 53.02N117.20W
Cadoux Australia **89** 30.47S117.05E
Caen France **18** 49.11N 0.21W
Caernarfon U.K. **12** 53.08N 4.17W
Caernarfon B. U.K. **12** 53.05N 4.25W
Caerphilly U.K. **13** 51.34N 3.13W
Caesarea *see* Horbat Qesari Israel **67**
Caeté Brazil **126** 19.54S 43.37W
Cafima Angola **78** 16.34S 16.30E
Cafu Angola **78** 16.30S 15.14E
Cagayan de Oro Phil. **59** 8.29N124.40E
Cagli Italy **30** 43.33N 12.39E
Cagliari Italy **32** 39.13N 9.06E
Cagliari, Golfo di *g.* Italy **32** 39.05N 9.10E
Cagnes France **21** 43.40N 7.09E
Caguán *r.* Colombia **122** 0.08S 74.18W
Caguas Puerto Rico **117** 18.08N 66.00W
Cahama Angola **78** 16.16S 14.23E
Caha Mts. Rep. of Ire. **15** 51.44N 9.45W
Cahelli Italy **30** 44.43N 8.17E
Caherciveen Rep. of Ire. **15** 51.51N 10.14W
Cahir Rep. of Ire. **15** 52.23N 7.56W
Cahora Bassa Dam Mozambique **79** 15.36S 32.41E
Cahore Pt. Rep. of Ire. **15** 52.34N 6.12W
Cahors France **20** 44.27N 1.26E
Cahuapanas Peru **122** 5.15S 77.00W
Caia *r.* Portugal **27** 38.50N 7.05W
Caianda Angola **78** 11.02S 23.29E
Caibarién Cuba **117** 22.31N 79.28W
Caicó Brazil **123** 6.25S 37.04W
Caicos Is. C. America **97** 21.30N 72.00W
Caicos Is. Turks & Caicos Is. **117** 21.30N 72.00W
Caird Coast *f.* Antarctica **128** 75.00S 20.00W
Cairngorms *mts.* U.K. **14** 57.04N 3.30W
Cairns Australia **90** 16.51S145.43E
Cairo *see* Al Qāhirah Egypt **66**
Cairo Ill. U.S.A. **111** 37.01N 89.09W
Cairo N.Y. U.S.A. **115** 42.18N 74.00W
Cairo W.Va. U.S.A. **114** 39.13N 81.09W
Cairo Montenotte Italy **30** 44.24N 8.16E
Caiundo Angola **78** 15.43S 17.30E
Caiwarro Australia **93** 28.38S144.45E
Caizhai China **54** 37.20N118.10E
Caizi Hu *l.* China **55** 30.50N117.06E
Cajamarca Peru **122** 7.09S 78.32W
Cajarc France **20** 44.29N 1.50E
Cajàzeiras Brazil **123** 6.52S 38.31W
Čajniče Bosnia-Herzegovina **31** 43.33N 19.04E
Cajuru Brazil **126** 21.15S 47.18W
Čakovec Croatia **31** 46.23N 16.26E
Cala, Embalse de *resr.* Spain **27** 37.45N 6.05W
Calabar Nigeria **77** 4.56N 8.22E
Calabogie Canada **105** 45.18N 76.43W
Calabozo Venezuela **122** 8.58N 67.28W
Calabria *d.* Italy **33** 39.25N 16.30E
Calacuccia France **21** 42.20N 9.03E
Calafat Romania **34** 43.58N 22.59E
Calafate Argentina **125** 50.20S 72.16W
Calahorra Spain **26** 42.18N 1.59W
Calais France **19** 50.57N 1.50E
Calama Brazil **122** 8.03S 62.53W
Calama Chile **121** 22.30S 68.55W
Calamar Colombia **122** 10.15N 74.55W
Calamian Group *is.* Phil. **59** 12.00N120.05E
Cala Millor Spain **25** 39.35N 3.22E
Calamocha Spain **25** 40.55N 1.18W
Calañas Spain **27** 37.39N 6.53W
Calanda Spain **25** 40.56N 0.14W
Calangianus Italy **32** 40.56N 9.12E
Calapan Phil. **59** 13.23N121.10E
Călăraşi Romania **37** 44.11N 27.21E
Calatafimi Italy **32** 37.55N 12.52E
Calatayud Spain **25** 41.21N 1.38W
Calatrava Equat. Guinea **78** 1.09N 9.24E
Calau Germany **38** 51.45N 13.56E
Calayan *i.* Phil. **55** 19.20N121.25E
Calbayog Phil. **59** 12.04N124.58E
Calbe Germany **38** 51.54N 11.46E
Calcutta India **63** 22.32N 88.22E
Caldaro Italy **30** 46.25N 11.14E
Caldas Colombia **122** 6.05N 75.36W
Caldas da Rainha Portugal **27** 39.24N 9.08W
Caldas de Reyes Spain **26** 42.36N 8.38W
Caldeirão, Serra do *mts.* Portugal **27** 37.25N 8.10W
Caldera Chile **124** 27.04S 70.50W
Caldwell Idaho U.S.A. **108** 43.40N116.41W
Caldwell Ohio U.S.A. **114** 39.45N 81.31W
Caledon *r.* R.S.A. **80** 30.27S 26.12E
Caledon B. Australia **90** 12.58S136.52E
Caledonia Canada **104** 43.04N 79.56W
Caledonia U.S.A. **114** 42.58N 77.51W
Caledonia Hills Canada **103** 45.40N 65.00W
Calella Spain **25** 41.37N 2.40E
Calexico Mexico **109** 32.40N115.30W
Calf of Man *i.* I.o.M. Europe **12** 54.03N 4.49W
Calgary Canada **100** 51.00N114.10W
Cali Colombia **122** 3.24N 76.30W
Caliente U.S.A. **108** 37.37N114.31W
California *d.* U.S.A. **108** 37.29N119.58W
California, G. of *see* California, Golfo de *g.* Mexico **116**
California, Golfo de *g.* Mexico **109** 28.00N112.00W
Calingasta Argentina **124** 31.15S 69.30W
Calingiri Australia **89** 31.07S116.27E
Calitri Italy **33** 40.54N 15.27E
Callabonna, L. Australia **92** 29.47S140.07E
Callabonna Creek *r.* Australia **92** 29.37S140.08E
Callac France **18** 48.24N 3.26W
Callander Canada **104** 46.13N 79.23W
Callander U.K. **14** 56.15N 4.13W
Callao Peru **124** 12.05S 77.08W
Callicoon U.S.A. **115** 41.46N 75.03W
Callosa de Ensarriá Spain **25** 38.39N 0.07W
Callosa de Segura Spain **25** 38.08N 0.52W
Caloocan Phil. **59** 14.38N120.58E
Caloundra Australia **91** 26.47S153.08E
Caltagirone Italy **33** 37.14N 14.31E
Caltanissetta Italy **33** 37.29N 14.04E
Caluire-et-Cuire France **21** 45.48N 4.51E
Calulo Angola **78** 10.05S 14.56E
Calumbo Angola **78** 9.08S 13.24E
Calumet Canada **105** 45.39N 74.41W
Calundau Angola **78** 12.05S 19.10E
Caluula Somali Rep. **71** 11.58N 50.48E
Calvados *d.* France **18** 49.10N 0.30W
Calvert I. Canada **100** 51.30N128.00W
Calverton U.S.A. **114** 39.03N 76.56W
Calvi France **21** 42.34N 8.45E
Calvinia R.S.A. **80** 31.29S 19.44E
Calvo, Monte *mtn.* Italy **33** 41.44N 15.46E
Calw Germany **39** 48.43N 8.44E
Cam *r.* U.K. **13** 52.34N 0.21E
Camabatela Angola **78** 8.20S 15.29E
Camacupa Angola **78** 12.01S 17.22E
Camagüey Cuba **117** 21.25N 77.55W
Camagüey, Archipiélago de Cuba **117** 22.30N 78.00W
Camaiore Italy **30** 43.56N 10.18E
Camarat, Cap *c.* France **21** 43.12N 6.41E
Camarès France **20** 43.49N 2.53E
Camaret-sur-Mer France **18** 48.16N 4.37W
Camargue *d.* France **21** 43.20N 4.38E
Camariñas Spain **26** 43.08N 9.12W
Camarón, C. Honduras **117** 15.59N 85.00W
Camaronero, Laguna *l.* Mexico **109** 23.00N106.07W
Camarones Argentina **125** 44.45S 65.40W
Camas Spain **27** 37.24N 6.02W
Camas U.S.A. **108** 45.35N122.24W
Cambados Spain **26** 42.30N 8.48W
Cambay India **62** 22.18N 72.37E
Camberg Germany **39** 50.18N 8.16E
Camberley U.K. **13** 51.21N 0.45W
Cambodia Asia **56** 12.45N105.00E
Camborne U.K. **13** 50.12N 5.19W
Cambrai Australia **92** 34.39S139.17E
Cambrai France **19** 50.10N 3.14E
Cambria U.S.A. **109** 35.34N121.05W
Cambrian Mts. U.K. **13** 52.33N 3.33W
Cambridge Canada **114** 43.22N 80.19W
Cambridge New Zealand **86** 37.53S175.29E
Cambridge U.K. **13** 52.13N 0.08E
Cambridge Idaho U.S.A. **108** 44.34N116.41W
Cambridge Mass. U.S.A. **115** 42.22N 71.06W
Cambridge Md. U.S.A. **115** 38.34N 76.04W
Cambridge Minn. U.S.A. **110** 45.31N 93.14W
Cambridge N.Y. U.S.A. **115** 43.02N 73.23W
Cambridge Ohio U.S.A. **114** 40.02N 81.35W
Cambridge Bay *town* Canada **98** 69.09N105.00W
Cambridge G. Australia **88** 15.00S128.05E
Cambridgeshire *d.* U.K. **13** 52.15N 0.05E
Cambridge Springs *town* U.S.A. **114** 41.48N 80.04W
Cambrils de Mer Spain **25** 41.04N 1.03E
Cambundi-Catembo Angola **78** 10.09S 17.35E
Camden U.K. **13** 51.33N 0.10W
Camden Ark. U.S.A. **111** 33.35N 92.50W
Camden N.J. U.S.A. **115** 39.57N 75.07W
Camden N.Y. U.S.A. **115** 43.20N 75.45W
Camden S.C. U.S.A. **113** 34.16N 80.36W
Cameia Nat. Park Angola **78** 12.00S 21.30E
Camelford U.K. **13** 50.37N 4.41W
Camerino Italy **30** 43.08N 13.04E
Cameron Canada **104** 44.27N 78.46W
Cameron Ariz. U.S.A. **109** 35.51N111.25W
Cameron La. U.S.A. **111** 29.48N 93.19W
Cameron Mo. U.S.A. **110** 39.44N 94.14W
Cameron Tex. U.S.A. **111** 30.51N 96.59W
Cameron W.Va. U.S.A. **114** 39.50N 80.34W
Cameron Hills Canada **100** 59.48N118.00W
Cameron Mts. New Zealand **86** 45.50S167.00E
Cameroon Africa **77** 6.00N 12.30E
Camerota Italy **33** 40.02N 15.23E
Cameroun, Mont *mtn.* Cameroon **77** 4.20N 9.05E
Cametá Brazil **123** 2.12S 49.30W
Caminha Portugal **26** 41.52N 8.50W
Camiri Bolivia **124** 20.03S 63.31W
Camocim Brazil **123** 2.55S 40.50W
Camooweal Australia **90** 19.55S138.07E
Camopi Guiana **123** 3.12N 52.15W
Campagna Italy **33** 40.40N 15.08E
Campana Argentina **125** 34.10S 58.57W
Campana, Isla *i.* Chile **125** 48.25S 75.20W
Campanario Spain **26** 38.52N 5.37W
Campania *d.* Italy **33** 40.50N 14.50E
Campbell U.S.A. **114** 41.05N 80.36W
Campbell, C. New Zealand **86** 41.45S174.15E
Campbellford Canada **105** 44.18N 77.48W
Campbell I. Pacific Oc. **84** 52.30S169.02E
Campbellpore Pakistan **62** 33.46N 72.22E
Campbell River *town* Canada **100** 50.05N125.20W
Campbells Bay *town* Canada **105** 45.44N 76.36W
Campbellsville U.S.A. **113** 37.20N 85.21W
Campbellton Canada **103** 48.00N 66.40W
Campbell Town Australia **93** 41.55S147.30E
Campbelltown Australia **93** 34.04S150.49E
Campbeltown U.K. **14** 55.25N 5.36W
Camp Borden Canada **104** 44.18N 79.52W
Campeche Mexico **116** 19.50N 90.30W
Campeche *d.* Mexico **116** 19.00N 90.00W
Campeche, Bahía de *b.* Mexico **116** 19.30N 94.00W
Campeche B. *see* Campeche, Bahía de *b.* Mexico **116**
Camperdown Australia **92** 38.15S143.14E
Cam Pha Vietnam **56** 21.07N107.19E
Campiglia Marittima Italy **30** 43.03N 10.37E
Campillo de Llerena Spain **26** 38.30N 5.50W
Campillos Spain **27** 37.03N 4.51W
Campina Grande Brazil **123** 7.15S 35.50W
Campinas Brazil **126** 22.54S 47.06W
Campo Cameroon **77** 2.22N 9.50E
Campo *r.* Cameroon **78** 2.21N 9.51E
Campo U.S.A. **111** 37.06N102.35W
Campobasso Italy **33** 41.34N 14.39E
Campobello di Mazara Italy **32** 37.38N 12.45E
Campo Belo Brazil **126** 20.52S 45.16W
Campo de Criptana Spain **27** 39.24N 3.07W
Campo Gallo Argentina **124** 26.35S 62.50W
Campo Grande Brazil **124** 20.24S 54.35W

Campo Maior to Cataluña

Campo Maior Brazil 123 4.50S 42.12W
Campo Maior Portugal 27 39.01N 7.04W
Campos Brazil 126 21.45S 41.18W
Campos Belos Brazil 123 13.09S 47.03W
Campos do Jordão Brazil 126 23.28S 46.10W
Campo Tures Italy 30 46.55N 11.57E
Campton U.S.A. 105 43.53N 71.38W
Camp Wood U.S.A. 111 29.40N100.01W
Cam Ranh Vietnam 56 11.54N109.14E
Camrose Canada 100 53.00N112.50W
Canaan Conn. U.S.A. 115 42.02N 73.20W
Canaan Vt. U.S.A. 105 45.00N 71.32W
Canada N. America 98 60.00N105.00W
Cañada de Gómez Argentina 124 32.49S 61.25W
Canadian U.S.A. 111 35.55N100.23W
Canadian r. U.S.A. 111 35.27N 95.03W
Canadian Shield f. Canada 96 50.00N 82.00W
Canajohaire U.S.A. 115 42.56N 74.38W
Çanakkale Turkey 34 40.09N 26.24E
Çanakkale Boğazi str. Turkey 34 40.15N 26.25E
Canal du Midi France 17 43.18N 2.00E
Canal Fulton U.S.A. 114 40.54N 81.36W
Canandaigua U.S.A. 114 42.54N 77.17W
Canandaigua L. U.S.A. 114 42.49N 77.16W
Cananea Mexico 109 30.57N110.18W
Canarias, Islas is. Atlantic Oc. 74 28.00N 15.00W
Canary Is. see Canarias, Islas is. Atlantic Oc. 74
Canaseraga U.S.A. 114 42.45N 77.50W
Canastota U.S.A. 115 43.10N 75.45W
Canastra, Serra da mts. Brazil 126 20.05S 46.30W
Canaveral, C. U.S.A. 113 28.27N 80.32W
Cañaveras Spain 26 40.22N 2.24W
Canavieiras Brazil 123 15.44S 38.58W
Canbelego Australia 93 31.33S146.19E
Canberra Australia 93 35.18S149.08E
Canby Calif. U.S.A. 108 41.27N120.52W
Canby Minn. U.S.A. 110 44.43N 96.16W
Cancale France 18 48.41N 1.51W
Canche r. France 19 50.31N 1.39E
Cancon France 20 44.32N 0.38E
Candás Spain 26 43.35N 5.46W
Candé France 18 47.34N 1.02W
Candeias Brazil 126 20.44S 45.18W
Candelaro r. Italy 33 41.34N 15.53E
Candeleda Spain 27 40.09N 5.14W
Candle L. Canada 101 53.50N105.18W
Candlewood, L. U.S.A. 115 41.32N 73.27W
Candor U.S.A. 115 42.14N 76.21W
Canelles, Embalse de resr. Spain 25 42.10N 0.30E
Canelli Italy 30 44.43N 8.17E
Canelones Uruguay 125 34.32S 56.17W
Cañete Peru 122 13.00S 76.30W
Cañete Spain 25 40.03N 1.35W
Canfield Canada 104 42.59N 79.43W
Canfranc Spain 25 42.43N 0.31W
Cangamba Angola 78 13.40S 19.50E
Cangas Spain 26 42.16N 8.47W
Cangas de Narcea Spain 26 43.11N 6.33W
Cangas de Onís Spain 26 43.21N 5.07W
Cangkuang, Tanjung c. Indonesia 59 6.45S105.15E
Cangombe Angola 78 14.27S 20.00E
Canguçu Brazil 124 31.24S 52.41W
Cangwu China 55 23.27N111.17E
Cangzhou China 54 38.15N116.58E
Caniapiscau r. Canada 103 57.40N 69.30W
Caniapiscau, Résr. l. Canada 103 54.10N 69.55W
Canicattì Italy 32 37.21N 13.51E
Canigou, Pic du mtn. France 20 42.30N 2.27E
Canisteo U.S.A. 114 42.07N 77.08W
Canisteo r. U.S.A. 105 42.07N 77.08W
Canjáyar Spain 27 37.00N 2.44W
Çankiri Turkey 64 40.35N 33.37E
Canna i. U.K. 14 57.03N 6.30W
Cannes France 21 43.33N 7.01E
Cannich U.K. 14 57.20N 4.45W
Cannington Canada 104 44.21N 79.02W
Cannock U.K. 13 52.42N 2.02W
Cann River town Australia 93 37.35S149.06E
Canôas Brazil 126 29.55S 51.10W
Canoe L. Canada 101 55.11N108.15W
Canojoharie U.S.A. 105 42.56N 74.38W
Canonba Australia 93 31.19S147.22E
Canon City U.S.A. 108 38.27N105.14W
Canonsburg U.S.A. 114 40.16N 80.11W
Canopus Australia 92 33.30S140.57E
Canora Canada 101 51.37N102.26W
Canosa Italy 33 41.13N 16.04E
Canossa site Italy 30 44.35N 10.27E
Canowindra Australia 93 33.34S148.30E
Canso Canada 103 45.20N 61.00W
Cantabria d. Spain 26 43.15N 4.00W
Cantabria, Sierra de mts. Spain 26 42.35N 2.30W
Cantábrica, Cordillera mts. Spain 26 43.00N 5.00W
Cantagalo Brazil 126 21.59S 42.22W
Cantal d. France 20 45.05N 2.45E
Cantalejo Spain 26 41.15N 3.55W
Cantanhede Portugal 26 40.21N 8.36W
Cantaura Venezuela 122 9.22N 64.24W
Canterbury d. New Zealand 86 43.30S172.00E
Canterbury U.K. 13 51.17N 1.05E
Canterbury Bight New Zealand 86 44.15S172.00E
Can Tho Vietnam 56 10.03N105.40E
Canton see Guangzhou China 55
Canton Miss. U.S.A. 111 32.37N 90.02W
Canton N.C. U.S.A. 113 35.33N 82.51W
Canton N.Y. U.S.A. 105 44.36N 75.10W
Canton Ohio U.S.A. 114 40.48N 81.22W
Canton Okla. U.S.A. 111 36.03N 98.35W
Canton Penn. U.S.A. 114 41.39N 76.51W
Cantù Italy 30 45.44N 9.08E
Cantua Creek town U.S.A. 109 36.30N120.19W
Cantung Canada 100 62.00N128.09W
Cañuelas Argentina 125 35.03S 58.44W
Canumã r. Brazil 122 3.55S 59.10W
Canutama Brazil 122 6.32S 64.20W
Canutillo Mexico 109 26.21N105.25W
Cany-Barville France 18 49.47N 0.38E
Canyon Tex. U.S.A. 111 34.59N101.55W
Canyon Wyo. U.S.A. 108 44.43N110.32W
Cao Bang Vietnam 55 22.37N106.18E
Caombo Angola 78 8.45S 16.50E
Caorle Italy 30 45.36N 12.53E
Capac U.S.A. 114 43.01N 82.56W
Capanema Brazil 123 1.08S 47.07W
Cap-Chat Canada 103 48.56N 66.53W
Cap de la Madeleine Canada 105 46.22N 72.31W
Cape Barren I. Australia 91 40.25S148.15E
Cape Basin f. Atlantic Oc. 127 38.00S 10.00E
Cape Breton Highlands Canada 103 46.45N 60.45W
Cape Breton I. Canada 103 46.00N 60.30W
Cape Coast town Ghana 76 5.10N 1.13W
Cape Cod B. U.S.A. 115 41.52N 70.22W
Cape Crawford town Australia 90 16.38S135.43E
Cape Croker town Canada 104 44.55N 81.01W
Cape Dyer town Canada 99 66.30N 61.20W
Cape Girardeau town U.S.A. 111 37.19N 89.32W
Cape Johnson Depth Pacific Oc. 59 10.20N127.20E
Capellen Lux. 16 49.39N 5.59E
Capelongo Angola 78 14.55S 15.03E
Cape May town U.S.A. 115 38.56N 74.55W
Cape Province d. R.S.A. 80 31.30S 23.30E
Cape Rise f. Indian Oc. 49 38.00S 27.00E
Capernaum see Kefar Nahum Israel 67
Cape Town R.S.A. 80 33.55S 18.27E
Cape Verde Atlantic Oc. 127 16.00N 24.00W
Cape Verde Basin f. Atlantic Oc. 127 15.00N 35.00W
Cape Vincent town U.S.A. 105 44.08N 76.20W
Cape York Pen. Australia 90 12.40S142.20E
Cap-Haïtien town Haiti 117 19.47N 72.17W
Capim r. Brazil 123 1.40S 47.47W
Capljina Bosnia-Herzegovina 31 43.07N 17.42E
Capon Bridge U.S.A. 114 39.21N 78.23W
Capoompeta, Mt. Australia 93 29.22S151.59E
Cappoquin Rep. of Ire. 15 52.09N 7.52W
Capraia i. Italy 30 43.03N 9.50E
Caprarola Italy 30 42.19N 12.14E
Capreol Canada 104 46.43N 80.56W
Caprera i. Italy 32 41.12N 9.28E
Capri i. Italy 33 40.33N 14.13E
Caprivi Strip f. Namibia 80 17.50S 23.10E
Captains Flat Australia 93 35.34S149.28E
Captieux France 20 44.18N 0.16W
Captiva U.S.A. 113 26.31N 82.12W
Capua Italy 33 41.06N 14.12E
Caqueta r. Colombia 122 1.20S 70.50W
Caracal Romania 37 44.08N 24.18E
Caracas Venezuela 122 10.35N 66.56W
Caragabal Australia 93 33.49S147.46E
Caraguatatuba Brazil 126 23.39S 45.26W
Carandaí Brazil 126 20.55S 43.46W
Carangola Brazil 126 20.44S 42.03W
Caransebeş Romania 37 45.25N 22.13E
Caratasca, Laguna de b. Honduras 117 15.10N 84.00W
Caratinga Brazil 126 19.50S 42.06W
Caravaca Spain 25 38.06N 1.51W
Caravaggio Italy 30 45.30N 9.38E
Caravelí Peru 122 15.45S 73.25W
Carballino Spain 26 42.26N 8.04W
Carballo Spain 26 43.13N 8.41W
Carbenyabba Creek r. Australia 92 29.02S143.28E
Carberry Canada 101 49.52N 99.20W
Carbonara, Capo c. Italy 32 39.06N 9.31E
Carbon-Blanc France 20 44.53N 0.31W
Carbondale Ill. U.S.A. 111 37.44N 89.13W
Carbondale Penn. U.S.A. 115 41.35N 75.30W
Carbonear Canada 103 47.45N 53.14W
Carboneras de Guadazaon Spain 25 39.53N 1.48W
Carbonia Italy 32 39.11N 8.32E
Carbonin Italy 30 46.37N 12.13E
Carcagente Spain 25 39.08N 0.27W
Carcajou Canada 100 57.47N117.06W
Carcans, Étang de b. France 20 45.08N 1.08W
Carcassonne France 20 43.13N 2.21E
Carcastillo Spain 25 42.23N 1.26W
Carcross Canada 100 60.13N134.45W
Cárdenas Cuba 117 23.02N 81.12W
Cárdenas Mexico 116 22.00N 99.40W
Cardenete Spain 25 39.46N 1.41W
Cardiff Canada 104 44.59N 78.01W
Cardiff U.K. 13 51.28N 3.11W
Cardigan U.K. 13 52.06N 4.41W
Cardigan B. U.K. 13 52.30N 4.30W
Cardigan State Park U.S.A. 105 43.38N 71.54W
Cardinal Canada 105 44.47N 75.23W
Cardington U.S.A. 114 40.30N 82.53W
Cardona Spain 25 41.56N 1.40E
Cardona Uruguay 125 33.53S 57.23W
Cardoner r. Spain 25 41.41N 1.51E
Cardwell Australia 90 18.21S146.04E
Carei Romania 37 47.42N 22.28E
Carentan France 18 49.18N 1.14W
Cares r. Spain 26 43.22N 4.31W
Carey U.S.A. 108 43.18N113.56W
Carey, L. Australia 89 29.05S122.15E
Carey L. Canada 101 62.12N102.55W
Carhaix France 18 48.17N 3.35W
Carhué Argentina 125 37.11S 62.45W
Cariati Italy 33 39.30N 16.56E
Caribbean Sea C. America 117 15.00N 75.00W
Cariboo Mts. Canada 100 53.00N121.00W
Caribou r. Man. Canada 101 59.20N 94.44W
Caribou r. N.W.T. Canada 100 61.27N125.45W
Caribou U.S.A. 112 46.52N 68.01W
Caribou Is. Canada 100 61.55N113.15W
Caribou Mts. Canada 100 59.12N115.40W
Carignan Canada 105 47.18N 72.47W
Carignan France 19 49.38N 5.10E
Carinda Australia 93 30.29S147.45E
Cariñena Spain 25 41.20N 1.13W
Carinhanha Brazil 123 14.18S 43.47W
Carini Italy 32 38.08N 13.11E
Caritianas Brazil 122 9.25S 63.06W
Carlentini Italy 33 37.16N 15.02E
Carlet Spain 25 39.14N 0.31W
Carleton Place Canada 105 45.08N 76.09W
Carlingford Rep. of Ire. 15 54.03N 6.12W
Carlingford Lough Rep. of Ire. 15 54.03N 6.09W
Carlinville U.S.A. 110 39.17N 89.52W
Carlisle U.K. 12 54.54N 2.55W
Carlisle U.S.A. 114 40.12N 77.12W
Carloforte Italy 32 39.08N 8.18E
Carlos Reyles Uruguay 125 33.03S 56.29W
Carlow Rep. of Ire. 15 52.50N 6.46W
Carlow d. Rep. of Ire. 15 52.43N 6.50W
Carlsbad Calif. U.S.A. 109 33.10N117.21W
Carlsbad N.Mex. U.S.A. 109 32.25N104.14W
Carlsberg Ridge f. Indian Oc. 49 4.00N 65.00E
Carlyle Canada 101 49.38N102.16W
Carmacks Canada 98 62.04N136.21W
Carmagnola Italy 30 44.51N 7.43E
Carman Canada 101 49.32N 98.00W
Carmarthen U.K. 13 51.52N 4.20W
Carmarthen B. U.K. 13 52.30N 4.30W
Carmaux France 20 44.03N 2.09E
Carmel U.S.A. 115 41.26N 73.41W
Carmel, Mt. see Karmel, Har mtn. Israel 67
Carmel Head U.K. 12 53.24N 4.35W
Carmelo Uruguay 125 34.00S 58.17W
Carmen Colombia 122 9.46N 75.06W
Carmen Mexico 116 18.38N 91.50W
Carmen Uruguay 125 33.15S 56.01W
Carmen, Isla i. Mexico 109 25.55N111.10W
Carmen, Isla del i. Mexico 116 18.35N 91.40W
Carmen de Areco Argentina 125 34.20S 59.50W
Carmen de Patagones Argentina 125 40.48S 63.00W
Carmi U.S.A. 110 38.05N 88.11W
Carmichael U.S.A. 108 38.38N121.19W
Carmila Australia 90 21.55S149.25E
Carmo Brazil 126 21.56S 42.37W
Carmody, L. Australia 89 32.27S119.20E
Carmona Spain 27 37.28N 5.38W
Carnac France 18 47.35N 3.05W
Carnarvon Australia 88 24.53S113.40E
Carnarvon Canada 104 45.03N 78.40W
Carnarvon R.S.A. 80 30.58S 22.07E
Carndonagh Rep. of Ire. 15 55.15N 7.15W
Carnegie Australia 88 25.43S122.59E
Carnegie, L. Australia 88 26.15S123.00E
Carnew Rep. of Ire. 15 52.43N 6.31W
Carniche, Alpi mts. Italy / Austria 30 46.35N 13.00E
Car Nicobar i. India 56 9.11N 92.45E
Carnot C.A.R. 77 4.59N 15.56E
Carnot, C. Australia 92 34.57S135.38E
Carnoustie U.K. 14 56.30N 2.44W
Carnsore Pt. Rep. of Ire. 15 52.10N 6.21W
Caro U.S.A. 104 43.29N 83.24W
Carolina Brazil 123 7.20S 47.25W
Carolina Puerto Rico 117 18.23N 65.57W
Carolina R.S.A. 80 26.04S 30.07E
Caroline I. Kiribati 85 10.00S150.30W
Caroline Is. Pacific Oc. 59 7.50N145.00E
Caroline-Solomon Ridge Pacific Oc. 84 8.00N150.00E
Caroní r. Venezuela 122 8.20N 62.42W
Carora Venezuela 122 10.12N 70.07W
Carp Canada 105 45.21N 76.02W
Carpathians mts. Europe 37 48.45N 23.45E
Carpaţii Meridionali mts. Romania 37 45.35N 24.40E
Carpentaria, G. of Australia 90 14.00S139.00E
Carpenter Ridge f. Indian Oc. 49 3.00N 90.00E
Carpentras France 21 44.03N 5.03E
Carpi Italy 30 44.47N 10.53E
Carpio Spain 26 41.13N 5.07W
Carquefou France 18 47.18N 1.30W
Carra, Lough Rep. of Ire. 15 53.41N 9.15W
Carrara Italy 30 44.05N 10.06E
Carrathool Australia 93 34.25S145.24E
Carrauntoohil mtn. Rep. of Ire. 15 52.00N 9.45W
Carrickfergus U.K. 15 54.43N 5.49W
Carrickmacross Rep. of Ire. 15 53.58N 6.43W
Carrick-on-Shannon Rep. of Ire. 15 53.57N 8.06W
Carrick-on-Suir Rep. of Ire. 15 52.21N 7.26W
Carrieton Australia 92 32.28S138.34E
Carrington U.S.A. 110 47.27N 99.08W
Carrión r. Spain 26 41.53N 4.32W
Carrión de los Condes Spain 26 42.20N 4.36W
Carrizo Spain 26 42.35N 5.50W
Carrizo Springs town U.S.A. 111 28.31N 99.52W
Carrizozo U.S.A. 109 33.38N105.53W
Carroll U.S.A. 110 42.04N 94.52W
Carrollton Mich. U.S.A. 104 43.27N 83.54W
Carrollton Mo. U.S.A. 110 39.22N 93.30W
Carrollton Ohio U.S.A. 114 40.34N 81.05W
Carrot r. Canada 101 53.50N101.17W
Carrowmore Lough Rep. of Ire. 15 54.11N 9.47W
Carrum Australia 93 38.05S145.08E
Çarşamba Turkey 64 41.13N 36.43E
Çarşamba r. Turkey 64 37.52N 31.48E
Carson U.S.A. 110 46.25N101.34W
Carson City U.S.A. 108 39.10N119.46W
Carstairs U.K. 14 55.42N 3.41W
Cartagena Colombia 122 10.24N 75.33W
Cartagena Spain 25 37.36N 0.59W
Cartago Colombia 122 4.45N 75.55W
Cartago Costa Rica 117 9.50N 83.52W
Cartaxo Portugal 27 39.09N 8.47W
Cartaya Spain 27 37.17N 7.09W
Carter U.S.A. 108 41.27N110.25W
Carteret France 18 49.22N 1.48W
Cartersville U.S.A. 113 34.09N 84.49W
Carterton New Zealand 86 41.01S175.31E
Carthage Tunisia 32 36.51N 10.21E
Carthage site Tunisia 32 36.52N 10.20E
Carthage Mo. U.S.A. 111 37.11N 94.19W
Carthage N.Y. U.S.A. 105 43.59N 75.37W
Carthage S.Dak. U.S.A. 110 44.10N 97.43W
Carthage Tex. U.S.A. 111 32.09N 94.20W
Cartier Canada 104 46.43N 81.34W
Cartwright Canada 103 53.50N 56.45W
Caruarú Brazil 123 8.15S 35.55W
Carúpano Venezuela 122 10.39N 63.14W
Caruthersville U.S.A. 111 36.11N 89.39W
Carvin France 19 50.29N 2.58E
Carvoeiro Brazil 122 1.24S 61.59W
Carvoeiro, Cabo c. Portugal 27 39.21N 9.24W
Caryapundy Swamp Australia 92 29.00S142.36E
Casablanca Morocco 74 33.39N 7.35W
Casa Branca Brazil 126 21.45S 47.06W
Casacalenda Italy 31 41.44N 14.51E
Casa Grande U.S.A. 109 32.53N111.45W
Casalbordino Italy 31 42.09N 14.35E
Casale Italy 30 45.08N 8.27E
Casarano Italy 33 40.00N 18.10E
Casar de Cáceres Spain 27 39.34N 6.25W
Casas Ibáñez Spain 25 39.17N 1.28W
Casasimarro Spain 25 39.22N 2.02W
Casavieja Spain 26 40.17N 4.46W
Cascade Idaho U.S.A. 108 44.31N116.02W
Cascade Mont. U.S.A. 108 47.16N111.42W
Cascade Pt. New Zealand 86 44.01S168.22E
Cascade Range mts. U.S.A. 108 46.15N121.00W
Cascina Italy 30 43.41N 10.33E
Caserta Italy 33 41.04N 14.20E
Caseville U.S.A. 104 43.56N 83.16W
Cashel Tipperary Rep. of Ire. 15 52.31N 7.54W
Casilda Argentina 125 33.03S 61.10W
Casimiro de Abreu Brazil 126 22.28S 42.12W
Casino Australia 93 28.50S153.02E
Casma Peru 122 9.30S 78.20W
Casoli Italy 31 42.07N 14.18E
Caspe Spain 25 41.14N 0.02W
Casper U.S.A. 108 42.51N106.19W
Caspian Depression f. Russian Fed. / Kazakhstan 45 47.00N 48.00E
Caspian Sea Europe / Asia 45 42.00N 51.00E
Cass r. U.S.A. 114 43.23N 83.59W
Cassai r. Angola 78 10.38S 22.15E
Cassano allo Ionio Italy 33 39.47N 16.20E
Cass City U.S.A. 114 43.36N 83.10W
Casselman Canada 105 45.19N 75.05W
Casselton U.S.A. 110 46.54N 97.13W
Cassiar Canada 100 59.16N129.40W
Cassiar Mts. Canada 100 59.00N129.00W
Cassilis Australia 93 32.01S149.59E
Cassino Italy 32 41.30N 13.49E
Cass Lake town U.S.A. 110 47.22N 94.35W
Casslar Mts. Canada 96 59.30N130.30W
Castanheira de Pêra Portugal 27 40.00N 8.13W
Castaños Mexico 111 26.48N101.26W
Castelbuono Italy 33 37.56N 14.06E
Castel del Piano Italy 30 42.53N 11.32E
Castelfiorentino Italy 30 43.36N 10.58E
Castelfranco Veneto Italy 30 45.40N 11.55E
Casteljaloux France 20 44.19N 0.05E
Castellammare Italy 33 40.42N 14.29E
Castellammare, Golfo di g. Italy 32 38.10N 12.55E
Castellammare del Golfo Italy 32 38.01N 12.53E
Castellana Grotte Italy 33 40.53N 17.11E
Castellaneta Italy 33 40.37N 16.57E
Castell' Arquato Italy 30 44.51N 9.52E
Castelli Argentina 125 36.07S 57.50W
Castellón Spain 25 39.59N 0.02W
Castellón d. Spain 25 40.20N 0.00
Castellote Spain 25 40.48N 0.19W
Castelmassa Italy 30 45.01N 11.18E
Castelmoron-sur-Lot France 20 44.24N 0.30E
Castelnaudary France 20 43.19N 1.57E
Castelnau-Montratier France 20 44.16N 1.21E
Castelnovo ne'Monti Italy 30 44.26N 10.24E
Castelnuovo di Garfagnana Italy 30 44.06N 10.24E
Castelo Brazil 126 20.33S 41.14W
Castelo Branco Portugal 27 39.49N 7.30W
Castelo Branco d. Portugal 27 40.00N 7.30W
Castel San Giovanni Italy 30 45.04N 9.26E
Castelsardo Italy 32 40.55N 8.42E
Castelsarrasin France 20 44.02N 1.06E
Casteltermini Italy 32 37.32N 13.39E
Castelvetrano Italy 32 37.41N 12.47E
Casterton Australia 92 37.35S141.25E
Castets France 20 43.53N 1.09W
Castiglion Fiorentino Italy 30 43.20N 11.55E
Castile U.S.A. 114 42.38N 78.03W
Castilla Peru 122 5.16S 80.36W
Castilla la Mancha d. Spain 27 39.50N 3.00W
Castilla y León d. Spain 26 41.20N 4.30W
Castilletes Colombia 122 11.55N 71.20W
Castillon-la-Bataille France 20 44.51N 0.03W
Castlebar Rep. of Ire. 15 53.52N 9.19W
Castleblayney Rep. of Ire. 15 54.08N 6.46W
Castle Douglas U.K. 14 54.56N 3.56W
Castleford U.K. 12 53.43N 1.21W
Castlegar Canada 100 49.20N117.40W
Castlegate U.S.A. 108 39.44N110.52W
Castle Harbour b. Bermuda 127 32.20N 64.40W
Castleisland Rep. of Ire. 15 52.13N 9.28W
Castlemaine Australia 92 37.05S144.19E
Castlerea Rep. of Ire. 15 53.45N 8.30W
Castlereagh r. Australia 93 30.12S147.32E
Castle Rock town Colo. U.S.A. 108 39.22N104.51W
Castle Rock town Wash. U.S.A. 108 46.17N122.54W
Castleton on Hudson U.S.A. 115 42.32N 73.45W
Castletown I.o.M. Europe 12 54.04N 4.38W
Castletownshend Rep. of Ire. 15 51.32N 9.12W
Castres France 20 43.36N 2.15E
Castries St. Lucia 117 14.01N 60.59W
Castro Chile 125 42.30S 73.46W
Castro Daire Portugal 26 40.54N 7.56W
Castro del Río Spain 27 37.41N 4.28W
Castrojeriz Spain 26 42.17N 4.08W
Castro Marim Portugal 27 37.13N 7.26W
Castronuño Spain 26 41.23N 5.16W
Castropol Spain 26 43.32N 7.02W
Castro Urdiales Spain 26 43.23N 3.13W
Castro Verde Portugal 26 37.42N 8.05W
Castrovillari Italy 33 39.49N 16.13E
Castuera Spain 26 38.43N 5.33W
Casula Mozambique 79 15.26S 33.32E
Cataguases Brazil 126 21.23S 42.39W
Çatalca Turkey 29 41.09N 28.29E
Catalina Pt. Guam 84 13.31N144.55E
Cataluña d. Spain 25 41.30N 1.00E

Catamarca to Cheboksary

Catamarca Argentina 124 28.30S 65.45W
Catamarca d. Argentina 124 27.45S 67.00W
Catanduanes i. Phil. 59 13.45N124.20E
Catanduva Brazil 126 21.03S 49.00W
Catania Italy 33 37.30N 15.06E
Catania, Golfo di g. Italy 33 37.25N 15.15E
Catanzaro Italy 33 38.54N 16.36E
Catarman Phil. 59 12.28N124.50E
Catarroja Spain 25 39.24N 0.24W
Catbalogan Phil. 59 11.46N124.55E
Catchacombe L. Canada 104 44.45N 78.20W
Catete Angola 78 9.09S 13.40E
Cathcart Australia 93 36.49S149.25E
Cathcart R.S.A. 80 32.17S 27.08E
Cat I. Bahamas 113 24.33N 75.36W
Cat L. Canada 102 51.40N 91.50W
Catoche, C. Mexico 117 21.38N 87.08W
Catonsville U.S.A. 114 39.16N 76.44W
Catriló Argentina 125 36.23S 63.24W
Catskill U.S.A. 115 42.13N 73.52W
Catskill Mts. U.S.A. 115 42.10N 74.30W
Catskill Park U.S.A. 115 42.10N 74.10W
Cattaraugus U.S.A. 114 42.20N 78.52W
Catterick U.K. 12 54.23N 1.38W
Cattolica Italy 30 43.58N 12.44E
Catuane Mozambique 81 26.49S 32.17E
Catus France 20 44.34N 1.20E
Cauca r. Colombia 122 8.57N 74.30W
Caucasus mts. Europe 45 43.00N 44.00E
Caudry France 19 50.07N 3.25E
Caulonia Italy 33 38.23N 16.25E
Caungula Angola 78 8.26S 18.35E
Cauquenes Chile 125 35.58S 72.21W
Caura r. Venezuela 122 7.38N 64.53W
Caussade France 20 44.10N 1.32E
Causse du Larzac f. France 20 44.00N 3.15E
Causse Méjean f. France 20 44.15N 3.30E
Cava Italy 33 40.42N 14.42E
Cávado r. Portugal 26 41.32N 8.48W
Cavaillon France 21 43.50N 5.02E
Cavalaire-sur-Mer France 21 43.10N 6.32E
Cavalese Italy 30 46.17N 11.27E
Cavalier U.S.A. 110 48.48N 97.37W
Cavally r. Ivory Coast 76 4.25N 7.39W
Cavan Rep. of Ire. 15 54.00N 7.22W
Cavan d. Rep. of Ire. 15 53.58N 7.10W
Cavarzere Italy 30 45.08N 12.05E
Caviana, Ilha i. Brazil 123 0.02N 50.00W
Cavtat Croatia 31 42.35N 18.13E
Cawndilla L. Australia 92 32.30S142.18E
Caxambu Brazil 126 21.59S 44.54W
Caxias Brazil 123 4.53S 43.20W
Caxias do Sul Brazil 126 29.14S 51.10W
Caxito Angola 78 8.32S 13.38E
Cayambe Ecuador 122 0.03N 78.08W
Cayenne Guiana 123 4.55N 52.18W
Caylus France 20 44.14N 1.46E
Cayman Brac i. Cayman Is. 117 19.44N 79.48W
Cayman Is. C. America 117 19.00N 81.00W
Cayman Trough Carib. Sea 127 18.00N 8.00W
Cayuga Canada 104 42.56N 79.51W
Cayuga L. U.S.A. 115 42.55N 76.44W
Cazalla de la Sierra Spain 27 37.56N 5.45W
Cazaux, Étang de b. France 20 44.30N 1.10W
Cazenovia U.S.A. 115 42.56N 75.51W
Cazères France 20 43.13N 1.05E
Čazma Croatia 31 45.45N 16.37E
Cazombo Angola 78 11.54S 22.56E
Cazorla Spain 27 37.55N 3.00W
Cea r. Spain 26 42.00N 5.36W
Ceara d. Brazil 123 4.50S 39.00W
Ceba Canada 101 53.07N102.14W
Ceballos Mexico 111 26.32N104.09W
Cebollera, Sierra de mts. Spain 26 41.55N 2.30W
Cebreros Spain 26 40.27N 4.28W
Cebu Phil. 59 10.17N123.56E
Cebu i. Phil. 59 10.15N123.45E
Ceccano Italy 32 41.34N 13.20E
Cecina Italy 30 43.19N 10.31E
Cecita, Lago di l. Italy 33 39.24N 16.30E
Cedar City U.S.A. 108 37.41N113.04W
Cedar Falls town U.S.A. 110 42.32N 92.27W
Cedar Grove U.S.A. 114 38.13N 81.26W
Cedar Key U.S.A. 113 29.08N 83.03W
Cedar L. Man. Canada 101 53.20N100.00W
Cedar L. Ont. Canada 104 46.02N 78.30W
Cedar Rapids town U.S.A. 110 41.59N 91.40W
Cedarville U.S.A. 115 39.20N 75.12W
Cedeira Spain 26 43.39N 8.03W
Cedillo, Embalse de resr. Spain / Portugal 27 39.40N 7.25W
Cedrino r. Italy 32 40.23N 9.44E
Cedrón r. Spain 27 39.57N 3.51W
Cedros, Isla i. Mexico 109 28.10N115.15W
Ceduna Australia 92 32.07S133.42E
Ceel Afweyne Somali Rep. 71 9.55N 47.14E
Ceel Buur Somali Rep. 71 4.40N 46.40E
Ceel Dhaab Somali Rep. 71 8.58N 46.38E
Ceel Dheere Somali Rep. 71 3.55N 47.10E
Ceel Xamurre Somali Rep. 71 7.11N 48.55E
Ceepeecee Canada 100 49.52N126.42W
Ceerigaabo Somali Rep. 71 10.40N 47.20E
Cefalù Italy 33 38.02N 14.01E
Cega r. Spain 26 41.33N 4.46W
Cegléd Hungary 37 47.10N 19.48E
Ceglie Italy 33 40.39N 17.31E
Cehegín Spain 25 38.06N 1.48W
Cela Angola 78 11.26S 15.05E
Celano Italy 31 42.05N 13.33E
Celanova Spain 26 42.09N 7.58W
Celaya Mexico 116 20.32N100.48W
Celebes i. see Sulawesi i. Indonesia 59
Celebes Sea Indonesia 59 3.00N122.00E
Celina U.S.A. 112 40.34N 84.35W
Celje Slovenia 31 46.14N 15.16E
Celle Germany 38 52.37N 10.05E
Celorico da Beira Portugal 26 40.38N 7.23W
Cemaes Head U.K. 13 52.08N 4.42W
Cenderawasih, Teluk b. Indonesia 59 2.20S135.50E
Ceno r. Italy 30 44.41N 10.05E
Centerburg U.S.A. 114 40.18N 82.42W
Center Cross U.S.A. 113 37.48N 76.48W
Centerville Iowa U.S.A. 110 40.43N 92.52W
Centerville S.Dak. U.S.A. 110 43.07N 96.58W
Centerville Tenn. U.S.A. 113 35.45N 87.29W
Cento Italy 30 44.43N 11.17E
Central d. Botswana 80 21.45S 26.15E
Central d. Ghana 76 5.30N 1.00W
Central d. Kenya 79 0.30S 37.00E
Central d. U.K. 14 56.10N 4.20W
Central d. Zambia 80 14.30S 29.30E
Central, Cordillera mts. Bolivia 124 18.30S 65.00W
Central, Cordillera mts. Colombia 120 6.00N 75.00W
Central African Republic Africa 70 7.00N 20.00E
Central Brāhui Range mts. Pakistan 62 29.15N 67.15E
Central City Ky. U.S.A. 113 37.17N 87.08W
Central City Nebr. U.S.A. 110 41.07N 98.00W
Central I. Kenya 79 3.30N 36.02E
Centralia Ill. U.S.A. 110 38.32N 89.08W
Centralia Wash. U.S.A. 108 46.43N122.58W
Central Makrān Range mts. Pakistan 62 26.30N 65.00E
Central Siberian Plateau see Sredne Sibirskoye Ploskogor'yee Ploskogor'ye Russian Fed. 51
Central Square U.S.A. 115 43.17N 76.09W
Centre d. Burkina 76 11.50N 1.10W
Centre d. France 19 47.40N 1.45E
Centre, Canal du France 19 46.27N 4.07E
Centre Est d. Burkina 76 11.20N 0.10W
Centre Nord d. Burkina 76 13.30N 1.00W
Centre Ouest d. Burkina 76 12.00N 2.20W
Centreville Ala. U.S.A. 113 32.57N 87.08W
Centreville Md. U.S.A. 115 39.03N 76.04W
Century Fla. U.S.A. 113 30.59N 87.18W
Century W.Va. U.S.A. 114 39.06N 80.11W
Cepu Indonesia 59 7.07S111.35E
Ceram i. see Seram i. Indonesia 59
Ceram Sea see Seram, Laut sea Pacific Oc. 59
Cère r. France 20 44.55N 1.53E
Ceres U.S.A. 108 37.35N120.57W
Ceresole Reale Italy 30 45.26N 7.15E
Céret France 20 42.29N 2.45E
Cereté Colombia 122 8.54N 75.51W
Cerignola Italy 33 41.16N 15.54E
Cérilly France 20 46.37N 2.49E
Cerisiers France 19 48.08N 3.29E
Cerknica Slovenia 31 45.48N 14.22E
Cernavodă Romania 37 44.20N 28.02E
Cernay France 19 47.49N 7.10E
Cerralvo, Isla i. Mexico 109 24.17N109.52W
Cërrik Albania 34 41.02N 19.57E
Cerritos Mexico 116 22.26N100.17W
Cerro de Pasco Peru 122 10.43S 76.15W
Cervaro r. Italy 33 41.30N 15.52E
Cervati, Monte mtn. Italy 33 40.17N 15.29E
Cervera Lérida Spain 25 41.40N 1.17E
Cervera Logroño Spain 26 42.01N 1.57W
Cervera de Pisuerga Spain 26 42.52N 4.30W
Cervia Italy 30 44.15N 12.22E
Cervialto, Monte mtn. Italy 33 40.47N 15.08E
Cervignano del Friuli Italy 30 45.49N 13.20E
Cervione France 21 42.20N 9.31E
Cervo Spain 26 43.40N 7.25W
Cesena Italy 30 44.08N 12.15E
Cesenatico Italy 30 44.12N 12.24E
Cēsis Latvia 44 57.18N 25.18E
Česká Kamenice Czech Republic 38 50.47N 14.26E
Česká Lípa Czech Republic 38 50.42N 14.32E
České Budějovice Czech Republic 36 49.00N 14.30E
Český Krumlov Czech Republic 39 48.49N 14.19E
Çeşme Turkey 35 38.18N 26.19E
Cessnock Australia 93 32.51S151.21E
Cetinje Yugo. 31 42.23N 18.55E
Ceuta Spain 27 35.53N 5.19W
Ceva Italy 30 44.23N 8.01E
Cévennes mts. France 21 44.00N 3.30E
Ceyhan Turkey 64 37.02N 35.48E
Ceyhan r. Turkey 64 36.54N 34.58E
Cèze r. France 21 44.06N 4.42E
Chabanais France 20 45.52N 0.43E
Chablis France 19 47.49N 3.48E
Chacabuco Argentina 125 34.38S 60.29W
Chachani mtn. Peru 122 16.12S 71.32W
Chachapoyas Peru 122 6.13S 77.54W
Chāchro Pakistan 62 25.07N 70.15E
Chaco d. Argentina 124 26.30S 60.00W
Chad Africa 70 16.00N 18.00E
Chad, L. Africa 77 13.30N 14.00E
Chadron U.S.A. 110 42.50N103.02W
Chafe Nigeria 77 11.56N 6.55E
Chāgai Pakistan 62 29.18N 64.42E
Chāgai Hills Pakistan 62 29.10N 63.35E
Chagda Russian Fed. 51 58.44N130.38E
'Chaghcharān Afghan. 62 34.32N 65.15E
Chagny France 19 46.55N 4.45E
Chagos Archipelago is. Indian Oc. 49 7.00S 72.00E
Chagrin Falls town U.S.A. 114 41.26N 81.24W
Cha'gyüngoinba China 63 31.10N 90.42E
Chahār Borjak Afghan. 62 30.17N 62.03E
Chāh Sandan well Pakistan 62 28.59N 63.27E
Chaibāsā India 63 22.34N 85.49E
Chaillé-les-Marais France 18 46.24N 1.01W
Chainat Thailand 56 15.10N100.10E
Chaiyaphum Thailand 56 15.46N101.57E
Chajarí Argentina 125 30.45S 57.59W
Chākāi India 63 24.34N 86.24E
Chākdaha India 63 23.05N 88.31E
Chake Chake Tanzania 79 5.13S 39.46E
Chakhānsūr Afghan. 62 31.10N 62.04E
Chakradharpur India 63 22.42N 85.38E
Chakwāl Pakistan 62 32.56N 72.52E
Chala Peru 122 15.48S 74.20W
Chalais France 20 45.16N 0.02E
Chaleur B. Canada 103 48.00N 65.45W
Chalhuanca Peru 122 14.20S 73.10W
Chālisgaon India 62 20.28N 75.01E
Chalk River town Canada 105 46.01N 77.27W
Challans France 18 46.51N 1.53W
Challenger Depth Pacific Oc. 59 11.19N142.15E
Challis U.S.A. 108 44.30N114.14W
Chalonnes-sur-Loire France 18 47.21N 0.46W
Châlons-sur-Marne France 19 48.57N 4.22E
Chalon-sur-Saône France 19 46.47N 4.51E
Chalosse d. France 20 43.45N 0.30W
Châlus France 20 45.39N 0.59E
Cham Germany 39 49.13N 12.41E
Chama U.S.A. 108 36.54N106.35W
Chama Zambia 79 11.09S 33.10E
Chaman Pakistan 62 30.55N 66.27E
Chamba India 62 32.34N 76.08E
Chambal r. India 63 26.29N 79.15E
Chamberlain U.S.A. 110 43.49N 99.20W
Chambersburg U.S.A. 114 39.56N 77.39W
Chambéry France 21 45.34N 5.56E
Chambeshi Zambia 79 10.57S 31.04E
Chambeshi r. Zambia 79 11.15S 30.37E
Chambley-Bussières France 19 49.03N 5.54E
Chambly Canada 105 45.27N 73.17W
Chambly France 19 49.10N 2.15E
Chambon-sur-Voueize France 20 46.11N 2.25E
Chamburi Kalāt Pakistan 62 26.09N 64.43E
Cha Messengue Angola 78 11.04S 18.56E
Chamical Argentina 124 30.22S 66.19W
Ch'amo Hāyk' l. Ethiopia 73 5.49N 37.35E
Chamoli India 63 30.24N 79.21E
Chamonix France 21 45.55N 6.52E
Chāmpa India 63 22.03N 82.39E
Champagne Canada 100 60.47N136.29W
Champagne-Ardenne d. France 19 49.00N 4.30E
Champagnole France 19 46.45N 5.55E
Champaign U.S.A. 110 40.07N 88.14W
Champdeniers France 18 46.29N 0.24W
Champdoré, Lac l. Canada 103 55.55N 65.50W
Champeix France 20 45.36N 3.08E
Champéry Switz. 39 46.10N 6.52E
Champlain Canada 105 46.27N 72.21W
Champlain U.S.A. 105 44.59N 73.27W
Champlain, L. U.S.A. 105 44.45N 73.15W
Champlitte-et-le-Prélot France 19 47.37N 5.31E
Champotón Mexico 116 19.21N 90.43W
Chāmpua India 63 22.05N 85.40E
Chamusca Portugal 27 39.21N 8.29W
Chañaral Chile 124 26.21S 70.37W
Chānasma India 62 23.43N 72.07E
Chandausi India 63 28.27N 78.46E
Chāndbāli India 63 20.46N 86.49E
Chandeleur Is. U.S.A. 111 29.48N 88.51W
Chandīgarh India 62 30.44N 76.47E
Chandīgarh d. India 62 30.45N 76.45E
Chāndil India 63 22.58N 86.03E
Chandler Canada 103 48.21N 64.41W
Chandler U.S.A. 111 35.42N 96.53W
Chāndor Hills India 62 20.30N 74.00E
Chandos L. Canada 105 44.49N 78.00W
Chāndpur Bangla. 61 22.08N 91.55E
Chāndpur Bangla. 63 23.13N 90.39E
Chāndpur India 63 29.09N 78.16E
Chandrapur India 63 19.57N 79.18E
Chāndvad India 62 20.20N 74.15E
Chānf Iran 65 26.40N 60.31E
Chang, Ko i. Thailand 56 12.04N102.23E
Changchun China 53 43.51N125.15E
Changde China 55 29.00N111.35E
Changfeng China 54 32.27N117.09E
Changhua Jiang r. China 55 19.20N108.38E
Chang Jiang r. China 55 31.40N121.15E
Changjin N. Korea 53 40.21N127.20E
Changle China 54 36.42N118.49E
Changli China 54 39.43N119.08E
Changling China 54 44.16N123.58E
Changning China 55 26.24N112.24E
Changping China 54 40.12N116.12E
Changsha China 55 28.09N112.59E
Changshan China 55 28.57N118.31E
Changshan Qundao is. China 54 39.20N123.00E
Changshou China 55 29.50N107.02E
Changshu China 55 31.48N120.52E
Changshun China 55 25.59N106.25E
Changting China 55 25.42N116.20E
Changyi China 54 36.51N119.23E
Changzhi China 54 36.10N113.00E
Changzhou China 55 31.46N119.58E
Channel Is. Europe 13 49.28N 2.13W
Channel Is. U.S.A. 109 34.00N120.00W
Channel-Port-aux-Basques town Canada 103 47.35N 59.11W
Channing Mich. U.S.A. 112 46.08N 88.06W
Channing Tex. U.S.A. 111 35.41N102.20W
Chantada Spain 26 42.37N 7.46W
Chanthaburi Thailand 56 12.35N102.05E
Chantilly France 19 49.12N 2.28E
Chanute U.S.A. 111 37.41N 95.27W
Chao'an China 55 23.40N116.32E
Chao Hu l. China 55 31.32N117.30E
Chaonde Mozambique 81 13.43S 40.31E
Chao Phraya r. Thailand 56 13.34N100.35E
Chao Xian China 55 31.36N117.52E
Chaoyang Guangdong China 55 23.25N116.31E
Chaoyang Liaoning China 54 41.35N120.20E
Chapada das Mangabeiras mts. Brazil 123 10.00S 46.30W
Chapada Diamantina Brazil 126 13.30S 42.30W
Chapala, Lago de l. Mexico 116 20.00N103.00W
Chapayevo Kazakhstan 45 50.12N 51.09E
Chapayevsk Russian Fed. 44 52.58N 49.44E
Chapeau Canada 105 45.54N 77.05W
Chapeau de Paille Canada 105 47.10N 73.30W
Chapelle-d'Angillon France 19 47.22N 2.26E
Chapicuy Uruguay 125 31.39S 57.54W
Chapleau Canada 102 47.50N 83.24W
Chāpra India 63 25.46N 84.45E
Chaqui Bolivia 124 19.36S 65.32W
Characot I. Antarctica 128 70.00S 75.00W
Charay Mexico 109 26.01N108.50W
Charcas Mexico 116 23.08N101.07W
Chard U.K. 13 50.52N 2.59W
Chardon U.S.A. 114 41.35N 81.12W
Charduār India 63 26.52N 92.46E
Chardzhou Turkmenistan 65 39.09N 63.34E
Charente d. France 20 45.40N 0.10E
Charente r. France 20 45.57N 1.05W
Charente-Maritime d. France 20 45.30N 0.45W
Charenton-du-Cher France 19 46.44N 2.38E
Chari r. Chad 77 13.00N 14.30E
Chari-Baguirmi d. Chad 77 12.20N 15.30E
Chārīkār Afghan. 62 35.01N 69.11E
Charing U.K. 13 51.12N 0.49E
Chariton U.S.A. 110 41.01N 93.19W
Charleroi Belgium 16 50.25N 4.27E
Charlesbourg Canada 105 46.51N 71.16W
Charles City U.S.A. 110 43.04N 92.40W
Charles Pt. Australia 88 12.23S130.37E
Charleston Miss. U.S.A. 111 34.00N 90.04W
Charleston S.C. U.S.A. 113 32.48N 79.58W
Charleston W.Va. U.S.A. 114 38.21N 81.38W
Charlestown Rep. of Ire. 15 53.57N 8.48W
Charlestown Ind. U.S.A. 112 38.28N 85.40W
Charlestown N.H. U.S.A. 115 43.14N 72.26W
Charles Town W.Va. U.S.A. 114 39.17N 77.52W
Charlesville Zaïre 78 5.27S 20.58E
Charleville Australia 90 26.25S146.13E
Charleville-Mézières France 19 49.46N 4.43E
Charlieu France 21 46.10N 4.10E
Charlotte N.C. U.S.A. 113 35.03N 80.50W
Charlotte Va. U.S.A. 113 37.03N 78.44W
Charlottenberg Sweden 43 59.53N 12.17E
Charlottesville U.S.A. 113 38.02N 78.29W
Charlottetown Canada 103 46.14N 63.08W
Charlton Australia 92 36.18S143.27E
Charlton I. Canada 102 52.00N 79.30W
Charly-sur-Marne France 19 48.58N 3.17E
Charmes France 19 48.22N 6.17E
Charny Canada 105 46.43N 71.16W
Charolles France 19 46.26N 4.17E
Charroux France 18 46.09N 0.24E
Chārsadda Pakistan 62 34.09N 71.44E
Charters Towers Australia 90 20.05S146.16E
Chartres France 18 48.27N 1.30E
Chascomús Argentina 125 35.35S 58.00W
Chase City U.S.A. 113 36.59N 78.30W
Châteaubriant France 18 47.43N 1.23W
Château-Chinon France 19 47.04N 3.56E
Château d'Oex Switz. 39 46.28N 7.08E
Château-du-Loir France 18 47.42N 0.25E
Châteaudun France 18 48.05N 1.20E
Chateaugay U.S.A. 105 44.56N 74.05W
Château Gontier France 18 47.50N 0.42W
Châteauguay, Lac l. Canada 103 56.27N 70.05W
Château Landon France 19 48.09N 2.42E
Château-la-Vallière France 18 47.33N 0.19E
Châteaulin France 18 48.12N 4.05W
Châteaumeillant France 19 46.34N 2.12E
Châteauneuf-de-Randon France 20 44.39N 3.40E
Châteauneuf-en-Thymerais France 18 48.35N 1.15E
Châteauneuf-sur-Charente France 20 45.36N 0.03W
Châteauneuf-sur-Loire France 19 47.52N 2.14E
Châteauneuf-sur-Sarthe France 18 47.41N 0.30W
Château-Porcien France 19 49.32N 4.15E
Château Renault France 18 47.35N 0.55E
Châteauroux France 19 46.49N 1.42E
Château-Salins France 19 48.49N 6.30E
Château-Thierry France 19 49.03N 3.24E
Châtelet Belgium 16 50.24N 4.32E
Châtellerault France 18 46.49N 0.33E
Châtel-sur-Moselle France 19 48.18N 6.24E
Châtelus-Malvaleix France 20 46.18N 2.01E
Chatham N.B. Canada 103 47.02N 65.28W
Chatham Ont. Canada 104 42.24N 82.11W
Chatham U.K. 13 51.23N 0.32E
Chatham Alas. U.S.A. 100 57.30N135.00W
Chatham Mass. U.S.A. 115 41.41N 69.58W
Chatham N.Y. U.S.A. 115 42.22N 73.36W
Chatham Is. Pacific Oc. 84 44.00S176.35W
Chatham Rise Pacific Oc. 84 43.30S178.00W
Chatham Str. U.S.A. 100 57.30N134.45W
Châtillon Italy 30 45.45N 7.37E
Châtillon-Coligny France 19 47.50N 2.51E
Châtillon-en-Bazois France 19 47.03N 3.49E
Châtillon-sur-Chalaronne France 21 46.07N 4.58E
Châtillon-sur-Indre France 18 46.59N 1.11E
Châtillon-sur-Seine France 19 47.51N 4.33E
Chatra India 63 24.13N 84.52E
Chatrapur India 63 19.21N 84.59E
Chātsu India 62 26.36N 75.57E
Chatsworth Canada 104 44.27N 80.54W
Chattahoochee U.S.A. 113 30.42N 84.51W
Chattahoochee r. U.S.A. 113 30.52N 84.57W
Chattanooga U.S.A. 113 35.02N 85.18W
Chatteris U.K. 13 52.27N 0.03E
Chaudes-Aigues France 20 44.51N 3.00E
Chauk Burma 56 20.52N 94.50E
Chaulnes France 19 49.49N 2.48E
Chaumont France 19 48.07N 5.08E
Chaumont-en-Vexin France 19 49.16N 1.53E
Chaungwabyin Burma 56 13.41N 98.22E
Chauny France 19 49.37N 3.13E
Chaupāran India 63 24.23N 85.15E
Chau Phu Vietnam 56 10.42N105.03E
Chaussin France 19 46.58N 5.25E
Chausy Belorussia 37 53.49N 30.57E
Chautauqua L. U.S.A. 114 42.12N 79.27W
Chauvigny France 18 46.34N 0.39E
Chavanges France 19 48.31N 4.34E
Chaves Brazil 123 0.10S 49.55W
Chaves Portugal 26 41.44N 7.28W
Chavuma Zambia 78 13.04S 22.43E
Chawang Thailand 56 8.25N 99.32E
Cheat r. U.S.A. 114 39.06N 79.33W
Cheat Mtn. U.S.A. 114 38.43N 79.51W
Cheb Czech Republic 39 50.01N 12.25E
Cheboksary Russian Fed. 44 56.08N 47.12E

Cheboygan to Ciudad Allende

Cheboygan U.S.A. 104 45.39N 84.29W
Chebsara Russian Fed. 44 59.14N 38.59E
Chebula Angola 78 12.27S 23.49E
Chech, Erg des. Mali / Algeria 74 24.30N 2.30W
Chechaouene Morocco 74 35.10N 5.16W
Chechersk Belorussia 37 52.54N 30.54E
Checiny Poland 37 50.48N 20.28E
Cheduba I. Burma 56 18.50N 93.35E
Chef-Boutonne France 18 46.07N 0.04W
Chegdomyn Russian Fed. 51 51.09N133.01E
Chegga well Mauritania 74 25.30N 5.46W
Chegutu Zimbabwe 80 18.09S 30.07E
Chehalis U.S.A. 108 46.40N122.58W
Cheil, Ras el c. Somali Rep. 71 7.45N 49.48E
Cheiron, Cime du mtn. France 21 43.49N 6.58E
Cheju S. Korea 53 33.31N126.29E
Cheju do i. S. Korea 53 33.20N126.30E
Cheleken Turkmenistan 65 39.26N 53.11E
Chelforó Argentina 125 39.04S 66.33W
Chelif, Oued r. Algeria 75 36.15N 2.05E
Chelkar Kazakhstan 50 47.48N 59.39E
Chelles France 19 48.53N 2.36E
Chełm Poland 37 51.10N 23.28E
Chelmer r. U.K. 11 51.43N 0.40E
Chelmsford Canada 104 46.35N 81.12W
Chelmsford U.K. 13 51.44N 0.28E
Chełmza Poland 37 53.12N 18.37E
Chelsea Canada 105 45.29N 75.48W
Chelsea Mich. U.S.A. 104 42.19N 84.01W
Chelsea Vt. U.S.A. 105 43.59N 72.27W
Cheltenham U.K. 13 51.53N 2.07W
Chelva Spain 25 39.45N 1.00W
Chelyabinsk Russian Fed. 9 55.12N 61.25E
Chelyuskin, Mys c. Russian Fed. 51 77.20N106.00E
Chemainus Canada 100 48.55N123.48W
Chemba Mozambique 79 17.11S 34.53E
Chemillé France 18 47.13N 0.44W
Chemnitz Germany 38 50.50N 12.55E
Chemult U.S.A. 108 43.13N121.47W
Chën, Gora mtn. Russian Fed. 51 65.30N141.20E
Chenāb r. Pakistan 62 29.23N 71.02E
Chenachane Algeria 74 26.00N 4.15W
Chenango r. U.S.A. 115 42.05N 75.55W
Chénéville Canada 105 45.53N 75.03W
Cheney U.S.A. 108 47.29N117.34W
Chengchow see Zhengzhou China 54
Chengde China 54 41.00N117.52E
Chengdu China 55 30.41N104.05E
Chenggu China 54 33.10N107.22E
Chenghai China 55 23.31N116.43E
Chengkou China 55 31.58N108.48E
Chengmai China 55 19.44N109.59E
Cheng Xian China 54 33.42N105.36E
Chenoa U.S.A. 110 40.44N 88.43W
Chen Xian China 55 25.45N113.00E
Chepelare Bulgaria 34 41.44N 24.41E
Chepén Peru 122 7.15S 79.20W
Chepstow U.K. 13 51.38N 2.40W
Cher d. France 19 47.05N 2.30E
Cher r. France 18 47.21N 0.29E
Cherbourg France 18 49.39N 1.39W
Cherdyn Russian Fed. 44 60.25N 55.22E
Cherelato Ethiopia 73 6.00N 38.10E
Cheremkhovo Russian Fed. 51 53.08N103.01E
Cherepovets Russian Fed. 44 59.05N 37.55E
Chergui, Chott ech f. Algeria 75 34.21N 0.30E
Cherikov Belorussia 37 53.35N 31.23E
Cherkassy Ukraine 45 49.27N 32.04E
Cherkessk Russian Fed. 45 44.14N 42.05E
Cherkovitsa Bulgaria 34 43.41N 24.49E
Cherlak Russian Fed. 50 54.10N 74.52E
Chernigov Ukraine 37 51.30N 31.18E
Chernikovsk Russian Fed. 44 54.51N 56.06E
Chernobyl Ukraine 37 51.17N 30.15E
Chernovtsy Ukraine 37 48.19N 25.52E
Chernyakhov Ukraine 37 50.30N 28.38E
Chernyakhovsk Russian Fed. 41 54.38N 21.49E
Cherokee Iowa U.S.A. 110 42.45N 95.33W
Cherokee Okla. U.S.A. 111 36.45N 98.21W
Cherquenco Chile 125 38.41S 72.00W
Cherrapunji India 63 25.18N 91.42E
Cherry Creek r. U.S.A. 110 44.36N101.30W
Cherry Creek town Nev. U.S.A. 108 39.54N113.53W
Cherry Creek town S.Dak. U.S.A. 110 44.36N101.26W
Cherry Valley town U.S.A. 115 42.48N 74.45W
Cherskogo, Khrebet mts. Russian Fed. 51 65.50N143.00E
Chertkovo Russian Fed. 45 49.22N 40.12E
Chertsey U.K. 13 51.23N 0.27W
Cherven-Bryag Bulgaria 34 43.17N 24.07E
Chervonograd Ukraine 37 50.25N 24.10E
Cherwell r. U.K. 13 51.44N 1.15W
Chesaning U.S.A. 104 43.11N 84.07W
Chesapeake Ohio U.S.A. 114 38.26N 82.28W
Chesapeake Va. U.S.A. 113 36.43N 76.15W
Chesapeake W.Va. U.S.A. 114 38.12N 81.33W
Chesapeake B. U.S.A. 115 38.40N 76.25W
Chesapeake Beach town U.S.A. 115 38.41N 76.32W
Chesham U.K. 13 51.43N 0.38W
Cheshire d. U.K. 12 53.14N 2.30W
Chëshskaya Guba g. Russian Fed. 44 67.20N 46.30E
Chesht-e Sharīf Afghan. 62 34.21N 63.44E
Chesil Beach f. U.K. 13 50.37N 2.33W
Chesley Canada 104 44.17N 81.05W
Chester U.K. 12 53.12N 2.53W
Chester Mont. U.S.A. 108 48.31N110.58W
Chester Penn. U.S.A. 115 39.51N 75.21W
Chester Vt. U.S.A. 115 43.16N 72.36W
Chesterfield U.K. 12 53.14N 1.26W
Chesterfield, Îles is. N. Cal. 84 20.00S159.00E
Chesterfield Inlet town Canada 99 63.00N 91.00W
Chestertown Md. U.S.A. 115 39.13N 76.04W
Chestertown N.Y. U.S.A. 115 43.38N 73.49W
Chesterville Canada 105 45.06N 75.14W
Chestnut Ridge mtn. U.S.A. 114 40.09N 79.24W
Chesuncook L. U.S.A. 112 46.00N 69.20W
Chéticamp Canada 103 46.38N 61.01W
Chetumal Mexico 117 18.30N 88.17W
Chetumal B. Mexico 117 18.30N 88.00W
Chetwynd Canada 100 55.45N121.45W
Cheviot New Zealand 86 42.49S173.16E
Cheviot U.S.A. 112 39.10N 84.32W
Ch'ew Bahir l. Ethiopia 73 4.40N 36.50E
Cheyenne Okla. U.S.A. 111 35.37N 99.40W
Cheyenne r. U.S.A. 110 44.40N101.15W
Cheyenne Wyo. U.S.A. 108 41.08N104.49W
Cheyne B. Australia 89 34.35S118.50E
Chhabra India 62 24.40N 76.50E
Chhātak Bangla. 63 25.02N 91.40E
Chhatarpur Bihār India 63 24.23N 84.11E
Chhatarpur Madhya P. India 63 24.54N 79.36E
Chhattīsgarh f. India 63 21.00N 82.00E
Chhindwāra India 63 22.04N 78.56E
Chhota-Chhindwāra India 63 23.03N 79.29E
Chhota Udepur India 62 22.19N 74.01E
Chiali Taiwan 55 23.10N120.11E
Chiang Mai Thailand 56 18.48N 98.59E
Chiapas d. Mexico 116 16.30N 93.00W
Chiaramonte Gulfi Italy 33 37.01N 14.43E
Chiaravalle Centrale Italy 33 38.41N 16.25E
Chiari Italy 30 45.32N 9.56E
Chiavari Italy 30 44.19N 9.19E
Chiavenna Italy 30 46.19N 9.24E
Chiba Japan 57 35.36N140.07E
Chiba d. Japan 57 35.10N140.00E
Chibemba Angola 80 15.43S 14.07E
Chibia Angola 78 15.10S 13.32E
Chibougamau Canada 102 49.56N 74.24W
Chibougamau Lac l. Canada 102 49.50N 74.20W
Chibougamau Prov. Park Canada 103 49.25N 73.50W
Chibuk Nigeria 77 10.52N 12.50E
Chibuto Mozambique 81 24.41S 33.32E
Chicago U.S.A. 110 41.50N 87.45W
Chichagof I. U.S.A. 100 57.55N135.45W
Chicheng China 54 40.52N115.50E
Chichester U.K. 13 50.50N 0.47W
Chichibu Japan 57 35.59N139.05E
Chickasha U.S.A. 111 35.02N 97.58W
Chiclana Spain 27 36.25N 6.08W
Chiclayo Peru 122 6.47S 79.47W
Chico r. Chubut Argentina 125 43.45S 66.10W
Chico r. Santa Cruz Argentina 125 50.03W 68.35W
Chico U.S.A. 108 39.44N121.50W
Chicomo Mozambique 81 24.33S 34.11E
Chicopee U.S.A. 115 42.10N 72.36W
Chicora U.S.A. 114 40.57N 79.45W
Chicoutimi-Jonquière Canada 103 48.26N 71.06W
Chicualacuala Mozambique 81 22.06S 31.42E
Chidambarum India 61 11.24N 79.42E
Chidembo Angola 78 14.34S 19.17E
Chidenguele Mozambique 81 24.54S 34.13E
Chidley, C. Canada 99 60.30N 65.00W
Chiemsee l. Germany 39 47.54N 12.29E
Chiengi Zambia 79 8.42S 29.07E
Chieri Italy 30 45.01N 7.49E
Chieti Italy 31 42.21N 14.10E
Chifeng China 54 42.13N118.56E
Chigasaki Japan 57 35.19N139.24E
Chignecto B. Canada 103 45.35N 64.45W
Chiguana Bolivia 124 21.05S 67.58W
Chigubo Mozambique 81 22.38S 33.18E
Chigu Co l. China 63 28.40N 91.50E
Chihuahua Mexico 109 28.38N106.05W
Chihuahua d. Mexico 109 28.40N106.00W
Chiili Kazakhstan 50 44.10N 66.37E
Chikhli India 62 20.21N 76.15E
Chikumbi Zambia 79 15.14S 28.21E
Chikwawa Malaŵi 79 16.00S 34.54E
Chil r. Iran 65 25.12N 61.30E
Chilanga Zambia 80 15.33S 28.17E
Chilapa Mexico 116 17.38N 99.11W
Chilcoot U.S.A. 108 39.49N120.08W
Childers Australia 90 25.14S152.17E
Childress U.S.A. 111 34.25N100.13W
Chile S. America 124 32.30S 71.00W
Chile Basin Pacific Oc. 85 34.20S 80.00W
Chile Chico Chile 125 46.33S 71.44W
Chilka L. India 63 19.46N 85.20E
Chilko L. Canada 98 51.20N124.05W
Chillagoe Australia 90 17.09S144.32E
Chillán Chile 125 36.36S 72.07W
Chillicothe Mo. U.S.A. 110 39.48N 93.33W
Chillicothe Ohio U.S.A. 112 39.20N 82.59W
Chilliwack Canada 100 49.10N122.00W
Chiloé, Isla de i. Chile 125 43.00S 73.00W
Chilonga Zambia 79 12.02S 31.17E
Chilpancingo Mexico 116 17.33N 99.30W
Chiltern Australia 93 36.11S146.36E
Chiltern Hills U.K. 13 51.40N 0.53W
Chilton U.S.A. 110 44.04N 88.10W
Chilumba Malaŵi 79 10.25S 34.18E
Chilwa, L. Malaŵi 79 15.15S 35.45E
Chimakela Angola 78 15.12S 16.58E
Chimanimani Zimbabwe 81 19.48S 32.52E
Chimay Belgium 16 50.03N 4.20E
Chimbas Argentina 124 31.28S 68.30W
Chimbay Uzbekistan 50 42.56N 59.46E
Chimborazo mtn. Ecuador 122 1.29S 78.52W
Chimbote Peru 122 9.04S 78.34W
Chimishliya Moldavia 37 46.30N 28.50E
Chimkent Kazakhstan 52 42.16N 69.05E
Chimoio Mozambique 81 19.04S 33.29E
Chin d. Burma 56 22.00N 93.30E
China Asia 52 33.00N103.00E
China Lake town U.S.A. 109 35.46N117.39W
Chinandega Nicaragua 117 12.35N 87.10W
Chinati Peak U.S.A. 109 29.57N104.29W
Chincha Alta Peru 122 13.25S 76.07W
Chinchaga r. Canada 100 58.50N118.20W
Chinchilla Australia 91 26.44S150.39E
Chinchón Spain 27 40.08N 3.25W
Chinchoua Gabon 78 0.00 9.48E
Chincilla de Monte Aragón Spain 25 38.55N 1.45W
Chincoteague U.S.A. 113 37.55N 75.23W
Chinde Mozambique 81 18.37S 36.24E
Chindio Mozambique 79 17.46S 35.23E
Chindwin r. Burma 56 21.30N 95.12E
Chinga Mozambique 79 15.14S 38.40E
Chingleput India 61 12.42N 79.59E
Chingola Zambia 79 12.29S 27.53E
Chingombe Zambia 79 14.25S 29.56E
Chingshui Taiwan 55 24.15N120.35E
Chin Hills Burma 56 22.30N 93.30E
Chinhoyi Zimbabwe 80 17.22S 30.10E
Chīni India 63 31.32N 78.15E
Chiniot Pakistan 62 31.43N 72.59E
Chinjan Pakistan 62 30.34N 67.58E
Chinkapook Australia 92 35.11S142.57E
Chinko r. C.A.R. 73 4.50N 23.53E
Chinle U.S.A. 109 36.09N109.33W
Chinon France 18 47.10N 0.15E
Chinook U.S.A. 108 48.35N109.14W
Chino Valley town U.S.A. 109 34.45N112.27W
Chinsali Zambia 79 10.33S 32.05E
Chintheche Malaŵi 79 11.50S 34.13E
Chiny Belgium 16 49.45N 5.20E
Chiôco Mozambique 79 16.27S 32.49E
Chioggia Italy 30 45.13N 12.17E
Chipata Zambia 79 13.37S 32.40E
Chipera Mozambique 79 15.20S 32.35E
Chipie r. Canada 102 51.25N 83.20W
Chipinge Zimbabwe 81 20.12S 32.38E
Chippenham U.K. 13 51.27N 2.07W
Chippewa r. U.S.A. 104 43.35N 84.17W
Chippewa Falls town U.S.A. 110 44.56N 91.24W
Chipping Norton U.K. 13 51.56N 1.32W
Chiquian Peru 122 10.10S 77.00W
Chiquinquirá Colombia 122 5.37N 73.50W
Chir r. Russian Fed. 45 48.34N 42.53E
Chirāwa India 62 28.15N 75.38E
Chirchik Uzbekistan 9 41.28N 69.31E
Chiredzi Zimbabwe 81 21.03S 31.39E
Chiredzi r. Zimbabwe 81 21.10S 31.50E
Chiricahua Peak mtn. U.S.A. 109 31.52N109.20W
Chiriquí mtn. Panama 117 8.49N 82.38W
Chiriquí, Laguna de b. Panama 117 9.00N 82.00W
Chiromo Malaŵi 79 16.28S 35.10E
Chirpan Bulgaria 34 42.10N 25.19E
Chirripó mtn. Costa Rica 117 9.31N 83.30W
Chirundu Zimbabwe 80 16.04S 28.51E
Chisamba Zambia 80 14.58S 28.23E
Chisasibi Canada 102 53.50N 79.00W
Chishan Taiwan 55 22.53N120.29E
Chisholm U.S.A. 110 47.29N 92.53W
Chisholm Mills Canada 100 54.55N114.09W
Chishtiān Mandi Pakistan 62 29.48N 72.52E
Chishui China 55 28.29N105.38E
Chişinau see Kishinev Moldavia 37
Chisone r. Italy 30 44.49N 7.25E
Chistopol Russian Fed. 44 55.25N 50.38E
Chita Russian Fed. 53 52.03N113.35E
Chitek L. Canada 101 52.25N 99.20W
Chitembo Angola 78 13.33S 16.47E
Chitipa Malaŵi 79 9.41S 33.19E
Chitorgarh India 62 24.53N 74.38E
Chitrakūt Dham India 63 25.11N 80.52E
Chitrāl Pakistan 60 35.52N 71.58E
Chitré Panama 97 7.58N 80.26W
Chittagong Bangla. 63 22.20N 91.50E
Chittenango U.S.A. 115 43.03N 75.52W
Chittoor India 61 13.13N 79.06E
Chiumbe r. Zaïre 78 6.37S 21.04E
Chiume Angola 78 15.08S 21.11E
Chiusi Italy 30 43.01N 11.57E
Chiuta, L. Malaŵi / Mozambique 79 14.45S 35.50E
Chiva Spain 25 39.28N 0.43W
Chivasso Italy 30 45.11N 7.53E
Chivhu Zimbabwe 80 19.01S 30.53E
Chivilcoy Argentina 125 34.52S 60.02W
Chiwanda Tanzania 79 11.21S 34.55E
Chobe d. Botswana 80 18.30S 25.15E
Chobe r. Namibia / Botswana 80 17.48S 25.12E
Chobe Swamp f. Namibia 80 18.20S 23.40E
Chocolate Mts. U.S.A. 109 33.20N115.15W
Chocope Peru 122 7.47S 79.12W
Choele-Choel Argentina 125 39.15S 65.30W
Chōfu Japan 57 35.39N139.33E
Chohtan India 62 25.29N 71.04E
Choix Mexico 109 26.43N108.17W
Chojnice Poland 37 53.42N 17.32E
Chokai zan mtn. Japan 57 39.08N140.04E
Ch'ok'ē Mts. Ethiopia 73 11.00N 37.30E
Cholet France 18 47.04N 0.53W
Cholon Vietnam 56 10.40N106.30E
Choluteca Honduras 117 13.16N 87.11W
Choma Zambia 79 16.51S 27.04E
Chomu India 62 27.10N 75.44E
Chomutov Czech Republic 39 50.28N 13.26E
Chon Buri Thailand 56 13.20N101.02E
Chone Ecuador 122 0.44S 80.04W
Chong'an China 55 27.46N118.01E
Ch'ŏngjin N. Korea 53 41.55N129.50E
Ch'ŏngju S. Korea 53 36.39N127.31E
Chŏng Kal Cambodia 56 13.57N103.35E
Chongming i. China 55 31.36N121.33E
Chongqing China 55 29.31N106.35E
Chongren China 55 27.44N116.02E
Chŏnju S. Korea 53 35.50N127.05E
Chonos, Archipelago de los is. Chile 125 45.00S 74.00W
Cho Oyu mtn. China / Nepal 63 28.06N 86.40E
Chopda India 62 21.15N 75.18E
Choptank r. U.S.A. 115 38.38N 76.13W
Chorges France 21 44.33N 6.17E
Chorley U.K. 12 53.39N 2.39W
Chorokh r. Georgia 45 41.36N 41.35E
Chortkov Ukraine 37 49.01N 25.42E
Chorzów Poland 37 50.19N 18.56E
Chosica Peru 122 11.55S 76.38W
Chos Malal Argentina 125 37.20S 70.15W
Choszczno Poland 36 53.10N 15.26E
Choteau U.S.A. 108 47.49N112.11W
Chotila India 62 22.25N 71.11E
Choum Mauritania 74 21.10N 13.00W
Chowchilla U.S.A. 108 37.07N120.16W
Christchurch New Zealand 86 43.33S172.40E
Christchurch U.K. 13 50.44N 1.47W
Christian I. Canada 104 44.50N 80.13W
Christian Sd. U.S.A. 100 55.56N134.40W
Christiansfeld Denmark 42 55.21N 9.29E
Christianshåb Greenland 99 68.50N 51.00W
Christie B. Canada 101 62.32N111.10W
Christina r. Canada 101 56.40N111.03W
Christmas Creek town Australia 88 18.55S125.56E
Christmas I. Indian Oc. 58 10.30S105.40E
Christmas I. see Kiritimati i. Kiribati 85
Chrudim Czech Republic 36 49.57N 15.48E
Chu r. Kazakhstan 52 42.30N 76.10E
Chuādānga Bangla. 63 23.38N 88.51E
Chubbuck U.S.A. 109 34.22N115.20W
Chūbu d. Japan 57 35.25N137.40E
Chubut d. Argentina 125 44.00S 68.00W
Chubut r. Argentina 125 43.18S 65.06W
Chu Chua Canada 100 51.22N120.10W
Chudleigh U.K. 13 50.35N 3.36W
Chudnov Ukraine 37 50.05N 28.01E
Chudovo Russian Fed. 44 59.10N 31.41E
Chūgoku d. Japan 57 35.00N133.00E
Chūgoku sanchi mts. Japan 57 35.30N133.00E
Chugwater U.S.A. 108 41.46N104.49W
Chuiquimula Guatemala 117 15.52N 89.50W
Chukai Malaysia 58 4.16N103.24E
Chukchi Sea Arctic Oc. 96 69.30N172.00W
Chukotskiy Poluostrov pen. Russian Fed. 51 66.00N174.30W
Chukudukraal Botswana 80 22.30S 23.22E
Chula Vista U.S.A. 109 32.39N117.05W
Chulman Russian Fed. 51 56.54N124.55E
Chulucanas Peru 122 5.08S 80.00W
Chulym Russian Fed. 50 55.09N 80.59E
Chum Russian Fed. 44 67.05N 63.15E
Chumbicha Argentina 124 28.50S 66.18W
Chumikan Russian Fed. 51 54.40N135.15E
Chumphon Thailand 56 10.34N 99.15E
Chuna r. Russian Fed. 51 58.00N 94.00E
Ch'unch'ŏn S. Korea 53 37.53N127.45E
Chungking see Chongqing China 55
Chunya Tanzania 79 8.31S 33.28E
Chuquicamata Chile 124 22.20S 68.56W
Chuquisaca d. Bolivia 124 21.00S 64.00W
Chur Switz. 39 46.51N 9.32E
Churchill Canada 101 58.46N 94.10W
Churchill r. Man. Canada 101 58.47N 94.12W
Churchill r. Nfld. Canada 103 53.20N 60.11W
Churchill, C. Canada 101 58.46N 93.12W
Churchill L. Canada 101 55.55N108.20W
Churchill Peak mtn. Canada 100 58.10N125.10W
Church Stretton U.K. 13 52.32N 2.49W
Churia Range mts. Nepal 63 28.40N 81.30E
Churu India 62 28.18N 74.57E
Chusovoy Russian Fed. 44 58.18N 57.50E
Chu Xian China 54 32.25N118.15E
Chuxiong China 61 25.03N101.33E
Chu Yang Sin mtn. Vietnam 56 12.25N108.25E
Ciamis Indonesia 59 7.20S108.21E
Cianjur Indonesia 59 6.50S107.09E
Cibatu Indonesia 59 7.10S107.59E
Ćićarija mts. Slovenia / Croatia 31 45.30N 14.00E
Cidacos r. Spain 25 42.21N 1.38W
Ciechanów Poland 37 52.53N 20.38E
Ciego de Avila Cuba 117 21.51N 78.47W
Ciempozuelos Spain 26 40.10N 3.37W
Ciénaga Colombia 122 11.11N 74.15W
Cienfuegos Cuba 117 22.10N 80.27W
Cíes, Islas is. Spain 26 42.13N 8.54W
Cieszyn Poland 37 49.45N 18.38E
Cieza Spain 25 38.14N 1.25W
Cifuentes Spain 26 40.47N 2.37W
Cigüela r. Spain 27 39.08N 3.44W
Cijara, Embalse de resr. Spain 27 39.18N 4.52W
Cijulang Indonesia 59 7.44S108.30E
Cikampek Indonesia 59 6.21S107.25E
Cilacap Indonesia 59 7.44S109.00E
Ciledug Indonesia 59 6.56S108.43E
Cili China 55 29.24N111.04E
Cilleruelo de Bezana Spain 26 43.00N 3.51W
Cimanuk r. Indonesia 59 6.20S108.12E
Cimarron U.S.A. 111 37.48N100.21W
Cimarron r. U.S.A. 111 36.10N 96.17W
Cimone, Monte mtn. Italy 30 44.12N 10.42E
Cîmpina Romania 29 45.08N 25.44E
Cîmpulung Romania 29 45.16N 25.03E
Cinca r. Spain 25 41.26N 0.21E
Cincar mtn. Bosnia-Herzegovina 31 43.54N 17.04E
Cincinnati U.S.A. 112 39.10N 84.30W
Ciney Belgium 16 50.17N 5.06E
Cingoli Italy 30 43.22N 13.13E
Cinto, Monte mtn. France 21 42.23N 8.56E
Cipolletti Argentina 125 38.56S 67.59W
Circeo, Parco Nazionale del Nat. Park Italy 32 41.17N 13.05E
Circle U.S.A. 108 47.25N105.35W
Circleville Ohio U.S.A. 112 39.36N 82.57W
Circleville Utah U.S.A. 108 38.10N112.16W
Cirebon Indonesia 59 6.46S108.33E
Cirencester U.K. 13 51.43N 1.59W
Cirey-sur-Vezouse France 19 48.35N 6.57E
Ciriè Italy 30 45.14N 7.36E
Cirò Marina Italy 33 39.22N 17.08E
Cisco U.S.A. 111 32.23N 98.59W
Ciskei Africa 80 32.45S 27.00E
Cisterna di Latina Italy 32 41.35N 12.49E
Cistierna Spain 26 42.48N 5.07W
Citlaltepetl mtn. Mexico 97 19.00N 97.18W
Citra U.S.A. 113 29.24N 82.06W
Cittadella Italy 30 45.39N 11.47E
Città di Castello Italy 30 43.27N 12.14E
Cittanova Italy 33 38.21N 16.05E
Ciudad Acuña Mexico 111 29.18N100.55W
Ciudad Allende Mexico 111 28.20N100.51W

Ciudad Bolívar to **Conroe**

Ciudad Bolívar Venezuela **122** 8.06N 63.36W
Ciudad Camargo Mexico **109** 27.40N105.10W
Ciudad Delicias Mexico **97** 28.13N105.28W
Ciudad de México Mexico **116** 19.25N 99.10W
Ciudadela Spain **25** 40.00N 3.50E
Ciudad Guayana Venezuela **122** 8.22N 62.40W
Ciudad Guerrero Mexico **116** 28.33N107.28W
Ciudad Guzmán Mexico **116** 19.41N103.29W
Ciudad Ixtepec Mexico **116** 16.32N 95.10W
Ciudad Jiménez Mexico **109** 27.08N104.55W
Ciudad Juárez Mexico **109** 31.44N106.29W
Ciudad Lerdo Mexico **111** 25.32N103.32W
Ciudad Madero Mexico **116** 22.19N 97.50W
Ciudad Mante Mexico **116** 22.44N 98.57W
Ciudad Melchor Múzquiz Mexico **111** 27.53N101.31W
Ciudad Mier Mexico **111** 26.26N 99.09W
Ciudad Obregón Mexico **109** 27.29N109.56W
Ciudad Ojeda Venezuela **122** 10.05N 71.17W
Ciudad Piar Venezuela **122** 7.27N 63.19W
Ciudad Real Spain **26** 38.59N 3.56W
Ciudad Real *d.* Spain **27** 38.50N 4.00W
Ciudad Rodrigo Spain **26** 40.36N 6.32W
Ciudad Victoria Mexico **116** 23.43N 99.10W
Ciurana *r.* Spain **25** 41.08N 0.39E
Civita Castellana Italy **30** 42.17N 12.25E
Civitanova Italy **31** 43.18N 13.44E
Civitavecchia Italy **30** 42.06N 11.48E
Civray France **18** 46.09N 0.18E
Çivril Turkey **64** 38.18N 29.43E
Ci Xian China **54** 36.22N114.23E
Cizre Turkey **64** 37.21N 42.11E
Clackline Australia **89** 31.43S116.31E
Clacton on Sea U.K. **13** 51.47N 1.10E
Clain *r.* France **18** 46.47N 0.32E
Claire, L. Canada **100** 58.30N112.00W
Clairton U.S.A. **114** 40.18N 79.53W
Clairvaux-les-Lacs France **19** 46.34N 5.45E
Claise *r.* France **18** 46.54N 0.45E
Clamecy France **19** 47.27N 3.31E
Clanton U.S.A. **113** 32.50N 86.38W
Clapperton I. Canada **104** 46.02N 82.13W
Clara Rep. of Ire. **15** 53.21N 7.37W
Clare N.S.W. Australia **92** 33.27S143.55E
Clare S.A. Australia **92** 33.50S138.38E
Clare *d.* Rep. of Ire. **15** 52.52N 8.55W
Clare *r.* Rep. of Ire. **15** 53.17N 9.04W
Clare U.S.A. **112** 43.49N 84.47W
Clare I. Rep. of Ire. **15** 53.48N 10.00W
Claremont U.S.A. **115** 43.23N 72.20W
Claremore U.S.A. **111** 36.19N 95.36W
Claremorris Rep. of Ire. **15** 53.44N 9.00W
Clarence *r.* Australia **93** 29.25S153.02E
Clarence *r.* New Zealand **86** 42.10S173.55E
Clarence U.S.A. **114** 41.03N 77.56W
Clarence I. Antarctica **128** 61.30S 53.50W
Clarence Str. Australia **88** 12.00S131.00E
Clarence Str. U.S.A. **100** 55.40N132.10W
Clarendon U.S.A. **111** 34.56N100.53W
Clarendon L. Canada **105** 44.52N 76.53W
Claresholm Canada **100** 50.00N113.45W
Clarie Coast *f.* Antarctica **128** 67.00S133.00E
Clarinda U.S.A. **110** 40.44N 95.02W
Clarington Ohio U.S.A. **114** 39.47N 80.53W
Clarington Penn. U.S.A. **114** 41.20N 79.07W
Clarion U.S.A. **114** 41.13N 79.24W
Clarion *r.* U.S.A. **114** 41.07N 79.41W
Clark, L. U.S.A. **98** 60.15N154.15W
Clark, Pt. *c.* Canada **104** 44.04N 81.45W
Clarke I. Australia **91** 40.30S148.10E
Clark Fork *r.* U.S.A. **108** 48.09N116.15W
Clarksburg U.S.A. **114** 39.17N 80.21W
Clarksdale U.S.A. **111** 34.12N 90.34W
Clarks Summit U.S.A. **115** 41.30N 75.42W
Clarkston U.S.A. **108** 46.26N117.02W
Clarksville Ark. U.S.A. **111** 35.28N 93.28W
Clarksville Tenn. U.S.A. **113** 36.31N 87.21W
Clarksville Tex. U.S.A. **111** 33.37N 95.03W
Clary France **19** 50.05N 3.24E
Clausthal-Zellerfeld Germany **38** 51.48N 10.20E
Clay U.S.A. **114** 38.28N 81.05W
Clayoquot Sd. Canada **100** 49.11N126.08W
Claysburg U.S.A. **114** 40.18N 78.27W
Claysville U.S.A. **114** 40.07N 80.25W
Clayton *r.* Australia **92** 29.06S137.59E
Clayton Idaho U.S.A. **108** 44.16N114.25W
Clayton N.J. U.S.A. **115** 39.39N 75.06W
Clayton N.Mex. U.S.A. **111** 36.27N103.11W
Clayton N.Y. U.S.A. **105** 44.14N 76.05W
Clear, C. Rep. of Ire. **11** 51.25N 9.32W
Clearfield Penn. U.S.A. **114** 41.02N 78.27W
Clearfield Utah U.S.A. **108** 41.07N112.01W
Clear I. Rep. of Ire. **15** 51.26N 9.30W
Clear L. U.S.A. **108** 39.02N122.50W
Clear Lake *town* Iowa U.S.A. **110** 43.08N 92.23W
Clear Lake *town* S.Dak. U.S.A. **110** 44.45N 96.41W
Clear Spring U.S.A. **114** 39.39N 77.55W
Clearwater Canada **100** 51.38N120.02W
Clearwater *r.* Canada **101** 56.40N109.30W
Clearwater U.S.A. **113** 27.57N 82.48W
Clearwater Mts. U.S.A. **108** 46.00N115.30W
Cle Elum U.S.A. **108** 47.12N120.56W
Cleethorpes U.K. **12** 53.33N 0.02W
Clefmont France **19** 48.06N 5.31E
Clelles France **21** 44.50N 5.37E
Clendenin U.S.A. **114** 38.29N 81.21W
Clermont Australia **90** 22.49S147.39E
Clermont France **19** 49.23N 2.24E
Clermont-en-Argonne France **19** 49.05N 5.05E
Clermont-Ferrand France **20** 45.47N 3.05E
Clervaux Lux. **16** 50.04N 6.01E
Cles Italy **30** 46.22N 11.02E
Cleve Australia **92** 33.37S136.32E
Clevedon U.K. **13** 51.26N 2.52W
Cleveland *d.* U.K. **12** 54.37N 1.08W
Cleveland Miss. U.S.A. **111** 33.45N 90.50W
Cleveland Ohio U.S.A. **114** 41.30N 81.41W
Cleveland Tenn. U.S.A. **113** 35.10N 84.51W
Cleveland Tex. U.S.A. **111** 30.21N 95.05W
Cleveland, C. Australia **90** 19.11S147.01E
Cleveland Heights *town* U.S.A. **114** 41.30N 81.34W
Cleveland Hills U.K. **12** 54.25N 1.10W
Cleveleys U.K. **12** 53.52N 3.01W
Clew B. Rep. of Ire. **15** 53.50N 9.47W
Clifden Rep. of Ire. **15** 53.29N 10.02W
Clifford Canada **104** 43.58N 80.58W
Clifford U.S.A. **114** 43.19N 83.11W
Cliffy Head Australia **89** 34.58S116.24E
Clifton Ariz. U.S.A. **109** 33.03N109.18W
Clifton N.J. U.S.A. **115** 40.53N 74.08W
Clifton Tex. U.S.A. **111** 31.47N 97.35W
Clifton Forge U.S.A. **113** 37.49N 79.49W
Climax Canada **101** 49.13N108.23W
Clint U.S.A. **109** 31.35N106.14W
Clinton B.C. Canada **100** 51.05N121.35W
Clinton Ont. Canada **104** 43.37N 81.32W
Clinton New Zealand **86** 46.13S169.23E
Clinton Ark. U.S.A. **111** 35.36N 92.38W
Clinton Conn. U.S.A. **115** 41.17N 72.32W
Clinton Ill. U.S.A. **110** 40.10N 88.59W
Clinton Iowa U.S.A. **110** 41.51N 90.12W
Clinton Mass. U.S.A. **115** 42.25N 71.41W
Clinton Mich. U.S.A. **104** 42.04N 83.58W
Clinton Mo. U.S.A. **110** 38.22N 93.46W
Clinton N.C. U.S.A. **113** 35.00N 78.20W
Clinton N.J. U.S.A. **115** 40.38N 74.55W
Clinton Okla. U.S.A. **111** 35.31N 98.59W
Clintwood U.S.A. **113** 37.09N 82.30W
Clio U.S.A. **104** 43.11N 83.44W
Clipperton *i.* Pacific Oc. **85** 10.17N109.13W
Clisham *mtn.* U.K. **14** 57.58N 6.50W
Clisson France **18** 47.05N 1.17W
Clive L. Canada **100** 63.13N118.54W
Cliza Bolivia **124** 17.36S 65.56W
Cloghan Offaly Rep. of Ire. **15** 53.13N 7.54W
Clogher Head Kerry Rep. of Ire. **15** 52.09N 10.28W
Clonakilty Rep. of Ire. **15** 51.37N 8.54W
Cloncurry Australia **90** 20.42S140.30E
Clones Rep. of Ire. **15** 54.11N 7.16W
Clonmel Rep. of Ire. **15** 52.21N 7.44W
Clonroche Rep. of Ire. **15** 52.27N 6.45W
Cloppenburg Germany **38** 52.50N 8.02E
Cloquet U.S.A. **110** 46.43N 92.28W
Clorinda Argentina **124** 25.20S 57.40W
Cloud Peak *mtn.* U.S.A. **108** 44.25N107.10W
Cloughton U.K. **12** 54.20N 0.27W
Cloverdale U.S.A. **108** 38.48N123.01W
Clovis Calif. U.S.A. **108** 36.49N119.42W
Clovis N.Mex. U.S.A. **111** 34.24N103.12W
Clowne U.K. **12** 53.18N 1.16W
Cluj-Napoca Romania **37** 46.47N 23.37E
Clunes Australia **92** 37.16S143.47E
Cluny France **19** 46.26N 4.39E
Cluses France **21** 46.04N 6.36E
Clusone Italy **30** 45.53N 9.57E
Clutha *r.* New Zealand **86** 46.18S169.05E
Clwyd *d.* U.K. **12** 53.07N 3.20W
Clwyd *r.* U.K. **12** 53.19N 3.30W
Clyde Canada **99** 70.30N 68.30W
Clyde New Zealand **86** 45.11S169.19E
Clyde *r.* U.K. **14** 55.58N 4.53W
Clyde N.Y. U.S.A. **114** 43.05N 76.52W
Clyde Ohio U.S.A. **114** 41.18N 82.59W
Clydebank U.K. **14** 55.53N 4.23W
Clyde Forks Canada **105** 45.07N 76.41W
Clymer U.S.A. **114** 40.40N 79.01W
Côa *r.* Portugal **26** 41.05N 7.05W
Coachella U.S.A. **109** 33.41N116.10W
Coahuila *d.* Mexico **111** 27.40N102.00W
Coal *r.* Canada **100** 59.39N126.57W
Coalgate U.S.A. **111** 34.32N 96.13W
Coal Grove U.S.A. **114** 38.30N 82.39W
Coalinga U.S.A. **109** 36.09N120.21W
Coalport U.S.A. **114** 40.45N 78.32W
Coalville U.K. **13** 52.43N 1.21W
Coast *d.* Kenya **79** 3.00S 39.30E
Coast Mts. Canada **100** 55.00N129.00W
Coast Range *mts.* U.S.A. **108** 42.40N123.30W
Coatbridge U.K. **14** 55.52N 4.02W
Coatesville U.S.A. **115** 39.59N 75.49W
Coaticook Canada **105** 45.08N 71.48W
Coats I. Canada **99** 62.30N 83.00W
Coats Land *f.* Antarctica **128** 77.00S 25.00W
Coatzacoalcos Mexico **116** 18.10N 94.25W
Cobalt Canada **104** 47.24N 79.41W
Cobán Guatemala **116** 15.28N 90.20W
Cobar Australia **93** 31.32S145.51E
Cobargo Australia **93** 36.24S149.52E
Cobden Australia **92** 38.21S143.07E
Cobden Canada **105** 45.38N 76.53W
Cobh Rep. of Ire. **15** 51.50N 8.18W
Cobham L. Australia **92** 30.09S142.05E
Cobija Bolivia **124** 11.02S 68.44W
Cobleskill U.S.A. **115** 42.41N 74.29W
Cobourg Canada **104** 43.58N 78.10W
Cobourg Pen. Australia **90** 11.20S132.15E
Cobram Australia **93** 35.56S145.40E
Cobre U.S.A. **108** 41.07N114.25W
Cobue Mozambique **79** 12.10S 34.50E
Coburg Germany **39** 50.15N 10.58E
Coburg I. Canada **99** 76.00N 79.25W
Cocentaina Spain **25** 38.45N 0.26W
Cochabamba Bolivia **124** 17.24S 66.09W
Cochabamba *d.* Bolivia **124** 17.30S 65.40W
Cochem Germany **39** 50.11N 7.09E
Cochise U.S.A. **109** 32.06N109.56W
Cochran U.S.A. **113** 32.22N 83.21W
Cochrane Alta. Canada **100** 51.11N114.30W
Cochrane Ont. Canada **102** 49.00N 81.00W
Cochrane Chile **125** 47.20S 72.30W
Cockaleechie Australia **92** 34.07S135.53E
Cockburn Australia **92** 32.05S141.00E
Cockburn I. Canada **104** 45.55N 83.24W
Cockburn Island *town* Canada **104** 45.58N 83.22W
Cockburnspath U.K. **14** 55.56N 2.22W
Cockeysville U.S.A. **115** 39.29N 76.39W
Cocklebiddy Australia **89** 32.02S126.05E
Cocksackie U.S.A. **115** 42.21N 73.48W
Coco *r.* Honduras **117** 14.58N 83.15W
Coco, Isla del *i.* Pacific Oc. **85** 5.32N 87.04W
Cocoa U.S.A. **113** 28.21N 80.46W
Cocoa Beach *town* U.S.A. **113** 28.19N 80.36W
Cocobeach Gabon **78** 0.59N 9.36E
Cocoparra Range *mts.* Australia **93** 34.00S146.00E
Cocos Is. Indian Oc. **49** 13.00S 96.00E
Cod, C. U.S.A. **115** 41.42N 70.15W
Codăeşti Romania **37** 46.52N 27.46E
Codajás Brazil **122** 3.55S 62.00W
Codigoro Italy **30** 44.49N 12.08E
Codó Brazil **123** 4.28S 43.51W
Codogno Italy **30** 45.09N 9.42E
Codroipo Italy **30** 45.58N 12.59E
Cody U.S.A. **108** 44.32N109.03W
Coen Australia **90** 13.56S143.12E
Coesfeld Germany **38** 51.56N 7.10E
Coeur d'Alene U.S.A. **106** 47.40N116.46W
Coevorden Neth. **16** 52.39N 6.45E
Coffeyville U.S.A. **111** 37.02N 93.37W
Coffin B. Australia **92** 34.27S135.19E
Coffin Bay Pen. Australia **92** 34.30S135.14E
Coff's Harbour Australia **93** 30.19S153.05E
Cofre de Perote *mtn.* Mexico **116** 19.30N 97.10W
Cofrentes Spain **25** 39.14N 1.04W
Coghinas *r.* Italy **32** 40.55N 8.48E
Coghinas, Lago di *l.* Italy **32** 40.43N 9.05E
Cognac France **20** 45.42N 0.20W
Cogolludo Spain **26** 40.57N 3.05W
Cohocton U.S.A. **114** 42.09N 77.05W
Cohoes U.S.A. **115** 42.46N 73.42W
Cohuna Australia **92** 35.47S144.15E
Coiba, Isla de *i.* Panama **117** 7.23N 81.45W
Coihaique Chile **125** 45.35S 72.08W
Coimbatore India **60** 11.00N 76.57E
Coimbra Brazil **126** 19.55S 57.47W
Coimbra Portugal **26** 40.12N 8.25W
Coimbra *d.* Portugal **26** 40.10N 8.20W
Coín Spain **27** 36.40N 4.45W
Cojimies Ecuador **122** 0.20N 80.00W
Cokeville U.S.A. **108** 42.05N110.57W
Colac Australia **92** 38.22S143.38E
Colares Portugal **27** 38.48N 9.27W
Colatina Brazil **126** 19.35S 40.37W
Colbeck, C. Antarctica **128** 77.20S159.00W
Colborne Canada **105** 44.00N 77.53W
Colby U.S.A. **110** 39.24N101.03W
Colchester U.K. **13** 51.54N 0.55E
Colchester U.S.A. **115** 41.34N 72.20W
Cold L. Canada **101** 54.33N110.05W
Cold Lake *town* Canada **101** 54.27N110.10W
Coldstream U.K. **14** 55.39N 2.15W
Coldwater Canada **104** 44.44N 79.39W
Coldwater U.S.A. **112** 41.57N 85.01W
Coldwell Canada **102** 48.45N 86.30W
Coleambally Australia **93** 34.48S145.53E
Colebrook U.S.A. **105** 44.54N 71.30W
Coleman *r.* Australia **90** 15.06S141.38E
Coleman Tex. U.S.A. **111** 31.50N 99.26W
Coleman Wisc. U.S.A. **110** 45.04N 88.02W
Colenso R.S.A. **80** 28.43S 29.49E
Coleraine Australia **92** 37.36S141.42E
Coleraine U.K. **15** 55.08N 6.40W
Colesberg R.S.A. **80** 30.43S 25.05E
Colfax U.S.A. **111** 31.31N 92.42W
Colgong India **63** 25.16N 87.13E
Colico Italy **30** 46.08N 9.22E
Colima Mexico **116** 19.14N103.41W
Colima *d.* Mexico **116** 19.05N104.00W
Colinas Brazil **123** 6.02S 44.14W
Coll *i.* U.K. **14** 56.38N 6.34W
Collarenebri Australia **93** 29.33S148.36E
College U.S.A. **98** 64.54N147.55W
College Park *town* Ga. U.S.A. **113** 33.39N 84.28W
College Park *town* Md. U.S.A. **114** 39.00N 76.55W
College Station *town* U.S.A. **111** 30.37N 96.21W
Collerina Australia **93** 29.22S146.32E
Collesalvetti Italy **30** 43.35N 10.28E
Collie N.S.W. Australia **93** 31.41S148.22E
Collie W.A. Australia **89** 33.21S116.09E
Collie Cardiff Australia **89** 33.27S116.09E
Collier B. Australia **88** 16.10S124.15E
Collingswood U.S.A. **115** 39.55N 75.04W
Collingwood Canada **104** 44.29N 80.13W
Collingwood New Zealand **86** 40.41S172.41E
Collingwood B. P.N.G. **90** 9.20S149.30E
Collinsville Australia **90** 20.34S147.51E
Collinsville U.S.A. **115** 41.49N 72.55W
Collin Top *mtn.* U.K. **15** 54.58N 6.08W
Collon Rep. of Ire. **15** 53.47N 6.30W
Collooney Rep. of Ire. **15** 54.11N 8.29W
Colmar France **19** 48.05N 7.22E
Colmars France **21** 44.11N 6.38E
Colmenar Spain **27** 36.54N 4.20W
Colmenar de Oreja Spain **27** 40.06N 3.23W
Colmenar Viejo Spain **26** 40.40N 3.46W
Colne *r.* Essex U.K. **13** 51.50N 0.59E
Colnett, Cabo *c.* Mexico **109** 31.00N116.20W
Colo *r.* Australia **93** 33.26S150.53E
Cologne *see* Köln Germany **38**
Colombey-les-Belles France **19** 48.32N 5.54E
Colombia S. America **122** 4.00N 72.30W
Colombian Basin *f.* Carib. Sea **127** 14.00N 76.00W
Colombo Sri Lanka **61** 6.55N 79.52E
Colón Argentina **125** 32.15S 58.10W
Colón Panama **122** 9.21N 79.54W
Colona Australia **91** 31.38S132.05E
Colonelganj India **63** 27.08N 81.42E
Colonia del Sacramento Uruguay **125** 34.28S 57.51W
Colonia Las Heras Argentina **125** 46.33S 68.57W
Colonia Lavelleja Uruguay **125** 31.06S 57.01W
Colonna, Capo *c.* Italy **33** 39.02N 17.11E
Colonsay *i.* U.K. **14** 56.04N 6.13W
Colorado *r.* Argentina **125** 39.50S 62.02W
Colorado *d.* U.S.A. **108** 39.07N105.27W
Colorado *r.* Ariz. U.S.A. **109** 31.45N114.40W
Colorado *r.* Tex. U.S.A. **111** 28.36N 95.58W
Colorado City U.S.A. **111** 32.24N100.52W
Colorado Plateau *f.* U.S.A. **109** 36.30N108.00W
Colorado Springs *town* U.S.A. **108** 38.50N104.49W
Colton N.Y. U.S.A. **105** 44.33N 74.56W
Colton S.Dak. U.S.A. **110** 43.47N 96.56W
Columbia La. U.S.A. **111** 32.06N 92.05W
Columbia Miss. U.S.A. **111** 31.15N 89.56W
Columbia Mo. U.S.A. **110** 38.57N 92.20W
Columbia *r.* U.S.A. **108** 46.15N124.05W
Columbia S.C. U.S.A. **113** 34.00N 81.00W
Columbia Tenn. U.S.A. **113** 35.37N 87.02W
Columbia, District of U.S.A. **114** 39.13N 76.52W
Columbia, Mt. Canada **100** 52.08N117.20W
Columbia, Sierra *mts.* Mexico **109** 29.30N114.50W
Columbia Basin *f.* U.S.A. **108** 46.55N117.36W
Columbia Falls *town* U.S.A. **108** 48.23N114.11W
Columbiana U.S.A. **114** 40.53N 80.42W
Columbia Plateau *f.* U.S.A. **108** 44.00N117.30W
Columbretes, Islas *is.* Spain **25** 39.52N 0.40E
Columbus Ga. U.S.A. **113** 32.28N 84.59W
Columbus Ind. U.S.A. **112** 39.12N 85.57W
Columbus Miss. U.S.A. **111** 33.30N 88.25W
Columbus Mont. U.S.A. **108** 45.38N109.15W
Columbus Nebr. U.S.A. **110** 41.25N 97.22W
Columbus N.Mex. U.S.A. **109** 31.50N107.38W
Columbus Ohio U.S.A. **114** 39.57N 83.00W
Columbus Tex. U.S.A. **111** 29.42N 96.33W
Colville *r.* U.S.A. **98** 70.06N151.30W
Colwyn Bay *town* U.K. **12** 53.18N 3.43W
Comacchio Italy **30** 44.42N 12.11E
Comacchio, Valli di *b.* Italy **30** 44.38N 12.06E
Comai China **63** 28.28N 91.33E
Comanche U.S.A. **111** 34.22N 97.58W
Comayagua Honduras **117** 14.30N 87.39W
Combeaufontaine France **19** 47.43N 5.53E
Comber Canada **104** 42.14N 82.33W
Combermere Canada **105** 45.22N 77.37W
Comblain-au-Pont Belgium **16** 50.29N 5.32E
Combles France **19** 50.01N 2.52E
Combourg France **18** 48.25N 1.45W
Comboyne Australia **93** 31.35S152.27E
Combronde France **20** 45.59N 3.05E
Comeragh Mts. Rep. of Ire. **15** 52.17N 7.34W
Comilla Bangla. **63** 23.28N 91.10E
Comino, Capo *c.* Italy **32** 40.31N 9.50E
Comiso Italy **33** 36.56N 14.37E
Comitán Mexico **116** 16.15N 92.08W
Commentry France **20** 46.17N 2.44E
Commerce U.S.A. **111** 33.15N 95.54W
Commercy France **19** 48.45N 5.35E
Comminges *f.* France **20** 43.15N 0.45E
Commonwealth Territory *d.* Australia **93** 35.00S151.00E
Como Italy **30** 45.48N 9.04E
Como, Lago di *l.* Italy **30** 46.00N 9.20E
Comodoro Rivadavia Argentina **125** 45.50S 67.30W
Comorin, C. India **48** 8.04N 77.35E
Comoros Africa **79** 12.15S 44.00E
Compiègne France **19** 49.25N 2.50E
Cona China **63** 27.59N 91.59E
Co Nag *l.* China **63** 32.00N 91.15E
Conakry Guinea **76** 9.30N 13.43W
Concarneau France **18** 47.52N 3.55W
Conceição Mozambique **81** 18.45S 36.10E
Conceição do Araguaia Brazil **123** 8.15S 49.17W
Concepción Argentina **124** 27.20S 65.36W
Concepción Chile **125** 36.50S 73.03W
Concepción *r.* Mexico **109** 30.32N112.59W
Concepción Paraguay **124** 23.22S 57.26W
Concepción del Oro Mexico **111** 24.38N101.25W
Concepción del Uruguay Argentina **125** 32.30S 58.14W
Conception, Pt. U.S.A. **109** 34.27N120.27W
Conception B. Namibia **80** 23.53S 14.28E
Conches France **18** 48.58N 0.58E
Conchillas Uruguay **125** 34.15S 58.04W
Conchos *r.* Mexico **109** 29.32N104.25W
Concord Mass. U.S.A. **115** 42.27N 71.21W
Concord N.C. U.S.A. **113** 35.25N 80.34W
Concord N.H. U.S.A. **115** 43.12N 71.32W
Concordia Argentina **125** 31.24S 58.02W
Concórdia Brazil **122** 4.35S 66.35W
Concordia Mexico **109** 23.17N106.04W
Concordia U.S.A. **110** 39.34N 97.39W
Condé France **18** 48.51N 0.33W
Condé-sur-l'Escaut France **19** 50.27N 3.36E
Condobolin Australia **93** 33.03S147.11E
Condom France **20** 43.58N 0.22E
Conegliano Italy **30** 45.53N 12.18E
Conemaugh River Resr. U.S.A. **114** 40.28N 79.17W
Confluence U.S.A. **114** 39.49N 79.21W
Confolens France **20** 46.01N 0.41E
Conghua China **55** 23.33N113.34E
Congleton U.K. **12** 53.10N 2.12W
Congo Africa **78** 1.00S 16.00E
Congo *r. see* Zaïre *r.* Zaïre **78**
Congo Basin *f.* Zaïre **70** 1.00N 21.00E
Congonhas Brazil **126** 20.30S 43.53W
Coningsby U.K. **12** 53.07N 0.09W
Coniston Canada **104** 46.29N 80.51W
Coniston U.K. **12** 54.22N 3.06W
Conkouati Congo **78** 4.00S 11.16E
Conn, Lough Rep. of Ire. **15** 54.01N 9.15W
Connah's Quay *town* U.K. **12** 53.13N 3.03W
Conneaut U.S.A. **114** 41.57N 80.34W
Conneaut Lake *town* U.S.A. **114** 41.36N 80.19W
Conneautville U.S.A. **114** 41.36N 80.18W
Connecticut *d.* U.S.A. **115** 41.45N 72.45W
Connecticut *r.* U.S.A. **115** 41.17N 72.21W
Connellsville U.S.A. **114** 40.01N 79.35W
Connemara *f.* Rep. of Ire. **15** 53.32N 9.56W
Conner, Mt. Australia **90** 25.35S131.49E
Conodoguinet *r.* U.S.A. **114** 40.17N 76.55W
Conon *r.* U.K. **14** 57.33N 4.33W
Conrad U.S.A. **108** 48.10N111.57W
Conroe U.S.A. **111** 30.19N 95.27W

Consecon to **Culebra, Sierra de la**

Consecon Canada 105 44.00N 77.31W
Conselheiro Lafaiete Brazil 126 20.40S 43.48W
Consett U.K. 12 54.52N 1.50W
Con Son *is.* Vietnam 56 8.45N106.38E
Constance, L. *see* Bodensee Europe 39
Constanța Romania 29 44.10N 28.31E
Constantia U.S.A. 115 43.15N 76.00W
Constantina Spain 27 37.52N 5.37W
Constantine Algeria 75 36.22N 6.38E
Constânzia Portugal 27 39.28N 8.20W
Constitución Chile 125 35.20S 72.25W
Constitución Uruguay 125 31.05S 57.50W
Consuegra Spain 27 39.28N 3.36W
Consul Canada 101 49.21N109.30W
Contact U.S.A. 108 41.48N114.46W
Contai India 63 21.47N 87.45E
Contamana Peru 122 7.19S 75.00W
Contas *r.* Brazil 123 14.15S 39.00W
Contreras, Embalse de *resr.* Spain 25 39.32N 1.30W
Contres France 18 47.25N 1.26E
Contwoyto L. Canada 98 65.42N110.50W
Conty France 19 49.44N 2.09E
Conversano Italy 33 40.58N 17.08E
Conway Ark. U.S.A. 111 35.05N 92.26W
Conway N.H. U.S.A. 112 43.59N 71.07W
Conway S.C. U.S.A. 113 33.51N 79.04W
Conway, L. Australia 92 28.17S135.35E
Conwy *r.* U.K. 11 53.17N 3.49W
Coober Pedy Australia 92 29.01S134.43E
Cooch Behār India 63 26.19N 89.26E
Cook, C. Canada 98 50.08N127.55W
Cook, Mt. New Zealand 86 43.45S170.12E
Cooke, Mt. Australia 89 32.26S116.18E
Cookeville U.S.A. 113 36.10N 85.30W
Cookhouse R.S.A. 80 32.44S 25.47E
Cook Inlet U.S.A. 98 60.30N152.00W
Cook Is. Pacific Oc. 84 15.00S160.00W
Cookshire Canada 105 45.25N 71.38W
Cookstown Canada 104 44.11N 79.42W
Cookstown U.K. 15 54.39N 6.46W
Cook Str. New Zealand 86 41.15S174.30E
Cooktown Australia 90 15.29S145.15E
Coolabah Australia 93 31.02S146.45E
Coolah Australia 93 31.48S149.45E
Coolamara Australia 92 31.59S143.42E
Coolamon Australia 93 34.48S147.12E
Coolangatta Australia 93 28.10S153.26E
Coolgardie Australia 89 31.01S121.12E
Coolidge U.S.A. 109 32.59N111.31W
Coolville U.S.A. 114 39.13N 81.49W
Cooma Australia 93 36.15S149.07E
Coombah Australia 92 32.58S141.39E
Coomberdale Australia 89 30.29S116.03E
Coonabarabran Australia 93 31.16S149.18E
Coonalpyn Australia 92 35.41S139.52E
Coonamble Australia 93 30.55S148.26E
Coonana Australia 89 31.01S123.05E
Coonawarra Australia 92 37.16S140.50E
Coondambo Australia 92 31.07S135.20E
Cooper Creek *r.* Australia 92 28.33S137.46E
Cooperstown U.S.A. 115 42.42N 74.56W
Coorow Australia 89 29.53S116.01E
Coos Bay *town* U.S.A. 108 43.22N124.13W
Cootamundra Australia 93 34.41S148.03E
Cootehill Rep. of Ire. 15 54.05N 7.05W
Copainalá Mexico 116 17.05N 93.12W
Copán *ruins* Honduras 117 14.52N 89.10W
Cope U.S.A. 108 39.40N102.51W
Copenhagen *see* København Denmark 43
Copertino Italy 33 40.16N 18.03E
Copiapó Chile 124 27.22S 70.20W
Copparo Italy 30 44.54N 11.49E
Copperbelt *d.* Zambia 80 13.00S 28.00E
Copper Belt *f.* Zambia 79 12.40S 28.00E
Copper Center U.S.A. 98 61.58N145.19W
Copper Cliff *town* Canada 104 46.28N 81.04W
Copper Harbor U.S.A. 112 47.28N 87.54W
Coppermine *r.* Canada 98 67.54N115.10W
Coppermine *see* Qurlurtuuq *town* Canada 98
Copper Mountain *town* Canada 100 49.20N120.30W
Copper Queen Zimbabwe 80 17.31S 29.20E
Copperton R.S.A. 80 30.00S 22.15E
Copp L. Canada 100 60.14N114.40W
Coqên China 63 31.13N 85.12E
Coquet *r.* U.K. 12 55.21N 1.35W
Coquille U.S.A. 108 43.11N124.11W
Coquimbo Chile 124 29.58S 71.21W
Corabia Romania 34 43.48N 24.30E
Coracora Peru 122 15.02S 73.48W
Coraki Australia 93 23.00S153.17E
Coral Bay *town* Australia 88 23.02S113.48E
Coral Harbour *town* Canada 99 64.10N 83.15W
Coral Sea Pacific Oc. 90 14.30S149.30E
Coral Sea Basin Pacific Oc. 84 14.00S152.00E
Corangamite, L. Australia 92 38.10S143.25E
Corato Italy 33 41.09N 16.25E
Corbeil Canada 104 46.17N 79.18W
Corbeil France 19 48.36N 2.29E
Corbeny France 19 49.28N 3.49E
Corbières *mts.* France 20 42.55N 2.38E
Corbigny France 19 47.15N 3.40E
Corbin U.S.A. 113 36.58N 84.06W
Corby U.K. 13 52.29N 0.41W
Corcubión Spain 26 42.57N 9.11W
Cordes France 20 44.04N 1.56E
Córdoba Argentina 124 31.25S 64.10W
Córdoba *d.* Argentina 124 30.30S 64.30W
Córdoba Mexico 116 18.55N 96.55W
Córdoba Spain 27 37.53N 4.46W
Córdoba *d.* Spain 27 38.10N 4.50W
Córdoba, Sierras de *mts.* Argentina 124 30.30S 64.40W
Cordova U.S.A. 98 60.33N139.44W
Corentyne *r.* Guyana 123 5.10N 57.20W
Corfield Australia 90 21.43S143.22E
Corfu *i. see* Kérkira *i.* Greece 34
Coria Spain 27 39.59N 6.32W
Coria del Río Spain 27 37.16N 6.03W
Coricudgy, Mt. Australia 93 32.51S150.25E
Corigliano Italy 33 39.36N 16.31E
Corindi Australia 93 30.00S153.21E
Corinne Canada 101 50.04N104.40W
Corinth Miss. U.S.A. 111 34.56N 88.31W
Corinth N.Y. U.S.A. 115 43.15N 73.49W
Corinth, G. of *see* Korinthiakos Kólpos *g.* Greece 35
Corinto Nicaragua 117 12.29N 87.14W
Cork Rep. of Ire. 15 51.54N 8.28W
Cork *d.* Rep. of Ire. 15 52.00N 8.40W
Cork Harbour *est.* Rep. of Ire. 15 51.50N 8.17W
Corlay France 18 48.19N 3.03W
Corleone Italy 32 37.49N 13.18E
Corleto Italy 33 40.23N 16.03E
Cormeilles France 18 49.15N 0.23E
Cormons Italy 31 45.58N 13.28E
Cormorant Canada 101 54.14N100.35W
Corner Brook *town* Canada 103 48.57N 57.57W
Corner Inlet *b.* Australia 93 38.43S146.20E
Corning Ark. U.S.A. 111 36.24N 90.35W
Corning N.Y. U.S.A. 114 42.09N 77.04W
Corning Ohio U.S.A. 114 39.36N 82.05W
Corno, Monte *mtn.* Italy 31 42.28N 13.34E
Cornwall Canada 105 45.02N 74.44W
Cornwall *d.* U.K. 13 50.26N 4.40W
Cornwallis I. Canada 99 75.00N 95.00W
Coro Venezuela 122 11.27N 69.41W
Coroatá Brazil 123 4.08S 44.08W
Coroico Bolivia 124 16.10S 67.44W
Coromandel New Zealand 86 36.46S175.30E
Coromandel Pen. New Zealand 86 36.45S175.30E
Corona U.S.A. 109 34.15N105.36W
Coronation G. Canada 98 68.00N112.00W
Coronation I. U.S.A. 100 55.52N134.20W
Coronda Argentina 125 31.55S 60.55W
Coronel Chile 125 37.01S 73.08W
Coronel Brandsen Argentina 125 35.10S 58.15W
Coronel Pringles Argentina 125 37.56S 61.25W
Coronel Suárez Argentina 125 37.30S 61.52W
Coropuna *mtn.* Peru 122 15.31S 72.45W
Corowa Australia 93 36.00S146.20E
Corozal Belize 117 18.23N 88.23W
Corpus Christi U.S.A. 111 27.48N 97.24W
Corral de Amalguer Spain 27 39.46N 3.11W
Correggio Italy 30 44.46N 10.47E
Correntes, Cabo das *c.* Mozambique 81 24.11S 35.35E
Corrèze *d.* France 20 45.20N 1.50E
Corrib, Lough Rep. of Ire. 15 53.26N 9.14W
Corrientes Argentina 124 27.30S 58.48W
Corrientes *d.* Argentina 124 28.00S 57.00W
Corrientes, Cabo *c.* Colombia 122 5.30N 77.34W
Corrigan U.S.A. 111 31.00N 94.50W
Corrigin Australia 89 32.21S117.52E
Corry U.S.A. 114 41.56N 79.39W
Corryong Australia 93 36.11S147.58E
Corse *d.* France 21 42.00N 9.00E
Corse *i.* France 21 42.00N 9.10E
Corse, Cap *c.* France 21 43.00N 9.25E
Corse-du-Sud *d.* France 21 41.45N 9.00E
Corsham U.K. 13 51.25N 2.11W
Corsica *i. see* Corse *i.* France 21
Corsicana U.S.A. 111 32.06N 96.28W
Corte France 21 42.18N 9.08E
Cortegana Spain 27 37.55N 6.49W
Cortez Colo. U.S.A. 108 37.21N108.35W
Cortez Nev. U.S.A. 108 40.09N116.38W
Cortina Italy 30 46.32N 12.08E
Cortland N.Y. U.S.A. 115 42.36N 76.11W
Cortland Ohio U.S.A. 114 41.20N 80.44W
Cortona Italy 30 43.16N 11.59E
Coruche Portugal 27 38.58N 8.31W
Çoruh Nehri *r.* Turkey *see* Chorokh *r.* Georgia 64
Çorum Turkey 64 40.31N 34.57E
Corumbá Brazil 124 19.00S 57.27W
Corumbá *r.* Brazil 126 18.15S 48.55W
Corunna U.S.A. 104 42.59N 84.07W
Corvallis U.S.A. 108 44.34N123.16W
Corwen U.K. 12 52.59N 3.23W
Cosenza Italy 33 39.17N 16.15E
Coshocton U.S.A. 114 40.16N 81.51W
Cosne France 19 47.24N 2.55E
Coso Junction U.S.A. 109 36.03N117.58W
Cosson *r.* France 19 47.30N 1.15E
Costa Blanca *f.* Spain 25 38.30N 0.05E
Costa Brava *f.* Spain 25 41.55N 3.15E
Costa del Sol *f.* Spain 27 36.30N 4.30W
Costa Mesa U.S.A. 109 33.39N117.55W
Costa Rica C. America 117 10.00N 84.00W
Costeşti Romania 29 44.40N 24.53E
Coswig Sachsen Germany 38 51.07N 13.34E
Coswig Sachsen-Anhalt Germany 38 51.53N 12.26E
Cotabato Phil. 59 7.14N124.15E
Cotagaita Bolivia 124 20.50S 65.41W
Côte d'Azur *f.* France 21 43.30N 7.00E
Côte d'Ivoire *see* Ivory Coast Africa 76
Côte-d'Or *d.* France 19 47.30N 4.50E
Côte d'Or *f.* France 19 47.10N 4.50E
Côtes d'Armor *d.* France 18 48.26N 2.40W
Cotonou Benin 77 6.24N 2.31E
Cotopaxi *mtn.* Ecuador 122 0.40S 78.28W
Cotswold Hills U.K. 13 51.50N 2.00W
Cottage Grove U.S.A. 108 43.48N123.03W
Cottbus Germany 38 51.45N 14.19E
Cottiennes, Alpes *mts.* France 21 44.45N 7.00E
Cottonvale Australia 93 28.32S151.57E
Cottonwood U.S.A. 109 34.45N112.01W
Cotulla U.S.A. 111 28.26N 99.14W
Coubre, Pointe de la *c.* France 20 45.41N 1.13W
Coucy France 19 49.31N 3.19E
Coudersport U.S.A. 114 41.46N 78.01W
Couer d'Alene U.S.A. 108 47.41N117.00W
Couesnon *r.* France 18 48.37N 1.31W
Couhé France 18 46.18N 0.11E
Coulagh B. Rep. of Ire. 15 51.42N 10.00W
Coulee City U.S.A. 108 47.37N119.17W
Coulommiers France 19 48.49N 3.05E
Coulon *r.* France 21 43.51N 5.00E
Coulonge *r.* Canada 105 45.51N 76.45W
Council U.S.A. 98 64.55N163.44W
Council Bluffs U.S.A. 110 41.16N 95.52W
Coupar Angus U.K. 14 56.33N 3.17W
Courçon France 20 46.15N 0.49W
Courland Lagoon Russian Fed./Lithuania 41 55.00N 21.00E
Courpière France 20 45.45N 3.33E
Courson-les-Carrières France 19 47.36N 3.30E
Courtalain France 18 48.05N 1.09E
Courtenay Canada 100 49.41N125.00W
Courtrai *see* Kortrijk Belgium 16
Coutances France 18 49.03N 1.26W
Coutras France 20 45.02N 0.08W
Couvin Belgium 16 50.03N 4.30E
Cové Benin 77 7.16N 2.20E
Cove City U.S.A. 113 35.11N 77.20W
Cove I. Canada 104 45.17N 81.44W
Coventry U.K. 13 52.25N 1.31W
Covilhã Portugal 26 40.17N 7.30W
Covington Ga. U.S.A. 113 33.35N 83.52W
Covington Ky. U.S.A. 112 39.04N 84.30W
Covington Okla. U.S.A. 111 36.18N 97.35W
Covington Tenn. U.S.A. 111 35.34N 89.38W
Covington Va. U.S.A. 113 37.48N 80.01W
Cowal, L. Australia 93 33.36S147.22E
Cowan Canada 101 52.05N100.45W
Cowan, L. Australia 89 32.00S122.00E
Cowangie Australia 92 35.14S141.28E
Cowansville Canada 105 45.12N 72.45W
Cowcowing Lakes Australia 89 31.01S117.18E
Cowdenbeath U.K. 14 56.07N 3.21W
Cowell Australia 92 33.41S136.55E
Cowen U.S.A. 114 38.25N 80.34W
Cowes Australia 93 38.27S145.15E
Cowes U.K. 13 50.45N 1.18W
Cowra Australia 93 33.50S148.45E
Cox *r.* Australia 90 15.19S135.25E
Coxim Brazil 124 18.28S 54.37W
Coxsackie U.S.A. 105 42.21N 73.48W
Cox's Bāzār Bangla. 63 21.26N 91.59E
Coyuca de Catalán Mexico 116 18.20N100.39W
Cozad U.S.A. 110 40.52N 99.59W
Cozes France 20 45.35N 0.50W
Cozumel, Isla de *i.* Mexico 117 20.30N 87.00W
Cradock Australia 92 31.59S138.34E
Cradock R.S.A. 80 32.10S 25.35E
Craig Alas. U.S.A. 100 55.29N133.09W
Craig Colo. U.S.A. 108 40.31N107.33W
Craigavon U.K. 15 54.28N 6.25W
Craignure U.K. 14 56.28N 5.42W
Craigsville U.S.A. 114 38.05N 79.23W
Crail U.K. 14 56.16N 2.38W
Crailsheim Germany 39 49.08N 10.04E
Craiova Romania 29 44.18N 23.46E
Cranberry L. U.S.A. 105 44.10N 74.50W
Cranbourne Australia 93 38.07S145.19E
Cranbrook Australia 89 34.15S117.32E
Cranbrook Canada 100 49.30N115.46W
Crane U.S.A. 108 43.25N118.34W
Cranston U.S.A. 115 41.47N 71.26W
Craon France 18 47.51N 0.57W
Craonne France 19 49.26N 3.47E
Craponne France 20 45.20N 3.51E
Craponne, Canal de France 21 43.40N 4.39E
Crater L. U.S.A. 108 42.56N122.06W
Crateús Brazil 123 5.10S 40.39W
Crati *r.* Italy 33 39.41N 16.30E
Crato Amazonas Brazil 122 7.25S 63.00W
Crato Ceará Brazil 123 7.10S 39.25W
Craughwell Rep. of Ire. 15 53.14N 8.44W
Crawford U.S.A. 110 42.41N103.25W
Crawfordsville U.S.A. 112 40.03N 86.54W
Crawfordville U.S.A. 113 30.12N 84.21W
Crawley U.K. 13 51.07N 0.10W
Crazy Mts. U.S.A. 108 46.08N110.20W
Crécy France 19 50.15N 1.53E
Crécy-sur-Serre France 19 49.42N 3.37E
Cree *r.* Canada 101 59.00N105.47W
Creede U.S.A. 108 37.51N106.56W
Cree L. Canada 101 57.30N106.30W
Creemore Canada 104 44.19N 80.06W
Creil France 19 49.16N 2.29E
Crema Italy 30 45.22N 9.41E
Cremona Italy 30 45.07N 10.02E
Crépy France 19 49.36N 3.31E
Crépy-en-Valois France 19 49.14N 2.54E
Cres *i.* Croatia 31 44.50N 14.25E
Cres *town* Croatia 31 44.58N 14.25E
Cresaptown U.S.A. 114 39.36N 78.50W
Crescent U.S.A. 108 43.29N121.41W
Crescent City U.S.A. 108 41.45N124.12W
Crescent Head *town* Australia 93 31.10S152.59E
Crespo Argentina 125 32.02S 60.20W
Cresson U.S.A. 114 40.28N 78.35W
Cressy Australia 92 38.02S143.38E
Crest France 21 44.44N 5.02E
Crestline U.S.A. 114 40.47N 82.44W
Creston Canada 100 49.10N116.31W
Creston Iowa U.S.A. 110 41.04N 94.22W
Creston Ohio U.S.A. 114 40.59N 81.54W
Creston Oriental de la Sierra Madre *mts.* Mexico 109 28.40N107.50W
Crestview U.S.A. 113 30.44N 86.34W
Creswick Australia 92 37.25S143.54E
Crete *i. see* Kríti *i.* Greece 35
Crete U.S.A. 110 40.38N 96.58W
Crete, Sea of *see* Kritikón Pélagos *sea* Greece 35
Crétéville Tunisia 32 36.40N 10.20E
Creus, Cabo de *c.* Spain 25 42.19N 3.19E
Creuse *d.* France 20 46.05N 2.00E
Creuse *r.* France 17 47.00N 0.35E
Creussen Germany 38 49.51N 11.37E
Crevillente Spain 25 38.15N 0.48W
Crewe U.K. 12 53.06N 2.28W
Crianlarich U.K. 14 56.23N 4.37W
Criccieth U.K. 12 52.55N 4.15W
Criciúma Brazil 126 28.40S 49.23W
Crieff U.K. 14 56.23N 3.52W
Crikvenica Croatia 31 45.11N 14.42E
Crillon, Mt. U.S.A. 100 58.39N137.14W
Crimea *pen. see* Krym *pen.* Ukraine 45
Crimmitschau Germany 38 50.49N 12.23E
Crinan U.K. 14 56.06N 5.34W
Cristóbal Colón *mtn.* Colombia 122 10.53N 73.48W
Crişu Alb *r.* Romania 37 46.42N 21.17E
Crivitz Germany 38 53.35N 11.38E
Crna *r.* Macedonia 34 41.35N 21.59E
Crna Gora *d.* Yugo. 31 42.55N 19.00E
Crnoljeva Planina *mts.* Yugo. 34 42.20N 21.00E
Črnomelj Slovenia 31 45.34N 15.11E
Croaghnameal *mtn.* Rep. of Ire. 15 54.40N 7.57W
Croatia Europe 31 45.35N 16.10E
Crockett U.S.A. 111 31.19N 95.28W
Crocodile *r.* Trans. R.S.A. 80 24.11S 26.48E
Croghan U.S.A. 105 43.54N 75.24W
Croker I. Australia 90 11.12S132.32E
Cromarty Canada 101 58.03N 94.09W
Cromarty U.K. 14 57.40N 4.02W
Cromarty Firth *est.* U.K. 14 57.41N 4.10W
Cromer U.K. 12 52.56N 1.18E
Cromwell New Zealand 86 45.03S169.14E
Crooked I. Bahamas 117 22.45N 74.00W
Crookhaven Rep. of Ire. 15 51.29N 9.45W
Crookston U.S.A. 110 47.47N 96.37W
Crooksville U.S.A. 114 39.46N 82.06W
Crookwell Australia 93 34.27S149.28E
Croom Rep. of Ire. 15 52.31N 8.43W
Croppa Creek *town* Australia 93 29.08S150.20E
Crosby I.o.M. Europe 12 54.11N 4.34W
Crosby U.S.A. 111 31.17N 91.04W
Cross City U.S.A. 113 29.39N 83.09W
Crossett U.S.A. 111 33.08N 91.58W
Cross Fell *mtn.* U.K. 12 54.43N 2.28W
Cross L. Canada 101 54.45N 97.30W
Cross River *d.* Nigeria 77 5.45N 8.25E
Crossroads U.S.A. 111 33.30N103.21W
Cross Sd. U.S.A. 100 58.10N136.30W
Crossville U.S.A. 113 35.57N 85.02W
Croswell U.S.A. 114 43.16N 82.37W
Crotone Italy 33 39.05N 17.07E
Crow *r.* Canada 100 59.41N124.20W
Crow Agency U.S.A. 108 45.36N107.27W
Crowell U.S.A. 111 33.59N 99.43W
Crowl Creek *r.* Australia 93 31.58S144.53E
Crown Point *town* U.S.A. 105 43.57N 73.25W
Crowsnest Pass Canada 100 49.40N114.40W
Croyde U.K. 13 51.07N 4.13W
Croydon Australia 90 18.12S142.14E
Croydon U.K. 13 51.23N 0.06W
Crozet, Îles *is.* Indian Oc. 49 46.00S 52.00E
Crozon France 18 48.15N 4.29W
Crucero U.S.A. 109 35.03N116.10W
Cruger U.S.A. 111 33.14N 90.14W
Cruz, Cabo *c.* Cuba 117 19.52N 77.44W
Cruz Alta Brazil 126 28.38S 53.38W
Cruz del Eje Argentina 124 30.44S 64.49W
Cruzeiro Brazil 126 22.33S 44.59W
Cruzeiro do Sul Brazil 122 7.40S 72.39W
Crvenka Yugo. 31 45.39N 19.28E
Crystal U.S.A. 110 45.00N 93.25W
Crystal Brook *town* Australia 92 33.21S138.13E
Crystal City U.S.A. 111 28.41N 99.50W
Crystal River *town* U.S.A. 113 28.54N 82.36W
Csongrád Hungary 31 46.43N 20.09E
Csongrád *d.* Hungary 31 46.25N 20.10E
Csorna Hungary 37 47.37N 17.16E
Csurgó Hungary 31 46.16N 17.06E
Cuamba Mozambique 79 14.48S 36.32E
Cuando *r.* Angola 80 18.30S 23.32E
Cuando-Cubango *d.* Angola 80 16.00S 20.00E
Cuangar Angola 78 17.34S 18.39E
Cuango *r. see* Kwango *r.* Zaïre 78
Cuanza *r.* Angola 78 9.20S 13.09E
Cuanza Norte *d.* Angola 78 8.45S 15.00E
Cuanza Sul *d.* Angola 78 11.00S 15.00E
Cua Rao Vietnam 56 19.16N104.27E
Cuaró Uruguay 125 30.37S 56.54W
Cuaró *r.* Uruguay 125 30.15S 57.01W
Cuauhtémoc Mexico 109 28.25N106.52W
Cuba C. America 117 22.00N 79.00W
Cuba Portugal 27 38.10N 7.53W
Cuba U.S.A. 109 36.01N107.04W
Cuballing Australia 89 32.50S117.07E
Cubango *r. see* Okavango *r.* Angola 78
Cubia *r.* Angola 78 16.00S 21.46E
Cubo Mozambique 81 23.48S 33.55E
Cuchi *r.* Angola 80 15.23S 17.12E
Cuckfield U.K. 13 51.00N 0.08W
Cucuí Brazil 122 1.12N 66.50W
Cúcuta Colombia 122 7.55N 72.31W
Cudahy U.S.A. 110 42.57N 87.52W
Cuddalore India 61 11.43N 79.46E
Cue Australia 88 27.25S117.54E
Cuéllar Spain 26 41.25N 4.19W
Cuenca Ecuador 122 2.54S 79.00W
Cuenca Spain 25 40.04N 2.08W
Cuenca *d.* Spain 27 40.00N 2.30W
Cuenca, Serranía de *mts.* Spain 25 40.00N 1.45W
Cuernavaca Mexico 116 18.57N 99.15W
Cuero U.S.A. 111 29.06N 97.18W
Cuers France 21 43.14N 6.04E
Cuervo U.S.A. 109 35.02N104.24W
Cuevas del Almanzora Spain 27 37.19N 1.52W
Cuglieri Italy 32 40.11N 8.34E
Cuiabá Brazil 123 15.32S 56.05W
Cuiabá *r.* Brazil 124 18.00S 57.25W
Cuidado, Punta *c.* I. de Pascua 85 27.08S109.19W
Cuillin Hills U.K. 14 57.12N 6.13W
Cuilo *r. see* Kwilu *r.* Zaïre 78
Cuiseaux France 19 46.30N 5.24E
Cuito *r.* Angola 78 18.01S 20.50E
Cuito Cuanavale Angola 80 15.11S 19.11E
Culbertson U.S.A. 108 48.09N104.31W
Culcairn Australia 93 35.40S147.03E
Culebra, Sierra de la *mts.* Spain 26 41.55N 6.30W

Culemborg to Dečani

Culemborg Neth. 16 51.57N 5.14E
Culgoa r. Australia 93 29.56S146.20E
Culiacán Mexico 109 24.48N107.24W
Culiacán r. Mexico 109 24.30N107.31W
Cúllar de Baza Spain 27 37.35N 2.34W
Cullen U.K. 14 57.41N 2.50W
Cullera Spain 25 39.10N 0.15W
Cullin Sd. U.K. 14 57.03N 6.13W
Culloden Moor U.K. 14 57.29N 3.55W
Culpeper U.S.A. 114 38.28N 77.53W
Culuene r. Brazil 123 12.56S 52.51W
Culver, Pt. Australia 89 32.52S124.41E
Cuma Angola 78 12.52S 15.05E
Cumali Turkey 35 36.42N 27.28E
Cumaná Venezuela 122 10.29N 64.12W
Cumberland Ky. U.S.A. 113 36.58N 82.59W
Cumberland Md. U.S.A. 114 39.39N 78.46W
Cumberland r. U.S.A. 113 37.09N 88.25W
Cumberland Va. U.S.A. 113 37.31N 78.16W
Cumberland Wisc. U.S.A. 110 45.32N 92.01W
Cumberland, C. Vanuatu 84 14.39S166.37E
Cumberland, L. U.S.A. 113 36.45N 84.51W
Cumberland I. U.S.A. 113 30.51N 81.27W
Cumberland L. Canada 101 54.02N102.17W
Cumberland Pen. Canada 99 66.50N 64.00W
Cumberland Plateau f. U.S.A. 113 36.00N 85.00W
Cumberland Sd. Canada 99 65.00N 65.30W
Cumbernauld U.K. 14 55.57N 4.00W
Cumbria d. U.K. 12 54.30N 3.00W
Cumbrian Mts. U.K. 12 54.32N 3.05W
Cuminá r. Brazil 123 1.30S 56.00W
Cummins Australia 92 34.16S135.44E
Cumnock Australia 93 32.56S148.46E
Cumnock U.K. 14 55.27N 4.15W
Cunderdin Australia 89 31.39S117.15E
Cunene d. Angola 78 16.00S 16.00E
Cunene r. Angola 78 17.15S 11.50E
Cuneo Italy 30 44.23N 7.32E
Cungena Australia 92 32.33S134.40E
Cunlhat France 20 45.38N 3.35E
Cunnamulla Australia 93 28.04S145.40E
Cuokkaraš'ša mtn. Norway 40 69.57N 24.32E
Cuorgnè Italy 30 45.23N 7.39E
Cupar U.K. 14 56.19N 3.01W
Cupica, Golfo de g. Colombia 122 6.35N 77.25W
Cuprija Yugo. 34 43.56N 21.23E
Curaçao i. Neth. Antilles 122 12.15N 69.00W
Curacautín Chile 125 38.26S 71.53W
Curaco r. Argentina 125 38.49S 65.01W
Curanilahue Chile 125 37.28S 73.21W
Curaray r. Peru 122 2.20S 74.05W
Curban Australia 93 31.33S148.36E
Curdlawidny L. Australia 92 30.16S136.20E
Cure r. France 19 47.40N 3.41E
Curiapo Venezuela 122 8.33N 61.05W
Curicó Chile 125 34.59S 71.14W
Curitiba Brazil 126 25.24S 49.16W
Curlewis Australia 93 31.08S150.16E
Curnamona Australia 92 31.40S139.35E
Currane, Lough Rep. of Ire. 15 51.50N 10.07W
Currant U.S.A. 108 38.44N115.30W
Curranyalpa Australia 93 30.57S144.33E
Currie Australia 91 39.56S143.52E
Currie U.S.A. 108 40.17N114.44W
Curtin Australia 89 30.50S122.05E
Curtis Spain 26 43.07N 8.03W
Curtis U.S.A. 110 40.38N100.31W
Curtis I. Australia 90 23.38S151.09E
Curuá r. Brazil 123 5.23S 54.22W
Čurug Yugo. 31 45.29N 20.04E
Cururupu Brazil 123 1.50S 44.52W
Curuzú Cuatiá Argentina 125 29.50S 58.05W
Curvelo Brazil 126 18.45S 44.27W
Curwensville U.S.A. 114 40.58N 78.32W
Cushendall U.K. 15 55.06N 6.05W
Cushing U.S.A. 111 35.59N 96.46W
Cusna, Monte mtn. Italy 30 44.17N 10.23E
Cut Bank U.S.A. 108 48.38N112.20W
Cutro Italy 33 39.02N 16.59E
Cuttaburra Creek r. Australia 93 29.18S145.00E
Cuttack India 63 20.30N 85.50E
Cuxhaven Germany 38 53.52N 8.42E
Cuyahoga Falls town U.S.A. 114 41.08N 81.29W
Cuyuni r. Guyana 122 6.24N 58.38W
Cuzco Peru 122 13.32S 71.57W
Cuzna r. Spain 26 38.04N 4.41W
Cwmbran U.K. 13 51.39N 3.01W
Cyclades is. see Kikládhes is. Greece 35
Cynthiana U.S.A. 112 38.22N 84.18W
Cypress Hills Canada 101 49.40N109.30W
Cyprus Asia 66 35.00N 33.00E
Cyrenaica f. see Barqah f. Libya 72
Czech Republic Europe 36 49.30N 15.00E
Czeremcha Poland 37 52.32N 23.15E
Czersk Poland 37 53.48N 18.00E
Częstochowa Poland 37 50.49N 19.07E

D

Dà r. Vietnam 56 21.20N105.24E
Da'an China 54 45.30N124.18E
Ḍab'ah Jordan 67 31.36N 36.04E
Dabakala Ivory Coast 76 8.19N 4.24W
Daba Shan mts. China 55 32.00N109.00E
Dabat Ethiopia 73 12.58N 37.48E
Dabbāgh, Jabal mtn. Saudi Arabia 66 27.51N 35.43E
Dabhoi India 62 22.11N 73.26E
Dabie Shan mts. China 55 31.15N115.20E
Dabola Guinea 76 10.48N 11.02W
Dabra India 63 25.54N 78.20E
Dabu Jiangxi China 55 26.47N116.04E
Dacca see Dhākā Bangla. 63
Dachau Germany 39 48.15N 11.26E
Dacre Canada 105 45.22N 76.59W
Dadanawa Guyana 122 2.30N 59.30W
Dade City U.S.A. 113 28.23N 82.11W
Dādhar Pakistan 62 29.28N 67.39E
Dādra & Nagar Haveli d. India 62 20.05N 73.00E
Dādu Pakistan 62 26.44N 67.47E
Dadu He r. China 61 28.47N104.40E
Daet Phil. 59 14.07N122.58E
Dagali Norway 41 60.25N 8.27E
Dagana Senegal 76 16.28N 15.35W
Daga Post Sudan 73 9.12N 33.58E
Dagash Sudan 72 19.22N 33.24E
Dagu China 54 38.58N117.40E
Dagua P.N.G. 59 3.25S143.20E
Daguan China 52 27.44N103.53E
Dagupan Phil. 59 16.02N120.21E
Daguragu Australia 88 17.33S130.30E
Dagzê China 63 29.45N105.45E
Dagzê Co l. China 63 31.45N 87.50E
Dahan-e Qowmghī Afghan. 62 34.28N 66.31E
Da Hinggan Ling mts. China 53 50.00N122.10E
Dahlak Archipelago is. Ethiopia 72 15.45N 40.30E
Dahlak Kebir I. Ethiopia 72 15.38N 40.11E
Dahlem Germany 39 50.23N 6.33E
Dahlgren U.S.A. 114 38.20N 77.03W
Dahme Germany 38 51.52N 13.25E
Dahra Senegal 76 15.21N 15.29W
Dahujiang China 55 26.06N114.58E
Dahūk Iraq 64 36.52N 43.00E
Daḥy, Nafūd ad f. Saudi Arabia 71 22.00N 45.25E
Ḍaḥyah, 'Urūq f. Yemen 71 18.45N 51.15E
Dai Hai l. China 54 40.31N112.43E
Dā'īl Syria 67 32.45N 36.08E
Dailekh Nepal 63 28.50N 81.43E
Daimiel Spain 27 39.04N 3.37W
Daitō Japan 57 34.42N135.38E
Daiyun Shan mtn. China 55 25.41N118.11E
Dājal Pakistan 62 29.33N 70.23E
Dajarra Australia 90 21.42S139.31E
Dajing China 55 28.25N121.10E
Dakar Senegal 76 14.38N 17.27W
Dakhal, Wādī ad r. Egypt 66 28.49N 32.45E
Dākhilah, Al Wāḥāt ad oasis Egypt 64 25.30N 28.10E
Dakhla W. Sahara 74 23.43N 15.57W
Dakhlet Nouadhibou d. Mauritania 74 20.30N 16.00W
Dakhovskaya Russian Fed. 23 44.13N 40.13E
Dakingari Nigeria 77 11.40N 4.06E
Dakota City U.S.A. 110 42.25N 96.25W
Dakovica Yugo. 34 42.22N 20.26E
Dakovo Croatia 31 45.19N 18.25E
Dal r. Sweden 41 60.38N 17.27E
Dala Congo 78 1.40N 16.39E
Dalaba Guinea 76 10.47N 12.12W
Dalai Nur l. China 54 43.27N116.25E
Dalandzadgad Mongolia 54 43.30N104.18E
Dalane f. Norway 42 58.35N 6.20E
Da Lat Vietnam 56 11.56N108.25E
Dālbandin Pakistan 62 28.53N 64.25E
Dalbeattie U.K. 14 54.55N 3.49W
Dalbosjön b. Sweden 43 58.45N 12.48E
Dalby Australia 91 27.11S151.12E
Dalby Sweden 43 55.40N 13.20E
Dale Hordaland Norway 41 60.35N 5.49E
Dale Sogn og Fj. Norway 41 61.22N 5.24E
Dalen Norway 42 59.27N 8.00E
Dalhart U.S.A. 111 36.04N102.31W
Dalhousie Canada 103 48.04N 66.23W
Dalhousie Jammu & Kashmir 62 32.32N 75.59E
Dali China 52 25.42N100.11E
Dali China 52 25.33N100.09E
Dalian China 54 38.49N121.48E
Dalías Spain 27 36.49N 2.52W
Dāliyat el Karmel Israel 67 32.42N 35.03E
Dalj Croatia 31 45.29N 18.59E
Dalkeith U.K. 14 55.54N 3.04W
Dallas Oreg. U.S.A. 108 44.55N123.19W
Dallas Tex. U.S.A. 111 32.47N 96.48W
Dallastown U.S.A. 115 39.54N 76.39W
Dall I. U.S.A. 100 55.00N133.00W
Dalli Rajhāra India 63 20.35N 81.04E
Dalmacija f. Croatia 31 43.33N 16.40E
Dalmally U.K. 14 56.25N 4.58W
Dalmas, Lac l. Canada 103 53.27N 71.50W
Dalmellington U.K. 14 55.19N 4.24W
Dalnerechensk Russian Fed. 53 45.55N133.45E
Daloa Ivory Coast 76 6.56N 6.28W
Dalou Shan mts. China 55 28.25N107.15E
Dalqū Sudan 72 20.07N 30.35E
Dalrymple, Mt. Australia 90 21.02S148.38E
Dalsingh Sarai India 63 25.40N 85.50E
Dalsland f. Sweden 43 59.00N 12.10E
Dalton Canada 102 48.10N 84.00W
Dalton U.S.A. 113 34.46N 84.59W
Daltonganj India 63 24.02N 84.04E
Dalupiri i. Phil. 55 19.05N121.13E
Dalvik Iceland 40 65.58N 18.28W
Dalwhinnie U.K. 14 56.56N 4.15W
Daly r. Australia 88 13.20S130.19E
Daly City U.S.A. 108 37.42N122.29W
Daly Waters town Australia 90 16.15S133.22E
Damā, Wādī r. Saudi Arabia 64 27.04N 35.48E
Damān India 62 20.25N 72.51E
Damān d. India 62 20.10N 73.00E
Damanhūr Egypt 66 31.03N 30.28E
Damar i. Indonesia 59 7.10S128.30E
Damascus see Dimashq Syria 66
Damaturu Nigeria 77 11.49N 11.50E
Damāvand, Qolleh-ye mtn. Iran 65 35.47N 52.04E
Damba Angola 78 6.44S 15.17E
Damen i. China 55 27.58N121.05E
Dāmghān Iran 65 36.09N 54.22E
Damiaoshan China 55 24.43N109.15E
Daming Shan mts. China 55 23.23N108.30E
Dāmiyā Jordan 67 32.06N 35.33E
Dammartin-en-Goële France 19 49.03N 2.41E
Dāmodar r. India 63 22.17N 88.05E
Damoh India 63 23.50N 79.27E
Damongo Ghana 76 9.06N 1.48W
Dampier Australia 88 20.40S116.42E
Dampier, Selat str. Pacific Oc. 59 0.30S130.50E
Dampier Land Australia 88 17.20S123.00E
Damqawt Yemen 71 16.34N 52.50E
Damxung China 63 30.32N 91.06E
Dan Israel 67 33.14N 35.39E
Dana Canada 101 52.18N105.42W
Danané Ivory Coast 76 7.21N 8.10W
Da Nang Vietnam 56 16.04N108.13E
Dānāpur India 63 25.38N 85.03E
Danba China 52 30.57N101.55E
Danbury Conn. U.S.A. 115 41.23N 73.27W
Danbury N.H. U.S.A. 115 43.32N 71.54W
Dand Afghan. 62 31.37N 65.41E
Dandaragan Australia 89 30.40S115.42E
Dande r. Angola 78 8.30S 13.23E
Dandeldhura Nepal 63 29.17N 80.36E
Dandenong Australia 93 37.59S145.14E
Dandong China 54 40.10N124.25E
Danger Is. Cook Is. 84 10.53S165.49W
Dangila Ethiopia 73 11.18N 36.54E
Dangqên China 63 31.41N 91.51E
Dangriga Belize 117 16.58N 88.13W
Dangshan China 54 34.25N116.24E
Dangyang China 55 30.52N111.40E
Daniel U.S.A. 108 42.52N110.04W
Daniel's Harbour Canada 103 50.14N 57.35W
Danielson U.S.A. 115 41.48N 71.53W
Danilov Russian Fed. 44 58.10N 40.12E
Daning China 54 36.32N110.47E
Danisa Hills Kenya 79 3.10N 39.37E
Danja Nigeria 77 11.29N 7.30E
Danjiangkou shuiku resr. China 54 32.42N111.20E
Danlí Honduras 117 14.02N 86.30W
Dannenberg Germany 38 53.06N 11.05E
Dannevirke New Zealand 86 40.12S176.08E
Dannhauser R.S.A. 80 28.00S 30.03E
Dansville U.S.A. 114 42.34N 77.42W
Dantewāra India 63 18.54N 81.21E
Danube r. Europe 31 45.20N 29.40E
Danube, Mouths of the see Dunării, Delta f. Romania 37
Danvers U.S.A. 115 42.34N 70.56W
Danville Canada 105 45.47N 72.01W
Danville Ill. U.S.A. 110 40.09N 87.37W
Danville Ky. U.S.A. 113 37.40N 84.49W
Danville Penn. U.S.A. 115 40.57N 76.37W
Danville Va. U.S.A. 113 36.34N 79.25W
Danville Vt. U.S.A. 105 44.25N 72.09W
Dan Xian China 55 19.30N109.35E
Dão r. Portugal 26 40.20N 8.11W
Daordeng China 54 40.47N119.05E
Daosa India 62 26.53N 76.20E
Daoukro Ivory Coast 76 7.10N 3.58W
Daoulas France 18 48.22N 4.15W
Dao Xian China 55 25.32N111.35E
Daozhen China 55 28.46N107.45E
Dapango Togo 76 10.51N 0.15E
Dapingfang China 54 41.25N120.07E
Da Qaidam China 52 37.44N 95.08E
Daqinggou China 54 41.22N114.13E
Daqing Shan mts. China 54 41.00N111.00E
Daqqāq Sudan 73 12.56N 26.58E
Daqq-e Patargān f. Iran 65 33.30N 60.40E
Dar'ā Syria 67 32.37N 36.06E
Dar'ā d. Syria 67 32.50N 36.10E
Dārāb Iran 65 28.45N 54.34E
Darāban Pakistan 62 31.44N 70.20E
Darabani Romania 37 48.11N 26.35E
Darakht-e Yahyā Afghan. 62 31.50N 68.08E
Darān Iran 65 33.00N 50.27E
Darband, Kūh-e mtn. Iran 65 31.33N 57.08E
Darbhanga India 63 26.10N 85.54E
Darby Mont. U.S.A. 108 46.01N114.11W
Darby Penn. U.S.A. 115 39.54N 75.15W
D'Arcy Canada 100 50.33N122.32W
Darda Croatia 31 45.37N 18.41E
Dardanelles see Çanakkale Bogazi str. Turkey 34
Dar es Salaam Tanzania 79 6.51S 39.18E
Dar es Salaam d. Tanzania 79 6.45S 39.10E
Dareton Australia 92 34.04S142.04E
Darfield New Zealand 86 43.29S172.07E
Dargan Ata Turkmenistan 50 40.30N 62.10E
Dargaville New Zealand 86 35.57S173.53E
Dargo Australia 93 37.30S147.16E
Darhan Mongolia 52 49.34N106.23E
Darie Hills Somali Rep. 71 8.15N 47.25E
Darien U.S.A. 115 41.05N 73.28W
Darién, Golfo del g. Colombia 122 9.20N 77.30W
Darjeeling India 63 27.02N 88.16E
Darkan Australia 89 33.19S116.42E
Darke Peak mtn. Australia 92 33.28S136.12E
Darling r. Australia 92 34.05S141.57E
Darling Downs f. Australia 91 28.00S149.45E
Darling Range mts. Australia 89 32.00S116.30E
Darlington U.K. 12 54.33N 1.33W
Darlington Point town Australia 93 34.36S146.01E
Darłowe Poland 36 54.26N 16.23E
Darmstadt Germany 39 49.53N 8.40E
Darnah Libya 72 32.45N 22.39E
Darnah d. Libya 72 31.30N 23.30E
Darnétal France 18 49.27N 1.09E
Darney France 19 48.05N 6.03E
Darnick Australia 92 32.55S143.39E
Darnley, C. Antarctica 128 68.00S 69.00E
Daroca Spain 25 41.07N 1.25W
Darreh Gaz Iran 65 37.22N 59.08E
Dar Rounga f. C.A.R. 73 9.25N 21.30E
Darsser Ort c. Germany 38 54.29N 12.31E
Dartmoor Australia 92 37.58S141.19E
Dartmoor Forest hills U.K. 13 50.33N 3.55W
Dartmouth Canada 103 44.40N 63.34W
Dartmouth U.K. 13 50.21N 3.35W
Dartmouth Resr. Australia 93 36.36S147.38E
Dartry Mts. Rep. of Ire. 15 54.23N 8.25W
Dartuch, Cabo c. Spain 25 39.56N 3.48E
Daru P.N.G. 90 9.04S143.12E
Daruvar Croatia 31 45.36N 17.13E
Darvaza Turkmenistan 50 40.12N 58.24E
Darvel, Teluk b. Malaysia 58 4.40N118.30E
Darwen U.K. 12 53.42N 2.29W
Dārwha India 63 20.19N 77.46E
Darwin Australia 90 12.23S130.44E
Daryācheh-ye Bakhtegān l. Iran 65 29.20N 54.05E
Daryācheh-ye Namak l. Iran 65 34.45N 51.36E
Daryācheh-ye Orūmīyeh l. Iran 65 37.40N 45.28E
Daryācheh-ye Sīstān f. Iran 65 31.00N 61.15E
Darya Khān Pakistan 62 31.48N 71.06E
Daryāpur India 62 20.56N 77.20E
Dasāda India 62 23.19N 71.50E
Dasht r. Pakistan 62 25.10N 61.40E
Dashte-e Mārgow des. Afghan. 65 30.45N 63.00E
Dasht-e Kavīr des. Iran 65 34.40N 55.00E
Dasht-e Lūt des. Iran 65 31.30N 58.00E
Dashui Nur China 54 42.45N116.47E
Daspalla India 63 20.21N 84.51E
Dassa-Zoumé Benin 77 7.50N 2.13E
Dassow Germany 38 53.50N 10.59E
Dastgardān Iran 65 34.19N 56.51E
Dastjerd Iran 65 34.33N 50.15E
Datça Turkey 35 36.46N 27.40E
Datia India 63 25.40N 78.28E
Datong China 54 40.10N113.15E
Datteln Germany 38 51.40N 7.23E
Datu, Tanjung c. Malaysia 58 2.00N109.30E
Datu Piang Phil. 59 7.02N124.30E
Daua r. Kenya see Dawa r. Ethiopia 73
Dāud Khel Pakistan 62 32.53N 71.34E
Daudnagar India 63 25.02N 84.24E
Daugavpils Latvia 44 55.52N 26.31E
Daun Germany 39 50.11N 6.50E
Dauphin Canada 101 51.09N100.03W
Dauphiné, Alpes du mts. France 21 44.35N 5.45E
Dauphin L. Canada 101 51.17N 99.48W
Daura Nigeria 77 13.05N 8.18E
Dāvangere India 60 14.30N 75.52E
Davao Phil. 59 7.05N125.38E
Davao G. Phil. 59 6.30N126.00E
Daveluyville Canada 105 46.12N 72.08W
Davenport U.S.A. 110 41.32N 90.36W
Daventry U.K. 13 52.16N 1.10W
Davenyns, L. Canada 105 47.05N 73.45W
David Panama 117 8.26N 82.26W
David-Gorodok Belorussia 37 52.04N 27.10E
Davis U.S.A. 108 38.33N121.44W
Davis Creek town U.S.A. 108 41.44N120.24W
Davison U.S.A. 104 43.02N 83.31W
Davis Sea Antarctica 128 66.00S 90.00E
Davis Str. N. America 99 66.00N 58.00W
Davlekanovo Russian Fed. 44 54.12N 55.00E
Davos Switz. 39 46.48N 9.50E
Davutlar Turkey 35 37.43N 27.17E
Dawa China 54 40.58N122.00E
Dawa r. Ethiopia 73 4.11N 42.06E
Dawaxung China 63 31.26N 85.06E
Dawei see Tavoy Burma 56
Dawei see Tavoy Burma 56
Dawlish U.K. 13 50.34N 3.28W
Dawna Range mts. Burma 56 17.00N 98.00E
Dawson Canada 98 64.04N139.24W
Dawson U.S.A. 113 31.47N 84.27W
Dawson Creek town Canada 100 55.45N120.15W
Dawson Range f. Canada 98 62.40N139.00W
Dawu China 52 31.00N101.09E
Dax France 20 43.43N 1.03W
Daxian China 55 31.10N107.28E
Daxing China 54 39.44N116.20E
Daylesford Australia 92 37.22S144.12E
Dayman r. Uruguay 125 31.25S 58.00W
Dayong Hunan China 55 29.06N110.24E
Dayr Abū Sa'īd Jordan 67 32.30N 35.41E
Dayr al Balaḥ Egypt 67 31.25N 34.21E
Dayr al Ghuṣūn Jordan 67 32.21N 35.05E
Dayr az Zawr Syria 64 35.20N 40.08E
Dayr Dibwān Jordan 67 31.55N 35.16E
Dayr Sharaf Jordan 67 32.15N 35.11E
Dayton N.Y. U.S.A. 114 42.25N 78.58W
Dayton Ohio U.S.A. 112 39.45N 84.10W
Dayton Penn. U.S.A. 114 40.53N 79.16W
Dayton Tenn. U.S.A. 113 35.30N 85.01W
Dayton Wash. U.S.A. 108 46.19N117.59W
Daytona Beach town U.S.A. 113 29.11N 81.01W
Dayu China 55 25.24N114.22E
Da Yunhe canal China 54 39.10N117.12E
Dazhu China 55 30.50N107.12E
De Aar R.S.A. 80 30.39S 24.01E
Dead Sea Jordan 67 31.25N 35.30E
Deal U.K. 13 51.13N 1.25E
De'an China 55 29.20N115.46E
Deán Funes Argentina 124 30.25S 64.20W
Dean Lake town Canada 104 46.13N 83.09W
Dearborn U.S.A. 104 42.18N 83.10W
Dease r. Canada 100 59.54N128.30W
Dease Arm b. Canada 98 66.52N119.37W
Dease L. Canada 100 58.05N130.04W
Death Valley f. U.S.A. 109 36.30N117.00W
Death Valley town U.S.A. 109 36.18N116.25W
Death Valley Nat. Monument U.S.A. 108 36.30N117.00W
Deauville France 18 49.22N 0.04E
Debar Macedonia 34 41.31N 20.30E
Debica Poland 37 50.04N 21.24E
Deblin Poland 37 51.35N 21.50E
Deborah, L. Australia 89 30.45S119.07E
Debre Birhan Ethiopia 73 9.40N 39.33E
Debrecen Hungary 37 47.30N 21.37E
Debre Tabor Ethiopia 73 11.50N 38.05E
Dečani Yugo. 34 42.30N 20.10E

Decatur to Djénne

Decatur Ala. U.S.A. 113 34.36N 87.00W
Decatur Ga. U.S.A. 113 33.45N 84.17W
Decatur Ill. U.S.A. 110 39.51N 89.32W
Decatur Ind. U.S.A. 112 40.50N 84.57W
Decazeville France 20 44.34N 2.15E
Deccan f. India 60 18.30N 77.30E
Decelles, Lac l. Canada 102 47.40N 78.10W
Dechu India 62 26.47N 72.20E
Decimomannu Italy 32 39.19N 8.58E
Děčín Czech Republic 38 50.48N 14.13E
Decize France 19 46.50N 3.27E
Deckerville U.S.A. 114 43.32N 82.44W
De Cocksdorp Neth. 16 53.12N 4.52E
Decorah U.S.A. 110 43.18N 91.48W
Decs Hungary 31 46.17N 18.46E
Deda Romania 37 46.57N 24.53E
Dédi Ivory Coast 76 8.34N 3.33W
Dediāpada India 62 21.35N 73.40E
Dedza Malaŵi 79 14.20S 34.24E
Dee r. D. and G. U.K. 14 54.50N 4.05W
Dee r. Grampian U.K. 14 57.07N 2.04W
Dee r. Wales U.K. 12 53.13N 3.05W
Deep B. Canada 100 61.15N116.35W
Deep Creek L. U.S.A. 114 39.30N 79.19W
Deep River town Canada 105 46.06N 77.30W
Deep River town U.S.A. 115 41.23N 72.26W
Deepwater Australia 93 29.26S151.51E
Deep Well Australia 90 24.25S134.05E
Deerfield r. U.S.A. 115 42.35N 72.35W
Deer Lake town Canada 103 49.07N 57.35W
Deer Lodge U.S.A. 108 46.24N112.44W
Deesa India 62 24.15N 72.10E
Deeth U.S.A. 108 41.04N115.18W
Deex Nugaaleed r. Somali Rep. 71 7.58N 49.52E
Defiance U.S.A. 112 41.17N 84.21W
De Funiak Springs town U.S.A. 113 30.41N 86.08W
Deganya Bet Israel 67 32.42N 35.35E
Degeberga Sweden 43 55.50N 14.05E
Degerby Finland 43 60.02N 20.23E
Degerfors Sweden 43 59.14N 14.26E
Degerhamn Sweden 43 56.21N 16.24E
Deggendorf Germany 39 48.51N 12.59E
De Grey r. Australia 88 20.12S119.11E
Deh Bīd Iran 65 30.38N 53.12E
Dehej India 62 21.42N 72.35E
Dehibat Tunisia 75 32.01N 10.42E
Dehra Dūn India 63 30.19N 78.02E
Dehri India 63 24.52N 84.11E
Deh Shū Afghan. 62 30.28N 63.25E
Dehua China 55 25.30N118.14E
Deinze Belgium 16 50.59N 3.32E
Dej Romania 37 47.08N 23.55E
Deje Sweden 43 59.36N 13.28E
Dejiang China 55 28.19N108.05E
Dek'emhāre Ethiopia 72 15.05N 39.02E
Dekese Zaïre 78 3.25S 21.24E
Dekina Nigeria 77 7.43N 7.04E
De Land U.S.A. 113 29.02N 81.18W
Delano U.S.A. 109 35.41N119.15W
Delārām Afghan. 62 32.11N 63.25E
Delaronde L. Canada 101 54.05N107.05W
Delaware d. U.S.A. 115 39.10N 75.30W
Delaware r. U.S.A. 115 39.20N 75.25W
Delaware town U.S.A. 112 40.18N 83.06W
Delaware, East Branch r. U.S.A. 115 41.55N 75.17W
Delaware, West Branch r. U.S.A. 115 41.56N 75.17W
Delaware B. U.S.A. 115 39.05N 75.15W
Delaware Water Gap town U.S.A. 115 40.59N 75.09W
Delaware Water Gap Nat. Recreation Area U.S.A. 115 41.07N 75.06W
Delčevo Macedonia 34 41.58N 22.46E
Delegate Australia 93 37.03S148.58E
Delémont Switz. 39 47.22N 7.21E
Delfinópolis Brazil 126 20.21S 46.51W
Delft Neth. 16 52.01N 4.23E
Delfzijl Neth. 16 53.20N 6.56E
Delgado, C. Mozambique 79 10.45S 40.38E
Delhi Canada 104 42.51N 80.30W
Delhi India 62 28.40N 77.13E
Delhi d. India 62 28.37N 77.10E
Delhi U.S.A. 115 42.17N 74.55W
Delicias Mexico 109 28.13N105.28W
Délimbé C.A.R. 73 9.53N 22.37E
Delingha China 52 37.16N 97.12E
Delitzsch Germany 38 51.31N 12.20E
Dell City U.S.A. 109 31.56N105.12W
Delle France 19 47.30N 7.00E
Delmar U.S.A. 115 38.27N 75.34W
Delmarva Pen. U.S.A. 115 38.48N 75.47W
Delmenhorst Germany 38 53.03N 8.38E
Delnice Croatia 31 45.24N 14.48E
De Long Mts. U.S.A. 98 68.20N162.00W
Delphos U.S.A. 112 40.50N 84.21W
Del Rio U.S.A. 111 29.22N100.54W
Delta d. Nigeria 77 5.30N 6.00E
Delta Colo. U.S.A. 108 38.44N108.04W
Delta Utah U.S.A. 108 39.21N112.35W
Delungra Australia 93 29.38S150.50E
Delvinë Albania 34 39.57N 20.06E
Demak Indonesia 59 6.53S110.40E
Demanda, Sierra de la mts. Spain 26 42.10N 3.00W
Demba Zaïre 78 5.28S 22.14E
Dembī Ethiopia 73 8.05N 36.27E
Dembia C.A.R. 73 5.07N 24.25E
Dembī Dolo Ethiopia 73 8.30N 34.48E
Demer r. Belgium 16 50.59N 4.42E
Deming U.S.A. 109 32.16N107.45W
Demmin Germany 36 53.54N 13.02E
Demmitt Canada 100 55.20N119.50W
Demonte Italy 30 44.19N 7.17E
Demopolis U.S.A. 111 32.31N 87.50W
Demotte U.S.A. 112 41.07N 87.14W
Dêmqog China 63 32.43N 79.29E
Denain France 19 50.20N 3.23E
Denakil f. Ethiopia 73 13.00N 41.00E
Denbigh Canada 105 45.08N 77.16W
Denbigh U.K. 12 53.11N 3.25W
Den Burg Neth. 16 53.03N 4.47E
Dendermonde Belgium 16 51.01N 4.07E
Dendre r. Belgium 16 51.01N 4.07E
Dengkou China 54 40.18N106.59E
Deng Xian China 54 32.44N112.00E
Denham Australia 88 25.54S113.35E
Denham Range mts. Australia 90 21.55S147.46E
Den Helder Neth. 16 52.58N 4.46E
Denia Spain 25 38.51N 0.07E
Deniliquin Australia 93 35.33S144.58E
Denison Iowa U.S.A. 110 42.01N 95.21W
Denison Tex. U.S.A. 111 33.45N 96.33W
Denizli Turkey 64 37.46N 29.05E
Denman Australia 93 32.23S150.42E
Denmark Australia 89 34.54S117.25E
Denmark Europe 42 56.05N 10.00E
Denmark Str. Greenland/Iceland 96 65.00N 30.00W
Dennison U.S.A. 114 40.24N 81.19W
Den Oever Neth. 16 52.56N 5.01E
Denpasar Indonesia 59 8.40S115.14E
Denton Mont. U.S.A. 108 47.19N109.57W
Denton Tex. U.S.A. 111 33.13N 97.08W
D'Entrecasteaux, Pt. Australia 89 34.50S116.00E
D'Entrecasteaux, Recifs reef N. Cal. 84 18.00S163.10E
D'Entrecasteaux Is. P.N.G. 90 9.30S150.40E
Denver U.S.A. 108 39.43N105.01W
Denys r. Canada 102 55.05N 77.22W
Denzlingen Germany 39 48.04N 7.52E
Deo r. Cameroon 77 8.33N 12.45E
Deogarh Madhya P. India 63 24.33N 78.15E
Deogarh mtn. India 63 23.32N 82.16E
Deogarh Orissa India 63 21.32N 84.44E
Deogarh Rāj. India 62 25.32N 73.54E
Deogarh Hills India 63 23.45N 82.30E
Deoghar India 63 24.29N 86.42E
Deolāli India 62 19.57N 73.50E
Deoli India 62 25.45N 75.23E
Deori India 63 23.08N 78.41E
Deoria India 63 26.31N 83.47E
Deori Khās India 63 23.24N 79.01E
Deosil India 63 23.42N 82.15E
De Peel f. Belgium 16 51.30N 5.50E
Depew U.S.A. 114 42.54N 78.42W
Deposit U.S.A. 115 42.04N 75.25W
Depot Harbour town Canada 104 45.19N 80.06W
Dêqên China 52 28.45N 98.58E
De Queen U.S.A. 111 34.02N 94.21W
De Quincy U.S.A. 111 30.27N 93.26W
Dera Bugti Pakistan 62 29.02N 69.09E
Dera Ghāzi Khān Pakistan 62 30.03N 70.38E
Dera Ismāil Khān Pakistan 62 31.50N 70.54E
Derazhnya Ukraine 37 49.18N 27.28E
Derbent Russian Fed. 65 42.03N 48.18E
Derby Tas. Australia 91 41.08S147.47E
Derby W.A. Australia 88 17.19S123.38E
Derby U.K. 12 52.55N 1.28W
Derby Conn. U.S.A. 115 41.19N 73.05W
Derby N.Y. U.S.A. 114 42.41N 78.58W
Derby Center U.S.A. 105 44.58N 72.09W
Derbyshire d. U.K. 12 52.55N 1.28W
Derg, Lough Donegal Rep. of Ire. 15 54.37N 7.55W
Derg, Lough Tipperary Rep. of Ire. 15 52.57N 8.18W
De Ridder U.S.A. 111 30.51N 93.17W
Dernieres, Isles is. U.S.A. 111 29.02N 90.47W
Déroute, Passage de la str. France/U.K. 13 49.10N 1.45W
Derry U.S.A. 115 42.53N 71.19W
Derrynasaggart Mts. Rep. of Ire. 15 51.58N 9.15W
Derryveagh Mts. Rep. of Ire. 15 55.00N 8.07W
Derudeb Sudan 72 17.32N 36.06E
De Ruyter U.S.A. 115 42.46N 75.53W
Derval France 18 47.40N 1.40W
Dervéni Greece 35 38.08N 22.25E
Derventa Bosnia-Herzegovina 31 44.58N 17.55E
Derwent r. Cumbria U.K. 12 54.38N 3.34W
Derwent r. Derbys. U.K. 11 52.52N 1.19W
Derwent r. N. Yorks. U.K. 12 53.44N 0.57W
Desaguadero r. Bolivia 124 18.24S 67.05W
Desappointement, Îles du is. Pacific Oc. 85 14.02S141.24W
Desaulniers Canada 104 46.34N 80.08W
Descanso Mexico 109 32.14N116.58W
Descartes France 18 46.58N 0.42E
Deschaillons Canada 105 46.32N 72.07W
Deschutes r. U.S.A. 108 45.38N120.54W
Desē Ethiopia 73 11.05N 39.41E
Deseado Argentina 125 47.39S 65.20W
Deseado r. Argentina 125 47.45S 65.50W
Desenzano del Garda Italy 30 45.28N 10.32E
Deseronto Canada 105 44.12N 77.03W
Deserta Grande is. Madeira Is. 127 32.32N 16.30W
Desert Center U.S.A. 109 33.44N115.25W
Desfiladero de Despeñaperros Spain 26 38.24N 3.30W
Deshnoke India 62 27.48N 73.21E
Des Moines Iowa U.S.A. 110 41.35N 93.37W
Des Moines N.Mex. U.S.A. 108 36.46N103.50W
Des Moines r. U.S.A. 110 40.22N 91.26W
Desna r. Ukraine 37 50.32N 30.37E
De Soto U.S.A. 111 38.08N 90.33W
Dessau Germany 38 51.50N 12.14E
Desvres France 19 50.40N 1.50E
Dete Zimbabwe 80 18.39S 26.49E
Detlor Canada 105 45.02N 77.45W
Detmold Germany 38 51.56N 8.52E
De Tour Village U.S.A. 104 46.00N 83.56W
Detroit U.S.A. 114 42.20N 83.03W
Detroit Lakes town U.S.A. 110 46.49N 95.51W
Deūlgaon Rāja India 62 20.01N 76.02E
Deurne Belgium 16 51.13N 4.26E
Deurne Neth. 16 51.29N 5.44E
Deutsche Bucht b. Germany 38 54.10N 8.00E
Deutschlandsberg Austria 31 46.49N 15.13E
Deux Rivières town Canada 104 46.15N 78.19W
Deux-Sevres d. France 18 46.30N 0.20W
Deva Romania 37 45.54N 22.55E
Deventer Neth. 16 52.15N 6.10E
Deveron r. U.K. 14 57.40N 2.30W
Devès, Monts du mts. France 20 45.00N 3.45E
Devīkot India 62 26.42N 71.12E
Devil's Bridge U.K. 13 52.23N 3.50W
Devils Lake town U.S.A. 110 48.07N 98.59W
Devin Bulgaria 34 41.44N 24.24E
Devizes U.K. 13 51.21N 2.00W
Devoll r. Albania 34 40.57N 20.15E
Devon d. U.K. 13 50.50N 3.40W
Devon I. Canada 99 75.00N 86.00W
Devonport Australia 91 41.09S146.16E
Devrez r. Turkey 64 41.07N 34.25E
Dewās India 62 22.58N 76.04E
De Witt U.S.A. 111 34.18N 91.20W
Dewsbury U.K. 12 53.42N 1.38W
Dexter Mich. U.S.A. 104 42.20N 83.53W
Dexter Mo. U.S.A. 111 36.48N 89.57W
Dexter N.Y. U.S.A. 105 44.01N 76.03W
Deyang China 55 31.05N104.18E
Dey-Dey L. Australia 91 29.12S131.02E
Dez r. Iran 65 31.38N 48.54E
Dezadeash L. Canada 100 60.28N136.58W
Dezfūl Iran 65 32.24N 48.27E
Dezhneva, Mys c. Russian Fed. 48 66.05N169.40W
Dezhou China 54 37.23N116.16E
Dezh Shāhpūr Iran 65 35.31N 46.10E
Dháfni Greece 35 37.48N 22.01E
Dhahab Egypt 66 28.30N 34.31E
Dhahran see Az̧ Z̧ahrān Saudi Arabia 65
Dhākā Bangla. 63 23.43N 90.25E
Dhamār Yemen 71 14.33N 44.24E
Dhamtari India 63 20.41N 81.34E
Dhānbād India 63 23.48N 86.27E
Dhandhuka India 62 22.22N 71.59E
Dhangarhi Nepal 63 28.41N 80.38E
Dhankuta Nepal 63 26.59N 87.21E
Dhār India 62 22.36N 75.18E
Dharampur India 62 20.32N 73.11E
Dharān Bāzār Nepal 63 26.49N 87.17E
Dharangaon India 62 21.01N 75.16E
Dhāri India 62 21.20N 71.01E
Dharmābād India 63 18.54N 77.51E
Dharmjaygarh India 63 22.28N 83.13E
Dharmsāla India 62 32.13N 76.19E
Dhārni India 62 21.33N 76.53E
Dhaulāgiri mtn. Nepal 63 28.42N 83.31E
Dhebar L. India 62 24.16N 74.00E
Dhenkānāl India 63 20.40N 85.36E
Dhenoúsa i. Greece 35 37.08N 25.48E
Dhërmiu site Albania 34 40.08N 19.42E
Dheskáti Greece 34 39.55N 21.49E
Dhestina Greece 35 38.25N 22.31E
Dhiavolítsion Greece 35 37.18N 21.58E
Dhībān Jordan 67 31.30N 35.47E
Dhidhimótikhon Greece 34 41.22N 26.29E
Dhiinsoor Somali Rep. 71 2.28N 43.00E
Dhíkti mtn. Greece 35 35.08N 25.22E
Dhílos site Greece 35 37.26N 25.16E
Dhimitsána Greece 35 37.37N 22.03E
Dhodhekánisos is. Greece 35 36.35N 27.10E
Dhodhóni site Greece 34 39.34N 20.47E
Dholiana Greece 34 39.54N 20.32E
Dholka India 62 22.43N 72.28E
Dholpur India 63 26.42N 77.54E
Dhomokós Greece 35 39.10N 22.18E
Dhorāji India 62 21.44N 70.27E
Dhoxáton Greece 34 41.05N 24.14E
Dhrāngadhra India 62 22.59N 71.28E
Dhrol India 62 22.34N 70.25E
Dhubri India 63 26.02N 89.58E
Dhule India 62 20.54N 74.47E
Dhuliān India 63 24.41N 87.58E
Dhuudo Somali Rep. 71 9.20N 50.14E
Día i. Greece 35 35.26N 25.13E
Dialakoro Mali 76 12.18N 7.54W
Diamante Argentina 125 32.05S 60.35W
Diamantina r. Australia 90 26.45S139.10E
Diamantina Brazil 126 18.17S 43.37W
Diamantina, Chapada hills Brazil 123 13.00S 42.30W
Diamantino Brazil 126 14.25S 56.29W
Diamond Harbour India 63 22.12N 88.12E
Dianalund Denmark 42 55.32N 11.30E
Diana's Peak mtn. St. Helena 127 15.58S 5.42W
Dianbai China 55 21.30N111.01E
Diane Bank is. Australia 90 15.50S149.48E
Dianjiang China 55 30.14N107.27E
Diapaga Burkina 77 12.04N 1.48E
Dibai India 63 28.13N 78.15E
Dibaya Zaïre 78 6.31S 22.57E
Dibi Cameroon 77 7.09N 13.43E
Dibrugarh India 61 27.29N 94.56E
Dibs Sudan 73 14.18N 24.23E
Dickinson U.S.A. 110 46.53N102.47W
Dicle r. Turkey see Dijlah r. Asia 64
Didcot U.K. 13 51.36N 1.14W
Didiéni Mali 76 14.05N 7.50W
Dīdwāna India 62 27.24N 74.34E
Didyma site Turkey 35 37.25N 27.16E
Die France 21 44.45N 5.22E
Dieburg Germany 39 49.54N 8.50E
Diefenbaker, L. Canada 101 51.00N106.55W
Diekirch Lux. 16 49.52N 6.10E
Diélette France 18 49.33N 1.52W
Diéma Mali 76 14.32N 9.03W
Diemen Neth. 16 52.22N 4.58E
Diemuchuoke Jammu & Kashmir 63 32.42N 79.29E
Dien Bien Phu Vietnam 56 21.23N103.02E
Diepholz Germany 38 52.35N 8.21E
Dieppe France 18 49.56N 1.05E
Dierdorf Germany 38 50.33N 7.39E
Dieren Neth. 16 52.03N 6.06E
Dierks U.S.A. 111 34.07N 94.01W
Diesdorf Germany 38 52.45N 10.52E
Diest Belgium 16 50.59N 5.03E
Dieulefit France 21 44.31N 5.04E
Dieuze France 19 48.49N 6.43E
Diez Germany 39 50.22N 8.01E
Dif Kenya 79 1.04N 40.57E
Diffa Niger 77 13.19N 12.35E
Diffa d. Niger 77 16.00N 13.00E
Dīg India 62 27.20N 77.25E
Digby Canada 103 44.30N 65.47W
Dighton U.S.A. 110 38.29N100.28W
Digne France 21 44.06N 6.14E
Digoin France 19 46.29N 3.59E
Digras India 63 20.07N 77.43E
Digri Pakistan 62 25.10N 69.07E
Digul r. Indonesia 59 7.10S139.08E
Dijlah r. Asia 65 31.00N 47.27E
Dijle r. Belgium 16 51.02N 4.25E
Dijon France 19 47.19N 5.01E
Dikhil Djibouti 73 11.06N 42.22E
Dikili Turkey 29 39.05N 26.52E
Dikirnis Egypt 66 31.05N 31.35E
Dikodougou Ivory Coast 76 9.00N 5.45W
Diksmuide Belgium 16 51.01N 2.52E
Dikwa Nigeria 77 12.01N 13.55E
Dili Indonesia 59 8.35S125.35E
Dillenburg Germany 38 50.44N 8.17E
Dilley U.S.A. 111 28.40N 99.10W
Dilling Sudan 73 12.03N 29.39E
Dillingen Germany 39 48.34N 10.29E
Dillingham U.S.A. 98 59.02N158.29W
Dillon U.S.A. 108 45.13N112.38W
Dillsburg U.S.A. 114 40.07N 77.02W
Dilolo Zaïre 78 10.39S 22.20E
Dimashq Syria 66 33.30N 36.19E
Dimbelenge Zaïre 78 5.32S 23.04E
Dimbokro Ivory Coast 76 6.43N 4.46W
Dimboola Australia 92 36.27S142.02E
Dîmboviţa r. Romania 37 44.13N 26.22E
Dimitrovgrad Bulgaria 34 42.05N 25.35E
Dimitrovo see Pernik Bulgaria 34
Dimona Israel 67 31.04N 35.01E
Dinagat i. Phil. 59 10.15N125.30E
Dinājpur Bangla. 63 25.38N 88.38E
Dinan France 18 48.27N 2.02W
Dinant Belgium 16 50.16N 4.55E
Dinar Turkey 64 38.05N 30.09E
Dīnār, Kūh-e mtn. Iran 65 30.45N 51.39E
Dinara Planina mts. Europe 31 43.40N 17.00E
Dinard France 18 48.38N 2.04W
Dinaric Alps mts. see Dinara Planina mts. Europe 31
Dindar r. Sudan 72 14.06N 33.40E
Dindar Nat. Park Sudan 73 12.00N 35.00E
Dindigul India 60 10.23N 78.00E
Dindori India 63 22.57N 81.05E
Dinga Pakistan 62 25.26N 67.10E
Dingbian China 54 37.36N107.38E
Dinggyê China 63 28.18N 88.06E
Dingle Rep. of Ire. 15 52.09N 10.17W
Dingle B. Rep. of Ire. 15 52.05N 10.12W
Dingmans Ferry town U.S.A. 115 41.14N 74.53W
Dingolfing Germany 39 48.38N 12.31E
Dinguiraye Guinea 76 11.19N 10.49W
Dingwall U.K. 14 57.35N 4.26W
Dingxi China 54 35.33N104.32E
Ding Xian China 54 38.30N115.00E
Dingxing China 54 39.17N115.46E
Dinkelsbühl Germany 39 49.04N 10.19E
Dinokwe Botswana 80 23.24S 26.40E
Dinuba U.S.A. 109 36.32N119.23W
Diö Sweden 43 56.38N 14.33E
Diodār India 62 24.06N 71.47E
Dioïla Mali 76 12.30N 6.49W
Diourbel Senegal 76 14.30N 16.10W
Diplo Pakistan 62 24.28N 69.35E
Dipolog Phil. 59 8.34N123.28E
Dirdal Norway 42 58.47N 6.14E
Diré Mali 76 16.16N 3.24W
Direction, C. Australia 90 12.51S143.32E
Dirē Dawa Ethiopia 73 9.35N 41.50E
Dirico Angola 78 17.58S 20.40E
Dirj Libya 75 30.09N 10.26E
Dirk Hartog I. Australia 88 25.50S113.00E
Dirranbandi Australia 93 28.35S148.10E
Disappointment, L. Australia 88 23.30S122.55E
Disaster B. Australia 93 37.20S149.58E
Discovery Canada 98 63.10N113.58W
Discovery B. Australia 92 38.12S141.07E
Disentis Switz. 39 46.43N 8.51E
Disko i. Greenland 99 69.45N 53.00W
Diss U.K. 13 52.23N 1.06E
District of Columbia d. U.S.A. 114 38.55N 77.00W
Distrito Federal d. Brazil 123 15.45S 47.50W
Distrito Federal d. Mexico 116 19.20N 99.10W
Disūq Egypt 66 31.09N 30.39E
Dithmarschen f. Germany 38 54.10N 9.15E
Diu India 62 20.42N 70.59E
Diu d. India 62 20.45N 70.59E
Diver Canada 104 46.42N 79.30W
Dives r. France 18 49.19N 0.05W
Divinópolis Brazil 126 20.08S 44.55W
Divnoye Russian Fed. 45 45.55N 43.21E
Divo Ivory Coast 76 5.48N 5.15W
Divriği Turkey 64 39.23N 38.06E
Dīwāl Qol Afghan. 62 34.19N 67.54E
Dixcove Ghana 76 4.49N 1.57W
Dixie U.S.A. 108 45.34N115.28W
Dix Milles, Lac l. Canada 105 46.46N 77.45W
Dixon Ill. U.S.A. 110 41.50N 89.29W
Dixon N.Mex. U.S.A. 109 36.12N105.33W
Dixon Entrance str. U.S.A./Canada 100 54.25N132.30W
Diyālā r. Iraq 65 33.13N 44.33E
Diyarbakır Turkey 64 37.55N 40.14E
Dja r. Cameroon 78 1.38N 16.03E
Djabéta Gabon 78 0.45N 14.00E
Djado Niger 77 21.00N 12.20E
Djado, Plateau du f. Niger 77 22.00N 12.30E
Djambala Congo 78 2.33S 14.38E
Djanet Algeria 75 24.34N 9.29E
Djebel Abiod Tunisia 32 36.58N 9.05E
Djelfa Algeria 75 34.40N 3.15E
Djema C.A.R. 73 6.03N 25.19E
Djénne Mali 76 13.55N 4.31W

Djerba, Île de to **Dun-le-Palestel**

Djerba, Île de *i.* Tunisia **75** 33.48N 10.54E
Djerid, Chott *f.* Tunisia **75** 33.42N 8.26E
Djibo Burkina **76** 14.09N 1.38W
Djibouti Africa **73** 12.00N 42.50E
Djibouti *town* Djibouti **73** 11.35N 43.11E
Djilbabo Plain *f.* Ethiopia **73** 4.00N 39.10E
Djolu Zaïre **78** 0.35N 22.28E
Djouah *r.* Gabon **78** 1.16N 13.12E
Djougou Benin **77** 9.40N 1.47E
Djugu Zaïre **79** 1.55N 30.31E
Djúpivogur Iceland **40** 64.41N 14.16W
Djurö *i.* Sweden **43** 58.52N 13.28E
Dmitriya Lapteva, Proliv *str.* Russian Fed. **51** 73.00N142.00E
Dnepr *r.* Ukraine *see* Dnieper *r.* Europe **37**
Dneprodzerzhinsk Ukraine **45** 48.30N 34.37E
Dnepropetrovsk Ukraine **45** 48.29N 35.00E
Dneprovskaya Nizmennost *f.* Belorussia **37** 52.30N 29.45E
Dneprovsko-Bugskiy Kanal Belorussia **37** 52.03N 25.35E
Dnestr *r.* Ukraine *see* Dniester *r.* Europe **37**
Dnieper *r.* Europe **37** 50.00N 31.00E
Dniester *r.* Europe **37** 46.21N 30.20E
Dno Russian Fed. **44** 57.50N 30.00E
Doba Chad **77** 8.40N 16.50E
Dobane C.A.R. **73** 6.24N 24.42E
Dobbiaco Italy **30** 46.44N 12.14E
Dobele Latvia **41** 56.37N 23.16E
Döbeln Germany **38** 51.07N 13.07E
Dobo Indonesia **59** 5.46S134.13E
Doboj Bosnia-Herzegovina **31** 44.44N 18.06E
Dobra *r.* Croatia **31** 45.33N 15.31E
Dobrich Bulgaria **29** 43.34N 27.52E
Dobrodzień Poland **37** 50.44N 18.27E
Dobruja *f.* Romania **37** 44.30N 28.15E
Dobrush Belorussia **37** 52.24N 31.19E
Dobryanka Russian Fed. **44** 58.30N 56.26E
Dobzha China **63** 28.28N 88.13E
Doce *r.* Brazil **126** 19.32S 39.57W
Docking U.K. **12** 52.55N 0.39E
Doda Jammu & Kashmir **62** 33.08N 75.34E
Doda, Lac *l.* Canada **102** 49.24N 75.14W
Dodecanese *is. see* Dhodhekánisos *is.* Greece **35**
Dodge City U.S.A. **111** 37.45N100.01W
Dodman Pt. U.K. **13** 50.13N 4.48W
Dodoma Tanzania **79** 6.10S 35.40E
Dodoma *d.* Tanzania **79** 6.00S 36.00E
Dodson U.S.A. **108** 48.24N108.15W
Doetinchem Neth. **16** 51.57N 6.17E
Dogai Coring *l.* China **61** 34.30N 89.00E
Doğanbey Turkey **35** 37.37N 27.11E
Dog Creek *town* Canada **100** 51.35N122.14W
Dogger Bank *f.* North Sea **11** 54.45N 2.00E
Doğubayazit Turkey **65** 39.32N 44.08E
Do'gyaling China **63** 31.58N 88.24E
Doha *see* Ad Dawḩah Qatar **65**
Dohad India **62** 22.50N 74.16E
Doheny Canada **105** 47.04N 72.36W
Dohhi India **63** 24.32N 84.54E
Doilungdêqên China **63** 30.06N 90.32E
Doiran, L. Greece / Macedonia **34** 41.13N 22.44E
Dokkum Neth. **16** 53.20N 6.00E
Dokri Pakistan **62** 27.23N 68.06E
Dolbeau Canada **103** 48.53N 72.14W
Dol-de-Bretagne France **18** 48.33N 1.45W
Dole France **19** 47.06N 5.30E
Dolgellau U.K. **13** 52.44N 3.53W
Dolina Ukraine **37** 49.00N 23.59E
Dolinskaya Ukraine **45** 48.06N 32.46E
Dollard *b.* Germany **38** 53.17N 7.10E
Dolni Dubnik Bulgaria **34** 43.24N 24.26E
Dolni Lom Bulgaria **34** 43.31N 22.47E
Dolny Kubín Slovakia **37** 49.12N 19.17E
Dolomiti *mts.* Italy **30** 46.15N 11.55E
Dolores Argentina **125** 36.19S 57.40W
Dolores Mexico **109** 28.53N108.27W
Dolores Spain **25** 38.08N 0.46W
Dolores Uruguay **125** 33.33S 58.13W
Dolores U.S.A. **108** 37.28N108.30W
Dolphin and Union Str. Canada **98** 69.20N118.00W
Doma Nigeria **77** 8.23N 8.21E
Domadare Somali Rep. **73** 1.48N 41.13E
Domažlice Czech Republic **38** 49.27N 12.56E
Dombås Norway **41** 62.05N 9.08E
Dombe Grande Angola **78** 13.00S 13.06E
Dombes *f.* France **21** 46.00N 5.03E
Dombey, C. Australia **92** 37.12S139.43E
Dombóvár Hungary **31** 46.23N 18.08E
Domburg Neth. **16** 51.35N 3.31E
Domfront France **18** 48.36N 0.39W
Dominica Windward Is. **117** 15.30N 61.30W
Dominican Republic C. America **117** 18.00N 70.00W
Dominion L. Canada **103** 52.40N 61.42W
Dommel *r.* Neth. **16** 51.44N 5.17E
Domo Ethiopia **71** 7.54N 46.52E
Domodossola Italy **30** 46.07N 8.17E
Dompierre-sur-Besbre France **20** 46.31N 3.41E
Domuyo *mtn.* Argentina **125** 36.37S 70.28W
Domvraína Greece **35** 38.15N 22.59E
Domžale Slovenia **31** 46.08N 14.36E
Don Mexico **109** 26.26N109.02W
Don *r.* Russian Fed. **45** 47.06N 39.16E
Don *r.* England U.K. **12** 53.41N 0.50W
Don *r.* Scotland U.K. **14** 57.10N 2.05W
Donaghadee U.K. **15** 54.39N 5.33W
Donald Australia **92** 36.25S143.04E
Donaldsonville U.S.A. **111** 30.06N 90.59W
Donau *r.* Germany *see* Danube *r.* Europe **36**
Donaueschingen Germany **39** 47.57N 8.29E
Donauwörth Germany **39** 48.43N 10.46E
Don Benito Spain **27** 38.53N 5.51W
Doncaster U.K. **12** 53.31N 1.09W
Dondaicha India **62** 21.20N 74.34E
Dondo Angola **78** 9.40S 14.25E
Dondo Mozambique **81** 19.39S 34.39E
Donegal Rep. of Ire. **15** 54.39N 8.06W
Donegal *d.* Rep. of Ire. **15** 54.52N 8.00W
Donegal U.S.A. **114** 40.07N 79.23W
Donegal B. Rep. of Ire. **15** 54.32N 8.18W
Donegal Pt. Rep. of Ire. **15** 52.43N 9.38W
Donetsk Ukraine **45** 48.00N 37.50E
Donga Nigeria **77** 7.45N 10.05E
Donga *r.* Nigeria **77** 8.20N 10.00E
Dongara Australia **89** 29.15S114.56E
Dongargarh India **63** 21.12N 80.44E
Dongbei Pingyuan *f.* China **54** 42.30N123.00E
Dongchuan China **52** 26.10N103.02E
Dongco China **63** 32.07N 84.35E
Dongfang China **55** 19.05N108.39E
Donggala Indonesia **58** 0.48S119.45E
Donggou China **54** 39.52N124.08E
Dongguang China **54** 37.53N116.32E
Donghai China **54** 34.35N118.49E
Donghai *i.* China **55** 21.02N110.25E
Dong Hoi Vietnam **56** 17.32N106.35E
Dong Jiang *r.* China **55** 23.00N113.33E
Dongkalang Indonesia **59** 0.12N120.07E
Dongling China **54** 41.44N123.32E
Dongou Congo **78** 2.05N 18.00E
Dongping Hu *l.* China **54** 35.55N116.15E
Dongqiao China **63** 31.57N 90.30E
Dongsheng China **54** 39.49N109.59E
Dongtai China **54** 32.42N120.26E
Dongting Hu *l.* China **55** 29.10N113.00E
Dongtou *i.* China **55** 27.50N121.08E
Dong Ujimqin Qi China **54** 45.33N116.50E
Dongxi China **55** 28.42N106.40E
Dongxing China **55** 21.33N107.58E
Donington U.K. **12** 52.55N 0.12W
Donja Stubica Croatia **31** 45.59N 15.58E
Donji Vakuf Bosnia-Herzegovina **31** 44.09N 17.25E
Dönna *i.* Norway **40** 66.05N 12.30E
Donnacona Canada **105** 46.40N 71.47W
Donnybrook Australia **89** 33.34S115.47E
Donnybrook R.S.A. **80** 29.55S 29.51E
Donora U.S.A. **114** 40.11N 79.52W
Donostia *see* San Sebastián Spain **26**
Doodlakine Australia **89** 31.41S117.23E
Doolow Somali Rep. **71** 4.13N 42.08E
Doon, Loch U.K. **14** 55.15N 4.23W
Dor Israel **67** 32.37N 34.55E
Dora, L. Australia **88** 22.05S122.55E
Dora Baltea *r.* Italy **30** 45.11N 8.05E
Doran L. Canada **101** 61.13N108.06W
Dora Riparia *r.* Italy **30** 45.05N 7.44E
Dorchester U.K. **13** 50.52N 2.28W
Dorchester, C. Canada **99** 65.29N 77.30W
Dordogne *d.* France **20** 45.10N 0.45E
Dordogne *r.* France **20** 45.02N 0.35W
Dordrecht Neth. **16** 51.48N 4.40E
Dordrecht R.S.A. **80** 31.22S 27.02E
Dore, Mont *mtn.* France **20** 45.35N 2.48E
Doré L. Canada **101** 54.46N107.17W
Dorfen Germany **39** 48.17N 12.08E
Dorgali Italy **32** 40.17N 9.35E
Dori Burkina **76** 14.03N 0.02W
Dorion Canada **105** 45.23N 74.03W
Dorking U.K. **13** 51.14N 0.20W
Dormagen Germany **38** 51.05N 6.50E
Dormans France **19** 49.04N 3.38E
Dornbirn Austria **39** 47.25N 9.44E
Dornie U.K. **14** 57.16N 5.31W
Dornoch U.K. **14** 57.52N 4.02W
Dornoch Firth *est.* U.K. **14** 57.50N 4.04W
Dornogovĭ *d.* Mongolia **54** 44.00N110.00E
Dornum Germany **38** 53.40N 7.28E
Doro Mali **76** 16.09N 0.51W
Dorohoi Romania **37** 47.57N 26.24E
Dörpen Germany **38** 52.57N 7.20E
Dorre I. Australia **88** 25.08S113.06E
Dorrigo Australia **93** 30.20S152.41E
Dorris U.S.A. **108** 41.58N121.55W
Dorset Canada **104** 45.14N 78.54W
Dorset *d.* U.K. **13** 50.48N 2.25W
Dorset U.S.A. **115** 43.15N 73.06W
Dorset, C. Canada **99** 64.10N 76.40W
Dorset Peak *mtn.* U.S.A. **115** 43.19N 73.02W
Dorsten Germany **38** 51.39N 6.58E
Dortmund Germany **38** 51.31N 7.28E
Dortmund-Ems Kanal Germany **38** 52.00N 7.36E
Dorval Canada **105** 45.27N 73.44W
Dos Bahías, C. Argentina **125** 44.55S 65.32W
Dos Hermanas Spain **27** 37.17N 5.55W
Dosquet Canada **105** 46.28N 71.33W
Dosse *r.* Germany **38** 53.13N 12.20E
Dosso Niger **77** 13.03N 3.10E
Dosso *d.* Niger **77** 13.00N 3.15E
Dossor Kazakhstan **45** 47.31N 53.01E
Dothan U.S.A. **113** 31.12N 85.25W
Douai France **19** 50.22N 3.04E
Douako Guinea **76** 9.45N 10.08W
Douala Cameroon **77** 4.05N 9.43E
Douarnenez France **18** 48.06N 4.20W
Double Mer *g.* Canada **103** 54.05N 59.00W
Doubs *d.* France **19** 47.10N 6.25E
Doubs *r.* France **19** 46.54N 5.02E
Doubtless B. New Zealand **86** 35.10S173.30E
Doudeville France **18** 49.43N 0.48E
Douentza Mali **76** 14.58N 2.48W
Douglas I.o.M. Europe **12** 54.09N 4.29W
Douglas R.S.A. **80** 29.03S 23.45E
Douglas Ariz. U.S.A. **109** 31.21N109.33W
Douglas Ga. U.S.A. **113** 31.30N 82.54W
Douglas Mich. U.S.A. **112** 42.38N 86.13W
Douglas Wyo. U.S.A. **108** 42.45N105.24W
Douglas Creek *r.* Australia **92** 28.35S136.50E
Douglas L. U.S.A. **104** 45.34N 84.39W
Douglas Pt. Canada **104** 44.20N 81.35W
Doulaincourt France **19** 48.19N 5.12E
Doulevant-le-Château France **19** 48.23N 4.55E
Doullens France **19** 50.09N 2.21E
Doumé Cameroon **77** 4.13N 13.30E
Douna Mali **76** 12.40N 6.00W
Dounreay U.K. **14** 58.35N 3.42W
Dourados Brazil **124** 22.09S 54.52W
Dourdan France **19** 48.32N 2.01E
Douro *r.* Portugal **26** 41.08N 8.40W
Douvres France **18** 49.17N 0.23W
Douze *r.* France **20** 43.54N 0.30W
Dove *r.* Derbys. U.K. **12** 52.50N 1.35W
Dover U.K. **13** 51.07N 1.19E
Dover Del. U.S.A. **115** 39.10N 75.32W
Dover N.H. U.S.A. **115** 43.12N 70.56W
Dover N.J. U.S.A. **115** 40.53N 74.34W
Dover Ohio U.S.A. **114** 40.32N 81.29W
Dover Tenn. U.S.A. **113** 36.30N 87.50W
Dover, Pt. Australia **89** 32.32S125.30E
Dover, Str. of U.K. **13** 51.00N 1.30E
Dovey *r.* U.K. **13** 52.33N 3.56W
Dovrefjell *mts.* Norway **41** 62.06N 9.25E
Dovsk Belorussia **37** 53.07N 30.29E
Dowa Malaŵi **79** 13.40S 33.55E
Dowagiac U.S.A. **112** 41.58N 86.06W
Dowerin Australia **89** 31.15S117.00E
Dowlatābād Iran **65** 28.19N 56.40E
Dowlat Yār Afghan. **62** 34.33N 65.47E
Down *d.* U.K. **15** 54.20N 6.00W
Downey U.S.A. **108** 42.26N112.07W
Downham Market U.K. **13** 52.36N 0.22E
Downpatrick U.K. **15** 54.21N 5.43W
Downpatrick Head Rep. of Ire. **15** 54.20N 9.22W
Downton, Mt. Canada **100** 52.42N124.51W
Dowra Rep. of Ire. **15** 54.11N 8.02W
Doylestown U.S.A. **115** 40.19N 75.08W
Dozois, Rés. Canada **105** 47.30N 77.05W
Drâa, Hamada du *f.* Algeria **74** 29.00N 6.00W
Drâa, Oued *wadi* Morocco **74** 28.40N 11.06W
Drac *r.* France **21** 45.13N 5.41E
Drachten Neth. **16** 53.05N 6.06E
Dragaš Yugo. **34** 42.05N 20.35E
Drăgăşani Romania **37** 44.40N 24.16E
Dragoman, Pasul *pass* Bulgaria / Yugo. **29** 42.56N 22.52E
Dragonera, Isla *i.* Spain **25** 39.35N 2.19E
Dragon's Mouth *str.* Trinidad **122** 11.00N 61.35W
Dragovishtitsa Bulgaria **34** 42.22N 22.39E
Draguignan France **21** 43.32N 6.28E
Drake Australia **93** 28.55S152.24E
Drake U.S.A. **110** 47.55N100.23W
Drakensberg *mts.* R.S.A. / Lesotho **80** 30.00S 29.05E
Drake Passage *str.* Atlantic Oc. **127** 59.00S 65.00W
Dráma Greece **34** 41.09N 24.08E
Drammen Norway **42** 59.44N 10.15E
Drās Jammu & Kashmir **62** 34.27N 75.46E
Drau *r.* Austria *see* Drava *r.* Slovenia / Croatia **30**
Drava *r.* Slovenia / Croatia **31** 45.33N 18.55E
Dravinja *r.* Slovenia **31** 46.22N 15.57E
Drayton Valley *town* Canada **100** 53.25N114.58W
Drenovets Bulgaria **34** 43.42N 22.59E
Drenthe *d.* Neth. **16** 52.52N 6.30E
Dresden Germany **38** 51.03N 13.44E
Dresden U.S.A. **114** 40.07N 82.01W
Dreux France **18** 48.44N 1.22E
Driftwood Canada **102** 49.08N 81.23W
Driftwood U.S.A. **114** 41.20N 78.08W
Drin *r.* Albania **34** 41.37N 20.28E
Drina *r.* Bosnia-Herzegovina **31** 44.53N 19.21E
Drniš Croatia **31** 43.51N 16.09E
Dröbak Norway **42** 59.39N 10.39E
Drocourt Canada **104** 45.47N 80.22W
Drogheda Rep. of Ire. **15** 53.42N 6.23W
Drogobych Ukraine **37** 49.10N 23.30E
Droitwich U.K. **13** 52.16N 2.10W
Drokiya Moldavia **37** 48.07N 27.49E
Drôme *d.* France **21** 44.35N 5.10E
Drôme *r.* France **21** 44.46N 4.46E
Dromedary, C. Australia **93** 36.18S150.15E
Dronero Italy **30** 44.28N 7.22E
Dronfield U.K. **12** 53.18N 1.29W
Dronne *r.* France **20** 45.02N 0.09W
Dronninglund Denmark **42** 57.09N 10.18E
Dronning Maud Land *f.* Antarctica **128** 74.00S 10.00E
Drumbo Canada **104** 43.14N 80.33W
Drumheller Canada **100** 51.25N112.40W
Drum Hills Rep. of Ire. **15** 52.03N 7.42W
Drummond U.S.A. **104** 46.02N 83.42W
Drummond I. U.S.A. **104** 46.00N 83.40W
Drummond Range *mts.* Australia **90** 23.30S147.15E
Drummondville Canada **105** 45.53N 72.29W
Drummore U.K. **14** 54.41N 4.54W
Druskininkai Lithuania **37** 53.48N 23.58E
Drut *r.* Belorussia **37** 53.03N 30.42E
Drvar Bosnia-Herzegovina **31** 44.22N 16.24E
Dryanovo Bulgaria **34** 42.58N 25.27E
Dry B. U.S.A. **100** 59.08N138.25W
Dryden Canada **102** 49.47N 92.50W
Dryden U.S.A. **115** 42.29N 76.18W
Drymen U.K. **14** 56.04N 4.27W
Drysdale *r.* Australia **88** 13.59S126.51E
Dschang Cameroon **77** 5.28N 10.02E
Dua *r.* Zaïre **78** 3.12N 20.55E
Du'an China **55** 24.01N108.06E
Duaringa Australia **90** 23.42S149.40E
Ḑubā Saudi Arabia **64** 27.21N 35.40E
Dubai *see* Dubayy U.A.E. **65**
Dubawnt *r.* Canada **99** 62.50N102.00W
Dubawnt L. Canada **101** 63.04N101.42W
Dubayy U.A.E. **65** 25.13N 55.17E
Dubbo Australia **93** 32.16S148.41E
Dubica Croatia **31** 45.11N 16.48E
Dublin Rep. of Ire. **15** 53.21N 6.18W
Dublin *d.* Rep. of Ire. **15** 53.20N 6.18W
Dublin U.S.A. **113** 32.31N 82.54W
Dublin B. Rep. of Ire. **15** 53.20N 6.09W
Dubno Ukraine **37** 50.28N 25.40E
Dubois Idaho U.S.A. **108** 44.10N112.14W
Du Bois Penn. U.S.A. **114** 41.07N 78.46W
Dubovka Russian Fed. **45** 49.04N 44.48E
Dubréka Guinea **76** 9.50N 13.32W
Dubrovitsa Ukraine **37** 51.38N 26.40E
Dubrovnik Croatia **31** 42.38N 18.07E
Dubuque U.S.A. **110** 42.30N 90.41W
Duchesne U.S.A. **108** 40.10N110.24W
Duchess Australia **90** 21.22S139.52E
Ducie I. Pacific Oc. **85** 24.40S124.48W
Du Coüedic, C. Australia **92** 36.00S136.10E
Duderstadt Germany **38** 51.31N 10.16E
Dudhnai India **63** 25.59N 90.44E
Dudinka Russian Fed. **51** 69.27N 86.13E
Dudley U.K. **13** 52.30N 2.05W
Dudna *r.* India **62** 19.07N 76.54E
Dudweiler Germany **39** 49.17N 7.02E
Duékoué Ivory Coast **76** 6.50N 7.22W
Duerna *r.* Spain **26** 42.19N 5.54W
Duero *r.* Spain *see* Douro *r.* Portugal **26**
Duff Creek *town* Australia **92** 28.28S135.51E
Dufftown U.K. **14** 57.27N 3.09W
Duga Poljana Yugo. **34** 43.15N 20.14E
Duga Resa Croatia **31** 45.27N 15.30E
Dugi *i.* Croatia **31** 44.00N 15.04E
Du Gué *r.* Canada **103** 57.20N 70.48W
Duifken Pt. Australia **90** 12.33S141.38E
Duisburg Germany **38** 51.25N 6.46E
Duitama Colombia **122** 5.50N 73.01W
Duiveland *i.* Neth. **16** 51.39N 4.00E
Dujuuma Somali Rep. **79** 1.14N 42.37E
Dukambiya Ethiopia **72** 14.42N 37.30E
Dukat Albania **34** 40.16N 19.32E
Duk Fadiat Sudan **73** 7.45N 31.25E
Duk Faiwil Sudan **73** 7.30N 31.29E
Dukhān Qatar **65** 25.24N 50.47E
Duki Pakistan **62** 30.09N 68.34E
Dukou China **52** 26.33N101.44E
Dukye Dzong Bhutan **63** 27.20N 89.30E
Dulce *r.* Argentina **124** 30.40S 62.00W
Duleek Rep. of Ire. **15** 53.39N 6.24W
Dülmen Germany **38** 51.51N 7.16E
Dulovo Bulgaria **37** 43.49N 27.09E
Duluth U.S.A. **110** 46.47N 92.06W
Dūmā Syria **66** 33.33N 36.24E
Dumaguete Phil. **59** 9.20N123.18E
Dumai Indonesia **58** 1.41N101.27E
Dumaran *i.* Phil. **58** 10.33N119.50E
Dumaresq *r.* Australia **93** 28.40S150.28E
Dumaring Indonesia **58** 1.36N118.12E
Dumas Ark. U.S.A. **111** 33.53N 91.29W
Dumas Tex. U.S.A. **111** 35.52N101.58W
Dumbarton U.K. **14** 55.57N 4.35W
Dumbleyung Australia **89** 33.18S117.42E
Dumbrăveni Romania **37** 46.14N 24.35E
Dum-Dum India **63** 22.35N 88.24E
Dumfries U.K. **14** 55.04N 3.37W
Dumfries and Galloway *d.* U.K. **14** 55.05N 3.40W
Dumka India **63** 24.16N 87.15E
Dumoine *r.* Canada **105** 46.13N 77.50W
Dumoine, Lac *l.* Canada **105** 46.53N 77.54W
Dumont, Lac *l.* Canada **105** 46.04N 76.28W
Dumraon India **63** 25.33N 84.09E
Dumyāţ Egypt **66** 31.26N 31.48E
Duna *r.* Hungary *see* Danube *r.* Europe **31**
Dunaföldvár Hungary **31** 46.48N 18.55E
Dunajec *r.* Poland **37** 50.15N 20.44E
Dunajská Streda Slovakia **37** 48.01N 17.35E
Dunany Pt. Rep. of Ire. **15** 53.51N 6.15W
Dunărea *r.* Romania *see* Danube *r.* Europe **37**
Dunării, Delta *f.* Romania **37** 45.05N 29.45E
Dunaújváros Hungary **31** 46.58N 18.57E
Dunav *r.* Yugo. *see* Danube *r.* Europe **37**
Dunav *r.* Bulgaria *see* Danube *r.* Europe **37**
Duna-völgyi-főcsatorno *r.* Hungary **31** 46.12N 18.56E
Dunbar U.K. **14** 56.00N 2.31W
Dunbar U.S.A. **114** 38.22N 81.45W
Dunblane U.K. **14** 56.12N 3.59W
Dunboyne Rep. of Ire. **15** 53.26N 6.30W
Duncan Canada **100** 48.45N123.40W
Duncan *r.* Canada **100** 50.11N116.57W
Duncan U.S.A. **111** 34.30N 97.57W
Duncan, C. Canada **102** 52.40N 80.48W
Duncan L. N.W.T. Canada **100** 62.51N113.58W
Duncan L. Que. Canada **102** 53.35N 77.55W
Duncannon U.S.A. **114** 40.23N 77.02W
Duncansby Head U.K. **14** 58.39N 3.01W
Dundalk Canada **104** 44.10N 80.24W
Dundalk Rep. of Ire. **15** 54.01N 6.25W
Dundalk U.S.A. **115** 39.15N 76.31W
Dundalk B. Rep. of Ire. **15** 53.55N 6.17W
Dundas Canada **104** 43.16N 79.58W
Dundas, L. Australia **89** 32.35S121.50E
Dundas I. Canada **100** 54.33N130.50W
Dundas Str. Australia **90** 11.20S131.35E
Dundee R.S.A. **80** 28.09S 30.14E
Dundee U.K. **14** 56.28N 3.00W
Dundee Mich. U.S.A. **104** 41.57N 83.40W
Dundee N.Y. U.S.A. **114** 42.31N 76.59W
Dundgovĭ *d.* Mongolia **54** 45.00N106.00E
Dundrum U.K. **15** 54.16N 5.51W
Dundrum B. U.K. **15** 54.12N 5.46W
Dunedin New Zealand **86** 45.52S170.30E
Dunedin U.S.A. **113** 28.02N 82.47W
Dunedoo Australia **93** 32.00S149.25E
Dunfermline U.K. **14** 56.04N 3.29W
Dungannon U.K. **15** 54.31N 6.47W
Dūngarpur India **62** 23.50N 73.43E
Dungarvan Rep. of Ire. **15** 52.06N 7.39W
Dungeness *c.* U.K. **13** 50.55N 0.58E
Dungiven U.K. **15** 54.56N 6.56W
Dungog Australia **93** 32.24S151.46E
Dungu Zaïre **79** 3.40N 28.40E
Dunhuang China **52** 40.00N 94.40E
Dunkeld Qld. Australia **91** 26.55S148.00E
Dunkeld Vic. Australia **92** 37.40S142.23E
Dunkeld U.K. **14** 56.34N 3.36W
Dunkerque France **16** 51.02N 2.23E
Dunk I. Australia **90** 17.56S146.10E
Dunkirk *see* Dunkerque France **16**
Dunkirk U.S.A. **114** 42.29N 79.20W
Dunkwa Central Ghana **76** 5.59N 1.45W
Dun Laoghaire Rep. of Ire. **15** 53.17N 6.09W
Dunlap U.S.A. **110** 41.51N 95.36W
Dunleer Rep. of Ire. **15** 53.49N 6.24W
Dun-le-Palestel France **20** 46.17N 1.48E

Dunmahon to **Elleker**

Dunmahon Rep. of Ire. **15** 52.09N 7.23W
Dunmarra Australia **90** 16.37S133.22E
Dunmore U.S.A. **115** 41.25N 75.38W
Dunnet Head U.K. **14** 58.40N 3.23W
Dunning U.S.A. **110** 41.50N100.06W
Dunnville Canada **104** 42.54N 79.36W
Dunolly Australia **92** 36.50S143.45E
Dunoon U.K. **14** 55.57N 4.57W
Dunqulah Sudan **72** 19.10N 30.29E
Dunqunâb Sudan **72** 21.06N 37.05E
Duns U.K. **14** 55.47N 2.20W
Dunsborough Australia **89** 33.37S115.06E
Dunshaughlin Rep. of Ire. **15** 53.30N 6.34W
Dunstable U.K. **13** 51.53N 0.32W
Dunstan Mts. New Zealand **86** 44.45S169.45E
Dunster Canada **100** 53.08N119.50W
Dun-sur-Auron France **19** 46.53N 2.34E
Dun-sur-Meuse France **19** 49.23N 5.11E
Dunyâpur Pakistan **62** 29.48N 71.44E
Duolun China **54** 42.09N116.21E
Duong Dong Vietnam **56** 10.12N103.57E
Dupont U.S.A. **112** 38.53N 85.30W
Duque de Caxias Brazil **126** 22.47S 43.18W
Duquesne U.S.A. **114** 40.21N 79.51W
Du Quoin U.S.A. **111** 38.01N 89.14W
Dūrâ Jordan **67** 31.30N 35.02E
Duran U.S.A. **109** 34.28N105.24W
Durance *r.* France **21** 43.55N 4.44E
Durand U.S.A. **104** 42.55N 83.59W
Durango Mexico **116** 24.01N104.00W
Durango *d.* Mexico **111** 24.30N104.00W
Durango Spain **26** 43.10N 2.37W
Durango U.S.A. **108** 37.16N107.53W
Durant U.S.A. **111** 34.00N 96.23W
Duras France **20** 44.41N 0.11E
Duraton *r.* Spain **26** 41.37N 4.07W
Durazno Uruguay **125** 33.22S 56.31W
Durban R.S.A. **80** 29.50S 30.59E
Durbe Latvia **41** 56.35N 21.21E
Durbin U.S.A. **114** 38.33N 79.50W
Durdevac Croatia **31** 46.03N 17.04E
Dureji Pakistan **62** 25.53N 67.18E
Düren Germany **38** 50.48N 6.28E
Durg India **63** 21.11N 81.17E
Durgâpur India **63** 23.29N 87.20E
Durham Canada **104** 44.10N 80.49W
Durham U.K. **12** 54.47N 1.34W
Durham *d.* U.K. **12** 54.42N 1.45W
Durham N.C. U.S.A. **113** 36.00N 78.54W
Durham N.H. U.S.A. **115** 43.08N 70.56W
Durham Sud Canada **105** 45.39N 72.19W
Durlston Head *c.* U.K. **13** 50.35N 1.58W
Durmitor *mtn.* Yugo. **31** 43.08N 19.01E
Durness U.K. **14** 58.33N 4.45W
Durrës Albania **34** 41.19N 19.26E
Durrow Rep. of Ire. **15** 52.51N 7.25W
Dursey Head Rep. of Ire. **15** 51.35N 10.15W
Durūz, Jabal ad *mtn.* Syria **66** 32.42N 36.42E
D'Urville I. New Zealand **86** 40.45S173.50E
Dushak Turkmenistan **50** 37.13N 60.01E
Dushan China **55** 25.50N107.30E
Dushanbe Tajikistan **52** 38.38N 68.51E
Dushore U.S.A. **115** 41.31N 76.24W
Duskotna Bulgaria **29** 42.52N 27.10E
Düsseldorf Germany **38** 51.12N 6.47E
Dutch Creek *town* Canada **100** 50.18N115.58W
Dutlhe Botswana **80** 23.55S 23.47E
Dutton Canada **104** 42.39N 81.30W
Dutton, L. Australia **92** 31.49S137.08E
Duxbury U.S.A. **115** 42.02N 70.40W
Duxun China **55** 23.57N117.37E
Duyun China **55** 26.12N107.29E
Dve Mogili Bulgaria **34** 43.36N 25.52E
Dvina *r.* Europe **9** 57.03N 24.00E
Dvinskaya Guba *b.* Russian Fed. **44** 64.40N 39.30E
Dwarda Australia **89** 32.45S116.23E
Dwârka India **62** 22.14N 68.58E
Dwellingup Australia **89** 32.42S116.04E
Dwight Canada **104** 45.21N 78.58W
Dyatlovichi Belorussia **37** 52.08N 30.49E
Dyatlovo Belorussia **37** 53.28N 25.28E
Dyer, C. Canada **99** 67.45N 61.45W
Dyer Bay *town* Canada **104** 45.10N 81.18W
Dyérem *r.* Cameroon **77** 6.36N 13.10E
Dyer Plateau Antarctica **128** 70.00S 65.00W
Dyersburg U.S.A. **111** 36.03N 89.23W
Dyfed *d.* U.K. **13** 52.00N 4.17W
Dykh Tau *mtn.* Russian Fed. **45** 43.04N 43.10E
Dymer Ukraine **37** 50.50N 30.20E
Dyulevo Bulgaria **29** 42.22N 27.10E
Dyultydag *mtn.* Russian Fed. **65** 41.55N 46.52E
Dzamïn Üüd Mongolia **54** 43.50N111.53E
Dzerzhinsk Belorussia **37** 53.40N 27.01E
Dzerzhinsk Russian Fed. **44** 56.15N 43.30E
Dzhambul Kazakhstan **52** 42.50N 71.25E
Dzhankoy Ukraine **23** 45.42N 34.23E
Dzhardzhan Russian Fed. **51** 68.49N124.08E
Dzhelinde Russian Fed. **51** 70.09N114.00E
Dzhetygara Kazakhstan **50** 52.14N 61.10E
Dzhezkazgan Kazakhstan **50** 47.48N 67.24E
Dzhizak Uzbekistan **50** 40.06N 67.45E
Dzhugdzhur, Khrebet *mts.* Russian Fed. **51** 57.30N138.00E
Dzhurin Ukraine **37** 48.40N 28.16E
Działdowo Poland **37** 53.15N 20.10E
Dzierżoniów Poland **36** 50.44N 16.39E
Dzodze Ghana **76** 6.14N 1.00E

E

Eabamet L. Canada **102** 51.30N 88.00W
Eads U.S.A. **110** 38.29N102.47W
Eagle *r.* Canada **103** 53.35N 57.25W
Eagle U.S.A. **110** 39.39N106.50W
Eagle Butte *town* U.S.A. **110** 45.00N101.14W
Eagle Grove U.S.A. **110** 42.40N 93.54W
Eagle L. U.S.A. **112** 46.17N 69.20W
Eagle Lake *town* Canada **104** 45.08N 78.29W
Eagle Lake *town* U.S.A. **112** 47.02N 68.36W
Eagle Pass *town* U.S.A. **111** 28.43N100.30W
Eagle River *town* U.S.A. **110** 45.55N 89.15W
Ealing U.K. **13** 51.31N 0.20W
Earlimart U.S.A. **109** 35.53N119.16W
Earlville U.S.A. **115** 42.44N 75.33W
Earn *r.* U.K. **14** 56.21N 3.18W
Earn, Loch U.K. **14** 56.23N 4.12W
Easingwold U.K. **12** 54.08N 1.11W
Easky Rep. of Ire. **15** 54.17N 8.58W
Easley U.S.A. **113** 34.50N 82.34W
East *r.* Canada **104** 45.20N 79.17W
East Alligator *r.* Australia **90** 12.25S132.58E
East Anglian Heights *hills* U.K. **13** 52.03N 0.15E
East Angus Canada **105** 45.29N 71.40W
East Aurora U.S.A. **114** 42.46N 78.37W
East B. U.S.A. **111** 29.30N 94.35W
Eastbourne U.K. **13** 50.46N 0.18E
East Brady U.S.A. **114** 40.59N 79.37W
East Broughton Canada **105** 46.14N 71.05W
East C. New Zealand **86** 37.45S178.30E
East Caroline Basin Pacific Oc. **84** 3.00N147.00E
East China Sea Asia **53** 29.00N125.00E
East Dereham U.K. **11** 52.40N 0.57E
Easter I. *see* Pascua, Isla de *i.* Pacific Oc. **85**
Eastern *d.* Ghana **76** 6.20N 0.45W
Eastern *d.* Kenya **79** 0.00 38.00E
Eastern Desert *see* Sharqīyah, Aş Şaḩrā' ash *des.* Egypt **66**
Eastern Ghâts *mts.* India **61** 16.30N 80.30E
Eastern-Indian-Antarctic Basin *f.* Indian Oc. **49** 56.00S110.00E
Easterville Canada **101** 53.06N 99.53W
East Falkland *i.* Falkland Is. **125** 51.45S 58.50W
East Grand Forks U.S.A. **110** 47.56N 96.55W
East Grinstead U.K. **13** 51.08N 0.01W
Easthampton Mass. U.S.A. **115** 42.16N 72.40W
East Hampton N.Y. U.S.A. **115** 40.58N 72.11W
East Hartford U.S.A. **115** 41.46N 72.39W
East Haven U.S.A. **115** 41.17N 72.52W
East Ilsley U.K. **13** 51.33N 1.15W
East Kilbride U.K. **14** 55.46N 4.09W
East Lansing U.S.A. **104** 42.44N 84.29W
Eastleigh U.K. **13** 50.58N 1.21W
East Liverpool U.S.A. **114** 40.38N 80.35W
East London R.S.A. **80** 33.00S 27.54E
Eastmain Canada **102** 52.15N 78.30W
Eastmain *r.* Canada **102** 52.15N 78.30W
Eastman Canada **105** 45.18N 72.19W
Easton Md. U.S.A. **115** 38.46N 76.04W
Easton Penn. U.S.A. **115** 40.42N 75.12W
Easton Wash. U.S.A. **108** 47.14N121.11W
East Orange U.S.A. **115** 40.46N 74.14W
East Pacific Ridge Pacific Oc. **85** 15.00S112.00W
East Palestine U.S.A. **114** 40.50N 80.33W
East Point *town* U.S.A. **113** 33.41N 84.29W
Eastport U.S.A. **115** 40.49N 72.44W
East Providence U.S.A. **115** 41.49N 71.23W
East Retford U.K. **12** 53.19N 0.55W
East Rochester U.S.A. **114** 43.07N 77.29W
East Springfield U.S.A. **114** 41.57N 80.28W
East St. Louis U.S.A. **110** 38.34N 90.04W
East Sussex *d.* U.K. **13** 50.56N 0.12E
East Sydenham *r.* Canada **104** 42.35N 82.23W
East Tawas U.S.A. **104** 44.17N 83.29W
Eaton U.S.A. **110** 40.32N104.42W
Eau Claire U.S.A. **110** 44.50N 91.30W
Eau-Claire, Lac à l' *l.* Canada **102** 56.10N 74.30W
Eauripik *i.* Federated States of Micronesia **59** 6.42N143.04E
Eaurpik-N. Guinea Rise Pacific Oc. **84** 2.00N141.00E
Eauze France **20** 43.52N 0.06E
Eban Nigeria **77** 9.41N 4.54E
Ebbw Vale U.K. **13** 51.47N 3.12W
Ebebiyin Equat. Guinea **78** 2.09N 11.20E
Ebeltoft Denmark **42** 56.12N 10.41E
Ebensburg U.S.A. **114** 40.29N 78.44W
Ebensee Austria **39** 47.48N 13.46E
Eberbach Germany **39** 49.28N 8.59E
Ebermannstadt Germany **38** 49.23N 11.13E
Ebern Germany **39** 50.05N 10.47E
Eberndorf Austria **31** 46.35N 14.38E
Ebersbach Germany **38** 51.00N 14.35E
Ebersberg Germany **39** 48.04N 11.59E
Eberstein Austria **31** 46.48N 14.34E
Eberswalde Germany **38** 52.50N 13.49E
Ebingen Germany **39** 48.13N 9.01E
Ebinur Hu *l.* China **52** 45.00N 83.00E
Ebola *r.* Zaïre **73** 3.20N 20.57E
Eboli Italy **33** 40.37N 15.04E
Ebolowa Cameroon **78** 2.56N 11.11E
Ebon *i.* Pacific Oc. **84** 4.38N168.43E
Ebony Namibia **80** 22.05S 15.15E
Ebro *r.* Spain **25** 40.43N 0.54E
Ebro, Delta del *f.* Spain **25** 40.43N 0.54E
Ebro, Embalse del *resr.* Spain **26** 43.00N 4.00W
Ecclefechan U.K. **12** 55.03N 3.18W
Eceabat Turkey **34** 40.11N 26.21E
Echeng China **55** 30.26N114.00E
Echo Bay *town* Canada **104** 46.29N 84.02W
Echternach Lux. **16** 49.49N 6.25E
Echuca Australia **93** 36.10S144.20E
Écija Spain **27** 37.32N 5.05W
Eckernförde Germany **38** 54.28N 9.50E
Écommoy France **18** 47.50N 0.16E
Ecuador S. America **122** 1.40S 79.00W
Écueillé France **18** 47.05N 1.21E
Ēd Ethiopia **72** 13.52N 41.40E
Ed Sweden **42** 58.55N 11.55E
Edam Neth. **16** 52.30N 5.02E
Eday *i.* U.K. **10** 59.11N 2.47W
Eddrachillis B. U.K. **14** 58.17N 5.15W
Eddystone Pt. Australia **91** 40.58S148.12E
Ede Neth. **16** 52.03N 5.40E
Ede Nigeria **77** 7.45N 4.26E
Edea Cameroon **78** 3.47N 10.15E
Edehon L. Canada **101** 60.25N 97.15W
Eden Australia **93** 37.04S149.54E
Eden Canada **104** 42.47N 80.46W
Eden *r.* Cumbria U.K. **12** 54.57N 3.02W
Eden U.S.A. **108** 42.03N109.26W
Edenburg R.S.A. **80** 29.44S 25.55E
Edendale New Zealand **86** 46.19S168.47E
Edenderry Rep. of Ire. **15** 53.21N 7.05W
Edenhope Australia **92** 37.04S141.20E
Edenton U.S.A. **113** 36.04N 76.39W
Edeowie Australia **92** 31.28S138.29E
Eder *r.* Germany **38** 51.13N 9.27E
Ederny U.K. **15** 54.32N 7.40W
Edgartown U.S.A. **115** 41.23N 70.31W
Edgeley U.S.A. **110** 46.22N 98.43W
Edgeöya *i.* Arctic Oc. **128** 77.45N 22.30E
Edgeworthstown Rep. of Ire. **15** 53.42N 7.38W
Edgington Canada **104** 45.23N 79.47W
Édhessa Greece **34** 40.48N 22.05E
Ediacara Australia **92** 30.18S137.50E
Edina Liberia **76** 6.01N 10.10W
Edinboro U.S.A. **114** 41.52N 80.08W
Edinburgh U.K. **14** 55.57N 3.13W
Edirne Turkey **34** 41.40N 26.34E
Edithburgh Australia **92** 35.06S137.44E
Edjudina Australia **89** 29.48S122.23E
Edmond U.S.A. **111** 35.39N 97.29W
Edmonton Canada **100** 53.30N113.30W
Edmundston Canada **103** 47.22N 68.20W
Edna U.S.A. **111** 28.59N 96.39W
Edo *r.* Japan **57** 35.37N139.53E
Edo *d.* Nigeria **77** 6.20N 5.55E
Edolo Italy **30** 46.11N 10.20E
Edounga Gabon **78** 0.03S 13.43E
Edremit Turkey **29** 39.35N 27.02E
Edremit Körfezi *b.* Turkey **34** 39.30N 26.45E
Edsbruk Sweden **43** 58.02N 16.28E
Edson Canada **100** 53.35N116.26W
Edward, L. Uganda / Zaïre **79** 0.30S 29.30E
Edwards Plateau *f.* U.S.A. **111** 31.20N101.00W
Eeklo Belgium **16** 51.11N 3.34E
Eel *r.* U.S.A. **108** 40.40N124.20W
Efate *i.* Vanuatu **84** 17.40S168.25E
Eferding Austria **39** 48.18N 14.02E
Effingham U.S.A. **110** 39.07N 88.33W
Ega *r.* Spain **25** 42.19N 1.55W
Egadi, Isole *is.* Italy **32** 38.00N 12.10E
Egaña Argentina **125** 36.57S 59.06W
Eganville Canada **105** 45.32N 77.06W
Egbe Nigeria **77** 8.13N 5.31E
Egeland U.S.A. **110** 48.38N 99.10W
Eger Hungary **37** 47.54N 20.23E
Egersund Norway **42** 58.27N 6.00E
Egerton, Mt. Australia **88** 24.44S117.40E
Eggenfelden Germany **39** 48.25N 12.46E
Egg Harbor U.S.A. **115** 39.32N 74.39W
Égletons France **20** 45.24N 2.03E
Egmont, Mt. New Zealand **86** 39.20S174.05E
Eğridir Turkey **64** 37.52N 30.51E
Eğridir Gölü *l.* Turkey **64** 38.04N 30.55E
Egtved Denmark **42** 55.37N 9.18E
Egypt Africa **72** 26.00N 30.00E
Ehingen Germany **39** 48.17N 9.43E
Eiao *i.* Îs. Marquises **85** 8.00S140.40W
Eibar Spain **26** 43.11N 2.28W
Eibiswald Austria **31** 46.41N 15.15E
Eichstätt Germany **38** 48.54N 11.12E
Eidsvåg Norway **40** 62.47N 8.03E
Eidsvold Australia **90** 25.23S151.08E
Eidsvoll Norway **42** 60.19N 11.14E
Eifel *f.* Germany **39** 50.10N 6.40E
Eigg *i.* U.K. **14** 56.53N 6.09W
Eighty Mile Beach *f.* Australia **88** 19.00S121.00E
Eil, Loch U.K. **14** 56.51N 5.12W
Eildon, L. Australia **93** 37.10S146.00E
Eilenburg Germany **38** 51.27N 12.37E
Einasleigh Australia **90** 18.31S144.05E
Einbeck Germany **38** 51.49N 9.52E
Eindhoven Neth. **16** 51.26N 5.30E
Einsiedeln Switz. **39** 47.08N 8.45E
Eirunepé Brazil **122** 6.40S 69.52W
Eiseb *r.* Namibia **80** 20.26S 20.05E
Eisenach Germany **38** 50.59N 10.19E
Eisenberg Germany **38** 50.58N 11.53E
Eisenerz Austria **36** 47.33N 14.53E
Eisenhut *mtn.* Austria **36** 47.00N 13.45E
Eisenhüttenstadt Germany **38** 52.10N 14.39E
Eisfeld Germany **39** 50.26N 10.54E
Eišiškes Lithuania **37** 54.09N 24.55E
Eisleben Germany **38** 51.31N 11.32E
Eitorf Germany **38** 50.46N 7.26E
Ejby Denmark **42** 55.26N 9.57E
Ejde Faroe Is. **10** 62.03N 7.06W
Ejea de los Caballeros Spain **25** 42.08N 1.08W
Ejin Qi China **52** 41.50N100.50E
Ejura Ghana **76** 7.24N 1.20W
Ekalaka U.S.A. **108** 45.53N104.33W
Eket Nigeria **77** 4.39N 7.56E
Eketahuna New Zealand **86** 40.39S175.44E
Ekhínos Greece **34** 41.17N 24.59E
Ekibastuz Kazakhstan **50** 51.45N 75.22E
Ekimchan Russian Fed. **51** 53.09N133.00E
Eksjö Sweden **43** 57.40N 14.57E
Ekträsk Sweden **40** 64.29N 19.50E
Ekuku Zaïre **78** 0.42S 21.38E
Ekwan *r.* Canada **102** 53.30N 84.00W
El Aaiún W. Sahara **74** 27.09N 13.12W
El Alia Tunisia **32** 37.10N 10.03E
Elands *r.* Trans. R.S.A. **80** 24.52S 29.20E
El Arahal Spain **27** 37.16N 5.33W
El Arco Mexico **109** 28.00N113.25W
El Arenal Spain **25** 39.30N 2.45E
El Asnam Algeria **75** 36.10N 1.20E
Elassón Greece **34** 39.54N 22.11E
Elat Israel **66** 29.33N 34.56E
Elâzig Turkey **64** 38.41N 39.14E
Elba *i.* Italy **30** 42.46N 10.17E
El Barco de Avilla Spain **26** 40.21N 5.31W
El Barco de Valdeorras Spain **26** 42.25N 6.59W
El Barril Mexico **109** 28.22N113.00W
Elbasan Albania **34** 41.09N 20.09E
Elbasan Berat *d.* Albania **34** 40.58N 20.00E
El Baúl Venezuela **122** 8.59N 68.16W
Elbe *r.* Germany **38** 53.50N 10.00E
Elbe-Havel-Kanal Germany **38** 52.23N 12.15E
Elbe-Lübeck-Kanal Germany **38** 53.50N 10.36E
El Beni *d.* Bolivia **124** 14.00S 65.30W
Elbert, Mt. U.S.A. **110** 39.07N106.27W
Elberton U.S.A. **113** 34.05N 82.54W
Elbeuf France **18** 49.17N 1.00E
Elbistan Turkey **64** 38.14N 37.11E
Elblag Poland **37** 54.10N 19.25E
El Bonillo Spain **26** 38.57N 2.32W
Elbrus *mtn.* Russian Fed. **45** 43.21N 42.29E
Elburg Neth. **16** 52.27N 5.50E
El Burgo de Osma Spain **26** 41.35N 3.04W
Elburz Mts. *see* Alborz, Reshteh-ye Kūhhā-ye *ye* Iran **65**
El Cajon U.S.A. **109** 32.48N116.58W
El Callao Venezuela **122** 7.18N 61.48W
El Campo U.S.A. **111** 29.12N 96.16W
El Casco Mexico **111** 25.34N104.35W
El Cenajo, Embalse de *resr.* Spain **27** 38.25N 2.00W
El Centro U.S.A. **109** 32.48N115.34W
Elche Spain **25** 38.15N 0.42W
Elche de la Sierra Spain **25** 38.27N 2.03W
Elcho U.S.A. **110** 45.26N 89.11W
Elcho I. Australia **90** 11.55S135.45E
El Corral Mexico **111** 25.09N 97.58W
El Cozón Mexico **109** 31.18N112.29W
El Cuy Argentina **125** 39.57S 68.20W
Elda Spain **25** 38.29N 0.47W
Elde *r.* Germany **36** 53.17N 12.40E
El Der Ethiopia **71** 5.08N 43.08E
Elder, L. Australia **92** 30.39S140.13E
El Desemboque Mexico **109** 29.30N112.27W
El Djouf *des.* Mauritania **74** 20.30N 7.30W
Eldon U.S.A. **110** 38.21N 93.35W
Eldorado Canada **101** 59.35N108.30W
El Dorado Ark. U.S.A. **111** 33.13N 92.40W
El Dorado Kans. U.S.A. **111** 37.49N 96.52W
El Dorado Venezuela **122** 6.45N 61.37W
Eldoret Kenya **79** 0.31N 35.17E
Eldsdro Sweden **43** 59.53N 18.33E
Electra U.S.A. **111** 34.02N 98.55W
El Eglab *f.* Algeria **74** 26.30N 4.15W
Elei, Wâdi Sudan **72** 22.04N 34.27E
Eleja Latvia **41** 56.26N 23.42E
Elektrosal Russian Fed. **44** 55.46N 38.30E
Elena Bulgaria **34** 42.56N 25.53E
Elephant Butte Resr. U.S.A. **109** 33.19N107.10W
Elephant I. Atlantic Oc. **121** 61.00S 55.00W
El Eulma Algeria **75** 36.09N 5.41E
Eleuthera I. Bahamas **113** 25.15N 76.20W
Elevsís Greece **35** 38.02N 23.33E
Elevtheroúpolis Greece **34** 40.55N 24.16E
El Ferrol Spain **26** 43.29N 8.14W
Elgå Norway **41** 62.11N 11.07E
Elgenfield Canada **104** 43.10N 81.22W
Elgin *l.* Ont. Canada **105** 44.36N 76.13W
Elgin *Man.* Canada **101** 49.26N100.15W
Elgin U.K. **14** 57.39N 3.20W
Elgin Ill. U.S.A. **110** 42.03N 88.19W
Elgin Nev. U.S.A. **108** 37.21N114.30W
Elgin Oreg. U.S.A. **108** 45.34N117.55W
Elgin Tex. U.S.A. **111** 30.21N 97.22W
El Golea Algeria **75** 30.34N 2.53E
Elgon, Mt. Kenya / Uganda **79** 1.07N 34.35E
El Grove Spain **26** 42.30N 8.52W
El Haouaria Tunisia **32** 37.03N 11.02E
Elida U.S.A. **111** 33.57N103.39W
Elim Namibia **80** 17.47S 15.30E
Elin Pelin Bulgaria **34** 42.40N 23.38E
Elista Russian Fed. **45** 46.18N 44.14E
Elizabeth Australia **92** 34.45S138.39E
Elizabeth N.J. U.S.A. **115** 40.40N 74.11W
Elizabeth W.Va. U.S.A. **114** 39.04N 81.24W
Elizabeth City U.S.A. **113** 36.18N 76.16W
Elizabethtown Ky. U.S.A. **113** 37.41N 85.51W
Elizabethtown N.Y. U.S.A. **105** 44.13N 73.36W
Elizabethtown Penn. U.S.A. **115** 40.09N 76.36W
El Jadida Morocco **74** 33.16N 8.30W
Elk *r.* Canada **100** 49.10N115.14W
Elk Poland **37** 53.50N 22.22E
Elk *r.* U.S.A. **114** 38.21N 81.38W
El Kairouan Tunisia **75** 35.41N 10.07E
El Kala Algeria **32** 36.50N 8.30E
El Kasserine Tunisia **75** 35.11N 8.48E
Elk City U.S.A. **111** 35.25N 99.25W
El Kef Tunisia **75** 36.11N 8.43E
El-Kelâa-des-Srarhna Morocco **74** 32.02N 7.23W
El Kerē Ethiopia **73** 5.48N 42.10E
Elkhart Ind. U.S.A. **110** 41.52N 85.56W
Elkhart Kans. U.S.A. **111** 37.00N101.54W
El Khnâchich *f.* Mali **76** 21.50N 3.45W
Elkhorn Canada **101** 49.58N101.14W
Elkhovo Bulgaria **34** 42.09N 26.36E
Elkins N.Mex. U.S.A. **109** 33.41N104.04W
Elkins W.Va. U.S.A. **114** 38.55N 79.51W
Elkland U.S.A. **114** 41.59N 77.21W
Elko U.S.A. **108** 40.50N115.46W
Elkton Md. U.S.A. **115** 39.36N 75.50W
Elkton Va. U.S.A. **114** 38.25N 78.38W
Elleker Australia **89** 34.55S117.40E

Ellen, Mt. to **Everett**

Ellen, Mt. U.S.A. **106** 38.06N110.50W
Ellenboro U.S.A. **114** 39.17N 81.04W
Ellenburg U.S.A. **105** 44.54N 73.51W
Ellendale Australia **88** 17.56S124.48E
Ellensburg U.S.A. **108** 47.00N120.32W
Ellenville U.S.A. **115** 41.43N 74.24W
Ellesmere I. Canada **99** 78.00N 82.00W
Ellesmere Port U.K. **12** 53.17N 2.55W
Ellicottville U.S.A. **114** 42.17N 78.40W
Elliot R.S.A. **80** 31.19S 27.49E
Elliot Lake *town* Canada **104** 46.23N 82.39W
Elliott Australia **90** 17.33S133.31E
Ellis U.S.A. **110** 38.56N 99.34W
Elliston Australia **92** 33.39S134.55E
Ellon U.K. **14** 57.22N 2.05W
Ellora India **62** 20.01N 75.10E
Ellwangen Germany **39** 48.57N 10.07E
Ellwood City U.S.A. **114** 40.50N 80.17W
Elm Switz. **39** 46.55N 9.11E
El Mahdía Tunisia **75** 35.30N 11.04E
Elmali Turkey **64** 36.43N 29.56E
El Maneadero Mexico **109** 31.45N116.35W
Elmer U.S.A. **115** 39.36N 75.10W
El Metlaoui Tunisia **75** 34.20N 8.24E
Elmhurst U.S.A. **110** 41.54N 87.56W
Elmina Ghana **76** 5.07N 1.21W
Elmira Canada **104** 43.36N 80.33W
Elmira U.S.A. **114** 42.06N 76.49W
El Molinillo Spain **27** 39.28N 4.13W
Elmore Australia **93** 36.30S144.40E
El Mreiti *well* Mauritania **74** 23.29N 7.52W
El Mreyyé *f.* Mauritania **74** 19.30N 7.00W
Elmshorn Germany **38** 53.45N 9.39E
Elmsta Sweden **43** 59.58N 18.45E
Elmvale Canada **104** 44.35N 79.52W
Elne France **20** 42.36N 2.58E
El Niybo Ethiopia **73** 4.32N 39.59E
El Ouassi *well* Mali **76** 20.23N 0.12E
El Oued Algeria **75** 33.20N 6.53E
Eloy U.S.A. **109** 32.45N111.33W
El Paso U.S.A. **109** 31.45N106.29W
El Portal U.S.A. **108** 37.41N119.47W
El Prat de Llobregat Spain **25** 41.20N 2.06E
El Puente del Arzobispo Spain **27** 39.48N 5.10W
El Quelite Mexico **109** 23.32N106.28W
El Real Panama **117** 8.06N 77.42W
El Reno U.S.A. **111** 35.32N 97.57W
El Roba Kenya **79** 3.57N 40.01E
Elrose Canada **101** 51.13N108.01W
El Salto Mexico **109** 23.47N105.22W
El Salvador C. America **117** 13.30N 89.00W
Elsas Canada **102** 48.32N 82.55W
Elsdorf Germany **16** 50.56N 6.35E
Elsfleth Germany **38** 53.14N 8.28E
Elsinore U.S.A. **108** 38.41N112.09W
Elspe Germany **38** 51.09N 8.04E
Elsterwerda Germany **38** 51.28N 13.31E
El Sueco Mexico **109** 29.54N106.24W
El Tabacal Argentina **124** 23.15S 64.14W
El Tarf Algeria **32** 36.45N 8.20E
El Tigre Venezuela **122** 8.44N 64.18W
Eltmann Germany **39** 49.58N 10.40E
Elton, Ozero *l.* Russian Fed. **45** 49.10N 46.34E
El Turbio Argentina **125** 51.41S 72.05W
Elūru India **61** 16.45N 81.10E
Elvas Portugal **27** 38.53N 7.10W
Elvdal Norway **41** 61.38N 11.56E
Elven France **18** 47.44N 2.35W
El Vendrell Spain **25** 41.13N 1.32E
Elverum Norway **41** 60.53N 11.34E
Elvira Argentina **125** 35.15S 59.30W
El Wak Kenya **79** 2.45N 40.52E
Elwood Nebr. U.S.A. **110** 40.36N 99.52W
Elwood N.J. U.S.A. **115** 39.35N 74.43W
Ely U.K. **11** 52.24N 0.16E
Ely Minn. U.S.A. **110** 47.53N 91.52W
Ely Nev. U.S.A. **108** 39.15N114.53W
Elyria U.S.A. **114** 41.22N 82.06W
Elz *f.* Germany **39** 48.07N 7.45E
Emae *i.* Vanuatu **84** 17.04S168.24E
Emāmshahr Iran **65** 36.25N 55.00E
Emån *r.* Sweden **43** 57.08N 16.30E
Emba Kazakhstan **50** 48.47N 58.05E
Emba *r.* Kazakhstan **45** 46.38N 53.00E
Embarcación Argentina **124** 23.15S 64.10W
Embid Spain **25** 40.58N 1.43W
Embleton U.K. **12** 55.30N 1.37W
Embrun France **21** 44.34N 6.30E
Embu Kenya **79** 0.32S 37.28E
Emden Germany **38** 53.22N 7.12E
'Emeq Yizre'el *f.* Israel **67** 32.36N 35.14E
Emerald Australia **90** 23.32S148.10E
Emerson Canada **101** 49.00N 97.12W
Emi Koussi *mtn.* Chad **77** 19.58N 18.30E
Emilia-Romagna *d.* Italy **30** 44.35N 11.00E
Emlenton U.S.A. **114** 41.11N 79.43W
Emlichheim Germany **38** 52.36N 6.50E
Emmaboda Sweden **43** 56.38N 15.32E
Emmaste Estonia **41** 58.42N 22.36E
Emmaus U.S.A. **115** 40.32N 75.30W
Emmaville Australia **93** 29.25S151.39E
Emme *r.* Switz. **39** 47.13N 7.34E
Emmeloord Neth. **16** 52.43N 5.46E
Emmen Neth. **16** 52.48N 6.55E
Emmendingen Germany **39** 48.07N 7.50E
Emmerich Germany **38** 51.50N 6.15E
Emmett U.S.A. **108** 43.52N116.30W
Emmitsburg U.S.A. **114** 39.42N 77.20W
Emory Peak *mtn.* U.S.A. **111** 29.13N103.17W
Empalme Mexico **109** 27.58N110.51W
Empangeni R.S.A. **81** 28.45S 31.54E
Empedrado Argentina **124** 27.59S 58.47W
Empoli Italy **30** 43.43N 10.57E
Emporia Kans. U.S.A. **110** 38.24N 96.11W
Emporia Va. U.S.A. **113** 36.42N 77.33W
Emporium U.S.A. **114** 41.31N 78.14W
Ems *r.* Germany **38** 53.14N 7.25E
Emsdale Canada **104** 45.32N 79.19W
Emsdetten Germany **38** 52.10N 7.31E
Ems-Jade Kanal Germany **38** 53.29N 7.35E
Emyvale Rep. of Ire. **15** 54.20N 6.59W
Enard B. U.K. **14** 58.05N 5.20W
Encarnación Paraguay **126** 27.20S 55.50W
Enchi Ghana **76** 5.53N 2.48W
Encinal U.S.A. **111** 28.02N 99.21W
Encino U.S.A. **109** 34.39N105.28W
Encontada, Cerro de la *mtn.* Mexico **109** 27.03N112.31W
Encontrados Venezuela **122** 9.03N 72.14W
Encounter B. Australia **92** 35.35S138.44E
Endeavour Str. Australia **90** 10.50S142.15E
Endeh Indonesia **59** 8.51S121.40E
Enderbury I. Kiribati **84** 3.08S171.05W
Enderby Canada **100** 50.35N119.10W
Enderby Land *f.* Antarctica **128** 67.00S 53.00E
Enderlin U.S.A. **110** 46.37N 97.36W
Endicott U.S.A. **115** 42.06N 76.03W
Endicott Arm *f.* U.S.A. **100** 57.38N133.22W
Endicott Mts. U.S.A. **98** 68.00N152.00W
Endola Namibia **80** 17.37S 15.50E
Eneabba Australia **89** 29.48S115.16E
Enewetak *i.* Pacific Oc. **84** 11.30N162.15E
Enez Turkey **34** 40.44N 26.04E
Enfida Tunisia **75** 36.08N 10.22E
Enfield U.K. **13** 51.40N 0.05W
Enfield U.S.A. **115** 41.58N 72.36W
Engaño, C. Phil. **59** 18.30N122.20E
Engcobo R.S.A. **80** 31.39S 28.01E
'En Gedi Israel **66** 31.28N 35.23E
Engel's Russian Fed. **45** 51.30N 46.07E
Enggano *i.* Indonesia **58** 5.20S102.15E
Enghershatu *mtn.* Ethiopia **72** 16.40N 38.20E
Enghien Belgium **16** 50.42N 4.02E
England U.K. **12** 53.00N 2.00W
Englewood Colo. U.S.A. **108** 39.39N104.59W
Englewood Fla. U.S.A. **113** 26.58N 82.21W
English Bāzār India **63** 25.00N 88.09E
English Channel U.K. **13** 50.15N 1.00W
English River *town* Canada **102** 49.20N 91.00W
Enguera Spain **25** 38.59N 0.41W
'En Harod Israel **67** 32.33N 35.23E
Enid U.S.A. **111** 36.19N 97.48W
Enkhuizen Neth. **16** 52.42N 5.17E
Enköping Sweden **43** 59.38N 17.04E
Enna Italy **33** 37.34N 14.17E
Ennadai Canada **101** 61.08N100.53W
Ennadai L. Canada **101** 61.00N101.00W
Ennedi *f.* Chad **72** 17.15N 22.00E
Enneri Yoo *wadi* Chad **77** 19.24N 16.38E
Enngonia Australia **93** 29.20S145.53E
Ennis Rep. of Ire. **15** 52.51N 9.00W
Ennis U.S.A. **111** 32.20N 96.38W
Enniscorthy Rep. of Ire. **15** 52.30N 6.35W
Enniskillen U.K. **15** 54.21N 7.40W
Ennistymon Rep. of Ire. **15** 52.56N 9.18W
Enns *r.* Austria **36** 48.14N 14.22E
Enontekiö Finland **40** 68.23N 23.38E
Enosburg Falls U.S.A. **105** 44.55N 72.48W
Enping China **55** 22.11N112.18E
Ensay Australia **93** 37.24S147.52E
Enschede Neth. **16** 52.13N 6.54E
Ensenada Argentina **125** 34.51S 57.55W
Ensenada Baja Calif. Norte Mexico **109** 31.52N116.37W
Ensenada Nuevo León Mexico **111** 25.56N 97.50W
Enshi China **55** 30.18N109.29E
Enshū-nada *sea* Japan **57** 34.30N137.30E
Entebbe Uganda **79** 0.08N 32.29E
Enterprise Canada **100** 60.47N115.45W
Entinas, Punta *c.* Spain **27** 36.41N 2.46W
Entraygues France **20** 44.39N 2.34E
Entrepeñas, Embalse de *resr.* Spain **26** 40.34N 2.42W
Entre Ríos *d.* Argentina **125** 32.10S 59.00W
Entre Rios de Minas Brazil **126** 20.39S 44.06W
Entrocamento Portugal **27** 39.28N 8.28W
Entwistle Canada **100** 53.30N115.00W
Enugu Nigeria **77** 6.20N 7.29E
Enugu *d.* Nigeria **77** 6.30N 7.30E
Envalira, Port d' *pass* France / Andorra **20** 42.35N 1.45E
Envermeu France **18** 49.54N 1.16E
Envigado Colombia **122** 6.09N 75.35W
Enza *r.* Italy **30** 44.54N 10.31E
Enzan Japan **57** 35.42N138.44E
Eo *r.* Spain **26** 43.32N 7.03W
Eolie, Isole *is.* Italy **33** 38.50N 15.00E
Epanomi Greece **34** 40.26N 22.56E
Epe Neth. **16** 52.21N 5.59E
Epernay France **19** 49.03N 3.57E
Ephesus *site* Turkey **35** 37.55N 27.17E
Ephraim U.S.A. **108** 39.22N111.35W
Ephrata Penn. U.S.A. **115** 40.11N 76.10W
Ephrata Wash. U.S.A. **108** 47.19N119.33W
Epi *i.* Vanuatu **84** 16.43S168.15E
Épila Spain **25** 41.36N 1.17W
Épinal France **19** 48.11N 6.27E
Epitálion Greece **35** 37.37N 21.30E
Epping U.K. **13** 51.42N 0.07E
Epping U.S.A. **115** 43.02N 71.04W
Epsom U.K. **13** 51.20N 0.16W
Epte *r.* France **19** 49.04N 1.37E
Equateur *d.* Zaïre **78** 0.00 21.00E
Equatorial Guinea Africa **78** 2.00N 10.00E
Equerdreville France **18** 49.40N 1.40W
Era, Ozero *l.* Russian Fed. **45** 47.38N 45.18E
Eraclea Italy **30** 45.35N 12.40E
Erbach Germany **39** 49.40N 8.59E
Erciyaş Dagi *mtn.* Turkey **64** 38.33N 35.25E
Erdevik Yugo. **31** 45.07N 19.25E
Erding Germany **39** 48.18N 11.54E
Erdre *r.* France **18** 47.11N 1.31W
Erebus, Mt. Antarctica **128** 77.40S167.20E
Erechim Brazil **126** 27.35S 52.15W
Eregli Konya Turkey **64** 37.30N 34.02E
Eregli Zonguldak Turkey **64** 41.17N 31.26E
Erei, Monti *mts.* Italy **33** 37.30N 14.10E
Erenhot China **54** 43.48N112.00E
Ērer *r.* Ethiopia **71** 7.35N 42.05E
Eresma *r.* Spain **26** 41.26N 4.45W
Eresós Greece **35** 39.11N 25.57E
Erétria Greece **35** 38.23N 23.50E
Erfoud Morocco **74** 31.28N 4.10W
Erft *r.* Germany **16** 51.12N 6.45E
Erfurt Germany **38** 50.58N 11.01E
Ergani Turkey **64** 38.17N 39.44E
Ergel Mongolia **54** 43.08N109.05E
Ergene *r.* Turkey **29** 41.02N 26.22E
Erges *r. see* Erjas *r.* Spain **27**
Ergig *r.* Chad **77** 11.30N 15.30E
Eria *r.* Spain **26** 42.03N 5.44W
Erica Neth. **16** 52.44N 6.56E
Erice Italy **32** 38.02N 12.36E
Ericeira Portugal **27** 38.59N 9.25W
Erie U.S.A. **114** 42.08N 80.04W
Erie, L. Canada / U.S.A. **114** 42.15N 81.00W
Erieau Canada **104** 42.16N 81.56W
Eriksdale Canada **101** 50.52N 98.06W
Erímanthos *mtn.* Greece **35** 37.59N 21.51E
Erimo misaki *c.* Japan **57** 41.55N143.13E
Eriskay *i.* U.K. **14** 57.04N 7.17W
Erithraí Greece **35** 38.13N 23.19E
Eritrea *see* Ērtra *d.* Ethiopia **72**
Eritrea *f.* Ethiopia **72** 15.30N 38.00E
Erjas *r.* Portugal **27** 39.47N 7.00W
Erkelenz Germany **38** 51.05N 6.19E
Erkner Germany **38** 52.25N 13.45E
Erlangen Germany **38** 49.36N 11.01E
Erldunda Australia **90** 25.14S133.12E
Ermelo Neth. **16** 52.19N 5.38E
Ermelo R.S.A. **80** 26.30S 29.59E
Ermidas Portugal **27** 38.00N 8.23W
Ermióni Greece **35** 37.23N 23.15E
Ermoúpolis Greece **35** 37.26N 24.56E
Erne *r.* Rep. of Ire. **11** 54.30N 8.17W
Ernée France **18** 48.18N 0.56W
Ernest U.S.A. **114** 40.41N 79.10W
Erode India **60** 11.21N 77.43E
Eromanga *i.* Vanuatu **84** 18.45S169.05E
Erota Ethiopia **72** 16.13N 37.57E
Er Rachidia Morocco **74** 31.58N 4.25W
Errego Mozambique **79** 16.02S 37.11E
Er Reina Israel **67** 32.43N 35.18E
Errenteria *see* Rentería Spain **26**
Errigal Mtn. Rep. of Ire. **15** 55.02N 8.08W
Erris Head Rep. of Ire. **15** 54.19N 10.00W
Erstein France **19** 48.26N 7.40E
Ertix He *r.* Kazakhstan **52** 48.00N 84.20E
Ērtra *d.* Ethiopia **72** 15.30N 39.00E
Erudina Australia **92** 31.30S139.23E
Ervy-le-Châtel France **19** 48.02N 3.55E
Erzgebirge *mts.* Germany **38** 50.34N 13.00E
Erzin Russian Fed. **52** 50.16N 95.14E
Erzincan Turkey **64** 39.44N 39.30E
Erzurum Turkey **64** 39.57N 41.17E
Esbjerg Denmark **42** 55.28N 8.27E
Esbo *see* Espoo Finland **41**
Esca *r.* Spain **25** 42.37N 1.03W
Escalante U.S.A. **108** 37.47N111.36W
Escalón Mexico **111** 26.45N104.20W
Escalona Spain **26** 40.10N 4.24W
Escanaba U.S.A. **112** 45.47N 87.04W
Escandón, Puerto de *pass* Spain **25** 40.17N 1.00W
Esch Lux. **16** 49.31N 5.59E
Eschau France **19** 48.29N 7.43E
Eschwege Germany **38** 51.11N 10.04E
Eschweiler Germany **38** 50.49N 6.16E
Escondido *r.* Nicaragua **117** 11.58N 83.45W
Escondido U.S.A. **109** 33.07N117.05W
Escuinapa Mexico **109** 22.51N105.48W
Escuintla Guatemala **116** 14.18N 90.47W
Esens Germany **38** 53.39N 7.37E
Ésera *r.* Spain **25** 42.06N 0.15E
Eşfahān Iran **65** 32.42N 51.40E
Esgueva *r.* Spain **26** 41.40N 4.43W
Eshbol Israel **67** 31.27N 34.40E
Esher U.K. **13** 51.23N 0.22W
Eshkanān Iran **65** 27.10N 53.38E
Eshowe R.S.A. **80** 28.53S 31.29E
Eshta'ol Israel **67** 31.47N 35.00E
Esk *r.* N. Yorks. U.K. **12** 54.29N 0.37W
Eskifjördhur *town* Iceland **40** 65.05N 14.00W
Eskilstrup Denmark **42** 54.51N 11.54E
Eskilstuna Sweden **43** 59.22N 16.30E
Eskimo Point *town* Canada **101** 61.10N 94.03W
Eskişehir Turkey **64** 39.46N 30.30E
Esla *r.* Spain **26** 41.29N 6.03W
Eslāmābād-e-Gharb Iran **65** 34.08N 46.35E
Eslöv Sweden **43** 55.50N 13.20E
Esmeraldas Ecuador **122** 0.56N 79.40W
Espalion France **20** 44.31N 2.46E
Espanola Canada **104** 46.15N 81.46W
Espe Kazakhstan **50** 43.50N 74.10E
Espejo Spain **27** 37.41N 4.33W
Espelkamp Germany **38** 52.25N 8.36E
Esperance Australia **89** 33.49S121.52E
Esperance B. Australia **89** 33.51S121.53E
Esperanza Argentina **125** 31.30S 61.00W
Esperanza Mexico **109** 27.35N109.56W
Espichel, Cabo *c.* Portugal **27** 38.25N 9.13W
Espinal Colombia **122** 4.08N 75.00W
Espinhaço, Serra do *mts.* Brazil **126** 17.15S 43.10W
Espinho Portugal **26** 41.00N 8.39W
Espírito Santo *d.* Brazil **126** 20.00S 40.30W
Espíritu Santo I. Vanuatu **84** 15.50S166.50E
Espoo Finland **41** 60.13N 24.40E
Esposende Portugal **26** 41.32N 8.47W
Espuña, Sierra de *mts.* Spain **25** 37.50N 1.40E
Espungabera Mozambique **81** 20.28S 32.48E
Esquel Argentina **125** 42.55S 71.20W
Esquimalt Canada **100** 48.30N123.23W
Esquina Argentina **125** 30.00S 59.30W
Essaouira Morocco **74** 31.30N 9.47W
Essen Germany **38** 51.28N 7.01E
Essequibo *r.* Guyana **122** 6.30N 58.40W
Essex Canada **104** 42.10N 82.49W
Essex *d.* U.K. **13** 51.46N 0.30E
Essex U.S.A. **109** 34.45N115.15W
Essex Junction U.S.A. **105** 44.29N 73.07W
Essexville U.S.A. **104** 43.37N 83.50W
Esslingen Germany **39** 48.45N 9.16E
Essonne *d.* France **19** 48.36N 2.20E
Essoyes France **19** 48.04N 4.32E
Essoyla Russian Fed. **44** 61.47N 33.11E
Es Suki Sudan **73** 13.24N 33.55E
Est *d.* Burkina **76** 12.45N 0.25E
Est, Pointe de l' *c.* Canada **103** 49.08N 61.41W
Estaca de Bares, Punta de la *c.* Spain **26** 43.46N 7.42W
Estacado, Llano *f.* U.S.A. **111** 33.30N102.40W
Estados, Isla de los *i.* Argentina **125** 54.45S 64.00W
Eşţahbānāt Iran **65** 29.05N 54.03E
Estaire Canada **104** 46.21N 80.47W
Estância Brazil **123** 11.15S 37.28W
Estand, Kūh-e *mtn.* Iran **65** 31.18N 60.03E
Estarreja Portugal **26** 40.45N 8.34W
Estats, Pic d' *mtn.* Spain **25** 42.40N 1.23E
Este Italy **30** 45.14N 11.39E
Estelí Nicaragua **97** 13.05N 86.23W
Estella Spain **26** 42.40N 2.02W
Estelline U.S.A. **111** 34.33N100.26W
Estepa Spain **27** 37.18N 4.54W
Estepona Spain **27** 36.26N 5.08W
Esternay France **19** 48.44N 3.34E
Estevan Canada **101** 49.07N103.05W
Estevan Is. Canada **100** 53.03N129.38W
Estevan Pt. Canada **100** 49.23N126.33W
Estherville U.S.A. **110** 43.24N 94.50W
Estissac France **19** 48.16N 3.49E
Estivane Mozambique **81** 24.07S 32.38E
Eston U.K. **12** 54.34N 1.07W
Estonia Europe **44** 59.00N 25.00E
Estoril Portugal **27** 38.42N 9.23W
Estrela *mtn.* Portugal **26** 40.19N 7.37W
Estrela, Serra da *mts.* Portugal **26** 40.20N 7.40W
Estremoz Portugal **27** 38.51N 7.35W
Esztergom Hungary **37** 47.48N 18.45E
Étables France **18** 48.38N 2.50W
Etadunna Australia **92** 28.43S138.38E
Etah India **63** 27.38N 78.40E
Étain France **19** 49.13N 5.38E
Etamamiou Canada **103** 50.16N 59.58W
Étampes France **19** 48.26N 2.09E
Étaples France **19** 50.31N 1.39E
Etāwah India **63** 26.46N 79.02E
Ethel Creek *town* Australia **88** 23.05S120.14E
Ethiopia Africa **73** 9.00N 39.00E
Etive, Loch U.K. **14** 56.27N 5.15W
Etna, Monte *mtn.* Italy **33** 37.46N 15.00E
Etne Norway **42** 59.40N 5.56E
Etolin I. U.S.A. **100** 56.10N132.30W
Etosha Game Res. Namibia **80** 18.50S 15.40E
Etosha Pan *f.* Namibia **80** 18.50S 16.20E
Etowah U.S.A. **113** 35.20N 84.30W
Étretat France **18** 49.42N 0.12E
Etropole Bulgaria **34** 42.50N 24.00E
Et Taiyiba Israel **67** 32.16N 35.01E
Ettelbrück Lux. **16** 49.51N 6.06E
Et Tira Israel **67** 32.14N 34.57E
Ettlingen Germany **39** 48.56N 8.24E
Eu France **18** 50.03N 1.25E
Eua *i.* Tonga **85** 21.23S174.55W
Euabalong Australia **93** 33.07S146.28E
Eubank U.S.A. **113** 37.16N 84.40W
Euboea *see* Évvoia *i.* Greece **35**
Eucla Australia **89** 31.40S128.51E
Euclid U.S.A. **114** 41.34N 81.32W
Eucumbene, L. Australia **93** 36.05S148.45E
Eudora U.S.A. **111** 33.07N 91.16W
Eudunda Australia **92** 34.09S139.04E
Eufaula Resr. U.S.A. **107** 35.15N 95.35W
Eugene U.S.A. **108** 44.02N123.05W
Eugenia, Punta *c.* Mexico **109** 27.50N115.03W
Eugowra Australia **93** 33.24S148.25E
Eume *r.* Spain **26** 43.25N 8.08W
Eunice La. U.S.A. **111** 30.30N 92.25W
Eunice N.Mex. U.S.A. **111** 32.26N103.09W
Eupen Belgium **16** 50.38N 6.04E
Euphrates *r. see* Nahr al Furāt *r.* Asia **65**
Eurdon U.S.A. **111** 33.55N 93.09W
Eure *d.* France **18** 49.10N 1.00E
Eure *r.* France **18** 49.18N 1.12E
Eure-et-Loire *d.* France **18** 48.30N 1.30E
Eureka Calif. U.S.A. **108** 40.47N124.09W
Eureka Kans. U.S.A. **111** 37.49N 96.17W
Eureka Nev. U.S.A. **108** 39.31N115.58W
Eureka Utah U.S.A. **108** 39.57N112.07W
Eurinilla *r.* Australia **92** 30.50S140.01E
Euriowie Australia **92** 31.22S141.42E
Euroa Australia **93** 36.46S145.35E
Euro Disneyland France **19** 48.50N 2.50E
Europa, Picos de *mts.* Spain **26** 43.10N 4.50W
Europa Pt. Gibraltar **27** 36.10N 5.22W
Europe **8**
Euskirchen Germany **38** 50.39N 6.47E
Euston Australia **92** 34.34S142.49E
Eutin Germany **38** 54.08N 10.37E
Eutsuk L. Canada **100** 53.20N126.45W
Evale Angola **78** 16.24S 15.50E
Evans, Lac *l.* Canada **102** 50.50N 77.00W
Evans Head *c.* Australia **93** 29.06S153.25E
Evanston Ill. U.S.A. **110** 42.02N 87.41W
Evanston Wyo. U.S.A. **108** 41.16N110.58W
Evansville U.S.A. **112** 38.00N 87.33W
Evelyn Creek *r.* Australia **92** 28.20S134.50E
Even Yehuda Israel **67** 32.16N 34.53E
Everard, C. Australia **93** 37.50S149.16E
Everard, L. Australia **92** 31.25S135.05E
Everard Range *mts.* Australia **91** 27.05S132.28E
Everest, Mt. China / Nepal **63** 27.59N 86.56E
Everett Penn. U.S.A. **114** 40.01N 78.23W
Everett Wash. U.S.A. **108** 47.59N122.13W

Everett, Mt. to **Flathead L.**

Everett, Mt. U.S.A. **115** 42.06N 73.25W
Everglades U.S.A. **113** 25.52N 81.23W
Everglades Nat. Park U.S.A. **113** 25.27N 80.53W
Everöd Sweden **43** 55.54N 14.06E
Evesham U.K. **13** 52.06N 1.57W
Évian-les-Bains France **21** 46.23N 6.35E
Evijärvi Finland **40** 63.22N 23.29E
Evinayong Equat. Guinea **78** 1.27N 10.34E
Evisa France **21** 42.15N 8.47E
Evje Norway **42** 58.36N 7.51E
Évora Portugal **27** 38.34N 7.54W
Évora *d.* Portugal **27** 38.40N 7.55W
Évreux France **18** 49.01N 1.09E
'Evron Israel **67** 32.59N 35.06E
Évros *r. see* Meriç *r.* Greece **34**
Evrótas *r.* Greece **35** 36.48N 22.40E
Évry France **19** 48.38N 2.27E
Évvoia *i.* Greece **35** 38.40N 24.00E
Ewe, Loch U.K. **14** 57.48N 5.38W
Ewing U.S.A. **110** 42.16N 98.21W
Ewo Congo **78** 0.48S 14.47E
Excelsior Springs *town* U.S.A. **110** 39.20N 94.13W
Exe *r.* U.K. **13** 50.40N 3.28W
Exeter Canada **104** 43.21N 81.29W
Exeter U.K. **13** 50.43N 3.31W
Exeter Nebr. U.S.A. **110** 40.39N 97.27W
Exeter N.H. U.S.A. **115** 42.59N 70.57W
Exmoor Forest *hills* U.K. **13** 51.08N 3.45W
Exmore U.S.A. **113** 37.32N 75.49W
Exmouth Australia **88** 21.54S114.10E
Exmouth U.K. **13** 50.37N 3.24W
Exmouth G. Australia **88** 22.00S114.20E
Expedition Range *mts.* Australia **90** 24.30S149.05E
Extremadura *d.* Spain **27** 39.25N 6.00W
Exuma Is. Bahamas **117** 24.00N 76.00W
Eyasi, L. Tanzania **79** 3.40S 35.00E
Eydehavn Norway **42** 58.31N 8.53E
Eye U.K. **13** 52.19N 1.09E
Eyemouth U.K. **14** 55.52N 2.05W
Eygurande France **20** 45.40N 2.26E
Eyjafjördhur *est.* Iceland **40** 65.54N 18.15W
Eyl Somali Rep. **71** 8.00N 49.51E
Eymet France **20** 44.40N 0.24E
Eymoutiers France **20** 45.44N 1.44E
Eyrarbakki Iceland **40** 63.52N 21.09W
Eyre *r.* Australia **90** 26.40S139.00E
Eyre, L. Australia **92** 28.30S137.25E
Eyre Pen. Australia **92** 34.00S135.45E
Ezequil Ramos Mexia, Embalse *resr.* Argentina **125** 39.20S 69.00W
Ezine Turkey **34** 39.48N 26.12E

F

Faaone Tahiti **85** 17.40S149.18W
Fåberg Norway **41** 61.10N 10.22E
Fåborg Denmark **42** 55.06N 10.15E
Fabre Canada **104** 47.12N 79.23W
Fabriano Italy **30** 43.20N 12.54E
Facatativá Colombia **122** 4.48N 74.32W
Facundo Argentina **125** 45.19S 69.59W
Fada Chad **72** 17.14N 21.33E
Fada-N'Gourma Burkina **76** 12.03N 0.22E
Fadd Hungary **31** 46.28N 18.50E
Faenza Italy **30** 44.17N 11.53E
Fafa Mali **76** 15.20N 0.43E
Fafe Portugal **26** 41.27N 8.10W
Fafen *r.* Ethiopia **71** 6.07N 44.20E
Fagamalo W. Samoa **84** 13.24S172.22W
Făgăraş Romania **37** 45.51N 24.58E
Fagernes Norway **41** 60.59N 9.17E
Fagersta Sweden **43** 60.00N 15.47E
Faguibine, Lac *l.* Mali **76** 16.45N 3.54W
Fagus Egypt **66** 30.44N 31.47E
Fâ'id Egypt **66** 30.19N 32.19E
Fairbanks U.S.A. **98** 64.50N147.50W
Fairborn U.S.A. **112** 39.48N 84.03W
Fairbury U.S.A. **110** 40.08N 97.11W
Fairfax U.S.A. **111** 36.34N 96.42W
Fairfield Ala. U.S.A. **113** 33.29N 86.59W
Fairfield Calif. U.S.A. **108** 38.15N122.03W
Fairfield Conn. U.S.A. **115** 41.09N 73.15W
Fairfield Ill. U.S.A. **110** 38.22N 88.23W
Fairfield Iowa U.S.A. **110** 40.56N 91.57W
Fairgrove U.S.A. **104** 43.31N 83.33W
Fairhaven Mass. U.S.A. **115** 41.39N 70.54W
Fair Haven N.Y. U.S.A. **114** 43.19N 76.42W
Fair Haven Vt. U.S.A. **115** 43.36N 73.16W
Fair Head U.K. **15** 55.13N 6.09W
Fair Isle U.K. **14** 59.32N 1.38W
Fairlie New Zealand **86** 44.06S170.50E
Fairmont Minn. U.S.A. **110** 43.39N 94.28W
Fairmont W.Va. U.S.A. **114** 39.29N 80.09W
Fairport U.S.A. **114** 43.06N 77.27W
Fairport Harbor U.S.A. **114** 41.45N 81.17W
Fairview Canada **100** 56.05N118.25W
Fairview Mich. U.S.A. **104** 44.44N 84.03W
Fairview Mont. U.S.A. **108** 47.51N104.03W
Fairview Okla. U.S.A. **111** 36.16N 98.29W
Fairview Penn. U.S.A. **114** 42.03N 80.13W
Fairview Utah U.S.A. **108** 39.38N111.26W
Fairweather, Mt. U.S.A. **100** 59.00N137.30W
Faisalābād Pakistan **62** 31.25N 73.05E
Faistós *site* Greece **35** 35.01N 24.48E
Faith U.S.A. **110** 45.02N102.02W
Faizābād India **63** 26.47N 82.08E
Fajr, Wādī *r.* Saudi Arabia **64** 30.00N 38.25E
Fakaofo Pacific Oc. **84** 9.30S171.15W
Fakenham U.K. **12** 52.50N 0.51E
Fakfak Indonesia **59** 2.55S132.17E
Fakse Denmark **43** 55.15N 12.08E
Fakse Bugte *b.* Denmark **43** 55.10N 12.15E
Falaise France **18** 48.54N 0.12W
Falakrón Óros *mts.* Greece **34** 41.15N 23.58E
Falam Burma **56** 22.58N 93.45E
Falcarragh Rep. of Ire. **15** 55.08N 8.06W
Falconara Marittima Italy **30** 43.37N 13.24E
Falconbridge Canada **104** 46.35N 80.48W
Falcone, Capo del *c.* Italy **32** 40.57N 8.12E
Falconer U.S.A. **114** 42.07N 79.12W
Falcon Resr. U.S.A. **111** 26.37N 99.11W
Falealupo W. Samoa **84** 13.29S172.47W
Falémé *r.* Senegal **76** 14.55N 12.00W
Faleshty Moldavia **37** 47.30N 27.45E
Falfurrias U.S.A. **111** 27.14N 98.09W
Falkenberg Germany **38** 51.35N 13.14E
Falkenberg Sweden **43** 56.54N 12.28E
Falkenhagen Germany **38** 53.12N 12.12E
Falkensee Germany **38** 52.33N 13.04E
Falkenstein Germany **39** 49.06N 12.30E
Falkirk U.K. **14** 56.00N 3.48W
Falkland Is. Atlantic Oc. **125** 51.45W 59.00W
Falkland Sd. *str.* Falkland Is. **125** 51.45W 59.25W
Falköping Sweden **43** 58.10N 13.31E
Fallbrook U.S.A. **109** 33.23N117.15W
Fallon U.S.A. **108** 46.50N105.07W
Fall River *town* U.S.A. **115** 41.43N 71.08W
Falls City U.S.A. **110** 40.03N 95.36W
Falmouth U.K. **13** 50.09N 5.05W
Falmouth Mass. U.S.A. **115** 41.34N 70.38W
Falmouth Va. U.S.A. **114** 38.19N 77.28W
False B. R.S.A. **80** 34.10S 18.40E
False C. U.S.A. **115** 38.29N 74.59W
False Pt. India **63** 20.22N 86.52E
Falset Spain **25** 41.08N 0.49E
Falster *i.* Denmark **41** 54.48N 11.58E
Falsterbo Sweden **43** 55.24N 12.50E
Fălticeni Romania **37** 47.28N 26.18E
Falun Sweden **41** 60.36N 15.38E
Famagusta *see* Ammókhostos Cyprus **66**
Family L. Canada **101** 51.54N 95.30W
Famoso U.S.A. **109** 35.36N119.14W
Fanárion Greece **34** 39.50N 21.47E
Fandriana Madagascar **81** 20.14S 47.23E
Fangak Sudan **73** 9.04N 30.53E
Fangcheng China **54** 33.16N112.59E
Fangdou Shan *mts.* China **55** 30.36N108.45E
Fang Xian China **55** 32.04N110.47E
Fanjing Shan *mtn.* China **55** 27.57N108.50E
Fannich, Loch U.K. **14** 57.38N 5.00W
Fanning I. *see* Tabuaeran *i.* Kiribati **85**
Fanö *i.* Denmark **42** 55.25N 8.25E
Fano Italy **30** 43.50N 13.00E
Fan Xian China **54** 35.59N115.31E
Faradje Zaïre **79** 3.45N 29.43E
Faradofay Madagascar **81** 25.02S 47.00E
Farafangana Madagascar **81** 22.49S 47.50E
Farāfirah, Wāḥāt al *oasis* Egypt **64** 27.15N 28.10E
Farāh Afghan. **62** 32.22N 62.07E
Farāh *d.* Afghan. **62** 33.00N 62.00E
Farāh *r.* Afghan. **62** 31.29N 61.24E
Faranah Guinea **76** 10.01N 10.47W
Farasān, Jazā'ir *is.* Saudi Arabia **72** 16.48N 41.54E
Faratsiho Madagascar **81** 19.24S 46.57E
Faraulep *is.* Federated States of Micronesia **59** 8.36N144.33E
Fardes *r.* Spain **27** 37.35N 3.00W
Fareara, Pt. Tahiti **85** 17.52S149.39W
Fareham U.K. **13** 50.52N 1.11W
Farewell, C. *see* Farvel, Kap *c.* Greenland **99**
Farewell, C. New Zealand **86** 40.30S172.35E
Färgelanda Sweden **42** 58.34N 11.59E
Fargo U.S.A. **110** 46.52N 96.48W
Fāri'ah *r.* Jordan **67** 32.06N 35.31E
Faribault U.S.A. **110** 44.18N 93.16W
Farīdpur Bangla. **63** 23.36N 89.50E
Farim Guinea Bissau **76** 12.30N 15.09W
Farina Australia **92** 30.05S138.20E
Färjestaden Sweden **43** 56.39N 16.27E
Farkwa Tanzania **79** 5.26S 35.15E
Farley Canada **105** 46.18N 76.00W
Farmerville U.S.A. **111** 32.47N 92.24W
Farmington Mo. U.S.A. **111** 37.47N 90.25W
Farmington N.H. U.S.A. **115** 43.24N 71.04W
Farmington N.Mex. U.S.A. **108** 36.44N108.12W
Farnborough U.K. **13** 51.17N 0.46W
Farne Is. U.K. **12** 55.38N 1.36W
Farnham Canada **105** 45.17N 72.59W
Farnham U.K. **13** 51.13N 0.49W
Faro Brazil **123** 2.11S 56.44W
Faro Portugal **27** 37.01N 7.56W
Faro *d.* Portugal **27** 37.15N 8.10W
Faroe Bank *f.* Atlantic Oc. **10** 61.00N 9.00W
Faroe Is. Europe **10** 62.00N 7.00W
Fårön *i.* Sweden **43** 57.56N 19.08E
Fårösund Sweden **43** 57.52N 19.03E
Farrell U.S.A. **114** 41.13N 80.30W
Farrukhābād India **63** 27.24N 79.34E
Fársala Greece **35** 39.18N 22.23E
Fārsī Afghan. **62** 33.47N 63.15E
Farsö Denmark **42** 56.47N 9.21E
Farsund Norway **42** 58.05N 6.48E
Fartak, Ra's *c.* Yemen **71** 15.38N 52.15E
Farvel, Kap *c.* Greenland **99** 60.00N 44.20W
Farwell U.S.A. **111** 34.23N103.02W
Fasā Iran **65** 28.55N 53.38E
Fasano Italy **33** 40.50N 17.22E
Fastov Ukraine **37** 50.08N 29.59E
Fatehābād India **62** 29.31N 75.28E
Fatehjang Pakistan **62** 33.34N 72.39E
Fatehpur Rāj. India **62** 27.59N 74.57E
Fatehpur Uttar P. India **63** 25.56N 80.48E
Fatehpur Pakistan **62** 31.10N 71.13E
Fatehpur Sīkri India **63** 27.06N 77.40E
Fatick Senegal **76** 14.19N 16.27W
Fátima Portugal **27** 39.37N 8.39W
Fatu Hiva *i.* Îs. Marquises **85** 10.27S138.39W
Fatwā India **63** 25.31N 85.19E
Faucilles, Monts *mts.* France **19** 48.07N 6.16E
Faulkton U.S.A. **110** 45.02N 99.08W
Faulquemont France **19** 49.03N 6.36E
Făurei Romania **37** 45.04N 27.15E
Fauske Norway **40** 67.17N 15.25E
Favara Italy **32** 37.19N 13.40E
Faverges France **21** 45.45N 6.18E
Favignana *i.* Italy **32** 37.56N 12.19E
Fawcett Canada **100** 54.34N114.06W
Fawcett L. Canada **102** 51.20N 91.46W
Fawn *r.* Canada **102** 55.20N 88.20W
Faxaflói *b.* Iceland **40** 64.30N 22.50W
Faxe *r.* Sweden **40** 63.15N 17.15E
Fayence France **21** 43.37N 6.41E
Fayette U.S.A. **113** 33.42N 87.50W
Fayetteville Ark. U.S.A. **111** 36.04N 94.10W
Fayetteville N.C. U.S.A. **113** 35.03N 78.53W
Fayetteville N.Y. U.S.A. **115** 43.02N 76.00W
Fayetteville Tenn. U.S.A. **113** 35.08N 86.33W
Fayl-Billot France **19** 47.47N 5.36E
Fāzilka India **62** 30.24N 74.02E
Fāzilpur Pakistan **62** 29.18N 70.27E
Fdérik Mauritania **74** 22.30N 12.30W
Feale *r.* Rep. of Ire. **15** 52.28N 9.37W
Fear, C. U.S.A. **113** 33.50N 77.58W
Fécamp France **18** 49.45N 0.22E
Federación Argentina **125** 31.00S 57.55W
Federal Argentina **125** 30.55S 58.45W
Federal Capital Territory *d.* Nigeria **77** 8.50N 7.00E
Federated States of Micronesia Pacific Oc. **84** 10.00N155.00E
Fedovo Russian Fed. **44** 62.22N 39.21E
Fedulki Russian Fed. **44** 65.00N 66.10E
Feeagh, Lough Rep. of Ire. **15** 53.56N 9.35W
Feerfeer Somali Rep. **71** 5.07N 45.07E
Fehmarn *i.* Germany **38** 54.28N 11.08E
Fehmarn Belt *str.* Germany **38** 54.33N 11.20E
Feia, Lagoa *l.* Brazil **126** 22.00S 41.20W
Feijó Brazil **122** 8.09S 70.21W
Feilding New Zealand **86** 40.10S175.25E
Feira Zambia **79** 15.30S 30.27E
Feira de Santana Brazil **123** 12.17S 38.53W
Felanitx Spain **25** 39.28N 3.08E
Feldbach Austria **31** 46.57N 15.54E
Feldberg *mtn.* Germany **39** 47.51N 8.02E
Feldkirch Austria **39** 47.14N 9.36E
Feldkirchen in Kärnten Austria **39** 46.43N 14.05E
Felixstowe U.K. **13** 51.58N 1.20E
Fellbach Germany **39** 48.48N 9.15E
Felletin France **20** 45.53N 2.10E
Feltre Italy **30** 46.01N 11.54E
Femunden *l.* Norway **41** 62.12N 11.52E
Femundsenden Norway **41** 61.55N 11.55E
Fenelon Falls Canada **104** 44.32N 78.45W
Fengcheng Jiangxi China **55** 28.10N115.45E
Fengcheng Liaoning China **54** 40.29N124.00E
Fengfeng China **54** 36.35N114.28E
Fenggang China **55** 27.58N107.47E
Fengjie China **55** 31.02N109.31E
Fengnan China **54** 39.30N117.58E
Fengpin Taiwan **55** 23.36N121.31E
Fengrun China **54** 39.51N118.08E
Fen He *r.* China **54** 35.30N110.38E
Feni Bangla. **63** 23.01N 91.20E
Feno, Capo di *c.* France **21** 41.57N 8.36E
Fenoarivo Madagascar **81** 18.26S 46.34E
Fenoarivo Atsinanana Madagascar **81** 17.22S 49.25E
Fensfjorden *est.* Norway **41** 60.51N 4.50E
Fenton U.S.A. **112** 42.48N 83.42W
Fenwick U.S.A. **114** 38.14N 80.35W
Fenyang China **54** 37.10N111.40E
Feodosiya Ukraine **45** 45.03N 35.23E
Ferdows Iran **65** 34.00N 58.10E
Fère-Champenoise France **19** 48.45N 3.59E
Fère-en-Tardenois France **19** 49.12N 3.31E
Ferentino Italy **32** 41.42N 13.15E
Fergana Uzbekistan **52** 40.23N 71.19E
Fergus Canada **104** 43.42N 80.22W
Fergus Falls *town* U.S.A. **110** 46.17N 96.04W
Ferguson U.S.A. **110** 38.46N 90.19W
Fergusson I. P.N.G. **90** 9.30S150.40E
Ferkéssédougou Ivory Coast **76** 9.30N 5.10W
Ferlach Austria **31** 46.31N 14.18E
Fermanagh *d.* U.K. **15** 54.21N 7.40W
Fermo Italy **31** 43.09N 13.43E
Fermoselle Spain **26** 41.19N 6.23W
Fermoy Rep. of Ire. **15** 52.08N 8.17W
Fernandina Beach *town* U.S.A. **113** 30.40N 81.26W
Fernando de Noronha *i* Atlantic Oc. **127** 3.50S 32.25W
Fernán-Núñez Spain **27** 37.40N 4.43W
Fernlee Australia **93** 28.12S147.05E
Férrai Greece **34** 40.53N 26.10E
Ferrandina Italy **33** 40.29N 16.28E
Ferrara Italy **30** 44.50N 11.35E
Ferrato, Capo *c.* Italy **32** 39.18N 9.38E
Ferreira do Alentejo Portugal **27** 38.03N 8.07W
Ferreñafe Peru **122** 6.42S 79.45W
Ferret, Cap *c.* France **20** 44.37N 1.15W
Ferriday U.S.A. **111** 31.38N 91.33W
Ferrières France **19** 48.05N 2.47E
Fès Morocco **74** 34.05N 4.57W
Feshi Zaïre **78** 6.08S 18.12E
Festubert Canada **105** 47.12N 72.40W
Festus U.S.A. **110** 38.13N 90.24W
Feteşti Romania **37** 44.23N 27.50E
Fethiye Turkey **64** 36.37N 29.06E
Fetlar *i.* U.K. **14** 60.37N 0.52W
Fetsund Norway **42** 59.56N 11.10E
Feucht Germany **38** 49.22N 11.13E
Feuchtwangen Germany **39** 49.10N 10.20E
Feuilles, Rivière aux *r.* Canada **99** 58.47N 70.06W
Feurs France **21** 45.45N 4.14E
Fevik Norway **42** 58.23N 8.42E
Fevzipaşa Turkey **64** 37.07N 36.38E
Fianarantsoa Madagascar **81** 21.26S 47.05E
Fichē Ethiopia **73** 9.52N 38.46E
Fichtel Gebirge *mts.* Germany **38** 50.00N 11.50E
Fidenza Italy **30** 44.52N 10.03E
Field Canada **104** 46.32N 80.03W
Fier Albania **34** 40.43N 19.33E
Fiesch Switz. **39** 46.20N 8.10E
Fife *d.* U.K. **14** 56.10N 3.10W
Fife Ness *c.* U.K. **14** 56.17N 2.36W
Figeac France **20** 44.37N 2.02E
Figeholm Sweden **43** 57.22N 16.33E
Figueira da Foz Portugal **26** 40.09N 8.52W
Figueras Spain **25** 42.16N 2.58E
Figueres *see* Figueras Spain **25**
Fihaonana Madagascar **81** 18.36S 47.12E
Fiherenana *r.* Madagascar **81** 23.19S 43.37E
Fiji Pacific Oc. **84** 18.00S178.00E
Fīk' Ethiopia **73** 8.10N 42.18E
Filabres, Sierra de los *mts.* Spain **27** 37.13N 2.20W
Filabusi Zimbabwe **80** 20.34S 29.20E
Filadelfia Italy **33** 38.48N 16.18E
Fildegrand *r.* Canada **105** 46.18N 77.51W
Filey U.K. **12** 54.13N 0.18W
Fili *site* Greece **35** 38.10N 23.40E
Filiaşi Romania **37** 44.33N 23.31E
Filiátes Greece **34** 39.38N 20.16E
Filiatrá Greece **35** 37.09N 21.35E
Filicudi, Isola *i.* Italy **33** 38.35N 14.34E
Filingué Niger **77** 14.21N 3.22E
Filippoi *site* Greece **34** 41.00N 24.16E
Filipstad Sweden **43** 59.43N 14.10E
Fillmore Canada **101** 49.50N103.25W
Fillmore Calif. U.S.A. **109** 34.24N118.55W
Fillmore N.Y. U.S.A. **114** 42.28N 78.07W
Filtu Ethiopia **73** 5.05N 40.42E
Fimi *r.* Zaïre **78** 3.00S 17.00E
Finale Emilia Italy **30** 44.50N 11.17E
Finale Ligure Italy **30** 44.10N 8.20E
Finarwa Ethiopia **73** 13.05N 38.58E
Finch Canada **105** 45.11N 75.07W
Findhorn *r.* U.K. **14** 57.38N 3.37W
Findlay U.S.A. **112** 41.02N 83.40W
Findlay, Mt. Canada **100** 50.04N116.10W
Finger Lakes U.S.A. **114** 42.55N 76.44W
Finistère *d.* France **18** 48.20N 4.00W
Finisterre, Cabo de *c.* Spain **26** 42.53N 9.16W
Finke Australia **90** 25.35S134.34E
Finke *r.* Australia **91** 27.00S136.10E
Finland Europe **44** 64.30N 27.00E
Finland, G. of Finland/Estonia **41** 59.30N 24.00E
Finlay *r.* Canada **100** 57.00N125.05W
Finley Australia **93** 35.40S145.34E
Finmark Canada **102** 48.36N 89.44W
Finn *r.* Rep. of Ire. **15** 54.50N 7.30W
Finnmark *d.* Norway **40** 70.10N 26.00E
Finschhafen P.N.G. **59** 6.35S147.51E
Finse Norway **41** 60.36N 7.30E
Finspång Sweden **43** 58.43N 15.47E
Finsterwalde Germany **38** 51.38N 13.42E
Fiora *r.* Italy **30** 42.20N 11.34E
Fiorenzuola d'Arda Italy **30** 44.56N 9.55E
Fīq Syria **67** 32.47N 35.42E
Firat *r.* Turkey *see* Al Furāt *r.* Asia **64**
Firebag *r.* Canada **101** 57.45N111.20W
Firedrake L. Canada **101** 61.25N104.30W
Firenze Italy **30** 43.46N 11.15E
Firenzuola Italy **30** 44.07N 11.23E
Firminy France **21** 45.23N 4.18E
Firozābād India **63** 27.09N 78.25E
Firozpur India **62** 30.55N 74.38E
Firozpur Jhirka India **62** 27.48N 76.57E
Firth of Clyde *est.* U.K. **14** 55.35N 4.53W
Firth of Forth *est.* U.K. **14** 56.05N 3.00W
Firth of Lorn *est.* U.K. **14** 56.20N 5.40W
Firth of Tay *est.* U.K. **14** 56.24N 3.08W
Fīrūzābād Iran **65** 28.50N 52.35E
Firyuza Turkmenistan **50** 37.55N 58.03E
Fish *r.* Namibia **80** 28.07S 17.45E
Fisher U.S.A. **111** 35.30N 90.58W
Fishers I. U.S.A. **115** 41.16N 72.02W
Fisher Str. Canada **99** 63.00N 84.00W
Fishguard U.K. **13** 51.59N 4.59W
Fiskárdhon Greece **35** 38.27N 20.35E
Fiskebäckskil Sweden **42** 58.15N 11.27E
Fiskenaesset Greenland **99** 63.05N 50.40W
Fiskivötn *f.* Iceland **40** 64.50N 20.45W
Fismes France **19** 49.18N 3.41E
Fitchburg U.S.A. **115** 42.35N 71.48W
Fitzgerald U.S.A. **113** 31.43N 83.16W
Fitz Roy Argentina **125** 47.00S 67.15W
Fitzroy *r.* Australia **88** 17.31S123.35E
Fitzroy Crossing Australia **88** 18.13S125.33E
Fitzwilliam I. Canada **104** 45.30N 81.45W
Fiuggi Italy **32** 41.48N 13.13E
Fiumicino Italy **32** 41.46N 12.14E
Fivizzano Italy **30** 44.14N 10.08E
Fizi Zaïre **79** 4.18S 28.56E
Fjällåsen Sweden **40** 67.29N 20.10E
Fjällbacka Sweden **42** 58.36N 11.17E
Fjällsjo *r.* Sweden **40** 63.27N 17.06E
Fjerritslev Denmark **42** 57.05N 9.16E
Fjugesta Sweden **43** 59.10N 14.52E
Flå Norway **41** 60.25N 9.26E
Flagler U.S.A. **108** 39.18N103.04W
Flagstaff U.S.A. **109** 35.12N111.39W
Flagstaff B. St. Helena **127** 15.55S 5.40W
Flåm Norway **41** 60.50N 7.07E
Flamborough Head U.K. **12** 54.06N 0.05W
Fläming *f.* Germany **38** 52.00N 13.00E
Flaming Gorge Resr. U.S.A. **108** 41.15N109.30W
Flandre *f.* Belgium **16** 50.52N 3.00E
Flannan Is. U.K. **14** 58.16N 7.40W
Flåren *l.* Sweden **43** 57.02N 14.06E
Flåsjön *l.* Sweden **40** 64.06N 15.51E
Flat *r.* Canada **100** 61.51N126.00W
Flathead L. U.S.A. **108** 47.52N114.08W

165

Fugou to **General Lavalle**

Fugou China **54** 34.04N114.23E
Fugu China **54** 39.02N111.03E
Fuji Japan **57** 35.09N138.39E
Fuji *r.* Japan **57** 35.07N138.38E
Fujian *d.* China **55** 26.00N118.00E
Fu Jiang *r.* China **55** 30.02N106.20E
Fujieda Japan **57** 34.52N138.16E
Fujin China **53** 47.15N131.59E
Fujinomiya Japan **57** 35.12N138.38E
Fuji san *mtn.* Japan **57** 35.22N138.44E
Fujisawa Japan **57** 35.21N139.29E
Fuji-yoshida Japan **57** 35.38N138.42E
Fukagawa Japan **57** 43.43N142.03E
Fukui Japan **57** 36.04N136.12E
Fukuoka Japan **57** 33.39N130.21E
Fukuroi Japan **57** 34.45N137.55E
Fukushima Japan **57** 37.44N140.28E
Fukuyama Japan **57** 34.29N133.21E
Fūlādī, Kūh-e *mtn.* Afghan. **62** 34.38N 67.32E
Fulda Germany **38** 50.33N 9.41E
Fulda *r.* Germany **38** 51.25N 9.39E
Fuling China **55** 29.40N107.20E
Fulton Mo. U.S.A. **110** 38.52N 91.57W
Fulton N.Y. U.S.A. **115** 43.19N 76.25W
Fumay France **19** 49.59N 4.42E
Fumel France **20** 44.29N 0.57E
Funabashi Japan **57** 35.42N139.59E
Funafuti Tuvalu **84** 8.31S179.13E
Funan Gaba Ethiopia **73** 4.22N 37.58E
Funchal Madeira Is. **127** 32.40N 16.55W
Fundão Portugal **27** 40.08N 7.30W
Fundy, B. of Canada **103** 45.00N 66.00W
Funing China **55** 23.37N105.36E
Funiu Shan *mts.* China **54** 33.40N112.20E
Funtua Nigeria **77** 11.34N 7.18E
Fuping China **54** 38.52N114.12E
Fuqing China **55** 25.43N119.22E
Furakawa Japan **57** 38.30N140.50E
Furancungo Mozambique **79** 14.51S 33.38E
Furculeşti Romania **34** 43.52N 25.09E
Fūrg Iran **65** 28.19N 55.10E
Furnas, Reprêsa de *resr.* Brazil **126** 20.45S 46.00W
Furneaux Group *is.* Australia **91** 40.15S148.15E
Furqlus Syria **66** 34.38N 37.08E
Fürstenau Germany **38** 52.31N 7.40E
Fürstenberg Germany **38** 52.11N 13.10E
Fürstenfeld Austria **31** 47.03N 16.05E
Fürstenfeldbruck Germany **39** 48.10N 11.15E
Fürstenwalde Germany **38** 52.21N 14.04E
Fürth Germany **39** 49.28N 10.59E
Furth im Wald Germany **39** 49.18N 12.51E
Furu-tone *r.* Japan **57** 35.58N139.51E
Fusagasugá Colombia **122** 4.22N 74.21W
Fushun China **54** 41.50N123.55E
Fusong China **53** 42.17N127.19E
Füssen Germany **38** 47.34N 10.42E
Fusui China **55** 22.35N107.57E
Fuwah Egypt **66** 31.12N 30.33E
Fu Xian Liaoning China **54** 39.35N122.07E
Fu Xian Shaanxi China **54** 36.00N109.20E
Fuxin China **54** 42.08N121.45E
Fuyang Anhui China **54** 32.52N115.52E
Fuyang Zhejiang China **55** 30.03N119.57E
Fuyang He *r.* China **54** 38.10N116.08E
Fuyu China **53** 45.12N124.49E
Fuyuan Heilongjiang China **53** 48.20N134.18E
Fuyuan Yunnan China **55** 25.40N104.14E
Fuzhou Fujian China **55** 26.09N119.21E
Fuzhou Jiangxi China **55** 28.01N116.13E
Fyn *i.* Denmark **42** 55.20N 10.30E
Fyne, Loch U.K. **14** 55.55N 5.23W
Fyresvatn *l.* Norway **42** 59.06N 8.12E

G

Ga Ghana **76** 9.48N 2.28W
Gaalkacyo Somali Rep. **71** 6.49N 47.23E
Gabare Bulgaria **34** 43.19N 23.55E
Gabas *r.* France **20** 43.46N 0.42W
Gabela Angola **78** 10.52S 14.24E
Gabès Tunisia **75** 33.53N 10.07E
Gabès, Golfe de *g.* Tunisia **75** 34.00N 10.25E
Gabir Sudan **73** 8.35N 24.40E
Gabon Africa **78** 0.00 12.00E
Gabon *r.* Gabon **78** 0.15N 10.00E
Gaborone Botswana **80** 24.45S 25.55E
Gabras Sudan **73** 10.16N 26.14E
Gabriels U.S.A. **105** 44.26N 74.13W
Gabriel y Galan, Embalse de *resr.* Spain **26** 40.15N 6.15W
Gabrovo Bulgaria **34** 42.52N 25.27E
Gacé France **18** 48.48N 0.18E
Gach Sārān Iran **65** 30.13N 50.49E
Gacko Bosnia-Herzegovina **31** 43.10N 18.32E
Gada Nigeria **77** 13.50N 5.40E
Gādarwāra India **63** 22.55N 78.47E
Gäddede Sweden **40** 64.30N 14.15E
Gádor Spain **27** 36.57N 2.29W
Gádor, Sierra de *mts.* Spain **27** 36.54N 2.47W
Gadot Israel **67** 33.01N 35.37E
Gadra Pakistan **62** 25.40N 70.37E
Gadsden U.S.A. **113** 34.00N 86.00W
Gaeta Italy **32** 41.12N 13.35E
Gaeta, Golfo di *g.* Italy **32** 41.06N 13.30E
Gaferut *i.* Federated States of Micronesia **59** 9.14N145.23E
Gaffney U.S.A. **113** 35.03N 81.40W
Gafsa Tunisia **75** 34.25N 8.48E
Gagarin Russian Fed. **44** 55.38N 35.00E
Gagetown U.S.A. **104** 43.44N 83.16W
Gagliano del Capo Italy **33** 39.50N 18.22E
Gagnoa Ivory Coast **76** 6.04N 5.55W
Gagnon Canada **103** 51.53N 68.10W
Gagnon, Lac *l.* Canada **105** 46.07N 75.07W
Gaibānda Bangla. **63** 25.19N 89.33E
Gaillac France **20** 43.54N 1.55E
Gaillon France **18** 49.10N 1.20E
Gailtaler Alpen *mts.* Austria **39** 46.42N 13.15E
Gaines U.S.A. **104** 42.52N 83.55W
Gainesville Fla. U.S.A. **113** 29.37N 82.21W
Gainesville Ga. U.S.A. **113** 34.17N 83.50W
Gainesville Mo. U.S.A. **111** 36.36N 92.26W
Gainesville Tex. U.S.A. **111** 33.37N 97.08W
Gainesville Va. U.S.A. **114** 38.48N 77.34W
Gainsborough U.K. **12** 53.23N 0.46W
Gairdner *r.* Australia **89** 34.20S119.30E
Gairdner, L. Australia **92** 31.30S136.00E
Gairloch U.K. **14** 57.43N 5.40W
Gaithersburg U.S.A. **114** 39.09N 77.12W
Gai Xian China **54** 40.25N122.15E
Gaj Croatia **31** 45.29N 17.02E
Gal, Punta de *c.* Spain **25** 39.10N 1.05E
Galana *r.* Kenya **79** 3.12S 40.09E
Galangue Angola **78** 13.40S 16.00E
Galapagos, Islas *is.* Ecuador **97** 0.20S 91.00W
Galaroza Spain **27** 37.55N 6.42W
Galashiels U.K. **14** 55.37N 2.49W
Galaţi Romania **37** 45.27N 27.59E
Galatina Italy **33** 40.10N 18.10E
Galaxídhion Greece **35** 38.22N 22.23E
Galdhöpiggen *mtn.* Norway **41** 61.37N 8.17E
Galeana Mexico **111** 24.50N100.04W
Galeh Dār Iran **65** 27.36N 52.42E
Galena Alas. U.S.A. **98** 64.43N157.00W
Galena Md. U.S.A. **115** 39.20N 75.55W
Galesburg U.S.A. **110** 40.57N 90.22W
Galeton U.S.A. **114** 41.44N 77.39W
Galich Russian Fed. **44** 58.20N 42.12E
Galicia *d.* Spain **26** 42.45N 8.00W
Galilee *see* HaGalil *f.* Israel **67**
Galilee, L. Australia **90** 22.21S145.48E
Galilee, Sea of *see* Yam Kinneret *l.* Israel **67**
Galion U.S.A. **114** 40.44N 82.47W
Galiuro Mts. U.S.A. **109** 32.40N110.20W
Gallarate Italy **30** 45.40N 8.47E
Gallatin U.S.A. **113** 36.22N 86.28W
Galle Sri Lanka **61** 6.01N 80.13E
Gállego *r.* Spain **25** 41.39N 0.51W
Gallegos *r.* Argentina **125** 51.35S 69.00W
Galley Head Rep. of Ire. **15** 51.32N 8.57W
Galliate Italy **30** 45.29N 8.42E
Gallinas, Punta *c.* Colombia **122** 12.20N 71.30W
Gallipoli Italy **33** 40.03N 18.00E
Gallipoli *see* Gelibolu Turkey **34**
Gallipolis U.S.A. **114** 38.49N 82.12W
Gällivare Sweden **40** 67.07N 20.45E
Gällö Sweden **40** 62.56N 15.15E
Gallo, Capo *c.* Italy **32** 38.13N 13.19E
Galloo I. U.S.A. **105** 43.54N 76.25W
Galloway *f.* U.K. **14** 55.00N 4.28W
Gallup U.S.A. **109** 35.32N108.44W
Gallur Spain **25** 41.52N 1.19W
Gal'on Israel **67** 31.38N 34.51E
Galong Australia **93** 34.37S148.34E
Galston U.K. **14** 55.36N 4.23W
Galt Canada **104** 43.21N 80.19W
Galtür Austria **39** 46.58N 10.11E
Galty Mts. Rep. of Ire. **15** 52.20N 8.10W
Galva U.S.A. **110** 41.10N 90.03W
Galveston U.S.A. **111** 29.18N 94.48W
Galveston B. U.S.A. **111** 29.36N 94.57W
Galvez Argentina **124** 32.03S 61.14W
Galway Rep. of Ire. **15** 53.17N 9.04W
Galway *d.* Rep. of Ire. **15** 53.25N 9.00W
Galway B. Rep. of Ire. **15** 53.12N 9.07W
Gam *r.* Vietnam **55** 18.47N105.40E
Gamagōri Japan **57** 34.50N137.14E
Gamawa Nigeria **77** 12.10N 10.31E
Gamba China **63** 28.18N 88.32E
Gambēla Ethiopia **73** 8.18N 34.37E
Gambia Africa **76** 13.10N 16.00W
Gambia *r.* Gambia **76** 13.28N 15.55W
Gambier, Îles *is.* Pacific Oc. **85** 23.10S135.00W
Gambier I. Australia **92** 35.12S136.32E
Gambo Canada **103** 48.46N 54.14W
Gamboli Pakistan **62** 29.50N 68.26E
Gamboma Congo **78** 1.50S 15.58E
Gamboula C.A.R. **77** 4.05N 15.10E
Gamia Benin **77** 10.24N 2.45E
Gamlakarleby *see* Kokkola Finland **40**
Gamleby Sweden **43** 57.54N 16.24E
Gamo Gofa *d.* Ethiopia **73** 6.00N 37.00E
Ganado U.S.A. **109** 35.43N109.33W
Gananoque Canada **105** 44.20N 76.10W
Ganbashao China **55** 26.37N107.41E
Ganda Angola **78** 12.58S 14.39E
Gandajika Zaïre **78** 6.46S 23.58E
Gandak *r.* India **63** 25.40N 85.13E
Gāndarbal Jammu & Kashmir **62** 34.14N 74.47E
Gandāva Pakistan **62** 28.37N 67.29E
Gander Canada **103** 48.57N 54.34W
Gander *r.* Canada **103** 49.15N 54.30W
Ganderkesee Germany **38** 53.02N 8.32E
Gander L. Canada **103** 48.55N 54.40W
Gandesa Spain **25** 41.03N 0.26E
Gandevi India **62** 20.49N 73.00E
Gāndhi Sāgar *resr.* India **62** 24.18N 75.21E
Gandía Spain **25** 38.58N 0.11W
Gandou Congo **78** 2.25N 17.25E
Ganga *r.* India **63** 23.22N 90.32E
Gangāpur Rāj. India **62** 25.13N 74.16E
Gangāpur Rāj. India **62** 26.29N 76.43E
Gangara Niger **77** 14.35N 8.40E
Gāngārāmpur India **63** 25.24N 88.31E
Gangdhār India **62** 23.57N 75.37E
Gangdisê Shan *mts.* China **63** 31.15N 82.00E
Ganges France **20** 43.56N 3.42E
Ganges *r. see* Ganga *r.* India **63**
Gangi Italy **33** 37.49N 14.13E
Gangotri India **63** 30.56N 79.02E
Gangtok India **63** 27.20N 88.37E
Gangu China **54** 34.30N105.30E
Gan Jiang *r.* China **55** 29.10N116.00E
Ganmain Australia **93** 34.47S147.01E
Gannat France **20** 46.06N 3.12E
Gannett Peak *mtn.* U.S.A. **108** 43.11N109.39W
Ganquan China **54** 36.19N109.19E
Gan Shemu'el Israel **67** 32.27N 34.57E
Gansu *d.* China **52** 36.00N103.00E
Ganta Liberia **76** 7.15N 8.59W
Gantheaume, C. Australia **92** 36.05S137.27E
Gan Yavne Israel **67** 31.47N 34.43E
Ganye Nigeria **77** 8.24N 12.02E
Ganyu China **54** 34.50N119.07E
Ganzhou China **55** 25.49N114.50E
Gao Mali **76** 16.19N 0.09W
Gao *d.* Mali **77** 17.20N 1.25E
Gao'an China **55** 28.25N115.22E
Gaohe China **55** 22.46N112.57E
Gaolan China **54** 36.23N103.55E
Gaolou Ling *mtn.* China **55** 24.47N106.48E
Gaomi China **54** 36.23N119.44E
Gaoping China **54** 35.48N112.55E
Gaotai China **52** 39.20N 99.58E
Gaoua Burkina **76** 10.20N 3.09W
Gaoual Guinea **76** 11.44N 13.14W
Gaoxiong Taiwan **55** 22.40N120.18E
Gaoyou China **54** 32.40N119.30E
Gaoyou Hu *l.* China **54** 32.50N119.25E
Gaozhou China **55** 21.58N110.59E
Gap France **21** 44.34N 6.05E
Gar China **63** 32.11N 79.59E
Gara, Lough Rep. of Ire. **15** 53.57N 8.27W
Garah Australia **93** 29.04S149.38E
Garanhuns Brazil **123** 8.53S 36.28W
Garba C.A.R. **73** 9.12N 20.30E
Gārbosh, Kūh-e *mtn.* Iran **65** 32.36N 50.02E
García de Sola, Embalse de *resr.* Spain **27** 39.15N 5.05W
Gard *r.* France **21** 43.51N 4.37E
Garda Italy **30** 45.34N 10.42E
Garda, Lago di *l.* Italy **30** 45.40N 10.41E
Gardelegen Germany **38** 52.31N 11.23E
Garden *r.* Canada **104** 46.32N 84.09W
Garden City Ala. U.S.A. **113** 34.01N 86.55W
Garden City Kans. U.S.A. **111** 37.58N100.53W
Garden Reach India **63** 22.33N 88.17E
Garden River *town* Canada **104** 46.33N 84.09W
Gardermoen Norway **42** 60.13N 11.06E
Gardēz Afghan. **62** 33.37N 69.07E
Gardiner U.S.A. **108** 45.02N110.42W
Gardiners I. U.S.A. **115** 41.05N 72.07W
Gardner U.S.A. **115** 42.34N 71.59W
Gardnerville U.S.A. **108** 38.56N119.45W
Gardone Val Trompia Italy **30** 45.41N 10.11E
Gardunha, Serra de *mts.* Portugal **27** 40.06N 7.30W
Garešnica Croatia **31** 45.35N 16.56E
Garessio Italy **30** 44.12N 8.02E
Garet el Djenoun *mtn.* Algeria **75** 25.05N 5.25E
Gargaliánoi Greece **35** 37.04N 21.38E
Gargano, Testa del *c.* Italy **33** 41.49N 16.12E
Garhākota India **63** 23.46N 79.09E
Garhi Khairo Pakistan **62** 28.04N 67.59E
Garibaldi Prov. Park Canada **100** 49.50N122.40W
Garies R.S.A. **80** 30.34S 18.00E
Garigliano *r.* Italy **28** 41.13N 13.45E
Gariglione, Monte *mtn.* Italy **33** 39.09N 16.41E
Garissa Kenya **79** 0.27S 39.49E
Garko Nigeria **77** 11.45N 8.53E
Garland Tex. U.S.A. **111** 32.54N 96.39W
Garland Utah U.S.A. **108** 41.45N112.10W
Garlasco Italy **30** 45.12N 8.55E
Garlin France **20** 43.34N 0.15W
Garm Āb Afghan. **62** 32.14N 65.01E
Garmisch Partenkirchen Germany **39** 47.29N 11.05E
Garmsār Iran **65** 35.15N 52.21E
Garnett U.S.A. **110** 38.17N 95.14W
Garo Hills India **63** 25.45N 90.30E
Garonne *r.* France **20** 45.02N 0.36W
Garoua Cameroon **77** 9.17N 13.22E
Garoua Boulaï Cameroon **77** 5.54N 14.33E
Garrel Germany **38** 52.57N 8.01E
Garrettsville U.S.A. **114** 41.17N 81.06W
Garrison U.S.A. **111** 31.49N 94.30W
Garrison Resr. U.S.A. **110** 48.00N102.30W
Garron Pt. U.K. **15** 55.03N 5.57W
Garrovillas Spain **27** 39.43N 6.33W
Garry L. Canada **99** 66.00N100.00W
Garson Canada **104** 46.34N 80.52W
Garub Namibia **80** 26.33S 16.00E
Garut Indonesia **59** 7.15S107.55E
Garvão Portugal **26** 37.42N 8.21W
Garve U.K. **14** 57.37N 4.41W
Garvie Mts. New Zealand **86** 45.15S169.00E
Garwa India **63** 24.11N 83.49E
Gary U.S.A. **112** 41.34N 87.20W
Garyarsa China **52** 31.30N 80.40E
Gar Zangbo *r.* China **63** 32.25N 79.40E
Garzón Colombia **122** 2.14N 75.37W
Gas City U.S.A. **112** 40.28N 85.37W
Gascogne, Golfe de *g.* France **17** 44.00N 2.40W
Gascony, G. of *see* Gascogne, Golfe de France **17**
Gascoyne *r.* Australia **88** 25.00S113.40E
Gascoyne Junction Australia **88** 25.02S115.15E
Gash *r.* Ethiopia *see* Qāsh *r.* Sudan **72**
Gashua Nigeria **77** 12.53N 11.02E
Gaspé Canada **103** 48.50N 64.30W
Gaspé, Cap de *c.* Canada **103** 48.45N 64.09W
Gaspé, Péninsule de *pen.* Canada **103** 48.30N 65.00W
Gaspésie Prov. Park Canada **103** 48.50N 65.45W
Gassaway U.S.A. **114** 38.40N 80.47W
Gassol Nigeria **77** 8.34N 10.25E
Gasteiz *see* Vitoria Spain **26**
Gastonia U.S.A. **113** 35.14N 81.12W
Gastoúni Greece **35** 37.51N 21.16E
Gastre Argentina **125** 42.17S 69.15W
Gata, Cabo de *c.* Spain **27** 36.44N 2.10W
Gata, Sierra de *mts.* Spain **26** 40.20N 6.35W
Gátas, Akrotírion *c.* Cyprus **66** 34.33N 33.03E
Gatchina Russian Fed. **44** 59.32N 30.05E
Gatehouse of Fleet U.K. **14** 54.53N 4.12W
Gateshead U.K. **12** 54.57N 1.35W
Gatesville U.S.A. **111** 31.26N 97.45W
Gâtine, Hauteurs de *hills* France **18** 46.40N 0.50W
Gatineau Canada **105** 45.29N 75.40W
Gatineau *r.* Canada **105** 45.27N 75.40W
Gatineau N.C.C. Park Canada **105** 45.30N 75.52W
Gattinara Italy **30** 45.37N 8.22E
Gatton Australia **91** 27.32S152.18E
Gatun L. Panama **117** 9.20N 80.00W
Gauchy France **19** 49.49N 3.13E
Gaucín Spain **27** 36.31N 5.19W
Gauer L. Canada **101** 57.00N 97.50W
Gauhāti India **63** 26.11N 91.44E
Gauley *r.* U.S.A. **114** 38.10N 81.12W
Gaurela India **63** 22.45N 81.54E
Gauri Sankar *mtn.* China / Nepal **63** 27.57N 86.21E
Gausta *mtn.* Norway **42** 59.50N 8.35E
Gauting Germany **39** 48.04N 11.23E
Gavá Spain **25** 41.18N 2.00E
Gavāter Iran **65** 25.10N 61.31E
Gávdhos *i.* Greece **35** 34.50N 24.06E
Gāv Koshī Iran **65** 28.39N 57.13E
Gävle Sweden **41** 60.40N 17.10E
Gävleborg *d.* Sweden **41** 61.30N 16.15E
Gavorrano Italy **30** 42.55N 10.54E
Gávrion Greece **35** 37.52N 24.46E
Gawachab Namibia **80** 27.03S 17.50E
Gāwīlgarh Hills India **62** 21.30N 77.00E
Gawler Australia **92** 34.38S138.44E
Gawler Ranges *mts.* Australia **92** 32.30S136.00E
Gaya India **63** 24.47N 85.00E
Gaya Niger **77** 11.53N 3.31E
Gay Head *c.* U.S.A. **115** 41.21N 70.49W
Gaylord U.S.A. **104** 45.02N 84.40W
Gayndah Australia **90** 25.37S151.36E
Gayny Russian Fed. **44** 60.17N 54.15E
Gaysin Ukraine **37** 48.50N 29.29E
Gayvoron Ukraine **37** 48.20N 29.52E
Gaza *see* Ghazzah Egypt **67**
Gaza *d.* Mozambique **81** 23.20S 32.35E
Gaza Strip *f.* Egypt **67** 31.20N 34.20E
Gaziantep Turkey **64** 37.04N 37.21E
Gbanhui Ivory Coast **76** 8.12N 3.02W
Gboko Nigeria **77** 7.22N 8.58E
Gcuwa R.S.A. **80** 32.20S 28.09E
Gdańsk Poland **37** 54.22N 18.38E
Gdansk, G. of Poland **37** 54.45N 19.15E
Gdov Russian Fed. **44** 58.48N 27.52E
Gdynia Poland **37** 54.31N 18.30E
Gebe *i.* Indonesia **59** 0.05S129.20E
Gebze Turkey **64** 40.48N 29.26E
Gech'a Ethiopia **73** 7.31N 35.22E
Gedera Israel **67** 31.48N 34.46E
Gediz *r.* Turkey **29** 38.37N 26.47E
Gedser Denmark **41** 54.35N 11.57E
Geel Belgium **16** 51.10N 5.00E
Geelong Australia **92** 38.10S144.26E
Geesthacht Germany **38** 53.26N 10.22E
Gê'gyai China **63** 32.25N 84.05E
Gehua P.N.G. **90** 10.20S150.25E
Geidam Nigeria **77** 12.55N 11.55E
Geikie *r.* Canada **101** 57.45N103.52W
Geilenkirchen Germany **16** 50.58N 6.08E
Geilo Norway **41** 60.31N 8.12E
Geisenfeld Germany **39** 48.41N 11.37E
Geisenheim Germany **39** 49.59N 7.58E
Geislingen Germany **39** 48.36N 9.50E
Gejiu China **52** 23.25N103.05E
Gela Italy **33** 37.03N 14.15E
Gela, Golfo di *g.* Italy **33** 37.00N 14.10E
Geladī Ethiopia **71** 6.58N 44.30E
Gelai *mtn.* Tanzania **79** 2.37S 36.07E
Gelderland *d.* Neth. **16** 52.05N 6.00E
Geldermalsen Neth. **16** 51.53N 5.17E
Geldern Germany **38** 51.31N 6.20E
Geldrop Neth. **16** 51.26N 5.31E
Geleen Neth. **16** 50.58N 5.51E
Gélengdeng Chad **77** 10.56N 15.32E
Gelibolu Turkey **34** 40.24N 26.40E
Gelibolu Yarimadasi *c.* Turkey **34** 40.20N 26.30E
Gélise *r.* France **20** 44.11N 0.17E
Gelligaer U.K. **13** 51.40N 3.18W
Gelsenkirchen Germany **38** 51.31N 7.07E
Gem Canada **100** 50.58N112.11W
Gemas Malaysia **58** 2.35N102.35E
Gembloux Belgium **16** 50.34N 4.42E
Gemena Zaïre **78** 3.14N 19.48E
Gemerek Turkey **64** 39.13N 36.05E
Gemla Sweden **43** 56.52N 14.38E
Gemlik Turkey **64** 40.26N 29.10E
Gemona del Friuli Italy **30** 46.16N 13.09E
Gemünden Germany **39** 50.03N 9.41E
Genalē *r.* Ethiopia **73** 4.15N 42.10E
Genappe Belgium **16** 50.37N 4.25E
Gençay France **18** 46.23N 0.24E
Gendringen Neth. **16** 51.52N 6.26E
General Acha Argentina **125** 37.20S 64.35W
General Alvear Buenos Aires Argentina **125** 36.00S 60.00W
General Alvear Mendoza Argentina **125** 34.59S 67.42W
General Belgrano Argentina **125** 35.45S 58.30W
General Campos Argentina **125** 31.30S 58.25W
General Conesa Argentina **125** 36.30S 57.19W
General Guido Argentina **125** 36.40S 57.45W
General Lavalle Argentina **125** 36.22S 56.55W

General Madariaga to Goñi

General Madariaga Argentina 125 37.00S 57.05W
General Paz Argentina 125 35.32S 58.18W
General Pico Argentina 125 35.38S 63.46W
General Roca Argentina 125 39.02S 67.33W
General Santos Phil. 59 6.05N125.15E
Genesee U.S.A. 114 41.59N 77.52W
Genesee r. U.S.A. 114 43.16N 77.36W
Geneseo Ill. U.S.A. 110 41.27N 90.09W
Geneseo N.Y. U.S.A. 114 42.48N 77.49W
Geneva see Genève Switz. 39
Geneva Nebr. U.S.A. 110 40.32N 97.36W
Geneva N.Y. U.S.A. 114 42.52N 77.00W
Geneva Ohio U.S.A. 114 41.48N 80.57W
Geneva, L. see Léman, Lac l. Switz. 39
Genève Switz. 39 46.12N 6.09E
Genève d. Switz. 39 46.15N 6.15E
Genichesk Ukraine 45 46.10N 34.49E
Genil r. Spain 27 37.42N 5.19W
Genk Belgium 16 50.58N 5.34E
Genlis France 19 47.14N 5.13E
Gennargentu, Monti del mts. Italy 32 39.59N 9.19E
Gennep Neth. 16 51.43N 5.58E
Gennes France 18 47.20N 0.14W
Genoa Australia 93 37.29S149.35E
Genoa see Genova Italy 30
Genoa U.S.A. 110 41.27N 97.44W
Genoa, G. of see Genova, Golfo di g. Italy 30
Genova Italy 30 44.25N 8.57E
Genova, Golfo di g. Italy 30 44.00N 9.00E
Gens de Terre r. Canada 105 46.53N 76.00W
Gent Belgium 16 51.02N 3.42E
Genthin Germany 38 52.24N 12.09E
Gentilly Canada 105 46.24N 72.17W
Gentioux France 20 45.47N 1.59E
Genzano di Roma Italy 32 41.42N 12.41E
Geographe B. Australia 89 33.35S115.15E
George r. Australia 92 28.24S136.39E
George r. Canada 99 58.30N 66.00W
George R.S.A. 80 33.57S 22.27E
George, L. N.S.W. Australia 93 35.07S149.22E
George, L. S.A. Australia 92 37.26S140.00E
George, L. Uganda 79 0.00 30.10E
George, L. Fla. U.S.A. 113 29.17N 81.36W
George, L. N.Y. U.S.A. 115 43.35N 73.35W
George B. Canada 103 45.50N 61.45W
George's Cove Canada 103 52.40N 55.50W
Georgetown Ascension 127 7.56S 14.25W
Georgetown Qld. Australia 90 18.18S143.33E
George Town Tas. Australia 91 41.04S146.48E
Georgetown Canada 103 46.11N 62.32W
Georgetown Cayman Is. 117 19.20N 81.23W
Georgetown Gambia 76 13.31N 14.50W
Georgetown Guyana 122 6.46N 58.10W
George Town Malaysia 58 5.30N100.16E
Georgetown Del. U.S.A. 115 38.42N 75.23W
Georgetown S.C. U.S.A. 113 33.23N 79.18W
Georgetown Tex. U.S.A. 111 30.38N 97.41W
George V Land f. Antarctica 128 69.00S145.00E
Georgia Europe 45 42.00N 43.30E
Georgia d. U.S.A. 113 32.50N 83.15W
Georgia, Str. of Canada 100 49.25N124.00W
Georgian B. Canada 104 45.15N 80.50W
Georgi Dimitrov Bulgaria 34 42.37N 23.04E
Georgina r. Australia 90 23.12S139.33E
Georgiyevsk Russian Fed. 45 44.10N 43.30E
Gera Germany 38 50.52N 12.04E
Geraardsbergen Belgium 16 50.47N 3.53E
Geral de Goiás, Serra mts. Brazil 123 13.00S 45.40W
Geraldine New Zealand 86 44.05S171.15E
Geral do Paranã, Serra mts. Brazil 123 14.40S 47.30W
Geraldton Australia 89 28.49S114.36E
Geraldton Canada 102 49.44N 86.59W
Gerar r. Israel 67 31.24N 34.26E
Gérardmer France 19 48.04N 6.53E
Gerede Turkey 64 40.48N 32.13E
Gereshk Afghan. 62 31.48N 64.34E
Gérgal Spain 27 37.07N 2.33W
Gering U.S.A. 110 41.50N103.40W
Gerlach U.S.A. 108 40.40N119.21W
Gerlachovsky mtn. Slovakia 37 49.10N 20.05E
Germania U.S.A. 114 41.39N 77.40W
Germany Europe 38 51.05N 9.45E
Germencik Turkey 35 37.51N 27.37E
Germersheim Germany 39 49.13N 8.22E
Germiston R.S.A. 80 26.14S 28.10E
Gerolstein Germany 39 50.13N 6.40E
Gerolzhofen Germany 39 49.54N 10.21E
Gerona Spain 25 41.59N 2.49E
Gerona see Girona Spain 25
Gerona see Girona d. Spain 25
Gerringong Australia 93 34.45S150.50E
Gers d. France 20 43.40N 0.30E
Gêrzê China 63 32.16N 84.12E
Gescher Germany 38 51.57N 6.59E
Geseke Germany 38 51.38N 8.31E
Getafe Spain 26 40.18N 3.43W
Gete r. Belgium 16 50.58N 5.07E
Gethsémani Canada 103 50.13N 60.40W
Getinge Sweden 43 56.49N 12.44E
Gettysburg Penn. U.S.A. 114 39.50N 77.14W
Gettysburg S.Dak. U.S.A. 110 45.01N 99.57W
Gevān Iran 65 26.03N 57.17E
Gevar'am Israel 67 31.35N 34.37E
Gevelsberg Germany 38 51.19N 7.20E
Gevgelija Macedonia 34 41.09N 22.30E
Gévora r. Spain 27 38.53N 6.57W
Gevulot Israel 67 31.12N 34.28E
Geyikli Turkey 34 39.50N 26.12E
Geysdorp R.S.A. 80 26.31S 25.17E
Geyser U.S.A. 108 47.16N110.30W
Geyve Turkey 64 40.32N 30.18E
Gezer Israel 67 31.52N 34.55E
Ghabāghib Syria 67 33.10N 36.13E
Ghābat al 'Arab Sudan 73 9.02N 29.29E
Ghadaf, Wādī al r. Jordan 66 31.46N 36.50E
Ghadāmis Libya 75 30.08N 9.30E
Ghaddūwah Libya 75 26.26N 14.18E
Ghāghra r. India 63 25.47N 84.37E
Ghana Africa 76 8.00N 1.00W
Ghanzi Botswana 80 21.42S 21.39E
Ghanzi d. Botswana 80 21.44S 21.38E
Gharb al Istiwā'īyah d. Sudan 73 5.25N 29.00E
Ghardaïa Algeria 75 32.29N 3.40E
Gharghoda India 63 22.10N 83.21E
Ghārib, Jabal mtn. Egypt 66 28.06N 32.54E
Gharīyat ash Sharqīyah Syria 67 32.40N 36.16E
Gharo Pakistan 62 24.44N 67.35E
Gharyān Libya 75 32.10N 13.01E
Gharyān d. Libya 75 30.35N 12.00E
Ghāt Libya 75 24.58N 10.11E
Ghātsīla India 63 22.36N 86.29E
Ghazāl, Baḩr al r. Sudan 73 9.31N 30.25E
Ghāziābād India 63 28.40N 77.26E
Ghāzīpur India 63 25.35N 83.34E
Ghazlūna Pakistan 62 31.24N 67.49E
Ghaznī Afghan. 62 33.33N 68.26E
Ghaznī d. Afghan. 62 32.45N 68.30E
Ghaznī r. Afghan. 62 32.35N 67.58E
Ghazzah Egypt 67 31.30N 34.28E
Ghedi Italy 30 45.24N 10.16E
Gheorghe-Gheorghiu-Dej Romania 37 46.14N 26.44E
Gheorgheni Romania 37 46.43N 25.36E
Gherla Romania 37 47.02N 23.55E
Ghisonàccia France 21 42.00N 9.25E
Ghotki Pakistan 62 28.01N 69.19E
Ghowr d. Afghan. 62 34.00N 64.15E
Ghubaysh Sudan 73 12.09N 27.21E
Ghudāf, Wādī al r. Iraq 64 32.54N 43.33E
Ghūriān Afghan. 62 34.21N 61.30E
Gia Dinh Vietnam 56 10.54N106.43E
Giarre Italy 33 37.43N 15.11E
Gibb River town Australia 88 16.29S126.20E
Gibeon Namibia 80 25.09S 17.44E
Gibraleón Spain 27 37.23N 6.58W
Gibraltar Europe 27 36.09N 5.21W
Gibraltar, Str. of Africa/Europe 24 36.00N 5.25W
Gibraltar Pt. U.K. 12 53.05N 0.20E
Gibson Australia 89 33.39S121.48E
Gibson Desert Australia 88 23.10S125.35E
Gīda Ethiopia 73 9.40N 35.16E
Giddings U.S.A. 111 30.11N 96.56W
Gien France 19 47.42N 2.38E
Giessen Germany 38 50.35N 8.40E
Gieten Neth. 16 53.01N 6.45E
Gifford r. Canada 99 70.21N 83.05W
Gifford U.S.A. 108 48.20N118.08W
Gifhorn Germany 38 52.29N 10.33E
Gifu Japan 57 35.25N136.45E
Gifu d. Japan 57 35.32N137.15E
Giganta, Sierra de la mts. Mexico 109 25.30N111.15W
Gigantes, Llanos de los f. Mexico 109 30.00N105.00W
Gigen Bulgaria 34 43.40N 24.28E
Gigha i. U.K. 14 55.41N 5.44W
Giglio i. Italy 30 42.21N 10.54E
Gijón Spain 26 43.32N 5.40W
Gila r. U.S.A. 109 32.43N114.33W
Gila Bend U.S.A. 109 32.57N112.43W
Gila Bend Mts. U.S.A. 109 33.10N113.10W
Gilardo Dam Canada 105 47.12N 73.48W
Gilat Israel 67 31.19N 34.40E
Gilbert r. Australia 90 16.35S141.15E
Gilbert Islands Kiribati 84 2.00S175.00E
Gildford U.S.A. 108 48.34N110.18W
Gilé Mozambique 81 16.10S 38.17E
Gilgandra Australia 93 31.42S148.40E
Gil Gil r. Australia 93 29.10S148.50E
Gilgil Kenya 79 0.29S 36.19E
Gilgit Jammu & Kashmir 60 35.54N 74.20E
Gilgunnia Australia 93 32.25S146.04E
Giljeva Planina mts. Yugo. 31 43.15N 19.55E
Gill, Lough Rep. of Ire. 15 54.15N 8.14W
Gilleleje Denmark 43 56.07N 12.19E
Gilles, L. Australia 92 32.50S136.45E
Gillette U.S.A. 108 44.18N105.30W
Gillingham Kent U.K. 13 51.24N 0.33E
Gill Pt. c. St. Helena 127 15.59S 5.38W
Gilmour Canada 105 44.48N 77.37W
Gīlo r. Ethiopia 73 8.10N 33.15E
Gimli Canada 101 50.39N 97.00W
Gimo Sweden 43 60.11N 18.11E
Gimone r. France 20 44.00N 1.06E
Gimont France 20 43.38N 0.53E
Gimzo Israel 67 31.56N 34.57E
Gingin Australia 89 31.21S115.42E
Ginīr Ethiopia 73 7.07N 40.46E
Ginnosar Israel 67 32.51N 35.31E
Ginosa Italy 33 40.34N 16.46E
Ginzo de Limia Spain 26 42.03N 7.43W
Gioia del Colle Italy 33 40.48N 16.56E
Gioia Tauro Italy 33 38.26N 15.54E
Gióna mtn. Greece 35 38.38N 22.14E
Girard Ohio U.S.A. 114 41.10N 80.42W
Girard Penn. U.S.A. 114 42.00N 80.19W
Girardot Colombia 122 4.19N 74.47W
Girdle Ness U.K. 14 57.06N 2.02W
Giresun Turkey 64 40.55N 38.25E
Gīr Hills India 62 21.10N 71.00E
Giri r. Zaïre 78 0.30N 17.58E
Girīdih India 63 24.11N 86.18E
Girilambone Australia 93 31.14S146.55E
Girna r. India 62 21.08N 75.19E
Giromagny France 19 47.45N 6.50E
Girona see Gerona Spain 25
Girona d. Spain 25 42.05N 2.50E
Gironde d. France 20 44.45N 0.35W
Gironde r. France 20 45.35N 1.00W
Girvan U.K. 14 55.15N 4.51W
Girwa r. India 63 27.20N 81.25E
Gisborne New Zealand 86 38.41S178.02E
Gisborne d. New Zealand 86 38.20S177.45E
Gislaved Sweden 43 57.18N 13.32E
Gisors France 19 49.17N 1.47E
Gitega Burundi 79 3.25S 29.58E
Giugliano Italy 33 40.56N 14.12E
Giulianova Italy 31 42.45N 13.57E
Giurgiu Romania 34 43.53N 25.57E
Giv'atayim Israel 67 32.04N 34.49E
Giv'at Brenner Israel 67 31.52N 34.48E
Give Denmark 42 55.51N 9.15E
Givet France 17 50.08N 4.49E
Givors France 21 45.35N 4.46E
Givry France 19 46.47N 4.45E
Gīzāb Afghan. 62 33.23N 65.55E
Gizhiga Russian Fed. 51 62.00N160.34E
Gizhiginskaya Guba g. Russian Fed. 51 61.00N158.00E
Giżycko Poland 37 54.03N 21.47E
Gjerstad Norway 42 58.54N 9.00E
Gjirokastër Albania 34 40.05N 20.10E
Gjoa Haven town Canada 99 68.39N 96.08W
Gjövik Norway 41 60.48N 10.42E
Glace Bay town Canada 103 46.12N 59.57W
Glacier Nat. Park Canada 100 51.15N117.30W
Glacier Peak mtn. U.S.A. 108 48.07N121.06W
Gladewater U.S.A. 111 32.33N 94.56W
Gladmar Canada 101 49.12N104.31W
Gladstone Qld. Australia 90 23.52S151.16E
Gladstone S.A. Australia 92 33.17S138.22E
Gladstone Mich. U.S.A. 112 45.52N 87.02W
Gladstone N.J. U.S.A. 115 40.43N 74.40W
Gladwin U.S.A. 104 43.59N 84.29W
Glafsfjorden l. Sweden 43 59.34N 12.37E
Glåma r. Norway 42 59.12N 10.57E
Glamoč Bosnia-Herzegovina 31 44.03N 16.51E
Glan r. Germany 16 49.46N 7.43E
Glan l. Sweden 43 58.37N 15.58E
Glanaman U.K. 13 51.49N 3.54W
Glandorf Germany 38 52.05N 7.59E
Glarner Alpen mts. Switz. 39 46.55N 9.00E
Glarus Switz. 39 47.02N 9.04E
Glarus d. Switz. 39 46.59N 9.05E
Glasco Kans. U.S.A. 110 39.22N 97.50W
Glasco N.Y. U.S.A. 115 42.03N 73.57W
Glasgow U.K. 14 55.52N 4.15W
Glasgow Ky. U.S.A. 113 36.59N 85.56W
Glasgow Mont. U.S.A. 108 48.12N106.38W
Glassboro U.S.A. 115 39.42N 75.07W
Glastonbury U.K. 13 51.09N 2.42W
Glauchau Germany 38 50.49N 12.32E
Glazov Russian Fed. 44 58.09N 52.42E
Gleisdorf Austria 31 47.06N 15.44E
Glen R.S.A. 80 28.57S 26.19E
Glen Affric f. U.K. 14 57.15N 5.03W
Glen Afton Canada 104 46.39N 80.17W
Glénans, Îles de is. France 18 47.43N 3.57W
Glenarm U.K. 15 54.57N 5.58W
Glenburnie Australia 92 37.49S140.56E
Glen Burnie U.S.A. 115 39.10N 76.37W
Glencoe Australia 92 37.41S140.05E
Glencoe Canada 104 42.45N 81.43W
Glen Coe f. U.K. 14 56.40N 5.03W
Glencoe U.S.A. 110 44.45N 94.10W
Glen Cove U.S.A. 115 40.52N 73.37W
Glendale Ariz. U.S.A. 109 33.32N112.11W
Glendale Calif. U.S.A. 109 34.10N118.17W
Glendale Oreg. U.S.A. 108 42.44N123.26W
Glen Davis Australia 93 33.07S150.22E
Glendive U.S.A. 108 47.06N104.43W
Glenelg r. Australia 92 38.03S141.00E
Glenfield U.S.A. 115 43.43N 75.24W
Glengarriff Rep. of Ire. 15 51.45N 9.33W
Glen Garry f. Highland U.K. 14 57.03N 5.04W
Glen Head Rep. of Ire. 15 54.44N 8.46W
Glen Helen town Australia 90 23.15S132.35E
Glen Innes Australia 93 29.42S151.45E
Glen Lyon U.S.A. 115 41.10N 76.05W
Glen Mòr f. U.K. 14 57.15N 4.30W
Glenmora U.S.A. 111 30.59N 92.35W
Glenmorgan Australia 91 27.19S149.40E
Glen Moriston U.K. 14 57.09N 4.50W
Glennie U.S.A. 104 44.33N 83.44W
Glenns Ferry U.S.A. 108 42.57N115.18W
Glenrock U.S.A. 108 42.52N105.52W
Glenrothes U.K. 14 56.12N 3.10W
Glenroy Australia 88 17.23S126.01E
Glens Falls town U.S.A. 115 43.19N 73.39W
Glenshee f. U.K. 14 56.45N 3.25W
Glen Spean f. U.K. 14 56.53N 4.40W
Glenville U.S.A. 114 38.56N 80.50W
Glenwood Ark. U.S.A. 111 34.20N 93.33W
Glenwood Iowa U.S.A. 110 41.03N 95.45W
Glenwood Oreg. U.S.A. 108 45.39N123.16W
Glenwood Springs town U.S.A. 108 39.33N107.19W
Glífa Greece 35 38.57N 22.58E
Glimåkra Sweden 43 56.18N 14.08E
Glimmingehus Sweden 43 55.30N 14.13E
Glina Croatia 31 45.20N 16.06E
Glina r. Croatia 31 45.26N 16.07E
Glittertind mtn. Norway 41 61.39N 8.33E
Gliwice Poland 37 50.17N 18.40E
Globe U.S.A. 109 33.24N110.47W
Głogów Poland 36 51.40N 16.06E
Glotovo Russian Fed. 44 63.25N 49.28E
Gloucester Australia 93 31.59S151.58E
Gloucester U.K. 13 51.52N 2.15W
Gloucester U.S.A. 115 42.41N 70.39W
Gloucester City U.S.A. 115 39.54N 75.07W
Gloucestershire d. U.K. 13 51.45N 2.00W
Glouster U.S.A. 114 39.30N 82.05W
Gloversville U.S.A. 115 43.03N 74.20W
Głubczyce Poland 37 50.13N 17.49E
Glücksburg Germany 38 54.50N 9.33E
Glückstadt Germany 38 53.47N 9.25E
Glusha Belorussia 37 53.03N 28.55E
Glyngöre Denmark 42 56.46N 8.52E
Gmünd Austria 31 46.54N 13.32E
Gmunden Austria 39 47.55N 13.48E
Gnadenhutten U.S.A. 114 40.22N 81.26W
Gnarp Sweden 41 62.03N 17.16E
Gnesta Sweden 43 59.03N 17.18E
Gniewkowo Poland 37 52.24N 18.25E
Gniezno Poland 37 52.32N 17.32E
Gnjilane Yugo. 34 42.28N 21.58E
Gnoien Germany 38 53.58N 12.42E
Gnosjö Sweden 43 57.22N 13.44E
Gnowangerup Australia 89 33.57S117.58E
Gnuca Australia 89 31.08S117.24E
Goa d. India 60 15.30N 74.00E
Goageb Namibia 80 26.45S 17.18E
Goālpāra India 63 26.10N 90.37E
Goat Fell mtn. U.K. 14 55.37N 5.12W
Goba Ethiopia 73 7.02N 40.00E
Goba Mozambique 81 26.11S 32.08E
Gobabis Namibia 80 22.28S 18.58E
Gobi des. Asia 54 45.00N108.00E
Goch Germany 38 51.41N 6.10E
Gochas Namibia 80 24.50S 18.48E
Godalming U.K. 13 51.11N 0.37W
Godar Pakistan 62 28.10N 63.14E
Godāvari r. India 61 16.40N 82.15E
Godbout Canada 103 49.19N 67.37W
Goderich Canada 104 43.45N 81.43W
Goderville France 18 49.39N 0.22E
Godhavn Greenland 99 69.20N 53.30W
Godhra India 62 22.45N 73.38E
Godoy Cruz Argentina 125 32.55S 68.50W
Gods r. Canada 101 56.22N 92.51W
Gods L. Canada 101 54.45N 94.00W
Godthåb Greenland 99 64.10N 51.40W
Goéland, Lac au l. Canada 102 49.47N 76.41W
Goélands, Lac aux l. Canada 103 55.25N 64.20W
Goes Neth. 16 51.30N 3.54E
Goffstown U.S.A. 115 43.01N 71.36W
Gogama Canada 102 47.35N 81.35W
Gogeh Ethiopia 73 8.12N 38.27E
Göggingen Germany 39 48.20N 10.52E
Gogonou Benin 77 10.50N 2.50E
Gogra r. see Ghāghra India 63
Gogrial Sudan 73 8.32N 28.07E
Goha Ethiopia 73 10.25N 34.38E
Gohad India 63 26.26N 78.27E
Goiana Brazil 123 7.30S 35.00W
Goiânia Brazil 123 16.43S 49.18W
Goiás Brazil 123 15.57S 50.07W
Goiás d. Brazil 123 15.00S 48.00W
Goichran India 63 31.04N 78.07E
Góis Portugal 26 40.09N 8.07W
Goito Italy 30 45.15N 10.40E
Gojam d. Ethiopia 73 11.10N 37.00E
Gojeb r. Ethiopia 73 7.10N 37.27E
Gojō Japan 57 34.21N135.42E
Gojra Pakistan 62 31.09N 72.41E
Gökçe Turkey 34 40.10N 25.57E
Gökçeada i. Turkey 34 40.10N 26.00E
Göksun Turkey 64 38.03N 36.30E
Gokteik Burma 61 22.26N 97.00E
Gokwe Zimbabwe 80 18.14S 28.54E
Gol Norway 41 60.42N 8.57E
Gola Gokaran Nath India 63 28.05N 80.28E
Golan Heights mts. Syria 67 32.55N 35.42E
Golconda U.S.A. 108 40.57N117.30W
Gold U.S.A. 114 41.52N 77.52W
Goldap Poland 37 54.19N 22.19E
Gold Beach town U.S.A. 108 42.25N124.25W
Golden Canada 100 51.20N117.00W
Golden Rep. of Ire. 15 52.30N 7.59W
Golden U.S.A. 108 39.46N105.13W
Golden B. New Zealand 86 40.45S172.50E
Goldendale U.S.A. 108 45.49N120.50W
Golden Hinde mtn. Canada 100 49.40N125.44W
Golden L. Canada 105 45.35N 77.20W
Golden Lake town Canada 105 45.35N 77.16W
Golden Ridge town Australia 89 30.51S121.42E
Golden Vale f. Rep. of Ire. 15 52.30N 8.07W
Goldfield U.S.A. 108 37.42N117.14W
Goldfields Canada 101 59.28N108.31W
Goldpines Canada 102 50.45N 93.05W
Goldsand L. Canada 101 56.58N101.02W
Goldsboro U.S.A. 113 35.23N 78.00W
Goldsworthy Australia 88 20.20S119.30E
Goleniów Poland 36 53.36N 14.50E
Golets Skalisty mtn. Russian Fed. 51 56.00N130.40E
Golfito Costa Rica 117 8.42N 83.10W
Golfo degli Aranci town Italy 32 41.00N 9.38E
Goliad U.S.A. 111 28.40N 97.23W
Goljam Perelik mtn. Bulgaria 34 41.36N 24.34E
Golling Austria 39 47.36N 13.10E
Golmud China 52 36.22N 94.55E
Golo r. France 21 42.31N 9.32E
Golovanevsk Ukraine 37 48.25N 30.30E
Golpāyegān Iran 65 33.23N 50.18E
Golspie U.K. 14 57.58N 3.58W
Goma Zaïre 79 1.37S 29.10E
Gomang Co l. China 63 31.10N 89.10E
Gombe Nigeria 77 10.17N 11.20E
Gombe r. Tanzania 79 4.43S 31.30E
Gomel Belorussia 37 52.25N 31.00E
Gomera i. Canary Is. 74 28.08N 17.14W
Gómez Palacio Mexico 111 25.34N103.30W
Gomīshān Iran 65 37.04N 54.06E
Gompa Jammu & Kashmir 62 35.02N 77.20E
Gonaïves Haiti 117 19.29N 72.42W
Gonâve, Golfe de la g. Haiti 117 19.20N 73.00W
Gonâve, Île de la i. Haiti 117 18.50N 73.00W
Gonbad-e Kāvūs Iran 65 37.15N 55.11E
Gonda India 63 27.08N 81.56E
Gondal India 62 21.58N 70.48E
Gonder Ethiopia 73 12.39N 37.29E
Gonder d. Ethiopia 73 12.30N 37.30E
Gondia India 63 21.27N 80.12E
Gondomar Portugal 26 41.09N 8.32W
Gondrecourt-le-Château France 19 48.31N 5.30E
Gonen Israel 67 33.08N 35.39E
Gongbo'gyamda China 63 29.56N 93.23E
Gonggar China 63 29.15N 90.50E
Gongga Shan mtn. China 52 29.30N101.30E
Gongola r. Nigeria 77 9.30N 12.06E
Gongolgon Australia 93 30.22S146.56E
Goñi Uruguay 125 33.31S 56.24W

Goniri to Grindavik

Goniri Nigeria 77 11.30N 12.15E
Gonnesa Italy 32 39.15N 8.28E
Gonzaga Italy 30 44.57N 10.49E
Gonzales U.S.A. 111 29.30N 97.27W
Good Hope, C. of R.S.A. 80 34.21S 18.28E
Good Hope Mtn. Canada 100 51.09N124.10W
Gooding U.S.A. 108 42.56N114.43W
Goodland U.S.A. 110 39.21N101.43W
Goodooga Australia 93 29.08S147.30E
Goodsprings U.S.A. 109 35.50N115.26W
Goole U.K. 12 53.42N 0.52W
Goolgowi Australia 93 33.59S145.42E
Goolma Australia 93 32.21S149.20E
Gooloogong Australia 93 33.36S148.27E
Goolwa Australia 92 35.31S138.45E
Goomalling Australia 89 31.19S116.49E
Goombalie Australia 93 29.59S145.24E
Goondiwindi Australia 93 28.30S150.17E
Goongarrie Australia 89 30.03S121.09E
Goor Neth. 16 52.16N 6.33E
Goose *r.* Canada 103 53.18N 60.23W
Goose Bay *town* Canada 103 53.19N 60.24W
Goose L. U.S.A. 108 41.57N120.25W
Gopālganj Bangla. 63 23.01N 89.50E
Gopālganj India 63 26.28N 84.26E
Göppingen Germany 39 48.42N 9.40E
Gorakhpur India 63 26.45N 83.22E
Goras India 62 25.32N 76.56E
Goražde Bosnia-Herzegovina 31 43.40N 18.56E
Gordon *r.* Australia 89 34.12S117.00E
Gordon U.S.A. 110 42.48N102.12W
Gordon Downs *town* Australia 88 18.43S128.33E
Gordon L. Canada 100 63.05N113.11W
Gordonvale Australia 90 17.05S145.47E
Goré Chad 77 7.57N 16.31E
Gorē Ethiopia 73 8.08N 35.33E
Gore New Zealand 86 46.06S168.58E
Gore Bay *town* Canada 104 45.55N 82.28W
Gore Mtn. U.S.A. 105 44.55N 71.48W
Gorgān Iran 65 36.50N 54.29E
Gorgān *r.* Iran 65 37.00N 54.00E
Gorgol *d.* Mauritania 74 15.45N 13.00W
Gori Georgia 65 41.59N 44.05E
Gorinchem Neth. 16 51.50N 4.59E
Gorizia Italy 31 45.57N 13.38E
Gorjani Croatia 31 45.24N 18.21E
Gorki *see* Nizhniy Novgorod Russian Fed. 44
Gorkovskoye Vodokhranilishche *resr.* Russian Fed. 44 56.49N 43.00E
Görlitz Germany 38 51.09N 14.59E
Gorlovka Ukraine 45 48.17N 38.05E
Gorna Oryakhovitsa Bulgaria 34 43.07N 25.40E
Gornja Radogna Slovenia 31 46.41N 16.00E
Gornji Grad Slovenia 31 46.18N 14.49E
Gornji Vakuf Bosnia-Herzegovina 31 43.56N 17.35E
Gorno Altaysk Russian Fed. 50 51.59N 85.56E
Gorno Filinskoye Russian Fed. 50 60.06N 69.58E
Gornyatskiy Russian Fed. 44 67.30N 64.03E
Goroch'an *mtn.* Ethiopia 73 9.22N 37.04E
Gorodenka Ukraine 37 48.40N 25.30E
Gorodishche Belorussia 37 53.18N 26.00E
Gorodishche Belorussia 37 53.45N 29.45E
Gorodnitsa Ukraine 37 50.50N 27.19E
Gorodnya Ukraine 37 51.54N 31.37E
Gorodok Ukraine 37 49.48N 23.39E
Goroka P.N.G. 59 6.02S145.22E
Goroke Australia 92 36.43S141.30E
Gorokhov Ukraine 37 50.30N 24.46E
Gorongosa *r.* Mozambique 81 20.29S 34.36E
Gorontalo Indonesia 59 0.33N123.05E
Gort Rep. of Ire. 15 53.04N 8.49W
Goryn Ukraine 37 52.08N 27.17E
Gorzów Wielkopolski Poland 36 52.42N 15.12E
Gosford Australia 93 33.25S151.18E
Goslar Germany 38 51.54N 10.25E
Gospić Croatia 31 44.33N 15.23E
Gosport U.K. 13 50.48N 1.08W
Gossi Mali 76 15.49N 1.17W
Gossinga Sudan 73 8.39N 25.59E
Gostivar Macedonia 34 41.47N 20.24E
Gostynin Poland 37 52.26N 19.29E
Göta *r.* Sweden 43 57.42N 11.52E
Göta Kanal Sweden 43 58.45N 14.05E
Göteborg Sweden 42 57.43N 11.58E
Göteborg och Bohus *d.* Sweden 42 58.30N 11.30E
Gotemba Japan 57 35.18N138.56E
Götene Sweden 43 58.32N 13.29E
Gotha Germany 38 50.57N 10.41E
Gothem Sweden 43 57.35N 18.43E
Gothenburg *see* Göteborg Sweden 42
Gothenburg U.S.A. 110 40.56N100.09W
Gothèye Niger 77 13.51N 1.31E
Gotland *d.* Sweden 43 57.25N 18.25E
Gotland *i.* Sweden 43 57.30N 18.33E
Gotse Delchev Bulgaria 34 41.34N 23.44E
Gotska Sandön *i.* Sweden 43 58.23N 19.16E
Gōtsu Japan 57 35.00N132.14E
Göttingen Germany 38 51.32N 9.55E
Götzis Austria 39 47.20N 9.38E
Gouarec France 18 48.13N 3.11W
Gouda Neth. 16 52.01N 4.43E
Gough I. Atlantic Oc. 127 40.20S 10.00W
Gouin, Résr. Canada 102 48.38N 74.54W
Goulais River *town* Canada 104 46.43N 84.18W
Goulburn Australia 93 34.47S149.43E
Goulburn *r.* Australia 93 36.08S144.30E
Goulburn Is. Australia 90 11.33S133.26E
Gould Canada 105 45.35N 71.24W
Goulimime Morocco 74 28.56N 10.04W
Gouménissa Greece 34 40.56N 22.37E
Goundam Mali 76 17.27N 3.39W
Gourdon France 20 44.44N 1.23E
Gouré Niger 77 13.59N 10.15E
Gourin France 18 48.08N 3.36W
Gourma-Rharous Mali 76 16.58N 1.50W
Gournay France 17 49.29N 1.44E
Gouro Chad 75 19.33N 19.33E
Gouverneur U.S.A. 105 44.20N 75.28W
Governador Valadares Brazil 126 18.51S 42.00W
Govind Balabh Pant Sāgar *resr.* India 63 24.05N 82.50E
Govind Sāgar *resr.* India 62 31.20N 76.45E
Gowanda U.S.A. 114 42.28N 78.56W
Goward Canada 104 47.08N 79.49W
Gowd-e Zereh *des.* Afghan. 65 30.00N 62.00E
Gower *pen.* U.K. 13 51.37N 4.10W
Gowmal *r.* Afghan. *see* Gumal *r.* Pakistan 62
Gowmal Kalay Afghan. 62 32.29N 68.55E
Goya Argentina 124 29.10S 59.20W
Goyder *r.* Australia 90 12.38S135.11E
Goz Béïda Chad 73 12.13N 21.25E
Gozo *i.* Malta 28 36.03N 14.16E
Graaff Reinet R.S.A. 80 32.15S 24.31E
Graben Germany 39 49.09N 8.29E
Grabow Germany 38 53.16N 11.34E
Gračac Croatia 31 44.18N 15.51E
Gračanica Bosnia-Herzegovina 31 44.42N 18.19E
Graçay France 19 47.08N 1.51E
Grace, L. Australia 89 33.18S118.15E
Gracefield Canada 105 46.06N 76.03W
Gracias á Dios, Cabo *c.* Honduras/Nicaragua 117 15.00N 83.10W
Gradačac Bosnia-Herzegovina 31 44.53N 18.26E
Grado Italy 30 45.40N 13.23E
Grado Spain 26 43.23N 6.04W
Grafenau Germany 39 48.52N 13.25E
Gräfenhainichen Germany 38 51.44N 12.27E
Grafing Germany 39 48.02N 11.59E
Gråfjell *mtn.* Norway 42 60.16N 9.29E
Grafton Australia 93 29.40S152.56E
Grafton Canada 104 44.00N 78.01W
Grafton Mass. U.S.A. 115 42.12N 71.41W
Grafton N.Dak. U.S.A. 110 48.25N 97.25W
Grafton Ohio U.S.A. 114 41.16N 82.04W
Grafton Wisc. U.S.A. 110 43.20N 87.58W
Grafton W.Va. U.S.A. 114 39.20N 80.01W
Graham *r.* Canada 100 56.31N122.17W
Graham U.S.A. 111 33.06N 98.35W
Graham, Mt. U.S.A. 109 32.42N109.52W
Graham I. Canada 100 53.40N132.30W
Graham Land *f.* Antarctica 128 67.00S 60.00W
Grahamstown R.S.A. 80 33.18S 26.30E
Graiguenamanagh Rep. of Ire. 15 52.33N 6.57W
Grajaú *r.* Brazil 123 3.41S 44.48W
Gram Denmark 42 55.17N 9.04E
Gramada Bulgaria 34 43.49N 22.39E
Gramat France 20 44.47N 1.43E
Grammichele Italy 33 37.13N 14.38E
Grámmos, Óros *mtn.* Greece 34 40.23N 20.45E
Grampian *d.* U.K. 14 57.22N 2.35W
Grampian Mts. U.K. 14 56.55N 4.00W
Grampians *mts.* Australia 92 37.12S142.34E
Gramsh Albania 34 40.52N 20.12E
Granada Nicaragua 117 11.58N 85.59W
Granada Spain 27 37.13N 3.41W
Granada *d.* Spain 27 37.30N 3.00W
Granby Canada 105 45.24N 72.44W
Gran Canaria *i.* Canary Is. 74 28.00N 15.30W
Gran Chaco *f.* S. America 124 22.00S 60.00W
Grand *r.* Canada 104 42.51N 79.34W
Grand *r.* Ohio U.S.A. 114 41.46N 81.17W
Grand *r.* S.Dak. U.S.A. 110 45.40N100.32W
Grandas Spain 26 43.13N 6.52W
Grandas de Salime, Embalse de *resr.* Spain 26 43.10N 6.45W
Grand Bahama I. Bahamas 113 26.40N 78.20W
Grand Ballon *mtn.* France 19 47.55N 7.08E
Grand Bank *town* Canada 103 47.06N 55.47W
Grand Bassam Ivory Coast 76 5.14N 3.45W
Grand Bend Canada 104 43.15N 81.45W
Grand Blanc U.S.A. 104 42.56N 83.38W
Grand Canal *see* Da Yunhe *canal* China 54
Grand Canyon *f.* U.S.A. 109 36.10N112.45W
Grand Canyon *town* U.S.A. 109 36.03N112.09W
Grand Canyon Nat. Park U.S.A. 109 36.15N112.58W
Grand Cayman *i.* Cayman Is. 117 19.20N 81.30W
Grand Centre Canada 101 54.25N110.13W
Grand Cess Liberia 76 4.40N 8.12W
Grand Couronne France 18 49.21N 1.00E
Grande *r.* Bolivia 124 15.10S 64.55W
Grande *r.* Bahia Brazil 123 11.05S 43.09W
Grande *r.* Minas Gerais Brazil 124 20.00S 51.00W
Grande *r.* Spain 25 39.07N 0.44W
Grande, Bahía *b.* Argentina 125 51.30S 67.30W
Grande, Ilha *i.* Brazil 126 23.07S 44.16W
Grande, Sierra *mts.* Mexico 109 29.35N104.55W
Grande Cascapédia Canada 103 48.19N 65.54W
Grande Comore *i.* Comoros 79 11.35S 43.20E
Grande do Gurupá, Ilha *i.* Brazil 123 1.00S 51.30W
Grande Prairie Canada 100 55.15N118.50W
Grand Erg de Bilma *des.* Niger 77 18.30N 14.00E
Grand Erg Occidental *des.* Algeria 74 30.10N 0.20E
Grand Erg Oriental *des.* Algeria 75 30.00N 7.00E
Grande Rivière *town* Canada 103 48.24N 64.30W
Grandes, Salinas *f.* Argentina 124 29.37S 64.56W
Grandes Bergeronnes Canada 103 48.15N 69.33W
Grande Vallée Canada 103 49.14N 65.08W
Grand Falls *town* N.B. Canada 103 46.55N 67.45W
Grand Falls *town* Nfld. Canada 103 48.56N 55.40W
Grand Forks Canada 100 49.00N118.30W
Grand Forks U.S.A. 110 47.55N 97.03W
Grand Fougeray France 18 47.44N 1.44W
Grand Gorge U.S.A. 115 42.22N 74.30W
Grand Hers *r.* France 20 43.47N 1.20E
Grand Island *town* U.S.A. 110 40.55N 98.21W
Grand Isle U.S.A. 105 44.44N 72.18W
Grand Junction U.S.A. 108 39.05N108.33W
Grand L. N.B. Canada 103 45.38N 67.38W
Grand L. Nfld. Canada 103 49.00N 57.25W
Grand L. U.S.A. 112 45.15N 67.50W
Grand Lahou Ivory Coast 76 5.09N 5.01W
Grand Lieu, Lac de *l.* France 18 47.06N 1.40W
Grand Manan I. Canada 103 44.40N 66.50W
Grand Marais U.S.A. 110 47.45N 90.20W
Grand' Mère Canada 105 46.37N 72.41W
Grandois Canada 103 51.07N 55.46W
Grândola Portugal 27 38.10N 8.34W
Grand Passage N. Cal. 84 18.45S163.10E
Grand Prairie *town* U.S.A. 111 32.45N 96.59W
Grand Rapids *town* Canada 101 53.08N 99.20W
Grand Rapids *town* Mich. U.S.A. 112 42.57N 85.40W
Grand Rapids *town* Minn. U.S.A. 110 47.14N 93.31W
Grand Récif de Cook *reef* N. Cal. 84 19.25S163.50E
Grand Remous Canada 105 46.37N 75.53W
Grandrieu France 20 44.47N 3.38E
Grand St. Bernard, Col du *pass* Italy/Switz. 30 45.52N 7.11E
Grand Teton *mtn.* U.S.A. 108 43.44N110.48W
Grand Teton Nat. Park U.S.A. 108 43.30N110.37W
Grand Traverse B. U.S.A. 112 45.02N 85.30W
Grand Valley Canada 104 43.54N 80.19W
Grand Valley *town* U.S.A. 108 39.27N108.03W
Grandville U.S.A. 112 42.54N 85.48W
Grañén Spain 25 41.56N 0.22W
Grangärde Sweden 43 60.16N 14.59E
Grangemouth U.K. 14 56.01N 3.44W
Granger U.S.A. 108 41.35N109.58W
Grängesberg Sweden 43 60.05N 14.59E
Grangeville U.S.A. 108 45.56N116.07W
Granite City U.S.A. 110 38.43N 90.04W
Granite Falls *town* U.S.A. 110 44.49N 95.31W
Granite Peak *town* Australia 88 25.38S121.21E
Granite Peak *mtn.* U.S.A. 106 45.10N109.50W
Granitola, Capo *c.* Italy 32 37.33N 12.40E
Granity New Zealand 86 41.38S171.51E
Granja Brazil 123 3.06S 40.50W
Gränna Sweden 43 58.01N 14.28E
Granollers Spain 25 41.37N 2.18E
Granön Sweden 40 64.15N 19.19E
Gran Paradiso *mtn.* Italy 30 45.32N 7.16E
Gran Sasso d'Italia *mts.* Italy 31 42.26N 13.35E
Gransee Germany 38 53.00N 13.09E
Grant Mich. U.S.A. 112 43.20N 85.49W
Grant Nebr. U.S.A. 110 40.50N101.56W
Grant City U.S.A. 110 40.29N 94.25W
Grantham U.K. 12 52.55N 0.39W
Grantown-on-Spey U.K. 14 57.20N 3.38W
Grant Range *mts.* U.S.A. 108 38.25N115.30W
Grants U.S.A. 109 35.09N107.52W
Grants Pass *town* U.S.A. 108 42.26N123.19W
Grantsville U.S.A. 114 38.55N 81.06W
Granville France 18 48.50N 1.36W
Granville N.Dak. U.S.A. 110 48.16N100.47W
Granville N.Y. U.S.A. 115 43.24N 73.16W
Granville L. Canada 101 56.18N100.30W
Gras, Lac de *l.* Canada 98 64.30N110.30W
Graskop R.S.A. 80 24.55S 30.50E
Grassano Italy 33 40.38N 16.18E
Grasse France 21 43.40N 6.55E
Grasset, L. Canada 102 49.55N 78.00W
Grass Lake *town* U.S.A. 104 42.15N 84.13W
Grass Valley *town* Calif. U.S.A. 108 39.13N121.04W
Grass Valley *town* Oreg. U.S.A. 108 45.22N120.47W
Gråsten Denmark 42 54.55N 9.36E
Grates Pt. Canada 103 48.09N 52.57W
Graubünden *d.* Switz. 39 46.42N 9.25E
Grave Neth. 16 51.45N 5.45E
Grave, Pointe de *c.* France 20 45.34N 1.04W
Gravelbourg Canada 101 49.53N106.34W
Gravenhurst Canada 104 44.55N 79.22W
Gravesend Australia 93 29.35S150.20E
Gravesend U.K. 13 51.27N 0.24E
Gravina in Puglia Italy 33 40.49N 16.25E
Gray France 19 47.27N 5.35E
Grayling U.S.A. 104 44.40N 84.43W
Grays U.K. 13 51.29N 0.20E
Graz Austria 31 47.05N 15.27E
Grazalema Spain 27 36.46N 5.22W
Grdelica Yugo. 34 42.54N 22.04E
Great Abaco I. Bahamas 113 26.25N 77.10W
Great Artesian Basin *f.* Australia 90 26.30S143.02E
Great Australian Bight Australia 89 33.10S129.30E
Great B. U.S.A. 115 39.30N 74.23W
Great Bahama Bank *f.* Bahamas 113 23.15N 78.00W
Great Barrier I. New Zealand 86 36.15S175.30E
Great Barrier Reef *f.* Australia 90 16.30S146.30E
Great Barrington U.S.A. 115 42.12N 73.22W
Great Basin *f.* U.S.A. 108 40.35N116.00W
Great Bear L. Canada 98 66.00N120.00W
Great Bend *town* U.S.A. 110 38.22N 98.46W
Great Bitter L. *see* Murrah al Kubrá, Al Buḩayrah al *h5ayrah al* Egypt 66
Great Blasket I. Rep. of Ire. 15 52.05N 10.32W
Great Cloche I. Canada 104 46.01N 81.54W
Great Coco *i.* Burma 56 14.06N 93.21E
Great Divide Basin *f.* U.S.A. 108 42.00N108.10W
Great Dividing Range *mts.* Australia 93 29.00S152.00E
Great Driffield U.K. 12 54.01N 0.26W
Great Duck I. Canada 104 45.40N 82.58W
Greater Antilles *is.* C. America 117 17.00N 70.00W
Greater London *d.* U.K. 13 51.31N 0.06W
Greater Manchester *d.* U.K. 12 53.30N 2.18W
Great Exuma *i.* Bahamas 117 23.00N 76.00W
Great Falls *town* U.S.A. 108 47.30N111.17W
Great Inagua I. Bahamas 117 21.00N 73.20W
Great Indian Desert *see* Thar Desert India/Pakistan 62
Great Karoo *f.* R.S.A. 80 32.40S 22.20E
Great Kei *r.* R.S.A. 80 32.39S 28.23E
Great L. Australia 91 41.50S146.43E
Great Malvern U.K. 13 52.07N 2.19W
Great Namaland *f.* Namibia 80 25.30S 17.20E
Great Nicobar *i.* India 56 7.00N 93.45E
Great Ouse *r.* U.K. 12 52.47N 0.23E
Great Pt. U.S.A. 115 41.23N 70.03W
Great Rift Valley *f.* Africa 70 8.00S 31.30E
Great Ruaha *r.* Tanzania 79 7.55S 37.52E
Great Sacandaga L. U.S.A. 115 43.08N 74.10W
Great Salt L. U.S.A. 108 41.10N112.30W
Great Salt Lake Desert U.S.A. 108 40.40N113.30W
Great Sand Hills Canada 101 50.35N109.05W
Great Sandy Desert Australia 88 20.30S123.35E
Great Sandy Desert *see* An Nafūd *des.* Saudi Arabia 64
Great Sea Reef Fiji 84 16.25S179.20E
Great Slave L. Canada 100 61.23N115.38W
Great Smoky Mountain Nat. Park U.S.A. 113 35.56N 82.48W
Great Sound *b.* Bermuda 127 32.18N 64.60W
Great Victoria Desert Australia 89 29.00S127.30E
Great Whernside *mtn.* U.K. 12 54.09N 1.59W
Great Yarmouth U.K. 13 52.40N 1.45E
Great Zimbabwe *ruins* Zimbabwe 80 20.30S 30.30E
Grebbestad Sweden 42 58.42N 11.15E
Gréboun, Mont *mtn.* Niger 75 20.01N 8.35E
Gredos, Sierra de *mts.* Spain 26 40.15N 5.20W
Greece Europe 34 40.00N 23.00E
Greeley U.S.A. 108 40.25N104.42W
Green *r.* U.S.A. 108 38.11N109.53W
Green B. U.S.A. 110 45.00N 87.30W
Green Bay *town* U.S.A. 110 44.30N 88.01W
Greenbush Mich. U.S.A. 104 44.34N 83.19W
Greenbush Minn. U.S.A. 110 48.42N 96.11W
Greenbushes Australia 89 33.50S116.00E
Greencastle Ind. U.S.A. 112 39.39N 86.51W
Greencastle Penn. U.S.A. 114 39.47N 77.44W
Greene U.S.A. 115 42.20N 75.46W
Greene I. Canada 104 45.51N 83.08W
Greeneville U.S.A. 113 36.10N 82.50W
Greenfield Ill. U.S.A. 110 39.21N 90.21W
Greenfield Iowa U.S.A. 110 41.18N 94.28W
Greenfield Mass. U.S.A. 115 42.36N 72.36W
Greenfield Mo. U.S.A. 111 37.25N 93.51W
Greenhills Australia 89 31.58S117.01E
Greening Canada 102 48.08N 74.55W
Greenland N. America 99 68.00N 45.00W
Greenlaw U.K. 14 55.43N 2.28W
Green Mts. U.S.A. 115 43.45N 72.45W
Greenock U.K. 14 55.57N 4.45W
Greenore Pt. Rep. of Ire. 15 52.14N 6.19W
Greenough *r.* Australia 89 29.22S114.34E
Greenport U.S.A. 115 41.06N 72.22W
Green River *town* Utah U.S.A. 108 38.59N110.10W
Green River *town* Wyo. U.S.A. 108 41.32N109.28W
Greensboro N.C. U.S.A. 113 36.04N 79.47W
Greensboro Vt. U.S.A. 105 44.32N 72.17W
Greensburg Ind. U.S.A. 112 39.20N 85.29W
Greensburg Penn. U.S.A. 114 40.18N 79.33W
Greenvale Australia 90 18.57S144.53E
Greenville Canada 100 55.03N129.33W
Greenville Liberia 76 5.01N 9.03W
Greenville Ala. U.S.A. 113 31.50N 86.40W
Greenville Mich. U.S.A. 112 43.11N 85.13W
Greenville Miss. U.S.A. 111 33.25N 91.05W
Greenville Mo. U.S.A. 111 37.08N 90.27W
Greenville N.C. U.S.A. 113 35.36N 77.23W
Greenville N.H. U.S.A. 115 42.46N 71.49W
Greenville Penn. U.S.A. 114 41.24N 80.23W
Greenville S.C. U.S.A. 113 34.52N 82.25W
Greenville Tex. U.S.A. 111 33.08N 96.07W
Greenwich Conn U.S.A. 115 41.01N 73.38W
Greenwich N.Y. U.S.A. 115 41.05N 73.30W
Greenwich Ohio U.S.A. 114 41.02N 82.31W
Greenwood Miss. U.S.A. 111 33.31N 90.11W
Greenwood N.Y. U.S.A. 114 42.08N 77.39W
Greenwood S.C. U.S.A. 113 34.11N 82.10W
Gregory *r.* Australia 90 17.53S139.17E
Gregory U.S.A. 110 43.14N 99.26W
Gregory, L. S.A. Australia 92 28.55S139.00E
Gregory L. W.A. Australia 88 20.10S127.20E
Gregory Range *mts.* Australia 90 19.00S143.05E
Greifswald Germany 38 54.05N 13.23E
Greifswalder Bodden *c.* Germany 38 54.15N 13.35E
Greiz Germany 38 50.39N 12.12E
Gremikha Russian Fed. 44 68.03N 39.38E
Grenå Denmark 42 56.25N 10.53E
Grenada C. America 117 12.07N 61.40W
Grenade France 20 43.47N 1.10E
Grenchen Switz. 39 47.11N 7.24E
Grenen *c.* Denmark 42 57.45N 10.40E
Grenfell Australia 93 33.53S148.11E
Grenoble France 21 45.10N 5.43E
Grenville, C. Australia 90 12.00S143.13E
Gréoux-les-Bains France 21 43.45N 5.53E
Gresik Indonesia 59 7.12S112.38E
Gretna U.K. 14 55.00N 3.04W
Gretna U.S.A. 111 29.55N 90.03W
Greven Germany 38 52.05N 7.36E
Grevená Greece 34 40.04N 21.25E
Grevenbroich Germany 16 51.07N 6.33E
Grevesmühlen Germany 38 53.51N 11.10E
Grey *r.* New Zealand 86 42.28S171.13E
Grey, C. Australia 90 13.00S136.40E
Greybull U.S.A. 108 44.30N108.03W
Grey Is. Canada 103 50.50N 55.37W
Greylock, Mt. U.S.A. 115 42.38N 73.10W
Greymouth New Zealand 86 42.28S171.12E
Grey Range *mts.* Australia 91 27.30S143.59E
Greystones Rep. of Ire. 15 53.09N 6.04W
Greytown R.S.A. 80 29.04S 30.36E
Griesbach Germany 39 48.28N 13.11E
Griesheim Germany 39 49.50N 8.34E
Griffin U.S.A. 107 33.15N 84.17W
Griffith Australia 93 34.18S146.04E
Griffith Canada 105 45.14N 77.12W
Griffith I. Canada 104 44.51N 80.54W
Griggsville U.S.A. 110 39.42N 90.43W
Grignan France 21 44.25N 4.54E
Grignols France 20 44.23N 0.03W
Grigoriopol Moldavia 37 47.08N 29.18E
Grim, C. Australia 91 40.45S144.45E
Grimari C.A.R. 73 5.44N 20.03E
Grimma Germany 38 51.14N 12.43E
Grimmen Germany 38 54.07N 13.02E
Grimsby Canada 104 43.12N 79.34W
Grimsby U.K. 12 53.35N 0.05W
Grimsel Pass Switz. 39 46.34N 8.21E
Grimstad Norway 42 58.20N 8.36E
Grimsvötn *mtn.* Iceland 40 64.30N 17.10W
Grindavik Iceland 40 63.50N 22.27W

Grindelwald to **Halden**

Grindelwald Switz. **39** 46.37N 8.02E
Grindsted Denmark **42** 55.45N 8.56E
Grinnell U.S.A. **110** 41.45N 92.43W
Grintavec *mtn.* Slovenia **31** 46.21N 14.32E
Griqualand East *f.* R.S.A. **80** 30.40S 29.10E
Griqualand West *f.* R.S.A. **80** 28.50S 23.30E
Gris-Nez, Cap *c.* France **18** 50.52N 1.35E
Grisslehamn Sweden **43** 60.06N 18.50E
Griva Russian Fed. **44** 60.35N 50.58E
Grmeč *mts.* Bosnia-Herzegovina **31** 44.40N 16.15E
Grobina Latvia **41** 56.33N 21.10E
Groblershoop R.S.A. **80** 28.55S 20.59E
Grodno Belorussia **37** 53.40N 23.50E
Grodzisk Poland **36** 52.14N 16.22E
Grodzyanka Belorussia **37** 53.30N 28.41E
Groenlo Neth. **16** 52.02N 6.36E
Groix, Île de *i.* France **18** 47.38N 3.27W
Gronau Germany **38** 52.13N 7.00E
Grong Norway **40** 64.27N 12.19E
Groningen Neth. **16** 53.13N 6.35E
Groningen *d.* Neth. **16** 53.15N 6.45E
Groom U.S.A. **111** 35.12N101.06W
Groot *r.* C.P. *r.* R.S.A. **80** 33.58S 25.03E
Groote Eylandt *i.* Australia **90** 14.00S136.40E
Grootfontein Namibia **80** 19.32S 18.07E
Groot Karasberge *mts.* Namibia **80** 27.20S 18.50E
Grootlaagte *r.* Botswana **80** 20.58S 21.42E
Groot Swartberge *mts.* R.S.A. **80** 33.20S 22.00E
Grossenbrode Germany **38** 54.22N 11.05E
Grossenhain Germany **38** 51.17N 13.31E
Grosser Arber *mtn.* Germany **39** 49.07N 13.07E
Grosser Priel *mtn.* Austria **39** 47.43N 14.04E
Grosseto Italy **30** 42.46N 11.08E
Gross-Gerau Germany **39** 49.55N 8.29E
Gross Glockner *mtn.* Austria **30** 47.04N 12.42E
Grossräschen Germany **38** 51.35N 14.00E
Gross Venediger *mtn.* Austria **30** 47.06N 12.21E
Groswater B. Canada **103** 54.20N 57.30W
Grote Nete *r.* Belgium **16** 51.07N 4.20E
Groton U.S.A. **115** 42.35N 76.22W
Grottaglie Italy **33** 40.32N 17.26E
Grottaminarda Italy **33** 41.04N 15.02E
Grottammare Italy **31** 42.59N 13.52E
Groundhog *r.* Canada **102** 49.40N 82.06W
Grouse Creek *town* U.S.A. **108** 41.22N113.53W
Grove City U.S.A. **114** 41.10N 80.05W
Grover City U.S.A. **109** 35.07N120.37W
Groves U.S.A. **111** 29.57N 93.55W
Groveton N.H. U.S.A. **105** 44.36N 71.31W
Groveton Tex. U.S.A. **111** 31.03N 95.08W
Groznyy Russian Fed. **45** 43.21N 45.42E
Grubišno Polje Croatia **31** 45.42N 17.10E
Grudziądz Poland **37** 53.29N 18.45E
Grumeti *r.* Tanzania **79** 2.05S 33.45E
Grumo Appula Italy **33** 41.01N 16.43E
Grums Sweden **43** 59.21N 13.06E
Grünau Austria **39** 47.51N 13.57E
Grünau Namibia **80** 27.44S 18.18E
Grundarfjördhur *town* Iceland **40** 64.55N 23.20W
Grundy U.S.A. **113** 37.13N 82.08W
Grungedal Norway **42** 59.44N 7.43E
Grünstadt Germany **39** 49.34N 8.10E
Gryazovets Russian Fed. **44** 58.52N 40.12E
Gryfice Poland **36** 53.56N 15.12E
Grythyttan Sweden **43** 59.42N 14.32E
Gstaad Switz. **39** 46.28N 7.17E
Guachipas Argentina **124** 25.31S 65.31W
Guacuí Brazil **126** 20.44S 41.40W
Guadajoz *r.* Spain **27** 37.50N 4.51W
Guadalajara Mexico **116** 20.30N103.20W
Guadalajara Spain **26** 40.38N 3.10W
Guadalajara *d.* Spain **26** 40.50N 2.50W
Guadalamar *r.* Spain **26** 38.05N 3.36W
Guadalaviar *r.* Spain **25** 40.21N 1.08W
Guadalcanal *i.* Solomon Is. **84** 9.32S160.12E
Guadalcanal Spain **26** 38.06N 5.49W
Guadalén Spain **26** 38.05N 3.32W
Guadalén, Embalse de *resr.* Spain **26** 38.25N 3.15W
Guadalete *r.* Spain **27** 36.35N 6.13W
Guadalmena *r.* Spain **26** 38.19N 2.56W
Guadalmez *r.* Spain **26** 38.46N 5.04W
Guadalope *r.* Spain **25** 41.15N 0.03W
Guadalquivir *r.* Spain **27** 36.47N 6.22W
Guadalupe Mexico **111** 25.41N100.15W
Guadalupe, Isla de *i.* Mexico **109** 29.00N118.16W
Guadalupe, Sierra de *mts.* Spain **27** 39.35N 5.25W
Guadarrama *r.* Spain **27** 39.53N 4.10W
Guadarrama, Puerto de *pass* Spain **26** 40.43N 4.10W
Guadarrama, Sierra de *mts.* Spain **26** 41.00N 3.50W
Guadazaón Spain **25** 39.42N 1.36W
Guadeloupe *i.* Leeward Is. **117** 16.20N 61.40W
Guadiana *r.* Portugal **27** 37.11N 7.24W
Guadiana Menor *r.* Spain **27** 37.56N 3.15W
Guadiaro *r.* Spain **27** 36.17N 5.17W
Guadix Spain **27** 37.18N 3.08W
Guafo, Golfo de *g.* Chile **125** 43.35S 74.15W
Guainía *r.* Colombia **122** 2.01N 67.07W
Guaíra Brazil **124** 24.04S 54.15W
Guajará Mirim Brazil **122** 10.48S 65.22W
Guajira, Península de la *pen.* Colombia **122** 12.00N 72.00W
Gualdo Tadino Italy **30** 43.14N 12.47E
Gualeguay Argentina **125** 33.10S 59.20W
Gualeguay *r.* Argentina **125** 33.18S 59.38W
Gualeguaychu Argentina **125** 33.00S 58.30W
Guam *i.* Mariana Is. **84** 13.30N144.40E
Guamal Colombia **122** 9.10N 74.15W
Guanajuato Mexico **116** 21.00N101.16W
Guanajuato *d.* Mexico **116** 21.00N101.00W
Guanare Venezuela **122** 9.04N 69.45W
Guanarito Venezuela **122** 8.43N 69.12W
Guane Cuba **117** 22.13N 84.07W
Guang'an China **55** 30.30N106.35E
Guangchang China **55** 26.50N116.16E
Guangdong *d.* China **55** 23.00N113.00E
Guanghan China **55** 30.59N104.15E
Guanghua *see* Laohekou China **54**
Guangji China **55** 29.42N115.39E
Guangming Ding *mtn.* China **55** 30.09N118.11E
Guangnan China **55** 24.03N105.03E
Guangrao China **54** 37.04N118.22E
Guangxi Zhuangzu *d.* China **55** 23.30N109.00E
Guangyuan China **54** 32.29N105.55E
Guangze China **55** 27.27N117.23E
Guangzhou China **55** 23.08N113.20E
Guanling China **55** 25.57N105.38E
Guantánamo Cuba **117** 20.09N 75.14W
Guan Xian Shandong China **54** 36.29N115.25E
Guan Xian Sichuan China **61** 30.59N103.40E
Guanyun China **54** 34.17N119.15E
Guaporé *r.* Bolivia / Brazil **124** 12.00S 65.15W
Guaqui Bolivia **124** 16.35S 68.51W
Guara, Sierra de *mts.* Spain **25** 42.20N 0.20W
Guarabira Brazil **123** 6.46S 35.25W
Guarapuava Brazil **126** 25.22S 51.28W
Guaratinguetá Brazil **126** 22.49S 45.09W
Guarda Portugal **26** 40.32N 7.16W
Guarda *d.* Portugal **26** 40.40N 7.15W
Guardavalle Italy **33** 38.30N 16.30E
Guardiagrele Italy **31** 42.11N 14.13E
Guardo Spain **26** 42.47N 4.50W
Guareim *r.* Uruguay *see* Quarí *r.* Brazil **125**
Guareña Spain **27** 38.51N 6.06W
Guareña *r.* Spain **26** 41.29N 5.23W
Guasave Mexico **109** 25.34N108.27W
Guasipati Venezuela **122** 7.28N 61.54W
Guastalla Italy **30** 44.55N 10.39E
Guatemala C. America **117** 15.40N 90.00W
Guatemala *town* Guatemala **116** 14.38N 90.22W
Guatemala Basin Pacific Oc. **85** 12.00N 95.00W
Guatemala Trench Pacific Oc. **85** 15.00N 93.00W
Guatire Venezuela **122** 10.28N 66.32W
Guaviare *r.* Colombia **122** 4.00N 67.35W
Guaxupé Brazil **126** 21.17S 46.44W
Guayaquil Ecuador **122** 2.13S 79.54W
Guayaquil, Golfo de *g.* Ecuador **122** 3.00S 80.35W
Guaymallén Argentina **125** 32.54S 68.47W
Guaymas Mexico **109** 27.56N110.54W
Guayquiraró *r.* Argentina **125** 30.25S 59.36W
Guba Zaïre **78** 10.40S 26.26E
Gubakha Russian Fed. **44** 58.55N 57.30E
Gubbio Italy **30** 43.21N 12.35E
Gubeikou China **54** 40.41N117.09E
Gubin Poland **36** 51.59N 14.42E
Gubio Nigeria **77** 12.31N 12.44E
Guchab Namibia **80** 19.40S 17.47E
Gucheng China **54** 37.20N115.57E
Gúdar, Sierra de *mts.* Spain **25** 40.30N 0.40W
Gudbrandsdalen *f.* Norway **41** 61.30N 10.00E
Gudhjem Denmark **43** 55.13N 14.59E
Gudvangen Norway **41** 60.52N 6.50E
Guebwiller France **19** 47.55N 7.12E
Guecho Spain **26** 43.22N 3.00W
Guékédou Guinea **76** 8.35N 10.11W
Guelma Algeria **75** 36.28N 7.26E
Guelph Canada **104** 43.33N 80.15W
Guelta Zemmur W. Sahara **74** 25.15N 12.20W
Guéméné-sur-Scorff France **18** 48.04N 3.12W
Guera *d.* Chad **77** 11.22N 18.00E
Guerande France **18** 47.20N 2.26W
Guérard, Lac *l.* Canada **103** 56.20N 65.35W
Guéret France **20** 46.10N 1.52E
Guernica Spain **26** 43.19N 2.40W
Guernsey *i.* Channel Is. Europe **13** 49.27N 2.35W
Guerra Mozambique **79** 13.05S 35.12E
Guerrero *d.* Mexico **116** 18.00N100.00W
Guiana S. America **123** 3.40N 53.00W
Guiana Highlands S. America **122** 4.00N 59.00W
Guichen France **18** 47.58N 1.48W
Guichón Uruguay **125** 32.21S 57.12W
Guidimaka *d.* Mauritania **74** 15.20N 12.00W
Guiding China **55** 26.32N107.15E
Guidong China **55** 26.12N114.00E
Guiers, Lac de *l.* Senegal **76** 16.12N 15.50W
Gui Jiang *r.* China **55** 23.25N111.20E
Guijuelo Spain **26** 40.33N 5.40W
Guildford Australia **89** 31.55S115.55E
Guildford U.K. **13** 51.14N 0.35W
Guildhall U.S.A. **105** 44.34N 71.34W
Guilin China **55** 25.20N110.10E
Guillaume-Delisle, Lac *l.* Canada **102** 56.20N 75.50W
Guillaumes France **21** 44.05N 6.51E
Guillestre France **21** 44.40N 6.39E
Guilvinec France **18** 47.47N 4.17W
Guimarães Brazil **123** 2.08S 44.36W
Guimarães Portugal **26** 41.27N 8.18W
Guimeng Ding *mtn.* China **54** 35.34N117.50E
Guinan China **52** 35.20N100.50E
Guinea Africa **76** 10.30N 11.30W
Guinea, G. of Africa **77** 3.00N 3.00E
Guinea Basin *f.* Atlantic Oc. **127** 0.00 5.00W
Guinea Bissau Africa **76** 11.30N 15.00W
Güines Cuba **117** 22.50N 82.02W
Guînes France **19** 50.52N 1.52E
Guingamp France **18** 48.33N 3.11W
Guinguinéo Senegal **76** 14.20N 15.57W
Guiping China **55** 23.20N110.02E
Guipúzcoa *d.* Spain **26** 43.00N 2.20W
Guir, Hammada du *f.* Morocco / Algeria **74** 31.00N 3.20W
Güiria Venezuela **122** 10.37N 62.21W
Guiscard France **19** 49.39N 3.03E
Guise France **19** 49.54N 3.38E
Guitiriz Spain **26** 43.11N 7.54W
Guitres France **20** 45.03N 0.11W
Guiuan Phil. **59** 11.02N125.44E
Guixi China **55** 28.12N117.10E
Gui Xian China **55** 23.02N109.40E
Guiyang China **55** 26.31N106.39E
Guizhou *d.* China **55** 27.00N107.00E
Gujarat *d.* India **62** 22.20N 70.30E
Gūjar Khān Pakistan **62** 33.16N 73.19E
Gujrānwāla Pakistan **62** 32.26N 74.33E
Gujrāt Pakistan **62** 32.34N 74.05E
Gulang Gansu China **54** 37.30N102.54E
Gulargambone Australia **93** 31.21S148.32E
Gulbarga India **60** 17.22N 76.47E
Gulfport U.S.A. **111** 30.22N 89.06W
Gulgong Australia **93** 32.20S149.49E
Gulin China **55** 28.07N105.51E
Gulistān Pakistan **62** 30.36N 66.35E
Gullholmen Sweden **42** 58.11N 11.24E
Gull Lake *town* Canada **101** 50.08N108.27W
Gullspång Sweden **43** 58.59N 14.06E
Güllük Turkey **35** 37.14N 27.36E
Gulma Nigeria **77** 12.41N 4.24E
Gülpinar Turkey **34** 39.32N 26.10E
Gulshad Kazakhstan **52** 46.37N 74.22E
Gulu Uganda **79** 2.46N 32.21E
Guluy Ethiopia **72** 14.43N 36.45E
Gulwe Tanzania **79** 6.27S 36.27E
Gulyantsi Bulgaria **34** 43.38N 24.42E
Gumal *r.* Pakistan **62** 32.08N 69.50E
Gumel Nigeria **77** 12.39N 9.23E
Gumla India **63** 23.03N 84.33E
Gummersbach Germany **38** 51.02N 7.34E
Gum Spring *town* U.S.A. **113** 37.47N 77.54W
Gümüşhane Turkey **64** 40.26N 39.26E
Guna India **62** 24.39N 77.19E
Gunbar Australia **93** 34.04S145.25E
Gundagai Australia **93** 35.07S148.05E
Gundlupet India **60** 11.48N 76.41E
Gungu Zaïre **78** 5.43S 19.20E
Gunisao *r.* Canada **101** 53.54N 97.58W
Gunisao L. Canada **101** 53.33N 96.15W
Gunnebo Sweden **43** 57.43N 16.32E
Gunnedah Australia **93** 30.59S150.15E
Gunning Australia **93** 34.46S149.17E
Gunnison Colo. U.S.A. **108** 38.33N106.56W
Gunnison *r.* U.S.A. **108** 39.03N108.35W
Gunnison Utah U.S.A. **108** 39.09N111.49W
Guntersville U.S.A. **113** 34.20N 86.18W
Guntersville L. U.S.A. **113** 34.45N 86.03W
Guntūr India **61** 16.20N 80.27E
Gunungsitoli Indonesia **58** 1.17N 97.37E
Gunupur India **63** 19.05N 83.49E
Günz *r.* Germany **39** 48.27N 10.16E
Günzburg Germany **39** 48.27N 10.16E
Gunzenhausen Germany **39** 49.07N 10.45E
Guochengyi China **54** 36.14N104.52E
Gurais Jammu & Kashmir **62** 34.38N 74.50E
Gura Portiţei *f.* Romania **37** 44.40N 29.00E
Gurban Obo China **54** 43.05N112.27E
Gurdāspur Jammu & Kashmir **62** 32.02N 75.31E
Gurgaon India **62** 28.28N 77.02E
Gurgueia *r.* Brazil **123** 6.45S 43.35W
Gūrha India **62** 25.14N 71.45E
Gurk *r.* Austria **31** 46.36N 14.31E
Gursköy *i.* Norway **40** 62.16N 5.42E
Gurué Mozambique **81** 15.30S 36.58E
Gürün Turkey **64** 38.44N 37.15E
Gurupá Brazil **123** 1.25S 51.39W
Gurupi *r.* Brazil **123** 1.13S 46.06W
Guru Sikhar *mtn.* India **62** 24.39N 72.46E
Guruve Zimbabwe **80** 16.42S 30.40E
Gurvan Sayhan Uul *mts.* Mongolia **54** 43.45N103.30E
Guryev Kazakhstan **45** 47.08N 51.59E
Gusau Nigeria **77** 12.12N 6.40E
Gusev Russian Fed. **37** 54.32N 22.12E
Gusong China **55** 28.25N105.12E
Guspini Italy **32** 39.32N 8.38E
Güssing Austria **31** 47.04N 16.20E
Gustav Holm, Kap *c.* Greenland **99** 67.00N 34.00W
Güstrow Germany **38** 53.48N 12.10E
Gusum Sweden **43** 58.16N 16.29E
Gütersloh Germany **38** 51.54N 8.23E
Guthrie Ky. U.S.A. **113** 36.40N 87.10W
Guthrie Okla. U.S.A. **111** 35.53N 97.25W
Guvrin, Nahal *wadi* Israel **67** 31.43N 34.42E
Guyana S. America **122** 4.40N 59.00W
Guyang China **54** 41.03N110.03E
Guymon U.S.A. **111** 36.41N101.29W
Guyra Australia **93** 30.14S151.40E
Guyuan Hebei China **54** 41.40N115.41E
Guyuan Ningxia Huizu China **54** 36.00N106.25E
Guzhen Anhui China **54** 33.19N117.19E
Guzman, Laguna de *l.* Mexico **109** 31.25N107.25W
Gwa Burma **61** 17.36N 94.35E
Gwabegar Australia **93** 30.34S149.00E
Gwadabawa Nigeria **77** 13.23N 5.15E
Gwādar Pakistan **62** 25.07N 62.19E
Gwagwada Nigeria **77** 10.15N 7.15E
Gwai Zimbabwe **80** 19.15S 27.42E
Gwai *r.* Zimbabwe **80** 17.59S 26.55E
Gwalior India **63** 26.13N 78.10E
Gwanda Zimbabwe **80** 20.59S 29.00E
Gwane Zaïre **73** 4.43N 25.50E
Gwasero Nigeria **77** 9.30N 8.30E
Gweebarra B. Rep. of Ire. **15** 54.52N 8.28W
Gwent *d.* U.K. **13** 51.44N 3.00W
Gweru Zimbabwe **80** 19.25S 29.50E
Gwydir *r.* Australia **93** 29.35S148.45E
Gwynedd *d.* U.K. **12** 53.00N 4.00W
Gy France **19** 47.24N 5.49E
Gyaca China **63** 29.05N 92.55E
Gyandzha Azerbaijan **65** 40.39N 46.20E
Gyangrang China **63** 30.47N 85.09E
Gyangzê China **63** 28.57N 89.38E
Gyaring Co *l.* China **63** 31.05N 88.00E
Gydanskiy Poluostrov *pen.* Russian Fed. **50** 70.00N 78.30E
Gyimda China **63** 31.03N 97.18E
Gyirong China **63** 29.00N 85.15E
Gympie Australia **90** 26.11S152.40E
Gyōda Japan **57** 36.08N139.28E
Gyöngyös Hungary **37** 47.47N 19.56E
Györ Hungary **37** 47.41N 17.40E
Gypsum Pt. Canada **100** 61.53N114.35W
Gypsumville Canada **101** 51.45N 98.35W
Gyueshovo Bulgaria **34** 42.14N 22.28E

H

Haag Germany **39** 48.10N 12.11E
Haan Germany **16** 51.10N 7.02E
Ha'apai Group *is.* Tonga **85** 19.50S174.30W
Haapajärvi Finland **40** 63.45N 25.20E
Haapamäki Finland **40** 62.15N 24.28E
Haapavesi Finland **40** 64.08N 25.22E
Haapsalu Estonia **41** 58.56N 23.33E
Haar Germany **39** 48.06N 11.44E
Hā Arava *r.* Israel / Jordan **66** 30.30N 35.10E
Haarlem Neth. **16** 52.22N 4.38E
Haarlem R.S.A. **80** 33.46S 23.28E
Hab *r.* Pakistan **62** 24.53N 66.41E
Habahe China **52** 47.53N 86.12E
Ḥabarūt Yemen **60** 17.18N 52.44E
Habaswein Kenya **79** 1.06N 39.26E
Habay-la-Neuve Belgium **16** 49.45N 5.38E
Ḥabbān Yemen **71** 14.21N 47.05E
Hab Chauki Pakistan **62** 25.01N 66.53E
Habiganj Bangla. **63** 24.23N 91.25E
Habikino Japan **57** 34.33N135.37E
Habo Sweden **43** 57.55N 14.04E
Hachinohe Japan **57** 40.30N141.30E
Hachiōji Japan **57** 35.39N139.20E
Hack, Mt. Australia **92** 30.44S138.45E
Hadāli Pakistan **62** 32.18N 72.12E
Hadano Japan **57** 35.22N139.14E
Ḥadāribah, Ra's al *c.* Sudan **72** 22.04N 36.54E
Hadarom *d.* Israel **67** 31.15N 34.50E
Ḥaḍbaram Oman **71** 17.27N 55.15E
Ḥadd, Ra's al *c.* Oman **65** 22.32N 59.49E
Haddington U.K. **14** 55.57N 2.47W
Hadejia Nigeria **77** 12.30N 10.03E
Hadejia *r.* Nigeria **77** 12.47N 10.44E
Hadera Israel **67** 32.26N 34.55E
Hadera *r.* Israel **67** 32.27N 35.53E
Haderslev Denmark **42** 55.15N 9.30E
Hadīboh Yemen **71** 12.39N 54.02E
Hadjer Mornou *mtn.* Chad **72** 17.12N 23.08E
Hadley N.Y. U.S.A. **115** 43.19N 73.51W
Hadley Penn. U.S.A. **114** 41.25N 80.14W
Ha Dong Vietnam **55** 20.40N105.58E
Ḥaḍramawt *f.* Yemen **71** 16.30N 49.30E
Hadsten Denmark **42** 56.20N 10.03E
Hadsund Denmark **42** 56.43N 10.07E
Haedo, Cuchilla de *mts.* Uruguay **125** 31.50S 56.10W
Haegeland Norway **42** 58.15N 7.47E
Haeju N. Korea **53** 38.04N125.40E
Haena Hawaiian Is. **85** 22.14N159.34W
Ḥafar al Bāṭin Saudi Arabia **65** 28.28N 46.00E
Ḥafīrah, Qā'al *f.* Jordan **67** 31.06N 36.14E
Hāfizābād Pakistan **62** 32.04N 73.41E
Hafnarfjördhur *town* Iceland **40** 64.04N 21.58W
Haft Gel Iran **65** 31.28N 49.35E
HaGalil *f.* Israel **67** 32.54N 35.20E
Hagen Germany **38** 51.22N 7.28E
Hagenow Germany **38** 53.26N 11.11E
Hagerman U.S.A. **109** 33.07N104.20W
Hagerstown U.S.A. **114** 39.39N 77.43W
Hagersville Canada **104** 42.58N 80.03W
Hagetmau France **20** 43.40N 0.35W
Hagfors Sweden **43** 60.02N 13.42E
Hagi Japan **57** 34.25N131.22E
Ha Giang Vietnam **55** 22.50N105.00E
Hagondange France **19** 49.15N 6.10E
Hags Head Rep. of Ire. **15** 52.56N 9.29W
Hague U.S.A. **115** 43.45N 73.31W
Hague, Cap de la *c.* France **18** 49.44N 1.56W
Haguenau France **19** 48.49N 7.47E
Hahn Germany **38** 50.31N 7.53E
Hai'an Shan *mts.* China **55** 23.00N115.30E
Haicheng China **54** 40.52N122.48E
Hai Duong Vietnam **56** 20.56N106.21E
Haifa *see* Hefa Israel **67**
Haifa, B. of *see* Mifraz Hefa Israel **67**
Haifeng China **55** 22.58N115.20E
Haikang China **55** 20.55N110.04E
Haikou China **55** 20.03N110.27E
Ḥā'il Saudi Arabia **64** 27.31N 41.45E
Hailākāndi India **63** 24.41N 92.34E
Hailar China **53** 49.15N119.41E
Haileybury Canada **104** 47.27N 79.38W
Hailong China **54** 42.39N125.49E
Hailsham U.K. **13** 50.52N 0.17E
Hailun China **53** 47.29N126.58E
Hailuoto *i.* Finland **40** 65.02N 24.42E
Haimen China **55** 28.41N121.30E
Hainan *d.* China **55** 19.00N109.30E
Hainaut *d.* Belgium **16** 50.30N 3.45E
Haines Alas. U.S.A. **100** 59.11N135.23W
Haines Oreg. U.S.A. **108** 44.55N117.56W
Haines Junction Canada **100** 60.45N137.30W
Haining China **55** 30.30N120.35E
Haiphong Vietnam **55** 20.48N106.40E
Haiti C. America **117** 19.00N 73.00W
Haiyang China **54** 36.46N121.09E
Haiyuan China **54** 36.35N105.40E
Ḥajar Banga Sudan **73** 11.30N 23.00E
Hajdúböszörmény Hungary **37** 47.41N 21.30E
Hajdúszoboszló Hungary **37** 47.27N 21.24E
Hajiki saki *c.* Japan **57** 38.25N138.32E
Hājīpur India **63** 25.41N 85.13E
Hakkâri Turkey **65** 37.36N 43.45E
Hakodate Japan **57** 41.46N140.44E
Hakupu Niue **84** 19.07S169.51W
Hala Pakistan **62** 25.49N 68.25E
Ḥalab Syria **64** 36.14N 37.10E
Ḥalabjah Iraq **65** 35.10N 45.59E
Ḥalā'ib Sudan **72** 22.13N 36.38E
Hålaveden *hills* Sweden **43** 58.05N 14.45E
Ḥalbā Lebanon **66** 34.34N 36.05E
Halberstadt Germany **38** 51.54N 11.02E
Halden Norway **42** 59.09N 11.23E

Haldensleben to **Heiligenhafen**

Haldensleben Germany **38** 52.18N 11.26E
Haldia India **63** 22.05N 88.03E
Haldwāni India **63** 29.13N 79.31E
Hale U.S.A. **104** 44.23N 83.48W
Haleyville U.S.A. **113** 34.12N 87.38W
Half Assini Ghana **76** 5.04N 2.53W
Halfmoon Bay *town* Canada **100** 49.31N123.54W
Halfmoon Bay *town* New Zealand **86** 46.45S168.08E
Ḩalḩūl Jordan **67** 31.35N 35.07E
Haliburton Canada **104** 45.03N 78.30W
Haliburton Highlands Canada **104** 45.16N 78.19W
Halicarnassus *site* Turkey **35** 37.03N 27.28E
Halifax Canada **103** 44.39N 63.36W
Halifax U.K. **12** 53.43N 1.51W
Halifax U.S.A. **113** 36.46N 78.57W
Halīl *r.* Iran **60** 27.35N 58.44E
Halkett, C. U.S.A. **98** 71.00N152.00W
Halkirk U.K. **14** 58.30N 3.30W
Halladale *r.* U.K. **14** 58.34N 3.54W
Halland *d.* Sweden **43** 56.48N 12.50E
Halland *f.* Sweden **43** 57.03N 12.45E
Hallands Väderö *i.* Sweden **43** 56.26N 12.33E
Halle Belgium **16** 50.45N 4.14E
Halle Germany **38** 51.29N 11.58E
Hällefors Sweden **43** 59.47N 14.30E
Hälleforsnäs Sweden **43** 59.10N 16.30E
Hallein Austria **39** 47.41N 13.06E
Halligen *is.* Germany **38** 54.35N 8.35E
Hallingdal *f.* Norway **41** 60.30N 9.00E
Hall Is. Pacific Oc. **84** 8.37N152.00E
Hall Lake *town* Canada **99** 68.40N 81.30W
Hällnäs Sweden **40** 64.19N 19.38E
Hall Pen. Canada **99** 63.30N 66.00W
Hallsberg Sweden **43** 59.04N 15.07E
Hall's Creek *town* Australia **88** 18.13S127.39E
Hallstahammar Sweden **43** 59.37N 16.13E
Hallstatt Austria **39** 47.33N 13.39E
Hallstavik Sweden **43** 60.03N 18.36E
Hallstead U.S.A. **115** 41.58N 75.45W
Hallton U.S.A. **114** 41.26N 78.56W
Halmahera *i.* Indonesia **59** 0.45N128.00E
Halmstad Sweden **43** 56.39N 12.50E
Halsa Norway **40** 63.03N 8.14E
Hälsingborg Sweden **43** 56.03N 12.42E
Haltern Germany **38** 51.46N 7.10E
Haltia Tunturi *mtn.* Finland **40** 69.17N 21.21E
Haltwhistle U.K. **12** 54.58N 2.27W
Ham France **19** 49.45N 3.04E
Ham, Mt. Canada **105** 45.47N 71.37W
Ḩamaḑ, Wādī al *r.* Saudi Arabia **64** 25.49N 36.37E
Hamada *f. see* Drâa, Hamada du *f.* W. Sahara **74**
Hamadān Iran **65** 34.47N 48.33E
Ḩamādat Marzūq *f.* Libya **75** 26.00N 12.30E
Ḩamāh Syria **66** 35.09N 36.44E
Hamakita Japan **57** 34.48N137.47E
Hamamatsu Japan **57** 34.42N137.44E
Hamar Norway **41** 60.48N 11.06E
Hamaröy Norway **40** 68.05N 15.40E
Ḩamāţah, Jabal *mtn.* Egypt **64** 24.11N 35.01E
Hamborn Germany **16** 51.29N 6.46E
Hamburg Germany **38** 53.33N 9.59E
Hamburg *d.* Germany **38** 53.35N 10.00E
Hamburg R.S.A. **80** 33.17S 27.27E
Hamburg N.J. U.S.A. **115** 41.09N 74.35W
Hamburg N.Y. U.S.A. **114** 42.43N 78.50W
Hamburg Penn. U.S.A. **115** 40.34N 75.59W
Hamburgsund Sweden **42** 58.33N 11.16E
Hamden U.S.A. **115** 41.21N 72.56W
Häme *d.* Finland **41** 61.20N 24.30E
Hämeenlinna Finland **41** 61.00N 24.27E
Hamelin B. Australia **89** 34.10S115.00E
Hameln Germany **38** 52.06N 9.21E
HaMerkaz *d.* Israel **67** 32.05N 34.55E
Hamer Koke Ethiopia **73** 5.12N 36.45E
Hamersley Range *mts.* Australia **88** 22.00S118.00E
Hamhŭng N. Korea **53** 39.54N127.35E
Hami China **52** 42.40N 93.30E
Hamidiye Turkey **34** 41.09N 26.40E
Hamilton Australia **92** 37.45S142.04E
Hamilton *r.* Australia **91** 27.12S135.28E
Hamilton Bermuda **127** 32.18N 64.48W
Hamilton Canada **104** 43.15N 79.51W
Hamilton New Zealand **86** 37.46S175.18E
Hamilton U.K. **14** 55.46N 4.10W
Hamilton Mont. U.S.A. **108** 46.15N114.09W
Hamilton N.Y. U.S.A. **115** 42.50N 75.33W
Hamilton Ohio U.S.A. **112** 39.23N 84.33W
Hamilton Tex. U.S.A. **111** 31.42N 98.07W
Hamley Bridge *town* Australia **92** 34.21S138.41E
Hamlin Tex. U.S.A. **111** 32.53N100.08W
Hamlin W.Va. U.S.A. **114** 38.17N 82.06W
Hamm Germany **38** 51.41N 7.49E
Hammamet, Golfe de *g.* Tunisia **75** 36.05N 10.40E
Hammam Lif Tunisia **32** 36.44N 10.20E
Ḩammān, Wādī al Jordan **67** 31.38N 36.00E
Ḩammār, Hawr al *l.* Iraq **65** 30.50N 47.00E
Hammel Denmark **42** 56.15N 9.52E
Hammelburg Germany **39** 50.07N 9.53E
Hammerdal Sweden **40** 63.35N 15.20E
Hammerfest Norway **40** 70.40N 23.42E
Hammond Australia **92** 32.33S138.20E
Hammond La. U.S.A. **111** 30.30N 90.28W
Hammond N.Y. U.S.A. **105** 44.27N 75.42W
Hammond B. U.S.A. **104** 45.33N 84.00W
Hammondsport U.S.A. **114** 42.25N 77.13W
Hammonton U.S.A. **115** 39.38N 74.48W
Ham Nord Canada **105** 45.54N 71.39W
Hamoir Belgium **16** 50.25N 5.32E
Hamoyet, Jabal *mtn.* Sudan **72** 17.33N 38.00E
Hampshire *d.* U.K. **13** 51.03N 1.20W
Hampton N.H. U.S.A. **115** 42.56N 70.50W
Hampton S.C. U.S.A. **113** 32.52N 81.06W
Hampton Va. U.S.A. **113** 37.02N 76.23W
Hampton Bays *town* U.S.A. **115** 40.53N 72.31W
Hamra, Saguia el *wadi* W. Sahara **74** 27.15N 13.21W
Ḩamrīn, Jabal *mts.* Iraq **65** 34.40N 44.10E
Ham Sud Canada **105** 45.46N 71.36W
Hāmūn-e Jaz Mūrīān *l.* Iran **60** 27.20N 58.55E
Hana Hawaiian Is. **85** 20.45N155.59W
Hanamaki Japan **57** 39.23N141.07E
Hanang *mtn.* Tanzania **79** 4.30S 35.21E
Hanau Germany **39** 50.08N 8.55E
Hancheng China **54** 35.29N110.30E
Hancock Md. U.S.A. **114** 39.42N 78.13W
Hancock Mich. U.S.A. **112** 47.08N 88.34W
Hancock N.Y. U.S.A. **115** 41.57N 75.17W
Handa Japan **57** 34.53N136.56E
Handa Somali Rep. **71** 10.39N 51.08E
Handan China **54** 36.37N114.26E
Handen Sweden **43** 59.10N 18.08E
Handeni Tanzania **79** 5.25S 38.04E
HaNegev *des.* Israel **66** 30.42N 34.55E
Hanford U.S.A. **109** 36.20N119.39W
Hanga Roa I. de Pascua **85** 27.09S109.26W
Hanggin Houqi China **54** 40.50N107.06E
Hanggin Qi China **54** 39.56N108.54E
Hangö Finland **41** 59.50N 22.57E
Hangu China **54** 39.11N117.45E
Hangu Pakistan **62** 33.32N 71.04E
Hangzhou China **55** 30.14N120.08E
Hangzhou Wan *b.* China **55** 30.25N121.00E
Hanita Israel **67** 33.05N 35.10E
Hanjiang China **55** 25.30N119.14E
Hankey R.S.A. **80** 33.50S 24.52E
Hankinson U.S.A. **110** 46.04N 96.55W
Hanksville U.S.A. **108** 38.21N110.44W
Hānle Jammu & Kashmir **63** 32.48N 79.00E
Hanmer Springs *town* New Zealand **86** 42.31S172.50E
Hann, Mt. Australia **88** 15.55S125.57E
Hanna Canada **101** 51.38N111.54W
Hannaford U.S.A. **110** 47.19N 98.11W
Hannah B. Canada **102** 51.20N 80.00W
Hannibal Mo. U.S.A. **107** 39.41N 91.25W
Hannibal Ohio U.S.A. **114** 39.39N 80.51W
Hannover Germany **38** 52.24N 9.44E
Hannut Belgium **16** 50.40N 5.05E
Hanöbukten *b.* Sweden **43** 55.47N 15.00E
Hanoi Vietnam **55** 21.01N105.53E
Hanover Canada **104** 44.09N 81.02W
Hanover R.S.A. **80** 31.04S 24.25E
Hanover Mass. U.S.A. **115** 42.07N 70.49W
Hanover N.H. U.S.A. **115** 43.42N 72.18W
Hanover Penn. U.S.A. **114** 39.48N 76.59W
Hanover, Isla *i.* Chile **125** 50.57S 74.40W
Han Pijesak Bosnia-Herzegovina **31** 44.04N 18.59E
Hānsdiha India **63** 24.36N 87.05E
Hanshou China **55** 28.55N111.58E
Han Shui *r.* China **55** 30.32N114.20E
Hānsi Haryana India **62** 29.06N 75.58E
Hansi Himachal P. India **63** 32.27N 77.50E
Hanson, L. Australia **92** 31.02S136.13E
Hanstholm Denmark **42** 57.07N 8.38E
Hantengri Feng *mtn.* China **52** 42.09N 80.12E
Han Ul China **54** 45.10N119.48E
Hanyang China **55** 30.42N113.50E
Hanyin China **54** 32.53N108.37E
Hanzhong China **54** 33.08N107.04E
Haouach, Ouadi *wadi* Chad **75** 16.45N 19.35E
Haparanda Sweden **40** 65.50N 24.10E
Happy Valley *town* Canada **103** 53.16N 60.14W
Hapsu N. Korea **53** 41.12N128.48E
Hāpur India **63** 28.43N 77.47E
Ḩaql Saudi Arabia **66** 29.14N 34.56E
Ḩaraḑ Saudi Arabia **65** 24.12N 49.08E
Harare Zimbabwe **81** 17.49S 31.04E
Har-Ayrag Mongolia **54** 45.42N109.14E
Haraze Chad **73** 9.55N 20.48E
Harbin China **53** 45.45N126.41E
Harboör Denmark **42** 56.37N 8.12E
Harbor Beach U.S.A. **104** 43.51N 82.39W
Harborcreek U.S.A. **114** 42.10N 79.57W
Harbour Deep *town* Canada **103** 50.22N 56.27W
Harbour Grace *town* Canada **103** 47.42N 53.13W
Harburg Germany **36** 53.27N 9.58E
Hårby Denmark **42** 55.13N 10.07E
Harda India **62** 22.20N 77.06E
Hardangerfjorden *est.* Norway **41** 60.10N 6.00E
Hardangerjökulen *mtn.* Norway **41** 60.33N 7.26E
Hardanger Vidda *f.* Norway **42** 60.15N 7.20E
Hardeeville U.S.A. **113** 32.18N 81.05W
Hardenberg Neth. **16** 52.36N 6.40E
Harderwijk Neth. **16** 52.21N 5.37E
Harding R.S.A. **80** 30.34S 29.52E
Hardman U.S.A. **108** 45.10N119.40W
Hardoi India **63** 27.25N 80.07E
Hardwār India **63** 29.58N 78.10E
Hardwick U.S.A. **105** 44.30N 72.22W
Hardwicke B. Australia **92** 34.52S137.10E
Hardy U.S.A. **111** 36.19N 91.29W
Hare B. Canada **103** 51.18N 55.50W
Haren Germany **38** 52.47N 7.14E
Hārer Ethiopia **73** 9.20N 42.10E
Hārergē *d.* Ethiopia **73** 8.00N 41.00E
Harfleur France **18** 49.30N 0.12E
Hargeysa Somali Rep. **71** 9.31N 44.02E
Har Hu *l.* China **52** 38.20N 97.40E
Hari *r.* Indonesia **58** 1.00S104.15E
Harima nada *str.* Japan **57** 34.30N134.30E
Harīpur Pakistan **62** 33.59N 72.56E
Ḩārim *r.* Syria **67** 32.45N 35.55E
Harīrūd *r.* Afghan. **60** 35.42N 61.12E
Harlan U.S.A. **110** 41.39N 95.19W
Harlech U.K. **12** 52.52N 4.08W
Harlem U.S.A. **108** 48.32N108.47W
Harlingen Neth. **16** 53.10N 5.25E
Harlingen U.S.A. **111** 26.11N 97.42W
Harlow U.K. **13** 51.47N 0.08E
Harlowton U.S.A. **108** 46.26N109.50W
Harman U.S.A. **114** 38.55N 79.32W
Harnai Pakistan **62** 30.06N 67.56E
Harnātānr India **63** 27.19N 84.01E
Harney Basin *f.* U.S.A. **108** 43.15N120.40W
Harney L. U.S.A. **108** 43.14N119.07W
Härnösand Sweden **40** 62.37N 17.55E
Har Nuur *l.* Mongolia **52** 48.00N 93.25E
Haro Spain **26** 42.35N 2.51W
Haroldswick U.K. **10** 60.47N 0.50W
Harper Liberia **76** 4.25N 7.43W
Harpers Ferry *town* U.S.A. **114** 39.13N 77.45W
Harrai India **63** 22.37N 79.13E
Harricana *r.* Canada **102** 51.10N 79.45W
Harrigan, C. Canada **103** 55.50N 60.21W
Harrington Australia **93** 31.50S152.43E
Harrington U.S.A. **115** 38.56N 75.35W
Harrington Harbour Canada **103** 50.31N 59.30W
Harris Canada **101** 51.44N107.35W
Harris *i.* U.K. **14** 57.50N 6.55W
Harris, L. Australia **92** 31.08S135.14E
Harris, Sd. of U.K. **14** 57.43N 7.05W
Harrisburg Ill. U.S.A. **111** 37.44N 88.33W
Harrisburg Oreg. U.S.A. **108** 44.16N123.10W
Harrisburg Penn. U.S.A. **114** 40.16N 76.52W
Harrismith Australia **89** 32.55S117.50E
Harrismith R.S.A. **80** 28.15S 29.07E
Harrison Ark. U.S.A. **111** 36.14N 93.07W
Harrison Nebr. U.S.A. **110** 42.41N103.53W
Harrison, C. Canada **103** 54.55N 57.55W
Harrisonburg U.S.A. **114** 38.27N 78.54W
Harrison L. Canada **100** 49.33N121.50W
Harrisonville U.S.A. **110** 38.39N 94.21W
Harrisville Mich. U.S.A. **104** 44.39N 83.17W
Harrisville N.Y. U.S.A. **105** 44.09N 75.19W
Harrisville *W.Va.* U.S.A. **114** 39.13N 81.03W
Harrodsburg U.S.A. **113** 37.46N 84.51W
Harrogate U.K. **12** 53.59N 1.32W
Harrow Canada **104** 42.02N 82.55W
Harrow U.K. **13** 51.35N 0.21W
Harrowsmith Canada **105** 44.24N 76.40W
Harstad Norway **40** 68.48N 16.30E
Harsūd India **62** 22.06N 76.44E
Hart, L. Australia **92** 31.08S136.24E
Ḩartā Jordan **67** 32.48N 36.34E
Hartford U.S.A. **115** 41.46N 72.41W
Hartland Canada **103** 46.18N 67.32W
Hartland U.K. **13** 50.59N 4.29W
Hartland Pt. U.K. **13** 51.01N 4.32W
Hartlepool U.K. **12** 54.42N 1.11W
Hartley Bay *town* Canada **100** 53.27N129.18W
Hartola Finland **41** 61.35N 26.01E
Hartshorne U.S.A. **111** 34.51N 95.33W
Harts Range *town* Australia **90** 23.06S134.55E
Hartsville U.S.A. **113** 34.23N 80.05W
Hārūnābād Pakistan **62** 29.37N 73.08E
Har Us Nuur *l.* Mongolia **52** 48.10N 92.10E
Hārūt *r.* Afghan. **62** 31.35N 61.18E
Harvey Australia **89** 33.06S115.50E
Harvey Ill. U.S.A. **110** 41.37N 87.39W
Harvey N.Dak. U.S.A. **110** 47.47N 99.56W
Harwich U.K. **13** 51.56N 1.18E
Haryana *d.* India **62** 29.15N 76.30E
Harz *mts.* Germany **38** 51.43N 10.40E
Ḩasā, Wādī al *r.* Jordan **66** 31.01N 35.29E
Hasa Oasis *see* Aḩsā', Wāḩat al *oasis* Saudi Arabia **65**
Hasdo *r.* India **63** 21.44N 82.44E
Hase *r.* Germany **38** 52.41N 7.18E
Haselünne Germany **38** 52.40N 7.29E
Hasenkamp Argentina **125** 31.30S 59.50W
Hashābah Sudan **72** 14.19N 32.19E
Ḩasharūd Iran **65** 37.29N 47.05E
Hashefela *f.* Israel **67** 31.40N 34.55E
Hashimoto Japan **57** 34.19N135.37E
Haskell U.S.A. **111** 33.10N 99.44W
Hasle Denmark **43** 55.11N 14.43E
Haslemere U.K. **13** 51.05N 0.41W
Haslev Denmark **42** 55.20N 11.58E
Hasselt Belgium **16** 50.56N 5.20E
Hassfurt Germany **39** 50.02N 10.31E
Hassi bel Guebbour Algeria **75** 28.30N 6.41E
Hassi er Rmel *well* Algeria **75** 32.57N 3.11E
Hassi Messaoud Algeria **75** 31.43N 6.03E
Hassi Tagsist *well* Algeria **74** 25.20N 1.35E
Hässleholm Sweden **43** 56.09N 13.46E
Hassloch Germany **39** 49.22N 8.16E
Hastings Australia **93** 38.18S145.12E
Hastings Canada **105** 44.18N 77.57W
Hastings New Zealand **86** 39.39S176.52E
Hastings U.K. **13** 50.51N 0.36E
Hastings Nebr. U.S.A. **110** 40.35N 98.23W
Hatch U.S.A. **109** 32.40N107.09W
Hatches Creek *town* Australia **90** 20.56S135.12E
Hatfield Australia **92** 33.53S143.47E
Hatfield U.K. **13** 51.46N 0.13W
Hāthras India **63** 27.36N 78.03E
Hātia I. Bangla. **63** 22.40N 90.55E
Ha Tinh Vietnam **56** 18.21N105.55E
Hatta India **63** 24.07N 79.36E
Hattah Australia **92** 34.52S142.23E
Hattem Neth. **16** 52.29N 6.06E
Hatteras, C. U.S.A. **113** 35.13N 75.32W
Hattiesburg U.S.A. **111** 31.19N 89.16W
Hattingen Germany **16** 51.24N 7.09E
Hatton U.S.A. **108** 46.46N118.49W
Hatutu *i.* Is. Marquises **85** 7.56S140.38W
Hatvan Hungary **37** 47.40N 19.41E
Hauge Norway **42** 58.18N 6.15E
Haugesund Norway **42** 59.25N 5.18E
Haugsdorf Austria **36** 48.42N 16.05E
Hauraki G. New Zealand **86** 36.30S175.00E
Hausach Germany **39** 48.17N 8.10E
Haut Atlas *mts.* Morocco **74** 31.30N 7.00W
Haute-Corse *d.* France **21** 42.30N 9.20E
Haute-Garonne *d.* France **20** 43.25N 1.30E
Haute Kotto *d.* C.A.R. **73** 7.15N 23.30E
Haute-Loire *d.* France **20** 45.05N 3.50E
Haute-Marne *d.* France **19** 48.05N 5.10E
Haute Maurice Prov. Park Canada **102** 48.38N 74.30W
Haute-Normandie *d.* France **18** 49.30N 1.00E
Haute-Pyrénées *d.* France **20** 43.00N 0.10E
Hauterive Canada **103** 49.11N 68.16W
Hautes-Alpes *d.* France **21** 44.40N 6.30E
Haute-Saône *d.* France **19** 47.40N 6.10E
Haute-Savoie *d.* France **21** 46.00N 6.20E
Haute-Vienne *d.* France **20** 45.50N 1.15E
Haut Mbomou *d.* C.A.R. **73** 6.25N 26.10E
Hautmont France **19** 50.15N 3.56E
Haut-Rhin *d.* France **19** 47.53N 7.13E
Hauts Bassins *d.* Burkina **76** 10.45N 4.30W
Hauts Plateau *f.* Morocco / Algeria **74** 34.00N 0.10W
Haut Zaïre *d.* Zaïre **79** 2.00N 27.00E
Havana *see* La Habana Cuba **117**
Havant U.K. **13** 50.51N 0.59W
Havel *r.* Germany **38** 52.53N 11.58E
Havelange Belgium **16** 50.23N 5.14E
Havelberg Germany **38** 52.50N 12.04E
Havelland *f.* Germany **38** 52.30N 12.35E
Havelock Canada **105** 44.26N 77.53W
Havelock New Zealand **86** 41.17S173.46E
Haverfordwest U.K. **13** 51.48N 4.59W
Haverhill U.K. **13** 52.06N 0.27E
Haverhill U.S.A. **115** 42.47N 71.05W
Havlíčkuv Brod Czech Republic **36** 49.38N 15.35E
Havre U.S.A. **108** 48.33N109.41W
Havre de Grace U.S.A. **115** 39.33N 76.06W
Havre St. Pierre Canada **103** 50.15N 63.36W
Hawaii *d.* U.S.A. **106** 21.00N156.00W
Hawaii *i.* Hawaii U.S.A. **106** 19.30N155.30W
Hawaiian Is. U.S.A. **106** 21.00N157.00W
Hawdon North, L. Australia **92** 37.09S139.54E
Hawea, L. New Zealand **86** 44.30S169.15E
Hawera New Zealand **86** 39.35S174.19E
Hawick U.K. **14** 55.25N 2.47W
Hawke B. New Zealand **86** 39.18S177.15E
Hawker Australia **92** 31.53S138.25E
Hawker Gate Australia **92** 29.46S141.00E
Hawke's Bay *d.* New Zealand **86** 39.00S176.35E
Hawkesbury Canada **105** 45.36N 74.37W
Hawks U.S.A. **104** 45.16N 83.53W
Hawley U.S.A. **115** 41.28N 75.11W
Ḩawrān, Wādī *r.* Iraq **64** 33.57N 42.35E
Ḩawsh 'Īsá Egypt **66** 30.55N 30.17E
Hawthorne U.S.A. **108** 38.32N118.38W
Hay Australia **93** 34.31S144.31E
Hay *r.* Australia **90** 25.00S138.00E
Hay *r.* Canada **100** 60.49N115.52W
Haya *r.* Japan **57** 35.30N138.26E
Hayange France **19** 49.20N 6.03E
Haybān Sudan **71** 11.13N 30.31E
Haydān, Wādī al Jordan **67** 31.27N 35.36E
Hayden U.S.A. **109** 33.00N110.47W
Hayes *r.* Canada **101** 57.03N 92.09W
Hayes Creek *town* Australia **88** 13.27S131.25E
Hayesville U.S.A. **114** 40.46N 82.16W
Hay-on-Wye U.K. **13** 52.04N 3.09W
Hay River *town* Canada **100** 60.51N115.44W
Hays U.S.A. **110** 38.53N 99.20W
Hayward U.S.A. **110** 46.02N 91.26W
Haywards Heath *f.* U.K. **13** 51.00N 0.05E
HaZafon *d.* Israel **67** 32.50N 35.20E
Hazārān, Kūh-e *mtn.* Iran **65** 29.30N 57.18E
Hazard U.S.A. **113** 37.14N 83.11W
Hazāribāgh India **63** 23.59N 85.21E
Hazel Hurst U.S.A. **114** 41.42N 78.35W
Hazelton Canada **100** 55.20N127.42W
Hazelton U.S.A. **110** 46.29N100.17W
Hazen U.S.A. **108** 39.34N119.03W
Hazerim Israel **67** 31.14N 34.43E
Hazlehurst Ga. U.S.A. **113** 31.53N 82.34W
Hazlehurst Miss. U.S.A. **111** 31.52N 90.24W
Hazleton U.S.A. **115** 40.58N 75.59W
Hazor Israel **67** 32.59N 35.33E
Hazor Ashdod Israel **67** 31.46N 34.43E
Head Waters U.S.A. **114** 38.20N 79.21W
Healdsburg U.S.A. **108** 38.37N122.52W
Healesville Australia **93** 37.40S145.31E
Healy U.S.A. **98** 63.52N148.58W
Heanor U.K. **12** 53.01N 1.20W
Heard I. Indian Oc. **49** 53.07S 73.20E
Hearne L. Canada **100** 62.20N113.10W
Hearst Canada **102** 49.40N 83.41W
Heathcote Australia **93** 36.54S144.42E
Hebei *d.* China **54** 39.00N116.00E
Hebel Australia **93** 28.55S147.49E
Heber Springs *town* U.S.A. **111** 35.30N 92.02W
Hebi China **54** 35.57N114.05E
Hebrides *is.* U.K. **8** 57.45N 7.00W
Hebrides, Sea of the U.K. **10** 57.00N 7.20W
Hebron Canada **99** 58.05N 62.30W
Hebron *see* Al Khalīl Jordan **67**
Hebron N.Dak. U.S.A. **110** 46.54N102.03W
Hebron Nebr. U.S.A. **110** 40.10N 97.35W
Heby Sweden **43** 59.56N 16.53E
Hecate Str. Canada **100** 53.00N131.00W
Hechi China **55** 24.42N108.02E
Hechingen Germany **39** 48.21N 8.58E
Hechtel Belgium **16** 51.07N 5.22E
Hechuan China **55** 30.05N106.14E
Hecla U.S.A. **110** 45.53N 98.09W
Hede Sweden **41** 62.25N 13.30E
Hedemora Sweden **43** 60.17N 15.59E
Hedensted Denmark **42** 55.46N 9.42E
Hedi Shuiku *resr.* China **55** 21.50N110.19E
Hedley U.S.A. **111** 34.52N100.39W
Hedmark *d.* Norway **41** 61.20N 11.30E
Heemstede Neth. **16** 52.21N 4.38E
Heerde Neth. **16** 52.23N 6.02E
Heerenveen Neth. **16** 52.57N 5.55E
Heerlen Neth. **16** 50.53N 5.59E
Hefa Israel **67** 32.49N 34.59E
Hefa *d.* Israel **67** 32.50N 35.00E
Hefei China **55** 31.50N117.16E
Hegang China **53** 47.36N130.30E
Heide Germany **38** 54.12N 9.06E
Heide *f.* Germany **38** 52.50N 10.30E
Heidelberg Germany **39** 49.25N 8.43E
Heidelberg C.P. R.S.A. **80** 34.05S 20.58E
Heidenheim Germany **39** 48.40N 10.08E
Heilbron R.S.A. **80** 27.16S 27.57E
Heilbronn Germany **39** 49.08N 9.13E
Heiligenblut Austria **39** 47.02N 12.50E
Heiligenhafen Germany **38** 54.22N 10.58E

Heiligenstadt to **Hornell**

Heiligenstadt Germany **38** 51.23N 10.09E
Heilongjiang *d.* China **53** 47.15N128.50E
Heiloo Neth. **16** 52.37N 4.43E
Heinola Finland **41** 61.13N 26.02E
Heinsberg Germany **38** 51.03N 6.05E
Heishan China **54** 41.40N122.03E
Heishui China **54** 42.03N119.21E
Heishuisi China **54** 36.01N108.56E
Hejaz *f.* see Al Ḥijāz *f.* Saudi Arabia **64**
Hejian China **54** 38.26N116.05E
Hejiang China **55** 28.48N105.47E
Hekinan Japan **57** 34.51N136.58E
Hekla, Mt. Iceland **40** 64.00N 19.45W
Hekou China **61** 22.39N103.57E
Hekura jima *i.* Japan **57** 37.52N136.56E
Helagsfjället *mtn.* Sweden **40** 62.58N 12.25E
Helan China **54** 38.35N106.16E
Helan Shan *mts.* China **54** 38.40N106.00E
Helbra Germany **38** 51.33N 11.29E
Helena U.S.A. **108** 46.36N112.01W
Helen Reef *i.* Pacific Oc. **59** 2.43N131.46E
Helensburgh U.K. **14** 56.01N 4.44W
Helensville New Zealand **86** 36.40S174.27E
Helez Israel **67** 31.35N 34.40E
Helgoland *i.* Germany **38** 54.12N 7.53E
Helgoländer Bucht *b.* Germany **38** 54.05N 8.15E
Hellendoorn Neth. **16** 52.24N 6.29E
Hellenthal Germany **38** 50.29N 6.26E
Hellesylt Norway **41** 62.05N 6.54E
Hellevoetsluis Neth. **16** 51.49N 4.08E
Hellín Spain **25** 38.31N 1.41W
Helmand *d.* Afghan. **62** 31.15N 64.00E
Helmand *r.* Asia **62** 31.12N 61.34E
Helmond Neth. **16** 51.28N 5.40E
Helmsdale U.K. **14** 58.07N 3.40W
Helmsdale *r.* U.K. **14** 58.05N 3.39W
Helmstedt Germany **38** 52.13N 11.00E
Helsingfors see Helsinki Finland **41**
Helsingör Denmark **43** 56.02N 12.37E
Helsinki Finland **41** 60.08N 25.00E
Helston U.K. **13** 50.07N 5.17W
Helvecia Argentina **125** 31.06S 60.05W
Hemaruka Canada **101** 51.48N111.10W
Hemau Germany **38** 49.03N 11.47E
Hemel Hempstead U.K. **13** 51.46N 0.28W
Hemingford U.S.A. **110** 42.19N103.04W
Hemmingford Canada **105** 45.03N 73.36W
Hempstead N.Y. U.S.A. **115** 40.42N 73.37W
Hempstead Tex. U.S.A. **111** 30.06N 96.05W
Hemse Sweden **43** 57.14N 18.22E
Hemsedal Norway **41** 60.52N 8.34E
Henan *d.* China **54** 34.00N114.00E
Henares *r.* Spain **26** 40.24N 3.30W
Henbury Australia **90** 24.35S133.15E
Hendaye France **20** 43.22N 1.46W
Henderson Ky. U.S.A. **113** 37.50N 87.35W
Henderson N.C. U.S.A. **113** 36.20N 78.26W
Henderson Nev. U.S.A. **109** 36.02N114.59W
Henderson N.Y. U.S.A. **105** 43.51N 76.11W
Henderson Tex. U.S.A. **111** 32.09N 94.48W
Henderson I. Pacific Oc. **85** 24.20S128.20W
Hendrik Verwoerd Dam R.S.A. **80** 30.37S 25.29E
Hendrina R.S.A. **80** 26.09S 29.42E
Hengelo Neth. **16** 52.16N 6.46E
Hengnan see Hengyang China **55**
Hengshan Hunan China **55** 27.14N112.52E
Hengshan Shaanxi China **54** 37.57N109.11E
Hengshui China **54** 37.40N115.48E
Heng Xian China **55** 22.35N109.26E
Hengyang China **55** 26.52N112.35E
Hénin-Beaumont France **19** 50.25N 2.56E
Henlopen, C. U.S.A. **115** 38.48N 75.05W
Hennebont France **18** 47.48N 3.17W
Hennigsdorf Germany **38** 52.38N 13.12E
Henniker U.S.A. **115** 43.11N 71.49W
Henrietta Maria, C. Canada **102** 55.00N 82.15W
Henryetta U.S.A. **111** 35.27N 95.59W
Henryville Canada **105** 45.08N 73.11W
Hentiesbaai Namibia **80** 22.10S 14.19E
Henty Australia **93** 35.30S147.03E
Henzada Burma **56** 17.36N 95.26E
Heppenheim Germany **39** 49.39N 8.38E
Heppner U.S.A. **108** 45.21N119.33W
Hepu China **55** 21.31N109.10E
Hepworth Canada **104** 44.37N 81.09W
Heqing China **61** 26.34N100.12E
Herāt Afghan. **62** 34.20N 62.12E
Herāt *d.* Afghan. **62** 34.10N 62.30E
Herault *r.* France **20** 43.17N 3.26E
Herbignac France **18** 47.27N 2.19W
Herborn Germany **38** 50.40N 8.17E
Herceg-Novi Yugo. **31** 42.27N 18.32E
Hereford U.K. **13** 52.04N 2.43W
Hereford Md. U.S.A. **115** 39.35N 76.40W
Hereford Tex. U.S.A. **111** 34.49N102.24W
Hereford and Worcester *d.* U.K. **13** 52.08N 2.30W
Herencia Spain **27** 39.21N 3.22W
Herentals Belgium **16** 51.12N 4.42E
Herford Germany **38** 52.06N 8.40E
Herington U.S.A. **110** 38.40N 96.57W
Herisau Switz. **39** 47.23N 9.17E
Herleshausen Germany **38** 51.00N 10.09E
Hermagor Austria **39** 46.37N 13.22E
Hermannsburg Australia **90** 23.56S132.46E
Hermanus R.S.A. **80** 34.24S 19.16E
Hermidale Australia **93** 31.33S146.44E
Hermiston U.S.A. **108** 45.51N119.17W
Hermosillo Mexico **109** 29.04N110.58W
Herndon U.S.A. **114** 40.43N 76.50W
Herne Germany **38** 51.32N 7.13E
Herne Bay *town* U.K. **13** 51.23N 1.10E
Herning Denmark **42** 56.08N 8.59E
Heron Bay *town* Canada **102** 48.40N 86.25W
Herrera del Duque Spain **27** 39.10N 5.03W
Herrera de Pisuerga Spain **26** 42.36N 4.20W
Herrljunga Sweden **43** 58.05N 13.02E
Hershey U.S.A. **115** 40.17N 76.39W
Herstal Belgium **16** 50.14N 5.38E
Herten Germany **38** 51.35N 7.07E
Hertford U.K. **13** 51.48N 0.05W
Hertfordshire *d.* U.K. **13** 51.51N 0.05W
Hervás Spain **26** 40.16N 5.51W
Hervey B. Australia **90** 25.00S153.00E
Herzberg Brandenburg Germany **38** 51.41N 13.14E
Herzberg Nschn. Germany **38** 51.39N 10.20E
Herzliyya Israel **67** 32.10N 34.50E
Hesbaye *f.* Belgium **16** 50.32N 5.07E
Hesdin France **19** 50.22N 2.02E
Hesel Germany **38** 53.18N 7.35E
Heshui China **54** 35.43N108.07E
Heshun China **54** 37.19N113.34E
Hesselö *i.* Denmark **42** 56.12N 11.43E
Hessen *d.* Germany **38** 50.44N 9.00E
Hesso Australia **92** 32.08S137.58E
Hetou China **55** 21.05N109.44E
Hettinger U.S.A. **110** 46.00N102.39W
Hettstedt Germany **38** 51.38N 11.30E
Hetzerath Germany **39** 49.52N 6.49E
Heuvelton U.S.A. **105** 44.37N 75.25W
Hevron, Nahal *wadi* Israel **67** 31.15N 34.50E
Hewett, C. Canada **99** 70.20N 68.00W
Hexham U.K. **12** 54.58N 2.06W
Hexi China **55** 24.51N117.13E
He Xian China **55** 24.25N111.31E
Hexigten Qi China **54** 43.17N117.24E
Heyrieux France **21** 45.38N 5.03E
Heysham U.K. **12** 54.03N 2.53W
Heyuan China **55** 23.42N114.48E
Heywood Australia **92** 38.08S141.38E
Heywood U.K. **12** 53.36N 2.13W
Heze China **54** 35.12N115.15E
Hezhang China **55** 27.08N104.43E
Hiawatha Kans. U.S.A. **110** 39.51N 95.32W
Hiawatha Utah U.S.A. **108** 39.29N111.01W
Hibbing U.S.A. **110** 47.25N 92.55W
Hickman, Mt. Canada **100** 57.11N131.10W
Hickory U.S.A. **113** 35.44N 81.23W
Hicks Bay *town* New Zealand **86** 37.35S178.18E
Hickson L. Canada **101** 56.17N104.25W
Hicksville U.S.A. **115** 40.46N 73.32W
Hidaka Sammyaku *mts.* Japan **57** 42.50N143.00E
Hidalgo *d.* Mexico **116** 20.50N 98.30W
Hidalgo Nuevo León Mexico **111** 25.59N100.27W
Hidalgo Tamaulipas Mexico **116** 24.15N 99.26W
Hidalgo del Parral Mexico **109** 26.56N105.40W
Hieradhsvotn *r.* Iceland **40** 65.45N 18.50W
Hierro *i.* Canary Is. **74** 27.45N 18.00W
Higashimatsuyama Japan **57** 36.02N139.24E
Higashimurayama Japan **57** 35.46N139.29E
Higashiōsaka Japan **57** 34.39N135.35E
Higgins U.S.A. **111** 36.07N100.02W
Higgins L. U.S.A. **104** 44.30N 84.45W
Higginsville Australia **89** 31.46S121.43E
Highgate Canada **104** 42.30N 81.49W
High Hill *r.* Canada **101** 55.52N 94.42W
High Knob *mtn.* U.S.A. **114** 39.08N 78.26W
Highland *d.* U.K. **14** 57.42N 5.00W
Highland *town* U.S.A. **115** 41.43N 73.58W
Highland Park *town* U.S.A. **114** 42.24N 83.06W
High Level Canada **100** 58.31N117.08W
Highmore U.S.A. **110** 44.31N 99.27W
High Peak *mtn.* U.K. **12** 53.22N 1.48W
High Point *town* U.S.A. **113** 35.58N 80.00W
High Prairie Canada **100** 55.30N116.30W
Highrock L. Man. Canada **101** 55.45N100.30W
Highrock L. Sask. Canada **101** 57.04N105.30W
High Willhays *mtn.* U.K. **13** 50.41N 4.00W
High Wycombe U.K. **13** 51.38N 0.46W
Hiiumaa *i.* Estonia **41** 58.52N 22.40E
Híjar Spain **25** 41.10N 0.27W
Ḥijāz, Jabal al *mts.* Saudi Arabia **72** 19.45N 41.55E
Hikone Japan **57** 35.15N136.15E
Hikurangi New Zealand **86** 35.36S174.17E
Hikurangi *mtn.* New Zealand **86** 37.50S178.10E
Hikutavake Niue **84** 18.57S169.53W
Hildburghausen Germany **39** 50.25N 10.44E
Hilden Germany **38** 51.10N 6.56E
Hildesheim Germany **38** 52.09N 9.57E
Hill City Kans. U.S.A. **110** 39.22N 99.51W
Hill City Minn. U.S.A. **110** 46.59N 93.44W
Hillegom Neth. **16** 52.19N 4.35E
Hill End Australia **93** 33.01S149.26E
Hilleröd Denmark **43** 55.56N 12.19E
Hill Island L. Canada **101** 60.30N109.50W
Hillman U.S.A. **104** 45.04N 83.54W
Hillsboro N.H. U.S.A. **115** 43.07N 71.54W
Hillsboro Oreg. U.S.A. **108** 45.31N122.59W
Hillsboro Tex. U.S.A. **111** 32.01N 97.08W
Hillsdale U.S.A. **112** 41.56N 84.37W
Hillsport Canada **102** 49.27N 85.34W
Hillston Australia **93** 33.30S145.33E
Hilo Hawaii U.S.A. **106** 19.42N155.04W
Hilton U.S.A. **114** 43.17N 77.48W
Hilton Beach Canada **104** 46.16N 83.56W
Hilton Head I. U.S.A. **113** 32.12N 80.45W
Hiltrup Germany **38** 51.54N 7.38E
Hilversum Neth. **16** 52.14N 5.12E
Himachal Pradesh *d.* India **62** 32.05N 77.15E
Himalaya *mts.* Asia **63** 29.00N 84.30E
Himanka Finland **40** 64.04N 23.39E
Himarë Albania **34** 40.08N 19.43E
Himatnagar India **62** 23.36N 72.57E
Himeji Japan **57** 34.50N134.40E
Himi Japan **57** 36.51N136.59E
Himmerland *f.* Denmark **42** 56.52N 9.30E
Ḥimş Syria **66** 34.44N 36.43E
Hinchinbrook I. Australia **90** 18.23S146.17E
Hinckley U.K. **13** 52.33N 1.21W
Hinckley Resr. U.S.A. **115** 43.20N 75.05W
Hindaun India **62** 26.43N 77.01E
Hindmarsh, L. Australia **92** 36.03S141.53E
Hindubāgh Pakistan **62** 30.49N 67.45E
Hindu Kush *mts.* Asia **60** 36.40N 70.00E
Hindupur India **60** 13.49N 77.29E
Hines Creek *town* Canada **100** 56.20N118.40W
Hinganghāt India **63** 20.34N 78.50E
Hingol *r.* Pakistan **62** 25.23N 65.28E
Hingoli India **62** 19.43N 77.09E
Hinnöy *i.* Norway **40** 68.35N 15.50E
Hinojosa Spain **26** 38.30N 5.09W
Hinsdale Mont. U.S.A. **108** 48.24N107.05W
Hinsdale N.H. U.S.A. **115** 42.47N 72.29W
Hinterrhein *r.* Switz. **39** 46.49N 9.25E
Hinton Canada **100** 53.25N117.34W
Hipólito Mexico **111** 25.41N101.26W
Hippolytushoef Neth. **16** 52.57N 4.58E
Hirakata Japan **57** 34.48N135.38E
Hīrākud India **63** 21.31N 83.57E
Hīrākud *resr.* India **63** 21.31N 83.52E
Hīrāpur India **63** 24.22N 79.13E
Hiratsuka Japan **57** 35.19N139.21E
Hīrmand *r.* see Helmand *r.* Iran **62**
Hirok Sāmi Pakistan **62** 26.02N 63.25E
Hirosaki Japan **57** 40.34N140.28E
Hiroshima Japan **57** 34.30N132.27E
Hirson France **19** 49.55N 4.05E
Hîrşova Romania **37** 44.41N 27.57E
Hirtshals Denmark **42** 57.35N 9.58E
Hisai Japan **57** 34.40N136.28E
Hisār India **62** 29.10N 75.43E
Ḥisbān Jordan **67** 31.48N 35.48E
Ḥismá *f.* Saudi Arabia **66** 28.45N 35.56E
Hispaniola *i.* C. America **117** 19.00N 71.00W
Hisua India **63** 24.50N 85.25E
Ḥisyah Syria **66** 34.24N 36.45E
Hīt Iraq **64** 33.38N 42.50E
Hitachi Japan **57** 36.35N140.40E
Hitchin U.K. **13** 51.57N 0.16W
Hitra *i.* Norway **40** 63.37N 8.46E
Hiva Oa *i.* Is. Marquises **85** 9.45S139.00W
Hixon Canada **100** 53.27N122.36W
Hjälmaren *l.* Sweden **43** 59.15N 15.45E
Hjalmar L. Canada **101** 61.33N109.25W
Hjelmelandsvågen Norway **42** 59.14N 6.11E
Hjo Sweden **43** 58.18N 14.17E
Hjörring Denmark **42** 57.28N 9.59E
Hlotse Lesotho **80** 28.52S 28.02E
Ho Ghana **76** 6.38N 0.38E
Hòa Bình Vietnam **55** 20.40N105.17E
Hoare B. Canada **99** 65.20N 62.30W
Hoarusib *r.* Namibia **80** 19.04S 12.33E
Hobart Australia **91** 42.54S147.18E
Hobart Ind. U.S.A. **112** 41.32N 87.14W
Hobart Okla. U.S.A. **111** 35.01N 99.06W
Hobbs U.S.A. **111** 32.42N103.08W
Hoboken Belgium **16** 51.11N 4.21E
Hoboken U.S.A. **115** 40.45N 74.03W
Hobq Shamo *des.* China **54** 40.00N109.00E
Hobro Denmark **42** 56.38N 9.48E
Hoburgen *c.* Sweden **43** 56.55N 18.07E
Hobyo Somali Rep. **71** 5.20N 48.30E
Hochgolling *mtn.* Austria **39** 47.16N 13.45E
Ho Chi Minh Vietnam **56** 10.46N106.43E
Höchstadt an der Aisch Germany **39** 49.42N 10.44E
Hockenheim Germany **39** 49.19N 8.33E
Hocking *r.* U.S.A. **114** 39.12N 81.45W
Hockley U.S.A. **111** 30.02N 95.51W
Hodal India **62** 27.54N 77.22E
Hodgson Canada **101** 51.13N 97.34W
Hod HaSharon Israel **67** 32.15N 34.55E
Hodh ech Chargui *d.* Mauritania **76** 19.00N 7.15W
Hodh el Gharbi *d.* Mauritania **76** 16.30N 10.00W
Hodiyya Israel **67** 31.41N 34.38E
Hódmezövásárhely Hungary **31** 46.25N 20.20E
Hodna, Monts du *mts.* Algeria **75** 35.50N 4.50E
Hoek van Holland Neth. **16** 51.59N 4.08E
Hoeryong N. Korea **57** 42.27N129.44E
Hof Germany **38** 50.18N 11.55E
Hofgeismar Germany **38** 51.30N 9.22E
Hofheim Bayern Germany **39** 50.08N 10.31E
Hofheim Hessen Germany **39** 50.07N 8.26E
Höfn Iceland **40** 64.16N 15.10W
Hofors Sweden **41** 60.33N 16.17E
Hofsjökull *mtn.* Iceland **40** 64.50N 19.00W
Hofsos Iceland **40** 65.53N 19.26W
Höganäs Sweden **43** 56.12N 12.33E
Hogansburg U.S.A. **105** 44.59N 74.40W
Hogeland U.S.A. **108** 48.51N108.39W
Hogem Ranges *f.* Canada **100** 55.40N126.00W
Högsby Sweden **43** 57.10N 16.02E
Hohe Acht *mtn.* Germany **39** 50.23N 7.00E
Hohenthurn Austria **39** 46.33N 13.40E
Hoher Dachstein *mtn.* Austria **39** 47.28N 13.35E
Hohhot China **54** 40.42N111.38E
Hoh Tolgoin Sum China **54** 44.27N112.41E
Hohultslätt Sweden **43** 56.58N 15.39E
Hoi An Vietnam **56** 15.54N108.19E
Hoima Uganda **79** 1.25N 31.22E
Hojāi India **63** 26.00N 92.51E
Höjer Denmark **42** 54.58N 8.43E
Hökensås *hills* Sweden **43** 58.11N 14.08E
Hokitika New Zealand **86** 42.42S170.59E
Hokkaidō *d.* Japan **57** 43.00N143.00E
Hokkaidō *i.* Japan **57** 43.00N144.00E
Hokksund Norway **42** 59.47N 9.59E
Hola Kenya **79** 1.29S 40.02E
Holbaek Denmark **42** 55.43N 11.43E
Holbrook Australia **93** 35.46S147.20E
Holbrook U.S.A. **109** 34.54N110.10W
Holdrege U.S.A. **110** 40.26N 99.22W
Holguín Cuba **117** 20.54N 76.15W
Höljes Sweden **41** 60.54N 12.36E
Hollabrunn Austria **36** 48.34N 16.05E
Holland Mich. U.S.A. **112** 42.46N 86.06W
Holland N.Y. U.S.A. **114** 42.38N 78.33W
Holland Centre Canada **104** 44.24N 80.48W
Hollidaysburg U.S.A. **114** 40.26N 78.23W
Holly Kans. U.S.A. **111** 38.03N102.07W
Holly Mich. U.S.A. **104** 42.48N 83.38W
Hollywood U.S.A. **113** 26.01N 80.09W
Holman Island *town* Canada **98** 70.43N117.43W
Holmavik Iceland **40** 65.43N 21.39W
Holmenkollen Norway **42** 59.58N 10.40E
Holmer, Lac *l.* Canada **103** 54.10N 71.44W
Holmestrand Norway **42** 59.29N 10.18E
Holmön *i.* Sweden **40** 63.47N 20.53E
Holmsund Sweden **40** 63.41N 20.20E
Holon Israel **67** 32.01N 34.46E
Holroyd *r.* Australia **90** 14.10S141.36E
Holstebro Denmark **42** 56.21N 8.38E
Holstein Canada **104** 44.03N 80.45W
Holsteinsborg Greenland **99** 66.55N 53.30W
Holsworthy U.K. **13** 50.48N 4.21W
Holt U.K. **12** 52.55N 1.04E
Holten Neth. **16** 52.18N 6.26E
Holwerd Neth. **16** 53.22N 5.54E
Holy Cross U.S.A. **98** 62.12N159.47W
Holyhead U.K. **12** 53.18N 4.38W
Holyhead B. U.K. **12** 53.22N 4.40W
Holy I. England U.K. **12** 55.41N 1.47W
Holy I. Wales U.K. **12** 53.15N 4.38W
Holyoke Colo. U.S.A. **110** 40.35N102.18W
Holyoke Mass. U.S.A. **115** 42.12N 72.37W
Holýšov Czech Republic **38** 49.36N 13.05E
Holywood U.K. **15** 54.38N 5.50W
Holzkirchen Germany **39** 47.52N 11.42E
Holzminden Germany **38** 51.50N 9.27E
Homberg Germany **38** 51.02N 9.24E
Hombori Mali **76** 15.20N 1.38W
Homburg Germany **39** 49.19N 7.20E
Home B. Canada **99** 69.00N 66.00W
Home Hill *town* Australia **90** 19.40S147.25E
Homer Alas. U.S.A. **98** 59.40N151.37W
Homer La. U.S.A. **111** 32.48N 93.04W
Homer N.Y. U.S.A. **115** 42.38N 76.11W
Homer Tunnel New Zealand **86** 44.40S168.15E
Homestead U.S.A. **113** 25.29N 80.29W
Hommersåk Norway **42** 58.58N 5.42E
Homoine Mozambique **81** 23.45S 35.09E
Homoljske Planina *f.* Yugo. **37** 44.20N 21.45E
Honda Colombia **122** 5.15N 74.50W
Hondeklipbaai R.S.A. **80** 30.19S 17.12E
Hondo *r.* Mexico **117** 18.33N 88.22W
Hondo U.S.A. **111** 29.21N 99.09W
Honduras C. America **117** 14.30N 87.00W
Honduras, G. of Carib. Sea **117** 16.20N 87.30W
Honesdale U.S.A. **115** 41.34N 75.16W
Honfleur France **18** 49.25N 0.14E
Höng Denmark **42** 55.31N 11.18E
Hong'an China **55** 31.18N114.33E
Hòn Gay Vietnam **55** 21.01N107.02E
Hong Hà *r.* Vietnam **56** 20.15N106.36E
Honghu China **55** 29.42N113.26E
Hong Hu *l.* China **55** 29.50N113.15E
Hongjiang China **55** 27.08N109.54E
Hongjian Nur *l.* China **54** 39.09N109.56E
Hong Kong Asia **55** 22.15N114.15E
Hongor Mongolia **54** 45.20N113.41E
Hongor Mongolia **54** 45.45N112.56E
Hongshui He *r.* China **55** 23.20N110.04E
Hongtong China **54** 36.15N111.37E
Honguedo, Détroit d' *str.* Canada **103** 49.25N 64.00W
Hongze China **54** 33.18N118.51E
Hongze Hu *l.* China **54** 33.15N118.40E
Honiton U.K. **13** 50.48N 3.13W
Honjō Japan **57** 39.23N140.03E
Honkajoki Finland **41** 62.00N 22.15E
Hönö Sweden **42** 57.42N 11.39E
Honokaa Hawaiian Is. **85** 20.05N155.28W
Honokahua Hawaiian Is. **85** 21.00N156.39W
Honolulu Hawaii U.S.A. **106** 21.19N157.50W
Honshū *i.* Japan **57** 36.00N138.00E
Hood, Mt. U.S.A. **108** 45.23N121.41W
Hood Pt. Australia **89** 34.23S119.34E
Hood Range *mts.* Australia **93** 28.35S144.30E
Hoogeveen Neth. **16** 52.44N 6.29E
Hoogezand Neth. **16** 53.10N 6.47E
Hooghly *r.* India **63** 21.55N 88.05E
Hoogstade Belgium **16** 50.59N 2.42E
Hooker U.S.A. **111** 36.52N101.13W
Hook Head Rep. of Ire. **15** 52.07N 6.55W
Hoopa U.S.A. **108** 41.03N123.40W
Hoopeston U.S.A. **110** 40.28N 87.41W
Hoopstad R.S.A. **80** 27.48S 25.52E
Höör Sweden **43** 55.56N 13.32E
Hoorn Neth. **16** 52.38N 5.03E
Hoosick Falls *town* U.S.A. **115** 42.54N 73.21W
Hoover Dam U.S.A. **109** 36.00N114.27W
Hope U.S.A. **111** 33.40N 93.36W
Hope, L. S.A. Australia **92** 28.23S139.19E
Hope, L. W.A. Australia **89** 32.31S120.25E
Hope, Pt. U.S.A. **96** 68.20N166.49W
Hopedale Canada **103** 55.50N 60.10W
Hopefield R.S.A. **80** 33.04S 18.19E
Hopetoun Vic. Australia **92** 35.43S142.20E
Hopetoun W.A. Australia **89** 33.57S120.05E
Hopetown R.S.A. **80** 29.37S 24.04E
Hopkins *r.* Australia **92** 38.25S142.00E
Hopkins, L. Australia **88** 24.15S128.50E
Hopkinsville U.S.A. **113** 36.50N 87.30W
Hopland U.S.A. **108** 38.58N123.07W
Hoquiam U.S.A. **108** 46.59N123.53W
Horažďovice Czech Republic **38** 49.20N 13.43E
Horb Germany **39** 48.26N 8.41E
Horbat Qesari *site* Israel **67** 32.30N 34.53E
Hörby Sweden **43** 55.51N 13.39E
Hordaland *d.* Norway **42** 60.00N 6.00E
Horde Germany **16** 51.29N 7.30E
Horgen Switz. **39** 47.15N 8.36E
Hörh Uul *mts.* Mongolia **54** 42.20N105.30E
Horinger China **54** 40.23N111.53E
Horizonte Mexico **111** 25.50N103.48W
Horlick Mts. Antarctica **128** 86.00S102.00W
Hormuz, Str. of Asia **65** 26.35N 56.20E
Horn Austria **36** 48.40N 15.40E
Horn *r.* Canada **100** 61.30N118.01W
Horn, C. see Hornos, Cabo de *c.* S. America **125**
Hornavan *l.* Sweden **40** 66.10N 17.30E
Horncastle U.K. **12** 53.13N 0.08W
Horndal Sweden **43** 60.18N 16.25E
Hornell U.S.A. **114** 42.19N 77.40W

Hornell L. to **Ilanz**

Hornell L. Canada **100** 62.20N119.25W
Hornepayne Canada **102** 49.14N 84.48W
Hornindal Norway **41** 61.58N 6.31E
Horn Mts. Canada **100** 62.15N119.15W
Hornos, Cabo de *c.* S. America **125** 55.47S 67.00W
Hornsby Australia **93** 33.11S151.06E
Hornsea U.K. **12** 53.55N 0.10W
Hornslet Denmark **42** 56.19N 10.20E
Hořovice Czech Republic **36** 49.50N 13.54E
Horqin Zuoyi Houqi China **54** 42.57N122.21E
Horqin Zuoyi Zhongqi China **54** 44.08N123.18E
Horru China **63** 30.30N 91.32E
Horse Creek *town* U.S.A. **108** 41.25N105.11W
Horseheads U.S.A. **114** 42.10N 76.50W
Horsens Denmark **42** 55.52N 9.52E
Horsham Australia **92** 36.45S142.15E
Horsham U.K. **13** 51.04N 0.20W
Hörsholm Denmark **43** 55.53N 12.30E
Horšovský Týn Czech Republic **38** 49.32N 12.56E
Horta *wadi* Chad **72** 17.15N 21.52E
Horten Norway **42** 59.25N 10.30E
Horton *r.* Canada **98** 70.00N127.00W
Horton L. Canada **98** 67.30N122.28W
Horvot Mezada *site* Israel **67** 31.19N 35.21E
Hosa'ina Ethiopia **73** 7.38N 37.52E
Hösbach Germany **39** 50.00N 9.12E
Hose, Pegunungan *mts.* Malaysia **58** 1.30N114.10E
Hoshāb Pakistan **62** 26.01N 63.56E
Hoshangābād India **63** 22.45N 77.43E
Hoshiārpur India **62** 31.32N 75.54E
Hôsh 'Isa Egypt **66** 30.55N 30.17E
Hoskins P.N.G. **87** 5.30S150.27E
Hospital de Orbigo Spain **26** 42.28N 5.53W
Hospitalet de Llobregat Spain **25** 41.22N 2.08E
Hossegor France **20** 43.40N 1.27W
Hoste, Isla *i.* Chile **125** 55.10S 69.00W
Hotan China **52** 37.07N 79.57E
Hotazel R.S.A. **80** 27.16S 22.57E
Hotham *r.* Australia **89** 32.58S116.22E
Hotham, Mt. Australia **93** 36.58S147.11E
Hoting Sweden **40** 64.07N 16.10E
Hotin Gol China **54** 38.58N104.14E
Hot Springs *town* Ark. U.S.A. **111** 34.30N 93.02W
Hot Springs *town* S.Dak. U.S.A. **110** 43.26N103.29W
Hottah L. Canada **98** 65.04N118.29W
Houailou N. Cal. **84** 21.17S165.38E
Houdan France **19** 48.47N 1.36E
Houeillès France **20** 44.12N 0.02E
Houffalize Belgium **16** 50.08N 5.50E
Houghton L. U.S.A. **112** 44.16N 84.48W
Houghton-le-Spring U.K. **12** 54.51N 1.28W
Houlton U.S.A. **112** 46.08N 67.51W
Houma China **54** 35.36N111.21E
Houma U.S.A. **111** 29.36N 90.43W
Houndé Burkina **76** 11.34N 3.31W
Hourn, Loch U.K. **14** 57.06N 5.33W
Housatonic *r.* U.S.A. **115** 41.10N 73.07W
Houston Mo. U.S.A. **111** 37.22N 91.58W
Houston Tex. U.S.A. **111** 29.46N 95.22W
Houtzdale U.S.A. **114** 40.49N 78.21W
Hova Sweden **43** 58.52N 14.13E
Hovd Mongolia **52** 46.40N 90.45E
Hove U.K. **13** 50.50N 0.10W
Hövsgöl Mongolia **54** 43.36N109.40E
Hövsgöl Nuur *l.* Mongolia **52** 51.00N100.30E
Howa, Ouadi *see* Howar, Wādī Chad **72**
Howar, Wādī Sudan **72** 17.30N 27.08E
Howard L. Canada **101** 62.15N105.57W
Howe, C. Australia **93** 37.30S149.59E
Howell U.S.A. **104** 42.36N 83.55W
Howick Canada **105** 45.11N 73.51W
Howitt, Mt. Australia **93** 37.15S146.40E
Howrah India **63** 22.35N 88.20E
Howth Head Rep. of Ire. **15** 53.22N 6.03W
Höxter Germany **38** 51.46N 9.23E
Hoy *i.* U.K. **14** 58.51N 3.17W
Höyanger Norway **41** 61.13N 6.05E
Hoyerswerda Germany **38** 51.26N 14.14E
Hoyos Spain **27** 40.10N 6.43W
Hradec Králové Czech Republic **36** 50.13N 15.50E
Hron *r.* Slovakia **37** 47.49N 18.45E
Hrubieszów Poland **37** 50.49N 23.55E
Hsenwi Burma **56** 23.18N 97.58E
Hsipaw Burma **56** 22.42N 97.21E
Hsuphāng Burma **56** 20.18N 98.42E
Huab *r.* Namibia **80** 20.55S 13.28E
Huabei Pingyuan *f.* China **54** 35.00N115.30E
Huachi China **54** 36.32N108.14E
Huacho Peru **122** 11.05S 77.36W
Huachuca City U.S.A. **109** 31.34N110.21W
Huade China **54** 41.57N114.04E
Hua Hin Thailand **56** 12.34N 99.58E
Huahine *i.* Îs. de la Société **85** 16.45S151.00W
Huai'an Hebei China **54** 40.40N114.18E
Huai'an Jiangsu China **54** 33.29N119.15E
Huaibei China **54** 33.58N116.50E
Huai He *r.* China **54** 32.58N118.18E
Huaiji China **55** 23.58N112.10E
Huailai China **54** 40.25N115.27E
Huainan China **54** 32.39N117.01E
Huaining China **55** 30.21N116.42E
Huairen China **54** 39.50N113.07E
Huairou China **54** 40.20N116.37E
Huaiyang China **54** 33.47N114.59E
Huaiyuan China **54** 32.57N117.12E
Huajuápan Mexico **116** 17.50N 97.48W
Hualian Taiwan **55** 24.00N121.39E
Huallaga *r.* Peru **122** 5.02S 75.30W
Huamanrazo *mtn.* Peru **122** 12.54S 75.04W
Huambo Angola **78** 12.47S 15.44E
Huambo *d.* Angola **78** 12.30S 15.45E
Huanan China **53** 46.13N130.31E
Huancané Peru **122** 15.10S 69.44W
Huancapi Peru **122** 13.35S 74.05W
Huancavelica Peru **122** 12.45S 75.03W
Huancayo Peru **122** 12.05S 75.12W
Huangchuan China **55** 32.07N115.02E
Huanggang China **55** 30.33N114.59E
Huanggang Shan *mtn.* China **55** 27.50N117.47E
Huang Hai *b.* N. Korea **54** 39.30N123.40E
Huang He *r.* China **54** 38.00N118.40E
Huanghe Kou *est.* China **54** 37.54N118.48E
Huanghua China **54** 38.22N117.20E
Huangling China **54** 35.36N109.17E
Huangpi China **55** 30.52N114.22E
Huangping China **55** 26.54N107.53E
Huangshan China **55** 29.41N118.22E
Huangshi China **55** 30.10N115.04E
Huang Xian China **54** 37.38N120.30E
Huangyan China **55** 28.42N121.25E
Huan Jiang *r.* China **54** 35.13N108.00E
Huanren China **54** 41.16N125.21E
Huanta Peru **122** 12.54S 74.13W
Huánuco Peru **122** 9.55S 76.11W
Huaráz Peru **122** 9.33S 77.31W
Huarmey Peru **122** 10.05S 78.05W
Huascaran *mtn.* Peru **122** 9.08S 77.36W
Huasco Chile **124** 28.28S 71.14W
Huatabampo Mexico **109** 26.50N109.38W
Huatong China **54** 40.03N121.56E
Hua Xian Guangdong China **55** 23.22N113.12E
Hua Xian Shaanxi China **54** 34.31N109.46E
Huayuan China **55** 28.37N109.28E
Hubbard L. U.S.A. **104** 44.49N 83.34W
Hubei *d.* China **55** 31.00N112.00E
Hubli India **60** 15.20N 75.14E
Hückelhoven Germany **38** 51.03N 6.13E
Hucknall U.K. **12** 53.03N 1.12W
Huddersfield U.K. **12** 53.38N 1.49W
Huddinge Sweden **43** 59.14N 17.59E
Hudiksvall Sweden **41** 61.44N 17.07E
Hudson Mich. U.S.A. **104** 41.51N 84.21W
Hudson N.Y. U.S.A. **115** 42.15N 73.47W
Hudson *r.* U.S.A. **115** 40.42N 74.02W
Hudson Wyo. U.S.A. **108** 42.54N108.35W
Hudson B. Canada **99** 58.00N 86.00W
Hudson Bay *town* Canada **101** 52.52N102.25W
Hudson Falls *town* U.S.A. **115** 43.18N 73.35W
Hudson Highlands U.S.A. **115** 41.24N 74.15W
Hudson Hope Canada **100** 56.03N121.59W
Hudson Mts. Antarctica **128** 76.00S 99.00W
Hudson Str. Canada **99** 62.00N 70.00W
Hue Vietnam **56** 16.28N107.40E
Huebra *r.* Spain **26** 41.02N 6.48W
Huedin Romania **37** 46.52N 23.02E
Huehuetenango Guatemala **116** 15.19N 91.26W
Huelgoat France **18** 48.22N 3.45W
Huelma Spain **27** 37.39N 3.27W
Huelva Spain **27** 37.16N 6.57W
Huelva *d.* Spain **27** 37.35N 7.10W
Huelva *r.* Spain **27** 37.27N 6.00W
Huércal-Overa Spain **27** 37.23N 1.57W
Huerva *r.* Spain **25** 41.39N 0.52W
Huesca Spain **25** 42.08N 0.25W
Huesca *d.* Spain **25** 42.20N 0.00
Huéscar Spain **27** 37.49N 2.32W
Huete Spain **26** 40.08N 2.41W
Ḥufrat an Naḥās Sudan **73** 9.45N 24.19E
Hugh *r.* Australia **90** 25.01S134.01E
Hughenden Australia **90** 20.51S144.12E
Hughes Australia **91** 30.40S129.32E
Hughes U.S.A. **98** 66.03N154.16W
Hugo U.S.A. **111** 34.01N 95.31W
Hugoton U.S.A. **111** 37.11N101.21W
Hugou China **54** 33.22N117.07E
Hui'an China **55** 25.02N118.48E
Huiarau Range *mts.* New Zealand **86** 38.20S177.15E
Huikou China **55** 29.49N116.15E
Huíla *d.* Angola **78** 15.10S 15.30E
Huilai China **55** 23.03N116.17E
Huimin China **54** 37.30N117.29E
Huining China **54** 35.42N105.06E
Huisne *r.* France **18** 47.59N 0.11E
Huixtla Mexico **116** 15.09N 92.30W
Huizen Neth. **16** 52.18N 5.12E
Huizhou China **55** 23.05N114.29E
Hukuntsi Botswana **80** 24.02S 21.48E
Ḥulayfā' Saudi Arabia **64** 26.00N 40.47E
Hulda Israel **67** 31.50N 34.53E
Hulín Czech Republic **37** 49.19N 17.28E
Hull Canada **105** 45.26N 75.43W
Hüls Germany **38** 51.22N 6.30E
Hulst Neth. **16** 51.18N 4.01E
Hultsfred Sweden **43** 57.29N 15.50E
Hulun Nur *l.* China **53** 49.00N117.27E
Ḥulwān Egypt **66** 29.51N 31.20E
Humaitá Brazil **122** 7.31S 63.02W
Humansdorp R.S.A. **80** 34.02S 24.45E
Ḥumaydah Sudan **72** 14.22N 22.31E
Humber *r.* U.K. **12** 53.40N 0.12W
Humberside *d.* U.K. **12** 53.48N 0.35W
Humble U.S.A. **111** 30.00N 95.16W
Humboldt Canada **101** 52.12N105.07W
Humboldt U.S.A. **111** 35.49N 88.55W
Humboldt *r.* U.S.A. **108** 40.02N118.31W
Hume, L. Australia **93** 36.06S147.05E
Hūmedān Iran **65** 25.24N 59.39E
Humenné Slovakia **37** 48.56N 21.55E
Humphreys Peak *mtn.* U.S.A. **109** 35.20N111.40W
Hūn Libya **75** 29.07N 15.56E
Húnaflói *b.* Iceland **40** 65.45N 20.50W
Hunan *d.* China **55** 27.30N111.30E
Hundested Denmark **42** 55.58N 11.52E
Hundred U.S.A. **114** 39.41N 80.28W
Hundred Mile House *town* Canada **100** 51.38N121.18W
Hunedoara Romania **37** 45.45N 22.54E
Hünfeld Germany **38** 50.40N 9.46E
Hungary Europe **37** 47.30N 19.00E
Hungerford Australia **92** 29.00S144.26E
Hungerford U.K. **13** 51.25N 1.30W
Hungfou Hsü *i.* Taiwan **55** 22.03N121.33E
Hŭngnam N. Korea **53** 39.49N127.40E
Hung Yen Vietnam **55** 20.38N106.05E
Huningue France **19** 47.36N 7.35E
Hunnebostrand Sweden **42** 58.27N 11.18E
Hunsberge *mts.* Namibia **80** 27.40S 17.12E
Hunse *r.* Neth. **16** 53.20N 6.18E
Hunsrück *mts.* Germany **39** 49.45N 7.00E
Hunstanton U.K. **12** 52.57N 0.30E
Hunte *r.* Germany **38** 53.14N 8.18E
Hunter *r.* Australia **93** 32.50S151.42E
Hunter I. Australia **91** 40.30S144.46E
Hunter I. Canada **100** 51.55N128.00W
Hunter Island Ridge Pacific Oc. **84** 21.30S175.00E
Huntingdon Canada **105** 45.05N 74.10W
Huntingdon U.K. **13** 52.20N 0.11W
Huntingdon Penn. U.S.A. **114** 40.29N 78.01W
Huntington Ind. U.S.A. **112** 40.54N 85.30W
Huntington Mass. U.S.A. **115** 42.14N 72.53W
Huntington N.Y. U.S.A. **115** 40.51N 73.25W
Huntington Oreg. U.S.A. **108** 44.21N117.16W
Huntington Utah U.S.A. **108** 39.20N110.58W
Huntington W.Va. U.S.A. **114** 38.25N 82.26W
Huntington Beach *town* U.S.A. **109** 33.39N118.01W
Huntly New Zealand **86** 37.35S175.10E
Huntly U.K. **14** 57.27N 2.47W
Huntsville Canada **104** 45.20N 79.14W
Huntsville Ala. U.S.A. **113** 34.44N 86.35W
Huntsville Tex. U.S.A. **111** 30.43N 95.33W
Hunyani *r.* Mozambique **81** 15.41S 30.38E
Hunyuan China **54** 39.45N113.35E
Huon Pen. P.N.G. **59** 6.00S147.00E
Huonville Australia **91** 43.01S147.01E
Huoshan China **55** 31.24N116.20E
Huqoq Israel **67** 32.53N 35.29E
Hurd, C. Canada **104** 45.13N 81.44W
Hure Qi China **54** 42.44N121.44E
Huretin Sum China **54** 40.19N103.02E
Huriel France **20** 46.23N 2.29E
Hurlock U.S.A. **115** 38.38N 75.52W
Hurmāgai Pakistan **62** 28.18N 64.26E
Huron Ohio U.S.A. **114** 41.24N 82.33W
Huron *r.* U.S.A. **104** 42.03N 83.14W
Huron S.Dak. U.S.A. **110** 44.22N 98.13W
Huron, L. Canada / U.S.A. **114** 44.30N 82.15W
Hurso Ethiopia **73** 9.38N 41.38E
Hurup Denmark **42** 56.45N 8.25E
Húsavík Iceland **40** 66.03N 17.21W
Husevig Faroe Is. **10** 61.49N 6.41W
Huşi Romania **37** 46.40N 28.04E
Huskvarna Sweden **43** 57.48N 14.16E
Husum Germany **38** 54.28N 9.03E
Hutchinson R.S.A. **80** 31.30S 23.10E
Hutchinson U.S.A. **111** 38.05N 97.56W
Hüttental Germany **38** 50.54N 8.02E
Huttig U.S.A. **111** 33.02N 92.11W
Huttonsville U.S.A. **114** 38.43N 80.00W
Hutuo He *r.* China **54** 39.10N117.12E
Hut Yanchi *l.* China **54** 39.24N105.01E
Ḥuwwārah Jordan **67** 32.09N 35.15E
Huy Belgium **16** 50.31N 5.14E
Hvar *i.* Croatia **31** 43.09N 16.45E
Hvar *town* Croatia **31** 43.10N 16.27E
Hvarski Kanal *str.* Croatia **31** 43.20N 16.45E
Hvide Sande Denmark **42** 55.59N 8.08E
Hvita *r.* Iceland **40** 64.33N 21.45W
Hvittingfoss Norway **42** 59.29N 10.01E
Hwange Zimbabwe **80** 18.20S 26.29E
Hwange Nat. Park Zimbabwe **80** 19.00S 26.30E
Hwang Ho *r. see* Huang He *r.* China **54**
Hyannis Mass. U.S.A. **115** 41.39N 70.17W
Hyannis Nebr. U.S.A. **110** 41.59N101.44W
Hyargas Nuur *l.* Mongolia **52** 49.30N 93.35E
Hydaburg U.S.A. **100** 55.15N132.50W
Hyde U.K. **12** 53.26N 2.06W
Hyden Australia **89** 32.27S118.53E
Hyde Park U.S.A. **105** 44.36N 72.37W
Hyde Park Corner *town* Canada **104** 43.00N 81.28W
Hyderābād India **61** 17.22N 78.26E
Hyderābād Pakistan **62** 25.22N 68.22E
Hydesville U.S.A. **108** 40.31N124.00W
Hydetown U.S.A. **114** 41.40N 79.44W
Hyères France **21** 43.07N 6.07E
Hyères, Îles d' *is.* France **21** 43.00N 6.20E
Hyland *r.* Canada **100** 59.50N128.10W
Hyland, Mt. Australia **93** 30.09S152.25E
Hyland Post Canada **100** 57.40N128.10W
Hylestad Norway **42** 59.05N 7.32E
Hyllestad Norway **41** 61.10N 5.18E
Hyltebruk Sweden **43** 57.00N 13.14E
Hyndman U.S.A. **114** 39.49N 78.44W
Hyndman Peak U.S.A. **108** 43.50N114.10W
Hysham U.S.A. **108** 46.18N107.14W
Hythe Kent U.K. **13** 51.04N 1.05E
Hyvinkää Finland **41** 60.38N 24.52E

I

Iakoro Madagascar **81** 23.06S 46.40E
Ialomiţa *r.* Romania **37** 44.41N 27.52E
Iar Connacht *f.* Rep. of Ire. **15** 53.21N 9.22W
Iaşi Romania **37** 47.09N 27.38E
Íasmos Greece **34** 41.07N 25.12E
Iauaretê Brazil **122** 0.36N 69.12W
Iaupolo P.N.G. **90** 9.34S150.30E
Ibadan Nigeria **77** 7.23N 3.56E
Ibagué Colombia **122** 4.25N 75.20W
Ibar *r.* Yugo. **34** 43.15N 20.40E
Ibaraki Japan **57** 34.49N135.34E
Ibarra Ecuador **122** 0.23N 78.05W
Ibb Yemen **71** 13.58N 44.11E
Ibba Sudan **73** 4.48N 29.06E
Ibba *wadi* Sudan **73** 7.09N 28.41E
Ibbenbüren Germany **38** 52.16N 7.43E
Iberville Canada **105** 45.18N 73.14W
Ibi *r.* Japan **57** 35.03N136.42E
Ibi Nigeria **77** 8.11N 9.44E
Ibiapaba, Serra da *mts.* Brazil **123** 5.30S 41.00W
Ibicaraí Brazil **123** 14.52S 39.37W
Ibicuy Argentina **125** 33.45S 59.13W
Ibina *r.* Zaïre **79** 1.00N 28.40E
Ibitinga Brazil **126** 21.43S 48.47W
Ibiza *i.* Spain **25** 39.00N 1.25E
Ibiza *town* Spain **25** 38.54N 1.26E
Iblei, Monti *mts.* Italy **33** 37.07N 14.40E
Ibor *r.* Spain **27** 39.49N 5.33W
Ibotirama Brazil **123** 12.13S 43.12W
Ibrah, Wadi Sudan **73** 10.36N 25.05E
'Ibrī Oman **71** 23.14N 56.30E
İbriktepe Turkey **34** 41.00N 26.30E
Ibshawāy Egypt **66** 29.21N 30.40E
Ibta' Syria **67** 32.47N 36.09E
Ibusuki Japan **57** 31.16N130.39E
Içá *r.* Brazil **122** 3.07S 67.58W
Ica Peru **122** 14.02S 75.48W
Içana Brazil **122** 0.21N 67.19W
Içana *r.* Brazil **122** 0.00 67.10W
Iceland Europe **40** 64.45N 18.00W
Ichchāpuram India **63** 19.07N 84.42E
Ichihara Japan **57** 35.31N140.05E
Ichikawa Japan **57** 35.44N139.55E
Ichinomiya Japan **57** 35.18N136.48E
Icoraci Brazil **123** 1.16S 48.28W
Icy Str. U.S.A. **100** 58.20N135.30W
Idabel U.S.A. **111** 33.54N 94.50W
Ida Grove U.S.A. **110** 42.21N 95.28W
Idah Nigeria **77** 7.05N 6.45E
Idaho *d.* U.S.A. **108** 44.58N115.56W
Idaho Falls *town* U.S.A. **108** 43.30N112.02W
Idanha-a-Nova Portugal **27** 39.55N 7.14W
Idar India **62** 23.50N 73.00E
Idar-Oberstein Germany **39** 49.42N 7.19E
Ideles Algeria **75** 23.49N 5.55E
Idfū Egypt **64** 24.58N 32.50E
Ídhi Óros *mtn.* Greece **35** 35.18N 24.43E
Ídhra *i.* Greece **35** 37.20N 23.32E
Ídhra *town* Greece **35** 37.20N 23.29E
Idiofa Zaïre **78** 4.58S 19.38E
Idmū Egypt **66** 28.09N 30.41E
Idnah Jordan **67** 31.34N 34.59E
Idre Sweden **41** 61.52N 12.43E
Idrija Slovenia **31** 46.00N 14.01E
Idstein Germany **39** 50.13N 8.16E
Ieper Belgium **16** 50.51N 2.53E
Ierápetra Greece **35** 35.00N 25.44E
Ierissós Greece **34** 40.24N 23.52E
Ierzu Italy **32** 39.48N 9.32E
Iesi Italy **30** 43.31N 13.14E
Iesolo Italy **30** 45.32N 12.38E
Ifakara Tanzania **79** 8.09S 36.41E
Ifalik *is.* Federated States of Micronesia **59** 7.15N144.27E
Ifanadiana Madagascar **81** 21.19S 47.39E
Ife Oyo Nigeria **77** 7.33N 4.34E
Iferouâne Niger **77** 19.04N 8.24E
Iga *r.* Japan **57** 34.45N136.01E
Igatpuri India **62** 19.42N 73.33E
Iggesund Sweden **41** 61.38N 17.04E
Iglesias Italy **32** 39.19N 8.32E
Igli Algeria **74** 30.27N 2.18W
Igloolik Island *town* Canada **99** 69.05N 81.25W
Ignace Canada **102** 49.30N 91.40W
Iğneada Burnu *c.* Turkey **29** 41.50N 28.05E
Igoumenítsa Greece **34** 39.30N 20.16E
Igra Russian Fed. **44** 57.31N 53.09E
Iguaçu *r.* Brazil **126** 25.33S 54.35W
Iguaçu, Saltos do *f.* Brazil / Argentina **126** 25.35S 54.22W
Iguala Mexico **116** 18.21N 99.31W
Igualada Spain **25** 41.35N 1.38E
Iguassu Falls *see* Iguaçu, Saltos do *f.* Brazil / Argentina **126**
Iguatu Brazil **123** 6.22S 39.20W
Iguéla Gabon **78** 1.57S 9.22E
Ihiala Nigeria **77** 5.51N 6.52E
Ihosy Madagascar **81** 22.24S 46.08E
Ihosy *r.* Madagascar **81** 21.58S 43.38E
Ii *r.* Finland **40** 65.19N 25.20E
Iida Japan **57** 35.31N137.50E
Iidaan Somali Rep. **71** 6.03N 49.01E
Iide yama *mtn.* Japan **57** 37.50N139.42E
Iisalmi Finland **40** 63.34N 27.11E
Ijebu Ode Nigeria **77** 6.47N 3.54E
Ijill, Kediet *mtn.* Mauritania **74** 22.38N 12.33W
IJmuiden Neth. **16** 52.28N 4.37E
IJssel *r.* Zuid Holland Neth. **16** 51.54N 4.32E
IJssel *r.* Overijssel Neth. **16** 52.34N 5.50E
IJsselmeer *l.* Neth. **16** 52.45N 5.20E
Ijuí Brazil **126** 28.23S 53.55W
Ijzendijke Neth. **16** 51.19N 3.37E
Ijzer *r.* Belgium **16** 51.09N 2.44E
Ikaría *i.* Greece **35** 37.41N 26.20E
Ikdū Egypt **66** 31.18N 30.18E
Ikela Zaïre **78** 1.06S 23.04E
Ikelemba Congo **78** 1.15N 16.38E
Ikelemba *r.* Zaïre **78** 0.08N 18.19E
Ikerre Nigeria **77** 7.30N 5.14E
Ikhast Denmark **42** 56.09N 9.08E
Ikhtiman Bulgaria **34** 42.27N 23.48E
Iki shima *i.* Japan **57** 33.47N129.43E
Ikopa *r.* Madagascar **81** 16.29S 46.43E
Ila Nigeria **77** 8.01N 4.55E
Ilagan Phil. **59** 17.07N121.53E
Īlām Iran **65** 33.27N 46.27E
Ilām Nepal **63** 26.55N 87.56E
Ilan Taiwan **55** 24.45N121.44E
Ilangali Tanzania **79** 6.50S 35.06E
Ilanz Switz. **39** 46.46N 9.12E

Ilaro to Iwo

Ilaro Nigeria 77 6.53N 3.03E
Iława Poland 37 53.37N 19.33E
Ilebo Zaïre 78 4.20S 20.35E
Ilek r. Russian Fed. 45 51.30N 54.00E
Ileret Kenya 79 4.22N 36.13E
Ilerh, Oued wadi Algeria 75 20.59N 2.14E
Îles, Lac des l. Canada 105 46.50N 77.10W
Ilesha Oyo Nigeria 77 7.39N 4.45E
Ilford Canada 101 56.04N 95.35W
Ilfracombe Australia 90 23.30S144.30E
Ilfracombe U.K. 13 51.13N 4.08W
Ilhabela Brazil 126 23.47S 45.20W
Ilha Grande, Baía da b. Brazil 126 23.09S 44.30W
Ilha Grande, Represa resr. Brazil 126 23.10S 53.40W
Ílhavo Portugal 26 40.36N 8.40W
Ilhéus Brazil 123 14.50S 39.06W
Ili r. Kazakhstan 52 45.00N 74.20E
Ilia Romania 37 45.56N 22.39E
Iliamna L. U.S.A. 98 59.30N155.00W
Ilich Russian Fed. 52 40.50N 68.29E
Iligan Phil. 59 8.12N124.13E
Ilintsy Ukraine 37 49.08N 29.11E
Ilion U.S.A. 115 43.01N 75.02W
Ilirska Bistrica Slovenia 31 45.34N 14.15E
Ilkley U.K. 12 53.56N 1.49W
Illapel Chile 124 31.38S 71.10W
Ille-et-Vilaine d. France 18 48.10N 1.30W
Illéla Niger 77 14.30N 5.09E
Iller r. Germany 39 48.23N 9.58E
Illeret Kenya 73 4.19N 36.13E
Illertissen Germany 39 48.13N 10.06E
Illescas Spain 27 40.07N 3.50W
Illiers France 18 48.18N 1.15E
Illinois d. U.S.A. 110 40.30N 89.30W
Illinois r. U.S.A. 110 38.58N 90.27W
Illizi Algeria 75 26.29N 8.28E
Ilmajoki Finland 40 62.44N 22.34E
Ilmenau r. Germany 38 53.23N 10.10E
Ilminster U.K. 13 50.55N 2.56W
Ilo Peru 124 17.38S 71.20W
Iloilo Phil. 59 10.45N122.33E
Ilorin Nigeria 77 8.32N 4.34E
Ilovlya Russian Fed. 45 49.19N 44.01E
Īlubabor d. Ethiopia 73 7.50N 34.55E
Imabari Japan 57 34.04N132.59E
Imala Mozambique 79 14.39S 39.34E
Imandra Russian Fed. 44 67.53N 33.30E
Imandra, Ozero l. Russian Fed. 44 67.30N 32.45E
Imbābah Egypt 66 30.05N 31.12E
Imese Zaïre 78 2.07N 18.06E
Īmī Ethiopia 73 6.28N 42.18E
Imlay City U.S.A. 114 43.02N 83.05W
Immenstadt Germany 38 47.33N 10.13E
Immingham U.K. 12 53.37N 0.12W
Immokalee U.S.A. 113 26.25N 81.26W
Imo d. Nigeria 77 5.30N 7.20E
Imola Italy 30 44.21N 11.42E
Imotski Croatia 31 43.27N 17.13E
Imperatriz Brazil 123 5.32S 47.28W
Imperia Italy 30 43.53N 8.03E
Imperial Calif. U.S.A. 109 32.51N115.34W
Imperial Nebr. U.S.A. 110 40.31N101.39W
Imperial Dam U.S.A. 109 32.55N114.30W
Imperial de Aragón, Canal Spain 25 41.37N 1.00W
Imperial Valley f. U.S.A. 109 32.50N115.30W
Impfondo Congo 78 1.36N 17.58E
Imphāl India 61 24.47N 93.55E
Imroz i. see Gökçeada i. Turkey 34
Imst Austria 39 47.14N 10.44E
Ina Japan 57 35.50N137.57E
Ina r. Japan 57 34.43N135.28E
In Abbangarit well Niger 77 17.49N 6.15E
Inaccessible I. Tristan da Cunha 127 37.19S 12.44W
I-n-Amguel Algeria 75 23.40N 5.08E
Inangahua Junction New Zealand 86 41.53S171.58E
Inanwatan Indonesia 59 2.08S132.10E
Inarajan Guam 84 13.16N144.45E
Inari l. Finland 40 69.00N 28.00E
Inari town Finland 40 68.54N 27.01E
Inazawa Japan 57 35.15N136.47E
I-n-Belbel Algeria 74 27.54N 1.10E
Inca Spain 25 39.43N 2.54E
Incesu Turkey 64 38.39N 35.12E
Inchiri d. Mauritania 74 20.10N 15.00W
Inch'on S. Korea 53 37.30N126.38E
Incudine, L' mtn. France 21 41.51N 9.12E
Indals r. Sweden 40 62.30N 17.20E
Indaw Burma 56 23.40N 94.46E
Independence Calif. U.S.A. 108 36.48N118.12W
Independence Kans. U.S.A. 111 37.13N 95.42W
Independence Mo. U.S.A. 110 39.05N 94.24W
Inderborskiy Kazakhstan 45 48.32N 51.44E
India Asia 61 23.00N 78.30E
Indian r. Canada 105 45.16N 76.14W
Indiana d. U.S.A. 112 40.00N 86.15W
Indiana town U.S.A. 114 40.37N 79.09W
Indian-Antarctic Ridge f. Indian Oc. 49 49.00S125.00E
Indianapolis U.S.A. 112 39.45N 86.10W
Indian Cabins Canada 100 59.52N117.02W
Indian Harbour Canada 103 54.25N 57.20W
Indian Head Canada 101 50.32N103.40W
Indian L. Canada 104 47.08N 82.08W
Indian L. U.S.A. 115 43.47N 74.16W
Indian Lake town U.S.A. 105 43.47N 74.16W
Indian Ocean 49
Indianola U.S.A. 110 41.22N 93.34W
Indian River town U.S.A. 104 45.25N 84.37W
Indian River B. U.S.A. 115 38.36N 75.05W
Indiga Russian Fed. 44 67.40N 49.00E
Indigirka r. Russian Fed. 51 71.00N148.45E
Indija Yugo. 31 45.03N 20.05E
Indio U.S.A. 109 33.43N116.13W
Indonesia Asia 58 6.00S118.00E
Indore India 62 22.43N 75.50E
Indragiri r. Indonesia 58 0.30S103.08E
Indramayu Indonesia 59 6.22S108.20E
Indrāvati r. India 63 18.44N 80.16E
Indre d. France 19 46.45N 1.30E
Indre r. France 18 47.16N 0.19E
Indre-et-Loire d. France 18 47.15N 0.45E
Indus r. Pakistan 62 24.20N 67.47E
Inebolu Turkey 64 41.57N 33.45E
Inegöl Turkey 64 40.06N 29.31E
I-n-Eker Algeria 75 24.01N 5.05E
I-n-Ezzane well Algeria 75 23.29N 11.15E
Infiesto Spain 26 43.21N 5.22W
I-n-Gall Niger 77 16.47N 6.56E
Ingatestone U.K. 13 51.41N 0.22E
Ingelstad Sweden 43 56.45N 14.55E
Ingende Zaïre 78 0.17S 18.58E
Ingenika r. Canada 100 56.43N125.07W
Ingersoll Canada 104 43.02N 80.53W
Inggen China 54 41.35N104.47E
Ingham Australia 90 18.35S146.12E
Ingleborough mtn. U.K. 12 54.10N 2.23W
Inglewood Qld Australia 93 28.25S151.02E
Inglewood Vic. Australia 92 36.33S143.53E
Inglewood Canada 104 43.47N 79.56W
Inglewood New Zealand 86 39.09S174.12E
Inglewood U.S.A. 109 33.58N118.21W
Ingolstadt Germany 39 48.46N 11.27E
Ingomar Australia 92 29.38S134.48E
Ingraham U.S.A. 105 44.47N 73.30W
Ingulets Ukraine 45 47.43N 33.16E
Ingwiller France 19 48.52N 7.29E
Inhambane Mozambique 81 23.51S 35.29E
Inhambane d. Mozambique 81 22.20S 34.00E
Inhaminga Mozambique 81 18.24S 35.00E
Inharrime Mozambique 81 24.29S 35.01E
Inhassoro Mozambique 81 21.32S 35.10E
Iniesta Spain 25 39.26N 1.45W
Inirida r. Colombia 122 3.59N 67.45W
Inishbofin i. Galway Rep. of Ire. 15 53.38N 10.14W
Inisheer i. Rep. of Ire. 15 53.04N 9.32W
Inishmaan i. Rep. of Ire. 15 53.06N 9.36W
Inishmore i. Rep. of Ire. 15 53.08N 9.43W
Inishowen Pen. Rep. of Ire. 15 55.08N 7.20W
Inishturk i. Rep. of Ire. 15 53.43N 10.08W
Injune Australia 90 25.51S148.34E
Inklin Canada 100 58.56N133.05W
Inklin r. Canada 100 58.50N133.10W
Inkster U.S.A. 104 42.17N 83.17W
Inn r. Europe 39 48.35N 13.28E
Innaminka Australia 91 27.43S140.46E
Inner Hebrides is. U.K. 14 56.50N 6.45W
Inner Mongolia d. see Nei Monggol Zizhiqu d. China 54
Inner Sd. U.K. 14 57.30N 5.55W
Innisfail Australia 90 17.32S146.02E
Innisfail Canada 100 52.00N113.57W
Innsbruck Austria 39 47.16N 11.24E
Innset Norway 40 68.41N 18.50E
Innviertel f. Austria 39 48.05N 13.08E
Inongo Zaïre 78 1.55S 18.20E
Inowrocław Poland 37 52.49N 18.12E
I-n-Salah Algeria 75 27.13N 2.28E
Insein Burma 56 16.54N 96.08E
In Tasik well Mali 77 18.03N 2.00E
Intepe Turkey 34 40.01N 26.19E
Interlaken Switz. 39 46.41N 7.51E
International Falls town U.S.A. 110 48.38N 93.26W
Intracoastal Waterway canal U.S.A. 111 28.45N 95.40W
Intute Mozambique 79 14.08S 39.55E
Inubō saki c. Japan 57 35.41N140.52E
Inukjuak Canada 99 58.25N 78.18W
Inuvik Canada 98 68.16N133.40W
Inuvik d. Canada 98 68.00N130.00W
Inuyama Japan 57 35.23N136.56E
Inveraray U.K. 14 56.24N 5.05W
Inverbervie U.K. 14 56.51N 2.17W
Invercargill New Zealand 86 46.26S168.21E
Inverell Australia 93 29.46S151.10E
Invergordon U.K. 14 57.42N 4.10W
Inverhuron Canada 104 44.17N 81.34W
Inverness U.K. 14 57.27N 4.15W
Inverurie U.K. 14 57.17N 2.23W
Inverway Australia 88 17.49S129.40E
Investigator Group is. Australia 92 33.45S134.30E
Investigator Str. Australia 92 35.25S137.10E
Invinheima r. Brazil 124 22.52S 53.20W
Inya Russian Fed. 50 50.24N 86.47E
Inyangani mtn. Zimbabwe 81 18.18S 32.50E
Inyonga Tanzania 79 6.43S 32.02E
Inzia r. Zaïre 78 3.47S 17.57E
Ioánnina Greece 34 39.39N 20.57E
Iola U.S.A. 111 37.55N 95.24W
Iona i. U.K. 14 56.20N 6.25W
Iongo Angola 78 9.11S 17.45E
Ionia U.S.A. 112 42.58N 85.06W
Ionian Is. see Iónioi Nísoi is. Greece 35
Ionian Sea Med. Sea 35 38.30N 18.45E
Iónioi Nísoi is. Greece 35 38.40N 20.08E
Íos i. Greece 35 36.44N 25.16E
Íos town Greece 35 36.44N 25.16E
Iowa d. U.S.A. 110 42.00N 93.30W
Iowa r. U.S.A. 110 41.10N 91.02W
Iowa City U.S.A. 110 41.40N 91.32W
Iowa Falls town U.S.A. 110 42.31N 93.16W
Ipati Greece 35 38.52N 22.14E
Ipatovo Russian Fed. 45 45.44N 42.56E
Ipeiros f. Greece 34 39.30N 20.30E
Ipiales Colombia 122 0.52N 77.38W
Ipiaú Brazil 123 14.07S 39.43W
Ipixuna Brazil 122 7.00S 71.30W
Ipoh Malaysia 58 4.36N101.02E
Ippa r. Belorussia 37 52.13N 29.08E
Ippy C.A.R. 73 6.15N 21.12E
İpsala Turkey 34 40.55N 26.23E
Ipswich Australia 93 27.38S152.40E
Ipswich U.K. 13 52.04N 1.09E
Ipu Brazil 123 4.23S 40.44W
Ipuh Indonesia 58 2.58S101.28E
Iquique Chile 124 20.13S 70.10W
Iquitos Peru 122 3.51S 73.13W
Irago-suidō str. Japan 57 34.35N137.00E
Iráklia i. Greece 35 36.50N 25.28E
Iráklion Greece 35 35.20N 25.09E
Iran Asia 65 32.00N 54.30E
Iran, Pegunungan mts. Indonesia/Malaysia 58 3.20N115.00E
Īrānshahr Iran 65 27.14N 60.42E
Irapuato Mexico 116 20.40N101.40W
Iraq Asia 64 33.00N 44.00E
Irauen, Wādī Libya 75 26.28N 12.00E
Irayel Russian Fed. 44 64.23N 55.25E
Irazú mtn. Costa Rica 117 9.59N 83.52W
Irbid Jordan 67 32.33N 35.51E
Irbid d. Jordan 67 32.27N 35.51E
Irbīl Iraq 65 36.12N 44.01E
Irdning Austria 39 47.33N 14.01E
Irebu Zaïre 78 0.37S 17.45E
Iregua r. Spain 26 42.27N 2.24W
Ireland I. Bermuda 127 32.19N 64.51W
Irgiz Kazakhstan 9 48.36N 61.14E
Irgiz r. Kazakhstan 9 48.00N 62.30E
Irharhar, Oued wadi Algeria 75 23.45N 5.55E
Irian Jaya d. Indonesia 59 4.00S138.00E
Iriba Chad 72 15.07N 22.15E
Irié Guinea 76 8.15N 9.10W
Iringa Tanzania 79 7.49S 35.39E
Iringa d. Tanzania 79 8.30S 35.00E
Iriomote jima i. Japan 53 24.30N124.00E
Iriri r. Brazil 123 3.50S 52.40W
Irish Sea U.K./Rep. of Ire. 15 53.30N 5.40W
Irkutsk Russian Fed. 52 52.18N104.15E
Iroise b. France 18 48.15N 4.55W
Iron Baron Australia 92 32.59S137.09E
Iron Bridge town Canada 104 46.17N 83.14W
Iron Gate f. Romania/Yugo. 37 44.40N 22.30E
Iron Knob Australia 92 32.44S137.08E
Iron Mountain town U.S.A. 112 45.51N 88.03W
Iron Mts. Rep. of Ire. 15 54.10N 7.56W
Iron River town U.S.A. 110 46.05N 88.38W
Irons U.S.A. 112 44.08N 85.55W
Ironton U.S.A. 114 38.31N 82.40W
Ironwood U.S.A. 112 46.25N 90.08W
Iroquois Canada 105 44.51N 75.19W
Iroquois Falls town Canada 102 48.40N 80.40W
Irosin Phil. 59 12.45N124.02E
Irō-zaki c. Japan 57 34.36N138.51E
Irpen Ukraine 37 50.31N 30.29E
Irrapatana Australia 92 29.03S136.28E
Irrawaddy d. Burma 56 17.00N 95.00E
Irrawaddy r. Burma 56 15.50N 95.00E
Irrawaddy Delta Burma 56 16.45N 95.00E
Irsha r. Ukraine 37 50.45N 29.30E
Irsina Italy 33 40.45N 16.15E
Irthing r. U.K. 11 54.55N 2.50W
Irtysh r. Russian Fed. 9 61.00N 69.00E
Iruma r. Japan 57 35.57N139.30E
Irumu Zaïre 79 1.29N 29.48E
Irún Spain 26 43.20N 1.48W
Iruñea see Pamplona Spain 25
Irurzun Spain 25 42.55N 1.50W
Irvine U.K. 14 55.37N 4.40W
Irvinestown U.K. 15 54.29N 7.40W
Irving U.S.A. 111 32.49N 96.56W
Irvona U.S.A. 114 40.46N 78.33W
Irwin, Pt. Australia 89 35.03S116.20E
Is, Jabal mtn. Sudan 72 22.03N 35.28E
Isa Nigeria 77 13.14N 6.24E
Isaac r. Australia 90 22.52S149.20E
Isaba Spain 25 42.52N 0.55W
Isabelia, Cordillera mts. Nicaragua 117 13.30N 85.00W
Isábena r. Spain 25 42.11N 0.21E
Ísafjördhur town Iceland 40 66.05N 23.06W
Isaka Tanzania 79 3.52S 32.54E
Isaka Bandundu Zaïre 78 2.35S 18.48E
Isaka Equateur Zaïre 78 1.49S 20.50E
Īsa Khel Pakistan 62 32.41N 71.17E
Isakogorka Russian Fed. 44 64.23N 40.31E
Isangi Zaïre 78 0.48N 24.03E
Isar r. Germany 39 48.49N 12.58E
Isbergues France 16 50.38N 2.24E
Ischia Italy 32 40.43N 13.57E
Ischia i. Italy 32 40.43N 13.54E
Ise Japan 57 34.29N136.42E
Isefjord b. Denmark 42 55.52N 11.49E
Iseo, Lago d' l. Italy 30 45.43N 10.04E
Isère d. France 21 45.10N 5.50E
Isère r. France 21 44.59N 4.51E
Iserlohn Germany 38 51.22N 7.41E
Isernia Italy 33 41.36N 14.14E
Ise-wan b. Japan 57 34.45N136.40E
Iseyin Nigeria 77 7.59N 3.36E
Isfahan see Eşfahān Iran 60
Ishikari r. Japan 57 43.15N141.21E
Ishikari wan b. Japan 57 43.15N141.20E
Ishim Russian Fed. 50 56.10N 69.30E
Ishim r. Russian Fed. 9 57.50N 71.00E
Ishinomaki Japan 57 38.25N141.18E
Ishpeming U.S.A. 112 46.29N 87.40W
Ishurdi Bangla. 63 24.09N 89.03E
Isigny France 18 49.18N 1.06W
Isiolo Kenya 79 0.20N 37.36E
Isipingo Beach town R.S.A. 80 30.00S 30.57E
Isiro Zaïre 79 2.50N 27.40E
Iskâr r. Bulgaria 34 43.44N 24.27E
Iskenderun Turkey 64 36.37N 36.08E
Iskenderun Körfezi g. Turkey 64 36.40N 35.50E
Iskilip Turkey 64 40.45N 34.28E
Iskûr r. Bulgaria 34 43.35N 24.20E
Iskûr, Yazovir l. Bulgaria 34 42.27N 23.38E
Isla r. U.K. 14 56.32N 3.22W
Isla Cristina town Spain 27 37.12N 7.19W
Islāmābād Pakistan 62 33.40N 73.10E
Islāmkot Pakistan 62 24.42N 70.11E
Islāmpur Bihār India 63 25.09N 85.12E
Islāmpur W. Bengal India 63 26.16N 88.12E
Island L. Australia 92 31.30S136.40E
Island L. Canada 101 53.47N 94.25W
Island Magee pen. U.K. 15 54.48N 5.44W
Islands, B. of Canada 103 49.10N 58.15W
Islands, B. of New Zealand 86 35.15S174.15E
Islay i. U.K. 14 55.45N 6.20W
Isle r. France 20 44.55N 0.15W
Isle of Portland f. U.K. 13 50.32N 2.25W
Isle of Wight d. U.K. 13 50.40N 1.17W
Isleta U.S.A. 109 34.55N106.42W
Ismael Cortinas Uruguay 125 33.58S 57.06W
Ismay U.S.A. 108 46.30N104.48W
Isnā Egypt 64 25.16N 32.30E
Isny Germany 38 47.41N 10.02E
Isoka Zambia 79 10.06S 32.39E
Isola della Scala Italy 32 45.16N 11.00E
Isola del Liri town Italy 31 41.41N 13.34E
Isola di Capo Rizzuto town Italy 33 38.58N 17.06E
Isparta Turkey 64 37.46N 30.32E
Isperikh Bulgaria 34 43.43N 26.50E
Ispica Italy 33 36.46N 14.55E
Ispikān Pakistan 62 26.14N 62.12E
Israel Asia 67 32.00N 34.50E
Israelite B. Australia 89 33.40S123.55E
Israelite Bay town Australia 89 33.37S123.48E
Issia Ivory Coast 76 6.33N 6.33W
Issigeac France 20 44.44N 0.36E
Issoire France 20 45.33N 3.15E
Issoudun France 19 46.57N 2.00E
Is-sur-Tille France 19 47.31N 5.06E
Issyk Kul l. Kyrgyzstan 52 43.30N 77.20E
Istanbul Turkey 29 41.02N 28.58E
Istanbul Boğazi str. Turkey 29 41.07N 29.04E
Isthmus of Kra Thailand 56 10.20N 99.10E
Istiaía Greece 35 38.57N 23.10E
Istok Yugo. 34 42.45N 20.24E
Istra pen. Croatia 31 45.10N 13.55E
Itabaiana Brazil 123 7.20S 35.20W
Itabira Brazil 126 19.39S 43.14W
Itabirito Brazil 126 20.21S 43.45W
Itabuna Brazil 123 14.48S 39.18W
Itacajuna r. Brazil 123 5.20S 49.08W
Itacoatiara Brazil 122 3.06S 58.22W
Itagüí Colombia 122 6.10N 75.36W
Itaí Brazil 126 23.23S 49.05W
Itaim r. Brazil 123 6.43S 42.48W
Itaipu, Represa resr. Brazil/Paraguay 126 24.30S 54.20W
Itaituba Brazil 123 4.17S 55.59W
Itajaí Brazil 126 26.50S 48.39W
Itajubá Brazil 126 22.24S 45.25W
Itaka Tanzania 79 8.51S 32.48E
Itálica site Spain 27 37.30N 6.05W
Italy Europe 28 43.00N 12.00E
Itami Japan 57 34.46N135.25E
Itapecerica Brazil 126 20.28S 45.09W
Itapecuru Mirim Brazil 123 3.24S 44.20W
Itaperuna Brazil 126 21.14S 41.51W
Itapetinga Brazil 123 15.17S 40.16W
Itapetininga Brazil 126 23.36S 48.07W
Itapeva Brazil 126 23.59S 48.59W
Itapicuru r. Brazil 123 11.50S 37.30W
Itapira Brazil 126 22.24S 46.56W
Itaqui Brazil 126 29.07S 56.33W
Itārsi India 63 22.37N 77.45E
Itatiba Brazil 126 22.59S 46.51W
Itatinga Brazil 126 23.06S 48.36W
Itatuba Brazil 122 5.40S 63.20W
Itaúna Brazil 126 20.04S 44.14W
Itbayat i. Phil. 55 20.45N121.50E
Itéa Greece 35 38.25N 22.25E
Ithaca U.S.A. 115 42.27N 76.30W
Itháki Greece 35 38.23N 20.42E
Itháki i. Greece 35 38.24N 20.42E
Itimbiri r. Zaïre 78 2.02N 22.47E
Itmurinkol, Ozero l. Kazakhstan 45 49.30N 52.17E
Itō Japan 57 34.58N139.05E
Itoko Zaïre 78 1.00S 21.45E
Iton r. France 18 49.09N 1.12E
Itsa Egypt 66 29.14N 30.47E
Ittel, Oued wadi Algeria 75 34.18N 6.02E
Ittiri Italy 32 40.36N 8.33E
Itu Brazil 126 23.17S 47.18W
Ituí r. Brazil 122 4.38S 70.19W
Ituiutaba Brazil 126 19.00S 49.25W
Ituri r. Zaïre 79 1.45N 27.06E
Iturup i. Russian Fed. 53 44.00N147.30E
Ituverava Brazil 126 20.22S 47.48W
Ituxi r. Brazil 122 7.20S 64.50W
Ityāy al Bārūd Egypt 66 30.53N 30.40E
Itzehoe Germany 38 53.55N 9.31E
Ivaí r. Brazil 126 23.20S 53.23W
Ivalo Finland 40 68.42N 27.30E
Ivalo r. Finland 40 68.43N 27.36E
Ivanec Croatia 31 46.13N 16.08E
Ivangrad Yugo. 31 42.50N 19.52E
Ivanhoe Australia 92 32.56S144.22E
Ivanhoe U.S.A. 110 44.28N 96.12W
Ivanić Grad Croatia 31 45.42N 16.24E
Ivanjica Yugo. 34 43.35N 20.14E
Ivano-Frankovsk Ukraine 37 48.55N 24.42E
Ivanovo Belorussia 37 52.10N 25.13E
Ivanovo Russian Fed. 44 57.00N 41.00E
Ivdel Russian Fed. 44 60.45N 60.30E
Ivenets Belorussia 37 53.50N 26.40E
Ivigtût Greenland 99 61.10N 48.00W
Ivindo Gabon 78 0.02S 12.13E
Ivittuut see Ivigtût Greenland 99
Iviza i. see Ibiza i. Spain 25
Ivohibe Madagascar 81 22.29S 45.52E
Ivory Coast Africa 76 8.00N 5.30W
Ivösjön l. Sweden 43 56.06N 14.27E
Ivrea Italy 30 45.28N 7.52E
Ivujivik Canada 99 62.24N 77.55W
Ivybridge U.K. 13 50.24N 3.56W
Ivydale U.S.A. 114 38.32N 81.03W
Iwaki Japan 57 36.58N140.58E
Iwaki r. Japan 57 41.20N140.00E
Iwakuni Japan 57 34.10N132.09E
Iwata Japan 57 34.42N137.48E
Iwo Nigeria 77 7.38N 4.11E

Ixiamas Bolivia **124** 13.45S 68.09W
Iyo nada *str.* Japan **57** 33.40N132.20E
Izabal, Lago de *l.* Guatemala **117** 15.30N 89.00W
Izberbash Russian Fed. **45** 42.31N 47.52E
Izhevsk Russian Fed. **44** 56.49N 53.11E
Izhma Russian Fed. **44** 65.03N 53.48E
Izhma *r.* Russian Fed. **44** 65.16N 53.18E
Izmail Ukraine **37** 45.20N 28.50E
Izmir Turkey **29** 38.24N 27.09E
Izmir Körfezi *g.* Turkey **29** 38.30N 26.45E
Izmit Turkey **64** 40.48N 29.55E
Iznajar, Embalse de *resr.* Spain **27** 37.15N 4.20W
Iznalloz Spain **27** 37.23N 3.31W
Izozog, Bañados de *f.* Bolivia **124** 18.30S 62.05W
Izozog Marshes *f.* *see* Izozog, Bañados de *f.* Bolivia **124**
Izra' Syria **67** 32.51N 36.15E
Izsák Hungary **31** 46.48N 19.22E
Iztochni Rodopi *mts.* Bulgaria **34** 41.44N 25.28E
Izu-hantō *pen.* Japan **57** 34.53N138.55E
Izuhara Japan **57** 34.12N129.17E
Izumi Japan **57** 34.29N135.26E
Izumi-ōtsu Japan **57** 34.30N135.24E
Izumi-sano Japan **57** 34.25N135.19E
Izumo Japan **57** 35.33N132.50E
Izumo *r.* Japan **57** 34.38N136.33E
Izyaslav Ukraine **37** 50.10N 26.46E
Izyum Ukraine **45** 49.12N 37.19E

J

Jaba Ethiopia **73** 6.17N 35.12E
Jaba' Jordan **67** 32.19N 35.13E
Jabā Syria **67** 33.10N 35.56E
Jabal, Baḩr al *r.* Sudan **73** 9.30N 30.30E
Jabal al Awliyā' Sudan **72** 15.14N 32.30E
Jabal Dūd Sudan **73** 13.22N 33.09E
Jabalón *r.* Spain **26** 38.53N 4.05W
Jabalpur India **63** 23.10N 79.57E
Jabālyah Egypt **67** 31.32N 34.29E
Jabbān, Arḑ al *f.* Jordan **66** 32.08N 36.35E
Jabiru Australia **90** 12.39S132.55E
Jabjabah, Wādī Egypt **72** 22.37N 33.17E
Jablah Syria **66** 35.22N 35.56E
Jablanac Croatia **31** 44.42N 14.54E
Jablanica Bosnia-Herzegovina **31** 43.39N 17.45E
Jablaničko Jezero *resr.* Bosnia-Herzegovina **31** 43.40N 17.50E
Jablonec nad Nisou Czech Republic **36** 50.44N 15.10E
Jabori Pakistan **62** 34.36N 73.16E
Jaboticabal Brazil **126** 21.15S 48.17W
Jabrat Sa'īd *wells* Sudan **72** 16.06N 31.50E
Jaca Spain **25** 42.34N 0.33W
Jacareí Brazil **126** 23.17S 45.57W
Jackman U.S.A. **112** 45.38N 70.16W
Jacks Mtn. U.S.A. **114** 40.45N 77.30W
Jackson Ky. U.S.A. **113** 37.32N 83.24W
Jackson Mich. U.S.A. **104** 42.15N 84.24W
Jackson Miss. U.S.A. **111** 32.18N 90.12W
Jackson Mo. U.S.A. **111** 37.23N 89.40W
Jackson Ohio U.S.A. **114** 39.03N 82.39W
Jackson Tenn. U.S.A. **111** 35.37N 88.49W
Jackson Wyo. U.S.A. **108** 43.29N110.38W
Jackson Bay *town* Canada **100** 50.32N125.57W
Jacksonville Fla. U.S.A. **113** 30.20N 81.40W
Jacksonville Ill. U.S.A. **110** 39.44N 90.14W
Jacksonville N.C. U.S.A. **113** 34.45N 77.26W
Jacksonville Tex. U.S.A. **111** 31.58N 95.17W
Jacksonville Beach *town* U.S.A. **113** 30.18N 81.24W
Jacobābād Pakistan **62** 28.17N 68.26E
Jacobina Brazil **123** 11.13S 40.30W
Jacob Lake *town* U.S.A. **109** 36.41N112.14W
Jacob's Well *see* Bi'r Yaqūb Jordan **67**
Jacques Cartier, Détroit de *str.* Canada **103** 50.00N 63.30W
Jacques Cartier, Mt. Canada **103** 48.59N 65.57W
Jacuí *r.* Brazil **126** 29.56S 51.13W
Jacundá *r.* Brazil **123** 1.57S 50.26W
Jaddi, Rās *c.* Pakistan **62** 25.14N 63.31E
Jade Germany **38** 53.20N 8.14E
Jadebusen *b.* Germany **38** 53.30N 8.10E
Jadraque Spain **26** 40.55N 2.55W
Jādū Libya **75** 31.57N 12.01E
Jaén Peru **122** 5.21S 78.28W
Jaén Spain **27** 37.46N 3.47W
Jaén *d.* Spain **27** 37.55N 3.30W
Jaeren *f.* Norway **42** 58.40N 5.45E
Jāfarābād India **62** 20.52N 71.22E
Jaffa *see* Tel Aviv-Yafo Israel **67**
Jaffa, C. Australia **92** 36.58S139.39E
Jaffna Sri Lanka **61** 9.38N 80.02E
Jaffrey U.S.A. **115** 42.50N 72.04W
Jagādhri India **62** 30.10N 77.18E
Jāgan Pakistan **62** 28.05N 68.30E
Jagatsingpur India **63** 20.16N 86.10E
Jagdalpur India **63** 19.04N 82.02E
Jaggang China **63** 32.52N 79.45E
Jagst *r.* Germany **39** 49.14N 9.11E
Jagtiāl India **63** 18.48N 78.56E
Jaguarão Brazil **126** 32.30S 53.25W
Jahānābād India **63** 25.13N 84.59E
Jahrom Iran **65** 28.30N 53.30E
Jailolo Indonesia **59** 1.05N127.29E
Jainti India **63** 26.42N 89.36E
Jaintiāpur Bangla. **63** 25.08N 92.07E
Jaipur India **62** 26.53N 75.50E
Jāis India **63** 26.15N 81.32E
Jaisalmer India **62** 26.55N 70.54E
Jājarkot Nepal **63** 28.42N 82.14E
Jajawijaya Mts. Asia **59** 4.20S139.10E
Jajce Bosnia-Herzegovina **31** 44.21N 17.16E
Jajjha Pakistan **62** 28.45N 70.34E
Jājpur India **63** 20.51N 86.20E
Jakarta Indonesia **59** 6.08S106.45E
Jakarta *d.* Indonesia **59** 6.10S106.48E
Jakhāu India **62** 23.13N 68.43E
Jäkkvik Sweden **40** 66.23N 17.00E
Jakobstad *see* Pietarsaari Finland **40**
Jakupica *mts.* Macedonia **34** 41.45N 21.22E
Jal U.S.A. **111** 32.07N103.12W
Jalālābād Afghan. **62** 34.26N 70.28E
Jalālah al Baḩrīyah, Jabal *mts.* Egypt **66** 29.20N 32.12E
Jalālat al Qiblīyah, Jabal al *mts.* Egypt **66** 28.42N 32.23E
Jalālpur India **63** 26.19N 82.44E
Jalapa Mexico **116** 19.45N 96.48W
Jālaun India **63** 26.09N 79.21E
Jaldak Afghan. **62** 31.58N 66.44E
Jalesar India **63** 27.29N 78.19E
Jaleswar India **63** 21.49N 87.13E
Jālgaon Mahār. India **62** 21.03N 76.32E
Jālgaon Mahār. India **62** 21.01N 75.34E
Jalingo Nigeria **77** 8.54N 11.21E
Jalisco *d.* Mexico **116** 21.00N103.00W
Jallas *r.* Spain **26** 42.54N 9.08W
Jālna India **62** 19.50N 75.53E
Jalón *r.* Spain **25** 41.47N 1.04W
Jālor India **62** 25.21N 72.37E
Jalpaiguri India **63** 26.31N 88.44E
Jālū Libya **75** 29.02N 21.33E
Jaluit *i.* Pacific Oc. **84** 6.00N169.35E
Jalūlā Iraq **65** 34.16N 45.10E
Jamaame Somali Rep. **79** 0.04N 42.46E
Jamaari Nigeria **77** 11.44N 9.53E
Jamaica C. America **117** 18.00N 77.00W
Jamālpur Bangla. **63** 24.55N 89.56E
Jamālpur India **63** 25.18N 86.30E
Jamanxim *r.* Brazil **123** 4.43S 56.18W
Jambes Belgium **16** 50.28N 4.52E
Jambi Indonesia **58** 1.36S103.39E
Jambi *d.* Indonesia **58** 2.00S102.30E
Jambusar India **62** 22.03N 72.48E
James *r.* S.Dak. U.S.A. **110** 42.55N 97.28W
James *r.* Va. U.S.A. **113** 36.57N 76.26W
James B. Canada **102** 53.30N 80.00W
James Bay Prov. Park Canada **102** 51.30N 79.00W
Jamestown Australia **92** 33.12S138.38E
Jamestown St. Helena **127** 15.56S 5.44W
Jamestown N.Dak. U.S.A. **110** 46.54N 98.42W
Jamestown N.Y. U.S.A. **114** 42.06N 79.14W
Jamestown Penn. U.S.A. **114** 41.29N 80.27W
Jamestown Tenn. U.S.A. **113** 36.24N 84.58W
Jamjodhpur India **62** 21.54N 70.01E
Jammerbught *b.* Denmark **42** 57.20N 9.30E
Jammu Jammu & Kashmir **62** 32.42N 74.52E
Jammu & Kashmir Asia **62** 34.45N 76.00E
Jāmnagar India **62** 22.28N 70.04E
Jamnotri India **63** 31.01N 78.27E
Jampang Kulon Indonesia **59** 7.18S106.33E
Jāmpur Pakistan **62** 28.45N 70.36E
Jamsah Egypt **66** 27.39N 33.35E
Jämsänkoski Finland **41** 61.55N 25.11E
Jamshedpur India **63** 22.48N 86.11E
Jämtland *d.* Sweden **40** 63.00N 14.30E
Jamūi India **63** 24.55N 86.13E
Jamuna *r.* Bangla. **63** 23.51N 89.45E
Jand Pakistan **62** 33.26N 72.01E
Janda, Laguna de la *l.* Spain **27** 36.15N 5.51W
Jandiāla India **62** 31.33N 75.02E
Jándula Spain **26** 38.03N 4.06W
Jándula, Embalse de *resr.* Spain **26** 38.30N 4.00W
Janesville U.S.A. **110** 42.42N 89.02W
Jangamo Mozambique **81** 24.06S 35.21E
Jangipur India **63** 24.28N 88.04E
Janīn Jordan **67** 32.28N 35.18E
Janja Bosnia-Herzegovina **31** 44.40N 19.15E
Janjevo Yugo. **34** 42.35N 21.19E
Janjina Croatia **31** 42.56N 17.26E
Jan Kempdorp R.S.A. **80** 27.55S 24.48E
Jan Mayen *i.* Arctic Oc. **96** 68.00N 8.00W
Jánoshalma Hungary **31** 46.18N 19.20E
Januária Brazil **126** 15.28S 44.23W
Janūb Dārfūr *d.* Sudan **73** 11.45N 25.00E
Janūb Kurdufān *d.* Sudan **73** 11.10N 30.00E
Janzé France **18** 47.58N 1.30W
Jaora India **62** 23.38N 75.08E
Japan Asia **57** 36.00N138.00E
Japan, Sea of Asia **57** 40.00N135.00E
Japan Trench Pacific Oc. **84** 33.00N142.00E
Japla India **63** 24.33N 84.01E
Japurá *r.* Brazil **122** 3.00S 64.50W
Jaraicejo Spain **27** 39.40N 5.49W
Jaraiz de la Vera Spain **27** 40.04N 5.45W
Jarales U.S.A. **109** 34.37N106.46W
Jarama *r.* Spain **26** 40.02N 3.39W
Jarandilla Spain **27** 40.08N 5.39W
Jarānwāla Pakistan **62** 31.20N 73.26E
Jarash Jordan **67** 32.17N 35.54E
Jardee Australia **89** 34.18S116.04E
Jardine *r.* Australia **90** 11.07S142.30E
Jardines de la Reina *is.* Cuba **117** 20.30N 79.00W
Jardinópolis Brazil **126** 20.59S 47.48W
Jargeau France **19** 47.52N 2.07E
Jāria Jhānjail Bangla. **63** 25.02N 90.39E
Jaridih India **63** 23.38N 86.04E
Järna Sweden **43** 59.06N 17.34E
Jarnac France **20** 45.41N 0.10W
Jarocin Poland **37** 51.59N 17.31E
Jarosław Poland **37** 50.02N 22.42E
Jarrāḩī *r.* Iran **65** 30.40N 48.23E
Jartai China **54** 39.45N105.46E
Jartai Yanchi *l.* China **54** 39.43N105.41E
Jarud Qi China **54** 44.30N120.35E
Järvenpää Finland **41** 60.28N 25.06E
Jarvis Canada **104** 42.53N 80.06W
Jarvis I. Pacific Oc. **84** 0.23S160.02W
Jasdan India **62** 22.02N 71.12E
Jāsk Iran **65** 25.40N 57.45E
Jasło Poland **37** 49.45N 21.29E
Jasper Canada **100** 52.55N118.05W
Jasper Ala. U.S.A. **113** 33.48N 87.18W
Jasper Fla. U.S.A. **113** 30.31N 82.58W
Jasper Tex. U.S.A. **111** 30.55N 94.01W
Jasper Nat. Park Canada **100** 52.50N118.08W
Jasra India **63** 25.17N 81.48E
Jastrebarsko Croatia **31** 45.40N 15.39E
Jastrowie Poland **36** 53.26N 16.49E
Jászberény Hungary **37** 47.30N 19.55E
Jataí Brazil **126** 17.58S 51.45W
Jāti Pakistan **62** 24.21N 68.16E
Jatibarang Indonesia **59** 6.26S108.18E
Jatinegara Indonesia **59** 6.12S106.51E
Játiva Spain **25** 38.59N 0.31W
Jatni India **63** 20.10N 85.42E
Jatt Israel **67** 32.24N 35.02E
Jaú Brazil **126** 22.11S 48.35W
Jauja Peru **122** 11.50S 75.15W
Jaunjelgava Latvia **44** 56.34N 25.02E
Jaunpur India **63** 25.44N 82.41E
Java *i.* *see* Jawa *i.* Indonesia **59**
Javalambre *mtn.* Spain **25** 40.06N 1.03W
Javari *r.* Peru **122** 4.30S 71.20W
Java Sea *see* Jawa, Laut *sea* Indonesia **58**
Java Trench *f.* Indonesia **58** 10.00S110.00E
Jávea Spain **25** 38.47N 0.10E
Jawa *i.* Indonesia **59** 7.25S110.00E
Jawa, Laut *sea* Indonesia **58** 5.00S111.00E
Jawa Barat *d.* Indonesia **59** 7.10S107.00E
Jawa Tengah *d.* Indonesia **59** 7.49S110.35E
Jawa Timur *d.* Indonesia **59** 8.42S113.10E
Jayah, Wādī al *see* Hā 'Arava Jordan/Israel **66**
Jayapura Indonesia **59** 2.28S140.38E
Jaynagar India **63** 26.32N 86.07E
Jay Peak *mtn.* U.S.A. **105** 44.55N 72.32W
Jazirah Doberai *f.* Indonesia **59** 1.10S132.30E
Jazzīn Lebanon **66** 33.32N 35.34E
Jean U.S.A. **109** 35.46N115.20W
Jeanerette U.S.A. **111** 29.55N 91.40W
Jean Marie River *town* Canada **98** 61.32N120.40W
Jebāl Bārez, Kūh-e *mts.* Iran **65** 28.40N 58.10E
Jebba Nigeria **77** 9.11N 4.49E
Jebri Pakistan **62** 27.18N 65.44E
Jedburgh U.K. **14** 55.29N 2.33W
Jedda *see* Jiddah Saudi Arabia **72**
Jedrzejów Poland **37** 50.39N 20.18E
Jefferson U.S.A. **114** 41.44N 80.46W
Jefferson, Mt. Nev. U.S.A. **108** 38.46N116.55W
Jefferson, Mt. Oreg. U.S.A. **108** 44.40N121.47W
Jefferson City U.S.A. **110** 38.34N 92.10W
Jeffersonville U.S.A. **112** 38.16N 85.45W
Jega Nigeria **77** 12.12N 4.23E
Jēkabpils Latvia **44** 56.28N 25.58E
Jelenia Góra Poland **36** 50.55N 15.45E
Jelgava Latvia **41** 56.39N 23.42E
Jelli Sudan **73** 5.22N 31.48E
Jelling Denmark **42** 55.45N 9.26E
Jember Indonesia **59** 8.07S113.45E
Jena Germany **38** 50.56N 11.35E
Jena U.S.A. **111** 31.41N 92.08W
Jenbach Austria **39** 47.24N 11.47E
Jendouba *d.* Tunisia **32** 36.45N 8.45E
Jennersdorf Austria **31** 46.57N 16.08E
Jenolan Caves *town* Australia **93** 33.53S150.03E
Jepara Indonesia **59** 6.32S110.40E
Jeparit Australia **92** 36.09S141.59E
Jeppo Finland **40** 63.24N 22.37E
Jequié Brazil **123** 13.52S 40.06W
Jequitinhonha *r.* Brazil **126** 16.46S 39.45W
Jerada Morocco **74** 34.17N 2.13W
Jerantut Malaysia **58** 3.56N102.22E
Jérémie Haiti **117** 18.40N 74.09W
Jerez Spain **27** 38.19N 6.46W
Jerez de la Frontera Spain **27** 36.41N 6.08W
Jericho *see* Arīḩā Jordan **67**
Jerilderie Australia **93** 35.23S145.41E
Jerome U.S.A. **108** 42.43N114.31W
Jerramungup Australia **89** 33.57S118.53E
Jersey *i.* Channel Is. Europe **13** 49.13N 2.08W
Jersey City U.S.A. **115** 40.44N 74.02W
Jersey Shore U.S.A. **114** 41.12N 77.16W
Jerseyville U.S.A. **110** 39.07N 90.20W
Jerusalem *see* Yerushalayim Israel/Jordan **67**
Jervis B. Australia **93** 35.05S150.44E
Jesenice Czech Republic **39** 50.04N 13.29E
Jesenice Slovenia **31** 46.27N 14.04E
Jessen Germany **38** 51.47N 12.58E
Jessore Bangla. **63** 23.10N 89.13E
Jesup U.S.A. **113** 31.36N 81.54W
Jesús Carranza Mexico **116** 17.26N 95.02W
Jetmore U.S.A. **111** 38.03N 99.54W
Jetpur India **62** 21.44N 70.37E
Jever Germany **38** 53.34N 7.54E
Jevnaker Norway **42** 60.15N 10.28E
Jewett Ohio U.S.A. **114** 40.22N 81.00W
Jewett Tex. U.S.A. **111** 31.22N 96.09W
Jewett City U.S.A. **115** 41.36N 71.59W
Jeypore India **63** 18.51N 82.35E
Jezerce *mtn.* Albania **34** 42.26N 19.49E
Jeziorak, Jezioro *l.* Poland **37** 53.40N 19.04E
Jhābua India **62** 22.46N 74.36E
Jhajha India **63** 24.46N 86.22E
Jhal Pakistan **62** 28.17N 67.27E
Jhālakāti Bangla. **63** 22.39N 90.12E
Jhālawār India **62** 24.36N 76.09E
Jhal Jhao Pakistan **62** 26.18N 65.35E
Jhālod India **62** 23.06N 74.09E
Jhang Sadar Pakistan **62** 31.16N 72.20E
Jhānsi India **63** 25.26N 78.35E
Jharia India **63** 23.45N 86.24E
Jhārsuguda India **63** 21.51N 84.02E
Jhawāni Nepal **63** 27.35N 84.38E
Jhelum Pakistan **62** 32.56N 73.44E
Jhelum *r.* Pakistan **62** 31.12N 72.08E
Jhinkpāni India **63** 22.25N 85.47E
Jhok Rind Pakistan **62** 31.27N 70.26E
Jhūnjhunu India **62** 28.08N 75.24E
Jiaganj India **63** 24.14N 88.16E
Jialing Jiang *r.* China **55** 29.30N106.35E
Jiamusi China **53** 46.50N130.21E
Ji'an China **55** 27.03N115.00E
Jianchang China **54** 40.50N119.50E
Jiange China **54** 32.04N105.26E
Jiangling China **55** 30.20N112.14E
Jiangmen China **55** 22.31N113.08E
Jiangshan China **55** 28.43N118.39E
Jiangsu *d.* China **54** 33.00N119.30E
Jiangxi *d.* China **55** 27.00N115.30E
Jiangyou China **55** 31.47N104.45E
Jianhe China **55** 26.39N108.35E
Jian'ou China **55** 27.04N118.17E
Jianping China **54** 41.23N119.40E
Jianshi China **55** 30.42N109.20E
Jianyang Fujian China **55** 27.19N118.01E
Jianyang Sichuan China **55** 30.25N104.32E
Jiaochangba Sichuan China **54** 32.05N103.43E
Jiaohe China **53** 43.42N127.19E
Jiaolai He *r.* China **54** 43.48N123.00E
Jiaoling China **55** 24.40N116.10E
Jiaonan China **54** 35.53N119.58E
Jiao Xian China **54** 36.16N120.00E
Jiaozou China **54** 35.11N113.27E
Jiashan China **54** 32.49N118.01E
Jiawang China **54** 34.27N117.27E
Jiaxian China **54** 38.02N110.29E
Jiaxing China **55** 30.52N120.45E
Jiayi Taiwan **55** 23.30N120.24E
Jiazi China **55** 22.57N116.01E
Jiddah Saudi Arabia **72** 21.30N 39.10E
Jiddat al Ḩarāsīs *f.* Oman **71** 19.45N 56.30E
Jiepai China **55** 31.11N113.42E
Jiexi China **55** 23.26N115.52E
Jiexiu China **54** 37.00N111.55E
Jieyang China **55** 23.29N116.19E
Jifnā Jordan **67** 31.58N 35.13E
Jigawa *d.* Nigeria **77** 12.30N 9.30E
Jihlava Czech Republic **36** 49.24N 15.35E
Jijel Algeria **75** 36.48N 5.46E
Jijiga Ethiopia **71** 9.22N 42.47E
Jijona Spain **25** 38.32N 0.30W
Jilib Somali Rep. **79** 0.28N 42.50E
Jilin China **53** 43.53N126.35E
Jilin *d.* China **53** 44.50N125.00E
Jiloca *r.* Spain **25** 41.21N 1.39W
Jilong Taiwan **55** 25.09N121.45E
Jīma Ethiopia **73** 7.36N 36.50E
Jimbe Angola **78** 10.20S 16.40E
Jimena de la Frontera Spain **27** 36.26N 5.27W
Jiménez Mexico **116** 27.08N104.55W
Jimeta Nigeria **77** 9.19N 12.25E
Jimo China **54** 36.23N120.27E
Jinan China **54** 36.40N117.01E
Jīnd India **62** 29.19N 76.19E
Jindabyne Australia **93** 36.24S148.37E
Jing'an China **55** 28.52N115.22E
Jingbian China **54** 37.33N108.36E
Jingchuan China **54** 35.15N107.22E
Jingde China **55** 30.19N118.31E
Jingdezhen China **55** 29.14N117.14E
Jingellic Australia **93** 35.54S147.44E
Jinggu Gansu China **54** 35.05N103.41E
Jinggu Yunnan China **61** 23.29N100.19E
Jinghai China **55** 23.02N116.31E
Jing He *r.* China **54** 34.26N109.00E
Jinghong China **52** 21.59N100.49E
Jingmen China **55** 31.02N112.06E
Jingning China **54** 35.30N105.45E
Jingou China **54** 41.37N120.33E
Jingtai China **54** 37.10N104.08E
Jingxi China **55** 23.03N106.36E
Jing Xian China **55** 26.35N109.41E
Jingyuan Gansu China **54** 36.40N104.40E
Jingyuan Ningxia Huizu China **54** 35.29N106.20E
Jinhua China **55** 29.05N119.40E
Jining Shantung China **54** 35.22N116.45E
Jining Nei Monggol Zizhiqu China **53** 40.56N113.00E
Jinja Uganda **79** 0.27N 33.10E
Jinotepe Nicaragua **117** 11.50N 86.10W
Jinsha Jiang *r.* China **61** 26.30N101.40E
Jinshi China **55** 29.35N111.56E
Jintang China **55** 30.51N104.27E
Jinxi Fujian China **55** 26.12N117.34E
Jinxi Liaoning China **54** 40.48N120.46E
Jinxian China **55** 28.13N116.34E
Jin Xian Liaoning China **54** 39.06N121.49E
Jin Xian Liaoning China **54** 41.10N121.20E
Jinxiang China **54** 35.08N116.20E
Jinzhou China **54** 41.06N121.05E
Jipijapa Ecuador **122** 1.23S 80.35W
Jire Somali Rep. **71** 5.22N 48.05E
Jirjā Egypt **72** 26.20N 31.53E
Jishui China **55** 27.13N115.07E
Jisr al Ḩusayn Jordan **67** 31.52N 35.32E
Jitarning Australia **89** 32.48S117.57E
Jiu *r.* Romania **29** 43.44N 23.52E
Jiuding Shan *mtn.* China **55** 31.36N103.54E
Jiudongshan China **55** 23.44N117.32E
Jiujiang China **55** 29.39N116.02E
Jiulian Shan *mts.* China **55** 24.40N115.00E
Jiuling Shan *mts.* China **55** 28.40N114.45E
Jiulong Jiang *r.* China **55** 24.30N117.47E
Jiuzhou Jiang *r.* China **55** 21.25N109.58E
Jixi China **53** 45.17N130.59E
Ji Xian Henan China **54** 35.25N114.05E
Ji Xian Tianjin China **54** 40.03N117.24E
Jīzān Saudi Arabia **72** 16.54N 42.32E
Jizl, Wādī al *r.* Saudi Arabia **64** 25.37N 38.20E
João Pessoa Brazil **123** 7.06S 34.53W

K

Kampar to **Kédhros**

Kampar *r.* Indonesia **58** 0.20N102.55E
Kampen Neth. **16** 52.33N 5.55E
Kampene Zaïre **78** 3.36S 26.40E
Kamphaeng Phet Thailand **56** 16.28N 99.31E
Kamp-Lintfort Germany **16** 51.34N 6.38E
Kamp 'O S. Korea **57** 35.48N129.29E
Kâmpóng Cham Cambodia **56** 11.59N105.26E
Kâmpóng Chhnăng Cambodia **56** 12.16N104.39E
Kâmpóng Saôm Cambodia **58** 10.38N103.30E
Kâmpóng Thum Cambodia **56** 12.42N104.52E
Kâmpôt Cambodia **56** 10.37N104.11E
Kampti Burkina **76** 10.07N 3.22W
Kamsack Canada **101** 51.34N101.54W
Kamskoye Vodokhranilishche *resr.* Russian Fed. **44** 58.55N 56.20E
Kāmthi India **63** 21.14N 79.12E
Kamui misaki *c.* Japan **57** 43.30N140.15E
Kamyshin Russian Fed. **45** 50.05N 45.24E
Kana *r.* Zimbabwe **80** 18.30S 26.50E
Kanaaupscow *r.* Canada **102** 53.40N 77.10W
Kanafis Sudan **73** 9.48N 25.40E
Kanagawa *d.* Japan **57** 35.25N139.10E
Kanairiktok *r.* Canada **103** 55.05N 60.20W
Kanākir Syria **67** 33.15N 36.05E
Kanália Greece **34** 39.30N 22.53E
Kananga Zaïre **78** 5.53S 22.26E
Kanash Russian Fed. **44** 55.30N 47.27E
Kanastraion, Ákra *c.* Greece **34** 39.56N 23.47E
Kanaudi India **63** 23.36N 81.23E
Kanawha *r.* U.S.A. **114** 38.50N 82.08W
Kanazawa Japan **57** 36.35N136.40E
Kanchanaburi Thailand **56** 14.02N 99.28E
Kānchenjunga *mtn.* Nepal / India **63** 27.44N 88.11E
Kānchipuram India **61** 12.50N 79.44E
Kandāhu Pakistan **62** 27.33N 69.24E
Kandalaksha Russian Fed. **44** 67.09N 32.31E
Kandalakshskaya Guba *g.* Russian Fed. **44** 66.30N 34.00E
Kandangan Indonesia **58** 2.50S115.15E
Kandavu *i.* Fiji **84** 19.05S178.15E
Kandavu Passage Fiji **84** 18.45S178.00E
Kandel Germany **39** 49.05N 8.11E
Kandhkot Pakistan **62** 28.14N 69.11E
Kandi Benin **77** 11.05N 2.59E
Kāndi India **63** 23.57N 88.02E
Kandiāro Pakistan **62** 27.04N 68.13E
Kandira Turkey **64** 41.05N 30.08E
Kandla India **62** 23.00N 70.10E
Kandos Australia **93** 32.53S149.59E
Kandrāch Pakistan **62** 25.29N 65.29E
Kandreho Madagascar **81** 17.29S 46.06E
Kandy Sri Lanka **61** 7.18N 80.43E
Kane U.S.A. **114** 41.40N 78.49W
Kanem *d.* Chad **77** 15.10N 15.30E
Kanevka Russian Fed. **44** 67.08N 39.50E
Kang Botswana **80** 23.43S 22.51E
Kangaarsussuaq *c.* see Parry, Kap *c.* Greenland **99**
Kangaba Mali **76** 11.56N 8.25W
Kangān Iran **65** 27.50N 52.07E
Kangar Malaysia **58** 6.28N100.10E
Kangaroo I. Australia **92** 35.50S137.06E
Kangding China **52** 30.05N102.04E
Kangean, Kepulauan *is.* Indonesia **59** 7.00S115.30E
Kangerlussuaq *see* Söndreströmfjord Greenland **99**
Kangikajiip Agpalia *see* Brewster, K. *c.* Greenland **96**
Kangiqsualujjuaq Canada **99** 58.35N 65.59W
Kangiqsujuaq Canada **99** 61.30N 72.00W
Kangirsuk Canada **99** 60.01N 70.01W
Kangle China **54** 35.16N103.39E
Kangmar Xizang China **63** 30.45N 85.43E
Kangmar Xizang Zizhiqu China **63** 28.30N 89.45E
Kango Gabon **78** 0.15N 10.14E
Kangping China **54** 42.45N123.20E
Kangrinboqê Feng Xizang Zizhiqu China **63** 31.05N 81.21E
Kangto *mtn.* China **63** 27.54N 92.32E
Kanhar *r.* India **63** 24.28N 83.08E
Kani Ivory Coast **76** 8.34N 6.35W
Kaniama Zaïre **78** 7.32S 24.11E
Kanin, Poluostrov *pen.* Russian Fed. **44** 68.00N 45.00E
Kaningo Kenya **79** 0.52S 38.31E
Kanin Nos, Mys *c.* Russian Fed. **44** 68.38N 43.20E
Kaniva Australia **92** 36.33S141.17E
Kanjiža Yugo. **31** 46.04N 20.04E
Kankakee U.S.A. **110** 41.08N 87.52W
Kankan Gabon **78** 0.03S 12.14E
Kankan Guinea **76** 10.22N 9.11W
Kānker India **63** 20.17N 81.29E
Kankossa Mauritania **74** 15.58N 11.31W
Kannack Vietnam **56** 14.07N108.36E
Kannapolis U.S.A. **113** 35.30N 80.36W
Kannauj India **63** 27.04N 79.55E
Kannod India **62** 22.40N 76.44E
Kano *r.* Japan **57** 35.05N138.52E
Kano Nigeria **77** 12.00N 8.31E
Kano *d.* Nigeria **77** 11.45N 8.30E
Kanona Zambia **79** 13.03S 30.37E
Kanowna Australia **89** 30.36S121.36E
Kanoya Japan **57** 31.22N130.50E
Kānpur India **63** 26.28N 80.21E
Kansas *d.* U.S.A. **110** 38.30N 99.00W
Kansas *r.* U.S.A. **110** 39.07N 94.36W
Kansas City Kans. U.S.A. **110** 39.07N 94.39W
Kansas City Mo. U.S.A. **110** 39.05N 94.35W
Kansenia Zaïre **78** 10.19S 26.02E
Kansk Russian Fed. **51** 56.11N 95.20E
Kansŏng S. Korea **53** 38.20N128.28E
Kantābānji India **63** 20.29N 82.55E
Kantché Niger **77** 13.31N 8.30E
Kantemirovka Russian Fed. **45** 49.40N 39.52E
Kantō *d.* Japan **57** 35.35N139.30E
Kantō-heiya *f.* Japan **57** 36.02N140.10E
Kantō-sanchi *mts.* Japan **57** 36.00N138.35E
Kanye Botswana **80** 24.58S 25.17E
Kanyu Botswana **80** 20.05S 24.39E
Kao *i.* Tonga **85** 19.40S175.01W
Kaohsiung Taiwan **48** 22.36N120.17E
Kaoko Veld *f.* Namibia **80** 18.30S 13.30E
Kaolack Senegal **76** 14.09N 16.08W
Kaoma Zambia **78** 14.55S 24.58E
Kapaa Hawaiian Is. **85** 22.05N159.19W
Kapadvanj India **62** 23.01N 73.04E
Kapanga Zaïre **78** 8.22S 22.37E
Kapaonik *mts.* Yugo. **34** 43.10N 21.00E
Kap Arkona *c.* Germany **38** 54.41N 13.26E
Kapchagay Kazakhstan **52** 43.51N 77.14E
Kapenguria Kenya **79** 1.13N 35.07E
Kapfenberg Austria **36** 47.27N 15.18E
Kapiri Mposhi Zambia **79** 13.59S 28.40E
Kapiskau Canada **102** 52.20N 82.01W
Kapiskau *r.* Canada **102** 52.20N 83.40W
Kapit Malaysia **58** 2.01N112.56E
Kapiti I. New Zealand **86** 40.50S174.50E
Kapoeta Sudan **73** 4.47N 33.35E
Kapongolo Zaïre **79** 7.51S 28.12E
Kapos *r.* Hungary **31** 46.44N 18.30E
Kaposvár Hungary **31** 46.22N 17.47E
Kappar Pakistan **62** 25.19N 62.42E
Kappeln Germany **38** 54.40N 9.56E
Kappelshamn Sweden **43** 57.52N 18.50E
Kapps Namibia **80** 22.22S 17.52E
Kapsabet Kenya **79** 0.12N 35.05E
Kaptai Bangla. **63** 22.21N 92.17E
Kaptol Croatia **31** 45.26N 17.44E
Kapuas *r.* Indonesia **58** 0.13S109.12E
Kapunda Australia **92** 34.21S138.54E
Kapūrthala India **62** 31.23N 75.23E
Kapuskasing Canada **102** 49.25N 82.30W
Kaputar, Mt. Australia **93** 30.20S150.10E
Kapuvár Hungary **37** 47.36N 17.02E
Kara Russian Fed. **50** 69.12N 65.00E
Kara-Bogaz Gol, Zaliv *b.* Turkmenistan **65** 41.20N 53.40E
Karabük Turkey **64** 41.12N 32.36E
Karabutak Kazakhstan **50** 49.55N 60.05E
Karāchi Pakistan **62** 24.52N 67.03E
Karād India **60** 17.17N 74.12E
Karaganda Kazakhstan **9** 49.53N 73.07E
Karaginskiy, Ostrov *i.* Russian Fed. **51** 59.00N165.00E
Karakas Kazakhstan **52** 48.20N 83.30E
Karakelong *i.* Indonesia **59** 4.20N126.50E
Karakoram Pass Asia **61** 35.33N 77.51E
Karakoram Range *mts.* Jammu & Kashmir **60** 35.30N 76.30E
Karakoro *r.* Mauritania **74** 14.43N 12.03W
Karaköse *see* Ağri Turkey **45**
Karakumskiy Kanal *canal* Turkmenistan **65** 37.30N 65.48E
Karakumy, Peski *f.* Turkmenistan **65** 37.45N 60.00E
Karakuwisa Namibia **80** 18.56S 19.43E
Karaman Turkey **64** 37.11N 33.13E
Karamay China **52** 45.48N 84.30E
Karamea New Zealand **86** 41.15S172.07E
Karamea Bight *b.* New Zealand **86** 41.15S171.30E
Karamürsel Turkey **64** 40.42N 29.37E
Karand Iran **65** 34.16N 46.15E
Kāranja India **63** 20.29N 77.29E
Karanjia India **63** 21.47N 85.58E
Karasburg Namibia **80** 28.00S 18.46E
Karasjok Norway **40** 69.27N 25.30E
Karasuk Russian Fed. **50** 53.45N 78.01E
Karatau, Khrebet *mts.* Kazakhstan **45** 44.15N 52.10E
Karatobe Kazakhstan **45** 49.44N 53.30E
Karaton Kazakhstan **45** 46.26N 53.32E
Karauli India **62** 26.30N 77.01E
Karawa Zaïre **78** 3.12N 20.20E
Karawanken *mts.* Austria **31** 46.30N 14.10E
Karazhal Kazakhstan **50** 48.00N 70.55E
Karbalā' Iraq **65** 32.37N 44.03E
Karcag Hungary **37** 47.19N 20.56E
Kardhámaina Greece **35** 36.47N 27.09E
Kardhamila Greece **35** 36.53N 22.14E
Kardhámilia Greece **35** 38.34N 26.05E
Kardhítsa Greece **35** 39.21N 21.55E
Kärdla Estonia **41** 59.00N 22.42E
Kareli India **63** 22.55N 79.04E
Karema Tanzania **79** 6.50S 30.25E
Karen India **61** 12.50N 92.55E
Karepino Russian Fed. **44** 61.05N 58.02E
Karesuando Finland **40** 68.25N 22.30E
Kargasok Russian Fed. **50** 59.07N 80.58E
Kargi Kenya **79** 2.31N 37.34E
Kargil Jammu & Kashmir **62** 34.34N 76.06E
Kargopol Russian Fed. **44** 61.32N 38.59E
Kari Nigeria **77** 11.17N 10.35E
Kariaí Greece **34** 40.16N 24.15E
Kariba Zimbabwe **80** 16.32S 28.50E
Kariba, L. Zimbabwe / Zambia **80** 16.50S 28.00E
Kariba Dam Zimbabwe / Zambia **80** 16.15S 28.55E
Karibib Namibia **80** 21.56S 15.52E
Kārikāl India **61** 10.58N 79.50E
Karimama Benin **77** 12.02N 3.15E
Karīmganj India **63** 24.52N 92.20E
Karin Somali Rep. **71** 10.51N 45.45E
Karis Finland **41** 60.05N 23.40E
Karisimbi, Mt. Zaïre / Rwanda **79** 1.31S 29.25E
Káristos Greece **35** 38.01N 24.25E
Kariya Japan **57** 34.59N136.59E
Kariyangwe Zimbabwe **80** 17.57S 27.30E
Karkaralinsk Kazakhstan **9** 49.21N 75.27E
Karkar I. P.N.G. **59** 4.40S146.00E
Karkas, Kūh-e *mtn.* Iran **65** 33.25N 51.40E
Karkheh *r.* Iran **65** 31.45N 47.52E
Karkinitskiy Zaliv *g.* Ukraine **45** 45.50N 32.45E
Karkoo Australia **92** 34.02S135.44E
Karkur Israel **67** 32.28N 35.00E
Karlino Poland **36** 54.03N 15.51E
Karl-Marx-Stadt *see* Chemnitz Germany **38**
Karlobag Croatia **31** 44.32N 15.05E
Karlovac Croatia **31** 45.29N 15.34E
Karlovo Bulgaria **34** 42.38N 24.48E
Karlovy Vary Czech Republic **39** 50.11N 12.52E
Karlsborg Sweden **43** 58.32N 14.31E
Karlshamn Sweden **43** 56.10N 14.51E
Karlskoga Sweden **43** 59.20N 14.31E
Karlskrona Sweden **43** 56.10N 15.35E
Karlsruhe Germany **39** 49.03N 8.24E
Karlstad Sweden **43** 59.22N 13.30E
Karlstad U.S.A. **110** 48.35N 96.31W
Karlstadt Germany **39** 49.57N 9.45E
Karmah Sudan **72** 19.38N 30.25E
Karmel, Har *mtn.* Israel **67** 32.44N 35.02E
Karmi'el Israel **67** 32.55N 35.18E
Karmöy *i.* Norway **42** 59.15N 5.15E
Karnafuli Resr. Bangla. **61** 22.40N 92.05E
Karnāl India **62** 29.41N 76.59E
Karnāli *r.* Nepal **63** 28.45N 81.16E
Karnaphuli Resr. Bangla. **63** 22.30N 92.20E
Karnataka *d.* India **60** 14.45N 76.00E
Karnes City U.S.A. **111** 28.53N 97.54W
Karnobat Bulgaria **29** 42.40N 27.00E
Kärnten *d.* Austria **39** 46.50N 13.30E
Karoi Zimbabwe **80** 16.51S 29.39E
Karokh Afghan. **62** 34.28N 62.35E
Karonga Malaŵi **79** 9.54S 33.55E
Karonie Australia **89** 30.58S122.32E
Karoonda Australia **92** 35.09S139.54E
Karor Pakistan **62** 31.13N 70.57E
Karora Sudan **72** 17.42N 38.22E
Káros *i.* Greece **35** 36.54N 25.40E
Karos Dam R.S.A. **80** 28.27S 21.39E
Karousádhes Greece **34** 39.47N 19.45E
Karpach Moldavia **37** 48.00N 27.10E
Kárpathos Greece **35** 35.40N 27.10E
Kárpathos *i.* Greece **35** 35.40N 27.10E
Karpenísion Greece **35** 38.55N 21.40E
Karpineny Moldavia **37** 46.46N 28.18E
Karpinsk Russian Fed. **44** 59.48N 59.59E
Karpogory Russian Fed. **44** 64.01N 44.30E
Karragullen Australia **89** 32.05S116.03E
Karratha Australia **88** 20.44S116.50E
Karridale Australia **89** 34.12S115.04E
Kars Turkey **64** 40.35N 43.05E
Karsakpay Kazakhstan **9** 47.47N 66.43E
Kärsämaki Finland **40** 63.58N 25.46E
Kārsava Russian Fed. **44** 56.45N 27.40E
Karskoye More *sea* Russian Fed. **50** 73.00N 65.00E
Karstädt Germany **38** 53.09N 11.44E
Kartaly Russian Fed. **50** 53.06N 60.37E
Karufa Indonesia **59** 3.50S133.27E
Karumba Australia **90** 17.28S140.50E
Kārūn *r.* Iran **65** 30.25N 48.12E
Karunga Kenya **73** 1.09S 36.49E
Karungi Sweden **40** 66.03N 23.55E
Karungu Kenya **79** 0.50S 34.09E
Karup Denmark **42** 56.18N 9.10E
Karviná Czech Republic **37** 49.50N 18.30E
Kasai *r.* Zaïre **78** 3.10S 16.13E
Kasai Occidental *d.* Zaïre **78** 5.00S 21.30E
Kasai Oriental *d.* Zaïre **78** 5.00S 24.00E
Kasaji Zaïre **78** 10.22S 23.27E
Kasama Zambia **79** 10.10S 31.11E
Kasane Botswana **80** 17.48S 25.09E
Kasanga Tanzania **79** 8.27S 31.10E
Kāsaragod India **60** 12.30N 75.00E
Kasba India **63** 25.51N 87.33E
Kasba L. Canada **101** 60.20N102.10W
Kasba-Tadla Morocco **22** 32.34N 6.18W
Kåseberga Sweden **43** 55.23N 14.04E
Kasempa Zambia **78** 13.28S 25.48E
Kasese Uganda **79** 0.07N 30.06E
Kāsganj India **63** 27.49N 78.39E
Kāshān Iran **65** 33.59N 51.31E
Kashi China **52** 39.29N 76.02E
Kashin Russian Fed. **44** 57.22N 37.39E
Kashipur India **63** 29.13N 78.57E
Kashiwa Japan **57** 35.52N139.59E
Kāshmar Iran **65** 35.12N 58.26E
Kashmor Pakistan **62** 28.26N 69.35E
Kasia India **63** 26.45N 83.55E
Kasimov Russian Fed. **44** 54.55N 41.25E
Kaskaskia *r.* U.S.A. **111** 37.59N 89.56W
Kaskattama *r.* Canada **101** 57.03N 90.07W
Kaskinen Finland **40** 62.23N 21.13E
Kaskö *see* Kaskinen Finland **40**
Kaslo Canada **100** 49.55N117.00W
Kasongo Zaïre **78** 4.32S 26.33E
Kasongo-Lunda Zaïre **78** 6.30S 16.47E
Kásos *i.* Greece **35** 35.22N 26.56E
Kassalā Sudan **72** 15.28N 36.24E
Kassalā *d.* Sudan **72** 15.30N 35.00E
Kassándra *pen.* Greece **34** 40.00N 23.30E
Kassel Germany **38** 51.19N 9.29E
Kastamonu Turkey **64** 41.22N 33.47E
Kastanéai Greece **34** 41.38N 26.28E
Kastl Germany **38** 49.22N 11.42E
Kastoría Greece **34** 40.30N 21.19E
Kastorías, Límni *l.* Greece **34** 40.30N 21.20E
Kastrávion, Tekhnití Límni *l.* Greece **35** 38.45N 21.20E
Kastrosikiá Greece **35** 39.09N 20.36E
Kasugai Japan **57** 35.14N136.58E
Kasukabe Japan **57** 35.58N139.45E
Kasulu Tanzania **79** 4.34S 30.06E
Kasumi Japan **57** 35.38N134.38E
Kasungu Malaŵi **79** 13.04S 33.29E
Kasūr Pakistan **62** 31.07N 74.27E
Kataba Zambia **78** 16.12S 25.05E
Katako Kombe Zaïre **78** 3.27S 24.21E
Katákolon Greece **35** 37.38N 21.19E
Katangi India **63** 23.27N 79.47E
Katanning Australia **89** 33.42S117.33E
Katanti Zaïre **79** 2.19S 27.08E
Katarniān Ghāt India **63** 28.20N 81.09E
Katchall *i.* India **61** 7.57N 93.22E
Katerini Greece **34** 40.16N 22.30E
Katete Zambia **79** 14.08S 31.50E
Katha Burma **56** 24.11N 95.20E
Katherine Australia **90** 14.29S132.20E
Kāthgodām India **63** 29.16N 79.32E
Kathla India **62** 32.00N 76.47E
Kathmandu Nepal **63** 27.42N 85.20E
Kathor India **62** 21.18N 72.57E
Kathrabbā Jordan **67** 31.08N 35.37E
Kathua Jammu & Kashmir **62** 32.22N 75.31E
Kati Mali **76** 12.41N 8.04W
Katihār India **63** 25.32N 87.35E
Katima Rapids *f.* Zambia **78** 17.15S 24.20E
Katiola Ivory Coast **76** 8.10N 5.10W
Kātlang Pakistan **62** 34.22N 72.05E
Katlanovo Macedonia **34** 41.52N 21.40E
Káto Akhaia Greece **35** 38.09N 21.32E
Kātol India **63** 21.16N 78.35E
Katonah U.S.A. **115** 41.16N 73.41W
Katonga *r.* Uganda **79** 0.03N 30.15E
Katoomba Australia **93** 33.42S150.23E
Katopa Zaïre **78** 2.45S 25.06E
Káto Stavrós Greece **34** 40.39N 23.43E
Katoúna Greece **35** 38.47N 21.07E
Katowice Poland **37** 50.15N 18.59E
Kātrīnā, Jabal *mtn.* Egypt **66** 28.30N 33.57E
Katrine, Loch U.K. **14** 56.15N 4.30W
Katrineholm Sweden **43** 59.00N 16.12E
Katsina Nigeria **77** 13.00N 7.32E
Katsina *d.* Nigeria **77** 12.25N 7.55E
Katsina Ala Nigeria **77** 7.10N 9.30E
Katsina Ala *r.* Nigeria **77** 7.50N 8.58E
Katsura *r.* Japan **57** 34.53N135.42E
Katsuura Japan **57** 35.08N140.18E
Kattaviá Greece **35** 35.57N 27.46E
Kattegat *str.* Denmark / Sweden **42** 57.25N 11.30E
Katthammarsvik Sweden **43** 57.26N 18.50E
Katul, Jabal *mtn.* Sudan **72** 14.16N 29.23E
Katumba Zaïre **78** 7.45S 25.18E
Kātwa India **63** 23.39N 88.08E
Katwijk aan Zee Neth. **16** 52.13N 4.27E
Katzenbuckel *mtn.* Germany **39** 49.28N 9.02E
Katzenfurt Germany **38** 50.37N 8.21E
Kauai *i.* Hawaii U.S.A. **106** 22.05N159.30W
Kaub Germany **39** 50.05N 7.46E
Kaufbeuren Germany **39** 47.53N 10.37E
Kauhajoki Finland **40** 62.26N 22.11E
Kauhava Finland **40** 63.06N 23.05E
Kaukauna U.S.A. **110** 44.20N 88.16W
Kaukauveld *mts.* Namibia **80** 20.00S 20.15E
Kauliranta Finland **40** 66.26N 23.40E
Kaumba Zaïre **78** 8.26S 24.40E
Kaunas Lithuania **41** 54.54N 23.54E
Kaura Namoda Nigeria **77** 12.39N 6.38E
Kautokeino Norway **40** 69.00N 23.02E
Kavadarci Macedonia **34** 41.26N 22.03E
Kavajë Albania **34** 41.11N 19.33E
Kavála Greece **34** 40.56N 24.25E
Kāvali India **61** 14.55N 80.01E
Kavarna Bulgaria **29** 43.26N 28.22E
Kavimba Botswana **80** 18.05S 24.34E
Kavkaz Russian Fed. **45** 45.20N 36.39E
Kävlinge Sweden **43** 55.48N 13.06E
Kavungo Angola **78** 11.28S 23.01E
Kaw Guiana **123** 4.29N 52.02W
Kawachi-nagano Japan **57** 34.25N135.32E
Kawagama L. Canada **104** 45.18N 78.45W
Kawagoe Japan **57** 35.55N139.29E
Kawaguchi Japan **57** 35.48N139.43E
Kawambwa Zambia **79** 9.47S 29.10E
Kawardha India **63** 22.01N 81.15E
Kawartha L. Canada **104** 44.40N 78.10W
Kawasaki Japan **57** 35.32N139.43E
Kawerau New Zealand **86** 38.05S176.42E
Kawhia New Zealand **86** 38.04S174.49E
Kawm Sudan **73** 13.31N 22.50E
Kawthaung Burma **56** 10.09N 98.33E
Kaya Burkina **76** 13.04N 1.04W
Kayah *d.* Burma **56** 19.15N 97.30E
Kayambi Zambia **79** 9.26S 32.01E
Kayan *r.* Indonesia **58** 2.47N117.46E
Kaycee U.S.A. **108** 43.43N106.38W
Kayenta U.S.A. **108** 36.44N110.17W
Kayes Congo **78** 4.25S 11.41E
Kayes Mali **76** 14.26N 11.28W
Kayes *d.* Mali **76** 14.00N 10.55W
Kayin *d.* Burma **56** 17.30N 97.45E
Kayonza Rwanda **73** 1.53S 30.31E
Kayseri Turkey **64** 38.42N 35.28E
Kaysville U.S.A. **108** 41.02N111.56W
Kazabazua Canada **105** 45.56N 76.01W
Kazachye Russian Fed. **51** 70.46N136.15E
Kazakhskiy Zaliv *b.* Kazakhstan **45** 42.43N 52.30E
Kazakhstan Asia **45** 48.00N 52.30E
Kazan Russian Fed. **44** 55.45N 49.10E
Kazanlŭk Bulgaria **34** 42.38N 25.35E
Kazatin Ukraine **37** 49.41N 28.49E
Kazaure Nigeria **77** 12.40N 8.25E
Kazbek *mtn.* Russian Fed. **45** 42.42N 44.30E
Kāzerūn Iran **65** 29.35N 51.39E
Kazhim Russian Fed. **44** 60.18N 51.34E
Kazima C.A.R. **73** 5.16N 26.11E
Kazincbarcika Hungary **37** 48.16N 20.37E
Kazo Japan **57** 36.07N139.36E
Kazumba Zaïre **78** 6.30S 22.02E
Kbal Dâmrei Cambodia **56** 14.03N105.20E
Kdyně Czech Republic **38** 49.23N 13.02E
Kéa Greece **35** 37.38N 24.21E
Kéa *i.* Greece **35** 37.34N 24.22E
Kearney U.S.A. **110** 40.42N 99.05W
Keban Turkey **64** 38.48N 38.45E
Kebbi *d.* Nigeria **77** 11.30N 3.45E
K'ebelē Ethiopia **73** 12.52N 40.40E
Kebili Tunisia **75** 33.42N 8.58E
Kebnekaise *mtn.* Sweden **40** 67.53N 18.33E
K'ebrī Dehar Ethiopia **71** 6.47N 44.17E
Kebumen Indonesia **59** 7.40S109.41E
Kecel Hungary **31** 46.32N 19.16E
Kech *r.* Pakistan **62** 26.00N 62.44E
Kechika *r.* Canada **100** 59.36N127.05W
Kecskemét Hungary **37** 46.54N 19.42E
Kedada Ethiopia **73** 5.20N 36.00E
Kedainiai Lithuania **41** 55.17N 24.00E
Kedgwick Canada **103** 47.39N 67.21W
Kédhros Greece **35** 39.13N 22.03E

Kediri to **Kingman Reef**

Kediri Indonesia 59 7.45S112.01E
Kédougou Senegal 76 12.35N 12.09W
Keefers Canada 100 50.00N121.40W
Keele Peak *mtn.* Canada 98 63.15N129.50W
Keene Canada 104 44.15N 78.10W
Keene U.S.A. 115 42.56N 72.17W
Keepit, L. Australia 93 30.52S150.30E
Keer-Weer, C. Australia 90 13.58S141.30E
Keeseville U.S.A. 105 44.30N 73.29W
Keetmanshoop Namibia 80 26.34S 18.07E
Keewatin Canada 102 49.46N 94.34W
Keewatin *d.* Canada 99 65.00N 90.00W
Kefa *d.* Ethiopia 73 7.00N 36.30E
Kefallinía *i.* Greece 35 38.15N 20.35E
Kefalos Greece 35 36.45N 27.00E
Kefar 'Eqron Israel 67 31.51N 34.49E
Kefar Gil'adi Israel 67 33.15N 35.34E
Kefar Nahum *site* Israel 67 32.53N 35.34E
Kefar Sava Israel 67 32.11N 34.54E
Kefar Szold Israel 67 33.11N 35.39E
Kefar Tavor Israel 67 32.41N 35.25E
Kefar Vitkin Israel 67 32.23N 34.53E
Kefar Yona Israel 67 32.19N 34.56E
Kefar Zekharya Israel 67 31.42N 34.57E
Kefar Zetim Israel 67 32.49N 35.28E
Keffi Nigeria 77 8.52N 7.53E
Keflavík Iceland 40 64.01N 22.35W
K'eftya Ethiopia 72 13.56N 37.13E
Keg River *town* Canada 100 57.54N117.07W
Kehsi Mānsām Burma 56 21.56N 97.51E
Keighley U.K. 12 53.52N 1.54W
Keila Estonia 41 59.18N 24.29E
Keimoes R.S.A. 80 28.41S 20.58E
Keitele *l.* Finland 40 62.55N 26.00E
Keith Australia 92 36.06S140.22E
Keith U.K. 14 57.32N 2.57W
Keith Arm *b.* Canada 98 65.20N122.15W
Kekri India 62 25.58N 75.09E
Kelang Malaysia 58 2.57N101.24E
Kelberg Germany 39 50.17N 6.55E
Kelem Ethiopia 73 4.48N 36.06E
Kelheim Germany 39 48.55N 11.54E
Kelibia Tunisia 32 36.51N 11.06E
Kelkit *r.* Turkey 64 40.46N 36.32E
Kelle Congo 78 0.05S 14.33E
Keller U.S.A. 108 48.03N118.40W
Kellerberrin Australia 89 31.38S117.43E
Kellet, C. Canada 98 71.59N125.34W
Kelleys I. U.S.A. 114 41.36N 82.42W
Kelloselkä Finland 44 66.55N 28.50E
Kells Meath Rep. of Ire. 15 53.44N 6.53W
Kelme Lithuania 41 55.38N 22.56E
Kélo Chad 77 9.21N 15.50E
Kelowna Canada 100 49.50N119.25W
Kelso U.K. 14 55.36N 2.26W
Kelso Calif. U.S.A. 109 35.01N115.39W
Kelso Wash. U.S.A. 108 46.09N122.54W
Keluang Malaysia 58 2.01N103.18E
Kelvedon U.K. 13 51.50N 0.43E
Kelvington Canada 101 52.10N103.30W
Kem Russian Fed. 44 64.58N 34.39E
Kema Indonesia 59 1.22N125.08E
Ke Macina Mali 76 14.05N 5.20W
Kemah Turkey 64 39.35N 39.02E
Kemaliye Turkey 64 39.16N 38.29E
Kemano Canada 100 53.35N128.00W
Kembolcha Ethiopia 73 11.02N 39.43E
Kemerovo Russian Fed. 50 55.25N 86.10E
Kemi Finland 40 65.49N 24.32E
Kemi *r.* Finland 40 65.47N 24.30E
Kemijärvi Finland 40 66.36N 27.24E
Kemmerer U.S.A. 108 41.48N110.32W
Kemnath Germany 38 49.52N 11.54E
Kempen *f.* Belgium 16 51.05N 5.00E
Kemp Land *f.* Antarctica 128 69.00S 57.00E
Kempsey Australia 93 31.05S152.50E
Kempt, Lac *l.* Canada 105 47.25N 74.22W
Kempten Germany 39 47.43N 10.19E
Kemptville Canada 105 45.01N 75.38W
Ken *r.* India 63 25.46N 80.31E
Kenai U.S.A. 98 60.33N151.15W
Kenai Pen. U.S.A. 96 64.40N150.18W
Kenamuke Swamp Sudan 73 5.55N 33.48E
Kenaston Canada 101 51.30N106.18W
Kendai India 63 22.45N 82.37E
Kendal Indonesia 59 6.56S110.14E
Kendal U.K. 12 54.19N 2.44W
Kendall Australia 93 31.28S152.40E
Kendall U.S.A. 114 43.20N 78.02W
Kendari Indonesia 59 3.57S122.36E
Kendenup Australia 89 34.28S117.35E
Kendrāpāra India 63 20.30N 86.25E
Kendrick U.S.A. 108 46.37N116.39W
Kenebri Australia 93 30.45S149.02E
Kenema Sierra Leone 76 7.57N 11.11W
Kenge Zaïre 78 4.56S 17.04E
Kengeja Tanzania 79 5.24S 39.45E
Keng Tung Burma 56 21.16N 99.39E
Kenhardt R.S.A. 80 29.21S 21.08E
Kenilworth U.K. 13 52.22N 1.35W
Kenitra Morocco 74 34.20N 6.34W
Kenli China 54 37.35N118.34E
Kenmare Rep. of Ire. 15 51.53N 9.36W
Kenmare U.S.A. 108 48.40N102.05W
Kenmore U.S.A. 114 42.58N 78.53W
Kennebec *r.* U.S.A. 112 44.00N 69.50W
Kennebunk U.S.A. 115 43.23N 70.33W
Kenner U.S.A. 111 29.59N 90.15W
Kennet *r.* U.K. 13 51.28N 0.57W
Kennett Square U.S.A. 115 39.51N 75.43W
Kennewick U.S.A. 108 46.12N119.07W
Kenogami *r.* Canada 102 50.24N 84.20W
Keno Hill *town* Canada 98 63.58N135.22W
Kenora Canada 102 49.47N 94.29W
Kenosha U.S.A. 110 42.35N 87.49W
Kenozero, Ozero *l.* Russian Fed. 44 62.20N 37.00E
Kent *d.* U.K. 13 51.12N 0.40E
Kent Ohio U.S.A. 114 41.09N 81.22W
Kent Tex. U.S.A. 109 31.04N104.13W
Kent Wash. U.S.A. 108 47.23N122.14W
Kentau Kazakhstan 9 43.28N 68.36E
Kentland U.S.A. 112 40.46N 87.26W
Kenton U.S.A. 112 40.38N 83.38W
Kent Pen. Canada 98 68.30N107.00W
Kentucky *d.* U.S.A. 113 37.30N 85.15W
Kentucky *r.* U.S.A. 113 38.40N 85.09W
Kentucky L. U.S.A. 111 36.25N 88.05W
Kentville Canada 103 45.05N 64.30W
Kenya Africa 79 1.00N 38.00E
Kenya, Mt. *see* Kirinyaga *mtn.* Kenya 79
Keokuk U.S.A. 110 40.24N 91.24W
Keonjhargarh India 63 21.38N 85.35E
Kepi Indonesia 59 6.32S139.19E
Kepno Poland 37 51.17N 17.59E
Keppel B. Australia 90 23.21S150.55E
Kerala *d.* India 60 10.30N 76.30E
Kerang Australia 92 35.42S143.59E
Keratéa Greece 35 37.48N 23.59E
Kerch Ukraine 45 45.22N 36.27E
Kerchenskiy Proliv *str.* Ukraine/Russian Fed. 45 45.15N 36.35E
Kerema P.N.G. 59 7.59S145.46E
Kerem Ben Zimra Israel 67 33.02N 35.28E
Kerem Maharal Israel 67 32.39N 34.59E
Keren Ethiopia 72 15.46N 38.28E
Kerguelen, Îles de *is.* Indian Oc. 49 49.15S 69.10E
Kerguelen Basin *f.* Indian Oc. 49 35.00S 65.00E
Kerguelen-Gaussberg Ridge *f.* Indian Oc. 49 55.00S 75.00E
Kericho Kenya 79 0.22S 35.19E
Kerinci, Gunung *mtn.* Indonesia 58 1.45S101.20E
Kerio *r.* Kenya 79 3.00N 36.14E
Keríon Greece 35 37.40N 20.48E
Kerkebet Ethiopia 72 16.13N 37.30E
Kerkenna, Îles *is.* Tunisia 75 34.44N 11.12E
Kerki Russian Fed. 44 63.40N 54.00E
Kerki Turkmenistan 50 37.53N 65.10E
Kerkinitis, Límni *l.* Greece 34 41.10N 23.08E
Kérkira Greece 34 39.36N 19.56E
Kérkira *i.* Greece 34 39.40N 19.42E
Kerkrade Neth. 16 50.52N 6.02E
Kermadec Is. Pacific Oc. 84 30.00S178.30W
Kermadec Trench Pacific Oc. 84 33.30S176.00W
Kermān Iran 65 30.18N 57.05E
Kermānshāh Iran 65 34.19N 47.04E
Kerme Körfezi *g.* Turkey 35 36.50N 28.00E
Kermit U.S.A. 111 31.51N103.06W
Kerouane Guinea 76 9.16N 9.00W
Kerpen Germany 16 50.52N 6.42E
Kerrobert Canada 101 51.55N109.08W
Kerrville U.S.A. 111 30.03N 99.08W
Kerry *d.* Rep. of Ire. 15 52.07N 9.35W
Kerry Head Rep. of Ire. 15 52.24N 9.56W
Kerteminde Denmark 42 55.27N 10.40E
Kerulen *r.* Mongolia 53 48.45N117.00E
Kesagami L. Canada 102 50.23N 80.15W
Keşan Turkey 34 40.51N 26.37E
Keshod India 62 21.18N 70.15E
Keskal India 63 20.03N 81.34E
Keski-Suomi *d.* Finland 40 62.30N 25.30E
Keswick U.K. 12 54.35N 3.09W
Keszthely Hungary 31 46.46N 17.15E
Ketapang Jawa Indonesia 59 6.56S113.14E
Ketapang Kalimantan Indonesia 58 1.50S110.02E
Ketchikan U.S.A. 100 55.25N131.40W
Ketchum U.S.A. 108 43.41N114.22W
Kete Krachi Ghana 76 7.50N 0.03W
Keti Bandar Pakistan 62 24.08N 67.27E
Ketrzyn Poland 37 54.06N 21.23E
Kettering U.K. 13 52.24N 0.44W
Kettering U.S.A. 112 39.41N 84.10W
Kettle *r.* Canada 101 56.55N 89.25W
Kettle Falls *town* U.S.A. 108 48.36N118.03W
Kettle Pt. Canada 104 43.11N 82.01W
Keuka L. U.S.A. 114 42.27N 77.10W
Keweenaw B. U.S.A. 112 46.46N 88.26W
Keweenaw Pen. U.S.A. 112 47.10N 88.30W
Key, Lough Rep. of Ire. 15 54.00N 8.15W
Keyala Sudan 73 4.27N 32.52E
Key Harbour Canada 104 45.53N 80.44W
Keynsham U.K. 13 51.25N 2.30W
Key West U.S.A. 113 24.33N 81.48W
Kezhma Russian Fed. 51 58.58N101.08E
Kežmarok Slovakia 37 49.08N 20.25E
Kgalagadi *d.* Botswana 80 25.00S 21.30E
Kgatleng *d.* Botswana 80 24.20S 26.20E
Khaanziir, Ras *c.* Somali Rep. 71 10.55N 45.47E
Khabab Syria 67 33.01N 36.16E
Khabarovsk Russian Fed. 53 48.32N135.08E
Khairāgarh India 63 21.25N 80.58E
Khairpur Punjab Pakistan 62 29.35N 72.14E
Khairpur Sind Pakistan 62 27.32N 68.46E
Khajrāho India 63 24.50N 79.58E
Khalatse Jammu & Kashmir 62 34.20N 76.49E
Khalkhāl Iran 65 37.36N 48.36E
Khálki Greece 34 39.36N 22.30E
Khálki *i.* Greece 35 36.17N 27.35E
Khalkidhikí *f.* Greece 23 40.25N 23.27E
Khalkís Greece 35 38.28N 23.36E
Khalmer Yu Russian Fed. 44 67.58N 64.48E
Khālsar Jammu & Kashmir 63 34.31N 77.41E
Khalturin Russian Fed. 44 58.38N 48.50E
Khalūf Oman 60 20.31N 58.04E
Khambhāliya India 62 22.12N 69.39E
Khambhāt, G. of India 62 20.30N 71.45E
Khāmgaon India 62 20.41N 76.34E
Khamkeut Laos 56 18.14N104.44E
Khānaqīn Iraq 65 34.22N 45.22E
Khān az Zabīb Jordan 67 31.28N 36.06E
Khandela India 62 27.36N 75.30E
Khandwa India 62 21.50N 76.20E
Khāneh Khvodī Iran 65 36.05N 56.04E
Khānewāl Pakistan 62 30.18N 71.56E
Khāngarh Punjab Pakistan 62 29.55N 71.10E
Khāngarh Punjab Pakistan 62 28.22N 71.43E
Khanh Hung Vietnam 56 9.36N105.55E
Khaniá Greece 35 35.31N 24.02E
Khanion, Kólpos *g.* Greece 35 35.34N 23.48E
Khanka, Ozero *l.* Russian Fed. 53 45.00N132.30E
Khankendy *see* Stepanakert Azerbaijan 65
Khanna India 62 30.42N 76.14E
Khannā, Qā' *f.* Jordan 67 32.04N 36.26E
Khānozai Pakistan 62 30.37N 67.19E
Khānpur Pakistan 62 28.39N 70.39E
Khanty-Mansiysk Russian Fed. 50 61.00N 69.00E
Khān Yūnus Egypt 67 31.21N 34.18E
Khapalu Jammu & Kashmir 62 35.10N 76.20E
Khapcheranga Russian Fed. 53 49.46N112.20E
Kharagpur India 63 22.20N 87.20E
Khārān *r.* Iran 65 27.37N 58.48E
Khārān Pakistan 62 28.35N 65.25E
Kharbatā Jordan 67 31.57N 35.04E
Khargon India 62 21.49N 75.36E
Khāriān Pakistan 62 32.49N 73.52E
Khariār Road *town* India 63 20.54N 82.31E
Khārijah, Al Wāḥāt al *oasis* Egypt 64 24.55N 30.35E
Kharkov Ukraine 45 50.00N 36.15E
Khār Kūh *mtn.* Iran 65 31.37N 53.47E
Kharmanli Bulgaria 34 41.56N 25.54E
Kharovsk Russian Fed. 44 59.67N 40.07E
Khartoum *see* Al Kharṭūm Sudan 72
Kharutayuvam Russian Fed. 44 66.51N 59.31E
Khasavyurt Russian Fed. 45 43.16N 46.36E
Khāsh Afghan. 62 31.31N 62.52E
Khāsh *r.* Afghan. 62 31.11N 61.50E
Khāsh Iran 65 28.14N 61.15E
Khāsh, Dasht-e *des.* Afghan. 62 31.50N 62.30E
Khashgort Russian Fed. 44 65.25N 65.40E
Khashm al Qirbah Sudan 72 14.58N 35.55E
Khaskovo Bulgaria 34 41.56N 25.33E
Khaskovo *d.* Bulgaria 34 41.57N 25.32E
Khatanga Russian Fed. 51 71.50N102.31E
Khatangskiy Zaliv *g.* Russian Fed. 51 75.00N112.10E
Khāvda India 62 23.51N 69.43E
Khawr Barakah *r.* Sudan 72 18.13N 37.35E
Khemisset Morocco 74 33.50N 6.03W
Khemmarat Thailand 56 16.00N105.10E
Khenchela Algeria 75 35.26N 7.08E
Khenifra Morocco 74 33.00N 5.40W
Khersān *r.* Iran 65 31.29N 48.53E
Kherson Ukraine 45 46.39N 32.38E
Kherwāra India 62 23.59N 73.35E
Khetia India 62 21.40N 74.35E
Khewāri Pakistan 62 26.36N 68.52E
Khiliomódhion Greece 35 37.48N 22.51E
Khíos Greece 35 38.22N 26.08E
Khíos *i.* Greece 35 38.22N 26.00E
Khipro Pakistan 62 25.50N 69.22E
Khirbat al Ghazālah Syria 67 32.44N 36.12E
Khisfin Syria 67 32.51N 35.49E
Khiva Uzbekistan 65 41.25N 60.49E
Khmelnik Ukraine 37 49.36N 27.59E
Khmelnitskiy Ukraine 37 49.25N 26.49E
Khodorov Ukraine 37 49.20N 24.19E
Khogali Sudan 73 6.08N 27.47E
Khok Kloi Thailand 56 8.19N 98.18E
Kholm Russian Fed. 44 57.10N 31.11E
Kholmogory Russian Fed. 44 63.51N 41.46E
Khomas-Hochland *mts.* Namibia 80 22.50S 16.25E
Khondmāl Hills India 63 20.15N 84.00E
Khonu Russian Fed. 51 66.29N143.12E
Khoper *r.* Russian Fed. 45 49.35N 42.17E
Khóra Greece 35 37.03N 21.42E
Khorāl India 62 26.30N 71.14E
Khóra Sfakíon Greece 35 35.12N 24.09E
Khorixas Namibia 80 20.24S 14.58E
Khorog Tajikistan 52 37.32N 71.32E
Khorramābād Iran 65 33.29N 48.21E
Khorramshahr Iran 65 30.26N 48.09E
Khotimsk Belorussia 37 53.24N 32.36E
Khotin Ukraine 37 48.30N 26.31E
Khouribga Morocco 74 32.54N 6.57W
Khowai India 63 24.06N 91.38E
Khowrnag, Kūh-e *mtn.* Iran 65 32.10N 54.38E
Khowst Afghan. 62 33.22N 69.57E
Khoyniki Belorussia 37 51.54N 30.00E
Khrisoúpolis Greece 34 40.58N 24.42E
Khudzhand Tajikistan 52 40.14N 69.40E
Khugīānī Afghan. 62 31.33N 66.15E
Khūgīānī Šānī Afghan. 62 31.31N 66.12E
Khūiāla India 62 27.15N 70.25E
Khuis Botswana 80 26.37S 21.45E
Khulga *r.* Russian Fed. 44 63.33N 61.53E
Khulna Bangla. 63 22.49N 89.34E
Khumbur Khule Ghar *mtn.* Afghan. 62 33.05N 69.00E
Khunti India 63 23.05N 85.17E
Khurai India 63 24.03N 78.19E
Khurda India 63 20.11N 85.37E
Khurja India 63 28.15N 77.51E
Khurli Pakistan 62 28.59N 65.52E
Khurr, Wādī al *r.* Iraq 71 31.02N 42.00E
Khurra Bārīk *r.* Iraq 64 32.00N 44.15E
Khushāb Pakistan 62 32.18N 72.21E
Khust Ukraine 37 48.11N 23.19E
Khuwayy Sudan 73 13.05N 29.14E
Khuzdār Pakistan 62 27.48N 66.37E
Khvājeh Ra'ūf Afghan. 62 33.19N 64.43E
Khvor Iran 65 33.47N 55.06E
Khvormuj Iran 65 28.40N 51.20E
Khvoy Iran 65 38.32N 45.02E
Khyber Pass Afghan./Pakistan 62 34.06N 71.05E
Kiama Australia 93 34.41S150.49E
Kiamika Canada 105 46.25N 75.23W
Kiáton Greece 35 38.01N 22.45E
Kibaek Denmark 42 56.02N 8.51E
Kibali *r.* Zaïre 79 3.37N 28.38E
Kibamba Zaïre 78 4.53S 26.33E
Kibar India 63 32.20N 78.01E
Kibenga Zaïre 78 7.55S 17.35E
Kibombo Zaïre 78 3.58S 25.57E
Kibondo Tanzania 79 3.35S 30.41E
Kibre Mengist Ethiopia 73 5.52N 39.00E
Kibungu Rwanda 79 2.10S 30.31E
Kibwesa Tanzania 79 6.30S 29.57E
Kibwezi Kenya 79 2.28S 37.57E
Kičevo Macedonia 34 41.34N 20.59E
Kichiga Russian Fed. 51 59.50N163.27E
Kicking Horse Pass Canada 100 51.27N116.25W
Kidal Mali 77 18.27N 1.25E
Kidderminster U.K. 13 52.24N 2.13W
Kidete Morogoro Tanzania 79 6.39S 36.42E
Kidsgrove U.K. 12 53.06N 2.15W
Kiefersfelden Austria 39 47.37N 12.11E
Kiel Germany 38 54.20N 10.08E
Kiel Canal *see* Nord-Ostsee-Kanal Germany 38
Kielce Poland 37 50.52N 20.37E
Kielder *resr.* U.K. 12 55.12N 2.30W
Kieler Bucht *b.* Germany 38 54.35N 10.35E
Kiev *see* Kiyev Ukraine 37
Kiffa Mauritania 74 16.38N 11.28W
Kifisiá Greece 35 38.04N 23.49E
Kifissós *r.* Greece 35 38.30N 23.00E
Kigali Rwanda 79 1.59S 30.05E
Kiglapatt, C. Canada 103 57.05N 61.05W
Kigoma Tanzania 79 4.52S 29.36E
Kigoma *d.* Tanzania 79 4.45S 30.00E
Kigosi *r.* Tanzania 79 4.37S 31.29E
Kiiminkin *r.* Finland 40 65.12N 25.18E
Kii sanchi *mts.* Japan 57 34.00N135.20E
Kii suidō *str.* Japan 57 34.00N135.00E
Kikinda Yugo. 37 45.51N 20.30E
Kikládhes *is.* Greece 35 37.30N 25.00E
Kikongo Zaïre 78 4.16S 17.11E
Kikori P.N.G. 59 7.25S144.13E
Kikori *r.* P.N.G. 59 7.10S144.05E
Kikwissi, L. Canada 104 47.00N 78.30W
Kikwit Zaïre 78 5.02S 18.51E
Kil Sweden 43 59.30N 13.19E
Kilafors Sweden 41 61.14N 16.34E
Kila Kila P.N.G. 59 9.31S147.10E
Kilchu N. Korea 53 40.55N129.21E
Kilcoy Australia 91 26.57S152.33E
Kilcullen Rep. of Ire. 15 53.08N 6.46W
Kildare Rep. of Ire. 15 53.10N 6.55W
Kildare *d.* Rep. of Ire. 15 53.10N 6.50W
Kildonan Zimbabwe 80 17.22S 30.33E
Kilfinan U.K. 14 55.58N 5.18W
Kilgore U.S.A. 111 32.23N 94.53W
Kilifi Kenya 79 3.30S 39.50E
Kilimanjaro *d.* Tanzania 79 3.45S 37.40E
Kilimanjaro *mtn.* Tanzania 79 3.02S 37.20E
Kilindoni Tanzania 79 7.55S 39.39E
Kilingi-Nõmme Estonia 41 58.09N 24.58E
Kilis Turkey 64 36.43N 37.07E
Kiliya Ukraine 37 45.30N 29.16E
Kilkee Rep. of Ire. 15 52.41N 9.40W
Kilkenny Rep. of Ire. 15 52.39N 7.16W
Kilkenny *d.* Rep. of Ire. 15 52.35N 7.15W
Kilkieran B. Rep. of Ire. 15 53.20N 9.42W
Kilkís Greece 34 41.00N 22.53E
Killala B. Rep. of Ire. 15 54.15N 9.10W
Killaloe Canada 105 45.33N 77.25W
Killard Pt. U.K. 15 54.19N 5.31W
Killarney Australia 93 28.18S152.15E
Killarney Man. Canada 101 49.12N 99.42W
Killarney Ont. Canada 104 45.58N 81.31W
Killarney Rep. of Ire. 15 52.04N 9.32W
Killarney Prov. Park Canada 104 46.05N 81.30W
Killary Harbour *est.* Rep. of Ire. 15 53.38N 9.56W
Killdeer U.S.A. 108 47.22N102.45W
Killeen U.S.A. 111 31.08N 97.44W
Killin U.K. 14 56.29N 4.19W
Killíni Greece 35 37.55N 21.09E
Killíni *mtn.* Greece 35 37.57N 22.23E
Killorglin Rep. of Ire. 15 52.07N 9.45W
Killybegs Rep. of Ire. 15 54.38N 8.27W
Killyleagh U.K. 15 54.24N 5.39W
Kilmarnock U.K. 14 55.37N 4.30W
Kilmichael Pt. Rep. of Ire. 15 52.44N 6.09W
Kilmore Australia 93 37.18S144.58E
Kilninver U.K. 14 56.21N 5.30W
Kilombero *r.* Tanzania 79 8.30S 37.28E
Kilosa Tanzania 79 6.49S 37.00E
Kilronan Rep. of Ire. 15 53.08N 9.41W
Kilrush Rep. of Ire. 15 52.39N 9.30W
Kilsyth U.K. 14 55.59N 4.04W
Kilvo Sweden 40 66.50N 21.04E
Kilwa Kivinje Tanzania 79 8.45S 39.21E
Kilwa Masoko Tanzania 79 8.55S 39.31E
Kimaan Indonesia 59 7.54S138.51E
Kimba Australia 92 33.09S136.25E
Kimball U.S.A. 110 41.14N103.40W
Kimberley Canada 100 49.40N115.59W
Kimberley R.S.A. 80 28.44S 24.44E
Kimberley Plateau Australia 88 17.20S127.20E
Kimch'aek N. Korea 57 40.41N129.12E
Kími Greece 35 38.38N 24.06E
Kimito *i.* Finland 41 60.10N 22.30E
Kímolos *i.* Greece 35 36.47N 24.35E
Kimparana Mali 76 12.52N 4.59W
Kimry Russian Fed. 44 56.51N 37.20E
Kimsquit Canada 100 52.45N126.57W
Kinabalu *mtn.* Malaysia 58 6.10N116.40E
Kincaid Canada 101 49.39N107.00W
Kincardine Canada 104 44.11N 81.38W
Kindersley Canada 101 51.27N109.10W
Kindia Guinea 76 10.03N 12.49W
Kindu Zaïre 78 3.00S 25.56E
Kinel Russian Fed. 44 53.17N 50.42E
Kineshma Russian Fed. 44 57.28N 42.08E
Kingaroy Australia 90 26.33S151.50E
King City U.S.A. 109 36.13N121.08W
Kingcome Inlet *town* Canada 100 50.58N125.15W
King Edward *r.* Australia 88 14.12S126.34E
King George Is. Canada 102 57.20N 78.25W
King George Sd. Australia 89 35.03S117.57E
King I. Australia 91 39.50S144.00E
King I. Canada 100 52.10N127.40W
King Leopold Range *mts.* Australia 88 17.00S125.30E
Kingman Ariz. U.S.A. 109 35.12N114.04W
Kingman Kans. U.S.A. 111 37.39N 98.07W
Kingman Reef Pacific Oc. 84 6.24N162.22W

Kingoonya to Kopervik

Kingoonya Australia 92 30.54S135.18E
Kingri Pakistan 62 30.27N 69.49E
Kings r. U.S.A. 109 36.03N119.49W
Kingsbridge U.K. 13 50.17N 3.46W
Kings Canyon Australia 90 24.15S131.33E
Kings Canyon Nat. Park U.S.A. 108 36.48N118.30W
Kingsclere U.K. 13 51.20N 1.14W
Kingscote Australia 92 35.40S137.38E
King Sd. Australia 88 17.00S123.30E
Kingsdown Kent U.K. 13 51.21N 0.17E
Kingsley Dam U.S.A. 106 41.15N101.30W
King's Lynn U.K. 12 52.45N 0.25E
Kingsmill Group is. Kiribati 84 1.00S175.00E
Kings Peaks mts. U.S.A. 108 40.46N110.23W
Kingsport U.S.A. 113 36.33N 82.34W
Kingston Canada 105 44.14N 76.30W
Kingston Jamaica 117 17.58N 76.48W
Kingston New Zealand 86 45.20S168.43E
Kingston N.H. U.S.A. 115 42.55N 71.02W
Kingston N.Y. U.S.A. 115 41.56N 74.00W
Kingston Penn. U.S.A. 115 41.16N 75.54W
Kingston W.Va. U.S.A. 113 37.58N 81.19W
Kingston S.E. Australia 92 36.50S139.50E
Kingston upon Hull U.K. 12 53.45N 0.20W
Kingstown St. Vincent 117 13.12N 61.14W
Kingstree U.S.A. 113 33.40N 79.50W
Kingsville Canada 104 42.02N 82.45W
Kingsville U.S.A. 111 27.31N 97.52W
Kingswood Avon U.K. 13 51.27N 2.29W
Kings Worthy U.K. 13 51.06N 1.18W
Kington U.K. 13 52.12N 3.02W
Kingurutik r. Canada 103 56.49N 62.00W
Kingussie U.K. 14 57.05N 4.04W
King William I. Canada 99 69.00N 97.30W
King William's Town R.S.A. 80 32.52S 27.23E
Kingwood U.S.A. 114 39.28N 79.41W
Kinki d. Japan 57 35.10N135.00E
Kinloch Rannoch U.K. 14 56.42N 4.11W
Kinmount Canada 104 44.47N 78.39W
Kinna Sweden 43 57.30N 12.41E
Kinnairds Head U.K. 14 57.42N 2.00W
Kinnegad Rep. of Ire. 15 53.28N 7.08W
Kinnekulle hill Sweden 43 58.35N 13.23E
Kinneret Israel 67 32.44N 35.34E
Kinneret-Negev Conduit canal Israel 67 32.52N 35.32E
Kino r. Japan 57 34.13N135.09E
Kinross U.K. 14 56.13N 3.27W
Kinsale Rep. of Ire. 15 51.42N 8.32W
Kinshasa Zaïre 78 4.18S 15.18E
Kinsley U.S.A. 111 37.55N 99.25W
Kintyre pen. U.K. 14 55.35N 5.35W
Kinuso Canada 100 55.25N115.25W
Kinvara Rep. of Ire. 15 53.08N 8.56W
Kinyeti mtn. Sudan 73 3.57N 32.54E
Kinzia Zaïre 78 3.36S 18.26E
Kiosk Canada 104 46.06N 78.53W
Kiowa Kans. U.S.A. 111 37.01N 98.29W
Kiowa Okla. U.S.A. 111 34.43N 95.54W
Kiparissía Greece 35 37.15N 21.40E
Kiparissiakós Kólpos g. Greece 35 37.14N 21.40E
Kipawa Canada 104 46.47N 79.00W
Kipawa, Lac l. Canada 104 46.55N 79.00W
Kipawa Prov. Park Canada 104 47.15N 78.15W
Kipengere Range mts. Tanzania 79 9.15S 34.15E
Kipili Tanzania 79 7.30S 30.39E
Kipini Kenya 79 2.31S 40.32E
Kippure mtn. Rep. of Ire. 15 53.11N 6.20W
Kipungo Angola 78 14.49S 14.34E
Kipushi Zaïre 79 11.46S 27.15E
Kirby U.S.A. 108 43.49N108.10W
Kirbyville U.S.A. 111 30.40N 93.54W
Kirchbach in Steiermark Austria 31 46.54N 15.44E
Kircheimbolanden Germany 39 49.39N 8.00E
Kirchheim Germany 39 48.39N 9.27E
Kirchmöser Germany 38 52.22N 12.25E
Kirensk Russian Fed. 51 57.45N108.00E
Kirgiziya Step f. Kazakhstan 45 50.00N 57.10E
Kirgiz Steppe see Kirgiziya Step f. Kazakhstan 45
Kiri Zaïre 78 1.23S 19.00E
Kiribati Pacific Oc. 84 6.00S170.00W
Kirikkale Turkey 64 39.51N 33.32E
Kirillov Russian Fed. 44 59.53N 38.21E
Kirínia Cyprus 66 35.20N 33.20E
Kirinyaga mtn. Kenya 79 0.10S 37.19E
Kiritimati i. Kiribati 85 1.52N157.20W
Kirkby Lonsdale U.K. 12 54.13N 2.36W
Kirkby Stephen U.K. 12 54.27N 2.23W
Kirkcaldy U.K. 14 56.07N 3.10W
Kirkcudbright U.K. 14 54.50N 4.03W
Kirkenes Norway 40 69.40N 30.03E
Kirkfield Canada 104 44.33N 79.00W
Kirkland Ariz. U.S.A. 109 34.26N112.43W
Kirkland Wash. U.S.A. 108 47.41N122.12W
Kirkland Lake town Canada 102 48.15N 80.00W
Kirklareli Turkey 29 41.44N 27.12E
Kirkpatrick, Mt. Antarctica 128 85.00S170.00E
Kirksville U.S.A. 110 40.12N 92.35W
Kirkūk Iraq 65 35.28N 44.26E
Kirkwall U.K. 14 58.59N 2.58W
Kirkwood R.S.A. 80 33.25S 25.24E
Kirkwood U.S.A. 110 38.35N 90.24W
Kirn Germany 39 49.47N 7.28E
Kirov Russian Fed. 44 58.38N 49.38E
Kirov Russian Fed. 44 53.59N 34.20E
Kirovakan Armenia 65 40.49N 44.30E
Kirovo-Chepetsk Russian Fed. 44 58.40N 50.02E
Kirovograd Ukraine 45 48.31N 32.15E
Kirovsk Russian Fed. 44 67.37N 33.39E
Kirovskiy Russian Fed. 51 54.25N155.37E
Kirriemuir Canada 101 51.56N110.20W
Kirriemuir U.K. 14 56.41N 3.01W
Kirs Russian Fed. 44 59.21N 52.10E
Kirsanoy Kazakhstan 45 51.29N 52.30E
Kirşehir Turkey 64 39.09N 34.08E
Kirthar Range mts. Pakistan 62 27.15N 67.00E
Kiruna Sweden 40 67.51N 20.16E
Kiryu Japan 57 36.26N139.18E
Kisa Sweden 43 57.59N 15.37E
Kisaga Tanzania 79 4.26S 34.26E
Kisangani Zaïre 78 0.33N 25.14E
Kisantu Zaïre 78 5.07S 15.05E
Kisaran Indonesia 58 2.47N 99.29E
Kisarazu Japan 57 35.23N139.55E
Kiselevsk Russian Fed. 50 54.01N 86.41E
Kishanganj India 63 26.07N 87.56E
Kishangarh Rāj. India 62 26.34N 74.52E
Kishangarh Rāj. India 62 27.52N 70.34E
Kishinev Moldavia 37 47.00N 28.50E
Kishiwada Japan 57 34.28N135.22E
Kishorganj Bangla. 63 24.26N 90.46E
Kishtwār Jammu & Kashmir 62 33.19N 75.46E
Kisii Kenya 79 0.40S 34.44E
Kisiju Tanzania 79 7.23S 39.20E
Kiskitto L. Canada 101 54.16N 98.34W
Kiskörös Hungary 31 46.38N 19.17E
Kiskunfélegyháza Hungary 31 46.43N 19.52E
Kiskunhalas Hungary 31 46.26N 19.30E
Kiskunmajsa Hungary 31 46.30N 19.45E
Kislovodsk Russian Fed. 45 43.56N 42.44E
Kismaayo Somali Rep. 79 0.25S 42.31E
Kiso Japan 57 35.02N136.45E
Kiso sammyaku mts. Japan 57 35.42N137.50E
Kissamos Greece 35 35.20N 23.38E
Kissidougou Guinea 76 9.48N 10.08W
Kissimmee U.S.A. 113 28.20N 81.24W
Kississing L. Canada 101 55.10N101.20W
Kissū, Jabal mtn. Sudan 72 21.35N 25.09E
Kistanje Croatia 31 43.59N 15.58E
Kistna r. see Krishna r. India 60
Kisumu Kenya 79 0.07S 34.47E
Kisvárda Hungary 37 48.13N 22.05E
Kita Mali 76 13.04N 9.29W
Kitab Uzbekistan 50 39.08N 66.51E
Kitabu Zaïre 78 6.31S 26.40E
Kitakyūshū Japan 57 33.50N130.50E
Kitale Kenya 79 1.01N 35.01E
Kit Carson U.S.A. 110 38.46N102.48W
Kitchener Australia 89 31.01S124.20E
Kitchener Canada 104 43.27N 80.29W
Kitchigama r. Canada 102 51.12N 78.55W
Kitgum Uganda 79 3.17N 32.54E
Kíthira Greece 35 36.09N 23.00E
Kíthira i. Greece 35 36.20N 22.58E
Kíthnos Greece 35 37.26N 24.26E
Kíthnos i. Greece 35 37.25N 24.28E
Kitikmeot d. Canada 98 80.00N105.00W
Kitimat Canada 100 54.05N128.38W
Kitinen r. Finland 40 67.20N 27.27E
Kítros Greece 34 40.22N 22.34E
Kitsman Ukraine 37 48.30N 25.50E
Kittakittaooloo, L. Australia 92 28.09S138.09E
Kittanning U.S.A. 114 40.49N 79.32W
Kittery U.S.A. 115 43.05N 70.45W
Kittilä Finland 40 67.40N 24.54E
Kitui Kenya 79 1.22S 38.01E
Kitunda Tanzania 79 6.48S 33.17E
Kitwe Zambia 79 12.50S 28.04E
Kitzbühel Austria 39 47.27N 12.23E
Kitzingen Germany 39 49.44N 10.09E
Kiumbi Zaïre 78 5.31S 26.34E
Kiunga Kenya 79 1.46S 41.30E
Kivijärvi l. Finland 40 63.10N 25.09E
Kivik Sweden 43 55.41N 14.15E
Kivotós Greece 34 40.13N 21.26E
Kivu d. Zaïre 79 3.00S 27.00E
Kivu, L. Rwanda / Zaïre 79 2.00S 29.10E
Kiyev Ukraine 37 50.28N 30.29E
Kiyevskoye Vodokhranilishche resr. Ukraine 37 51.00N 30.25E
Kizel Russian Fed. 44 59.01N 57.42E
Kizema Russian Fed. 44 61.12N 44.52E
Kizil r. Turkey 64 41.45N 35.57E
Kizlyar Russian Fed. 45 43.51N 46.43E
Kizlyarskiy Zaliv b. Russian Fed. 45 44.33N 47.00E
Kizu r. Japan 57 34.53N135.42E
Kizyl-Arvat Turkmenistan 65 39.00N 56.23E
Kizyl Atrek Turkey 65 37.37N 54.49E
Kladanj Bosnia-Herzegovina 31 44.13N 18.41E
Kladno Czech Republic 38 50.08N 14.05E
Klagenfurt Austria 31 46.38N 14.18E
Klaipeda Lithuania 41 55.43N 21.07E
Klakah Indonesia 59 7.55S113.12E
Klaksvig Faroe Is. 10 62.13N 6.34W
Klamath r. U.S.A. 108 41.33N124.04W
Klamath Falls town U.S.A. 108 42.14N121.47W
Klamath Mts. U.S.A. 108 41.40N123.20W
Klamono Indonesia 59 1.08S131.28E
Klar r. Sweden 43 59.23N 13.32E
Klatovy Czech Republic 38 49.24N 13.18E
Klawer R.S.A. 80 31.48S 18.34E
Klawock U.S.A. 100 55.33N133.06W
Kleena Kleene Canada 100 51.58N124.50W
Kleinsee R.S.A. 80 29.41S 17.04E
Klekovača mtn. Bosnia-Herzegovina 31 44.26N 16.31E
Klerksdorp R.S.A. 80 26.51S 26.38E
Klevan Ukraine 37 50.44N 25.50E
Kleve Germany 38 51.48N 6.09E
Klickitat U.S.A. 108 45.49N121.09W
Klimovichi Belorussia 37 53.36N 31.58E
Klimpfjäll Sweden 40 65.04N 14.52E
Klin Russian Fed. 44 56.20N 36.45E
Klinaklini r. Canada 100 51.21N125.40W
Klingenthal Germany 39 51.21N 12.28E
Klintehamn Sweden 43 57.24N 18.12E
Klintsy Russian Fed. 37 52.45N 32.15E
Klipdale R.S.A. 80 34.18S 19.58E
Klippan Sweden 43 56.08N 13.06E
Klipplaat R.S.A. 80 33.01S 24.19E
Klisura Bulgaria 34 42.40N 24.28E
Klitmöller Denmark 42 57.02N 8.31E
Kłobuck Poland 37 50.55N 18.57E
Klock Canada 104 46.18N 78.36W
Kłodzko Poland 36 50.27N 16.39E
Klöfta Norway 42 60.04N 11.09E
Klondike Canada 98 64.02N139.24W
Klosters Switz. 39 46.54N 9.53E
Kloten Switz. 39 47.27N 8.35E
Klötze Germany 38 52.38N 11.10E
Kluane Nat. Park Canada 100 60.32N139.40W
Kluczbork Poland 37 50.59N 18.13E
Klukwan U.S.A. 100 59.25N135.55W
Klungkung Indonesia 59 8.32S115.25E
Knäred Sweden 43 56.32N 13.19E
Knaresborough U.K. 12 54.01N 1.29W
Knezha Bulgaria 34 43.30N 23.56E
Knić Yugo. 34 43.55N 20.43E
Knight Inlet f. Canada 100 50.45N125.40W
Knighton U.K. 13 52.21N 3.02W
Knin Croatia 31 44.02N 16.12E
Knislinge Sweden 43 56.11N 14.05E
Knivsta Sweden 43 59.43N 17.48E
Knjaževac Yugo. 34 43.35N 22.18E
Knobly Mtn. U.S.A. 114 39.21N 79.32W
Knobs Mtn. U.S.A. 114 41.12N 78.26W
Knockadoon Head Rep. of Ire. 15 51.52N 7.52W
Knockalongy mtn. Rep. of Ire. 15 54.12N 8.45W
Knockmealdown Mts. Rep. of Ire. 15 52.15N 7.55W
Knokke Belgium 16 51.21N 3.17E
Knolls U.S.A. 108 40.44N113.18W
Knossos site Greece 35 35.20N 25.10E
Knox U.S.A. 114 41.14N 79.32W
Knox, C. Canada 100 54.11N133.04W
Knox City U.S.A. 111 33.25N 99.49W
Knoxville U.S.A. 113 36.00N 83.57W
Knutsford U.K. 12 53.18N 2.22W
Knyazhevo Russian Fed. 44 59.40N 43.51E
Knysna R.S.A. 80 34.02S 23.03E
Kobarid Slovenia 31 46.15N 13.35E
Kobar Sink f. Ethiopia 72 14.00N 40.30E
Kōbe Japan 57 34.41N135.10E
København Denmark 43 55.40N 12.35E
Koblenz Germany 39 50.21N 7.35E
Kobowen Swamp Sudan 73 5.38N 33.54E
Kobrin Belorussia 37 52.16N 24.22E
Kobroor i. Indonesia 59 6.10S134.30E
Kočani Macedonia 34 41.55N 22.25E
Koçarli Turkey 35 37.45N 27.42E
Kočevje Slovenia 31 45.38N 14.52E
Kocher r. Germany 39 49.14N 9.12E
Kochi India 60 9.56N 76.15E
Kōchi Japan 57 33.33N133.52E
Kochkoma Russian Fed. 44 64.03N 34.14E
Kochmes Russian Fed. 44 66.12N 60.48E
Kodaira Japan 57 35.44N139.29E
Kodari Nepal 63 27.56N 85.56E
Kodarma India 63 24.28N 85.36E
Kodiak U.S.A. 98 57.49N152.30W
Kodiak I. U.S.A. 98 57.00N153.50W
Kodima Russian Fed. 44 62.24N 43.57E
Kodinār India 62 20.47N 70.42E
Kodok Sudan 73 9.53N 32.07E
Kodyma Ukraine 37 48.06N 29.04E
Koekelare Belgium 16 51.08N 2.59E
Koekenaap R.S.A. 80 31.30S 18.18E
Koersel Belgium 16 51.04N 5.19E
Koës Namibia 80 25.58S 19.07E
Koffiefontein R.S.A. 80 29.24S 25.00E
Köflach Austria 31 47.04N 15.05E
Koforidua Ghana 76 6.01N 0.12W
Kōfu Japan 57 35.39N138.35E
Koga Tanzania 79 6.10S 32.21E
Kogaluk r. Canada 103 56.12N 61.45W
Køge Denmark 43 55.27N 12.11E
Køge Bugt b. Denmark 43 55.30N 12.20E
Køge Bugt b. Greenland 99 65.00N 40.30W
Kogi d. Nigeria 77 7.15N 7.00E
Kohak Pakistan 62 25.44N 62.33E
Kohāt Pakistan 62 33.35N 71.26E
Kohīma India 61 25.40N 94.08E
Kohler Range mts. Antarctica 128 77.00S110.00W
Kohtla-Järve Estonia 44 59.28N 27.20E
Koidu Sierra Leone 76 8.41N 10.55W
Koito r. Japan 57 35.21N139.52E
Kojonup Australia 89 33.50S117.05E
Kokand Uzbekistan 52 40.33N 70.55E
Kökar i. Finland 43 59.56N 20.55E
Kokas Indonesia 59 2.45S132.26E
Kokchetav Kazakhstan 9 53.18N 69.25E
Kokemäki Finland 41 61.15N 22.21E
Kokenau Indonesia 59 4.42S136.25E
Kokka Sudan 72 20.00N 30.35E
Kokkola Finland 40 63.50N 23.07E
Koko Sokoto Nigeria 77 11.27N 4.35E
Kokoda P.N.G. 90 8.50S147.45E
Kokomo U.S.A. 112 40.30N 86.09W
Kokpekty Kazakhstan 52 48.45N 82.25E
Koksoak r. Canada 99 58.30N 68.15W
Kokstad R.S.A. 80 30.32S 29.25E
Kokuora Russian Fed. 51 71.33N144.50E
Kolāchi r. Pakistan 62 26.25N 67.50E
Kolahun Liberia 76 8.24N 10.02W
Kolaka Indonesia 59 4.04S121.38E
Kolan Australia 90 24.42S152.10E
Kola Pen. see Kolskiy Poluostrov pen. Russian Fed. 44
Kolār India 61 13.10N 78.10E
Kolāras India 63 25.14N 77.36E
Kolari Finland 40 67.20N 23.48E
Kolašin Yugo. 31 42.49N 19.31E
Kolāyat India 62 27.50N 72.57E
Kolbäck Sweden 43 59.34N 16.15E
Kolbio Kenya 79 1.11S 41.10E
Kolbotn Norway 42 59.49N 10.48E
Kolda Senegal 76 12.56N 14.55W
Kolding Denmark 42 55.31N 9.29E
Kole H.Zaïre Zaïre 78 2.07N 25.26E
Kole K.Oriental Zaïre 78 3.28S 22.29E
Kolepom i. see Yos Sudarsa, Pulau i. Indonesia 59
Kolguyev, Ostrov i. Russian Fed. 44 69.00N 49.00E
Kolhāpur India 60 16.43N 74.15E
Kolia Ivory Coast 76 9.46N 6.28W
Kolín Czech Republic 36 50.02N 15.10E
Kolka Latvia 41 57.45N 22.35E
Kolki Ukraine 37 51.09N 25.40E
Kollam India 60 8.53N 76.38E
Kolmården Sweden 43 58.41N 16.45E
Köln Germany 38 50.56N 6.59E
Kolno Poland 37 53.25N 21.56E
Koło Poland 37 52.12N 18.37E
Kołobrzeg Poland 36 54.10N 15.35E
Kologriv Russian Fed. 44 58.49N 44.19E
Kolokani Mali 76 13.35N 7.45W
Kololo Ethiopia 73 7.29N 41.58E
Kolomna Russian Fed. 44 55.05N 38.45E
Kolomyya Ukraine 37 48.31N 25.00E
Kolondiéba Mali 76 11.05N 6.54W
Kolosib India 63 24.14N 92.42E
Kolpashevo Russian Fed. 50 58.21N 82.59E
Kolpino Russian Fed. 44 59.44N 30.39E
Kolskiy Poluostrov pen. Russian Fed. 44 67.00N 38.00E
Kolsva Sweden 43 59.36N 15.50E
Kolubara r. Yugo. 31 44.40N 20.15E
Koluszki Poland 37 51.44N 19.49E
Kolvereid Norway 40 64.53N 11.35E
Kolwezi Zaïre 78 10.44S 25.28E
Kolyma r. Russian Fed. 51 68.50N161.00E
Kolymskiy, Khrebet mts Russian Fed. 51 63.00N160.00E
Kom r. Cameroon 78 2.20N 10.38E
Kom Kenya 79 1.06N 38.00E
Koma Ethiopia 73 8.25N 36.53E
Komadugu Gana r. Nigeria 77 13.06N 12.23E
Komadugu Yobe r. Niger / Nigeria 77 13.43N 13.19E
Komagane Japan 57 35.43N137.55E
Komaga-take mtn. Japan 57 35.47N137.48E
Komaki Japan 57 35.17N136.55E
Komandorskiye Ostrova is. Russian Fed. 84 55.00N167.00E
Komárno Slovakia 37 47.45N 18.09E
Komarom Hungary 37 47.44N 18.08E
Komatipoort R.S.A. 81 25.25S 31.55E
Komatsu Japan 57 36.24N136.27E
Komba Zaïre 78 2.52N 24.03E
Komló Hungary 31 46.12N 18.16E
Kommunarsk Ukraine 23 48.30N 38.47E
Kommunizma, Pik mtn. Tajikistan 52 38.39N 72.01E
Komotiní Greece 34 41.08N 25.25E
Komrat Moldavia 37 46.18N 28.40E
Komsberg mtn. R.S.A. 80 32.40S 20.48E
Komsomolets, Ostrov i. Russian Fed. 51 80.20N 96.00E
Komsomolets, Zaliv g. Kazakhstan 45 45.17N 53.30E
Komsomolsk-na-Amure Russian Fed. 51 50.32N136.59E
Kōnan Japan 57 35.20N136.53E
Konar r. Afghan. 62 34.26N 70.32E
Konārak India 63 19.54N 86.07E
Konar-e Khās Afghan. 62 34.39N 70.54E
Konch India 63 25.59N 79.09E
Kondagaon India 63 19.36N 81.40E
Kondakovo Russian Fed. 51 69.38N152.00E
Kondinin Australia 89 32.33S118.13E
Kondoa Tanzania 79 4.54S 35.49E
Kondopoga Russian Fed. 44 62.12N 34.17E
Kondratyevo Russian Fed. 51 57.22N 98.15E
Kondut Australia 89 30.44S117.06E
Koné N. Cal. 84 21.04S164.52E
Konevo Russian Fed. 9 62.09N 39.22E
Kōng r. Cambodia 56 13.32N105.57E
Kong Ivory Coast 76 8.54N 4.36W
Kong Christian den IX Land f. Greenland 99 68.20N 37.00W
Kong Christian den X Land f. Greenland 96 73.00N 26.00W
Kong Frederik den VIII Land f. Greenland 96 77.30N 25.00W
Kong Frederik den VI Kyst f. Greenland 99 63.00N 44.00W
Kong Haakon VII Hav sea Antarctica 128 65.00S 25.00E
Kongolo Zaïre 79 5.20S 27.00E
Kongor Sudan 73 7.10N 31.21E
Kongsberg Norway 42 59.39N 9.39E
Kongsvinger Norway 43 60.12N 12.00E
Kongur Shan mtn. China 52 38.40N 75.30E
Kongwa Tanzania 79 6.13S 36.28E
Königsmoor f. Germany 38 53.15N 9.57E
Königs Wusterhausen Germany 38 52.18N 13.37E
Konin Poland 37 52.13N 18.16E
Kónitsa Greece 34 40.02N 20.45E
Konjic Bosnia-Herzegovina 31 43.39N 17.57E
Könkämä r. Sweden / Finland 40 68.29N 22.30E
Konkouré r. Guinea 76 9.55N 13.45W
Konongo Ghana 76 6.38N 1.12W
Konosha Russian Fed. 44 60.58N 40.08E
Kōnosu Japan 57 36.03N139.31E
Konotop Ukraine 45 51.15N 33.14E
Końskie Poland 37 51.12N 20.26E
Konstanz Germany 39 47.40N 9.10E
Kontagora Nigeria 77 10.24N 5.22E
Kontcha Cameroon 77 7.59N 12.15E
Kontiomäki Finland 44 64.21N 28.10E
Kontum Vietnam 56 14.23N108.00E
Kontum, Plateau du f. Vietnam 56 14.00N108.00E
Konya Turkey 64 37.51N 32.30E
Konz Germany 39 49.42N 6.34E
Konza Kenya 79 1.45S 37.07E
Koolkootinnie L. Australia 92 27.58S137.47E
Koolyanobbing Australia 89 30.48S119.29E
Koondrook Australia 92 35.39S144.11E
Koongawa Australia 92 33.11S135.52E
Koorawatha Australia 93 34.02S148.33E
Koorda Australia 89 30.50S117.51E
Kootenay L. Canada 100 49.45N117.00W
Kootenay Nat. Park Canada 100 51.00N116.00W
Kootjieskolk R.S.A. 80 31.14S 20.18E
Kopāganj India 63 26.01N 83.34E
Kopargaon India 62 19.53N 74.29E
Kópavogur Iceland 40 64.06N 21.53W
Koper Slovenia 31 45.33N 13.44E
Kopervik Norway 42 59.17N 5.18E

Kopet Dag, Khrebet to Kwamouth

Kopet Dag, Khrebet *mts.* Turkmenistan **65** 38.00N 58.00E
Kopeysk Russian Fed. **9** 55.07N 61.37E
Köping Sweden **41** 59.31N 16.00E
Koplik Albania **34** 42.13N 19.26E
Koppány Hungary **31** 46.35N 18.26E
Kopparberg *d.* Sweden **41** 60.50N 15.00E
Koppom Sweden **43** 59.43N 12.09E
Koprivnica Croatia **31** 46.10N 16.50E
Kopychintsy Ukraine **37** 49.10N 25.58E
Kor *r.* Iran **65** 29.40N 53.17E
Koralpe *mts.* Austria **31** 46.40N 15.00E
Koraput India **63** 18.49N 82.43E
Koratla India **63** 18.49N 78.43E
Korba India **63** 22.21N 82.41E
Korbach Germany **38** 51.16N 8.52E
Korbous Tunisia **32** 36.49N 10.35E
Korçë Albania **34** 40.37N 20.50E
Korçë *d.* Albania **34** 40.40N 20.50E
Korčula Croatia **31** 42.58N 17.08E
Korčula *i.* Croatia **31** 42.57N 16.50E
Korčulanski Kanal *str.* Croatia **31** 43.03N 16.40E
Kord Kūy Iran **65** 36.48N 54.07E
Korea Str. S. Korea / Japan **53** 35.00N129.20E
Korem Ethiopia **73** 12.30N 39.30E
Korets Ukraine **37** 50.39N 27.10E
Korhogo Ivory Coast **76** 9.22N 5.31W
Korim Indonesia **59** 0.58S136.10E
Korinthiakós Kólpos *g.* Greece **35** 38.16N 22.30E
Kórinthos Greece **35** 37.56N 22.56E
Korinthou, Dhiórix *canal* Greece **35** 37.57N 22.56E
Kōriyama Japan **57** 37.23N140.22E
Korma Belorussia **37** 53.08N 30.47E
Körmend Hungary **31** 47.01N 16.37E
Kornat *i.* Croatia **31** 43.50N 15.16E
Korneshty Moldavia **37** 47.21N 28.00E
Kornsjö Norway **42** 58.57N 11.39E
Koro *i.* Fiji **84** 17.22S179.25E
Koro Ivory Coast **76** 8.36N 7.28W
Koro Mali **76** 14.01N 2.58W
Korocha Russian Fed. **45** 50.50N 37.13E
Korogwe Tanzania **79** 5.10S 38.35E
Koroit Australia **92** 38.17S142.26E
Korong Vale *town* Australia **92** 36.22S143.45E
Koróni Greece **35** 36.48N 21.56E
Koronia, Límni *l.* Greece **34** 40.41N 23.05E
Koropíon Greece **35** 37.54N 23.53E
Koror *i.* Palau **59** 7.30N134.30E
Koro Sea Fiji **84** 18.00S179.00E
Korosten Ukraine **37** 51.00N 28.30E
Korostyshev Ukraine **37** 50.19N 29.03E
Koro Toro Chad **77** 16.05N 18.30E
Korsör Denmark **42** 55.20N 11.09E
Korsze Poland **37** 54.10N 21.09E
Kortrijk Belgium **16** 50.49N 3.17E
Koryakskiy Khrebet *mts.* Russian Fed. **51** 62.20N171.00E
Koryazhma Russian Fed. **44** 61.19N 47.12E
Kos Greece **35** 36.53N 27.18E
Kos *i.* Greece **35** 36.50N 27.10E
Kosa Ethiopia **73** 7.51N 36.51E
Kościan Poland **36** 52.06N 16.38E
Kościerzyna Poland **37** 54.08N 18.00E
Kosciusko U.S.A. **111** 32.58N 89.35W
Kosciusko, Mt. Australia **93** 36.28S148.17E
Kosha Sudan **72** 20.49N 30.32E
Koshikijima rettō *is.* Japan **57** 31.45N129.49E
Koshk-e Kohneh Afghan **65** 34.52N 62.29E
Košice Slovakia **37** 48.44N 21.15E
Koski Finland **41** 60.39N 23.09E
Koslan Russian Fed. **44** 63.29N 48.59E
Kossanto Senegal **76** 13.12N 11.56W
Kossovo Belorussia **37** 52.40N 25.18E
Kosta Sweden **43** 56.51N 15.23E
Kostajnica Croatia **31** 45.14N 16.33E
Koster R.S.A. **80** 25.51S 26.52E
Kostopol Ukraine **37** 50.51N 26.22E
Kostroma Russian Fed. **44** 57.46N 40.59E
Kostrzyn Poland **36** 52.24N 17.11E
Kostyukovichi Belorussia **37** 53.20N 32.01E
Kosyu Russian Fed. **44** 65.36N 59.00E
Koszalin Poland **36** 54.12N 16.09E
Kota Madhya P. India **63** 22.18N 82.02E
Kota Rāj. India **62** 25.11N 75.50E
Kota Baharu Malaysia **58** 6.07N102.15E
Kota Belud Malaysia **58** 6.00N116.00E
Kotabumi Indonesia **58** 4.52S104.59E
Kot Addu Pakistan **62** 30.28N 70.58E
Kota Kinabalu Malaysia **58** 5.59N116.04E
Kotari *mts.* Croatia **31** 44.05N 15.17E
Kotelnich Russian Fed. **44** 58.20N 48.10E
Kotelnikovo Russian Fed. **45** 47.39N 43.08E
Kotel'nyy, Ostrov *i.* Russian Fed. **51** 75.30N141.00E
Köthen Germany **38** 51.45N 11.58E
Kotka Finland **44** 60.26N 26.55E
Kot Kapūra India **62** 30.35N 74.49E
Kotlas Russian Fed. **44** 61.15N 46.28E
Kotli Jammu & Kashmir **62** 33.31N 73.55E
Kotlik U.S.A. **98** 63.02N163.33W
Kotor Yugo. **31** 42.25N 18.46E
Kotoriba Croatia **31** 46.21N 16.49E
Kotor Varoš Bosnia-Herzegovina **31** 44.37N 17.23E
Kotovsk Moldavia **37** 46.50N 28.31E
Kotovsk Ukraine **37** 47.42N 29.30E
Kot Pūtli India **62** 27.43N 76.12E
Kotra India **62** 24.22N 73.10E
Kotri Pakistan **62** 25.22N 68.18E
Kotri Allāhrakhio Pakistan **62** 24.24N 67.50E
Kötschach Austria **39** 46.40N 13.00E
Kottagūdem India **61** 17.32N 80.39E
Kotto *r.* C.A.R. **73** 4.14N 22.02E
Kotuy *r.* Russian Fed. **51** 71.40N103.00E
Kotzebue U.S.A. **98** 66.51N162.40W
Kotzebue Sd. U.S.A. **98** 66.20N163.00W
Kötzting Germany **39** 49.11N 12.52E
Kouango C.A.R. **73** 4.58N 20.00E
Koudougou Burkina **76** 12.15N 2.21W
Kouibli Ivory Coast **76** 7.09N 7.16W
Kouki C.A.R. **77** 7.09N 17.13E
Koúklia Cyprus **66** 34.42N 32.34E
Koula Moutou Gabon **78** 1.12S 12.29E
Koulikoro Mali **76** 12.55N 7.31W
Koumac N. Cal. **84** 20.33S164.17E
Koumankou Mali **76** 11.58N 6.06W
Koumbal C.A.R. **73** 9.26N 22.39E
Koumbia Burkina **76** 11.18N 3.38W
Koumbia Guinea **76** 11.54N 13.40W
Koumbisaleh *site* Mauritania **74** 15.55N 8.05W
Koumongou Togo **76** 10.10N 0.29E
Koumra Chad **77** 8.56N 17.32E
Koupéla Burkina **76** 12.09N 0.22W
Kouroussa Guinea **76** 10.40N 9.50W
Kousseri Chad **77** 12.05N 14.56E
Koutiala Mali **76** 12.20N 5.23W
Kouto Ivory Coast **76** 9.53N 6.25W
Kouvola Finland **44** 60.54N 26.45E
Kouyou *r.* Congo **78** 0.40S 16.37E
Kovdor Russian Fed. **44** 67.33N 30.30E
Kovel Ukraine **37** 51.12N 24.48E
Kovpyta Ukraine **37** 51.22N 30.51E
Kovrov Russian Fed. **44** 56.23N 41.21E
Kovzha *r.* Russian Fed. **44** 61.05N 36.27E
Kowanyama Australia **90** 15.29S141.44E
Kowloon Hong Kong **55** 22.19N114.12E
Kowt-e 'Ashrow Afghan. **62** 34.27N 68.48E
Koyukuk *r.* U.S.A. **98** 64.50N157.30W
Kozan Turkey **64** 37.27N 35.47E
Kozáni Greece **34** 40.19N 21.47E
Kozara *mts.* Bosnia-Herzegovina **31** 45.05N 16.50E
Kozarac Bosnia-Herzegovina **31** 44.58N 16.51E
Kozelets Ukraine **37** 50.54N 31.09E
Kozhikode India **60** 11.15N 75.45E
Kozhim Russian Fed. **44** 65.45N 59.30E
Kozhposelok Russian Fed. **44** 63.10N 38.10E
Kpandu Ghana **76** 7.02N 0.17E
Kpessi Togo **77** 8.07N 1.17E
Krabi Thailand **56** 8.08N 98.52E
Krâchéh Cambodia **56** 12.30N106.00E
Kragan Indonesia **59** 6.40S111.33E
Kragerö Norway **42** 58.52N 9.25E
Kragujevac Yugo. **29** 44.01N 20.55E
Kraków Poland **37** 50.03N 19.55E
Kraljevica Croatia **31** 45.16N 14.34E
Kraljevo Yugo. **34** 43.43N 20.41E
Kralovice Czech Republic **38** 49.59N 13.29E
Kralupy nad Vltavou Czech Republic **38** 50.11N 14.18E
Kramatorsk Ukraine **45** 48.43N 37.33E
Kramer U.S.A. **110** 48.20N100.42W
Kramfors Sweden **40** 62.55N 17.50E
Kranídhion Greece **35** 37.22N 23.10E
Kranj Slovenia **31** 46.15N 14.21E
Kranskop R.S.A. **80** 28.58S 30.52E
Krapina Croatia **31** 46.10N 15.52E
Krapkowice Poland **37** 50.29N 17.56E
Krasavino Russian Fed. **44** 60.58N 46.25E
Krasilov Ukraine **37** 49.39N 26.59E
Kraskino Russian Fed. **53** 42.42N130.48E
Krasnaya Gora Russian Fed. **37** 53.00N 31.36E
Kraśnik Poland **37** 50.56N 22.13E
Krasnodar Russian Fed. **45** 45.02N 39.00E
Krasnograd Ukraine **45** 49.22N 35.28E
Krasnokamsk Russian Fed. **44** 58.05N 55.49E
Krasnoperekopsk Ukraine **45** 45.56N 33.47E
Krasnoselkup Russian Fed. **50** 65.45N 82.31E
Krasnoturinsk Russian Fed. **44** 59.46N 60.10E
Krasnoufimsk Russian Fed. **44** 56.40N 57.49E
Krasnouralsk Russian Fed. **50** 58.25N 60.00E
Krasnovishersk Russian Fed. **44** 60.25N 57.02E
Krasnovodsk Turkmenistan **65** 40.01N 53.00E
Krasnovodskiy Poluostrov *pen.* Turkmenistan **65** 40.30N 53.10E
Krasnovodskiy Zaliv *g.* Turkmenistan **65** 39.50N 53.15E
Krasnoyarsk Russian Fed. **51** 56.05N 92.46E
Krasnyy Yar Russian Fed. **45** 46.32N 48.21E
Kratovo Macedonia **34** 42.06N 22.10E
Krawang Indonesia **59** 6.15S107.15E
Krefeld Germany **38** 51.20N 6.34E
Kremastón, Tekhnití Límni *l.* Greece **35** 38.52N 21.30E
Kremenchug Ukraine **45** 49.03N 33.25E
Kremenchugskoye Vodokhranilishche *resr.* Ukraine **45** 49.20N 32.30E
Kremenets Ukraine **37** 50.05N 25.48E
Kremmling U.S.A. **108** 40.03N106.24W
Krems Austria **36** 48.25N 15.36E
Krestovka Russian Fed. **44** 66.24N 52.31E
Kretinga Lithuania **41** 55.53N 21.13E
Kría Vrísi Greece **34** 40.41N 22.18E
Kribi Cameroon **77** 2.56N 9.56E
Krichev Belorussia **37** 53.40N 31.44E
Krichim Bulgaria **34** 42.08N 24.32E
Kriens Switz. **39** 47.02N 8.17E
Krimml Austria **39** 47.13N 12.11E
Krionéri Greece **35** 38.20N 21.35E
Krishna *r.* India **61** 16.00N 81.00E
Krishnanagar India **63** 23.24N 88.30E
Kristdala Sweden **43** 57.24N 16.11E
Kristianopel Sweden **43** 56.15N 16.02E
Kristiansand Norway **42** 58.10N 8.00E
Kristianstad Sweden **43** 56.02N 14.08E
Kristianstad *d.* Sweden **43** 56.10N 13.40E
Kristiansund Norway **40** 63.07N 7.45E
Kristiinankaupunki Finland **41** 62.17N 21.23E
Kristinehamn Sweden **43** 59.20N 14.07E
Kristinestad *see* Kristiinankaupunki Finland **41**
Kristinovka Ukraine **37** 48.50N 29.58E
Kríti *i.* Greece **35** 35.29N 24.42E
Kritikón Pélagos *sea* Greece **35** 35.46N 23.54E
Kriva *r.* Macedonia **34** 42.12N 22.18E
Krivaja *r.* Bosnia-Herzegovina **31** 44.27N 18.09E
Kriva Palanka Macedonia **34** 42.12N 22.20E
Krivodol Bulgaria **34** 43.23N 23.29E
Krivoy Rog Ukraine **45** 47.55N 33.24E
Križevci Croatia **31** 46.02N 16.33E
Krk *i.* Croatia **31** 45.05N 14.35E
Krnov Czech Republic **37** 50.05N 17.41E
Kröderen *l.* Norway **42** 60.15N 9.38E
Krokek Sweden **43** 58.40N 16.24E
Kroken Norway **40** 65.23N 14.15E
Krokom Sweden **40** 63.20N 14.30E
Krokowa Poland **43** 54.48N 18.11E
Kronach Germany **38** 50.14N 11.20E
Krông Kaôh Kông Cambodia **56** 11.37N102.59E
Kronoberg *d.* Sweden **43** 56.40N 14.35E
Kronprins Olav Kyst *f.* Antarctica **128** 69.00S 42.00E
Kronshtadt Russian Fed. **44** 60.00N 29.40E
Kroonstad R.S.A. **80** 27.38S 27.12E
Kropotkin Russian Fed. **45** 45.25N 40.35E
Kropperfjäll *hill* Sweden **43** 58.40N 12.13E
Krosno Poland **37** 49.42N 21.46E
Krotoszyn Poland **37** 51.42N 17.26E
Kroya Indonesia **59** 7.37S109.13E
Krško Slovenia **31** 45.58N 15.29E
Kruger Nat. Park R.S.A. **81** 24.10S 31.36E
Krugersdorp R.S.A. **80** 26.06S 27.46E
Krujë Albania **34** 41.30N 19.48E
Krumbach Germany **39** 48.14N 10.22E
Krumovgrad Bulgaria **34** 41.29N 25.38E
Krung Thep *see* Bangkok Thailand **56**
Krupki Belorussia **37** 54.19N 29.05E
Kruševac Yugo. **34** 43.35N 21.20E
Kruševo Macedonia **34** 41.23N 21.19E
Krušnéhory *mts. see* Erzgebirge *mts.* Czech Republic **38**
Krylbo Sweden **43** 60.08N 16.13E
Krym *pen.* Ukraine **45** 45.30N 34.00E
Krymsk Russian Fed. **45** 44.56N 38.00E
Krzyz Poland **36** 52.54N 16.01E
Ksar el Boukhari Algeria **75** 35.53N 2.45E
Ksar-el-Kebir Morocco **74** 35.01N 5.54W
Ksar Rhilane Tunisia **75** 33.00N 9.38E
Ksel, Djebel *mtn.* Algeria **75** 33.44N 1.10E
Kuala Dungun Malaysia **58** 4.47N103.26E
Kualakapuas Indonesia **58** 3.01S114.21E
Kuala Lipis Malaysia **58** 4.11N102.00E
Kuala Lumpur Malaysia **58** 3.08N101.42E
Kuala Trengganu Malaysia **58** 5.10N103.10E
Kuancheng China **54** 40.36N118.27E
Kuandang Indonesia **59** 0.53N122.58E
Kuandian China **54** 40.47N124.43E
Kuantan Malaysia **58** 3.50N103.19E
Kuba Azerbaijan **65** 41.23N 48.33E
Kuban *r.* Russian Fed. **45** 45.20N 37.17E
Kubbum Sudan **73** 11.47N 23.47E
Kubrat Bulgaria **34** 43.49N 26.31E
Kuchaiburi India **63** 22.16N 86.10E
Kuchāman India **62** 27.09N 74.52E
Kuching Malaysia **58** 1.32N110.20E
Kuchinoerabu jima *i.* Japan **57** 30.30N130.20E
Küchnay Darvīshān Afghan. **62** 30.59N 64.11E
Kuçovë Albania **34** 40.48N 19.54E
Küçükbahce Turkey **35** 38.33N 26.24E
Kūd Jammu & Kashmir **62** 33.05N 75.17E
Kudat Malaysia **58** 6.45N116.47E
Kudus Indonesia **59** 6.46S110.48E
Kufrinjah Jordan **67** 32.18N 35.42E
Kufrinjah, Wādī Jordan **67** 32.16N 35.33E
Kufstein Austria **39** 47.35N 12.10E
Kūhpāyeh Iran **65** 32.42N 52.25E
Kūhrān, Kūh-e *mtn.* Iran **65** 26.46N 58.15E
Kuito Angola **78** 12.25S 16.58E
Kuiu I. U.S.A. **100** 56.40N134.00W
Kuivaniemi Finland **40** 65.35N 25.11E
Kujū san *mtn.* Japan **57** 33.08N131.10E
Kuke Botswana **80** 23.19S 24.29E
Kukerin Australia **89** 33.11S118.03E
Kukës Albania **34** 42.05N 20.20E
Kukshi India **62** 22.12N 74.45E
Kūl *r.* Iran **65** 28.00N 55.45E
Kula Bulgaria **34** 43.52N 22.36E
Kula Turkey **64** 38.33N 28.38E
Kula Yugo. **31** 45.36N 19.32E
Kulāchi Pakistan **62** 31.56N 70.27E
Kulakshi Kazakhstan **45** 47.09N 55.22E
Kulal, Mt. Kenya **79** 2.44N 36.56E
Kulaura Bangla. **63** 24.30N 92.03E
Kuldīga Latvia **41** 56.58N 21.59E
Kulen Vakuf Bosnia-Herzegovina **31** 44.34N 16.06E
Kulgera Australia **90** 25.50S133.18E
Kulin Australia **89** 32.40S118.10E
Kulja Australia **89** 30.28S117.17E
Kulkyne *r.* Australia **93** 30.16S144.12E
Kulmbach Germany **38** 50.06N 11.27E
Kulpara Australia **92** 34.07S137.59E
Kulsary Kazakhstan **45** 46.59N 54.02E
Kulu India **62** 31.58N 77.07E
Kulu Turkey **45** 39.06N 33.02E
Kulunda Russian Fed. **50** 52.34N 78.58E
Kulwin Australia **92** 35.02S142.40E
Kulyab Tajikistan **52** 37.55N 69.47E
Kuma *r.* Russian Fed. **45** 44.40N 46.55E
Kumagaya Japan **57** 36.08N139.23E
Kumai Indonesia **58** 2.45S111.44E
Kumamoto Japan **57** 32.50N130.42E
Kumanovo Macedonia **34** 42.08N 21.43E
Kumara New Zealand **86** 42.38S171.11E
Kumarl Australia **89** 32.47S121.33E
Kumasi Ghana **76** 6.45N 1.35W
Kumayri Armenia **65** 40.47N 43.49E
Kumba Cameroon **77** 4.39N 9.26E
Kumbakonam India **61** 10.59N 79.24E
Kum Dag Turkmenistan **65** 39.14N 54.33E
Kumdah Saudi Arabia **71** 20.23N 45.05E
Kumertau Russian Fed. **44** 52.48N 55.46E
Kumi Uganda **79** 1.26N 33.54E
Kumla Sweden **43** 59.08N 15.08E
Kummerower See *l.* Germany **38** 53.49N 12.52E
Kumon Range *mts.* Burma **56** 26.30N 97.15E
Kunashir *i.* Russian Fed. **53** 44.25N146.00E
Kunchha Nepal **63** 28.08N 84.22E
Kundam India **63** 23.13N 80.21E
Kundelungu Mts. Zaïre **79** 9.30S 27.50E
Kundiān Pakistan **62** 32.27N 71.28E
Kundip Australia **89** 33.44S120.11E
Kundla India **62** 21.20N 71.18E
Kungälv Sweden **42** 57.52N 11.58E
Kungsbacka Sweden **43** 57.29N 12.04E
Kungshamn Sweden **42** 58.22N 11.15E
Kungsör Sweden **43** 59.25N 16.05E
Kungu Zaïre **78** 2.47N 19.12E
Kungur Russian Fed. **44** 57.27N 56.50E
Kuningan Indonesia **59** 7.02S108.30E
Kunkuri India **63** 22.45N 83.57E
Kunlong Burma **56** 23.25N 98.39E
Kunlun Shan *mts.* China **52** 36.40N 88.00E
Kunming China **52** 25.04N102.41E
Kunö *i.* Faroe Is. **10** 62.20N 6.39W
Kunsan S. Korea **53** 35.57N126.42E
Kunshan China **55** 31.24N121.08E
Kunszentmárton Hungary **31** 46.51N 20.18E
Kuntair Gambia **76** 13.36N 16.20W
Kununoppin Australia **89** 31.09S117.53E
Kununurra Australia **87** 15.42S128.50E
Kunyo Ethiopia **71** 6.20N 42.32E
Künzelsau Germany **39** 49.16N 9.41E
Kuolayarvi Russian Fed. **40** 66.58N 29.12E
Kuopio Finland **44** 62.51N 27.30E
Kupa *r.* Croatia **31** 45.28N 16.24E
Kupang Indonesia **59** 10.13S123.38E
Küplü Turkey **34** 41.07N 26.21E
Kupreanof I. U.S.A. **100** 56.50N133.30W
Kupres Bosnia-Herzegovina **31** 44.00N 17.17E
Kupyansk Ukraine **45** 49.41N 37.37E
Kuqa China **52** 41.43N 82.58E
Kura *r.* Azerbaijan **65** 39.18N 49.22E
Kurashiki Japan **57** 34.36N133.43E
Kuraymah Sudan **72** 18.33N 31.51E
Kurayyimah Jordan **67** 32.16N 35.36E
Kurchum Kazakhstan **52** 48.35N 83.39E
Kurdistan *f.* Asia **65** 37.00N 43.30E
Kūrdzhali Bulgaria **34** 41.39N 25.22E
Kure Japan **57** 34.20N132.40E
Kuressaare Estonia **41** 58.12N 22.30E
Kurgaldzhino Kazakhstan **50** 50.35N 70.03E
Kurgan Russian Fed. **9** 55.30N 65.20E
Kurīgrām Bangla. **63** 25.49N 89.39E
Kurikka Finland **40** 62.37N 22.25E
Kuril Ridge Pacific Oc. **84** 46.10N152.30E
Kurilskiye Ostrova *is.* Russian Fed. **53** 46.00N150.30E
Kuril Trench Pacific Oc. **84** 46.00N155.00E
Kuring Kuru Namibia **80** 17.36S 18.36E
Kurlovski Russian Fed. **44** 55.26N 40.40E
Kurmuk Sudan **73** 10.33N 34.17E
Kurnool India **61** 15.51N 78.01E
Kurow New Zealand **86** 44.44S170.28E
Kurram Pakistan **62** 30.06N 66.31E
Kurri Kurri Australia **93** 32.49S151.29E
Kurseong India **63** 26.53N 88.17E
Kursk Russian Fed. **45** 51.45N 36.14E
Kuršumlija Yugo. **34** 43.09N 21.19E
Kūrtī Sudan **72** 18.07N 31.33E
Kuru Finland **41** 61.52N 23.44E
Kuru Sudan **73** 7.43N 26.31E
Kuruman R.S.A. **80** 27.28S 23.25E
Kuruman *r.* R.S.A. **80** 26.53S 20.38E
Kurume Japan **57** 33.20N130.29E
Kurur, Jabal *mtn.* Sudan **72** 20.31N 31.32E
Kuşadasi Turkey **35** 37.51N 27.15E
Kusadasi Körfezi *b.* Greece **35** 37.50N 27.08E
Kusatsu Japan **57** 35.02N135.57E
Kusel Germany **39** 49.32N 7.24E
Kushālgarh India **62** 23.10N 74.27E
Kushchevskaya Russian Fed. **45** 46.34N 39.39E
Kushida *r.* Japan **57** 34.36N136.34E
Kushiro Japan **57** 42.58N144.24E
Kushka Turkmenistan **65** 35.14N 62.15E
Kushtia Bangla. **63** 23.55N 89.07E
Kusiyāra *r.* Bangla. **63** 24.36N 91.44E
Kuskokwim B. U.S.A. **98** 59.45N162.25W
Kuskokwim Mts. U.S.A. **98** 62.50N156.00W
Kusma Nepal **63** 28.13N 83.41E
Kussharo ko *l.* Japan **57** 43.40N144.20E
Küssnacht Switz. **39** 47.05N 8.27E
Kustanay Kazakhstan **50** 53.15N 63.40E
Küstenkanal Germany **38** 53.08N 8.00E
Kūstī Sudan **73** 13.10N 32.40E
Kütahya Turkey **64** 39.25N 29.56E
Kutaisi Georgia **45** 42.15N 42.44E
Kutina Croatia **31** 45.29N 16.46E
Kutiyāna India **62** 21.38N 69.59E
Kutná Hora Czech Republic **36** 49.57N 15.16E
Kutno Poland **37** 52.15N 19.23E
Kutu Zaïre **78** 2.42S 18.09E
Kutubdia I. Bangla. **63** 21.50N 91.52E
Kutum Sudan **72** 14.12N 24.40E
Kutztown U.S.A. **115** 40.31N 75.47W
Kuujjuaq Canada **99** 58.10N 68.15W
Kuujjuarapik Canada **102** 55.25 77.45W
Kuusamo Finland **44** 65.57N 29.15E
Kuvango Angola **78** 14.28S 16.25E
Kuwait Asia **65** 29.20N 47.40E
Kuwait *town see* Al Kuwayt Kuwait **65**
Kuwana Japan **57** 35.04N136.42E
Kuybyshev *see* Samara Russian Fed. **44**
Kuybyshevskoye Vodokhranilishche *resr.* Russian Fed. **44** 55.00N 49.00E
Kuyeda Russian Fed. **44** 56.25N 55.33E
Kuzey Anadolu Daglari *mts.* Turkey **64** 40.32N 38.00E
Kuznetsk Russian Fed. **44** 53.08N 46.36E
Kuzomen Russian Fed. **44** 66.15N 36.51E
Kuzreka Russian Fed. **44** 66.35N 34.48E
Kvaenangen *est.* Norway **40** 69.50N 21.30E
Kvarner *g.* Croatia **31** 45.00N 14.10E
Kvarnerić *str.* Croatia **31** 44.45N 14.35E
Kvenna *r.* Norway **42** 60.01N 7.56E
Kvina *r.* Norway **42** 58.17N 6.56E
Kwale Kenya **79** 4.20S 39.25E
Kwamouth Zaïre **78** 3.11S 16.16E

Kwangju to Langkawi

Kwangju S. Korea 53 35.07N126.52E
Kwango r. Zaïre 78 3.20S 17.23E
Kwara d. Nigeria 77 8.20N 5.35E
Kwatisore Indonesia 59 3.18S134.50E
Kwa Zulu f. R.S.A. 80 27.30S 32.00E
Kwekwe Zimbabwe 80 18.59S 29.46E
Kweneng d. Botswana 80 24.30S 25.40E
Kwenge r. Zaïre 78 4.53S 18.47E
Kwethluk U.S.A. 98 60.49N161.27W
Kwidzyn Poland 37 53.45N 18.56E
Kwigillingok U.S.A. 98 59.51N163.08W
Kwiguk U.S.A. 98 62.45N164.28W
Kwilu r. Zaïre 78 3.18S 17.22E
Kwinana Australia 89 32.15S115.48E
Kwoka mtn. Indonesia 59 1.30S132.30E
Kyabé Chad 77 9.28N 18.54E
Kyabram Australia 93 36.18S145.05E
Kyaiklat Burma 56 16.25N 95.42E
Kyaikto Burma 56 17.16N 97.01E
Kyaka Tanzania 79 1.16S 31.27E
Kyakhta Russian Fed. 52 50.22N106.30E
Kyalite Australia 92 34.57S143.31E
Kyancutta Australia 92 33.08S135.34E
Kyaukpadaung Burma 56 20.50N 95.08E
Kyaukpyu Burma 56 19.20N 93.33E
Kybybolite Australia 92 36.54S140.58E
Kychema Russian Fed. 44 65.32N 42.42E
Kyle of Lochalsh town U.K. 14 57.17N 5.43W
Kyll r. Germany 16 49.48N 6.42E
Kyllburg Germany 39 50.02N 6.35E
Kyluchevskaya mtn. Russian Fed. 51 56.00N160.30E
Kyneton Australia 92 37.14S144.28E
Kynnefjäll hill Sweden 42 58.42N 11.41E
Kynuna Australia 90 21.35S141.55E
Kyoga, L. Uganda 79 1.30N 33.00E
Kyogle Australia 93 28.36S152.59E
Kyong Burma 56 20.49N 96.40E
Kyonpyaw Burma 56 17.18N 95.12E
Kyotera Uganda 79 0.40S 31.31E
Kyōto Japan 57 35.00N135.45E
Kyōto d. Japan 57 34.55N135.35E
Kyrgyzstan Asia 52 41.30N 75.00E
Kyritz Germany 38 52.56N 12.23E
Kyrkheden Sweden 43 60.10N 13.29E
Kyrön r. Finland 40 63.14N 21.45E
Kyrta Russian Fed. 44 64.02N 57.40E
Kyshtym Russian Fed. 9 55.43N 60.32E
Kyūshū d. Japan 57 32.00N130.00E
Kyūshū i. Japan 57 32.00N130.00E
Kyushu Palau Ridge Pacific Oc. 84 15.00N135.00E
Kyūshū sanchi mts. Japan 57 32.20N131.20E
Kyustendil Bulgaria 34 42.25N 22.41E
Kywong Australia 93 35.01S146.45E
Kyyiv see Kiyev Ukraine 37
Kyyjärvi Finland 40 63.02N 24.34E
Kyzyl Russian Fed. 52 51.42N 94.28E
Kyzyl Kum, Peski f. Uzbekistan 9 42.00N 64.30E
Kzyl Orda Kazakhstan 9 44.52N 65.28E
K2 mtn. Asia 52 35.53N 76.32E

L

La Alagaba Spain 27 37.28N 6.01W
La Albuera Spain 27 38.43N 6.49W
La Albufera l. Spain 25 39.20N 0.22W
La Almarcha Spain 27 39.41N 2.22W
La Almunia de Doña Godina Spain 25 41.29N 1.22W
Laas Caanood Somali Rep. 71 8.26N 47.24E
Laas Dawaco Somali Rep. 71 10.22N 49.03E
Laas Dhaareed Somali Rep. 71 10.10N 46.01E
Laas Qoray Somali Rep. 71 11.10N 48.16E
La Asunción Venezuela 122 11.06N 63.53W
Laâyoune see El Aaiún W. Sahara 74
La Baleine r. Canada 99 58.00N 57.50W
La Banda Argentina 124 27.44S 64.15W
La Bañeza Spain 26 42.18N 5.54W
Labao Indonesia 59 8.12S122.49E
La Barca Mexico 116 20.20N102.33W
La Barge U.S.A. 108 42.16N110.12W
La Bassée France 19 50.32N 2.48E
Labastide-Murat France 20 44.39N 1.34E
La Baule France 18 47.17N 2.24W
Labbezanga Mali 76 14.57N 0.42E
Labe r. Czech. see Elbe r. Germany 38
Labé Guinea 76 11.17N 12.11W
Labelle Canada 105 46.16N 74.44W
La Belle U.S.A. 113 26.43N 81.27W
Labelle Prov. Park Canada 105 46.13N 75.19W
Laberge, L. Canada 100 61.11N135.12W
Labin Croatia 31 45.05N 14.07E
Labinsk Russian Fed. 45 44.39N 40.44E
La Bisbal Spain 25 41.57N 3.03E
La Blanquilla i. Venezuela 117 11.53N 64.38W
Laboe Germany 38 54.24N 10.15E
Labouheyre France 20 44.13N 0.55W
Laboulaye Argentina 125 34.05S 63.25W
Labrador f. Canada 103 53.00N 62.00W
Labrador Basin f. Atlantic Oc. 127 55.00N 45.00W
Labrador City Canada 103 52.57N 66.54W
Labrador Sea Canada/Greenland 99 57.00N 53.00W
Lábrea Brazil 122 7.16S 64.47W
Labrède France 20 44.41N 0.31W
Labrit France 20 44.07N 0.33W
Labuan Indonesia 59 6.25S105.49E
Labuan i. Malaysia 58 5.20N115.15E
Labuha Indonesia 59 0.37S127.29E
Labutta Burma 56 16.09N 94.46E
Labyrinth, L. Australia 92 30.43S135.07E
Laç Albania 34 41.38N 19.40E
Lac d. Chad 77 13.30N 14.35E
La Calera Chile 125 32.47S 71.12W
La Campana Spain 27 37.34N 5.26W
Lacanau France 20 44.59N 1.05W
Lacanau, Étang de b. France 20 44.58N 1.07W
La Cañiza Spain 26 42.13N 8.16W
La Canourgue France 20 44.26N 3.13E
La Capelle France 19 49.58N 3.55E
Lacapelle-Marival France 20 44.44N 1.54E
La Carlota Argentina 125 33.25S 63.18W
La Carolina Spain 26 38.15N 3.37W
Lacaune France 20 43.43N 2.42E
Lacaune, Monts de mts. France 20 43.43N 2.50E
Lac aux Sables town Canada 105 46.52N 72.24W
Lacedonia Italy 33 41.03N 15.25E
La Ceiba Honduras 117 15.45N 86.45W
Lacepede B. Australia 92 36.47S139.45E
Lac Gatineau town Canada 105 46.34N 75.44W
Lac Giao Vietnam 56 12.41N108.02E
Lacha, Ozero l. Russian Fed. 44 61.25N 39.00E
La Chaise-Dieu France 20 45.19N 3.42E
La Chambre France 21 45.22N 6.18E
La Charité France 19 47.11N 3.01E
La Chartre France 18 47.44N 0.35E
La Châtaigneraie France 18 46.39N 0.44W
La Châtre France 19 46.35N 1.59E
La Chaux-de-Fonds Switz. 39 47.06N 6.50E
Lach Dera r. Somali Rep. 79 0.01S 42.45E
Lachhmangarh India 62 27.49N 75.02E
Lachine Canada 105 45.26N 73.40W
Lachine U.S.A. 104 45.26N 83.40W
Lachlan r. Australia 92 34.21S143.58E
Lachute Canada 105 45.38N 74.20W
La Ciotat France 21 43.10N 5.36E
Lackan Resr. Rep. of Ire. 15 53.09N 6.31W
Lackawanna U.S.A. 114 42.49N 78.50W
Läckö Sweden 43 58.41N 13.13E
Lac la Biche town Canada 101 54.46N111.58W
Lac la Ronge Prov. Park Canada 101 55.14N104.45W
La Clayette France 19 46.18N 4.19E
La Cocha Argentina 124 27.45S 65.35W
Lacolle Canada 105 45.05N 73.22W
Lacombe Canada 100 52.30N113.44W
La Concepción Venezuela 122 10.25N 71.41W
La Concordia Mexico 116 16.05N 92.38W
Laconia U.S.A. 115 43.31N 71.29W
La Coruña Spain 26 43.22N 8.23W
La Coruña d. Spain 26 43.10N 8.30W
La Courtine le-Trucq France 20 45.42N 2.16E
Lac Rémi town Canada 105 46.01N 74.47W
La Crosse Kans. U.S.A. 110 38.32N 99.18W
La Crosse Wisc. U.S.A. 110 43.48N 91.15W
La Cruz Mexico 109 27.50N105.11W
La Cruz Uruguay 125 33.56S 56.15W
Lac St. Paul town Canada 105 46.44N 75.18W
Ladākh Range mts. Jammu & Kashmir 63 34.15N 78.00E
La Demanda, Sierra de mts. Spain 24 42.10N 3.20W
Ládhi Greece 34 41.28N 26.15E
Ladhón r. Greece 35 37.40N 21.50E
Ladismith R.S.A. 80 33.29S 21.15E
Ladispoli Italy 32 41.56N 12.05E
Lādīz Iran 65 28.57N 61.18E
Lādnun India 62 27.39N 74.23E
Ladoga l. see Ladozhskoye Ozero l. Russian Fed. 44
La Dorada Colombia 122 5.27N 74.40W
Ladozhskoye Ozero l. Russian Fed. 44 61.00N 32.00E
La Dura Mexico 109 28.22N109.33W
Ladushkin Russian Fed. 37 54.30N 20.05E
Ladva Vetka Russian Fed. 44 61.16N 34.23E
Ladybrand R.S.A. 80 29.11S 27.26E
Lady Evelyn L. Canada 104 47.20N 80.10W
Ladysmith Canada 100 49.58N123.49W
Ladysmith R.S.A. 80 28.32S 29.47E
Ladysmith U.S.A. 110 45.27N 91.07W
Lae P.N.G. 59 6.45S146.30E
Lae Thailand 56 19.25N101.00E
Laesö i. Denmark 42 57.16N 11.01E
La Estrada Spain 26 42.41N 8.29W
La Fayette Ga. U.S.A. 113 34.42N 85.18W
Lafayette Ind. U.S.A. 112 40.25N 86.54W
Lafayette La. U.S.A. 111 30.14N 92.01W
Lafayette, Mt. U.S.A. 105 44.10N 71.38W
La Fère France 19 49.40N 3.22E
La Ferté-Bernard France 18 48.11N 0.40E
La Ferté-Gaucher France 19 48.47N 3.18E
La Ferté-Macé France 18 48.36N 0.22W
La Ferté-St. Aubin France 19 47.43N 1.56E
Lafia Nigeria 77 8.35N 8.34E
Lafiagi Nigeria 77 8.50N 5.23E
La Flèche France 18 47.42N 0.05W
Lafollette U.S.A. 113 36.23N 84.09W
Laforest Canada 104 47.02N 81.13W
La Fregeneda Spain 26 40.59N 6.52W
La Fuente de San Esteban Spain 26 40.48N 6.15W
La Galite i. Tunisia 32 37.32N 8.56E
La Galite, Canal de str. Tunisia 32 37.20N 9.15E
La Gallega Spain 26 41.54N 3.16W
Lagan Sweden 43 56.55N 13.59E
Lagan r. Sweden 43 56.33N 12.56E
Lagan r. U.K. 15 54.37N 5.44W
La Garde, Lac l. Canada 104 46.46N 78.14W
Lage Spain 26 43.13N 9.00W
Lågen r. Akershus Norway 41 60.10N 11.28E
Lågen r. Vestfold Norway 42 59.03N 10.05E
Laghouat Algeria 75 33.49N 2.55E
Lago Dilolo town Angola 78 11.27S 22.03E
Lagonegro Italy 33 40.07N 15.46E
Lagos Mexico 116 21.21N101.55W
Lagos Nigeria 77 6.27N 3.28E
Lagos d. Nigeria 77 6.32N 3.30E
Lagos Portugal 27 37.06N 8.40W
La Goulette Tunisia 32 36.49N 10.18E
La Granadella Spain 25 41.21N 0.40E
La Grand'Combe France 20 44.13N 4.02E
La Grande r. Canada 102 53.50N 79.00W
La Grande U.S.A. 108 45.20N118.05W
La Grande Résr. 2 Canada 102 53.35N 77.10W
La Grande Résr. 3 Canada 102 53.35N 74.55W
La Grande Résr. 4 Canada 102 53.50N 73.30W
Lagrange Australia 88 18.46S121.49E
La Grange U.S.A. 113 33.02N 85.02W
La Grave France 21 45.03N 6.18E
La Guaira Venezuela 122 10.38N 66.55W
La Guardia Pontevedra Spain 26 41.54N 8.51W
Laguardia Vascongadas Spain 26 42.33N 2.35W
La Gudiña Spain 26 42.04N 7.08W
La Guerche-de-Bretagne France 18 47.56N 1.14W
La Guerche-sur-l'Aubois France 19 46.57N 2.57E
Laguiole France 20 44.41N 2.51E
Laguna Brazil 124 28.29S 48.47W
Laguna Dam U.S.A. 109 32.55N114.25W
Lagunas Chile 124 20.59S 69.37W
Lagunas Peru 122 5.10S 73.35W
La Habana Cuba 117 23.07N 82.25W
Lahad Datu Malaysia 58 5.05N118.20E
La Harpe U.S.A. 110 40.35N 90.57W
Lahat Indonesia 58 3.46S103.32E
La Haye-du-Puits France 18 49.18N 1.33W
Laḥij Yemen 71 13.04N 44.53E
Lāhījān Iran 65 37.12N 50.00E
Lahn r. Germany 16 50.18N 7.36E
Lahnstein Germany 39 50.18N 7.37E
Laholm Sweden 43 56.31N 13.02E
Laholmsbukten b. Sweden 43 56.35N 12.50E
Lahore Pakistan 62 31.35N 74.18E
Lahr Germany 39 48.20N 7.52E
Lahri Pakistan 62 29.11N 68.13E
Lahti Finland 41 60.58N 25.40E
Laï Chad 77 9.22N 16.14E
Laiagam P.N.G. 59 5.31S143.39E
Laibin China 55 23.42N109.16E
Lai Chau Vietnam 56 22.04N103.12E
L'Aigle r. Canada 105 46.28N 76.01W
L'Aigle France 18 48.45N 0.38E
Laignes France 19 47.50N 4.22E
Laihia Finland 40 62.58N 22.01E
Lainá Greece 34 41.03N 26.19E
Laingsburg R.S.A. 80 33.11S 20.49E
Laingsburg U.S.A. 104 42.54N 84.21W
Lainio r. Sweden 40 67.28N 22.50E
Lairg U.K. 14 58.01N 4.25W
Laisamis Kenya 79 1.38N 37.47E
Laissac France 20 44.23N 2.49E
Laitila Finland 41 60.53N 21.41E
Laiyuan China 54 39.19N114.41E
Laizhou Wan b. China 54 37.30N119.30E
La Jarrie France 20 46.08N 1.00W
La Javie France 21 44.10N 6.21E
Lajes Brazil 126 27.48S 50.20W
La Junta U.S.A. 108 37.59N103.33W
Lakaband Pakistan 62 31.00N 69.30E
Lak Bor r. Kenya 73 1.18N 40.40E
Lak Bor r. Somali Rep. 79 0.32N 42.05E
Lake Biddy town Australia 89 33.01S118.51E
Lake Boga town Australia 92 35.27S143.39E
Lake Brown town Australia 89 30.57S118.19E
Lake Cargelligo town Australia 93 33.19S146.23E
Lake Charles town U.S.A. 111 30.13N 93.12W
Lake City U.S.A. 113 30.12N 82.39W
Lake Clear town Canada 105 45.27N 77.17W
Lake District f. U.K. 12 54.30N 3.10W
Lakefield Canada 104 44.26N 78.16W
Lake George town Colo. U.S.A. 108 38.58N105.23W
Lake George town N.Y. U.S.A. 115 43.26N 73.43W
Lake Grace town Australia 89 33.06S118.28E
Lake Harbour town Canada 99 62.50N 69.50W
Lake King town Australia 89 33.05S119.40E
Lakeland town U.S.A. 113 28.02N 81.59W
Lake Mead Nat. Recreation Area U.S.A. 109 36.00N114.30W
Lake Nash town Australia 90 21.00S137.55E
Lake Orion town U.S.A. 114 42.47N 83.14W
Lakepa Niue 84 19.01S169.49W
Lake Placid town U.S.A. 112 44.17N 73.59W
Lake River town Canada 102 54.30N 82.30W
Lakes Entrance town Australia 93 37.53S147.59E
Lakeshore U.S.A. 108 37.15N119.12W
Lakeside Ohio U.S.A. 114 41.32N 82.45W
Lakeside Utah U.S.A. 108 41.13N112.54W
Lake Superior Prov. Park Canada 102 47.30N 84.50W
Lakeview U.S.A. 108 42.11N120.21W
Lake Village U.S.A. 111 33.20N 91.17W
Lakewood N.J. U.S.A. 115 40.06N 74.13W
Lakewood N.Mex. U.S.A. 109 32.39N104.39W
Lakewood N.Y. U.S.A. 114 42.06N 79.20W
Lakewood Ohio U.S.A. 114 41.29N 81.48W
Lākheri India 62 25.40N 76.10E
Lakhīmpur India 63 27.57N 80.46E
Lakhish, Nahal wadi Israel 67 31.37N 34.46E
Lakhnādon India 63 22.36N 79.36E
Lakhpat India 62 23.49N 68.47E
Lakonikós Kólpos g. Greece 35 36.25N 22.37E
Lakota Ivory Coast 76 5.50N 5.30W
Lakota U.S.A. 110 48.02N 98.21W
Laksefjorden est. Norway 40 70.58N 27.00E
Lakselv Norway 40 70.03N 24.55E
Lakshadweep Is. Indian Oc. 60 11.00N 72.00E
Lala India 63 24.25N 92.40E
Lāla Mūsa Pakistan 62 32.42N 73.58E
Lalaua Mozambique 79 14.20S 38.30E
Lalbenque France 20 44.20N 1.33E
Lālehzār, Kūh-e mtn. Iran 65 29.26N 56.48E
Lālganj India 63 25.52N 85.11E
Lalībela Ethiopia 73 12.02N 39.02E
La Libertad El Salvador 117 13.28N 89.20W
Lalín Spain 26 42.39N 8.07W
Lalinde France 20 44.51N 0.44E
La Línea Spain 27 36.10N 5.19W
Lalitpur India 63 24.41N 78.25E
Lalitpur Nepal 63 27.41N 85.20E
Lālmanir Hāt Bangla. 63 25.54N 89.27E
La Loche Canada 101 56.29N109.27W
La Loche, Lac l. Canada 101 56.25N109.30W
La Loupe France 18 48.28N 1.01E
La Louvière Belgium 16 50.29N 4.11E
Lālpur India 62 22.12N 69.58E
Lālsot India 62 26.34N 76.20E
La Maddalena Italy 32 41.13N 9.24E
Lamar U.S.A. 110 38.05N102.37W
Lamarche France 19 48.04N 5.47E
La Marsa Tunisia 32 36.53N 10.20E
Lamastre France 21 44.59N 4.35E
Lamballe France 18 48.28N 2.31W
Lambaréné Gabon 78 0.40S 10.15E
Lambasa Fiji 84 16.25S179.24E
Lambayeque Peru 122 6.36S 79.50W
Lambay I. Rep. of Ire. 15 53.29N 6.01W
Lambert's Bay town R.S.A. 80 32.06S 18.16E
Lámbia Greece 35 37.52N 21.53E
Lamé Chad 77 9.14N 14.33E
Lame Nigeria 77 10.27N 9.12E
Lamego Portugal 26 41.06N 7.49W
Lameroo Australia 92 35.20S140.33E
La Mesa Calif. U.S.A. 109 32.46N117.01W
Lamesa Tex. U.S.A. 111 32.44N101.57W
Lamía Greece 35 38.54N 22.26E
La Minerve Canada 105 46.15N 74.56W
Lammermuir Hills U.K. 14 55.51N 2.40W
Lammhult Sweden 43 57.10N 14.35E
Lamoille r. U.S.A. 105 44.35N 73.10W
Lamongan Indonesia 59 7.05S112.26E
Lamont U.S.A. 108 42.12N107.28W
La Mothe-Achard France 18 46.37N 1.40W
Lamotrek i. Federated States of Micronesia 59 7.28N146.23E
Lamotte-Beuvron France 19 47.36N 2.01E
La Motte-Chalençon France 21 44.29N 5.23E
La Motte du-Claire France 21 44.21N 6.02E
La Moure U.S.A. 110 46.21N 98.18W
Lampa Peru 122 15.10S 70.30W
Lampasas U.S.A. 111 31.04N 98.12W
Lampazos Mexico 111 27.00N100.30W
Lampedusa i. Italy 28 35.30N 12.35E
Lampertheim Germany 39 49.35N 8.28E
Lampeter U.K. 13 52.06N 4.06W
Lampinoú Greece 34 39.22N 23.10E
Lampione i. Italy 28 35.33N 12.18E
Lamu Kenya 79 2.20S 40.54E
La Mure France 21 44.54N 5.47E
Lana Italy 30 46.37N 11.09E
Lanai i. Hawaiian Is. 85 20.50N156.55W
Lanai City Hawaiian Is. 85 20.50N156.55W
La Nao, Cabo de Spain 24 38.42N 0.15E
Lanark U.K. 14 55.41N 3.47W
La Nava de Ricomalillo Spain 27 39.39N 4.59W
Lancang Jiang r. China see Mekong r. Asia 56
Lancashire d. U.K. 12 53.53N 2.30W
Lancaster Canada 105 45.08N 74.30W
Lancaster U.K. 12 54.03N 2.48W
Lancaster Calif. U.S.A. 109 34.42N118.08W
Lancaster N.H. U.S.A. 105 44.29N 71.34W
Lancaster N.Y. U.S.A. 114 42.54N 78.40W
Lancaster Ohio U.S.A. 114 39.43N 82.36W
Lancaster Penn. U.S.A. 115 40.02N 76.19W
Lancaster S.C. U.S.A. 113 34.43N 80.47W
Lancaster Tex. U.S.A. 111 32.36N 96.46W
Lancaster Sd. Canada 99 74.00N 85.00W
Lancelin Australia 89 31.01S115.19E
Lanchow see Lanzhou China 54
Lanciano Italy 31 42.14N 14.23E
Lancun China 54 36.24N120.10E
Landau Bayern Germany 39 48.40N 12.43E
Landau Rhein.-Pfalz. Germany 39 49.12N 8.07E
Landay Afghan. 62 30.31N 63.47E
Landeck Austria 39 47.08N 10.34E
Landen Belgium 16 50.46N 5.04E
Lander r. Australia 90 20.25S132.00E
Lander U.S.A. 108 42.50N108.44W
Landerneau France 18 48.27N 4.15W
Landes d. France 20 44.20N 1.00W
Landes f. France 20 44.00N 1.00W
Landete Spain 25 39.56N 1.25W
Landisville U.S.A. 115 39.31N 74.55W
Landivisiau France 18 48.31N 4.04W
Landor Australia 88 25.06S116.50E
Landquart Switz. 39 46.58N 9.33E
Landrecies France 19 50.08N 3.42E
Landsberg Germany 39 48.05N 10.55E
Landsbro Sweden 43 57.22N 14.54E
Lands End c. Canada 96 76.10N123.00W
Land's End c. U.K. 13 50.03N 5.45W
Landshut Germany 39 48.33N 12.09E
Landskrona Sweden 43 55.52N 12.50E
Lanett U.S.A. 113 32.52N 85.12W
Langå Denmark 42 56.23N 9.55E
La'nga Co l. China 63 30.45N 81.15E
Langadhás Greece 34 40.45N 23.04E
Langádhia Greece 35 37.41N 22.02E
Langanes c. Iceland 40 66.30N 14.30W
Langao China 54 33.22N109.04E
Långban Sweden 43 59.51N 14.15E
Langdon U.S.A. 110 48.46N 98.22W
Langeac France 20 45.06N 3.30E
Langeais France 18 47.20N 0.24E
L'Ange Gardien Canada 105 46.55N 71.07W
Langeland i. Denmark 42 55.00N 10.50E
Längelmävesi l. Finland 41 61.32N 24.22E
Langen Germany 39 49.59N 8.41E
Längenfeld Austria 39 47.04N 10.58E
Langenhagen Germany 38 52.27N 9.44E
Langenthal Switz. 39 47.13N 7.47E
Langeoog i. Germany 38 53.46N 7.32E
Langesund Norway 42 59.00N 9.45E
Langholm U.K. 14 55.09N 3.00W
Langjökull ice cap Iceland 40 63.43N 20.03W
Langkawi i. Malaysia 58 6.20N 99.30E

Langlade to Lepontine, Alpi

Langlade Canada 102 48.14N 76.00W
Langnau Switz. 39 46.57N 7.47E
Langogne France 20 44.43N 3.51E
Langon France 20 44.33N 0.15W
Langöy i. Norway 40 68.45N 15.00E
Langres France 19 47.52N 5.20E
Langres, Plateau de f. France 19 47.41N 5.03E
Langsa Indonesia 58 4.28N 97.59E
Langshan China 54 41.02N107.27E
Lang Shan mts. China 54 41.30N107.10E
Lang Son Vietnam 55 21.49N106.45E
Langtry U.S.A. 111 29.48N101.34W
Languedoc-Roussillon d. France 20 43.50N 3.30E
Langxi China 55 31.08N119.10E
Laniel Canada 104 47.04N 79.18W
Lannemezan France 20 43.08N 0.23E
Lannilis France 18 48.34N 4.31W
Lannion France 18 48.44N 3.28W
L'Annonciation Canada 105 46.25N 74.52W
Lanoraie Canada 105 45.58N 73.13W
Lansdale U.S.A. 115 40.15N 75.17W
Lansdowne India 63 29.50N 78.41E
L'Anse au Loup Canada 103 51.34N 56.48W
Lansing U.S.A. 112 42.44N 84.34W
Lanslebourg France 21 45.17N 6.52E
Lantewa Nigeria 77 12.15N 11.45E
Lanusei Italy 32 39.52N 9.34E
Lanxi China 55 29.17N119.31E
Lanzarote i. Canary Is. 74 29.00N 13.40W
Lanzhou China 54 36.01N103.46E
Lanzo Torinese Italy 30 45.16N 7.28E
Laoag Phil. 59 18.14N120.36E
Lào Cai Vietnam 56 22.30N104.00E
Laochang China 55 25.12N104.35E
Laoha He r. China 54 43.30N120.42E
Laohekou China 54 32.26N111.41E
Laois d. Rep. of Ire. 15 53.00N 7.20W
Laojun Shan mtn. China 54 33.45N111.38E
Laon France 19 49.34N 3.40E
Laona U.S.A. 102 45.35N 88.40W
La Orotava Canary Is. 127 28.26N 16.30W
La Oroya Peru 122 11.36S 75.54W
Laos Asia 56 18.30N104.00E
Lapalisse France 20 46.15N 3.38E
La Palma i. Canary Is. 74 28.50N 18.00W
La Palma Spain 27 37.23N 6.33W
La Pampa d. Argentina 125 37.00S 66.00W
La Paragua Venezuela 122 6.53N 63.22W
La Paz Entre Ríos Argentina 125 30.45S 59.38W
La Paz Mendoza Argentina 125 33.28S 67.34W
La Paz Bolivia 124 16.30S 68.09W
La Paz d. Bolivia 124 16.00S 68.10W
La Paz Mexico 109 24.10N110.18W
La Paz, Bahía de b. Mexico 109 24.15N110.30W
La Pedrera Colombia 122 1.18S 69.43W
Lapeer U.S.A. 104 43.03N 83.19W
La Peña, Sierra de mts. Spain 24 42.30N 0.50W
La Perouse Str. Russian Fed. 51 45.50N142.30E
La Pine U.S.A. 108 43.40N121.30W
Lapinjärvi Finland 41 60.38N 26.13E
Lapland f. Sweden/Finland 40 68.10N 24.10E
La Plata Argentina 125 34.55S 57.57W
La Plata Md. U.S.A. 114 38.32N 76.59W
La Plata Mo. U.S.A. 110 40.02N 92.29W
La Plata, Río de est. Argentina/Uruguay 125 35.15S 56.45W
Lapointe, Lac l. Canada 103 53.32N 68.56W
Laporte U.S.A. 115 41.25N 76.30W
Lappajärvi l. Finland 40 63.08N 23.40E
Lappeenranta Finland 44 61.04N 28.05E
Lappi d. Finland 40 67.20N 26.00E
Laptevykh, More sea Russian Fed. 51 74.30N125.00E
Lapua Finland 40 62.57N 23.00E
La Puebla Spain 25 39.46N 3.01E
La Puebla de Cazalla Spain 27 37.14N 5.19W
La Puebla de Montalbán Spain 27 39.52N 4.21W
La Push U.S.A. 108 47.55N124.38W
La Quiaca Argentina 124 22.05S 65.36W
L'Aquila Italy 30 42.22N 13.22E
Lār Iran 65 27.37N 54.16E
Lara Australia 92 38.01S144.26E
Laracha Spain 26 43.15N 8.35W
Larache Morocco 74 35.12N 6.10W
Laragne-Montéglin France 21 44.19N 5.49E
La Rambla Spain 27 37.36N 4.44W
Laramie U.S.A. 108 41.19N105.35W
Laramie Mts. U.S.A. 108 42.00N105.40W
L'Arbresle France 21 45.50N 4.37E
Lärbro Sweden 43 57.47N 18.47E
Larche, Col de pass France/Italy 21 44.25N 6.53E
Laredo Spain 26 43.24N 3.25W
Laredo U.S.A. 111 27.31N 99.30W
Laredo Sd. Canada 100 52.30N128.53W
La Réole France 20 44.35N 0.02E
Largeau Chad 77 17.55N 19.07E
L'Argentière-la-Bessée France 21 44.47N 6.33E
Largs U.K. 14 55.48N 4.52W
Lariang Indonesia 58 1.35S119.25E
Lárimna Greece 35 38.34N 23.17E
Larino Italy 33 41.48N 14.54E
La Rioja Argentina 124 29.25S 66.50W
La Rioja d. Argentina 124 29.00S 66.00W
La Rioja d. Spain 26 42.25N 2.30W
Lárisa Greece 34 39.38N 22.28E
Lark r. U.K. 13 52.26N 0.20E
Lārkāna Pakistan 62 27.33N 68.13E
Larkspur U.S.A. 108 39.13N104.54W
Larnaca see Lárnax Cyprus 66
Lárnax Cyprus 66 34.54N 33.39E
Larne U.K. 15 54.51N 5.49W
La Robla Spain 26 42.48N 5.37W
La Roca de la Sierra Spain 27 39.07N 6.41W
La Roche Belgium 16 50.11N 5.35E
La Roche-Bernard France 18 47.31N 2.18W
La Rochelle France 20 46.10N 1.10W
La Roche-sur-Yon France 18 46.40N 1.26W
La Roda Spain 27 39.13N 2.09W
La Romana Dom. Rep. 117 18.27N 68.57W
La Ronge Canada 101 55.06N105.17W
La Ronge, Lac l. Canada 98 55.07N105.15W
Laroquebrou France 20 44.58N 2.11E
Larrimah Australia 90 15.35S133.12E
Larvik Norway 42 59.04N 10.00E
La Sagra mtn. Spain 27 37.57N 2.34W
La Salle U.S.A. 110 41.20N 89.06W
Las Animas U.S.A. 108 38.04N103.13W
La Sarre Canada 102 48.45N 79.15W
Las Cabezas de San Juan Spain 27 36.59N 5.56W
Las Casitas, Cerro mtn. Mexico 109 23.32N109.59W
L'Ascension Canada 105 46.33N 74.50W
Las Cruces U.S.A. 109 32.23N106.29W
Las Cuevas Mexico 111 29.38N101.19W
La Seine, Baie de France 17 49.40N 0.30W
La Serena Chile 124 29.54S 71.16W
La Seu d'Urgell Spain 25 42.22N 1.23E
La Seyne France 21 43.06N 5.53E
Las Flores Argentina 125 36.02S 59.07W
Lāsh-e Joveyn Afghan. 62 31.43N 61.37E
Las Heras Argentina 125 32.50S 68.50W
Lashio Burma 56 22.58N 96.51E
Lashkar Gāh Afghan. 62 31.30N 64.21E
Laško Slovenia 31 46.09N 15.14E
Las Lomitas Argentina 124 24.43S 60.35W
Las Marismas f. Spain 27 37.05N 6.20W
La Solana Spain 26 38.56N 3.14W
L'Asomption r. Canada 105 45.43N 73.29W
Las Palmas de Gran Canaria Canary Is. 74 28.08N 15.27W
Las Palomas Mexico 109 31.44N107.37W
Las Perlas, Archipelago de Panama 117 8.45N 79.30W
La Spezia Italy 30 44.07N 9.50E
Las Piedras Uruguay 125 34.44S 56.13W
Las Plumas Argentina 125 43.40S 67.15W
Lassay France 18 48.26N 0.30W
Lassen Peak mtn. U.S.A. 108 40.29N121.31W
L'Assomption Canada 105 45.50N 73.25W
Last Chance U.S.A. 108 39.45N103.36W
Last Mountain L. Canada 101 51.05N105.10W
Lastoursville Gabon 78 0.50S 12.47E
Lastovo i. Croatia 31 42.45N 16.53E
Lastovski Kanal str. Croatia 31 42.50N 16.59E
Las Tres Vírgenes, Volcán mtn. Mexico 109 27.27N112.37W
Lastrup Germany 38 52.48N 7.52E
La Suze France 18 47.54N 0.02E
Las Vegas Nev. U.S.A. 109 36.11N115.08W
Las Vegas N.Mex. U.S.A. 109 35.36N105.13W
Latacunga Ecuador 122 0.58S 78.36W
La Tagua Colombia 122 0.03S 74.40W
Latakia see Al Lādhiqīyah Syria 66
Latambar Pakistan 62 33.07N 70.52E
Latchford Canada 104 47.20N 79.48W
Late i. Tonga 85 18.49S174.40W
Lātēhar India 63 23.45N 84.30E
La Teste-de-Buch France 20 44.38N 1.09W
Lathen Germany 38 52.52N 7.19E
Lāthi India 62 21.43N 71.23E
Latina Italy 32 41.28N 12.52E
Latisana Italy 30 45.47N 13.00E
La Tortuga i. Venezuela 122 11.00N 65.20W
La Tour-d'Auvergne France 20 45.32N 2.41E
La Tour-du-Pin France 21 45.34N 5.27E
La Tremblade France 20 45.46N 1.08W
La Trimouille France 18 46.28N 1.02E
Latrobe U.S.A. 114 40.19N 79.23W
La Trobe, Mt. Australia 93 39.03S146.25E
La Truite, Lac à l. Canada 104 47.16N 78.17W
Laṭrūn Jordan 67 31.50N 34.59E
La Tuque Canada 103 47.27N 72.47W
Latvia Europe 44 56.45N 25.00E
Lau Nigeria 77 9.14N 11.15E
Lauchhammer Germany 38 51.30N 13.47E
Lauenburg Germany 38 53.22N 10.33E
Lauf an der Pegnitz Germany 38 49.30N 11.17E
Laughlen, Mt. Australia 90 23.23S134.23E
Lau Group is. Fiji 84 19.00S178.30W
Launceston Australia 91 41.25S147.07E
Launceston U.K. 13 50.38N 4.21W
La Unión Chile 125 40.15S 73.02W
La Unión Spain 25 37.37N 0.52W
Laupheim Germany 39 48.14N 9.52E
Laura Australia 92 33.08S138.19E
La Urbana Venezuela 122 7.08N 66.56W
Laureana di Borrello Italy 33 38.30N 16.05E
Laurel Del. U.S.A. 115 38.33N 75.34W
Laurel Miss. U.S.A. 111 31.42N 89.08W
Laurel Mont. U.S.A. 108 45.40N108.46W
Laurel Hill mtn. U.S.A. 114 40.02N 79.17W
Laurel Ridge mtn. U.S.A. 114 39.20N 79.53W
Laurelville U.S.A. 114 39.28N 82.44W
Laurencekirk U.K. 14 56.50N 2.29W
Laurens U.S.A. 113 34.29N 82.01W
Laurentians mts. Canada 105 45.43N 75.52W
Laurentides mts. Canada 105 46.25N 73.28W
Laurentides Prov. Park Canada 103 47.30N 71.30W
Lauria Italy 33 40.02N 15.50E
Laurier Canada 105 46.32N 71.38W
Laurière France 20 46.05N 1.28E
Laurieton Australia 93 31.38S152.46E
Laurinburg U.S.A. 113 34.46N 79.29W
Lauro, Monte mtn. Italy 33 37.08N 14.47E
Lausanne Switz. 39 46.31N 6.38E
Laut i. Indonesia 58 3.45S116.20E
Lauta Germany 38 51.27N 14.04E
Lautaro Chile 125 38.31S 72.27W
Lauterbach Germany 38 50.38N 9.24E
Lauterbrunnen Switz. 39 46.36N 7.55E
Lauterecken Germany 39 49.39N 7.35E
Lautoka Fiji 84 17.37S177.27E
Lauzerte France 20 44.15N 1.08E
Lauzon Canada 105 46.50N 71.10W
Lauzun France 20 44.38N 0.28E
Lavagh More mtn. Rep. of Ire. 15 54.45N 8.07W
Lava Hot Springs town U.S.A. 108 42.37N112.01W
Laval Canada 105 45.35N 73.45W
Laval France 18 48.04N 0.46W
Lávara Greece 34 41.19N 26.22E
Lavardac France 20 44.11N 0.18E
La Vecilla de Curueño Spain 26 42.51N 5.24W
La Vega Dom. Rep. 117 19.15N 70.33W
La Vela Venezuela 122 11.27N 69.34W
Lavelanet France 20 42.56N 1.51E
Lavello Italy 33 41.03N 15.48E
La Verendrye Prov. Park Canada 105 47.30N 77.30W
Laverlochère Canada 104 47.26N 79.19W
Laverne U.S.A. 111 36.43N 99.54W
Laverton Australia 89 28.49S122.25E
Lavi Israel 67 32.47N 35.26E
Lavia Finland 41 61.36N 22.36E
Lavielle, L. Canada 104 45.51N 78.14W
Lavigne Canada 104 46.20N 80.05W
Lavik Norway 41 61.06N 5.30E
La Voulte-sur-Rhône France 21 44.48N 4.47E
Lavras Brazil 126 21.15S 44.59W
Lávrion Greece 35 37.44N 24.04E
Lawra Ghana 76 10.40N 2.49W
Lawrence New Zealand 86 45.55S169.42E
Lawrence Kans. U.S.A. 110 38.58N 95.14W
Lawrence Mass. U.S.A. 115 42.42N 71.09W
Lawrenceburg U.S.A. 113 35.16N 87.20W
Lawrenceville Canada 105 45.25N 72.19W
Lawrenceville Penn. U.S.A. 114 42.00N 77.08W
Lawton Okla. U.S.A. 111 34.37N 98.25W
Lawton Penn. U.S.A. 115 41.46N 76.05W
Lawz, Jabal al mtn. Saudi Arabia 66 28.40N 35.20E
Laxå Sweden 43 58.59N 14.37E
Lay r. France 18 46.20N 1.18W
Laysan i. Hawaiian Is. 84 25.46N171.44W
Laytonville U.S.A. 108 39.41N123.29W
Lazio d. Italy 30 42.05N 12.20E
Lead U.S.A. 110 44.21N103.46W
Leader Canada 101 50.53N109.31W
Leadhills U.K. 14 55.25N 3.46W
Leamington Canada 104 42.03N 82.36W
Leamington U.S.A. 108 39.31N112.17W
Learmonth Australia 88 22.13S114.04E
Leavenworth U.S.A. 110 39.19N 94.55W
Lebak Phil. 59 6.32N124.03E
Lebane Yugo. 34 42.56N 21.44E
Lebango Congo 78 0.24N 14.44E
Lebanon Asia 66 34.00N 36.00E
Lebanon Ind. U.S.A. 112 40.02N 87.28W
Lebanon Kans. U.S.A. 110 39.49N 98.33W
Lebanon Ky. U.S.A. 113 37.33N 85.15W
Lebanon Mo. U.S.A. 111 37.41N 92.40W
Lebanon N.H. U.S.A. 115 43.38N 72.15W
Lebanon Oreg. U.S.A. 108 44.32N122.54W
Lebanon Penn. U.S.A. 115 40.20N 76.25W
Lebanon Tenn. U.S.A. 113 36.11N 86.19W
Lebec U.S.A. 109 34.50N118.52W
Lebesby Norway 40 70.34N 27.00E
Le Blanc France 18 46.38N 1.04E
Lebork Poland 37 54.33N 17.44E
Le Bourg-d'Oisans France 21 45.03N 6.02E
Lebrija Spain 27 36.55N 6.04W
Lebu Chile 125 37.37S 73.39W
Le Bugue France 20 44.55N 0.56E
Le Cannet France 21 43.34N 7.01E
Le Cateau France 19 50.06N 3.33E
Le Catelet France 19 50.00N 3.15E
Lecce Italy 33 40.23N 18.11E
Lecco Italy 30 45.51N 9.23E
Lech r. Germany 39 48.44N 10.56E
Lechang China 55 25.08N113.20E
Le Château d'Oléron France 20 45.53N 1.11W
Le Châtelet France 19 46.39N 2.17E
Le Chesne France 19 49.31N 4.46E
Le Cheylard France 21 44.54N 4.25E
Lechiguanas, Islas de las is. Argentina 125 33.26S 59.42W
Lechtaler Alpen mts. Austria 39 47.15N 10.33E
Le Conquet France 18 48.22N 4.46W
L'Écorce, Lac de l. Canada 105 47.05N 76.24W
Le Creusot France 19 46.48N 4.26E
Le Croisic France 18 47.18N 2.31W
Lectoure France 20 43.56N 0.38E
Ledbury U.K. 13 52.03N 2.25W
Ledesma Spain 26 41.05N 6.00W
Le Donjon France 20 46.21N 3.48E
Le Dorat France 20 46.13N 1.05E
Leduc Canada 100 53.20N113.30W
Lee r. Rep. of Ire. 15 51.53N 8.25W
Lee U.S.A. 115 42.19N 73.15W
Leechburg U.S.A. 114 40.38N 79.36W
Leech L. U.S.A. 110 47.09N 94.23W
Leedey U.S.A. 111 35.52N 99.21W
Leeds Canada 105 46.16N 71.22W
Leeds U.K. 12 53.48N 1.34W
Leeds U.S.A. 113 33.32N 86.31W
Leek U.K. 12 53.07N 2.02W
Leer Germany 38 53.14N 7.26E
Leesburg Fla. U.S.A. 113 28.49N 81.54W
Leesburg Va. U.S.A. 114 39.07N 77.34W
Leeston New Zealand 86 43.46S172.18E
Leeton Australia 93 34.33S146.24E
Leeuwarden Neth. 16 53.12N 5.48E
Leeuwin, C. Australia 89 34.22S115.08E
Leeward Is. C. America 117 18.00N 61.00W
Lefroy, L. Australia 89 31.15S121.40E
Legazpi Phil. 59 13.10N123.45E
Legges Tor mtn. Australia 91 41.32S147.40E
Legget U.S.A. 108 39.52N123.34W
Leghorn see Livorno Italy 30
Legion Mine Zimbabwe 80 21.23S 28.33E
Legionowo Poland 37 52.25N 20.56E
Legnago Italy 30 45.11N 11.18E
Legnano Italy 30 45.36N 8.54E
Legnica Poland 36 51.12N 16.10E
Le Grand-Lucé France 18 47.52N 0.28E
Le Grand-Quevilly France 18 49.25N 1.02E
Le Grau-du-Roi France 21 43.32N 4.08E
Leh Jammu & Kashmir 63 34.10N 77.35E
Le Havre France 18 49.30N 0.08E
Lehighton U.S.A. 115 40.49N 75.45W
Lehrte Germany 38 52.22N 9.59E
Lehututu Botswana 80 23.54S 21.52E
Leiah Pakistan 62 30.58N 70.56E
Leibnitz Austria 31 46.48N 15.32E
Leicester U.K. 13 52.39N 1.09W
Leicestershire d. U.K. 13 52.29N 1.10W
Leichardt r. Australia 90 17.35S139.48E
Leiden Neth. 16 52.10N 4.30E
Leie r. Belgium 16 51.03N 3.44E
Leifeng China 55 25.35N118.17E
Leigh Creek r. Australia 92 29.49S138.10E
Leigh Creek town Australia 92 30.31S138.25E
Leighton Buzzard U.K. 13 51.55N 0.39W
Leikanger Norway 41 61.10N 6.52E
Leine Germany 38 52.41N 9.36E
Leinster Australia 89 27.59S120.30E
Leipzig Germany 38 51.19N 12.20E
Leiria Portugal 27 39.45N 8.48W
Leiria d. Portugal 27 39.50N 8.50W
Leirvik Norway 42 59.45N 5.30E
Lei Shui r. China 55 26.57N112.33E
Leithbridge Canada 100 49.40N112.45W
Leitrim d. Rep. of Ire. 15 54.08N 8.00W
Leiyang China 55 26.30N112.42E
Leizhou Bandao pen. China 55 21.00N110.00E
Lek r. Neth. 16 51.55N 4.29E
Lekhainá Greece 35 37.56N 21.17E
Leksvik Norway 40 63.40N 10.40E
Leland U.S.A. 111 33.24N 90.54W
Leland Lakes Canada 101 60.00N110.59W
Lelång l. Sweden 43 59.08N 12.10E
Lelchitsy Belorussia 37 51.48N 28.20E
Leleque Argentina 125 42.24S 71.04W
Leling China 54 37.45N117.13E
Le Lion-d'Angers France 18 47.38N 0.43W
Le Locle Switz. 39 47.03N 6.45E
Le Lude France 18 47.39N 0.09E
Lelystad Neth. 16 52.32N 5.29E
Le Madonie Italy 33 37.55N 14.00E
Léman, Lac l. Switz. 39 46.25N 6.30E
Le Mans France 18 48.00N 0.12E
Le Mars U.S.A. 110 42.47N 96.10W
Le Mayet-de-Montagne France 20 46.05N 3.40E
Leme Brazil 126 22.10S 47.23W
Le Merlerault France 18 48.42N 0.18E
Lemesós Cyprus 66 34.40N 33.03E
Lemgo Germany 38 52.02N 8.54E
Lemhi Range mts. U.S.A. 108 44.30N113.25W
Lemland i. Finland 43 60.03N 20.10E
Lemmer Neth. 16 52.50N 5.43E
Lemmon U.S.A. 110 45.56N102.10W
Le Monastier France 20 44.56N 4.00E
Le Montet France 20 46.25N 3.03E
Lemsid W. Sahara 74 26.32N 13.49W
Lemvig Denmark 42 56.32N 8.18E
Lena r. Russian Fed. 51 72.00N127.10E
Lena U.S.A. 111 31.47N 92.48W
Lenakel Vanuatu 84 19.32S169.16E
Lenart Slovenia 31 46.35N 15.50E
Lencloître France 18 46.49N 0.20E
Lendery Russian Fed. 44 63.24N 31.04E
Lendinara Italy 30 45.05N 11.36E
Lengerich Germany 38 52.11N 7.50E
Lengoue r. Congo 78 1.15S 16.42E
Lenhovda Sweden 43 57.00N 15.17E
Lenina, Kanal canal Russian Fed. 45 43.46N 45.00E
Lenina, Pik mtn. Tajikistan 52 40.14N 69.40E
Leningrad see Sankt-Peterburg Russian Fed. 44
Leninogorsk Kazakhstan 50 50.23N 83.32E
Leninsk Russian Fed. 45 48.42N 45.14E
Leninsk Kuznetskiy Russian Fed. 50 54.44N 86.13E
Lenk Switz. 39 46.28N 7.27E
Lenkoran Azerbaijan 65 38.45N 48.50E
Lenmalu Indonesia 59 1.58S130.00E
Lenne r. Germany 38 51.25N 7.30E
Lennoxville Canada 105 45.22N 71.51W
Lenoir U.S.A. 113 35.56N 81.31W
Lenora Czech Republic 38 48.56N 13.48E
Lenora U.S.A. 110 39.38N100.03W
Lenore L. Canada 101 52.30N105.00W
Lenox U.S.A. 115 42.22N 73.17W
Lens France 19 50.26N 2.50E
Lenti Hungary 31 46.37N 16.33E
Lentini Italy 33 37.17N 15.00E
Lenvik Norway 40 69.22N 18.10E
Léo Burkina 76 11.05N 2.06W
Leoben Austria 36 47.23N 15.06E
Leominster U.K. 13 52.15N 2.43W
Leominster U.S.A. 115 42.32N 71.45W
Léon France 20 43.53N 1.18W
León Mexico 116 21.10N101.42W
León d. Mexico 111 25.00N100.20W
León Nicaragua 117 12.24N 86.52W
León Spain 26 42.36N 5.34W
Leon U.S.A. 110 40.44N 93.45W
León, Montes de mts. Spain 26 42.30N 6.15W
Leonardtown U.S.A. 115 38.17N 76.38W
Leonardville Namibia 80 23.31S 18.47E
Leonárison Cyprus 66 35.28N 34.08E
Leonberg Germany 39 48.48N 9.01E
Leondári Greece 35 39.11N 22.08E
Leonforte Italy 33 37.39N 14.24E
Leongatha Australia 93 38.29S145.57E
Leonídhion Greece 35 37.10N 22.52E
Leonora Australia 89 28.54S121.20E
Leopoldina Brazil 126 21.30S 42.38W
Leopoldsburg Belgium 16 51.08N 5.13E
Leovo Moldavia 37 46.29N 28.12E
Le Palais France 18 47.21N 3.09W
Lepe Spain 27 37.15N 7.12W
Lepel Russian Fed. 44 54.48N 28.40E
Le Pellerin France 18 47.12N 1.45W
Leping China 55 28.58N117.08E
L'Epiphanie Canada 105 45.51N 73.30W
Le Pont-de-Beauvoisin France 21 45.32N 5.40E
Lepontine, Alpi mts. Switz. 39 46.20N 8.37E

Le Puy to Livno

Le Puy France 20 45.02N 3.53E
Lequeitio Spain 26 43.22N 2.30W
Le Quesnoy France 19 50.15N 3.38E
Lerbäck Sweden 43 58.56N 15.02E
Lercara Friddi Italy 32 37.45N 13.36E
Léré Chad 77 9.41N 14.17E
Lerici Italy 30 44.04N 9.55E
Lérida Spain 25 41.37N 0.37E
Lérida see Lleida Spain 25
Lérida see Lleida d. Spain 25
Lerma Spain 26 42.02N 3.45W
Le Rochefoucauld France 20 45.45N 0.23E
Léros Greece 35 37.10N 26.50E
Leross Canada 101 51.17N103.53W
Le Roy Kans. U.S.A. 111 38.05N 95.38W
Le Roy Mich. U.S.A. 112 44.03N 85.29W
Le Roy N.Y. U.S.A. 114 42.59N 77.59W
Lerwick U.K. 14 60.09N 1.09W
Les Aix-d'Angillon France 19 47.12N 2.34E
Les Andelys France 18 49.15N 1.25E
Les Borges Blanques Spain 25 41.31N 0.52E
Les Cayes Haiti 117 18.15N 73.46W
Leschenault, C. Australia 89 31.50S115.23E
Les Échelles France 21 45.26N 5.45E
Les Ecrins mtn. France 21 44.50N 6.20E
Les Essarts France 18 46.46N 1.14W
Lesh Albania 34 41.46N 19.39E
Leshan China 55 29.30N103.45E
Les Herbiers France 18 46.52N 1.01W
Leshukonskoye Russian Fed. 44 64.55N 45.50E
Lesina, Lago di l. Italy 31 41.53N 15.26E
Lesjaskog Norway 41 62.15N 8.22E
Lesjöfors Sweden 43 59.59N 14.11E
Leskovac Yugo. 34 42.59N 21.57E
Leslie Ark. U.S.A. 111 35.50N 92.34W
Leslie Mich. U.S.A. 104 42.27N 84.26W
Lešnica Yugo. 31 44.39N 19.19E
Lesotho Africa 80 29.00S 28.00E
Lesozavodsk Russian Fed. 53 45.30N133.29E
Les Pieux France 18 49.31N 1.48W
Les Riceys France 19 47.59N 4.22E
Les Sables d'Olonne France 18 46.30N 1.47W
Lessay France 18 49.13N 1.32W
Lessebo Sweden 43 56.45N 15.16E
Lesser Antilles is. C. America 117 13.00N 65.00W
Lesser Slave L. Canada 100 55.30N115.25W
Lesser Sunda Is. see Nusa Tenggara is. Indonesia 58
Lessines Belgium 16 50.43N 3.50E
Lesti r. Finland 40 64.04N 23.38E
Le Sueur U.S.A. 110 44.27N 93.54W
Les Vans France 21 44.24N 4.08E
Lésvos i. Greece 35 39.10N 25.50E
Leszno Poland 36 51.51N 16.35E
Letchworth U.K. 13 51.58N 0.13W
Letchworth State Park U.S.A. 114 42.42N 77.56W
Letenye Hungary 31 46.26N 16.43E
Lethbridge Canada 98 49.43N112.48W
Lethem Guyana 122 3.18N 59.46W
Le Thillot France 19 47.53N 6.46E
Leti, Kepulauan is. Indonesia 59 8.20S128.00E
Letiahau r. Botswana 80 21.16S 24.00E
Leticia Colombia 122 4.09S 69.57W
Leting China 54 39.26N118.56E
Letohatchee U.S.A. 113 32.08N 86.30W
Le Trayas France 21 43.28N 6.55E
Le Tréport France 18 50.04N 1.22E
Letterkenny Rep. of Ire. 15 54.56N 7.45W
Leucate, Étang de b. France 20 42.51N 3.00E
Leuk Switz. 39 46.19N 7.38E
Leuser mtn. Indonesia 58 3.50N 97.10E
Leutkirch Germany 39 47.49N 10.01E
Leuven Belgium 16 50.53N 4.45E
Leuze Hainaut Belgium 16 50.36N 3.37E
Leuze Namur Belgium 16 50.34N 4.53E
Levack Canada 104 46.38N 81.23W
Levádhia Greece 35 38.27N 22.54E
Levanger Norway 40 63.45N 11.19E
Levanto Italy 30 44.10N 9.38E
Levanzo, Isola di i. Italy 32 38.00N 12.20E
Levelland U.S.A. 111 33.35N102.23W
Lévêque, C. Australia 88 16.25S123.00E
Le Verdon France 20 45.33N 1.04W
Leverkusen Germany 38 51.03N 6.59E
Levice Slovakia 37 48.13N 18.37E
Levier France 19 46.57N 6.08E
Levin New Zealand 86 40.37S175.18E
Lévis Canada 105 46.48N 71.11W
Levittown U.S.A. 115 40.41N 73.31W
Lévka Cyprus 66 35.06N 32.51E
Lévka Óri mtn. Greece 35 35.18N 24.01E
Levkás Greece 35 38.48N 20.43E
Levkás i. Greece 35 38.39N 20.27E
Levkimni Greece 34 39.25N 20.04E
Levkosía Cyprus 66 35.11N 33.23E
Levroux France 19 46.59N 1.37E
Levski Bulgaria 34 43.21N 25.10E
Lewes U.K. 13 50.53N 0.02E
Lewes U.S.A. 115 38.47N 75.08W
Lewis i. U.K. 14 58.10N 6.40W
Lewisburg U.S.A. 114 40.58N 76.53W
Lewis Pass f. New Zealand 86 42.30S172.15E
Lewisporte Canada 103 49.15N 55.04W
Lewis Range mts. U.S.A. 108 48.30N113.15W
Lewiston Idaho U.S.A. 108 46.25N117.01W
Lewiston Maine U.S.A. 112 44.06N 70.13W
Lewiston Mich. U.S.A. 104 44.53N 84.18W
Lewistown Mont. U.S.A. 108 47.04N109.26W
Lewistown Penn. U.S.A. 114 40.36N 77.31W
Lexington Ky. U.S.A. 113 38.03N 84.30W
Lexington Mich. U.S.A. 114 43.16N 82.32W
Lexington Miss. U.S.A. 111 33.07N 90.03W
Lexington Nebr. U.S.A. 110 40.47N 99.45W
Lexington Oreg. U.S.A. 108 45.27N119.41W
Leyburn U.K. 12 54.19N 1.50W
Leydsdorp R.S.A. 80 23.59S 30.32E
Leyre r. France 20 44.39N 1.01W
Leyte i. Phil. 59 10.40N124.50E
Lezignan France 20 43.12N 2.46E
Lhari China 63 30.47N 93.24E
Lhasa China 63 29.39N 91.06E
Lhasa He r. China 63 29.21N 90.45E
Lhazê China 63 29.10N 87.45E
Lhazhong China 63 32.02N 86.34E
Lhokseumawe Indonesia 58 5.09N 97.09E
Lhozhag China 63 28.23N 90.49E
Lhuntsi Dzong Bhutan 63 27.39N 91.09E
Lhünzê China 63 28.26N 92.27E
Lhünzhub China 63 30.00N 91.12E
Li Thailand 56 17.50N 98.55E
Liancheng China 55 25.47N116.48E
Liangcheng China 54 40.31N112.29E
Liangdang China 54 33.59N106.23E
Lianjiang Fujian China 55 26.10N119.33E
Lianjiang Guangdong China 55 21.33N110.19E
Lianshan China 55 24.37N112.02E
Lianshui China 54 33.46N119.18E
Lian Xian China 55 24.52N112.27E
Lianyungang China 54 34.36N119.10E
Liaocheng China 54 36.25N115.58E
Liaodong Bandao pen. China 54 40.00N122.20E
Liaodong Wan b. China 54 40.00N121.00E
Liao He r. China 54 40.40N122.20E
Liaoning d. China 54 41.40N121.20E
Liaoyang China 54 41.17N123.13E
Liaoyuan China 54 42.50N125.08E
Liapádhes Greece 34 39.40N 19.44E
Liard r. Canada 100 61.51N121.18W
Liāri Pakistan 62 25.41N 66.29E
Liart France 19 49.46N 4.20E
Libby U.S.A. 108 48.23N115.33W
Libenge Zaïre 78 3.39N 18.39E
Liberal U.S.A. 111 37.02N100.55W
Liberdade Brazil 126 22.01S 44.22W
Liberec Czech Republic 36 50.48N 15.05E
Liberia Africa 76 6.30N 9.30W
Liberia Costa Rica 117 10.39N 85.28W
Liberty N.Y. U.S.A. 115 41.48N 74.45W
Liberty Tex. U.S.A. 111 30.03N 94.47W
Lībīyah, Aş Şahrā' al des. Africa 64 24.00N 25.30E
Libo China 55 25.25N107.53E
Libourne France 20 44.55N 0.14W
Libramont Belgium 16 49.56N 5.22E
Librazhd Albania 34 41.12N 20.22E
Libreville Gabon 78 0.25N 9.30E
Libya Africa 75 26.30N 17.00E
Libyan Desert see Lībīyah, Aş Şahrā' al a-' al Africa 64
Libyan Plateau see Aḑ Ḑiffah f. Africa 64
Licantén Chile 125 34.59S 72.00W
Licata Italy 32 37.05N 13.56E
Lich Germany 38 50.33N 8.50E
Lichfield U.K. 13 52.40N 1.50W
Lichinga Mozambique 79 13.09S 35.17E
Lichtenburg R.S.A. 80 26.08S 26.09E
Lichtenfels Germany 38 50.09N 11.04E
Lichtenvoorde Neth. 16 51.59N 6.32E
Lichuan Hubei China 55 30.18N108.51E
Lichuan Jiangxi China 55 27.22N116.59E
Lickdale U.S.A. 115 40.28N 76.31W
Lickershamn Sweden 43 57.50N 18.31E
Licko Polje f. Croatia 31 44.35N 15.25E
Lida Belorussia 37 53.50N 25.19E
Lida U.S.A. 108 37.29N117.29W
Lidan r. Sweden 43 58.31N 13.09E
Lidhorikion Greece 35 38.28N 22.12E
Lidingö Sweden 43 59.22N 18.08E
Lidköping Sweden 43 58.30N 13.10E
Liechtenstein Europe 39 47.09N 9.32E
Liège Belgium 16 50.38N 5.35E
Liège d. Belgium 16 50.32N 5.35E
Lien-Huong Vietnam 56 11.13N108.48E
Lienz Austria 30 46.50N 12.47E
Liepāja Latvia 41 56.31N 21.01E
Lier Belgium 16 51.08N 4.35E
Lierneux Belgium 16 50.18N 5.50E
Liestal Switz. 39 47.29N 7.44E
Lieşti Romania 37 45.38N 27.32E
Lietariegos, Puerto de pass Spain 26 43.00N 6.25W
Liévin France 19 50.25N 2.46E
Lièvre, Rivière du r. Canada 105 45.31N 75.26W
Liffey r. Rep. of Ire. 15 53.21N 6.14W
Liffré France 18 48.13N 1.30W
Lifjell mtn. Norway 42 59.30N 8.52E
Lifou, Île i. N. Cal. 84 20.53S167.13E
Lightning Ridge town Australia 93 29.27S148.00E
Lignières France 19 46.45N 2.11E
Ligny-en-Barrois France 19 48.41N 5.20E
Ligoúrion Greece 35 37.37N 23.02E
Ligueil France 18 47.03N 0.49E
Liguria d. Italy 30 44.30N 8.50E
Ligurian Sea Med. Sea 30 43.40N 9.00E
Lihou Reef and Cays Australia 90 17.25S151.40E
Lihue Hawaiian Is. 85 21.59N159.23W
Lihula Estonia 41 58.41N 23.50E
Lijiang China 61 26.50N100.15E
Lijin China 54 37.29N118.16E
Likasi Zaïre 78 10.58S 26.50E
Likati Zaïre 78 3.21N 23.53E
Liknes Norway 42 58.19N 6.59E
Likona r. Congo 78 0.11N 16.25E
Likouala r. Congo 78 0.51S 17.17E
Liku Niue 84 19.03S169.48W
L'Île Bouchard France 18 47.07N 0.25E
L'Île Rousse France 21 42.38N 8.56E
Lilla Edet Sweden 43 58.08N 12.08E
Lille France 19 50.38N 3.04E
Lille Baelt str. Denmark 42 55.20N 9.45E
Lillebonne France 18 49.31N 0.33E
Lillehammer Norway 41 61.08N 10.30E
Lillers France 19 50.34N 2.29E
Lillesand Norway 42 58.15N 8.24E
Lilleström Norway 42 59.57N 11.05E
Lillhärdal Sweden 41 61.51N 14.04E
Lillo Spain 27 39.43N 3.18W
Lillooet Canada 100 50.42N121.56W
Lillooet r. Canada 100 49.15N121.57W
Lilongwe Malaŵi 79 13.58S 33.49E
Liloy Phil. 59 8.08N122.40E
Lilydale Australia 92 32.58S139.59E
Lim r. Bosnia-Herzegovina 31 43.45N 19.13E
Lima Peru 122 12.06S 77.03W
Lima r. Portugal 26 41.41N 8.50W
Lima Sweden 41 60.56N 13.26E
Lima Mont. U.S.A. 108 44.38N112.36W
Lima Ohio U.S.A. 112 40.43N 84.06W
Limassol see Lemesós Cyprus 66
Limavady U.K. 15 55.03N 6.57W
Limay r. Argentina 125 39.02S 68.07W
Limbang Malaysia 58 4.50N115.00E
Limbara, Monte mtn. Italy 32 40.51N 9.11E
Limbdi India 62 22.34N 71.48E
Limbe Cameroon 77 4.01N 9.12E
Limbourg Belgium 16 50.36N 5.57E
Limburg d. Belgium 16 50.36N 5.57E
Limburg d. Neth. 16 51.15N 5.45E
Limburg an der Lahn Germany 39 50.23N 8.04E
Limeira Brazil 126 22.34S 47.25W
Limerick Rep. of Ire. 15 52.40N 8.37W
Limerick d. Rep. of Ire. 15 52.40N 8.37W
Limfjorden str. Denmark 42 56.55N 9.10E
Liminka Finland 40 64.49N 25.24E
Limmared Sweden 43 57.32N 13.21E
Limmen Bight Australia 90 14.45S135.40E
Límni Greece 35 38.43N 23.18E
Límnos i. Greece 34 39.54N 25.21E
Limoges France 20 45.50N 1.16E
Limogne France 20 44.24N 1.46E
Limón Costa Rica 117 10.00N 83.01W
Limon U.S.A. 108 39.16N103.41W
Limone Piemonte Italy 30 44.12N 7.34E
Limousin d. France 20 45.45N 1.30E
Limousin, Plateaux du f. France 20 45.30N 1.15E
Limoux France 20 43.04N 2.14E
Limpopo r. Mozambique 81 25.14S 33.33E
Līnah Saudi Arabia 65 28.48N 43.45E
Linakhamari Russian Fed. 44 69.39N 31.21E
Linares Chile 125 35.51S 71.36W
Linares Mexico 111 24.52N 99.34W
Linares Spain 26 38.05N 3.38W
Linariá Greece 35 38.50N 24.32E
Lincang China 52 24.00N100.10E
Lincheng China 54 37.26N114.34E
Lincoln Argentina 125 34.55S 61.30W
Lincoln New Zealand 86 43.38S172.29E
Lincoln U.K. 12 53.14N 0.32W
Lincoln Ill. U.S.A. 110 40.10N 89.21W
Lincoln Mich. U.S.A. 104 44.41N 83.25W
Lincoln Nebr. U.S.A. 110 40.48N 96.42W
Lincoln N.H. U.S.A. 105 44.03N 71.40W
Lincoln City U.S.A. 108 44.59N124.00W
Lincoln Park town U.S.A. 114 42.14N 83.09W
Lincoln Sea Greenland 128 82.00N 55.00W
Lincolnshire d. U.K. 12 53.14N 0.32W
Lincoln Wolds hills U.K. 12 53.22N 0.08W
Lindau Germany 39 47.33N 9.41E
Lindeman Group is. Australia 90 20.28S149.05E
Linden Ala. U.S.A. 111 32.18N 87.47W
Linden Penn. U.S.A. 114 41.14N 77.08W
Lindenhurst U.S.A. 115 40.41N 73.22W
Linderödsåsen hills Sweden 43 55.44N 13.06E
Lindesberg Sweden 43 59.35N 15.15E
Lindesnes c. Norway 42 58.00N 7.02E
Líndhos Greece 35 36.06N 28.04E
Líndhos site Greece 35 36.06N 28.05E
Lindi Tanzania 79 10.00S 39.41E
Lindi r. Zaïre 78 0.30N 25.06E
Lindome Sweden 43 57.34N 12.05E
Lindsay Canada 104 44.21N 78.44W
Lindsay U.S.A. 109 36.12N119.05W
Line Is. Pacific Oc. 85 3.00S155.00W
Linesville U.S.A. 114 41.39N 80.26W
Linfen China 54 36.07N111.34E
Lingao China 55 19.54N109.40E
Lingayen Phil. 59 16.02N120.14E
Lingbo Sweden 41 61.03N 16.41E
Lingchuan China 55 25.25N110.20E
Lingen Germany 38 52.31N 7.19E
Lingga i. Indonesia 58 0.20S104.30E
Lingling China 55 26.12N111.30E
Lingshan China 55 22.17N109.27E
Lingshui China 55 18.31N110.00E
Linguère Senegal 76 15.22N 15.11W
Linhai China 55 28.49N121.08E
Linhe China 54 40.50N107.30E
Linköping Sweden 43 58.25N 15.37E
Linnhe, Loch U.K. 14 56.35N 5.25W
Linosa i. Italy 28 35.52N 12.50E
Linquan China 54 33.03N115.17E
Linru China 54 34.12N112.45E
Lins Brazil 126 21.40S 49.44W
Linshui China 55 30.18N106.55E
Lintan China 54 34.33N103.40E
Lintao China 54 35.20N104.00E
Linthal Switz. 39 46.55N 9.00E
Linton Canada 105 47.16N 72.15W
Linton Ind. U.S.A. 112 39.01N 87.10W
Linton N.Dak. U.S.A. 110 46.16N100.14W
Lintong China 54 34.24N109.13E
Lintorf Germany 38 51.20N 6.49E
Linwood U.S.A. 114 43.44N 83.59W
Linxe France 20 43.56N 1.10W
Linxi China 54 43.31N118.02E
Linxia China 54 35.30N103.10E
Lin Xian China 54 37.57N110.57E
Linyi Shandong China 54 35.08N118.20E
Linyi Shanxi China 54 35.12N110.45E
Linz Austria 39 48.18N 14.18E
Linz Germany 38 50.34N 7.17E
Linzgau f. Germany 39 47.50N 9.20E
Lion, Golfe du g. France 20 43.00N 4.00E
Lions, G. of see Lion, Golfe du g. France 20
Lion's Head town Canada 104 44.59N 81.15W
Liouesso Congo 78 1.12N 15.47E
Lipari, Isola i. Italy 33 38.30N 14.57E
Lipéité Congo 78 3.09N 17.22E
Lipetsk Russian Fed. 44 52.37N 39.36E
Liphook U.K. 13 51.05N 0.49W
Liping China 55 26.16N109.08E
Lipkany Moldavia 37 48.18N 26.48E
Lipova Romania 37 46.05N 21.40E
Lipovets Ukraine 37 49.11N 29.01E
Lippe r. Germany 38 51.39N 6.38E
Lippstadt Germany 38 51.40N 8.19E
Lipsoí i. Greece 35 37.19N 26.50E
Liptovský Mikuláš Slovakia 37 49.06N 19.37E
Liptrap, C. Australia 93 38.53S145.55E
Lipu China 55 24.28N110.12E
Lira Uganda 79 2.15N 32.55E
Liranga Congo 78 0.43S 17.32E
Liri r. Italy 32 41.25N 13.52E
Liria Spain 25 39.38N 0.36W
Liria Sudan 73 4.38N 32.05E
Lisala Zaïre 78 2.13N 21.37E
Lisboa Portugal 27 38.43N 9.08W
Lisboa d. Portugal 27 39.05N 9.00W
Lisbon see Lisboa Portugal 27
Lisbon N.Dak. U.S.A. 110 46.27N 97.41W
Lisbon Ohio U.S.A. 114 40.47N 80.46W
Lisburn U.K. 15 54.30N 6.03W
Lisburne, C. U.S.A. 98 69.00N165.50W
Liscannor B. Rep. of Ire. 15 52.55N 9.24W
Liscia r. Italy 32 41.05N 9.17E
Lishi China 54 37.30N111.07E
Lishui China 55 28.28N119.59E
Lisianski i. Hawaiian Is. 84 26.04N173.58W
Lisichansk Ukraine 45 48.53N 38.25E
Lisieux France 18 49.09N 0.14E
Liskeard U.K. 13 50.27N 4.29W
Liski Russian Fed. 45 51.00N 39.30E
L'Isle Jourdain H.-Gar. France 20 43.37N 1.05E
L'Isle Jourdain Poit.-Char. France 18 46.14N 0.41E
L'Isle-sur-le-Doubs France 19 47.27N 6.35E
Lismore N.S.W. Australia 93 28.48S153.17E
Lismore Vic. Australia 92 37.58S143.22E
Lismore Rep. of Ire. 15 52.08N 7.57W
Liss U.K. 13 51.03N 0.53W
Lisse Neth. 16 52.18N 4.33E
Lista f. Norway 42 58.07N 6.40E
Lištica Bosnia-Herzegovina 31 43.23N 17.36E
Listowel Canada 104 43.44N 80.57W
Listowel Rep. of Ire. 15 52.27N 9.30W
Litang China 55 23.09N109.09E
Litang Qu r. China 61 28.09N101.30E
Litchfield Conn. U.S.A. 115 41.45N 73.11W
Litchfield Ill. U.S.A. 110 39.11N 89.40W
Litchfield Minn. U.S.A. 110 45.08N 94.31W
Litchfield Nebr. U.S.A. 110 41.09N 99.09W
Lithgow Australia 93 33.30S150.09E
Líthinon, Ákra c. Greece 35 34.55N 24.44E
Lithuania Europe 44 55.30N 24.00E
Lititz U.S.A. 115 40.09N 76.18W
Litókhoron Greece 34 40.06N 22.30E
Litoměřice Czech Republic 38 50.35N 14.09E
Little Andaman i. India 56 10.40N 92.24E
Little Bahama Bank f. Bahamas 113 26.40N 78.00W
Little Belt Mts. U.S.A. 108 46.45N110.35W
Little Cayman i. Cayman Is. 117 19.40N 80.00W
Little Coco i. Burma 56 13.59N 93.12E
Little Colorado r. U.S.A. 109 36.11N111.48W
Little Current r. Canada 102 50.00N 84.35W
Little Current town Canada 104 45.58N 81.56W
Little Falls town Minn. U.S.A. 110 45.59N 94.21W
Little Falls town N.Y. U.S.A. 115 43.03N 74.52W
Littlefield U.S.A. 111 33.55N102.20W
Little Grand Rapids town Canada 101 52.05N 95.29W
Littlehampton U.K. 13 50.48N 0.32W
Little Inagua i. Bahamas 117 21.30N 73.00W
Little Kanawha r. U.S.A. 114 39.16N 81.34W
Little Karoo f. R.S.A. 80 33.40S 21.40E
Little Lake town U.S.A. 109 35.58N117.53W
Little Mecatina r. Canada 103 50.28N 59.35W
Little Missouri r. U.S.A. 110 47.30N102.25W
Little Nicobar i. India 61 7.20N 93.40E
Little Ouse r. U.K. 13 52.34N 0.20E
Little Quill L. Canada 101 51.55N104.05W
Little Rann of Kachchh f. India 62 23.25N 71.30E
Little Rock town U.S.A. 111 34.44N 92.15W
Little Smoky r. Canada 100 55.42N117.38W
Littlestown U.S.A. 114 39.45N 77.05W
Littleton Colo. U.S.A. 108 39.37N105.01W
Littleton N.H. U.S.A. 105 44.18N 71.46W
Little Topar Australia 92 31.44S142.14E
Little Valley town U.S.A. 114 42.15N 78.48W
Little White r. Canada 104 46.21N 83.20W
Litvínov Czech Republic 38 50.37N 13.36E
Liuba China 54 33.37N106.55E
Liucheng China 55 24.39N109.14E
Liuchong He r. China 55 26.50N106.04E
Liuli Tanzania 79 11.07S 34.34E
Liulin China 54 37.26N110.52E
Liuzhou China 55 24.19N109.12E
Livadherón Greece 34 40.02N 21.57E
Livanátai Greece 35 38.42N 23.03E
Livanjsko Polje f. Bosnia-Herzegovina 31 44.00N 16.40E
Livarot France 18 49.01N 0.09E
Lively Canada 104 46.26N 81.09W
Live Oak U.S.A. 113 30.19N 82.59W
Livermore, Mt. U.S.A. 109 30.39N104.11W
Liverpool Australia 93 33.57S150.52E
Liverpool Canada 103 44.02N 64.43W
Liverpool U.K. 12 53.25N 3.00W
Liverpool U.S.A. 115 43.06N 76.13W
Liverpool, C. Canada 99 73.38N 78.06W
Liverpool B. U.K. 12 53.30N 3.10W
Liverpool Range mts. Australia 93 31.45S150.45E
Livigno Italy 30 46.32N 10.04E
Livingston U.K. 14 55.54N 3.31W
Livingston Mont. U.S.A. 108 45.40N110.34W
Livingston Tex. U.S.A. 111 30.43N 94.56W
Livingstone see Maramba Zambia 80
Livingstonia Malaŵi 79 10.35S 34.10E
Livno Bosnia-Herzegovina 31 43.50N 17.01E

Livo to Lucin

Livo r. Finland 40 65.24N 26.48E
Livonia Mich. U.S.A. 104 42.25N 83.23W
Livonia N.Y. U.S.A. 114 42.49N 77.40W
Livorno Italy 30 43.33N 10.19E
Liwale Tanzania 79 9.47S 38.00E
Liwan Sudan 73 4.55N 35.41E
Li Xian Gansu China 54 34.11N105.02E
Li Xian Hunan China 55 29.38N111.45E
Lixoúrion Greece 35 38.14N 20.24E
Liyujiang China 55 25.59N113.12E
Lizard U.K. 13 49.58N 5.12W
Lizard I. Australia 90 14.39S145.28E
Lizard Pt. U.K. 13 49.57N 5.15W
Lizarra see Estella Spain 26
Lizemores U.S.A. 114 38.20N 81.12W
Ljan Norway 42 59.51N 10.48E
Ljubija Bosnia-Herzegovina 31 44.56N 16.37E
Ljubinje Bosnia-Herzegovina 31 42.57N 18.05E
Ljubljana Slovenia 31 46.03N 14.31E
Ljubovija Yugo. 31 44.11N 19.22E
Ljubški Bosnia-Herzegovina 31 43.12N 17.33E
Ljugarn Sweden 43 57.19N 18.42E
Ljungan r. Sweden 41 62.19N 17.23E
Ljungby Sweden 43 56.50N 13.56E
Ljungbyholm Sweden 43 56.38N 16.10E
Ljungdalen Sweden 40 62.54N 12.45E
Ljungsbro Sweden 43 58.31N 15.30E
Ljusdal Sweden 41 61.50N 16.05E
Ljusnan r. Sweden 41 61.12N 17.08E
Ljusne Sweden 41 61.13N 17.08E
Ljusterö i. Sweden 43 59.31N 18.37E
Ljutomer Slovenia 31 46.31N 16.12E
Llança Spain 25 42.22N 3.09E
Llandeilo U.K. 13 51.54N 4.00W
Llandovery U.K. 13 51.59N 3.49W
Llandrindod Wells U.K. 13 52.15N 3.23W
Llandudno U.K. 12 53.19N 3.49W
Llanelli U.K. 13 51.41N 4.11W
Llanes Spain 26 43.25N 4.45W
Llangadfan U.K. 13 52.41N 3.28W
Llangollen U.K. 12 52.58N 3.10W
Llanidloes U.K. 13 52.28N 3.31W
Llanos f. S. America 122 7.30N 70.00W
Llanwrtyd Wells U.K. 13 52.06N 3.39W
Lleida see Lérida Spain 25
Lleida d. Spain 25 42.00N 1.10E
Llentrisca, Cabo de c. Spain 25 38.51N 1.14E
Llerena Spain 26 38.14N 6.01W
Llobregat r. Spain 25 41.19N 2.09E
Lloret de Mar Spain 25 41.42N 2.53E
Lloydminster Canada 101 53.17N110.00W
Lluchmayor Spain 25 39.29N 2.54E
Loange r. Zaïre 78 4.18S 20.05E
Lobatse Botswana 80 25.12S 25.39E
Löbau Germany 38 51.05N 14.40E
Lobaye r. C.A.R. 77 3.40N 18.35E
Lobería Argentina 125 38.08S 58.48W
Lobito Angola 78 12.20S 13.34E
Lobonäs Sweden 41 61.33N 15.20E
Lobos Argentina 125 35.10S 59.05W
Locarno Switz. 39 46.10N 8.48E
Lochboisdale town U.K. 14 57.09N 7.19W
Lochem Neth. 16 52.10N 6.25E
Loches France 18 47.08N 1.00E
Lochgilphead U.K. 14 56.02N 5.26W
Lochinver U.K. 14 58.09N 5.15W
Lochmaddy town U.K. 14 57.36N 7.10W
Lochnagar mtn. U.K. 14 56.57N 3.15W
Lochranza U.K. 14 55.42N 5.18W
Loch Raven Resr. U.S.A. 115 39.27N 76.36W
Lochy, Loch U.K. 14 56.58N 4.55W
Lock Australia 92 33.34S135.46E
Lockeport Canada 103 43.42N 65.07W
Lockerbie U.K. 14 55.07N 3.21W
Lockhart Australia 93 35.16S146.42E
Lockhart U.S.A. 111 29.53N 97.41W
Lockhart, L. Australia 89 33.27S119.00E
Lockhart River town Australia 90 12.58S143.29E
Lock Haven U.S.A. 114 41.08N 77.27W
Löcknitz Germany 38 53.27N 14.12E
Lockport U.S.A. 114 43.10N 78.42W
Loc Ninh Vietnam 56 11.51N106.35E
Locri Italy 33 38.14N 16.16E
Lod Israel 67 31.57N 34.54E
Lodalskåpa mtn. Norway 41 61.47N 7.13E
Loddon r. Australia 92 35.40S143.59E
Lodève France 20 43.43N 3.19E
Lodeynoye Pole Russian Fed. 44 60.43N 33.30E
Lodge Grass U.S.A. 108 45.19N107.22W
Lodhrān Pakistan 62 29.32N 71.38E
Lodi Italy 30 45.19N 9.30E
Lodi Calif. U.S.A. 108 38.08N121.16W
Lodi Ohio U.S.A. 114 41.03N 82.01W
Lodja Zaïre 78 3.29S 23.33E
Lodosa Spain 25 42.25N 2.05W
Lodwar Kenya 79 3.06N 35.38E
Łódź Poland 37 51.49N 19.28E
Loei Thailand 56 17.32N101.34E
Lofer Austria 39 47.35N 12.41E
Lofoten is. Norway 8 68.15N 13.50E
Lofoten Vesterålen is. Norway 40 68.15N 13.50E
Log Russian Fed. 45 49.28N 43.51E
Loga Niger 77 13.40N 3.15E
Logan N.Mex. U.S.A. 109 35.22N103.25W
Logan Ohio U.S.A. 114 39.32N 82.25W
Logan Utah U.S.A. 108 41.44N111.50W
Logan, Mt. Canada 100 60.34N140.24W
Logansport U.S.A. 112 40.45N 86.25W
Loganton U.S.A. 114 41.02N 77.18W
Loge r. Angola 78 7.52S 13.08E
Logone r. Cameroon/Chad 77 12.10N 15.00E
Logone Occidental d. Chad 77 8.40N 15.50E
Logone Oriental d. Chad 77 8.10N 16.00E
Logoysk Belorussia 37 54.08N 27.42E
Logroño Spain 25 42.28N 2.27W
Logrosán Spain 27 39.20N 5.29W
Løgstør Denmark 42 56.58N 9.15E
Løgumkloster Denmark 42 55.03N 8.57E
Lohārdaga India 63 23.26N 84.41E
Lohāru India 62 28.27N 75.49E
Lohja Finland 41 60.15N 24.05E
Lohjanjärvi l. Finland 41 60.15N 23.55E
Lohne Germany 38 52.42N 8.12E
Lohr Germany 39 50.00N 9.34E
Loikaw Burma 56 19.40N 97.17E
Loimaa Finland 41 60.51N 23.03E
Loir r. France 18 47.33N 0.32W
Loire d. France 21 45.30N 4.00E
Loire r. France 18 47.16N 2.11W
Loire-Atlantique d. France 18 47.20N 1.35W
Loiret d. France 19 47.55N 2.20E
Loir-et-Cher d. France 18 47.30N 1.30E
Loja Ecuador 122 3.59S 79.16W
Loja Spain 27 37.10N 4.09W
Loka Sudan 73 4.16N 31.01E
Loka Zaïre 78 0.20N 17.57E
Løken Norway 42 59.48N 11.29E
Loken tekojärvi resr. Finland 40 67.55N 27.40E
Lokeren Belgium 16 51.06N 3.59E
Loket Czech Republic 39 50.09N 12.43E
Lokichar Kenya 79 2.23N 35.39E
Lokitaung Kenya 79 4.15N 35.45E
Lokka Finland 40 67.49N 27.44E
Løkken Denmark 42 57.22N 9.43E
Løkken Norway 40 63.06N 9.43E
Loknya Russian Fed. 44 56.49N 30.00E
Lokoja Nigeria 77 7.49N 6.44E
Lokolo r. Zaïre 78 0.45S 19.36E
Lokoro r. Zaïre 78 1.40S 18.29E
Lol r. Sudan 73 9.11N 29.12E
Lolland i. Denmark 41 54.46N 11.30E
Lom Bulgaria 34 43.49N 23.14E
Lom Norway 41 61.50N 8.33E
Loma U.S.A. 108 47.57N110.30W
Lomami r. Zaïre 78 0.45N 24.10E
Lomas de Zamora Argentina 125 34.46S 58.24W
Lombardia d. Italy 30 45.45N 9.00E
Lombok i. Indonesia 58 8.30S116.20E
Lombok, Selat str. Indonesia 59 8.38S115.40E
Lomé Togo 77 6.10N 1.21E
Lomela Zaïre 78 2.15S 23.15E
Lomela r. Zaïre 78 0.14S 20.45E
Lomié Cameroon 77 3.09N 13.35E
Lomme France 19 50.39N 2.59E
Lommel Belgium 16 51.15N 5.18E
Lomond Canada 100 50.21N112.39W
Lomond, Loch U.K. 14 56.07N 4.36W
Lompoc U.S.A. 109 34.38N120.27W
Łomża Poland 37 53.11N 22.04E
Lonaconing U.S.A. 114 39.34N 78.59W
Londinières France 18 49.50N 1.24E
London Canada 104 42.59N 81.14W
London Kiribati 85 1.58N157.28W
London U.K. 13 51.32N 0.06W
Londonderry U.K. 15 55.00N 7.21W
Londonderry d. U.K. 15 55.00N 7.00W
Londonderry, C. Australia 88 13.58S126.55E
Londonderry, Isla i. Chile 125 55.03S 70.40W
Londrina Brazil 124 23.30S 51.13W
Lonely I. Canada 104 45.34N 81.29W
Lone Pine U.S.A. 109 36.36N118.04W
Long, L. Canada 105 47.05N 74.06W
Longa r. Angola 78 16.15S 19.07E
Longá Greece 35 36.53N 21.55E
Longa, Proliv str. Russian Fed. 51 70.00N178.00E
Long'an China 55 23.11N107.41E
Longarone Italy 30 46.16N 12.18E
Long Beach town Calif. U.S.A. 109 33.46N118.11W
Long Beach town N.Y. U.S.A. 115 40.35N 73.41W
Long Branch U.S.A. 115 40.18N 74.00W
Longchamps Belgium 16 50.05N 5.42E
Longchang China 55 29.18N105.20E
Longchuan China 55 24.12N115.25E
Long Creek town U.S.A. 108 44.43N119.06W
Long Eaton U.K. 12 52.54N 1.16W
Longeau France 19 47.46N 5.18E
Longford Rep. of Ire. 15 53.44N 7.48W
Longford d. Rep. of Ire. 15 53.42N 7.45W
Longhua Hebei China 54 41.17N117.37E
Long I. Bahamas 117 23.00N 75.00W
Long I. Canada 102 54.55N 79.30W
Long I. U.S.A. 115 40.50N 73.00W
Longido Tanzania 79 2.43S 36.41E
Longiram Indonesia 58 0.05S115.45E
Long Island Sd. U.S.A. 115 41.05N 72.58W
Long Jiang r. China 55 24.12N109.30E
Long L. Canada 102 49.30N 86.50W
Long L. U.S.A. 105 44.04N 74.20W
Longlac town Canada 102 49.45N 86.25W
Long Lake town U.S.A. 105 43.58N 74.25W
Longli China 55 26.29N107.59E
Longlin China 55 24.43N105.26E
Longmeadow U.S.A. 115 42.03N 72.34W
Longmont U.S.A. 108 40.10N105.06W
Longnan China 55 24.54N114.47E
Longnawan Indonesia 58 1.54N114.53E
Longniddry U.K. 14 55.58N 2.53W
Long Point B. Canada 104 42.40N 80.14W
Long Pt. Canada 104 42.33N 80.04W
Longquan China 55 28.05N119.07E
Long Range Mts. Nfld. Canada 103 48.00N 58.30W
Long Range Mts. Nfld. Canada 103 50.00N 57.00W
Longreach Australia 90 23.26S144.15E
Long Sault Canada 105 45.00N 74.55W
Longsheng China 55 25.59N110.01E
Longs Peak U.S.A. 108 40.15N105.37W
Longtown U.K. 12 55.01N 2.58W
Longué France 18 47.23N 0.06W
Longueuil Canada 105 45.32N 73.30W
Longuyon France 19 49.26N 5.36E
Longview Tex. U.S.A. 111 32.30N 94.44W
Longview Wash. U.S.A. 108 46.08N122.57W
Longwood St. Helena 127 15.57S 5.42W
Longwy France 19 49.31N 5.46E
Longxi China 54 34.59N104.45E
Long Xian China 54 34.52N106.50E
Long Xuyen Vietnam 56 10.23N105.23E
Longyan China 55 25.10N117.02E
Longzhou China 55 22.24N106.50E
Lonigo Italy 30 45.23N 11.23E
Löningen Germany 38 52.44N 7.46E
Lonja r. Croatia 31 45.30N 16.40E
Lönsboda Sweden 43 56.24N 14.19E
Lönsdal Norway 40 66.46N 15.26E
Lonsdale, L. Australia 92 37.05S142.15E
Lons-le-Saunier France 19 46.40N 5.33E
Looc Phil. 59 12.20N122.05E
Looe U.K. 13 50.51N 4.26W
Lookout, C. U.S.A. 113 34.35N 76.32W
Loolmalassin mtn. Tanzania 79 3.00S 35.45E
Loon Lake Mts. U.S.A. 105 44.35N 74.08W
Loop Head Rep. of Ire. 15 52.33N 9.56W
Lopari Zaïre 73 1.15N 19.59E
Lopari r. Zaïre 78 1.20N 20.22E
Lop Buri Thailand 56 14.49N100.37E
Lopez, C. Gabon 78 0.36S 8.40E
Lopi Congo 78 2.57N 16.47E
Lop Nur l. China 52 40.30N 90.30E
Lopphavet est. Norway 40 70.30N 20.00E
Lopydino Russian Fed. 44 61.10N 52.02E
Lora, Hāmūn-i- l. Pakistan 62 29.20N 64.50E
Lora Creek r. Australia 92 28.10S135.22E
Lora del Río Spain 27 37.39N 5.32W
Lorain U.S.A. 114 41.28N 82.10W
Loralai Pakistan 62 30.22N 68.36E
Lorca Spain 25 37.40N 1.42W
Lord Howe I. Pacific Oc. 84 31.28S159.09E
Lord Howe Rise Pacific Oc. 84 29.00S162.30E
Lordsburg U.S.A. 109 32.21N108.43W
Lorena Brazil 126 22.44S 45.07W
Lorengau P.N.G. 59 2.01S147.15E
Lorenzo Geyres Uruguay 125 32.05S 57.55W
Loreto Brazil 123 7.05S 45.09W
Loreto Italy 31 43.26N 13.36E
Loreto Mexico 109 26.01N111.21W
Loretteville Canada 105 46.51N 71.21W
Lorian Swamp Kenya 79 0.35N 39.40E
Lorient France 18 47.45N 3.22W
Loriol France 21 44.45N 4.49E
Lormes France 19 47.17N 3.49E
Lorne Australia 92 38.34S144.01E
Lörrach Germany 39 47.37N 7.40E
Lorraine d. France 19 49.00N 6.00E
Lorrainville Canada 104 47.20N 79.21W
Lorris France 19 47.53N 2.31E
Lorsch Germany 39 49.39N 8.34E
Lorup Germany 38 52.55N 7.38E
Los Alamos Mexico 111 28.40N103.30W
Los Alamos U.S.A. 109 35.53N106.19W
Los Andes Chile 125 32.50S 70.37W
Los Angeles Chile 125 37.28S 72.21W
Los Angeles U.S.A. 106 34.00N118.17W
Los Bajíos Mexico 109 28.31N108.25W
Los Banos U.S.A. 108 37.04N120.51W
Los Blancos Argentina 124 23.40S 62.35W
Los Blancos Spain 25 37.38N 0.49W
Los Canarreos, Archipiélago de Cuba 117 21.40N 82.30W
Los Herreras Mexico 111 25.55N 99.24W
Lošinj i. Croatia 31 44.36N 14.24E
Losinovka Ukraine 37 50.50N 31.57E
Los Llanos de Aridane Canary Is. 127 28.39N 17.54W
Los Lunas U.S.A. 109 34.48N106.44W
Los Mochis Mexico 116 25.45N108.57W
Los Navalmorales Spain 27 39.43N 4.38W
Los Olivos U.S.A. 109 34.40N120.06W
Los Palacios y Villafranca Spain 27 37.10N 5.56W
Los Roques is. Venezuela 122 12.00N 67.00W
Los Santos de Maimona Spain 27 38.27N 6.23W
Lossiemouth U.K. 14 57.43N 3.18W
Lost r. U.S.A. 114 39.05N 78.36W
Lost Cabin U.S.A. 108 43.19N107.36W
Lost City U.S.A. 114 38.55N 78.51W
Los Teques Venezuela 122 10.25N 67.01W
Lost River town U.S.A. 114 38.57N 78.50W
Los Vilos Chile 124 31.55S 71.31W
Los Yébenes Spain 27 39.34N 3.53W
Lot d. France 20 44.35N 1.40E
Lot r. France 20 44.18N 0.20E
Lota Chile 125 37.05S 73.10W
Lot-et-Garonne d. France 20 44.20N 0.20E
Lothian d. U.K. 14 55.50N 3.00W
Lotoi r. Zaïre 78 1.30S 18.30E
Lotsani r. Botswana 80 22.42S 28.11E
Lötschberg Tunnel Switz. 38 46.25N 7.53E
Lotuke mtn. Sudan 73 4.07N 33.48E
Louang Namtha Laos 56 20.57N101.25E
Louangphrabang Laos 56 19.53N102.10E
Loubomo Congo 78 4.09S 12.40E
Loudéac France 18 48.10N 2.45W
Loudima Congo 78 4.06S 13.05E
Loudonville U.S.A. 114 40.38N 82.14W
Loudun France 18 47.01N 0.05E
Loué France 18 48.00N 0.09W
Loue r. France 19 47.04N 6.10E
Louga Senegal 76 15.37N 16.13W
Loughborough U.K. 12 52.47N 1.11W
Loughrea Rep. of Ire. 15 53.12N 8.35W
Loughros More B. Rep. of Ire. 15 54.48N 8.32W
Louhans France 19 46.38N 5.13E
Louisburgh Rep. of Ire. 15 53.46N 9.49W
Louiseville Canada 105 46.14N 72.56W
Louisiade Archipelago is. P.N.G. 90 11.00S153.00E
Louisiana d. U.S.A. 111 30.60N 92.30W
Louis Trichardt R.S.A. 80 23.03S 29.54E
Louisville Ky. U.S.A. 112 38.13N 85.48W
Louisville Miss. U.S.A. 111 33.07N 89.03W
Louisville Ohio U.S.A. 114 40.50N 81.16W
Louis XIV, Pointe c. Canada 102 54.35N 79.50W
Loukhi Russian Fed. 44 66.05N 33.04E
Loukouo Congo 78 3.38S 14.39E
Loulé Portugal 27 37.08N 8.00W
Loum Cameroon 77 4.46N 9.45E
Louny Czech Republic 39 50.19N 13.46E
Lourches France 19 50.19N 3.21E
Lourdes France 20 43.06N 0.03W
Loures Portugal 27 38.50N 9.10W
Lourinhã Portugal 27 39.14N 9.19W
Lourosa Portugal 26 40.19N 7.56W
Lousã Portugal 27 40.07N 8.15W
Louth Australia 93 30.34S145.09E
Louth d. Rep. of Ire. 15 53.55N 6.30W
Louth U.K. 12 53.23N 0.00
Loutra Greece 35 37.51N 21.06E
Loutrá Aidhipsoú Greece 35 38.54N 23.02E
Louviers France 18 49.13N 1.10E
Louvigné-du-Désert France 18 48.29N 1.08W
Lövånger Sweden 40 64.22N 21.18E
Lovat r. Russian Fed. 44 58.06N 31.37E
Lovech Bulgaria 34 43.08N 24.43E
Lovech d. Bulgaria 34 43.10N 25.00E
Loveland U.S.A. 108 40.24N105.05W
Lovell U.S.A. 108 44.50N108.24W
Lovelock U.S.A. 108 40.11N118.28W
Love Point town U.S.A. 115 39.02N 76.18W
Lovere Italy 30 45.49N 10.04E
Lovington U.S.A. 111 32.57N103.21W
Lovoi r. Zaïre 79 8.14S 26.40E
Lovosice Czech Republic 38 50.31N 14.03E
Lovozero Russian Fed. 44 68.01N 35.08E
Lovrin Romania 37 45.58N 20.48E
Lovua r. Zaïre 78 6.08S 20.35E
Low Canada 105 45.48N 75.57W
Lowa Zaïre 78 1.24S 25.51E
Lowa r. Kivu Zaïre 78 1.25S 25.55E
Lowell U.S.A. 115 42.39N 71.18W
Löwenberg Germany 38 52.54N 13.08E
Lower Arrow L. Canada 100 49.40N118.05W
Lower California pen. see Baja California pen. Mexico 116
Lower Egypt see Mişr Baḩrī f. Egypt 66
Lower Hutt New Zealand 86 41.13S174.55E
Lower Lough Erne U.K. 15 54.28N 7.48W
Lower Pen. f. U.S.A. 104 44.34N 84.28W
Lower Post Canada 100 59.55N128.30W
Lower Red L. U.S.A. 110 48.00N 94.50W
Lowestoft U.K. 13 52.29N 1.44E
Lowgar d. Afghan. 62 34.10N 69.20E
Lowicz Poland 37 52.06N 19.55E
Lowrah r. Afghan. see Pishīn Lora r. Pakistan 62
Lowville U.S.A. 105 43.47N 75.29W
Loxton Australia 92 34.38S140.38E
Loyalsock r. U.S.A. 114 41.14N 76.56W
Loyalty Is. see Loyauté, Îles is. N. Cal. 84
Loyauté, Îles is. N. Cal. 84 21.00S167.00E
Loyoro Uganda 79 3.22N 34.16E
Lozère d. France 20 44.30N 3.30E
Loznica Yugo. 31 44.32N 19.13E
Lozoyuela Spain 26 40.55N 3.37W
Lua r. Zaïre 78 2.45N 18.28E
Luabo Mozambique 81 18.30S 36.10E
Luachimo Angola 78 7.25S 20.43E
Lualaba r. Zaïre 78 0.18N 25.32E
Luama r. Zaïre 79 4.45S 26.55E
Luampa Zambia 78 15.04S 24.20E
Lu'an China 55 31.47N116.30E
Luancheng Guang. Zhuang. China 55 22.48N108.55E
Luancheng Hebei China 54 37.53N114.39E
Luanda Angola 78 8.50S 13.20E
Luanda d. Angola 78 9.00S 13.20E
Luando Game Res. Angola 78 11.00S 17.45E
Luanginga r. Zambia 78 15.11S 23.05E
Luangwa r. Central Zambia 79 15.32S 30.28E
Luan He r. China 54 39.25N119.10E
Luanping China 54 40.55N117.17E
Luanshya Zambia 79 13.09S 28.24E
Luan Xian China 54 39.45N118.44E
Luapula r. Zambia 79 9.25S 28.36E
Luarca Spain 26 43.32N 6.32W
Luau Angola 78 10.41S 22.09E
Lubalo Angola 78 9.13S 19.21E
Lubango Angola 78 14.52S 13.30E
Lubao Zaïre 78 5.19S 25.43E
Lübben Germany 38 51.56N 13.53E
Lübbenau Germany 38 51.52N 13.57E
Lubbock U.S.A. 111 33.35N101.51W
Lubeck Australia 92 36.47S142.38E
Lübeck Germany 38 53.52N 10.40E
Lübecker Bucht b. Germany 38 54.10N 11.20E
Lubefu r. Zaïre 78 4.05S 23.00E
Lubenka Kazakhstan 45 50.22N 54.13E
Lubersac France 20 45.27N 1.24E
Lubia Angola 78 11.01S 17.06E
Lubika Zaïre 79 7.50S 29.12E
Lubilash r. Zaïre 78 4.59S 23.25E
Lubin Poland 36 51.24N 16.13E
Lublin Poland 37 51.18N 22.31E
Lubliniec Poland 37 50.40N 18.41E
Lubny Ukraine 45 50.01N 33.00E
Lübtheen Germany 38 53.18N 11.04E
Lubudi r. K.Occidental Zaïre 78 4.00S 21.23E
Lubudi Zaïre 78 9.57S 25.59E
Lubudi r. Shaba Zaïre 78 9.13S 25.40E
Lubumbashi Zaïre 79 11.44S 27.29E
Lubutu Zaïre 78 0.48S 26.19E
Lübz Germany 38 53.27N 12.01E
Lucas González Argentina 125 32.25S 59.33W
Lucca Italy 30 43.50N 10.29E
Luce B. U.K. 14 54.45N 4.47W
Lucena Phil. 59 13.56N121.37E
Lucena Spain 27 37.24N 4.29W
Lucena del Cid Spain 25 40.08N 0.17W
Lucenay-l'Évêque France 19 47.05N 4.15E
Luc-en-Diois France 21 44.37N 5.27E
Lučenec Slovakia 37 48.20N 19.40E
Lucera Italy 33 41.30N 15.20E
Lucerne U.S.A. 108 48.12N120.36W
Lucero Mexico 109 30.49N106.30W
Luchena r. Spain 25 37.44N 1.50W
Lüchow Germany 38 52.58N 11.10E
Lucin U.S.A. 108 41.22N113.55W

Lucindale to **Magude**

Lucindale Australia **92** 36.59S140.25E
Lucira Angola **78** 13.51S 12.31E
Luckau Germany **38** 51.51N 13.43E
Luckeesarai India **63** 25.11N 86.05E
Luckenwalde Germany **38** 52.05N 13.10E
Lucknow Canada **104** 43.57N 81.31W
Lucknow India **63** 26.51N 80.55E
Luçon France **18** 46.27N 1.10W
Lucy Creek *town* Australia **90** 22.25S136.20E
Lüda *see* Dalian China **54**
Luda Kamchiya *r.* Bulgaria **34** 42.50N 27.00E
Ludbreg Croatia **31** 46.15N 16.37E
Lüdenscheid Germany **38** 51.13N 7.38E
Lüderitz Namibia **80** 26.37S 15.09E
Ludgate Canada **104** 45.54N 80.32W
Ludhiāna India **62** 30.55N 75.51E
Lüdinghausen Germany **16** 51.46N 7.27E
Ludington U.S.A. **112** 43.58N 86.27W
Ludlow U.K. **13** 52.23N 2.42W
Ludlow Penn. U.S.A. **114** 41.44N 78.57W
Ludlow Vt. U.S.A. **115** 43.24N 72.42W
Ludogorie *mts.* Bulgaria **37** 43.45N 27.00E
Luduş Romania **37** 46.29N 24.05E
Ludvika Sweden **43** 60.09N 15.11E
Ludwigsburg Germany **39** 48.53N 9.11E
Ludwigsfelde Germany **38** 52.17N 13.16E
Ludwigshafen Germany **39** 49.29N 8.26E
Ludwigslut Germany **38** 53.19N 11.30E
Luebo Zaïre **78** 5.16S 21.27E
Luena Angola **78** 11.46S 19.55E
Luena *r.* Angola **78** 12.30S 22.37E
Luena Zaïre **78** 9.27S 25.47E
Luena Zambia **79** 10.40S 30.21E
Luena *r.* Western Zambia **78** 14.47S 23.05E
Luengue *r.* Angola **78** 16.58S 21.15E
Luenha *r.* Mozambique **81** 16.29S 33.40E
Lüeyang China **54** 33.20N106.03E
Lufeng China **55** 23.01N115.35E
Lufira *r.* Zaïre **78** 8.15S 26.30E
Lufkin U.S.A. **107** 31.21N 94.47W
Luga Russian Fed. **44** 58.42N 29.49E
Lugano Switz. **39** 46.01N 8.58E
Lugano, Lago di *l.* Switz./Italy **39** 46.00N 9.00E
Lugansk Ukraine **45** 48.35N 39.20E
Luganville Vanuatu **84** 15.32S167.08E
Lugela Mozambique **81** 16.25S 36.42E
Lugenda *r.* Mozambique **79** 11.23S 38.30E
Luginy Ukraine **37** 51.05N 28.21E
Lugnaquilla Mtn. Rep. of Ire. **15** 52.58N 6.28W
Lugo Italy **30** 44.25N 11.54E
Lugo Spain **26** 43.02N 7.34W
Lugo *d.* Spain **26** 42.55N 7.30W
Lugoj Romania **37** 45.42N 21.56E
Luiana Angola **78** 17.08S 22.59E
Luiana *r.* Angola **78** 17.28S 23.02E
Luilaka *r.* Zaïre **78** 0.15S 19.00E
Luilu *r.* Zaïre **78** 6.22S 23.53E
Luino Italy **30** 46.00N 8.44E
Luiro *r.* Finland **40** 67.18N 27.28E
Luisa Zaïre **78** 7.15S 22.27E
Lujiang China **55** 31.14N117.17E
Lukala Zaïre **78** 5.23S 13.02E
Lukanga Swamp *f.* Zambia **79** 14.15S 27.30E
Lukenie *r.* Zaïre **78** 2.43S 18.12E
Lukka Sudan **72** 14.33N 23.42E
Lukovit Bulgaria **34** 43.12N 24.10E
Łuków Poland **37** 51.56N 22.23E
Lukoyanov Russian Fed. **44** 55.03N 44.29E
Lukuga *r.* Zaïre **79** 5.37S 26.58E
Lukula *r.* Zaïre **78** 4.15S 17.59E
Lukulu Zambia **78** 14.35S 23.25E
Lukumbule Tanzania **79** 11.34S 37.24E
Lule *r.* Sweden **40** 65.35N 22.03E
Luleå Sweden **40** 65.34N 22.10E
Lüleburgaz Turkey **29** 41.25N 27.23E
Lüliang Shan *mts.* China **54** 37.00N111.20E
Lulonga *r.* Zaïre **78** 0.42N 18.26E
Lulu *r.* Zaïre **78** 1.18N 23.42E
Lulua *r.* Zaïre **78** 5.03S 21.07E
Lumai Angola **78** 13.13S 21.13E
Lumajangdong Co *l.* China **63** 34.02N 81.40E
Lumbala Kaquengue Angola **78** 12.37S 22.33E
Lumbala N'guimbo Angola **78** 14.02S 21.35E
Lumberton Miss. U.S.A. **111** 31.00N 89.27W
Lumberton N.Mex. U.S.A. **108** 36.55N106.56W
Lumbrales Spain **26** 40.56N 6.43W
Lumbres France **19** 50.42N 2.08E
Lumsden New Zealand **86** 45.44S168.26E
Lūnāvāda India **62** 23.08N 73.37E
Lund Sweden **43** 55.42N 13.11E
Lund Nev. U.S.A. **108** 38.52N115.00W
Lund Utah U.S.A. **108** 38.01N113.28W
Lunda Norte *d.* Angola **78** 8.30S 19.00E
Lunda Sul *d.* Angola **78** 11.00S 20.00E
Lundazi Zambia **79** 12.19S 33.11E
Lundevatn *l.* Norway **42** 58.22N 6.36E
Lundy *i.* U.K. **13** 51.10N 4.41W
Lune *r.* U.K. **12** 54.03N 2.49W
Lüneburg Germany **38** 53.15N 10.23E
Lüneburger *f.* Germany **38** 53.06N 10.30E
Lunel France **21** 43.41N 4.08E
Lünen Germany **16** 51.37N 7.31E
Lunenburg U.S.A. **105** 44.28N 71.39W
Lunéville France **19** 48.36N 6.30E
Lunga *r.* Zambia **78** 14.28S 26.27E
Lunge Angola **78** 12.13S 16.07E
Lunggar China **63** 31.10N 84.01E
Lungwebungu *r.* Zambia **78** 14.20S 23.15E
Lūni India **62** 26.00N 73.00E
Lūni *r.* India **62** 24.41N 71.15E
Luninets Belorussia **37** 52.18N 26.50E
Luning U.S.A. **108** 38.30N118.10W
Lūnkaransar India **62** 28.32N 73.50E
Luocheng China **55** 24.47N108.54E
Luodian China **55** 25.29N106.39E
Luoding China **55** 22.44N111.32E
Luofo Zaïre **79** 0.12S 29.15E
Luogosanto Italy **32** 41.04N 9.12E
Luohe China **54** 33.30N114.04E
Luo He *r.* China **54** 34.40N110.15E
Luonan China **54** 34.06N110.10E
Luoyang China **54** 34.48N112.25E
Lupilichi Mozambique **79** 11.45S 35.15E
Luquan China **61** 25.35N102.30E
Luque Spain **27** 37.33N 4.16W
Lūrah *r.* Afghan. **62** 31.20N 65.45E
Luray U.S.A. **114** 38.40N 78.28W
Lure France **19** 47.41N 6.30E
Lurgan U.K. **15** 54.28N 6.21W
Lurio Mozambique **79** 13.30S 40.30E
Lurio *r.* Mozambique **79** 13.32S 40.31E
Lusaka Zambia **79** 15.20S 28.14E
Lusambo Zaïre **78** 4.59S 23.26E
Luscar Canada **100** 53.05N117.26W
Lu Shan *mtn.* China **54** 36.18N118.03E
Lüshi China **54** 34.04N111.02E
Lushnje Albania **34** 40.55N 19.41E
Lushoto Tanzania **79** 4.48S 38.20E
Lüshun China **54** 38.42N121.15E
Lusignan France **18** 46.26N 0.07E
Lusk U.S.A. **108** 42.46N104.27W
Lussac-les-Châteaux France **18** 46.24N 0.44E
Luton U.K. **13** 51.53N 0.25W
Lutsk Ukraine **37** 50.42N 25.15E
Lutterworth U.K. **13** 52.28N 1.12W
Lützow Germany **38** 53.40N 11.11E
Luud *r.* Somali Rep. **71** 10.25N 51.05E
Luuq Somali Rep. **79** 3.56N 42.32E
Luverne U.S.A. **110** 43.39N 96.13W
Luvua *r.* Zaïre **79** 6.45S 27.00E
Luwegu *r.* Tanzania **79** 8.30S 37.28E
Luwingu Zambia **79** 10.13S 30.05E
Luxembourg *d.* Belgium **16** 49.58N 5.30E
Luxembourg Europe **16** 49.50N 6.15E
Luxembourg *town* Lux. **16** 49.37N 6.08E
Luxeuil-les-Bains France **19** 47.49N 6.23E
Luxi China **55** 28.17N110.10E
Luxor *see* Al Uqşur Egypt **64**
Luy de Béarn *r.* France **20** 43.36N 0.44W
Luy de France *r.* France **20** 43.38N 0.47W
Luza Russian Fed. **44** 60.41N 47.12E
Luza *r.* Russian Fed. **44** 60.45N 46.25E
Luzarches France **19** 49.07N 2.25E
Luzern Switz. **39** 47.03N 8.18E
Luzern *d.* Switz. **39** 47.12N 8.05E
Luzhai China **55** 24.29N109.29E
Luzhou China **55** 28.48N105.23E
Luziânia Brazil **123** 16.18S 47.57W
Luzon *i.* Phil. **59** 17.50N121.00E
Luzon Str. Pacific Oc. **59** 20.20N122.00E
Luzy France **19** 46.48N 3.58E
Lvov Ukraine **37** 49.50N 24.00E
Lyantonde Uganda **79** 0.26S 31.08E
Lybster U.K. **14** 58.18N 3.18W
Lyckeby Sweden **43** 56.12N 15.39E
Lycksele Sweden **40** 64.36N 18.40E
Lydenburg R.S.A. **80** 25.06S 30.27E
Lyell I. Canada **100** 52.40N131.35W
Lygnern *l.* Sweden **43** 57.29N 12.20E
Lykens U.S.A. **114** 40.34N 76.43W
Lyme B. U.K. **13** 50.40N 2.55W
Lyme Regis U.K. **13** 50.44N 2.57W
Lymington U.K. **13** 50.46N 1.32W
Łyna *r.* Poland **37** 54.37N 21.14E
Lynchburg U.S.A. **113** 37.24N 79.10W
Lynden Canada **104** 43.14N 80.09W
Lyndhurst Australia **92** 30.19S138.24E
Lyndonville U.S.A. **114** 43.19N 78.23W
Lyngdal Norway **42** 58.08N 7.05E
Lyngen Norway **40** 69.36N 20.10E
Lyngen *est.* Norway **40** 69.35N 20.20E
Lynn U.S.A. **115** 42.28N 70.57W
Lynn, L. U.S.A. **114** 39.41N 79.55W
Lynn Canal U.S.A. **100** 58.38N135.08W
Lynn Lake *town* Canada **101** 56.51N101.03W
Lynton U.K. **13** 51.14N 3.50W
Lynx Canada **102** 50.08N 85.55W
Lyon France **21** 45.45N 4.51E
Lyon Mountain *town* U.S.A. **105** 44.43N 73.55W
Lyonnais, Monts du *mts.* France **21** 45.40N 4.30E
Lyons Australia **92** 30.34S133.50E
Lyons *r.* Australia **88** 25.02S115.09E
Lyons U.S.A. **114** 43.04N 77.00W
Lyons Falls U.S.A. **115** 43.37N 75.22W
Lysefjorden *est.* Norway **42** 59.00N 6.14E
Lysekil Sweden **42** 58.16N 11.26E
Lyster Canada **105** 46.22N 71.38W
Lysva Russian Fed. **44** 58.07N 57.49E
Lysyanka Ukraine **37** 49.16N 30.49E
Lysyye Gory Russian Fed. **45** 51.32N 44.48E
Lytham St. Anne's U.K. **12** 53.45N 3.01W
Lyubar Ukraine **37** 49.58N 27.41E
Lyubech Ukraine **37** 51.42N 30.41E
Lyubertsy Russian Fed. **44** 55.38N 37.58E
Lyubeshov Ukraine **37** 51.42N 25.32E
Lyubimets Bulgaria **34** 41.50N 26.05E
Lyushcha Belorussia **37** 52.28N 26.41E

M

Ma *r.* Vietnam **55** 19.48N105.55E
Ma, Oued el- *wadi* Mauritania **74** 24.30N 9.10W
Ma'ād Jordan **67** 32.36N 35.37E
Maamakeogh *mtn.* Rep. of Ire. **15** 54.17N 9.29W
Maamturk Mts. Rep. of Ire. **15** 53.32N 9.42W
Ma'ān Jordan **66** 30.11N 35.43E
Ma'anshan China **55** 31.47N118.33E
Maarianhamina Finland **43** 60.06N 19.57E
Maas *r.* Neth. **16** 51.44N 4.42E
Maaseik Belgium **16** 51.08N 5.48E
Maassluis Neth. **16** 51.58N 4.12E
Maastricht Neth. **16** 50.51N 5.42E
Maave Mozambique **81** 21.06S 34.48E
Maaza Plateau Egypt **66** 27.39N 31.45E
Mabalane Mozambique **81** 23.49S 32.36E
Ma'barot Israel **67** 32.22N 34.54E
Maberly Canada **105** 44.50N 76.36W
Mablethorpe U.K. **12** 53.21N 0.14E
Mabrouk Mali **76** 19.29N 1.15W
Macá *mtn.* Chile **125** 45.06S 73.12W
Macaé Brazil **126** 22.21S 41.48W
Macalister *r.* Australia **93** 37.55S146.50E
Macão Portugal **27** 39.33N 8.00W
Macapá Brazil **123** 0.04N 51.04W
Macarthur Australia **92** 38.01S142.01E
Macau Asia **55** 22.11N113.33E
Macau Brazil **123** 5.05S 36.37W
Macclesfield U.K. **12** 53.16N 2.09W
Macdiarmid Canada **102** 49.27N 88.08W
Macdoel U.S.A. **108** 41.50N122.00W
Macdonald, L. Australia **88** 23.30S129.00E
Macdonnell Ranges *mts.* Australia **90** 23.45S133.20E
Macduff U.K. **14** 57.40N 2.29W
Macedo de Cavaleiros Portugal **26** 41.32N 6.58W
Macedon, Mt. Australia **93** 37.27S144.34E
Macedonia Europe **34** 41.53N 21.40E
Maceió Brazil **123** 9.40S 35.44W
Macenta Guinea **76** 8.31N 9.32W
Macerata Italy **31** 43.18N 13.27E
MacFarlane *r.* Canada **101** 59.12N107.58W
Macfarlane, L. Australia **92** 31.55S136.42E
Macgillycuddy's Reeks *mts.* Rep. of Ire. **15** 52.00N 9.43W
Machado Brazil **126** 21.39S 45.33W
Machala Ecuador **122** 3.20S 79.57W
Machattie, L. Australia **90** 24.50S139.48E
Machece Mozambique **81** 19.17S 35.33E
Machecoul France **18** 47.00N 1.50W
Macheke Zimbabwe **81** 18.08S 31.49E
Macheng China **55** 31.11N115.02E
Machevna Russian Fed. **51** 60.46N171.40E
Machias Maine U.S.A. **112** 44.43N 67.28W
Machias N.Y. U.S.A. **114** 42.25N 78.30W
Machichaco, Cabo *c.* Spain **26** 43.27N 2.45W
Machichi *r.* Canada **101** 57.03N 92.06W
Machida Japan **57** 35.32N139.27E
Machilīpatnam India **61** 16.13N 81.12E
Machiques Venezuela **122** 10.04N 72.37W
Machiya *r.* Japan **57** 35.01N136.42E
Machrihanish U.K. **14** 55.25N 5.44W
Machynlleth U.K. **13** 52.35N 3.51W
Maciá Argentina **125** 32.11S 59.25W
Macia Mozambique **81** 25.03S 33.10E
Macintyre *r.* Australia **93** 28.50S150.50E
Mackay Australia **90** 21.09S149.11E
MacKay U.S.A. **108** 43.55N113.37W
Mackay, L. Australia **88** 22.30S129.10E
Mackenzie *r.* Australia **90** 22.48S149.15E
Mackenzie *r.* Canada **98** 69.20N134.00W
Mackenzie King I. Canada **98** 77.30N112.00W
Mackenzie Mts. Canada **98** 64.00N130.00W
Mackinac I. U.S.A. **104** 45.51N 84.38W
Mackinaw City U.S.A. **104** 45.47N 84.44W
Mackinnon Road *town* Kenya **79** 3.50S 39.03E
Macklin Canada **101** 52.20N109.56W
Macksville Australia **93** 30.43S152.55E
Maclean Australia **91** 29.27S153.14E
Maclear R.S.A. **80** 31.04S 28.21E
Macleay *r.* Australia **93** 30.52S153.01E
MacLeod, L. Australia **88** 24.10S113.35E
Maçobere Mozambique **81** 21.14S 32.50E
Macomer Italy **32** 40.16N 8.46E
Mâcon France **21** 46.18N 4.50E
Macon Ga. U.S.A. **113** 32.49N 83.37W
Macon Mo. U.S.A. **110** 39.44N 92.28W
Mâconnais, Monts du *mts.* France **19** 46.18N 4.45E
Macquarie *r.* Australia **93** 30.07S147.24E
Macquarie, L. Australia **93** 33.05S151.35E
Macquarie-Balleny Ridge Pacific Oc. **84** 58.00S160.00E
Macquarie I. Pacific Oc. **84** 54.29S158.58E
Macquarie Marshes Australia **93** 30.50S147.32E
MacRobertson Land *f.* Antarctica **128** 69.30S 64.00E
Macroom Rep. of Ire. **15** 51.54N 8.58W
Mac Tier Canada **104** 45.08N 79.47W
Macumba *r.* Australia **91** 27.55S137.15E
Ma'dabā Jordan **67** 31.44N 35.48E
Madagascar Africa **81** 17.00S 46.00E
Madan Bulgaria **34** 41.30N 24.57E
Madang P.N.G. **59** 5.14S145.45E
Madaoua Niger **77** 14.05N 6.27E
Mādārīpur Bangla. **63** 23.10N 90.12E
Madawaska Canada **105** 45.30N 77.59W
Madawaska *r.* Canada **105** 45.27N 76.21W
Madawaska U.S.A. **112** 47.21N 68.20W
Maddalena *i.* Italy **32** 41.13N 9.24E
Maddaloni Italy **33** 41.02N 14.23E
Madeira *r.* Brazil **122** 3.20S 59.00W
Madeira *i.* Madeira Is. **127** 32.45N 17.00W
Madeira, Arquipélago da *is.* Atlantic Oc. **127** 32.45N 17.00W
Madeira Is. *see* Madeira, Arquipélago da *is.* Atlantic Oc. **127**
Mädelegabel *mtn.* Austria **39** 47.18N 10.18E
Madeleine, Îles de la *is.* Canada **103** 47.20N 61.50W
Madera U.S.A. **108** 36.57N120.03W
Madera, Sierra de la *mts.* Mexico **109** 30.20N109.00W
Madgaon India **60** 15.26N 73.50E
Madhubani India **63** 26.22N 86.05E
Madhupur India **63** 24.16N 86.39E
Madhya Pradesh *d.* India **63** 23.30N 78.30E
Madibira Tanzania **79** 8.13S 34.47E
Madigan G. Australia **92** 28.55S137.48E
Madill U.S.A. **111** 34.06N 96.46W
Madīnat ash Sha'b Yemen **71** 12.50N 44.56E
Madingley Rise *f.* Indian Oc. **49** 5.00S 62.00E
Madison Fla. U.S.A. **107** 30.29N 83.39W
Madison Ind. U.S.A. **112** 38.46N 85.22W
Madison N.J. U.S.A. **115** 40.46N 74.25W
Madison Ohio U.S.A. **114** 41.47N 81.04W
Madison S.Dak. U.S.A. **110** 44.00N 97.07W
Madison Tenn. U.S.A. **113** 36.16N 86.44W
Madison Va. U.S.A. **114** 38.23N 78.15W
Madison Wisc. U.S.A. **110** 43.05N 89.22W
Madison W.Va. U.S.A. **113** 38.03N 81.50W
Madison Junction U.S.A. **108** 44.39N110.51W
Madisonville Ky. U.S.A. **113** 37.20N 87.30W
Madisonville Tex. U.S.A. **111** 30.57N 95.55W
Madiun Indonesia **59** 7.37S111.33E
Madoc Canada **105** 44.30N 77.28W
Mado Gashi Kenya **79** 0.40N 39.11E
Madoi China **52** 34.28N 98.56E
Madonna di Campiglio Italy **30** 46.14N 10.49E
Madrakah, Ra's al *c.* Oman **60** 19.00N 57.50E
Madras India **61** 13.05N 80.18E
Madras U.S.A. **108** 44.38N121.08W
Madre, Laguna *b.* Mexico **111** 25.00N 97.40W
Madre, Laguna *b.* U.S.A. **111** 27.00N 97.35W
Madre, Sierra *mts.* Mexico/Guatemala **116** 15.20N 92.20W
Madre de Dios *r.* Bolivia **122** 10.24S 65.30W
Madre del Sur, Sierra *mts.* Mexico **116** 17.00N100.00W
Madre Occidental, Sierra *mts.* Mexico **109** 25.00N105.00W
Madre Oriental, Sierra *mts.* Mexico **111** 28.10N102.10W
Madrid Spain **26** 40.24N 3.41W
Madrid *d.* Spain **26** 40.15N 3.30W
Madridejos Spain **27** 39.28N 3.32W
Madrigalejo Spain **27** 39.09N 5.37W
Madrona, Sierra *mts.* Spain **26** 38.30N 3.00W
Madroñera Spain **27** 39.26N 5.46W
Madukani Tanzania **79** 3.57S 35.49E
Madura *i.* Indonesia **59** 7.02S113.22E
Madurai India **48** 9.55N 78.07E
Maebashi Japan **57** 36.30N139.04E
Mae Klong *r.* Thailand **56** 13.21N100.00E
Mae Sot Thailand **56** 16.40N 98.35E
Maestra, Sierra *mts.* Cuba **117** 20.10N 76.30W
Maestu Spain **26** 42.44N 2.27W
Maevatanana Madagascar **81** 16.56S 46.49E
Maewo *i.* Vanuatu **84** 15.10S168.10E
Mafeking Canada **101** 52.43N100.59W
Mafeteng Lesotho **80** 29.51S 27.13E
Maffra Australia **93** 37.58S146.59E
Mafia I. Tanzania **79** 7.50S 39.50E
Mafikeng R.S.A. **80** 25.52S 25.36E
Mafra Portugal **27** 38.56N 9.20W
Magadan Russian Fed. **51** 59.38N150.50E
Magadi Kenya **79** 1.53S 36.18E
Magallanes, Estrecho de *str.* Chile **125** 53.00S 71.00W
Magallan's Str. *see* Magellanes, Estrecho de*str.* Chile **125**
Magalluf Spain **25** 39.30N 2.30E
Magangué Colombia **122** 9.14N 74.46W
Magazine U.S.A. **111** 35.10N 93.40W
Magburaka Sierra Leone **76** 8.44N 11.57W
Magdalena Argentina **125** 35.04S 57.32W
Magdalena Bolivia **124** 13.50S 64.08W
Magdalena *r.* Colombia **122** 10.56N 74.58W
Magdalena Mexico **109** 30.38N110.59W
Magdalena, Isla *i.* Chile **125** 44.42S 73.10W
Magdalena, Llano de la *f.* Mexico **109** 24.55N111.40W
Magdalene *mtn.* Malaysia **58** 4.25N117.55E
Magdeburg Germany **38** 52.08N 11.38E
Magé Brazil **126** 22.37S 43.03W
Magee U.S.A. **111** 31.52N 89.44W
Magelang Indonesia **59** 7.28S110.11E
Magen Israel **67** 31.18N 34.26E
Magenta Italy **30** 45.28N 8.53E
Magenta, L. Australia **89** 33.26S119.10E
Mageröya *i.* Norway **40** 71.03N 25.45E
Maggiorasca, Monte *mtn.* Italy **30** 44.33N 9.29E
Maggiore, Lago *l.* Italy **30** 46.00N 8.40E
Maghâghah Egypt **66** 28.39N 30.50E
Maghār Israel **67** 32.53N 35.24E
Magherafelt U.K. **15** 54.45N 6.38W
Magina *mtn.* Spain **27** 37.44N 3.28W
Magione Italy **30** 43.08N 12.12E
Maglaj Bosnia-Herzegovina **31** 44.33N 18.06E
Magna U.S.A. **108** 40.42N112.06W
Magnetawan Canada **104** 45.40N 79.38W
Magnetawan *r.* Canada **104** 45.46N 80.37W
Magnetic I. Australia **90** 19.08S146.50E
Magnitogorsk Russian Fed. **44** 53.28N 59.06E
Magnolia Ark. U.S.A. **111** 33.16N 93.14W
Magnolia Miss. U.S.A. **111** 31.09N 90.28W
Magnolia Tex. U.S.A. **111** 30.13N 95.45W
Magny-en-Vexin France **19** 49.09N 1.47E
Magog Canada **105** 45.16N 72.09W
Magoye Zambia **79** 16.00S 27.38E
Magpie *r.* Canada **103** 50.18N 64.28W
Magrath Canada **100** 49.25N112.50W
Magro *r.* Spain **25** 39.11N 0.25W
Magude Mozambique **81** 25.01S 32.39E

Magué to **Manturovo**

Magué Mozambique **79** 15.46S 31.42E
Maguse River *town* Canada **101** 61.20N 94.25W
Magwe Burma **56** 20.08N 95.00E
Magwe *d.* Burma **56** 23.00N 95.00E
Mahābād Iran **65** 36.44N 45.44E
Mahābhārat Range *mts.* Nepal **63** 28.00N 84.30E
Mahabo Madagascar **81** 20.23S 44.40E
Mahadday Weyne Somali Rep. **79** 2.58N 45.32E
Mahādeo Hills India **63** 22.15N 78.30E
Mahaffey U.S.A. **114** 40.53N 78.44W
Mahagi Zaïre **79** 2.16N 30.59E
Mahajamba *r.* Madagascar **81** 15.33S 47.08E
Mahājan India **62** 28.47N 73.50E
Mahajanga Madagascar **81** 15.43S 46.19E
Mahajilo *r.* Madagascar **81** 19.42S 45.22E
Maḩajjah Syria **67** 32.57N 36.14E
Mahalapye Botswana **80** 23.04S 26.47E
Mahalás Greece **35** 38.41N 21.11E
Maḩallāt Iran **65** 33.54N 50.28E
Mahānadi India **63** 20.19N 86.45E
Mahānadi *r.* India **61** 20.17N 86.43E
Mahanoro Madagascar **81** 19.54S 48.48E
Mahanoy City U.S.A. **115** 40.49N 76.08W
Mahārājpur India **63** 25.01N 79.44E
Mahārāshtra *d.* India **62** 19.40N 76.00E
Mahāsamund India **63** 21.06N 82.06E
Maha Sarakham Thailand **56** 15.50N 103.47E
Mahavavy *r.* Madagascar **81** 15.57S 45.54E
Mahbés W. Sahara **74** 27.13N 9.44W
Mahd adh Dhahab Saudi Arabia **64** 23.30N 40.52E
Mahdia Guyana **122** 5.10N 59.12W
Mahendraganj India **63** 25.20N 89.45E
Mahenge Tanzania **79** 8.46S 36.38E
Mahi *r.* India **62** 22.30N 72.58E
Mahia Pen. New Zealand **86** 39.10S 177.50E
Mahmūdābād India **63** 27.18N 81.07E
Mahmūd-e 'Erāqī Afghan. **62** 35.01N 69.20E
Mahnomen U.S.A. **110** 47.19N 96.01W
Maho Sri Lanka **61** 7.49N 80.17E
Mahoba India **63** 25.17N 79.52E
Mahón Spain **25** 39.53N 4.15E
Mahone B. Canada **103** 44.30N 64.15W
Mahora Spain **25** 39.13N 1.44W
Mahroni India **63** 24.35N 78.43E
Mahuva India **62** 21.05N 71.48E
Maia Portugal **26** 41.14N 8.37W
Maiao *i.* Îs. de la Société **85** 17.23S 150.37W
Maîche France **19** 47.15N 6.48E
Maidenhead U.K. **13** 51.32N 0.44W
Maidstone U.K. **13** 51.17N 0.32E
Maiduguri Nigeria **77** 11.53N 13.16E
Maignelay France **19** 49.33N 2.31E
Maihar India **63** 24.16N 80.45E
Maikala Range *mts.* India **63** 21.45N 81.00E
Maiko *r.* Zaïre **78** 0.15N 25.35E
Maillezais France **18** 46.22N 0.44W
Main *r.* Germany **39** 50.00N 8.18E
Mā'īn Jordan **67** 31.41N 35.44E
Mainburg Germany **39** 48.38N 11.47E
Main Camp Kiribati **85** 2.01N 157.25W
Main Centre Canada **101** 50.38N 107.20W
Main Channel *str.* Canada **104** 45.22N 81.50W
Mai Ndombe *l.* Zaïre **78** 2.00S 18.20E
Main Duck I. Canada **105** 43.56N 76.37W
Maine *d.* U.S.A. **112** 45.15N 69.15W
Maine-et-Loire *d.* France **18** 47.25N 0.30W
Mainhardt Germany **39** 49.04N 9.33E
Mainland *i.* Orkney Is. U.K. **14** 59.00N 3.10W
Mainoru Australia **90** 14.02S 134.05E
Mainpuri India **63** 27.14N 79.01E
Maintenon France **19** 48.35N 1.35E
Maintirano Madagascar **81** 18.03S 44.01E
Mainz Germany **39** 50.01N 8.16E
Maipo *mtn.* Argentina **125** 34.10S 69.50W
Maipú Argentina **125** 36.52S 57.54W
Maiquetía Venezuela **122** 10.03N 66.57W
Maiskhāl I. Bangla. **63** 21.36N 91.56E
Maitland N.S.W. Australia **93** 32.33S 151.33E
Maitland S.A. Australia **92** 34.21S 137.42E
Maitland *r.* Canada **104** 43.45N 81.43W
Maizhokunggar China **63** 29.50N 91.44E
Maizuru Japan **57** 35.30N 135.20E
Majd el Kurūm Israel **67** 32.55N 35.15E
Majeigha Sudan **73** 11.33N 24.40E
Majene Indonesia **58** 3.33S 118.59E
Majī Ethiopia **73** 6.11N 35.38E
Majiahewan China **54** 37.12N 105.48E
Majiang China **55** 26.30N 107.35E
Majorca *i. see* Mallorca *i.* Spain **25**
Majrūr Sudan **72** 14.01N 30.27E
Majuba Hill R.S.A. **80** 27.26S 29.48E
Majuro *i.* Pacific Oc. **84** 7.09N 171.12E
Makabana Congo **78** 3.25S 12.41E
Makale Indonesia **58** 3.06S 119.53E
Makalu *mtn.* China / Nepal **63** 27.54N 87.06E
Makarikha Russian Fed. **44** 66.17N 58.28E
Makarska Croatia **31** 43.18N 17.02E
Makaryev Russian Fed. **44** 57.52N 43.40E
Makasar, Selat *str.* Indonesia **58** 3.00S 118.00E
Makassar Str. *see* Makasar, Selat *str.* Indonesia **58**
Makat Kazakhstan **45** 47.38N 53.16E
Makaw Burma **56** 26.27N 96.42E
Makay, Massif du *mts.* Madagascar **81** 21.15S 45.15E
Makaya Zaïre **78** 3.22S 18.02E
Makedonija *see* Macedonia Europe **34**
Makefu Niue **84** 19.01S 169.55W
Makeni Sierra Leone **76** 8.57N 12.02W
Makere Tanzania **79** 4.15S 30.26E
Makeyevka Ukraine **45** 48.01N 38.00E
Makgadikgadi Salt Pan *f.* Botswana **80** 20.50S 25.45E
Makhachkala Russian Fed. **45** 42.59N 47.30E
Makham Thailand **56** 12.40N 102.12E
Makhfar al Quwayrah Jordan **66** 29.49N 35.18E
Makhrūq, Wādī al *r.* Jordan **66** 31.30N 37.10E
Makinsk Kazakhstan **9** 52.37N 70.26E
Makkah Saudi Arabia **72** 21.26N 39.49E
Makkovik Canada **103** 55.00N 59.10W
Makó Hungary **37** 46.13N 20.30E
Mako Senegal **76** 13.00N 12.26W
Makobe L. Canada **104** 47.27N 80.25W
Makokou Gabon **78** 0.38N 12.47E
Makoua Congo **78** 0.01S 15.40E
Makrai India **62** 22.04N 77.06E
Makran *f.* Asia **65** 26.30N 61.20E
Makrāna India **62** 27.03N 74.43E
Makrān Coast Range *mts.* Pakistan **62** 25.30N 64.30E
Maksamaa Finland **40** 63.14N 22.05E
Makuliro Tanzania **79** 9.34S 37.26E
Makurdi Nigeria **77** 7.44N 8.35E
Māl India **63** 26.52N 88.44E
Malabo Equat. Guinea **77** 3.45N 8.48E
Malacca *see* Melaka Malaysia **58**
Malacca, Str. of Indian Oc. **58** 3.00N 100.30E
Malad City U.S.A. **108** 42.12N 112.15W
Málaga Spain **27** 36.43N 4.25W
Málaga *d.* Spain **27** 36.45N 4.40W
Malaga U.S.A. **109** 32.14N 104.04W
Malagón Spain **27** 39.35N 3.51W
Malagón *r.* Spain **27** 37.35N 7.29W
Malaimbandy Madagascar **81** 20.20S 45.36E
Malaita Solomon Is. **84** 9.00S 161.00E
Malakāl Sudan **73** 9.31N 31.39E
Malakand Pakistan **62** 34.34N 71.56E
Mala Kapela *mts.* Croatia **31** 45.00N 15.20E
Malam Chad **73** 11.27N 20.59E
Malang Indonesia **59** 7.59S 112.45E
Malangwa Nepal **63** 26.52N 85.34E
Malanje Angola **78** 9.36S 16.21E
Malanje *d.* Angola **78** 8.40S 16.50E
Mälaren *l.* Sweden **43** 59.30N 17.12E
Malartic Canada **102** 48.09N 78.09W
Malatya Turkey **64** 38.22N 38.18E
Malaucène France **21** 44.10N 5.08E
Malaut India **62** 30.11N 74.30E
Malaŵi Africa **79** 12.00S 34.00E
Malaŵi, L. Africa **79** 12.00S 34.30E
Malaya Vishera Russian Fed. **44** 58.53N 32.08E
Malāyer Iran **65** 34.19N 48.51E
Malaysia Asia **58** 5.00N 110.00E
Malazgirt Turkey **64** 39.09N 42.31E
Malbaie *r.* Canada **103** 47.40N 70.05W
Malbaie, Baie de *b.* Canada **103** 48.35N 64.16W
Malbooma Australia **92** 30.41S 134.11E
Malbork Poland **37** 54.02N 19.01E
Malchin Germany **38** 53.44N 12.46E
Malchow Germany **38** 53.28N 12.25E
Malcolm Australia **89** 28.56S 121.30E
Malcolm, Pt. Australia **89** 33.47S 123.44E
Malden Mo. U.S.A. **111** 36.34N 89.57W
Malden I. Kiribati **85** 4.03S 154.49W
Maldive Ridge *f.* Indian Oc. **49** 0.00 73.00E
Maldives Indian Oc. **60** 6.20N 73.00E
Maldon U.K. **13** 51.43N 0.41E
Maldonado Uruguay **126** 34.57S 54.59W
Male Italy **30** 46.21N 10.55E
Maléa, Ákra *c.* Greece **35** 36.26N 23.12E
Malebo Pool *f.* Zaïre **78** 4.15S 15.25E
Mālegaon India **62** 20.33N 74.32E
Malek Sudan **73** 6.04N 31.36E
Malek Dīn Afghan. **62** 32.25N 68.04E
Malekula *i.* Vanuatu **84** 16.15S 167.30E
Malema Mozambique **79** 14.55S 37.09E
Malenga Russian Fed. **44** 63.50N 36.50E
Malente Germany **38** 54.10N 10.33E
Māler Kotla India **62** 30.32N 75.53E
Malesherbes France **19** 48.18N 2.25E
Malesína Greece **35** 38.37N 23.15E
Malestroit France **18** 47.49N 2.23W
Malgomaj *l.* Sweden **40** 64.47N 16.12E
Malheur L. U.S.A. **108** 43.20N 118.45W
Mali Africa **76** 17.30N 2.30E
Mali *r.* Burma **56** 25.43N 97.29E
Malik, Wādī al Sudan **72** 18.02N 30.58E
Malili Indonesia **59** 2.38S 121.06E
Målilla Sweden **43** 57.23N 15.48E
Malin Ukraine **37** 50.48N 29.08E
Malinau Indonesia **58** 3.35N 116.38E
Malindi Kenya **79** 3.14S 40.08E
Malingping Indonesia **59** 6.45S 106.01E
Malin Head Rep. of Ire. **15** 55.23N 7.24W
Malin More Rep. of Ire. **15** 54.42N 8.48W
Malipo China **55** 23.11N 104.41E
Maliqi Albania **34** 40.45N 20.48E
Mali Rajinac Croatia **31** 44.48N 15.02E
Malita Phil. **59** 6.19N 125.39E
Māliya India **62** 23.05N 70.46E
Malkāpur India **62** 20.53N 76.12E
Mallacoota Australia **93** 37.34S 149.43E
Mallacoota Inlet *b.* Australia **93** 37.34S 149.43E
Mallaig U.K. **14** 57.00N 5.50W
Mallawī Egypt **66** 27.44N 30.50E
Mallersdorf Germany **39** 48.47N 12.16E
Mallnitz Austria **30** 46.59N 13.10E
Mallorca *i.* Spain **25** 39.30N 3.00E
Mallow Rep. of Ire. **15** 52.08N 8.39W
Malm Norway **40** 64.04N 11.12E
Malmbäck Sweden **43** 57.35N 14.28E
Malmberget Sweden **40** 67.10N 20.40E
Malmédy Belgium **16** 50.25N 6.02E
Malmesbury R.S.A. **80** 33.28S 18.43E
Malmö Sweden **43** 55.36N 13.00E
Malmöhus *d.* Sweden **43** 55.45N 13.30E
Malmslätt Sweden **43** 58.25N 15.30E
Malmyzh Russian Fed. **44** 56.34N 50.41E
Maloja Switz. **39** 46.24N 9.41E
Malolos Guam **84** 13.18N 144.46E
Malone U.S.A. **105** 44.51N 74.17W
Malonga Zaïre **78** 10.26S 23.10E
Malorita Belorussia **37** 51.50N 24.08E
Målöy Norway **41** 61.56N 5.07E
Malozemelskaya Tundra *f.* Russian Fed. **44** 67.40N 50.10E
Malpartida de Plasencia Spain **27** 39.59N 6.02W
Malpas Australia **92** 34.44S 140.43E
Malta Europe **28** 35.55N 14.25E
Malta Mont. U.S.A. **108** 48.21N 107.52W
Malta Ohio U.S.A. **114** 39.39N 81.52W
Malta Channel Med. Sea **28** 36.20N 14.45E
Maltby U.K. **12** 53.25N 1.12W
Malton U.K. **12** 54.09N 0.48W
Maluku *d.* Indonesia **59** 4.00S 129.00E
Maluku, Laut *sea* Pacific Oc. **59**
Malumfashi Nigeria **77** 11.48N 7.36E
Malundo Angola **78** 14.51S 22.00E
Malung Sweden **41** 60.40N 13.44E
Malūţ Sudan **73** 10.26N 32.12E
Malvinas, Islas *see* Falkland Is. Atlantic Ocean **125**
Mama Russian Fed. **51** 58.20N 112.55E
Mamadysh Russian Fed. **44** 55.43N 51.20E
Mamaia Romania **37** 44.15N 28.37E
Mambasa Zaïre **79** 1.20N 29.05E
Mamberamo *r.* Indonesia **59** 1.45S 137.25E
Mambéré *r.* C.A.R. **77** 3.30N 16.08E
Mambilima Falls *town* Zambia **79** 10.32S 28.45E
Mamers France **18** 48.21N 0.23E
Mamfe Cameroon **77** 5.46N 9.18E
Mamonovo Russian Fed. **37** 54.30N 19.59E
Mamore *r.* Bolivia **124** 12.00S 65.15W
Mamou Guinea **76** 10.24N 12.05W
Mampika Congo **78** 2.58S 14.38E
Mampikony Madagascar **81** 16.06S 47.38E
Mampong Ghana **76** 7.06N 1.24W
Mamry, Jezioro *l.* Poland **37** 54.08N 21.42E
Mamuju Indonesia **58** 2.41S 118.55E
Ma'mūn Sudan **73** 12.15N 22.41E
Man Ivory Coast **76** 7.31N 7.37W
Man Jammu & Kashmir **63** 33.51N 78.32E
Man, Isle of Europe **12** 54.15N 4.30W
Mana *r.* Guiana **123** 5.35N 53.55W
Mana Hawaiian Is. **85** 22.02N 156.46W
Manacapuru Brazil **122** 3.16S 60.37W
Manacor Spain **25** 39.34N 3.12E
Manado Indonesia **59** 1.30N 124.58E
Managua Nicaragua **117** 12.06N 86.18W
Managua, Lago de *l.* Nicaragua **117** 12.10N 86.30W
Manahawkin U.S.A. **115** 39.42N 74.16W
Manakara Madagascar **81** 22.08S 48.01E
Manāli India **62** 32.16N 77.10E
Manambao *r.* Madagascar **81** 17.43S 43.57E
Mananara Madagascar **81** 16.10S 49.46E
Mananara *r.* Madagascar **81** 23.21S 47.42E
Manangatang Australia **92** 35.02S 142.54E
Mananjary Madagascar **81** 21.13S 48.20E
Manankoro Mali **76** 10.25N 7.26W
Manantali, Lac de *l.* Mali **76** 13.00N 10.20W
Manantenina Madagascar **81** 24.17S 47.19E
Manapouri, L. New Zealand **86** 45.30S 167.00E
Manār *r.* India **62** 18.39N 77.44E
Manāslu *mtn.* Nepal **63** 28.33N 84.35E
Manasquan U.S.A. **115** 40.07N 74.03W
Manassas U.S.A. **114** 38.45N 77.28W
Manau P.N.G. **59** 8.02S 148.00E
Manaus Brazil **122** 3.06S 60.00W
Manāwar India **62** 22.14N 75.05E
Manawatu-Wanganui *d.* New Zealand **86** 39.00S 175.25E
Mancelona U.S.A. **112** 44.54N 85.03W
Mancha Real Spain **27** 37.47N 3.37W
Manche *d.* France **18** 49.00N 1.10W
Mancherāl India **63** 18.52N 79.26E
Manchester U.K. **12** 53.30N 2.15W
Manchester Conn. U.S.A. **115** 41.47N 72.31W
Manchester Mich. U.S.A. **104** 42.09N 84.02W
Manchester N.H. U.S.A. **115** 42.59N 71.28W
Manchester N.Y. U.S.A. **114** 42.58N 77.14W
Manchurian Plain *f. see* Dongbei Pingyuan *f.* China **53**
Manciano Italy **30** 42.35N 11.31E
Mand *r.* Iran **65** 28.09N 51.16E
Manda Iringa Tanzania **79** 10.30S 34.37E
Manda Mbeya Tanzania **79** 7.59S 32.27E
Manda, Jabal *mtn.* Sudan **73** 8.39N 24.27E
Mandabe Madagascar **81** 21.03S 44.55E
Mandal Norway **42** 58.02N 7.27E
Mandala Peak Indonesia **59** 4.45S 140.15E
Mandalay Burma **56** 21.58N 96.04E
Mandalay *d.* Burma **56** 22.00N 96.00E
Mandalgovi Mongolia **54** 45.40N 106.10E
Mandals *r.* Norway **42** 58.02N 7.28E
Mandalya Körfezi *b.* Turkey **35** 37.12N 27.20E
Mandan U.S.A. **110** 46.50N 100.54W
Mandara Mts. Nigeria / Cameroon **77** 10.30N 13.30E
Mandas Italy **32** 39.39N 9.08E
Mandasor India **62** 24.04N 75.04E
Mandeb, Bāb el *str.* Asia **73** 13.00N 43.10E
Mandel Afghan. **62** 33.17N 61.52E
Mandera Kenya **79** 3.55N 41.50E
Mandi India **62** 31.42N 76.55E
Mandiana Guinea **76** 10.37N 8.39W
Mandi Būrewāla Pakistan **62** 30.09N 72.41E
Mandi Dabwāli India **62** 29.58N 74.42E
Mandji Gabon **78** 1.37S 10.53E
Mandla India **63** 22.36N 80.23E
Mandora Australia **88** 19.45S 120.50E
Mandoto Madagascar **81** 19.34S 46.17E
Mandoúdhion Greece **35** 38.48N 23.29E
Mandra Pakistan **62** 33.22N 73.14E
Mandritsara Madagascar **81** 15.50S 48.49E
Māndu India **62** 22.22N 75.23E
Mandurah Australia **89** 32.31S 115.41E
Manduria Italy **33** 40.24N 17.38E
Māndvi India **62** 22.50N 69.22E
Mandya India **60** 12.33N 76.54E
Måne *r.* Norway **42** 59.00N 9.40E
Manendragarh India **63** 23.13N 82.13E
Manerbio Italy **32** 45.21N 10.08E
Manevichi Ukraine **37** 51.19N 25.35E
Manfredonia Italy **33** 41.38N 15.55E
Manfredonia, Golfo di *g.* Italy **33** 41.35N 16.05E
Mangaia I. Cook Is. **85** 21.56S 157.56W
Mangaldai India **63** 26.26N 92.02E
Mangalia Romania **37** 43.50N 28.35E
Mangalore India **60** 12.54N 74.51E
Mangando Angola **78** 8.02S 17.08E
Mangareva *i.* Pacific Oc. **85** 23.07S 134.57W
Mangawān India **63** 24.41N 81.33E
Mangaweka New Zealand **86** 38.49S 175.48E
Mangeigne Chad **73** 10.31N 21.19E
Mangnai China **52** 37.52N 91.26E
Mango Togo **76** 10.23N 0.30E
Mangochi Malaŵi **79** 14.29S 35.15E
Mangoky *r.* Madagascar **81** 21.29S 43.41E
Mangombe Zaïre **79** 1.23S 26.50E
Mangonui New Zealand **86** 35.00S 173.34E
Mangoro *r.* Madagascar **81** 20.00S 48.45E
Māngrol India **62** 21.07N 70.07E
Mangualde Portugal **26** 40.36N 7.46W
Mangueira, L. Brazil **126** 33.06S 52.48W
Mangum U.S.A. **111** 34.53N 99.30W
Mangyshlak, Poluostrov *pen.* Kazakhstan **45** 44.00N 52.30E
Manhattan U.S.A. **110** 39.11N 96.35W
Manhiça Mozambique **81** 25.24S 32.49E
Manhuaçu Brazil **126** 20.16S 42.01W
Manhumirim Brazil **126** 20.22S 41.57W
Mania *r.* Madagascar **81** 19.42S 45.22E
Maniago Italy **30** 46.10N 12.43E
Maniamba Mozambique **79** 12.30S 35.05E
Manica Mozambique **81** 19.00S 33.00E
Manica *d.* Mozambique **81** 20.00S 34.00E
Manicoré Brazil **122** 5.49S 61.17W
Manicouagan *r.* Canada **103** 49.15N 68.20W
Manicouagan, Résr. Canada **103** 51.20N 68.48W
Maniitsoq *see* Sukkertoppen Greenland **99**
Mānikganj Bangla. **63** 23.19N 87.03E
Mānikpur India **63** 25.04N 81.07E
Manila Phil. **59** 14.36N 120.59E
Manila U.S.A. **108** 40.59N 109.43W
Manildra Australia **93** 33.12S 148.41E
Manilla Australia **93** 30.45S 150.45E
Maningory *r.* Madagascar **81** 17.13S 49.28E
Manipur *d.* India **61** 25.00N 93.40E
Manisa Turkey **29** 38.37N 27.28E
Manistee U.S.A. **112** 44.14N 86.20W
Manistee *r.* U.S.A. **112** 44.14N 86.20W
Manistique U.S.A. **112** 45.58N 86.17W
Manitoba *d.* Canada **101** 55.00N 96.00W
Manitoba, L. Canada **101** 51.00N 98.45W
Manitou L. Canada **104** 45.48N 82.00W
Manitoulin I. Canada **104** 45.45N 82.30W
Manitowaning Canada **104** 45.45N 81.49W
Manitowoc U.S.A. **110** 44.06N 87.40W
Maniwaki Canada **105** 46.23N 75.58W
Manizales Colombia **122** 5.03N 75.32W
Manjā Jordan **67** 31.45N 35.51E
Manja Madagascar **81** 21.26S 44.20E
Manjakandriana Madagascar **81** 18.55S 47.47E
Mānjhand Pakistan **62** 25.55N 68.14E
Manjīl Iran **65** 36.44N 49.29E
Manjimup Australia **89** 34.14S 116.06E
Mankato U.S.A. **110** 44.10N 94.01W
Mankera Pakistan **62** 31.23N 71.26E
Mankono Ivory Coast **76** 8.01N 6.09W
Manlléu Spain **25** 42.00N 2.17E
Manly Australia **93** 33.47S 151.17E
Manmād India **62** 20.15N 74.27E
Mann *r.* Australia **90** 12.20S 134.07E
Mann *r.* N.S.W. Australia **93** 29.38S 152.21E
Mān Na Burma **56** 23.27N 97.14E
Manna Indonesia **58** 4.27S 102.55E
Mannahill Australia **92** 32.26S 139.59E
Mannar Sri Lanka **61** 8.59N 79.54E
Mannar, G. of India / Sri Lanka **61** 8.20N 79.00E
Mannessier, Lac *l.* Canada **103** 55.28N 70.38W
Mannheim Germany **39** 49.29N 8.29E
Mannin B. Rep. of Ire. **15** 53.28N 10.06W
Manning Canada **100** 56.53N 117.39W
Manning U.S.A. **113** 33.42N 80.12W
Mannington U.S.A. **114** 39.32N 80.20W
Manns Choice U.S.A. **114** 40.01N 78.39W
Mannsville U.S.A. **115** 43.43N 76.04W
Mannu *r.* Sardegna Italy **32** 39.16N 9.00E
Mannu *r.* Sardegna Italy **32** 40.50N 8.23E
Mannum Australia **92** 34.50S 139.20E
Mano Sierra Leone **76** 8.04N 12.02W
Manoharpur India **63** 22.23N 85.12E
Manokwari Indonesia **59** 0.53S 134.05E
Manolás Greece **35** 38.04N 21.21E
Manombo Madagascar **81** 22.57S 43.28E
Manono Zaïre **79** 7.18S 27.24E
Manorhamilton Rep. of Ire. **15** 54.18N 8.10W
Manosque France **21** 43.50N 5.47E
Manouane Canada **105** 47.14N 74.25W
Manouane *r.* Canada **103** 49.29N 71.13W
Manouane, Lac *l.* Canada **103** 50.40N 70.45W
Manouba Tunisia **32** 36.50N 10.06E
Mānpur India **63** 20.22N 80.43E
Manresa Spain **25** 41.44N 1.50E
Mānsa Gujarat India **62** 23.26N 72.40E
Mānsa Punjab India **62** 29.59N 75.23E
Mansa Zambia **79** 11.10S 28.52E
Mānsehra Pakistan **62** 34.20N 73.12E
Mansel I. Canada **99** 62.00N 80.00W
Mansfield U.K. **12** 53.08N 1.12W
Mansfield La. U.S.A. **111** 32.02N 93.43W
Mansfield Mass. U.S.A. **115** 42.02N 71.13W
Mansfield Ohio U.S.A. **114** 40.46N 82.31W
Mansfield Penn. U.S.A. **114** 41.48N 77.05W
Mansfield, Mt. U.S.A. **105** 44.33N 72.49W
Mansle France **20** 45.53N 0.11E
Manso *r.* Brazil **124** 11.59S 50.25W
Mansôa Guinea Bissau **76** 12.08N 15.18W
Mansūrah Syria **67** 33.08N 35.48E
Manta Ecuador **122** 0.59S 80.44W
Mantaro *r.* Peru **122** 12.00S 74.00W
Manteca U.S.A. **108** 37.48N 121.13W
Mantes France **19** 48.59N 1.43E
Mantiqueira, Serra da *mts.* Brazil **126** 22.25S 45.00W
Mantova Italy **30** 45.09N 10.48E
Mänttä Finland **41** 62.02N 24.38E
Mantua U.S.A. **114** 41.17N 81.14W
Manturovo Russian Fed. **44** 58.20N 44.42E

Mäntyluoto to **Matochkin Shar**

Mäntyluoto Finland **41** 61.35N 21.29E
Manú Peru **122** 12.14S 70.51W
Manua Is. Samoa **84** 14.13S169.35W
Manuel Benavides Mexico **111** 29.05N103.55W
Manui *i.* Indonesia **59** 3.35S123.08E
Manukau New Zealand **86** 36.59S174.53E
Manukau Harbour *est.* New Zealand **86** 37.10S174.00E
Manunda Creek *r.* Australia **92** 32.50S138.58E
Manus *i.* P.N.G. **59** 2.00S147.00E
Manville U.S.A. **108** 42.47N104.37W
Manyane Botswana **80** 23.23S 21.44E
Manyara, L. Tanzania **79** 3.40S 35.50E
Manych *r.* Russian Fed. **45** 47.14N 40.20E
Manych Gudilo, Ozero *l.* Russian Fed. **45** 46.20N 42.45E
Manyinga *r.* Zambia **80** 13.28S 24.25E
Manyoni Tanzania **79** 5.46S 34.50E
Mânzai Pakistan **62** 30.07N 68.52E
Manzanares Spain **27** 39.00N 3.22W
Manzanillo Cuba **117** 20.21N 77.21W
Manzanillo Mexico **97** 19.00N104.20W
Manzano Mts. U.S.A. **109** 34.48N106.12W
Manzhouli China **53** 49.36N117.28E
Manzil Pakistan **62** 29.15N 63.05E
Manzilah, Buḩayrat al *l.* Egypt **66** 31.20N 32.00E
Manzini Swaziland **80** 26.29S 31.24E
Mao Chad **77** 14.06N 15.11E
Maobitou *c.* Taiwan **55** 22.00N120.45E
Maoke, Pegunungan *mts.* Indonesia **59** 4.00S137.30E
Maokui Shan *mtn.* China **54** 33.55N111.33E
Maoming China **55** 21.50N110.58E
Maoniu Shan *mtn.* China **54** 33.00N103.56E
Mapai Mozambique **81** 22.51S 32.00E
Mapam Yumco *l.* China **63** 30.40N 81.20E
Mapi Indonesia **59** 7.06S139.23E
Mapia, Kepulauan *is.* Indonesia **59** 1.00N134.15E
Mapimí, Bolsóne de *des.* Mexico **111** 27.30N103.15W
Mapinhane Mozambique **81** 22.19S 35.03E
Mapire Venezuela **122** 7.46N 64.41W
Maple Creek *town* Canada **101** 49.55N109.27W
Maprik P.N.G. **59** 3.38S143.02E
Mapuera *r.* Brazil **123** 2.00S 55.40W
Maputo Mozambique **81** 25.58S 32.35E
Maputo *d.* Mozambique **81** 26.00S 32.30E
Maqnâ Saudi Arabia **66** 28.26N 34.44E
Maqu China **61** 34.05N102.15E
Maquan He *r.* China **63** 29.35N 84.10E
Maqueda Spain **27** 40.04N 4.22W
Maquela do Zombo Angola **78** 6.06S 15.12E
Maquinchao Argentina **125** 41.15S 68.44W
Maquoketa U.S.A. **110** 42.04N 90.40W
Mar, Serra do *mts.* Brazil **126** 23.00S 44.40W
Mara Tanzania **79** 1.30S 34.31E
Mara *d.* Tanzania **79** 1.45S 34.30E
Mara *r.* Tanzania **79** 1.30S 33.52E
Maraâ Brazil **122** 1.50S 65.22W
Maraa Tahiti **85** 17.46S149.34W
Marabá Brazil **123** 5.23S 49.10W
Marabastad R.S.A. **80** 23.58S 29.21E
Maracaibo Venezuela **122** 10.44N 71.37W
Maracaibo, Lago de *l.* Venezuela **122** 9.50N 71.30W
Maracaju, Serra de *mts.* Brazil **126** 21.38S 55.10W
Maracay Venezuela **122** 10.20N 67.28W
Marâdah Libya **75** 29.14N 19.13E
Maradi Niger **77** 13.29N 7.10E
Maradi *d.* Niger **77** 14.00N 8.10E
Marâgheh Iran **65** 37.25N 46.13E
Maragogipe Brazil **123** 12.48S 38.59W
Marahuaca, Cerro *mtn.* Venezuela **122** 3.37N 65.25W
Marajó, Ilha de *i.* Brazil **123** 1.00S 49.40W
Maralal Kenya **79** 1.15N 36.48E
Maralinga Australia **89** 30.13S131.32E
Maramba Zambia **78** 17.40S 25.50E
Maramsilli Resr. India **63** 20.32N 81.41E
Mârân, Koh-i- *mtn.* Pakistan **62** 29.33N 66.53E
Marana U.S.A. **109** 32.27N111.13W
Maranchón Spain **26** 41.03N 2.12W
Marand Iran **65** 38.25N 45.50E
Maranhão *d.* Brazil **123** 6.00S 45.30W
Maranoa *r.* Australia **91** 27.55S148.30E
Marañón *r.* Peru **122** 4.40S 73.20W
Marans France **20** 46.19N 1.00W
Marão Mozambique **81** 24.21S 34.07E
Marapi *mtn.* Indonesia **58** 0.20S100.45E
Mărăşeşti Romania **37** 45.52N 27.14E
Maratea Italy **33** 39.59N 15.45E
Marathón Greece **35** 38.09N 23.57E
Marathon N.Y. U.S.A. **115** 42.26N 76.02W
Marathon Tex. U.S.A. **111** 30.12N103.15W
Maratua *i.* Indonesia **58** 2.10N118.35E
Marâveh Tappeh Iran **65** 37.55N 55.57E
Marav L. Pakistan **62** 29.04N 69.18E
Marawī Sudan **72** 18.29N 31.49E
Marbella Spain **27** 36.31N 4.53W
Marble Bar Australia **88** 21.16S119.45E
Marburg Germany **38** 50.49N 8.46E
Marcali Hungary **31** 46.35N 17.25E
Marcaria Italy **32** 45.07N 10.32E
Marcellus U.S.A. **115** 42.59N 76.20W
March U.K. **13** 52.33N 0.05E
Marche Belgium **16** 50.13N 5.21E
Marche *d.* Italy **30** 43.35N 13.00E
Marchena Spain **27** 37.20N 5.24W
Mar Chiquita *l.* Argentina **124** 30.42S 62.36W
Marcigny France **19** 46.17N 4.02E
Marcos Paz Argentina **125** 34.49S 58.51W
Marcounda C.A.R. **77** 7.37N 16.59E
Marcq-en-Baroeul France **16** 50.40N 3.01E
Marcus Hook U.S.A. **115** 39.49N 75.25W
Marcus I. Pacific Oc. **84** 24.18N153.58E
Marcy, Mt. U.S.A. **105** 44.07N 73.56W
Mardân Pakistan **62** 34.12N 72.02E
Mar del Plata Argentina **125** 38.00S 57.32W
Marden U.K. **13** 51.11N 0.30E
Mardie Australia **88** 21.14S115.57E
Mardin Turkey **64** 37.19N 40.43E
Maré, Île *i.* N. Cal. **84** 21.30S168.00E
Maree, Loch U.K. **14** 57.41N 5.28W
Mareeba Australia **90** 17.00S145.26E
Marennes France **20** 45.50N 1.06W
Marettimo *i.* Italy **32** 37.58N 12.04E
Mareuil-sur-Belle France **20** 45.28N 0.28E
Marfa U.S.A. **111** 30.18N104.01W
Margai Caka *l.* China **61** 35.11N 86.57E
Margaret *r.* Australia **92** 29.26S137.00E
Margaret Bay *town* Canada **100** 51.20N127.20W
Margaret L. Canada **100** 58.56N115.25W
Margaret River *town* W. Aust. Australia **89** 33.57S115.04E
Margaret River *town* W. Aust. Australia **88** 18.38S126.52E
Margarita, Isla de *i.* Venezuela **122** 11.00N 64.00W
Margarítion Greece **34** 39.22N 20.26E
Margate R.S.A. **80** 30.51S 30.22E
Margate U.K. **13** 51.23N 1.24E
Margeride, Monts de la *mts.* France **20** 44.50N 3.30E
Margherita di Savoia Italy **33** 41.23N 16.09E
Mārgow, Dasht-e *des.* Afghan. **62** 30.45N 63.10E
Maria Elena Chile **124** 22.21S 69.40W
Maria Gail Austria **39** 46.36N 13.52E
Mariager Denmark **42** 56.39N 10.00E
María Grande Argentina **125** 31.40S 59.55W
Maria I. Australia **90** 14.52S135.40E
Mariana Brazil **126** 20.23S 43.23W
Marianao Cuba **117** 23.03N 82.29W
Mariana Ridge Pacific Oc. **84** 17.00N146.00E
Mariana Trench Pacific Oc. **84** 16.00N148.00E
Marianna Ark. U.S.A. **111** 34.46N 90.46W
Marianna Fla. U.S.A. **113** 30.45N 85.15W
Mariannelund Sweden **43** 57.37N 15.34E
Mariánské Lázně Czech Republic **39** 49.59N 12.43E
Marias *r.* U.S.A. **108** 47.56N110.30W
Maribo Denmark **41** 54.46N 11.31E
Maribor Slovenia **31** 46.33N 15.39E
Marico *r.* R.S.A. **80** 24.12S 26.57E
Maricopa U.S.A. **109** 35.03N119.24W
Marīdī Sudan **73** 4.55N 29.28E
Marīdī *r.* Sudan **73** 6.55N 29.00E
Marié *r.* Brazil **122** 0.27S 66.26W
Marieburg Belgium **16** 50.07N 4.30E
Mariefred Sweden **43** 59.18N 17.15E
Marie-Galante *i.* Guadeloupe **117** 15.54N 61.11W
Mariehamn *see* Maarianhamina Finland **43**
Mariemberg Neth. **16** 52.32N 6.35E
Mariental Namibia **80** 24.38S 17.58E
Marienville U.S.A. **114** 41.28N 79.07W
Mariestad Sweden **43** 58.43N 13.51E
Marietta Ga. U.S.A. **113** 33.57N 84.34W
Marietta Ohio U.S.A. **114** 39.25N 81.27W
Marieville Canada **105** 45.26N 73.10W
Mariga *r.* Nigeria **77** 9.37N 5.55E
Marignane France **21** 43.25N 5.13E
Marijampolė Lithuania **41** 54.33N 23.21E
Marília Brazil **126** 22.13S 50.20W
Marín Spain **26** 42.23N 8.42W
Marina di Gioiosa Ionica Italy **33** 38.18N 16.20E
Marina di Ravenna Italy **30** 44.29N 12.17E
Marine City U.S.A. **114** 42.43N 82.30W
Marineland U.S.A. **113** 29.39N 81.13W
Marinette U.S.A. **110** 45.06N 87.38W
Maringá Brazil **126** 23.36S 52.02W
Maringa Zaïre **73** 1.14N 20.00E
Maringa *r.* Zaïre **78** 1.13N 19.50E
Maringue Mozambique **81** 17.55S 34.24E
Marinha Grande Portugal **27** 39.45N 8.56W
Marion Canada **104** 47.00N 84.10W
Marion Ill. U.S.A. **111** 37.44N 88.56W
Marion Ind. U.S.A. **112** 40.33N 85.40W
Marion Iowa U.S.A. **110** 42.02N 91.36W
Marion Ohio U.S.A. **112** 40.35N 83.08W
Marion S.C. U.S.A. **113** 34.11N 79.23W
Marion Va. U.S.A. **113** 36.51N 81.30W
Marion, L. U.S.A. **113** 33.30N 80.25W
Marion Bay *town* Australia **92** 35.13S137.00E
Marion Reef Australia **90** 19.10S152.17E
Mariposa U.S.A. **108** 37.29N119.58W
Mariscal Estigarribia Paraguay **126** 22.03S 60.35W
Maritimes, Alpes *mts.* France **21** 44.15N 7.10E
Maritsa Bulgaria **34** 42.02N 25.50E
Maritsa *r.* Bulgaria **34** 42.15N 24.00E
Maritsa *r.* Turkey **29** 41.00N 26.15E
Mariupol' Ukraine **45** 47.05N 37.34E
Mārkâ Jordan **67** 31.59N 35.59E
Marka Somali Rep. **79** 1.42N 44.47E
Markaryd Sweden **43** 56.26N 13.36E
Markdale Canada **104** 44.19N 80.39W
Marked Tree U.S.A. **111** 35.32N 90.25W
Marken *i.* Neth. **16** 52.28N 5.03E
Markerwaard *f.* Neth. **16** 52.30N 5.15E
Market Drayton U.K. **12** 52.55N 2.30W
Market Harborough U.K. **13** 52.29N 0.55W
Market Rasen U.K. **12** 53.24N 0.20W
Market Weighton U.K. **12** 53.52N 0.04W
Markha *r.* Russian Fed. **51** 63.37N119.00E
Markham Canada **104** 43.52N 79.16W
Markham, Mt. Antarctica **128** 83.00S164.00E
Markoupolon Greece **35** 37.53N 23.57E
Marks Russian Fed. **45** 51.43N 46.45E
Markstay Canada **104** 46.29N 80.33W
Marktheidenfeld Germany **39** 49.50N 9.36E
Marktoberdorf Germany **39** 47.47N 10.37E
Marktredwitz Germany **39** 50.00N 12.06E
Marl Germany **38** 51.38N 7.05E
Marla Australia **90** 27.22S133.48E
Marlboro U.S.A. **115** 42.21N 71.33W
Marlborough Australia **90** 22.51S149.50E
Marlborough U.K. **13** 51.26N 1.44W
Marlborough U.S.A. **105** 42.21N 71.33W
Marle France **19** 49.44N 3.46E
Marlette U.S.A. **114** 43.20N 83.05W
Marlin U.S.A. **111** 31.18N 96.53W
Marlo Australia **93** 37.50S148.35E
Marmande France **20** 44.30N 0.10E
Marmara *i.* Turkey **29** 40.38N 27.37E
Marmara, Sea of *see* Marmara Denizi *sea* Turkey **29**
Marmara Denizi *sea* Turkey **29** 40.45N 28.15E
Marmaris Turkey **35** 36.50N 28.14E
Marmarth U.S.A. **110** 46.18N103.54W
Marmet U.S.A. **114** 38.15N 81.04W
Marmion L. Canada **102** 48.55N 91.25W
Marmolada *mtn.* Italy **30** 46.26N 11.51E
Marmora Canada **105** 44.29N 77.41W
Marnay France **19** 47.17N 5.46E
Marne *d.* France **19** 48.55N 4.10E
Marne *r.* France **19** 48.49N 2.24E
Marne Germany **38** 53.57N 9.00E
Marne à la Saône, Canal de la France **19** 49.44N 4.36E
Marne au Rhin, Canal de la France **19** 48.35N 7.47E
Marnoo Australia **92** 36.40S142.55E
Maroantsetra Madagascar **81** 15.26S 49.44E
Marobi Pakistan **62** 32.36N 69.52E
Marolambo Madagascar **81** 20.02S 48.07E
Maromme France **18** 49.28N 1.02E
Marondera Zimbabwe **81** 18.11S 31.31E
Maroni *r.* Guiana **123** 5.30N 54.00W
Maronne *r.* France **20** 45.07N 1.57E
Maroochydore Australia **91** 26.40S153.07E
Maros *r.* Hungary **31** 46.15N 20.13E
Maroua Cameroon **77** 10.35N 14.20E
Marovoay Madagascar **81** 16.06S 46.39E
Marquard R.S.A. **80** 28.39S 27.25E
Marquesas Is. *see* Marquises, Îles *is.* Pacific Oc. **85**
Marquette U.S.A. **112** 46.33N 87.23W
Marquina-Jemein Spain **26** 43.16N 2.30W
Marquise France **19** 50.49N 1.42E
Marquises, Îles *is.* Pacific Oc. **85** 9.00S139.30W
Marra Australia **92** 31.11S144.03E
Marra *r.* Australia **93** 30.05S147.05E
Marracuene Mozambique **81** 25.44S 32.41E
Marradi Italy **30** 44.04N 11.37E
Marrah, Jabal *mtn.* Sudan **73** 13.10N 24.22E
Marrakech Morocco **74** 31.49N 8.00W
Marrawah Australia **91** 40.55S144.42E
Marree Australia **92** 29.40S138.04E
Marromeu Mozambique **81** 18.20S 35.56E
Marrupa Mozambique **79** 13.10S 37.30E
Marsá al Burayqah Libya **72** 30.25N 19.35E
Marsabit Kenya **79** 2.20N 37.59E
Marsala Italy **32** 37.48N 12.26E
Marsá Maţrūḩ Egypt **64** 31.21N 27.14E
Marsciano Italy **30** 42.54N 12.20E
Marsden Australia **93** 33.46S147.35E
Marseille France **21** 43.18N 5.24E
Marseille-en-Beauvaisis France **19** 49.35N 1.57E
Marsfjället *mtn.* Sweden **40** 65.05N 15.28E
Marshall Liberia **76** 6.10N 10.23W
Marshall Ark. U.S.A. **111** 35.55N 92.38W
Marshall Minn. U.S.A. **110** 44.27N 95.47W
Marshall Mo. U.S.A. **110** 39.07N 93.12W
Marshall Tex. U.S.A. **111** 32.33N 94.23W
Marshall Va. U.S.A. **114** 38.52N 77.52W
Marshall Is. Pacific Oc. **84** 10.00N172.00E
Marshalltown U.S.A. **110** 42.03N 92.55W
Marshyhope Creek *r.* U.S.A. **115** 38.32N 75.45W
Märsta Sweden **43** 59.37N 17.51E
Marstrand Sweden **42** 57.53N 11.35E
Martaban Burma **56** 16.32N 97.35E
Martaban, G. of Burma **56** 15.10N 96.30E
Martapura Indonesia **58** 3.22S114.56E
Marte Nigeria **77** 12.23N 13.46E
Martelange Belgium **16** 49.50N 5.44E
Marten River *town* Canada **104** 46.42N 79.41W
Martés, Sierra *mts.* Spain **25** 39.20N 1.10W
Marthaguy Creek *r.* Australia **93** 30.16S147.35E
Martha's Vineyard *i.* U.S.A. **115** 41.25N 70.40W
Martigny Switz. **39** 46.06N 7.04E
Martigues France **21** 43.24N 5.03E
Martin Slovakia **37** 49.05N 18.55E
Martín *r.* Spain **25** 41.18N 0.19W
Martin U.S.A. **110** 43.10N101.44W
Martina Franca Italy **33** 40.42N 17.21E
Martinique *i.* Windward Is. **117** 14.40N 61.00W
Martin L. U.S.A. **113** 32.50N 85.55W
Martin Pt. U.S.A. **98** 70.10N143.50W
Martinsburg Penn. U.S.A. **114** 40.19N 78.20W
Martinsburg W.Va. U.S.A. **114** 39.27N 77.58W
Martins Ferry *town* U.S.A. **114** 40.06N 80.44W
Martinsville Ind. U.S.A. **112** 39.25N 86.25W
Martinsville Va. U.S.A. **113** 36.43N 79.53W
Martin Vaz *is.* Atlantic Oc. **127** 20.30S 28.51W
Marton New Zealand **86** 40.04S175.25E
Martos Spain **27** 37.43N 3.58W
Martre, Lac la *l.* Canada **100** 63.15N116.55W
Martti Finland **40** 67.28N 28.28E
Marudi Malaysia **58** 4.15N114.19E
Ma'rūf Afghan. **62** 31.34N 67.03E
Marula Zimbabwe **80** 20.26S 28.06E
Marum Neth. **16** 53.06N 6.16E
Marvejols France **20** 44.33N 3.18E
Marvel Loch *town* Australia **89** 31.31S119.30E
Marviken Sweden **43** 58.34N 16.51E
Mārwār India **62** 25.44N 73.36E
Mary Turkmenistan **50** 37.42N 61.54E
Maryborough Qld. Australia **90** 25.32S152.36E
Maryborough Vic. Australia **92** 37.05S143.47E
Marydale R.S.A. **80** 29.24S 22.06E
Mary Frances L. Canada **101** 63.19N106.13W
Maryland *d.* U.S.A. **114** 39.00N 76.45W
Maryland Beach *town* U.S.A. **115** 38.26N 74.59W
Maryport U.K. **12** 54.43N 3.30W
Mary's Harbour Canada **103** 52.18N 55.51W
Marystown Canada **103** 47.11N 55.10W
Marysvale U.S.A. **108** 38.27N112.11W
Marysville Kans. U.S.A. **110** 39.51N 96.39W
Marysville Mich. U.S.A. **114** 42.54N 82.29W
Marysville Penn. U.S.A. **114** 40.20N 76.56W
Maryvale Australia **90** 24.41S134.04E
Maryville Mo. U.S.A. **110** 40.21N 94.52W
Maryville Tenn. U.S.A. **113** 35.45N 83.59W
Marzūq Libya **75** 25.55N 13.55E
Marzūq, Şaḩrā' *des.* Libya **75** 24.30N 13.00E
Mas'adah Syria **67** 33.14N 35.45E
Masāhīm, Kūh-e *mtn.* Iran **65** 30.26N 55.08E
Masai Steppe *f.* Tanzania **79** 4.30S 37.00E
Masaka Uganda **79** 0.20S 31.46E
Masan S. Korea **53** 35.10N128.35E
Masasi Tanzania **79** 10.43S 38.48E
Masba Nigeria **77** 10.35N 13.01E
Masbate *i.* Phil. **59** 12.00N123.30E
Mascara Algeria **74** 35.24N 0.08E
Mascarene Basin *f.* Indian Oc. **49** 17.00S 55.00E
Mascarene Is. Indian Oc. **49** 21.00S 56.00E
Mascarene Ridge *f.* Indian Oc. **49** 10.00S 60.00E
Maseru Lesotho **80** 29.18S 27.28E
Mashhad Iran **65** 36.16N 59.34E
Mashkai *r.* Pakistan **62** 26.02N 65.19E
Māshkel *r.* Pakistan **62** 28.02N 63.25E
Māshkel, Hāmūn-i- *l.* Pakistan **62** 28.15N 63.00E
Mashki Chāh Pakistan **62** 29.01N 62.27E
Mashonaland *f.* Zimbabwe **81** 18.20S 32.00E
Mashūray Afghan. **62** 32.12N 68.21E
Masi Norway **40** 69.26N 23.40E
Masīlah, Wādī al *f.* Yemen **71** 15.10N 51.08E
Masi-Manimba Zaïre **78** 4.47S 17.54E
Masindi Uganda **79** 1.41N 31.45E
Maşīrah *i.* Oman **60** 20.30N 58.50E
Maşīrah, Khalīj *b.* Oman **71** 20.10N 58.10E
Masjed Soleymān Iran **65** 31.59N 49.18E
Mask, Lough Rep. of Ire. **15** 53.38N 9.22W
Maskinongé Canada **105** 46.35N 73.30W
Mason Mich. U.S.A. **104** 42.35N 84.26W
Mason Tex. U.S.A. **111** 30.45N 99.14W
Mason W.Va. U.S.A. **114** 39.00N 82.02W
Mason City U.S.A. **110** 43.09N 93.12W
Masontown U.S.A. **114** 39.51N 79.54W
Maspalomas Canary Is. **127** 27.42N 15.34W
Masqaţ Oman **65** 23.36N 58.37E
Massa Italy **30** 44.01N 10.09E
Massachusetts *d.* U.S.A. **115** 42.15N 71.50W
Massachusetts B. U.S.A. **115** 42.20N 70.50W
Massafra Italy **33** 40.35N 17.07E
Massakory Chad **77** 13.02N 15.43E
Massa Marittima Italy **30** 43.03N 10.53E
Massangena Mozambique **81** 21.31S 33.03E
Massangulo Mozambique **81** 13.54S 35.24E
Massarosa Italy **30** 43.52N 10.20E
Massena U.S.A. **105** 44.56N 74.54W
Massenya Chad **77** 11.21N 16.09E
Masset Canada **100** 54.00N132.09W
Masseube France **20** 43.26N 0.35E
Massey Canada **104** 46.12N 82.05W
Massiac France **20** 45.15N 3.12E
Massif Central *mts.* France **20** 45.00N 3.10E
Massillon U.S.A. **114** 40.48N 81.32W
Massinga Mozambique **81** 23.20S 35.25E
Massingir Mozambique **81** 23.49S 32.04E
Masterton New Zealand **86** 40.57S175.39E
Mastic Beach *town* U.S.A. **115** 40.45N 72.50W
Mastigouche Prov. Park Canada **105** 46.39N 73.24W
Mastung Pakistan **62** 29.48N 66.51E
Mastūrah Saudi Arabia **64** 23.06N 38.50E
Masuda Japan **57** 34.40N131.51E
Masvingo Zimbabwe **80** 20.10S 30.49E
Maşyāf Syria **66** 35.03N 36.21E
Mat *r.* Albania **34** 41.40N 20.00E
Matabeleland *f.* Zimbabwe **80** 19.50S 28.15E
Matabuena Spain **26** 41.06N 3.48W
Matachel *r.* Spain **26** 38.50N 6.17W
Matachewan Canada **102** 47.56N 80.39W
Matadi Zaïre **78** 5.50S 13.36E
Matagami Canada **102** 49.45N 77.34W
Matagami, L. Canada **102** 49.50N 77.40W
Matagorda B. U.S.A. **111** 28.35N 96.20W
Matakana Australia **93** 32.59S145.53E
Matakana I. New Zealand **86** 37.35S176.15E
Matala Angola **78** 14.45S 15.02E
Matam Senegal **74** 15.40N 13.15W
Matamata New Zealand **86** 37.49S175.46E
Matameye Niger **77** 13.26N 8.28E
Matamoros Coahuila Mexico **111** 25.32N103.15W
Matamoros Tamaulipas Mexico **111** 25.53N 97.30W
Ma'ţan Bishrah *well* Libya **72** 22.58N 22.39E
Matandu *r.* Tanzania **79** 8.44S 39.22E
Matane Canada **103** 48.51N 67.32W
Matang China **55** 29.30N113.08E
Matankari Niger **77** 13.47N 4.00E
Matanzas Cuba **117** 23.04N 81.35W
Mataram Indonesia **59** 8.36S116.07E
Matarani Peru **124** 16.58S 72.07W
Mataranka Australia **88** 14.56S133.07E
Mataró Spain **25** 41.32N 2.27E
Matarraña *r.* Spain **25** 41.14N 0.22E
Matatiele R.S.A. **80** 30.19S 28.48E
Matatula, C. Samoa **84** 14.15S170.35W
Mataura *r.* New Zealand **86** 46.34S168.45E
Matautu W. Samoa **84** 13.57S171.56W
Matavera Rarotonga Cook Is. **84** 21.13S159.44W
Matawai New Zealand **86** 38.21S177.32E
Matawin *r.* Canada **105** 46.50N 72.45W
Maţāy Egypt **66** 28.25N 30.46E
Matehuala Mexico **116** 23.40N100.40W
Mateke Hills Zimbabwe **80** 21.48S 31.00E
Matelica Italy **30** 43.15N 13.00E
Matera Italy **33** 40.40N 16.37E
Matetsi Zimbabwe **80** 18.17S 25.57E
Mateur Tunisia **32** 37.03N 9.40E
Matfors Sweden **41** 62.21N 17.02E
Matha France **20** 45.52N 0.19W
Mathews Peak *mtn.* Kenya **79** 1.18N 37.20E
Mathis U.S.A. **111** 28.06N 97.50W
Mathoura Australia **93** 35.49S144.54E
Mathura India **63** 27.30N 77.41E
Mati Phil. **59** 6.55N126.15E
Matias Barbosa Brazil **126** 21.52S 43.21W
Matignon France **18** 48.36N 2.18W
Matinenda L. Canada **104** 46.22N 82.57W
Matipó Brazil **126** 20.16S 42.17W
Mātli Pakistan **62** 25.02N 68.39E
Matlock U.K. **12** 53.09N 1.32W
Matochkin Shar Russian Fed. **50** 73.15N 56.35E

Mato Grosso to **Merrill**

Mato Grosso *d.* Brazil **124** 13.00S 55.00W
Mato Grosso *town* Brazil **124** 15.05S 59.57W
Mato Grosso, Planalto do *f.* Brazil **124** 16.00S 54.00W
Mato Grosso do Sul *d.* Brazil **124** 20.00S 54.30W
Matope Malaŵi **79** 15.20S 34.57E
Matopo Hills Zimbabwe **80** 20.45S 28.30E
Matosinhos Portugal **26** 41.11N 8.42W
Maṭraḥ Oman **65** 23.37N 58.33E
Matrei in Osttirol Austria **39** 47.00N 12.32E
Matsena Nigeria **77** 13.13N 10.04E
Matsiatra *r.* Madagascar **81** 21.25S 45.33E
Matsubara Japan **57** 34.34N135.33E
Matsudo Japan **57** 35.47N139.54E
Matsue Japan **57** 35.29N133.00E
Matsumae Japan **57** 41.26N140.07E
Matsumoto Japan **57** 36.18N137.58E
Matsusaka Japan **57** 34.34N136.32E
Matsuyama Japan **57** 33.50N132.47E
Mattagami *r.* Canada **102** 50.43N 81.29W
Mattawa Canada **104** 46.19N 78.42W
Mattawamkeag U.S.A. **112** 45.31N 68.21W
Mattawin Canada **105** 46.55N 72.55W
Matterhorn *mtn.* Switz./Italy **39** 45.59N 7.43E
Matterhorn *mtn.* U.S.A. **108** 41.49N115.23W
Matthews Ridge *town* Guyana **122** 7.30N 60.10W
Matthew Town Bahamas **117** 20.57N 73.40W
Mattice Canada **102** 49.39N 83.20W
Mattighofen Austria **39** 48.06N 13.09E
Mattmar Sweden **40** 63.19N 13.45E
Mattoon U.S.A. **110** 39.29N 88.21W
Matua Indonesia **58** 2.58S110.52E
Maturín Venezuela **122** 9.45N 63.10W
Maua Mozambique **81** 13.53S 37.10E
Mau Aimma India **63** 25.42N 81.55E
Maubeuge France **19** 50.17N 3.58E
Maudaha India **63** 25.41N 80.07E
Maude Australia **92** 34.27S144.21E
Maués Brazil **123** 3.24S 57.42W
Mauganj India **63** 24.41N 81.53E
Maui *i.* Hawaii U.S.A. **106** 20.45N156.15W
Mauléon France **18** 46.56N 0.45W
Mauléon-Licharre France **20** 43.14N 0.54W
Maulvi Bāzār Bangla. **63** 24.29N 91.42E
Maumee U.S.A. **112** 41.34N 83.41W
Maumee *r.* U.S.A. **112** 41.40N 83.35W
Maumere Indonesia **59** 8.35S122.13E
Maun Botswana **80** 19.52S 23.40E
Maunaloa Hawaiian Is. **85** 21.08N157.13W
Mauna Loa *mtn.* Hawaiian Is. **85** 19.29N155.36W
Maunath Bhanjan India **63** 25.57N 83.33E
Mau Rānīpur India **63** 25.15N 79.08E
Maure-de-Bretagne France **18** 47.54N 1.59W
Maures *mts.* France **21** 43.16N 6.23E
Mauriac France **20** 45.13N 2.20E
Maurice, L. Australia **91** 29.28S130.58E
Maurice Nat. Park Canada **105** 46.42N 73.00W
Mauritania Africa **74** 20.00N 10.00W
Mauritius Indian Oc. **49** 20.10S 58.00E
Mauritius Basin *f.* Indian Oc. **49** 26.00S 55.00E
Mauron France **18** 48.05N 2.18W
Maurs France **20** 44.43N 2.11E
Mauston U.S.A. **110** 43.48N 90.05W
Mauvezin France **20** 43.44N 0.55E
Mavinga Angola **78** 15.47S 20.21E
Mavqi'im Israel **67** 31.37N 34.35E
Mavuradonha Mts. Zimbabwe **81** 16.30S 31.20E
Mawjib, Wādī al Jordan **67** 31.28N 35.34E
Mawlaik Burma **56** 23.50N 94.30E
Mawlamyine *see* Moulmein Burma **56**
Maxcanú Mexico **116** 20.35N 89.59W
Maxville Canada **105** 45.17N 74.51W
May, C. U.S.A. **115** 38.56N 74.55W
Maya Spain **26** 43.12N 1.29W
Mayaguana I. Bahamas **117** 22.30N 73.00W
Mayagüez Puerto Rico **117** 18.13N 67.09W
Mayāmey Iran **65** 36.27N 55.40E
Maya Mts. Belize **117** 16.30N 89.00W
Maybole U.K. **14** 55.21N 4.41W
Maych'ew Ethiopia **71** 13.02N 39.34E
Maydena Australia **91** 42.45S146.38E
Maydh Somali Rep. **71** 10.57N 47.06E
Mayen Germany **39** 50.19N 7.13E
Mayenne France **18** 48.18N 0.37W
Mayenne *d.* France **18** 48.05N 0.40W
Mayenne *r.* France **18** 47.30N 0.33W
Mayerthorpe Canada **100** 53.57N115.08W
Mayfield U.S.A. **111** 36.44N 88.38W
Maykop Russian Fed. **45** 44.37N 40.48E
Maymyo Burma **56** 22.05N 96.28E
Maynooth Canada **105** 45.13N 77.57W
Maynooth Rep. of Ire. **15** 53.23N 6.37W
Mayo *r.* Mexico **109** 26.45N109.47W
Mayo *d.* Rep. of Ire. **15** 53.47N 9.07W
Mayo, Plains of *f.* Rep. of Ire. **15** 53.46N 9.05W
Mayo Daga Nigeria **77** 6.59N 11.25E
Mayo Landing Canada **98** 63.45N135.45W
Mayor I. New Zealand **86** 37.15S176.15E
Mayotte, Île *i.* Comoros **79** 12.50S 45.10E
May Pen Jamaica **117** 17.58N 77.14W
Maysah, Tall al *mtn.* Jordan **67** 31.08N 35.40E
Mays Landing U.S.A. **115** 39.27N 74.44W
Maysville U.S.A. **112** 38.38N 83.46W
Maythalūn Jordan **67** 32.21N 35.16E
Mayumba Gabon **78** 3.23S 10.38E
Mayville Mich. U.S.A. **104** 43.20N 83.21W
Mayville N.Dak. U.S.A. **110** 47.30N 97.19W
Mayville N.Y. U.S.A. **114** 42.15N 79.30W
Mazabuka Zambia **79** 15.50S 27.47E
Mazagão Brazil **123** 0.07S 51.17W
Mazamba Mozambique **81** 18.32S 34.50E
Mazamet France **20** 43.30N 2.24E
Mazán Peru **122** 3.15S 73.00W
Mazara del Vallo Italy **32** 37.39N 12.36E
Mazarredo Argentina **125** 47.00S 66.45W
Mazarrón Spain **25** 37.36N 1.19W
Mazarrón, Golfo de *g.* Spain **25** 37.30N 1.18W
Mazatenango Guatemala **116** 14.31N 91.30W
Mazatlán Mexico **109** 23.13N106.25W
Mažeikiai Lithuania **41** 56.19N 22.20E
Mazinaw L. Canada **105** 44.55N 77.12W
Mazirbe Latvia **41** 57.41N 22.21E
Mazowe *r.* Mozambique **81** 16.32S 33.25E
Mazowe Zimbabwe **81** 17.30S 30.58E
Mazu Liedao *is.* China **53** 26.12N120.00E
Mazunga Zimbabwe **80** 21.45S 29.52E
Mazurski, Pojezierze *lakes* Poland **37** 53.50N 21.00E
Mbabane Swaziland **80** 26.19S 31.08E
Mbagne Mauritania **74** 16.06N 14.47W
M'Baiki C.A.R. **77** 3.53N 18.01E
Mbala C.A.R. **73** 7.48N 20.51E
Mbala Zambia **79** 8.50S 31.24E
Mbale Uganda **79** 1.04N 34.12E
Mbalmayo Cameroon **77** 3.35N 11.31E
Mbamba Bay *town* Tanzania **79** 11.18S 34.50E
Mbandaka Zaïre **78** 0.03N 18.21E
Mbanza Congo Angola **78** 6.18S 14.16E
Mbarara Uganda **79** 0.36S 30.40E
Mbari *r.* C.A.R. **73** 4.34N 22.43E
Mbeya Tanzania **79** 8.54S 33.29E
Mbeya *d.* Tanzania **79** 8.30S 32.30E
Mbinda Congo **78** 2.11S 12.55E
Mbogo Tanzania **79** 7.26S 33.26E
Mbomou *d.* C.A.R. **73** 5.10N 23.00E
Mbomou *r.* C.A.R. **73** 4.08N 22.26E
Mboro Sudan **73** 6.18N 28.45E
M'Bour Senegal **76** 14.22N 16.54W
Mbout Mauritania **74** 16.02N 12.35W
M'bridge *r.* Angola **78** 7.12S 12.55E
Mbua Fiji **84** 16.48S178.37E
Mbuji Mayi Zaïre **78** 6.08S 23.39E
Mbulamuti Uganda **79** 0.50N 33.05E
Mbura Tanzania **79** 11.14S 35.25E
Mbutha Fiji **84** 16.39S179.50E
Mbuzi Zambia **79** 12.20S 32.17E
McAlester U.S.A. **111** 34.56N 95.46W
McAllen U.S.A. **111** 26.12N 98.15W
McArthur *r.* Australia **90** 15.54S136.40E
McArthur U.S.A. **114** 39.15N 82.29W
McArthurs Mills Canada **105** 45.06N 77.38W
McBride Canada **100** 53.20N120.10W
McCamey U.S.A. **111** 31.08N102.13W
McClintock Canada **101** 57.50N 94.10W
McClintock Channel Canada **99** 71.20N102.00W
McClure U.S.A. **114** 40.42N 77.19W
McClure Str. Canada **98** 74.30N116.00W
McComb U.S.A. **111** 31.14N 90.27W
McConaughy, L. U.S.A. **110** 41.15N102.00W
McConnel Creek *town* Canada **100** 56.53N126.30W
McConnellsburg U.S.A. **114** 39.57N 78.01W
McConnelsville U.S.A. **114** 39.39N 81.51W
McCook U.S.A. **110** 40.12N100.38W
McDermitt U.S.A. **108** 41.59N117.36W
McDouall Peak Australia **92** 29.51S134.55E
McGrath U.S.A. **98** 62.58N155.40W
McGregor U.S.A. **110** 46.36N 93.19W
McHenry U.S.A. **110** 42.21N 88.16W
Mchinja Tanzania **79** 9.44S 39.45E
Mchinji Malaŵi **79** 13.48S 32.55E
McIlwraith Range *mts.* Australia **90** 14.00S143.10E
McKeesport U.S.A. **114** 40.21N 79.52W
McKees Rocks *town* U.S.A. **114** 40.28N 80.10W
Mckellar Canada **104** 45.30N 79.55W
McKenzie U.S.A. **111** 36.08N 88.31W
McKerrow Canada **104** 46.18N 81.44W
McKinley, Mt. U.S.A. **98** 63.00N151.00W
McKinney U.S.A. **111** 33.12N 96.37W
McKittrick U.S.A. **109** 35.18N119.37W
McLaughlin U.S.A. **110** 45.49N100.49W
McLennan Canada **100** 55.42N116.50W
McLeod *r.* Canada **100** 54.08N115.42W
McLeod B. Canada **101** 62.53N110.00W
Mcleod Lake *town* Canada **100** 54.58N123.00W
M'Clintock Canada **100** 60.35N134.25W
McMinnville Oreg. U.S.A. **108** 45.13N123.12W
McMinnville Tenn. U.S.A. **113** 35.40N 85.49W
McNary U.S.A. **109** 34.04N109.51W
McPherson U.S.A. **110** 38.22N 97.40W
McPherson Range *mts.* Australia **93** 28.15S153.00E
Mdantsane R.S.A. **80** 32.54S 27.24E
Mead, L. U.S.A. **109** 36.05N114.25W
Meade U.S.A. **111** 37.17N100.20W
Meadow Lake *town* Canada **101** 54.07N108.20W
Meadville U.S.A. **114** 41.38N 80.09W
Meaford Canada **104** 44.36N 80.35W
Mealhada Portugal **26** 40.22N 8.27W
Meander River *town* Canada **100** 59.02N117.42W
Mearim *r.* Brazil **123** 3.20S 44.20W
Meath *d.* Rep. of Ire. **15** 53.32N 6.40W
Meaux France **19** 48.57N 2.52E
Mécatina, Cap *c.* Canada **103** 50.45N 59.01W
Mecca *see* Makkah Saudi Arabia **72**
Mecca U.S.A. **109** 33.35N116.03W
Mechanicsville U.S.A. **114** 38.26N 76.44W
Mechanicville U.S.A. **115** 42.54N 73.42W
Mechelen Belgium **16** 51.01N 4.28E
Mecheria Algeria **74** 33.33N 0.17W
Mecidiye Turkey **34** 40.38N 26.32E
Mecklenburger Bucht *b.* Germany **38** 54.20N 11.50E
Mecklenburg-Vorpommern *d.* Germany **38** 53.36N 12.45E
Meconta Mozambique **79** 15.00S 39.50E
Mecsek *mts.* Hungary **31** 46.15N 18.05E
Mecufi Mozambique **79** 13.20S 40.32E
Meda Portugal **26** 40.58N 7.16W
Medan Indonesia **58** 3.35N 98.39E
Mede Italy **30** 45.06N 8.44E
Médéa Algeria **75** 36.15N 2.48E
Mededsiz *mtn.* Turkey **64** 37.33N 34.38E
Medegue Gabon **78** 0.37N 10.08E
Medellín Colombia **122** 6.15N 75.36W
Medemblik Neth. **16** 52.48N 5.06E
Médenine Tunisia **75** 33.21N 10.30E
Mederdra Mauritania **76** 17.02N 15.41W
Medevi Sweden **43** 58.40N 14.57E
Medford Mass. U.S.A. **115** 42.25N 71.07W
Medford Oreg. U.S.A. **108** 42.19N122.52W
Medford Wisc. U.S.A. **110** 45.09N 90.20W
Medgidia Romania **37** 44.15N 28.16E
Medi Sudan **73** 5.04N 30.44E
Media U.S.A. **115** 39.54N 75.23W
Mediaş Romania **37** 46.10N 24.21E
Medicina Italy **30** 44.28N 11.38E
Medicine Bow Mts. U.S.A. **108** 41.10N106.10W
Medicine Bow Peak *mtn.* U.S.A. **108** 41.21N106.19W
Medicine Hat Canada **101** 50.03N110.40W
Medicine Lake *town* U.S.A. **108** 48.30N104.30W
Medicine Lodge U.S.A. **111** 37.17N 98.35W
Medina *see* Al Madīnah Saudi Arabia **64**
Medina N.Dak. U.S.A. **110** 46.54N 99.18W
Medina N.Y. U.S.A. **114** 43.13N 78.23W
Medina Ohio U.S.A. **114** 41.08N 81.52W
Medinaceli Spain **26** 41.10N 2.26W
Medina del Campo Spain **26** 41.18N 4.55W
Medina de Rioseco Spain **26** 41.53N 5.02W
Medina-Sidonia Spain **27** 36.27N 5.55W
Mediterranean Sea 23 36.00N 16.00E
Medjerda, Monts de la *mts.* Tunisia **32** 36.40N 8.40E
Medjerda, Oued *r.* Tunisia **32** 37.07N 10.13E
Medjez el Bab Tunisia **32** 36.39N 9.37E
Medoc *d.* France **20** 45.20N 1.00W
Mêdog China **52** 29.19N 95.19E
Medstead Canada **101** 53.19N108.02W
Medveda Yugo. **34** 42.50N 21.32E
Medveditsa *r.* Russian Fed. **45** 49.35N 42.45E
Medvezhyegorsk Russian Fed. **44** 62.56N 34.28E
Medvin Ukraine **37** 49.25N 30.48E
Medway *r.* U.K. **13** 51.24N 0.31E
Medzhibozh Ukraine **37** 49.29N 27.28E
Meeberrie Australia **88** 26.58S115.51E
Meekatharra Australia **88** 26.35S118.30E
Meeker U.S.A. **108** 40.02N107.55W
Meer Belgium **16** 51.27N 4.46E
Meerane Germany **38** 50.51N 12.28E
Meerhusener Moor *f.* Germany **38** 53.35N 7.30E
Meersburg Germany **39** 47.41N 9.16E
Meerut India **63** 28.59N 77.42E
Mefallesim Israel **67** 31.30N 34.34E
Mēga Ethiopia **73** 4.07N 38.16E
Megalon Khorion Greece **35** 36.27N 27.24E
Megalópolis Greece **35** 37.24N 22.08E
Mégara Greece **35** 38.00N 23.20E
Megasini *mtn.* India **63** 21.38N 86.21E
Meghalaya *d.* India **63** 25.30N 91.00E
Meghna *r.* Bangla. **63** 22.50N 90.50E
Mégiscane *r.* Canada **102** 48.36N 76.00W
Mehadia Romania **37** 44.55N 22.22E
Mehar Pakistan **62** 27.11N 67.49E
Mehekar India **62** 20.09N 76.34E
Mehidpur India **62** 23.49N 75.40E
Mehndāwal India **63** 26.59N 83.07E
Mehsāna India **62** 23.36N 72.24E
Mehtar Lām Afghan. **62** 34.39N 70.10E
Mehun-sur-Yèvre France **19** 47.09N 2.13E
Meiktila Burma **56** 20.53N 95.50E
Meiningen Germany **38** 50.34N 10.25E
Meira, Sierra de *mts.* Spain **26** 43.15N 7.15W
Meiringen Switz. **39** 46.43N 8.12E
Me'ir Shefeya Israel **67** 32.35N 34.57E
Meishan China **55** 30.02N103.50E
Meissen Germany **38** 51.10N 13.28E
Meixian *see* Meizhou China **55**
Meiyino Sudan **73** 6.12N 34.40E
Meizhou China **55** 24.20N116.15E
Mekatina Canada **104** 47.05N 84.07W
Mekdela Ethiopia **73** 11.28N 39.23E
Mek'elē Ethiopia **73** 13.33N 39.30E
Mekerrhane, Sebkha *f.* Algeria **74** 26.22N 1.20E
Mekhtar Pakistan **62** 30.28N 69.22E
Mekinac, L. Canada **105** 47.05N 73.39W
Meknès Morocco **74** 33.53N 5.37W
Mekong *r.* Asia **56** 10.00N106.40E
Mekong Delta Vietnam **56** 10.00N105.40E
Mekongga *mtn.* Indonesia **59** 3.39S121.15E
Mékôngk *r.* Cambodia *see* Mekong *r.* Asia **56**
Mékrou *r.* Benin **77** 12.20N 2.47E
Melaka Malaysia **58** 2.11N102.16E
Melanesia *is.* Pacific Oc. **84** 5.00N165.00E
Melbourne Australia **93** 37.45S144.58E
Melbourne U.S.A. **113** 28.04N 80.38W
Meldorf Germany **38** 54.05N 9.05E
Meldrum Bay *town* Canada **104** 45.56N 83.07W
Mélé C.A.R. **73** 9.46N 21.33E
Melegnano Italy **30** 45.21N 9.19E
Meleuz Russian Fed. **44** 52.58N 55.56E
Mélèzes, Rivière aux *r.* Canada **103** 57.40N 69.29W
Melfi Chad **77** 11.04N 18.03E
Melfi Italy **33** 40.59N 15.40E
Melfort Canada **101** 52.52N104.36W
Melgaço Portugal **26** 42.07N 8.16W
Melilla Spain **24** 35.17N 2.57W
Melilot Israel **67** 31.23N 34.36E
Melipilla Chile **125** 33.42S 71.13W
Melito di Porto Salvo Italy **33** 37.56N 15.47E
Melitopol Ukraine **45** 46.51N 35.22E
Melk Austria **36** 48.14N 15.20E
Melle France **18** 46.13N 0.09W
Mellen U.S.A. **110** 46.20N 90.40W
Mellerud Sweden **43** 58.42N 12.28E
Mellid Spain **26** 42.55N 8.00W
Mellit Sudan **72** 14.08N 25.33E
Melmore Pt. Rep. of Ire. **15** 55.15N 7.49W
Melnik Bulgaria **34** 41.58N 23.25E
Mělník Czech Republic **36** 50.20N 14.29E
Melo Uruguay **126** 32.22S 54.10W
Melrhir, Chott *f.* Algeria **75** 34.20N 6.20E
Melrose U.K. **14** 55.36N 2.43W
Melrose Mont. U.S.A. **108** 45.37N112.41W
Melrose N.Mex U.S.A. **109** 34.26N103.38W
Melstone U.S.A. **108** 46.36N107.52W
Melsungen Germany **38** 51.08N 9.32E
Meltaus Finland **40** 66.54N 25.22E
Melton Australia **93** 37.41S144.36E
Melton Mowbray U.K. **12** 52.46N 0.53W
Melun France **19** 48.32N 2.40E
Melvich U.K. **14** 58.33N 3.55W
Melville Canada **101** 50.55N102.48W
Melville, C. Australia **90** 14.11S144.30E
Melville, L. Canada **103** 53.45N 59.30W
Melville B. Australia **90** 12.10S136.32E
Melville Hills Canada **98** 69.20N122.00W
Melville I. Australia **90** 11.30S131.00E
Melville I. Canada **98** 75.30N110.00W
Melville Pen. Canada **99** 68.00N 84.00W
Melvin, Lough Rep. of Ire./U.K. **15** 54.26N 8.12W
Mélykút Hungary **31** 46.13N 19.24E
Melzo Italy **30** 45.30N 9.25E
Mêmar Co *l.* China **63** 34.10N 82.15E
Memba Mozambique **81** 14.16S 40.30E
Memboro Indonesia **58** 9.22S119.32E
Memmingen Germany **39** 47.59N 10.11E
Memphis *ruins* Egypt **66** 29.52N 31.12E
Memphis Mich. U.S.A. **114** 42.54N 82.46W
Memphis Tenn. U.S.A. **111** 35.08N 90.03W
Memphremagog, L. Canada **105** 45.05N 72.15W
Mena Ukraine **37** 51.30N 32.15E
Mena U.S.A. **111** 34.35N 94.15W
Menai Str. U.K. **12** 53.17N 4.20W
Ménaka Mali **75** 15.55N 2.24E
Mènam Khong *r.* Laos *see* Mekong *r.* Asia **56**
Menarandra *r.* Madagascar **81** 25.17S 44.30E
Menard U.S.A. **111** 30.55N 99.47W
Menawashei Sudan **73** 12.40N 24.59E
Mendawai *r.* Indonesia **58** 3.17S113.20E
Mende France **20** 44.30N 3.30E
Mendebo Mts. Ethiopia **73** 7.00N 39.30E
Mendi P.N.G. **59** 6.13S143.39E
Mendip Hills U.K. **13** 51.15N 2.40W
Mendocino, C. U.S.A. **108** 40.25N124.25W
Mendooran Australia **93** 31.48S149.08E
Mendoza Argentina **125** 32.54S 68.50W
Mendoza *d.* Argentina **125** 34.30S 68.00W
Mendung Indonesia **58** 0.31N103.12E
Ménéac France **18** 48.09N 2.28W
Mene Grande Venezuela **122** 9.51N 70.57W
Menemen Turkey **64** 38.34N 27.03E
Menen Belgium **16** 50.48N 3.07E
Menfi Italy **32** 37.36N 12.59E
Mengcheng China **54** 33.16N116.33E
Mengzi China **61** 23.20N103.21E
Menihek Lakes Canada **103** 54.00N 66.35W
Menindee Australia **92** 32.23S142.30E
Menindee L. Australia **92** 32.21S142.20E
Menominee U.S.A. **110** 45.07N 87.37W
Menomonie U.S.A. **110** 44.53N 91.55W
Menongue Angola **78** 14.40S 17.41E
Menor, Mar *b.* Spain **25** 37.43N 0.48W
Menorca *i.* Spain **25** 40.00N 4.00E
Mens France **21** 44.49N 5.45E
Mentawai, Kepulauan *is.* Indonesia **58** 2.50S 99.00E
Mentekab Malaysia **58** 3.29N102.21E
Mentok Indonesia **58** 2.04S105.12E
Menton France **21** 43.47N 7.30E
Mentor U.S.A. **114** 41.40N 81.20W
Menyapa, Gunung *mtn.* Indonesia **58** 1.00N116.20E
Menzel Bourguiba Tunisia **32** 37.10N 9.48E
Menzel Bou Zelfa Tunisia **32** 36.41N 10.36E
Menzel Djemil Tunisia **32** 37.14N 9.55E
Menzel Temime Tunisia **32** 36.47N 10.59E
Menzies Australia **89** 29.41S121.02E
Menzies, Mt. Antarctica **128** 71.50S 61.00E
Me'ona Israel **67** 33.01N 35.16E
Meppel Neth. **16** 52.42N 6.12E
Meppen Germany **38** 52.41N 7.17E
Mer France **18** 47.42N 1.30E
Merambéllou, Kólpos *g.* Greece **35** 35.14N 25.47E
Merano Italy **30** 46.40N 11.09E
Merauke Indonesia **90** 8.30S140.22E
Merbein Australia **92** 34.11S142.04E
Mercato Saraceno Italy **30** 43.57N 12.12E
Merced U.S.A. **108** 37.18N120.29W
Mercedes Buenos Aires Argentina **125** 34.40S 59.25W
Mercedes Corrientes Argentina **124** 29.15S 58.05W
Mercedes San Luis Argentina **125** 33.40S 65.30W
Mercedes Uruguay **125** 33.16S 58.01W
Mercer U.S.A. **114** 41.14N 80.15W
Mercy, C. Canada **99** 65.00N 63.30W
Mere U.K. **13** 51.05N 2.16W
Meredith Australia **92** 37.50S144.05E
Meredith, L. U.S.A. **111** 35.36N101.42W
Mereeg Somali Rep. **71** 3.47N 47.18E
Merefa Ukraine **45** 49.49N 36.05E
Mereke C.A.R. **73** 7.34N 23.09E
Mergenevo Kazakhstan **45** 49.59N 51.19E
Mergui Burma **56** 12.26N 98.38E
Mergui Archipelago *is.* Burma **56** 11.15N 98.00E
Meribah Australia **92** 34.42S140.53E
Meriç *r.* Turkey **34** 40.52N 26.12E
Mérida Mexico **117** 20.59N 89.39W
Mérida Spain **27** 38.55N 6.20W
Mérida Venezuela **122** 8.24N 71.08W
Mérida, Cordillera de *mts.* Venezuela **122** 8.30N 71.00W
Meriden U.S.A. **115** 41.32N 72.48W
Meridian U.S.A. **111** 32.22N 88.42W
Mérignac France **20** 44.50N 0.42W
Merigur Australia **92** 34.21S141.23E
Merikarvia Finland **41** 61.51N 21.30E
Merimbula Australia **93** 36.52S149.55E
Merino Australia **92** 37.45S141.35E
Merir *i.* Pacific Oc. **59** 4.19N132.18E
Merirumã Brazil **123** 1.15N 54.50W
Merizo Guam **84** 13.16N144.40E
Merkendorf Germany **39** 49.12N 10.42E
Merksem Belgium **16** 51.14N 4.25E
Merlin Canada **104** 42.14N 82.14W
Merlo Argentina **125** 34.40S 58.45W
Meron, Har *mtn.* Israel **67** 33.00N 35.25E
Merredin Australia **89** 31.29S118.16E
Merrick *mtn.* U.K. **14** 55.08N 4.29W
Merrickville Canada **105** 44.55N 75.50W
Merrill Oreg. U.S.A. **108** 42.01N121.36W

Merrill to **Mitla, Mamarr**

Merrill Wisc. U.S.A. **110** 45.11N 89.41W
Merriman U.S.A. **110** 42.55N101.42W
Merritt Canada **100** 50.10N120.45W
Merriwa Australia **93** 32.08S150.20E
Mersa Fatma Ethiopia **72** 14.55N 40.20E
Mersch Lux. **16** 49.44N 6.05E
Mersea I. U.K. **13** 51.47N 0.58E
Merseburg Germany **38** 51.21N 11.59E
Mersey *r.* U.K. **12** 53.22N 2.37W
Merseyside *d.* U.K. **12** 53.28N 3.00W
Mersin Turkey **64** 36.47N 34.37E
Mersing Malaysia **58** 2.25N103.50E
Merta India **62** 26.39N 74.02E
Merta Road *town* India **62** 26.43N 73.55E
Merthyr Tydfil U.K. **13** 51.45N 3.23W
Mértola Portugal **27** 37.38N 7.40W
Merton U.K. **13** 51.25N 0.12W
Mertzon U.S.A. **111** 31.16N100.49W
Méru France **19** 49.14N 2.08E
Meru *mtn.* Tanzania **79** 3.15S 36.44E
Méry France **19** 48.30N 3.53E
Merzifon Turkey **64** 40.52N 35.28E
Merzig Germany **39** 49.27N 6.36E
Mesa *r.* Spain **25** 41.15N 1.48W
Mesa U.S.A. **109** 33.25N111.50W
Mesagne Italy **33** 40.33N 17.49E
Mesarás, Kólpos *g.* Greece **35** 34.58N 24.36E
Meschede Germany **38** 51.20N 8.17E
Meshoppen U.S.A. **115** 41.34N 76.03W
Meslay-du-Maine France **18** 47.57N 0.33W
Mesocco Switz. **39** 46.23N 9.14E
Mesolóngion Greece **35** 38.21N 21.17E
Mesopotamia *f.* Iraq **65** 33.30N 44.30E
Messalo *r.* Mozambique **79** 11.38S 40.27E
Messina Italy **33** 38.11N 15.33E
Messina R.S.A. **80** 22.20S 30.03E
Messina, Stretto di *str.* Italy **33** 38.10N 15.35E
Messines Canada **105** 46.14N 76.01W
Messíni Greece **35** 37.03N 22.00E
Messíni *site* Greece **35** 37.11N 21.57E
Messiniakós, Kólpos *g.* Greece **35** 36.58N 22.00E
Messkirch Germany **39** 47.59N 9.07E
Mestá Greece **35** 38.16N 25.53E
Mesta *r.* Bulgaria *see* Néstos *r.* Greece **34**
Mestre Italy **30** 45.29N 12.15E
Meta *r.* Venezuela **122** 6.10N 67.30W
Metagama Canada **104** 47.05N 81.57W
Metallifere, Colline *mts.* Italy **30** 43.15N 11.00E
Metán Argentina **124** 25.30S 65.00W
Metangula Mozambique **79** 12.41S 34.51E
Metapontum *site* Italy **33** 40.24N 16.49E
Metéora *site* Greece **34** 39.46N 21.36E
Methóni Greece **35** 36.50N 21.43E
Methuen U.S.A. **115** 42.44N 71.11W
Metkovets Bulgaria **34** 43.37N 23.10E
Metković Croatia **31** 43.03N 17.39E
Metlakatla U.S.A. **100** 55.09N131.35W
Metlika Slovenia **31** 45.39N 15.19E
Métsovon Greece **34** 39.46N 21.11E
Metulla Israel **67** 33.16N 35.35E
Metz France **19** 49.08N 6.10E
Metzingen Germany **39** 48.32N 9.17E
Meu *r.* France **18** 48.02N 1.47W
Meulaboh Indonesia **58** 4.10N 96.09E
Meulan France **19** 49.01N 1.54E
Meurthe *r.* France **19** 48.47N 6.09E
Meurthe-et-Moselle *d.* France **19** 48.35N 6.10E
Meuse *d.* France **19** 49.00N 5.30E
Meuse *r.* Belgium *see* Maas *r.* Neth. **16**
Meuselwitz Germany **38** 51.02N 12.17E
Mexia U.S.A. **111** 31.41N 96.29W
Mexicali Mexico **109** 32.40N115.29W
Mexico C. America **116** 20.00N100.00W
México *d.* Mexico **116** 19.45N 99.30W
Mexico Mo. U.S.A. **110** 39.10N 91.53W
Mexico N.Y. U.S.A. **115** 43.28N 76.14W
Mexico, G. of N. America **116** 25.00N 90.00W
Mexico B. U.S.A. **115** 43.31N 76.17W
Mexico City *see* Ciudad de México Mexico **116**
Meximieux France **21** 45.54N 5.12E
Meydān Kalay Afghan. **62** 32.25N 66.44E
Meydān Khvolah Afghan. **62** 33.36N 69.51E
Meyenburg Germany **38** 53.18N 12.14E
Meyersdale U.S.A. **114** 39.45N 79.05W
Meymac France **20** 45.32N 2.09E
Meymaneh Afghan. **60** 35.54N 64.43E
Meyrueis France **20** 44.10N 3.26E
Mezdra Bulgaria **34** 43.12N 23.35E
Mèze France **20** 43.25N 3.36E
Mézel France **21** 43.59N 6.12E
Mezen Russian Fed. **44** 65.50N 44.20E
Mezen *r.* Russian Fed. **44** 65.50N 44.18E
Mézenc, Mont *mtn.* France **21** 44.55N 4.11E
Mezenskaya Guba *g.* Russian Fed. **44** 66.30N 44.00E
Mezer Israel **67** 32.26N 35.03E
Mézières-en-Brenne France **18** 46.49N 1.13E
Mézin France **20** 44.03N 0.16E
Mezökövesd Hungary **37** 47.50N 20.34E
Mezzolombardo Italy **30** 46.13N 11.05E
M'goun, Irhil *mtn.* Morocco **22** 31.31N 6.25W
Mhow India **62** 22.33N 75.46E
Miahuatlán Mexico **116** 16.20N 96.36W
Miajadas Spain **27** 39.09N 5.54W
Miājlar India **62** 26.15N 70.23E
Miami Fla. U.S.A. **113** 25.45N 80.15W
Miami Okla. U.S.A. **111** 36.53N 94.53W
Miami Tex. U.S.A. **111** 35.42N100.38W
Miami Beach *town* U.S.A. **113** 25.47N 80.07W
Mīāndow Āb Iran **65** 36.57N 46.06E
Miandrivazo Madagascar **81** 19.31S 45.28E
Mīāneh Iran **65** 37.23N 47.45E
Miang, Phukao *mtn.* Thailand **56** 16.55N101.00E
Miāni India **62** 21.51N 69.23E
Miāni Hōr *b.* Pakistan **62** 25.34N 66.19E
Miānwāli Pakistan **62** 32.35N 71.33E
Mianyang Hubei China **55** 30.25N113.30E
Mianyang Sichuan China **55** 31.26N104.45E
Miao'er Shan *mtn.* China **55** 25.50N110.22E
Miaoli Taiwan **55** 24.34N120.48E
Miarinarivo Madagascar **81** 18.57S 46.55E
Miass Russian Fed. **50** 55.00N 60.00E
Mibu *r.* Japan **57** 35.49N137.57E
Mica R.S.A. **80** 24.09S 30.49E
Micang Shan *mts.* China **54** 32.40N107.28E
Michael, L. Canada **103** 54.32N 58.15W
Michalovce Slovakia **37** 48.45N 21.55E
Michelson, Mt. U.S.A. **98** 69.19N144.17W
Michigan *d.* U.S.A. **112** 44.00N 85.00W
Michigan, L. U.S.A. **112** 44.00N 87.00W
Michigan Center U.S.A. **104** 42.14N 84.20W
Michigan City U.S.A. **112** 41.43N 86.54W
Michipicoten Canada **102** 47.59N 84.55W
Michipicoten I. Canada **102** 47.40N 85.50W
Michoacán *d.* Mexico **116** 19.20N101.00W
Michurin Bulgaria **29** 42.09N 27.51E
Michurinsk Russian Fed. **44** 52.54N 40.30E
Micronesia *is.* Pacific Oc. **84** 8.00N160.00E
Midale Canada **101** 49.22N103.27W
Mid Atlantic Ridge *f.* Atlantic Oc. **127** 20.00N 45.00W
Middelburg Neth. **16** 51.30N 3.36E
Middelburg C.P. R.S.A. **80** 31.29S 25.00E
Middelburg Trans. R.S.A. **80** 25.45S 29.27E
Middelfart Denmark **42** 55.30N 9.45E
Middelharnis Neth. **16** 51.46N 4.09E
Middenmeer Neth. **16** 52.51N 4.59E
Middleboro Canada **101** 49.01N 95.21W
Middleboro U.S.A. **115** 41.49N 70.55W
Middleburg N.Y. U.S.A. **115** 42.36N 74.20W
Middleburg Va. U.S.A. **114** 38.58N 77.44W
Middlebury U.S.A. **105** 44.01N 73.10W
Middlefield U.S.A. **114** 41.28N 81.05W
Middle I. Australia **89** 34.07S123.12E
Middle Loup *r.* U.S.A. **110** 41.17N 98.23W
Middleport N.Y. U.S.A. **114** 43.13N 78.29W
Middleport Ohio U.S.A. **114** 39.00N 82.03W
Middlesboro U.S.A. **113** 36.37N 83.43W
Middlesbrough U.K. **12** 54.34N 1.13W
Middleton Canada **103** 44.57N 65.04W
Middleton Reef Pacific Oc. **84** 29.28S159.06E
Middletown Conn. U.S.A. **115** 41.33N 72.39W
Middletown Del. U.S.A. **115** 39.25N 75.47W
Middletown Ind. U.S.A. **112** 39.31N 84.13W
Middletown N.Y. U.S.A. **115** 41.27N 74.25W
Middletown Penn. U.S.A. **114** 40.12N 76.44W
Middletown R.I. U.S.A. **115** 41.32N 71.17W
Mid Glamorgan *d.* U.K. **13** 51.38N 3.25W
Midi, Canal du France **20** 43.26N 1.58E
Midi de Bigorre, Pic du *mtn.* France **20** 42.56N 0.08E
Mid-Indian Basin *f.* Indian Oc. **49** 15.00S 80.00E
Mid-Indian Ridge *f.* Indian Oc. **49** 30.00S 75.00E
Midi-Pyrénées *d.* France **20** 44.10N 2.00E
Midland Canada **104** 44.45N 79.53W
Midland Mich. U.S.A. **104** 43.37N 84.14W
Midland Tex. U.S.A. **111** 32.00N102.05W
Midland Junction Australia **89** 31.54S115.57E
Midleton Rep. of Ire. **15** 51.55N 8.10W
Midnapore India **63** 22.26N 87.20E
Midongy-Sud Madagascar **81** 23.35S 47.01E
Midou *r.* France **20** 43.54N 0.30W
Midway Is. Hawaiian Is. **84** 28.15N177.25W
Midwest U.S.A. **108** 43.25N106.16W
Midwest City U.S.A. **111** 35.27N 97.24W
Midyan *f.* Saudi Arabia **66** 27.50N 35.30E
Midye Turkey **29** 41.37N 28.07E
Midžor *mtn.* Bulgaria / Yugo. **34** 43.24N 22.40E
Mie *d.* Japan **57** 34.42N136.08E
Miechów Poland **37** 50.23N 20.01E
Miedzychód Poland **36** 52.36N 15.55E
Miélan France **20** 43.26N 0.19E
Mielec Poland **37** 50.18N 21.25E
Mien *l.* Sweden **43** 56.25N 14.51E
Mienga Angola **78** 17.16S 19.50E
Mieres Spain **26** 43.15N 5.46W
Miesbach Germany **39** 47.47N 11.50E
Mifflin U.S.A. **114** 40.34N 77.24W
Mifraz Hefa *b.* Israel **67** 32.52N 35.03E
Migang Shan *mtn.* China **54** 35.32N106.13E
Migdal Israel **67** 32.50N 35.30E
Migdal Ha'Emeq Israel **67** 32.41N 35.15E
Miguel Hidalgo, Presa *resr.* Mexico **109** 26.41N108.19W
Migyaunglaung Burma **56** 14.40N 98.09E
Mijares *r.* Spain **25** 39.55N 0.01W
Mikhaylov Russian Fed. **44** 54.14N 39.00E
Mikhaylovgrad Bulgaria **34** 43.27N 23.16E
Mikhaylovka Russian Fed. **45** 50.05N 43.15E
Miki Japan **57** 34.48N134.59E
Mikínai Greece **35** 37.43N 22.46E
Mikindani Tanzania **79** 10.16S 40.05E
Mikjaylovgrad *d.* Bulgaria **34** 43.25N 23.11E
Mikkeli Finland **44** 61.44N 27.15E
Mikkwa *r.* Canada **100** 58.25N114.46W
Míkonos Greece **35** 37.30N 25.25E
Míkonos *i.* Greece **35** 37.29N 25.25E
Mikre Bulgaria **34** 43.02N 24.31E
Mikumi Tanzania **79** 7.22S 37.00E
Mikun Russian Fed. **44** 62.20N 50.01E
Mikuni sammyaku *mts.* Japan **57** 37.00N139.20E
Milagro Ecuador **122** 2.11S 79.36W
Milan *see* Milano Italy **30**
Milan Mich. U.S.A. **104** 42.05N 83.40W
Milan Mo. U.S.A. **110** 40.12N 93.07W
Milange Mozambique **79** 16.09S 35.44E
Milano Italy **30** 45.28N 9.12E
Milâs Turkey **35** 37.19N 27.47E
Milazzo Italy **33** 38.14N 15.15E
Milbank U.S.A. **110** 45.14N 96.38W
Milbanke Sd. Canada **100** 52.18N128.33W
Mildenhall U.K. **13** 52.20N 0.30E
Mildmay Canada **104** 44.03N 81.07W
Mildura Australia **92** 34.14S142.13E
Miléai Greece **35** 39.20N 23.09E
Miles Australia **90** 26.40S150.11E
Miles City U.S.A. **108** 46.25N105.51W
Miletto, Monte *mtn.* Italy **33** 41.27N 14.22E
Miletus *site* Turkey **35** 37.30N 27.18E
Milevsko Czech Republic **39** 49.27N 14.22E
Milford Conn. U.S.A. **115** 41.13N 73.04W
Milford Del. U.S.A. **115** 38.55N 75.25W
Milford Mass. U.S.A. **115** 42.08N 71.32W
Milford Mich. U.S.A. **104** 42.35N 83.36W
Milford N.H. U.S.A. **115** 42.50N 71.39W
Milford N.Y. U.S.A. **115** 42.35N 74.57W
Milford Penn. U.S.A. **115** 41.19N 74.48W
Milford Utah U.S.A. **108** 38.24N113.01W
Milford Haven *town* U.K. **13** 51.43N 5.02W
Milford Sound *town* New Zealand **86** 44.41S167.56E
Miliana Algeria **75** 27.21N 2.28E
Miling Australia **89** 30.27S116.20E
Milk *r.* U.S.A. **108** 48.05N106.15W
Millau France **20** 44.06N 3.05E
Millbrook Canada **104** 44.09N 78.27W
Millbrook U.S.A. **115** 41.47N 73.42W
Mille Lacs, Lac des *l.* Canada **102** 48.45N 90.35W
Mille Lacs L. U.S.A. **110** 46.10N 93.45W
Miller *r.* Australia **92** 30.05S136.07E
Millerovo Russian Fed. **45** 48.55N 40.25E
Millers *r.* U.S.A. **115** 42.35N 72.30W
Millersburg Mich. U.S.A. **104** 45.20N 84.04W
Millersburg Ohio U.S.A. **114** 40.33N 81.55W
Millersburg Penn. U.S.A. **114** 40.33N 76.58W
Millerton U.S.A. **115** 41.57N 73.31W
Milleur Pt. U.K. **14** 55.01N 5.07W
Millicent Australia **92** 37.36S140.22E
Millington U.S.A. **115** 39.16N 75.50W
Millinocket U.S.A. **112** 45.39N 68.43W
Millmerran Australia **91** 27.51S151.17E
Millom U.K. **12** 54.13N 3.16W
Mills L. Canada **100** 61.30N118.10W
Millstatt Austria **31** 46.48N 13.35E
Millville U.S.A. **115** 39.24N 75.02W
Milne Inlet *town* Canada **99** 72.30N 80.59W
Milnet Canada **104** 46.49N 80.59W
Milo *r.* Guinea **76** 11.05N 9.05W
Mílos Greece **35** 36.45N 24.27E
Mílos *i.* Greece **35** 36.41N 24.15E
Milparinka Australia **92** 29.45S141.55E
Milroy U.S.A. **114** 40.43N 77.35W
Miltenberg Germany **39** 49.42N 9.15E
Milton Australia **93** 35.19S150.24E
Milton Canada **104** 43.31N 79.53W
Milton Del. U.S.A. **115** 38.47N 75.19W
Milton Mass. U.S.A. **115** 42.15N 71.05W
Milton N.H. U.S.A. **115** 43.23N 70.59W
Milton Penn. U.S.A. **114** 41.01N 76.51W
Milton Vt. U.S.A. **105** 44.38N 73.07W
Milton W.Va. U.S.A. **114** 38.26N 82.08W
Milton Keynes U.K. **13** 52.03N 0.42W
Miltou Chad **77** 10.10N 17.30E
Miluo China **55** 28.50N113.05E
Milverton Canada **104** 43.34N 80.55W
Milwaukee U.S.A. **110** 43.02N 87.55W
Milwaukie U.S.A. **108** 45.27N122.38W
Milyatino Russian Fed. **44** 54.30N 34.20E
Mim Ghana **76** 6.55N 2.34W
Miminiska L. Canada **102** 51.32N 88.33W
Mimizan France **20** 44.12N 1.14W
Mina U.S.A. **108** 38.24N118.07W
Mīnā 'al Aḥmadī Kuwait **60** 29.04N 48.08E
Mīnāb Iran **65** 27.07N 57.05E
Mīnā Baranis Egypt **72** 23.55N 35.28E
Minaki Canada **102** 50.00N 94.48W
Minamata Japan **57** 32.13N130.24E
Minas Uruguay **125** 34.23S 55.14W
Minas Basin *b.* Canada **103** 45.20N 64.00W
Minas Channel *str.* Canada **103** 45.15N 64.45W
Minas de Corrales Uruguay **125** 31.35S 55.28W
Minas de Riotinto Spain **27** 37.42N 6.22W
Minas Gerais *d.* Brazil **126** 18.00S 45.00W
Minatitlán Mexico **116** 17.59N 94.32W
Minbu Burma **56** 20.09N 94.52E
Mindanao *i.* Phil. **59** 7.30N125.00E
Mindanao Sea Phil. **59** 9.10N124.25E
Mindarie Australia **92** 34.51S140.12E
Mindemoya Canada **104** 45.44N 82.10W
Minden Canada **104** 44.55N 78.43W
Minden Germany **38** 52.17N 8.55E
Minden U.S.A. **111** 32.37N 93.17W
Minden City U.S.A. **104** 43.40N 82.47W
Mindif Cameroon **77** 10.25N 14.23E
Mindiptana Indonesia **59** 5.45S140.22E
Mindona L. Australia **92** 33.09S142.09E
Mindoro *i.* Phil. **59** 13.00N121.00E
Mindoro Str. Pacific Oc. **59** 12.30N120.10E
Mindra *mtn.* Romania **37** 45.20N 23.32E
Minehead U.K. **13** 51.12N 3.29W
Mineola U.S.A. **111** 32.40N 95.29W
Minerva Australia **90** 24.00S148.05E
Minerva U.S.A. **114** 40.44N 81.06W
Minervino Murge Italy **33** 41.05N 16.05E
Mingan Canada **103** 50.18N 64.02W
Mingary Australia **92** 32.09S140.46E
Mingela Australia **90** 19.53S146.40E
Mingenew Australia **89** 29.11S115.26E
Mingin Burma **56** 22.52N 94.39E
Mingin Range *mts.* Burma **56** 24.00N 95.45E
Minglanilla Spain **25** 39.32N 1.36W
Mingorría Spain **26** 40.45N 4.40W
Minhe China **54** 36.12N102.59E
Minho *r. see* Miño *r.* Portugal **26**
Minićevo Yugo. **34** 43.42N 22.18E
Minidoka U.S.A. **108** 42.46N113.30W
Minigwal, L. Australia **89** 29.35S123.12E
Min Jiang *r.* China **55** 26.06N119.15E
Minlaton Australia **92** 34.46S137.37E
Minna Nigeria **77** 9.39N 6.32E
Minneapolis Kans. U.S.A. **110** 39.08N 97.42W
Minneapolis Minn. U.S.A. **110** 44.59N 93.13W
Minnedosa Canada **101** 50.14N 99.51W
Minnesota *d.* U.S.A. **110** 46.00N 94.00W
Minnesota *r.* U.S.A. **110** 44.54N 93.10W
Minnesota Lake *town* U.S.A. **110** 43.51N 93.50W
Minnipa Australia **92** 32.51S135.09E
Minnitaki L. Canada **102** 50.00N 91.50W
Mino Japan **57** 35.34N136.56E
Miño *r.* Spain **26** 41.52N 8.51W
Minobu-sanchi *mts.* Japan **57** 35.05N138.15E
Mino-kamo Japan **57** 35.26N137.01E
Mino-mikawa-kōgen *mts.* Japan **57** 35.16N137.10E
Minorca *i. see* Menorca *i.* Spain **25**
Minot U.S.A. **110** 48.16N101.19W
Minqin China **54** 38.42N103.11E
Minsen Germany **38** 53.42N 7.58E
Min Shan *mts.* China **54** 32.40N104.40E
Minsk Belorussia **37** 53.51N 27.30E
Minta Cameroon **77** 4.37N 12.47E
Minto, Lac *l.* Canada **102** 57.15N 74.50W
Minturno Italy **32** 41.15N 13.45E
Minûf Egypt **66** 30.28N 30.56E
Min Xian China **54** 34.26N104.02E
Minyâ al Qamḥ Egypt **66** 30.31N 31.21E
Minyar Russian Fed. **44** 55.06N 57.29E
Mio U.S.A. **104** 44.39N 84.08W
Mionica Yugo. **31** 44.15N 20.05E
Miquelon Canada **102** 49.25N 76.32W
Mira Italy **30** 45.26N 12.08E
Mira Portugal **26** 40.26N 8.44W
Mira *r.* Portugal **27** 37.43N 8.47W
Mīrābād Afghan. **62** 30.25N 61.50E
Miracema Brazil **126** 21.22S 42.09W
Mirah, Wādī al *r.* Iraq **64** 32.27N 41.21E
Miraj India **60** 16.51N 74.42E
Miramas France **21** 43.35N 5.00E
Mirambeau France **20** 45.23N 0.34W
Miramichi B. Canada **103** 47.08N 65.08W
Mīram Shāh Pakistan **62** 33.01N 70.04E
Mīrān Pakistan **62** 31.24N 70.43E
Miranda de Ebro Spain **26** 42.41N 2.57W
Miranda do Douro Portugal **26** 41.30N 6.16W
Mirande France **20** 43.31N 0.25E
Mirandela Portugal **26** 41.29N 7.11W
Mirando City U.S.A. **111** 27.26N 99.00W
Mirandola Italy **30** 44.53N 11.04E
Miravete, Puerto de *pass* Spain **27** 39.43N 5.43W
Mīr Bachcheh Kūt Afghan. **62** 34.45N 69.08E
Mirbāṭ Oman **60** 17.00N 54.45E
Mirebeau-sur-Bèze France **19** 47.24N 5.19E
Mirecourt France **19** 48.18N 6.08E
Miri Malaysia **58** 4.28N114.00E
Mirim, L. Brazil **126** 33.10S 53.30W
Mírina Greece **34** 39.52N 25.04E
Mirintu Creek *r.* Australia **92** 28.58S143.18E
Mironovka Ukraine **37** 49.40N 30.59E
Miroşi Romania **37** 44.25N 24.58E
Mirow Germany **38** 53.16N 12.49E
Mīrpur Jammu & Kashmir **62** 33.15N 73.55E
Mīrpur Batoro Pakistan **62** 24.44N 68.16E
Mīrpur Khās Pakistan **60** 25.33N 69.05E
Mīrpur Sakro Pakistan **62** 24.33N 67.37E
Mirtóön Pélagos *sea* Greece **35** 36.51N 23.18E
Miryeny Moldavia **37** 47.00N 29.06E
Mirzāpur India **63** 25.09N 82.35E
Mi saki *c.* Japan **57** 40.09N141.52E
Misawa Japan **57** 40.41N141.24E
Miscou I. Canada **103** 47.57N 64.33W
Mishawaka U.S.A. **112** 41.38N 86.10W
Mishima Japan **57** 35.07N138.55E
Mishkino Russian Fed. **44** 55.34N 56.00E
Mishmar Ayyalon Israel **67** 31.52N 34.57E
Mishmar Ha'Emeq Israel **67** 32.36N 35.09E
Mishmar HaNegev Israel **67** 31.21N 34.43E
Mishmar Hayarden Israel **67** 33.00N 35.36E
Mishomis Canada **105** 47.11N 75.40W
Misilmeri Italy **32** 38.01N 13.27E
Misima I. P.N.G. **90** 10.40S152.45E
Misiones *d.* Argentina **124** 27.00S 54.40W
Miskī Sudan **72** 14.51N 24.13E
Miskolc Hungary **37** 48.07N 20.47E
Mismâr Sudan **72** 18.13N 35.38E
Misool *i.* Indonesia **59** 1.50S130.10E
Mişr al Jadīdah Egypt **66** 30.06N 31.20E
Mişrātah Libya **75** 32.23N 15.06E
Mişrātah *d.* Libya **75** 30.30N 17.00E
Mişr Bahrī *f.* Egypt **66** 30.30N 31.00E
Missinaibi *r.* Canada **102** 50.44N 81.29W
Mission U.S.A. **110** 43.18N100.40W
Mississagi *r.* Canada **104** 46.10N 83.01W
Mississagi Prov. Park Canada **104** 46.35N 82.30W
Mississauga Canada **104** 43.35N 79.37W
Mississippi *r.* Canada **105** 45.26N 76.16W
Mississippi *d.* U.S.A. **111** 32.40N 90.00W
Mississippi *r.* U.S.A. **111** 29.00N 89.15W
Mississippi Delta U.S.A. **111** 29.10N 89.15W
Mississippi L. Canada **105** 45.05N 76.12W
Mississippi Sd. U.S.A. **111** 30.15N 88.40W
Missoula U.S.A. **108** 46.52N114.01W
Missouri *d.* U.S.A. **110** 38.30N 92.00W
Missouri *r.* U.S.A. **110** 38.50N 90.08W
Missouri Valley *town* U.S.A. **110** 41.33N 95.53W
Mistake Creek *town* Australia **88** 17.06S129.04E
Mistassini Canada **103** 48.54N 72.13W
Mistassini *r.* Canada **103** 48.53N 72.14W
Mistassini, Lac *l.* Canada **103** 51.15N 73.10W
Mistassini Prov. Park Canada **103** 51.30N 73.20W
Mistastin Canada **103** 55.55N 63.30W
Misterbianco Italy **33** 37.31N 15.01E
Mistinibi, L. Canada **103** 55.55N 64.10W
Mistretta Italy **33** 37.56N 14.22E
Mitchell Australia **90** 26.29S147.58E
Mitchell *r.* Qld. Australia **90** 15.12S141.35E
Mitchell *r.* Vic. Australia **93** 37.53S147.41E
Mitchell Canada **104** 43.28N 81.12W
Mitchell Oreg. U.S.A. **108** 44.34N120.09W
Mitchell S.Dak. U.S.A. **110** 43.40N 98.00W
Mitchell, Mt. U.S.A. **113** 35.47N 82.16W
Mitchells Bay *town* Canada **104** 42.28N 82.26W
Mitchelstown Rep. of Ire. **15** 52.16N 8.17W
Mīt Ghamr Egypt **66** 30.43N 31.16E
Mithapur India **62** 22.25N 69.00E
Mithi Pakistan **62** 24.44N 69.48E
Mitilíni Greece **35** 39.00N 26.20E
Mitla, Mamarr *pass* Egypt **66** 30.00N 32.53E

Mitla Pass to **Morehead City**

Mitla Pass see Mitla, Mamarr pass Egypt **66**
Mito Japan **57** 36.30N140.29E
Mitri Prespa, Límni l. Greece **34** 40.55N 21.00E
Mitrovica Yugo. **34** 42.54N 20.52E
Mitsinjo Madagascar **81** 16.01S 45.52E
Mits'iwa Ethiopia **72** 15.36N 39.29E
Mits'iwa Channel Ethiopia **72** 15.30N 40.00E
Mittagong Australia **93** 34.27S150.25E
Mittelandkanal Germany **38** 52.23N 8.00E
Mittenwald Germany **39** 47.27N 11.15E
Mittersill Austria **39** 47.16N 12.29E
Mittweida Germany **38** 50.59N 12.59E
Mitú Colombia **122** 1.08N 70.03W
Mitumba, Monts mts. Zaïre **79** 3.00S 28.30E
Mitwaba Zaïre **79** 8.32S 27.20E
Mitzic Gabon **78** 0.48N 11.30E
Miura Japan **57** 35.08N139.37E
Mivtahim Israel **67** 31.14N 34.23E
Miya r. Japan **57** 34.32N136.44E
Miyako Japan **57** 39.40N141.59E
Miyako jima i. Japan **53** 24.45N125.25E
Miyakonojō Japan **57** 31.43N131.02E
Miyazaki Japan **57** 31.58N131.50E
Mizdah Libya **75** 31.26N 12.59E
Mizen Head Rep. of Ire. **15** 51.27N 9.50W
Mizil Romania **37** 45.00N 26.26E
Mizoch Ukraine **37** 50.30N 25.50E
Mizoram d. India **61** 23.40N 92.40E
Mizpa Israel **67** 32.47N 35.31E
Mizpe Ramon Israel **66** 30.36N 34.48E
Mizra' Israel **67** 32.39N 35.17E
Mizukaidō Japan **57** 36.01N139.59E
Mizunami Japan **57** 35.22N137.15E
Mizusawa Japan **57** 39.08N141.08E
Mjölby Sweden **43** 58.19N 15.08E
Mjöndalen Norway **42** 59.45N 10.01E
Mjörn l. Sweden **43** 57.54N 12.25E
Mjösa l. Norway **41** 60.40N 11.00E
Mkata Tanga Tanzania **79** 5.47S 38.18E
Mkushi Zambia **79** 13.40S 29.26E
Mkuze R.S.A. **81** 27.10S 32.00E
Mkwaja Tanzania **79** 5.46S 38.51E
Mkwiti Tanzania **79** 10.27S 39.18E
Mladá Boleslav Czech Republic **36** 50.26N 14.55E
Mława Poland **37** 53.06N 20.23E
Mljet i. Croatia **29** 42.45N 17.30E
Mljet i. Croatia **31** 42.45N 17.30E
Mljetski Kanal str. Croatia **31** 42.48N 17.35E
Mneni Zimbabwe **80** 20.38S 30.03E
Moab U.S.A. **108** 38.35N109.33W
Moa I. Australia **90** 10.12S142.16E
Moama Australia **93** 36.05S144.50E
Moamba Mozambique **81** 25.35S 32.13E
Moanda Gabon **78** 1.25S 13.18E
Moapa U.S.A. **109** 36.40N114.39W
Moatize Mozambique **81** 16.10S 33.40E
Moba Zaïre **79** 7.03S 29.42E
Mobara Japan **57** 35.25N140.18E
Mobaye C.A.R. **73** 4.19N 21.11E
Moberly U.S.A. **110** 39.25N 92.26W
Mobert Canada **102** 48.41N 85.40W
Mobile U.S.A. **111** 30.42N 88.05W
Mobile B. U.S.A. **111** 30.25N 88.00W
Mobridge U.S.A. **110** 45.32N100.26W
Mobutu Sese Seko, L. see Albert, L. Uganda/Zaïre **79**
Moçambique town Mozambique **79** 15.00S 40.47E
Mocimboa da Praia Mozambique **79** 11.19S 40.19E
Mocimboa do Ruvuma Mozambique **79** 11.05S 39.15E
Möckeln l. Sweden **43** 56.40N 14.10E
Moclips U.S.A. **108** 47.14N124.13W
Mococa Brazil **126** 21.28S 47.00W
Moctezuma Mexico **109** 30.10N106.28W
Mocuba Mozambique **79** 16.52S 37.02E
Moćurica r. Bulgaria **34** 42.31N 26.32E
Modane France **21** 45.12N 6.40E
Modāsa India **62** 23.28N 73.18E
Modder r. R.S.A. **80** 29.03S 23.56E
Modena Italy **30** 44.40N 10.54E
Modena U.S.A. **108** 37.48N113.57W
Modesto U.S.A. **108** 37.39N121.00W
Modica Italy **33** 36.51N 14.47E
Modjamboli Zaïre **78** 2.28N 22.06E
Modriča Bosnia-Herzegovina **31** 44.57N 18.18E
Moe Australia **93** 38.10S146.15E
Moebase Mozambique **81** 17.04S 38.41E
Moelv Norway **41** 60.56N 10.42E
Moffat U.K. **14** 55.20N 3.27W
Moga India **62** 30.48N 75.10E
Mogadishu see Muqdisho Somali Rep. **79**
Mogadouro Portugal **26** 41.20N 6.39W
Mogaung Burma **56** 25.15N 96.54E
Mogi das Cruzes Brazil **126** 23.33S 46.14W
Mogi-Guaçu Brazil **126** 20.55S 48.06W
Mogilev Belorussia **37** 53.54N 30.20E
Mogilev Podolskiy Ukraine **37** 48.29N 27.49E
Mogilno Poland **37** 52.40N 17.58E
Mogi-Mirim Brazil **126** 22.29S 46.55W
Mogincual Mozambique **79** 15.33S 40.29E
Mogliano Veneto Italy **30** 45.33N 12.14E
Mogok Burma **56** 23.00N 96.30E
Mogollon Rim f. U.S.A. **109** 32.30N111.00W
Moguer Spain **27** 37.16N 6.50W
Mogumber Australia **89** 31.01S116.02E
Mohács Hungary **31** 45.59N 18.42E
Mohammedia Morocco **74** 33.44N 7.24W
Mohana India **63** 25.54N 77.45E
Mohawk Ariz. U.S.A. **109** 32.41N113.47W
Mohawk N.Y. U.S.A. **115** 43.00N 75.00W
Mohawk r. U.S.A. **115** 42.47N 73.42W
Moheda Sweden **43** 57.00N 14.34E
Mohéli i. Comoros **79** 12.22S 43.45E
Mohon France **19** 49.45N 4.44E
Mohoro Tanzania **79** 8.09S 39.07E
Mohoru Kenya **79** 1.01S 34.07E
Moi Norway **42** 58.28N 6.32E
Moincêr China **63** 31.10N 80.52E
Moindi Gabon **78** 3.24S 11.43E
Mointy Kazakhstan **9** 47.10N 73.18E
Moira r. Canada **105** 44.09N 77.23W
Moira U.S.A. **105** 44.50N 74.34W
Mo-i-Rana Norway **40** 66.19N 14.10E
Mõisaküla Estonia **41** 58.06N 25.11E
Moisdon France **18** 47.37N 1.22W
Moisie r. Canada **103** 50.13N 66.02W
Moissac France **20** 44.06N 1.05E
Moïssala Chad **77** 8.20N 17.40E
Moita Portugal **27** 38.39N 8.59W
Mojácar Spain **27** 37.09N 1.50W
Mojave U.S.A. **109** 35.03N118.10W
Mojave Desert U.S.A. **109** 35.00N117.00W
Mojokerto Indonesia **59** 7.25S112.31E
Mokameh India **63** 25.24N 85.55E
Mokau New Zealand **86** 38.41S174.37E
Mokmer Indonesia **59** 1.13S136.13E
Mokpo S. Korea **53** 34.50N126.25E
Mokra Gora mts. Yugo. **34** 42.50N 20.30E
Mokren Bulgaria **34** 42.45N 26.39E
Mol Belgium **16** 51.11N 5.09E
Mola di Bari Italy **33** 41.04N 17.05E
Moláoi Greece **35** 36.48N 22.52E
Molat i. Croatia **31** 44.15N 14.49E
Molchanovo Russian Fed. **50** 57.39N 83.45E
Mold U.K. **12** 53.10N 3.08W
Moldavia Europe **37** 47.30N 28.30E
Molde Norway **40** 62.44N 7.08E
Molepolole Botswana **80** 24.26S 25.34E
Molfetta Italy **33** 41.12N 16.36E
Molihong Shan mtn. China **54** 42.11N124.43E
Molina de Aragón Spain **25** 40.51N 1.53W
Molina de Segura Spain **25** 38.04N 1.12W
Moline U.S.A. **110** 41.30N 90.30W
Molinella Italy **30** 44.37N 11.40E
Molino Lacy Mexico **109** 30.05N114.24W
Molins Spain **25** 41.25N 2.01E
Moliro Zaïre **79** 8.11S 30.29E
Molise d. Italy **33** 41.40N 14.30E
Molkom Sweden **43** 59.36N 13.43E
Mölle Sweden **43** 56.17N 12.29E
Mollendo Peru **124** 17.02S 72.01W
Mölln Germany **38** 53.37N 10.41E
Mollösund Sweden **42** 58.04N 11.28E
Mölndal Sweden **43** 57.39N 12.01E
Molodechno Belorussia **37** 54.16N 26.50E
Molokai i. Hawaii U.S.A. **106** 21.20N157.00W
Molong Australia **93** 33.08S148.53E
Molopo r. R.S.A. **80** 28.30S 20.22E
Mólos Greece **35** 38.47N 22.37E
Moloundou Cameroon **78** 2.55N 12.01E
Molsheim France **19** 48.32N 7.29E
Molson L. Canada **101** 54.12N 96.45W
Molt U.S.A. **110** 46.22N102.20W
Molteno R.S.A. **80** 31.23S 26.21E
Moluccas is. Indonesia **59** 4.00S128.00E
Molucca Sea see Maluku, Laut sea Pacific Oc. **59**
Moma Mozambique **79** 16.40S 39.10E
Mombasa Kenya **79** 4.04S 39.40E
Mombuey Spain **26** 42.02N 6.20W
Momchilgrad Bulgaria **34** 41.32N 25.25E
Momi Zaïre **79** 1.42S 27.03E
Mommark Denmark **36** 54.55N 10.03E
Mompós Colombia **122** 9.15N 74.29W
Mon d. Burma **56** 16.45N 97.25E
Møn i. Denmark **43** 55.00N 12.20E
Mona i. Puerto Rico **117** 18.06N 67.54W
Monaco Europe **21** 43.40N 7.25E
Monadhliath Mts. U.K. **14** 57.09N 4.08W
Monaghan Rep. of Ire. **15** 54.15N 6.58W
Monaghan d. Rep. of Ire. **15** 54.10N 7.00W
Monahans U.S.A. **111** 31.36N102.54W
Monarch Mt. Canada **100** 51.55N125.57W
Monastir Tunisia **75** 35.35N 10.50E
Moncalieri Italy **30** 45.00N 7.40E
Moncão Portugal **26** 42.05N 8.29W
Moncayo, Sierra del mts. Spain **25** 41.48N 1.50W
Monchegorsk Russian Fed. **44** 67.55N 33.01E
Mönchen Gladbach Germany **38** 51.12N 6.28E
Monchique Portugal **27** 37.19N 8.33W
Monclova Mexico **111** 26.54N101.25W
Moncontour France **18** 48.21N 2.39W
Moncton Canada **103** 46.06N 64.47W
Mondego r. Portugal **26** 40.09N 8.52W
Mondego, Cabo c. Portugal **26** 40.11N 8.55W
Mondo Tanzania **79** 5.00S 35.54E
Mondoñedo Spain **26** 43.26N 7.22W
Mondoubleau France **18** 47.59N 0.54E
Mondovì Italy **30** 44.23N 7.49E
Mondragone Italy **32** 41.07N 13.53E
Mondrain I. Australia **89** 34.08S122.15E
Monemvasía Greece **35** 36.41N 23.03E
Monessen U.S.A. **114** 40.09N 79.53W
Monesterio Spain **26** 38.05N 6.16W
Monet Canada **102** 48.10N 75.40W
Monett U.S.A. **111** 36.55N 93.55W
Monfalcone Italy **31** 45.49N 13.32E
Monflanquin France **20** 44.32N 0.46E
Monforte Portugal **27** 39.03N 7.26W
Monforte Spain **26** 42.31N 7.33W
Monga Zaïre **73** 4.12N 22.49E
Mongala r. Zaïre **78** 1.58N 19.55E
Mongalla Sudan **73** 5.12N 31.46E
Mong Cai Vietnam **55** 21.36N107.55E
Mongers L. Australia **89** 29.15S117.05E
Monghyr India **63** 25.23N 86.28E
Mongo Chad **77** 12.14N 18.45E
Mongolia Asia **52** 46.30N104.00E
Mongororo Chad **73** 12.01N 22.28E
Mongu Zambia **78** 15.10S 23.09E
Monheim Germany **39** 48.50N 10.51E
Monifieth U.K. **14** 56.29N 2.50W
Monistrol-sur-Loire France **21** 45.17N 4.10E
Monitor Range mts. U.S.A. **108** 38.45N116.30W
Monkoto Zaïre **73** 1.38S 20.39E
Monmouth U.K. **13** 51.48N 2.43W
Monmouth Ill. U.S.A. **110** 40.54N 90.39W
Monmouth Oreg. U.S.A. **108** 44.51N123.14W
Monocacy r. U.S.A. **114** 39.13N 77.27W
Mono L. U.S.A. **108** 38.00N119.00W
Monomoy Pt. U.S.A. **115** 41.33N 70.02W
Monongahela r. U.S.A. **114** 40.27N 80.00W
Monopoli Italy **33** 40.57N 17.19E
Monor Hungary **37** 47.21N 19.27E
Monóvar Spain **25** 38.25N 0.47W
Monreal Spain **25** 42.42N 1.30W
Monreal del Campo Spain **25** 40.47N 1.21W
Monreale Italy **32** 38.05N 13.17E
Monroe La. U.S.A. **111** 32.33N 92.07W
Monroe Mich. U.S.A. **104** 41.55N 83.24W
Monroe N.C. U.S.A. **113** 35.00N 80.35W
Monroe N.Y. U.S.A. **115** 41.20N 74.11W
Monroe Wisc. U.S.A. **110** 42.36N 89.38W
Monroe City U.S.A. **110** 39.39N 91.44W
Monroeville U.S.A. **113** 31.32N 87.21W
Monrovia Liberia **76** 6.20N 10.46W
Mons Belgium **16** 50.27N 3.57E
Monselice Italy **30** 45.14N 11.45E
Mönsterås Sweden **43** 57.02N 16.26E
Montabaur Germany **39** 50.26N 7.50E
Montagnana Italy **30** 45.14N 11.28E
Montague Canada **103** 46.10N 62.39W
Montaigu France **18** 46.59N 1.19W
Montaigut-en-Combraille France **20** 46.11N 2.38E
Montalbán Spain **25** 40.50N 0.48W
Montalbano di Elicona Italy **33** 38.02N 15.02E
Montalbano Ionico Italy **33** 40.17N 16.34E
Montalcino Italy **30** 43.03N 11.29E
Montalegre Portugal **26** 41.49N 7.48W
Montalto mtn. Italy **33** 38.10N 15.55E
Montalto di Castro Italy **30** 42.21N 11.37E
Montalto Uffugo Italy **33** 39.25N 16.09E
Montana Switz. **39** 46.18N 7.29E
Montana d. U.S.A. **108** 47.14N109.26W
Montánchez Spain **27** 39.13N 6.09W
Montargil Portugal **27** 39.05N 8.10W
Montargis France **19** 48.00N 2.45E
Montauban France **20** 44.01N 1.21E
Montauk U.S.A. **115** 41.03N 71.57W
Montbard France **19** 47.37N 4.20E
Montbarrey France **19** 47.01N 5.39E
Montbéliard France **19** 47.31N 6.48E
Montblanch Spain **25** 41.22N 1.10E
Montbrison France **21** 45.36N 4.03E
Montbron France **20** 45.40N 0.30E
Montceau-les-Mines France **19** 46.40N 4.22E
Mont Cenis, Col du pass France **21** 45.15N 6.54E
Montcerf Canada **105** 46.32N 76.02W
Montchannin France **19** 46.45N 4.27E
Montcornet France **19** 49.41N 4.01E
Mont de Marsan town France **20** 43.53N 0.30W
Montdidier France **19** 49.39N 2.34E
Monte Alegre town Brazil **123** 2.01S 54.04W
Monte Azul town Brazil **126** 15.53S 42.53W
Montebello Canada **105** 45.39N 74.56W
Montebello Iónico Italy **33** 37.59N 15.45E
Monte Carlo Monaco **21** 43.44N 7.25E
Monte Caseros Argentina **125** 30.15S 57.38W
Montecatini Terme Italy **30** 43.53N 10.46E
Montecristo i. Italy **30** 42.20N 10.19E
Montefalco Italy **30** 42.54N 12.39E
Montefrío Spain **27** 37.19N 4.01W
Montego Bay town Jamaica **117** 18.27N 77.56W
Montejicar Spain **27** 37.34N 3.30W
Montélimar France **21** 44.34N 4.45E
Montellano Spain **27** 37.00N 5.34W
Montemor-o-Novo Portugal **27** 38.39N 8.13W
Montemor-o-Velho Portugal **26** 40.10N 8.41W
Montemura mtn. Portugal **26** 40.59N 7.59W
Montendre France **20** 45.17N 0.24W
Montenegro see Crna Gora d. Yugo. **31**
Montenero di Bisaccia Italy **33** 41.57N 14.47E
Montepuez Mozambique **81** 13.09S 39.33E
Montepulciano Italy **30** 43.05N 11.47E
Montereau France **19** 48.23N 2.57E
Monterey Calif. U.S.A. **108** 36.37N121.55W
Monterey Va. U.S.A. **114** 38.25N 79.35W
Monterey B. U.S.A. **108** 36.45N121.55W
Montería Colombia **122** 8.45N 75.54W
Montero Bolivia **124** 17.20S 63.15W
Monteros Argentina **124** 27.10S 65.30W
Monterotondo Italy **30** 42.03N 12.37E
Monterrey Mexico **111** 25.40N100.19W
Montesano Italy **33** 40.16N 15.43E
Monte Sant 'Angelo Italy **33** 41.42N 15.59E
Monte Santu, Capo di c. Italy **32** 40.05N 9.44E
Montesarchio Italy **33** 41.04N 14.38E
Montes Claros Brazil **126** 16.45S 43.52W
Montevarchi Italy **30** 43.31N 11.34E
Montevideo Uruguay **125** 34.53S 56.11W
Montevideo U.S.A. **110** 44.57N 95.43W
Montezuma U.S.A. **111** 37.36N100.26W
Montfaucon France **21** 45.10N 4.18E
Montfort-sur-Meu France **18** 48.08N 1.58W
Montgomery U.K. **13** 52.34N 3.09W
Montgomery Ala. U.S.A. **113** 32.22N 86.20W
Montgomery Penn. U.S.A. **114** 41.10N 76.52W
Montguyon France **20** 45.13N 0.11W
Monthey Switz. **39** 46.15N 6.57E
Monthois France **19** 49.19N 4.43E
Monticello Ark. U.S.A. **111** 33.38N 91.47W
Monticello Miss. U.S.A. **111** 31.33N 90.07W
Monticello N.Y. U.S.A. **115** 41.39N 74.42W
Monticello Utah U.S.A. **108** 37.52N109.21W
Montichiari Italy **30** 45.25N 10.23E
Montiel, Campo de f. Spain **26** 38.46N 2.45W
Montignac France **20** 45.04N 1.10E
Montigny-le-Roi France **19** 48.00N 5.30E
Montijo Portugal **27** 38.42N 8.58W
Montijo Spain **27** 38.55N 6.37W
Montijo Dam Spain **24** 38.52N 6.20W
Montilla Spain **27** 37.35N 4.38W
Montivilliers France **18** 49.33N 0.12E
Mont Joli town Canada **103** 48.35N 68.14W
Mont Laurier town Canada **105** 46.33N 75.30W
Mont Louis town Canada **103** 49.15N 65.46W
Mont-Louis France **20** 42.31N 2.07E
Montluçon France **20** 46.21N 2.36E
Montmagny Canada **103** 46.59N 70.33W
Montmédy France **19** 49.31N 5.22E
Montmirail France **19** 48.52N 3.32E
Montmoreau St. Cybard France **20** 45.24N 0.08E
Montmorillon France **18** 46.26N 0.52E
Montmort France **19** 48.55N 3.49E
Monto Australia **90** 24.52S151.07E
Montorio al Vomano Italy **31** 42.35N 13.38E
Montoro Spain **26** 38.01N 4.23W
Montour Falls town U.S.A. **114** 42.21N 76.51W
Montoursville U.S.A. **114** 41.15N 76.55W
Montpelier Idaho U.S.A. **108** 42.20N111.20W
Montpelier Vt. U.S.A. **105** 44.16N 72.35W
Montpellier France **20** 43.36N 3.53E
Montpon-sur-l'Isle France **20** 45.00N 0.10E
Montreal Canada **105** 45.31N 73.34W
Montreal r. Canada **104** 47.14N 84.39W
Montreal L. Canada **101** 54.20N105.40W
Montreal Lake town Canada **101** 54.03N105.46W
Montréal-Nord Canada **105** 45.36N 73.38W
Montreal River town Canada **104** 46.41N 79.50W
Montrejeau France **20** 43.05N 0.33E
Montrésor France **18** 47.09N 1.12E
Montreuil France **19** 50.28N 1.46E
Montreuil-Bellay France **18** 47.08N 0.09W
Montreux Switz. **39** 46.26N 6.55E
Montrevel France **21** 46.20N 5.08E
Montrichard France **18** 47.21N 1.11E
Montrose U.K. **14** 56.43N 2.29W
Montrose Colo. U.S.A. **108** 38.29N107.53W
Montrose Penn. U.S.A. **115** 41.50N 75.56W
Montserrat i. Leeward Is. **117** 16.45N 62.14W
Montserrat, Serra de mts. Spain **25** 41.15N 0.55E
Mont Tremblant Prov. Park Canada **105** 46.42N 74.20W
Montuenga Spain **26** 41.03N 4.37W
Montville U.S.A. **115** 41.27N 72.08W
Monument Valley f. U.S.A. **108** 36.50N110.20W
Monveda Zaïre **78** 2.57N 21.27E
Monywa Burma **56** 22.05N 95.15E
Monza Italy **30** 45.35N 9.16E
Monze Zambia **79** 16.16S 27.28E
Monzón Spain **25** 41.55N 0.12E
Moolawatana Australia **92** 29.55S139.43E
Mooloogool Australia **88** 26.06S119.05E
Moomba Australia **91** 28.08S140.16E
Moomin Creek r. Australia **93** 29.35S148.45E
Moonbi Range mts. Australia **93** 31.00S151.10E
Moonie Australia **91** 27.40S150.19E
Moonie r. Australia **91** 29.30S148.40E
Moonta Australia **92** 34.04S137.37E
Moora Australia **89** 30.40S116.01E
Moorarie Australia **88** 25.56S117.35E
Moorcroft U.S.A. **108** 44.16N104.57W
Moore r. Australia **89** 31.22S115.29E
Moore, L. Australia **89** 29.30S117.30E
Mooréa i. Is. de la Société **85** 17.32S149.50W
Moorefield U.S.A. **114** 39.04N 78.58W
Moorefield r. U.S.A. **114** 39.04N 78.58W
Moorfoot Hills U.K. **14** 55.43N 3.03W
Moorhead U.S.A. **110** 46.53N 96.45W
Moor Lake town Canada **105** 46.09N 77.42W
Moornanyah L. Australia **92** 33.02S143.58E
Mooroopna Australia **93** 36.24S145.22E
Moosburg Germany **39** 48.29N 11.57E
Moose Creek town Canada **105** 45.15N 74.58W
Moosehead L. U.S.A. **112** 45.40N 69.40W
Moose Jaw Canada **101** 50.23N105.32W
Moose Lake town U.S.A. **110** 46.26N 92.45W
Moosomin Canada **101** 50.07N101.40W
Moosonee Canada **102** 51.17N 80.39W
Mootwingee Australia **92** 31.52S141.14E
Mopanzhang China **54** 33.07N117.22E
Mopêia Velha Mozambique **81** 17.58S 35.40E
Mopti Mali **76** 14.29N 4.10W
Mopti d. Mali **74** 15.30N 3.40W
Moqor Afghan. **62** 32.55N 67.40E
Moquegua Peru **124** 17.20S 70.55W
Mora Cameroon **77** 11.02N 14.07E
Mora Portugal **27** 38.56N 8.10W
Mora Spain **27** 39.41N 3.46W
Mora Sweden **41** 61.00N 14.33E
Mora U.S.A. **110** 45.53N 93.18W
Morādābād India **63** 28.50N 78.47E
Mora de Rubielos Spain **25** 40.15N 0.45W
Morafenobe Madagascar **81** 17.49S 44.45E
Mórahalom Hungary **31** 46.13N 19.54E
Moralana Australia **92** 31.42S138.12E
Moral de Calatrava Spain **26** 38.50N 3.35W
Moramanga Madagascar **81** 18.56S 48.12E
Moran U.S.A. **104** 46.00N 84.50W
Morar, Loch U.K. **14** 56.56N 4.00W
Morasverdes Spain **26** 40.36N 6.16W
Moratalla Spain **25** 38.12N 1.53W
Morava r. Czech Republic **37** 48.10N 16.59E
Morava r. Yugo. **37** 44.43N 21.02E
Moravia U.S.A. **115** 42.43N 76.25W
Moravské Budějovice Czech Republic **36** 49.03N 15.49E
Morawhanna Guyana **122** 8.17N 59.44W
Moray Firth est. U.K. **14** 57.35N 5.15W
Morbach Germany **39** 49.48N 7.07E
Morbegno Italy **30** 46.08N 9.34E
Morbihan d. France **18** 47.55N 2.50W
Mörbylånga Sweden **43** 56.31N 16.23E
Morcenx France **20** 44.02N 0.55W
Morden Australia **92** 30.30S142.23E
Morden Canada **101** 49.11N 98.05W
Mordovo Russian Fed. **45** 52.06N 40.45E
Moreau r. U.S.A. **110** 45.18N100.43W
Morecambe U.K. **12** 54.03N 2.52W
Morecambe B. U.K. **12** 54.05N 3.00W
Moree Australia **93** 29.29S149.53E
Morée France **18** 47.54N 1.14E
Morehead U.S.A. **113** 38.11N 83.27W
Morehead City U.S.A. **113** 34.43N 76.44W

Morelia to Müritzsee

Morelia Mexico 116 19.40N101.11W
Morella Spain 25 40.37N 0.06W
Morelos *d.* Mexico 116 18.40N 99.00W
Morena India 63 26.30N 78.09E
Morena, Sierra *mts.* Spain 27 38.20N 4.25W
Morenci U.S.A. 109 33.05N109.22W
Moreno Mexico 109 28.29N110.41W
Möre og Romsdal *d.* Norway 40 63.00N 9.00E
Moresby I. Canada 100 52.30N131.40W
Moreton I. Australia 91 27.10S153.25E
Morez France 19 46.31N 6.02E
Mórfou Cyprus 66 35.12N 33.00E
Mórfou, Kólpos *b.* Cyprus 66 35.15N 32.50E
Morgan Australia 92 34.02S139.40E
Morgan U.S.A. 111 32.01N 97.37W
Morgan City U.S.A. 111 29.42N 91.12W
Morganfield U.S.A. 113 37.41N 87.55W
Morgantown U.S.A. 114 39.38N 79.57W
Morghāb *r.* Afghan. 60 36.50N 63.00E
Morgongåva Sweden 43 59.56N 16.57E
Moriki Nigeria 77 12.55N 6.30E
Moringen Germany 38 51.42N 9.52E
Morin Heights Canada 105 45.54N 74.21W
Morioka Japan 57 39.43N141.10E
Morisset Australia 93 33.06S151.29E
Moriyama Japan 57 35.04N135.59E
Morlaix France 18 48.35N 3.50W
Mörlunda Sweden 43 57.19N 15.51E
Mormanno Italy 33 39.53N 16.00E
Mormon Range *mts.* U.S.A. 108 37.08N114.20W
Mornington I. Australia 90 16.33S139.24E
Mornington Mission Australia 90 16.40S139.10E
Morobe P.N.G. 59 7.45S147.35E
Morocco Africa 74 32.30N 5.00W
Moro G. Phil. 59 6.30N123.20E
Morogoro Tanzania 79 6.47S 37.40E
Morogoro *d.* Tanzania 79 8.30S 37.00E
Moroleón Mexico 116 20.08N101.12W
Morombe Madagascar 81 21.45S 43.22E
Morón Argentina 125 34.39S 58.37W
Morón Cuba 117 22.08N 78.39W
Mörön Mongolia 52 49.36N100.08E
Morón Spain 27 37.08N 5.27W
Morondava Madagascar 81 20.17S 44.17E
Morón de Almazán Spain 25 41.25N 2.25W
Moroni Comoros 79 11.40S 43.19E
Morotai *i.* Indonesia 59 2.10N128.30E
Moroto Uganda 79 2.32N 34.41E
Moroto, Mt. Uganda 79 2.30N 34.46E
Morpeth U.K. 12 55.10N 1.40W
Morrilton U.S.A. 111 35.09N 92.45W
Morrinsville New Zealand 86 37.39S175.32E
Morris Minn. U.S.A. 110 45.35N 95.55W
Morris Penn. U.S.A. 114 41.36N 77.18W
Morrisburg Canada 105 44.54N 75.11W
Morristown Ariz. U.S.A. 109 33.51N112.37W
Morristown N.J. U.S.A. 115 40.48N 74.29W
Morristown N.Y. U.S.A. 105 44.35N 75.39W
Morristown S.Dak. U.S.A. 110 45.56N101.43W
Morristown Tenn. U.S.A. 113 36.13N 83.18W
Morrisville N.Y. U.S.A. 115 42.54N 75.39W
Morrisville Vt. U.S.A. 105 44.34N 72.44W
Mörrum Sweden 43 56.11N 14.45E
Morrumbene Mozambique 81 23.41S 35.25E
Mörrumsån *r.* Sweden 43 56.09N 14.44E
Mors *i.* Denmark 42 56.50N 8.45E
Morsbach Germany 38 50.52N 7.43E
Morsi India 63 21.21N 78.00E
Mortagne France 18 48.31N 0.33E
Mortagne *r.* France 19 48.33N 6.27E
Mortagne-sur-Sèvre France 18 47.00N 0.57W
Mortain France 18 48.39N 0.56W
Mortara Italy 30 45.15N 8.44E
Morteau France 19 47.04N 6.37E
Mortes *r. see* Manso *r.* Brazil 124
Mortes *r.* Brazil 126 21.09S 45.06W
Mortlake *town* Australia 92 38.05S142.48E
Morundah Australia 93 34.56S146.18E
Moruya Australia 93 35.56S150.06E
Morvan, Monts du *mts.* France 19 47.05N 4.00E
Morven Australia 90 26.25S147.05E
Morvern *f.* U.K. 14 56.37N 5.45W
Morvi India 62 22.49N 70.50E
Morwell Australia 93 38.14S146.25E
Morzhovets *i.* Russian Fed. 44 66.45N 42.30E
Mosbach Germany 39 49.21N 9.08E
Mosby Norway 42 58.14N 7.54E
Moscow *see* Moskva Russian Fed. 44
Moscow U.S.A. 108 46.44N117.00W
Mosel *r.* Germany 39 50.22N 7.36E
Moselle *d.* France 19 49.00N 6.30E
Moselle *r. see* Mosel *r.* France 19
Moses Lake *town* U.S.A. 108 47.08N119.17W
Mosgiel New Zealand 86 45.53S170.22E
Moshi Tanzania 79 3.20S 37.21E
Mosjöen Norway 40 65.50N 13.10E
Moskenes Norway 40 67.55N 13.00E
Moskenesöy *i.* Norway 40 67.55N 13.00E
Moskva Russian Fed. 44 55.45N 37.42E
Moskva *r.* Russian Fed. 44 55.08N 38.50E
Mosquera Colombia 122 2.30N 78.29W
Mosquero U.S.A. 109 35.47N103.58W
Mosquitia Plain Honduras 117 15.00N 84.00W
Mosquito Creek Resr. U.S.A. 114 41.10N 80.45W
Mosquitos, Costa de *f.* Nicaragua 117 13.00N 84.00W
Mosquitos, Golfo de los *g.* Panama 117 9.00N 81.00W
Moss Norway 42 59.26N 10.42E
Mossaka Congo 78 1.20S 16.44E
Mossburn New Zealand 86 45.41S168.15E
Mosselbaai R.S.A. 80 34.11S 22.08E
Mossendjo Congo 78 2.52S 12.46E
Mossgiel Australia 93 33.18S144.05E
Mossman Australia 90 16.28S145.22E
Mossoró Brazil 123 5.10S 37.18W
Mossuril Mozambique 81 14.58S 40.42E
Moss Vale *town* Australia 93 34.33S150.24E
Most Czech Republic 38 50.32N 13.39E
Mostaganem Algeria 74 35.56N 0.05E
Mostar Bosnia-Herzegovina 31 43.20N 17.49E
Mösting, Kap *c.* Greenland 99 64.00N 41.00W
Mostiska Ukraine 37 49.48N 23.05E
Mosul *see* Al Mawṣil Iraq 64
Mösvatnet *l.* Norway 42 59.52N 8.05E
Mota del Cuervo Spain 27 39.30N 2.52W
Mota del Marqués Spain 26 41.38N 5.10W
Motagua *r.* Guatemala 117 15.56N 87.45W
Motala Sweden 43 58.33N 15.03E
Moth India 63 25.43N 78.57E
Motherwell U.K. 14 55.48N 4.00W
Motīhāri India 63 26.39N 84.55E
Motilla del Palancar Spain 25 39.34N 1.53W
Motloutse *r.* Botswana 80 22.15S 29.00E
Motol Belorussia 37 52.25N 25.05E
Motou China 54 32.17N120.35E
Motril Spain 27 36.45N 3.31W
Mott U.S.A. 108 46.22N102.20W
Mottola Italy 33 40.38N 17.03E
Motueka New Zealand 86 41.08S173.01E
Motu Iti *i.* Îs. de la Société 85 16.15S151.50W
Motutapu Niue 84 19.02S169.52W
Mouali Congo 78 0.10N 15.33E
Mouchalagane *r.* Canada 103 53.32N 69.00W
Moúdhros Greece 34 39.52N 25.16E
Moudjéria Mauritania 74 17.53N 12.20W
Moudon Switz. 39 46.40N 6.48E
Mouhoun *r.* Burkina *see* Black Volta *r.* Ghana 76
Mouila Gabon 78 1.50S 11.02E
Mouka C.A.R. 73 7.16N 21.52E
Moulamein Australia 92 35.03S144.05E
Moulhoulé Djibouti 73 12.36N 43.12E
Moulins France 20 46.34N 3.20E
Moulins-la-Marche France 18 48.39N 0.29E
Moulmein Burma 56 16.55N 97.49E
Moulouya, Oued *r.* Morocco 74 35.05N 2.25W
Moultrie U.S.A. 113 31.11N 83.47W
Moultrie, L. U.S.A. 113 33.20N 80.05W
Mound City U.S.A. 110 40.07N 95.14W
Moundou Chad 77 8.36N 16.02E
Moundsville U.S.A. 114 39.55N 80.44W
Moundville U.S.A. 111 32.59N 87.38W
Mountain Ash U.K. 13 51.42N 3.22W
Mountain City U.S.A. 108 41.50N115.58W
Mountain Grove Canada 105 44.44N 76.51W
Mountain Home Ark. U.S.A. 111 36.20N 92.23W
Mountain Home Idaho U.S.A. 108 43.08N115.41W
Mountain Nile *r. see* Jabal, Baḩr al *r.* Sudan 73
Mountain Village U.S.A. 98 62.05N163.44W
Mount Airy *town* Md. U.S.A. 114 39.23N 77.09W
Mount Airy *town* N.C. U.S.A. 113 36.31N 80.38W
Mount Barker *town* S.A. Australia 92 35.06S138.52E
Mount Barker *town* W.A. Australia 89 34.36S117.37E
Mount Beauty *town* Australia 93 36.43S147.11E
Mount Bellew *town* Rep. of Ire. 15 53.28N 8.30W
Mount Brydges *town* Canada 104 42.54N 81.29W
Mount Carmel *town* Ill. U.S.A. 110 38.25N 87.46W
Mount Carmel *town* Penn. U.S.A. 115 40.48N 76.25W
Mount Clemens *town* U.S.A. 114 42.36N 82.53W
Mount Darwin *town* Zimbabwe 81 16.46S 31.36E
Mount Drysdale *town* Australia 93 31.11S145.51E
Mount Eba *town* Australia 92 30.12S135.33E
Mount Fletcher *town* R.S.A. 80 30.41S 28.30E
Mount Forest *town* Canada 104 43.59N 80.44W
Mount Gambier *town* Australia 92 37.51S140.50E
Mount Gilead *town* U.S.A. 114 40.33N 82.50W
Mount Hagen *town* P.N.G. 59 5.54S144.13E
Mount Holly *town* U.S.A. 115 39.59N 74.47W
Mount Holly Springs *town* U.S.A. 114 40.07N 77.11W
Mount Hope *town* N.S.W. Australia 93 32.49S145.48E
Mount Hope *town* S.A. Australia 92 34.07S135.23E
Mount Hopeless *town* Australia 92 29.42S139.41E
Mount Isa *town* Australia 90 20.50S139.29E
Mount Lebanon *town* U.S.A. 114 40.23N 80.03W
Mount Lofty Range *mts.* Australia 92 34.40S139.03E
Mount Magnet *town* Australia 89 28.06S117.50E
Mount Manara *town* Australia 92 32.28S143.59E
Mountmellick Rep. of Ire. 15 53.08N 7.21W
Mount Morgan *town* Australia 90 23.39S150.23E
Mount Morris *town* Mich. U.S.A. 104 43.07N 83.42W
Mount Morris *town* N.Y. U.S.A. 114 42.44N 77.53W
Mount Morris *town* Penn. U.S.A. 114 39.44N 80.02W
Mount Murchison *town* Australia 92 31.23S143.42E
Mount Pleasant *town* Canada 104 43.05N 80.19W
Mount Pleasant *town* Mich. U.S.A. 112 43.36N 84.46W
Mount Pleasant *town* S.C. U.S.A. 113 32.48N 79.54W
Mount Pleasant *town* Tex. U.S.A. 111 33.09N 94.58W
Mount Robson *town* Canada 100 52.56N119.15W
Mount Savage *town* U.S.A. 114 39.42N 78.53W
Mount's B. U.K. 13 50.05N 5.25W
Mount Sterling *town* U.S.A. 113 38.03N 83.56W
Mount Union *town* U.S.A. 114 40.23N 77.53W
Mount Upton *town* U.S.A. 115 42.26N 75.23W
Mount Vernon *town* Australia 88 24.09S118.10E
Mount Vernon *town* Ill. U.S.A. 110 38.19N 88.52W
Mount Vernon *town* N.Y. U.S.A. 115 40.54N 73.50W
Mount Vernon *town* Ohio U.S.A. 114 40.23N 82.29W
Mount Vernon *town* Wash. U.S.A. 108 48.25N122.20W
Mount Walker *town* Australia 89 27.47S152.32E
Mount Willoughby Australia 92 27.58S134.08E
Moura Australia 90 24.33S149.58E
Moura Brazil 122 1.27S 61.38W
Moura Chad 72 13.47N 21.13E
Moura Portugal 27 38.08N 7.27W
Mourdi, Dépression de *f.* Chad 72 18.10N 23.00E
Mourdiah Mali 76 14.35N 7.25W
Mourne *r.* U.K. 11 54.50N 7.29W
Mourne Mts. U.K. 15 54.10N 6.02W
Mouscron Belgium 16 50.46N 3.10E
Moussoro Chad 77 13.41N 16.31E
Mouth of Seneca U.S.A. 114 38.52N 79.21W
Moutier Switz. 39 47.17N 7.23E
Moûtiers France 21 45.29N 6.32E
Mouzákion Greece 34 39.26N 21.40E
Moxico Angola 78 11.50S 20.05E
Moxico *d.* Angola 78 13.00S 21.00E
Moy *r.* Rep. of Ire. 15 54.10N 9.09W
Moyale Kenya 79 3.31N 39.04E
Moyamba Sierra Leone 76 8.04N 12.03W
Moyen Atlas *mts.* Morocco 74 33.30N 5.00W
Moyen-Chari *d.* Chad 77 9.20N 17.35E
Moyeni Lesotho 80 30.24S 27.41E
Moyeuvre-Grande France 19 49.15N 6.02E
Moyie Canada 100 49.17N115.50W
Moyobamba Peru 122 6.04S 76.56W
Moyowosi *r.* Tanzania 79 4.59S 30.58E
Moza Israel 67 31.47N 35.09E
Mozambique Africa 81 17.30S 35.45E
Mozambique Channel Indian Oc. 81 16.00S 42.30E
Mozdok Russian Fed. 45 43.45N 44.43E
Mozyr Belorussia 37 52.02N 29.10E
Mpala Zaïre 79 6.45S 29.31E
M'Pama *r.* Congo 78 0.59S 15.40E
Mpanda Tanzania 79 6.21S 31.01E
Mpésoba Mali 76 12.31N 5.39W
Mphoengs Zimbabwe 80 21.10S 27.51E
Mpika Zambia 79 11.52S 31.30E
Mponela Malaŵi 79 13.32S 33.43E
Mporokoso Zambia 79 9.22S 30.06E
M'Pouya Congo 78 2.38S 16.08E
Mpunde *mtn.* Tanzania 79 6.12S 33.48E
Mpwapwa Tanzania 79 6.23S 36.38E
M'qoun, Irhil *mtn.* Morocco 74 31.31N 6.25W
Mrhila, Djebel *mtn.* Tunisia 75 35.25N 9.14E
Mrkonjić Grad Bosnia-Herzegovina 31 44.25N 17.05E
Mrkopalj Croatia 31 45.19N 14.51E
Msaken Tunisia 22 35.42N 10.33E
Mseleni R.S.A. 81 27.21S 32.33E
Msingu Tanzania 79 4.52S 39.08E
Msta *r.* Russian Fed. 44 58.28N 31.20E
Mtakuja Tanzania 79 7.21S 30.37E
Mtama Tanzania 79 10.20S 39.19E
Mtito Andei Kenya 79 2.32S 38.10E
Mtsensk Russian Fed. 44 53.18N 36.35E
Mtwara Tanzania 79 10.17S 40.11E
Mtwara *d.* Tanzania 79 10.00S 38.30E
Mu *r.* Japan 57 42.30N142.20E
Muaná Brazil 123 1.32S 49.13W
Muangangia Angola 78 13.33S 18.04E
Muang Chiang Rai Thailand 56 19.56N 99.51E
Muang Khammouan Laos 56 17.22N104.50E
Muang Khon Kaen Thailand 56 16.25N102.52E
Muang Lampang Thailand 56 18.16N 99.30E
Muang Lamphun Thailand 56 18.36N 99.02E
Muang Nakhon Phanom Thailand 56 17.22N104.45E
Muang Nakhon Sawan Thailand 56 15.42N100.04E
Muang Nan Thailand 56 18.47N100.50E
Muang Ngoy Laos 56 20.43N102.41E
Muang Pak Lay Laos 56 18.12N101.25E
Muang Phaya Thailand 56 19.10N 99.55E
Muang Phetchabun Thailand 56 16.25N101.08E
Muang Phichit Thailand 56 16.29N100.21E
Muang Phitsanulok Thailand 56 16.45N100.18E
Muang Phrae Thailand 56 18.07N100.09E
Muang Sakon Nakhon Thailand 56 17.10N104.08E
Muang Sing Laos 56 21.11N101.09E
Muang Soum Laos 56 18.46N102.36E
Muang Ubon Thailand 56 15.15N104.50E
Muar Malaysia 58 2.01N102.35E
Muara Brunei 58 5.01N115.01E
Muara Indonesia 58 0.32S101.20E
Muarakaman Indonesia 58 0.02S116.45E
Muaratewe Indonesia 58 0.57S114.53E
Muāri, Rās *c.* Pakistan 62 24.49N 66.40E
Mubende Uganda 79 0.30N 31.24E
Mubi Nigeria 77 10.16N 13.17E
Mucanona Angola 78 8.13S 16.39E
Muchea Australia 89 31.36S115.57E
Mücheln Germany 38 51.18N 11.48E
Muchinga Mts. Zambia 79 12.15S 31.00E
Muck *i.* U.K. 14 56.50N 6.14W
Mucojo Mozambique 79 12.05S 40.26E
Muconda Angola 78 10.31S 21.20E
Mudanjiang China 53 44.36N129.42E
Mudaysīsāt, Jabal al *mtn.* Jordan 67 31.39N 36.14E
Mudgee Australia 93 32.37S149.36E
Mudon Burma 56 16.15N 97.44E
Mudyuga Russian Fed. 44 63.45N 39.29E
Muèda Mozambique 79 11.40S 39.31E
Muene Quibau Angola 78 11.27S 19.14E
Mufulira Zambia 79 12.30S 28.12E
Mufu Shan *mts.* China 55 29.30N114.45E
Muganskaya Ravnina *f.* Azerbaijan 65 39.40N 48.30E
Mughr Syria 67 33.05N 35.43E
Mughshin, Wādī Oman 71 19.44N 55.15E
Mugi Japan 57 33.40N134.25E
Mugia Spain 26 43.06N 9.10W
Muğla Turkey 29 37.12N 28.22E
Muhamdi India 63 27.57N 80.13E
Muḩammad, Ra's *c.* Egypt 66 27.42N 34.13E
Mühlacker Germany 39 48.57N 8.50E
Mühldorf Germany 39 48.15N 12.32E
Mühlhausen Germany 38 51.12N 10.27E
Mühlig Hofmann fjella *mts.* Antarctica 128 72.30S 5.00E
Muhola Finland 40 63.20N 25.05E
Muhos Finland 40 64.48N 25.59E
Muhu *i.* Estonia 41 58.32N 23.20E
Muhuru Kenya 73 1.01S 34.07E
Muhu Väin *str.* Estonia 41 58.45N 23.30E
Mui Ca Mau *c.* Vietnam 56 8.30N104.35E
Muine Bheag *town* Rep. of Ire. 15 52.42N 6.58W
Muir, L. Australia 89 34.30S116.30E
Mukachevo Ukraine 37 48.26N 22.45E
Mukah Malaysia 58 2.56N112.02E
Mukallik, Wādī al Jordan 67 31.46N 35.29E
Mukandwara India 62 24.49N 75.59E
Mukawa P.N.G. 90 9.48S150.00E
Mukāwir *site* Jordan 67 31.34N 35.38E
Mukeriān India 62 31.57N 75.37E
Mukinbudin Australia 89 30.52S118.08E
Muko *r.* Japan 57 34.41N135.23E
Mukoba Zaïre 78 6.50S 20.50E
Mukongo Zaïre 78 6.32S 23.30E
Muktsar India 62 30.28N 74.31E
Mukwela Zambia 78 17.00S 26.40E
Mūl India 63 20.04N 79.40E
Mula *r.* India 62 19.35N 74.50E
Mūla *r.* Pakistan 62 27.57N 67.37E
Mula Spain 25 38.03N 1.30W
Mulanje Mts. Malaŵi 79 15.57S 35.33E
Mulchén Chile 125 37.43S 72.14W
Mulde *r.* Germany 38 51.10N 12.48E
Mulgathing Australia 92 30.15S134.00E
Mulgrave Canada 103 45.37N 61.23W
Mulhacén *mtn.* Spain 27 37.03N 3.19W
Mülheim N.-Westfalen Germany 38 51.24N 6.54E
Mülheim N.-Westfalen Germany 38 50.58N 7.00E
Mulhouse France 19 47.45N 7.20E
Mull *i.* U.K. 14 56.28N 5.56W
Mull, Sd. of *str.* U.K. 14 56.32N 5.55W
Mullaghanattin *mtn.* Rep. of Ire. 15 51.56N 9.51W
Mullaghareirk Mts. Rep. of Ire. 15 52.19N 9.06W
Mullaghmore *mtn.* U.K. 15 54.51N 6.51W
Mullaley Australia 93 31.06S149.55E
Mullen U.S.A. 110 42.03N101.01W
Mullengudgery Australia 93 31.40S147.23E
Mullens U.S.A. 113 37.35N 81.25W
Mullet Pen. Rep. of Ire. 15 54.12N 10.04W
Mullett L. U.S.A. 104 45.30N 84.30W
Mullewa Australia 89 28.33S115.31E
Müllheim Germany 39 47.48N 7.38E
Mullingar Rep. of Ire. 15 53.31N 7.21W
Mull of Galloway *c.* U.K. 14 54.39N 4.52W
Mull of Kintyre *c.* U.K. 14 55.17N 5.45W
Mullovka Russian Fed. 44 54.12N 49.26E
Mullsjö Sweden 43 57.55N 13.53E
Mullumbimby Australia 93 28.32S153.30E
Mulobezi Zambia 80 16.49S 25.09E
Muloorina Australia 92 29.10S137.51E
Multai India 63 21.46N 78.15E
Multān Pakistan 62 30.11N 71.29E
Multyfarnham Rep. of Ire. 15 53.37N 7.25W
Mulyungarie Australia 92 31.30S140.45E
Mumbai *see* Bombay India 62
Mumbwa Zambia 79 14.57S 27.01E
Mumcular Turkey 35 37.05N 27.40E
Mun *r.* Thailand 56 15.15N104.50E
Mun, Jabal *mtn.* Sudan 72 14.08N 22.42E
Muna *i.* Indonesia 59 5.00S122.30E
Munābāo India 62 25.45N 70.17E
Munan Pass China / Vietnam 55 22.06N106.46E
Münchberg Germany 38 50.11N 11.47E
München Germany 39 48.08N 11.34E
Muncho Lake *town* Canada 100 59.00N125.50W
Muncie U.S.A. 112 40.11N 85.23W
Mundaring Weir Australia 89 31.59S116.13E
Münden Germany 38 51.25N 9.39E
Mundiwindi Australia 88 23.50S120.07E
Mundo *r.* Spain 25 38.19N 1.40W
Mundra India 62 22.51N 69.44E
Munera Spain 27 39.02N 2.28W
Mungari Mozambique 81 17.12S 33.31E
Mungbere Zaïre 79 2.40N 28.25E
Mungeli India 63 22.04N 81.41E
Mungeranie Australia 92 28.00S138.36E
Mungindi Australia 93 28.58S148.56E
Munhango Angola 78 12.10S 18.36E
Munich *see* München Germany 39
Muniesa Spain 25 41.02N 0.48W
Muniz Freire Brazil 126 20.25S 41.23W
Munkedal Sweden 42 58.29N 11.41E
Munkfors Sweden 43 59.50N 13.32E
Munning *r.* Australia 93 31.50S152.30E
Münsingen Germany 39 48.25N 9.29E
Münsingen Switz. 39 46.53N 7.34E
Munster France 19 48.03N 7.08E
Munster Nschn. Germany 38 52.59N 10.05E
Münster N.-Westfalen Germany 38 51.57N 7.37E
Muntadgin Australia 89 31.41S118.32E
Munuscong L. U.S.A. 104 46.10N 84.08W
Munyati *r.* Zimbabwe 80 17.32S 29.23E
Muong Hinh Vietnam 55 19.49N105.03E
Muonio Finland 40 67.57N 23.42E
Muonio *r.* Finland / Sweden 40 67.10N 23.40E
Mupa Angola 80 16.07S 15.45E
Mupa *r.* Mozambique 81 19.07S 35.50E
Muping China 54 37.23N121.35E
Muqaddam, Wādī Sudan 72 18.04N 31.30E
Muqdisho Somali Rep. 79 2.02N 45.21E
Mur *r.* Austria *see* Mura *r.* Croatia 31
Mura *r.* Croatia 31 46.18N 16.53E
Murallón *mtn.* Argentina / Chile 125 49.48S 73.25W
Muranga Kenya 79 0.43S 37.10E
Murashi Russian Fed. 44 59.20N 48.59E
Murat France 20 45.07N 2.52E
Murau Austria 39 47.07N 14.10E
Muravera Italy 32 39.25N 9.35E
Murça Portugal 26 41.24N 7.27W
Murchison Australia 93 36.36S145.14E
Murchison *r.* Australia 88 27.30S114.10E
Murchison New Zealand 86 41.48S172.20E
Murcia Spain 25 37.59N 1.07W
Murcia *d.* Spain 25 37.55N 1.40W
Mur-de-Barrez France 20 44.51N 2.39E
Murdo U.S.A. 110 43.53N100.43W
Mureș *r.* Romania 37 46.16N 20.10E
Muret France 20 43.28N 1.21E
Murewa Zimbabwe 81 17.40S 31.47E
Murfreesboro U.S.A. 113 35.50N 86.25W
Murg *r.* Germany 39 48.55N 8.10E
Murgha Faqīrzai Pakistan 62 31.03N 67.48E
Murgha Kibzai Pakistan 62 30.44N 69.25E
Murgon Australia 90 26.15S151.57E
Murguia Spain 26 42.57N 2.49W
Muri Cook Is. 84 21.14S159.43W
Muria, Gunung *mtn.* Indonesia 59 6.39S110.51E
Muriaé Brazil 126 21.08S 42.33W
Murias de Paredes Spain 26 42.51N 6.11W
Müritzsee *l.* Germany 38 53.25N 12.43E

Murjek to **Naryn**

Murjek Sweden **40** 66.29N 20.50E
Murliganj India **63** 25.54N 86.59E
Murmansk Russian Fed. **44** 68.59N 33.08E
Murnau Germany **39** 47.40N 11.12E
Murnei Sudan **73** 12.57N 22.52E
Muro, Capo di *c.* France **21** 41.44N 8.40E
Muro Lucano Italy **33** 40.45N 15.30E
Murom Russian Fed. **44** 55.04N 42.04E
Muroran Japan **57** 42.21N140.59E
Muros Spain **26** 42.47N 9.02W
Muros y Noya, Ría de *est.* Spain **26** 42.45N 9.00W
Murrah al Kubrá, Al Buḩayrah al *l.* Egypt **66** 30.20N 32.20E
Murra Murra Australia **93** 28.18S146.48E
Murray *r.* S.A. Australia **92** 35.23S139.20E
Murray *r.* W.A. Australia **89** 32.35S115.46E
Murray *r.* Canada **100** 56.11N120.45W
Murray Ky. U.S.A. **111** 36.37N 88.19W
Murray Utah U.S.A. **108** 40.40N111.53W
Murray, L. P.N.G. **59** 7.00S141.30E
Murray, L. U.S.A. **113** 34.04N 81.23W
Murray Bridge *town* Australia **92** 35.10S139.17E
Murrayville Australia **92** 35.16S141.14E
Murree Pakistan **62** 33.54N 73.24E
Murrhardt Germany **39** 48.59N 9.34E
Murringo Australia **93** 34.19S148.36E
Murrumbidgee *r.* Australia **92** 34.38S143.10E
Murrumburrah Australia **93** 34.33S148.21E
Murrurundi Australia **93** 31.47S150.51E
Murshidābād India **63** 24.11N 88.16E
Murska Sobota Slovenia **31** 46.40N 16.10E
Murten Switz. **39** 46.56N 7.07E
Murtoa Australia **92** 36.40S142.31E
Murtosa Portugal **26** 40.44N 8.38W
Murud *mtn.* Malaysia **58** 3.45N115.30E
Murwāra India **63** 23.51N 80.24E
Murwillumbah Australia **93** 28.20S153.24E
Muş Turkey **64** 38.45N 41.30E
Mūsá, Jabal *mtn.* Egypt **66** 28.31N 33.59E
Musadi Zaïre **78** 2.31S 22.50E
Mūsa Khel Pakistan **62** 32.38N 71.44E
Mūsa Khel Bāzār Pakistan **62** 30.52N 69.49E
Musala *mtn.* Bulgaria **34** 42.13N 23.37E
Musan N. Korea **57** 42.14N129.13E
Mūsā Qal 'eh Afghan. **62** 32.05N 64.51E
Mūsā Qal 'eh *r.* Afghan. **62** 32.22N 64.46E
Musay'īd Qatar **65** 24.47N 51.36E
Mūsāzai Pakistan **62** 30.23N 66.32E
Muscat *see* Masqaţ Oman **65**
Muscatine U.S.A. **110** 41.25N 91.03W
Müsgebi Turkey **35** 37.02N 27.21E
Musgrave Australia **90** 14.47S143.30E
Musgrave Ranges *mts.* Australia **88** 26.10S131.50E
Mushāsh, Wādī al Jordan **67** 31.35N 35.22E
Mushie Zaïre **78** 2.59S 16.55E
Mushima Zambia **80** 14.13S 25.05E
Mushin Nigeria **77** 6.33N 3.22E
Musi *r.* Indonesia **58** 2.20S104.57E
Muskegon U.S.A. **112** 43.13N 86.15W
Muskegon *r.* U.S.A. **112** 43.13N 86.16W
Muskegon Heights *town* U.S.A. **112** 43.03N 86.16W
Muskingum *r.* U.S.A. **114** 40.03N 81.59W
Muskö *i.* Sweden **43** 59.00N 18.06E
Muskogee U.S.A. **111** 35.45N 95.22W
Muskoka, L. Canada **104** 45.00N 79.25W
Muskwa *r.* Alta. Canada **100** 56.16N114.06W
Muskwa *r.* B.C. Canada **100** 58.47N122.48W
Musoma Tanzania **79** 1.31S 33.48E
Mussari Angola **80** 13.07S 17.56E
Musselburgh U.K. **14** 55.57N 3.04W
Musselkanaal Neth. **16** 52.57N 7.01E
Musselshell *r.* U.S.A. **108** 47.21N107.58W
Mussende Angola **78** 10.33S 16.02E
Musserra Angola **78** 7.31S 13.02E
Mussidan France **20** 45.02N 0.22E
Mussomeli Italy **32** 37.35N 13.46E
Mustahil Ethiopia **71** 5.12N 44.17E
Mustāng Nepal **63** 29.11N 83.57E
Mustjala Estonia **41** 58.28N 22.14E
Muswellbrook Australia **93** 32.17S150.55E
Mūţ Egypt **72** 25.29N 28.59E
Mut Turkey **64** 36.38N 33.27E
Mutala Mozambique **81** 15.54S 37.51E
Mutalau Niue **84** 18.58S169.50W
Mutanda Zambia **78** 12.23S 26.16E
Mutare Zimbabwe **81** 18.59S 32.40E
Mutbin Syria **67** 33.09N 36.15E
Mutoko Zimbabwe **81** 17.23S 32.13E
Mutooroo Australia **92** 32.30S140.58E
Mutoray Russian Fed. **51** 61.20N100.32E
Mutshatsha Zaïre **78** 10.39S 24.27E
Mutsu Japan **57** 41.17N141.10E
Mutsu wan *b.* Japan **57** 41.10N141.05E
Mutton Bay *town* Canada **103** 50.47N 59.02W
Muwale Tanzania **79** 6.22S 33.46E
Muxima Angola **78** 9.33S 13.58E
Muya Russian Fed. **51** 56.28N115.50E
Muyinga Burundi **79** 2.48S 30.21E
Muzaffarābād Jammu & Kashmir **62** 34.22N 73.28E
Muzaffargarh Pakistan **62** 30.04N 71.12E
Muzaffarnagar India **63** 29.28N 77.41E
Muzaffarpur India **63** 26.07N 85.24E
Muzhi Russian Fed. **44** 65.25N 64.40E
Muzillac France **18** 47.33N 2.29W
Muzoka Zambia **80** 16.43S 27.18E
Muztag *mtn.* China **52** 36.25N 87.25E
Mvadhi Gabon **78** 1.13N 13.10E
Mvolo Sudan **73** 6.03N 29.56E
Mvomero Tanzania **79** 6.18S 37.26E
Mvuma Zimbabwe **80** 19.16S 30.30E
Mvurwi Range *mts.* Zimbabwe **80** 17.10S 30.45E
Mwali *see* Mohéli *i.* Comoros **79**
Mwanza Tanzania **79** 2.30S 32.54E
Mwanza *d.* Tanzania **79** 3.00S 32.30E
Mwanza Zaïre **78** 7.51S 26.43E
Mwaya Mbeya Tanzania **79** 9.33S 33.56E
Mweka Zaïre **78** 4.51S 21.34E
Mwene Ditu Zaïre **78** 7.04S 23.27E
Mwenezi *r.* Mozambique **81** 22.42S 31.45E
Mwenezi Zimbabwe **80** 21.22S 30.45E
Mweru, L. Zaïre / Zambia **79** 9.00S 28.40E
Mwingi Kenya **79** 1.00S 38.04E
Mwinilunga Zambia **78** 11.44S 24.24E
Mya, Oued *wadi* Algeria **75** 31.40N 5.15E
Myanaung Burma **61** 18.25N 95.10E
Myanma *see* Burma Asia **56**
Myaungmya Burma **56** 16.33N 94.55E
Myingyan Burma **56** 21.22N 95.28E
Myinkyado Burma **56** 20.56N 96.42E
Myinmu Burma **56** 21.58N 95.43E
Myitkyinā Burma **56** 25.24N 97.25E
Mymensingh Bangla. **63** 24.45N 90.24E
Myrdal Norway **41** 60.44N 7.08E
Myrdalsjökull *ice cap* Iceland **40** 63.40N 19.06W
Myrtle Beach *town* U.S.A. **113** 33.42N 78.54W
Myrtle Creek *town* U.S.A. **108** 43.01N123.17W
Myrtleford Australia **93** 36.35S146.44E
Myrtle Point *town* U.S.A. **108** 43.04N124.08W
Mysen Norway **42** 59.33N 11.20E
Myślenice Poland **37** 49.51N 19.56E
Mysore India **60** 12.18N 76.37E
Mystic U.S.A. **115** 41.21N 71.58W
My Tho Vietnam **56** 10.27N106.20E
Mytishchi Russian Fed. **44** 55.54N 37.47E
Mziha Tanzania **79** 5.53S 37.48E
Mzimba Malaŵi **79** 12.00S 33.39E

N

Naab *r.* Germany **39** 49.01N 12.02E
Naalehu Hawaiian Is. **85** 19.04N155.35W
Na'âm *r.* Sudan **73** 6.48N 29.57E
Na'an Israel **67** 31.53N 34.51E
Naantali Finland **41** 60.27N 22.02E
Naas Rep. of Ire. **15** 53.13N 6.41W
Näätämö *r.* Norway **40** 69.40N 29.30E
Nabā, Jabal *mtn.* Jordan **67** 31.46N 35.45E
Nababeep R.S.A. **80** 29.36S 17.44E
Nabadwīp India **63** 23.25N 88.22E
Nabari *r.* Japan **57** 34.45N136.01E
Naberezhnyye Chelny Russian Fed. **44** 55.42N 52.20E
Nabeul Tunisia **75** 36.28N 10.44E
Nabeul *d.* Tunisia **32** 36.45N 10.45E
Nābha India **62** 30.22N 76.09E
Nabingora Uganda **79** 0.31N 31.11E
Nabī Shu'ayb, Jabal an *mtn.* Yemen **71** 15.17N 43.59E
Naboomspruit R.S.A. **80** 24.31S 28.24E
Nabq Egypt **66** 28.04N 34.26E
Nābulus Jordan **67** 32.13N 35.16E
Nābulus *d.* Jordan **67** 32.15N 35.17E
Nacala Mozambique **81** 14.34S 40.41E
Nacchio Ethiopia **73** 7.30N 40.15E
Nachikapau L. Canada **103** 56.44N 68.00W
Nachingwea Tanzania **79** 10.21S 38.46E
Nāchna India **62** 27.30N 71.43E
Nacka Sweden **43** 59.18N 18.10E
Naco Mexico **109** 31.20N109.56W
Nacogdoches U.S.A. **111** 31.36N 94.39W
Nadela Spain **26** 42.58N 7.30W
Nadiād India **62** 22.42N 72.52E
Nador Morocco **74** 35.12N 2.55W
Nadūshan Iran **65** 32.03N 53.33E
Nadvoitsy Russian Fed. **44** 63.56N 34.20E
Nadvornaya Ukraine **37** 48.37N 24.30E
Nadym Russian Fed. **50** 65.25N 72.40E
Naenwa India **62** 25.46N 75.51E
Naerbö Norway **42** 58.40N 5.39E
Naeröy Norway **40** 64.48N 11.17E
Naestved Denmark **42** 55.14N 11.46E
Nafada Nigeria **77** 11.08N 11.20E
Nafīshah Egypt **66** 30.34N 32.15E
Naft-e Safīd Iran **65** 31.38N 49.20E
Nāg Pakistan **62** 27.24N 65.08E
Naga Phil. **59** 13.36N123.12E
Nāgāland *d.* India **61** 26.10N 94.30E
Nagambie Australia **93** 36.48S145.12E
Nagano Japan **57** 36.39N138.10E
Nagano *d.* Japan **57** 35.33N137.50E
Nagaoka Japan **57** 37.30N138.50E
Nāgappattinam India **61** 10.45N 79.50E
Nagara *r.* Japan **57** 35.01N136.43E
Nagar Pārkar Pakistan **62** 24.22N 70.45E
Nagarzê China **63** 28.58N 90.24E
Nagasaki Japan **57** 32.45N129.52E
Nāgaur India **62** 27.12N 73.44E
Nāgāvali *r.* India **63** 18.13N 83.56E
Nāgda India **62** 23.27N 75.25E
Nagele Neth. **16** 52.39N 5.43E
Nāgercoil India **60** 8.11N 77.30E
Nagichot Sudan **73** 4.16N 33.34E
Nagīna India **63** 29.27N 78.27E
Nagles Mts. Rep. of Ire. **15** 52.06N 8.26W
Nagold Germany **39** 48.33N 8.43E
Nagorskoye Russian Fed. **44** 58.18N 50.50E
Nagoya Japan **57** 35.10N136.55E
Nāgpur India **63** 21.09N 79.06E
Nagqên China **61** 32.15N 96.13E
Nagqu China **63** 31.30N 92.00E
Nagyatád Hungary **31** 46.14N 17.22E
Nagybajom Hungary **31** 46.23N 17.31E
Nagykanizsa Hungary **31** 46.27N 16.59E
Naha Japan **53** 26.10N127.40E
Nahalal Israel **67** 32.41N 35.12E
Nāhan India **63** 30.33N 77.18E
Nahanni Butte *town* Canada **98** 61.03N123.31W
Nahariyya Israel **67** 33.01N 35.05E
Nahāvand Iran **65** 34.13N 48.23E
Nahe *r.* Germany **39** 49.58N 7.57E
Nahf Israel **67** 32.56N 35.19E
Nahr al Furāt *r.* Asia **65** 31.00N 47.27E
Nahunta U.S.A. **113** 31.12N 82.00W
Nai Ga Burma **56** 27.48N 97.30E
Naila Germany **38** 50.19N 11.42E
Naiman Qi China **54** 42.53N120.40E
Nain Canada **103** 57.00N 61.40W
Nā'īn Iran **65** 32.52N 53.05E
Naini Tāl India **63** 29.23N 79.27E
Nainpur India **63** 22.26N 80.07E
Nairn Canada **104** 46.21N 81.36W
Nairn U.K. **14** 57.35N 3.52W
Nairobi Kenya **79** 1.17S 36.50E
Naita *mtn.* Ethiopia **73** 5.31N 35.18E
Naivasha Kenya **79** 0.44S 36.26E
Najac France **20** 44.17N 2.00E
Najd *f.* Saudi Arabia **64** 25.00N 45.00E
Nájera Spain **26** 42.25N 2.44W
Naj 'Hammādī Egypt **64** 26.04N 32.13E
Najrān *see* Abā as Su'ūd Saudi Arabia **71**
Nāka Khārari Pakistan **62** 25.15N 66.44E
Nakambe *r.* Burkina *see* White Volta *r.* Ghana **76**
Nakaminato Japan **57** 36.21N140.36E
Nakano shima *i.* Japan **57** 29.55N129.55E
Nakape Sudan **73** 5.47N 28.38E
Nakatsu Japan **57** 33.37N131.11E
Nakatsugawa Japan **57** 35.29N137.30E
Nak'fa Ethiopia **72** 16.43N 38.32E
Nakhichevan Azerbaijan **65** 39.12N 45.24E
Nakhodka Russian Fed. **53** 42.53N132.54E
Nakhola India **63** 26.07N 92.11E
Nakhon Pathom Thailand **56** 13.50N100.01E
Nakhon Ratchasima Thailand **56** 14.58N102.06E
Nakhon Si Thammarat Thailand **56** 8.24N 99.58E
Nakhtarana India **62** 23.20N 69.15E
Nakina Canada **102** 50.10N 86.40W
Nakło Poland **37** 53.08N 17.35E
Naknek U.S.A. **98** 58.45N157.00W
Nakop Namibia **80** 28.05S 19.57E
Nakskov Denmark **41** 54.50N 11.09E
Näkten *l.* Sweden **40** 65.50N 14.35E
Nakuru Kenya **79** 0.16S 36.04E
Nāl *r.* Pakistan **62** 26.02N 65.19E
Nalbāri India **63** 26.26N 91.30E
Nalchik Russian Fed. **45** 43.31N 43.38E
Nalón *r.* Spain **26** 43.32N 6.04W
Nālūt Libya **75** 31.52N 10.59E
Namacurra Mozambique **79** 17.35S 37.00E
Namakī *r.* Iran **65** 31.02N 55.20E
Namanga Kenya **79** 2.33S 36.48E
Namangan Uzbekistan **52** 40.59N 71.41E
Namanyere Tanzania **79** 7.34S 31.00E
Namapa Mozambique **81** 13.48S 39.44E
Namaponda Mozambique **81** 15.51S 39.52E
Namari Senegal **74** 15.05N 13.39W
Namarroi Mozambique **81** 15.58S 36.55E
Namatele Tanzania **79** 10.01S 38.26E
Namba Angola **78** 11.32S 15.33E
Nambala Zambia **80** 15.07S 27.02E
Nambour Australia **91** 26.36S152.59E
Nambucca Heads *town* Australia **93** 30.38S152.59E
Namco China **63** 30.53N 91.06E
Nam Co *l.* China **63** 30.45N 90.30E
Nam Dinh Vietnam **55** 20.21N106.09E
Namecala Mozambique **81** 12.50S 39.38E
Nametil Mozambique **81** 15.41S 39.30E
Namib Desert Namibia **80** 23.00S 15.20E
Namibe Angola **78** 15.10S 12.10E
Namibe *d.* Angola **80** 15.30S 12.30E
Namibia Africa **80** 21.30S 16.45E
Namīn Iran **65** 38.25N 48.30E
Namlea Indonesia **59** 3.15S127.07E
Namling China **63** 29.40N 89.03E
Namoi *r.* Australia **93** 30.14S148.28E
Namonuito *i.* Pacific Oc. **84** 8.46N150.02E
Namous, Oued *wadi* Algeria **74** 30.28N 0.14W
Nampa Canada **100** 56.02N117.07W
Nampa U.S.A. **108** 43.44N116.34W
Nam Phan *f.* Vietnam **56** 10.40N106.00E
Nam Phong Thailand **56** 16.45N102.52E
Namp'o N. Korea **53** 38.40N125.30E
Nampula Mozambique **81** 15.09S 39.14E
Nampula *d.* Mozambique **81** 15.00S 39.00E
Namsen *r.* Norway **40** 64.27N 12.19E
Namsos Norway **40** 64.28N 11.30E
Namtu Burma **56** 23.04N 97.26E
Namu Canada **100** 51.52N127.41W
Namuchabawashan *mtn.* China **61** 29.30N 95.10E
Namungua Mozambique **79** 13.11S 40.30E
Namur Belgium **16** 50.28N 4.52E
Namur *d.* Belgium **16** 50.20N 4.45E
Namur Canada **105** 45.54N 74.56W
Namutoni Namibia **80** 18.48S 16.58E
Namwala Zambia **78** 15.44S 26.25E
Nanaimo Canada **100** 49.10N124.00W
Nanam N. Korea **57** 41.43N129.41E
Nanango Australia **91** 26.42S151.58E
Nanao Japan **57** 37.03N136.58E
Nanchang China **55** 28.37N115.57E
Nancheng China **55** 27.35N116.33E
Nanchong China **55** 30.53N106.05E
Nanchuan China **55** 29.12N107.30E
Nancy France **19** 48.41N 6.12E
Nanda Devi *mtn.* India **63** 30.23N 79.59E
Nandan China **55** 24.59N107.32E
Nānded India **62** 19.09N 77.20E
Nandewar Range *mts.* Australia **93** 30.20S150.45E
Nāndgaon India **62** 20.19N 74.39E
Nandi Fiji **84** 17.48S177.25E
Nandu Jiang *r.* China **55** 20.04N110.20E
Nandurbār India **62** 21.22N 74.15E
Nandyāl India **61** 15.29N 78.29E
Nanfeng China **55** 27.10N116.24E
Nanga Eboko Cameroon **77** 4.41N 12.21E
Nānga Parbat *mtn.* Jammu & Kashmir **60** 35.10N 74.35E
Nangapinoh Indonesia **58** 0.20S111.44E
Nangola Mali **76** 12.41N 6.35W
Nangqên China **52** 32.15N 96.13E
Nangrūl Pīr India **62** 20.19N 77.21E
Nang Xian China **63** 29.03N 93.12E
Nanhui China **55** 31.03N121.46E
Nanjiang China **54** 32.21N106.50E
Nanjing China **55** 32.02N118.52E
Nanking *see* Nanjing China **55**
Nanling China **55** 30.56N118.19E
Nan Ling *mts.* China **55** 25.10N110.00E
Nannine Australia **88** 26.53S118.20E
Nanning China **55** 22.48N108.18E
Nannup Australia **89** 33.57S115.42E
Nanortalik Greenland **99** 60.09N 45.15W
Nānpāra India **63** 27.52N 81.30E
Nanpi China **54** 38.02N116.42E
Nanping Fujian China **55** 26.38N118.10E
Nanpu Xi *r.* China **55** 26.38N118.10E
Nanri *i.* China **55** 25.13N119.30E
Nansa *r.* Spain **26** 43.22N 4.29W
Nansei shotō *is.* Japan **53** 26.30N125.00E
Nansei-Shotō Trench Pacific Oc. **84** 25.00N129.00E
Nanshan *is.* S. China Sea **58** 10.30N116.00E
Nant France **20** 44.01N 3.18E
Nantes France **18** 47.13N 1.33W
Nanteuil-le-Haudouin France **19** 49.08N 2.48E
Nanticoke U.S.A. **115** 41.12N 76.00W
Nanton Canada **100** 50.21N113.46W
Nantong China **54** 32.02N120.55E
Nantou Taiwan **55** 23.54N120.41E
Nantua France **21** 46.09N 5.37E
Nantucket U.S.A. **115** 41.17N 70.06W
Nantucket I. U.S.A. **115** 41.16N 70.03W
Nantucket Sd. U.S.A. **115** 41.30N 70.15W
Nantwich U.K. **12** 53.05N 2.31W
Nanumea *i.* Tuvalu **84** 5.40S176.10E
Nanwan Shuiku *resr.* China **55** 32.05N113.55E
Nanxi China **55** 28.52N104.59E
Nan Xian China **55** 29.22N112.25E
Nanxiong China **55** 25.10N114.16E
Nanyang China **54** 33.07N112.30E
Nanyō Japan **57** 38.03N140.10E
Nanzhang China **55** 31.47N111.42E
Nao, Cabo de la *c.* Spain **25** 38.44N 0.14E
Naococane, Lac *l.* Canada **103** 52.50N 70.40W
Naogaon Bangla. **63** 24.47N 88.56E
Naokot Pakistan **62** 24.51N 69.27E
Náousa Greece **34** 40.37N 22.05E
Napa U.S.A. **108** 38.18N122.17W
Napadogan Canada **103** 46.24N 67.01W
Napanee Canada **105** 44.15N 76.57W
Napè Laos **56** 18.18N105.07E
Napier New Zealand **86** 39.29S176.58E
Napierville Canada **105** 45.11N 73.25W
Naples *see* Napoli Italy **33**
Naples Fla. U.S.A. **113** 26.09N 81.48W
Naples N.Y. U.S.A. **114** 42.37N 77.25W
Napo China **55** 23.23N105.48E
Napo *r.* Peru **122** 3.30S 73.10W
Napoleon U.S.A. **112** 41.24N 84.09W
Napoli Italy **33** 40.51N 14.17E
Napoli, Golfo di *g.* Italy **33** 40.45N 14.15E
Naqb Ishtar Jordan **66** 30.00N 35.30E
Nār, Wādī an Jordan **67** 31.40N 35.27E
Nara Japan **57** 34.41N135.50E
Nara *d.* Japan **57** 34.27N135.55E
Nara Mali **74** 15.13N 7.20W
Nāra Pakistan **62** 24.07N 69.07E
Naracoorte Australia **92** 36.58S140.46E
Naradhan Australia **93** 33.39S146.20E
Naraini India **63** 25.11N 80.29E
Narathiwat Thailand **56** 6.25N101.48E
Nara Visa U.S.A. **111** 35.37N103.06W
Nārāyanganj Bangla. **63** 23.37N 90.30E
Narbada *r. see* Narmada *r.* India **62**
Narbonne France **20** 43.11N 3.00E
Narcea Spain **26** 43.28N 6.06W
Nardò Italy **33** 40.11N 18.02E
Narembeen Australia **89** 32.04S118.23E
Nares Str. Canada **99** 78.30N 75.00W
Naretha Australia **89** 31.01S124.50E
Nāri *r.* Pakistan **62** 29.10N 67.50E
Naria Bangla. **63** 23.18N 90.25E
Narita Japan **57** 35.47N140.19E
Närke *f.* Sweden **43** 59.03N 14.55E
Narmada *r.* India **62** 21.40N 73.00E
Nārnaul India **62** 28.03N 76.06E
Narni Italy **30** 42.31N 12.31E
Naro Italy **32** 37.17N 13.48E
Nāro, Koh-i- *mtn.* Pakistan **62** 29.15N 63.30E
Narodichi Ukraine **37** 51.11N 29.01E
Narodnaya *mtn.* Russian Fed. **44** 65.00N 61.00E
Narok Kenya **79** 1.04S 35.54E
Narón Spain **26** 43.32N 8.10W
Narooma Australia **93** 36.15S150.06E
Narrabri Australia **93** 30.20S149.49E
Narrabri West Australia **93** 30.22S149.47E
Narran *r.* Australia **93** 29.45S147.20E
Narrandera Australia **93** 34.36S146.34E
Narran L. Australia **93** 29.40S147.25E
Narrogin Australia **89** 32.58S117.10E
Narromine Australia **93** 32.17S148.20E
Narsimhapur India **63** 22.57N 79.12E
Narsingdi Bangla. **63** 23.55N 90.43E
Narsinghgarh India **62** 23.42N 77.06E
Narubis Namibia **80** 26.56S 18.36E
Narva Russian Fed. **44** 59.22N 28.17E
Narvik Norway **40** 68.26N 17.25E
Narwāna India **62** 29.37N 76.07E
Naryan Mar Russian Fed. **44** 67.37N 53.02E
Naryilco Australia **92** 28.41S141.50E
Naryn Kyrgyzstan **50** 41.24N 76.00E

Nasa to **Newtown**

Nasa *mtn.* Norway **40** 66.29N 15.23E
Nasarawa Nigeria **77** 8.35N 7.44E
Nasbinals France **20** 44.40N 3.03E
Naseby New Zealand **86** 45.01S170.09E
Nashua Iowa U.S.A. **110** 42.57N 92.32W
Nashua Mont. U.S.A. **108** 48.08N106.22W
Nashua N.H. U.S.A. **115** 42.46N 71.27W
Nashville U.S.A. **113** 36.10N 86.50W
Naşīb Syria **67** 32.33N 36.11E
Našice Croatia **31** 45.29N 18.06E
Näsijärvi *l.* Finland **41** 61.37N 23.42E
Nāsik India **62** 19.59N 73.48E
Nāşir Sudan **73** 8.36N 33.04E
Nāşir, Buḩayrat *l.* Egypt **72** 22.40N 32.00E
Nasīrābād India **62** 26.18N 74.44E
Nasīrābād Pakistan **62** 28.23N 68.24E
Naskaupi *r.* Canada **103** 53.45N 60.50W
Naşr Egypt **66** 30.36N 30.23E
Nass *r.* Canada **100** 55.00N129.50W
Nassau Bahamas **113** 25.05N 77.21W
Nassau I. Cook Is. **84** 11.33S165.25W
Nasser, L. *see* Nāşir, Buḩayrat *l.* Egypt **72**
Nassereith Austria **39** 47.19N 10.50E
Nassian Ivory Coast **76** 8.33N 3.18W
Nässjö Sweden **43** 57.39N 14.41E
Nastapoca *r.* Canada **102** 56.55N 76.33W
Nastapoka Is. Canada **102** 57.00N 77.00W
Nata Botswana **80** 20.12S 26.12E
Natal Brazil **123** 5.46S 35.15W
Natal Indonesia **58** 0.35N 99.07E
Natal *d.* R.S.A. **80** 28.30S 30.30E
Natal Basin *f.* Indian Oc. **49** 35.00S 39.00E
Natanes Plateau *f.* U.S.A. **109** 33.35N110.15W
Naţanz Iran **65** 33.30N 51.57E
Natashquan Canada **103** 50.11N 61.49W
Natashquan *r.* Canada **103** 50.06N 61.49W
Natchez U.S.A. **111** 31.34N 91.23W
Natchitoches U.S.A. **111** 31.46N 93.05W
Nathalia Australia **93** 36.02S145.14E
Nāthdwāra India **62** 24.56N 73.49E
National City U.S.A. **109** 32.40N117.06W
Natitingou Benin **77** 10.17N 1.19E
Natl Jordan **67** 31.39N 35.52E
Natoma U.S.A. **110** 39.11N 99.01W
Natron, L. Tanzania **79** 2.18S 36.05E
Naţrūn, Wādī an *f.* Egypt **66** 30.25N 30.18E
Natuna Besar *i.* Indonesia **58** 4.00N108.20E
Naturaliste, C. Australia **89** 33.32S115.01E
Naubinway U.S.A. **112** 46.05N 85.27W
Naucelle France **20** 44.12N 2.20E
Nauders Austria **39** 46.53N 10.30E
Nauen Germany **38** 52.36N 12.52E
Naugatuck U.S.A. **115** 41.30N 73.04W
Naumburg Germany **38** 51.09N 11.48E
Nā'ūr Jordan **67** 31.53N 35.50E
Nauroz Kalāt Pakistan **62** 28.47N 65.38E
Nauru Pacific Oc. **84** 0.32S166.55E
Naushahro Fīroz Pakistan **62** 26.50N 68.07E
Naustdal Norway **41** 61.31N 5.43E
Nauta Peru **122** 4.30S 73.40W
Nautanwa India **63** 27.26N 83.25E
Nautla Mexico **116** 20.13N 96.47W
Nava Mexico **111** 28.25N100.46W
Nava *r.* Zaïre **79** 1.45N 27.06E
Nava del Rey Spain **26** 41.20N 5.05W
Navahermosa Spain **27** 39.38N 4.28W
Navalcarnero Spain **26** 40.18N 4.00W
Navalmoral de la Mata Spain **27** 39.54N 5.32W
Navalvillar de Pela Spain **27** 39.06N 5.28W
Navan Rep. of Ire. **15** 53.39N 6.42W
Navāpur India **62** 21.15N 73.55E
Navarra *d.* Spain **25** 42.45N 1.30W
Navarre Australia **92** 36.54S143.09E
Navarre U.S.A. **114** 40.43N 81.32W
Navarro Argentina **125** 35.00S 59.10W
Navasota U.S.A. **111** 30.23N 96.05W
Naver *r.* U.K. **14** 58.32N 4.14W
Navia Spain **26** 43.32N 6.43W
Navia *r.* Spain **26** 43.33N 6.44W
Navlya Russian Fed. **44** 52.51N 34.30E
Navoi Uzbekistan **9** 40.04N 65.20E
Navojoa Mexico **109** 27.06N109.26W
Návpaktos Greece **35** 38.23N 21.50E
Návplion Greece **35** 37.34N 22.48E
Navrongo Ghana **76** 10.51N 1.03W
Navsāri India **62** 20.57N 72.59E
Nawá Syria **67** 32.53N 36.03E
Nawābganj Bangla. **63** 24.36N 88.17E
Nawābganj India **63** 26.56N 81.13E
Nawābshāh Pakistan **62** 26.15N 68.25E
Nawāda India **63** 24.53N 85.32E
Nāwah Afghan. **62** 32.19N 67.53E
Nawākot Nepal **63** 27.55N 85.10E
Nawa Kot Pakistan **62** 28.20N 71.22E
Nawalgarh India **62** 27.51N 75.16E
Nawāpāra India **63** 20.58N 81.51E
Naxi China **55** 28.44N105.27E
Náxos Greece **35** 37.06N 25.23E
Náxos *i.* Greece **35** 37.02N 25.35E
Nayāgarh India **63** 20.08N 85.06E
Nayak Afghan. **62** 34.44N 66.57E
Nayarit *d.* Mexico **116** 21.30N104.00W
Nāy Band Iran **65** 32.20N 57.34E
Nāy Band Iran **65** 27.23N 52.38E
Nāy Band, Kūh-e *mtn.* Iran **65** 32.25N 57.30E
Nayoro Japan **57** 44.21N142.28E
Nazaré Brazil **123** 13.00S 39.00W
Nazaré Portugal **27** 39.36N 9.04W
Nazareth *see* Nazerat Israel **67**
Nazareth Trough *f.* Indian Oc. **49** 15.00S 64.00E
Nazarovka Russian Fed. **44** 54.19N 41.20E
Nazas *r.* Mexico **116** 25.34N103.25W
Nazca Peru **122** 14.53S 74.54W
Nazerat Israel **67** 32.41N 35.16E
Nazilli Turkey **64** 37.55N 28.20E
Nazinon *r.* Burkina *see* Red Volta *r.* Ghana **76**
Nāzir Hāt Bangla. **63** 22.38N 91.47E
Nazrēt Ethiopia **73** 8.32N 39.22E
Nazuo China **55** 24.06N105.19E
Nchanga Zambia **79** 12.30S 27.55E
Ncheu Malaŵi **79** 14.50S 34.45E
N'dalatando Angola **78** 9.12S 14.54E
Ndali Benin **77** 9.53N 2.45E
Ndasegera *mtn.* Tanzania **79** 1.58S 35.41E
Ndélé C.A.R. **73** 8.24N 20.39E
Ndélélé Cameroon **77** 4.03N 14.55E
N'Dendé Gabon **78** 2.20S 11.23E
Ndikiniméki Cameroon **77** 4.46N 10.49E
N'Djamena Chad **77** 12.10N 14.59E
Ndjolé Gabon **78** 0.07S 10.45E
Ndola Zambia **80** 12.58S 28.39E
Ndoro Gabon **78** 0.24S 12.34E
Ndrhamcha, Sebkha de *f.* Mauritania **74** 18.45N 15.48W
Ndungu Tanzania **79** 4.25S 38.04E
Nea *r.* Norway **40** 63.15N 11.00E
Neagh, Lough U.K. **15** 54.36N 6.25W
Néa Kallikrátia Greece **34** 40.21N 23.01E
Neale, L. Australia **90** 24.21S130.04E
Néa Páfos Cyprus **66** 34.45N 32.25E
Neápolis Greece **34** 40.20N 21.24E
Neápolis Greece **35** 36.31N 23.03E
Neápolis Kriti Greece **35** 35.15N 25.37E
Neath U.K. **13** 51.39N 3.49W
Nebit-Dag Turkmenistan **65** 39.31N 54.24E
Nebraska *d.* U.S.A. **110** 41.50N100.06W
Nebraska City U.S.A. **110** 40.41N 95.52W
Nebrodi, Monti *mts.* Italy **33** 37.55N 14.35E
Nechako *r.* Canada **100** 53.30N122.44W
Neches *r.* U.S.A. **111** 29.55N 93.50W
Neckar *r.* Germany **39** 49.31N 8.26E
Neckarsulm Germany **39** 49.12N 9.13E
Necochea Argentina **125** 38.31S 58.46W
Necuto Angola **78** 4.55S 12.38E
Nêdong China **63** 29.14N 91.48E
Nedroma Algeria **74** 35.00N 1.44W
Nedstrand Norway **42** 59.21N 5.51E
Needles U.S.A. **109** 34.51N114.37W
Neepawa Canada **101** 50.13N 99.29W
Neerpelt Belgium **16** 51.13N 5.28E
Nefta Tunisia **75** 33.52N 7.33E
Neftegorsk Russian Fed. **45** 44.21N 39.44E
Nefyn U.K. **12** 52.55N 4.31W
Negara Indonesia **59** 8.21S114.35E
Negaunee U.S.A. **112** 46.31N 87.37W
Negba Israel **67** 31.40N 34.41E
Negele Ethiopia **73** 5.20N 39.36E
Negev *des. see* HaNegev *des.* Israel **66**
Negoiu *mtn.* Romania **37** 45.36N 24.32E
Negomano Mozambique **79** 11.26S 38.30E
Negombo Sri Lanka **61** 7.13N 79.50E
Negotin Yugo. **37** 44.14N 22.33E
Negra, Punta *c.* Peru **120** 6.06S 81.09W
Negrais, C. Burma **56** 16.00N 94.12E
Negreira Spain **26** 42.54N 8.44W
Negritos Peru **122** 4.42S 81.18W
Negro *r.* Argentina **125** 40.50S 63.00W
Negro *r.* Brazil **122** 3.00S 59.55W
Negro *r.* Uruguay **125** 33.27S 58.20W
Negro, Baia del *b.* Somali Rep. **71** 7.52N 49.50E
Negros *i.* Phil. **59** 10.00N123.00E
Negru-Vodă Romania **37** 43.50N 28.12E
Neheim-Hüsten Germany **38** 51.27N 7.57E
Neijiang China **55** 29.29N105.03E
Nei Monggol Zizhiqu *d.* China **54** 41.50N112.30E
Neisse *r.* Germany **38** 52.04N 14.46E
Neiva Colombia **122** 2.58N 75.15W
Nejanilini L. Canada **101** 59.33N 97.48W
Nejdek Czech Republic **39** 50.17N 12.42E
Nejo Ethiopia **73** 9.30N 35.30E
Nek'emtē Ethiopia **73** 9.02N 36.31E
Neksö Denmark **43** 55.04N 15.09E
Nelidovo Russian Fed. **44** 56.13N 32.46E
Neligh U.S.A. **110** 42.08N 98.02W
Nelkan Russian Fed. **51** 57.40N136.04E
Nelligen Australia **93** 35.39S150.06E
Nellore India **61** 14.29N 80.00E
Nelson Australia **92** 38.04S141.05E
Nelson Canada **100** 49.30N117.20W
Nelson *r.* Canada **101** 57.04N 92.30W
Nelson New Zealand **86** 41.18S173.17E
Nelson U.K. **12** 53.50N 2.14W
Nelson U.S.A. **109** 35.30N113.16W
Nelson, C. Australia **92** 38.27S141.35E
Nelson, Estrecho *str.* Chile **125** 51.33S 74.40W
Nelson Bay *town* Australia **93** 32.43S152.08E
Nelson Forks Canada **100** 59.30N124.00W
Nelson-Marlborough *d.* New Zealand **86** 41.40S173.40E
Nelsonville U.S.A. **114** 39.27N 82.14W
Nelspoort R.S.A. **80** 32.07S 23.00E
Nelspruit R.S.A. **80** 25.27S 30.58E
Néma Mauritania **74** 16.40N 7.15W
Nembe Nigeria **77** 4.32N 6.25E
Neméa Greece **35** 37.49N 22.40E
Nemours France **19** 48.16N 2.42E
Nemunas *r.* Lithuania **41** 55.18N 21.23E
Nemuro Japan **57** 43.22N145.36E
Nemuro kaikyō *str.* Japan **57** 44.00N145.50E
Nenagh Rep. of Ire. **15** 52.52N 8.13W
Nenana U.S.A. **98** 64.35N149.20W
Nene *r.* U.K. **12** 52.49N 0.12E
Nenjiang China **53** 49.10N125.15E
Neodesha U.S.A. **111** 37.25N 95.41W
Néon Karlovásion Greece **35** 37.47N 26.40E
Néon Petrítsi Greece **34** 41.16N 23.15E
Neosho U.S.A. **111** 36.52N 94.22W
Neosho *r.* U.S.A. **110** 35.48N 95.18W
Nepal Asia **63** 28.00N 84.00E
Nepālganj Nepal **63** 28.03N 81.38E
Nepa Nagar India **62** 21.28N 76.23E
Nephi U.S.A. **108** 39.43N111.50W
Nephin Beg *mtn.* Rep. of Ire. **15** 54.02N 9.38W
Nephin Beg Range *mts.* Rep. of Ire. **15** 54.00N 9.37W
Nepomuk Czech Republic **38** 49.29N 13.36E
Nera Italy **30** 42.26N 12.24E
Nera *r.* Italy **28** 42.33N 12.43E
Nérac France **20** 44.08N 0.20E
Nerekhta Russian Fed. **44** 57.30N 40.40E
Néret, Lac *l.* Canada **103** 54.45N 70.50W
Neretva *r.* Bosnia-Herzegovina **31** 43.01N 17.27E
Neriquinha Angola **80** 15.50S 21.40E
Nerja Spain **27** 36.44N 3.52W
Nero Deep Pacific Oc. **59** 12.40N145.50E
Néronde France **17** 45.50N 4.14E
Nérondes France **19** 47.00N 2.49E
Nerva Spain **27** 37.42N 6.32W
Nes Neth. **16** 53.27N 5.46E
Nesbyen Norway **41** 60.34N 9.09E
Nesher Israel **67** 32.46N 35.03E
Nesle France **19** 49.46N 2.55E
Nesna Norway **40** 66.13N 13.04E
Nesöy *i.* Norway **40** 66.35N 12.40E
Ness, Loch U.K. **14** 57.16N 4.30W
Nesselwang Germany **38** 47.37N 10.30E
Nestaocano *r.* Canada **103** 48.40N 73.25W
Nesterov Ukraine **37** 50.04N 24.00E
Nestórion Greece **34** 40.24N 21.02E
Néstos *r.* Greece **34** 40.41N 24.44E
Nesttun Norway **42** 60.19N 5.23E
Nesvizh Belorussia **37** 53.16N 26.40E
Nes Ziyyona Israel **67** 31.55N 34.48E
Netanya Israel **67** 32.20N 34.51E
Netcong U.S.A. **115** 40.54N 74.42W
Netherlands Europe **16** 52.00N 5.30E
Netherlands Antilles S. America **117** 12.30N 69.00W
Neto *r.* Italy **33** 39.13N 17.08E
Netolice Czech Republic **39** 49.03N 14.12E
Netrakona Bangla. **63** 24.53N 90.43E
Nettilling L. Canada **99** 66.30N 70.40W
Nettuno Italy **32** 41.27N 12.39E
Neubrandenburg Germany **38** 53.33N 13.15E
Neuburg an der Donau Germany **39** 48.44N 11.11E
Neuchâtel Switz. **39** 46.59N 6.56E
Neuchâtel *d.* Switz. **39** 47.02N 6.50E
Neuchâtel, Lac de *l.* Switz. **39** 46.52N 6.50E
Neuenhagen Germany **38** 52.32N 13.41E
Neuenhaus Germany **38** 52.30N 6.59E
Neuf-Brisach France **19** 48.01N 7.32E
Neufchâteau Belgium **16** 49.51N 5.26E
Neufchâteau France **19** 48.21N 5.42E
Neufchâtel France **18** 49.44N 1.27E
Neuhausen Switz. **39** 47.41N 8.37E
Neuillé-Pont-Pierre France **18** 47.33N 0.33E
Neu-Isenberg Germany **39** 50.03N 8.41E
Neumarkt Austria **39** 48.16N 13.45E
Neumarkt Germany **38** 49.16N 11.28E
Neumarkt in Steiermark Austria **31** 47.05N 14.26E
Neumarkt-Sankt-Veit Germany **39** 48.22N 12.30E
Neumünster Germany **38** 54.04N 9.59E
Neunkirchen Germany **39** 49.30N 7.29E
Neuquén Argentina **125** 39.00S 68.05W
Neuquén *d.* Argentina **125** 38.30S 70.00W
Neuquén *r.* Argentina **125** 39.02S 68.07W
Neuruppin Germany **38** 52.55N 12.48E
Neuse *r.* U.S.A. **113** 35.06N 76.30W
Neusiedler See *l.* Austria **36** 47.52N 16.45E
Neuss Germany **38** 51.12N 6.41E
Neustadt Bayern Germany **39** 49.34N 10.37E
Neustadt Bayern Germany **39** 49.44N 12.11E
Neustadt B.-Würt. Germany **39** 47.54N 8.13E
Neustadt Sch.-Hol. Germany **38** 54.06N 10.48E
Neustadt Thüingen Germany **38** 50.44N 11.44E
Neustadt an der Weinstrasse Germany **39** 49.21N 8.08E
Neustadt bei Coburg Thüingen Germany **38** 50.19N 11.07E
Neustrelitz Germany **38** 53.21N 13.04E
Neu-Ulm Germany **39** 48.23N 10.01E
Neuvic France **20** 45.23N 2.16E
Neuville-de-Poitou France **18** 46.41N 0.15E
Neuville-sur-Saône France **21** 45.52N 4.51E
Neuwied Germany **39** 50.25N 7.27E
Nevada U.S.A. **111** 37.51N 94.22W
Nevada *d.* U.S.A. **108** 39.50N116.10W
Nevada, Sierra *mts.* Spain **27** 37.05N 3.10W
Nevada, Sierra *mts.* U.S.A. **106** 37.30N119.00W
Nevanka Russian Fed. **51** 56.31N 98.57E
Nevatim Israel **67** 31.13N 34.54E
Nevel Russian Fed. **44** 56.00N 29.59E
Nevers France **19** 47.00N 3.09E
Nevertire Australia **93** 31.52S147.47E
Nevesinje Bosnia-Herzegovina **31** 43.15N 18.07E
Nevinnomyssk Russian Fed. **45** 44.38N 41.59E
Nevlunghamn Norway **42** 58.58N 9.52E
Nevşehir Turkey **64** 38.38N 34.43E
Newala Tanzania **79** 10.56S 39.15E
New Albany Ind. U.S.A. **112** 38.17N 85.50W
New Albany Miss. U.S.A. **111** 34.29N 89.00W
New Amsterdam Guyana **123** 6.18N 57.30W
New Angledool Australia **93** 29.06S147.57E
Newark Del. U.S.A. **115** 39.41N 75.45W
Newark N.J. U.S.A. **115** 40.44N 74.10W
Newark N.Y. U.S.A. **114** 43.03N 77.06W
Newark Ohio U.S.A. **114** 40.04N 82.24W
Newark-on-Trent U.K. **12** 53.06N 0.48E
Newark Valley *town* U.S.A. **115** 42.14N 76.11W
New Athens U.S.A. **110** 38.19N 89.53W
New Bedford U.S.A. **115** 41.38N 70.56W
Newberg U.S.A. **108** 45.18N122.58W
New Berlin U.S.A. **115** 42.38N 75.20W
New Bern U.S.A. **113** 35.05N 77.04W
Newberry Mich. U.S.A. **112** 46.22N 85.30W
Newberry S.C. U.S.A. **113** 34.17N 81.39W
New Bethlehem U.S.A. **114** 41.00N 79.20W
Newbiggin-by-the-Sea U.K. **12** 55.11N 1.30W
New Bloomfield U.S.A. **114** 40.25N 77.11W
Newboro Canada **105** 44.39N 76.19W
Newboro L. Canada **105** 44.38N 76.20W
New Boston U.S.A. **105** 43.47N 75.45W
New Braunfels U.S.A. **111** 29.42N 98.08W
New Britain *i.* P.N.G. **87** 6.00S150.00E
New Britain U.S.A. **115** 41.40N 72.47W
New Brunswick *d.* Canada **103** 46.50N 66.00W
New Brunswick U.S.A. **115** 40.29N 74.27W
Newburgh U.S.A. **115** 41.30N 74.01W
Newbury U.K. **13** 51.24N 1.19W
Newburyport U.S.A. **115** 42.49N 70.53W
New Bussa Nigeria **77** 9.53N 4.29E
New Caledonia *is. see* Nouvelle Calédonie *is.* Pacific Oc. **84**
Newcastle Australia **93** 32.55S151.46E
Newcastle N.B. Canada **103** 47.00N 65.34W
Newcastle Ont. Canada **104** 43.55N 78.35W
Newcastle R.S.A. **80** 27.44S 29.55E
Newcastle U.K. **15** 54.13N 5.53W
New Castle Penn. U.S.A. **114** 41.00N 80.20W
Newcastle Wyo. U.S.A. **108** 43.50N104.11W
Newcastle B. Australia **90** 10.50S142.37E
Newcastle Emlyn U.K. **13** 52.02N 4.29W
Newcastle-under-Lyme U.K. **12** 53.02N 2.15W
Newcastle upon Tyne U.K. **12** 54.58N 1.36W
Newcastle Waters *town* Australia **90** 17.24S133.24E
Newcastle West Rep. of Ire. **15** 52.26N 9.04W
New City U.S.A. **115** 41.09N 73.59W
Newcomerstown U.S.A. **114** 40.16N 81.36W
New Concord U.S.A. **114** 40.00N 81.44W
New Cumberland U.S.A. **114** 40.30N 80.36W
Newdegate Australia **89** 33.06S119.01E
New Delhi India **62** 28.36N 77.12E
New Denver Canada **100** 50.00N117.25W
New England U.S.A. **110** 46.32N102.52W
New England Range *mts.* Australia **93** 30.30S151.50E
Newenham, C. U.S.A. **98** 58.37N162.12W
Newent U.K. **13** 51.56N 2.24W
Newfane U.S.A. **114** 43.17N 78.43W
New Forest *f.* U.K. **13** 50.50N 1.35W
Newfoundland *d.* Canada **103** 54.00N 60.10W
Newfoundland *i.* Canada **103** 48.30N 56.00W
New Freedom U.S.A. **115** 39.44N 76.42W
New Galloway U.K. **14** 55.05N 4.09W
Newgate Canada **100** 49.01N115.08W
New Glasgow Canada **103** 45.35N 62.39W
New Guinea *i.* Austa. **59** 5.00S140.00E
New Hamburg Canada **104** 43.23N 80.42W
New Hampshire *d.* U.S.A. **112** 43.35N 71.40W
New Hanover *i.* Pacific Oc. **87** 2.00S150.00E
Newhaven U.K. **13** 50.47N 0.04E
New Haven U.S.A. **115** 41.18N 72.56W
New Hebrides Basin Pacific Oc. **84** 16.00S162.00E
New Holland U.S.A. **115** 40.06N 76.05W
New Iberia U.S.A. **111** 30.00N 91.49W
New Ireland *i.* P.N.G. **87** 2.30S151.30E
New Jersey *d.* U.S.A. **115** 40.15N 74.30W
New Kensington U.S.A. **114** 40.34N 79.46W
New Lexington U.S.A. **114** 39.43N 82.31W
New Liskeard Canada **102** 47.31N 79.41W
New London Conn. U.S.A. **115** 41.21N 72.07W
New London Minn. U.S.A. **110** 45.18N 94.56W
New London Ohio U.S.A. **114** 41.05N 82.24W
Newman Australia **88** 23.22S119.43E
Newman U.S.A. **109** 31.55N106.20W
Newman, Mt. Australia **88** 23.15S119.33E
Newmarket Canada **104** 44.03N 79.28W
Newmarket Rep. of Ire. **15** 52.13N 9.00W
Newmarket U.K. **13** 52.15N 0.23E
Newmarket U.S.A. **115** 43.05N 70.56W
Newmarket on Fergus Rep. of Ire. **15** 52.46N 8.55W
New Marshfield U.S.A. **114** 39.20N 82.15W
New Martinsville U.S.A. **114** 39.39N 80.52W
New Matamoras U.S.A. **114** 39.31N 81.06W
New Meadows U.S.A. **108** 44.58N116.32W
New Mexico *d.* U.S.A. **108** 33.30N106.00W
New Milford Conn. U.S.A. **115** 41.35N 73.25W
New Milford Penn. U.S.A. **115** 41.52N 75.44W
Newnan U.S.A. **113** 33.23N 84.48W
New Norcia Australia **89** 30.58S116.15E
New Norfolk Australia **91** 42.46S147.02E
New Orleans U.S.A. **111** 29.58N 90.07W
New Oxford U.S.A. **114** 39.52N 77.04W
New Philadelphia U.S.A. **114** 40.30N 81.27W
New Plymouth New Zealand **86** 39.03S174.04E
Newport Mayo Rep. of Ire. **15** 53.53N 9.34W
Newport Tipperary Rep. of Ire. **15** 52.42N 8.25W
Newport Dyfed U.K. **13** 52.01N 4.51W
Newport Essex U.K. **13** 51.58N 0.13E
Newport Gwent U.K. **13** 51.34N 2.59W
Newport Hants. U.K. **13** 50.43N 1.18W
Newport Ark. U.S.A. **111** 35.35N 91.16W
Newport Maine U.S.A. **112** 44.50N 69.17W
Newport N.H. U.S.A. **115** 43.21N 72.09W
Newport N.Y. U.S.A. **115** 43.11N 75.01W
Newport Oreg. U.S.A. **108** 44.38N124.03W
Newport Penn. U.S.A. **114** 40.29N 77.08W
Newport R.I. U.S.A. **115** 41.13N 71.18W
Newport Vt. U.S.A. **105** 44.57N 72.12W
Newport News U.S.A. **113** 36.59N 76.26W
New Providence I. Bahamas **113** 25.25N 78.35W
Newquay U.K. **13** 50.24N 5.06W
New Quay U.K. **13** 52.13N 4.22W
New Radnor U.K. **13** 52.15N 3.10W
New Rochelle U.S.A. **115** 40.55N 73.47W
New Rockford U.S.A. **110** 47.41N 99.15W
New Romney U.K. **13** 50.59N 0.58E
New Ross Rep. of Ire. **15** 52.24N 6.57W
Newry U.K. **15** 54.11N 6.21W
New Scone U.K. **14** 56.25N 3.25W
New Smyrna Beach *town* U.S.A. **113** 29.01N 80.56W
New South Wales *d.* Australia **93** 32.40S147.40E
Newton Ill. U.S.A. **110** 38.59N 88.10W
Newton Iowa U.S.A. **110** 41.42N 93.03W
Newton Kans. U.S.A. **111** 38.03N 97.21W
Newton Mass. U.S.A. **115** 42.21N 71.11W
Newton Miss. U.S.A. **111** 32.19N 89.10W
Newton N.J. U.S.A. **115** 41.03N 74.45W
Newton Abbot U.K. **13** 50.32N 3.37W
Newton Aycliffe U.K. **12** 54.36N 1.34W
Newton Falls *town* N.Y. U.S.A. **105** 44.13N 74.59W
Newton Falls *town* Ohio U.S.A. **114** 41.11N 80.59W
Newtonmore U.K. **14** 57.04N 4.08W
Newton Stewart U.K. **14** 54.57N 4.29W
Newtown U.K. **13** 52.31N 3.19W

Newtownabbey to North Olmsted

Newtownabbey U.K. 15 54.39N 5.57W
Newtownards U.K. 15 54.35N 5.41W
Newtown Butler U.K. 15 54.12N 7.22W
Newtown St. Boswells U.K. 14 55.35N 2.40W
Newtownstewart U.K. 15 54.43N 7.25W
New Washington U.S.A. 114 40.58N 82.51W
New Waterford Canada 103 46.15N 60.05W
New Westminster Canada 100 49.10N122.52W
New York U.S.A. 115 40.43N 74.01W
New York d. U.S.A. 115 40.43N 74.01W
New York State Barge Canal U.S.A. 114 43.05N 78.43W
New Zealand Austa. 86 41.00S175.00E
New Zealand Plateau Pacific Oc. 84 50.00S170.00E
Nexon France 20 45.41N 1.11E
Neya Russian Fed. 44 58.18N 43.40E
Neyagawa Japan 57 34.46N135.38E
Neyrīz Iran 65 29.12N 54.17E
Neyshābūr Iran 65 36.13N 58.49E
Nezhin Ukraine 37 51.03N 31.54E
Ngala Nigeria 77 12.21N 14.10E
Ngambwe Rapids f. Zambia 78 17.08S 24.10E
Ngami, L. Botswana 80 20.32S 22.38E
Ngamiland d. Botswana 80 19.40S 22.00E
Ngamiland f. Botswana 80 20.00S 22.30E
Ngamring China 63 29.14N 87.10E
Ngangla Ringco l. China 63 31.40N 83.00E
Nganglong Kangri mtn. China 63 32.40N 81.00E
Nganglong Kangri mts. China 63 32.15N 82.00E
Ngangzê Co l. China 63 31.00N 87.00E
Nganjuk Indonesia 59 7.36S111.56E
N'Gao Congo 78 2.28S 15.40E
Ngaoundéré Cameroon 77 7.20N 13.35E
Ngara-Binsam Congo 78 1.36N 13.30E
Ngardiam C.A.R. 73 9.00N 20.58E
Ngaruawahia New Zealand 86 37.40S175.09E
Ngaruroro r. New Zealand 86 39.34S176.54E
Ngatangiia Rarotonga Cook Is. 84 21.14S159.44W
Ngau i. Fiji 84 18.02S179.18E
Ngauruhoe mtn. New Zealand 86 39.10S175.35E
Ngawi Indonesia 59 7.23S111.22E
Ngaya mtn. C.A.R. 73 9.18N 23.28E
Ng'iro, Mt. Kenya 79 2.06N 36.44E
N'Giva Angola 80 17.03S 15.47E
Ngoc Linh mtn. Vietnam 56 15.04N107.59E
Ngoma Zambia 78 16.04S 26.06E
Ngomba Tanzania 79 8.16S 32.51E
Ngomeni Kenya 79 3.00S 40.11E
Ngong Kenya 79 1.22S 36.40E
Ngonye Falls f. Zambia 78 16.35S 23.39E
Ngorongoro Crater f. Tanzania 79 3.13S 35.32E
Ngouo, Mont mtn. C.A.R. 73 7.55N 24.38E
Ngozi Burundi 79 2.52S 29.50E
Nguigmi Niger 77 14.00N 13.11E
Nguru Nigeria 77 12.53N 10.30E
Nguruka Tanzania 79 5.08S 30.58E
Ngwaketse d. Botswana 80 25.10S 25.00E
Ngwerere Zambia 79 15.18S 28.20E
Nhaccongo Mozambique 81 24.18S 35.14E
Nhachengue Mozambique 81 22.52S 35.10E
Nhandugue r. Mozambique 81 18.47S 34.30E
Nha Trang Vietnam 56 12.15N109.10E
Nhill Australia 92 36.20S141.40E
Nhulunbuy Australia 90 12.11S136.46E
Nhungo Angola 80 13.17S 20.06E
Niafounké Mali 74 15.56N 4.00W
Niagara Canada 104 43.05N 79.20W
Niagara Escarpment f. Canada 104 44.25N 80.30W
Niagara Falls town Canada 104 43.06N 79.04W
Niagara Falls town U.S.A. 114 43.06N 79.02W
Niah Malaysia 58 3.52N113.44E
Niamey Niger 77 13.32N 2.05E
Niamey d. Niger 77 14.00N 1.40E
Nianforando Guinea 76 9.37N 10.36W
Niangara Zaïre 79 3.47N 27.54E
Nia-Nia Zaïre 79 1.30N 27.41E
Niapa, Gunung mtn. Indonesia 58 1.45N117.30E
Nias i. Indonesia 58 1.05N 97.30E
Niassa d. Mozambique 79 13.00S 36.30E
Nibe Denmark 42 56.59N 9.38E
Nicaragua C. America 117 13.00N 85.00W
Nicaragua, Lago de l. Nicaragua 117 11.30N 85.30W
Nicastro Italy 33 38.59N 16.20E
Nice France 21 43.42N 7.16E
Nichelino Italy 30 44.59N 7.38E
Nicholson Australia 88 18.02S128.54E
Nicholson r. Australia 90 17.31S139.36E
Nicholson U.S.A. 115 41.38N 75.47W
Nicholson L. Canada 101 62.40N102.35W
Nicobar Is. India 56 8.00N 93.30E
Nicolet Canada 105 46.13N 72.37W
Nicolet r. Canada 105 46.14N 72.39W
Nicolls Town Bahamas 117 25.08N 78.00W
Nicosia see Levkosía Cyprus 66
Nicosia Italy 33 37.45N 14.24E
Nicotera Italy 33 38.34N 15.57E
Nicoya, Golfo de g. Costa Rica 117 9.30N 85.00W
Nicoya, Península de pen. Costa Rica 117 10.30N 85.30W
Nid r. Norway 42 58.24N 8.48E
Nida r. Poland 37 50.18N 20.52E
Nido, Sierra de mts. Mexico 109 29.30N107.00W
Nidzica Poland 37 53.22N 20.26E
Niebüll Germany 38 54.48N 8.50E
Niederbronn-les-Bains France 19 48.57N 7.38E
Niederösterreich d. Austria 36 48.20N 15.50E
Niedersachsen d. Germany 38 52.53N 9.30E
Niekerkshoop R.S.A. 80 29.19S 22.48E
Niéllé Ivory Coast 76 10.05N 5.28W
Nienburg Germany 38 52.38N 9.13E
Niéré Chad 72 14.30N 21.09E
Niers r. Neth. 16 51.43N 5.56E
Niesky Germany 38 51.17N 14.49E
Nieuw Nickerie Surinam 123 5.57N 56.59W
Nieuwpoort Belgium 16 51.08N 2.45E
Nièvre d. France 19 47.05N 3.30E
Nifi Ya'qūb Jordan 67 31.50N 35.14E
Nigde Turkey 64 37.58N 34.42E
Niger Africa 70 17.00N 10.00E
Niger d. Nigeria 77 9.50N 6.00E
Niger r. Nigeria 77 4.15N 6.05E
Niger Delta Nigeria 77 4.00N 6.10E
Nigeria Africa 77 9.00N 9.00E
Nightcaps New Zealand 86 45.58S168.02E
Nightingale I. Tristan da Cunha 127 37.28S 12.32W
Nigrita Greece 34 40.55N 23.30E
Nihing r. Pakistan 62 26.00N 62.44E
Nihoa i. Hawaiian Is. 84 23.03N161.55W
Niigata Japan 57 37.58N139.02E
Niihama Japan 57 33.57N133.15E
Niihau i. Hawaiian Is. 85 21.55N160.10W
Niiza Japan 57 35.48N139.34E
Níjar Spain 27 36.58N 2.11W
Nijmegen Neth. 16 51.50N 5.52E
Nikel Russian Fed. 40 69.20N 30.00E
Nikiniki Indonesia 88 9.49S124.29E
Nikki Benin 77 9.55N 3.18E
Nikolayev Ukraine 45 46.57N 32.00E
Nikolayevskiy Russian Fed. 45 50.05N 45.32E
Nikolayevsk-na-Amure Russian Fed. 51 53.20N140.44E
Nikolsk Russian Fed. 44 59.33N 45.30E
Nikopol Bulgaria 34 43.43N 24.54E
Nikopol Ukraine 45 47.34N 34.25E
Niksar Turkey 64 40.35N 36.59E
Nīkshahr Iran 65 26.14N 60.15E
Nikšić Yugo. 31 42.46N 18.56E
Nikumaroro i. Kiribati 84 4.40S174.32W
Nīl, An r. Egypt 66 31.30N 30.25E
Nila i. Indonesia 59 6.45S129.30E
Nile r. see Nīl, An r. Egypt 66
Nile Delta Egypt 66 31.00N 31.00E
Niles Mich. U.S.A. 112 41.51N 86.15W
Niles Ohio U.S.A. 114 41.11N 80.45W
Nilgaut, Lac l. Canada 105 46.36N 77.15W
Nīlgiri India 63 21.28N 86.46E
Nilgiri Hills India 60 11.30N 77.30E
Nīmach India 62 24.28N 74.52E
Nimai r. Burma 56 25.44N 97.30E
Nimba, Mt. Guinea 76 7.35N 8.28W
Nimbin Australia 93 28.35S153.12E
Nîmes France 21 43.50N 4.21E
Nimfaíon, Ákra c. Greece 34 40.05N 24.20E
Nīm Ka Thāna India 62 27.44N 75.48E
Nīmrūz d. Afghan. 62 30.40N 62.15E
Nimule Sudan 73 3.36N 32.03E
Nindigully Australia 93 28.20S148.47E
Ninety-East Ridge f. Indian Oc. 49 21.00S 89.00E
Ninety Mile Beach f. Australia 93 38.07S147.30E
Ninety Mile Beach f. New Zealand 86 34.45S173.00E
Nineveh ruins Iraq 64 36.24N 43.08E
Ningbo China 55 29.56N121.32E
Ningde China 55 26.41N119.32E
Ningdu China 55 26.29N115.46E
Ninggang China 55 26.45N113.58E
Ningguo China 55 30.38N118.58E
Ningming China 55 22.04N107.02E
Ningnan China 52 27.03N102.46E
Ningqiang China 54 32.49N106.13E
Ningwu China 54 38.59N112.12E
Ningxia Huizu d. China 54 37.00N105.00E
Ning Xian China 54 35.27N107.50E
Ningxiang China 55 28.15N112.33E
Ninh Binh Vietnam 56 20.14N106.00E
Ninove Belgium 16 50.50N 4.02E
Niobrara U.S.A. 110 42.45N 98.02W
Niobrara r. U.S.A. 110 42.45N 98.00W
Nioki Zaïre 78 2.43S 17.41E
Nioro Mali 74 15.12N 9.35W
Nioro du Rip Senegal 76 13.40N 15.50W
Niort France 18 46.19N 0.27W
Niout well Mauritania 74 16.03N 6.52W
Nipāni India 60 16.24N 74.23E
Nipigon Canada 102 49.00N 88.17W
Nipigon, L. Canada 102 49.50N 88.30W
Nipigon B. Canada 102 48.55N 88.00W
Nipissing Canada 104 46.06N 79.30W
Nipissing r. Canada 104 46.00N 78.30W
Nipissing, L. Canada 104 46.17N 80.00W
Niquelândia Brazil 126 14.27S 48.27W
Nirasaki Japan 57 35.42N138.27E
Nirim Israel 67 31.20N 34.24E
Nirmal India 63 19.06N 78.21E
Nirmali India 63 26.19N 86.35E
Nirwāno Pakistan 62 26.22N 62.43E
Nir Yisra'el Israel 67 31.41N 34.38E
Niš Yugo. 34 43.19N 21.58E
Nisa Portugal 27 39.31N 7.39W
Nisava r. Yugo. 34 43.20N 22.10E
Niscemi Italy 33 37.08N 14.24E
Nishi China 55 29.54N110.38E
Nishinomiya Japan 57 34.43N135.20E
Nísiros i. Greece 35 36.35N 27.10E
Niška Banja Yugo. 34 43.17N 22.02E
Niskibi r. Canada 102 56.28N 88.10W
Nisko Poland 37 50.35N 22.07E
Nissan r. Sweden 43 56.40N 12.51E
Nissedal Norway 42 59.15N 8.30E
Nisser l. Norway 42 59.10N 8.30E
Nissum Bredning b. Denmark 42 56.38N 8.22E
Nissum Fjord est. Denmark 42 56.21N 8.14E
Niṭā' Saudi Arabia 65 27.13N 48.25E
Nitchequon Canada 103 53.12N 70.47W
Niterói Brazil 126 22.54S 43.06W
Nith r. Canada 104 43.12N 80.22W
Nith r. U.K. 14 55.00N 3.35W
Nitra Slovakia 37 48.20N 18.05E
Nitro Canada 104 46.51N 81.42W
Nitro U.S.A. 114 38.25N 81.50W
Nittedal Norway 42 60.04N 10.53E
Niue i. Cook Is. 84 19.02S169.52W
Niut, Gunung mtn. Indonesia 58 1.00N110.00E
Nivala Finland 40 63.55N 24.58E
Nivelles Belgium 16 50.36N 4.20E
Nixon U.S.A. 111 29.16N 97.46W
Nizāmābād India 61 18.40N 78.05E
Nīzgān r. Afghan. 62 33.05N 63.20E
Nizhneangarsk Russian Fed. 51 55.48N109.35E
Nizhnekamskoye Vodokhranilishche Russian Fed. 44 55.45N 53.50E
Nizhne Kolymsk Russian Fed. 51 68.34N160.58E
Nizhneudinsk Russian Fed. 51 54.55N 99.00E
Nizhnevartovsk Russian Fed. 50 60.57N 76.40E
Nizhniy Novgorod Russian Fed. 44 56.20N 44.00E
Nizhniy Tagil Russian Fed. 44 58.00N 60.00E
Nizhnyaya Tunguska r. Russian Fed. 51 65.50N 88.00E
Nizhnyaya Tura Russian Fed. 44 58.40N 59.48E
Nizke Tatry mts. Slovakia 37 48.54N 19.40E
Nizza Monferrato Italy 30 44.46N 8.21E
Nizzanim Israel 67 31.43N 34.38E
Njazídja see Grande Comore i. Comoros 79
Njombe Tanzania 79 9.20S 34.47E
Njombe r. Tanzania 79 7.02S 35.55E
Njoro Tanzania 79 5.16S 36.30E
Nkalagu Nigeria 77 6.28N 7.46E
Nkawkaw Ghana 76 6.35N 0.47W
Nkayi Zimbabwe 80 19.00S 28.54E
Nkhata Bay town Malaŵi 79 11.37S 34.20E
Nkhotakota Malaŵi 79 12.55S 34.19E
Nkongsamba Cameroon 77 4.59N 9.53E
Nkungwe Mt. Tanzania 79 6.15S 29.54E
Noākhāli Bangla. 63 22.51N 91.06E
Noatak U.S.A. 98 67.34N162.59W
Nobel Canada 104 45.25N 80.06W
Nobeoka Japan 57 32.36N131.40E
Noboribetsu Japan 57 42.27N141.11E
Noce r. Italy 30 46.09N 11.04E
Nocera Italy 33 40.44N 14.39E
Noci Italy 33 40.48N 17.08E
Noelville Canada 104 46.09N 80.26W
Nogales Mexico 109 31.20N110.56W
Nogara Italy 32 45.11N 11.04E
Nogaro France 20 43.46N 0.02W
Nogayskiye Step f. Russian Fed. 45 44.25N 45.30E
Nogent-le-Rotrou France 18 48.19N 0.50E
Nogent-sur-Seine France 19 48.29N 3.30E
Nogoyá Argentina 125 32.22S 59.49W
Noguera Pallarese r. Spain 25 42.15N 0.54E
Noguera Ribagorçana r. Spain 25 41.40N 0.43E
Nohar India 62 29.11N 74.46E
Nohta India 63 23.40N 79.34E
Noire r. Que. Canada 105 45.55N 76.56W
Noire r. Que. Canada 105 45.33N 72.58W
Noire, Montagne mtn. France 18 48.11N 3.40W
Noire, Montagne mts. France 20 43.26N 2.12E
Noirétable France 20 45.49N 3.46E
Noirmoutier France 18 47.00N 2.14W
Noirmoutier, Île de i. France 18 47.00N 2.15W
Nojima-zaki c. Japan 57 34.56N139.53E
Nokha India 62 27.35N 73.29E
Nokia Finland 41 61.28N 23.30E
Nok Kundi Pakistan 62 28.46N 62.46E
Nokomis Canada 101 51.30N105.00W
Nokou Chad 77 14.35N 14.47E
Nola C.A.R. 77 3.28N 16.08E
Nola Italy 33 40.55N 14.33E
Nolinsk Russian Fed. 44 57.38N 49.52E
Noman L. Canada 101 62.15N108.55W
Noma Omuramba r. Botswana 80 19.14S 22.15E
Nombre de Dios Mexico 109 28.41N106.05W
Nome U.S.A. 98 64.30N165.30W
Nomgon Mongolia 54 42.50N105.13E
Nominingue Canada 105 46.24N 75.02W
Nomuka Group is. Tonga 85 20.15S174.46W
Nonancourt France 18 48.46N 1.12E
Nonburg Russian Fed. 44 65.32N 50.37E
Nong Khai Thailand 56 17.50N102.46E
Nongoma R.S.A. 81 27.58S 31.35E
Nongpoh India 63 25.54N 91.53E
Nongstoin India 63 25.31N 91.16E
Nonning Australia 92 32.30S136.30E
Nono Ethiopia 73 8.31N 37.30E
Nonthaburi Thailand 56 13.48N100.11E
Nontron France 20 45.32N 0.40E
Noojee Australia 93 37.57S146.00E
Noonamah Australia 88 12.35S131.03E
Noonan U.S.A. 110 48.54N103.01W
Noongaar Australia 89 31.21S118.55E
Noonkanbah Australia 88 18.30S124.50E
Noonthorangee Range mts. Australia 92 31.00S142.20E
Noorama Creek r. Australia 93 28.05S145.55E
Noord Beveland i. Neth. 16 51.35N 3.45E
Noord Brabant d. Neth. 16 51.37N 5.00E
Noord Holland d. Neth. 16 52.37N 4.50E
Noordoost-Polder f. Neth. 16 52.45N 5.45E
Noordwijk Neth. 16 52.16N 4.29E
Noorvik U.S.A. 98 66.50N161.14W
Noosa Heads town Australia 90 26.23S153.07E
Nootka I. Canada 100 49.32N126.42W
Noqui Angola 78 5.51S 13.25E
Nora Sweden 43 59.31N 15.02E
Noranda Canada 102 48.20N 79.00W
Norberg Sweden 43 60.04N 15.56E
Norcia Italy 30 42.48N 13.05E
Nord d. Burkina 76 13.50N 2.20W
Nord d. France 19 50.20N 3.40E
Nordaustlandet i. Arctic Oc. 128 79.55N 23.00E
Nordborg Denmark 42 55.03N 9.45E
Norddeich Germany 38 53.37N 7.10E
Nordegg Canada 100 52.29N116.05W
Norden Germany 38 53.36N 7.12E
Nordenham Germany 38 53.29N 8.28E
Norderney Germany 38 53.42N 7.08E
Norderney i. Germany 38 53.42N 7.10E
Norderstedt Germany 38 53.43N 9.59E
Nordfjord est. Norway 41 61.54N 5.12E
Nordfjordeid Norway 41 61.54N 6.00E
Nordfold Norway 40 67.48N 15.20E
Nordfriesische Inseln is. Germany 38 54.35N 8.30E
Nordhausen Germany 38 51.30N 10.47E
Nordhorn Germany 38 52.27N 7.05E
Nordkapp c. Norway 40 71.11N 25.48E
Nordkinnhalvöya pen. Norway 40 70.55N 27.45E
Nordland d. Norway 40 66.50N 14.50E
Nördlingen Germany 39 48.51N 10.30E
Nord-Ostsee-Kanal Germany 38 54.10N 9.25E
Nordreisa Norway 40 69.46N 21.00E
Nordrhein-Westfalen d. Germany 38 52.04N 7.20E
Nordstrand i. Germany 38 54.30N 8.53E
Nord Tröndelag d. Norway 40 64.20N 12.00E
Nordvik Russian Fed. 51 73.40N110.50E
Nore Norway 42 60.10N 9.01E
Nore r. Rep. of Ire. 15 52.25N 6.58W
Norfolk d. U.K. 13 52.39N 1.00E
Norfolk Conn. U.S.A. 115 41.59N 73.12W
Norfolk Nebr. U.S.A. 110 42.02N 97.25W
Norfolk Va. U.S.A. 113 36.54N 76.18W
Norfolk Broads f. U.K. 12 52.43N 1.35E
Norfolk I. Pacific Oc. 84 29.02S167.57E
Norfolk Island Ridge Pacific Oc. 84 29.00S167.00E
Norheimsund Norway 41 60.22N 6.08E
Norilsk Russian Fed. 51 69.21N 88.02E
Norland Canada 104 44.43N 78.49W
Normal U.S.A. 110 40.31N 89.00W
Norman r. Australia 90 17.28S140.49E
Norman U.S.A. 111 35.13N 97.26W
Normanby r. Australia 90 14.25S144.08E
Normanby New Zealand 86 39.32S174.16E
Normanby I. P.N.G. 90 10.05S151.05E
Normandie, Collines de hills France 18 48.55N 0.45W
Normanton Australia 90 17.40S141.05E
Norman Wells Canada 98 65.19N126.46W
Nornalup Australia 89 34.58S116.49E
Norquinco Argentina 125 41.50S 70.55W
Norrahammar Sweden 43 57.42N 14.06E
Norra Kvarken str. Sweden / Finland 40 63.36N 20.43E
Norra Storfjället mtn. Sweden 40 65.52N 15.18E
Norrbotten d. Sweden 40 67.00N 19.50E
Nörresundby Denmark 42 57.04N 9.55E
Norris L. U.S.A. 113 36.18N 83.58W
Norristown U.S.A. 115 40.07N 75.21W
Norrköping Sweden 43 58.36N 16.11E
Norrsundet Sweden 41 60.56N 17.08E
Norrtälje Sweden 43 59.46N 18.42E
Norseman Australia 89 32.15S121.47E
Norsjå l. Norway 42 59.18N 9.20E
Norsk Russian Fed. 51 52.22N129.57E
Norte d. W. Sahara 74 26.50N 11.15W
Norte, C. Brazil 123 1.40N 49.55W
Norte, Cabo c. I. de Pascua 85 27.03S109.24W
Norte, Punta c. Argentina 125 36.17S 56.46W
Norte Interior d. Portugal 26 41.30N 7.00W
Norte Litoral d. Portugal 26 41.00N 8.25W
North, C. Canada 103 47.01N 60.28W
North Adams U.S.A. 115 42.42N 73.07W
Northallerton U.K. 12 54.20N 1.26W
Northam Australia 89 31.41S116.40E
North America 96
Northampton Australia 89 28.21S114.37E
Northampton U.K. 13 52.14N 0.54W
Northampton Mass. U.S.A. 115 42.19N 72.38W
Northampton Penn. U.S.A. 115 40.41N 75.30W
Northamptonshire d. U.K. 13 52.18N 0.55W
North Augusta Canada 105 44.44N 75.45W
North Battleford Canada 101 52.47N108.17W
North Bay town Canada 104 46.19N 79.28W
North Bend Penn. U.S.A. 114 41.21N 77.42W
North Berwick U.K. 14 56.04N 2.43W
North Bourke Australia 93 30.01S145.59E
North Bradley U.S.A. 104 43.44N 84.31W
North C. Antarctica 128 71.00S166.00E
North C. New Zealand 86 34.28S173.00E
North Canadian r. U.S.A. 111 35.17N 95.31W
North Caribou L. Canada 102 52.50N 90.50W
North Carolina d. U.S.A. 113 35.30N 80.00W
North Channel str. Canada 104 46.02N 82.50W
North Channel U.K. 15 55.15N 5.52W
North Chicago U.S.A. 110 42.20N 87.51W
North China Plain f. see Huabei Pingyuan f. China 54
Northcliffe Australia 89 34.36S116.04E
North Creek town U.S.A. 115 43.42N 73.59W
North Dakota d. U.S.A. 110 47.00N100.00W
North Dorset Downs hills U.K. 13 50.46N 2.25W
North Downs hills U.K. 13 51.18N 0.40E
North East d. Botswana 80 20.45S 27.05E
North East U.S.A. 114 42.13N 79.50W
North Eastern d. Kenya 79 1.00N 40.00E
North Eastern Atlantic Basin f. Atlantic Oc. 127 45.00N 17.00W
North East Pt. Kiribati 85 1.57N157.16W
Northeim Germany 38 51.42N 10.00E
Northern d. Ghana 76 9.00N 1.30W
Northern Indian L. Canada 101 57.20N 97.20W
Northern Ireland d. U.K. 15 54.40N 6.45W
Northern Marianas is. Pacific Oc. 84 15.00N145.00E
Northern Territory d. Australia 90 20.00S133.00E
North Esk r. U.K. 14 56.45N 2.25W
Northfield U.S.A. 105 44.09N 72.40W
North Fiji Basin Pacific Oc. 84 17.00S173.00E
North Foreland c. U.K. 13 51.23N 1.26E
North French r. Canada 102 51.04N 80.46W
North Frisian Is. see Nordfriesische Inseln is. Germany 36
North Gower Canada 105 45.08N 75.43W
North Head c. Canada 103 53.42N 56.24W
North Henik L. Canada 101 61.45N 97.40W
North Horr Kenya 79 3.19N 37.00E
North I. Kenya 73 4.04N 36.03E
North I. New Zealand 86 39.00S175.00E
Northiam U.K. 13 50.59N 0.39E
North Knife r. Canada 101 58.53N 94.45W
North Korea Asia 53 40.00N128.00E
Northland d. New Zealand 86 35.25S174.00E
North Las Vegas U.S.A. 109 36.12N115.07W
North Little Rock U.S.A. 111 34.46N 92.14W
North Loup r. U.S.A. 110 41.17N 98.23W
North Mankato U.S.A. 110 44.15N 94.06W
North Nahanni r. Canada 100 62.15N123.20W
North Ogden U.S.A. 108 41.18N112.00W
North Olmsted U.S.A. 114 41.25N 81.56W

Northome to **Offa**

Northome U.S.A. **110** 47.52N 94.17W
North Platte U.S.A. **110** 41.08N100.46W
North Platte *r.* U.S.A. **110** 41.15N100.45W
Northport U.S.A. **113** 33.14N 87.33W
North Powder U.S.A. **108** 45.13N117.55W
North Pt. Canada **103** 47.05N 64.00W
North Pt. U.S.A. **104** 45.02N 83.16W
North Rona *i.* U.K. **10** 59.09N 5.43W
North Ronaldsay *i.* U.K. **14** 59.23N 2.26W
North Saskatchewan *r.* Canada **101** 53.15N105.06W
North Sea Europe **36** 54.00N 4.00E
North Seal *r.* Canada **101** 58.50N 98.10W
North Sporades *see* Voríai Sporádhes *is.* Greece **35**
North Stratford U.S.A. **105** 44.46N 71.36W
North Sydney Canada **103** 46.13N 60.15W
North Syracuse U.S.A. **115** 43.08N 76.08W
North Taranaki Bight *b.* New Zealand **86** 38.45S174.15E
North Tawton U.K. **13** 50.48N 3.55W
North Thames *r.* Canada **104** 42.59N 81.16W
North Thompson *r.* Canada **100** 50.40N120.20W
North Tonawanda U.S.A. **114** 43.02N 78.53W
North Troy U.S.A. **105** 45.00N 72.24W
North Twin I. Canada **102** 53.20N 80.00W
North Uist *i.* U.K. **14** 57.35N 7.20W
Northumberland *d.* U.K. **12** 55.12N 2.00W
Northumberland U.S.A. **114** 40.49N 76.39W
Northumberland, C. Australia **92** 38.04S140.40E
Northumberland Is. Australia **90** 21.40S150.00E
Northumberland Str. Canada **103** 46.00N 63.30W
Northville U.S.A. **115** 43.13N 74.11W
North Wabasca L. Canada **100** 56.00N113.55W
North Walsham U.K. **12** 52.49N 1.22E
Northway U.S.A. **98** 62.58N142.00W
North West C. Australia **88** 21.48S114.10E
North West Chile Ridge Pacific Oc. **85** 42.00S 90.00W
North Western *d.* Zambia **80** 13.00S 25.00E
North Western Atlantic Basin *f.* Atlantic Oc. **127** 33.00N 55.00W
Northwest Frontier *d.* Pakistan **62** 33.45N 71.00E
North West Highlands U.K. **14** 57.30N 5.15W
Northwest Providence Channel Bahamas **113** 26.10N 78.20W
North West Pt. Kiribati **85** 2.02N157.29W
North West River *town* Canada **103** 53.32N 60.09W
Northwest Territories *d.* Canada **99** 66.00N 95.00W
Northwich U.K. **12** 53.16N 2.30W
Northwood Iowa U.S.A. **110** 43.27N 93.13W
Northwood N.Dak. U.S.A. **110** 47.44N 97.34W
North Woodstock U.S.A. **105** 44.02N 71.41W
North York Moors *hills* U.K. **12** 54.21N 0.50W
North Yorkshire *d.* U.K. **12** 54.14N 1.14W
Norton Kans. U.S.A. **110** 39.50N 99.53W
Norton W.Va. U.S.A. **114** 38.58N 79.55W
Norton Sound *b.* U.S.A. **98** 63.50N164.00W
Nortorf Germany **38** 54.10N 9.50E
Nort-sur-Erdre France **18** 47.26N 1.30W
Norwalk Conn. U.S.A. **115** 41.07N 73.27W
Norwalk Ohio U.S.A. **114** 41.15N 82.37W
Norway Europe **40** 65.00N 13.00E
Norway House *town* Canada **101** 53.59N 97.50W
Norwegian Dependency Antarctica **128** 77.00S 10.00E
Norwegian Sea Europe **128** 65.00N 5.00E
Norwich Canada **104** 42.59N 80.36W
Norwich U.K. **13** 52.38N 1.17E
Norwich Conn. U.S.A. **115** 41.32N 72.05W
Norwich N.Y. U.S.A. **115** 42.32N 75.31W
Norwood Canada **105** 44.23N 77.59W
Norwood Mass. U.S.A. **115** 42.11N 71.12W
Norwood N.Y. U.S.A. **105** 44.45N 75.00W
Norwood Ohio U.S.A. **112** 39.12N 84.21W
Nosbonsing, L. Canada **104** 46.12N 79.13W
Noshiro Japan **57** 40.12N140.02E
Noshul Russian Fed. **44** 60.04N 49.30E
Nosovka Ukraine **37** 50.55N 31.37E
Noşratābād Iran **65** 29.54N 59.58E
Nossebro Sweden **43** 58.11N 12.43E
Noss Head U.K. **14** 58.28N 3.03W
Nosy Be *i.* Madagascar **81** 13.20S 48.15E
Nosy Boraha *i.* Madagascar **81** 16.50S 49.55E
Nosy Varika Madagascar **81** 20.35S 48.32E
Noteć *r.* Poland **36** 52.44N 15.26E
Notera Israel **67** 33.06N 35.38E
Noto Italy **33** 36.53N 15.05E
Noto, Golfo di *g.* Italy **33** 36.50N 15.15E
Notodden Norway **42** 59.34N 9.17E
Notre Dame, Monts *mts.* Canada **103** 48.00N 69.00W
Notre Dame B. Canada **103** 49.45N 55.15W
Notre Dame de la Salette Canada **105** 45.46N 75.35W
Notre Dame du Lac *town* Canada **104** 46.19N 80.10W
Notre Dame du Laus Canada **105** 46.05N 75.37W
Nottawasaga *r.* Canada **104** 44.32N 80.01W
Nottawasaga B. Canada **104** 44.40N 80.30W
Nottaway *r.* Canada **102** 51.25N 78.50W
Nottingham U.K. **12** 52.57N 1.10W
Nottinghamshire *d.* U.K. **12** 53.10N 1.00W
Notwani *r.* Botswana **80** 23.46S 26.57E
Nouadhibou Mauritania **74** 20.54N 17.01W
Nouakchott Mauritania **74** 18.09N 15.58W
Nouméa N.Cal. **84** 22.16S166.27E
Nouna Burkina **76** 12.44N 3.54W
Noupoort R.S.A. **80** 31.11S 24.56E
Nouvelle Anvers Zaïre **78** 1.38N 19.10E
Nouvelle Calédonie *is.* Pacific Oc. **84** 21.30S165.30E
Nouzonville France **19** 49.49N 4.45E
Nova Caipemba Angola **78** 7.25S 14.36E
Novafeltria Bagnodi Romagna Italy **30** 43.53N 12.17E
Nova Friburgo Brazil **126** 22.16S 42.32W
Nova Gradiška Croatia **31** 45.16N 17.23E
Nova Iguaçu Brazil **126** 22.45S 43.27W
Nova Lamego Guinea Bissau **76** 12.19N 14.11W
Nova Lima Brazil **126** 19.59S 43.51W
Novara Italy **30** 45.28N 8.38E
Nova Scotia *d.* Canada **103** 45.00N 63.30W
Nova Sofala Mozambique **81** 20.09S 34.24E
Novato U.S.A. **108** 38.06N122.34W
Nova Varoš Yugo. **31** 43.28N 19.48E
Novaya Ladoga Russian Fed. **44** 60.09N 32.15E
Novaya Lyalya Russian Fed. **50** 59.02N 60.38E
Novaya Sibir, Ostrov *i.* Russian Fed. **51** 75.20N148.00E
Novaya Ushitsa Ukraine **37** 48.50N 27.12E
Novaya Zemlya *i.* Russian Fed. **50** 74.00N 56.00E
Nova Zagora Bulgaria **34** 42.29N 26.01E
Novelda Spain **25** 38.23N 0.46W
Nové Zámky Slovakia **37** 47.59N 18.11E
Novgorod Russian Fed. **44** 58.30N 31.20E
Novgorod Severskiy Belorussia **44** 52.00N 33.15E
Novi Bečej Yugo. **31** 45.36N 20.08E
Novi di Modena Italy **30** 44.54N 10.54E
Novigrad Croatia **31** 45.19N 13.34E
Novi Ligure Italy **30** 44.46N 8.47E
Novi Pazar Yugo. **34** 43.08N 20.31E
Novi Sad Yugo. **31** 45.15N 19.50E
Novi Vinodolski Croatia **31** 45.08N 14.48E
Novoalekseyevka Ukraine **45** 46.14N 34.36E
Novoanninskiy Russian Fed. **45** 50.32N 42.42E
Novo Arkhangel'sk Ukraine **37** 48.34N 30.50E
Novocherkassk Russian Fed. **45** 47.25N 40.05E
Novofedorovka Ukraine **45** 47.04N 35.18E
Novograd Volynskiy Ukraine **37** 50.34N 27.32E
Novogrudok Belorussia **37** 53.35N 25.50E
Novo Hamburgo Brazil **126** 29.37S 51.07W
Novokazalinsk Kazakhstan **9** 45.48N 62.06E
Novokuznetsk Russian Fed. **50** 53.45N 87.12E
Novo Mesto Slovenia **31** 45.48N 15.10E
Novomoskovsk Russian Fed. **44** 54.06N 38.15E
Novomoskovsk Ukraine **45** 48.38N 35.15E
Novorossiysk Russian Fed. **45** 44.44N 37.46E
Novoshakhtinsk Russian Fed. **45** 47.46N 39.55E
Novosibirsk Russian Fed. **9** 55.04N 83.05E
Novosibirskiye Ostrova *is.* Russian Fed. **51** 76.00N144.00E
Novouzensk Russian Fed. **45** 50.29N 48.08E
Novo-Vyatsk Russian Fed. **44** 58.30N 49.40E
Novozybkov Russian Fed. **37** 52.31N 31.58E
Novska Croatia **31** 45.21N 16.59E
Nový Bor Czech Republic **38** 50.40N 14.33E
Nový Jičín Czech Republic **37** 49.36N 18.00E
Novyy Bykhov Belorussia **37** 53.20N 30.21E
Novyy Port Russian Fed. **50** 67.38N 72.33E
Nowa Ruda Poland **36** 50.34N 16.30E
Nowa Sól Poland **36** 51.49N 15.41E
Nowendoc Australia **93** 31.35S151.45E
Nowgong Assam India **63** 26.21N 92.40E
Nowgong Madhya P. India **63** 25.04N 79.27E
Nowingi Australia **92** 34.36S142.15E
Nowra Australia **93** 35.54S150.36E
Nowrangapur India **63** 19.14N 82.33E
Nowshera Pakistan **62** 34.01N 71.59E
Nowy Dwór Mazowiecki Poland **37** 52.26N 20.43E
Nowy Korczyn Poland **37** 50.19N 20.48E
Nowy Sacz Poland **37** 49.39N 20.40E
Nowy Targ Poland **37** 49.29N 20.02E
Nowy Tomśyl Poland **36** 52.20N 16.07E
Now Zād Afghan. **62** 32.24N 64.28E
Noxon U.S.A. **108** 48.01N115.47W
Noya Spain **26** 42.47N 8.53W
Noya *r.* Spain **25** 41.28N 1.56E
Noyant France **18** 47.31N 0.08E
Noyes I. U.S.A. **100** 55.30N133.40W
Noyon France **19** 49.35N 3.00E
Nozay France **18** 47.34N 1.38W
Nsanje Malaŵi **79** 16.55S 35.12E
Nsawam Ghana **76** 5.49N 0.20W
Nsok Equat. Guinea **78** 1.10N 11.19E
Nsombo Zambia **79** 10.50S 29.56E
Nsukka Nigeria **77** 6.51N 7.29E
Nuatja Togo **77** 6.59N 1.11E
Nubian Desert Sudan **72** 20.30N 34.00E
Nueces *r.* U.S.A. **111** 27.50N 97.30W
Nueces Plains *f.* U.S.A. **111** 28.30N 99.15W
Nueltin L. Canada **101** 60.30N 99.30W
Nueva Casas Grandes Mexico **109** 30.25N107.55W
Nueva Gerona Cuba **117** 21.53N 82.49W
Nueva Helvecia Uruguay **125** 34.19S 57.13W
Nueva Palmira Uruguay **125** 33.53S 58.25W
Nueva Rosita Mexico **111** 27.57N101.13W
Nueve de Julio Argentina **125** 35.30S 60.50W
Nuevitas Cuba **117** 21.34N 77.18W
Nuevo *d.* Mexico **111** 26.00N100.00W
Nuevo, Golfo *g.* Argentina **125** 42.42S 64.35W
Nuevo Berlín Uruguay **125** 32.59S 58.03W
Nuevo Laredo Mexico **111** 27.30N 99.31W
Nuevo León *d.* Mexico **116** 26.00N 99.00W
Nuevo Rocafuerte Ecuador **122** 0.56S 75.24W
Nūh, Rās *c.* Pakistan **62** 25.05N 62.24E
Nui *i.* Tuvalu **84** 7.12S177.10E
Nuits-St. Georges France **19** 47.08N 4.57E
Nu Jiang *r.* China *see* Salween *r.* Burma **61**
Nukha Azerbaijan **65** 41.12N 47.10E
Nukhaylah Sudan **72** 19.03N 26.19E
Nuku'alofa Tonga **85** 21.07S175.12W
Nuku Hiva *i.* Îs. Marquises **85** 8.56S140.00W
Nukunonu Pacific Oc. **84** 9.10S171.55W
Nulato U.S.A. **98** 64.43N158.06W
Nules Spain **25** 39.51N 0.09W
Nullagine Australia **88** 21.56S120.06E
Nullarbor Australia **89** 31.26S130.55E
Nullarbor Plain *f.* Australia **89** 31.30S128.00E
Numalla, L. Australia **92** 28.45S144.21E
Numan Nigeria **77** 9.30N 12.01E
Numancia *site* Spain **25** 41.48N 2.25W
Numazu Japan **57** 35.06N138.52E
Numedal *f.* Norway **42** 60.06N 9.06E
Numurkah Australia **93** 36.05S145.26E
Nunavik *c.* Greenland **99** 71.55N 55.00W
Nunda U.S.A. **114** 42.35N 77.57W
Nundle Australia **93** 31.28S151.08E
Nuneaton U.K. **13** 52.32N 1.29W
Nungo Mozambique **81** 13.25S 37.45E
Nunivak I. U.S.A. **98** 60.00N166.30W
Nunkun *mtn.* Jammu & Kashmir **62** 33.59N 76.01E
Nuoro Italy **32** 40.19N 9.20E
Nuqūb Yemen **71** 14.59N 45.48E
Nurallao Italy **32** 39.46N 9.05E
Nürburg Germany **39** 50.21N 6.57E
Nure *r.* Italy **30** 45.03N 9.49E
Nuriootpa Australia **92** 34.27S139.02E
Nürnberg Germany **38** 49.27N 11.04E
Nurri Italy **32** 39.42N 9.14E
Nurri, Mt. Australia **93** 31.44S146.04E
Nürtingen Germany **39** 48.38N 9.20E
Nusa Tenggara *is.* Indonesia **58** 8.30S118.00E
Nusa Tenggara Barat *d.* Indonesia **58** 8.50S117.30E
Nusa Tenggara Timur *d.* Indonesia **59** 9.30S122.00E
Nusaybin Turkey **64** 37.05N 41.11E
Nushki Pakistan **62** 29.33N 66.01E
Nutak Canada **103** 57.39N 61.50W
Nutter Fort U.S.A. **114** 39.20N 80.19W
Nuuk *see* Godthåb Greenland **99**
Nuwākot Nepal **63** 28.08N 83.53E
Nuwaybi'al Muzayyinah Egypt **66** 28.58N 34.38E
Nuweveldberge *mts.* R.S.A. **80** 32.15S 21.50E
Nuyts, Pt. Australia **89** 35.02S116.32E
Nuyts Archipelago *is.* Australia **91** 32.35S133.17E
Nxaunxau Botswana **80** 18.19S 21.04E
Nyaake Liberia **76** 4.52N 7.37W
Nyabing Australia **89** 33.32S118.09E
Nyahua Tanzania **79** 5.25S 33.16E
Nyahururu Falls *town* Kenya **79** 0.04N 36.22E
Nyah West Australia **92** 35.11S143.21E
Nyainqêntanglha Feng *mtn.* China **63** 30.27N 90.33E
Nyainqêntanglha Shan *mts.* China **63** 30.00N 90.00E
Nyainrong China **63** 32.02N 92.15E
Nyakanazi Tanzania **79** 3.05S 31.16E
Nyaksimvol Russian Fed. **44** 62.30N 60.52E
Nyala Sudan **73** 12.03N 24.53E
Nyalam China **63** 28.12N 85.58E
Nyamandhlovu Zimbabwe **80** 19.50S 28.15E
Nyamapanda Zimbabwe **81** 16.59S 32.50E
Nyamlell Sudan **73** 9.07N 26.58E
Nyamtukusa Tanzania **79** 3.03S 32.44E
Nyandoma Russian Fed. **44** 61.33N 40.05E
Nyanga *r.* Gabon **78** 3.00S 10.17E
Nyang Qu *r.* China **63** 29.19N 88.52E
Nyanza *d.* Kenya **79** 0.30S 34.30E
Nyanza Rwanda **79** 2.20S 29.42E
Nyashabozh Russian Fed. **44** 65.28N 53.42E
Nyaunglebin Burma **56** 17.57N 96.44E
Nyaungu Burma **56** 21.12N 94.55E
Nyborg Denmark **42** 55.19N 10.48E
Nybro Sweden **43** 56.45N 15.54E
Nyda Russian Fed. **50** 66.35N 72.58E
Nyêmo China **63** 29.25N 90.15E
Nyeri Kenya **79** 0.22S 36.56E
Nyerol Sudan **73** 8.41N 32.02E
Nyhammar Sweden **43** 60.17N 14.58E
Nyika Plateau *f.* Malaŵi **79** 10.25S 33.50E
Nyima China **63** 31.50N 87.48E
Nyimba Zambia **79** 14.33S 30.49E
Nyíregyháza Hungary **37** 47.59N 21.43E
Nyköbing Falster Denmark **41** 54.46N 11.53E
Nykøbing Jylland Denmark **42** 56.48N 8.52E
Nykøbing Sjælland Denmark **42** 55.55N 11.41E
Nyköping Sweden **43** 58.45N 17.00E
Nykroppa Sweden **43** 59.38N 14.18E
Nylstroom R.S.A. **80** 24.42S 28.24E
Nymagee Australia **93** 32.05S146.20E
Nymboida Australia **93** 29.57S152.32E
Nymboida *r.* Australia **93** 29.39S152.30E
Nymburk Czech Republic **36** 50.11N 15.03E
Nynäshamn Sweden **43** 58.54N 17.57E
Nyngan Australia **93** 31.34S147.14E
Nyngynderry Australia **92** 32.16S143.22E
Nyoma Jammu & Kashmir **63** 33.11N 78.38E
Nyon Switz. **39** 46.23N 6.14E
Nyong *r.* Cameroon **77** 3.15N 9.55E
Nyons France **21** 44.22N 5.08E
Nýřany Czech Republic **38** 49.43N 13.13E
Nýrsko Czech Republic **38** 49.18N 13.09E
Nysa Poland **37** 50.29N 17.20E
Nysa Kłodzka *r.* Poland **37** 50.49N 17.50E
Nyssa U.S.A. **108** 43.53N117.00W
Nyuksenitsa Russian Fed. **44** 60.24N 44.08E
Nyunzu Zaïre **79** 5.55S 28.00E
Nyurba Russian Fed. **51** 63.18N118.28E
Nyuri India **63** 27.42N 92.13E
Nzega Tanzania **79** 4.13S 33.09E
N'zérékoré Guinea **76** 7.49N 8.48W
N'zeto Angola **78** 7.13S 12.56E
Nzwani *see* Anjouan *i.* Comoros **79** 12.12S 44.28E

O

Oahe Resr. U.S.A. **110** 45.30N100.25W
Oahu *i.* Hawaiian Is. **85** 21.30N158.00W
Oakbank Australia **92** 33.07S140.33E
Oakdale U.S.A. **111** 30.49N 92.40W
Oakesdale U.S.A. **108** 47.08N117.15W
Oakey Australia **91** 27.26S151.43E
Oak Harbour U.S.A. **108** 48.18N122.39W
Oak Hill *town* Fla. U.S.A. **113** 28.52N 80.52W
Oak Hill *town* Ohio U.S.A. **114** 38.54N 82.34W
Oakland Calif. U.S.A. **108** 37.47N122.13W
Oakland Md. U.S.A. **114** 39.25N 79.24W
Oakland Oreg. U.S.A. **108** 43.25N123.18W
Oaklands Australia **93** 35.25S146.15E
Oakley U.S.A. **108** 42.15N113.53W
Oakover *r.* Australia **88** 20.49S120.40E
Oak Ridge *f.* Canada **104** 44.01N 79.19W
Oakridge U.S.A. **108** 43.45N122.28W
Oak Ridge *town* U.S.A. **113** 36.02N 84.12W
Oakvale Australia **92** 33.01S140.41E
Oakville Canada **104** 43.27N 79.41W
Oamaru New Zealand **86** 45.07S170.58E
Oates Land *f.* Antarctica **128** 70.00S155.00E
Oaxaca Mexico **116** 17.05N 96.41W
Oaxaca *d.* Mexico **116** 17.30N 97.00W
Ob *r.* Russian Fed. **44** 66.50N 69.00E
Oba Canada **102** 49.04N 84.07W
Oba *i.* Vanuatu **84** 15.25S167.50E
Oban U.K. **14** 56.26N 5.28W
Oberá Argentina **124** 27.30S 55.07W
Oberammergau Germany **39** 47.35N 11.04E
Oberdrauburg Austria **39** 46.45N 12.58E
Obergurgl Austria **39** 46.52N 11.01E
Oberhausen Germany **38** 51.28N 6.50E
Oberkirch Germany **39** 48.31N 8.05E
Oberlin Kans. U.S.A. **110** 39.49N100.32W
Oberlin Ohio U.S.A. **114** 41.18N 82.13W
Obernai France **19** 48.28N 7.29E
Oberon Australia **93** 33.41S149.52E
Oberösterreich *d.* Austria **39** 48.05N 13.40E
Oberpfälzer Wald *mts.* Germany **39** 49.35N 12.15E
Oberursel Germany **39** 50.11N 8.35E
Obervellach Austria **39** 46.56N 13.12E
Obi *i.* Indonesia **59** 1.45S127.30E
Obidos Brazil **123** 1.55S 55.31W
Obihiro Japan **57** 42.55N143.00E
Obing Germany **39** 48.00N 12.24E
Obitsu *r.* Japan **57** 35.24N139.54E
Obnova Bulgaria **34** 43.26N 24.59E
Obo C.A.R. **73** 5.24N 26.30E
Obock Djibouti **73** 11.59N 43.16E
Obodovka Ukraine **37** 48.28N 29.10E
Oboyan Russian Fed. **45** 51.13N 36.17E
Obozerskiy Russian Fed. **44** 63.28N 40.29E
Obregón, Presa *resr.* Mexico **109** 28.00N109.50W
Obrenovac Yugo. **31** 44.39N 20.12E
Obrovac Croatia **31** 44.12N 15.41E
Obruk Platosu *f.* Turkey **64** 38.00N 33.30E
Obskaya Guba *g.* Russian Fed. **50** 68.30N 74.00E
Ōbu Japan **57** 35.00N136.58E
Obuasi Ghana **76** 6.15N 1.36W
Obudu Nigeria **77** 6.42N 9.07E
Ocala U.S.A. **113** 29.11N 82.09W
Ocaña Colombia **122** 8.16N 73.21W
Ocaña Spain **27** 39.56N 3.31W
Occidental, Cordillera *mts.* Colombia **122** 5.00N 76.15W
Occidental, Cordillera *mts.* S. America **124** 17.00S 69.00W
Ocean City Md. U.S.A. **115** 38.20N 75.05W
Ocean City N.J. U.S.A. **115** 39.16N 74.36W
Ocean Falls *town* Canada **100** 52.25N127.40W
Ocean I. *see* Banaba *i.* Kiribati **84**
Oceanside Calif. U.S.A. **109** 33.12N117.23W
Oceanside N.Y. U.S.A. **115** 40.38N 73.38W
Ochamchire Georgia **45** 42.44N 41.30E
Ochil Hills U.K. **14** 56.16N 3.25W
Ochsenfurt Germany **39** 49.40N 10.03E
Ockelbo Sweden **41** 60.53N 16.43E
Öckerö Sweden **42** 57.43N 11.39E
Ocmulgee *r.* U.S.A. **113** 31.58N 82.32W
Oconee *r.* U.S.A. **113** 31.58N 82.32W
Oconto U.S.A. **110** 44.55N 87.52W
Ocotal Nicaragua **117** 13.37N 86.31W
Ocotlán Mexico **116** 20.21N102.42W
Ocreza, Ribeira da *r.* Portugal **27** 39.32N 7.50W
Octeville France **18** 49.37N 1.39W
Ocua Mozambique **81** 13.40S 39.46E
Oda Ghana **76** 5.55N 0.56W
Oda, Jabal *mtn.* Sudan **72** 20.21N 36.39E
Ódádhahraun *mts.* Iceland **40** 65.00N 17.30W
Ōdate Japan **57** 40.16N140.34E
Odawara Japan **57** 35.15N139.10E
Odda Norway **42** 60.04N 6.33E
Odder Denmark **42** 55.58N 10.10E
Ödeborg Sweden **43** 58.30N 12.01E
Odeleite *r.* Portugal **27** 37.21N 7.27W
Odemira Portugal **27** 37.36N 8.38W
Ödemiş Turkey **29** 38.12N 28.00E
Odense Denmark **42** 55.24N 10.23E
Odenwald *mts.* Germany **39** 49.35N 9.05E
Oder *r.* Germany *see* Odra *r.* Poland **36**
Oderberg Germany **38** 52.52N 14.02E
Oderhaff *b.* Germany **38** 53.46N 14.14E
Oder-Havel-Kanal Germany **38** 52.51N 13.30E
Oder-Spree-Kanal Germany **38** 52.16N 14.30E
Oderzo Italy **30** 45.47N 12.29E
Ödeshög Sweden **43** 58.14N 14.39E
Odessa Ukraine **37** 46.30N 30.46E
Odessa N.Y. U.S.A. **114** 42.20N 76.48W
Odessa Tex. U.S.A. **111** 31.51N102.22W
Odiel *r.* Spain **27** 37.10N 6.55W
Odienné Ivory Coast **76** 9.36N 7.32W
Odorhei Romania **37** 46.18N 25.18E
Odra *r.* Poland **36** 53.30N 14.36E
Odžaci Yugo. **31** 45.30N 19.16E
Odžak Bosnia-Herzegovina **31** 45.03N 18.18E
Odzi *r.* Zimbabwe **81** 19.46S 32.22E
Oebisfelde Germany **38** 52.25N 10.59E
Oegstgeest Neth. **16** 52.12N 4.31E
Oeiras Brazil **123** 7.00S 42.07W
Oelde Germany **38** 51.59N 8.08E
Oelrichs U.S.A. **110** 43.10N103.13W
Oelsnitz Germany **39** 50.24N 12.10E
Oelwein U.S.A. **110** 42.41N 91.55W
Oeno I. Pacific Oc. **85** 23.55S130.45W
Oettingen in Bayern Germany **39** 48.57N 10.36E
Oetz Austria **39** 47.12N 10.54E
Ofanto *r.* Italy **33** 41.22N 16.13E
Ofaqim Israel **67** 31.19N 34.37E
Offa Nigeria **77** 8.09N 4.44E

Offaly to **Osečina**

Offaly d. Rep. of Ire. 15 53.15N 7.30W
Offenbach Germany 39 50.08N 8.47E
Offenburg Germany 39 48.28N 7.57E
Offerdal Sweden 40 63.28N 14.03E
Offida Italy 31 42.56N 13.41E
Offranville France 18 49.52N 1.03E
Ofir Portugal 26 41.31N 8.47W
Ofotfjorden est. Norway 40 68.25N 17.00E
Ofu i. Samoa 84 14.11S169.40W
Ōfunato Japan 57 39.04N141.43E
Oga Japan 57 39.53N139.51E
Ogadēn f. Ethiopia 71 7.50N 45.40E
Ōgaki Japan 57 35.21N136.37E
Ogallala U.S.A. 110 41.08N101.43W
Ogbomosho Nigeria 77 8.05N 4.11E
Ogden Iowa U.S.A. 110 42.02N 94.02W
Ogden Utah U.S.A. 108 41.14N111.58W
Ogdensburg U.S.A. 105 44.42N 75.29W
Ogeechee r. U.S.A. 113 31.51N 81.06W
Ogilvie Mts. Canada 98 65.00N139.30W
Oginskiy, Kanal canal Belorussia 37 52.25N 25.55E
Oglio r. Italy 30 45.02N 10.39E
Ognon r. France 19 47.20N 5.29E
Ogoja Nigeria 77 6.40N 8.45E
Ogoki Canada 102 51.35N 86.00W
Ogoki r. Canada 102 51.35N 86.00W
Ogoki Resr. Canada 102 51.00N 88.15W
Ogooué r. Gabon 78 1.00S 9.05E
Ogosta r. Bulgaria 34 43.35N 23.35E
Ogr Sudan 73 12.02N 27.06E
Ograzden mts. Bulgaria / Macedonia 34 41.30N 22.50E
Ogulin Croatia 31 45.16N 15.14E
Ogun d. Nigeria 77 6.50N 3.20E
Ogunquit U.S.A. 115 43.15N 70.36W
Ohai New Zealand 86 45.56S167.57E
Ohanet Algeria 75 28.40N 8.50E
Ohey Belgium 16 50.26N 5.06E
O'Higgins, Cabo c. I. de Pascua 85 27.05S109.15W
O'Higgins, L. Chile 125 48.03S 73.10W
Ohio d. U.S.A. 112 40.15N 82.45W
Ohio r. U.S.A. 112 36.59N 89.08W
Ōhito Japan 57 34.59N138.56E
Ohne Germany 38 52.42N 8.12E
Ohře r. Czech Republic 39 50.32N 14.08E
Ohrid Macedonia 34 41.07N 20.47E
Ohrid, L. Albania / Macedonia 34 41.08N 20.52E
Öhringen Germany 39 49.12N 9.29E
Ōi r. Japan 57 34.45N138.18E
Oil City U.S.A. 114 41.26N 79.42W
Oise d. France 19 49.30N 2.30E
Oise r. France 19 49.00N 2.04E
Oisterwijk Neth. 16 51.34N 5.10E
Oita Japan 57 33.15N131.40E
Ojai U.S.A. 109 34.27N119.15W
Ojika zan pen. Japan 57 38.20N141.32E
Ojocaliente Mexico 116 22.35N102.18W
Ojo de Agua Argentina 124 29.30S 63.44W
Ojos del Salado mtn. Argentina / Chile 124 27.05S 68.05W
Oka Canada 105 45.29N 74.06W
Oka Nigeria 77 7.28N 5.48E
Oka r. Russian Fed. 44 56.09N 43.00E
Okaba Indonesia 59 8.06S139.46E
Okahandja Namibia 80 21.58S 16.44E
Okanagan L. Canada 100 50.00N119.30W
Okanogan U.S.A. 108 48.39N120.41W
Okanogan r. U.S.A. 108 48.22N119.35W
Okaputa Namibia 80 20.08S 16.58E
Okāra Pakistan 62 30.49N 73.27E
Okarito New Zealand 86 43.14S 170.07
Okaukuejo Namibia 80 19.12S 15.56E
Okavango r. Botswana 80 18.30S 22.04E
Okavango Basin f. Botswana 80 19.30S 22.30E
Okayama Japan 57 34.40N133.54E
Okeechobee U.S.A. 113 27.14N 80.50W
Okeechobee, L. U.S.A. 113 26.55N 80.45W
Okefenokee Swamp f. U.S.A. 113 30.42N 82.20W
Okehampton U.K. 13 50.44N 4.01W
Okere r. Uganda 79 1.37N 33.53E
Okha Russian Fed. 51 53.35N142.50E
Okhaldhunga Nepal 63 27.19N 86.31E
Okhansk Russian Fed. 44 57.42N 55.20E
Okhotsk Russian Fed. 51 59.20N143.15E
Okhotsk, Sea of Russian Fed. 51 55.00N150.00E
Okhotskiy Perevoz Russian Fed. 51 61.55N135.40E
Okiep R.S.A. 80 29.36S 17.49E
Oki guntō is. Japan 57 36.10N133.10E
Okinawa jima i. Japan 53 26.30N128.00E
Okipoko r. Namibia 80 18.40S 16.03E
Okitipupa Nigeria 77 6.31N 4.50E
Oklahoma d. U.S.A. 111 35.20N 98.00W
Oklahoma City U.S.A. 111 35.28N 97.32W
Okmulgee U.S.A. 111 35.37N 95.58W
Oknitsa Moldavia 37 48.22N 27.30E
Oko, Wādī Sudan 72 21.15N 35.56E
Okola Cameroon 77 4.03N 11.23E
Okolona U.S.A. 111 34.00N 88.45W
Okondja Gabon 78 0.03S 13.45E
Okoyo Congo 78 1.28S 15.00E
Oksböl Denmark 42 55.38N 8.17E
Oksskolten mtn. Norway 40 65.59N 14.15E
Oktyabr'sk Kazakhstan 45 49.30N 57.22E
Oktyabrskiy Belorussia 37 52.35N 28.45E
Oktyabrskiy Russian Fed. 44 54.30N 53.30E
Oktyabr'skoy Revolyutsii, Ostrov i. Russian Fed. 51 79.30N 96.00E
Okučani Croatia 31 45.16N 17.12E
Okuru New Zealand 86 43.56S168.55E
Okushiri tō i. Japan 57 42.00N139.50E
Okuta Nigeria 77 9.13N 3.12E
Ola U.S.A. 111 35.02N 93.13W
Ólafsvík Iceland 40 64.53N 23.44W
Olancha U.S.A. 109 36.17N118.01W
Öland i. Sweden 43 56.45N 16.38E
Olary Australia 92 32.18S140.19E
Olascoaga Argentina 125 35.14S 60.37W
Olavarría Argentina 125 36.57S 60.20W
Oława Poland 37 50.57N 17.17E
Olbia Italy 32 40.55N 9.29E
Old Bar Australia 93 31.59S152.35E
Old Crow Canada 98 67.34N139.43W
Oldenburg f. Germany 38 53.06N 8.25E
Oldenburg Nschn. Germany 38 53.08N 8.13E
Oldenburg Sch.-Hol. Germany 38 54.17N 10.52E
Oldenzaal Neth. 16 52.19N 6.55E
Old Forge N.Y. U.S.A. 115 43.43N 74.58W
Old Forge Penn. U.S.A. 115 41.22N 75.44W
Old Fort r. Canada 101 58.30N110.30W
Old Gumbiro Tanzania 79 10.00S 35.24E
Oldham U.K. 12 53.33N 2.08W
Old Head of Kinsale c. Rep. of Ire. 15 51.37N 8.33W
Oldman r. Canada 101 49.56N111.42W
Old Moolawatana Australia 92 30.04S140.02E
Olds Canada 100 51.50N114.10W
Old Saybrook U.S.A. 115 41.18N 72.23W
Old Town U.S.A. 112 44.56N 68.39W
Olean U.S.A. 114 42.05N 78.26W
Olecko Poland 37 54.03N 22.30E
Olekma r. Russian Fed. 51 60.20N120.30E
Olekminsk Russian Fed. 51 60.25N120.00E
Olema Russian Fed. 44 64.25N 40.15E
Ølen Norway 42 59.36N 5.48E
Olenëk Russian Fed. 51 68.38N112.15E
Olenëk r. Russian Fed. 51 73.00N120.00E
Olenëkskiy Zaliv g. Russian Fed. 51 74.00N120.00E
Oléron, Île d' i. France 20 45.56N 1.15W
Oleśnica Poland 37 51.13N 17.23E
Olevsk Ukraine 37 51.12N 27.35E
Olga Russian Fed. 53 43.46N135.14E
Olga, Mt. Australia 90 25.18S130.44E
Olga L. Canada 102 49.44N 77.18W
Ölgiy Mongolia 52 48.54N 90.00E
Ølgod Denmark 42 55.49N 8.37E
Olgopol Ukraine 37 48.10N 29.30E
Olhão Portugal 27 37.02N 8.50W
Olib i. Croatia 31 44.22N 14.48E
Oliena Italy 32 40.16N 9.24E
Olifants r. Namibia 80 25.28S 19.23E
Olifants r. C.P. R.S.A. 80 31.42S 18.10E
Olifants r. Trans. R.S.A. 80 24.08S 32.39E
Olimbía site Greece 35 37.38N 21.41E
Ólimbos mtn. Cyprus 66 34.55N 32.52E
Ólimbos Greece 35 35.44N 27.11E
Ólimbos mtn. Greece 34 40.05N 22.21E
Olinda Brazil 123 8.00S 34.51W
Olite Spain 25 42.29N 1.39W
Oliva Argentina 124 32.05S 63.35W
Oliva Spain 25 38.55N 0.07W
Oliva de la Frontera Spain 27 38.16N 6.55W
Olivares Spain 27 39.46N 2.20W
Oliveira Brazil 126 20.39S 44.47W
Olivenza Spain 27 38.41N 7.06W
Olmedillo de Roa Spain 26 41.47N 3.56W
Olmedo Spain 26 41.23N 4.41W
Olney U.K. 13 52.09N 0.42W
Olney U.S.A. 110 38.45N 88.05W
Olofström Sweden 43 56.16N 14.30E
Olomouc Czech Republic 37 49.36N 17.16E
Olonets Russian Fed. 44 61.00N 32.59E
Oloron France 20 43.12N 0.36W
Oloron, Gave d' r. France 20 43.33N 1.05W
Olosega i. Samoa 84 14.12S169.38W
Olot Spain 25 42.11N 2.29E
Olovyannaya Russian Fed. 53 50.58N115.35E
Olshammar Sweden 43 58.45N 14.48E
Olsztyn Poland 37 53.48N 20.29E
Olsztynek Poland 37 53.36N 20.17E
Olt r. Romania 34 43.43N 24.51E
Olten Switz. 39 47.21N 7.54E
Oltenița Romania 37 44.05N 26.31E
Olteț r. Romania 37 44.13N 24.28E
Olvera Spain 27 36.56N 5.16W
Olympia U.S.A. 108 47.03N122.53W
Olympic Mts. U.S.A. 108 47.50N123.45W
Olympic Nat. Park U.S.A. 108 47.48N123.30W
Olympus mtn. see Ólimbos mtn. Greece 34
Olympus, Mt. U.S.A. 108 47.48N123.43W
Oma China 63 32.30N 83.14E
Omae-zaki c. Japan 57 34.36N138.14E
Omagh U.K. 15 54.36N 7.20W
Omaha U.S.A. 110 41.16N 95.57W
Oman Asia 60 22.30N 57.30E
Oman, G. of Asia 65 25.00N 58.00E
Omarama New Zealand 86 44.29S169.58E
Omaruru Namibia 80 21.25S 15.57E
Omate Peru 124 16.40S 70.58W
Omberg hill Sweden 43 58.20N 14.39E
Omboué Gabon 78 1.38S 9.20E
Ombrone r. Italy 30 42.39N 11.00E
Ombu China 63 31.20N 86.34E
Omdurman see Umm Durmān Sudan 72
Omegna Italy 30 45.53N 8.24E
Omeo Australia 93 37.05S147.37E
'Omer Israel 67 31.17N 34.51E
Omer U.S.A. 104 44.03N 83.50W
Ometepec Mexico 116 16.41N 98.25W
Om Hājer Ethiopia 72 14.24N 36.46E
Ōmi-hachiman Japan 57 35.08N136.06E
Omineca r. Canada 100 56.05N124.30W
Omišalj Croatia 31 45.13N 14.34E
Omitara Namibia 80 22.18S 18.01E
Ōmiya Japan 57 35.54N139.38E
Ommen Neth. 16 52.32N 6.25E
Ömnögovi d. Mongolia 54 43.00N105.00E
Omo r. Ethiopia 73 4.51N 36.55E
Omolon r. Russian Fed. 51 68.50N158.30E
Omomee Canada 104 44.19N 78.31W
Omono r. Japan 57 39.44N140.05E
Ompah Canada 105 45.00N 76.49W
Omsk Russian Fed. 9 55.00N 73.22E
Omulew r. Poland 37 53.05N 21.32E
Omuramba Omatako r. Namibia 80 18.19S 19.52E
Omurtag Bulgaria 34 43.08N 26.26E
Ōmuta Japan 57 33.02N130.26E
Oña Spain 26 42.43N 3.25W
Onaga U.S.A. 110 39.29N 96.10W
Onai Angola 80 16.43S 17.33E
Onancock U.S.A. 113 37.43N 75.46W
Onaping L. Canada 104 46.57N 81.30W
Onaway U.S.A. 104 45.21N 84.14W
Oncocua Angola 80 16.40S 13.25E
Onda Spain 25 39.58N 0.15W
Ondangua Namibia 80 17.59S 16.02E
Ondo d. Nigeria 77 7.10N 5.20E
Onega Russian Fed. 44 63.57N 38.11E
Onega r. Russian Fed. 44 63.59N 38.11E
Oneida U.S.A. 115 43.06N 75.39W
Oneida L. U.S.A. 115 43.13N 76.00W
O'Neill U.S.A. 110 42.27N 98.39W
Oneonta U.S.A. 115 42.27N 75.04W
Onezhskaya Guba b. Russian Fed. 44 63.55N 37.30E
Onezhskoye Ozero l. Russian Fed. 44 62.00N 35.30E
Ongerup Australia 89 33.58S118.29E
Ongiyn Gol r. Mongolia 54 43.40N103.45E
Ongniud Qi China 54 43.00N118.43E
Ongole India 61 15.31N 80.04E
Onilahy r. Madagascar 81 23.34S 43.45E
Onitsha Nigeria 77 6.10N 6.47E
Ons, Isla de i. Spain 26 42.23N 8.56W
Onslow Australia 88 21.41S115.12E
Onslow B. U.S.A. 113 34.20N 77.20W
Onstwedde Neth. 16 53.04N 7.02E
Ontake san mtn. Japan 57 35.55N137.29E
Ontario d. Canada 102 51.00N 88.00W
Ontario Calif. U.S.A. 109 34.04N117.39W
Ontario Oreg. U.S.A. 108 44.02N116.58W
Ontario, L. Canada / U.S.A. 114 43.45N 78.00W
Onteniente Spain 25 38.49N 0.37W
Ontonagon U.S.A. 112 46.52N 89.18W
Oodnadatta Australia 91 27.30S135.27E
Ooldea Australia 91 30.27S131.50E
Oostelijk-Flevoland f. Neth. 16 52.30N 5.40E
Oostende Belgium 16 51.13N 2.55E
Oosterhout Neth. 16 51.38N 4.50E
Oosterschelde est. Neth. 16 51.35N 3.57E
Oosthuizen Neth. 16 52.33N 5.00E
Oostmalle Belgium 16 51.18N 4.45E
Oost Vlaanderen d. Belgium 16 51.00N 3.45E
Oost Vlieland Neth. 16 53.18N 5.04E
Ootsa L. Canada 100 53.50N126.20W
Opaka Bulgaria 34 43.28N 26.10E
Opal Mexico 111 24.18N102.22W
Opala Russian Fed. 51 51.58N156.30E
Opala Zaïre 78 0.42S 24.15E
Oparino Russian Fed. 44 59.53N 48.10E
Opasatika Canada 102 49.30N 82.50W
Opasatika r. Canada 102 50.24N 82.26W
Opasquia Canada 102 53.16N 93.34W
Opatija Croatia 31 45.21N 14.19E
Opava Czech Republic 37 49.56N 17.54E
Opelousas U.S.A. 111 30.32N 92.05W
Opeongo L. Canada 104 45.42N 78.23W
Opheim U.S.A. 108 48.51N106.24W
Opinaca r. Canada 102 52.20N 78.00W
Opinnagau r. Canada 102 54.12N 82.21W
Opiscotéo, Lac l. Canada 103 53.10N 68.10W
Opochka Russian Fed. 44 56.41N 28.42E
Opole Poland 37 50.40N 17.56E
Oporto see Porto Portugal 26
Opotiki New Zealand 86 38.00S177.18E
Opp U.S.A. 113 31.16N 86.18W
Oppdal Norway 40 62.36N 9.41E
Oppido Mamertina Italy 33 38.16N 16.00E
Oppland d. Norway 41 61.30N 9.00E
Opportunity U.S.A. 108 47.39N117.15W
Opunake New Zealand 86 39.27S173.51E
Ora Italy 30 46.21N 11.18E
Ora Banda Australia 89 30.27S121.04E
Oradea Romania 37 47.03N 21.55E
Öraefajökull mtn. Iceland 40 64.02N 16.39W
Orahovica Croatia 31 45.31N 17.53E
Orai India 63 25.59N 79.28E
Oran Algeria 74 35.42N 0.38W
Orán Argentina 124 23.07S 64.16W
Orange Australia 93 33.19S149.10E
Orange France 21 44.08N 4.48E
Orange r. R.S.A. 80 28.38S 16.38E
Orange Mass. U.S.A. 115 42.35N 72.19W
Orange N.J. U.S.A. 115 40.46N 74.14W
Orange Tex. U.S.A. 111 30.01N 93.44W
Orange, C. Brazil 123 4.25N 51.32W
Orangeburg U.S.A. 113 33.28N 80.53W
Orange Free State d. R.S.A. 80 28.00S 28.00E
Orangevale U.S.A. 108 38.41N121.13W
Orangeville Canada 104 43.55N 80.06W
Oranienburg Germany 38 52.45N 13.14E
Oranjefontein R.S.A. 80 23.27S 27.40E
Oranjemund Namibia 80 28.35S 16.26E
Or 'Aqiva Israel 67 32.30N 34.55E
Orarak Sudan 73 6.15N 32.23E
Oras Phil. 59 12.09N125.22E
Orbe Switz. 39 46.43N 6.32E
Orbetello Italy 30 42.27N 11.13E
Orbieu r. France 20 43.14N 2.54E
Orbigo r. Spain 26 41.58N 5.40W
Orbisonia U.S.A. 114 40.15N 77.54W
Orbost Australia 93 37.42S148.30E
Örbyhus Sweden 41 60.14N 17.42E
Orcera Spain 26 38.19N 2.39W
Orchies France 19 50.28N 3.14E
Orchila i. Venezuela 117 11.52N 66.10W
Orco r. Italy 30 45.10N 7.52E
Ord r. Australia 88 15.30S128.30E
Ordenes Spain 26 43.04N 8.24W
Ordu Turkey 64 41.00N 37.52E
Orduña Spain 26 42.58N 2.58W
Örebro Sweden 43 59.17N 15.13E
Örebro d. Sweden 43 59.30N 15.00E
Oregon d. U.S.A. 108 43.49N120.36W
Oregon City U.S.A. 108 45.21N122.36W
Öregrund Sweden 41 60.20N 18.26E
Orekhovo-Zuyevo Russian Fed. 44 55.47N 39.00E
Orel Russian Fed. 44 52.58N 36.04E
Orellana, Embalse de resr. Spain 27 39.00N 5.25W
Orem U.S.A. 108 40.19N111.42W
Orenburg Russian Fed. 44 51.50N 55.00E
Orense Spain 26 42.20N 7.51W
Orense d. Spain 26 42.15N 7.40W
Oressa r. Belorussia 37 52.33N 28.45E
Orestiás Greece 34 41.30N 26.31E
Orfanoú, Kólpos g. Greece 34 40.33N 24.00E
Orford U.S.A. 105 43.54N 72.10W
Orford, Mt. Canada 105 45.18N 72.08W
Orford Ness c. Australia 90 11.22S142.50E
Orford Ness c. U.K. 13 52.05N 1.36E
Orgaz Spain 27 39.39N 3.54W
Orgelet France 19 46.31N 5.37E
Orgeyev Moldavia 37 47.24N 28.50E
Orgūn Afghan. 62 32.55N 69.10E
Orick U.S.A. 108 41.17N124.04W
Oriental, Cordillera mts. Bolivia 124 17.00S 65.00W
Oriental, Cordillera mts. Colombia 122 5.00N 74.30W
Origny France 19 49.54N 3.30E
Orihuela Spain 25 38.05N 0.57W
Orillia Canada 104 44.37N 79.25W
Orimattila Finland 41 60.48N 25.45E
Orinduik Guyana 122 4.42N 60.01W
Orinoco r. Venezuela 122 9.00N 61.30W
Orinoco, Delta del f. Venezuela 122 9.00N 61.00W
Orissa d. India 63 20.20N 84.00E
Oristano Italy 32 39.54N 8.35E
Oristano, Golfo di g. Italy 32 39.50N 8.30E
Orizaba Mexico 116 18.51N 97.08W
Ørje Norway 42 59.29N 11.39E
Orjen mtn. Yugo. 31 42.30N 18.38E
Orjiva Spain 27 36.53N 3.24W
Orkanger Norway 40 63.17N 9.52E
Orkney Is. d. U.K. 14 59.00N 3.00W
Orlândia Brazil 126 20.55S 47.54W
Orlando U.S.A. 113 28.33N 81.21W
Orléans Canada 105 45.28N 75.31W
Orléans France 19 47.55N 1.54E
Orleans Mass. U.S.A. 115 41.47N 70.00W
Orleans N.H. U.S.A. 105 44.49N 72.12W
Orléans, Canal d' France 19 47.54N 1.55E
Ormāra Pakistan 62 25.12N 64.38E
Ormāra, Rās c. Pakistan 62 25.09N 64.35E
Ormilia Greece 34 40.16N 23.33E
Ormoc Phil. 59 11.00N124.37E
Ormond New Zealand 86 38.35S177.58E
Ormond Beach town U.S.A. 113 29.26N 81.03W
Ormož Slovenia 31 46.25N 16.09E
Ormskirk U.K. 12 53.35N 2.53W
Ormstown Canada 105 45.08N 74.00W
Ornans France 19 47.06N 6.09E
Orne d. France 18 48.40N 0.05E
Orne r. France 18 49.17N 0.11W
Ornö i. Sweden 43 59.04N 18.24E
Örnsköldsvik Sweden 40 63.17N 18.50E
Orobie, Alpi mts. Italy 30 46.03N 10.00E
Orocué Colombia 122 4.48N 71.20W
Orodara Burkina 76 11.00N 4.54W
Orogrande U.S.A. 109 32.23N106.28W
Orohena mtn. Tahiti 85 17.37S149.28W
Oromocto Canada 103 45.51N 66.29W
Oron Israel 66 30.55N 35.01E
Oron Nigeria 77 4.49N 8.15E
Orona i. Kiribati 84 4.29S172.10W
Orono Canada 104 43.59N 78.37W
Orono U.S.A. 112 44.53N 68.40W
Orosei Italy 32 40.23N 9.42E
Orosei, Golfo di g. Italy 32 40.10N 9.50E
Orosháza Hungary 37 46.34N 20.40E
Orote Pen. Guam 84 13.26N144.38E
Orotukan Russian Fed. 51 62.16N151.43E
Oroville Calif. U.S.A. 108 39.31N121.33W
Oroville Wash. U.S.A. 108 48.56N119.26W
Orrefors Sweden 43 56.50N 15.45E
Orroroo Australia 92 32.46S138.39E
Orrville U.S.A. 114 40.50N 81.46W
Orsa Sweden 41 61.07N 14.37E
Orsha Belorussia 44 54.30N 30.23E
Orsières Switz. 39 46.02N 7.09E
Orsk Russian Fed. 44 51.13N 58.35E
Orşova Romania 37 44.42N 22.22E
Ortaklar Turkey 35 37.53N 27.30E
Orta Nova Italy 33 41.19N 15.42E
Ortegal, Cabo c. Spain 26 43.45N 7.53W
Orthez France 20 43.29N 0.46W
Ortigueira Spain 26 43.41N 7.51W
Ortigueira, Ría de est. Spain 26 43.45N 7.50W
Ortisei Italy 30 46.34N 11.40E
Ortona Italy 31 42.21N 14.24E
Ortonville U.S.A. 110 45.18N 96.28W
Orūmīyeh Iran 65 37.32N 45.02E
Oruro Bolivia 124 17.59S 67.09W
Oruro d. Bolivia 124 18.00S 72.30W
Orust i. Sweden 42 58.10N 11.38E
Orūzgān Afghan. 62 32.56N 66.38E
Orūzgān d. Afghan. 62 33.40N 66.00E
Orvieto Italy 30 42.43N 12.07E
Orwell U.S.A. 114 41.32N 80.52W
Oryakhovo Bulgaria 34 43.40N 23.57E
Or Yehuda Israel 67 32.01N 34.51E
Orzinuovi Italy 30 45.24N 9.55E
Os Norway 40 62.31N 11.11E
Osa, Península de pen. Costa Rica 117 8.20N 83.30W
Osage Iowa U.S.A. 110 43.17N 92.49W
Osage r. U.S.A. 107 38.35N 91.57W
Osage Wyo. U.S.A. 108 43.59N104.25W
Ōsaka Japan 57 34.40N135.30E
Ōsaka d. Japan 57 34.24N135.25E
Ōsaka-wan b. Japan 57 34.30N135.18E
Osborne U.S.A. 110 39.26N 98.42W
Osby Sweden 43 56.22N 13.59E
Osceola Iowa U.S.A. 110 41.02N 93.46W
Osceola Mo. U.S.A. 111 38.03N 93.42W
Osceola Mills U.S.A. 114 40.51N 78.16W
Oschatz Germany 38 51.18N 13.07E
Oschersleben Germany 38 52.01N 11.13E
Oscoda U.S.A. 104 44.26N 83.20W
Osečina Yugo. 31 44.23N 19.36E

Osen Norway **40** 64.18N 10.32E
Osh Kyrgyzstan **50** 40.37N 72.49E
Oshawa Canada **104** 43.54N 78.51W
Ō shima *i.* Hokkaido Japan **57** 41.40N139.40E
Ō shima *i.* Tosan Japan **57** 34.43N139.24E
Oshkosh Nebr. U.S.A. **110** 41.24N102.21W
Oshmyany Belorussia **37** 54.22N 25.52E
Oshnovīyeh Iran **65** 37.03N 45.05E
Oshogbo Nigeria **77** 7.50N 4.35E
Oshtorān, Kūh *mtn.* Iran **65** 33.18N 49.15E
Oshvor Russian Fed. **44** 66.59N 62.59E
Oshwe Zaïre **78** 3.27S 19.32E
Osiān India **62** 26.43N 72.55E
Osijek Croatia **31** 45.33N 18.41E
Osilo Italy **32** 40.44N 8.39E
Osimo Italy **31** 43.29N 13.29E
Osipovichi Belorussia **37** 53.19N 28.36E
Oskaloosa U.S.A. **110** 41.18N 92.39W
Oskarshamn Sweden **43** 57.16N 16.26E
Oskarström Sweden **43** 56.48N 12.58E
Oskol *r.* Ukraine **45** 49.08N 37.10E
Oslo Norway **42** 59.55N 10.45E
Oslofjorden *est.* Norway **42** 59.20N 10.35E
Osmancik Turkey **64** 40.58N 34.50E
Osmaniye Turkey **64** 37.04N 36.15E
Ösmo Sweden **43** 58.59N 17.54E
Osnabrück Germany **38** 52.16N 8.02E
Osogovska Planina *mts.* Macedonia **34** 42.08N 22.18E
Osorno Chile **125** 40.35S 73.14W
Osorno Spain **26** 42.24N 4.22W
Osöyra Norway **42** 60.11N 5.28E
Osprey Reef Australia **90** 13.55S146.38E
Oss Neth. **16** 51.46N 5.31E
Ossa *mtn.* Greece **34** 39.47N 22.42E
Ossa, Mt. Australia **91** 41.52S146.04E
Ossabaw I. U.S.A. **113** 31.47N 81.06W
Osse *r.* France **20** 44.07N 0.17E
Osse *r.* Nigeria **77** 5.55N 5.15E
Ossineke U.S.A. **104** 44.54N 83.27W
Ossining U.S.A. **115** 41.10N 73.52W
Ossokmanuan L. Canada **103** 53.25N 65.00W
Ostaboningue, L. Canada **104** 47.09N 78.53W
Ostashkov Russian Fed. **44** 57.09N 33.10E
Oste *r.* Germany **38** 53.33N 9.10E
Ostend *see* Oostende Belgium **16**
Oster Ukraine **37** 50.55N 30.53E
Oster *r.* Ukraine **37** 53.47N 31.46E
Osterburg Germany **38** 52.47N 11.44E
Österbybruk Sweden **43** 60.12N 17.54E
Österbymo Sweden **43** 57.50N 15.16E
Österdal *r.* Sweden **41** 61.03N 14.30E
Österdalen *f.* Norway **41** 61.15N 11.10E
Östergötland *d.* Sweden **43** 58.20N 16.00E
Östergötland *f.* Sweden **43** 58.17N 15.40E
Osterholz-Scharmbeck Germany **38** 53.14N 8.47E
Österö *i.* Faroe Is. **10** 62.16N 6.54W
Osterode Germany **38** 51.43N 10.14E
Osteröy *i.* Norway **41** 60.33N 5.35E
Östersund Sweden **40** 63.10N 14.40E
Östervåla Sweden **43** 60.11N 17.11E
Osterwieck Germany **38** 51.58N 10.42E
Østfold *d.* Norway **42** 59.20N 11.25E
Ostfriesische Inseln *is.* Germany **38** 53.44N 7.25E
Östhammar Sweden **41** 60.16N 18.22E
Ostia Italy **32** 41.44N 12.14E
Östmark Sweden **43** 60.17N 12.45E
Ostrava Czech Republic **37** 49.50N 18.15E
Ostróda Poland **37** 53.43N 19.59E
Ostrog Ukraine **37** 50.20N 26.29E
Ostrołeka Poland **37** 53.06N 21.34E
Ostrov Czech Republic **39** 50.17N 12.57E
Ostrov Russian Fed. **44** 57.22N 28.22E
Ostrowiec-Świetokrzyski Poland **37** 50.57N 21.23E
Ostrów Mazowiecka Poland **37** 52.50N 21.51E
Ostrów Wielkopolski Poland **37** 51.39N 17.49E
Ostuni Italy **33** 40.44N 17.35E
Osum *r.* Albania **34** 40.40N 20.10E
Osŭm *r.* Bulgaria **29** 43.41N 24.51E
Ōsumi kaikyō *str.* Japan **57** 31.30N131.00E
Ōsumi shotō *is.* Japan **53** 30.30N131.00E
Osun *d.* Nigeria **77** 7.15N 4.30E
Osuna Spain **27** 37.14N 5.07W
Oswego U.S.A. **115** 43.27N 76.31W
Oswestry U.K. **12** 52.52N 3.03W
Otago *d.* New Zealand **86** 45.10S169.20E
Otago Pen. New Zealand **86** 45.48S170.45E
Otaki New Zealand **86** 40.45S175.08E
Otaru Japan **57** 43.14N140.59E
Otavalo Ecuador **122** 0.14N 78.16W
Otavi Namibia **80** 19.37S 17.21E
Ōtawara Japan **57** 36.52N140.02E
Otelec Romania **37** 45.36N 20.50E
Otematata New Zealand **86** 44.37S170.11E
Othonoí *i.* Greece **33** 39.50N 19.26E
Óthris, Óros *mtn.* Greece **35** 39.04N 22.42E
Oti *r.* Ghana **76** 8.43N 0.10E
Otira New Zealand **86** 42.51S171.33E
Otish, Monts *mts.* Canada **103** 52.22N 70.30W
Otisville U.S.A. **115** 41.28N 74.32W
Otiwarongo Namibia **80** 20.30S 16.39E
Otjiwero Namibia **80** 17.59S 13.22E
Otju Namibia **80** 18.15S 13.18E
Otočac Croatia **31** 44.52N 15.14E
Otog Qi China **54** 39.05N107.59E
Otosquen Canada **101** 53.17N102.01W
Otra *r.* Norway **42** 58.09N 8.00E
Otradnyy Russian Fed. **44** 53.26N 51.30E
Otranto Italy **33** 40.09N 18.30E
Otranto, Str. of Med. Sea **33** 40.00N 19.00E
Otrokovice Czech Republic **37** 49.13N 17.31E
Otsego U.S.A. **112** 42.26N 85.42W
Otsego L. U.S.A. **115** 42.45N 74.52W
Otsego Lake *town* U.S.A. **104** 44.55N 84.41W
Ōtsu Japan **57** 35.02N135.52E
Ōtsuki Japan **57** 35.36N138.57E
Otta Norway **41** 61.46N 9.32E
Ottawa Canada **105** 45.25N 75.42W
Ottawa *r.* Canada **105** 45.20N 73.58W
Ottawa Ill. U.S.A. **110** 41.21N 88.51W
Ottawa Kans. U.S.A. **110** 38.37N 95.16W
Ottawa Is. Canada **99** 59.50N 80.00W
Ottenby Sweden **43** 56.14N 16.25E
Otter *r.* U.K. **13** 50.38N 3.19W
Otterbäcken Sweden **43** 58.57N 14.02E
Otterburn U.K. **12** 55.14N 2.10W
Otter Creek *r.* U.S.A. **105** 44.13N 73.17W
Otter L. Canada **101** 55.35N104.39W
Otter Lake *town* Canada **105** 45.51N 76.26W
Otterndorf Germany **38** 53.48N 8.53E
Otteröy *i.* Norway **40** 62.45N 6.50E
Otterup Denmark **42** 55.31N 10.24E
Ottosdal R.S.A. **80** 26.48S 26.00E
Ottumwa U.S.A. **110** 41.01N 92.25W
Oturkpo Nigeria **77** 7.13N 8.10E
Otway, C. Australia **92** 38.51S143.34E
Ötztaler Alpen *mts.* Austria / Italy **30** 46.52N 10.50E
Ou *r.* Laos **56** 20.03N102.19E
Ouachita *r.* U.S.A. **111** 31.38N 91.49W
Ouachita, L. U.S.A. **111** 34.40N 93.25W
Ouachita Mts. U.S.A. **111** 34.40N 94.25W
Ouada, Djebel *mtn.* C.A.R. **73** 8.56N 23.26E
Ouadane Mauritania **74** 20.56N 11.37W
Ouadda C.A.R. **73** 8.04N 22.24E
Ouaddaï *d.* Chad **73** 13.00N 21.00E
Ouagadougou Burkina **76** 12.20N 1.40W
Ouahigouya Burkina **76** 13.31N 2.21W
Ouaka *d.* C.A.R. **73** 6.00N 21.00E
Oualâta Mauritania **74** 17.18N 7.02W
Ouallam Niger **77** 14.23N 2.09E
Ouallene Algeria **74** 24.35N 1.17E
Ouanda Djallé C.A.R. **73** 8.54N 22.48E
Ouarane *f.* Mauritania **74** 21.00N 9.30W
Ouararda, Passe de *pass* Mauritania **74** 21.01N 13.03W
Ouareau *r.* Canada **105** 45.56N 73.25W
Ouargla Algeria **75** 31.57N 5.20E
Ouarra *r.* C.A.R. **73** 5.05N 24.26E
Ouarzazate Morocco **74** 30.57N 6.50W
Ouassouas *well* Mali **74** 16.01N 1.26E
Ouche *r.* France **19** 47.06N 5.16E
Ouddorp Neth. **16** 51.49N 3.57E
Oudenaarde Belgium **16** 50.50N 3.37E
Oudenbosch Neth. **16** 51.35N 4.30E
Oude Rijn *r.* Neth. **16** 52.14N 4.26E
Oudon *r.* France **18** 47.47N 1.02W
Oudtshoorn R.S.A. **80** 33.35S 22.11E
Oued Zarga Tunisia **32** 36.40N 9.25E
Oued-Zem Morocco **74** 32.55N 6.30W
Ouellé Ivory Coast **76** 7.26N 4.01W
Ouenza Algeria **75** 35.57N 8.07E
Ouessant, Île d' *i.* France **18** 48.28N 5.05W
Ouesso Congo **78** 1.38N 16.03E
Ouezzane Morocco **74** 34.52N 5.35W
Oughter, Lough Rep. of Ire. **15** 54.01N 7.28W
Ouham *r.* Chad **77** 9.15N 18.13E
Ouimet Canada **102** 48.43N 88.35W
Ouistreham France **18** 49.17N 0.15W
Oujda Morocco **74** 34.41N 1.45W
Oulu Finland **40** 65.01N 25.28E
Oulu *d.* Finland **40** 65.00N 27.00E
Oulu *r.* Finland **40** 65.01N 25.25E
Oulujärvi *l.* Finland **40** 64.20N 27.15E
Oum Chalouba Chad **75** 15.48N 20.46E
Oumé Ivory Coast **76** 6.25N 5.23W
Oum er Rbia, Oued *r.* Morocco **74** 33.19N 8.21W
Oumm ed Droûs Guebli, Sebkhet *f.* Mauritania **74** 24.03N 11.45W
Oumm ed Droûs Telli, Sebkhet *f.* Mauritania **74** 24.20N 11.30W
Ounas *r.* Finland **40** 66.30N 25.45E
Oundle U.K. **13** 52.28N 0.28W
Ounianga Kébir Chad **75** 19.04N 20.29E
Our *r.* Lux. **16** 49.53N 6.16E
Ouray U.S.A. **108** 40.06N109.40W
Ourcq *r.* France **19** 49.01N 3.01E
Ourense *see* Orense Spain **26**
Ouri Chad **75** 21.34N 19.13E
Ourinhos Brazil **126** 23.00S 49.54W
Ourique Portugal **26** 37.39N 8.13W
Ouro Fino Brazil **126** 22.16S 46.25W
Ouro Prêto Brazil **126** 20.54S 43.30W
Ourthe *r.* Belgium **16** 50.38N 5.36E
Ouse *r.* Humber. U.K. **12** 53.41N 0.42W
Oust *r.* France **18** 47.39N 2.06W
Outardes, Rivière aux *r.* Canada **103** 49.04N 68.25W
Outer Hebrides *is.* U.K. **14** 57.40N 7.35W
Outjo Namibia **80** 20.07S 16.10E
Outlook U.S.A. **108** 48.53N104.47W
Ouvèze *r.* France **21** 43.59N 4.51E
Ouyen Australia **92** 35.06S142.22E
Ouzouer-le-Marché France **19** 47.55N 1.32E
Ouzzal, Oued I-n- *wadi* Algeria **75** 20.54N 2.28E
Ovalle Chile **124** 30.36S 71.12W
Ovamboland *f.* Namibia **80** 17.45S 16.00E
Ovar Portugal **26** 40.52N 8.38W
Ovens *r.* Australia **93** 36.20S146.18E
Overath Germany **16** 50.56N 7.18E
Overflakkee *i.* Neth. **16** 51.45N 4.08E
Overijssel *d.* Neth. **16** 52.25N 6.30E
Överkalix Sweden **40** 66.21N 22.56E
Overland Park *town* U.S.A. **110** 38.59N 94.40W
Overton U.S.A. **109** 36.33N114.27W
Övertorneå Sweden **40** 66.23N 23.40E
Överum Sweden **43** 57.59N 16.19E
Ovid Mich. U.S.A. **104** 43.01N 84.22W
Ovid N.Y. U.S.A. **114** 42.41N 76.49W
Ovidiopol Ukraine **37** 46.18N 30.28E
Oviedo Spain **26** 43.22N 5.50W
Ovinishche Russian Fed. **44** 58.20N 37.00E
Övörhangay *d.* Mongolia **54** 45.00N103.00E
Ovruch Ukraine **37** 51.20N 28.50E
Owaka New Zealand **86** 46.27S169.40E
Owando Congo **78** 0.30S 15.48E
Owase Japan **57** 34.04N136.12E
Owatonna U.S.A. **110** 44.06N 93.10W
Owbeh Afghan. **62** 34.22N 63.10E
Owego U.S.A. **115** 42.06N 76.16W
Owel, Lough Rep. of Ire. **15** 53.34N 7.24W
Owen Channel Canada **104** 45.31N 81.48W
Owen Falls Dam Uganda **79** 0.30N 33.07E
Owensboro U.S.A. **113** 37.46N 87.07W
Owen Sd. *b.* Canada **104** 44.40N 80.55W
Owens L. U.S.A. **109** 36.25N117.56W
Owen Sound *town* Canada **104** 44.34N 80.56W
Owen Stanley Range *mts.* P.N.G. **90** 9.30S148.00E
Owerri Nigeria **77** 5.29N 7.02E
Owl *r.* Canada **101** 57.51N 92.44W
Owo Nigeria **77** 7.10N 5.39E
Owosso U.S.A. **104** 43.00N 84.10W
Owyhee *r.* U.S.A. **108** 43.46N117.02W
Oxelösund Sweden **43** 58.40N 17.06E
Oxford U.K. **13** 51.45N 1.15W
Oxford Md. U.S.A. **115** 38.42N 76.10W
Oxford Mich. U.S.A. **104** 42.49N 83.16W
Oxford Penn. U.S.A. **115** 39.47N 75.59W
Oxfordshire *d.* U.K. **13** 51.46N 1.10W
Oxley Australia **92** 34.11S144.10E
Oxnard U.S.A. **109** 34.12N119.11W
Oxtongue Lake *town* Canada **104** 45.22N 78.55W
Oyapock *r.* Guiana **123** 4.10N 51.40W
Oyem Gabon **78** 1.34N 11.31E
Oyen Canada **101** 51.22N110.28W
Öyer Norway **41** 61.12N 10.22E
Öyeren *l.* Norway **42** 59.48N 11.14E
Oykel *r.* U.K. **14** 57.53N 4.21W
Oymyakon Russian Fed. **51** 63.30N142.44E
Oyo Nigeria **77** 7.50N 3.55E
Oyo *d.* Nigeria **77** 8.10N 3.40E
Oyonnax France **21** 46.15N 5.40E
Ozamiz Phil. **59** 8.09N123.59E
Ozarichi Belorussia **37** 52.28N 29.12E
Ozark Ala. U.S.A. **113** 31.27N 85.40W
Ozark Ark. U.S.A. **111** 35.29N 93.50W
Ozark Mo. U.S.A. **111** 37.01N 93.12W
Ozark Plateau U.S.A. **111** 37.00N 93.00W
Ózd Hungary **37** 48.14N 20.18E
Ozernoye Russian Fed. **44** 51.45N 51.29E
Ozersk Russian Fed. **37** 54.26N 22.00E
Ozieri Italy **32** 40.35N 9.00E
Ozinki Russian Fed. **45** 51.11N 49.43E
Ozona U.S.A. **111** 30.43N101.12W

P

Paamiut *see* Frederikshåb Greenland **99**
Pa-an Burma **56** 16.51N 97.37E
Paarl R.S.A. **80** 33.44S 18.58E
Pabianice Poland **37** 51.40N 19.22E
Pābna Bangla. **63** 24.00N 89.15E
Pacaraima, Sierra *mts.* Venezuela **122** 4.00N 62.30W
Pacasmayo Peru **122** 7.27S 79.33W
Pachino Italy **33** 36.42N 15.06E
Pachmarhi India **63** 22.28N 78.26E
Pāchora India **62** 20.40N 75.21E
Pachuca Mexico **116** 20.10N 98.44W
Pacific-Antarctic Basin Pacific Oc. **85** 58.00S 98.00W
Pacific-Antarctic Ridge Pacific Oc. **85** 57.00S145.00W
Pacific Ocean 85
Pacitan Indonesia **59** 8.12S111.05E
Packsaddle Australia **92** 30.28S141.28E
Packwood U.S.A. **108** 46.36N121.40W
Pacy-sur-Eure France **18** 49.01N 1.23E
Padam Jammu & Kashmir **62** 33.28N 76.53E
Padampur India **63** 20.59N 83.04E
Padang Indonesia **58** 0.55S100.21E
Padangpanjang Indonesia **58** 0.30S100.26E
Padangsidempuan Indonesia **58** 1.20N 99.11E
Padany Russian Fed. **44** 63.12N 33.20E
Padauari *r.* Brazil **122** 0.15S 64.05W
Paden City U.S.A. **114** 39.36N 80.56W
Paderborn Germany **38** 51.43N 8.45E
Padilla Bolivia **124** 19.19S 64.20W
Padlei Canada **101** 62.10N 97.05W
Padloping Island *town* Canada **99** 67.00N 62.50W
Padova Italy **32** 45.25N 11.53E
Pādra India **62** 22.14N 73.05E
Padrauna India **63** 26.55N 83.59E
Padre I. U.S.A. **111** 27.00N 97.15W
Padrón Spain **26** 42.44N 8.40W
Padstow U.K. **13** 50.33N 4.57W
Padthaway Australia **92** 36.37S140.28E
Padua *see* Padova Italy **32**
Paducah U.S.A. **111** 37.05N 88.36W
Paeroa New Zealand **86** 37.23S175.41E
Paestum *site* Italy **33** 40.25N 15.00E
Pafúri Mozambique **81** 22.27S 31.21E
Pag Croatia **31** 44.27N 15.04E
Pag *i.* Croatia **31** 44.30N 15.00E
Pagadian Phil. **59** 7.50N123.30E
Pagai Selatan *i.* Indonesia **58** 3.00S100.18E
Pagai Utara *i.* Indonesia **58** 2.42S100.05E
Pagan Burma **56** 21.07N 94.53E
Pagasitikós Kólpos *b.* Greece **35** 39.15N 23.12E
Page U.S.A. **108** 36.57N111.27W
Pager *r.* Uganda **79** 3.05N 32.28E
Paget Canada **104** 46.18N 80.48W
Paghmān Afghan. **62** 34.36N 68.57E
Pago Pago Samoa **84** 14.16S170.42W
Pagosa Springs *town* U.S.A. **108** 37.16N107.01W
Pagri China **63** 27.45N 89.10E
Paguchi L. Canada **102** 49.38N 91.40W
Pagwa River *town* Canada **102** 50.02N 85.14W
Pahala Hawaii U.S.A. **106** 19.12N155.28W
Pahiatua New Zealand **86** 40.26S175.49E
Paible U.K. **14** 57.35N 7.27W
Paide Estonia **41** 58.54N 25.33E
Paihia New Zealand **86** 35.16S174.05E
Päijänne *l.* Finland **41** 61.35N 25.30E
Paikü Co *l.* China **63** 28.48N 85.36E
Paimboeuf France **18** 47.17N 2.02W
Paimpol France **18** 48.46N 3.03W
Painan Indonesia **58** 1.21S100.34E
Painesville U.S.A. **114** 41.43N 81.15W
Pains Brazil **126** 20.23S 45.38W
Paintsville U.S.A. **113** 37.49N 82.48W
Paisley Canada **104** 44.18N 81.16W
Paisley U.K. **14** 55.50N 4.26W
País Vasco *d.* Spain **26** 43.00N 2.25W
Paiton Indonesia **59** 7.42S113.30E
Pajala Sweden **40** 67.11N 23.22E
Pajares, Puerto de *pass* Spain **26** 43.00N 5.46W
Pajule Uganda **79** 2.58N 32.53E
Pakaraima Mts. Guyana **122** 5.00N 60.00W
Pakaur India **63** 24.38N 87.51E
Pakenham Canada **105** 45.20N 76.17W
Paki Nigeria **77** 11.33N 8.08E
Pakistan Asia **62** 29.00N 67.00E
Pakokku Burma **56** 21.20N 95.10E
Pākpattan Pakistan **62** 30.21N 73.24E
Paks Hungary **31** 46.39N 18.53E
Paktīā *d.* Afghan. **62** 33.25N 69.30E
Pakwach Uganda **79** 2.27N 31.18E
Pakxé Laos **56** 15.07N105.47E
Pala Chad **77** 9.25N 15.05E
Palagonia Italy **33** 37.19N 14.45E
Palaiá Epídhavros Greece **35** 37.38N 23.09E
Palaia Kórinthos *site* Greece **35** 37.54N 22.56E
Palaiá Psará Greece **35** 38.46N 25.36E
Palaiokhóra Greece **35** 35.14N 23.41E
Pálairos Greece **35** 38.45N 20.51E
Palaiseau France **19** 48.43N 2.15E
Palamás Greece **34** 39.26N 22.04E
Palamós Spain **25** 41.51N 3.08E
Palana Russian Fed. **51** 59.05N159.59E
Palangkaraya Indonesia **58** 2.16S113.56E
Palanguinos Spain **24** 42.27N 5.31W
Pālanpur India **62** 24.10N 72.26E
Palanquinos Spain **26** 42.27N 5.30W
Palapye Botswana **80** 22.33S 27.07E
Palas del Rey Spain **26** 42.52N 7.52W
Palatka U.S.A. **113** 29.38N 81.40W
Palau *is.* Pacific Oc. **59** 7.00N134.25E
Palaw Burma **56** 12.58N 98.39E
Palawan *i.* Phil. **58** 9.30N118.30E
Palazzolo Acreide Italy **33** 37.03N 14.54E
Palazzo San Gervasio Italy **33** 40.56N 16.00E
Paldiski Estonia **41** 59.20N 24.06E
Paleleh Indonesia **59** 1.04N121.57E
Palembang Indonesia **58** 2.59S104.50E
Palena Italy **33** 41.59N 14.08E
Palencia Spain **26** 42.01N 4.32W
Palencia *d.* Spain **26** 42.30N 4.40W
Palenque Mexico **116** 17.32N 91.59W
Palermo Italy **32** 38.07N 13.21E
Palermo, Golfo di *g.* Italy **32** 38.10N 13.30E
Palestine U.S.A. **111** 31.46N 95.38W
Palestrina Italy **32** 41.50N 12.53E
Paletwa Burma **56** 21.25N 92.49E
Pāli India **62** 25.46N 73.20E
Palimé Togo **76** 6.55N 0.38E
Palinges France **19** 46.33N 4.13E
Palisades Resr. U.S.A. **108** 43.15N111.05W
Pālitāna India **62** 21.31N 71.50E
Palizada Mexico **116** 18.15N 92.05W
Palk Str. India / Sri Lanka **61** 10.00N 79.40E
Pallës, Bishti i *c.* Albania **34** 41.24N 19.24E
Pallinup *r.* Australia **89** 34.29S118.54E
Palliser, C. New Zealand **86** 41.35S175.15E
Pallu India **62** 28.56N 74.13E
Palma Mozambique **79** 10.48S 40.25E
Palma Spain **25** 39.33N 2.39E
Palma, Bahía de *b.* Spain **25** 39.27N 2.35E
Palma del Río Spain **27** 37.42N 5.17W
Palma di Montechiaro Italy **32** 37.11N 13.46E
Palmahim Israel **67** 31.56N 34.42E
Palmanova Italy **30** 45.54N 13.19E
Palmares Brazil **123** 8.41S 35.36W
Palmas, C. Liberia **76** 4.30N 7.55W
Palmas, Golfo di *g.* Italy **32** 39.00N 8.30E
Palm Beach *town* U.S.A. **113** 26.41N 80.02W
Palmeira dos Indios Brazil **123** 9.25S 36.38W
Palmeirinhas, Punta das Angola **78** 9.09S 12.58E
Palmer *r.* Australia **88** 24.46S133.25E
Palmer U.S.A. **98** 61.36N149.07W
Palmer Land Antarctica **128** 74.00S 61.00W
Palmerston Canada **104** 43.50N 80.51W
Palmerston New Zealand **86** 45.29S170.43E
Palmerston, C. Australia **90** 21.32S149.29E
Palmerston Atoll Cook Is. **84** 18.04S163.10W
Palmerston North New Zealand **86** 40.20S175.39E
Palmerton U.S.A. **115** 40.48N 75.37W
Palmetto U.S.A. **113** 27.31N 82.32W
Palmi Italy **33** 38.21N 15.51E
Palmira Colombia **122** 3.33N 76.17W
Palm Is. Australia **90** 18.48S146.37E
Palms U.S.A. **114** 43.37N 82.46W
Palm Springs *town* U.S.A. **109** 33.50N116.33W
Palmyra I. Pacific Oc. **84** 5.52N162.05W
Palmyras Pt. India **63** 20.46N 87.02E
Paloh Indonesia **58** 1.46N109.17E
Paloich Sudan **73** 10.28N 32.32E
Palojoensuu Finland **40** 68.17N 23.05E
Palomani *mtn.* Bolivia **124** 14.38S 69.14W
Palopo Indonesia **59** 3.01S120.12E
Palos, Cabo de *c.* Spain **25** 37.38N 0.41W
Pålsboda Sweden **43** 59.04N 15.20E
Palu Turkey **64** 38.43N 39.56E

Palwal to **Pendálofon**

Palwal India **62** 28.09N 77.20E
Pama Burkina **76** 11.15N 0.44E
Pamanukan Indonesia **59** 6.16S107.46E
Pamekasan Indonesia **59** 7.11S113.30E
Pameungpeuk Indonesia **59** 7.39S107.40E
Pamiers France **20** 43.07N 1.36E
Pamir *mts.* Tajikistan **52** 37.50N 73.30E
Pamlico Sd. U.S.A. **113** 35.20N 75.55W
Pampa U.S.A. **111** 35.32N100.58W
Pampas *f.* Argentina **125** 34.00S 64.00W
Pamplona Colombia **122** 7.24N 72.38W
Pamplona Spain **25** 42.49N 1.38W
Pana U.S.A. **110** 39.23N 89.05W
Panaca U.S.A. **108** 37.47N114.23W
Panache, L. Canada **104** 46.15N 81.20W
Panagyurishte Bulgaria **34** 42.39N 24.15E
Panaji India **60** 15.29N 73.50E
Panama C. America **117** 9.00N 80.00W
Panamá *town* Panama **117** 8.57N 79.30W
Panama Sri Lanka **61** 6.46N 81.47E
Panamá, Golfo de *g.* Panama **117** 8.30N 79.00W
Panama City U.S.A. **113** 30.10N 85.41W
Panamint Range *mts.* U.S.A. **109** 36.30N117.20W
Panarea, Isola *i.* Italy **33** 38.38N 15.05E
Panaro *r.* Italy **30** 44.55N 11.25E
Panay *i.* Phil. **59** 11.10N122.30E
Panayía Greece **34** 39.56N 25.20E
Pandan Phil. **59** 11.45N122.10E
Pandaria India **63** 22.14N 81.25E
Pandeglang Indonesia **59** 6.19S106.05E
Pāndharkawada India **63** 20.01N 78.32E
Pāndhurna India **63** 21.36N 78.31E
Pando *d.* Bolivia **124** 11.20S 67.40W
Pando Uruguay **125** 34.43S 55.57W
Panevežys Lithuania **41** 55.44N 24.21E
Panfilov Kazakhstan **52** 44.10N 80.01E
Panga Zaïre **78** 1.51N 26.25E
Pangaíon Óros *mts.* Greece **34** 40.50N 24.00E
Pangandaran Indonesia **59** 7.41S108.40E
Pangani Tanga Tanzania **79** 5.21S 39.00E
Pangi Zaïre **78** 3.10S 26.38E
Pangkalpinang Indonesia **58** 2.05S106.09E
Pang Long Burma **61** 23.11N 98.45E
Pangnirtung Canada **99** 66.05N 65.45W
Panīpat India **62** 29.23N 76.58E
Panjāb Afghan. **62** 34.22N 67.01E
Panjgūr Pakistan **62** 26.58N 64.06E
Panjpāi Pakistan **62** 29.55N 66.30E
Pankshin Nigeria **77** 9.22N 9.25E
Panna India **63** 24.43N 80.12E
Pannawonica Australia **88** 21.42S116.22E
Páno Lévkara Cyprus **66** 34.55N 33.10E
Páno Plátres Cyprus **66** 34.53N 32.52E
Pánormos Greece **35** 37.38N 25.02E
Panshan China **54** 41.10N122.01E
Pantano del Esla *l.* Spain **24** 41.40N 5.50W
Pantelleria Italy **32** 36.49N 11.57E
Pantelleria *i.* Italy **32** 36.47N 12.00E
Panton *r.* Australia **88** 17.05S128.46E
Pánuco Mexico **116** 22.03N 98.10W
Panvel India **62** 18.59N 73.06E
Pan Xian China **55** 25.46N104.39E
Panyu China **55** 23.00N113.30E
Paola Italy **33** 39.22N 16.03E
Paola U.S.A. **110** 38.35N 94.53W
Paoua C.A.R. **77** 7.09N 16.20E
Paôy Pêt Thailand **56** 13.41N102.34E
Papa Hawaiian Is. **85** 19.12N155.53W
Pápa Hungary **37** 47.19N 17.28E
Papa Stour *i.* U.K. **10** 60.20N 1.42W
Papa Westray *i.* U.K. **10** 59.22N 2.54W
Papeete Tahiti **85** 17.32S149.34W
Papenburg Germany **38** 53.05N 7.23E
Papenoo Tahiti **85** 17.30S149.25W
Papetoai Îs. de la Société **85** 17.29S149.52W
Paphos *see* Néa Páfos Cyprus **66**
Papigochic *r.* Mexico **109** 29.09N109.40W
Papillion U.S.A. **110** 41.09N 96.04W
Papineau, Lac *l.* Canada **105** 45.48N 74.46W
Papineau Prov. Park Canada **105** 45.55N 75.20W
Papineauville Canada **105** 45.37N 75.01W
Papua, G. of P.N.G. **90** 8.30S145.00E
Papua New Guinea Austa. **87** 6.00S144.00E
Papun Burma **56** 18.05N 97.26E
Papunya Australia **90** 23.15S131.53E
Para *d.* Brazil **123** 4.00S 53.00W
Paraburdoo Australia **88** 23.12S117.40E
Paracatu Brazil **126** 17.14S 46.52W
Paracatu *r.* Brazil **126** 16.30S 45.10W
Paracel Is. S. China Sea **58** 16.20N112.00E
Parachilna Australia **92** 31.09S138.24E
Pārachinār Pakistan **62** 33.54N 70.06E
Paraćin Yugo. **34** 43.52N 21.24E
Pará de Minas Brazil **126** 19.53S 44.35W
Paradip India **63** 20.15N 86.35E
Paradise *r.* Canada **103** 53.23N 57.18W
Paradise Calif. U.S.A. **108** 39.46N121.37W
Paradise Nev. U.S.A. **109** 36.09N115.10W
Paragonah U.S.A. **108** 37.53N112.46W
Paragould U.S.A. **111** 36.03N 90.29W
Paragua *r.* Venezuela **122** 6.55N 62.55W
Paraguaçu *r.* Brazil **123** 12.35S 38.59W
Paraguaná, Península de *pen.* Venezuela **122** 11.50N 69.59W
Paraguarí Paraguay **126** 25.36S 57.06W
Paraguay *r.* Argentina **126** 27.30S 58.50W
Paraguay S. America **126** 23.00S 57.00W
Paraíba *d.* Brazil **123** 7.30S 36.30W
Paraíba *r.* Brazil **126** 21.45S 41.10W
Paraibuna Brazil **126** 23.29S 45.32W
Paraisópolis Brazil **126** 22.33S 45.48W
Parakou Benin **77** 9.23N 2.40E
Parálion Astrous Greece **35** 37.25N 22.45E
Paramagudi India **61** 9.33N 78.36E
Paramaribo Surinam **123** 5.52N 55.14W
Paramithiá Greece **34** 39.30N 20.35E
Paramonga Peru **122** 10.42S 77.50W
Paraná Argentina **125** 31.45S 60.30W
Paraná *r.* Argentina **125** 34.00S 58.30W
Paranã Brazil **123** 12.33S 47.48W
Paraná *d.* Brazil **126** 24.30S 52.00W
Paraná *r.* Brazil **126** 21.30S 52.00W
Paranã *r.* Brazil **123** 12.30S 48.10W
Paranaguá Brazil **126** 25.32S 48.36W
Paranaíba Brazil **126** 19.44S 51.12W
Paranaíba *r.* Brazil **126** 20.00S 51.00W
Paranapanema *r.* Brazil **126** 22.30S 53.03W
Paranapiacaba, Serra *mts.* Brazil **126** 24.30S 49.15W
Paranavaí Brazil **126** 23.02S 52.36W
Paranéstion Greece **34** 41.16N 24.32E
Parangaba Brazil **123** 3.45S 38.33W
Paraparaumu New Zealand **86** 40.55S175.00E
Paratoo Australia **92** 32.46S139.40E
Paray-le-Monial France **19** 46.27N 4.07E
Pārbati *r.* India **62** 25.51N 76.36E
Pārbatipur Bangla. **63** 25.39N 88.55E
Parbhani India **62** 19.16N 76.47E
Parchim Germany **38** 53.25N 11.51E
Parczew Poland **37** 51.39N 22.54E
Pardes Hanna Israel **67** 32.28N 34.58E
Pārdi India **62** 20.31N 72.57E
Pardo *r.* Bahia Brazil **126** 15.40S 39.38W
Pardo *r.* Mato Grosso Brazil **126** 21.56S 52.07W
Pardo *r.* São Paulo Brazil **126** 20.10S 48.36W
Pardubice Czech Republic **36** 50.03N 15.45E
Parecis, Serra dos *mts.* Brazil **122** 13.30S 58.30W
Paredes de Nava Spain **26** 42.09N 4.41W
Pareloup, Lac de *l.* France **20** 44.15N 2.45E
Parent Canada **102** 47.55N 74.35W
Parent, Lac *l.* Canada **102** 48.40N 77.03W
Parentis-en-Born France **20** 44.21N 1.05W
Parepare Indonesia **58** 4.03S119.40E
Párga Greece **35** 39.17N 20.23E
Pargas Finland **41** 60.18N 22.18E
Paria, Golfo de *g.* Venezuela **122** 10.30S 62.00W
Paria, Península de *pen.* Venezuela **122** 10.45N 62.30W
Pariaguán Venezuela **122** 8.51N 64.43W
Pariaman Indonesia **58** 0.36S100.09E
Parichi Belorussia **37** 52.48N 29.25E
Parigi Indonesia **59** 0.49S120.10E
Parika Guyana **122** 6.51N 58.25W
Parima, Sierra *mts.* Venezuela **122** 2.30N 64.00W
Parinari Peru **122** 4.35S 74.25W
Paringa Australia **92** 34.10S140.49E
Parintins Brazil **123** 2.36S 56.44W
Paris Canada **104** 43.12N 80.23W
Paris France **19** 48.52N 2.20E
Paris Kiribati **85** 1.56N157.29W
Paris Ill. U.S.A. **110** 39.35N 87.41W
Paris Ky. U.S.A. **112** 38.13N 84.15W
Paris Tenn. U.S.A. **111** 36.19N 88.20W
Paris Tex. U.S.A. **111** 33.40N 95.33W
Parish U.S.A. **115** 43.24N 76.08W
Parisienne *d.* France **19** 48.30N 2.30E
Parisienne, Île *i.* Canada **104** 46.40N 84.44W
Parkano Finland **41** 62.01N 23.01E
Parkbeg Canada **101** 50.28N106.18W
Parker Ariz. U.S.A. **109** 34.09N114.17W
Parker Penn. U.S.A. **114** 41.06N 79.41W
Parker, C. Canada **99** 75.04N 79.40W
Parker Dam U.S.A. **109** 34.18N114.10W
Parkersburg U.S.A. **114** 39.17N 81.32W
Parkes Australia **93** 33.10S148.13E
Park Falls *town* U.S.A. **110** 45.56N 90.32W
Park Forest *town* U.S.A. **110** 41.35N 87.41W
Parkhill Canada **104** 43.09N 81.41W
Parkland U.S.A. **108** 47.09N122.26W
Park Range *mts.* U.S.A. **108** 40.00N106.30W
Parkton U.S.A. **115** 39.38N 76.40W
Parlākimidi India **63** 18.46N 84.05E
Parma Italy **30** 44.48N 10.20E
Parma *r.* Italy **30** 44.56N 10.26E
Parma U.S.A. **114** 41.22N 81.43W
Parnaguá Brazil **123** 10.17S 44.39W
Parnaíba Brazil **123** 2.58S 41.46W
Parnaíba *r.* Brazil **123** 2.58S 41.47W
Parnassós *mtn.* Greece **35** 38.17N 21.30E
Parndana Australia **92** 35.44S137.14E
Párnis *mtn.* Greece **35** 38.11N 23.42E
Párnon Óros *mts.* Greece **35** 37.18N 22.35E
Pärnu Estonia **41** 58.24N 24.32E
Pärnu *r.* Estonia **41** 58.23N 24.29E
Pārola India **62** 20.53N 75.07E
Paroo *r.* Australia **92** 31.30S143.34E
Páros Greece **35** 37.04N 25.08E
Páros *i.* Greece **35** 37.08N 25.12E
Parrakie Australia **92** 35.18S140.12E
Parral Chile **125** 36.09S 71.50W
Parramatta Australia **93** 33.50S150.57E
Parras Mexico **111** 25.30N102.11W
Parras, Sierra de *mts.* Mexico **111** 25.20N102.10W
Parrett *r.* U.K. **13** 51.10N 3.00W
Parry Canada **101** 49.47N104.41W
Parry, Kap *c.* Greenland **99** 76.50N 71.00W
Parry I. Canada **104** 45.18N 80.10W
Parry Is. Canada **99** 76.00N102.00W
Parry Sound *town* Canada **104** 45.21N 80.02W
Parsad India **62** 24.11N 73.42E
Parsęta *r.* Poland **36** 54.12N 15.33E
Parsnip *r.* Canada **100** 55.10N123.02W
Parsons Kans. U.S.A. **111** 37.20N 95.16W
Parsons W.Va. U.S.A. **114** 39.06N 79.41W
Partanna Italy **32** 37.43N 12.53E
Parthenay France **18** 46.39N 0.15W
Partille Sweden **43** 57.44N 12.07E
Partinico Italy **32** 38.03N 13.07E
Partry Mts. Rep. of Ire. **15** 53.40N 9.30W
Paru *r.* Brazil **123** 1.33S 52.38W
Pārvatipuram India **63** 18.47N 83.26E
Paryang China **63** 30.04N 83.28E
Parys R.S.A. **80** 26.54S 27.26E
Pasadena Calif. U.S.A. **109** 34.09N118.09W
Pasadena Tex. U.S.A. **111** 29.42N 95.13W
Pasaje Ecuador **122** 3.23S 79.50W
Pasawng Burma **56** 18.52N 97.18E
Pasay Phil. **59** 14.33N121.00E
Pascagoula U.S.A. **111** 30.23N 88.31W
Paşcani Romania **37** 47.15N 26.44E
Pasco U.S.A. **108** 46.14N119.06W
Pascoag U.S.A. **115** 41.57N 71.42W
Pascua, Isla de *i.* Pacific Oc. **85** 27.08S109.23W
Pas-de-Calais *d.* France **19** 50.30N 2.20E
Pasewalk Germany **38** 53.30N 14.00E
Pasfield L. Canada **101** 58.25N105.20W
Pasinler Turkey **64** 39.59N 41.41E
Pasir Puteh Malaysia **58** 5.50N102.24E
Påskallavik Sweden **43** 57.10N 16.27E
Pasley, C. Australia **89** 33.55S123.30E
Pašman *i.* Croatia **31** 43.58N 15.21E
Pasmore *r.* Australia **92** 31.07S139.48E
Pasni Pakistan **62** 25.16N 63.28E
Paso de Bermejo *f.* Argentina **121** 32.50S 70.00W
Paso de los Libres *town* Argentina **125** 29.45S 57.05W
Paso de los Toros *town* Uruguay **125** 32.49S 56.31W
Paso Robles U.S.A. **109** 35.38N120.41W
Paso Socompa *f.* Chile **121** 24.27S 68.18W
Paspébiac Canada **103** 48.01N 65.20W
Pasquia Hills Canada **101** 53.13N102.37W
Pasrūr Pakistan **62** 32.16N 74.40E
Passaic U.S.A. **115** 40.51N 74.08W
Passau Germany **39** 48.35N 13.28E
Passero, Capo *c.* Italy **33** 36.40N 15.09E
Passo Fundo Brazil **126** 28.16S 52.20W
Passos Brazil **126** 20.45S 46.38W
Pastaza *r.* Peru **122** 4.50S 76.25W
Pasto Colombia **122** 1.12N 77.17W
Pastrana Spain **26** 40.25N 2.55W
Pasuquin Phil. **55** 18.25N120.37E
Pasuruan Indonesia **59** 7.38S112.54E
Patagonia *f.* Argentina **125** 42.20S 67.00W
Pātan India **62** 23.50N 72.07E
Patchewollock Australia **92** 35.25S142.14E
Patchogue U.S.A. **115** 40.46N 73.00W
Patea New Zealand **86** 39.46S174.29E
Pategi Nigeria **77** 8.44N 5.47E
Pate I. Kenya **79** 2.08S 41.02E
Paterna Spain **25** 39.30N 0.26W
Paternion Austria **39** 46.43N 13.38E
Paternò Italy **33** 37.34N 14.54E
Paterson U.S.A. **115** 40.55N 74.10W
Pathānkot India **62** 32.17N 75.39E
Pathein *see* Bassein Burma **56**
Pathfinder Resr. U.S.A. **108** 42.30N106.50W
Pathiong Sudan **73** 6.46N 30.54E
Pati Indonesia **59** 6.45S111.00E
Patía *r.* Colombia **122** 1.54N 78.30W
Patiāla India **62** 30.19N 76.23E
Pati Pt. Guam **84** 13.36N144.57E
Patkai Hills Burma **56** 26.30N 95.30E
Pátmos *i.* Greece **35** 37.20N 26.33E
Patna India **63** 25.36N 85.07E
Patnāgarh India **63** 20.43N 83.09E
Patos Brazil **123** 6.55S 37.15W
Patos, Lagoa dos *l.* Brazil **126** 31.00S 51.10W
Patos de Minas Brazil **126** 18.35S 46.32W
Patquía Argentina **124** 30.02S 66.55W
Pátrai Greece **35** 38.15N 21.44E
Patraïkós Kólpos *g.* Greece **35** 38.14N 21.15E
Patrasuy Russian Fed. **44** 63.35N 61.50E
Patrickswell Rep. of Ire. **15** 52.36N 8.43W
Pattada Italy **32** 40.35N 9.07E
Pattani Thailand **56** 6.51N101.16E
Pattaya Thailand **56** 12.57N100.53E
Patterson Creek *r.* U.S.A. **114** 39.34N 78.23W
Patti Italy **33** 38.09N 14.58E
Patti, Golfo di *g.* Italy **33** 38.12N 15.05E
Pattoki Pakistan **62** 31.01N 73.51E
Patton U.S.A. **114** 40.38N 78.39W
Patuākhāli Bangla. **63** 22.21N 90.21E
Patuca *r.* Honduras **117** 15.50N 84.18W
Pātūr India **62** 20.27N 76.56E
Patuxent *r.* U.S.A. **115** 38.18N 76.25W
Pau France **20** 43.18N 0.22W
Pau, Gave de *r.* France **20** 43.33N 1.12W
Pauillac France **20** 45.12N 0.44W
Paúl do Mar Madeira Is. **127** 32.45N 17.14W
Paulhan France **20** 43.32N 3.27E
Paulina U.S.A. **108** 44.09N119.58W
Paulistana Brazil **123** 8.09S 41.09W
Paulo Afonso Brazil **123** 9.25S 38.15W
Paulsboro U.S.A. **115** 39.50N 75.15W
Pauls Valley *town* U.S.A. **111** 34.44N 97.13W
Paungde Burma **56** 18.30N 95.30E
Pauni India **63** 20.47N 79.38E
Pauri Madhya P. India **62** 25.32N 77.21E
Pauri Uttar P. India **63** 30.09N 78.47E
Pavia Italy **30** 45.10N 9.10E
Pavilly France **18** 49.34N 0.58E
Pavlikeni Bulgaria **34** 43.14N 25.20E
Pavlodar Kazakhstan **9** 52.21N 76.59E
Pavlograd Ukraine **45** 48.34N 35.50E
Pavlovo Russian Fed. **44** 55.58N 43.05E
Pavlovsk Russian Fed. **45** 50.28N 40.07E
Pavlovskaya Russian Fed. **45** 46.18N 39.48E
Pavullo nel Frignano Italy **30** 44.20N 10.50E
Pawnee U.S.A. **111** 36.20N 96.48W
Pawtucket U.S.A. **115** 41.53N 71.23W
Paxoí *i.* Greece **35** 39.14N 20.12E
Paxton U.S.A. **110** 41.07N101.21W
Payerne Switz. **39** 46.49N 6.56E
Payette U.S.A. **108** 44.05N116.56W
Payne, L. Canada **99** 59.25N 74.00W
Paynes Find Australia **89** 29.15S117.41E
Paysandú Uruguay **125** 32.19S 58.05W
Pays de Caux *f.* France **18** 49.40N 0.40E
Pays de la Loire *d.* France **18** 47.30N 1.00W
Pazardzhik Bulgaria **34** 42.12N 24.20E
Pazin Croatia **31** 45.14N 13.56E
Pčinja *r.* Yugo. **34** 42.00N 21.45E
Peace *r.* Canada **100** 59.00N111.25W
Peace River *town* Canada **100** 56.15N117.18W
Peach Springs *town* U.S.A. **109** 35.32N113.25W
Peacock Hills Canada **98** 66.05N110.45W
Peak, The *mtn.* Ascension **127** 7.57S 14.21W
Peake Creek *r.* Australia **92** 28.05S136.07E
Peak Hill *town* N.S.W. Australia **93** 32.47S148.13E
Peak Range *mts.* Australia **90** 23.18S148.30E
Peale, Mt. U.S.A. **108** 38.26N109.14W
Pearl *r.* U.S.A. **111** 30.11N 89.32W
Pearland U.S.A. **111** 29.34N 95.17W
Pearsall U.S.A. **111** 28.53N 99.06W
Peary Land *f.* Greenland **96** 83.00N 35.00W
Pebane Mozambique **81** 17.14S 38.10E
Pebas Peru **122** 3.17S 71.55W
Peć Yugo. **34** 42.40N 20.17E
Pechenga Russian Fed. **44** 69.28N 31.04E
Pechora Russian Fed. **44** 65.14N 57.18E
Pechora *r.* Russian Fed. **44** 68.10N 54.00E
Pechorskaya Guba *g.* Russian Fed. **44** 69.00N 56.00E
Pechorskoye More *sea* Russian Fed. **44** 69.00N 55.00E
Pecoraro, Monte *mtn.* Italy **33** 38.32N 16.20E
Pecos U.S.A. **111** 31.25N103.30W
Pecos *r.* U.S.A. **111** 29.42N101.22W
Pécs Hungary **31** 46.05N 18.13E
Pécs *d.* Hungary **31** 46.05N 18.10E
Peddie R.S.A. **80** 33.12S 27.07E
Pedras Salgadas Portugal **26** 41.32N 7.36W
Pedregulho Brazil **126** 20.15S 47.29W
Pedreiras Brazil **123** 4.32S 44.40W
Pedrinhas Brazil **123** 11.12S 37.41W
Pedro Afonso Brazil **123** 8.59S 48.11W
Pedro de Valdivia Chile **124** 22.36S 69.40W
Pedrógão Grande Portugal **27** 39.55N 8.09W
Pedro Juan Caballero Paraguay **126** 22.30S 55.44W
Pedro Muñoz Spain **27** 39.24N 2.58W
Peduyim Israel **67** 31.20N 34.37E
Peebinga Australia **92** 34.55S140.57E
Peebles U.K. **14** 55.39N 3.12W
Peebles U.S.A. **112** 38.57N 83.14W
Peekskill U.S.A. **115** 41.17N 73.55W
Peel *r.* Canada **98** 68.13N135.00W
Peel I.o.M. Europe **12** 54.14N 4.42W
Peel Inlet Australia **89** 32.35S115.44E
Peel Pt. Canada **98** 73.22N114.35W
Peene *r.* Germany **38** 54.09N 13.46E
Peera Peera Poolanna L. Australia **90** 26.43S137.42E
Peerless L. Canada **100** 56.37N114.35W
Pegasus B. New Zealand **86** 43.15S173.00E
Pegin Albania **34** 41.04N 19.44E
Pegnitz Germany **38** 49.45N 11.33E
Pegnitz *r.* Germany **38** 49.29N 11.00E
Pego Spain **25** 38.51N 0.07W
Pegu Burma **56** 17.20N 96.36E
Pegu *d.* Burma **56** 17.30N 96.30E
Pegunungan Van Rees *mts.* Indonesia **59** 2.35S138.15E
Pegu Yoma *mts.* Burma **56** 18.30N 96.00E
Pehčevo Macedonia **34** 41.41N 23.03E
Pehuajó Argentina **125** 35.50S 61.50W
Peikang Taiwan **55** 23.35N120.19E
Peine Germany **38** 52.19N 10.13E
Peipus, L. Estonia / Russian Fed. **44** 58.30N 27.30E
Peissenberg Germany **39** 47.48N 11.04E
Peixe Brazil **123** 12.03S 48.32W
Pei Xian China **54** 34.44N116.55E
Pekalongan Indonesia **59** 6.54S109.37E
Pekanbaru Indonesia **58** 0.33N101.20E
Pekin U.S.A. **110** 40.34N 89.40W
Peking *see* Beijing China **54**
Pelabuanratu Indonesia **59** 7.00S106.32E
Pelat, Mont *mtn.* France **21** 44.16N 6.42E
Peleaga *mtn.* Romania **37** 45.22N 22.54E
Pelee, Pt. Canada **114** 41.54N 82.30W
Pelee I. Canada **114** 41.46N 82.39W
Peleng *i.* Indonesia **59** 1.30S123.10E
Peleniya Moldavia **37** 47.58N 27.48E
Pelican U.S.A. **100** 57.55N136.10W
Pelister *mtn.* Macedonia **34** 41.00N 21.12E
Pelješac, Poluotok *pen.* Croatia **31** 42.58N 17.20E
Pelkum Germany **38** 51.39N 7.45E
Pélla *site* Greece **34** 40.45N 22.33E
Pelleg i Drinit *b.* Albania **34** 41.45N 19.28E
Pellegrino, Cozzo *mtn.* Italy **33** 39.45N 16.03E
Pello Finland **40** 66.47N 24.00E
Pellston U.S.A. **104** 45.33N 84.47W
Pellworm *i.* Germany **38** 54.31N 8.38E
Pelly *r.* Canada **98** 62.50N137.35W
Pelly Bay *town* Canada **99** 68.38N 89.45W
Pelly L. Canada **99** 65.59N101.12W
Peloncillo Mts. U.S.A. **109** 32.16N109.00W
Peloponnisos *f.* Greece **35** 37.30N 22.00E
Peloritani, Monti *mts.* Italy **33** 38.00N 15.25E
Pelotas Brazil **126** 31.45S 52.20W
Pelvoux, Massif du *f.* France **21** 44.55N 6.20E
Pemalang Indonesia **59** 6.53S109.21E
Pematangsiantar Indonesia **58** 2.59N 99.01E
Pemba Mozambique **81** 13.02S 40.30E
Pemba Zambia **79** 16.33S 27.20E
Pemba I. Tanzania **79** 5.10S 39.45E
Pemberton Australia **89** 34.28S116.01E
Pemberton Canada **100** 50.20N122.48W
Pembina *r.* Canada **100** 54.45N114.15W
Pembroke Canada **105** 45.49N 77.07W
Pembroke U.K. **13** 51.41N 4.57W
Pembroke U.S.A. **113** 32.09N 81.39W
Peña, Sierra de la *mts.* Spain **25** 42.30N 0.50W
Penacook U.S.A. **115** 43.17N 71.37W
Penafiel Portugal **26** 41.12N 8.17W
Peñafiel Spain **26** 41.36N 4.07W
Peñagolosa *mtn.* Spain **25** 40.13N 0.21W
Peñalara *mtn.* Spain **26** 40.51N 3.57W
Penang *see* Pinang, Pulau *i.* Malaysia **58**
Peñaranda de Bracamonte Spain **26** 40.54N 5.12W
Pen Argyl U.S.A. **115** 40.52N 75.16W
Peñarroya *mtn.* Spain **25** 40.24N 0.40W
Peñarroya-Pueblonuevo Spain **26** 38.18N 5.16W
Penarth U.K. **13** 51.26N 3.11W
Peñas, Cabo de *c.* Spain **26** 43.39N 5.51W
Penas, Golfo de *g.* Chile **125** 47.20S 75.00W
Pendálofon Greece **34** 40.14N 21.12E

Pende to **Pitt I.**

Pende *r.* Chad **77** 7.30N 16.20E
Pendembu Eastern Sierra Leone **76** 8.09N 10.42W
Pendine U.K. **13** 51.44N 4.33W
Pendleton U.S.A. **108** 45.40N118.47W
Penedo Brazil **123** 10.16S 36.33W
Penedono Portugal **26** 40.59N 7.24W
Penela Portugal **27** 40.02N 8.23W
Penetanguishene Canada **104** 44.47N 79.55W
Penfield U.S.A. **114** 41.13N 78.34W
Penganga *r.* India **63** 19.53N 79.09E
Penge Zaïre **78** 5.31S 24.37E
Penghu Liedao *is.* Taiwan **55** 23.35N119.32E
Pengshui China **55** 29.17N108.13E
Peniche Portugal **27** 39.21N 9.23W
Penicuik U.K. **14** 55.49N 3.13W
Peninsular Malaysia *d.* Malaysia **58** 5.00N102.00E
Peñíscola Spain **25** 40.21N 0.25E
Penmarc'h, Pointe de *c.* France **18** 47.48N 4.22W
Penne Italy **31** 42.27N 13.55E
Penne-d'Agenais France **20** 44.23N 0.49E
Penneshaw Australia **92** 35.42S137.55E
Pennsauken U.S.A. **115** 39.58N 75.04W
Pennsboro U.S.A. **114** 39.17N 80.58W
Penns Grove U.S.A. **115** 39.43N 75.28W
Pennsylvania *d.* U.S.A. **114** 40.45N 77.30W
Penn Yan U.S.A. **114** 42.40N 77.03W
Penny Highland *mtn.* Canada **99** 67.10N 66.50W
Penobscot *r.* U.S.A. **112** 44.30N 68.50W
Penola Australia **92** 37.23S140.21E
Penong Australia **89** 31.55S133.01E
Penonomé Panama **117** 8.30N 80.20W
Penrhyn Atoll Cook Is. **85** 9.00S158.00W
Penrith Australia **93** 33.47S150.44E
Penrith U.K. **12** 54.40N 2.45W
Penryn U.K. **13** 50.10N 5.07W
Pensacola U.S.A. **113** 30.26N 87.12W
Pensacola Mts. Antarctica **128** 84.00S 45.00W
Penshurst Australia **92** 37.52S142.20E
Pentecost I. Vanuatu **84** 15.42S168.10E
Penticton Canada **100** 49.30N119.30W
Pentland Australia **90** 20.32S145.24E
Pentland Firth *str.* U.K. **14** 58.40N 3.00W
Pentland Hills U.K. **14** 55.50N 3.20W
Penylan L. Canada **101** 61.50N106.20W
Penza Russian Fed. **44** 53.11N 45.00E
Penzance U.K. **13** 50.07N 5.32W
Penzberg Germany **39** 47.45N 11.23E
Penzhinskaya Guba *g.* Russian Fed. **51** 61.00N163.00E
Peoria Ariz. U.S.A. **109** 33.35N112.14W
Peoria Ill. U.S.A. **110** 40.43N 89.38W
Pepacton Resr. U.S.A. **115** 42.06N 74.54W
Peper Sudan **73** 7.04N 33.00E
Pepperell U.S.A. **115** 42.40N 71.35W
Perabumulih Indonesia **58** 3.29S104.14E
Perales de Alfambra Spain **25** 40.38N 1.00W
Perche, Collines du *hills* France **18** 48.25N 0.40E
Percival Lakes Australia **88** 21.25S125.00E
Perdido, Monte *mtn.* Spain **25** 42.40N 0.05E
Pereira Colombia **122** 4.47N 75.46W
Perekop Ukraine **45** 46.10N 33.42E
Perené *r.* Peru **124** 11.02S 74.19W
Perevolotskiy Russian Fed. **44** 51.10N 54.15E
Pereyaslav-Khmelnitskiy Ukraine **37** 50.05N 31.28E
Pergamino Argentina **125** 33.53S 60.35W
Pergine Valsugana Italy **30** 46.04N 11.14E
Pergola Italy **30** 43.34N 12.50E
Perham U.S.A. **110** 46.36N 95.34W
Péribonca *r.* Canada **103** 48.45N 72.05W
Pericos Mexico **109** 25.03N107.42W
Périers France **18** 49.11N 1.25W
Périgueux France **20** 45.11N 0.43E
Perija, Sierra de *mts.* Venezuela **122** 10.30N 72.30W
Peri L. Australia **92** 30.44S143.34E
Perleberg Germany **38** 53.04N 11.51E
Perm Russian Fed. **44** 58.01N 56.10E
Përmet Albania **34** 40.15N 20.21E
Pernambuco *d.* Brazil **123** 8.00S 39.00W
Pernatty L. Australia **92** 31.31S137.14E
Pernik Bulgaria **34** 42.36N 23.02E
Perniö Finland **41** 60.12N 23.08E
Péronne France **19** 49.56N 2.56E
Perosa Argentina Italy **30** 44.58N 7.10E
Pérouse, Bahía la *b.* I. de Pascua **85** 27.04S109.20W
Perpendicular, Pt. Australia **93** 35.03S150.50E
Perpignan France **20** 42.41N 2.53E
Perranporth U.K. **13** 50.21N 5.09W
Perro, Punta del *c.* Spain **27** 36.45N 6.26W
Perros-Guirec France **18** 48.49N 3.27W
Perry Fla. U.S.A. **113** 30.08N 83.36W
Perry Iowa U.S.A. **110** 41.50N 94.06W
Perry Mich. U.S.A. **104** 42.50N 84.13W
Perry Okla. U.S.A. **111** 36.17N 97.17W
Perryton U.S.A. **111** 36.24N100.48W
Perryville U.S.A. **111** 37.43N 89.52W
Persberg Sweden **43** 59.45N 14.15E
Persepolis *ruins* Iran **65** 29.55N 53.00E
Perth Australia **89** 31.58S115.49E
Perth Canada **105** 44.54N 76.15W
Perth U.K. **14** 56.24N 3.28W
Perth Amboy U.S.A. **115** 40.31N 74.16W
Pertuis France **21** 43.41N 5.30E
Peru S. America **122** 10.00S 75.00W
Peru Ill. U.S.A. **110** 41.19N 89.11W
Peru Basin Pacific Oc. **85** 19.00S 96.00W
Peru-Chile Trench Pacific Oc. **121** 23.00S 71.30W
Perugia Italy **30** 43.08N 12.22E
Perušić Croatia **31** 44.39N 15.23E
Péruwelz Belgium **16** 50.32N 3.36E
Pervomaysk Ukraine **37** 48.03N 30.50E
Pervouralsk Russian Fed. **44** 56.59N 59.58E
Pesaro Italy **30** 43.54N 12.55E
Pescara Italy **31** 42.28N 14.13E
Pescara *r.* Italy **31** 42.28N 14.13E
Pescia Italy **30** 43.54N 10.41E
Peshāwar Pakistan **62** 34.01N 71.33E
Peshīn Jān Afghan. **62** 33.25N 61.28E
Peshkopi Albania **34** 41.41N 20.25E
Peshtera Bulgaria **34** 42.02N 24.18E
Pesmes France **19** 47.17N 5.34E
Peso da Régua Portugal **26** 41.10N 7.47W
Pesqueira Brazil **123** 8.24S 36.38W
Pesqueria *r.* Mexico **111** 25.55N 99.28W
Pessac France **20** 44.48N 0.38W
Peşteana Jiu Romania **37** 44.50N 23.15E
Pestovo Russian Fed. **44** 58.32N 35.42E
Petah Tiqwa Israel **67** 32.05N 34.53E
Petalídhion Greece **35** 36.57N 21.55E
Petalión, Kólpos *g.* Greece **35** 37.59N 24.02E
Petaluma U.S.A. **108** 38.14N122.39W
Pétange Lux. **16** 49.32N 5.56E
Petare Venezuela **122** 10.31N 66.50W
Petatlán Mexico **116** 17.31N101.16W
Petauke Zambia **79** 14.16S 31.21E
Petawawa Canada **105** 45.54N 77.17W
Petawawa *r.* Canada **105** 45.55N 77.15W
Peterborough S.A. Australia **92** 33.00S138.51E
Peterborough Vic. Australia **92** 38.36S142.55E
Peterborough Canada **104** 44.18N 78.19W
Peterborough U.K. **13** 52.35N 0.14W
Peterborough U.S.A. **115** 42.53N 71.57W
Peterhead U.K. **14** 57.30N 1.46W
Peterlee U.K. **12** 54.45N 1.18W
Petermann Ranges *mts.* Australia **88** 25.00S129.46E
Peter Pond L. Canada **101** 55.55N108.44W
Petersburg Alas. U.S.A. **100** 56.49N132.58W
Petersburg Va. U.S.A. **113** 37.14N 77.24W
Petersburg W.Va. U.S.A. **114** 39.00N 79.09W
Petersfield U.K. **13** 51.00N 0.56W
Petilia Policastro Italy **33** 39.07N 16.47E
Petitot *r.* Canada **100** 60.14N123.29W
Petitsikapau L. Canada **103** 54.45N 66.25W
Petit St. Bernard, Col du *pass* France / Italy **30** 45.40N 6.53E
Petlād India **62** 22.30N 72.45E
Petoskey U.S.A. **112** 45.22N 84.59W
Petra *ruins* Jordan **66** 30.19N 35.26E
Petre, Pt. Canada **105** 43.50N 77.09W
Petrich Bulgaria **34** 41.24N 23.13E
Petrikov Belorussia **37** 52.09N 28.30E
Petrinja Croatia **31** 45.26N 16.17E
Petrodvorets Russian Fed. **44** 59.50N 29.57E
Petrolia Canada **104** 42.52N 82.09W
Petrolina Brazil **123** 9.22S 40.30W
Petropavlovsk Kazakhstan **9** 54.53N 69.13E
Petropavlovsk Kamchatskiy Russian Fed. **51** 53.03N158.43E
Petrópolis Brazil **126** 22.30S 43.06W
Petroşani Romania **37** 45.25N 23.22E
Petrovaradin Yugo. **31** 45.16N 19.55E
Petrovsk Russian Fed. **44** 52.20N 45.24E
Petrovsk Zabaykal'skiy Russian Fed. **51** 51.20N108.55E
Petrozavodsk Russian Fed. **44** 61.46N 34.19E
Petrus Steyn R.S.A. **80** 27.38S 28.08E
Peuerbach Austria **39** 48.21N 13.56E
Peureulak Indonesia **58** 4.48N 97.45E
Pevek Russian Fed. **51** 69.41N170.19E
Peyruis France **21** 44.02N 5.56E
Pézenas France **20** 43.27N 3.25E
Pezinok Slovakia **37** 48.18N 17.17E
Pezmog Russian Fed. **44** 61.50N 51.45E
Pezu Pakistan **62** 32.19N 70.44E
Pfaffenhofen Germany **39** 48.31N 11.30E
Pfalzel Germany **39** 49.47N 6.41E
Pfarrkirchen Germany **39** 48.27N 12.56E
Pforzheim Germany **39** 48.54N 8.42E
Pfronten Germany **38** 47.34N 10.33E
Pfunds Austria **39** 46.58N 10.33E
Pfungstadt Germany **39** 49.48N 8.36E
Phagwāra India **62** 31.13N 75.47E
Phalodi India **62** 27.08N 72.22E
Phalsbourg France **19** 48.46N 7.16E
Phangan, Ko *i.* Thailand **58** 9.50N100.00E
Phangnga Thailand **56** 8.29N 98.31E
Phan Rang Vietnam **56** 11.34N109.00E
Phan Thiet Vietnam **56** 11.00N108.06E
Pharenda India **63** 27.06N 83.17E
Phariāro Pakistan **62** 27.12N 68.59E
Phat Diem Vietnam **55** 20.06N106.07E
Phatthalung Thailand **56** 7.38N100.04E
Phelps U.S.A. **114** 42.57N 77.03W
Phelps L. Canada **101** 59.15N103.15W
Phenix City U.S.A. **113** 32.28N 85.01W
Phet Buri Thailand **56** 13.00N 99.58E
Philadelphia Miss. U.S.A. **111** 32.46N 89.07W
Philadelphia N.Y. U.S.A. **105** 44.09N 75.43W
Philadelphia Penn. U.S.A. **115** 39.57N 75.07W
Philippeville Belgium **16** 50.12N 4.32E
Philippi U.S.A. **114** 39.09N 80.02W
Philippines Asia **59** 13.00N123.00E
Philippine Sea Pacific Oc. **84** 18.00N135.00E
Philippine Trench Pacific Oc. **59** 8.45N127.20E
Philipsburg Canada **105** 45.02N 73.05W
Philipsburg U.S.A. **114** 40.45N 78.14W
Philip Smith Mts. U.S.A. **96** 68.30N147.00W
Philipstown R.S.A. **80** 30.25S 24.26E
Phillip U.S.A. **110** 44.02N101.40W
Phillip Edward I. Canada **104** 45.58N 81.17W
Phillip I. Australia **93** 38.29S145.14E
Phillips *r.* Australia **89** 33.55S120.01E
Phillips Maine U.S.A. **112** 44.49N 70.21W
Phillips Wisc. U.S.A. **110** 45.41N 90.24W
Phillipsburg Kans. U.S.A. **110** 39.45N 99.19W
Phillipsburg N.J. U.S.A. **115** 40.42N 75.12W
Phillipson, L. Australia **92** 29.28S134.28E
Philo U.S.A. **114** 39.52N 81.55W
Phnom Penh Cambodia **56** 11.35N104.55E
Phoenicia U.S.A. **115** 42.05N 74.19W
Phoenix Ariz. U.S.A. **109** 33.27N112.05W
Phoenix N.Y. U.S.A. **115** 43.14N 76.18W
Phoenix Is. Kiribati **84** 4.00S172.00W
Phoenixville Conn. U.S.A. **115** 41.51N 72.03W
Phoenixville Penn. U.S.A. **115** 40.08N 75.31W
Phon Thailand **56** 15.50N102.35E
Phôngsali Laos **56** 21.40N102.11E
Phou Loi *mtn.* Laos **56** 20.16N103.18E
Phu Huu Vietnam **55** 19.00N105.35E
Phukao Miang *mtn.* Thailand **61** 16.50N101.00E
Phuket Thailand **56** 7.55N 98.23E
Phuket, Ko *i.* Thailand **56** 8.10N 98.20E
Phu Ly Vietnam **55** 20.30N105.58E
Phumi Chuuk Vietnam **56** 10.50N104.28E
Phumĭ Sâmraông Cambodia **56** 14.12N103.31E
Phu Quoc *i.* Cambodia **56** 10.20N104.00E
Phu Tho Vietnam **56** 21.23N105.13E
Phu Vinh Vietnam **56** 9.57N106.20E
Piacá Brazil **123** 7.42S 47.18W
Piacenza Italy **30** 45.01N 9.40E
Pialba Australia **90** 25.13S152.55E
Pian *r.* Australia **93** 30.03S148.18E
Piana France **21** 42.14N 8.38E
Pianella Italy **31** 42.24N 14.02E
Piangil Australia **91** 35.04S143.20E
Pianoro Italy **30** 44.22N 11.20E
Pianosa *i.* Italy **30** 42.36N 10.04E
Piatra-Neamţ Romania **37** 46.56N 26.22E
Piauí *d.* Brazil **123** 7.45S 42.30W
Piauí *r.* Brazil **123** 6.14S 42.51W
Piave *r.* Italy **30** 45.32N 12.44E
Piawaning Australia **89** 30.51S116.22E
Piazza Armerina Italy **33** 37.23N 14.22E
Pibor *r.* Sudan **73** 8.26N 33.13E
Pibor Post Sudan **73** 6.48N 33.08E
Pic *r.* Canada **102** 48.38N 86.25W
Picardie *d.* France **19** 49.42N 2.40E
Pickens U.S.A. **114** 38.39N 80.13W
Pickerel *r.* Canada **104** 45.55N 80.50W
Pickerel River *town* Canada **104** 46.01N 80.45W
Pickering U.K. **12** 54.15N 0.46W
Pickford U.S.A. **104** 46.10N 84.22W
Pickle Crow Canada **102** 51.30N 90.04W
Pickwick L. *resr.* U.S.A. **111** 34.55N 88.10W
Picos Brazil **123** 7.05S 41.28W
Picos Ancares, Sierra de *mts.* Spain **26** 42.51N 6.52W
Picquigny France **19** 49.57N 2.09E
Picton Australia **93** 34.12S150.35E
Picton Canada **105** 44.00N 77.08W
Picton New Zealand **86** 41.17S174.02E
Picún Leufú Argentina **125** 39.30S 69.15W
Pidálion, Akrotírion *c.* Cyprus **66** 34.56N 34.05E
Pidarak Pakistan **62** 25.51N 63.14E
Piedecuesta Colombia **122** 6.59N 73.03W
Piedicroce France **21** 42.23N 9.23E
Piedimonte Matese Italy **33** 41.21N 14.22E
Piedmont U.S.A. **113** 33.55N 85.39W
Piedrabuena Spain **27** 39.02N 4.10W
Piedrafita, Puerto de *pass* Spain **26** 42.40N 7.01W
Piedrahita Spain **26** 40.28N 5.19W
Piedras *r.* Peru **122** 12.30S 69.10W
Piedras, Punta *c.* Argentina **125** 35.25S 57.07W
Piedras Negras Mexico **111** 28.40N100.32W
Piedra Sola Uruguay **125** 32.04S 56.21W
Pielavesi Finland **40** 63.14N 26.45E
Pielinen *l.* Finland **44** 63.20N 29.50E
Piemonte *d.* Italy **30** 44.55N 8.00E
Pienza Italy **30** 43.04N 11.41E
Pierce U.S.A. **108** 46.29N115.48W
Pierr-Buffière France **20** 45.42N 1.21E
Pierre U.S.A. **110** 44.22N100.21W
Pierreville Canada **105** 46.04N 72.49W
Piesseville Australia **89** 33.11S117.12E
Piešt'any Slovakia **37** 48.36N 17.50E
Pietarsaari Finland **40** 63.40N 22.42E
Pietermaritzburg R.S.A. **80** 29.36S 30.23E
Pietersburg R.S.A. **80** 23.54S 29.27E
Pietrasanta Italy **30** 43.57N 10.14E
Piet Retief R.S.A. **80** 27.00S 30.49E
Pietrosu *mtn.* Romania **37** 47.36N 24.38E
Pietrosul *mtn.* Romania **37** 47.08N 25.11E
Pieve di Cadore Italy **30** 46.26N 12.22E
Pigailoe *i.* Federated States of Micronesia **59** 8.08N146.40E
Pigeon U.S.A. **104** 43.50N 83.16W
Pigeon L. Canada **104** 44.30N 78.30W
Pigna Italy **30** 43.56N 7.40E
Pigón, Limni Greece **34** 39.45N 21.15E
Pihtipudas Finland **40** 63.23N 25.34E
Pikalevo Russian Fed. **44** 59.35N 34.07E
Pikangikum Canada **102** 51.49N 94.00W
Pikes Peak *mtn.* U.S.A. **108** 38.51N105.03W
Pikesville U.S.A. **114** 39.25N 77.25W
Piketberg R.S.A. **80** 32.54S 18.43E
Piketon U.S.A. **112** 39.03N 83.01W
Pikeville U.S.A. **113** 37.29N 82.33W
Pila Argentina **125** 36.00S 58.10W
Piła Poland **36** 53.09N 16.44E
Pilar Paraguay **126** 26.52S 58.23W
Pilar do Sul Brazil **126** 23.48S 47.45W
Pilcomayo *r.* Argentina / Paraguay **124** 25.15S 57.43W
Pīlībhīt India **63** 28.38N 79.48E
Pilica *r.* Poland **37** 51.52N 21.17E
Pilliga Australia **93** 30.23S148.55E
Pílos Greece **35** 36.55N 21.43E
Pilot Point *town* U.S.A. **111** 33.24N 96.58W
Pilsum Germany **38** 53.29N 7.04E
Pimba Australia **92** 31.18S136.47E
Pimenta Bueno Brazil **122** 11.40S 61.14W
Pina Spain **25** 41.29N 0.32W
Pinang, Pulau *i.* Malaysia **58** 5.30N100.10E
Pinar Turkey **35** 37.02N 27.57E
Pinarbaşi Turkey **64** 38.43N 36.23E
Pinar del Río Cuba **117** 22.24N 83.42W
Pincher Creek *town* Canada **100** 49.30N113.57W
Pinconning U.S.A. **104** 43.51N 83.59W
Píndhos Óros *mts.* Greece **34** 39.49N 21.14E
Pindiga Nigeria **77** 9.58N 10.53E
Pindi Gheb Pakistan **62** 33.14N 72.16E
Pindus Mts. *see* Píndhos Óros *mts.* Greece **34**
Pindwāra India **62** 24.48N 73.04E
Pine *r.* Canada **100** 56.08N120.41W
Pine *r.* U.S.A. **104** 43.35N 84.08W
Pine, C. Canada **103** 46.37N 53.30W
Pine Bluff *town* U.S.A. **111** 34.13N 92.01W
Pine Bluffs *town* U.S.A. **108** 41.11N104.04W
Pine City U.S.A. **110** 45.50N 92.59W
Pine Creek *town* Australia **88** 13.51S131.50E
Pine Creek *r.* U.S.A. **114** 41.10N 77.16W
Pinega Russian Fed. **44** 64.42N 43.28E
Pinega *r.* Russian Fed. **44** 63.51N 41.48E
Pine Grove U.S.A. **115** 40.33N 76.23W
Pinehouse L. Canada **101** 55.32N106.35W
Pine Is. U.S.A. **113** 26.35N 82.06W
Pine Point *town* Canada **100** 60.50N114.28W
Pine River *town* Canada **101** 51.45N100.40W
Pine River *town* U.S.A. **110** 46.43N 94.24W
Pinerolo Italy **30** 44.53N 7.21E
Pinetown R.S.A. **80** 29.49S 30.52E
Pineville U.S.A. **111** 31.19N 92.26W
Piney France **19** 48.22N 4.20E
Ping *r.* Thailand **56** 15.47N100.05E
Pingaring Australia **89** 34.45S118.34E
Pingba China **55** 26.25N106.15E
Pingdingshan Henan China **54** 33.38N113.30E
Pingdingshan Liaoning China **54** 41.28N124.45E
Pingdong Taiwan **55** 22.44N120.30E
Pingelap *i.* Pacific Oc. **84** 6.15N160.40E
Pingelly Australia **89** 32.34S117.04E
Pingle China **55** 24.38N110.38E
Pingliang China **54** 35.21N107.12E
Pingluo China **54** 38.56N106.34E
Pingnan China **55** 23.33N110.23E
Pingrup Australia **89** 33.33S118.30E
Pingtan *i.* China **55** 25.36N119.48E
Pingwu China **54** 32.25N104.36E
Pingxiang Guang. Zhuang. China **55** 22.07N106.42E
Pingxiang Jiangxi China **55** 27.36N113.48E
Pingyang China **55** 27.40N120.33E
Pingyao China **54** 37.12N112.08E
Pingyi China **54** 35.30N117.36E
Pingyuan China **55** 24.34N115.54E
Pinhal Brazil **126** 22.10S 46.46W
Pinhal Novo Portugal **27** 38.38N 8.55W
Pinhel Portugal **26** 40.46N 7.04W
Pini *i.* Indonesia **58** 0.10N 98.30E
Piniós *r.* Greece **34** 39.54N 22.45E
Pinjarra Australia **89** 32.37S115.53E
Pinnaroo Australia **92** 35.18S140.54E
Pinneberg Germany **38** 53.40N 9.47E
Pinos, Isla de *i.* Cuba **117** 21.40N 82.40W
Pinos-Puente Spain **27** 37.15N 3.45W
Pinrang Indonesia **58** 3.48S119.41E
Pins, Île des *i.* N. Cal. **84** 22.37S167.30E
Pins, Pointe aux *c.* Canada **104** 42.15N 81.51W
Pinsk Belorussia **37** 52.08N 26.01E
Pinto Argentina **124** 29.09S 62.38W
Pinto Butte *mtn.* Canada **101** 49.22N107.25W
Pinyug Russian Fed. **44** 60.10N 47.43E
Pinzgau *f.* Austria **39** 47.09N 12.30E
Piombino Italy **30** 42.55N 10.32E
Piorini, L. Brazil **122** 3.34S 63.15W
Piotrków Trybunalski Poland **37** 51.25N 19.42E
Piove di Sacco Italy **30** 45.18N 12.02E
Pipār India **62** 26.23N 73.32E
Piparia India **63** 22.45N 78.21E
Pipestone *r.* Ont. Canada **102** 52.48N 89.35W
Pipestone *r.* Sask. Canada **101** 58.40N105.45W
Pipestone U.S.A. **110** 43.58N 96.10W
Pipinas Argentina **125** 35.30S 57.19W
Piplān Pakistan **62** 32.17N 71.21E
Pipmouacane, Résr. Canada **103** 49.35N 70.30W
Piqua U.S.A. **112** 40.08N 84.14W
Piracicaba Brazil **126** 22.45S 47.40W
Piracicaba *r.* Brazil **126** 22.35S 48.14W
Piracuruca Brazil **123** 3.56S 41.42W
Piraeus *see* Piraiévs Greece **35**
Piraiévs Greece **35** 37.57N 23.38E
Piram I. India **62** 21.36N 72.41E
Piran Slovenia **31** 45.32N 13.34E
Pirassununga Brazil **126** 21.59S 47.25W
Pirdop Bulgaria **34** 42.42N 24.11E
Pírgos Greece **35** 37.41N 21.28E
Pírgos Greece **35** 36.38N 22.22E
Pirin Planina *mts.* Bulgaria **34** 41.40N 23.30E
Pirmasens Germany **39** 49.12N 7.36E
Pirna Germany **38** 50.58N 13.56E
Pirojpur Bangla. **63** 22.34N 89.59E
Pirón *r.* Spain **26** 41.23N 4.31W
Pirot Yugo. **34** 43.09N 22.39E
Pīr Panjāl Range *mts.* Jammu & Kashmir **62** 33.50N 74.30E
Piryatin Ukraine **45** 50.14N 32.31E
Pisa Italy **30** 43.43N 10.23E
Pisciotta Italy **33** 40.07N 15.12E
Pisco Peru **122** 13.46S 76.12W
Piseco L. U.S.A. **115** 43.24N 74.33W
Písek Czech Republic **39** 49.19N 14.10E
Pishan China **52** 37.30N 78.20E
Pishīn Pakistan **62** 30.35N 67.00E
Pishīn Lora *r.* Pakistan **62** 29.09N 64.55E
Pissos France **20** 44.19N 0.47W
Pisticci Italy **33** 40.23N 16.34E
Pistoia Italy **30** 43.55N 10.54E
Pisuerga *r.* Spain **26** 41.33N 4.52W
Pisz Poland **37** 53.38N 21.49E
Pita Guinea **76** 11.05N 12.15W
Pitalito Colombia **122** 1.51N 76.01W
Pitarpunga, L. Australia **92** 34.23S143.32E
Pitcairn I. Pacific Oc. **85** 25.04S130.06W
Pite *r.* Sweden **40** 65.14N 21.32E
Piteå Sweden **40** 65.20N 21.30E
Piteşti Romania **37** 44.52N 24.51E
Pithāpuram India **61** 17.07N 82.16E
Píthion Greece **34** 41.24N 26.40E
Pithiviers France **19** 48.10N 2.15E
Pithoragarh India **63** 29.35N 80.13E
Piti Guam **84** 13.28N144.41E
Pitigliano Italy **30** 42.38N 11.40E
Pitlochry U.K. **14** 56.43N 3.45W
Pitomača Croatia **31** 45.59N 17.14E
Pitt I. Canada **100** 53.35N129.45W

Porto Torres to Puy-de-Dôme

Porto Torres Italy 32 40.50N 8.23E
Pôrto Valter Brazil 122 8.15S 72.45W
Porto-Vecchio France 21 41.35N 9.16E
Pôrto Velho Brazil 122 8.45S 63.54W
Portoviejo Ecuador 122 1.07S 80.28W
Portpatrick U.K. 14 54.51N 5.07W
Port Perry Canada 104 44.06N 78.57W
Port Phillip B. Australia 93 38.05S144.50E
Port Pirie Australia 92 33.11S138.01E
Port Radium Canada 98 66.05N118.02W
Portree U.K. 14 57.24N 6.12W
Port Renfrew Canada 100 48.30N124.20W
Port Rowan Canada 104 42.37N 80.28W
Port Rupert see Waskaganish Canada 102
Portrush U.K. 15 55.12N 6.40W
Port Said see Būr Sa'īd Egypt 66
Port-Sainte-Marie France 20 44.15N 0.24E
Port Sanilac U.S.A. 114 43.26N 82.33W
Port Saunders Canada 103 50.39N 57.18W
Portsea Australia 93 38.19S144.43E
Port Severn Canada 104 44.47N 79.42W
Port Shepstone R.S.A. 80 30.44S 30.27E
Port Simpson Canada 100 54.32N130.25W
Portsmouth U.K. 13 50.48N 1.06W
Portsmouth N.H. U.S.A. 115 43.04N 70.46W
Portsmouth Ohio U.S.A. 112 38.45N 82.59W
Portsmouth Va. U.S.A. 113 36.50N 76.20W
Portsoy U.K. 14 57.41N 2.41W
Port Stanley Canada 104 42.40N 81.13W
Portstewart U.K. 15 55.11N 6.43W
Port St. Joe U.S.A. 113 29.49N 85.19W
Port St. Louis France 21 43.23N 4.48E
Port Sudan see Būr Sūdān Sudan 72
Port Talbot U.K. 13 51.35N 3.48W
Porttipahdan tekojärvi resr. Finland 40 68.08N 26.40E
Port Townsend U.S.A. 108 48.07N122.46W
Portugal Europe 24 39.30N 8.05W
Portugalete Spain 26 43.19N 3.01W
Portumna Rep. of Ire. 11 53.06N 8.14W
Port Vendres France 20 42.31N 3.07E
Port Victoria Australia 92 34.30S137.30E
Portville U.S.A. 114 42.02N 78.20W
Port Wakefield Australia 92 34.12S138.11E
Port Warrender Australia 88 14.30S125.50E
Porvenir Chile 125 53.18S 70.22W
Porz Germany 38 50.53N 7.03E
Porzuna Spain 27 39.09N 4.09W
Posada Italy 32 40.38N 9.43E
Posada r. Italy 32 40.39N 9.45E
Posadas Argentina 124 27.25S 55.48W
Posavina f. Croatia 31 45.20N 17.00E
Poschiavo Switz. 39 46.18N 10.04E
Posen U.S.A. 104 45.16N 83.42W
Posets, Pico de mtn. Spain 25 42.39N 0.25E
Posht r. Iran 65 29.09N 58.09E
Positano Italy 33 40.38N 14.29E
Poso Indonesia 59 1.23S120.45E
Posse Brazil 126 14.05S 46.22W
Possidhonia site Greece 35 37.40N 24.00E
Pössneck Germany 38 50.42N 11.37E
Post U.S.A. 111 33.12N101.23W
Postavy Lithuania 44 55.07N 26.50E
Poste Maurice Cortier Algeria 74 22.18N 1.05E
Poste Weygand Algeria 74 24.29N 0.40E
Postmasburg R.S.A. 80 28.19S 23.03E
Postojna Slovenia 31 45.47N 14.13E
Postoli Belorussia 37 52.30N 28.00E
Potamós Greece 35 36.38N 22.59E
Potchefstroom R.S.A. 80 26.42S 27.05E
Poteau U.S.A. 111 35.03N 94.37W
Potelu, Lacul l. Romania 34 43.44N 24.20E
Potenza Italy 33 40.38N 15.49E
Potes Spain 26 43.09N 4.37W
Potgietersrus R.S.A. 80 24.11S 29.00E
Poti r. Brazil 123 5.01S 42.48W
Poti Georgia 45 42.11N 41.41E
Potiskum Nigeria 77 11.40N 11.03E
Potomac r. U.S.A. 114 38.00N 76.18W
Potomac, North Branch r. U.S.A. 114 39.15N 79.21W
Potomac, South Branch r. U.S.A. 114 39.04N 78.59W
Potosí Bolivia 124 19.35S 65.45W
Potosí d. Bolivia 124 21.00S 67.00W
Potosi Cerro mtn. Mexico 111 24.50N100.15W
Pototan Phil. 59 10.54N122.38E
Potsdam Germany 38 52.24N 13.04E
Potsdam U.S.A. 105 44.40N 74.59W
Pottstown U.S.A. 115 40.15N 75.38W
Pottsville U.S.A. 115 40.41N 76.12W
Pouancé France 18 47.44N 1.11W
Poughkeepsie U.S.A. 115 41.42N 73.56W
Poultney U.S.A. 115 43.31N 73.14W
Pournári, Tekhnití Límni l. Greece 35 39.15N 21.00E
Pouso Alegre Brazil 126 22.13S 45.49W
Pouté Senegal 74 15.42N 14.10W
Poŭthĭsăt Cambodia 56 12.27N103.50E
Pouzauges France 18 46.47N 0.50W
Povenets Russian Fed. 44 62.52N 34.05E
Póvoa de Varzim Portugal 26 41.23N 8.46W
Povorino Russian Fed. 45 51.12N 42.15E
Powassan Canada 104 46.05N 79.22W
Powder r. U.S.A. 108 46.44N105.26W
Powder River town U.S.A. 108 43.03N106.58W
Powell U.S.A. 108 44.45N108.46W
Powell, L. U.S.A. 108 37.25N110.45W
Powell River town Canada 100 49.22N124.31W
Powers U.S.A. 102 45.42N 87.31W
Powers Lake town U.S.A. 110 48.34N102.39W
Powhatan Point town U.S.A. 114 39.52N 80.49W
Pownal U.S.A. 115 42.46N 73.14W
Powys d. U.K. 13 52.26N 3.26W
Poyang Hu l. China 55 29.10N116.20E
Požarevac Yugo. 37 44.38N 21.12E
Poza Rica de Hidalgo Mexico 116 20.34N 97.26W
Požega Yugo. 34 43.50N 20.02E
Poznań Poland 36 52.25N 16.53E
Pozo Alcón Spain 27 37.42N 2.56W
Pozoblanco Spain 26 38.22N 4.51W
Pozo-Cañada Spain 25 38.48N 1.45W
Pozuela de Alarcón Spain 26 40.26N 3.49W
Pozzallo Italy 33 36.43N 14.52E
Pozzuoli Italy 33 40.49N 14.07E
Prachatice Czech Republic 38 49.01N 14.00E
Prachin Buri Thailand 56 14.02N101.23E
Prachuap Khiri Khan Thailand 56 11.50N 99.49E
Pradera Colombia 122 3.23N 76.11W
Prades France 20 42.38N 2.25E
Praestö Denmark 43 55.07N 12.03E
Prague see Praha Czech Republic 39
Praha Czech Republic 38 50.05N 14.26E
Praha d. Czech Republic 39 50.05N 14.25E
Praha mtn. Czech Republic 39 49.40N 13.49E
Prainha Amazonas Brazil 122 7.16S 60.23W
Prainha Para Brazil 123 1.48S 53.29W
Prairie City U.S.A. 108 44.28N118.43W
Prairie du Chien town U.S.A. 110 43.03N 91.09W
Prairie Village U.S.A. 110 39.01N 94.38W
Pramánda Greece 34 39.32N 21.08E
Prang Ghana 76 8.02N 0.58W
Prasónisi, Ákra c. Greece 35 35.42N 27.46E
Pratāpgarh India 62 24.02N 74.47E
Prato Italy 30 43.53N 11.06E
Pratt U.S.A. 111 37.39N 98.44W
Pravia Spain 26 43.29N 6.07W
Predazzo Italy 30 46.19N 11.36E
Predejane Yugo. 34 42.51N 22.09E
Predlitz Austria 39 47.04N 13.55E
Pré-en-Pail France 18 48.27N 0.12W
Preesall U.K. 12 53.55N 2.58W
Preetz Germany 38 54.14N 10.16E
Pregel r. Russian Fed. 37 54.41N 20.22E
Preko Croatia 31 44.05N 15.11E
Premer Australia 93 31.26S149.54E
Premier Canada 100 56.04N129.56W
Premnitz Germany 38 52.32N 12.19E
Premuda i Croatia 31 44.20N 14.37E
Prenjas Albania 34 41.06N 20.32E
Prentice U.S.A. 110 45.33N 90.17W
Prenzlau Germany 38 53.19N 13.52E
Preparis i. Burma 56 14.51N 93.38E
Přerov Czech Republic 37 49.27N 17.27E
Prescott Canada 105 44.43N 75.31W
Prescott Ariz. U.S.A. 109 34.33N112.28W
Prescott Ark. U.S.A. 111 33.48N 93.23W
Preševo Yugo. 34 42.19N 21.39E
Presho U.S.A. 110 43.54N100.04W
Presidencia Roque Sáenz Peña Argentina 124 26.50S 60.30W
Presidente Epitácio Brazil 126 21.56S 52.07W
Presidente Hermes Brazil 124 11.17S 61.55W
Presidente Prudente Brazil 126 22.09S 51.24W
Presidio U.S.A. 111 29.33N104.23W
Preslav Bulgaria 34 43.10N 26.52E
Prešov Slovakia 37 49.00N 21.15E
Prespa, L. Macedonia / Greece 34 40.45N 21.00E
Presque Isle town Maine U.S.A. 112 46.41N 68.01W
Presque Isle town Mich. U.S.A. 104 45.16N 83.29W
Prestea Ghana 76 5.26N 2.07W
Presteigne U.K. 13 52.17N 3.00W
Přeštice Czech Republic 38 49.34N 13.20E
Preston Canada 104 43.23N 80.21W
Preston U.K. 12 53.46N 2.42W
Preston Idaho U.S.A. 108 42.06N111.53W
Preston Minn. U.S.A. 110 43.40N 92.04W
Prestonpans U.K. 14 55.57N 3.00W
Prestwick U.K. 14 55.30N 4.36W
Prêto r. Brazil 126 22.00S 43.21W
Pretoria R.S.A. 80 25.43S 28.11E
Préveza Greece 35 38.57N 20.44E
Prey Vêng Cambodia 56 11.29N105.19E
Priboj Yugo. 31 43.35N 19.31E
Příbram Czech Republic 39 49.42N 14.01E
Price Md. U.S.A. 115 39.06N 75.58W
Price Utah U.S.A. 108 39.36N110.48W
Prichard U.S.A. 111 30.44N 88.07W
Priego Spain 26 40.27N 2.18W
Priego de Córdoba Spain 27 37.26N 4.11W
Prien Germany 39 47.51N 12.20E
Prieska R.S.A. 80 29.40S 22.43E
Prieta, Peña mtn. Spain 26 43.01N 4.44W
Prijedor Bosnia-Herzegovina 31 44.59N 16.43E
Prijepolje Yugo. 31 43.23N 19.39E
Prikaspiyskaya Nizmennost see Caspian Depression Russian Fed. / Kazakhstan 45
Prilep Macedonia 34 41.20N 21.33E
Priluki Russian Fed. 44 63.05N 42.05E
Priluki Ukraine 45 50.35N 32.24E
Primorsk Russian Fed. 44 60.18N 28.35E
Primorsk Russian Fed. 43 54.44N 20.01E
Primorskiy Russian Fed. 57 43.10N131.40E
Primor'ye Russian Fed. 43 54.57N 20.02E
Primrose L. Canada 101 54.55N109.45W
Primstal Germany 39 49.32N 6.58E
Prince Albert Canada 101 53.12N105.46W
Prince Albert R.S.A. 80 33.14S 22.02E
Prince Albert Nat. Park Canada 101 54.00N106.25W
Prince Albert Sd. Canada 98 70.25N115.00W
Prince Alfred C. Canada 98 74.30N125.00W
Prince Charles I. Canada 99 67.50N 76.00W
Prince Edward B. Canada 105 43.57N 76.57W
Prince Edward-Crozet Ridge f. Indian Oc. 49 45.00S 42.00E
Prince Edward I. Canada 96 46.15N 63.00W
Prince Edward Is. Indian Oc. 49 46.35S 37.56E
Prince Edward Island d. Canada 103 46.45N 63.00W
Prince Frederick U.S.A. 115 38.33N 76.35W
Prince George Canada 100 53.50N122.50W
Prince of Wales, C. U.S.A. 98 66.00N168.30W
Prince of Wales I. Australia 90 10.40S142.10E
Prince of Wales I. Canada 99 73.00N 99.00W
Prince of Wales I. U.S.A. 100 55.00N132.30W
Prince Patrick I. Canada 98 77.00N120.00W
Prince Regent Inlet str. Canada 99 73.00N 90.30W
Prince Rupert Canada 100 54.09N130.20W
Princess Charlotte B. Australia 90 14.25S144.00E
Princess Royal I. Canada 100 53.00N128.40W
Princeton Ind. U.S.A. 112 38.21N 87.33W
Princeton Ky. U.S.A. 113 37.06N 87.55W
Princeton Mo. U.S.A. 110 40.24N 93.35W
Princeton N.J. U.S.A. 115 40.21N 74.40W
Príncipe i. São Tomé & Príncipe 77 1.37N 7.27E
Príncipe da Beira Brazil 122 12.23S 64.28W
Prinzapolca Nicaragua 117 13.19N 83.35W
Prior, Cabo c. Spain 26 43.34N 8.19W
Priozersk Russian Fed. 44 61.01N 30.08E
Pripet r. Europe 37 51.08N 30.30E
Pripet Marshes see Polesye f. Belorussia 37
Pripyat r. Belorussia see Pripet r. Europe 37
Priština Yugo. 34 42.40N 21.13E
Pritzwalk Germany 38 53.09N 12.10E
Privas France 21 44.44N 4.36E
Priverno Italy 32 41.28N 13.11E
Privolzhskaya Vozvyshennost f. Russian Fed. 44 53.15N 45.45E
Prizren Yugo. 34 42.13N 20.45E
Prizzi Italy 32 37.43N 13.26E
Prnjavor Bosnia-Herzegovina 31 44.52N 17.40E
Probolinggo Indonesia 59 7.45S113.09E
Probstzella Germany 38 50.32N 11.22E
Proctor U.S.A. 115 43.40N 73.02W
Proddatūr India 61 14.44N 78.33E
Proença-a-Nova Portugal 27 39.45N 7.55W
Progreso Mexico 117 21.20N 89.40W
Prokletije mts. Albania 34 42.30N 19.45E
Prokopyevsk Russian Fed. 50 53.55N 86.45E
Prokuplje Yugo. 34 43.16N 21.36E
Prome see Pyè Burma 56
Prophet r. Canada 100 58.48N122.40W
Propriá Brazil 123 10.15S 36.51W
Propriano France 21 41.40N 8.55E
Proserpine Australia 90 20.24S148.34E
Prosotsáni Greece 34 41.10N 23.59E
Prostějov Czech Republic 37 49.29N 17.07E
Protection U.S.A. 111 37.12N 99.29W
Protville Tunisia 32 36.54N 10.01E
Provence-Côte d'Azur d. France 21 43.45N 6.00E
Providence U.S.A. 115 41.50N 71.25W
Providence Bay town Canada 104 45.41N 82.16W
Providence Mts. U.S.A. 109 34.55N115.35W
Providencia, Isla de i. Colombia 117 13.21N 81.22W
Provincetown U.S.A. 115 42.03N 70.11W
Provins France 19 48.33N 3.18E
Provo U.S.A. 108 40.14N111.39W
Prozor Bosnia-Herzegovina 31 43.49N 17.37E
Prudhoe Bay town U.S.A. 98 70.20N148.25W
Prüm Germany 39 50.12N 6.25E
Prüm r. Germany 16 49.50N 6.29E
Pruszcz Gdański Poland 37 54.17N 18.40E
Pruszków Poland 37 52.11N 20.48E
Prut r. Romania / Ukraine 37 45.29N 28.14E
Prutz Austria 39 47.05N 10.40E
Pruzhany Belorussia 37 52.23N 24.28E
Prydz B. Antarctica 128 68.30S 74.00E
Pryor U.S.A. 111 36.19N 95.19W
Przemyśl Poland 37 49.48N 22.48E
Przeworsk Poland 37 50.05N 22.29E
Przhevalsk Kyrgyzstan 52 42.31N 78.22E
Psakhná Greece 35 38.34N 23.35E
Psará i. Greece 35 38.35N 25.37E
Psárion Greece 35 37.20N 21.51E
Psel r. Ukraine 45 49.00N 33.30E
Pskov Russian Fed. 44 57.48N 28.00E
Pskovskoye, Ozero l. Russian Fed. 44 58.00N 27.55E
Pteleón Greece 35 39.03N 22.57E
Ptich Belorussia 37 52.15N 28.49E
Ptich r. Belorussia 37 52.09N 28.52E
Ptolemaís Greece 34 40.30N 21.43E
Ptuj Slovenia 31 46.25N 15.52E
Puán Argentina 125 37.30S 62.45W
Pu'an China 55 25.47N104.57E
Puapua W. Samoa 84 13.34S172.12W
Pucallpa Peru 122 8.21S 74.33W
Pucarani Bolivia 124 16.23S 68.30W
Pucheng China 55 27.56N118.32E
Pučišća Croatia 31 43.21N 16.44E
Pudasjärvi Finland 40 65.25N 26.50E
Pūdeh Tal r. Afghan. 62 31.00N 61.50E
Pudozh Russian Fed. 44 61.50N 36.32E
Pudozhgora Russian Fed. 44 62.18N 35.54E
Puebla Mexico 116 19.03N 98.10W
Puebla d. Mexico 116 18.30N 98.00W
Puebla de Alcocer Spain 26 38.59N 5.15W
Puebla de Don Fadrique Spain 27 37.58N 2.26W
Puebla de Don Rodrigo Spain 27 39.05N 4.37W
Puebla de Sanabria Spain 26 42.03N 6.38W
Puebla de Trives Spain 26 42.20N 7.15W
Pueblo U.S.A. 108 38.16N104.37W
Pueblo Hundido Chile 124 26.23S 70.03W
Puelches Argentina 125 38.09S 65.58W
Puelén Argentina 125 37.32S 67.38W
Puente Alta Chile 125 33.37S 70.35W
Puenteareas Spain 26 42.11N 8.30W
Puente-Caldelas Spain 26 42.23N 8.30W
Puentedeume Spain 26 43.24N 8.10W
Puente-Genil Spain 27 37.23N 4.47W
Puente la Reina Spain 25 42.40N 1.49W
Puerto Aisén Chile 125 45.27S 72.58W
Puerto Ángel Mexico 116 15.40N 96.29W
Puerto Armuelles Panama 117 8.19N 82.15W
Puerto Ayacucho Venezuela 122 5.39N 67.32W
Puerto Barrios Guatemala 117 15.41N 88.32W
Puerto Bermúdez Peru 122 10.20S 75.00W
Puerto Berrío Colombia 122 6.28N 74.28W
Puerto Cabello Venezuela 122 10.29N 68.02W
Puerto Cabezas Nicaragua 117 14.02N 83.24W
Puerto Carreño Colombia 122 6.08N 67.27W
Puerto Casado Paraguay 124 22.20S 57.55W
Puerto Coig Argentina 125 50.54S 69.15W
Puerto Cortés Costa Rica 117 8.58N 83.32W
Puerto Cortés Honduras 117 15.50N 87.55W
Puerto de Nutrias Venezuela 122 8.07N 69.18W
Puerto de Pollensa Spain 25 39.55N 3.05E
Puerto de Santa Maria Spain 27 36.36N 6.13W
Puerto Heath Bolivia 122 12.30S 68.40W
Puerto Juárez Mexico 117 21.26N 86.51W
Puerto La Cruz Venezuela 122 10.14N 64.40W
Puerto Leguízamo Colombia 122 0.12S 74.46W
Puertollano Spain 26 38.41N 4.07W
Puerto Lobos Argentina 125 42.01S 65.04W
Puerto Madryn Argentina 125 42.46S 65.02W
Puerto Maldonado Peru 122 12.37S 69.11W
Puerto Melendez Peru 122 4.30S 77.30W
Puerto Montt Chile 125 41.28S 73.00W
Puerto Natales Chile 125 51.44S 72.31W
Puerto Páez Venezuela 122 6.13N 67.28W
Puerto Peñasco Mexico 109 31.20N113.33W
Puerto Pinasco Paraguay 126 22.36S 57.53W
Puerto Plata Dom. Rep. 117 19.48N 70.41W
Puerto Princesa Phil. 58 9.46N118.45E
Puerto Quepos Costa Rica 117 9.28N 84.10W
Puerto Real Spain 27 36.32N 6.11W
Puerto Rey Colombia 122 8.48N 76.34W
Puerto Rico C. America 117 18.20N 66.30W
Puerto Rico Trench Atlantic Oc. 117 19.50N 66.00W
Puerto Saavedra Chile 125 38.47S 73.24W
Puerto Santa Cruz Argentina 125 50.03S 68.35W
Puerto Sastre Paraguay 126 22.02S 58.00W
Puerto Siles Bolivia 124 12.48S 65.05W
Puerto Suspiro del Moro Spain 27 37.03N 3.43W
Puerto Tejado Colombia 122 3.16N 76.22W
Puerto Vallarta Mexico 116
Puerto Varas Chile 125 41.20S 73.00W
Pugachev Russian Fed. 44 52.02N 48.49E
Puget-Théniers France 21 43.57N 6.54E
Puglia d. Italy 33 41.00N 16.40E
Puig Major mtn. Spain 25 39.48N 2.48E
Puigmal mtn. Spain 25 42.23N 2.07E
Puisaye, Collines de la hills France 19 47.34N 3.28E
Pujehun Sierra Leone 76 7.23N 11.44W
Pukaki, L. New Zealand 86 44.00S170.10E
Pukatawagan Canada 101 55.45N101.20W
Pukë Albania 34 42.03N 19.54E
Pukekohe New Zealand 86 37.12S174.56E
Pukeuri New Zealand 86 45.02S171.02E
Pukhovichi Belorussia 37 53.28N 28.18E
Pula Croatia 31 44.52N 13.50E
Pulacayo Bolivia 124 20.25S 66.41W
Pulaski N.Y. U.S.A. 115 43.34N 76.08W
Pulaski Tenn. U.S.A. 113 35.11N 87.02W
Pulaski Va. U.S.A. 113 37.03N 80.47W
Puławy Poland 37 51.25N 21.57E
Pulgaon India 63 20.44N 78.20E
Pulkkila Finland 40 64.16N 25.52E
Pullman U.S.A. 108 46.44N117.10W
Pulog mtn. Phil. 59 16.50N120.50E
Pulozero Russian Fed. 44 68.22N 33.15E
Pulpito, Punta c. Mexico 109 26.31N111.28W
Pulsano Italy 33 40.23N 17.22E
Pułtusk Poland 37 52.42N 21.02E
Puma Tanzania 79 5.02S 34.46E
Puma Yumco l. China 63 28.35N 90.20E
Punaauia Tahiti 85 17.38S149.36W
Punakha Bhutan 63 27.37N 89.52E
Puncak Jaya mtn. Indonesia 59 4.00S137.15E
Pūnch Jammu & Kashmir 62 33.46N 74.06E
Pune India 60 18.34N 73.58E
Punjab d. India 62 30.45N 75.30E
Punjab d. Pakistan 62 30.25N 72.30E
Puno Peru 122 15.53S 70.03W
Punta Alta town Argentina 125 38.50S 62.00W
Punta Arenas town Chile 125 53.10S 70.56W
Puntabie Australia 92 32.15S134.13E
Punta Delgada town Argentina 125 42.43S 63.38W
Punta Gorda town Belize 117 16.10N 88.45W
Punta Gorda town U.S.A. 113 26.56N 82.01W
Puntarenas Costa Rica 117 10.00N 84.50W
Punto Fijo Venezuela 122 11.50N 70.16W
Punxsutawney U.S.A. 114 40.57N 78.59W
Puolanka Finland 40 64.52N 27.40E
Puqi China 55 29.40N113.52E
Puquio Peru 122 14.44S 74.07W
Pur r. Russian Fed. 50 67.30N 75.30E
Pūranpur India 63 28.31N 80.09E
Purari r. P.N.G. 59 7.49S145.10E
Purcell U.S.A. 111 35.01N 97.22W
Purchena Spain 27 37.21N 2.22W
Purgatoire r. U.S.A. 108 38.04N103.10W
Puri India 63 19.48N 85.51E
Purisima, Sierra de la mts. Mexico 111 26.28N101.45W
Purli India 62 18.51N 76.32E
Pūrna r. India 62 19.07N 77.02E
Purnea India 63 25.47N 87.31E
Purros Namibia 80 18.38S 12.59E
Purūlia India 63 23.20N 86.22E
Purus r. Brazil 122 3.58S 61.25W
Pŭrvomay Bulgaria 34 42.08N 25.17E
Purwakarta Indonesia 59 6.30S107.25E
Purwodadi Indonesia 59 7.05S110.53E
Purwokerto Indonesia 59 7.28S109.09E
Purworejo Indonesia 59 7.45S110.04E
Pusad India 63 19.54N 77.35E
Pusan S. Korea 53 35.05N129.02E
Pushkar India 62 26.30N 74.33E
Pushkin Russian Fed. 44 59.43N 30.22E
Pushkino Russian Fed. 45 51.16N 47.09E
Püspökladány Hungary 37 47.19N 21.07E
Pustoshka Russian Fed. 44 56.20N 29.20E
Putao Burma 56 27.22N 97.27E
Putaruru New Zealand 86 38.03S175.47E
Putian China 55 25.29N119.04E
Puting, Tanjung c. Indonesia 58 3.35S111.52E
Putney U.S.A. 115 42.59N 72.31W
Putorana, Gory mts. Russian Fed. 51 68.30N 96.00E
Putsonderwater R.S.A. 80 29.14S 21.50E
Puttalam Sri Lanka 61 8.02N 79.50E
Puttgarden Germany 38 54.30N 11.13E
Putumayo r. Brazil 122 3.05S 68.10W
Puulavesi l. Finland 41 61.50N 26.42E
Puyallup U.S.A. 108 47.11N122.18W
Puyang China 54 35.40N115.02E
Puy-de-Dôme d. France 20 45.45N 3.05E

Puy de Dôme to **Ramillies**

Puy de Dôme *mtn.* France 20 45.47N 2.58E
Puy de Sancy *mtn.* France 20 45.32N 2.49E
Puylaurens France 20 43.34N 2.01E
Puy L'Évèque France 20 44.30N 1.08E
Puymorens, Col de *pass* France 20 42.30N 1.50E
Puysegur Pt. New Zealand 86 46.10S166.35E
Pūzak, Jehīl-e *l.* Afghan. 62 31.30N 61.45E
Pwani *d.* Tanzania 79 7.00S 39.00E
Pweto Zaïre 79 8.27S 28.52E
Pwllheli U.K. 12 52.53N 4.25W
Pyaozero, Ozero *l.* Russian Fed. 44 66.00N 31.00E
Pyapon Burma 56 16.15N 95.40E
Pyasina *r.* Russian Fed. 51 73.10N 84.55E
Pyatigorsk Russian Fed. 45 44.04N 43.06E
Pyè Burma 56 18.50N 95.14E
Pyhä *r.* Finland 40 64.28N 24.13E
Pyhäjärvi *l.* Oulu Finland 40 63.35N 25.57E
Pyhäjärvi *l.* Turku-Pori Finland 41 61.00N 22.20E
Pyhäjoki Finland 40 64.28N 24.14E
Pyinmana Burma 56 19.45N 96.12E
Pymatuning Resr. U.S.A. 114 41.37N 80.30W
Pyongyang N. Korea 53 39.00N125.47E
Pyramid U.S.A. 108 40.05N119.43W
Pyramid Hill *town* Australia 92 36.03S144.24E
Pyramid Hills Canada 103 57.35N 65.00W
Pyramid L. U.S.A. 108 40.00N119.35W
Pyramids Egypt 72 29.52N 31.00E
Pyrénées *mts.* France / Spain 25 42.40N 0.00
Pyrénées-Atlantiques *d.* France 20 43.15N 1.00W
Pyrénées Orientales *d.* France 20 42.30N 2.20E
Pyrzyce Poland 36 53.10N 14.55E
Pythonga, Lac *l.* Canada 105 46.23N 76.26W
Pytteggja *mtn.* Norway 41 62.13N 7.42E
Pyu Burma 56 18.29N 96.26E

Q

Qaanaaq *see* Thule Greenland 99
Qabalān Jordan 67 32.06N 35.17E
Qabātiyah Jordan 67 32.25N 35.17E
Qā'emshahr Iran 65 36.28N 52.53E
Qagan Nur *l.* China 54 43.30N114.35E
Qagbasêrag China 63 30.51N 92.42E
Qagcaka China 63 32.32N 81.52E
Qahā Egypt 66 30.17N 31.12E
Qalāt Afghan. 62 32.07N 66.54E
Qal'at Bīshah Saudi Arabia 72 19.50N 42.36E
Qal 'eh Kāh Afghan. 62 32.18N 61.31E
Qal'eh-ye Now Afghan 65 34.58N 63.04E
Qal'eh-ye Sāber Afghan. 62 34.02N 69.01E
Qallābāt Sudan 73 12.58N 36.09E
Qalqīlyah Jordan 67 32.11N 34.58E
Qalyūb Egypt 66 30.11N 31.12E
Qam Jordan 67 32.35N 35.44E
Qamar, Ghubbat al *b.* Yemen 71 16.00N 52.30E
Qamdo China 52 31.11N 97.18E
Qamīnis Libya 72 31.40N 20.01E
Qamr-ud-dīn Kārez Pakistan 62 31.39N 68.25E
Qānā Lebanon 67 33.13N 35.18E
Qan'abah Syria 67 33.08N 35.40E
Qanâtir Muhammad 'Alī Egypt 66 30.12N 31.08E
Qanayah Syria 67 33.01N 36.11E
Qandahār Afghan. 62 31.32N 65.30E
Qandahār *d.* Afghan. 62 31.00N 65.30E
Qandala Somali Rep. 71 11.23N 49.53E
Qaqortoq *see* Julianehåb Greenland 99
Qarā, Jabal al *mts.* Oman 71 17.15N 54.15E
Qārah Egypt 64 27.37N 26.30E
Qārat Khazzī *hill* Libya 72 21.26N 24.30E
Qardho Somali Rep. 71 9.30N 49.03E
Qareh Sū Iran 65 34.52N 51.25E
Qareh Sū *r.* Iran 65 35.58N 56.25E
Qarqan He *r.* China 52 40.56N 86.27E
Qārūn, Birkat *l.* Egypt 66 29.30N 30.40E
Qaryat al Qaddāḩīyah Libya 75 31.22N 15.14E
Qāsh *r.* Sudan 72 16.48N 35.51E
Qasigiannguit *see* Christianshåb Greenland 99
Qāsim Syria 67 32.59N 36.05E
Qaşr al Farāfirah Egypt 64 27.15N 28.10E
Qaşr al Mushāsh *ruin* Jordan 67 31.49N 36.19E
Qaşr al Mushattá *site* Jordan 67 31.44N 36.01E
Qaşr al Qarābūllī Libya 75 32.45N 13.43E
Qaşr-e Qand Iran 65 26.13N 60.37E
Qa'ţabah Yemen 71 13.51N 44.42E
Qatanā Syria 66 33.27N 36.04E
Qatar Asia 65 25.20N 51.10E
Qaţrānī, Jabal *mts.* Egypt 66 29.40N 30.36E
Qattara Depression *see* Qaţţārah, Munkhafaḑ al *f.* Egypt 64
Qaţţārah, Munkhafaḑ al *f.* Egypt 64 29.40N 27.30E
Qawz Rajab Sudan 72 16.04N 35.34E
Qāyen Iran 65 33.44N 59.07E
Qaysān Sudan 73 10.45N 34.48E
Qāzigund Jammu & Kashmir 62 33.38N 75.09E
Qazvīn Iran 65 36.16N 50.00E
Qeqertarsuaq *see* Godhavn Greenland 99
Qeqertarsuatsiaat *see* Fiskenaesset Greenland 99
Qeshm Iran 65 26.58N 57.17E
Qeshm *i.* Iran 65 26.48N 55.48E
Qezel Owzan *r.* Iran 65 36.44N 49.27E
Qezi'ot Israel 66 30.52N 34.28E
Qian'an China 54 45.00N124.00E
Qianjiang China 55 29.28N108.43E
Qianxi China 54 40.10N118.19E
Qianyang China 55 27.22N110.14E
Qiaotou China 54 42.56N118.54E
Qibyā Jordan 67 31.59N 35.01E
Qidong Hunan China 55 26.47N112.07E
Qidong Jiangsu China 55 31.49N121.40E
Qiemo China 52 38.08N 85.33E
Qijiang China 55 29.00N106.40E
Qila Abdullāh Pakistan 62 30.43N 66.38E
Qila Lādgasht Pakistan 62 27.54N 62.57E
Qila Saifullāh Pakistan 62 30.43N 68.21E
Qilian Shan *mts.* China 52 38.30N 99.20E
Qimantag *mts.* China 52 37.45N 89.40E
Qimen China 55 29.50N117.38E
Qinā Egypt 64 26.10N 32.43E
Qinā, Wādī *r.* Egypt 64 26.07N 32.42E
Qingdao China 54 36.02N120.25E
Qinghai *d.* China 63 34.20N 91.00E
Qinghai Hu *l.* China 52 36.40N100.00E
Qingjian China 54 37.02N110.06E
Qingjiang China 55 28.01N115.30E
Qing Jiang Shuiku *resr.* China 55 30.00N112.12E
Qinglong Guizhou China 55 25.47N105.12E
Qinglong Hebei China 54 40.24N118.53E
Qingshui Jiang *r.* China 55 28.08N110.06E
Qing Xian China 54 38.35N116.48E
Qingxu China 54 37.36N112.21E
Qingyang China 54 36.03N107.52E
Qingyuan Guangdong China 55 23.42N113.00E
Qingyuan Jilin China 54 42.05N125.01E
Qingyuan Zhejiang China 55 27.37N119.03E
Qing Zang Gaoyuan *f.* China 52 33.40N 86.00E
Qinhuangdao China 54 39.52N119.42E
Qin Ling *mts.* China 54 33.30N109.00E
Qin Xian China 54 36.45N112.41E
Qinyang China 54 35.06N112.57E
Qinzhou China 55 21.58N108.34E
Qionghai China 55 19.12N110.31E
Qiongshan China 55 19.59N110.30E
Qiongzhou Haixia *str.* China 55 20.09N110.20E
Qipanshan China 54 42.05N117.37E
Qiqihar China 53 47.23N124.00E
Qira China 52 37.02N 80.53E
Qiryat Ata Israel 67 32.48N 35.06E
Qiryat Bialik Israel 67 32.50N 35.05E
Qiryat Gat Israel 67 31.37N 34.47E
Qiryat Motzkin Israel 67 32.50N 35.04E
Qiryat Shemona Israel 67 33.13N 35.35E
Qiryat Tiv'on Israel 67 32.43N 35.08E
Qiryat Yam Israel 67 32.51N 35.04E
Qishn Yemen 60 15.25N 51.40E
Qishon *r.* Israel 67 32.49N 35.02E
Qiuxizhen China 55 29.54N104.40E
Qi Xian Henan China 54 35.35N114.08E
Qi Xian Henan China 54 34.30N114.50E
Qom Iran 65 34.40N 50.57E
Qonggyai China 63 29.03N 91.41E
Qornet'es Sauda *mtn.* Lebanon 66 34.17N 36.04E
Qoţūr Iran 65 38.28N 44.25E
Quabbin Resr. U.S.A. 115 42.22N 72.18W
Quadeville Canada 105 45.18N 77.24W
Quairading Australia 89 32.00S117.22E
Quakenbrück Germany 38 52.40N 7.57E
Quakertown U.S.A. 115 40.26N 75.21W
Qu'ali China 55 29.46N117.15E
Quambatook Australia 92 35.52S143.36E
Quambone Australia 93 30.54S147.55E
Quang Ngai Vietnam 56 15.09N108.50E
Quang Tri Vietnam 56 16.44N107.10E
Quang Yen Vietnam 56 20.56N106.49E
Quan Long Vietnam 56 9.11N105.09E
Quannan China 55 24.45N114.32E
Quantico U.S.A. 114 38.31N 77.17W
Quanzhou Fujian China 55 24.57N118.36E
Quanzhou Guang. Zhuang. China 55 26.00N111.00E
Qu'Appelle *r.* Canada 101 50.33N101.20W
Quaqtaq Canada 99 61.05N 69.36W
Quaraí Brazil 125 30.23S 56.27W
Quaraí *r.* Brazil 125 30.12S 57.36W
Quarryville U.S.A. 115 39.54N 76.10W
Quartu Sant'Elena Italy 32 39.14N 9.11E
Quartzsite U.S.A. 109 33.40N114.13W
Quatsino Sd. Canada 100 50.42N127.58W
Qūchān Iran 65 37.04N 58.29E
Queanbeyan Australia 93 35.24S149.17E
Québec Canada 105 46.50N 71.20W
Québec *d.* Canada 103 51.20N 68.45W
Quebracho Uruguay 125 31.57S 57.53W
Quedlinburg Germany 38 51.48N 11.09E
Queen Anne U.S.A. 115 38.55N 75.57W
Queen Charlotte Canada 100 53.18N132.04W
Queen Charlotte Is. Canada 100 53.00N132.00W
Queen Charlotte Sd. Canada 100 51.30N129.30W
Queen Charlotte Str. Canada 100 51.00N128.00W
Queen Elizabeth Is. Canada 99 78.30N 99.00W
Queen Maud G. Canada 99 68.30N 99.00W
Queen Maud Range *mts.* Antarctica 128 86.20S165.00W
Queens Channel Australia 88 14.46S129.24E
Queenscliff Australia 93 38.17S144.42E
Queensland *d.* Australia 90 23.30S144.00E
Queenstown Australia 91 42.07S145.33E
Queenstown New Zealand 86 45.03S168.41E
Queenstown R.S.A. 80 31.52S 26.51E
Queenstown U.S.A. 115 38.59N 76.09W
Queguay Grande *r.* Uruguay 125 32.09S 58.09W
Queimadas Brazil 123 10.58S 39.38W
Quela Angola 78 9.18S 17.05E
Quelimane Mozambique 79 17.53S 36.57E
Quemado U.S.A. 109 34.20N108.30W
Quemoy *i.* China 55 24.30N118.20E
Quetico Prov. Park Canada 102 48.20N 91.30W
Quequén Argentina 125 38.34S 58.42W
Querétaro Mexico 116 20.38N100.23W
Querétaro *d.* Mexico 116 21.03N100.00W
Querobabi Mexico 109 30.03N111.01W
Quesada Spain 27 37.51N 3.04W
Queshan China 54 32.48N114.01E
Quesnel Canada 100 53.05N122.30W
Quesnel *r.* Canada 100 52.58N122.29W
Questembert France 18 47.40N 2.27W
Quetta Pakistan 62 30.12N 67.00E
Quettehou France 18 49.36N 1.18W
Quevedo Ecuador 122 0.59S 79.27W
Quezaltenango Guatemala 116 14.50N 91.30W
Quezon City Phil. 59 14.39N121.01E
Quibala Angola 78 10.48S 14.56E
Quibaxi Angola 78 8.34S 14.37E
Quibdó Colombia 122 5.40N 76.38W
Quiberon France 18 47.29N 3.07W
Quibocolo Angola 78 6.20S 15.05E
Quicama Nat. Park Angola 78 9.40S 13.30E
Quiet L. Canada 100 61.05N133.05W
Quilán, C. Chile 125 43.16S 74.27W
Quilengues Angola 78 14.09S 14.04E
Quillabamba Peru 122 12.50S 72.50W
Quillacollo Bolivia 124 17.26S 66.17W
Quillan France 20 42.52N 2.11E
Quillota Chile 125 32.53S 71.16W
Quilpie Australia 90 26.37S144.15E
Quilpué Chile 125 33.03S 71.27W
Quimbele Angola 78 6.29S 16.25E
Quimilí Argentina 124 27.35S 62.25W
Quimper France 18 48.00N 4.06W
Quimperlé France 18 47.52N 3.33W
Quincy Ill. U.S.A. 110 39.56N 91.23W
Quincy Mass. U.S.A. 115 42.15N 71.01W
Quincy Wash. U.S.A. 108 47.14N119.51W
Qui Nhon Vietnam 56 13.47N109.11E
Quintanar de la Orden Spain 27 39.34N 3.03W
Quintana Roo *d.* Mexico 117 19.00N 88.00W
Quinte, B. of Canada 105 44.07N 77.15W
Quinter U.S.A. 110 39.04N100.14W
Quintin France 18 48.24N 2.55W
Quinto Spain 25 41.25N 0.29W
Quinzau Angola 78 6.51S 12.46E
Quionga Mozambique 79 10.37S 40.31E
Quipar *r.* Spain 25 38.14N 1.36W
Quirigua *ruins* Guatemala 117 15.20N 89.25W
Quirimbo Angola 78 10.41S 14.16E
Quirindi Australia 93 31.30S150.42E
Quiroga Spain 26 42.29N 7.16W
Quiros, C. Vanuatu 84 14.55S167.01E
Quissanga Mozambique 79 12.24S 40.33E
Quissico Mozambique 81 24.42S 34.44E
Quitapa Angola 78 10.10S 18.16E
Quiterajo Mozambique 79 11.46S 40.25E
Quito Ecuador 122 0.14S 78.30W
Qu Jiang *r.* China 55 30.02N106.20E
Qumigxung China 63 30.53N 86.38E
Qumrān *site* Jordan 67 31.44N 35.27E
Quorn Australia 92 32.20S138.02E
Qurayyah, Wādī *r.* Egypt 66 30.26N 34.01E
Qurdūd Sudan 73 10.17N 29.56E
Qurlurtuuq Canada 98 67.49N115.12W
Quşrah Jordan 67 32.05N 35.20E
Qū' Wishām *f.* Oman 71 18.55N 55.55E
Quxian China 55 30.50N106.54E
Qu Xian China 55 28.59N118.56E
Quyon Canada 105 45.31N 76.14W
Qūzū China 63 29.21N 90.39E

R

Raab *r.* *see* Rába *r.* Austria 31
Raahe Finland 40 64.41N 24.29E
Raalte Neth. 16 52.22N 6.17E
Ra'anana Israel 67 32.11N 34.53E
Raasay *i.* U.K. 14 57.25N 6.05W
Raas Caseyr *c.* Somali Rep. 71 11.48N 51.22E
Rab Croatia 31 44.46N 14.46E
Rab *i.* Croatia 31 44.45N 14.45E
Rába *r.* Hungary 31 47.42N 17.38E
Raba Indonesia 58 8.27S118.45E
Rabaçal *r.* Portugal 26 41.30N 7.12W
Rábade Spain 26 43.07N 7.37W
Rabak Sudan 73 13.09N 32.44E
Rabang China 63 33.03N 80.29E
Rabat Morocco 74 34.02N 6.51W
Rabbit Flat *town* Australia 88 20.10S129.53E
Rabbit L. Canada 104 47.00N 79.37W
Rabbitskin *r.* Canada 100 61.47N120.42W
Rābor Iran 65 29.18N 56.56E
Rabyānah Libya 72 24.14N 21.59E
Rabyānah, Şahrā' *f.* Libya 75 24.30N 21.00E
Racconigi Italy 30 44.46N 7.46E
Raccoon Creek U.S.A. 114 40.02N 82.24W
Race, C. Canada 103 46.40N 53.10W
Race Pt. U.S.A. 115 42.04N 70.14W
Rach Gia Vietnam 56 10.02N105.05E
Racibórz Poland 37 50.06N 18.13E
Racine U.S.A. 110 42.42N 87.50W
Raco U.S.A. 104 46.24N 84.31W
Rădăuţi Romania 37 47.51N 25.55E
Råde Norway 42 59.21N 10.51E
Radeberg Germany 38 51.13N 13.43E
Radebeul Germany 38 51.06N 13.40E
Radeče Slovenia 31 46.04N 15.11E
Radekhov Ukraine 37 50.18N 24.35E
Radford U.S.A. 113 37.07N 80.34W
Rādhanpur India 62 23.50N 71.36E
Radium Hill *town* Australia 92 32.30S140.32E
Radium Hot Springs *town* Canada 100 50.48N116.12W
Radnevo Bulgaria 34 42.18N 25.56E
Radnice Czech Republic 38 49.51N 13.37E
Radom Poland 37 51.26N 21.10E
Radomir Bulgaria 34 42.37N 23.04E
Radomsko Poland 37 51.05N 19.25E
Radomyshl Ukraine 37 50.30N 29.14E
Radotín Czech Republic 38 50.00N 14.22E
Radoviš Macedonia 34 41.38N 22.28E
Radovljica Slovenia 31 46.21N 14.11E
Radöy *i.* Norway 41 60.38N 5.05E
Radstadt Austria 39 47.23N 13.27E
Radstock U.K. 13 51.17N 2.25W
Radstock, C. Australia 92 33.11S134.21E
Radville Canada 101 49.27N104.17W
Raḑwá, Jabal *mtn.* Saudi Arabia 64 24.36N 38.18E
Rae Canada 100 62.50N116.03W
Rāe Bareli India 63 26.13N 81.14E
Raeren Germany 38 50.41N 6.07E
Raeside, L. Australia 89 29.30S122.00E
Rafaela Argentina 124 31.16S 61.44W
Rafaḩ Egypt 67 31.18N 34.15E
Rafaï C.A.R. 73 4.58N 23.56E
Raffadali Italy 32 37.24N 13.33E
Raffili Mission Sudan 73 6.53N 27.58E
Rafḩā Saudi Arabia 64 29.38N 43.30E
Rafsanjān Iran 65 30.24N 56.00E
Raga Sudan 73 8.28N 25.41E
Ragged, Mt. Australia 89 33.27S123.27E
Ragunda Sweden 40 63.06N 16.23E
Ragusa Italy 33 36.55N 14.44E
Raha Indonesia 59 4.50S122.43E
Raḩá, Ḩarrat ar *f.* Saudi Arabia 66 28.00N 36.35E
Rahad *r.* Sudan 72 14.28N 33.31E
Rahad al Bardī Sudan 73 11.18N 23.53E
Rahīm Ki Bāzār Pakistan 62 24.19N 69.09E
Rahīmyār Khān Pakistan 62 28.25N 70.18E
Raiatea *i.* Is. de la Société 85 16.50S151.25W
Rāichūr India 60 16.15N 77.20E
Raiganj India 63 25.37N 88.07E
Raigarh India 63 21.54N 83.24E
Rainbow Australia 92 35.56S142.01E
Rainelle U.S.A. 113 37.58N 80.47W
Rainier, Mt. U.S.A. 108 46.52N121.46W
Rainy L. Canada / U.S.A. 102 48.42N 93.10W
Rainy River *town* Canada 102 48.43N 94.29W
Raipur India 63 21.14N 81.38E
Raipur Uplands *mts.* India 63 20.45N 82.30E
Rairākhol India 63 21.03N 84.23E
Ra'īs Saudi Arabia 64 23.35N 38.36E
Raisen India 63 23.20N 77.48E
Raisin *r.* U.S.A. 104 41.53N 83.20W
Raivavae *i.* Pacific Oc. 85 23.52S147.40W
Rājahmundry India 61 17.01N 81.52E
Rajāj Sudan 73 10.55N 24.43E
Rajang *r.* Malaysia 58 2.10N112.45E
Rājanpur Pakistan 62 29.06N 70.19E
Rājapālaiyam India 60 9.26N 77.36E
Rājasthān *d.* India 62 26.15N 74.00E
Rājasthān Canal India 62 31.10N 75.00E
Rājbāri Bangla. 63 23.46N 89.39E
Rāj Gāngpur India 63 22.11N 84.36E
Rājgarh Madhya P. India 62 23.56N 76.58E
Rājgarh Rāj. India 62 27.14N 76.38E
Rājgarh Rāj. India 62 28.38N 75.23E
Rājkot India 62 22.18N 70.47E
Rāj-Nāndgaon India 63 21.06N 81.02E
Rājpīpla India 62 21.47N 73.34E
Rājpur India 62 21.56N 75.08E
Rājshāhi Bangla. 63 24.22N 88.36E
Rājula India 62 21.01N 71.34E
Rakahanga Atoll Cook Is. 84 10.03S161.06W
Rakaia New Zealand 86 43.45S172.01E
Rakaia *r.* New Zealand 86 43.52S172.13E
Raka Zangbo *r.* China 63 29.24N 87.58E
Rakhni Pakistan 62 30.03N 69.55E
Rakhov Ukraine 37 48.02N 24.10E
Rakhshān *r.* Pakistan 62 27.10N 63.25E
Rākīn Jordan 67 31.14N 35.42E
Rakitnoye Ukraine 37 51.18N 27.10E
Rakkestad Norway 42 59.26N 11.21E
Rakops Botswana 80 21.00S 24.32E
Rakov Belorussia 37 53.58N 26.59E
Rakovník Czech Republic 39 50.05N 13.43E
Rakovski Bulgaria 34 42.18N 24.58E
Rakulka Russian Fed. 44 62.19N 46.52E
Råkvåg Norway 40 63.47N 10.10E
Rakvere Estonia 44 59.22N 26.28E
Raleigh U.S.A. 113 35.46N 78.39W
Raleigh B. U.S.A. 113 35.47N 76.09W
Ralik Chain *is.* Pacific Oc. 84 8.00N168.00E
Ram *r.* Canada 100 62.01N123.41W
Rama Israel 67 32.56N 35.22E
Rama Nicaragua 117 12.09N 84.15W
Ramacca Italy 33 37.23N 14.42E
Rāmah Saudi Arabia 65 25.33N 47.08E
Ramales de la Victoria Spain 26 43.15N 3.27W
Rām Allāh Jordan 67 31.55N 35.12E
Ramallo Argentina 125 33.28S 60.02W
Rāmānuj Ganj India 63 23.48N 83.42E
Ramat Dawid Israel 67 32.40N 35.12E
Ramat Gan Israel 67 32.05N 34.48E
Ramat HaSharon Israel 67 32.09N 34.50E
Ramat HaShofet Israel 67 32.37N 35.06E
Ramat Yishay Israel 67 32.42N 35.10E
Ramat Yohanan Israel 67 32.47N 35.07E
Rambau, Lac *l.* Canada 103 53.40N 70.10W
Rambervillers France 19 48.21N 6.38E
Rambla del Judío *r.* Spain 25 38.15N 1.27W
Rambouillet France 19 48.39N 1.50E
Rām Dās India 62 31.58N 74.55E
Rame Head Australia 93 37.50S149.25E
Rame Head U.K. 13 50.18N 4.13W
Ramelton Rep. of Ire. 15 55.02N 7.40W
Rāmgarh Bangla. 63 22.59N 91.43E
Rāmgarh Bihār India 63 23.38N 85.31E
Rāmgarh Rāj. India 62 27.22N 70.30E
Rāmgarh Rāj. India 62 27.15N 75.11E
Rāmhormoz Iran 65 31.14N 49.37E
Ramillies Belgium 16 50.39N 4.56E

Ramingstein to **Rift Valley**

Ramingstein Austria **39** 47.04N 13.50E
Ramīs *r.* Ethiopia **73** 7.59N 41.34E
Ramla Israel **67** 31.56N 34.52E
Ramlu *mtn.* Ethiopia **73** 13.20N 41.45E
Rāmnagar India **63** 25.17N 83.02E
Ramnäs Sweden **43** 59.46N 16.12E
Ramo Ethiopia **73** 6.50N 41.15E
Ramona Calif. U.S.A. **109** 33.08N116.52W
Ramona Okla. U.S.A. **111** 36.32N 95.55W
Ramore Canada **102** 48.30N 80.25W
Ramos Arizpe Mexico **111** 25.33N100.58W
Ramot Naftali Israel **67** 33.06N 35.33E
Rāmpur Himachal P. India **63** 31.27N 77.38E
Rāmpur Uttar P. India **63** 28.49N 79.02E
Rampura India **62** 24.28N 75.26E
Ramree I. Burma **56** 19.06N 93.48E
Ramsey I.o.M. Europe **12** 54.19N 4.23W
Ramsey England U.K. **13** 52.27N 0.06W
Ramsey L. Canada **104** 47.15N 82.16W
Ramsgate U.K. **13** 51.20N 1.25E
Rāmshīr Iran **65** 30.54N 49.24E
Ramsjö Sweden **41** 62.11N 15.39E
Rāmtek India **63** 21.24N 79.20E
Ramu *r.* P.N.G. **59** 4.00S144.40E
Ramusio, Lac *l.* Canada **103** 55.04N 63.40W
Ranau Malaysia **58** 5.58N116.41E
Rancagua Chile **125** 34.10S 70.45W
Rance *r.* France **18** 48.31N 1.59W
Rancheria *r.* Canada **100** 60.13N129.07W
Rānchī India **63** 23.21N 85.20E
Rand Australia **93** 35.34S146.35E
Randalstown U.K. **15** 54.45N 6.20W
Randan France **20** 46.01N 3.21E
Randazzo Italy **33** 37.53N 14.57E
Randburg R.S.A. **80** 26.07S 28.02E
Rānder India **62** 21.14N 72.47E
Randers Denmark **42** 56.28N 10.03E
Randolph Kans. U.S.A. **110** 39.27N 96.44W
Randolph N.Y. U.S.A. **114** 42.10N 78.59W
Randolph Vt. U.S.A. **105** 43.55N 72.40W
Randsburg U.S.A. **109** 35.22N117.39W
Randsfjorden *l.* Norway **41** 60.25N 10.24E
Råne *r.* Sweden **40** 65.52N 22.19E
Råneå Sweden **40** 65.52N 22.18E
Rāner India **62** 28.53N 73.17E
Ranfurly New Zealand **86** 45.08S170.08E
Rangdong China **54** 32.51N112.18E
Rangely U.S.A. **108** 40.05N108.48W
Ranger U.S.A. **113** 38.07N 82.10W
Ranger L. Canada **104** 46.54N 83.35W
Ranger Lake *town* Canada **104** 46.52N 83.36W
Rangia India **63** 26.28N 91.38E
Rangiora New Zealand **86** 43.18S172.38E
Rangiroa *i.* Pacific Oc. **85** 15.00S147.40W
Rangitaiki *r.* New Zealand **86** 37.55S176.50E
Rangkasbitung Indonesia **59** 6.21S106.12E
Rangoon *see* Yangon Burma **56**
Rangpur Bangla. **63** 25.45N 89.15E
Rānīganj India **63** 23.37N 87.08E
Rānīkhet India **63** 29.39N 79.25E
Rāniwāra India **62** 24.45N 72.13E
Rankin Inlet *town* Canada **99** 62.52N 92.00W
Rankins Springs *town* Australia **93** 33.52S146.18E
Rannoch, Loch U.K. **14** 56.41N 4.20W
Rann of Kachchh *f.* India **62** 23.50N 69.50E
Ranohira Madagascar **81** 22.29S 45.24E
Rano Kao *mtn.* I. de Pascua **85** 27.11S109.27W
Ranong Thailand **56** 9.59N 98.40E
Ransäter Sweden **43** 59.46N 13.26E
Rantauprapat Indonesia **58** 2.05N 99.46E
Rantekombola *mtn.* Indonesia **58** 3.30S119.58E
Råö Sweden **42** 57.24N 11.56E
Rao Co *mtn.* Laos **56** 18.10N105.25E
Raoping China **55** 23.45N117.05E
Raoul *i.* Pacific Oc. **84** 29.15S177.55W
Rapa *i.* Pacific Oc. **85** 27.35S144.20W
Rapallo Italy **30** 44.21N 9.14E
Rāpar India **62** 23.34N 70.38E
Rapidan *r.* U.S.A. **114** 38.22N 77.37W
Rapid Bay *town* Australia **92** 35.33S138.09E
Rapid City U.S.A. **110** 44.05N103.14W
Rapides des Joachims *town* Canada **105** 46.13N 77.43W
Rappahannock *r.* U.S.A. **114** 37.34N 76.18W
Rapperswil Switz. **39** 47.14N 8.50E
Rapsáni Greece **34** 39.54N 22.33E
Raquette *r.* U.S.A. **105** 45.00N 74.42W
Raquette L. U.S.A. **105** 43.52N 74.38W
Raquette Lake *town* U.S.A. **105** 43.49N 74.41W
Rarotonga *i.* Cook Is. **84** 21.14S159.46W
Ra's al Ḩadd *c.* Oman **60** 22.32N 59.49E
Ra's al Khaymah U.A.E. **65** 25.48N 55.56E
Ra's al Unūf Libya **75** 30.31N 18.34E
Ra's an Naqb *town* Egypt **66** 29.36N 34.51E
Ra's an Naqb *town* Jordan **66** 30.30N 35.29E
Ras Dashen *mtn.* Ethiopia **73** 13.20N 38.10E
Ras Djebel Tunisia **32** 37.13N 10.09E
Râs Ghârib Egypt **66** 28.22N 33.04E
Rashād Sudan **73** 11.51N 31.04E
Rashid Egypt **66** 31.25N 30.25E
Rashīd Qal 'eh Afghan. **62** 31.31N 67.31E
Rasht Iran **65** 37.18N 49.38E
Rasina *r.* Yugo. **34** 43.38N 21.21E
Raška Yugo. **34** 43.17N 20.37E
Rās Koh *mtn.* Pakistan **62** 28.50N 65.12E
Rason L. Australia **89** 28.46S124.20E
Rasra India **63** 25.51N 83.51E
Rastatt Germany **39** 48.51N 8.12E
Rastede Germany **38** 53.15N 8.11E
Rasu, Monte *mtn.* Italy **32** 40.25N 9.00E
Ratak Chain *is.* Pacific Oc. **84** 8.00N172.00E
Ratangarh India **62** 28.05N 74.36E
Rat Buri Thailand **56** 13.30N 99.50E
Ratcatchers L. Australia **92** 32.40S143.13E
Rāth India **63** 25.35N 79.34E
Rathcormack Rep. of Ire. **15** 52.05N 8.18W
Rathdrum Rep. of Ire. **15** 52.56N 6.15W
Rathenow Germany **38** 52.36N 12.20E
Rathlin I. U.K. **15** 55.17N 6.15W
Rath Luirc Rep. of Ire. **15** 52.21N 8.41W
Rathmullen Rep. of Ire. **15** 55.06N 7.32W
Ratlām India **62** 23.19N 75.04E
Ratnāgiri India **60** 16.59N 73.18E
Ratno Ukraine **37** 51.40N 24.32E
Ratodero Pakistan **62** 27.48N 68.18E
Raton U.S.A. **108** 36.54N104.24W
Rats, Rivière aux *r.* Canada **105** 47.12N 72.52W
Rattlesnake Range *mts.* U.S.A. **108** 42.45N107.10W
Rattray Head U.K. **14** 57.37N 1.50W
Rättvik Sweden **41** 60.53N 15.06E
Ratzeburg Germany **38** 53.42N 10.46E
Ratzeburger See *l.* Germany **38** 53.45N 10.47E
Rauch Argentina **125** 36.47S 59.05W
Raufoss Norway **41** 60.43N 10.37E
Raul Soares Brazil **126** 20.04S 42.27W
Rauma Finland **41** 61.08N 21.30E
Rauma *r.* Norway **40** 62.32N 7.43E
Raung, Gunung *mtn.* Indonesia **59** 8.07S114.03E
Raurkela India **63** 22.13N 84.53E
Rautas Sweden **40** 68.00N 19.55E
Ravalgaon India **62** 20.38N 74.25E
Ravanusa Italy **32** 37.16N 13.58E
Rāvar Iran **65** 31.14N 56.51E
Rava-Russkaya Ukraine **37** 50.15N 23.36E
Ravena U.S.A. **115** 42.29N 73.49W
Ravenna Italy **30** 44.25N 12.12E
Ravenna U.S.A. **114** 41.09N 81.15W
Ravensburg Germany **39** 47.47N 9.37E
Ravenshoe Australia **90** 17.37S145.29E
Ravensthorpe Australia **89** 33.35S120.02E
Ravenswood U.S.A. **114** 38.57N 81.46W
Rāver India **62** 21.15N 76.05E
Rāvi *r.* Pakistan **60** 30.30N 72.13E
Ravna Gora Croatia **31** 45.23N 14.57E
Rawaki *i.* Kiribati **84** 3.43S170.43W
Rāwalpindi Pakistan **62** 33.36N 73.04E
Rawāndūz Iraq **65** 36.38N 44.32E
Rawdon Canada **105** 46.03N 73.44W
Rawene New Zealand **86** 35.24S173.30E
Rawicz Poland **36** 51.37N 16.52E
Rawlinna Australia **89** 31.00S125.21E
Rawlins U.S.A. **108** 41.47N107.14W
Rawson Argentina **125** 34.40S 60.02W
Raxaul India **63** 26.59N 84.51E
Ray U.S.A. **110** 48.21N103.10W
Ray, C. Canada **103** 47.40N 59.18W
Raya *mtn.* Indonesia **58** 0.45S112.45E
Rāyagada India **63** 19.10N 83.25E
Rāyen Iran **65** 29.34N 57.26E
Raymond Canada **100** 49.30N112.35W
Raymond U.S.A. **108** 46.41N123.44W
Raymond Terrace Australia **93** 32.47S151.45E
Raymondville U.S.A. **111** 26.29N 97.47W
Rayong Thailand **56** 12.43N101.20E
Raz, Pointe du *c.* France **18** 48.02N 4.44W
Razan Iran **65** 35.22N 49.02E
Razanj Yugo. **34** 43.40N 21.31E
Razdelnaya Ukraine **37** 46.50N 30.02E
Razgrad Bulgaria **34** 43.33N 26.34E
Razgrad *d.* Bulgaria **34** 43.32N 26.10E
Razlog Bulgaria **34** 41.53N 23.28E
Ré, Île de *i.* France **20** 46.10N 1.26W
Reading U.K. **13** 51.27N 0.57W
Reading U.S.A. **115** 40.20N 75.56W
Readsboro U.S.A. **115** 42.46N 72.57W
Realicó Argentina **125** 35.02S 64.14W
Réalmont France **20** 43.47N 2.12E
Reay Forest *f.* U.K. **14** 58.17N 4.48W
Rebecca, L. Australia **89** 30.07S122.32E
Rebi Indonesia **59** 6.24S134.07E
Rebiana Sand Sea *see* Rabyānah, Ṣaḩrā'f. *f.* Libya **75**
Reboly Russian Fed. **44** 63.50N 30.49E
Rebun jima *i.* Japan **57** 45.25N141.04E
Recalde Argentina **125** 36.39S 61.05W
Recanati Italy **31** 43.24N 13.32E
Rechāh Lām Afghan. **62** 34.58N 70.51E
Recherche, Archipelago of the *is.* Australia **89** 34.05S122.45E
Rechitsa Belorussia **37** 52.21N 30.24E
Recife Brazil **123** 8.06S 34.53W
Recklinghausen Germany **38** 51.36N 7.13E
Recknitz *r.* Germany **38** 54.14N 12.28E
Reconquista Argentina **124** 29.08S 59.38W
Recreo Argentina **124** 29.20S 65.04W
Red *r.* Canada **101** 50.20N 96.50W
Red *r.* U.S.A. **111** 31.00N 91.40W
Red *r. see* Hong Hà *r.* Vietnam **56**
Red Bank U.S.A. **115** 40.21N 74.03W
Red Basin *f. see* Sichuan Pendi *f.* China **55**
Red Bay *town* Canada **103** 51.44N 56.45W
Red Bluff U.S.A. **108** 40.11N122.15W
Redcar U.K. **12** 54.37N 1.04W
Red Cliffs *town* Australia **92** 34.22S142.13E
Red Cloud U.S.A. **110** 40.04N 98.31W
Red Deer Canada **100** 52.20N113.50W
Red Deer *r.* Canada **101** 50.56N109.54W
Redding U.S.A. **108** 40.35N122.24W
Redditch U.K. **13** 52.18N 1.57W
Rede *r.* U.K. **12** 55.08N 2.13W
Redfield U.S.A. **110** 44.53N 98.31W
Redhill *town* Australia **92** 33.34S138.12E
Red Hook U.S.A. **115** 41.55N 73.53W
Red Indian L. Canada **103** 48.40N 56.50W
Red L. U.S.A. **107** 48.00N 95.00W
Red Lake *town* Canada **102** 51.03N 93.49W
Redlands U.S.A. **109** 34.03N117.11W
Red Lion U.S.A. **115** 39.54N 76.36W
Red Lodge U.S.A. **108** 45.11N109.15W
Redmond U.S.A. **108** 44.17N121.11W
Rednitz *r.* Germany **38** 49.28N 10.59E
Red Oak U.S.A. **110** 41.01N 95.14W
Redon France **18** 47.39N 2.05W
Redondela Spain **26** 42.17N 8.36W
Redondo Portugal **27** 38.39N 7.33W
Redondo Beach *town* U.S.A. **109** 33.51N118.23W
Red Rock Canada **100** 53.39N122.41W
Redrock U.S.A. **109** 32.35N111.19W
Redruth U.K. **13** 50.14N 5.14W
Red Sea Africa / Asia **71** 20.00N 39.00E
Redstone Canada **100** 52.13N123.50W
Red Sucker L. Canada **101** 54.09N 93.40W
Red Volta *r.* Ghana **76** 10.32N 0.31W
Redwater Alta. Canada **100** 53.55N113.06W
Redwater Ont. Canada **104** 46.54N 79.34W
Red Wing U.S.A. **110** 44.33N 92.31W
Redwood City U.S.A. **108** 37.29N122.13W
Ree, Lough Rep. of Ire. **15** 53.31N 7.58W
Reed City U.S.A. **112** 43.54N 85.31W
Reeder U.S.A. **110** 46.06N102.57W
Reedsport U.S.A. **108** 43.42N124.06W
Reedy U.S.A. **114** 38.54N 81.26W
Reefton New Zealand **86** 42.07S171.52E
Reese *r.* U.S.A. **108** 40.39N116.54W
Reftele Sweden **43** 57.11N 13.35E
Refuge Cove *town* Canada **100** 50.07N124.50W
Refugio U.S.A. **111** 28.18N 97.17W
Rega *r.* Poland **36** 54.10N 15.18E
Regavim Israel **67** 32.32N 35.02E
Regen Germany **39** 48.59N 13.07E
Regen *r.* Germany **39** 49.01N 12.06E
Regensburg Germany **39** 49.01N 12.06E
Reggane Algeria **74** 26.42N 0.10E
Reggello Italy **30** 43.41N 11.32E
Reggio Calabria Italy **33** 38.07N 15.39E
Reggio Emilia-Romagna Italy **30** 44.43N 10.36E
Reghin Romania **37** 46.47N 24.42E
Regina Canada **101** 50.25N104.39W
Regiwar Pakistan **62** 25.57N 65.44E
Regnéville France **18** 49.01N 1.33W
Reguengos de Monsaraz Portugal **27** 38.25N 7.32W
Rehau Germany **39** 50.15N 12.02E
Rehoboth Namibia **80** 23.19S 17.10E
Rehoboth B. U.S.A. **115** 38.40N 75.06W
Rehoboth Beach *town* U.S.A. **115** 38.43N 75.05W
Rehovot Israel **67** 31.54N 34.46E
Reichenbach Germany **38** 50.37N 12.18E
Reidsville U.S.A. **113** 36.21N 79.40W
Reigate U.K. **13** 51.14N 0.13W
Reims France **19** 49.15N 4.02E
Reinach Switz. **39** 47.30N 7.35E
Reindeer L. Canada **101** 57.15N102.40W
Reinosa Spain **26** 43.00N 4.08W
Reisterstown U.S.A. **114** 39.28N 76.50W
Rejmyra Sweden **43** 58.50N 15.55E
Rekovac Yugo. **34** 43.51N 21.03E
Relizane Algeria **75** 35.45N 0.33E
Remanso Brazil **123** 9.41S 42.04W
Remarkable, Mt. Australia **92** 32.48S138.10E
Rembang Indonesia **59** 6.45S111.22E
Remeshk Iran **65** 26.52N 58.46E
Remich Lux. **16** 49.34N 6.23E
Remington U.S.A. **114** 38.32N 77.49W
Remiremont France **19** 48.01N 6.35E
Remoulins France **21** 43.56N 4.34E
Remscheid Germany **38** 51.11N 7.11E
Remsen U.S.A. **115** 43.19N 75.11W
Rena Norway **41** 61.08N 11.22E
Rende Italy **33** 39.19N 16.11E
Rendina Greece **35** 39.04N 21.58E
Rendsburg Germany **38** 54.18N 9.40E
Renfrew Canada **105** 45.28N 76.41W
Rengat Indonesia **58** 0.26S102.35E
Rengo Chile **125** 34.25S 70.52W
Renheji China **55** 31.56N115.07E
Reni India **62** 28.41N 75.02E
Reni Ukraine **37** 45.28N 28.17E
Renkum Neth. **16** 51.59N 5.46E
Renmark Australia **92** 34.10S140.45E
Rennell Sd. Canada **100** 53.23N132.35W
Renner Springs *town* Australia **90** 18.20S133.48E
Rennes France **18** 48.05N 1.41W
Reno *r.* Italy **30** 44.37N 12.17E
Reno U.S.A. **108** 39.31N119.48W
Renovo U.S.A. **114** 41.20N 77.38W
Rensselaer U.S.A. **115** 42.39N 73.44W
Rentería Spain **26** 43.19N 1.54W
Renton U.S.A. **108** 47.30N122.11W
Ren Xian China **54** 37.07N114.41E
Réo Burkina **76** 12.20N 2.27W
Repki Ukraine **37** 51.47N 31.06E
Republic Penn. U.S.A. **114** 39.56N 79.55W
Republic Wash. U.S.A. **108** 48.39N118.44W
Republican *r.* U.S.A. **110** 39.03N 96.48W
Republic of Ireland Europe **15** 53.00N 8.00W
Republic of South Africa Africa **80** 28.30S 24.50E
Repulse B. Australia **90** 20.36S148.43E
Repulse Bay *town* Canada **99** 66.35N 86.20W
Requa U.S.A. **108** 41.34N124.05W
Requena Peru **122** 5.05S 73.52W
Requena Spain **25** 39.29N 1.06W
Réquista France **20** 44.02N 2.31E
Resadiye Karimadasi *pen.* Turkey **35** 36.45N 27.40E
Reschenpass Italy / Austria **39** 46.50N 10.30E
Resen Macedonia **34** 41.05N 21.00E
Reserve Canada **101** 52.28N102.39W
Resistencia Argentina **124** 27.28S 59.00W
Reşiţa Romania **37** 45.17N 21.53E
Resolute Canada **99** 74.40N 95.00W
Resolution I. Canada **99** 61.30N 65.00W
Resolution I. New Zealand **86** 45.40S166.30E
Restigouche *r.* Canada **103** 48.04N 66.20W
Restoule Canada **104** 46.03N 79.47W
Rethel France **19** 49.31N 4.22E
Réthimnon Greece **35** 35.22N 24.29E
Réunion *i.* Indian Oc. **49** 22.00S 55.00E
Reus Spain **25** 41.09N 1.07E
Reusel Neth. **16** 51.21N 5.09E
Reuterstadt Stavenhagen Germany **38** 53.40N 12.54E
Reutlingen Germany **39** 48.29N 9.11E
Reutte Austria **39** 47.29N 10.43E
Revda Russian Fed. **44** 56.49N 59.58E
Revelstoke Canada **100** 51.00N118.00W
Revigny-sur-Ornain France **19** 48.50N 4.59E
Revilla del Campo Spain **26** 42.13N 3.32W
Revilla Gigedo, Islas de *is.* Mexico **116** 19.00N111.00W
Revillagigedo I. U.S.A. **100** 55.50N131.20W
Revin France **19** 49.56N 4.38E
Revue *r.* Mozambique **81** 19.58S 34.40E
Rewa India **63** 24.32N 81.18E
Rewāri India **62** 28.11N 76.37E
Rexburg U.S.A. **108** 43.49N111.47W
Rexford U.S.A. **108** 48.53N115.13W
Rey Iran **65** 35.35N 51.27E
Reykjavík Iceland **40** 64.09N 21.58W
Reynoldsville U.S.A. **114** 41.06N 78.53W
Reynosa Mexico **111** 26.07N 98.18W
Rezé France **18** 47.12N 1.34W
Rēzekne Latvia **44** 56.30N 27.22E
Rhaetian Alps *mts.* Switz. **39** 46.45N 9.55E
Rhayader U.K. **13** 52.19N 3.30W
Rheda-Wiedenbrück Schloss Germany **38** 51.51N 8.17E
Rheden Neth. **16** 52.01N 6.02E
Rhein *r.* Europe **16** 51.53N 6.03E
Rheinbach Germany **38** 50.37N 6.57E
Rheine Germany **38** 52.17N 7.26E
Rheinfelden Germany **39** 47.33N 7.47E
Rheinland-Pfalz *d.* Germany **39** 49.50N 7.30E
Rheinsberg Germany **38** 53.06N 12.53E
Rhenen Neth. **16** 51.58N 5.34E
Rheydt Germany **38** 51.10N 6.25E
Rhine *see* Rhein *r.* Europe **16**
Rhinebeck U.S.A. **115** 41.56N 73.55W
Rhinelander U.S.A. **110** 45.39N 89.23W
Rhino Camp *town* Uganda **79** 2.58N 31.20E
Rhir, Cap *c.* Morocco **74** 30.38N 9.55W
Rho Italy **30** 45.32N 9.02E
Rhode Island *d.* U.S.A. **115** 41.40N 71.30W
Rhode Island Sd. U.S.A. **115** 41.25N 71.15W
Rhodes *i. see* Ródhos *i.* Greece **35**
Rhodope Mts. *see* Rhodopi Planina *mts.* Bulgaria **34**
Rhodopi Planina *mts.* Bulgaria **34** 41.40N 24.20E
Rhondda U.K. **13** 51.39N 3.30W
Rhône *d.* France **21** 45.54N 4.35E
Rhône *r.* France **21** 43.20N 4.50E
Rhône-Alpes *d.* France **21** 45.20N 5.45E
Rhône au Rhin, Canal du France **19** 47.06N 5.19E
Rhosneigr U.K. **12** 53.14N 4.31W
Rhue *r.* France **20** 45.23N 2.29E
Rhyl U.K. **12** 53.19N 3.29W
Riachão Brazil **123** 7.22S 46.37W
Riāng India **63** 27.32N 92.56E
Riánsares *r.* Spain **27** 39.32N 3.18W
Riāsi Jammu & Kashmir **62** 33.05N 74.50E
Riau *d.* Indonesia **58** 0.00 102.35E
Riau, Kepulauan *is.* Indonesia **58** 0.50N104.00E
Riaza Spain **26** 41.17N 3.28W
Riaza *r.* Spain **26** 41.42N 3.55W
Ribadeo Spain **26** 43.33N 7.02W
Ribadesella Spain **26** 43.28N 5.04W
Ribarroja, Embalse de *resr.* Spain **25** 41.12N 0.20E
Ribauè Mozambique **79** 14.57S 38.27E
Ribble *r.* U.K. **12** 53.45N 2.44W
Ribe Denmark **42** 55.21N 8.46E
Ribeauvillé France **19** 48.12N 7.19E
Ribécourt France **19** 49.31N 2.55E
Ribeirão Prêto Brazil **126** 21.09S 47.48W
Ribera Italy **32** 37.30N 13.16E
Ribérac France **20** 45.14N 0.22E
Riberalta Bolivia **124** 10.59S 66.06W
Ribnica Slovenia **31** 45.44N 14.44E
Ribnitz-Damgarten Germany **38** 54.15N 12.28E
Ribstone Creek *r.* Canada **101** 52.51N110.05W
Riccia Italy **33** 41.29N 14.50E
Riccione Italy **30** 43.59N 12.39E
Rice U.S.A. **109** 34.06N114.50W
Rice L. Canada **104** 44.08N 78.13W
Rice Lake *town* U.S.A. **110** 45.30N 91.43W
Rich, C. Canada **104** 44.43N 80.38W
Richard's Bay *town* R.S.A. **81** 28.47S 32.06E
Richardson *r.* Canada **101** 58.30N111.30W
Richardson U.S.A. **111** 32.57N 96.44W
Richelieu *r.* Canada **105** 46.03N 73.07W
Richelieu France **18** 47.01N 0.19E
Richfield Idaho U.S.A. **108** 43.03N114.09W
Richfield Utah U.S.A. **108** 38.46N112.05W
Richfield Springs U.S.A. **115** 42.51N 74.59W
Richford U.S.A. **105** 45.00N 72.40W
Rich Hill *town* U.S.A. **111** 38.06N 94.22W
Richibucto Canada **103** 46.41N 64.52W
Richland U.S.A. **108** 46.17N119.18W
Richmond Qld. Australia **90** 20.44S143.08E
Richmond Ont. Canada **105** 45.11N 75.50W
Richmond Que. Canada **105** 45.40N 72.09W
Richmond New Zealand **86** 41.20S173.10E
Richmond C.P. R.S.A. **80** 31.24S 23.56E
Richmond U.K. **12** 54.24N 1.43W
Richmond Ind. U.S.A. **112** 39.50N 84.51W
Richmond Utah U.S.A. **108** 41.55N111.48W
Richmond Va. U.S.A. **113** 37.34N 77.27W
Richmond Dale U.S.A. **114** 39.13N 82.54W
Richmond Hill Canada **104** 43.52N 79.27W
Richmond Range *mts.* Australia **93** 29.00S152.48E
Richwood U.S.A. **114** 38.14N 80.32W
Ricobayo, Embalse de *resr.* Spain **26** 41.30N 5.55W
Ridderkerk Neth. **16** 51.53N 4.39E
Rideau *r.* Canada **105** 45.27N 75.42W
Rideau Hills Canada **105** 44.37N 77.00W
Rideau Lakes Canada **105** 44.45N 76.17W
Ridgetown Canada **104** 42.26N 81.54W
Ridgway U.S.A. **114** 41.26N 78.44W
Riding Mtn. Canada **101** 50.37N 99.50W
Riding Mtn. Nat. Park Canada **101** 50.55N100.25W
Ried Austria **39** 48.13N 13.30E
Riemst Belgium **16** 50.49N 5.38E
Riesa Germany **38** 51.18N 13.17E
Riesi Italy **33** 37.17N 14.05E
Rieti Italy **30** 42.24N 12.51E
Rifle U.S.A. **108** 39.32N107.47W
Rift Valley *d.* Kenya **79** 1.00N 36.00E

Riga to Rovaniemi

Riga Latvia 41 56.53N 24.08E
Riga, G. of Latvia / Estonia 41 57.30N 23.35E
Rīgān Iran 65 28.40N 58.58E
Rigas Jūras Līcis see Riga, G. of g. Latvia 41
Rīgestān f. Afghan. 62 30.35N 65.00E
Riggins U.S.A. 108 45.25N116.19W
Rig Matī Iran 65 27.40N 58.11E
Rigo P.N.G. 90 9.50S147.35E
Rigolet Canada 103 54.20N 58.35W
Riia Laht g. see Riga, G. of Estonia 41
Riihimäki Finland 41 60.45N 24.46E
Riiser-Larsenhalvöya pen. Antarctica 128 68.00S 35.00E
Riječki Zaljev b. Croatia 31 45.15N 14.25E
Rijeka Croatia 31 45.20N 14.27E
Rijssen Neth. 16 52.19N 6.31E
Rijswijk Neth. 16 52.03N 4.22E
Rila Planina mts. Bulgaria 34 42.10N 23.30E
Riley U.S.A. 108 43.31N119.28W
Rimah, Wādī ar r. Saudi Arabia 64 26.10N 44.00E
Rimavská Sobota Slovakia 37 48.23N 20.02E
Rimbo Sweden 43 59.45N 18.22E
Rimersburg U.S.A. 114 41.02N 79.30W
Rimforsa Sweden 43 58.08N 15.40E
Rimini Italy 30 44.04N 12.34E
Rîmnicu-Sărat Romania 37 45.24N 27.06E
Rîmnicu-Vîlcea Romania 37 45.06N 24.22E
Rimouski Canada 103 48.27N 68.32W
Rinbung China 63 29.16N 89.54E
Rinconada Argentina 124 22.26S 66.10W
Rindal Norway 40 63.04N 9.13E
Ringe Denmark 42 55.14N 10.29E
Ringebu Norway 41 61.31N 10.10E
Ringerike Norway 42 60.10N 10.18E
Ringim Nigeria 77 12.09N 9.08E
Ringköbing Denmark 42 56.05N 8.15E
Ringköbing Fjord est. Denmark 42 56.00N 8.15E
Ringling U.S.A. 108 46.16N110.49W
Ringsted Denmark 42 55.27N 11.49E
Rīngus India 62 27.21N 75.34E
Ringvassöy i. Norway 40 69.55N 19.10E
Ringwood U.K. 13 50.50N 1.48W
Rintein Germany 38 52.11N 9.04E
Riobamba Ecuador 122 1.44S 78.40W
Rio Branco Brazil 122 9.59S 67.49W
Rio Bueno Chile 125 40.20S 72.55W
Rio Casca Brazil 126 20.13S 42.38W
Rio Claro Brazil 126 22.19S 47.35W
Río Cuarto Argentina 125 33.08S 64.20W
Rio de Janeiro Brazil 126 22.53S 43.17W
Rio de Janeiro d. Brazil 126 22.00S 42.30W
Río Gallegos Argentina 125 51.37S 69.10W
Rio Grande town Argentina 125 53.50S 67.40W
Rio Grande town Brazil 126 32.03S 52.08W
Rio Grande r. Mexico / U.S.A. 111 25.57N 97.09W
Río Grande r. Nicaragua 117 12.48N 83.30W
Rio Grande City U.S.A. 111 26.23N 98.49W
Rio Grande do Norte d. Brazil 123 6.00S 36.30W
Rio Grande do Sul d. Brazil 126 30.15S 53.30W
Ríohacha Colombia 122 11.34N 72.58W
Rio Largo Brazil 123 9.28S 35.50W
Riom France 20 45.54N 3.07E
Río Negro d. Argentina 125 40.00S 67.00W
Rio Negro Brazil 126 26.06S 49.48W
Río Negro, Embalse del resr. Uruguay 125 32.45S 56.00W
Rionero in Vulture Italy 33 40.56N 15.41E
Rio Novo Brazil 126 21.15S 43.09W
Riópar Spain 26 38.30N 2.27W
Rio Piracicaba Brazil 126 19.54S 43.10W
Rio Pomba Brazil 126 21.15S 43.12W
Rio Prêto Brazil 126 22.06S 43.52W
Ríosucio Colombia 122 7.27N 77.07W
Río Tercero Argentina 124 32.10S 64.05W
Rio Verde town Brazil 124 17.50S 50.55W
Rioz France 19 47.25N 6.04E
Ripatransone Italy 31 43.00N 13.46E
Ripley Canada 104 44.04N 81.34W
Ripley N.Y. U.S.A. 114 42.16N 79.43W
Ripley W.Va. U.S.A. 114 38.49N 81.43W
Ripoll Spain 25 42.12N 2.12E
Ripon Canada 105 45.47N 75.06W
Ripon U.K. 12 54.08N 1.31W
Riposto Italy 33 37.45N 15.12E
Rirapora Brazil 126 17.20S 45.02W
Risbäck Sweden 40 64.42N 15.32E
Riscle France 20 43.40N 0.05W
Rishā, Wādī ar r. Saudi Arabia 65 25.40N 44.08E
Rishikesh India 63 30.07N 78.42E
Rishiri tō i. Japan 57 45.11N141.15E
Rishon LeZiyyon Israel 67 31.57N 34.48E
Rishpon Israel 67 32.12N 34.49E
Risle r. France 18 49.26N 0.23E
Risnjak mtn. Croatia 31 45.26N 14.37E
Rison U.S.A. 111 33.58N 92.11W
Risör Norway 42 58.43N 9.14E
Rissani Morocco 74 31.23N 4.09W
Riti Nigeria 77 7.57N 9.41E
Ritidian Pt. Guam 84 13.39N144.51E
Rittman U.S.A. 114 40.58N 81.47W
Ritzville U.S.A. 108 47.08N118.23W
Riva Italy 30 45.53N 10.50E
Rivadavia Argentina 124 24.11S 62.53W
Rivarolo Canavese Italy 30 45.19N 7.43E
Rivas Nicaragua 117 11.26N 85.50W
Rive-de-Gier France 21 45.32N 4.37E
Rivera Uruguay 125 30.54S 55.31W
River Cess town Liberia 76 5.28N 9.32W
Rivergaro Italy 30 44.55N 9.36E
Riverhead U.S.A. 115 40.55N 72.40W
Riverina f. Australia 93 34.30S145.20E
Rivers Canada 101 50.02N100.12W
Rivers d. Nigeria 77 4.45N 6.35E
Riversdale R.S.A. 80 34.05S 21.15E
Riverside U.S.A. 109 33.59N117.22W
Rivers Inlet town Canada 100 51.40N127.20W
Riverton Australia 92 34.08S138.24E
Riverton Canada 101 50.59N 96.59W
Riverton New Zealand 86 46.21S168.01E
Riverton U.S.A. 108 43.02N108.23W
River Valley town Canada 104 46.35N 80.10W
Rivesaltes France 20 42.46N 2.52E
Rivesville U.S.A. 114 39.32N 80.07W
Riviera di Levante f. Italy 30 44.00N 9.40E
Riviera di Ponente f. Italy 30 43.40N 8.00E
Riviere à Pierre town Canada 105 46.59N 72.11W
Rivière aux Rats town Canada 105 47.13N 72.54W
Rivière-du-Loup town Canada 103 47.50N 69.32W
Rivière Pentecôte town Canada 103 49.47N 67.10W
Rivoli Italy 30 45.04N 7.31E
Riyadh see Ar Riyāḑ Saudi Arabia 65
Rize Turkey 64 41.03N 40.31E
Rizhao China 54 35.26N119.27E
Rizokárpason Cyprus 66 35.35N 34.24E
Rizzuto, Capo c. Italy 33 38.54N 17.06E
Rjukan Norway 42 59.52N 8.34E
Roa Norway 42 60.17N 10.37E
Roa Spain 26 41.42N 3.55W
Roag, Loch U.K. 14 58.14N 6.50W
Roanne France 21 46.02N 4.04E
Roanoke Ala. U.S.A. 113 33.09N 85.24W
Roanoke r. U.S.A. 113 35.56N 76.43W
Roanoke Va. U.S.A. 113 37.15N 79.58W
Roanoke Rapids town U.S.A. 113 36.28N 77.40W
Roaring Branch U.S.A. 114 41.34N 76.57W
Roaring Spring U.S.A. 114 40.20N 78.24W
Roaring Springs U.S.A. 111 33.54N100.52W
Robāţ Iran 65 30.04N 54.49E
Robe Australia 92 37.11S139.45E
Robe, Mt. Australia 92 31.39S141.16E
Röbel Germany 38 53.23N 12.35E
Robertsdale U.S.A. 114 40.11N 78.07W
Robertsganj India 63 24.42N 83.04E
Robertson R.S.A. 80 33.48S 19.52E
Robertsport Liberia 76 6.45N 11.22W
Robertstown Australia 92 33.59S139.03E
Roberval Canada 103 48.31N 72.13W
Robin Hood's Bay town U.K. 12 54.26N 0.31W
Robinson r. Australia 90 16.03S137.16E
Robinson Range mts. Australia 88 25.45S119.00E
Robinvale Australia 92 34.37S142.50E
Robleda Spain 26 40.23N 6.36W
Robledo Spain 26 38.46N 2.26W
Roblin Man. Canada 101 51.17N101.28W
Roblin Ont. Canada 105 44.21N 77.01W
Roboré Bolivia 124 18.20S 59.45W
Robson, Mt. Canada 100 53.10N119.10W
Rocas i. Atlantic Oc. 127 3.50S 33.50W
Roccadaspide Italy 33 40.26N 15.12E
Roccastrada Italy 30 43.00N 11.10E
Roccella Italy 29 38.19N 16.24E
Rocciamelone mtn. Italy 30 45.12N 7.05E
Rocella Italy 33 38.20N 16.24E
Rocha Uruguay 126 34.30S 54.22W
Rocha da Gale, Barragem resr. Portugal 27 38.20N 7.25W
Rochdale U.K. 12 53.36N 2.10W
Rochechouart France 20 45.50N 0.50E
Rochefort Belgium 16 50.10N 5.13E
Rochefort France 20 45.57N 0.58W
Rochefort-Montagne France 20 45.41N 2.48E
Rochelle U.S.A. 110 41.55N 89.05W
Rocher River town Canada 100 61.23N112.44W
Rochester Australia 93 36.22S144.42E
Rochester Kent U.K. 13 51.22N 0.30E
Rochester Minn. U.S.A. 110 44.01N 92.27W
Rochester N.H. U.S.A. 115 43.18N 70.59W
Rochester N.Y. U.S.A. 114 43.10N 77.36W
Rochester Penn. U.S.A. 114 40.43N 80.17W
Rochfort Bridge Rep. of Ire. 15 53.25N 7.19W
Rochlitz Germany 38 51.03N 12.47E
Rock r. Canada 100 60.07N127.07W
Rock U.S.A. 112 46.03N 87.10W
Rockall i. U.K. 10 57.39N 13.44W
Rockall Bank f. Atlantic Oc. 10 57.30N 14.00W
Rock Creek town U.S.A. 114 41.40N 80.52W
Rockdale U.S.A. 114 39.21N 76.46W
Rockefeller Plateau Antarctica 128 80.00S140.00W
Rockford U.S.A. 110 42.17N 89.06W
Rock Hall U.S.A. 115 39.08N 76.14W
Rockhampton Australia 90 23.22S150.32E
Rock Hill town U.S.A. 113 34.55N 81.01W
Rockingham Australia 89 32.16S115.21E
Rockingham U.S.A. 113 34.56N 79.47W
Rock Island town Canada 105 45.01N 72.06W
Rock Island town U.S.A. 110 41.30N 90.34W
Rockland Canada 105 45.32N 75.19W
Rockland Idaho U.S.A. 108 42.34N112.53W
Rockland Maine U.S.A. 112 44.06N 69.06W
Rockland Mich. U.S.A. 112 46.44N 89.12W
Rocklands Resr. Australia 92 37.13S141.52E
Rockport Canada 105 44.22N 75.58W
Rockport U.S.A. 108 39.45N123.47W
Rock Rapids town U.S.A. 110 43.26N 96.10W
Rock Sound town Bahamas 117 24.54N 76.11W
Rocksprings Tex. U.S.A. 111 30.01N100.13W
Rock Springs Wyo. U.S.A. 108 41.35N109.13W
Rockville U.S.A. 114 39.05N 77.09W
Rockwood Mich. U.S.A. 104 42.10N 83.15W
Rockwood Penn. U.S.A. 114 39.54N 79.09W
Rockwood Tenn. U.S.A. 113 35.52N 84.40W
Rocky Ford U.S.A. 106 38.03N103.44W
Rocky Gully town Australia 89 34.31S117.01E
Rocky Island L. Canada 104 46.56N 83.04W
Rocky Mount town U.S.A. 113 35.56N 77.48W
Rocky Mountain Foothills f. Canada 100 57.17N123.21W
Rocky Mountain Nat. Park U.S.A. 108 40.19N105.42W
Rocky Mountain Trench f. Canada 100 56.45N124.47W
Rocky Mts. N. America 108 43.21N109.50W
Rocky Pt. Namibia 80 19.00S 12.29E
Rocky River town U.S.A. 114 41.30N 81.40W
Rocroi France 19 49.55N 4.31E
Rod Pakistan 62 28.06N 63.12E
Rodalben Germany 39 49.14N 7.38E
Rodalquilar Spain 27 37.40N 2.08W
Rödberg Norway 42 60.16N 8.58E
Rödby Denmark 41 54.42N 11.24E
Roddickton Canada 103 50.52N 56.08W
Rödekro Denmark 42 55.04N 9.21E
Rodel U.K. 14 57.44N 6.58W
Rodeo Mexico 111 25.11N104.34W
Rodewisch Germany 39 50.32N 12.24E
Rodez France 20 44.21N 2.35E
Ródhos i. Greece 35 36.10N 28.00E
Ródhos town Greece 35 36.26N 28.13E
Rodi Garganico Italy 31 41.55N 15.53E
Roding Germany 39 49.12N 12.32E
Rodney Canada 104 42.34N 81.41W
Rodonit, Kep-i- c. Albania 34 41.32N 19.30E
Rodrigues i. Indian Oc. 49 19.42S 63.25E
Roe, L. Australia 89 30.40S122.10E
Roebourne Australia 88 20.45S117.08E
Roebuck B. Australia 88 19.04S122.17E
Roermond Neth. 16 51.12N 6.00E
Roeselare Belgium 16 50.57N 3.06E
Rogachev Belorussia 37 53.05N 30.02E
Rogaland d. Norway 42 59.10N 6.25E
Rogaška Slatina Slovenia 31 46.14N 15.38E
Rogatica Bosnia-Herzegovina 31 43.48N 19.00E
Rogers, Mt. U.S.A. 113 36.35N 81.32W
Rogers City U.S.A. 104 45.25N 83.49W
Rogerson U.S.A. 108 42.14N114.47W
Roggan r. Canada 102 54.24N 78.05W
Roggan L. Canada 102 54.10N 77.58W
Roggan River town Canada 102 54.24N 78.05W
Roggeveen, Cabo c. I. de Pascua 85 27.06S109.16W
Roggiano Gravina Italy 33 39.37N 16.09E
Rogliano France 21 42.57N 9.25E
Rogliano Italy 33 39.11N 16.20E
Rogue r. U.S.A. 108 42.26N124.25W
Rohri Pakistan 62 27.41N 68.54E
Rohtak India 62 28.54N 76.34E
Rojas Argentina 125 34.15S 60.44W
Rokan r. Indonesia 58 2.00N101.00E
Rokel r. Sierra Leone 76 8.36N 12.55W
Rokycany Czech Republic 38 49.45N 13.36E
Rola Co l. China 61 35.26N 88.24E
Röldal Norway 42 59.49N 6.48E
Roldskov f. Denmark 42 56.46N 9.50E
Rolette U.S.A. 110 48.40N 99.51W
Rolla Mo. U.S.A. 111 37.57N 91.46W
Rolla N.Dak. U.S.A. 110 48.52N 99.37W
Rolle Switz. 39 46.28N 6.20E
Rolleston Australia 90 24.25S148.35E
Rolleville Bahamas 117 23.41N 76.00W
Rolvsöya i. Norway 40 70.58N 24.00E
Roma Australia 90 26.35S148.47E
Roma Italy 32 41.54N 12.29E
Roma Sweden 43 57.32N 18.28E
Romain, C. U.S.A. 113 33.00N 79.22W
Romaine r. Canada 103 50.18N 63.47W
Roman Romania 37 46.55N 26.56E
Romanche r. France 21 45.05N 5.43E
Romang i. Indonesia 59 7.45S127.20E
Romania Europe 37 46.30N 24.00E
Romano, C. U.S.A. 113 25.50N 81.41W
Romans France 21 45.03N 5.03E
Romanshorn Switz. 39 47.34N 9.22E
Rome see Roma Italy 32
Rome Ga. U.S.A. 113 34.01N 85.02W
Rome N.Y. U.S.A. 115 43.13N 75.27W
Romeleåsen f. Sweden 43 55.34N 13.33E
Romeo U.S.A. 114 42.48N 83.01W
Romilly France 19 48.31N 3.43E
Romney Marsh f. U.K. 13 51.03N 0.55E
Römö i. Denmark 42 55.08N 8.31E
Romont Switz. 39 46.42N 6.55E
Romorantin France 19 47.22N 1.45E
Rona i. U.K. 14 57.33N 5.58W
Ronan U.S.A. 108 47.32N114.06W
Ronas Hill U.K. 10 60.32N 1.26W
Roncesvalles Spain 25 43.01N 1.19W
Ronchamp France 19 47.42N 6.39E
Ronda Spain 27 36.44N 5.10W
Ronda, Serranía de mts. Spain 27 36.44N 5.05W
Rondane mtn. Norway 41 61.55N 9.45E
Rönde Denmark 42 56.18N 10.29E
Rondônia d. Brazil 122 12.10S 62.30W
Rondonópolis Brazil 123 16.29S 54.37W
Rondout Resr. U.S.A. 115 41.50N 74.29W
Ronehamn Sweden 43 57.10N 18.29E
Rongcheng China 54 37.09N122.23E
Ronge, Lac la l. Canada 101 55.07N104.45W
Rongjiang China 55 25.56N108.31E
Rongxar China 63 28.14N 87.44E
Rong Xian China 55 29.28N104.32E
Roniu mtn. Tahiti 85 17.49S149.12W
Rönne Denmark 43 55.06N 14.42E
Ronneby Sweden 43 56.12N 15.18E
Ronse Belgium 16 50.45N 3.36E
Ronuro r. Brazil 123 11.56S 53.33W
Roof Butte mtn. U.S.A. 109 36.28N109.05W
Roorkee India 63 29.52N 77.53E
Roosendaal Neth. 16 51.32N 4.28E
Roosevelt r. Brazil 122 7.35S 60.20W
Roosevelt U.S.A. 108 40.18N109.59W
Roosevelt I. Antarctica 128 79.00S161.00W
Root r. Canada 100 62.50N123.40W
Ropcha Russian Fed. 44 62.50N 51.55E
Roper r. Australia 90 14.40S135.30E
Roquefort France 20 44.02N 0.19W
Roquemaure France 21 44.03N 4.47E
Roque Pérez Argentina 125 35.23S 59.22W
Roraima d. Brazil 122 2.00N 62.00W
Roraima, Mt. Guyana 122 5.14N 60.44W
Rörholtfjorden l. Norway 42 59.01N 9.15E
Rorketon Canada 101 51.26N 99.32W
Röros Norway 40 62.35N 11.23E
Rorschach Switz. 39 47.29N 9.30E
Rosa, Cap c. Algeria 32 36.58N 8.15E
Rosa, Monte mtn. Italy / Switz. 39 45.57N 7.53E
Rosamond U.S.A. 109 34.52N118.10W
Rosans France 21 44.23N 5.28E
Rosario Argentina 125 32.57S 60.40W
Rosário Brazil 123 3.00S 44.15W
Rosario Mexico 109 23.00N105.52W
Rosario Uruguay 125 34.19S 57.21W
Rosario de la Frontera Argentina 124 25.50S 64.55W
Rosario del Tala Argentina 125 32.20S 59.10W
Rosário do Sul Brazil 126 30.15S 54.55W
Rosarito Mexico 109 28.38N114.04W
Rosarito, Embalse de resr. Spain 27 40.05N 5.15W
Rosarno Italy 33 38.29N 15.59E
Roscoe N.Y. U.S.A. 115 41.56N 74.55W
Roscoe S.Dak. U.S.A. 110 45.27N 99.20W
Roscoff France 18 48.44N 4.00W
Roscommon Rep. of Ire. 15 53.38N 8.13W
Roscommon d. Rep. of Ire. 15 53.38N 8.11W
Roscommon U.S.A. 104 44.30N 84.35W
Roscrea Rep. of Ire. 15 52.57N 7.49W
Roseau r. Canada 101 49.10N 97.20W
Roseau Dominica 117 15.18N 61.23W
Roseau U.S.A. 110 48.51N 95.46W
Rose Blanche Canada 103 47.37N 58.43W
Rosebud Australia 93 38.21S144.54E
Rosebud r. Canada 100 51.25N112.37W
Roseburg U.S.A. 108 43.13N123.20W
Rose City U.S.A. 104 44.25N 84.07W
Rose Harbour Canada 100 52.15N131.10W
Rosenberg U.S.A. 111 29.33N 95.48W
Rosendal Norway 42 59.59N 6.01E
Rosenheim Germany 39 47.51N 12.07E
Roses Spain 25 42.19N 3.10E
Roses, Golf de g. Spain 25 42.10N 3.15E
Roseto degli Abruzzi Italy 31 42.41N 14.00E
Rosetown Canada 101 51.33N108.00W
Rosetta R.S.A. 80 29.18S 29.58E
Roseville Calif. U.S.A. 108 38.45N121.17W
Roseville Mich. U.S.A. 114 42.30N 82.56W
Roshage c. Denmark 42 57.08N 8.37E
Rosh Ha'Ayin Israel 67 32.06N 34.57E
Rosh Pinna Israel 67 32.58N 35.32E
Rosières France 19 49.49N 2.43E
Rosignano Marittimo Italy 30 43.24N 10.28E
Roşiori-de-Vede Romania 37 44.07N 25.00E
Rositsa Bulgaria 37 43.57N 27.57E
Roska r. Ukraine 37 49.27N 29.45E
Roskilde Denmark 43 55.39N 12.05E
Roslagen f. Sweden 43 59.40N 18.30E
Roslags-Näsby Sweden 43 59.26N 18.04E
Roslavl Russian Fed. 44 53.55N 32.53E
Roslev Denmark 42 56.42N 8.59E
Rosporden France 18 47.58N 3.50W
Ross New Zealand 86 42.54S170.49E
Rossano Italy 33 39.35N 16.39E
Ross Dependency Antarctica 128 75.00S170.00W
Rosseau, L. Canada 104 45.10N 79.35W
Rossignol, L. Canada 103 44.10N 65.10W
Rossing Namibia 80 22.31S 14.52E
Rossiter U.S.A. 114 40.53N 78.56W
Rosslare Rep. of Ire. 15 52.17N 6.23W
Rosslau Germany 38 51.53N 12.14E
Rossmore Canada 105 44.06N 77.23W
Rosso Mauritania 74 16.30N 15.49W
Rosso, Cap c. France 21 42.14N 8.33E
Ross-on-Wye U.K. 13 51.55N 2.36W
Rossosh Russian Fed. 45 50.12N 39.35E
Ross River town Canada 100 62.30N131.30W
Rössvatnet l. Norway 40 65.45N 14.00E
Rosta Norway 40 68.59N 19.40E
Rosthern Canada 101 52.40N106.17W
Rostock Germany 38 54.05N 12.07E
Rostov Russian Fed. 45 47.15N 39.45E
Rostov Russian Fed. 44 57.11N 39.23E
Roswell Ga. U.S.A. 113 34.02N 84.21W
Roswell N.Mex. U.S.A. 109 33.24N104.32W
Rota Spain 27 36.37N 6.21W
Rotem Belgium 16 51.04N 5.44E
Rotenburg Hessen Germany 38 51.00N 9.45E
Rotenburg Nschn. Germany 38 53.06N 9.24E
Roth Germany 38 49.14N 11.04E
Rothaargebirge mts. Germany 38 51.05N 8.15E
Rothbury U.K. 12 55.19N 1.54W
Rothenburg ob der Tober Germany 39 49.23N 10.10E
Rother r. U.K. 11 50.56N 0.46E
Rotherham U.K. 12 53.26N 1.21W
Rothes U.K. 14 57.31N 3.13W
Rothesay Canada 103 45.23N 66.00W
Rothesay U.K. 14 55.50N 5.03W
Roti i. Indonesia 88 10.30S123.10E
Roto Australia 93 33.04S145.27E
Rotondella Italy 33 40.10N 16.32E
Rotondo, Monte mtn. France 21 42.13N 9.03E
Rotorua New Zealand 86 38.07S176.17E
Rotorua, L. New Zealand 86 38.00S176.00E
Rottenburg Germany 39 48.28N 8.56E
Rottenburg an der Laaber Germany 39 48.42N 12.02E
Rotterdam Neth. 16 51.55N 4.29E
Rottnest I. Australia 89 32.01S115.28E
Rottweil Germany 39 48.10N 8.37E
Roubaix France 16 50.42N 3.10E
Roudnice Czech Republic 38 50.22N 14.16E
Rouen France 18 49.26N 1.05E
Rouge r. Canada 105 45.39N 74.41W
Rougé France 18 47.47N 1.27W
Rougemont France 19 47.29N 6.21E
Rouillac France 20 45.47N 0.04W
Rouku P.N.G. 90 8.40S141.35E
Round I. U.S.A. 104 45.51N 84.37W
Round L. Canada 105 45.38N 77.32W
Round Mt. Australia 93 30.26S152.15E
Round Pond l. Canada 103 48.10N 56.00W
Roundup U.S.A. 108 46.27N108.33W
Rousay i. U.K. 14 59.10N 3.02W
Roussillon f. France 20 42.30N 2.30E
Rouyn Canada 102 48.20N 79.00W
Rovaniemi Finland 40 66.30N 25.40E

Rovato to St. George

Rovato Italy **30** 45.34N 10.00E
Rovereto Italy **30** 45.53N 11.02E
Roverud Norway **43** 60.15N 12.03E
Rovigo Italy **32** 45.04N 11.47E
Rovinj Croatia **31** 45.05N 13.38E
Rovno Ukraine **37** 50.39N 26.10E
Rowanton Canada **105** 46.24N 77.46W
Rowena Australia **93** 29.49S148.54E
Rowlesburg U.S.A. **114** 39.21N 79.40W
Rowley Shoals *f.* Australia **88** 17.30S119.00E
Roxboro U.S.A. **113** 36.24N 79.00W
Roxburgh New Zealand **86** 45.33S169.19E
Roxbury U.S.A. **115** 42.17N 74.34W
Roxby Downs *town* Australia **92** 30.42S136.46E
Roxen *l.* Sweden **43** 58.30N 15.41E
Roxo, Barragem do *resr.* Portugal **27** 38.00N 8.10W
Roxton Canada **105** 45.29N 72.36W
Roy U.S.A. **109** 35.57N104.12W
Royale, Isle *i.* U.S.A. **112** 48.00N 89.00W
Royal L. Canada **101** 56.00N103.15W
Royal Leamington Spa U.K. **13** 52.18N 1.32W
Royal Oak U.S.A. **104** 42.30N 83.08W
Royalton U.S.A. **114** 41.18N 81.45W
Royal Tunbridge Wells U.K. **13** 51.07N 0.16E
Royan France **20** 45.37N 1.01W
Roye France **19** 49.42N 2.48E
Royston U.K. **13** 52.03N 0.01W
Rožaj Yugo. **34** 42.50N 20.15E
Rozhishche Ukraine **37** 50.58N 25.15E
Rožňava Slovakia **37** 48.40N 20.32E
Roztoky Czech Republic **38** 50.09N 14.22E
Rrëshen Albania **34** 41.47N 19.54E
Rrogozhinë Albania **34** 41.04N 19.19E
Rtishchevo Russian Fed. **44** 52.16N 43.45E
Ruahine Range *mts.* New Zealand **86** 40.00S176.00E
Ruapehu *mtn.* New Zealand **86** 39.20S175.30E
Ruapuke I. New Zealand **86** 46.45S168.30E
Rub 'al Khali *des. see* Ar Rub 'al Khālī *des.* Saudi Arabia **60**
Rubbestadneset Norway **42** 59.49N 5.17E
Rubi *r.* Zaïre **78** 2.50N 24.06E
Rubino Ivory Coast **76** 6.04N 4.18W
Rubio Colombia **122** 7.42N 72.23W
Rubryn Belorussia **37** 51.52N 27.30E
Rubtsovsk Russian Fed. **50** 51.29N 81.10E
Ruby Mts. U.S.A. **108** 40.25N115.35W
Rūdān *r.* Iran **65** 27.02N 56.53E
Rudauli India **63** 26.45N 81.45E
Rūdbār Afghan. **62** 30.09N 62.36E
Rüdersdorf Germany **38** 52.29N 13.47E
Rudewa Tanzania **79** 6.40S 37.08E
Rudki Ukraine **37** 49.40N 23.28E
Rudköbing Denmark **42** 54.56N 10.43E
Rudnaya Pristan Russian Fed. **53** 44.18N135.51E
Rudnichnyy Russian Fed. **44** 59.10N 52.28E
Rudnik Poland **37** 50.28N 22.15E
Rudnyy Kazakhstan **50** 53.00N 63.05E
Rudo Bosnia-Herzegovina **31** 43.37N 19.22E
Rudolstadt Germany **38** 50.43N 11.20E
Rudozem Bulgaria **34** 41.29N 24.51E
Rudrón *r.* Spain **26** 42.44N 3.25W
Rudyard U.S.A. **104** 46.14N 84.36W
Rue France **19** 50.16N 1.40E
Ruel Canada **104** 47.16N 81.29W
Ruen *mtn.* Bulgaria / Macedonia **34** 42.10N 22.31E
Rufā'ah Sudan **72** 14.46N 33.22E
Ruffec France **20** 46.02N 0.42E
Ruffieux France **21** 45.51N 5.50E
Rufiji *r.* Tanzania **79** 8.02S 39.19E
Rufino Argentina **125** 34.16S 62.45W
Rufisque Senegal **76** 14.43N 17.16W
Rufunsa Zambia **79** 15.02S 29.35E
Rugao China **54** 32.25N120.40E
Rugby U.K. **13** 52.23N 1.16W
Rugby U.S.A. **110** 48.22N100.00W
Rügen *i.* Germany **38** 54.25N 13.24E
Ruhpolding Germany **39** 47.45N 12.38E
Ruhr *f.* Germany **38** 51.21N 7.26E
Ruhr *r.* Germany **38** 51.27N 6.44E
Rui'an China **55** 26.50N120.40E
Ruijin China **55** 25.49N116.00E
Ruinen Neth. **16** 52.47N 6.21E
Rukwa *d.* Tanzania **79** 7.05S 31.25E
Rukwa, L. Tanzania **79** 8.00S 32.20E
Rum *i.* U.K. **14** 57.00N 6.20W
Ruma Yugo. **31** 45.00N 19.49E
Rumaysh Lebanon **67** 33.05N 35.22E
Rumbek Sudan **73** 6.48N 29.41E
Rum Cay *i.* Bahamas **117** 23.41N 74.53W
Rumford U.S.A. **112** 44.33N 70.33W
Rummāna Israel **67** 32.47N 35.18E
Rummānah Egypt **66** 31.01N 32.40E
Rumney U.S.A. **105** 43.58N 71.49W
Rumoi Japan **57** 43.56N141.39E
Runcorn U.K. **12** 53.20N 2.44W
Runde *r.* Zimbabwe **81** 21.20S 32.23E
Rundvik Sweden **40** 63.30N 19.24E
Rungāni Pakistan **62** 26.38N 65.43E
Rungwa *r.* Tanzania **79** 7.38S 31.55E
Rungwa Singida Tanzania **79** 6.57S 33.35E
Rungwe Mt. Tanzania **79** 9.10S 33.40E
Runka Nigeria **77** 12.28N 7.20E
Ruoqiang China **52** 39.00N 88.00E
Ruo Shui *r.* China **52** 42.15N101.03E
Rūpar India **62** 30.58N 76.32E
Rupert *r.* Canada **102** 51.30N 78.45W
Rupununi *r.* Guyana **122** 4.00N 58.30W
Ruqqad *r.* Syria **67** 32.44N 35.46E
Rur *r.* Neth. **16** 51.12N 5.58E
Rurutu *i.* Pacific Oc. **85** 22.25S151.20W
Rusape Zimbabwe **81** 18.30S 32.08E
Ruşayriş, Khazzān ar *resr.* Sudan **73** 11.40N 34.20E
Ruse Bulgaria **34** 43.48N 25.59E
Rusera India **63** 25.45N 86.02E
Rushan China **54** 36.54N121.30E
Rushden U.K. **13** 52.17N 0.37W
Rush Springs *town* U.S.A. **111** 34.47N 97.58W
Rushworth Australia **93** 36.38S145.02E
Rusken *l.* Sweden **43** 57.17N 14.20E
Russell Canada **105** 45.17N 75.17W
Russell U.S.A. **105** 44.26N 75.11W
Russellkonda India **63** 19.56N 84.35E
Russell L. Man. Canada **101** 56.15N101.30W
Russell L. N.W.T. Canada **100** 63.05N115.44W
Russell Pt. Canada **98** 73.30N115.00W
Russell Range *mts.* Australia **89** 33.15S123.30E
Russellville U.S.A. **111** 35.17N 93.08W
Rüsselsheim Germany **39** 50.00N 8.25E
Russian Federation Europe / Asia **50** 62.00N 80.00E
Russkaya Polyana Russian Fed. **50** 53.48N 73.54E
Rustavi Georgia **45** 41.34N 45.03E
Rustenburg R.S.A. **80** 25.39S 27.13E
Ruston U.S.A. **111** 32.32N 92.38W
Rutana Burundi **79** 3.58S 30.00E
Rutanzige, L. *see* Edward, L. Uganda / Zaïre **79**
Rütenbrock Germany **38** 52.50N 7.10E
Ruteng Indonesia **59** 8.35S120.28E
Rutenga Zimbabwe **80** 21.15S 30.46E
Ruth U.S.A. **108** 39.17N114.59W
Rutherglen Canada **104** 46.16N 79.04W
Ruthin U.K. **12** 53.07N 3.18W
Rutland U.S.A. **115** 43.36N 72.59W
Rutledge *r.* Canada **101** 61.04N112.00W
Rutledge L. Canada **101** 61.33N110.47W
Rutog China **63** 33.27N 79.43E
Rutshuru Zaïre **79** 1.10S 29.26E
Rutter Canada **104** 46.06N 80.40W
Ruvu Coast Tanzania **79** 6.50S 38.42E
Ruvuma *r.* Mozambique / Tanzania **79** 10.30S 40.30E
Ruvuma *d.* Tanzania **79** 10.45S 36.15E
Ruwaybah *wells* Sudan **72** 15.39N 28.45E
Ruwayfi, Jabal ar *mtn.* Jordan **67** 31.12N 36.00E
Ruwenzori Range *mts.* Uganda / Zaïre **79** 0.30N 30.00E
Ruyigi Burundi **79** 3.26S 30.14E
Ruzayevka Russian Fed. **44** 54.04N 44.55E
Ruzitgort Russian Fed. **44** 62.51N 64.52E
Ružomberok Slovakia **37** 49.06N 19.18E
Rwanda Africa **79** 2.00S 30.00E
Ryan, Loch U.K. **14** 54.56N 5.02W
Ryasna Belorussia **37** 54.00N 31.14E
Ryazan Russian Fed. **44** 54.37N 39.43E
Ryazhsk Russian Fed. **44** 53.40N 40.07E
Rybachiy, Poluostrov *pen.* Russian Fed. **44** 69.45N 32.30E
Rybachye Kazakhstan **52** 46.27N 81.30E
Rybinsk Russian Fed. **44** 58.01N 38.52E
Rybinskoye Vodokhranilishche *resr.* Russian Fed. **44** 58.30N 38.25E
Rybnik Poland **37** 50.06N 18.32E
Rybnitsa Moldavia **37** 47.42N 29.00E
Ryd Sweden **43** 56.28N 14.41E
Rydaholm Sweden **43** 56.59N 14.16E
Rye U.K. **13** 50.57N 0.46E
Rye *r.* U.K. **12** 54.10N 0.44W
Ryfylke *f.* Norway **42** 59.30N 5.30E
Rygnestad Norway **42** 59.16N 7.29E
Ryki Poland **37** 51.39N 21.56E
Rylstone Australia **93** 32.48S149.58E
Ryōtsu Japan **57** 38.05N138.26E
Ryūgasaki Japan **57** 35.54N140.11E
Ryukyu Is. *see* Nansei shotō *is.* Japan **53**
Rzeszów Poland **37** 50.04N 22.00E
Rzhev Russian Fed. **44** 56.15N 34.18E

S

Saa Cameroon **77** 4.24N 11.25E
Sa'ad Israel **67** 31.28N 34.32E
Saale *r.* Germany **38** 51.57N 11.55E
Saales France **19** 48.21N 7.07E
Saalfeld Germany **38** 50.39N 11.22E
Saanich Canada **100** 48.28N123.22W
Saar *r.* Germany **39** 49.42N 6.34E
Saarbrücken Germany **39** 49.14N 6.59E
Saarburg Germany **39** 49.36N 6.33E
Saaremaa *i.* Estonia **41** 58.25N 22.30E
Saarijärvi Finland **40** 62.43N 25.16E
Saariselkä *mts.* Finland **40** 68.15N 28.30E
Saarland *d.* Germany **39** 49.25N 6.45E
Saarlouis Germany **39** 49.21N 6.45E
Saba *i.* Leeward Is. **117** 17.42N 63.26W
Šabac Yugo. **31** 44.45N 19.42E
Sabadell Spain **25** 41.33N 2.06E
Sabah *d.* Malaysia **58** 5.30N117.00E
Sabalān, Kūhhā-ye *mts.* Iran **65** 38.15N 47.50E
Sabana, Archipiélago de Cuba **117** 23.30N 80.00W
Sabanalarga Colombia **122** 10.38N 75.00W
Sabastīyah Jordan **67** 32.17N 35.12E
Sab'atayn, Ramlat as *f.* Yemen **71** 15.30N 46.10E
Sabatini, Monti *mts.* Italy **30** 42.10N 12.15E
Sabaudia Italy **32** 41.18N 13.01E
Sabbioneta Italy **32** 45.00N 10.39E
Sabhā Libya **75** 27.02N 14.26E
Sabhā *d.* Libya **75** 27.02N 15.30E
Sabiñánigo Spain **25** 42.31N 0.22W
Sabinas Mexico **111** 27.51N101.07W
Sabinas Hidalgo Mexico **111** 26.30N100.10W
Sabine *r.* U.S.A. **111** 30.00N 93.45W
Sabine L. U.S.A. **111** 29.50N 93.50W
Sabini, Monti *mts.* Italy **30** 42.13N 12.50E
Sabkhat al Bardawīl *l.* Egypt **66** 31.10N 33.15E
Sablayan Phil. **59** 12.50N120.50E
Sable, C. Canada **103** 43.25N 65.35W
Sable, C. U.S.A. **113** 25.05N 65.50W
Sable I. Canada **103** 43.55N 59.50W
Sablé-sur-Sarthe France **18** 47.50N 0.20W
Sabon Birni Nigeria **77** 13.37N 6.15E
Sabongidda Nigeria **77** 6.54N 5.56E
Sabor *r.* Portugal **26** 41.10N 7.07W
Sabres France **20** 44.09N 0.44W
Sabrina Coast *f.* Antarctica **128** 67.00S120.00E
Sabugal Portugal **26** 40.21N 7.05W
Şabyā Saudi Arabia **72** 17.09N 42.37E
Sabzevār Iran **65** 36.13N 57.38E
Sacaca Bolivia **124** 18.05S 66.25W
Sacajawea *mtn.* U.S.A. **108** 45.15N117.17W
Sacandica Angola **78** 5.58S 15.56E
Sac City U.S.A. **110** 42.25N 95.00W
Sacedón Spain **26** 40.29N 2.43W
Sachigo *r.* Canada **102** 55.00N 89.00W
Sachigo L. Canada **102** 53.50N 92.00W
Sachsen *d.* Germany **38** 50.59N 13.15E
Sachsen *f.* Germany **38** 52.20N 11.20E
Sachsen-Anhalt *d.* Germany **38** 51.58N 11.30E
Sachsenburg Austria **39** 46.50N 13.21E
Sackets Harbor U.S.A. **105** 43.57N 76.07W
Säckingen Germany **39** 47.43N 7.56E
Sackville Canada **103** 45.54N 64.22W
Saco U.S.A. **115** 43.29N 70.28W
Sacramento Brazil **126** 19.51S 26.47W
Sacramento U.S.A. **108** 38.35N121.30W
Sacramento *r.* U.S.A. **108** 38.03N121.56W
Sacramento Mts. U.S.A. **109** 33.10N105.50W
Sacramento Valley *f.* U.S.A. **108** 39.15N122.00W
Sada Spain **26** 43.21N 8.15W
Sádaba Spain **25** 42.17N 1.16W
Sadani Tanzania **79** 6.00S 38.40E
Sadda Pakistan **62** 33.42N 70.20E
Sa Dec Vietnam **56** 10.19N105.45E
Sādiqābād Pakistan **62** 28.18N 70.08E
Sadiya India **61** 27.49N 95.38E
Sado *i.* Japan **57** 38.00N138.20E
Sado *r.* Portugal **27** 38.29N 8.55W
Sādri India **62** 25.11N 73.26E
Sadulgarh India **62** 29.35N 74.19E
Saeby Denmark **42** 57.20N 10.32E
Saegertown U.S.A. **114** 41.43N 80.09W
Şafājah *des.* Saudi Arabia **64** 26.30N 39.30E
Şafāniyah Egypt **66** 28.49N 30.48E
Şafarābād Iran **65** 38.59N 47.25E
Säffle Sweden **43** 59.08N 12.56E
Saffron Walden U.K. **13** 52.02N 0.15E
Safi Morocco **74** 32.20N 9.17W
Safīd *r.* Iran **65** 37.23N 50.11E
Safonovo Russian Fed. **44** 65.40N 48.10E
Safonovo Russian Fed. **44** 55.08N 33.16E
Saga China **63** 29.30N 85.09E
Saga Japan **57** 33.08N130.30E
Sagaing Burma **56** 22.00N 96.00E
Sagaing *d.* Burma **56** 24.00N 95.00E
Sagala Mali **76** 14.09N 6.38W
Sagami *r.* Japan **57** 35.14N139.23E
Sagamihara Japan **57** 35.32N139.23E
Sagami-nada *b.* Japan **57** 34.55N139.30E
Sagamore Mass. U.S.A. **115** 41.45N 70.33W
Sagamore Penn. U.S.A. **114** 40.47N 79.14W
Sāgar India **63** 23.50N 78.43E
Sagara Japan **57** 34.41N138.12E
Sage U.S.A. **108** 41.49N110.59W
Sag Harbor U.S.A. **115** 41.00N 72.18W
Saginaw U.S.A. **104** 43.25N 83.58W
Saginaw *r.* U.S.A. **104** 43.39N 83.51W
Saginaw B. U.S.A. **104** 43.50N 83.40W
Sagiz Kazakhstan **45** 47.31N 54.55E
Sagres Portugal **27** 37.00N 8.56W
Saguache U.S.A. **108** 38.05N106.08W
Sagua la Grande Cuba **117** 22.55N 80.05W
Saguenay *r.* Canada **103** 48.10N 69.43W
Sagunto Spain **25** 39.41N 0.16W
Sāgwāra India **62** 23.41N 74.01E
Sa'gya China **63** 28.55N 88.03E
Saḥāb Jordan **67** 31.53N 36.00E
Sahaba Sudan **72** 18.55N 30.28E
Sahagún Spain **26** 42.22N 5.02W
Saḥam Jordan **67** 32.42N 35.47E
Saḥam al Jawlān Syria **67** 32.46N 35.56E
Sahand, Kūh-e *mtn.* Iran **65** 37.37N 46.27E
Sahara *des.* Africa **75** 22.30N 3.00E
Sahāranpur India **63** 29.58N 77.33E
Saharsa India **63** 25.53N 86.36E
Sahaswān India **63** 28.05N 78.45E
Sahbā, Wādī as *r.* Saudi Arabia **65** 23.48N 49.50E
Sahel *d.* Burkina **76** 14.00N 0.50W
Sāhibganj India **63** 25.15N 87.39E
Sāhīwāl Punjab Pakistan **62** 31.58N 72.20E
Sāhīwāl Punjab Pakistan **62** 30.40N 73.06E
Sahtaneh *r.* Canada **100** 59.02N122.28W
Sahuarita U.S.A. **109** 31.57N110.58W
Sahwat al Qamḥ Syria **67** 32.36N 36.23E
Saibai *i.* Australia **90** 9.24S142.40E
Sa'īdābād Iran **65** 29.28N 55.43E
Saidpur Bangla. **63** 25.47N 88.54E
Saidu Pakistan **62** 34.45N 72.21E
Saigon *see* Ho Chi Minh Vietnam **56**
Saillans France **21** 44.42N 5.11E
Saimaa *l.* Finland **44** 61.20N 28.00E
Saimbeyli Turkey **64** 38.07N 36.08E
Saindak Pakistan **62** 29.17N 61.34E
St. Abb's Head U.K. **14** 55.54N 2.07W
St. Afrique France **20** 43.57N 2.53E
St. Agapit Canada **105** 46.34N 71.27W
St. Agathe des Monts Canada **105** 46.03N 74.17W
St. Agrève France **21** 45.01N 4.24E
St. Alban's Canada **103** 47.52N 55.51W
St. Albans U.K. **13** 51.46N 0.21W
St. Albans Vt. U.S.A. **105** 44.49N 73.05W
St. Albans W.Va. U.S.A. **114** 38.23N 81.49W
St. Albert Canada **100** 53.37N113.40W
St. Alexis des Monts Canada **105** 46.28N 73.08W
St. Amand France **19** 50.26N 3.26E
St. Amand-Mont-Rond France **19** 46.44N 2.30E
St. Ambroix France **21** 44.15N 4.11E
St. Amour France **19** 46.26N 5.21E
St. André-les-Alpes France **21** 43.58N 6.30E
St. Andrews U.K. **14** 56.20N 2.48W
St. Andries Belgium **16** 51.12N 3.10E
St. Anicet Canada **105** 45.07N 74.20W
St. Ann's Bay *town* Jamaica **117** 18.26N 77.12W
St. Anthony Canada **103** 51.22N 55.35W
St. Anthony U.S.A. **106** 43.59N111.40W
St. Antoine Canada **105** 46.39N 71.34W
St. Antonin France **20** 44.09N 1.45E
St. Arnaud Australia **92** 36.40S143.20E
St. Astier France **20** 45.09N 0.32E
St. Auban France **21** 43.51N 6.44E
St. Augustin *r.* Canada **103** 51.14N 58.41W
St. Augustine U.S.A. **113** 29.54N 81.19W
St. Augustin Saguenay Canada **103** 51.14N 58.39W
St. Aulaye France **20** 45.12N 0.08E
St. Austell U.K. **13** 50.20N 4.48W
St. Avold France **19** 49.06N 6.42E
St. Barthélemy Canada **105** 46.12N 73.08W
St. Barthélemy *i.* Leeward Is. **117** 17.55N 62.50W
St. Basile de Portneuf Canada **105** 46.45N 71.49W
St. Béat France **20** 42.55N 0.42E
St. Bees Head U.K. **12** 54.31N 3.39W
St. Benoît-du-Sault France **18** 46.27N 1.23E
St. Boniface Canada **101** 49.55N 97.06W
St. Bonnet-de-Joux France **19** 46.29N 4.27E
St. Brides B. U.K. **13** 51.48N 5.03W
St. Brieuc France **18** 48.31N 2.47W
St. Bruno de Guigues Canada **104** 47.27N 79.26W
St. Calais France **18** 47.55N 0.45E
St. Casimir Canada **105** 46.40N 72.08W
St. Catharines Canada **104** 43.10N 79.15W
St. Catherine's Pt. U.K. **13** 50.34N 1.18W
St. Céré France **20** 44.52N 1.53E
St. Chamond France **21** 45.28N 4.30E
St. Charles Mich. U.S.A. **104** 43.18N 84.09W
St. Charles Mo. U.S.A. **110** 38.47N 90.29W
St. Chély d'Apcher France **20** 44.48N 3.17E
St. Ciers-sur-Gironde France **20** 45.18N 0.37W
St. Clair *r.* Canada **104** 42.37N 82.31W
St. Clair U.S.A. **114** 42.49N 82.30W
St. Clair, L. Canada **104** 42.25N 82.41W
St. Clair Shores *town* U.S.A. **114** 42.30N 82.54W
St. Clairsville U.S.A. **114** 40.05N 80.54W
St. Claud France **20** 45.53N 0.23E
St. Claude Canada **105** 45.40N 72.00W
St. Claude France **19** 46.23N 5.52E
St. Cloud U.S.A. **110** 45.33N 94.10W
St. Croix *i.* U.S.V.Is. **117** 17.45N 64.35W
St. Cyprien France **20** 44.52N 1.02E
St. Cyrille de Wendover Canada **105** 45.56N 72.26W
St. David's U.K. **13** 51.54N 5.16W
St. David's I. Bermuda **127** 32.23N 64.42W
St. Denis France **19** 48.56N 2.22E
St. Dié France **19** 48.17N 6.57E
St. Dizier France **19** 48.38N 4.57E
St. Donat Canada **105** 46.19N 74.13W
Sainte-Agathe-des-Monts Canada **102** 46.03N 74.17W
Sainte Anne, Rivière *r.* Canada **105** 46.52N 71.49W
Sainte Anne de Beaupré Canada **105** 47.02N 70.56W
Sainte Anne de la Pérade Canada **105** 46.35N 72.12W
Sainte-Anne-des-Monts Canada **103** 49.07N 66.29W
Sainte Anne du Lac Canada **105** 46.52N 75.21W
Sainte Croix Canada **105** 46.38N 71.44W
Sainte-Croix Switz. **39** 46.49N 6.31E
Sainte Emelie Canada **105** 46.19N 73.39W
Sainte Famille d'Aumond Canada **105** 46.27N 75.52W
Sainte Foy la Grande France **20** 44.50N 0.13E
Sainte Hermine France **18** 46.33N 1.04W
St. Elias, Mt. U.S.A. **100** 60.18N140.55W
St. Elias Mts. Canada **100** 60.30N139.30W
St. Éloi Canada **103** 48.02N 69.13W
Sainte-Lucia France **21** 41.42N 9.22E
Sainte Lucie Canada **105** 46.07N 74.13W
Sainte Marguerite Canada **105** 46.03N 74.05W
Sainte Marguerite *r.* Canada **103** 50.10N 66.40W
Sainte-Marie-aux-Mines France **19** 48.15N 7.11E
Sainte-Mathieu, Pointe de *c.* France **18** 48.20N 4.46W
Sainte Maure de Touraine France **18** 47.07N 0.37E
Sainte-Maxime France **21** 43.18N 6.38E
Sainte Menehould France **19** 49.05N 4.54E
Sainte Mère-Église France **18** 49.24N 1.19W
St. Enimie France **20** 44.22N 3.26E
Saintes France **20** 45.44N 0.38W
Saintes-Maries-de-la-Mer France **21** 43.27N 4.26E
St. Espirit Canada **105** 45.56N 73.40W
Sainte Thècle Canada **105** 46.49N 72.31W
Sainte-Thérèse-de-Blainville Canada **105** 45.38N 73.51W
St. Étienne France **21** 45.26N 4.24E
St. Fargeau France **19** 47.38N 3.04E
St. Faustin Canada **105** 46.07N 74.30W
St. Félix Canada **105** 46.10N 73.26W
Saintfield U.K. **15** 54.28N 5.50W
St. Fintan's Canada **103** 48.10N 58.50W
St. Florent France **21** 42.41N 9.18E
St. Florentin France **19** 48.00N 3.44E
St. Florent-sur-Cher France **19** 46.59N 2.15E
St. Flour France **20** 45.02N 3.05E
St. Francis U.S.A. **110** 39.47N101.47W
St. Francisville U.S.A. **111** 30.47N 91.23W
St. Francois *r.* Canada **105** 46.07N 72.55W
St. François, Lac *l.* Canada **105** 45.55N 71.10W
St. Gabriel Canada **105** 46.17N 73.23W
St. Gallen Switz. **39** 47.25N 9.23E
St. Gallen *d.* Switz. **39** 47.00N 9.15E
St. Gaudens France **20** 43.07N 0.44E
St. Gaultier France **18** 46.38N 1.25E
St. Genis-de-Saintonge France **20** 45.29N 0.34W
St. George Australia **91** 28.03S148.30E
St. George Bermuda **127** 32.24N 64.42W

St. George to **San Blas, C.**

St. George N.B. Canada **103** 45.11N 66.57W
St. George Ont. Canada **104** 43.15N 80.15W
St. George U.S.A. **108** 37.06N113.35W
St. George, C. U.S.A. **113** 29.35N 85.04W
St. Georges Belgium **16** 50.37N 5.20E
St. Georges Canada **105** 46.37N 72.40W
St. George's Grenada **117** 12.04N 61.44W
St. Georges Guiana **123** 3.54N 51.48W
St. George's B. Canada **103** 48.20N 59.00W
St. George's Channel Rep. of Ire./U.K. **15** 51.30N 6.20W
St. George's I. Bermuda **127** 32.24N 64.42W
St. Germain France **19** 48.54N 2.05E
St. Germain de Grantham Canada **105** 45.50N 72.34W
St. Germain-du-Bois France **19** 46.45N 5.15E
St. Germain-Lembron France **20** 45.28N 3.14E
St. Germain-l'Herm France **20** 45.28N 3.33E
St. Gervais d'Auvergne France **20** 46.02N 2.49E
St. Géry France **20** 44.29N 1.35E
St. Gheorghe's Mouth *est.* Romania **29** 44.51N 29.37E
St. Gilles-Croix-de-Vie France **18** 46.42N 1.57W
St. Girons France **20** 42.59N 1.09E
St. Gotthard Pass Switz. **17** 46.30N 8.55E
St. Govan's Head U.K. **13** 51.36N 4.55W
St. Grégoire Canada **105** 46.16N 72.30W
St. Guénolé France **18** 47.49N 4.20W
St. Guillaume d'Upton Canada **105** 45.53N 72.46W
St. Helena *i.* Atlantic Oc. **127** 15.58S 5.43W
St. Helena B. R.S.A. **80** 32.35S 18.05E
St. Helens U.K. **12** 53.28N 2.43W
St. Helens U.S.A. **108** 45.52N122.48W
St. Helens, Mt. U.S.A. **108** 46.12N122.11W
St. Helier Channel Is. Europe **13** 49.12N 2.07W
St. Hilaire-du-Harcouët France **18** 48.35N 1.06W
St. Hippolyte France **19** 47.19N 6.49E
St. Hubert Belgium **16** 50.02N 5.22E
St. Hyacinthe Canada **105** 45.37N 72.57W
St. Ignace U.S.A. **104** 45.52N 84.43W
St. Ignace du Lac Canada **105** 46.43N 73.49W
St. Ives U.K. **13** 50.13N 5.29W
St. Jacobs Canada **104** 43.32N 80.33W
St. Jacques Canada **105** 45.57N 73.34W
St. Jean Canada **105** 45.19N 73.16W
St. Jean *r.* Canada **103** 50.17N 64.20W
St. Jean France **21** 45.17N 6.21E
St. Jean, Lac *l.* Canada **103** 48.35N 72.00W
St. Jean-d'Angély France **20** 45.57N 0.31W
St. Jean-de-Bournay France **21** 45.29N 5.08E
St. Jean-de-Losne France **19** 47.06N 5.15E
St. Jean-de-Luz France **20** 43.23N 1.40W
St. Jean de Matha Canada **105** 46.14N 73.33W
St. Jean-de-Monts France **18** 46.48N 2.03W
St. Jean-du-Gard France **20** 44.06N 3.53E
St. Jean Pied-de-Port France **20** 43.10N 1.14W
St. Jérôme Canada **105** 45.47N 74.00W
St. John Canada **103** 45.16N 66.03W
St. John *r.* Canada **103** 45.16N 66.04W
St. John U.S.A. **111** 38.00N 98.46W
St. John, C. Canada **103** 50.00N 55.32W
St. John B. Canada **103** 50.40N 57.08W
St. John's Antigua **117** 17.07N 61.51W
St. John's Canada **103** 47.34N 52.43W
St. Johns U.S.A. **109** 34.30N109.22W
St. Johns *r.* U.S.A. **113** 30.24N 81.24W
St. Johnsbury U.S.A. **105** 44.25N 72.01W
St. John's Pt. U.K. **15** 54.14N 5.39W
St. Jordi, Golf de *g.* Spain **25** 40.53N 1.00E
St. Joseph La. U.S.A. **111** 31.55N 91.14W
St. Joseph Mich. U.S.A. **112** 42.05N 86.30W
St. Joseph Mo. U.S.A. **110** 39.46N 94.51W
St. Joseph, L. Canada **102** 51.05N 90.35W
St. Joseph I. Canada **104** 46.13N 83.57W
St. Jovite Canada **105** 46.07N 74.36W
St. Jude Canada **105** 45.46N 72.59W
St. Julien-en-Born France **20** 44.04N 1.14W
St. Julien-en-Genevois France **21** 46.08N 6.05E
St. Junien France **20** 45.53N 0.54E
St. Just-en-Chaussée France **19** 49.30N 2.26E
St. Just-en-Chevalet France **20** 45.55N 3.50E
St. Kilda *i.* U.K. **10** 57.55N 8.20W
St. Kitts-Nevis Leeward Is. **117** 17.20N 62.45W
St. Lambert Canada **105** 45.30N 73.30W
St. Laurent Man. Canada **101** 50.24N 97.56W
St. Laurent Que. Canada **105** 45.30N 73.40W
St. Laurent du Maroni Guiana **123** 5.30N 54.02W
St. Laurent-et-Benon France **20** 45.09N 0.49W
St. Lawrence *r.* Canada **105** 44.15N 76.10W
St. Lawrence, G. of Canada **103** 48.00N 62.00W
St. Lawrence I. U.S.A. **98** 63.00N170.00W
St. Léonard d'Aston Canada **105** 46.06N 72.22W
St. Lewis Sd. Canada **103** 52.20N 55.40W
St. Lin Canada **105** 45.51N 73.45W
St. Lô France **18** 49.07N 1.05W
St. Louis Senegal **76** 16.01N 16.30W
St. Louis U.S.A. **110** 38.38N 90.11W
St. Louis Park *town* U.S.A. **110** 44.56N 93.22W
St. Loup-sur-Semouse France **19** 47.53N 6.16E
St. Lucia Windward Is. **117** 14.05N 61.00W
St. Lucia, L. R.S.A. **81** 28.05S 32.26E
St. Magnus B. U.K. **10** 60.25N 1.35W
St. Maixent France **18** 46.25N 0.12W
St. Malo Canada **105** 45.12N 71.30W
St. Malo France **18** 48.39N 2.01W
St. Malo, Golfe de *g.* France **18** 48.45N 2.00W
St. Mamert France **21** 43.53N 4.12E
St.-Marc Haiti **117** 19.08N 72.41W
St. Marc des Carrières Canada **105** 46.41N 72.03W
St. Marcellin France **21** 45.09N 5.19E
St. Margaret's Hope U.K. **14** 58.49N 2.57W
St. Maries U.S.A. **108** 47.19N116.35W
St. Martin Channel Is. Europe **13** 49.27N 2.34W
St. Martin *i.* Leeward Is. **117** 18.05N 63.05W
St. Martin, L. Canada **101** 51.37N 98.29W
St. Martin B. U.S.A. **104** 45.57N 84.35W
St. Martin-de-Londres France **20** 43.47N 3.44E
St. Martin d'Hères France **21** 45.10N 5.46E
St. Martin's *i.* U.K. **13** 49.57N 6.16W
St. Mary Channel Is. Europe **13** 49.14N 2.10W
St. Mary *r.* U.S.A. **104** 46.30N 84.36W
St. Mary Peak Australia **92** 31.30S138.35E
St. Marys Australia **91** 41.33S148.12E
St. Mary's Canada **104** 43.16N 81.08W
St. Mary's *r.* Canada **103** 45.02N 61.54W
St. Mary's *i.* U.K. **13** 49.55N 6.16W
St. Marys Penn. U.S.A. **114** 41.26N 78.34W
St. Marys W.Va. U.S.A. **114** 39.23N 81.12W
St. Mary's, C. Canada **103** 46.49N 54.12W
St. Mary's B. Canada **103** 46.50N 53.47W
St. Mathieu France **20** 45.42N 0.46E
St. Matthew I. U.S.A. **98** 60.30N172.45W
St. Maur France **19** 48.48N 2.30E
St. Maurice *r.* Canada **105** 46.21N 72.31W
St. Maurice Prov. Park Canada **105** 46.52N 73.10W
St. Méen-le-Grand France **18** 48.11N 2.12W
St. Michel des Saints Canada **105** 46.41N 73.55W
St. Mihiel France **19** 48.54N 5.33E
St. Moritz Switz. **39** 46.30N 9.50E
St. Nazaire France **18** 47.17N 2.12W
St. Neots U.K. **13** 52.14N 0.16W
St. Niklaas Belgium **16** 51.10N 4.09E
St. Omer France **19** 50.45N 2.15E
St. Pacôme Canada **103** 47.24N 69.57W
St. Pascal Canada **103** 47.32N 69.48W
St. Patrick, Lac *l.* Canada **105** 46.21N 77.18W
St. Paul *r.* Canada **103** 51.26N 57.40W
St. Paul A.H.Prov. France **21** 44.31N 6.45E
St. Paul Pyr. Or. France **20** 42.49N 2.29E
St. Paul Ark. U.S.A. **111** 35.50N 93.48W
St. Paul Minn. U.S.A. **110** 45.00N 93.10W
St. Paul Nebr. U.S.A. **110** 41.13N 98.27W
St. Paul, Île *i.* Indian Oc. **49** 38.43S 77.29E
St. Paul de Chester Canada **105** 45.57N 71.49W
St. Paul du Nord Canada **103** 48.27N 69.15W
St. Paulien France **20** 45.08N 3.49E
St. Paulin Canada **105** 46.25N 73.01W
St. Paul Rocks *is.* Atlantic Oc. **127** 1.00N 29.23W
St. Peter U.S.A. **110** 44.17N 93.57W
St. Peter Port Channel Is. Europe **13** 49.27N 2.32W
St. Petersburg U.S.A. **113** 27.45N 82.40W
St. Pierre Char. Mar. France **20** 45.59N 1.14W
St. Pierre S.Mar. France **18** 49.48N 0.29E
St. Pierre, Lac *l.* Canada **105** 46.12N 72.52W
St. Pierre and Miquelon *is.* N. America **103** 46.55N 56.10W
St. Pierre-Église France **18** 49.40N 1.24W
St. Pierre le Moûtier France **19** 46.48N 3.07E
St. Pierreville France **21** 44.49N 4.29E
St. Pol-de-Leon France **18** 48.41N 3.59W
St. Pol-sur-Ternoise France **19** 50.23N 2.20E
St. Pölten Austria **36** 48.13N 15.37E
St. Polycarpe Canada **105** 45.18N 74.18W
St. Pons France **20** 43.29N 2.46E
St. Pourçain France **20** 46.19N 3.17E
St. Priest France **21** 45.42N 4.57E
St. Quentin France **19** 49.51N 3.17E
St. Raphaël France **21** 43.25N 6.46E
St. Raymond Canada **105** 46.54N 71.50W
St. Regis Falls U.S.A. **105** 44.40N 74.33W
St. Rémy France **21** 43.47N 4.50E
St. Renan France **18** 48.26N 4.37W
St. Roch de Mekinac Canada **105** 46.48N 72.44W
St. Savin France **18** 46.34N 0.52E
St. Savinien France **20** 45.53N 0.40W
St. Seine-l'Abbaye France **19** 47.26N 4.47E
St. Siméon Canada **103** 47.55N 69.58W
St. Stephen Canada **103** 45.12N 67.17W
St. Sulpice les Feuilles France **20** 46.19N 1.22E
St. Symphorien France **20** 44.26N 0.30W
St. Thomas Canada **104** 42.47N 81.12W
St. Thomas *i.* U.S.V.Is. **117** 18.22N 64.57W
St. Tite Canada **105** 46.44N 72.34W
St. Tropez France **21** 43.16N 6.38E
St. Truiden Belgium **16** 50.49N 5.11E
St. Ubald Canada **105** 46.45N 72.16W
St. Valéry France **18** 49.52N 0.44E
St. Valéry-sur-Somme France **19** 50.11N 1.38E
St. Vallier France **21** 45.10N 4.49E
St. Vallier-de-Thiey France **21** 43.42N 6.51E
St. Varent France **18** 46.53N 0.14W
St. Vincent, G. Australia **92** 35.00S138.05E
St. Vincent and the Grenadines Windward Is. **117** 13.00N 61.15W
St. Vincent-de-Tyrosse France **20** 43.40N 1.18W
St. Vith Belgium **16** 50.15N 6.08E
St. Vivien-de-Médoc France **20** 45.26N 1.02W
St. Wendel Germany **39** 49.28N 7.10E
St. Yrieix France **20** 45.31N 1.12E
St. Zénon Canada **105** 46.33N 73.49W
Sairs, L. Canada **104** 46.51N 78.12W
Saitama *d.* Japan **57** 35.55N139.00E
Sajama *mtn.* Bolivia **124** 18.06S 69.00W
Saka Kenya **79** 0.09S 39.18E
Sakai Japan **57** 34.35N135.28E
Sakākah Saudi Arabia **64** 29.59N 40.12E
Sakakawea, L. *see* Garrison Resr. U.S.A. **110**
Sakami *r.* Canada **102** 53.40N 76.40W
Sakami, Lac *l.* Canada **102** 53.10N 77.00W
Sâkâne, Erg i-n *f.* Mali **74** 21.00N 1.00W
Sakania Zaïre **79** 12.44S 28.34E
Sakarya *r.* Turkey **64** 41.08N 30.36E
Sakata Japan **57** 38.55N139.51E
Sakété Benin **77** 6.45N 2.45E
Sakhalin *i.* Russian Fed. **53** 50.00N143.00E
Sākhar Afghan. **62** 32.57N 65.32E
Sakhi Sarwar Pakistan **62** 29.59N 70.18E
Sakhnīn Israel **67** 32.52N 35.17E
Sakht-Sar Iran **65** 36.54N 50.41E
Sākib Jordan **67** 32.17N 35.49E
Sākoli India **63** 21.05N 79.59E
Sakrand Pakistan **62** 26.08N 68.16E
Sakri India **62** 21.02N 74.40E
Sakrivier R.S.A. **80** 30.53S 20.24E
Sakti India **63** 22.02N 82.58E
Sakuma Japan **57** 35.05N137.48E
Sal *r.* Russian Fed. **45** 47.33N 40.40E
Sala Ethiopia **72** 16.58N 37.27E
Sala Sweden **43** 59.55N 16.36E
Salaca *r.* Latvia **41** 57.45N 24.21E
Salacgriva Latvia **41** 57.45N 24.21E
Sala Consilina Italy **33** 40.24N 15.36E
Salado *r.* Buenos Aires Argentina **125** 35.44S 57.22W
Salado *r.* Santa Fé Argentina **125** 31.40S 60.41W
Salado *r.* La Pampa Argentina **125** 36.15S 66.55W
Salado *r.* Mexico **111** 26.50N 99.17W
Salaga Ghana **76** 8.36N 0.32W
Salailua W. Samoa **84** 13.42S172.35W
Salālah Oman **60** 17.00N 54.04E
Salālah Sudan **72** 21.19N 36.13E
Salamanca Spain **26** 40.58N 5.39W
Salamanca *d.* Spain **26** 40.45N 6.00W
Salamanca U.S.A. **114** 42.09N 78.43W
Salamat *d.* Chad **73** 11.00N 20.40E
Salāmbek Pakistan **62** 28.18N 65.09E
Salamina Colombia **122** 5.24N 75.31W
Salamís *i.* Greece **35** 37.54N 23.26E
Salamís *town* Greece **35** 37.59N 23.28E
Salām Khān Afghan. **62** 31.47N 66.45E
Salani W. Samoa **84** 14.02S171.35W
Salar de Uyuni *l.* Bolivia **121** 20.30S 67.45W
Salas de los Infantes Spain **26** 42.01N 3.17W
Salatiga Indonesia **59** 7.15S110.34E
Salāya India **62** 22.19N 69.35E
Sala y Gomez *i.* Pacific Oc. **85** 26.28S105.28W
Salbris France **19** 47.26N 2.03E
Salcia Romania **34** 43.57N 24.56E
Salcombe U.K. **13** 50.14N 3.47W
Saldaña Spain **26** 42.31N 4.44W
Saldanha R.S.A. **80** 33.00S 17.56E
Saldanha B. R.S.A. **80** 33.05S 17.50E
Saldus Latvia **41** 56.40N 22.30E
Sale Australia **93** 38.06S147.06E
Salé Morocco **74** 34.04N 6.50W
Salekhard Russian Fed. **44** 66.33N 66.35E
Salelologa W. Samoa **84** 13.43S172.13W
Salem India **61** 11.38N 78.08E
Salem Ind. U.S.A. **112** 38.38N 86.06W
Salem Mass. U.S.A. **115** 42.31N 70.55W
Salem Mo. U.S.A. **111** 37.39N 91.32W
Salem N.H. U.S.A. **115** 42.47N 71.12W
Salem N.J. U.S.A. **115** 39.34N 75.28W
Salem N.Y. U.S.A. **115** 43.10N 73.20W
Salem Ohio U.S.A. **114** 40.54N 80.52W
Salem Oreg. U.S.A. **108** 44.57N123.01W
Salem Va. U.S.A. **113** 37.17N 80.04W
Salem W.Va. U.S.A. **114** 39.17N 80.34W
Salemi Italy **32** 37.49N 12.49E
Sälen Sweden **41** 61.10N 13.16E
Salerno Italy **33** 40.41N 14.47E
Salerno, Golfo di *g.* Italy **33** 40.32N 14.42E
Salers France **20** 45.08N 2.30E
Salfīt Jordan **67** 32.05N 35.11E
Salford U.K. **12** 53.30N 2.17W
Salgótarján Hungary **37** 48.07N 19.48E
Salgueiro Brazil **123** 8.04S 39.05W
Sali Croatia **31** 43.56N 15.10E
Salies-de-Béarn France **20** 43.29N 0.55W
Salignac Eyvignes France **20** 44.59N 1.19E
Salima Malaŵi **79** 13.45S 34.29E
Salim's Tanzania **79** 10.37S 36.33E
Salina U.S.A. **110** 38.50N 97.37W
Salina, Isola *i.* Italy **33** 38.34N 14.51E
Salina Cruz Mexico **116** 16.11N 95.12W
Salinas Ecuador **122** 2.13S 80.58W
Salinas U.S.A. **108** 36.40N121.38W
Salinas *r.* U.S.A. **106** 36.45N121.48W
Salinas, Cabo de *c.* Spain **25** 39.16N 3.03E
Saline U.S.A. **104** 42.10N 83.47W
Saline *r.* U.S.A. **110** 38.51N 97.30W
Salineville U.S.A. **114** 40.37N 80.51W
Salinópolis Brazil **123** 0.37S 47.20W
Salins France **19** 46.57N 5.53E
Salisbury U.K. **13** 51.04N 1.48W
Salisbury Md. U.S.A. **115** 38.22N 75.36W
Salisbury N.C. U.S.A. **113** 35.20N 80.30W
Salisbury Plain *f.* U.K. **13** 51.15N 1.55W
Salisbury Sd. U.S.A. **100** 57.30N135.56W
Şalkhad Syria **66** 32.29N 36.42E
Sallanches France **21** 45.56N 6.38E
Salles-Curan France **20** 44.11N 2.47E
Salling *f.* Denmark **42** 56.40N 9.00E
Sallisaw U.S.A. **111** 35.28N 94.47W
Salluit Canada **99** 62.10N 75.40W
Sallyāna Nepal **63** 28.22N 82.12E
Salmās Iran **65** 38.13N 44.50E
Salmi Russian Fed. **44** 61.19N 31.46E
Salmon *r.* Canada **100** 54.03N122.40W
Salmon U.S.A. **108** 45.11N113.55W
Salmon *r.* U.S.A. **108** 45.51N116.46W
Salmon Gums Australia **89** 32.59S121.39E
Salmon River Mts. U.S.A. **108** 44.45N115.30W
Salo Finland **41** 60.23N 23.08E
Salò Italy **30** 45.36N 10.31E
Salobreña Spain **27** 36.44N 3.35W
Salome U.S.A. **109** 33.47N113.37W
Salon France **21** 43.38N 5.06E
Salonga *r.* Zaïre **78** 0.09S 19.52E
Salonika *see* Thessaloníki Greece **34**
Salonta Romania **37** 46.48N 21.40E
Salor *r.* Spain **27** 39.39N 7.03W
Salsk Russian Fed. **45** 46.30N 41.33E
Salso *r.* Italy **32** 37.05N 13.57E
Salsomaggiore Terme Italy **30** 44.49N 9.59E
Salt *r.* U.S.A. **109** 33.23N112.18W
Salta Argentina **124** 24.47S 65.24W
Salta *d.* Argentina **124** 25.00S 65.00W
Saltdal Norway **40** 67.06N 15.25E
Saltee Is. Rep. of Ire. **15** 52.08N 6.36W
Saltfjorden *est.* Norway **40** 67.15N 14.10E
Saltfleet U.K. **12** 53.25N 0.11E
Salt Fork *r.* U.S.A. **107** 36.41N 97.05W
Saltillo Mexico **111** 25.30N101.00W
Salt Lake City U.S.A. **108** 40.46N111.53W
Salto Argentina **125** 34.17S 60.15W
Salto Brazil **126** 23.10S 47.16W
Salto *r.* Italy **30** 42.23N 12.54E
Salto Uruguay **125** 31.23S 57.58W
Salto da Divisa Brazil **123** 16.04S 40.00W
Salto Grande, Embalse de *resr.* Argentina/Uruguay **125** 31.00S 57.50W
Salton Sea *l.* U.S.A. **109** 33.19N115.50W
Salūmbar India **62** 24.08N 74.03E
Saluzzo Italy **30** 44.39N 7.29E
Salvador Brazil **123** 12.58S 38.29W
Salvador Canada **101** 52.12N109.32W
Salvaterra de Magos Portugal **27** 39.01N 8.48W
Salversville U.S.A. **113** 37.43N 83.06W
Salviac France **20** 44.41N 1.16E
Salween *r.* Burma **56** 16.32N 97.35E
Salyany Azerbaijan **65** 39.36N 48.59E
Salzach *r.* Austria **39** 48.12N 12.56E
Salzbrunn Namibia **80** 24.23S 18.00E
Salzburg Austria **39** 47.48N 13.02E
Salzburg *d.* Austria **39** 47.15N 13.00E
Salzgitter Germany **38** 52.02N 10.22E
Salzkammergut *f.* Austria **39** 47.38N 13.30E
Salzwedel Germany **38** 52.51N 11.09E
Sam India **62** 26.50N 70.31E
Sama Spain **26** 43.18N 5.41W
Samalambo Angola **78** 14.16S 17.53E
Samālūt Egypt **66** 28.18N 30.43E
Samaná Dom. Rep. **117** 19.14N 69.20W
Samana Cay *i.* Bahamas **117** 23.05N 73.45W
Samanga Tanzania **79** 8.24S 39.18E
Samannūd Egypt **66** 30.58N 31.14E
Samar Jordan **67** 32.41N 35.47E
Samar *i.* Phil. **59** 11.45N125.15E
Samara Russian Fed. **44** 53.10N 50.15E
Samara *r.* Russian Fed. **44** 53.17N 50.42E
Samarai P.N.G. **90** 10.37S150.40E
Samaria *see* As Sāmirah *f.* Jordan **67**
Samarinda Indonesia **58** 0.30S117.09E
Samarkand Uzbekistan **9** 39.40N 66.57E
Sāmarrā Iraq **65** 34.13N 43.52E
Samāstipur India **63** 25.51N 85.47E
Samawāri Pakistan **62** 28.34N 66.46E
Samba Zaïre **78** 0.14N 21.19E
Sambalpur India **63** 21.27N 83.58E
Sambao *r.* Madagascar **81** 16.40S 44.26E
Sambava Madagascar **81** 14.16S 50.10E
Sambāza Pakistan **62** 31.46N 69.20E
Sambhal India **63** 28.35N 78.33E
Sāmbhar India **62** 26.55N 75.12E
Sāmbhar L. India **62** 26.58N 75.05E
Sambor Ukraine **37** 49.31N 23.10E
Samborombón, Bahía *b.* Argentina **125** 36.00S 57.00W
Sambre *r.* Belgium **16** 50.29N 4.52E
Samburu Kenya **79** 3.46S 39.17E
Samch'ŏk S. Korea **53** 37.30N129.10E
Samdari India **62** 25.49N 72.35E
Same Tanzania **79** 4.10S 37.43E
Samnū Libya **75** 27.16N 14.54E
Samoa *is.* Pacific Oc. **84** 14.20S170.00W
Samoa Is. Pacific Oc. **84** 14.00S171.00W
Samobor Slovenia **36** 45.48N 15.43E
Samokov Bulgaria **34** 42.20N 23.33E
Samorogouan Burkina **76** 11.21N 4.57W
Sámos *i.* Greece **35** 37.45N 26.50E
Sámos *town* Greece **35** 37.45N 27.00E
Samothráki *i.* Greece **34** 40.30N 25.32E
Samothráki *town* Greece **34** 40.28N 25.31E
Sampang Indonesia **59** 7.13S113.15E
Sampit Indonesia **58** 2.34S112.59E
Sampson U.S.A. **114** 42.44N 76.54W
Sam Rayburn Resr. U.S.A. **111** 31.27N 94.37W
Samsang China **63** 30.22N 82.57E
Samsö Denmark **42** 55.52N 10.37E
Sam Son Vietnam **55** 19.44N105.53E
Samsun Turkey **64** 41.17N 36.22E
Samtredia Georgia **45** 42.10N 42.22E
Samui, Ko *i.* Thailand **56** 9.30N100.00E
Samur *r.* Russian Fed. **45** 42.00N 48.20E
Samut Prakan Thailand **56** 13.32N100.35E
Samut Sakhon Thailand **56** 13.31N100.13E
San *r.* Cambodia **56** 13.32N105.57E
San Mali **76** 13.21N 4.57W
San *r.* Poland **37** 50.25N 22.20E
Sana *r.* Bosnia-Herzegovina **31** 45.03N 16.23E
Şan'ā' Yemen **71** 15.23N 44.14E
Sana *see* Şan'ā' Yemen **71**
Sanaba Burkina **76** 12.25N 3.47W
Sanaga *r.* Cameroon **77** 3.35N 9.40E
San Ambrosio *i.* Chile **121** 26.28S 79.53W
Sānand India **62** 22.59N 72.23E
Sanandaj Iran **65** 35.18N 47.01E
San Andreas U.S.A. **108** 38.12N120.41W
San Andrés, Isla de *i.* Colombia **117** 12.33N 81.42W
San Andrés Tuxtla Mexico **116** 18.27N 95.13W
San Angelo U.S.A. **111** 31.28N100.26W
San Antonio Chile **125** 33.35S 71.38W
San Antonio N.Mex. U.S.A. **109** 33.55N106.52W
San Antonio Tex. U.S.A. **111** 29.28N 98.31W
San Antonio, C. Cuba **117** 21.50N 84.57W
San Antonio, Cabo *c.* Argentina **125** 36.40S 56.42W
San Antonio, Punta *c.* Mexico **109** 29.45N115.41W
San Antonio, Sierra de *mts.* Mexico **109** 30.00N110.10W
San Antonio Abad Spain **25** 38.59N 1.18E
San Antonio de Areco Argentina **125** 34.16S 59.30W
San Antonio Oeste Argentina **125** 40.44S 64.57W
San Augustine U.S.A. **111** 31.32N 94.07W
Sanāwad India **62** 22.11N 76.04E
San Bartolomeo Italy **33** 41.24N 15.01E
San Benedetto Italy **31** 42.57N 13.53E
San Benedetto Po Italy **30** 45.02N 10.55E
San Benito Guatemala **117** 16.55N 89.54W
San Benito U.S.A. **111** 26.08N 97.38W
San Bernardino U.S.A. **109** 34.06N117.17W
San Bernardo Chile **125** 33.36S 70.43W
San Blas, C. U.S.A. **113** 29.40N 85.22W

San Bonifacio to São Pedro do Sul

San Bonifacio Italy 30 45.24N 11.16E
Sanbornville U.S.A. 115 43.30N 70.57W
San Candido Italy 30 46.44N 12.17E
San Carlos Chile 125 36.25S 71.58W
San Carlos Mexico 111 29.01N100.51W
San Carlos Nicaragua 117 11.07N 84.47W
San Carlos Phil. 59 15.59N120.22E
San Carlos Venezuela 122 1.55N 67.04W
San Carlos Venezuela 122 9.39N 68.35W
San Carlos de Bariloche Argentina 125 41.08S 71.15W
San Carlos del Zulia Venezuela 122 9.01N 71.55W
San Cataldo Italy 32 37.29N 14.00E
Sancergues France 19 47.09N 2.55E
Sancerre France 19 47.20N 2.51E
Sancerrois, Collines du hills France 19 47.25N 2.45E
Sancha He r. China 55 26.50N106.04E
San Clemente Spain 27 39.24N 2.26W
San Clemente U.S.A. 109 33.26N117.37W
San Clemente i. U.S.A. 109 32.54N118.29W
Sancoins France 19 46.50N 2.55E
San Cristóbal Argentina 124 30.20S 61.41W
San Cristóbal Dom. Rep. 117 18.27N 70.07W
San Cristóbal Venezuela 122 7.46N 72.15W
Sancti Spíritus Cuba 117 21.55N 79.28W
Sand Norway 42 59.29N 6.15E
Sanda i. U.K. 14 55.17N 5.34W
Sandakan Malaysia 58 5.52N118.04E
Sandanski Bulgaria 34 41.34N 23.17E
Sandaré Mali 76 14.40N 10.15W
Sandared Sweden 43 57.43N 12.47E
Sanday i. U.K. 14 59.15N 2.33W
Sandbach U.K. 12 53.09N 2.23W
Sandefjord Norway 42 59.08N 10.14E
Sanders U.S.A. 109 35.13N109.20W
Sanderson U.S.A. 111 30.09N102.24W
Sandersville U.S.A. 113 32.59N 82.49W
Sandgate Australia 93 27.18S153.00E
Sandhammaren c. Denmark 43 55.23N 14.12E
Sandhornöy i. Norway 40 67.05N 14.10E
Sāndi India 63 27.18N 79.57E
Sandia Peru 122 14.14S 69.25W
San Diego U.S.A. 109 32.43N117.09W
San Diego, C. Argentina 125 54.38S 65.05W
Sandīla India 63 27.05N 80.31E
Sand Lake town Canada 102 47.45N 84.30W
Sandnes Norway 42 58.51N 5.44E
Sandness U.K. 14 60.18N 1.38W
Sandö i. Faroe Is. 10 61.50N 6.45W
Sandoa Zaïre 78 9.41S 22.56E
Sandomierz Poland 37 50.41N 21.45E
San Donà di Piave Italy 30 45.38N 12.34E
Sandover r. Australia 90 21.43S136.32E
Sandoway Burma 56 18.28N 94.20E
Sandown U.K. 13 50.39N 1.09W
Sandpoint town U.S.A. 108 48.17N116.34W
Sandringham U.K. 12 52.50N 0.30E
Sandstone Australia 89 27.59S119.17E
Sandu Shuizu Zizhixian China 55 25.59N107.52E
Sandusky Mich. U.S.A. 114 43.25N 82.50W
Sandusky Ohio U.S.A. 114 41.27N 82.42W
Sandveld f. Namibia 80 21.25S 20.00E
Sandvika Norway 42 59.54N 10.31E
Sandviken Sweden 41 60.37N 16.46E
Sandwich B. Canada 103 53.35N 57.15W
Sandwip I. Bangla. 63 22.29N 91.26E
Sandy U.S.A. 108 40.35N111.53W
Sandy B. St. Helena 127 16.02S 5.42W
Sandy Bight b. Australia 89 33.53S123.25E
Sandy C. Australia 90 24.42S153.17E
Sandy Creek town U.S.A. 115 43.39N 76.05W
Sandy Desert Pakistan 62 28.00N 65.00E
Sandy Hook f. U.S.A. 115 40.27N 74.00W
Sandy L. Nfld. Canada 103 49.16N 57.00W
Sandy L. Ont. Canada 102 53.00N 93.00W
Sandy Lake town Ont. Canada 102 53.00N 93.00W
Sandy Lake town Sask. Canada 101 57.00N107.15W
San Enrique Argentina 125 35.47S 60.22W
San Esteban, Isla i. Mexico 109 28.41N112.35W
San Esteban de Gormaz Spain 26 41.35N 3.12W
San Felipe Chile 125 32.45S 70.44W
San Felipe Colombia 122 1.55N 67.06W
San Felipe Mexico 109 31.00N114.52W
San Felipe Venezuela 122 10.25N 68.40W
San Félix i. Chile 121 26.23S 80.05W
San Fernando Argentina 125 34.26S 58.34W
San Fernando Chile 125 34.35S 71.00W
San Fernando r. Mexico 111 24.55N 97.40W
San Fernando Phil. 59 16.39N120.19E
San Fernando Spain 27 36.28N 6.12W
San Fernando Trinidad 122 10.16N 61.28W
San Fernando de Apure Venezuela 122 7.35N 67.15W
San Fernando de Atabapo Venezuela 122 4.03N 67.45W
Sanford r. Australia 88 27.22S115.53E
Sanford Fla. U.S.A. 113 28.49N 81.17W
Sanford Maine U.S.A. 115 43.26N 70.46W
Sanford N.C. U.S.A. 113 35.29N 79.10W
San Francisco Argentina 124 31.29S 62.06W
San Francisco Mexico 109 30.50N112.40W
San Francisco U.S.A. 108 37.48N122.24W
San Francisco r. U.S.A. 109 32.59N109.22W
San Francisco, C. Ecuador 122 0.50N 80.05W
San Francisco del Oro Mexico 109 26.52N105.51W
San Francisco de Macorís Dom. Rep. 117 19.19N 70.15W
San Fratelo Italy 33 38.01N 14.36E
Sanga Angola 78 11.09S 15.21E
Sanga-Tolon Russian Fed. 51 61.44N149.30E
San Gavino Monreale Italy 32 39.33N 8.48E
Sang-e Māsheh Afghan. 62 33.08N 67.27E
Sangerhausen Germany 38 51.28N 11.17E
Sanggan He r. China 54 40.23N115.18E
Sangha r. Congo 78 1.10S 16.47E
Sanghar Pakistan 62 26.02N 68.57E
Sangihe i. Indonesia 59 3.30N125.30E
Sangihe, Kepulauan is. Indonesia 59 2.45N125.20E
San Gil Colombia 122 6.35N 73.08W
San Gimignano Italy 30 43.28N 11.02E
San Giovanni in Fiore Italy 33 39.16N 16.42E
San Giovanni in Persiceto Italy 30 44.38N 11.11E
San Giovanni Rotondo Italy 31 41.42N 15.44E
San Giovanni Valdarno Italy 30 43.34N 11.32E
Sangkulirang Indonesia 58 1.00N117.58E
Sāngli India 60 16.55N 74.37E
Sangmélima Cameroon 77 2.55N 12.01E
Sangonera r. Spain 25 37.59N 1.04W
San Gottardo, Passo del pass Switz. 39 46.33N 8.34E
Sangre de Cristo Mts. U.S.A. 108 37.30N105.15W
San Gregorio Uruguay 125 32.37S 55.40W
Sangri China 63 29.18N 92.05E
Sangro r. Italy 31 42.14N 14.32E
Sangrūr India 62 30.14N 75.51E
Sangsues, Lac aux l. Canada 105 46.29N 77.57W
Sangüesa Spain 25 42.35N 1.17W
Sangzhi China 55 29.24N110.09E
Sanhala Ivory Coast 76 10.01N 6.48W
San Ignacio Bolivia 124 16.23S 60.59W
San Ignacio Mexico 109 27.27N112.51W
San Ignacio Paraguay 124 26.52S 57.03W
San Ignacio, Laguna l. Mexico 109 26.50N113.11W
San Ildefonso o La Granja Spain 26 40.54N 4.00W
San Isidro Argentina 125 34.29S 58.31W
Sanīyah, Hawr as l. Iraq 65 31.52N 46.50E
San Javier Argentina 125 30.40S 59.55W
San Javier Bolivia 124 16.22S 62.38W
San Javier Chile 125 35.35S 71.45W
Sanjāwi Pakistan 62 30.17N 68.21E
Sanjō Japan 57 37.37N138.57E
San Joaquin r. U.S.A. 108 38.03N121.50W
San Jorge, Bahía de b. Mexico 109 31.08N113.15W
San Jorge, Golfo g. Argentina 125 46.00S 66.00W
San José Costa Rica 117 9.59N 84.04W
San José Guatemala 116 13.58N 90.50W
San José Mexico 109 27.32N110.09W
San Jose U.S.A. 108 37.20N121.53W
San José, Isla i. Mexico 109 25.00N110.38W
San José de Chiquitos Bolivia 124 17.53S 60.45W
San José de Feliciano Argentina 125 30.25S 58.45W
San José de Guanipa Venezuela 122 8.54N 64.09W
San José del Cabo town Mexico 109 23.03N109.41W
San José del Guaviare Colombia 122 2.35N 72.38W
San José de Mayo Uruguay 125 34.20S 56.42W
San José de Ocuné Colombia 122 4.15N 70.20W
San Juan Argentina 124 31.30S 68.30W
San Juan d. Argentina 124 31.00S 68.30W
San Juan r. Costa Rica 117 10.50N 83.40W
San Juan Dom. Rep. 117 18.40N 71.05W
San Juan Peru 124 15.20S 75.09W
San Juan Phil. 59 8.25N126.22E
San Juan Puerto Rico 117 18.29N 66.08W
San Juan r. U.S.A. 108 37.18N110.28W
San Juan, C. Argentina 125 54.45S 63.50W
San Juan, Embalse de resr. Spain 26 40.25N 4.25W
San Juan Bautista Spain 25 39.05N 1.30E
San Juan de Guadalupe Mexico 111 24.38N102.44W
San Juan del Norte Nicaragua 117 10.58N 83.40W
San Juan de los Morros Venezuela 122 9.53N 67.23W
San Juan del Río Durango Mexico 111 24.47N104.27W
San Juan del Río Querétaro Mexico 116 20.23N100.00W
San Juan Mts. U.S.A. 108 37.35N107.10W
San Julián Argentina 121 49.19S 67.40W
San Justo Argentina 125 30.47S 60.35W
Sankh r. India 63 22.15N 84.48E
Sankheda India 62 22.10N 73.35E
Sānkra India 63 20.18N 82.03E
Sankt Anton Austria 39 47.08N 10.16E
Sankt Gilgen Austria 39 47.46N 13.22E
Sankt Ingbert Germany 39 49.17N 7.06E
Sankt Johann im Pongau Austria 39 47.21N 13.12E
Sankt Johann in Tirol Austria 39 47.31N 12.26E
Sankt Niklaus Switz. 39 46.11N 7.48E
Sankt Paul Austria 31 46.42N 14.52E
Sankt Peter Germany 38 54.18N 8.38E
Sankt-Peterburg Russian Fed. 44 59.55N 30.25E
Sankt Veit an der Glan Austria 31 46.46N 14.21E
Sankt Wolfgang Austria 39 47.44N 13.27E
Sankuru r. Zaïre 78 4.20S 20.27E
San Lázaro, Cabo c. Mexico 109 24.50N112.18W
San Lázaro, Sierra de mts. Mexico 109 23.20N110.00W
San Leonardo Spain 26 41.51N 3.05W
San Leonardo in Passiria Italy 30 46.49N 11.15E
Sanliurfa Turkey 64 37.08N 38.45E
San Lorenzo Argentina 125 32.45S 60.44W
San Lorenzo mtn. Chile 125 47.37S 72.19W
San Lorenzo Ecuador 122 1.17N 78.50W
San Lorenzo r. Mexico 109 24.15N107.25W
San Lorenzo de El Escorial Spain 26 40.35N 4.09W
San Lorenzo de la Parrilla Spain 27 39.51N 2.22W
Sanlúcar de Barrameda Spain 27 36.47N 6.21W
Sanlúcar la Mayor Spain 27 37.23N 6.12W
San Lucas Bolivia 124 20.06S 65.07W
San Lucas, Cabo c. Mexico 109 22.50N109.55W
San Luis Argentina 125 33.20S 66.20W
San Luis d. Argentina 125 34.00S 66.00W
San Luis Cuba 117 20.13N 75.50W
San Luis Obispo U.S.A. 109 35.17N120.40W
San Luis Potosí Mexico 116 22.10N101.00W
San Luis Potosí d. Mexico 116 23.00N100.00W
San Luis Rio Colorado Mexico 109 32.29N114.48W
San Luis Valley f. U.S.A. 108 37.25N106.00W
Sanluri Italy 32 39.33N 8.54E
San Marco Spain 26 43.13N 8.17W
San Marcos U.S.A. 111 29.53N 97.57W
San Marino Europe 30 43.56N 12.25E
San Marino town San Marino 30 43.55N 12.28E
San Martín r. Bolivia 124 12.25S 64.25W
San Martín de Valdeiglesias Spain 26 40.21N 4.24W
San Mateo Spain 25 40.28N 0.11E
San Mateo U.S.A. 108 37.35N122.19W
San Matías Bolivia 122 16.22S 58.24W
San Matías, Golfo g. Argentina 125 41.30S 64.00W
Sanmenxia China 54 35.45N111.22E
Sanmenxia Shuiku resr. China 54 34.38N111.05E
San Miguel r. Bolivia 124 12.25S 64.25W
San Miguel El Salvador 117 13.28N 88.10W
San Miguel del Monte Argentina 125 35.25S 58.49W
San Miguel de Tucumán Argentina 124 26.49S 65.13W
San Miguelito Panama 117 9.02N 79.30W
Sanming China 55 26.25N117.35E
San Miniato Italy 30 43.41N 10.51E
Sannār Sudan 73 13.33N 33.38E
Sannicandro Italy 31 41.50N 15.34E
San Nicolas Argentina 125 33.20S 60.13W
Sanniquellie Liberia 76 7.24N 8.45W
Sanok Poland 37 49.35N 22.10E
San Pablo Phil. 59 13.58N121.10E
San Pedro Buenos Aires Argentina 125 33.40S 59.41W
San Pedro Jujuy Argentina 124 24.14S 64.50W
San Pedro Dom. Rep. 117 18.30N 69.18W
San Pedro Ivory Coast 76 4.45N 6.37W
San Pedro Sonora Mexico 109 27.00N109.53W
San Pedro Paraguay 126 24.08S 57.08W
San Pedro, Punta c. Costa Rica 117 8.38N 83.45W
San Pedro, Sierra de mts. Spain 27 39.20N 6.40W
San Pedro de las Colonais Mexico 111 25.45N102.59W
San Pedro Mártir, Sierra mts. Mexico 109 30.45N115.30W
San Pedro Sula Honduras 117 15.26N 88.01W
San Pellegrino Terme Italy 30 45.50N 9.40E
San Pietro i. Italy 28 39.09N 8.16E
Sanquhar U.K. 14 55.22N 3.56W
San Quintín Mexico 109 30.28N115.58W
San Rafael U.S.A. 108 37.59N122.31W
San Raphael Argentina 125 34.40S 68.21W
San Remo Italy 30 43.49N 7.46E
San Roque Spain 27 36.13N 5.24W
San Salvador Argentina 125 31.37S 58.30W
San Salvador i. Bahamas 117 24.00N 74.32W
San Salvador El Salvador 117 13.40N 89.10W
San Salvador de Jujuy Argentina 124 24.10S 65.20W
San Sebastián Argentina 125 53.15S 68.30W
San Sebastián Spain 26 43.19N 1.59W
Sansepolcro Italy 30 43.34N 12.08E
San Severino Marche Italy 30 43.13N 13.10E
San Severo Italy 31 41.41N 15.23E
Sanshui China 55 23.09N112.52E
San Simon U.S.A. 109 32.16N109.14W
Sanski Most Bosnia-Herzegovina 31 44.46N 16.40E
Santa r. Peru 122 9.00S 78.35W
Santa Amalia Spain 26 39.01N 6.01W
Santa Ana Argentina 124 27.20S 65.35W
Santa Ana Bolivia 124 13.45S 65.35W
Santa Ana El Salvador 117 14.00N 89.31W
Santa Ana Mexico 109 30.33N111.07W
Santa Ana U.S.A. 109 33.44N117.54W
Santa Bárbara Mexico 109 26.48N105.49W
Santa Barbara U.S.A. 109 34.25N119.42W
Santa Catalina de Armara Spain 26 43.02N 8.49W
Santa Catarina d. Brazil 126 27.00S 52.00W
Santa Catarina Mexico 111 25.41N100.28W
Santa Cesarea Terme Italy 33 40.02N 18.29E
Santa Clara Cuba 117 22.25N 79.58W
Santa Clara Calif. U.S.A. 108 37.21N121.57W
Santa Clara Utah U.S.A. 108 37.08N113.39W
Santa Clotilde Peru 122 2.25S 73.35W
Santa Coloma de Farners Spain 25 41.52N 2.40E
Santa Comba Dão Portugal 26 40.24N 8.08W
Santa Cruz d. Argentina 125 48.00S 69.30W
Santa Cruz r. Argentina 125 50.03S 68.35W
Santa Cruz Bolivia 124 17.45S 63.14W
Santa Cruz d. Bolivia 124 17.45S 62.00W
Santa Cruz Madeira Is. 127 32.41N 16.48W
Santa Cruz U.S.A. 108 36.58N122.08W
Santa Cruz i. U.S.A. 109 34.01N119.45W
Santa Cruz de la Zarza Spain 27 39.58N 3.10W
Santa Cruz de Mudela Spain 26 38.38N 3.28W
Santa Cruz de Tenerife Canary Is. 74 28.28N 16.15W
Santa Cruz Is. Solomon Is. 84 10.30S166.00E
Santa Domingo Mexico 109 25.32N112.02W
Santa Elena Argentina 125 31.00S 59.50W
Santa Elena U.S.A. 111 26.46N 98.30W
Santa Elena, C. Costa Rica 117 10.54N 85.56W
Santa Eufemia Spain 26 38.36N 4.52W
Santa Eugenia Spain 26 42.33N 9.00W
Santa Eulalia Spain 25 40.34N 1.19W
Santa Eulalia del Río Spain 25 38.59N 1.31E
Santa Fé Argentina 125 31.40S 60.40W
Santa Fé d. Argentina 124 30.00S 61.00W
Santa Fe Spain 27 37.11N 3.43W
Santa Fe U.S.A. 109 35.42N106.57W
Santa Filomena Brazil 123 9.07S 45.56W
Sant'Agata di Militello Italy 33 38.04N 14.38E
Santai China 55 31.10N105.02E
Santa Inés, Isla i. Chile 125 53.40S 73.00W
Santa Isabel Argentina 125 36.15S 66.55W
Santa Isabel do Morro Brazil 123 11.36S 50.37W
Sāntalpur India 62 23.45N 71.10E
Santa Lucía Uruguay 125 34.27S 56.24W
Santa Lucía r. Uruguay 125 34.48S 56.22W
Santa Lucia Range mts. U.S.A. 109 36.00N121.20W
Santa Luzia Portugal 26 37.44N 8.24W
Santa Margarita, Isla de i. Mexico 109 24.25N111.50W
Santa Margarita, Sierra de mts. Mexico 109 30.00N110.00W
Santa Margherita Ligure Italy 30 44.20N 9.12E
Santa María Brazil 126 29.40S 53.47W
Santa Maria U.S.A. 109 34.57N120.26W
Santa María, Cabo de c. Portugal 27 36.58N 7.54W
Santa María, Laguna de l. Mexico 109 31.07N107.17W
Santa Maria Capua Vetere Italy 33 41.05N 14.15E
Santa Maria di Leuca, Capo c. Italy 33 39.47N 18.22E
Santa María la Real de Nieva Spain 26 41.04N 4.24W
Santa Maria Madalena Brazil 126 21.58S 42.02W
Santa-Maria-Siché France 30 41.52N 8.59E
Santa Marinella Italy 30 42.02N 11.51E
Santa Marta Colombia 122 11.18N 74.10W
Santa Marta, Sierra Nevada de mts. Colombia 122 11.20N 73.00W
Santa Monica U.S.A. 109 34.01N118.30W
Santana Madeira Is. 127 32.48N 16.54W
Santana do Livramento Brazil 125 30.53S 55.31W
Santander Colombia 122 3.00N 76.25W
Santander Spain 26 43.28N 3.48W
Sant'Angelo dei Lombardi Italy 33 40.56N 15.11E
Santanoni Pk. U.S.A. 105 44.08N 74.11W
Sant'Antioco Italy 32 39.02N 8.30E
Sant'Antioco, Isola di i. Italy 32 39.00N 8.25E
Santañy Spain 25 39.22N 3.07E
Santa Pola, Cabo de c. Spain 25 38.12N 0.31W
Sant'Arcangelo Italy 33 40.15N 16.17E
Santarém Brazil 123 2.26S 54.41W
Santarém Portugal 27 39.14N 8.41W
Santarém d. Portugal 27 39.10N 8.40W
Santa Rosa Argentina 125 36.00S 64.40W
Santa Rosa Bolivia 122 10.36S 67.25W
Santa Rosa Brazil 126 27.52S 54.29W
Santa Rosa Honduras 117 14.47N 88.46W
Santa Rosa Calif. U.S.A. 108 38.26N122.34W
Santa Rosa i. U.S.A. 109 33.58N120.06W
Santa Rosa N.Mex. U.S.A. 109 34.57N104.41W
Santa Rosa, Mt. Guam 84 13.32N144.55E
Santa Rosa de Cabal Colombia 122 4.52N 75.37W
Santa Rosalía Mexico 109 27.19N112.17W
Santa Rosa Range mts. U.S.A. 108 41.00N117.40W
Santa Teresa Mexico 111 25.19N 97.50W
Santa Teresa, Embalse de resr. Spain 26 40.40N 5.37W
Santa Teresa Gallura Italy 32 41.15N 9.12E
Santa Vitória do Palmar Brazil 126 33.31S 53.21W
Sant Boi de Llobregat Spain 25 41.21N 2.03E
Sant Carles de la Ràpita Spain 25 40.37N 0.36E
San Telmo Mexico 109 31.00N116.06W
Sant'Eufemia, Golfo di g. Italy 33 38.50N 16.00E
Sant Feliu de Guíxols Spain 25 41.47N 3.02E
Santhià Italy 30 45.22N 8.10E
Santiago Chile 125 33.27S 70.40W
Santiago Dom. Rep. 117 19.30N 70.42W
Santiago Panama 117 8.08N 80.59W
Santiago r. Peru 122 4.30S 77.48W
Santiago de Compostela Spain 26 42.53N 8.33W
Santiago de Cuba Cuba 117 20.00N 75.49W
Santiago del Estero Argentina 124 27.50S 64.15W
Santiago del Estero d. Argentina 124 27.40S 63.30W
Santiago do Cacém Portugal 27 38.01N 8.42W
Santiago Vázquez Uruguay 125 34.48S 56.21W
Sāntipur India 63 23.15N 88.26E
Säntis mtn. Switz. 39 47.15N 9.21E
Santisteban del Puerto Spain 26 38.15N 3.12W
Santo Amaro Brazil 123 12.35S 38.41W
Santo André Brazil 126 23.39S 46.29W
Santo Angelo Brazil 126 28.18S 54.16W
Santo Antônio do Içá Brazil 122 3.05S 67.57W
Santo Domingo Dom. Rep. 117 18.30N 69.57W
Santo Domingo de la Calzada Spain 26 42.26N 2.57W
Santo Domingo Pueblo U.S.A. 109 35.31N106.22W
Santolea, Embalse de resr. Spain 25 40.47N 0.19W
Santoña Spain 26 43.27N 3.27W
Santos Brazil 126 23.56S 46.22W
Santos Dumont Brazil 126 21.30S 43.34W
Santo Tirso Portugal 26 41.21N 8.28W
Santo Tomás Peru 122 14.34S 72.30W
Santo Tomé Argentina 124 28.31S 56.03W
Santpoort Neth. 16 52.27N 4.38E
Şanūr Jordan 67 32.21N 35.15E
San Valentin, Cerro mtn. Chile 125 46.40S 73.25W
San Vicente El Salvador 117 13.38N 88.42W
San Vicente de Alcántara Spain 27 39.21N 7.08W
San Vicente de la Barquera Spain 26 43.23N 4.24W
San Vincenzo Italy 30 43.06N 10.32E
San Vito Italy 32 39.27N 9.32E
San Vito, Capo c. Italy 32 38.11N 12.43E
San Vito al Tagliamento Italy 30 45.54N 12.52E
San Vito dei Normanni Italy 33 40.39N 17.42E
Sanya China 55 18.19N109.32E
Sanyuan China 54 34.30N108.52E
Sanza Pombo Angola 78 7.20S 16.12E
São Borja Brazil 126 28.35S 56.01W
São Bras de Alportel Portugal 27 37.08N 7.58W
São Caetano do Sul Brazil 126 23.36S 46.34W
São Carlos Brazil 126 22.01S 47.54W
São Domingos Guinea Bissau 76 12.22N 16.08W
São Francisco r. Brazil 123 10.20S 36.20W
São Francisco do Sol Brazil 126 26.17S 48.39W
São Gabriel Brazil 126 30.20S 54.19W
São Gonçalo do Sapucaí Brazil 126 21.54S 45.35W
Sao Hill town Tanzania 79 8.21S 35.10E
São João da Boa Vista Brazil 126 21.59S 46.45W
São João da Madeira Portugal 26 40.54N 8.30W
São João del Rei Brazil 126 21.08S 44.15W
São João do Piauí Brazil 123 8.21S 42.15W
São Joaquim da Barra Brazil 126 20.36S 47.51W
São José do Calçado Brazil 126 21.01S 41.37W
São José do Rio Prêto Brazil 126 20.50S 49.20W
São José dos Campos Brazil 126 23.07S 45.52W
São Leopoldo Brazil 126 29.46S 51.09W
São Lourenço Brazil 126 22.08S 45.05W
São Luís Brazil 123 2.34S 44.16W
São Manuel Brazil 126 22.40S 48.35W
São Manuel r. see Teles Pires r. Brazil 123
São Miguel d'Oeste Brazil 126 26.45S 53.34W
Saona i. Dom. Rep. 117 18.09N 68.42W
Saône r. France 21 45.44N 4.50E
Saône-et-Loire d. France 19 46.42N 4.45E
Saoner India 63 21.23N 78.54E
São Paulo Brazil 126 23.33S 46.39W
São Paulo d. Brazil 126 22.05S 48.00W
São Paulo de Olivença Brazil 122 3.34S 68.55W
São Pedro do Sul Portugal 26 40.45N 8.04W

São Roque to **Seminoe Resr.**

São Roque Brazil **126** 23.31S 47.09W
São Roque, Cabo de *c.* Brazil **121** 5.00S 35.00W
São Sebastião Brazil **126** 23.48S 45.26W
São Sebastião, Ilha de *i.* Brazil **126** 23.53S 45.17W
São Sebastião do Paraíso Brazil **126** 20.54S 46.59W
São Tiago Brazil **126** 20.54S 44.30W
São Tomé & Príncipe Africa **70** 0.19N 6.05E
Saoura, Oued *wadi* Algeria **74** 28.48N 0.50W
São Vicente Brazil **126** 23.57S 46.23W
São Vicente, Cabo de *c.* Portugal **27** 37.01N 8.59W
São Vicente de Minas Brazil **126** 21.40S 44.26W
Sápai Greece **34** 41.02N 25.41E
Sapé Brazil **123** 7.06S 35.13W
Sapele Nigeria **77** 5.53N 5.41E
Sapelo I. U.S.A. **113** 31.28N 81.15W
Sapporo Japan **57** 43.05N141.21E
Sapri Italy **33** 40.04N 15.38E
Sapt Kosi *r.* Nepal **63** 26.30N 86.55E
Sapu Angola **78** 12.28S 19.26E
Sapulpa U.S.A. **111** 36.00N 96.06W
Saqin Sum China **54** 42.06N111.03E
Saqqârah Egypt **66** 29.51N 31.13E
Saqqez Iran **65** 36.14N 46.15E
Sarâb Iran **65** 37.56N 47.35E
Sarâbiyûm Egypt **66** 30.23N 32.17E
Sara Buri Thailand **56** 14.30N100.59E
Saragossa *see* Zaragoza Spain **25**
Sarâi Naurang Pakistan **62** 32.50N 70.47E
Sarajevo Bosnia-Herzegovina **31** 43.52N 18.26E
Saranac L. U.S.A. **105** 44.20N 74.10W
Saranac Lake *town* U.S.A. **105** 44.20N 74.08W
Sarandë Albania **34** 39.52N 20.00E
Sarandí del Yi Uruguay **125** 33.21S 55.38W
Sarandí Grande Uruguay **125** 33.44S 56.20W
Sârangarh India **63** 21.36N 83.05E
Sârangpur India **62** 23.34N 76.28E
Saranley Somali Rep. **73** 2.28N 42.08E
Saranpaul Russian Fed. **44** 64.15N 60.58E
Saransk Russian Fed. **44** 54.12N 45.10E
Sarapul Russian Fed. **44** 56.30N 53.49E
Sarar Plain Somali Rep. **71** 9.35N 46.15E
Sarasota U.S.A. **113** 27.20N 82.32W
Sarata Ukraine **37** 46.00N 29.40E
Saratoga U.S.A. **108** 37.16N122.02W
Saratoga Springs U.S.A. **115** 43.05N 73.47W
Saratov Russian Fed. **45** 51.30N 45.55E
Saravan Laos **56** 15.43N106.24E
Sarawak *d.* Malaysia **58** 2.00N113.00E
Sarayakpinar Turkey **34** 41.46N 26.29E
Saraychik Kazakhstan **45** 47.29N 51.42E
Sarbâz Iran **65** 26.39N 61.20E
Sárbogárd Hungary **31** 46.53N 18.38E
Sarcelles France **19** 49.00N 2.23E
Sardâr Châh Pakistan **62** 27.58N 64.50E
Sardârpur India **62** 22.39N 74.59E
Sardârshahr India **62** 28.26N 74.29E
Sardegna *d.* Italy **32** 40.15N 9.00E
Sardegna *i.* Italy **32** 40.00N 9.00E
Sardinia *i. see* Sardegna *i.* Italy **32**
Sarek *mtn.* Sweden **40** 67.25N 17.46E
Sareks Nat. Park Sweden **40** 67.15N 17.30E
Sargasso Sea Atlantic Oc. **127** 28.00N 60.00W
Sargodha Pakistan **60** 32.01N 72.40E
Sarh Chad **77** 9.08N 18.22E
Sarhro, Jbel *mts.* Morocco **74** 31.00N 5.55W
Sarī Iran **65** 36.33N 53.06E
Saría *i.* Greece **35** 35.50N 27.15E
Sarikamiş Turkey **64** 40.19N 42.35E
Sarikei Malaysia **58** 2.07N111.31E
Sarina Australia **90** 21.26S149.13E
Sariñena Spain **25** 41.48N 0.10W
Sarita U.S.A. **111** 37.13N 97.47W
Sark *i.* Channel Is. Europe **13** 49.26N 2.22W
Sarlat France **20** 44.53N 1.13E
Sârmasu Romania **37** 46.46N 24.11E
Sármellék Hungary **31** 46.44N 17.10E
Sarmi Indonesia **59** 1.51S138.45E
Sarmiento Argentina **125** 45.35S 69.05W
Särna Sweden **41** 61.41N 13.08E
Sarnen Switz. **39** 46.54N 8.15E
Sarnia Canada **104** 42.58N 82.23W
Sarno Italy **33** 40.49N 14.37E
Sarny Ukraine **37** 51.21N 26.31E
Saronikós Kólpos *g.* Greece **35** 37.54N 23.12E
Saronno Italy **30** 45.38N 9.02E
Saros Körfezi *g.* Turkey **34** 40.30N 26.20E
Sárospatak Hungary **37** 48.19N 21.34E
Šar Planina *mts.* Macedonia / Yugo. **34** 42.10N 21.00E
Sarpsborg Norway **42** 59.17N 11.07E
Sarralbe France **19** 49.00N 7.01E
Sarre *r. see* Saar *r.* France **19**
Sarrebourg France **19** 48.44N 7.03E
Sarreguemines France **19** 49.06N 7.03E
Sarre-Union France **19** 48.56N 7.05E
Sarria Spain **26** 42.47N 7.24W
Sarro Mali **76** 13.40N 5.05W
Sartène France **21** 41.36N 8.59E
Sarthe *d.* France **18** 48.00N 0.05E
Sarthe *r.* France **18** 47.30N 0.32W
Sartilly France **18** 48.45N 1.27W
Sartynya Russian Fed. **50** 63.22N 63.11E
Şarūr Oman **65** 23.25N 58.10E
Sárvár Hungary **36** 47.15N 16.57E
Sárvíz *r.* Hungary **31** 46.24N 18.41E
Saryshagan Kazakhstan **52** 46.08N 73.32E
Sarzana Italy **30** 44.07N 9.58E
Sarzeau France **18** 47.32N 2.46W
Sasa Israel **67** 33.02N 35.24E
Sasabeneh Ethiopia **71** 7.55N 43.39E
Sasarâm India **63** 24.57N 84.02E
Sasebo Japan **57** 33.10N129.42E
Saseginaga, L. Canada **104** 47.06N 78.35W
Saser *mtn.* Jammu & Kashmir **63** 34.50N 77.50E
Saskatchewan *d.* Canada **101** 55.00N106.00W
Saskatchewan *r.* Canada **101** 53.12N 99.16W
Saskatoon Canada **101** 52.07N106.38W
Sasovo Russian Fed. **44** 54.21N 41.58E
Sassandra Ivory Coast **76** 4.58N 6.08W
Sassandra *r.* Ivory Coast **76** 5.00N 6.04W
Sassari Italy **32** 40.44N 8.33E
Sassnitz Germany **38** 54.31N 13.38E
Sassoferrato Italy **30** 43.26N 12.51E
Sasso Marconi Italy **30** 44.24N 11.15E
Sassuolo Italy **30** 44.33N 10.47E
Sastown Liberia **76** 4.44N 8.01W
Sasyk, Ozero *l.* Ukraine **37** 45.38N 29.38E
Satadougou Mali **76** 12.30N 11.30W
Satâna India **62** 20.35N 74.12E
Satanta U.S.A. **111** 37.26N100.59W
Sátão Portugal **26** 40.44N 7.44W
Sâtâra India **60** 17.43N 74.05E
Satīt *r.* Sudan **72** 14.20N 35.50E
Satkânia Bangla. **63** 22.04N 92.03E
Satna India **63** 24.35N 80.50E
Sátoraljaújhely Hungary **37** 48.24N 21.39E
Sâtpura Range *mts.* India **62** 21.30N 76.00E
Satu Mare Romania **37** 47.48N 22.52E
Satun Thailand **56** 6.38N100.05E
Sauce Argentina **125** 30.05S 58.45W
Sauda Norway **42** 59.39N 6.20E
Saudi Arabia Asia **64** 26.00N 44.00E
Sauerland *f.* Germany **38** 51.23N 8.20E
Saugeen *r.* Canada **104** 44.30N 81.22W
Saujon France **20** 45.40N 0.56W
Sauk Centre U.S.A. **110** 45.44N 94.57W
Saulgau Germany **39** 48.01N 9.30E
Saulieu France **19** 47.16N 4.14E
Sault-de-Vaucluse France **21** 44.05N 5.25E
Sault Sainte Marie Canada **104** 46.31N 84.20W
Sault Sainte Marie U.S.A. **104** 46.30N 84.21W
Saumarez Reef Australia **90** 21.50S153.40E
Saumlaki Indonesia **90** 7.59S131.22E
Saumur France **18** 47.16N 0.05W
Saurimo Angola **78** 9.38S 20.20E
Sausar India **63** 21.42N 78.52E
Sauveterre-de-Béarn France **20** 43.29N 0.56W
Sauveterre-en-Guyenne France **20** 44.42N 0.05W
Sava *r.* Europe **31** 44.50N 20.26E
Sava Italy **33** 40.24N 17.34E
Savage U.S.A. **108** 47.27N104.21W
Savai'i *i.* W. Samoa **84** 13.36S172.27W
Savalou Benin **77** 7.55N 1.59E
Savanna U.S.A. **110** 42.06N 90.07W
Savannah Ga. U.S.A. **113** 32.04N 81.05W
Savannah *r.* U.S.A. **113** 32.02N 80.53W
Savannah Tenn. U.S.A. **111** 35.14N 88.14W
Savannakhét Laos **56** 16.34N104.48E
Savant L. Canada **102** 50.48N 90.20W
Savant Lake *town* Canada **102** 50.20N 90.40W
Savé Benin **77** 8.04N 2.37E
Save *r.* France **20** 43.47N 1.17E
Save *r.* Mozambique **81** 20.59S 35.02E
Save *r.* Zimbabwe **81** 21.16S 32.20E
Sâveh Iran **65** 35.03N 50.25E
Savelugu Ghana **76** 9.39N 0.48W
Savenay France **18** 47.22N 1.57W
Saverdun France **20** 43.14N 1.35E
Saverne France **19** 48.44N 7.22E
Savigliano Italy **30** 44.38N 7.40E
Savigny-sur-Braye France **18** 47.53N 0.49E
Šavnik Yugo. **31** 42.57N 19.05E
Savoie *d.* France **21** 45.30N 6.25E
Savona Italy **30** 44.17N 8.30E
Savonlinna Finland **44** 61.52N 28.51E
Savoonga U.S.A. **98** 63.42N170.27W
Sävsjö Sweden **43** 57.25N 14.40E
Savu Sea *see* Sawu, Laut *sea* Pacific Oc. **59**
Sawai Mâdhopur India **62** 25.59N 76.22E
Sawâkin Sudan **72** 19.07N 37.20E
Sawatch Range *mts.* U.S.A. **110** 39.10N106.25W
Sawbridgeworth U.K. **13** 51.50N 0.09W
Sawdā', Jabal as *hills* Libya **75** 28.40N 15.00E
Sawdā', Qurnat as *mtn.* Lebanon **66** 34.17N 36.04E
Sawdirī Sudan **72** 14.25N 29.05E
Sawfajjīn, Wādī Libya **75** 31.54N 15.07E
Sawhâj Egypt **64** 26.33N 31.42E
Şawqirah, Ghubbat *b.* Oman **71** 18.35N 57.00E
Sawston U.K. **13** 52.07N 0.11E
Sawtell Australia **93** 30.21S153.05E
Sawtooth Mts. U.S.A. **108** 44.03N114.35W
Sawu *i.* Indonesia **59** 10.30S121.50E
Sawu, Laut *sea* Pacific Oc. **59** 9.30S122.30E
Saxmundham U.K. **13** 52.13N 1.29E
Saxon Switz. **39** 46.09N 7.11E
Saxton U.S.A. **114** 40.13N 78.15W
Say Mali **76** 13.50N 4.57W
Say Niger **77** 13.08N 2.22E
Sayama Japan **57** 35.51N139.24E
Şaydā Lebanon **66** 33.32N 35.22E
Sayers Lake *town* Australia **92** 32.46S143.20E
Saylūn *site* Jordan **67** 32.03N 35.17E
Saynshand Mongolia **54** 44.58N110.12E
Saynshand Mongolia **54** 43.33N102.13E
Sayre U.S.A. **115** 41.59N 76.32W
Sayula Mexico **116** 19.52N103.36W
Sayville U.S.A. **115** 40.44N 73.05W
Sâzava *r.* Czech Republic **36** 49.53N 14.21E
Sazliyka *r.* Bulgaria **34** 42.15N 25.50E
Sbaa Algeria **74** 28.13N 0.10W
Scaër France **18** 48.02N 3.42W
Scafell Pike *mtn.* U.K. **12** 54.27N 3.12W
Scalea Italy **33** 39.49N 15.48E
Scalloway U.K. **14** 60.08N 1.17W
Scammon Bay *town* U.S.A. **98** 61.50N165.35W
Scansano Italy **30** 42.41N 11.20E
Scapa Flow *str.* U.K. **14** 58.53N 3.05W
Scarborough Canada **104** 43.44N 79.16W
Scarborough Tobago **122** 11.11N 60.45W
Scarborough U.K. **12** 54.17N 0.24W
Scenic U.S.A. **108** 43.46N102.32W
Schaalsee *l.* Germany **38** 53.35N 10.57E
Schaerbeek Belgium **16** 50.54N 4.20E
Schaffhausen Switz. **39** 47.42N 8.38E
Schaffhausen *d.* Switz. **39** 47.40N 8.36E
Schagen Neth. **16** 52.47N 4.47E
Schärding Austria **39** 48.27N 13.26E
Schefferville Canada **99** 54.50N 67.00W
Scheinfeld Germany **39** 49.40N 10.27E
Schelde *r.* Belgium **16** 51.13N 4.25E
Schell Creek Range *mts.* U.S.A. **108** 39.10N114.40W
Schenectady U.S.A. **115** 42.47N 73.53W
Schesslitz Germany **38** 49.59N 11.01E
Scheveningen Neth. **16** 52.07N 4.16E
Schiedam Neth. **16** 51.55N 4.25E
Schiermonnikoog *i.* Neth. **16** 53.28N 6.15E
Schiltigheim France **19** 48.36N 7.45E
Schio Italy **30** 45.43N 11.21E
Schkeuditz Germany **38** 51.24N 12.13E
Schladming Austria **39** 47.23N 13.41E
Schleiden Germany **38** 50.31N 6.28E
Schleswig Germany **38** 54.31N 9.33E
Schleswig-Holstein *d.* Germany **38** 54.39N 9.30E
Schleusingen Germany **39** 50.31N 10.45E
Schlitz Germany **38** 50.40N 9.33E
Schlüchtern Germany **39** 50.20N 9.31E
Schmalkalden Germany **38** 50.43N 10.26E
Schmidmühlen Germany **38** 49.16N 11.56E
Schmölln Germany **38** 50.53N 12.20E
Schmutter *r.* Germany **39** 48.43N 10.47E
Schneeberg *mtn.* Germany **38** 50.03N 11.51E
Schneverdingen Germany **38** 53.07N 9.47E
Schoharie U.S.A. **115** 42.40N 74.19W
Schoharie Creek *r.* U.S.A. **115** 42.57N 74.18W
Schönebeck Germany **38** 52.01N 11.45E
Schongau Germany **39** 47.49N 10.54E
Schopfheim Germany **39** 47.39N 7.49E
Schorndorf Germany **39** 48.48N 9.31E
Schouten, Kepulauan *is.* Indonesia **59** 0.45S135.50E
Schouwen *i.* Neth. **16** 51.42N 3.45E
Schramberg Germany **39** 48.13N 8.23E
Schreiber Canada **102** 48.45N 87.20W
Schrobenhausen Germany **39** 48.33N 11.17E
Schroon Lake *town* U.S.A. **105** 43.47N 73.46W
Schuler Canada **101** 50.22N110.05W
Schuylkill *r.* U.S.A. **115** 39.53N 75.12W
Schuylerville U.S.A. **115** 43.06N 73.35W
Schuylkill Haven U.S.A. **115** 40.38N 76.12W
Schwabach Germany **38** 49.20N 11.01E
Schwaben *f.* Germany **39** 48.10N 10.50E
Schwäbische Alb *mts.* Germany **39** 48.30N 9.38E
Schwäbisch Gmünd Germany **39** 48.48N 9.47E
Schwäbisch Hall Germany **39** 49.07N 9.44E
Schwabmünchen Germany **39** 48.11N 10.45E
Schwandorf Germany **39** 49.20N 12.08E
Schwaner, Pegunungan *mts.* Indonesia **58** 0.45S113.20E
Schwarze Elster *r.* Germany **38** 51.49N 12.51E
Schwarzenburg Switz. **39** 46.49N 7.21E
Schwarzrand *mts.* Namibia **80** 25.40S 16.53E
Schwarzwald *f.* Germany **36** 48.00N 7.45E
Schwaz Austria **39** 47.20N 11.42E
Schwedt Germany **38** 53.03N 14.17E
Schweich Germany **39** 49.49N 6.45E
Schweinfurt Germany **39** 50.03N 10.14E
Schweitzingen Germany **39** 49.23N 8.34E
Schwelm Germany **38** 51.17N 7.17E
Schwenningen Germany **39** 48.04N 8.32E
Schwerin Germany **38** 53.38N 11.25E
Schweriner See *l.* Germany **38** 53.45N 11.28E
Schwyz Switz. **39** 47.02N 8.40E
Schwyz *d.* Switz. **39** 47.00N 8.45E
Schyan Canada **105** 46.10N 77.00W
Sciacca Italy **32** 37.30N 13.06E
Scicli Italy **33** 36.47N 14.43E
Scilla Italy **33** 38.15N 15.44E
Scilly, Isles of U.K. **13** 49.55N 6.20W
Šćit *mtn.* Bosnia-Herzegovina **31** 44.02N 17.47E
Scituate U.S.A. **115** 42.12N 70.44W
Scobey U.S.A. **108** 48.47N105.25W
Scone Australia **93** 32.01S150.53E
Scordia Italy **33** 37.18N 14.51E
Scorno, Punta di *c.* Italy **32** 41.07N 8.19E
Scotia Calif. U.S.A. **108** 40.26N123.31W
Scotia N.Y. U.S.A. **115** 42.47N 73.59W
Scotia Ridge *f.* Atlantic Oc. **127** 60.00S 35.00W
Scotia Sea Atlantic Oc. **127** 57.00S 45.00W
Scotland U.K. **14** 55.30N 4.00W
Scotsbluff U.S.A. **110** 41.52N103.40W
Scotstown Canada **105** 45.32N 71.17W
Scott Canada **105** 46.30N 71.04W
Scottburgh R.S.A. **80** 30.17S 30.45E
Scott City U.S.A. **110** 38.29N100.54W
Scottdale U.S.A. **114** 40.06N 79.35W
Scott Is. Canada **100** 50.48N128.40W
Scott L. Canada **101** 59.55N106.18W
Scott Reef Australia **88** 14.00S121.50E
Scottsbluff U.S.A. **108** 41.52N103.40W
Scottsboro U.S.A. **111** 34.40N 86.02W
Scottsdale Australia **91** 41.09S147.31E
Scottsdale U.S.A. **109** 33.30N111.56W
Scottsville U.S.A. **111** 36.45N 86.11W
Scranton U.S.A. **115** 41.24N 75.40W
Scugog, L. Canada **104** 44.10N 78.51W
Scunthorpe U.K. **12** 53.35N 0.38W
Scuol Switz. **39** 46.48N 10.18E
Scutari, L. Yugo. / Albania **34** 42.17N 19.17E
Seabrook, L. Australia **89** 30.56S119.40E
Seaford U.S.A. **115** 38.39N 75.37W
Seaforth Canada **104** 43.33N 81.24W
Seagroves U.S.A. **111** 32.57N102.34W
Seahouses U.K. **12** 55.35N 1.38W
Sea Isle City U.S.A. **115** 39.09N 74.42W
Seal *r.* Canada **101** 59.04N 94.48W
Sea Lake *town* Australia **92** 35.31S142.54E
Seal Bight Canada **103** 52.27N 55.40W
Searchlight U.S.A. **109** 35.28N114.55W
Seascale U.K. **12** 54.24N 3.29W
Seaside Calif. U.S.A. **108** 36.37N121.50W
Seaside Oreg. U.S.A. **108** 46.02N123.55W
Seaton U.K. **13** 50.43N 3.05W
Seattle U.S.A. **108** 47.36N122.20W
Seaview Range *mts.* Australia **90** 18.56S146.00E
Sebastian U.S.A. **113** 27.50N 80.29W
Sebastián Vizcaíno, Bahía *b.* Mexico **109** 28.00N114.30W
Sebba Burkina **76** 13.27N 0.33E
Sebeş Romania **37** 45.58N 23.34E
Sebewaing U.S.A. **104** 43.44N 83.27W
Sebidiro P.N.G. **59** 9.00S142.15E
Sebinkarahisar Turkey **64** 40.19N 38.25E
Sebnitz Germany **38** 50.58N 14.16E
Sebou, Oued *r.* Morocco **74** 34.15N 6.40W
Sebring U.S.A. **113** 27.30N 81.28W
Sechura, Desierto de *des.* Peru **122** 6.00S 80.30W
Seclin France **16** 50.34N 3.01E
Sêda *r.* Portugal **27** 38.55N 8.01W
Sedalia U.S.A. **110** 38.42N 93.14W
Sedan France **19** 49.42N 4.57E
Sedan U.S.A. **111** 37.08N 96.11W
Sedano Spain **26** 42.43N 3.45W
Seddon New Zealand **86** 41.40S174.04E
Séderon France **21** 44.12N 5.32E
Sederot Israel **67** 31.31N 34.35E
Sedgewick Canada **101** 52.46N111.41W
Sédhiou Senegal **76** 12.44N 15.30W
Sedini Italy **32** 40.50N 8.49E
Sedom Israel **66** 31.04N 35.23E
Sedot Yam Israel **67** 32.29N 34.53E
Seefeld Austria **39** 47.20N 11.11E
Seehausen Germany **38** 52.53N 11.45E
Seeheim Namibia **80** 26.50S 17.45E
Seeleys Bay *town* Canada **105** 44.29N 76.14W
Seelow Germany **38** 52.32N 14.23E
Sées France **18** 48.36N 0.10E
Seesen Germany **38** 51.53N 10.10E
Seevetal Germany **38** 53.26N 9.58E
Sefrou Morocco **74** 33.50N 4.50W
Segbwema Sierra Leone **76** 8.00N 11.00W
Segesta *site* Italy **32** 37.56N 12.50E
Segguer, Oued es *wadi* Algeria **75** 31.44N 2.18E
Segni Italy **30** 41.41N 13.01E
Ségou Mali **76** 13.28N 6.18W
Ségou *d.* Mali **76** 13.55N 6.20W
Segovia Spain **26** 40.57N 4.07W
Segovia *d.* Spain **26** 41.10N 4.00W
Segozero, Ozero *l.* Russian Fed. **44** 63.15N 33.40E
Segré France **18** 47.41N 0.53W
Segre *r.* Spain **25** 41.40N 0.43E
Séguédine Niger **77** 20.12N 12.59E
Séguéla Ivory Coast **76** 7.58N 6.44W
Seguin U.S.A. **111** 29.34N 97.58W
Segura Portugal **27** 39.50N 6.59W
Segura *r.* Spain **25** 38.06N 0.38W
Segura, Sierra de *mts.* Spain **27** 38.15N 2.30W
Sehore India **62** 23.12N 77.05E
Sehwân Pakistan **62** 26.26N 67.52E
Seia Portugal **26** 40.25N 7.42W
Seiches-sur-le-Loir France **18** 47.35N 0.22W
Seiland *i.* Norway **40** 70.25N 23.10E
Seilhac France **20** 45.22N 1.42E
Seille *r.* France **19** 49.07N 6.11E
Seinäjoki Finland **40** 62.47N 22.50E
Seine *r.* France **18** 49.26N 0.26E
Seine, Baie de la *b.* France **18** 49.25N 0.15E
Seine-et-Marne *d.* France **19** 48.30N 3.00E
Seine-Maritime *d.* France **18** 49.45N 1.00E
Seixal Portugal **27** 38.38N 9.06W
Sejerö *i.* Denmark **42** 55.53N 11.09E
Sekayu Indonesia **58** 2.58S103.58E
Seki Japan **57** 35.29N136.55E
Sekoma Botswana **80** 24.41S 23.50E
Sekondi-Takoradi Ghana **76** 4.57N 1.44W
Sek'ot'a Ethiopia **73** 12.38N 39.03E
Seküheh Iran **65** 30.45N 61.29E
Selaru *i.* Indonesia **90** 8.09S131.00E
Selatan, Tanjung *c.* Indonesia **58** 4.20S114.45E
Selatan Natuna, Kepulauan *is.* Indonesia **58** 3.00N108.50E
Selayar *i.* Indonesia **59** 6.07S120.28E
Selb Germany **39** 50.10N 12.08E
Selbu Norway **40** 63.14N 11.03E
Selby U.K. **12** 53.47N 1.05W
Selby U.S.A. **110** 45.31N100.02W
Selbyville U.S.A. **115** 38.28N 75.13W
Seldovia U.S.A. **98** 59.27N151.43W
Sele *r.* Italy **33** 40.27N 14.58E
Selenga *r.* Russian Fed. **52** 52.20N106.20E
Selenge Mörön *r. see* Selenga Mongolia **52**
Selenicë Albania **34** 40.33N 19.39E
Sélestat France **19** 48.16N 7.27E
Seligman U.S.A. **109** 35.20N112.53W
Selimiye Turkey **35** 37.24N 27.40E
Sélingue, Lac de *l.* Mali **76** 11.25N 8.15W
Selinoús Greece **35** 37.35N 21.37E
Selinsgrove U.S.A. **114** 40.48N 76.52W
Selinunte *site* Italy **32** 37.35N 12.50E
Seljord Norway **42** 59.29N 8.37E
Selkirk Man. Canada **101** 50.09N 96.52W
Selkirk Ont. Canada **104** 42.49N 79.56W
Selkirk U.K. **14** 55.33N 2.51W
Selkirk Mts. Canada **100** 50.02N116.20W
Selles-sur-Cher France **19** 47.16N 1.33E
Sells U.S.A. **109** 31.55N111.53W
Selma Ala. U.S.A. **111** 32.25N 87.01W
Selma Calif. U.S.A. **109** 36.34N119.37W
Selmer U.S.A. **111** 35.11N 88.36W
Selseleh ye Safīd Kūh *mts.* Afghan **65** 34.30N 63.30E
Selsey Bill *c.* U.K. **13** 50.44N 0.47W
Selty Russian Fed. **44** 57.19N 52.12E
Séune *r.* France **18** 48.35N 1.15W
Selva Argentina **126** 29.50S 62.02W
Selvas *f.* Brazil **122** 6.00S 65.00W
Selwyn L. Canada **101** 60.00N104.30W
Selwyn Mts. Canada **98** 63.00N130.00W
Selwyn Range *mts.* Australia **90** 21.35S140.35E
Seman *r.* Albania **34** 40.45N 19.50E
Semara W. Sahara **74** 26.44N 14.41W
Semarang Indonesia **59** 6.58S110.29E
Sembabule Uganda **79** 0.08S 31.27E
Semeru, Gunung *mtn.* Indonesia **59** 8.04S112.53E
Seminoe Resr. U.S.A. **108** 42.00N106.50W

Seminole to **Shiquan**

Seminole U.S.A. 111 32.43N102.39W
Semiozernoye Kazakhstan 50 52.22N 64.06E
Semipalatinsk Kazakhstan 9 50.26N 80.16E
Semīrom Iran 65 31.31N 52.10E
Semiyarka Kazakhstan 50 50.52N 78.23E
Semliki *r.* Zaïre 79 1.12N 30.27E
Semmering Pass Austria 36 47.40N 16.00E
Semnān Iran 65 35.31N 53.24E
Semois *r.* France 16 49.53N 4.45E
Semporna Malaysia 58 4.27N118.36E
Semu *r.* Tanzania 79 3.57S 34.20E
Semur-en-Auxois France 19 47.29N 4.20E
Sena Mozambique 79 17.36S 35.00E
Senador Pompeu Brazil 123 5.30S 39.25W
Senaja Malaysia 58 6.49N117.02E
Sena Madureira Brazil 122 9.04S 68.40W
Senanga Zambia 78 15.52S 23.19E
Senatobia U.S.A. 111 34.39N 89.58W
Sendai Kyushu Japan 57 31.49N130.18E
Sendai Tōfuku Japan 57 38.20N140.50E
Sendenhorst Germany 38 51.50N 7.49E
Sendhwa India 62 21.41N 75.06E
Sendurjana India 63 21.32N 78.17E
Seneca Oreg. U.S.A. 108 44.08N118.58W
Seneca S.C. U.S.A. 113 34.41N 82.59W
Seneca Falls *town* U.S.A. 114 42.55N 76.48W
Seneca L. U.S.A. 114 42.40N 76.57W
Senegal Africa 76 14.30N 14.30W
Sénégal *r.* Senegal / Mauritania 76 16.00N 16.28W
Senekal R.S.A. 80 28.18S 27.37E
Senetosa, Punta di *c.* France 21 41.33N 8.47E
Senftenberg Germany 38 51.31N 14.00E
Senhor do Bonfim Brazil 123 10.28S 40.11W
Senica Slovakia 37 48.41N 17.22E
Senigallia Italy 30 43.43N 13.13E
Senise Italy 33 40.09N 16.18E
Senj Croatia 31 44.59N 14.54E
Senja *i.* Norway 40 69.15N 17.20E
Senlis France 19 49.12N 2.35E
Senmonoron Vietnam 56 12.27N107.12E
Sennan Japan 57 34.22N135.17E
Sennen U.K. 13 50.04N 5.42W
Sennestadt Germany 38 51.57N 8.31E
Senneterre Canada 102 48.25N 77.15W
Sennori Italy 32 40.48N 8.34E
Sens France 19 48.12N 3.17E
Senta Yugo. 31 45.56N 20.04E
Sentinel U.S.A. 109 32.53N113.12W
Šentjur Slovenia 31 46.13N 15.24E
Senāth *r.* India 63 21.44N 82.28E
Seoni India 63 22.05N 79.32E
Seoni Mālwa India 63 22.27N 77.28E
Seorīnārāyan India 63 21.44N 82.35E
Seoul *see* Sŏul S. Korea 53
Sepik *r.* P.N.G. 59 3.54S144.30E
Sepopa Botswana 80 18.45S 22.11E
Sept Îles *town* Canada 103 50.12N 66.23W
Sepúlveda Spain 26 41.18N 3.45W
Sequeros Spain 26 40.31N 6.01W
Seraing Belgium 16 50.37N 5.33E
Seram *i.* Indonesia 59 3.10S129.30E
Seram, Laut *sea* Pacific Oc. 59 2.50S128.00E
Serang Indonesia 59 6.07S106.09E
Serbia *d. see* Srbija *d.* Yugo. 31
Serdo Ethiopia 73 11.59N 41.30E
Seremban Malaysia 58 2.42N101.54E
Serengeti Nat. Park Tanzania 79 2.30S 35.00E
Serengeti Plain *f.* Tanzania 79 3.00S 35.00E
Serenje Zambia 79 13.12S 30.50E
Sergach Russian Fed. 44 55.32N 45.27E
Sergipe *d.* Brazil 123 11.00S 37.00W
Sergiyev Posad Russian Fed. 44 56.20N 38.10E
Sergiyevsk Russian Fed. 44 53.56N 50.01E
Seria Brunei 58 4.39N114.23E
Serian Malaysia 58 1.10N110.35E
Sericho Kenya 73 1.05N 39.05E
Sérifos Greece 35 37.09N 24.31E
Sérifos *i.* Greece 35 37.11N 24.31E
Sérigny *r.* Canada 103 55.59N 68.43W
Serkout, Djebel *mtn.* Algeria 75 23.40N 6.48E
Serle, Mt Australia 92 30.34S138.55E
Sermata *i.* Indonesia 59 8.30S129.00E
Serodino Argentina 125 32.37S 60.57W
Serov Russian Fed. 44 59.42N 60.32E
Serowe Botswana 80 22.22S 26.42E
Serpa Portugal 27 37.56N 7.36W
Serpeddi, Punta *mtn.* Italy 32 39.22N 9.18E
Serpentine *r.* Australia 89 32.33S115.46E
Serpent's Mouth *str.* Venezuela 122 9.50N 61.00W
Serpis *r.* Spain 25 38.59N 0.09W
Serpukhov Russian Fed. 44 54.53N 37.25E
Serra do Navio Brazil 123 0.59N 52.03W
Sérrai Greece 34 41.05N 23.32E
Serramanna Italy 32 39.25N 8.54E
Serra San Bruno Italy 33 38.35N 16.20E
Serrat, Cap *c.* Tunisia 32 37.14N 9.13E
Serra Talhada Brazil 123 8.01S 38.17W
Serravalle Scrivia Italy 30 44.43N 8.51E
Serre *r.* France 16 49.40N 3.22E
Serres France 21 44.26N 5.43E
Serri Italy 32 39.41N 9.09E
Serrières France 21 45.19N 4.45E
Serrinha Brazil 123 11.38S 38.56W
Sersale Italy 33 39.01N 16.44E
Sertã Portugal 27 39.48N 8.06W
Sēru Ethiopia 73 7.50N 40.28E
Serui Indonesia 59 1.53S136.15E
Serule Botswana 80 21.54S 27.17E
Sérvia Greece 34 40.09N 21.58E
Serviceton Australia 92 36.22S141.02E
Şes, Munţii *mts.* Romania 37 47.05N 22.30E
Seseganaga L. Canada 102 50.00N 90.10W
Sese Is. Uganda 79 0.20S 32.30E
Sesepe Indonesia 59 1.30S127.59E
Sesheke Zambia 78 17.14S 24.22E
Sesia *r.* Italy 30 45.05N 8.37E
Sesimbra Portugal 24 38.26N 9.06W
Sessa Aurunca Italy 32 41.14N 13.56E
Sestao Spain 26 43.18N 3.00W
Sestri Levante Italy 30 44.16N 9.24E
Setana Japan 57 42.26N139.51E
Sète France 20 43.24N 3.41E
Sete Lagoas Brazil 126 19.29S 44.15W
Setesdal *f.* Norway 42 59.25N 7.25E
Sétif Algeria 22 36.10N 5.26E
Seto Japan 57 35.14N137.06E
Settat Morocco 74 33.04N 7.37W
Setté Cama Gabon 78 2.32S 9.46E
Settimo Torinese Italy 30 45.09N 7.46E
Settle U.K. 12 54.05N 2.18W
Settlement of Edinburgh Tristan da Cunha 127 37.03S 12.18W
Setúbal Portugal 27 38.32N 8.54W
Setúbal *d.* Portugal 27 38.15N 8.35W
Setúbal, Baía de *b.* Portugal 27 38.20N 9.00W
Seugne *r.* France 20 45.41N 0.34W
Seui Italy 32 39.50N 9.20E
Seul, Lac *l.* Canada 102 50.20N 92.30W
Seurre France 19 47.00N 5.09E
Sevagram India 63 20.45N 78.30E
Sevan, Ozero *l.* Armenia 65 40.22N 45.20E
Sevastopol' Ukraine 45 44.36N 33.31E
Sevenoaks U.K. 13 51.16N 0.12E
Seven Sisters Peaks *mts.* Canada 100 54.56N128.10W
Sévérac France 20 44.19N 3.04E
Severn *r.* Australia 93 29.08S150.50E
Severn *r.* Canada 102 56.00N 87.38W
Severn *r.* U.K. 13 51.50N 2.21W
Severnaya Zemlya *is.* Russian Fed. 51 80.00N 96.00E
Severn Falls Canada 104 44.51N 79.38W
Severnyy Russian Fed. 44 69.55N 49.01E
Severnyy Donets *r.* Ukraine 45 49.08N 37.28E
Severnyy Dvina *r.* Russian Fed. 44 57.03N 24.00E
Severočeský *d.* Czech Republic 39 50.26N 13.45E
Severodvinsk Russian Fed. 44 64.35N 39.50E
Severomorsk Russian Fed. 44 69.05N 33.30E
Severskiy Donets *r.* Russian Fed. / Ukraine 23 47.35N 40.55E
Sevier *r.* U.S.A. 108 39.04N113.06W
Sevier L. U.S.A. 108 38.55N113.09W
Sevilla Spain 27 37.23N 5.59W
Sevilla *d.* Spain 27 37.35N 6.00W
Sevlievo Bulgaria 34 43.01N 25.06E
Sèvre-Nantaise *r.* France 18 47.08N 1.26W
Sèvre Niortaise *r.* France 20 46.20N 1.09W
Sewa *r.* Sierra Leone 76 7.15N 12.08W
Seward Alas. U.S.A. 98 60.05N149.34W
Seward Nebr. U.S.A. 110 40.55N 97.06W
Seward Penn. U.S.A. 114 40.25N 79.01W
Seward Pen. U.S.A. 98 65.00N164.10W
Seychelles Indian Oc. 49 5.00S 55.00E
Seydhisfjördhur *town* Iceland 40 65.16N 14.02W
Seylac Somali Rep. 71 11.21N 43.30E
Seym *r.* Ukraine 45 51.30N 32.30E
Seymour Australia 93 37.01S145.10E
Seymour U.S.A. 111 33.35N 99.16W
Seyne France 21 44.21N 6.21E
Seyssel France 21 45.57N 5.49E
Sežana Slovenia 31 45.42N 13.52E
Sézanne France 19 48.43N 3.43E
Sezimbra Portugal 27 38.26N 9.06W
Sezze Italy 32 41.30N 13.03E
Sfax Tunisia 22 34.45N 10.43E
Sfîntu-Gheorghe Romania 37 45.52N 25.50E
Sforströmmen *str.* Denmark 42 54.58N 11.55E
'sGravenhage Neth. 16 52.05N 4.16E
Shaanxi *d.* China 54 35.00N108.30E
Shaba *d.* Zaïre 79 8.00S 27.00E
Shabeelle *r.* Somali Rep. 79 0.30N 43.10E
Shabunda Zaïre 79 2.42S 27.20E
Shache China 52 38.27N 77.16E
Shafter U.S.A. 109 35.30N119.16W
Shaftesbury U.K. 13 51.00N 2.12W
Shagamu *r.* Canada 102 55.50N 86.48W
Shāhābād India 63 27.39N 79.57E
Shāhāda India 62 21.28N 74.18E
Shahbā' Syria 66 32.51N 36.37E
Shāhbandar Pakistan 62 24.10N 67.54E
Shāhbāz Kalāt Pakistan 62 26.42N 63.58E
Shahdād Iran 65 30.27N 57.44E
Shāhdādkot Pakistan 62 27.51N 67.54E
Shāhdādpur Pakistan 62 25.56N 68.37E
Shahdol India 63 23.17N 81.21E
Shāhganj India 63 26.03N 82.41E
Shāhgarh India 62 27.07N 69.54E
Shaḥḥāt Libya 72 32.50N 21.52E
Shāh Jahān, Kūh-e *mts.* Iran 65 37.00N 58.00E
Shāhjahānpur India 63 27.53N 79.55E
Shāh Jūy Afghan. 62 32.31N 67.25E
Shāh Kot Pakistan 62 31.34N 73.29E
Shāh Kūh *mtn.* Iran 65 31.38N 59.16E
Shāhpur Pakistan 62 28.43N 68.25E
Shāhpura India 62 25.35N 75.00E
Shāhpur Chākar Pakistan 62 26.09N 68.39E
Shahrak Afghan. 62 34.06N 64.18E
Shahr-e Bābak Iran 65 30.08N 55.04E
Shahrestān Afghan. 62 34.22N 66.47E
Shahrezā Iran 65 32.00N 51.52E
Shahr Kord Iran 65 32.40N 50.52E
Sha'īb Abā al Qūr *wadi* Saudi Arabia 64 31.02N 42.00E
Shaikhpura India 63 25.09N 85.51E
Shājāpur India 62 23.26N 76.16E
Shakawe Botswana 80 18.22S 21.50E
Shaker Heights *town* U.S.A. 114 41.29N 81.36W
Shakhty Russian Fed. 23 47.43N 40.16E
Shakhunya Russian Fed. 44 57.41N 46.46E
Shaki Nigeria 77 8.41N 3.24E
Shakshūk Egypt 66 29.28N 30.42E
Shala Hāyk' *l.* Ethiopia 73 7.25N 38.30E
Shalingzi China 54 40.42N114.55E
Shallotte U.S.A. 113 33.58N 78.25W
Shalwa Israel 67 31.34N 34.46E
Shām, Jabal ash *mtn.* Oman 65 23.14N 57.17E
Shamāl Dārfūr *d.* Sudan 72 17.15N 25.30E
Shamāl Kurdufān *d.* Sudan 72 14.00N 29.00E
Shāmat al Akbād *des.* Saudi Arabia 64 28.15N 43.05E
Shamir Israel 67 33.10N 35.39E
Shāmli India 62 29.27N 77.19E
Shamokin U.S.A. 115 40.47N 76.34W
Shamrock U.S.A. 111 35.13N100.15W
Shamva Zimbabwe 79 17.20S 31.38E
Shan *d.* Burma 56 22.00N 98.00E
Shandī Sudan 72 16.42N 33.26E
Shandong *d.* China 54 36.00N119.00E
Shandong Bandao *pen.* China 54 37.00N121.30E
Shangcheng China 55 31.48N115.24E
Shangdu China 54 41.33N113.31E
Shanggao China 55 28.15N114.55E
Shanghai China 55 31.18N121.50E
Shanghai *d.* China 55 31.00N121.30E
Shanglin China 55 23.26N108.36E
Shangqiu China 54 34.21N115.40E
Shangrao China 55 28.24N117.56E
Shangshui China 54 33.31N114.39E
Shangxian *see* Shangzhou China 54
Shangyi China 54 41.06N114.00E
Shangyou Shuiku *resr.* China 55 25.52N114.21E
Shangyu China 55 30.01N120.52E
Shangzhou China 54 33.49N109.56E
Shanhaiguan China 54 39.58N119.45E
Shannon *r.* Rep. of Ire. 15 52.39N 8.43W
Shannon, Mouth of the *est.* Rep. of Ire. 15 52.29N 9.57W
Shan Plateau Burma 56 18.50N 98.00E
Shanshan China 52 42.52N 90.10E
Shantarskiy Ostrova *is.* Russian Fed. 51 55.00N138.00E
Shantou China 55 23.22N116.39E
Shanwa Tanzania 79 3.09S 33.48E
Shanxi *d.* China 54 37.00N112.00E
Shanyin China 54 39.30N112.50E
Shaoguan China 55 24.53N113.31E
Shaoxing China 55 30.01N120.40E
Shaoyang China 55 27.10N111.14E
Shap U.K. 12 54.32N 2.40W
Shapinsay *i.* U.K. 14 59.03N 2.51W
Shapur *ruins* Iran 65 29.42N 51.30E
Shaqrā Lebanon 67 33.12N 35.28E
Shaqrā' Saudi Arabia 65 25.17N 45.14E
Shaqrā' Syria 67 32.54N 36.14E
Shaqrā' Yemen 71 13.21N 45.42E
Sharan Jogīzai Pakistan 62 31.02N 68.33E
Sharbot Lake *town* Canada 105 44.46N 76.41W
Shark B. Australia 88 25.30S113.30E
Sharlyk Russian Fed. 44 52.58N 54.46E
Sharm ash Shaykh Egypt 66 27.51N 34.16E
Sharon U.S.A. 114 41.14N 80.31W
Sharon Springs *town* U.S.A. 110 38.54N101.45W
Sharq al Istiwā'īyah *d.* Sudan 73 5.00N 33.00E
Sharqī, Al Jabal ash *mts.* Lebanon 66 34.00N 36.25E
Sharqīyah, Aş Şaḥrā' ash *des.* Egypt 66 27.40N 32.00E
Sharya Russian Fed. 44 58.22N 45.50E
Shashi *r.* Botswana / Zimbabwe 80 22.10S 29.15E
Shashi China 55 30.18N112.20E
Shasta, Mt. U.S.A. 108 41.20N122.20W
Shatt al Arab *r.* Iraq 65 30.00N 48.30E
Shaunavon Canada 101 49.40N108.25W
Shawanaga Canada 104 45.32N 80.24W
Shawangunk Mts. U.S.A. 115 41.35N 74.30W
Shawano U.S.A. 102 44.46N 88.38W
Shawbridge Canada 105 45.52N 74.05W
Shaw I. Australia 90 20.29S149.05E
Shawinigan Canada 105 46.33N 72.45W
Shawinigan Sud Canada 105 46.30N 72.45W
Shawnee Ohio U.S.A. 114 39.36N 82.13W
Shawnee Okla. U.S.A. 111 35.20N 96.55W
Shawville Canada 105 45.36N 76.29W
Sha Xi *r.* China 55 26.38N118.10E
Sha Xian China 55 26.27N117.42E
Shayang China 55 30.42N112.29E
Shay Gap *town* Australia 88 20.28S120.05E
Shaykh, Jabal ash *mtn.* Lebanon 66 33.24N 35.52E
Shaykh 'Uthmān Yemen 71 12.52N 44.59E
Shchara *r.* Belorussia 37 53.27N 24.45E
Shchelyayur Russian Fed. 44 65.16N 53.17E
Shchors Ukraine 37 51.50N 31.59E
Sheboygan U.S.A. 110 43.46N 87.36W
Shebshi Mts. Nigeria 77 8.30N 11.45E
Shediac Canada 103 46.13N 64.32W
Sheeffry Hills Rep. of Ire. 15 53.41N 9.42W
Sheelin, Lough Rep. of Ire. 15 53.48N 7.20W
Sheep Range *mts.* U.S.A. 109 36.45N115.05W
Sheet Harbour Canada 103 44.55N 62.32W
Shefar'am Israel 67 32.48N 35.10E
Sheffield U.K. 12 53.23N 1.28W
Sheffield Ala. U.S.A. 113 34.46N 87.40W
Sheffield Penn. U.S.A. 114 41.42N 79.02W
Sheffield Tex. U.S.A. 111 30.41N101.49W
Shefford U.K. 13 52.02N 0.20W
Shegaon India 62 20.47N 76.41E
Sheguiandah Canada 104 45.53N 81.57W
Shekatika Bay *town* Canada 103 51.17N 58.20W
Shekhābād Afghan. 62 34.05N 68.45E
Shek Hasan Ethiopia 73 12.09N 35.54E
Shekhūpura Pakistan 62 31.42N 73.59E
Sheki Azerbaijan 45 41.12N 47.10E
Sheksna *r.* Russian Fed. 44 60.00N 37.49E
Shelburne N.S. Canada 103 43.46N 65.19W
Shelburne Ont. Canada 104 44.04N 80.12W
Shelburne U.S.A. 105 44.22N 73.15W
Shelburne B. Australia 90 11.49S143.00E
Shelby Mich. U.S.A. 112 43.36N 86.22W
Shelby Mont. U.S.A. 108 48.30N111.51W
Shelby Ohio U.S.A. 114 40.53N 82.40W
Shelbyville Ind. U.S.A. 112 39.31N 85.46W
Shelbyville Tenn. U.S.A. 113 35.29N 86.30W
Sheldon Iowa U.S.A. 110 43.11N 95.51W
Sheldon N.Dak. U.S.A. 110 46.35N 97.30W
Sheldrake Canada 103 50.20N 64.51W
Shelikof Str. U.S.A. 98 58.00N153.45W
Shelley U.S.A. 108 43.23N112.07W
Shellharbour Australia 93 34.35S150.52E
Shell Lake *town* Canada 101 53.18N107.07W
Shelton U.S.A. 108 47.13N123.06W
Shenandoah Iowa U.S.A. 110 40.46N 95.22W
Shenandoah Penn. U.S.A. 115 40.49N 76.12W
Shenandoah *r.* U.S.A. 114 38.56N 78.12W
Shenandoah Va. U.S.A. 114 38.29N 78.37W
Shenandoah, North Fork *r.* U.S.A. 114 38.57N 78.12W
Shenandoah, South Fork *r.* U.S.A. 114 38.57N 78.12W
Shenandoah Mts. U.S.A. 114 38.55N 78.56W
Shenandoah Nat. Park U.S.A. 114 38.48N 78.12W
Shenandoah Tower *mtn.* U.S.A. 114 38.30N 79.09W
Shenandoah Valley *f.* U.S.A. 114 38.42N 78.48W
Shenchi China 54 39.08N112.10E
Shëngjin Albania 34 41.50N 19.35E
Shengze China 55 30.53N120.40E
Shenkursk Russian Fed. 44 62.05N 42.58E
Shenmu China 54 38.54N110.24E
Shennongjia China 55 31.44N110.44E
Shen Xian China 54 36.15N115.40E
Shenyang China 54 41.48N123.27E
Shenzhen China 55 22.32N114.08E
Sheo India 62 26.11N 71.15E
Sheoganj India 62 25.09N 73.04E
Sheopur India 62 25.40N 76.42E
Shepetovka Ukraine 37 50.12N 27.01E
Shepherd Is. Vanuatu 84 16.55S168.36E
Shepparton Australia 93 36.25S145.26E
Sheppey, Isle of U.K. 13 51.24N 0.50E
Sherada Ethiopia 73 7.21N 36.32E
Sherborne U.K. 13 50.56N 2.31W
Sherbro I. Sierra Leone 76 7.30N 12.50W
Sherbrooke Canada 105 45.24N 71.54W
Sherburne U.S.A. 115 42.41N 75.30W
Sheridan U.S.A. 108 44.48N106.58W
Sheringa Australia 92 33.51S135.15E
Sheringham U.K. 12 52.56N 1.11E
Sherkin I. Rep. of Ire. 15 51.28N 9.25W
Sherman N.Y. U.S.A. 114 42.10N 79.36W
Sherman Tex. U.S.A. 111 33.38N 96.36W
Sherman Mills U.S.A. 112 45.52N 68.23W
Sherridon Canada 101 55.07N101.05W
'sHertogenbosch Neth. 16 51.42N 5.19E
Shesh Gāv Afghan. 62 33.45N 68.33E
Shetland Is. *d.* U.K. 14 60.20N 1.15W
Shetpe Kazakhstan 45 44.09N 52.06E
Shetrunji *r.* India 62 21.20N 72.05E
Shevchenko Kazakhstan 45 43.37N 51.11E
Shewa *d.* Ethiopia 73 8.40N 38.00E
Shewa Gīmīra Ethiopia 73 7.00N 35.50E
Sheyang China 54 33.47N120.19E
Sheyenne *r.* U.S.A. 110 47.05N 96.50W
Shiawassee *r.* U.S.A. 104 43.06N 84.10W
Shibām Yemen 71 15.56N 48.38E
Shibecha Japan 57 43.17N144.36E
Shibīn al Kawm Egypt 66 30.33N 31.00E
Shibīn al Qanāṭir Egypt 66 30.19N 31.19E
Shibogama L. Canada 102 53.35N 88.10W
Shickshinny U.S.A. 115 41.09N 76.09W
Shidao China 54 36.52N122.26E
Shiel, Loch U.K. 14 56.48N 5.33W
Shiga *d.* Japan 57 34.55N136.00E
Shigaib Sudan 72 15.01N 23.36E
Shihpao Shan *mts.* China 55 30.00N112.00E
Shijak Albania 34 41.21N 19.33E
Shijiazhuang China 54 38.03N114.26E
Shijiu Hu *l.* China 55 31.20N118.48E
Shikārpur Pakistan 62 27.57N 68.38E
Shikohābād India 63 27.06N 78.36E
Shikoku *d.* Japan 57 33.30N133.00E
Shikoku *i.* Japan 57 33.30N133.00E
Shikoku sanchi *mts.* Japan 57 34.00N134.00E
Shikotsu ko *l.* Japan 57 43.50N141.26E
Shilabo Ethiopia 71 6.05N 44.48E
Shilka Russian Fed. 53 51.55N116.01E
Shilka *r.* Russian Fed. 53 53.20N121.10E
Shillington U.S.A. 115 40.18N 75.58W
Shillo *r.* Israel 67 32.07N 34.53E
Shillong India 63 25.34N 91.53E
Shiloh *see* Saylūn Jordan 67
Shilong China 55 23.02N113.50E
Shima Japan 57 34.13N136.51E
Shimada Japan 57 34.49N138.11E
Shima-hantō *pen.* Japan 57 34.25N136.45E
Shimizu Japan 57 35.01N138.29E
Shimoda Japan 57 34.40N138.57E
Shimoga India 60 13.56N 75.31E
Shimo jima *i.* Japan 57 32.10N130.30E
Shimo Koshiki jima *i.* Japan 57 31.50N130.00E
Shimonoseki Japan 57 34.02N130.58E
Shimpek Kazakhstan 52 44.50N 74.10E
Shin, Loch U.K. 14 58.06N 4.32W
Shinano *r.* Japan 57 37.58N139.02E
Shīndand Afghan. 62 33.18N 62.08E
Shinglehouse U.S.A. 114 41.58N 78.12W
Shingleton U.S.A. 112 46.21N 86.28W
Shingū Japan 57 33.44N135.59E
Shīnkay Afghan. 62 31.57N 67.26E
Shīn Naray Afghan. 62 31.19N 66.43E
Shinnston U.S.A. 114 39.24N 80.18W
Shinshār Syria 66 34.36N 36.45E
Shinshiro Japan 57 34.54N137.30E
Shinyanga Tanzania 79 3.40S 33.20E
Shinyanga *d.* Tanzania 79 3.30S 33.00E
Shiono zaki *c.* Japan 57 33.28N135.47E
Ship Bottom U.S.A. 115 39.39N 74.11W
Shipka Pass Bulgaria 34 42.46N 25.33E
Shippegan Canada 103 47.45N 64.42W
Shippensburg U.S.A. 114 40.03N 77.31W
Shiprock U.S.A. 108 36.47N108.41W
Shipston on Stour U.K. 13 52.04N 1.38W
Shiqian China 55 27.20N108.10E
Shiqiao China 55 31.19N111.59E
Shiqizhen China 55 22.22N113.21E
Shiqma *r.* Israel 67 31.36N 34.30E
Shiquan China 54 33.03N108.17E

Shiquan He to **Slatina**

Shiquan He *r.* China **63** 32.30N 79.40E
Shirakawa Japan **57** 37.10N140.15E
Shirakskaya Step *f.* Georgia **65** 41.40N 46.20E
Shirane san *mtn.* Japan **57** 35.40N138.15E
Shīrāz Iran **65** 29.36N 52.33E
Shirbīn Egypt **66** 31.13N 31.31E
Shire *r.* Mozambique **79** 17.46S 35.20E
Shiriya saki *c.* Japan **57** 41.24N141.30E
Shīr Kūh *mtn.* Iran **65** 31.38N 54.07E
Shiroishi Japan **57** 38.00N140.37E
Shirpur India **62** 21.21N 74.53E
Shīrvān Iran **65** 37.24N 57.55E
Shivpuri India **63** 25.26N 77.39E
Shiwan Dashan *mts.* China **55** 21.48N107.50E
Shiyan Hubei China **54** 32.38N110.47E
Shizuishan China **54** 39.14N106.47E
Shizuoka Japan **57** 34.58N138.23E
Shizuoka *d.* Japan **57** 35.00N138.00E
Shklov Belorussia **37** 54.16N 30.16E
Shkodër Albania **34** 42.05N 19.30E
Shkodër *d.* Albania **34** 42.10N 19.40E
Shkumbin *r.* Albania **34** 41.01N 19.26E
Shoal C. Australia **89** 33.51S121.10E
Shoalhaven *r.* Australia **93** 34.51S150.40E
Sholāpur India **60** 17.43N 75.56E
Shomera Israel **67** 33.05N 35.17E
Shonai *r.* Japan **57** 35.04N136.50E
Shoshone Calif. U.S.A. **109** 35.58N116.17W
Shoshone Idaho U.S.A. **108** 42.57N114.25W
Shoshone Mts. U.S.A. **108** 39.25N117.15W
Shoshoni U.S.A. **108** 43.14N108.07W
Shostka Belorussia **44** 51.53N 33.30E
Shou Xian China **54** 32.30N116.35E
Shouyang China **54** 37.55N113.10E
Show Low U.S.A. **109** 34.15N110.02W
Shpola Ukraine **37** 49.00N 31.25E
Shreve U.S.A. **114** 40.41N 82.01W
Shreveport U.S.A **111** 32.30N 93.45W
Shrewsbury U.K. **13** 52.42N 2.45W
Shropshire *d.* U.K. **13** 52.35N 2.40W
Shuangliao China **54** 43.28N123.27E
Shuangyashan China **53** 46.37N131.22E
Shu'ayb, Wādī Jordan **67** 31.54N 35.38E
Shubenacadie Canada **103** 45.05N 63.25W
Shubrā al Khaymah Egypt **66** 30.06N 31.15E
Shuicheng China **55** 26.36N104.51E
Shujāābād Pakistan **62** 29.53N 71.18E
Shujālpur India **62** 23.24N 76.43E
Shuksan U.S.A. **108** 48.55N121.43W
Shule China **52** 39.25N 76.06E
Shumagin Is. U.S.A. **98** 55.00N160.00W
Shumerlya Russian Fed. **44** 55.30N 46.25E
Shumikha Russian Fed. **50** 55.15N 63.14E
Shumyachi Russian Fed. **37** 53.52N 32.25E
Shūnat Nimrīn Jordan **67** 31.54N 35.37E
Shunayn, Sabkhat *f.* Libya **72** 30.10N 21.00E
Shunchang China **55** 26.48N117.47E
Shunde China **55** 22.40N113.20E
Shuo Xian China **54** 39.19N112.25E
Shūr *r.* Khorāsān Iran **65** 34.11N 60.07E
Shūr *r.* Kermān Iran **65** 30.45N 57.55E
Shūr *r.* Kermān Iran **65** 31.14N 55.29E
Shūrāb Iran **65** 28.09N 60.18E
Shūrāb *r.* Iran **65** 31.30N 55.18E
Shurugwi Zimbabwe **80** 19.40S 30.00E
Shūshtar Iran **65** 32.04N 48.53E
Shuswap L. Canada **100** 50.55N119.03W
Shuwak Sudan **72** 14.23N 35.52E
Shuya Russian Fed. **44** 56.49N 41.23E
Shwebo Burma **56** 22.35N 95.42E
Shyok Jammu & Kashmir **63** 34.11N 78.08E
Siāhān Range *mts.* Pakistan **62** 27.30N 64.30E
Siālkot Pakistan **62** 32.30N 74.31E
Sian *see* Xi'an China **54**
Siargao *i.* Phil. **59** 9.55N126.05E
Siari Jammu & Kashmir **62** 34.56N 76.44E
Siasconset U.S.A. **115** 41.16N 69.58W
Siátista Greece **34** 40.15N 21.33E
Siau *i.* Indonesia **59** 2.42N125.24E
Siauliai Lithuania **41** 55.56N 23.19E
Sibasa R.S.A. **80** 22.56S 30.28E
Šibenik Croatia **31** 43.44N 15.54E
Siberut *i.* Indonesia **58** 1.30S 99.00E
Sibi Pakistan **62** 29.33N 67.53E
Sibiti Congo **78** 3.40S 13.24E
Sibiti *r.* Tanzania **79** 3.47S 34.45E
Sibiu Romania **29** 45.47N 24.09E
Sibley U.S.A. **110** 43.25N 95.43W
Sibolga Indonesia **58** 1.42N 98.48E
Sibu Malaysia **58** 2.18N111.49E
Sibut C.A.R. **77** 5.46N 19.06E
Sicasica Bolivia **124** 17.22S 67.45W
Siccus *r.* Australia **92** 31.26S139.30E
Sichuan *d.* China **52** 30.30N103.00E
Sichuan Pendi *f.* China **55** 31.00N106.00E
Sicié, Cap *c.* France **21** 43.03N 5.51E
Sicilia *d.* Italy **33** 37.45N 14.00E
Sicilia *i.* Italy **33** 37.30N 14.00E
Sicily *i. see* Sicilia *i.* Italy **33**
Sicuani Peru **122** 14.21S 71.13W
Šid Yugo. **31** 45.08N 19.13E
Sidamo *d.* Ethiopia **73** 4.30N 39.00E
Sidaouet Niger **77** 18.34N 8.03E
Siderno Italy **33** 38.16N 16.18E
Sídheros, Ákra *c.* Greece **35** 35.19N 26.19E
Sidhi India **63** 24.25N 81.53E
Sidhirókastron Greece **34** 41.14N 23.22E
Sidhpur India **62** 23.55N 72.23E
Sīdī Barrānī Egypt **64** 31.38N 25.58E
Sidi bel Abbès Algeria **74** 35.12N 0.38W
Sidi Daoud Tunisia **32** 37.01N 10.55E
Sidi Ifni Morocco **74** 29.24N 10.12W
Sidi-Kacem Morocco **74** 34.15N 5.39W
Sīdī Sālim Egypt **66** 31.16N 30.47E
Sidi Smaïl Morocco **74** 32.49N 8.30W
Sidlaw Hills U.K. **14** 56.31N 3.10W
Sidley, Mt. Antarctica **128** 77.30S125.00W
Sidmouth U.K. **13** 50.40N 3.13W
Sidney Canada **100** 48.39N123.24W
Sidney Mont. U.S.A. **108** 47.43N104.09W
Sidney Nebr. U.S.A. **110** 41.09N102.59W
Sidney N.Y. U.S.A. **115** 42.19N 75.24W
Sidney Ohio U.S.A. **112** 40.16N 84.10W
Sidon *see* Şaydā Lebanon **66**
Sidra, G. of *see* Surt, Khalīj *g.* Libya **75**
Siedlce Poland **37** 52.10N 22.18E
Sieg *r.* Germany **16** 50.49N 7.11E
Siegburg Germany **38** 50.47N 7.12E
Siegen Germany **38** 50.52N 8.02E
Siemiatycze Poland **37** 52.26N 22.53E
Siĕmréab Cambodia **56** 13.21N103.50E
Siena Italy **30** 43.19N 11.21E
Sieradz Poland **37** 51.36N 18.45E
Sierck-les-Bains France **19** 49.26N 6.21E
Sierpc Poland **37** 52.52N 19.41E
Sierra Blanca *town* U.S.A. **109** 31.11N105.12W
Sierra Colorada Argentina **125** 40.35S 67.50W
Sierra de Outes *town* Spain **26** 42.51N 8.54W
Sierra Leone Africa **76** 9.00N 12.00W
Sierra Mojada *town* Mexico **111** 27.17N103.42W
Sierra Nevada *mts.* U.S.A. **108** 37.45N119.30W
Sierre Switz. **39** 46.18N 7.32E
Sīfenī Ethiopia **73** 12.20N 40.24E
Sífnos *i.* Greece **35** 36.59N 24.40E
Sig Algeria **74** 35.32N 0.11W
Sig Russian Fed. **44** 65.31N 34.16E
Sigean France **20** 43.02N 2.59E
Sighetul Marmaţiei Romania **37** 47.56N 23.54E
Sighişoara Romania **37** 46.13N 24.49E
Sigli Indonesia **58** 5.23N 95.57E
Siglufjördhur Iceland **40** 66.12N 18.55W
Sigmaringen Germany **39** 48.05N 9.13E
Signy France **19** 49.42N 4.25E
Sigtuna Sweden **43** 59.37N 17.43E
Sigüenza Spain **26** 41.04N 2.38W
Sigües Spain **25** 42.38N 1.00W
Siguiri Guinea **76** 11.28N 9.07W
Sihor India **62** 21.42N 71.58E
Sihorā India **63** 23.29N 80.07E
Siikka *r.* Finland **40** 64.50N 24.44E
Si'īr Jordan **67** 31.35N 35.09E
Siirt Turkey **64** 37.56N 41.56E
Sikanni Chief *r.* Canada **100** 58.20N121.50W
Sīkar India **62** 27.37N 75.09E
Sikasso Mali **76** 11.18N 5.38W
Sikasso *d.* Mali **76** 11.20N 6.05W
Sikeston U.S.A. **111** 36.53N 89.35W
Sikhote Alin *mts.* Russian Fed. **53** 44.00N135.00E
Sikiá Greece **34** 40.02N 23.56E
Síkinos *i.* Greece **35** 36.39N 25.06E
Sikión *site* Greece **35** 37.59N 22.44E
Sikkim *d.* India **63** 27.30N 88.30E
Sil *r.* Spain **26** 42.27N 7.43W
Silandro Italy **30** 46.38N 10.46E
Silba Croatia **31** 44.23N 14.42E
Silba *i.* Croatia **31** 44.23N 14.42E
Silchar India **61** 24.49N 92.47E
Silcox Canada **101** 57.12N 94.10W
Silet Algeria **75** 22.39N 4.35E
Silgarhi-Doti Nepal **63** 29.16N 80.58E
Silghāt India **63** 26.37N 92.56E
Silifke Turkey **64** 36.22N 33.57E
Silīguri India **63** 26.42N 88.26E
Siliil Somali Rep. **71** 10.59N 43.31E
Siling Co *l.* China **63** 31.45N 88.50E
Silistra Bulgaria **29** 44.07N 27.17E
Šiljak *mtn.* Yugo. **34** 43.45N 21.50E
Siljan *l.* Sweden **41** 60.50N 14.45E
Silkeborg Denmark **42** 56.10N 9.34E
Sillé-le-Guillaume France **18** 48.12N 0.08W
Sillian Austria **39** 46.45N 12.25E
Sillian Italy **30** 46.45N 12.25E
Sillon de Talbert *c.* France **18** 48.53N 3.05W
Silloth U.K. **12** 54.53N 3.25W
Silogui Indonesia **58** 1.10S 98.46E
Silsbee U.S.A **111** 30.21N 94.11W
Silvassa India **62** 20.17N 73.00E
Silver Bow U.S.A. **108** 46.00N112.40W
Silver City U.S.A. **109** 32.46N108.17W
Silver Creek *town* U.S.A. **114** 42.33N 79.10W
Silverdalen Sweden **43** 57.32N 15.44E
Silver Lake *town* U.S.A. **108** 43.08N120.56W
Silver Spring *town* U.S.A. **114** 39.02N 77.03W
Silverstone U.K. **13** 52.05N 1.03W
Silverthrone Mtn. Canada **100** 51.31N126.06W
Silverton Australia **92** 31.53S141.13E
Silverton U.S.A. **108** 45.01N122.47W
Silves Portugal **27** 37.11N 8.26W
Silvi Italy **31** 42.34N 14.05E
Simanggang Malaysia **58** 1.10N111.32E
Simàrd, Lac *l.* Canada **102** 47.40N 78.40W
Simav *r.* Turkey **29** 40.24N 28.31E
Simba Kenya **79** 2.10S 37.37E
Simba Zaïre **78** 0.36N 22.55E
Simbach Germany **39** 48.34N 12.45E
Simcoe Canada **104** 42.50N 80.18W
Simcoe, L. Canada **104** 44.20N 79.20W
Simdega India **63** 22.37N 84.31E
Simenga Russian Fed. **51** 62.42N108.25E
Simeria Romania **29** 45.51N 23.01E
Simeto *r.* Italy **33** 37.24N 15.06E
Simeulue *i.* Indonesia **58** 2.30N 96.00E
Simferopol' Ukraine **45** 44.57N 34.05E
Simi Greece **35** 36.35N 27.50E
Simi *i.* Greece **35** 36.35N 27.50E
Simikot Nepal **63** 29.58N 81.51E
Simitli Bulgaria **34** 41.52N 23.07E
Simiyu *r.* Tanzania **79** 2.32S 33.25E
Simla India **62** 31.06N 77.09E
Simleul Silvaniei Romania **37** 47.14N 22.48E
Simmern Germany **39** 49.59N 7.31E
Simo *r.* Finland **40** 65.37N 25.03E
Simojärvo *l.* Finland **40** 66.06N 27.03E
Simon, Lac *l.* Canada **105** 45.58N 75.05W
Simon's Town R.S.A. **80** 34.12S 18.26E
Simoom Sound *town* Canada **98** 50.45N126.45W
Simplon Pass Switz. **39** 46.15N 8.02E
Simplon Tunnel Switz. **39** 46.15N 8.10E
Simpson Desert Australia **90** 25.00S136.50E
Simrishamn Sweden **43** 55.33N 14.20E
Simuco Mozambique **79** 14.00S 40.35E
Sīnā', Shibh Jazīrat *pen.* Egypt **66** 29.00N 34.00E
Sinadhago Somali Rep. **71** 5.22N 46.22E
Sinai *see* Sīnā', Shibh Jazīrat *pen.* Egypt **66**
Sinaloa *d.* Mexico **109** 25.00N107.30W
Sinaloa *r.* Mexico **109** 25.18N108.30W
Sinalunga Italy **30** 43.12N 11.44E
Sinan China **55** 27.51N108.24E
Sīnāwin Libya **75** 31.02N 10.36E
Sincelejo Colombia **122** 9.17N 75.23W
Sinclair U.S.A. **108** 41.47N107.07W
Sinclair Mills Canada **100** 54.05N121.40W
Sind *r.* India **63** 26.26N 79.13E
Sindal Denmark **42** 57.28N 10.13E
Sindara Gabon **78** 1.07S 10.41E
Sindari India **62** 25.35N 71.55E
Sindelfingen Germany **39** 48.42N 9.00E
Sindh *d.* Pakistan **62** 26.45N 69.00E
Sindhūli Garhi Nepal **63** 27.16N 85.58E
Sindri India **63** 23.45N 86.42E
Sines Portugal **26** 37.57N 8.52W
Sines, Cabo de *c.* Portugal **26** 37.57N 8.53W
Sinfåis Portugal **26** 41.04N 8.05W
Sinfra Ivory Coast **76** 6.35N 5.56W
Singālila *mtn.* India **63** 27.13N 88.01E
Singapore Asia **58** 1.20N103.45E
Singapore *town* Singapore **58** 1.20N103.45E
Singaraja Indonesia **59** 8.06S115.07E
Singatoka Fiji **84** 18.08S177.30E
Sing Buri Thailand **56** 14.56N100.21E
Singida Tanzania **79** 4.45S 34.42E
Singida *d.* Tanzania **79** 6.00S 34.30E
Singing India **61** 28.53N 94.47E
Singitikós Kólpos *g.* Greece **34** 40.06N 24.00E
Singkaling Hkāmti Burma **61** 26.00N 95.42E
Singkang Indonesia **59** 4.09S120.02E
Singkawang Indonesia **58** 0.57N108.57E
Singkep *i.* Indonesia **58** 0.30S104.20E
Singleton Australia **93** 32.33S151.11E
Singoli India **62** 25.00N 75.25E
Singosan N. Korea **53** 38.50N127.27E
Siniscola Italy **32** 40.34N 9.41E
Sinj Croatia **31** 43.42N 16.38E
Sinjah Sudan **73** 13.09N 33.56E
Sinjajevina *mts.* Yugo. **31** 43.00N 19.15E
Sinjil Jordan **67** 32.02N 35.16E
Sinkāt Sudan **72** 18.50N 36.50E
Sinkiang *d. see* Xinjiang Uygur Zizhiqu *d.* China **52**
Sinnai Italy **32** 39.18N 9.12E
Sinnar India **62** 19.51N 74.00E
Sinnemahoning *r.* U.S.A. **114** 41.19N 78.06W
Sinnes Norway **42** 58.56N 6.50E
Sinni *r.* Italy **33** 40.09N 16.42E
Sînnicolau Mare Romania **29** 46.05N 20.38E
Sinnūris Egypt **66** 29.25N 30.52E
Sinop Turkey **64** 42.02N 35.09E
Sinsheim Germany **39** 49.16N 8.53E
Sintang Indonesia **58** 0.03N111.31E
Sint Eustatius *i.* Leeward Is. **117** 17.33N 63.00W
Sint Maarten *i. see* St. Martin *i.* Leeward Is. **117**
Sinton U.S.A. **111** 29.41N 95.58W
Sintra Portugal **27** 38.48N 9.23W
Sinŭiju N. Korea **53** 40.04N124.25E
Sinyavka Belorussia **37** 52.58N 26.30E
Sinyukha *r.* Ukraine **37** 48.03N 30.51E
Sió *r.* Hungary **31** 46.20N 18.55E
Siocon Phil. **59** 7.42N122.08E
Siófok Hungary **31** 46.54N 18.04E
Sion Switz. **39** 46.14N 7.21E
Sioux City U.S.A. **110** 42.30N 96.23W
Sioux Falls *town* U.S.A. **110** 43.32N 96.44W
Sioux Lookout *town* Canada **102** 50.06N 91.55W
Siphaqeni R.S.A. **80** 31.05S 29.29E
Siping Hubei China **55** 31.58N111.10E
Siping Jilin China **54** 43.10N124.24E
Sipiwesk L. Canada **101** 55.05N 97.35W
Sipura *i.* Indonesia **58** 2.10S 99.40E
Sira Norway **42** 58.25N 6.38E
Sira *r.* Norway **42** 58.17N 6.24E
Siracusa Italy **33** 37.04N 15.17E
Sirājganj Bangla. **63** 24.27N 89.43E
Sirakoro Mali **76** 12.41N 9.14W
Sirasso Ivory Coast **76** 9.16N 6.06W
Sirdalsvatn *l.* Norway **42** 58.33N 6.41E
Sīrē Ethiopia **73** 9.00N 36.55E
Sir Edward Pellew Group *is.* Australia **90** 15.40S136.48E
Siret *r.* Romania **29** 45.28N 27.56E
Sirevåg Norway **42** 58.30N 5.47E
Sirha Nepal **63** 26.39N 86.12E
Sirḩān, Wādī as *f.* Saudi Arabia **64** 31.00N 37.30E
Sir James MacBrien, Mt. Canada **100** 62.07N127.41W
Sir Joseph Banks Group *is.* Australia **92** 34.35S136.12E
Sirohi India **62** 24.53N 72.52E
Sironj India **63** 24.06N 77.42E
Síros *i.* Greece **35** 37.26N 24.54E
Sirrah, Wādī as *r.* Saudi Arabia **65** 23.10N 44.22E
Sirsa India **62** 29.32N 75.02E
Sir Wilfrid, Mt. Canada **105** 46.41N 75.35W
Sisak Croatia **31** 45.29N 16.23E
Sisaket Thailand **56** 15.08N104.18E
Sishen R.S.A. **80** 27.46S 22.59E
Sisimiut *see* Holsteinsborg Greenland **99**
Sisipuk L. Canada **101** 55.45N101.50W
Sisŏphŏn Cambodia **56** 13.37N102.58E
Sissach Switz. **39** 47.28N 7.49E
Sisseton U.S.A. **110** 45.40N 97.03W
Sissonne France **19** 49.34N 3.54E
Sistema Central *mts.* Spain **26** 41.00N 3.30W
Sistema Ibérico *mts.* Spain **26** 41.00N 2.25W
Sistemas Béticos *mts.* Spain **27** 37.20N 3.00W
Sisteron France **21** 44.12N 5.56E
Sītāmarhi India **63** 26.36N 85.29E
Sītāpur India **63** 27.34N 80.41E
Sithonía *pen.* Greece **34** 40.00N 23.45E
Sitía Greece **35** 35.13N 26.06E
Sitka U.S.A. **100** 57.05N135.20W
Sitnica *r.* Yugo. **34** 42.45N 21.01E
Sittang *r.* Burma **56** 17.25N 96.50E
Sittard Neth. **16** 51.00N 5.52E
Sittensen Germany **38** 53.17N 9.30E
Sittwe Burma **56** 20.09N 92.50E
Situbondo Indonesia **59** 7.40S114.01E
Siuruan *r.* Finland **40** 65.20N 25.55E
Sīvan *r.* Iran **65** 29.50N 52.47E
Sivas Turkey **64** 39.44N 37.01E
Sivomaskinskiy Russian Fed. **44** 66.45N 62.44E
Sivrihisar Turkey **64** 39.29N 31.32E
Sīwah Egypt **64** 29.12N 25.31E
Sīwah, Wāḩat *oasis* Egypt **64** 29.10N 25.40E
Siwalik Range *mts.* India **63** 31.15N 77.45E
Siwān India **63** 26.13N 84.22E
Siwa Oasis *see* Sīwah, Wāḩat *oasis* Egypt **64**
Sixmilecross U.K. **15** 54.34N 7.08W
Siya Russian Fed. **44** 63.38N 41.40E
Sizun France **18** 48.24N 4.05W
Sjaelland *i.* Denmark **42** 55.30N 11.45E
Sjaellands Odde *c.* Denmark **42** 55.58N 11.22E
Sjenica Yugo. **34** 43.16N 20.00E
Sjeništa *mtn.* Bosnia-Herzegovina **31** 43.42N 18.37E
Sjöbo Sweden **43** 55.38N 13.42E
Sjötorp Sweden **43** 58.50N 13.59E
Skaelskör Denmark **42** 55.15N 11.19E
Skaerbaek Denmark **42** 55.09N 8.46E
Skagafjördhur *est.* Iceland **40** 65.55N 19.35W
Skagen Denmark **42** 57.44N 10.36E
Skagern *l.* Sweden **43** 58.59N 14.17E
Skagerrak *str.* Norway / Denmark **42** 58.00N 9.30E
Skagway U.S.A. **100** 59.23N135.20W
Skaill U.K. **14** 58.56N 2.43W
Skala Greece **35** 36.51N 22.40E
Skála Oropoú Greece **35** 38.20N 23.46E
Skala Podolskaya Ukraine **37** 48.51N 26.11E
Skalat Ukraine **37** 49.20N 25.59E
Skalderviken *b.* Sweden **43** 56.18N 12.38E
Skanderborg Denmark **42** 56.02N 9.56E
Skåne *f.* Sweden **43** 55.59N 13.30E
Skaneateles U.S.A. **115** 42.57N 76.26W
Skånevik Norway **42** 59.44N 5.59E
Skanör Sweden **43** 55.25N 12.52E
Skara Sweden **43** 58.22N 13.25E
Skaraborg *d.* Sweden **43** 58.20N 13.30E
Skärhamn Sweden **42** 58.00N 11.33E
Skarnes Norway **42** 60.15N 11.41E
Skarżysko-Kamienna Poland **37** 51.08N 20.53E
Skead Canada **104** 46.40N 80.45W
Skeena *r.* Canada **100** 54.09N130.02W
Skeena Mts. Canada **100** 57.00N128.30W
Skegness U.K. **12** 53.09N 0.20E
Skeleton L. Canada **104** 45.15N 79.27W
Skellefte *r.* Sweden **40** 64.42N 21.06E
Skellefteå Sweden **40** 64.46N 20.57E
Skelleftehamn Sweden **40** 64.41N 21.14E
Skelmersdale U.K. **12** 53.34N 2.49W
Skene Sweden **43** 57.29N 12.38E
Skerries Rep. of Ire. **15** 53.35N 6.07W
Skhíza *i.* Greece **35** 36.43N 21.46E
Ski Norway **42** 59.43N 10.50E
Skíathos Greece **35** 39.10N 23.29E
Skíathos *i.* Greece **35** 39.12N 23.30E
Skiddaw *mtn.* U.K. **12** 54.40N 3.09W
Skidel Belorussia **37** 53.37N 24.19E
Skien Norway **42** 59.12N 9.36E
Skierniewice Poland **37** 51.58N 20.08E
Skikda Algeria **75** 36.53N 6.54E
Skillingaryd Sweden **43** 57.26N 14.05E
Skinners Eddy U.S.A. **115** 41.37N 76.08W
Skinnskatteberg Sweden **43** 59.50N 15.41E
Skipness U.K. **14** 56.45N 5.22W
Skipton U.K. **12** 53.57N 2.01W
Skíros Greece **35** 38.55N 24.34E
Skíros *i.* Greece **35** 38.53N 24.32E
Skive Denmark **42** 56.34N 9.02E
Skjálfanda Fljót *r.* Iceland **40** 65.55N 17.30W
Skjálfandi *est.* Iceland **40** 66.08N 17.38W
Skjern Denmark **42** 55.57N 8.30E
Skjönsta Norway **40** 67.12N 15.45E
Škofja Loka Slovenia **31** 46.10N 14.18E
Skoghall Sweden **43** 59.19N 13.26E
Skole Ukraine **37** 49.00N 23.30E
Skópelos Greece **35** 39.09N 26.47E
Skópelos Greece **35** 39.07N 23.43E
Skópelos *i.* Greece **35** 39.10N 23.40E
Skopje Macedonia **34** 42.01N 21.32E
Skörping Denmark **42** 56.50N 9.53E
Skotfoss Norway **42** 59.12N 9.30E
Skotterud Norway **43** 59.59N 12.07E
Skövde Sweden **43** 58.24N 13.50E
Skovorodino Russian Fed. **51** 54.00N123.53E
Skradin Croatia **31** 43.49N 15.56E
Skreia Norway **41** 60.39N 10.56E
Skruv Sweden **43** 56.41N 15.22E
Skudeneshavn Norway **42** 59.09N 5.17E
Skull Rep. of Ire. **15** 51.32N 9.33W
Skultorp Sweden **43** 58.21N 13.49E
Skultuna Sweden **43** 59.43N 16.25E
Skuodas Lithuania **41** 56.16N 21.32E
Skurup Sweden **43** 55.28N 13.30E
Skutskär Sweden **41** 60.38N 17.25E
Skvira Ukraine **37** 49.42N 29.40E
Skye *i.* U.K. **14** 57.20N 6.15W
Slagelse Denmark **42** 55.24N 11.22E
Slalowa Wola Poland **37** 50.40N 22.05E
Slamet *mtn.* Indonesia **59** 7.14S109.10E
Slaney *r.* Rep. of Ire. **15** 52.21N 6.30W
Slano Croatia **31** 42.47N 17.54E
Slantsy Russian Fed. **44** 59.09N 28.09E
Slaný Czech Republic **38** 50.11N 14.04E
Slatina Romania **29** 44.26N 24.23E
Slatina Yugo. **34** 43.04N 20.58E

Slaton to **South West Peru Ridge**

Slaton U.S.A. **111** 33.26N101.39W
Slave *r.* Canada **100** 61.18N113.39W
Slavgorod Belorussia **37** 53.25N 31.00E
Slavgorod Russian Fed. **9** 53.01N 78.37E
Slavonski Požega Croatia **31** 45.20N 17.41E
Slavuta Ukraine **37** 50.20N 26.58E
Slavyansk Ukraine **45** 48.51N 37.36E
Sławno Poland **36** 54.22N 16.40E
Sleaford U.K. **12** 53.00N 0.22W
Sleaford B. Australia **92** 35.00S136.50E
Sleat, Sd. of *str.* U.K. **14** 57.05N 5.48W
Sledge U.S.A. **111** 34.26N 90.13W
Sledmere U.K. **12** 54.04N 0.35W
Sleeper Is. Canada **102** 56.50N 80.30W
Sleetmute U.S.A. **98** 61.40N157.11W
Slide Mtn. U.S.A. **115** 42.00N 74.23W
Sliedrecht Neth. **16** 51.48N 4.46E
Slieve Aughty Mts. Rep. of Ire. **15** 53.05N 8.31W
Slieve Bloom Mts. Rep. of Ire. **15** 53.03N 7.35W
Slieve Callan *mtn.* Rep. of Ire. **15** 52.51N 9.18W
Slieve Donard *mtn.* U.K. **15** 54.11N 5.56W
Slieve Gamph *mts.* Rep. of Ire. **15** 54.06N 8.52W
Slievekimalta *mtn.* Rep. of Ire. **15** 52.45N 8.17W
Slieve Mish *mts.* Rep. of Ire. **15** 52.48N 9.48W
Slieve Miskish *mts.* Rep. of Ire. **15** 51.41N 9.56W
Slievenamon *mtn.* Rep. of Ire. **15** 52.25N 7.34W
Slieve Snaght *mtn.* Donegal Rep. of Ire. **15** 55.12N 7.20W
Sligo Rep. of Ire. **15** 54.17N 8.28W
Sligo *d.* Rep. of Ire. **15** 54.10N 8.35W
Sligo U.S.A. **114** 41.07N 79.29W
Sligo B. Rep. of Ire. **15** 54.18N 8.40W
Slippery Rock *town* U.S.A. **114** 41.04N 80.03W
Slite Sweden **43** 57.43N 18.48E
Sliven Bulgaria **34** 42.42N 26.19E
Slivnitsa Bulgaria **34** 42.50N 23.00E
Sloan U.S.A. **110** 42.14N 96.14W
Slobodka Ukraine **37** 47.56N 29.18E
Slobodskoy Russian Fed. **44** 58.42N 50.10E
Slobozia Romania **34** 43.52N 25.55E
Slonim Belorussia **37** 53.05N 25.21E
Slough U.K. **13** 51.30N 0.35W
Slovakia Europe **37** 48.25N 19.20E
Slovechna *r.* Belorussia **37** 51.41N 29.41E
Slovechno Ukraine **37** 51.23N 28.20E
Slovenia Europe **31** 46.00N 15.00E
Slovenjgradec Slovenia **31** 46.31N 15.05E
Slovenska Bistrica Slovenia **31** 46.23N 15.34E
Słubice Poland **36** 52.20N 14.32E
Sluch *r.* Belorussia **37** 52.08N 27.31E
Sluis Neth. **16** 51.18N 3.23E
Slunj Croatia **31** 45.07N 15.35E
Słupsk Poland **37** 54.28N 17.01E
Slurry R.S.A. **80** 25.48S 25.49E
Slutsk Belorussia **37** 53.02N 27.31E
Slyne Head Rep. of Ire. **15** 53.25N 10.12W
Slyudyanka Russian Fed. **52** 51.40N103.40E
Småland *f.* Sweden **43** 57.20N 15.00E
Smålandsfarvandet *str.* Denmark **42** 55.05N 11.20E
Smålandsstenar Sweden **43** 57.10N 13.24E
Smallwood Resr. Canada **103** 54.00N 64.00W
Smeaton Canada **101** 53.30N104.49W
Smederevo Yugo. **29** 44.40N 20.56E
Smela Ukraine **45** 49.15N 31.54E
Smethport U.S.A. **114** 41.49N 78.27W
Smilde Neth. **16** 52.58N 6.28E
Smilovichi Belorussia **37** 53.45N 28.00E
Smith Canada **100** 55.10N114.00W
Smith Arm *b.* Canada **98** 66.15N124.00W
Smithers Canada **100** 54.45N127.10W
Smithfield R.S.A. **80** 30.11S 26.31E
Smiths Falls *town* Canada **105** 44.54N 76.01W
Smithton Australia **91** 40.52S145.07E
Smithtown Australia **93** 31.03S152.53E
Smithville U.S.A. **114** 39.04N 81.06W
Smoke Hole U.S.A. **114** 38.52N 79.18W
Smoky *r.* Canada **100** 56.10N117.21W
Smoky Bay *town* Australia **92** 32.22S133.56E
Smoky C. Australia **93** 30.55S153.05E
Smoky Hill *r.* U.S.A. **110** 39.03N 96.48W
Smöla *i.* Norway **40** 63.20N 8.00E
Smolensk Russian Fed. **44** 54.49N 32.04E
Smolevichi Belorussia **37** 54.00N 28.01E
Smólikas *mtn.* Greece **34** 40.06N 20.52E
Smolyan Bulgaria **34** 41.36N 24.38E
Smorgon Belorussia **37** 54.28N 26.20E
Smygehuk *c.* Sweden **43** 55.21N 13.23E
Smyrna U.S.A. **115** 39.18N 75.36W
Snaefell *mtn.* I.o.M. Europe **12** 54.16N 4.28W
Snaefell *mtn.* Iceland **40** 64.48N 15.34W
Snake *r.* Idaho U.S.A. **106** 43.50N117.05W
Snake *r.* Wash. U.S.A. **108** 46.12N119.02W
Snake Range *mts.* U.S.A. **108** 39.00N114.15W
Snake River *town* U.S.A. **108** 44.10N110.40W
Snake River Plain *f.* U.S.A. **108** 43.00N113.00W
Snåsa Norway **40** 64.15N 12.23E
Snåsavatn *l.* Norway **40** 64.05N 12.00E
Snedsted Denmark **42** 56.54N 8.32E
Sneek Neth. **16** 53.03N 5.40E
Sneem Rep. of Ire. **15** 51.50N 9.54W
Sneeuwberg *mtn.* R.S.A. **80** 32.30S 19.09E
Snežnik *mtn.* Slovenia **31** 45.35N 14.27E
Śniardwy, Jezioro *l.* Poland **37** 53.46N 21.44E
Snina Slovakia **37** 48.59N 22.07E
Snizort, Loch U.K. **14** 57.35N 6.30W
Snöhetta *mtn.* Norway **41** 62.20N 9.17E
Snov *r.* Ukraine **37** 51.45N 31.45E
Snowbird L. Canada **101** 60.45N103.00W
Snowdon *mtn.* U.K. **12** 53.05N 4.05W
Snowdrift Canada **101** 62.24N110.44W
Snowdrift *r.* Canada **101** 62.24N110.44W
Snowflake U.S.A. **109** 34.30N110.05W
Snow Hill *town* U.S.A. **113** 38.11N 75.23W
Snowtown Australia **92** 33.47S138.13E
Snowy *r.* Australia **93** 37.48S148.30E
Snowy Mts. Australia **93** 36.30S148.20E
Snyatyn Ukraine **37** 48.30N 25.50E
Snyder U.S.A. **111** 32.44N100.05W
Soacha Colombia **122** 4.35N 74.13W
Soalala Madagascar **81** 16.06S 45.20E
Soanierana-Ivongo Madagascar **81** 16.55S 49.35E
Soasiu Indonesia **59** 0.40N127.25E
Soavinandriana Madagascar **81** 19.09S 46.45E
Sob *r.* Ukraine **37** 48.42N 29.17E
Sobat *r.* Sudan **73** 9.30N 31.30E
Sobernheim Germany **39** 49.47N 7.38E
Soboko C.A.R. **73** 6.49N 24.50E
Sobradinho, Represa de *resr.* Brazil **123** 10.00S 42.30W
Sobrado Portugal **26** 41.02N 8.16W
Sobral Brazil **123** 3.45S 40.20W
Sochi Russian Fed. **45** 43.35N 39.46E
Société, Îles de la *is.* Pacific Oc. **85** 17.00S150.00W
Society Is. *see* Société, Îles de la *is.* Pacific Oc. **85**
Socorro Colombia **122** 6.30N 73.16W
Socorro U.S.A. **109** 34.04N106.54W
Socorro, Isla *i.* Mexico **116** 18.45N110.58W
Socotra *i. see* Suquṭrá *i.* Yemen **71**
Socuéllamos Spain **27** 39.17N 2.48W
Sodankylä Finland **40** 67.29N 26.32E
Söderhamn Sweden **41** 61.18N 17.03E
Söderköping Sweden **43** 58.29N 16.18E
Södermanland *d.* Sweden **43** 59.12N 16.49E
Södermanland *f.* Sweden **43** 58.56N 16.50E
Södertälje Sweden **43** 59.12N 17.37E
Sodium R.S.A. **80** 30.10S 23.08E
Sodo Ethiopia **73** 6.52N 37.47E
Södra Vi Sweden **43** 57.45N 15.48E
Sodražica Slovenia **31** 45.46N 14.38E
Sodus U.S.A. **114** 43.14N 77.04W
Sodus Point *town* U.S.A. **114** 43.16N 76.59W
Soest Germany **38** 51.34N 8.07E
Sofádhes Greece **35** 39.20N 22.06E
Sofala Australia **93** 33.05S149.42E
Sofala *d.* Mozambique **81** 19.00S 34.39E
Sofia *see* Sofiya Bulgaria **34**
Sofia *r.* Madagascar **81** 15.27S 47.23E
Sofikon Greece **35** 37.47N 23.03E
Sofiya Bulgaria **34** 42.41N 23.19E
Sofiya *d.* Bulgaria **34** 42.02N 23.05E
Sofiysk Russian Fed. **51** 52.19N133.55E
Sofporog Russian Fed. **44** 65.47N 31.30E
Sogamoso Colombia **122** 5.43N 72.56W
Sögel Germany **38** 52.50N 7.31E
Sögne Norway **42** 58.05N 7.49E
Sognefjorden *est.* Norway **41** 61.06N 5.10E
Sogn og Fjordane *d.* Norway **41** 61.30N 6.50E
Sögüt Turkey **64** 40.02N 30.10E
Sog Xian China **63** 31.51N 93.40E
Sohāgpur India **63** 22.42N 78.12E
Soignies Belgium **16** 50.35N 4.04E
Soissons France **19** 49.22N 3.20E
Sojat India **62** 25.55N 73.40E
Sokal Ukraine **37** 50.30N 24.10E
Söke Turkey **35** 37.45N 27.24E
Sokhós Greece **34** 40.48N 23.22E
Sokna Norway **42** 60.14N 9.54E
Soko Banja Yugo. **34** 43.40N 21.51E
Sokodé Togo **77** 8.59N 1.11E
Sokol Russian Fed. **44** 59.28N 40.04E
Sokółka Poland **37** 53.25N 23.31E
Sokolo Mali **76** 14.53N 6.11W
Sokolov Czech Republic **39** 50.09N 12.40E
Sokoto Nigeria **77** 13.02N 5.15E
Sokoto *d.* Nigeria **77** 11.50N 5.05E
Sokoto *r.* Nigeria **77** 13.05N 5.13E
Sola Norway **42** 58.53N 5.36E
Solbad Hall Austria **39** 47.17N 11.31E
Solec Kujawski Poland **37** 53.06N 18.14E
Soledad Venezuela **122** 8.10N 63.34W
Solesmes France **19** 50.11N 3.30E
Solginskiy Russian Fed. **44** 61.07N 41.30E
Solheim Norway **41** 60.53N 5.27E
Soligalich Russian Fed. **44** 59.02N 42.15E
Solihull U.K. **11** 52.26N 1.47W
Solikamsk Russian Fed. **44** 59.40N 56.45E
Sol-Iletsk Russian Fed. **44** 51.09N 55.00E
Soliman Tunisia **32** 36.42N 10.30E
Solingen Germany **38** 51.10N 7.05E
Sollefteå Sweden **40** 63.12N 17.20E
Sollentuna Sweden **43** 59.28N 17.54E
Sóller Spain **25** 39.46N 2.42E
Sollia Norway **41** 61.47N 10.24E
Solling *mts.* Germany **38** 51.45N 9.35E
Solna Sweden **43** 59.22N 18.01E
Solola Somali Rep. **73** 0.08N 41.30E
Solomon Is. Pacific Oc. **84** 8.00S160.00E
Solomons U.S.A. **115** 38.21N 76.29W
Solomon Sea Pacific Oc. **87** 7.00S150.00E
Solomon's Pool *see* Birak Sulaymān *site* Jordan **67**
Solon U.S.A. **112** 44.57N 69.52W
Solon Springs U.S.A. **110** 46.22N 91.48W
Solopaca Italy **33** 41.11N 14.33E
Solothurn Switz. **39** 47.13N 7.32E
Solothurn *d.* Switz. **39** 47.20N 7.45E
Solovetskiye, Ostrova *is.* Russian Fed. **44** 65.05N 35.30E
Solsona Spain **25** 41.59N 1.31E
Solt Hungary **31** 46.48N 19.00E
Šolta *i.* Croatia **31** 43.23N 16.15E
Solṭānābād Iran **65** 36.25N 58.02E
Soltau Germany **38** 52.59N 9.49E
Sölvesborg Sweden **43** 56.03N 14.33E
Solway Firth *est.* U.K. **12** 54.50N 3.30W
Solwezi Zambia **78** 12.11S 26.23E
Solzach *r.* Austria **36** 48.35N 13.30E
Soma Turkey **29** 39.11N 27.36E
Somabhula Zimbabwe **80** 19.40S 29.38E
Somali Basin *f.* Indian Oc. **49** 0.00 55.00E
Somali Republic Africa **71** 5.30N 47.00E
Sombor Yugo. **31** 45.46N 19.07E
Sombrerete Mexico **116** 23.38N103.39W
Somerset *d.* U.K. **13** 51.09N 3.00W
Somerset Ky. U.S.A. **113** 37.05N 84.38W
Somerset Ohio U.S.A. **114** 39.48N 82.18W
Somerset Penn. U.S.A. **114** 40.01N 79.05W
Somerset East R.S.A. **80** 32.43S 25.33E
Somerset I. Bermuda **127** 32.18N 64.53W
Somerset I. Canada **99** 73.00N 93.30W
Somerset Resr. U.S.A. **115** 43.00N 72.56W
Somers Point *town* U.S.A. **115** 39.20N 74.36W
Somersworth U.S.A. **115** 43.16N 70.52W
Somerville Mass. U.S.A. **115** 42.23N 71.06W
Somerville N.J. U.S.A. **115** 40.34N 74.37W
Somes *r.* Hungary **37** 48.40N 22.30E
Somme *d.* France **19** 49.55N 2.30E
Somme *r.* France **19** 50.11N 1.39E
Sommen *l.* Sweden **43** 58.01N 15.15E
Sömmerda Germany **38** 51.10N 11.07E
Somogy *d.* Hungary **31** 46.30N 17.40E
Somosierra, Puerto de *pass* Spain **26** 41.09N 3.35W
Sompeta India **63** 18.56N 84.36E
Somport, Puerto de *pass* Spain **25** 42.48N 0.31W
Sompuis France **19** 48.41N 4.23E
Son *r.* India **63** 25.42N 84.52E
Sonāmarg Jammu & Kashmir **62** 34.18N 75.18E
Sonāmura India **63** 23.29N 91.17E
Sonbong N. Korea **53** 42.19N130.24E
Sönderborg Denmark **42** 54.55N 9.47E
Sönder Omme Denmark **42** 55.50N 8.54E
Sondershausen Germany **38** 51.22N 10.52E
Söndreströmfjord Greenland **99** 66.30N 50.52W
Sondrio Italy **30** 46.10N 9.52E
Sonepur India **63** 20.50N 83.55E
Songa *r.* Norway **42** 59.47N 7.41E
Song-Cau Vietnam **56** 13.27N109.13E
Songe Norway **42** 58.41N 9.00E
Songea Tanzania **79** 10.42S 35.39E
Songhua Jiang *r.* China **53** 47.46N132.30E
Songjiang China **55** 31.01N121.20E
Songkhla Thailand **56** 7.12N100.35E
Songololo Zaïre **78** 5.40S 14.05E
Songpan China **54** 32.36N103.36E
Songtao Miaozu Zizhixian China **55** 28.12N109.12E
Song Xian China **54** 34.02N111.48E
Sonid Youqi China **54** 42.44N112.40E
Sonid Zuoqi China **54** 43.58N113.59E
Sonīpat India **62** 28.59N 77.01E
Son La Vietnam **56** 21.20N103.55E
Sonmiāni Pakistan **62** 25.26N 66.36E
Sonmiāni B. Pakistan **62** 25.15N 66.30E
Sonneberg Germany **39** 50.22N 11.10E
Sonoita Mexico **109** 31.51N112.50W
Sonora *d.* Mexico **109** 29.30N110.40W
Sonora *r.* Mexico **109** 28.50N111.33W
Sonora U.S.A. **111** 30.34N100.39W
Sonseca Spain **27** 39.42N 3.57W
Sonsorol *i.* Pacific Oc. **59** 5.20N132.13E
Son Tay Vietnam **55** 21.15N105.17E
Sonthofen Germany **38** 47.31N 10.17E
Sopi Indonesia **59** 2.40N128.28E
Sopo *r.* Sudan **73** 8.51N 26.11E
Sopot Poland **37** 54.28N 18.34E
Sopotskin Belorussia **37** 53.49N 23.42E
Soppero Sweden **40** 68.07N 21.40E
Sopron Hungary **36** 47.41N 16.36E
Sop's Arm *town* Canada **103** 49.46N 56.56W
Sopur Jammu & Kashmir **62** 34.18N 74.28E
Sor, Ribeira de *r.* Portugal **27** 39.00N 8.17W
Sora Italy **31** 41.43N 13.37E
Sorada India **63** 19.45N 84.26E
Sorbas Spain **27** 37.06N 2.07W
Sore France **20** 44.20N 0.35W
Sorel Canada **105** 46.02N 73.07W
Soreq *r.* Israel **67** 31.56N 34.42E
Sörfjorden Norway **40** 66.29N 13.20E
Sörfold Norway **40** 67.30N 15.30E
Sorgono Italy **32** 40.01N 9.06E
Sorgues France **21** 44.00N 4.52E
Soria Spain **26** 41.46N 2.28W
Soria *d.* Spain **26** 41.40N 2.45W
Soriano Uruguay **125** 33.24S 58.19W
Sor Kvalöy *i.* Norway **40** 69.40N 18.30E
Sörli Norway **40** 64.15N 13.50E
Sor Mertvyy Kultuk *f.* Kazakhstan **45** 45.30N 54.00E
Sorö Denmark **42** 55.26N 11.34E
Soro India **63** 21.17N 86.40E
Sorocaba Brazil **126** 23.29S 47.27W
Sorochinsk Russian Fed. **44** 52.29N 53.15E
Soroki Moldavia **37** 48.08N 28.12E
Sorol *i.* Federated States of Micronesia **59** 8.09N140.25E
Soron India **63** 27.53N 78.45E
Sorong Indonesia **59** 0.50S131.17E
Soroti Uganda **79** 1.40N 33.37E
Söröya *i.* Norway **40** 70.35N 22.30E
Sorraia *r.* Portugal **24** 39.00N 8.51W
Sorrento Italy **33** 40.37N 14.22E
Sör-Rondane *mts.* Antarctica **128** 72.30S 22.00E
Sorsele Sweden **40** 65.30N 17.30E
Sort Spain **25** 42.24N 1.08E
Sortavala Russian Fed. **44** 61.40N 30.40E
Sortland Norway **40** 68.44N 15.25E
Sör Tröndelag *d.* Norway **40** 63.00N 10.20E
Sorūbī Afghan. **62** 34.36N 69.43E
Sos del Rey Católico Spain **25** 42.30N 1.13W
Sosnogorsk Russian Fed. **44** 63.32N 53.55E
Sosnovo Russian Fed. **44** 60.33N 30.11E
Sosnovyy Russian Fed. **44** 66.01N 32.40E
Sosnowiec Poland **37** 50.18N 19.08E
Šoštanj Slovenia **31** 46.23N 15.03E
Sosva Russian Fed. **44** 59.10N 61.50E
Sosyka Russian Fed. **45** 46.11N 38.49E
Sotik Kenya **79** 0.40S 35.08E
Sotonera, Embalse de la *resr.* Spain **25** 42.05N 0.48W
Sotra *i.* Norway **42** 60.18N 5.05E
Sotteville France **18** 49.25N 1.06E
Soubré Ivory Coast **76** 5.50N 6.35W
Souderton U.S.A. **115** 40.19N 75.19W
Souflay Congo **78** 2.00N 14.54E
Souflíon Greece **34** 41.12N 26.18E
Souillac France **20** 44.54N 1.29E
Souilly France **19** 49.01N 5.17E
Souk Ahras Algeria **75** 36.17N 7.57E
Souk-el-Arba-du-Rharb Morocco **74** 34.43N 6.01W
Sŏul S. Korea **53** 37.30N127.00E
Soulac-sur-Mer France **20** 45.31N 1.07W
Soúnion, Ákra *c.* Greece **35** 37.37N 24.01E
Sources, Mont-aux- *mtn.* Lesotho **80** 28.44S 28.52E
Soure Portugal **27** 40.03N 8.38W
Souris Man. Canada **101** 49.38N100.15W
Souris P.E.I. Canada **103** 46.21N 62.15W
Souris *r.* Canada **101** 49.39N 99.34W
Soúrpi Greece **35** 39.06N 22.54E
Sous, Oued *wadi* Morocco **74** 30.27N 9.31W
Sousa Brazil **123** 6.41S 38.14W
Sousel Portugal **27** 38.57N 7.40W
Sous le Vent, Îles *is.* Îs. de la Société **85** 16.30S151.30W
Sousse Tunisia **75** 35.48N 10.38E
Soustons France **20** 43.45N 1.19W
South Alligator *r.* Australia **90** 12.53S132.29E
South America 120
Southampton Canada **104** 44.29N 81.23W
Southampton U.K. **13** 50.54N 1.23W
Southampton U.S.A. **115** 40.53N 72.24W
Southampton I. Canada **99** 64.30N 84.00W
South Atlantic Ocean 121
South Aulatsivik I. Canada **103** 56.45N 61.30W
South Australia *d.* Australia **92** 30.00S137.00E
South Australian Basin *f.* Indian Oc. **49** 40.00S130.00E
South Baymouth Canada **104** 45.33N 82.01W
South Bend Ind. U.S.A. **112** 41.40N 86.15W
South Bend Wash. U.S.A. **108** 46.40N123.48W
South Boston U.S.A. **113** 36.42N 78.58W
South Branch U.S.A. **104** 44.27N 83.53W
Southbridge U.S.A. **115** 42.05N 72.02W
South Carolina *d.* U.S.A. **113** 34.00N 81.00W
South Cerney U.K. **13** 51.40N 1.55W
South Charleston U.S.A. **114** 38.22N 81.44W
South China Sea Asia **58** 12.30N115.00E
South Dakota *d.* U.S.A. **110** 45.00N100.00W
South Dorset Downs *hills* U.K. **13** 50.40N 2.25W
South Downs *hills* U.K. **13** 50.04N 0.34W
South East *d.* Botswana **80** 25.00S 25.45E
South East C. Australia **91** 43.38S146.48E
South Eastern Atlantic Basin *f.* Atlantic Oc. **127** 20.00S 0.00
South East Head *c.* Ascension **127** 7.58S 14.18W
South East Indian Basin *f.* Indian Oc. **49** 35.00S105.00E
South-East Indian Ridge *f.* Indian Oc. **49** 32.00S 96.00E
South East Is. Australia **89** 34.23S123.30E
South East Pt. Kiribati **85** 1.40N157.10W
Southend-on-Sea U.K. **13** 51.32N 0.43E
Southern *d.* Zambia **80** 16.30S 26.40E
Southern Alps *mts.* New Zealand **86** 43.20S170.45E
Southern Cross Australia **89** 31.14S119.16E
Southern Indian L. Canada **101** 57.10N 98.40W
Southern Lueti *r.* Zambia **80** 16.15S 23.12E
Southern Ocean Pacific Oc. **84** 44.00S130.00E
Southern Pines U.S.A. **113** 35.12N 79.23W
Southern Uplands *hills* U.K. **14** 55.30N 3.30W
South Esk *r.* U.K. **14** 56.43N 2.32W
South Esk Tablelands *f.* Australia **88** 20.50S126.40E
Southey Canada **101** 50.56N104.30W
South Fiji Basin Pacific Oc. **84** 27.00S176.00E
South Georgia *i.* Atlantic Oc. **121** 54.00S 37.00W
South Glamorgan *d.* U.K. **13** 51.27N 3.22W
South-haa U.K. **14** 60.34N 1.17W
South Hātia I. Bangla. **63** 22.19N 91.07E
South Haven U.S.A. **112** 42.25N 86.16W
South Henik L. Canada **101** 61.30N 97.30W
South Honshu Ridge Pacific Oc. **84** 22.00N141.00E
South Horr Kenya **79** 2.10N 36.45E
South I. Kenya **79** 2.36N 36.38E
South I. New Zealand **86** 43.00S171.00E
South Knife *r.* Canada **101** 58.55N 94.37W
South Korea Asia **53** 36.00N128.00E
South Lake Tahoe *town* U.S.A. **108** 38.57N119.57W
Southland *d.* New Zealand **86** 45.40S168.00E
South Loup *r.* U.S.A. **110** 41.04N 98.40W
South Lyon U.S.A. **104** 42.28N 83.39W
South Molton U.K. **13** 51.01N 3.50W
South Nahanni *r.* Canada **100** 61.03N123.21W
South Nation *r.* Canada **105** 45.35N 75.06W
South Orkney Is. Atlantic Oc. **121** 60.50S 45.00W
South Platte *r.* U.S.A. **110** 41.07N100.42W
Southport Qld. Australia **93** 27.58S153.20E
Southport Tas. Australia **91** 43.25S146.59E
Southport U.K. **12** 53.38N 3.01W
Southport U.S.A. **113** 33.55N 78.00W
South River *town* Canada **104** 45.45N 79.25W
South River *town* U.S.A. **115** 40.27N 74.23W
South Ronaldsay *i.* U.K. **14** 58.47N 2.56W
South Sandwich Is. Atlantic Oc. **121** 58.00S 27.00W
South Sandwich Trench *f.* Atlantic Oc. **121** 57.00S 25.00W
South Saskatchewan *r.* Canada **101** 53.15N105.05W
South Seal *r.* Canada **101** 58.48N 98.08W
South Shields U.K. **12** 55.00N 1.24W
South Sioux City U.S.A. **110** 42.28N 96.24W
South Tasmania Ridge *f.* Pac. Oc./Ind. Oc. **84** 46.00S147.00E
South Thompson *r.* Canada **100** 50.40N120.20W
South Tucson U.S.A. **109** 32.12N110.58W
South Twin I. Canada **102** 53.00N 79.50W
South Tyne *r.* U.K. **14** 54.59N 2.08W
South Uist *i.* U.K. **14** 57.15N 7.20W
South Wabasca L. Canada **100** 55.54N113.45W
South West Australian Ridge *f.* Indian Oc. **49** 38.00S112.00E
Southwest C. New Zealand **86** 47.15S167.30E
South Western Pacific Basin Pacific Oc. **85** 39.00S148.00W
South-West Indian Ridge *f.* Indian Oc. **49** 33.00S 56.00E
South West Peru Ridge Pacific Oc. **85** 20.00S 82.00W

South West Pt. to Stuttgart

South West Pt. *c.* Kiribati **85** 1.52N157.33W
South West Pt. *c.* St. Helena **127** 16.00S 5.48W
South Windham U.S.A. **112** 43.44N 70.26W
Southwold U.K. **13** 52.19N 1.41E
South Yorkshire *d.* U.K. **12** 53.28N 1.25W
Soutpansberg *mts.* R.S.A. **80** 22.58S 29.50E
Souvigny France **20** 46.32N 3.11E
Soverato Italy **33** 38.41N 16.33E
Sovetsk Lithuania **41** 55.05N 21.53E
Sovetsk Russian Fed. **44** 57.39N 48.59E
Sovetskaya Gavan Russian Fed. **51** 48.57N140.16E
Soweto R.S.A. **80** 26.16S 27.51E
Soyo Angola **78** 6.12S 12.25E
Soyopa Mexico **109** 28.47N109.39W
Sozh *r.* Belorussia **37** 51.57N 30.48E
Spa Belgium **16** 50.29N 5.52E
Spain Europe **24** 40.00N 4.00W
Spalding Australia **92** 33.29S138.40E
Spalding U.K. **12** 52.47N 0.09W
Spalding U.S.A. **110** 41.41N 98.22W
Spandau Germany **38** 52.32N 13.12E
Spanish Canada **104** 46.12N 82.21W
Spanish *r.* Canada **104** 46.21N 81.52W
Spanish Fork U.S.A. **108** 40.07N111.39W
Sparks U.S.A. **108** 39.32N119.45W
Sparreholm Sweden **43** 59.04N 16.49E
Sparrows Point *town* U.S.A. **115** 39.13N 76.29W
Sparta Ga. U.S.A. **113** 33.17N 82.58W
Sparta N.J. U.S.A. **115** 41.02N 74.38W
Sparta Wisc. U.S.A. **110** 43.57N 90.47W
Spartanburg U.S.A. **113** 34.56N 81.57W
Spárti Greece **35** 37.05N 22.27E
Spartivento, Capo *c.* Calabria Italy **33** 37.56N 16.04E
Spartivento, Capo *c.* Sardegna Italy **32** 38.53N 8.50E
Spátha, Ákra *c.* Greece **35** 35.42N 23.44E
Spatsizi Plateau Wilderness Prov. Park Canada **100** 57.13N127.53W
Spearman U.S.A. **111** 36.12N101.12W
Speculator U.S.A. **115** 43.30N 74.23W
Speke G. Tanzania **79** 2.20S 33.30E
Spello Italy **30** 43.00N 12.40E
Spence Canada **104** 45.34N 79.40W
Spence Bay *town* Canada **99** 69.30N 93.20W
Spencer Idaho U.S.A. **108** 44.21N112.11W
Spencer Iowa U.S.A. **110** 43.09N 95.09W
Spencer Mass. U.S.A. **115** 42.15N 71.59W
Spencer S.Dak. U.S.A. **110** 43.44N 97.36W
Spencer W.Va. U.S.A. **114** 38.48N 81.21W
Spencer, C. Australia **92** 35.18S136.53E
Spencer G. Australia **92** 34.00S137.00E
Spencerville Canada **105** 44.51N 75.33W
Spences Bridge *town* Canada **100** 50.25N121.20W
Sperkhiós *r.* Greece **35** 38.57N 22.03E
Sperrin Mts. U.K. **15** 54.49N 7.06W
Sperryville U.S.A. **114** 38.39N 78.14W
Spétsai *i.* Greece **35** 37.16N 23.09E
Spey *r.* U.K. **14** 57.40N 3.06W
Speyer Germany **39** 49.19N 8.26E
Spezzano Albanese Italy **33** 39.40N 16.19E
Spiekeroog *i.* Germany **38** 53.46N 7.42E
Spiez Switz. **39** 46.41N 7.39E
Spilimbergo Italy **30** 46.07N 12.54E
Spilsby U.K. **12** 53.10N 0.06E
Spina *ruins* Italy **30** 44.42N 12.08E
Spinazzola Italy **33** 40.58N 16.06E
Spīn Būldak Afghan. **62** 31.01N 66.24E
Spincourt France **19** 49.20N 5.40E
Spirit River *town* Canada **100** 55.45N118.50W
Spišská Nová Ves Slovakia **37** 48.57N 20.34E
Spithead *str.* U.K. **13** 50.45N 1.05W
Spitsbergen *is.* Europe **48** 78.00N 17.00E
Spittal an der Drau Austria **39** 46.48N 13.30E
Split Croatia **31** 43.31N 16.27E
Split L. Canada **101** 56.08N 96.15W
Splügen Switz. **39** 46.33N 9.20E
Spofford U.S.A. **111** 29.11N100.25W
Spokane U.S.A. **108** 47.40N117.23W
Spokane *r.* U.S.A. **108** 47.44N118.20W
Spoleto Italy **30** 42.44N 12.44E
Spooner U.S.A. **110** 45.50N 91.53W
Spragge Canada **104** 46.13N 82.40W
Spratly *i.* S. China Sea **58** 8.45N111.54E
Spray U.S.A. **108** 44.50N119.48W
Spreča *r.* Bosnia-Herzegovina **31** 44.45N 18.06E
Spree *r.* Germany **36** 52.32N 13.15E
Spremberg Germany **38** 51.34N 14.22E
Springbok R.S.A. **80** 29.40S 17.50E
Springdale Canada **103** 49.30N 56.04W
Springe Germany **38** 52.12N 9.32E
Springer U.S.A. **108** 36.22N104.36W
Springerville U.S.A. **109** 34.08N109.17W
Springfield New Zealand **86** 43.20S171.56E
Springfield Colo. U.S.A. **111** 37.24N102.37W
Springfield Ill. U.S.A. **110** 39.49N 89.39W
Springfield Mass. U.S.A. **115** 42.07N 72.36W
Springfield Miss. U.S.A. **107** 37.11N 93.19W
Springfield Mo. U.S.A. **111** 37.14N 93.17W
Springfield Ohio U.S.A. **112** 39.55N 83.48W
Springfield Oreg. U.S.A. **108** 44.03N123.01W
Springfield Tenn. U.S.A. **113** 36.30N 86.54W
Springfield Vt. U.S.A. **115** 43.18N 72.29W
Springfield W.Va. U.S.A. **114** 39.26N 78.48W
Springfontein R.S.A. **80** 30.15S 25.41E
Spring Grove U.S.A. **114** 39.52N 76.52W
Springhill Canada **103** 45.39N 64.03W
Springs *town* R.S.A. **80** 26.16S 28.27E
Springsure Australia **90** 24.07S148.05E
Springvale U.S.A. **115** 43.28N 70.48W
Spring Valley *town* U.S.A. **110** 43.41N 92.23W
Springville N.Y. U.S.A. **114** 42.31N 78.40W
Springville Utah U.S.A. **108** 40.10N111.37W
Spruce Knob *mtn.* U.S.A. **114** 38.42N 79.32W
Spruce Knob-Seneca Rocks Nat. Recreation Area U.S.A. **114** 38.50N 79.20W
Spry U.S.A. **108** 37.55N112.28W
Spulico, Capo *c.* Italy **33** 39.58N 16.39E
Spurn Head U.K. **12** 53.35N 0.08E
Spuzzum Canada **100** 49.37N121.23W
Squamish Canada **100** 49.45N123.10W
Squaw Rapids *town* Canada **101** 53.41N103.20W
Squillace Italy **33** 38.46N 16.31E
Squillace, Golfo di *g.* Italy **33** 38.50N 16.50E
Squinzano Italy **33** 40.26N 18.03E
Sragen Indonesia **59** 7.24S111.00E
Srbija *d.* Yugo. **31** 44.30N 19.30E
Srbobran Yugo. **31** 45.33N 19.48E
Sredna Gora *mts.* Bulgaria **34** 42.40N 25.00E
Srednekolymsk Russian Fed. **51** 67.27N153.35E
Sredne Russkaya Vozvyshennost *f.* Russian Fed. **44** 53.00N 37.00E
Sredne Sibirskoye Ploskogor'ye *f.* Russian Fed. **51** 66.00N108.00E
Sredni Rodopi *mts.* Bulgaria **34** 41.40N 24.45E
Srê Moat Cambodia **56** 13.15N107.10E
Sremska Mitrovica Yugo. **31** 44.59N 19.37E
Sremski Karlovci Yugo. **31** 45.12N 19.57E
Srêpôk *r.* Cambodia **56** 13.33N106.16E
Sretensk Russian Fed. **53** 52.15N117.52E
Sri Dūngargarh India **62** 28.05N 74.00E
Sri Gangānagar India **62** 29.55N 73.52E
Srīkākulam India **61** 18.18N 83.54E
Sri Lanka Asia **61** 7.30N 80.50E
Sri Mohangarh India **62** 27.17N 71.14E
Srīnagar Jammu & Kashmir **62** 34.05N 74.49E
Srīpur Bangla. **63** 24.12N 90.29E
Srirampur India **62** 19.30N 74.30E
Srnetica Bosnia-Herzegovina **31** 44.26N 16.40E
Staaten *r.* Australia **90** 16.24S141.17E
Stade Germany **38** 53.36N 9.28E
Stadskanaal Neth. **16** 53.02N 6.55E
Stadt Allendorf Germany **38** 50.50N 9.01E
Stadthagen Germany **38** 52.19N 9.13E
Stadtkyll Germany **39** 50.21N 6.32E
Stadtlohn Germany **38** 51.59N 6.55E
Stadtoldendorf Germany **38** 51.53N 9.37E
Staffa *i.* U.K. **14** 56.26N 6.21W
Staffelstein Germany **38** 50.06N 11.00E
Stafford U.K. **12** 52.49N 2.09W
Stafford U.S.A. **114** 38.09N 76.51W
Staffordshire *d.* U.K. **12** 52.40N 1.57W
Staines U.K. **13** 51.26N 0.31W
Stainforth U.K. **12** 53.37N 1.01W
Stainz Austria **31** 46.54N 15.16E
Stakhanov Ukraine **45** 48.34N 38.40E
Stalać Yugo. **34** 43.43N 21.28E
Stalina Kanal *canal* Russian Fed. **44** 64.33N 34.48E
Ställdalen Sweden **43** 59.56N 14.56E
Stamford U.K. **13** 52.39N 0.28W
Stamford Conn. U.S.A. **115** 41.03N 73.32W
Stamford N.Y. U.S.A. **115** 42.25N 74.37W
Stamford Tex. U.S.A. **111** 32.57N 99.48W
Stanardsville U.S.A. **114** 38.18N 78.26W
Stanberry U.S.A. **110** 40.13N 94.35W
Standerton R.S.A. **80** 26.57S 29.14E
Standish U.S.A. **104** 43.59N 83.57W
Stanger R.S.A. **80** 29.20S 31.17E
Stanke Dimitrov Bulgaria **34** 42.27N 23.09E
Stanley Canada **98** 55.45N104.55W
Stanley Falkland Is. **125** 51.42W 57.51W
Stanley U.K. **12** 54.53N 1.42W
Stanley Idaho U.S.A. **108** 44.13N114.35W
Stanley Wisc. U.S.A. **110** 44.58N 90.56W
Stanley Mission Canada **101** 55.27N104.33W
Stanovoy Khrebet *mts.* Russian Fed. **51** 56.00N125.40E
Stanthorpe Australia **93** 28.37S151.52E
Stanton U.S.A. **111** 32.08N101.48W
Stapleton U.S.A. **110** 41.29N100.31W
Starachowice Poland **37** 51.03N 21.04E
Stara Dorogi Belorussia **37** 53.02N 28.18E
Stara Pazova Yugo. **31** 44.59N 20.10E
Stara Planina *mts.* Bulgaria **34** 43.15N 25.00E
Staraya Russa Russian Fed. **44** 58.00N 31.22E
Staraya Sinyava Ukraine **37** 49.38N 27.39E
Stara Zagora Bulgaria **34** 42.26N 25.39E
Starbuck I. Kiribati **85** 5.37S155.55W
Stargard Szczeciński Poland **36** 53.21N 15.01E
Stari Bar Yugo. **31** 42.06N 19.08E
Stari Grad Croatia **31** 43.11N 16.36E
Staritsa Russian Fed. **44** 56.29N 34.59E
Starke U.S.A. **113** 29.55N 82.06W
Starkville U.S.A. **111** 33.28N 88.48W
Starnberg Germany **39** 48.00N 11.20E
Starnberger See *l.* Germany **39** 47.55N 11.18E
Starobin Belorussia **37** 52.40N 27.29E
Starogard Gdański Poland **37** 53.59N 18.33E
Starokonstantinov Ukraine **37** 49.48N 27.10E
Start Pt. U.K. **13** 50.13N 3.38W
Staryy Oskol Russian Fed. **45** 51.20N 37.50E
Stassfurt Germany **38** 51.51N 11.34E
State College U.S.A. **114** 40.48N 77.52W
Staten I. *see* Estados, Isla de los *i.* Argentina **125**
Statesville U.S.A. **113** 35.46N 80.54W
Staunton U.S.A. **113** 38.09N 79.04W
Stavanger Norway **42** 58.58N 5.45E
Stavelot Belgium **16** 50.23N 5.54E
Staveren Neth. **16** 52.53N 5.21E
Stavern Norway **42** 59.00N 10.02E
Stavropol' Russian Fed. **45** 45.03N 41.59E
Stavropolskaya Vozvyshennost *mts.* Russian Fed. **45** 45.00N 42.30E
Stavrós Greece **34** 39.18N 22.15E
Stavroúpolis Greece **34** 41.12N 24.45E
Stawell Australia **92** 37.06S142.52E
Stawiski Poland **37** 53.23N 22.09E
Stayner Canada **104** 44.25N 80.05W
Stayton U.S.A. **108** 44.48N122.48W
Steamboat Springs *town* U.S.A. **108** 40.29N106.50W
Steele U.S.A. **110** 46.51N 99.55W
Steelpoort R.S.A. **80** 24.44S 30.13E
Steelton U.S.A. **114** 40.14N 76.49W
Steenbergen Neth. **16** 51.36N 4.19E
Steenvoorde France **19** 50.48N 2.35E
Steenwijk Neth. **16** 52.47N 6.07E
Steep Rock Lake *town* Canada **102** 48.50N 91.38W
Stege Denmark **43** 54.59N 12.18E
Stegeborg Sweden **43** 58.26N 16.35E
Steiermark *d.* Austria **36** 47.10N 15.10E
Steilloopbrug R.S.A. **80** 23.26S 28.37E
Steinach Austria **39** 47.05N 11.28E
Steinbach Canada **101** 49.32N 96.41W
Steinhuder Meer *l.* Germany **38** 52.28N 9.19E
Steinkjer Norway **40** 64.00N 11.30E
Steinkopf R.S.A. **80** 29.16S 17.41E
Stella R.S.A. **80** 26.32S 24.51E
Stellarton Canada **103** 45.34N 62.40W
Stellenbosch R.S.A. **80** 33.56S 18.51E
Stelvio, Passo dello *pass* Italy **30** 46.32N 10.27E
Stenay France **19** 49.29N 5.11E
Stendal Germany **38** 52.36N 11.51E
Stenstorp Sweden **43** 58.16N 13.43E
Stenstrup Denmark **42** 56.59N 9.52E
Stenträsk Sweden **40** 66.20N 19.50E
Stepan Ukraine **37** 51.09N 26.18E
Stepanakert Azerbaijan **65** 39.48N 46.45E
Stephens City U.S.A. **114** 39.05N 78.13W
Stephens Passage *str.* U.S.A. **100** 57.50N133.50W
Stephenville Canada **103** 48.33N 58.35W
Stephenville U.S.A. **111** 32.13N 98.12W
Stepnyak Kazakhstan **50** 52.52N 70.49E
Steps Pt. *c.* Samoa **84** 14.22S170.45W
Sterkstroom R.S.A. **80** 31.32S 26.31E
Sterling Colo. U.S.A. **108** 40.37N103.13W
Sterling Ill. U.S.A. **110** 41.48N 89.43W
Sterling Mich. U.S.A. **104** 44.02N 84.02W
Sterling Run U.S.A. **114** 41.25N 78.12W
Sterlitamak Russian Fed. **44** 53.40N 55.59E
Šternberk Czech Republic **37** 49.44N 17.18E
Stettler Canada **100** 52.19N112.40W
Steuben U.S.A. **112** 46.12N 86.27W
Steubenville U.S.A. **114** 40.22N 80.37W
Stevenage U.K. **13** 51.54N 0.11W
Stevenson L. Canada **101** 53.56N 96.09W
Stevens Point *town* U.S.A. **110** 44.32N 89.33W
Stevenston U.K. **14** 55.39N 4.45W
Stewart Canada **100** 55.56N130.01W
Stewart I. New Zealand **86** 47.00S168.00E
Stewart River *town* Canada **98** 63.19N139.26W
Stewartstown U.S.A. **105** 45.01N 71.30W
Steynsburg R.S.A. **80** 31.17S 25.48E
Steyr Austria **36** 48.04N 14.25E
Stigliano Italy **33** 40.24N 16.14E
Stigtomta Sweden **43** 58.48N 16.47E
Stikine *r.* Canada / U.S.A. **100** 56.40N132.30W
Stikine Mts. Canada **98** 59.00N129.00W
Stikine Plateau *f.* Canada **100** 58.45N130.00W
Stiklestad Norway **40** 63.48N 11.22E
Stilbaai R.S.A. **80** 34.22S 21.22E
Stilís Greece **35** 38.55N 22.36E
Stillwater U.S.A. **111** 36.07N 97.04W
Stillwater Range *mts.* U.S.A. **108** 39.50N118.15W
Stillwater Resr. U.S.A. **105** 43.57N 74.58W
Stilo, Punta *c.* Italy **33** 38.28N 16.36E
Stilton U.K. **13** 52.29N 0.17W
Stimson Canada **102** 48.58N 80.36W
Stinchar *r.* U.K. **14** 55.06N 5.00W
Stînisoara, Munţii *mts.* Romania **37** 47.10N 26.00E
Štip Macedonia **34** 41.42N 22.10E
Stira Greece **35** 38.09N 24.14E
Stirling Canada **105** 44.18N 77.33W
Stirling U.K. **14** 56.07N 3.57W
Stirling Range *mts.* Australia **89** 34.23S117.50E
Stjernöya *i.* Norway **40** 70.17N 22.40E
Stjördalshalsen Norway **40** 63.29N 10.51E
Stobi *site* Macedonia **34** 41.34N 21.58E
Stockach Germany **39** 47.51N 9.00E
Stockaryd Sweden **43** 57.18N 14.35E
Stockbridge U.K. **13** 51.07N 1.30W
Stockbridge U.S.A. **104** 42.27N 84.11W
Stockdale U.S.A. **111** 29.14N 97.58W
Stockerau Austria **36** 48.23N 16.13E
Stockett U.S.A. **108** 47.21N111.10W
Stockholm Sweden **43** 59.20N 18.03E
Stockholm *d.* Sweden **43** 59.20N 18.03E
Stockinbingal Australia **93** 34.03S147.53E
Stockport U.K. **12** 53.25N 2.11W
Stocksbridge U.K. **12** 53.30N 1.36W
Stockton Calif. U.S.A. **108** 37.57N121.17W
Stockton Kans. U.S.A. **110** 39.26N 99.16W
Stockton-on-Tees U.K. **12** 54.34N 1.20W
Stoeng Tréng Cambodia **56** 13.31N105.59E
Stoffberg R.S.A. **80** 25.25S 29.49E
Stogovo *mts.* Macedonia **34** 41.31N 20.38E
Stoke-on-Trent U.K. **12** 53.01N 2.11W
Stokes Bay *town* Canada **104** 45.00N 81.23W
Stokhod *r.* Ukraine **37** 51.52N 25.38E
Stokksund Norway **40** 64.03N 10.05E
Stolac Bosnia-Herzegovina **31** 43.05N 17.58E
Stolberg Germany **38** 50.46N 6.13E
Stolbtsy Belorussia **37** 53.30N 26.44E
Stolin Belorussia **37** 51.52N 26.51E
Ston Croatia **31** 42.50N 17.42E
Stone U.K. **12** 52.55N 2.10W
Stoneboro U.S.A. **114** 41.20N 80.07W
Stonecliffe Canada **105** 46.12N 77.54W
Stone Harbor U.S.A. **115** 39.03N 74.45W
Stonehaven U.K. **14** 56.58N 2.13W
Stony I. Canada **103** 53.00N 55.48W
Stony L. Canada **104** 44.33N 78.05W
Stony Pt. *c.* U.S.A. **105** 43.52N 76.15W
Stony Rapids *town* Canada **101** 59.16N105.50W
Stooping *r.* Canada **102** 52.08N 82.00W
Storå *r.* Denmark **42** 56.19N 8.19E
Stora Gla *l.* Sweden **43** 59.30N 12.30E
Stora Le *l.* Sweden **42** 59.05N 11.53E
Stora Lulevatten *l.* Sweden **40** 67.10N 19.16E
Stora Möja Sweden **43** 59.26N 18.55E
Stora Sjöfallets Nat. Park Sweden **40** 67.44N 18.16E
Storavan *l.* Sweden **40** 65.40N 18.15E
Storby Finland **41** 60.13N 19.34E
Stord *i.* Norway **42** 59.53N 5.25E
Store Baelt *str.* Denmark **42** 55.30N 11.00E
Store Heddinge Denmark **43** 55.19N 12.25E
Stor Elvdal Norway **41** 61.32N 11.02E
Stören Norway **40** 63.03N 10.18E
Storfors Sweden **43** 59.32N 14.16E
Storlien Sweden **40** 63.20N 12.05E
Storm Lake *town* U.S.A. **110** 42.39N 95.10W
Stornoway U.K. **14** 58.12N 6.23W
Storozhevsk Russian Fed. **44** 62.00N 52.20E
Storozhinets Ukraine **37** 48.11N 25.40E
Storsjön *l.* Sweden **40** 63.10N 14.20E
Storuman Sweden **40** 65.06N 17.06E
Storuman *l.* Sweden **40** 65.10N 16.40E
Storvreta Sweden **43** 59.58N 17.42E
Stouffville Canada **104** 43.59N 79.15W
Stoughton U.S.A. **110** 42.55N 89.13W
Stour *r.* Dorset U.K. **13** 50.43N 1.47W
Stour *r.* Kent U.K. **13** 51.19N 1.22E
Stour *r.* Suffolk U.K. **13** 51.56N 1.03E
Stourport-on-Severn U.K. **13** 52.21N 2.16W
Stowmarket U.K. **13** 52.11N 1.00E
Stow on the Wold U.K. **13** 51.55N 1.42W
Strabane U.K. **15** 54.50N 7.30W
Stradbally Laois Rep. of Ire. **15** 53.01N 7.09W
Stradbroke I. Australia **91** 27.38S153.45E
Stradella Italy **30** 45.05N 9.18E
Straelen Germany **38** 51.27N 6.16E
Strahan Australia **91** 42.08S145.21E
Strakonice Czech Republic **38** 49.16N 13.55E
Stralsund Germany **38** 54.19N 13.05E
Strand R.S.A. **80** 34.07S 18.50E
Stranda Norway **40** 62.19N 6.58E
Strangford Lough U.K. **15** 54.28N 5.35W
Strangways *town* Australia **92** 29.08S136.35E
Stranraer U.K. **14** 54.54N 5.02W
Strasbourg France **19** 48.35N 7.45E
Strasburg Germany **38** 53.30N 13.44E
Strasburg N.Dak. U.S.A. **110** 46.08N100.10W
Strasburg Ohio U.S.A. **114** 40.36N 81.32W
Stråssa Sweden **43** 59.45N 15.13E
Strasswalchen Austria **39** 47.59N 13.15E
Stratford Australia **93** 37.57S147.05E
Stratford Canada **104** 43.22N 80.57W
Stratford New Zealand **86** 39.20S174.18E
Stratford Conn. U.S.A. **115** 41.14N 73.07W
Stratford N.H. U.S.A. **105** 44.40N 71.34W
Stratford Tex. U.S.A. **111** 36.20N102.04W
Stratford-upon-Avon U.K. **13** 52.12N 1.42W
Strathalbyn Australia **92** 35.16S138.54E
Strathclyde *d.* U.K. **14** 55.45N 4.45W
Strathcona Prov. Park Canada **100** 49.38N125.40W
Strathmore *f.* Tayside U.K. **14** 56.44N 2.45W
Strathroy Canada **104** 42.57N 81.38W
Strathspey *f.* U.K. **14** 57.25N 3.25W
Stratton U.S.A. **110** 39.18N102.36W
Stratton Mtn. U.S.A. **115** 43.05N 72.56W
Straubing Germany **39** 48.53N 12.34E
Straumnes *c.* Iceland **40** 66.30N 23.05W
Strausberg Germany **38** 52.35N 13.53E
Strawn U.S.A. **111** 32.33N 98.30W
Streaky B. Australia **92** 32.36S134.08E
Streaky Bay *town* Australia **92** 32.48S134.13E
Streator U.S.A. **110** 41.07N 88.53W
Street U.K. **13** 51.07N 2.43W
Streeter U.S.A. **110** 46.39N 99.21W
Streetsville Canada **104** 43.35N 79.42W
Stresa Italy **30** 45.53N 8.32E
Stretton Australia **89** 32.30S117.42E
Striberg Sweden **43** 59.33N 14.56E
Strimon *r.* Greece **34** 40.47N 23.51E
Stromboli *i.* Italy **33** 38.48N 15.13E
Stromeferry U.K. **14** 57.21N 5.34W
Stromness U.K. **14** 58.57N 3.18W
Strömö *i.* Faroe Is. **10** 62.08N 7.00W
Strömsbruk Sweden **41** 61.53N 17.19E
Strömstad Sweden **42** 58.56N 11.10E
Strömsund Sweden **40** 63.51N 15.35E
Strömsvattudal *f.* Sweden **40** 64.15N 15.00E
Strongfield Canada **101** 51.20N106.36W
Strongoli Italy **33** 39.15N 17.03E
Stronsay *i.* U.K. **14** 59.07N 2.36W
Stroud Australia **93** 32.25S151.58E
Stroud U.K. **13** 51.44N 2.12W
Stroudsburg U.S.A. **115** 40.59N 75.12W
Struan Australia **92** 37.08S140.49E
Struer Denmark **42** 56.29N 8.37E
Struga Macedonia **34** 41.11N 20.40E
Struma *r.* Bulgaria *see* Strimon *r.* Greece **34**
Strumica Macedonia **34** 41.28N 22.41E
Struthers U.S.A. **114** 41.04N 80.38W
Stryama *r.* Bulgaria **34** 42.40N 24.28E
Strydenburg R.S.A. **80** 29.56S 23.39E
Stryker U.S.A. **108** 48.40N114.44W
Stryy Ukraine **37** 49.16N 23.51E
Strzelecki Creek *r.* Australia **92** 29.37S139.59E
Strzelno Poland **37** 52.38N 18.11E
Stuart Fla. U.S.A. **113** 27.12N 80.16W
Stuart Nebr. U.S.A. **110** 42.36N 99.08W
Stuart Creek *town* Australia **92** 29.43S137.01E
Stuart L. Canada **100** 54.30N124.30W
Stuart Range *mts.* Australia **92** 29.10S134.56E
Stuart Town Australia **93** 32.51S149.08E
Stubbeköbing Denmark **43** 54.53N 12.03E
Studenica Yugo. **34** 43.21N 20.35E
Studen Kladenets, Yazovir *l.* Bulgaria **34** 41.37N 25.29E
Studsvik Sweden **43** 58.46N 17.23E
Stupart *r.* Canada **101** 56.00N 93.22W
Sturgeon *r.* Canada **104** 46.19N 79.58W
Sturgeon Bay *town* U.S.A. **110** 44.50N 87.23W
Sturgeon Falls *town* Canada **104** 46.22N 79.55W
Sturgeon L. Ont. Canada **102** 50.00N 90.40W
Sturgeon L. Ont. Canada **104** 44.28N 78.42W
Sturgis U.S.A. **110** 44.25N103.31W
Sturminster Newton U.K. **13** 50.56N 2.18W
Sturt B. Australia **92** 35.24S137.32E
Sturt Creek *r.* Australia **88** 20.08S127.24E
Sturt Desert Australia **92** 28.30S141.12E
Sturt Plain *f.* Australia **90** 17.00S132.48E
Stutterheim R.S.A. **80** 32.32S 27.25E
Stuttgart Germany **39** 48.46N 9.11E

Stviga to Taiyuan

Stviga *r.* Belorussia **37** 52.04N 27.54E
Stykkishólmur Iceland **40** 65.06N 22.48W
Styr *r.* Belorussia **37** 52.07N 26.35E
Suao Taiwan **55** 24.36N121.51E
Subarnarekha *r.* India **63** 21.34N 87.24E
Subay', 'Urūq *f.* Saudi Arabia **72** 22.15N 43.05E
Subei Guangai Zongqu *canal* China **54** 34.06N120.19E
Subiaco Italy **30** 41.55N 13.06E
Subotica Yugo. **31** 46.06N 19.39E
Suceava Romania **37** 47.39N 26.19E
Suchan Russian Fed. **57** 43.03N133.05E
Suck *r.* Rep. of Ire. **15** 53.16N 8.04W
Suckling, Mt. P.N.G. **90** 9.45S148.55E
Sucre Bolivia **124** 19.02S 65.17W
Sucuriu *r.* Brazil **126** 20.44S 51.40W
Sudalsvatnet *l.* Norway **42** 59.35N 6.45E
Sudan Africa **72** 14.30N 29.00E
Sudan U.S.A. **111** 34.04N102.32W
Sudbury Canada **104** 46.30N 81.00W
Sudbury U.K. **13** 52.03N 0.45E
Sude *r.* Germany **38** 53.22N 10.45E
Sudety *mts.* Czech Republic / Poland **36** 50.30N 16.30E
Sudirman, Pegunungan *mts.* Indonesia **59** 3.50S136.30E
Sud Ouest *d.* Burkina **76** 10.45N 3.10W
Sudzukhe Russian Fed. **57** 42.50N133.43E
Sueca Spain **25** 39.12N 0.19W
Suez *see* As Suways Egypt **66**
Suez, G. of *see* Suways, Khalīj as *g.* Egypt **66**
Suez Canal *see* Suways, Qanāt as *canal* Egypt **66**
Sūf Jordan **67** 32.19N 35.50E
Şufaynah Saudi Arabia **64** 23.09N 40.32E
Suffolk *d.* U.K. **13** 52.16N 1.00E
Suffolk U.S.A. **113** 36.44N 76.37W
Sugargrove U.S.A. **114** 41.59N 79.21W
Sugar I. U.S.A. **104** 46.25N 84.12W
Suhaia, Lacul *l.* Romania **34** 43.45N 25.15E
Şuḩār Oman **65** 24.23N 56.43E
Sühbaatar *d.* Mongolia **54** 45.30N114.00E
Suhl Germany **38** 50.37N 10.41E
Suhopolje Croatia **31** 45.48N 17.30E
Sūi Pakistan **62** 28.37N 69.19E
Suibin China **53** 47.19N131.49E
Suichang China **55** 28.36N119.16E
Suichuan China **55** 26.24N114.31E
Suide China **54** 37.35N110.08E
Suihua China **53** 46.39N126.59E
Suileng China **53** 47.15N127.05E
Suining Jiangsu China **54** 33.54N117.56E
Suining Sichuan China **55** 30.31N105.32E
Suipacha Argentina **125** 34.47S 59.40W
Suippes France **19** 49.08N 4.32E
Suir *r.* Rep. of Ire. **15** 52.17N 7.00W
Suita Japan **57** 34.45N135.32E
Sui Xian Henan China **54** 34.25N115.04E
Sui Xian Hubei China **55** 31.45N113.30E
Suiyang Guizhou China **55** 27.57N107.11E
Suizhong China **54** 40.25N120.25E
Suj China **54** 42.02N107.58E
Sūjāngarh India **62** 27.42N 74.28E
Sujāwal Pakistan **62** 24.36N 68.05E
Sukabumi Indonesia **59** 6.55S106.50E
Sukadana Indonesia **58** 1.15S110.00E
Sukaraja Indonesia **58** 2.23S110.35E
Sukhinichi Russian Fed. **44** 54.07N 35.21E
Sukhona *r.* Russian Fed. **44** 61.30N 46.28E
Sukhumi Georgia **45** 43.01N 41.01E
Sukkertoppen Greenland **99** 65.40N 53.00W
Sukkur Pakistan **62** 27.42N 68.52E
Sukoharjo Indonesia **59** 7.40S110.50E
Sukumo Japan **57** 32.56N132.44E
Sul *d.* Portugal **27** 38.50N 8.05W
Sula *i.* Norway **41** 61.08N 4.55E
Sula, Kepulauan *is.* Indonesia **59** 1.50S125.10E
Sulaimān Range *mts.* Pakistan **62** 30.00N 69.50E
Sulak *r.* Russian Fed. **45** 43.18N 47.35E
Sulawesi *i.* Indonesia **59** 2.00S120.30E
Sulawesi Selatan *d.* Indonesia **59** 3.45S120.30E
Sulawesi Utara *d.* Indonesia **59** 1.45S120.30E
Sulechów Poland **36** 52.06N 15.37E
Sulejów Poland **37** 51.22N 19.53E
Sulina Romania **29** 45.08N 29.40E
Sulingen Germany **38** 52.41N 8.47E
Sulitjelma Norway **40** 67.10N 16.05E
Sullana Peru **122** 4.52S 80.39W
Sullivan U.S.A. **110** 38.13N 91.10W
Sully France **19** 47.46N 2.22E
Sulmona Italy **31** 42.03N 13.55E
Sulphur U.S.A. **111** 34.31N 96.58W
Sultan Canada **102** 47.36N 82.47W
Sultan Hamud Kenya **79** 2.02S 37.20E
Sultānpur India **63** 26.16N 82.04E
Sulu Archipelago Phil. **59** 5.30N121.00E
Sulūq Libya **75** 31.40N 20.15E
Sulu Sea Pacific Oc. **59** 8.00N120.00E
Sulzbach-Rosenburg Germany **38** 49.30N 11.45E
Sumatera *i.* Indonesia **58** 2.00S102.00E
Sumatera Barat *d.* Indonesia **58** 1.00S100.00E
Sumatera Selatan *d.* Indonesia **58** 3.00S104.00E
Sumatera Utara *d.* Indonesia **58** 2.00N 99.00E
Sumatra *see* Sumatera *i.* Indonesia **58**
Sumatra U.S.A. **108** 46.38N107.31W
Sumba *i.* Indonesia **58** 9.30S119.55E
Sumbar *r.* Turkmenistan **65** 38.00N 55.20E
Sumbawa *i.* Indonesia **58** 8.45S117.50E
Sumbawanga Tanzania **79** 7.58S 31.36E
Sumbe Angola **78** 11.11S 13.52E
Sumbilla Spain **25** 43.10N 1.40W
Sumburgh Head U.K. **14** 59.51N 1.16W
Sumedang Indonesia **59** 6.54S107.55E
Sümeg Hungary **31** 46.59N 17.17E
Šumen Bulgaria **29** 43.15N 26.55E
Sumenep Indonesia **59** 7.01S113.51E
Sumgait Azerbaijan **65** 40.35N 49.38E
Summerland Canada **100** 49.32N119.41W
Summerside Canada **103** 46.24N 63.47W
Summersville U.S.A. **114** 38.17N 80.51W
Summerville Ga. U.S.A. **113** 34.29N 85.21W
Summerville S.C. U.S.A. **113** 33.02N 80.11W
Šumperk Czech Republic **36** 49.58N 16.58E
Sumprabum Burma **56** 26.33N 97.34E
Sumuştā al Waqf Egypt **66** 28.55N 30.51E
Sumy Ukraine **45** 50.55N 34.49E
Sunagawa Japan **57** 43.30N141.55E
Sunām India **62** 30.08N 75.48E
Sunāmganj Bangla. **63** 25.04N 91.24E
Sunart, Loch U.K. **14** 56.43N 5.45W
Sunburst U.S.A. **108** 48.53N111.55W
Sunbury Australia **93** 37.36S144.45E
Sunbury Ohio U.S.A. **114** 40.14N 82.52W
Sunbury Penn. U.S.A. **114** 40.52N 76.47W
Sunda, Selat *str.* Indonesia **58** 6.00S105.50E
Sundance U.S.A. **108** 44.24N104.23W
Sundarbans *f.* India / Bangla. **63** 21.45N 89.00E
Sundargarh India **63** 22.07N 84.02E
Sundays *r.* R.S.A. **80** 33.43S 25.50E
Sundbyberg Sweden **43** 59.22N 17.58E
Sunde Norway **42** 59.50N 5.43E
Sunderland Canada **104** 44.16N 79.04W
Sunderland U.K. **12** 54.55N 1.22W
Sundridge Canada **104** 45.46N 79.24W
Sundsvall Sweden **41** 62.23N 17.18E
Sungai Kolok Thailand **56** 6.02N101.58E
Sungaipakning Indonesia **58** 1.19N102.00E
Sungaipenuh Indonesia **58** 2.00S101.28E
Sungguminasa Indonesia **58** 5.14S119.27E
Sungurlu Turkey **64** 40.10N 34.23E
Sunjikāy Sudan **73** 12.20N 29.46E
Sunne Sweden **43** 59.50N 13.09E
Sunnersta Sweden **43** 59.48N 17.39E
Sunnyside U.S.A. **108** 46.20N120.00W
Suntar Russian Fed. **51** 62.10N117.35E
Suntsar Pakistan **62** 25.31N 62.00E
Sun Valley *town* U.S.A. **106** 43.42N114.21W
Sunwu China **53** 49.40N127.10E
Sunyani Ghana **76** 7.22N 2.18W
Suō nada *str.* Japan **57** 33.45N131.30E
Suoyarvi Russian Fed. **44** 62.02N 32.20E
Supaul India **63** 26.07N 86.36E
Superior Mont. U.S.A. **108** 47.12N114.53W
Superior Wisc. U.S.A. **110** 46.42N 92.05W
Superior Wyo. U.S.A. **108** 41.46N108.58W
Superior, L. Canada / U.S.A. **112** 48.00N 88.00W
Supetar Croatia **31** 43.23N 16.33E
Suphan Buri Thailand **56** 14.14N100.07E
Suphan Buri *r.* Thailand **56** 13.34N100.15E
Süphan Dagi *mtn.* Turkey **45** 38.55N 42.55E
Suqian China **54** 33.59N118.25E
Suquţrá *i.* Yemen **71** 12.30N 54.00E
Şūr Lebanon **67** 33.16N 35.12E
Şūr Oman **65** 22.23N 59.32E
Sur *d.* W. Sahara **74** 23.40N 14.15W
Sur, Cabo *c.* I. de Pascua **85** 27.12S109.26W
Sur, Punta *c.* Argentina **125** 36.53S 56.41W
Sura Russian Fed. **44** 53.52N 45.45E
Sūrāb Pakistan **62** 28.29N 66.16E
Surabaya Indonesia **59** 7.14S112.45E
Surakarta Indonesia **59** 7.32S110.50E
Şūrān Syria **66** 35.18N 36.44E
Šurany Slovakia **37** 48.06N 18.14E
Surat Australia **91** 27.09S149.05E
Surat India **62** 21.12N 72.50E
Sūratgarh India **62** 29.18N 73.54E
Surat Thani Thailand **56** 9.09N 99.23E
Surazh Russian Fed. **37** 53.00N 32.22E
Surdulica Yugo. **34** 42.41N 22.10E
Sûre *r.* Lux. **16** 49.43N 6.31E
Sureau, Lac *l.* Canada **103** 53.10N 70.50W
Surendranagar India **62** 22.42N 71.41E
Surfer's Paradise Australia **93** 27.58S153.26E
Surgères France **20** 46.07N 0.45W
Surgut Russian Fed. **9** 61.13N 73.20E
Sūri India **63** 23.55N 87.32E
Şūrīf Jordan **67** 31.39N 35.04E
Surigao Phil. **59** 9.47N125.29E
Surin Thailand **56** 14.58N103.33E
Surinam S. America **123** 4.00N 56.00W
Suriname *r.* Surinam **123** 5.52N 55.14W
Surrey *d.* U.K. **13** 51.16N 0.30W
Sursee Switz. **39** 47.10N 8.06E
Surt Libya **75** 31.13N 16.35E
Surt, Khalīj *g.* Libya **75** 31.45N 17.50E
Surtanāhu Pakistan **62** 26.22N 70.00E
Surte Sweden **43** 57.49N 12.01E
Surtsey *i.* Iceland **40** 63.18N 20.30W
Surud Ad *mtn.* Somali Rep. **71** 10.41N 47.18E
Suruga-wan *b.* Japan **57** 34.45N138.30E
Susa Italy **30** 45.08N 7.03E
Susak *i.* Croatia **31** 44.31N 14.18E
Susanino Russian Fed. **51** 52.46N140.09E
Susanville U.S.A. **108** 40.25N120.39W
Sušice Czech Republic **38** 49.14N 13.32E
Susquehanna U.S.A. **115** 41.57N 75.36W
Susquehanna *r.* U.S.A. **115** 39.33N 76.05W
Susquehanna, West Branch *r.* U.S.A. **114** 40.53N 76.47W
Sussex N.J. U.S.A. **115** 41.13N 74.36W
Sussex Wyo. U.S.A. **108** 43.42N106.19W
Sutak Jammu & Kashmir **63** 33.12N 77.28E
Sutherland Australia **93** 34.02S151.04E
Sutherland R.S.A. **80** 32.23S 20.38E
Sutherlin U.S.A. **108** 43.25N123.19W
Sutlej *r.* Pakistan **62** 29.23N 71.02E
Sutton Canada **104** 44.18N 79.22W
Sutton *r.* Canada **102** 55.22N 83.48W
Sutton England U.K. **13** 51.22N 0.12W
Sutton Nebr. U.S.A. **110** 40.36N 97.52W
Sutton W. Va. U.S.A. **114** 38.40N 80.43W
Sutton in Ashfield U.K. **12** 53.08N 1.16W
Suva Fiji **84** 18.08S178.25E
Suva Planina *mts.* Yugo. **34** 43.10N 22.05E
Suva Reka Yugo. **34** 42.21N 20.50E
Suwa Ethiopia **72** 14.16N 41.10E
Suwałki Poland **37** 54.07N 22.56E
Suwanee *r.* U.S.A. **113** 29.18N 83.09W
Şuwayliḩ Jordan **67** 32.02N 35.50E
Suwaymah Jordan **67** 31.47N 35.36E
Suways, Khalīj as *g.* Egypt **66** 28.48N 33.00E
Suways, Qanāt as *canal* Egypt **66** 30.40N 32.20E
Suwon S. Korea **53** 37.16N126.59E
Suzhou China **55** 31.22N120.45E
Suzu Japan **57** 37.25N137.17E
Suzuka Japan **57** 34.51N136.35E
Suzuka *r.* Japan **57** 34.54N136.39E
Suzuka-sammyaku *mts.* Japan **57** 35.00N136.20E
Suzu misaki *c.* Japan **57** 37.30N137.21E
Suzzara Italy **30** 45.00N 10.45E
Svalyava Ukraine **37** 48.33N 23.00E
Svaneke Denmark **43** 55.08N 15.09E
Svanskog Sweden **43** 59.11N 12.33E
Svanvik Norway **40** 69.25N 30.00E
Svappavaara Sweden **40** 67.39N 21.04E
Svarhofthalvöya Norway **40** 70.35N 26.00E
Svartå Sweden **43** 59.08N 14.31E
Svartån *r.* Sweden **43** 59.37N 16.33E
Svartisen *mtn.* Norway **40** 66.40N 13.56E
Svatovo Ukraine **45** 49.24N 38.11E
Svay Riěng Cambodia **56** 11.05N105.48E
Svedala Sweden **43** 55.30N 13.14E
Sveg Sweden **41** 62.02N 14.21E
Svelgen Norway **41** 61.47N 5.15E
Svelvik Norway **42** 59.37N 10.24E
Svendborg Denmark **42** 55.03N 10.37E
Svenljunga Sweden **43** 57.30N 13.07E
Svenstrup Denmark **42** 56.59N 9.52E
Sverdlovsk *see* Yekaterinburg Russian Fed. **44**
Sveti Nikole Macedonia **34** 41.51N 21.56E
Svetlograd Russian Fed. **45** 45.25N 42.58E
Svetogorsk Russian Fed. **44** 61.07N 28.50E
Svetozarevo Yugo. **34** 43.58N 21.16E
Svilengrad Bulgaria **34** 41.49N 26.12E
Svindal Norway **42** 58.30N 7.28E
Svinesund Sweden **42** 59.06N 11.16E
Svinninge Denmark **42** 55.43N 11.28E
Svinö *i.* Faroe Is. **10** 62.17N 6.18W
Svir *r.* Russian Fed. **44** 60.09N 32.15E
Svishtov Bulgaria **34** 43.36N 25.23E
Svisloch Belorussia **37** 53.28N 29.00E
Svitavy Czech Republic **36** 49.45N 16.27E
Svobodnyy Russian Fed. **53** 51.24N128.05E
Svoge Bulgaria **34** 42.58N 23.21E
Svolvaer Norway **40** 68.15N 14.40E
Swaffham U.K. **13** 52.38N 0.42E
Swain Reefs Australia **90** 21.40S152.15E
Swains I. Samoa **84** 11.03S171.06W
Swakop *r.* Namibia **80** 22.38S 14.32E
Swakopmund Namibia **80** 22.40S 14.34E
Swale *r.* U.K. **12** 54.05N 1.20W
Swan *r.* Australia **89** 32.03S115.45E
Swanage U.K. **13** 50.36N 1.59W
Swan Hill *town* Australia **92** 35.23S143.37E
Swan Hills Canada **100** 54.42N115.24W
Swan L. Canada **101** 52.30N100.45W
Swan River *town* Canada **101** 52.10N101.17W
Swansea Australia **91** 42.08S148.00E
Swansea U.K. **13** 51.37N 3.57W
Swanton U.S.A. **105** 44.55N 73.07W
Swastika Canada **102** 48.07N 80.06W
Swatow *see* Shantou China **55**
Swaziland Africa **80** 26.30S 32.00E
Sweden Europe **40** 63.00N 16.00E
Swedru Ghana **76** 5.31N 0.42W
Sweetwater U.S.A. **111** 32.28N100.25W
Swidnica Poland **36** 50.51N 16.29E
Swiebodzin Poland **36** 52.15N 15.32E
Świetokrzyskie, Góry *mts.* Poland **37** 51.00N 20.30E
Swift Current *town* Canada **101** 50.17N107.50W
Swilly, Lough Rep. of Ire. **15** 55.10N 7.32W
Swindon U.K. **13** 51.33N 1.47W
Świnoujście Poland **36** 53.55N 14.18E
Switzerland Europe **39** 46.45N 8.30E
Swords Rep. of Ire. **11** 53.27N 6.15W
Syderö *i.* Faroe Is. **10** 61.30N 6.50W
Sydney Australia **93** 33.55S151.10E
Sydney Canada **103** 46.09N 60.11W
Sydney Mines *town* Canada **103** 46.14N 60.14W
Sydpröven Greenland **99** 60.30N 45.35W
Syke Germany **38** 52.54N 8.49E
Syktyvkar Russian Fed. **44** 61.42N 50.45E
Sylacauga U.S.A. **113** 33.10N 86.15W
Sylhet Bangla. **63** 24.54N 91.52E
Sylt *i.* Germany **38** 54.54N 8.20E
Sylte Norway **40** 62.31N 7.07E
Sylvan Lake *town* Canada **100** 52.20N114.10W
Syracuse *see* Siracusa Italy **33**
Syracuse Kans. U.S.A. **111** 37.59N101.45W
Syracuse N.Y. U.S.A. **115** 43.03N 76.09W
Syr Darya *r.* Kazakhstan **9** 46.00N 61.21E
Syria Asia **64** 35.00N 38.00E
Syriam Burma **58** 16.45N 96.17E
Syrian Desert *see* Bādiyat ash Shām *des.* Asia **64**
Syzran Russian Fed. **44** 53.10N 48.29E
Szarvas Hungary **37** 46.52N 20.34E
Szczecin Poland **36** 53.25N 14.32E
Szczecinek Poland **36** 53.42N 16.41E
Szczytno Poland **37** 53.34N 21.00E
Szécsény Hungary **37** 48.06N 19.31E
Szeged Hungary **31** 46.15N 20.09E
Székesfehérvár Hungary **37** 47.12N 18.25E
Szekszárd Hungary **31** 46.21N 18.42E
Szentes Hungary **31** 46.39N 20.16E
Szentgotthárd Hungary **31** 46.57N 16.18E
Szolnok Hungary **37** 47.10N 20.12E
Szombathely Hungary **36** 47.12N 16.38E
Sztutowo Poland **37** 54.20N 19.15E

T

Tabagne Ivory Coast **76** 7.59N 3.04W
Ţābah Saudi Arabia **64** 27.02N 42.10E
Tábara Spain **26** 41.49N 5.57W
Tabarka Tunisia **32** 36.57N 8.45E
Ţabas Khorāsān Iran **65** 32.48N 60.14E
Ţabas Khorāsān Iran **65** 33.36N 56.55E
Tabasco *d.* Mexico **116** 18.30N 93.00W
Tābask, Kūh-e *mtn.* Iran **65** 29.51N 51.52E
Tabelbala Algeria **74** 29.24N 3.15W
Taber Canada **100** 49.47N112.08W
Tabernes de Valldigna Spain **25** 39.04N 0.16W
Tabili Zaïre **79** 0.04N 28.01E
Table B. R.S.A. **80** 33.52S 18.26E
Tábor Czech Republic **36** 49.25N 14.41E
Tabora Tanzania **79** 5.02S 32.50E
Tabora *d.* Tanzania **79** 5.30S 32.50E
Tabou Ivory Coast **76** 4.28N 7.20W
Tabrīz Iran **65** 38.05N 46.18E
Tabuaço Portugal **26** 41.07N 7.34W
Tabuaeran *i.* Kiribati **85** 3.52N159.20W
Tabūk Saudi Arabia **66** 28.23N 36.36E
Tabulam Australia **93** 28.50S152.35E
Ţabūt Yemen **71** 15.57N 52.09E
Tachia Taiwan **55** 24.21N120.37E
Tachikawa Japan **57** 35.42N139.25E
Tachov Czech Republic **38** 49.48N 12.38E
Tacloban Phil. **59** 11.15N124.59E
Tacna Peru **124** 18.01S 70.15W
Tacoma U.S.A. **108** 47.15N122.27W
Taconic Mts. U.S.A. **115** 42.36N 73.14W
Taconic State Park U.S.A. **115** 42.05N 73.34W
Tacora *mtn.* Chile **124** 17.40S 69.45W
Tacuarembó Uruguay **125** 31.44S 55.59W
Tademaït, Plateau du *f.* Algeria **75** 28.30N 2.15E
Tadjetaret, Oued Algeria **75** 21.00N 7.30E
Tadjmout Algeria **75** 25.30N 3.42E
Tadjoura, Golfe de *g.* Djibouti **71** 11.42N 43.00E
Tadmor New Zealand **86** 41.26S172.47E
Tadmur Syria **64** 34.36N 38.15E
Tadoule L. Canada **101** 58.36N 98.20W
Tadoussac Canada **103** 48.09N 69.43W
Taegu S. Korea **53** 35.52N128.36E
Taejin S. Korea **57** 36.34N129.24E
Taejōn S. Korea **53** 36.20N127.26E
Tafalla Spain **25** 42.31N 1.40W
Ţafas Syria **67** 32.44N 36.04E
Tafassasset, Oued *wadi* Niger **75** 22.00N 9.55E
Tafassasset, Ténéré du *des.* Niger **77** 21.00N 11.00E
Taffanel, Lac *l.* Canada **103** 53.22N 70.56W
Tafí Viejo Argentina **124** 26.45S 65.15W
Tafraout Morocco **74** 29.40N 8.58W
Taftān, Kūh-e *mtn.* Iran **65** 28.38N 61.08E
Taga W. Samoa **84** 13.47S172.30W
Taganrog Russian Fed. **45** 47.14N 38.55E
Taganrogskiy Zaliv *g.* Ukraine / Russian Fed. **45** 47.00N 38.30E
Tagant *d.* Mauritania **74** 18.30N 10.30W
Tagant *f.* Mauritania **74** 18.20N 11.00W
Tagaytay City Phil. **59** 14.07N120.58E
Tagbilaran Phil. **59** 9.38N123.53E
Tagish Canada **100** 60.19N134.16W
Tagliacozzo Italy **30** 42.04N 13.14E
Tagliamento *r.* Italy **30** 45.38N 13.06E
Taglio di Po Italy **30** 45.00N 12.12E
Tagounit Morocco **74** 29.58N 5.36W
Tagula I. P.N.G. **90** 11.30S153.30E
Tagum Phil. **59** 7.33N125.53E
Tagus *r.* Portugal / Spain *see* Tejo *r.* Portugal **27**
Tahaa *i.* Îs. de la Société **85** 16.38S151.30W
Tahara Japan **57** 34.40N137.16E
Tahat *mtn.* Algeria **75** 23.18N 5.32E
Tahe China **53** 52.35N124.48E
Tahiti *i.* Îs. de la Société **85** 17.37S149.27W
Tahiti, Archipel de *is.* Îs. de la Société **85** 17.00S149.35W
Tahlequah U.S.A. **111** 35.55N 94.58W
Tahoe, L. U.S.A. **108** 39.07N120.03W
Tahoua Niger **77** 14.57N 5.16E
Tahoua *d.* Niger **77** 15.38N 4.50E
Ţahţā Egypt **64** 26.46N 31.30E
Tahuna Indonesia **59** 3.37N125.29E
Taï Ivory Coast **76** 5.52N 7.28W
Tai'an China **54** 36.16N117.13E
Taiarapu, Presqu'île de *pen.* Tahiti **85** 17.47S149.14W
Taibai China **54** 36.08N108.41E
Taibai Shan *mtn.* China **54** 33.55N107.45E
Taibus Qi China **54** 41.55N115.23E
Taidong Taiwan **55** 22.49N121.10E
Taigu China **54** 37.23N112.34E
Taihang Shan *mts.* China **54** 36.00N113.35E
Taihape New Zealand **86** 39.40S175.48E
Taihe Anhui China **54** 33.10N115.36E
Taihe Jiangxi China **55** 26.48 114.56E
Tai Hu *l.* China **55** 31.15N120.10E
Tailai China **53** 46.23N123.24E
Tailem Bend *town* Australia **92** 35.14S139.29E
Tain U.K. **14** 57.48N 4.04W
Tainan Taiwan **55** 23.01N120.12E
Taínaron, Ákra *c.* Greece **35** 36.22N 22.30E
Tai-o-haé Îs. Marquises **85** 8.55S140.04W
Taipei Taiwan **55** 25.05N121.30E
Taiping Anhui China **55** 30.18N118.06E
Taiping Malaysia **58** 4.54N100.42E
Taishan China **55** 22.10N112.57E
Taito, Península de *pen.* Chile **125** 46.30S 74.25W
Taitze He *r.* China **54** 41.07N122.43E
Taivalkoski Finland **40** 65.34N 28.15E
Taiwan Asia **55** 24.00N121.00E
Taiwan Str. China / Taiwan **55** 24.30N119.30E
Taiyetos Óros *mts.* Greece **35** 37.16N 22.12E
Taiyuan China **54** 37.48N112.33E

Taiyue Shan to **Tekamah**

Taiyue Shan *mts.* China **54** 36.40N112.00E
Taizhong Taiwan **55** 24.11N120.40E
Taizhou China **54** 32.22N119.58E
Ta'izz Yemen **71** 13.35N 44.02E
Tajarhī Libya **75** 24.21N 14.28E
Tajikistan Asia **52** 39.00N 70.30E
Tajimi Japan **57** 35.19N137.08E
Tajitos Mexico **109** 30.58N112.18W
Tajo *r.* Spain *see* Tejo *r.* Portugal **27**
Tajrīsh Iran **65** 35.48N 51.20E
Tajuna *r.* Spain **24** 40.10N 3.35W
Tak Thailand **56** 16.51N 99.08E
Takaka New Zealand **86** 40.51S172.48E
Takalar Indonesia **58** 5.29S119.26E
Takamatsu Japan **57** 34.28N134.05E
Takaoka Japan **57** 36.47N137.00E
Takapuna New Zealand **86** 36.48S174.47E
Takarazuka Japan **57** 34.49N135.21E
Takasaki Japan **57** 36.20N139.00E
Takatsuki Japan **57** 34.51N135.37E
Takayama Japan **57** 36.08N137.15E
Tåkern *l.* Sweden **43** 58.21N 14.48E
Tākestān Iran **65** 36.02N 49.40E
Takêv Cambodia **56** 11.00N104.46E
Takhādīd *well* Iraq **65** 29.59N 44.30E
Takla L. Canada **100** 55.15N125.45W
Taklimakan Shamo *des.* China **52** 38.10N 82.00E
Taku *r.* Canada / U.S.A. **100** 58.30N133.50W
Talā Egypt **66** 30.41N 30.56E
Tala Uruguay **125** 34.21S 55.46W
Talagang Pakistan **62** 32.55N 72.25E
Talagante Chile **125** 33.40S 70.56W
Talāja India **62** 21.21N 72.03E
Tālāla India **62** 21.02N 70.32E
Talangbetutu Indonesia **58** 2.48S104.42E
Talara Peru **122** 4.38S 81.18W
Talarrubias Spain **27** 39.02N 5.14W
Talasskiy Alatau *mts.* Kyrgyzstan **52** 42.20N 73.20E
Talata Mafara Nigeria **77** 12.37N 6.05E
Talaud, Kepulauan *is.* Indonesia **59** 4.20N126.50E
Talavera de la Reina Spain **27** 39.57N 4.50W
Talawdī Sudan **73** 10.38N 30.23E
Talbragar *r.* Australia **93** 32.12S148.37E
Talca Chile **125** 35.26S 71.40W
Talcahuano Chile **125** 36.43S 73.07W
Tālcher India **63** 20.57N 85.13E
Taldom Russian Fed. **44** 56.49N 37.30E
Taldy Kurgan Kazakhstan **52** 45.02N 78.23E
Taleex *well* Somali Rep. **71** 9.12N 48.23E
Talia Australia **92** 33.16S134.53E
Taliabu *i.* Indonesia **59** 1.50S124.55E
Tali Post Sudan **73** 5.54N 30.47E
Talkeetna U.S.A. **98** 62.20N150.09W
Ţalkhā Egypt **66** 31.04N 31.22E
Tallahassee U.S.A. **113** 30.26N 84.19W
Tallangatta Australia **93** 36.14S147.19E
Tallard France **21** 44.28N 6.03E
Tallinn Estonia **41** 59.22N 24.48E
Tall Kalakh Syria **66** 34.40N 36.18E
Tall Kūshik Syria **64** 36.48N 42.04E
Tall Salḩab Syria **66** 35.15N 36.22E
Tallulah U.S.A. **111** 32.25N 91.11W
Ţallūzā Jordan **67** 32.16N 35.18E
Talmont France **18** 46.28N 1.37W
Talnoye Ukraine **37** 48.55N 30.40E
Taloda India **62** 21.34N 74.13E
Talofofo Guam **84** 13.21N144.45E
Talsi Latvia **41** 57.15N 22.36E
Taltal Chile **124** 25.24S 70.29W
Talvik Norway **40** 70.05N 22.52E
Talwood Australia **93** 28.29S149.25E
Talyawalka *r.* Australia **92** 31.49S143.25E
Tama *r.* Japan **57** 35.32N139.47E
Tamala Australia **88** 26.42S113.47E
Tamale Ghana **76** 9.26N 0.49W
Tamanar Morocco **74** 31.00N 9.35W
Tamanrasset Algeria **75** 22.47N 5.31E
Tamanrasset, Oued *wadi* Algeria **74** 21.24N 1.00E
Tamanthi Burma **56** 25.19N 95.18E
Tamaqua U.S.A. **115** 40.48N 75.58W
Tamar *r.* U.K. **13** 50.28N 4.13W
Tamarite de Litera Spain **25** 41.52N 0.26E
Tamási Hungary **31** 46.38N 18.18E
Tamaské Niger **77** 14.55N 5.55E
Tamaulipas *d.* Mexico **111** 24.30N 98.50W
Tamazunchale Mexico **116** 21.16N 98.47W
Tambacounda Senegal **76** 13.45N 13.40W
Tambara Mozambique **79** 16.42S 34.17E
Tambar Springs *town* Australia **93** 31.20S149.50E
Tambellup Australia **89** 34.03S117.36E
Tambo Australia **90** 24.53S146.15E
Tambo *r.* Australia **93** 37.51S147.48E
Tambohorano Madagascar **81** 17.30S 43.58E
Tambor Mexico **109** 25.08N105.27W
Tambov Russian Fed. **44** 52.44N 41.28E
Tambre *r.* Spain **26** 42.49N 8.53W
Tambura Sudan **73** 5.36N 27.28E
Tamchaket Mauritania **74** 17.25N 10.40W
Tâmega *r.* Portugal **26** 41.05N 8.21W
Tamil Nadu *d.* India **61** 11.15N 79.00E
Ţāmiyah Egypt **66** 29.29N 30.58E
Tamkuhi India **63** 26.41N 84.11E
Tam Ky Vietnam **56** 15.34N108.29E
Tammisaari Finland **41** 59.58N 23.26E
Ţammūn Jordan **67** 32.17N 35.23E
Tämnaren *l.* Sweden **43** 60.10N 17.20E
Tampa U.S.A. **113** 27.58N 82.38W
Tampa B. U.S.A. **113** 27.45N 82.35W
Tampere Finland **41** 61.30N 23.45E
Tampico Mexico **116** 22.18N 97.52W
Tamra Hazafon Israel **67** 32.38N 35.24E
Tamra Hazafon Israel **67** 32.51N 35.12E
Tamri Morocco **74** 30.43N 9.43W
Tamsagbulag Mongolia **53** 47.10N117.21E
Tamworth Australia **93** 31.07S150.57E
Tamworth Canada **105** 44.29N 77.00W
Tamworth U.K. **13** 52.38N 1.42W
Tana *r.* Kenya **79** 2.32S 40.32E
Tana Norway **40** 70.26N 28.14E
Tana *r.* Norway **40** 69.45N 28.15E
Tana *i.* Vanuatu **84** 19.30S169.20E
Tanacross U.S.A. **98** 63.12N143.30W
Tanafjorden Norway **40** 70.54N 28.40E
T'ana Hāyk' *l.* Ethiopia **73** 12.00N 37.20E
Tanahgrogot Indonesia **58** 1.55S116.12E
Tanahmerah Indonesia **59** 6.08S140.18E
Tanakpur India **63** 29.05N 80.07E
Tanami Desert Australia **88** 19.50S130.50E
Tanana U.S.A. **98** 65.11N152.10W
Tanana *r.* U.S.A. **98** 65.09N151.55W
Tananarive *see* Antananarivo Madagascar **81**
Tanaro *r.* Italy **30** 45.01N 8.47E
Tanch 'On N. Korea **57** 40.27N128.54E
Tānda India **63** 26.33N 82.39E
Tanda Ivory Coast **76** 7.48N 3.10W
Tandaltī Sudan **73** 13.01N 31.50E
Tăndărei Romania **37** 44.38N 27.40E
Tandil Argentina **125** 37.18S 59.10W
Tandjilé *d.* Chad **77** 9.45N 16.28E
Tando Ādam Pakistan **62** 25.46N 68.40E
Tando Allāhyār Pakistan **62** 25.28N 68.43E
Tando Bāgo Pakistan **62** 24.47N 68.58E
Tando Muhammad Khan Pakistan **62** 25.08N 68.32E
Tandou L. Australia **92** 32.38S142.05E
Tandula Tank *resr.* India **63** 20.40N 81.12E
Tanega shima *i.* Japan **57** 30.32N131.00E
Taneytown U.S.A. **114** 39.40N 77.10W
Tanezrouft *des.* Algeria **74** 22.25N 0.30E
Tanga Tanzania **79** 5.07S 39.05E
Tanga *d.* Tanzania **79** 5.20S 38.30E
Tangalla Sri Lanka **61** 6.02N 80.47E
Tanganyika, L. Africa **79** 6.00S 29.30E
Tanger Morocco **74** 35.48N 5.45W
Tangerhütte Germany **38** 52.26N 11.48E
Tangermünde Germany **38** 52.32N 11.58E
Tanggo China **63** 31.37N 93.18E
Tanggu China **54** 39.01N117.43E
Tanggula Shan *mts.* China **63** 33.00N 90.00E
Tanggula Shankou *pass* China **63** 32.45N 92.24E
Tanggulashanqu China **63** 34.10N 92.23E
Tanghe China **54** 32.41N112.49E
Tāngi India **63** 19.57N 85.30E
Tangi Pakistan **62** 34.18N 71.40E
Tangier *see* Tanger Morocco **74**
Tangmarg Jammu & Kashmir **62** 34.02N 74.26E
Tangra Yumco *l.* China **63** 31.00N 86.15E
Tangshan China **54** 39.32N118.08E
Tangtse Jammu & Kashmir **63** 34.02N 78.11E
Tanguiéta Benin **77** 10.37N 1.18E
Tanimbar, Kepulauan *is.* Indonesia **59** 7.50S131.30E
Taninges France **21** 46.07N 6.36E
Tanintharyi *see* Tenasserim Burma **56**
Tanishpa *mtn.* Pakistan **62** 31.10N 68.24E
Tanjay Phil. **59** 9.31N123.10E
Tanjona Ankaboa *c.* Madagascar **81** 21.57S 43.16E
Tanjona Bobaomby *c.* Madagascar **81** 11.57S 49.17E
Tanjona Masoala *c.* Madagascar **81** 15.59S 50.13E
Tanjona Vilanandro *c.* Madagascar **81** 16.11S 44.27E
Tanjona Vohimena *c.* Madagascar **81** 25.36S 45.08E
Tanjung Indonesia **58** 2.10S115.25E
Tanjungbalai Indonesia **58** 2.59N 99.46E
Tanjungkarang Indonesia **58** 5.28S105.16E
Tanjungpandan Indonesia **58** 2.44S107.36E
Tanjungredeb Indonesia **58** 2.09N117.29E
Tānk Pakistan **62** 32.13N 70.23E
Tankapirtti Finland **40** 68.16N 27.20E
Tännäs Sweden **41** 62.27N 12.40E
Tannersville U.S.A. **115** 42.12N 74.08W
Tannin Canada **102** 49.40N 91.00W
Tannis Bugt *b.* Denmark **42** 57.40N 10.15E
Tannu Ola *mts.* Russian Fed. **51** 51.00N 93.30E
Tannūrah, Ra's *c.* Saudi Arabia **71** 26.39N 50.10E
Tano *r.* Ghana **76** 5.07N 2.54W
Tanout Niger **77** 14.55N 8.49E
Ţanţā Egypt **66** 30.48N 31.00E
Tanumshede Sweden **42** 58.44N 11.19E
Tanzania Africa **79** 5.00S 35.00E
Tao'an China **54** 45.20N122.48E
Taole China **54** 38.50N106.40E
Taormina Italy **33** 37.52N 15.17E
Taoudenni Mali **76** 22.45N 4.00W
Tapachula Mexico **116** 14.54N 92.15W
Tapajós *r.* Brazil **123** 2.25S 54.40W
Tapaktuan Indonesia **58** 3.30N 97.10E
Tapalquén Argentina **125** 36.20S 60.02W
Tapanahoni *r.* Surinam **123** 4.20N 54.25W
Tapanlieh Taiwan **55** 21.58N120.47E
Tapanui New Zealand **86** 45.57S169.16E
Tapauá *r.* Brazil **122** 5.40S 64.20W
Tapeta Liberia **76** 6.25N 8.47W
Tapirapecó, Serra *mts.* Venezuela / Brazil **122** 1.00N 64.30W
Tāplejung Nepal **63** 27.21N 87.40E
Tapolca Hungary **31** 46.53N 17.27E
Tāpti *r.* India **62** 21.05N 72.40E
Tapurucuara Brazil **122** 0.24S 65.02W
Taquari *r.* Brazil **126** 19.00S 57.27W
Taquaritinga Brazil **126** 21.23S 48.33W
Tar *r.* U.S.A. **113** 35.33N 77.05W
Tara Canada **104** 44.28N 81.09W
Tara Russian Fed. **9** 56.55N 74.24E
Tara *r.* Russian Fed. **50** 56.30N 74.40E
Tara *r.* Yugo. **31** 43.21N 18.51E
Taraba *d.* Nigeria **77** 8.15N 11.00E
Tarabine, Oued Ti-n- *wadi* Algeria **75** 21.16N 7.24E
Tarabuco Bolivia **124** 19.10S 64.57W
Ţarābulus Lebanon **66** 34.27N 35.50E
Ţarābulus *d.* Libya **75** 32.40N 13.15E
Ţarābulus *f.* Libya **75** 31.00N 13.30E
Ţarābulus *town* Libya **75** 32.58N 13.12E
Tarago Australia **93** 35.05S149.10E
Tarakan Indonesia **58** 3.20N117.38E
Taranaki *d.* New Zealand **86** 39.00S174.30E
Tarancón Spain **27** 40.01N 3.01W
Taranto Italy **33** 40.28N 17.15E
Taranto, Golfo di *g.* Italy **33** 40.00N 17.10E
Tarapacá Colombia **122** 2.52S 69.44W
Tarapoto Peru **122** 6.31S 76.23W
Tarare France **21** 45.54N 4.26E
Tarascon Ariège France **20** 42.51N 1.36E
Tarascon Vaucluse France **21** 43.48N 4.40E
Tarashcha Ukraine **37** 49.35N 30.20E
Tarasovo Russian Fed. **44** 66.14N 46.43E
Tarauacá Brazil **122** 8.10S 70.46W
Tarauacá *r.* Brazil **122** 6.42S 69.48W
Taravao, Isthme de Tahiti **85** 17.43S149.19W
Taravo *r.* France **21** 41.42N 8.49E
Tarawa *i.* Kiribati **84** 1.25N173.00E
Tarawera New Zealand **86** 39.02S176.36E
Tarazona Spain **25** 41.54N 1.44W
Tarazona de la Mancha Spain **25** 39.15N 1.55W
Tarbagatay, Khrebet *mts.* Kazakhstan **52** 47.00N 83.00E
Tarbat Ness *c.* U.K. **14** 57.52N 3.46W
Tarbert Rep. of Ire. **15** 52.34N 9.24W
Tarbert Strath. U.K. **14** 55.51N 5.25W
Tarbert W. Isles U.K. **14** 57.54N 6.49W
Tarbes France **20** 43.14N 0.05E
Tarcento Italy **30** 46.13N 13.13E
Tarcoola S.A. Australia **92** 30.41S134.33E
Tarcoon Australia **93** 30.19S146.43E
Tarcutta Australia **93** 35.17S147.45E
Tardajos Spain **26** 42.21N 3.49W
Taree Australia **93** 31.54S152.26E
Tarella Australia **92** 30.55S143.06E
Tärendö Sweden **40** 67.10N 22.38E
Tarentum U.S.A. **114** 40.36N 79.45W
Ţarfā, Wādī aţ *r.* Egypt **66** 28.36N 30.50E
Tarfaya Morocco **74** 27.58N 12.55W
Targon France **20** 44.44N 0.16W
Tarhjicht Morocco **74** 29.05N 9.24W
Tarifa Spain **27** 36.01N 5.36W
Tarifa, Punta de *c.* Spain **27** 36.00N 5.37W
Tarija Bolivia **124** 21.31S 64.45W
Tarija *d.* Bolivia **124** 21.40S 64.20W
Tarīm Yemen **71** 16.03N 49.00E
Tarim He *r.* China **52** 41.00N 83.30E
Tarīn Kowt Afghan. **62** 32.52N 65.38E
Taritatu *r.* Indonesia **59** 2.54S138.27E
Tarka La *mtn.* Bhutan **63** 27.05N 89.40E
Tarkwa Ghana **76** 5.16N 1.59W
Tarlac Phil. **59** 15.29N120.35E
Tarm Denmark **42** 55.55N 8.32E
Tarma Peru **122** 11.28S 75.41W
Tarn *d.* France **20** 43.50N 2.00E
Tarn *r.* France **20** 44.05N 1.06E
Tärnaby Sweden **40** 65.43N 15.16E
Tarnak *r.* Afghan. **62** 31.26N 65.31E
Tarn-et-Garonne *d.* France **20** 44.05N 1.20E
Tarnica *mtn.* Poland **37** 49.05N 22.44E
Tarnobrzeg Poland **37** 50.35N 21.41E
Tarnów Poland **37** 50.01N 20.59E
Tärnsjö Sweden **43** 60.09N 16.56E
Taro *r.* Italy **30** 45.00N 10.15E
Taroom Australia **90** 25.39S149.49E
Tarouca Portugal **26** 41.00N 7.40W
Taroudannt Morocco **74** 30.31N 8.55W
Tarpon Springs *town* U.S.A. **113** 28.08N 82.45W
Tarquinia Italy **30** 42.15N 11.45E
Tarqūmiyah Jordan **67** 31.35N 35.01E
Tarragona Spain **25** 41.07N 1.15E
Tarragona *d.* Spain **25** 41.10N 0.40E
Tarran Hills Australia **93** 32.27S146.27E
Tarrasa Spain **25** 41.34N 2.01E
Tárrega Spain **25** 41.39N 1.09E
Tarrytown U.S.A. **115** 41.05N 73.52W
Tarso Ahon *mtn.* Chad **77** 20.23N 18.18E
Tarso Ouri *mtn.* Chad **77** 21.25N 18.56E
Tarsus Turkey **64** 36.52N 34.52E
Tartagal Argentina **124** 22.32S 63.50W
Tartas France **20** 43.50N 0.48W
Tartu Estonia **44** 58.20N 26.44E
Ţarţūs Syria **66** 34.55N 35.52E
Tarutino Ukraine **37** 46.09N 29.04E
Tarutung Indonesia **58** 2.01N 98.54E
Tarvisio Italy **31** 46.30N 13.35E
Tashan China **54** 40.51N120.56E
Tashauz Uzbekistan **9** 41.49N 59.58E
Tashi Gang Dzong Bhutan **63** 27.19N 91.34E
Tashkent Kyrgyzstan **9** 41.16N 69.13E
Tasiilaq *see* Ammassalik Greenland **99**
Tasikmalaya Indonesia **59** 7.20S108.16E
Tasīl Syria **67** 32.50N 35.58E
Tåsinge *i.* Denmark **42** 55.00N 10.36E
Tåsjön Sweden **40** 64.15N 15.47E
Tasman B. New Zealand **86** 41.00S173.15E
Tasmania *d.* Australia **91** 42.00S147.00E
Tasman Mts. New Zealand **86** 41.00S172.40E
Tasman Pen. Australia **91** 43.08S147.51E
Tasman Sea Pacific Oc. **84** 38.00S162.00E
Tassili-n-Ajjer *f.* Algeria **75** 26.05N 7.00E
Tassili oua-n-Ahaggar *f.* Algeria **75** 20.30N 5.00E
Tataa, Pt. Tahiti **85** 17.33S149.36W
Tatabánya Hungary **37** 47.34N 18.26E
Tatarsk Russian Fed. **50** 55.14N 76.00E
Tatarskiy Proliv *g.* Russian Fed. **51** 47.40N141.00E
Tateyama Japan **57** 34.59N139.52E
Tathlina L. Canada **100** 60.32N117.32W
Tathra Australia **93** 36.44S149.58E
Tatinnai L. Canada **101** 60.55N 97.40W
Tatnam, C. Canada **101** 57.16N 91.00W
Tatong Australia **93** 36.46S146.03E
Tatta Pakistan **62** 24.45N 67.55E
Tatvan Turkey **64** 38.31N 42.15E
Tau Norway **42** 59.04N 5.54E
Tau *i.* Samoa **84** 14.15S169.30W
Taubaté Brazil **126** 23.00S 45.36W
Tauber *r.* Germany **39** 49.46N 9.31E
Tauberbischofsheim Germany **39** 49.37N 9.40E
Taulihawa Nepal **63** 27.32N 83.05E
Taumarunui New Zealand **86** 38.53S175.16E
Taumaturgo Brazil **122** 8.57S 72.48W
Taung R.S.A. **80** 27.32S 24.46E
Taungdwingyi Burma **56** 20.00N 95.30E
Taung-gyi Burma **56** 20.49N 97.01E
Taungup Burma **56** 18.51N 94.14E
Taunoa Tahiti **85** 17.45S149.21W
Taunsa Pakistan **62** 30.42N 70.39E
Taunton U.K. **13** 51.01N 3.07W
Taunton U.S.A. **115** 41.54N 71.06W
Taunus *mts.* Germany **36** 50.07N 7.48E
Taupo New Zealand **86** 38.42S176.06E
Taupo, L. New Zealand **86** 38.45S175.30E
Taurage Lithuania **41** 55.15N 22.17E
Tauranga New Zealand **86** 37.42S176.11E
Taureau, Résr. Canada **105** 46.46N 73.50W
Taurianova Italy **33** 38.21N 16.01E
Taurus Mts. *see* Toros Dağlari *mts.* Turkey **64**
Tauste Spain **25** 41.55N 1.15W
Tautira Tahiti **85** 17.45S149.10W
Tavani Canada **101** 62.10N 93.30W
Tavda Russian Fed. **50** 58.04N 65.12E
Tavda *r.* Russian Fed. **50** 57.40N 67.00E
Taveta Kenya **79** 3.23S 37.42E
Taveuni *i.* Fiji **84** 16.56S179.58W
Tavira Portugal **27** 37.07N 7.39W
Tavistock Canada **104** 43.19N 80.50W
Tavistock U.K. **13** 50.33N 4.09W
Tavor, Har *mtn.* Israel **67** 32.41N 35.23E
Távora *r.* Portugal **26** 41.08N 7.35W
Tavoy Burma **56** 14.02N 98.12E
Tavropoú, Tekhnití Límni *l.* Greece **35** 39.20N 21.45E
Taw *r.* U.K. **13** 51.05N 4.05W
Tawas City U.S.A. **104** 44.16N 83.31W
Tawau Malaysia **58** 4.16N117.54E
Tawitawi *i.* Phil. **59** 5.10N120.05E
Ţawkar Sudan **72** 18.26N 37.44E
Tawu Taiwan **55** 22.22N120.54E
Tāwurghā', Sabkhat *f.* Libya **22** 31.10N 15.15E
Tay *r.* U.K. **14** 56.21N 3.18W
Tay, L. Australia **89** 33.00S120.52E
Tay, Loch U.K. **14** 56.32N 4.08W
Tayabamba Peru **122** 8.15S 77.15W
Tayan Indonesia **58** 0.02S110.05E
Tayeegle Somali Rep. **71** 4.02N 44.36E
Taylor Tex. U.S.A. **111** 30.34N 97.25W
Taylor, Mt. U.S.A. **109** 35.14N107.37W
Taylors Island *town* U.S.A. **115** 38.28N 76.18W
Taymā' Saudi Arabia **64** 27.37N 38.30E
Taymyr, Ozero *l.* Russian Fed. **51** 74.20N101.00E
Taymyr, Poluostrov *pen.* Russian Fed. **51** 75.30N 99.00E
Tay Ninh Vietnam **56** 11.21N106.02E
Tayport U.K. **14** 56.27N 2.53W
Tayshet Russian Fed. **51** 55.56N 98.01E
Tayside *d.* U.K. **14** 56.35N 3.28W
Taytay Phil. **58** 10.47N119.32E
Taz *r.* Russian Fed. **50** 67.30N 78.50E
Taza Morocco **74** 34.16N 4.01W
Tazawa ko *l.* Japan **57** 39.43N140.40E
Tazenakht Morocco **74** 30.35N 7.12W
Tazin L. Canada **101** 59.40N109.00W
Tāzirbū Libya **72** 25.45N 21.00E
Tazovskiy Russian Fed. **50** 67.28N 78.43E
Tbilisi Georgia **65** 41.43N 44.48E
Tchad, Lac *see* Chad, L. Africa **77**
Tchamba Togo **77** 9.05N 1.27E
Tchibanga Gabon **78** 2.52S 11.07E
Tchien Liberia **76** 6.00N 8.10W
Tchigaï, Plateau du *f.* Niger / Chad **77** 21.30N 14.50E
Tcholliré Cameroon **77** 8.25N 14.10E
Tczew Poland **37** 54.06N 18.47E
Te Anau New Zealand **86** 45.25S167.43E
Te Anau, L. New Zealand **86** 45.10S167.15E
Teaneck U.S.A. **115** 40.53N 74.01W
Teano Italy **33** 41.15N 14.04E
Teapa Mexico **116** 17.33N 92.57W
Te Araroa New Zealand **86** 37.38S178.25E
Teba Spain **27** 36.58N 4.56W
Tébessa Algeria **75** 35.22N 8.08E
Tebingtinggi Sumatera Utara Indonesia **58** 3.20N 99.08E
Tebingtinggi Sumatera Selatan Indonesia **58** 3.37S103.09E
Tébourba Tunisia **32** 36.49N 9.51E
Teboursouk, Monts de *mts.* Tunisia **32** 36.45N 9.20E
Tebulos Mta *mtn.* Georgia **45** 42.34N 45.17E
Tech *r.* France **20** 42.36N 3.03E
Techiman Ghana **76** 7.36N 1.55W
Tecuci Romania **37** 45.49N 27.27E
Tecumseh U.S.A. **104** 42.00N 83.57W
Tedesa Ethiopia **73** 5.07N 37.45E
Tees *r.* U.K. **12** 54.35N 1.11W
Tefé Brazil **122** 3.24S 64.45W
Tefé *r.* Brazil **122** 3.35S 64.47W
Tegal Indonesia **59** 6.52S109.07E
Tegelen Neth. **16** 51.20N 6.08E
Tegernsee Germany **39** 47.43N 11.45E
Tegina Nigeria **77** 10.06N 6.11E
Tego Australia **93** 28.48S146.47E
Tegouma *well* Niger **77** 15.33N 9.19E
Tegucigalpa Honduras **117** 14.05N 87.14W
Teguidda I-n-Tessoum Niger **77** 17.21N 6.32E
Tehamiyam Sudan **72** 18.20N 36.32E
Tehata Bangla. **63** 23.43N 88.32E
Téhini Ivory Coast **76** 9.39N 3.32W
Tehkummah Canada **104** 45.39N 81.59W
Tehrān Iran **65** 35.40N 51.26E
Tehri India **63** 30.23N 78.29E
Tehuacán Mexico **116** 18.30N 97.26W
Tehuantepec Mexico **116** 16.21N 95.13W
Tehuantepec, Golfo de *g.* Mexico **116** 16.00N 95.00W
Tehuantepec, Istmo de *f.* Mexico **116** 17.00N 94.30W
Teifi *r.* U.K. **13** 52.05N 4.41W
Teignmouth U.K. **13** 50.33N 3.30W
Teixeiras Brazil **126** 20.37S 42.52W
Tejakula Indonesia **59** 8.09S115.19E
Tejo *r.* Portugal **27** 38.40N 9.24W
Te Kaha New Zealand **86** 37.44S177.52E
Tekamah U.S.A. **110** 41.47N 96.13W

Tekapo, L. to **Tinahely**

Tekapo, L. New Zealand **86** 43.35S170.30E
Tekax Mexico **117** 20.12N 89.17W
Teke Burnu *c.* Turkey **34** 40.02N 26.10E
Tekezē *r.* Ethiopia *see* Satīt *r.* Sudan **72**
Tekirdag Turkey **29** 40.59N 27.30E
Tekkali India **63** 18.37N 84.14E
Tekouiat, Oued *wadi* Algeria **75** 22.20N 2.30E
Tekro *well* Chad **72** 19.30N 20.58E
Te Kuiti New Zealand **86** 38.20S175.10E
Tel *r.* India **63** 20.50N 83.54E
Tela Honduras **117** 15.56N 87.25W
Tel 'Adashim Israel **67** 32.39N 35.18E
Tel Arshaf *site* Israel **67** 32.12N 34.48E
Tel Ashqelon *site* Israel **67** 31.39N 34.32E
Telavåg Norway **42** 60.16N 4.49E
Telavi Georgia **65** 41.56N 45.30E
Tel Aviv *d.* Israel **67** 32.05N 34.48E
Tel Aviv-Yafo Israel **67** 32.05N 34.46E
Tele *r.* Zaïre **78** 2.48N 24.00E
Telegraph Creek *town* Canada **100** 57.55N131.10W
Telemark *d.* Norway **42** 59.40N 8.45E
Teleneshty Moldavia **37** 47.35N 28.17E
Teles Pires *r.* Brazil **123** 7.20S 57.30W
Telfer Australia **88** 21.42S122.13E
Telford U.K. **13** 52.42N 2.30W
Telfs Austria **39** 47.18N 11.04E
Telgte Germany **38** 51.59N 7.47E
Tel Hazor *site* Israel **67** 33.01N 35.34E
Télimélé Guinea **76** 10.54N 13.02W
Tel Lakhish *site* Israel **67** 31.34N 34.51E
Tell Atlas *mts.* Algeria **75** 36.00N 1.00E
Tell City U.S.A. **113** 37.56N 86.46W
Teller U.S.A. **98** 65.16N166.22N
Tel Mediggo *site* Israel **67** 32.35N 35.11E
Tel Mond Israel **67** 32.15N 34.56E
Telpos-Iz *mtn.* Russian Fed. **44** 63.56N 59.02E
Telsen Argentina **125** 42.25S 67.00W
Telšiai Lithuania **41** 55.59N 22.15E
Telti Italy **32** 40.52N 9.21E
Teltow Germany **38** 52.23N 13.16E
Telukbetung Indonesia **58** 5.28S105.16E
Teluk Intan Malaysia **58** 4.00N101.00E
Tema Ghana **76** 5.41N 0.01W
Temagami, L. Canada **104** 47.00N 80.05W
Te Manga *mtn.* Rarotonga Cook Is. **84** 21.13S159.45W
Temaverachi, Sierra *mts.* Mexico **109** 29.30N109.30W
Tembleque Spain **27** 39.42N 3.30W
Tembo Aluma Angola **78** 7.42S 17.15E
Teme *r.* U.K. **13** 52.10N 2.13W
Temerin Yugo. **31** 45.24N 19.53E
Temir Kazakhstan **45** 49.09N 57.06E
Temirtau Kazakhstan **9** 50.05N 72.55E
Témiscaming Canada **104** 46.43N 79.06W
Temora Australia **93** 34.27S147.35E
Tempe U.S.A. **109** 33.25N111.56W
Tempino Indonesia **58** 1.55S103.23E
Tempio Italy **32** 40.54N 9.07E
Temple U.S.A. **111** 31.06N 97.21W
Temple B. Australia **90** 12.10S143.04E
Templemore Rep. of Ire. **15** 52.48N 7.51W
Templin Germany **38** 53.07N 13.30E
Temuco Chile **125** 38.44S 72.36W
Tenabo Mexico **116** 20.03N 90.14W
Tenaha U.S.A. **111** 31.57N 94.15W
Tenasserim Burma **56** 12.05N 99.00E
Tenasserim *d.* Burma **56** 13.00N 99.00E
Tenby U.K. **13** 51.40N 4.42W
Tenby Bay *town* Canada **104** 46.06N 83.56W
Tendaho Ethiopia **73** 11.48N 40.52E
Tende France **21** 44.05N 7.36E
Tende, Col de *pass* France / Italy **30** 44.09N 7.34E
Ten Degree Channel Indian Oc. **56** 10.00N 93.00E
Tendrara Morocco **74** 33.04N 1.59W
Tenenkou Mali **76** 14.25N 4.58W
Tenerife *i.* Canary Is. **74** 28.10N 16.30W
Ténès Algeria **75** 36.31N 1.18E
Teng *r.* Burma **56** 19.50N 97.40E
Tengchong China **61** 25.02N 98.28E
Tengger Shamo *des.* China **54** 39.00N104.10E
Tengiz, Ozero *l.* Kazakhstan **9** 50.30N 69.00E
Teng Xian China **54** 35.08N117.20E
Tenke Zaïre **78** 10.34S 26.07E
Tenkodogo Burkina **76** 11.47N 0.19W
Tenna *r.* Italy **31** 43.14N 13.47E
Tennant Creek *town* Australia **90** 19.31S134.15E
Tennessee *d.* U.S.A. **113** 35.50N 85.30W
Tennessee *r.* U.S.A. **113** 37.04N 88.33W
Tenosique Mexico **116** 17.29N 91.26W
Tenryū Japan **57** 34.52N137.49E
Tenryū *r.* Japan **57** 34.39N137.47E
Tensift, Oued *r.* Morocco **74** 32.02N 9.22W
Tenterfield Australia **93** 29.01S152.04E
Teófilo Otoni Brazil **126** 17.52S 41.31W
Tepa Indonesia **59** 7.52S129.31E
Tepa Pt. Niue **84** 19.07S169.56W
Tepelenë Albania **34** 40.18N 20.01E
Tepic Mexico **116** 21.30N104.51W
Teplice Czech Republic **38** 50.39N 13.48E
Ter *r.* Spain **25** 42.01N 3.12E
Téra Niger **76** 14.01N 0.45E
Tera *r.* Portugal **27** 38.55N 8.04W
Tera *r.* Spain **26** 41.54N 5.44W
Teramo Italy **31** 42.39N 13.42E
Terang Australia **92** 38.13S142.56E
Tercan Turkey **64** 39.47N 40.23E
Terebovlya Ukraine **37** 49.18N 25.44E
Terekhova Belorussia **37** 52.13N 31.28E
Teresina Brazil **123** 5.09S 42.46W
Teresópolis Brazil **126** 22.26S 42.59W
Terevaka *mtn.* I. de Pascua **85** 27.05S109.23W
Tergnier France **19** 49.39N 3.18E
Terhazza Mali **76** 23.45N 4.59W
Termez Uzbekistan **50** 37.15N 67.15E
Termination I. Australia **89** 34.25S121.53E
Termini Italy **28** 37.59N 13.42E
Termini Imerese Italy **32** 37.59N 13.42E
Termini Imerese, Golfo di *g.* Italy **32** 38.05N 13.50E
Términos, Laguna de *b.* Mexico **116** 18.30N 91.30W
Termoli Italy **33** 41.58N 14.59E
Ternate Indonesia **59** 0.48N127.23E
Terneuzen Neth. **16** 51.20N 3.50E
Terni Italy **30** 42.34N 12.37E
Ternopol Ukraine **37** 49.35N 25.39E
Terra Alta U.S.A. **114** 39.25N 79.35W
Terra Bella U.S.A. **109** 35.58N119.03W
Terrace Canada **100** 54.31N128.35W
Terracina Italy **32** 41.17N 13.15E
Terralba Italy **32** 39.43N 8.38E
Terrassa *see* Tarrasa Spain **25**
Terrasson-la-Villedieu France **20** 45.08N 1.18E
Terre Adélie *f.* Antarctica **128** 80.00S140.00E
Terrebonne Canada **105** 45.42N 73.38W
Terre Haute U.S.A. **112** 39.27N 87.24W
Terrenceville Canada **103** 47.42N 54.43W
Terry U.S.A. **108** 46.47N105.19W
Terschelling *i.* Neth. **16** 53.25N 5.25E
Teruel Spain **25** 40.21N 1.06W
Teruel *d.* Spain **25** 40.40N 1.00W
Tervola Finland **40** 66.05N 24.48E
Tešanj Bosnia-Herzegovina **31** 44.37N 18.00E
Tesaret, Oued *wadi* Algeria **75** 25.32N 2.52E
Teshio Japan **57** 44.53N141.44E
Teshio *r.* Japan **57** 44.53N141.44E
Teslić Bosnia-Herzegovina **31** 44.37N 17.51E
Teslin Canada **100** 60.10N132.43W
Teslin *r.* Canada **100** 61.34N134.54W
Teslin L. Canada **100** 60.15N132.57W
Tessalit Mali **76** 20.12N 1.00E
Tessaoua Niger **77** 13.46N 7.55E
Tessy-sur-Vire France **18** 48.58N 1.04W
Test *r.* U.K. **13** 50.55N 1.29W
Testa, Capo *c.* Italy **32** 41.14N 9.09E
Têt *r.* France **20** 42.44N 3.02E
Tetachuck L. Canada **100** 53.18N125.55W
Tete Mozambique **81** 16.10S 33.30E
Tete *d.* Mozambique **79** 15.30S 33.00E
Teterev *r.* Ukraine **37** 51.03N 30.30E
Teterow Germany **38** 53.46N 12.34E
Teteven Bulgaria **34** 42.58N 24.17E
Tethul *r.* Canada **100** 60.35N112.12W
Tetiaora *i.* Îs. de la Société **85** 17.05S149.32W
Tetica de Bacares *mtn.* Spain **27** 37.16N 2.26W
Tetiyev Ukraine **37** 49.22N 29.40E
Tétouan Morocco **74** 35.34N 5.23W
Tetovo Macedonia **34** 42.01N 21.02E
Tetuan *see* Tétouan Morocco **74**
Tetyukhe Pristan Russian Fed. **57** 44.31N135.31E
Teulada Italy **32** 38.58N 8.46E
Teulada, Capo *c.* Italy **32** 38.52N 8.39E
Teun *i.* Indonesia **59** 6.59S129.08E
Teutoburger Wald Germany **38** 52.10N 8.15E
Teuva Finland **40** 62.29N 21.44E
Tevere *r.* Italy **30** 41.44N 12.14E
Teverya Israel **67** 32.48N 35.32E
Teviot *r.* U.K. **14** 55.36N 2.27W
Teviotdale *f.* U.K. **12** 55.26N 2.46W
Teviothead U.K. **14** 55.20N 2.56W
Tewkesbury U.K. **13** 51.59N 2.09W
Tewksburg U.S.A. **115** 42.37N 71.14W
Texarkana Ark. U.S.A. **111** 33.26N 94.02W
Texarkana Tex. U.S.A. **111** 33.26N 94.03W
Texarkana, L. U.S.A. **111** 33.16N 94.14W
Texas Australia **93** 28.50S151.09E
Texas *d.* U.S.A. **111** 31.30N100.00W
Texas *town* U.S.A. **115** 43.30N 76.16W
Texas City U.S.A. **111** 29.23N 94.54W
Texel *i.* Neth. **16** 53.05N 4.47E
Texoma, L. U.S.A. **111** 33.55N 96.37W
Texon U.S.A. **111** 31.13N101.43W
Teyea *site* Greece **35** 37.29N 22.24E
Teyvareh Afghan. **62** 33.21N 64.25E
Tezpur India **63** 26.38N 92.48E
Tha-anne *r.* Canada **101** 60.31N 94.37W
Thabana Ntlenyana *mtn.* Lesotho **80** 29.28S 29.17E
Thabazimbi R.S.A. **80** 24.36S 27.23E
Thādiq Saudi Arabia **65** 25.18N 45.52E
Thai Binh Vietnam **55** 20.30N106.26E
Thailand Asia **56** 17.00N101.30E
Thailand, G. of Asia **56** 11.00N101.00E
Thai Nguyen Vietnam **55** 21.46N105.52E
Thak Pakistan **62** 30.32N 70.13E
Thal Pakistan **62** 33.22N 70.33E
Thal Desert Pakistan **62** 31.30N 71.40E
Thale Luang *l.* Thailand **56** 7.40N100.20E
Thallon Australia **93** 28.39S148.49E
Thalwil Switz. **39** 47.17N 8.34E
Thamarīt Oman **60** 17.39N 54.02E
Thames *r.* Canada **104** 42.19N 82.28W
Thames New Zealand **86** 37.08S175.35E
Thames *r.* U.K. **13** 51.30N 0.05E
Thamesford Canada **104** 43.04N 81.00W
Thamesville Canada **104** 42.33N 81.59W
Thāna India **62** 19.12N 72.58E
Thāna Pakistan **62** 28.55N 63.45E
Thanh Hóa Vietnam **55** 19.47N105.49E
Thanjāvūr India **61** 10.46N 79.09E
Thann France **19** 47.49N 7.05E
Thāno Bula Khān Pakistan **62** 25.22N 67.50E
Tharād India **62** 24.24N 71.38E
Thar Desert Pakistan / India **62** 28.00N 72.00E
Thargomindah Australia **91** 27.59S143.45E
Tharrawaddy Burma **56** 17.37N 95.48E
Tharthār, Wādī ath *r.* Iraq **64** 34.18N 43.07E
Thásos Greece **34** 40.47N 24.42E
Thásos *i.* Greece **34** 40.41N 24.47E
Thatcher U.S.A. **109** 32.51N109.56W
Thaton Burma **56** 16.50N 97.21E
Thau, Bassin de *b.* France **20** 43.23N 3.36E
Thaungdut Burma **56** 24.26N 94.45E
Thayer U.S.A. **111** 36.31N 91.33W
Thayetmyo Burma **56** 19.20N 95.10E
Thazi Burma **56** 20.51N 96.05E
Theano Pt. Canada **104** 47.11N 84.43W
Thebes *ruins* Egypt **64** 25.41N 32.40E
The Bight *town* Bahamas **117** 24.19N 75.24W
The Cherokees, L. O' U.S.A. **111** 36.45N 94.50W
The Cheviot *mtn.* U.K. **12** 55.29N 2.10W
The Cheviot Hills U.K. **12** 55.22N 2.24W
The Coorong *g.* Australia **92** 36.00S139.30E
The Dalles *town* U.S.A. **108** 45.36N121.10W
Thedford Canada **104** 43.09N 81.51W
Thedford U.S.A. **110** 41.59N100.35W
The Everglades *f.* U.S.A. **113** 26.00N 80.40W
The Fens *f.* U.K. **13** 55.10N 4.13W
The Gulf Asia **65** 27.00N 50.00E
The Hague *see* 's Gravenhage Neth. **16**
Thekulthili L. Canada **101** 61.03N110.00W
The Little Minch *str.* U.K. **14** 57.40N 6.45W
Thelon *r.* Canada **99** 64.23N 96.15W
The Machers *f.* U.K. **14** 54.45N 4.28W
The Minch *str.* U.K. **14** 58.10N 5.50W
The Needles *c.* U.K. **13** 50.39N 1.35W
Thénezay France **18** 46.43N 0.02W
Theodore Australia **90** 24.57S150.05E
Theodore Roosevelt L. U.S.A. **109** 33.30N110.57W
Theog India **62** 31.07N 77.21E
Theólogos Greece **34** 40.39N 24.41E
The Pas Canada **101** 53.50N101.15W
The Pennines *hills* U.K. **12** 55.40N 2.20W
Thérain *r.* France **19** 49.15N 2.27E
Theresa U.S.A. **105** 44.13N 75.48W
The Rhinns *f.* U.K. **14** 54.50N 5.02W
Thermaïkós Kólpos *g.* Greece **34** 40.23N 22.47E
Thermopolis U.S.A. **108** 43.39N108.13W
Thermopylae Pass Greece **35** 38.48N 22.33E
The Rock *town* Australia **93** 35.16S147.07E
The Salt L. Australia **92** 30.05S142.10E
The Snares *is.* New Zealand **84** 48.00S166.30E
The Solent *str.* U.K. **13** 50.45N 1.20W
The Sound *str.* Denmark / Sweden **43** 55.30N 12.40E
Thesprotikón Greece **35** 39.15N 20.47E
Thessalía *f.* Greece **34** 39.30N 22.00E
Thessalon Canada **104** 46.15N 83.34W
Thessaloníki Greece **34** 40.38N 22.56E
Thetford U.K. **13** 52.25N 0.44E
Thetford Mines *town* Canada **105** 46.05N 71.18W
The Twins *town* Australia **92** 30.00S135.16E
The Wash *b.* U.K. **12** 52.55N 0.15E
The Weald *f.* U.K. **13** 51.05N 0.20E
Thibodaux U.S.A. **111** 29.48N 90.49W
Thicket Portage Canada **101** 55.19N 97.42W
Thief River Falls *town* U.S.A. **110** 48.07N 96.10W
Thiene Italy **30** 45.42N 11.29E
Thiers France **20** 45.51N 3.34E
Thiès Senegal **76** 14.50N 16.55W
Thiesi Italy **32** 40.31N 8.43E
Thika Kenya **79** 1.04S 37.04E
Thimbu Bhutan **63** 27.28N 89.39E
Thingvallavatn *l.* Iceland **40** 64.10N 21.10W
Thionville France **19** 49.22N 6.10E
Thíra *i.* Greece **35** 36.24N 25.29E
Thíra *town* Greece **35** 36.24N 25.27E
Thirsk U.K. **12** 54.15N 1.20W
Thiruvananthapuram India **60** 8.41N 76.57E
Thisted Denmark **42** 56.57N 8.42E
Thistilfjördhur *b.* Iceland **40** 66.11N 15.20W
Thistle I. Australia **92** 35.00S136.09E
Thívai Greece **35** 38.21N 23.19E
Thiviers France **20** 45.25N 0.56E
Thjórsá *r.* Iceland **40** 63.53N 20.38W
Thoa *r.* Canada **101** 60.31N109.47W
Thoen Thailand **56** 17.41N 99.14E
Tholen *i.* Neth. **16** 51.34N 4.07E
Thomas U.S.A. **114** 39.09N 79.30W
Thomaston U.S.A. **113** 32.55N 84.20W
Thomasville Ala. U.S.A. **111** 31.55N 87.51W
Thomasville Fla. U.S.A. **113** 30.50N 83.59W
Thompson Canada **101** 55.45N 97.52W
Thompson Utah U.S.A. **108** 38.58N109.43W
Thompson Landing Canada **101** 62.56N110.40W
Thompsonville U.S.A. **112** 44.32N 85.57W
Thomson *r.* Australia **90** 25.11S142.53E
Thonburi Thailand **56** 13.43N100.27E
Thonon-les-Bains France **21** 46.22N 6.29E
Thórisvatn *l.* Iceland **40** 64.15N 18.50W
Thornbury Canada **104** 44.34N 80.26W
Thornton U.S.A. **114** 39.22N 79.56W
Thorshavn Faroe Is. **10** 62.02N 6.47W
Thorshöfn Iceland **40** 66.12N 15.17W
Thouars France **18** 46.59N 0.13W
Thousand Is. Canada **105** 44.15N 76.12W
Thowa *r.* Kenya **73** 1.33S 40.03E
Thrace *f.* Greece **34** 41.10N 25.30E
Thrakikón Pélagos *f.* Greece **34** 40.15N 24.28E
Thrapston U.K. **13** 52.24N 0.32W
Three Forks U.S.A. **108** 45.54N111.33W
Three Hills *town* Canada **100** 51.43N113.15W
Three Kings Is. New Zealand **84** 34.09S172.09E
Three Rivers *town* Australia **88** 25.07S119.09E
Three Rivers *town* U.S.A. **111** 28.28N 98.11W
Three Sisters Mt. U.S.A. **108** 44.10N121.46W
Thueyts France **21** 44.41N 4.13E
Thuin Belgium **16** 50.21N 4.20E
Thul Pakistan **62** 28.14N 68.46E
Thule Greenland **99** 77.30N 69.29W
Thun Switz. **39** 46.45N 7.37E
Thunder B. U.S.A. **104** 44.58N 83.24W
Thunder Bay *town* Canada **102** 48.25N 89.14W
Thunder Bay *r.* U.S.A. **104** 45.04N 83.25W
Thunder Hills Canada **101** 54.30N106.00W
Thunersee *l.* Switz. **39** 46.40N 7.45E
Thung Song Thailand **56** 8.10N 99.41E
Thunkar Bhutan **63** 27.55N 91.00E
Thurgau *d.* Switz. **39** 47.30N 9.10E
Thüringen *d.* Germany **38** 50.50N 10.35E
Thüringen *f.* Germany **38** 50.57N 11.30E
Thüringer Wald *mts.* Germany **38** 50.40N 10.52E
Thurles Rep. of Ire. **15** 52.41N 7.50W
Thurloo Downs *town* Australia **92** 29.18S143.30E
Thurmont U.S.A. **114** 39.37N 77.25W
Thursday I. Australia **84** 10.35S142.13E
Thursday Island *town* Australia **90** 10.34S142.14E
Thurso U.K. **14** 58.35N 3.32W
Thurso *r.* U.K. **10** 58.35N 3.32W
Thury-Harcourt France **18** 48.59N 0.29W
Thusis Switz. **39** 46.42N 9.26E
Thy *f.* Denmark **42** 57.00N 8.30E
Thyborön Denmark **42** 56.42N 8.13E
Thysville Zaïre **78** 5.15S 14.52E
Tiandong China **55** 23.36N107.08E
Tian'e China **55** 25.00N107.10E
Tian Head Canada **100** 53.47N133.06W
Tianjin China **54** 39.07N117.08E
Tianjin *d.* China **54** 39.30N117.20E
Tianjun China **52** 37.16N 98.52E
Tianlin China **55** 24.18N106.13E
Tianmen China **55** 30.40N113.25E
Tian Shan *mts.* Asia **52** 42.00N 80.30E
Tianshui China **54** 34.25N105.58E
Tiantai China **55** 29.09N121.02E
Tianyang China **55** 23.45N106.54E
Tiarei Tahiti **85** 17.32S149.20W
Tiaret Algeria **75** 35.28N 1.21E
Tiavea W. Samoa **84** 13.57S171.28W
Tibasti, Sarīr *des.* Libya **75** 24.00N 17.00E
Tibati Cameroon **77** 6.25N 12.33E
Tiber *r.* *see* Tevere *r.* Italy **30**
Tiberias *see* Teverya Israel **67**
Tiberias, L. *see* Yam Kinneret *l.* Israel **67**
Tibesti *mts.* Chad **77** 21.00N 17.30E
Tibet *d.* *see* Xizang *d.* China **63**
Tibetan Plateau *see* Qing Zang Gaoyuan *f.* China **52**
Tibooburra Australia **92** 29.28S142.04E
Tibro Sweden **43** 58.26N 14.10E
Tiburón, Isla Mexico **109** 29.00N112.20W
Tichborne Canada **105** 44.40N 76.41W
Tīchīt Mauritania **74** 18.28N 9.30W
Tichla W. Sahara **74** 21.35N 14.58W
Ticino *r.* Italy **30** 45.09N 9.14E
Ticino *d.* Switz. **39** 46.20N 8.45E
Ticonderoga U.S.A. **105** 43.51N 73.26W
Tidaholm Sweden **43** 58.11N 13.57E
Tidikelt *f.* Algeria **75** 27.00N 1.30E
Tidioute U.S.A. **114** 41.41N 79.24W
Tidirhine, Jbel *mtn.* Morocco **74** 34.50N 4.30W
Tidjikdja Mauritania **74** 18.29N 11.31W
Tiel Neth. **16** 51.53N 5.26E
Tieling China **54** 42.13N123.48E
Tielt Belgium **16** 51.00N 3.20E
Tienen Belgium **16** 50.49N 4.56E
Tiénigbé Ivory Coast **76** 8.11N 5.43W
Tientsin *see* Tianjin China **54**
Tierga Spain **25** 41.37N 1.36W
Tierp Sweden **41** 60.20N 17.30E
Tierra Amarilla U.S.A. **108** 36.42N106.33W
Tierra Blanca Mexico **116** 18.28N 96.12W
Tierra del Fuego *d.* Argentina **125** 54.30S 67.00W
Tierra del Fuego *i.* Argentina / Chile **125** 54.00S 69.00W
Tietar *r.* Spain **27** 39.50N 6.01W
Tietê Brazil **126** 23.04S 47.41W
Tifrah Israel **67** 31.20N 34.40E
Tifton U.S.A. **113** 31.27N 83.31W
Tiger U.S.A. **108** 48.42N117.24W
Tiger Hills Canada **101** 49.25N 99.30W
Tigil Russian Fed. **51** 57.49N158.40E
Tiglit Morocco **74** 28.31N 10.15W
Tignère Cameroon **77** 7.23N 12.37E
Tignish Canada **103** 46.57N 64.02W
Tigray *d.* Ethiopia **72** 14.10N 39.35E
Tigre *r.* Venezuela **122** 9.20N 62.30W
Tigris *r.* *see* Dijlah *r.* Asia **65**
Tih, Jabal at *f.* Egypt **66** 28.50N 34.00E
Tihāmah *f.* Saudi Arabia **72** 19.00N 41.00E
Tijesno Croatia **31** 43.48N 15.39E
Tijuana Mexico **109** 32.32N117.01W
Tikamgarh India **63** 24.44N 78.50E
Tikaré Burkina **76** 13.16N 1.44W
Tikhoretsk Russian Fed. **45** 45.52N 40.07E
Tikhvin Russian Fed. **44** 59.35N 33.29E
Tikitiki New Zealand **86** 37.47S178.25E
Tiksha Russian Fed. **44** 64.04N 32.35E
Tiksi Russian Fed. **51** 71.40N128.45E
Tilburg Neth. **16** 51.34N 5.05E
Tilbury Canada **104** 42.16N 82.26W
Tilbury U.K. **13** 51.28N 0.23E
Tilemsi, Vallée du *f.* Mali **76** 16.15N 0.02E
Tilghman U.S.A. **115** 38.42N 76.20W
Tilhar India **63** 27.59N 79.44E
Till *r.* Northum. U.K. **12** 55.41N 2.12W
Tillabéri Niger **77** 14.28N 1.27E
Tillamook U.S.A. **108** 45.27N123.51W
Tillsonburg Canada **104** 42.51N 80.44W
Tílos *i.* Greece **35** 36.25N 27.25E
Tilpa Australia **92** 30.57S144.24E
Tilton U.S.A. **115** 43.27N 71.35W
Timagami Canada **104** 47.05N 79.50W
Timanskiy Kryazh *mts.* Russian Fed. **44** 66.00N 49.00E
Timaru New Zealand **86** 44.23S171.41E
Timashevsk Russian Fed. **45** 45.38N 38.56E
Timbákion Greece **35** 35.04N 24.45E
Timbédra Mauritania **74** 16.17N 8.16W
Timber Creek *town* Australia **88** 15.38S130.28E
Timboon Australia **92** 38.32S143.02E
Timbuktu *see* Tombouctou Mali **76**
Timfi Óros *mtn.* Greece **34** 39.59N 20.45E
Timimoun Algeria **74** 29.15N 0.15E
Timimoun, Sebkha de *f.* Algeria **74** 29.10N 0.05E
Timiris, Cap *c.* Mauritania **76** 19.23N 16.32W
Timiş *r.* Yugo. / Romania **37** 44.49N 20.28E
Timiskaming, L. Canada **104** 47.35N 79.35W
Timişoara Romania **37** 45.47N 21.15E
Timmernabben Sweden **43** 56.58N 16.26E
Timmins Canada **102** 48.28N 81.25W
Timok *r.* Yugo. **34** 44.10N 22.40E
Timor *i.* Indonesia **88** 9.30S125.00E
Timor Sea Austa. **88** 11.00S127.00E
Timor Timur *d.* Indonesia **59** 9.00S125.00E
Timpahute Range *mts.* U.S.A. **108** 37.38N115.34W
Tinahely Rep. of Ire. **15** 52.48N 6.19W

Tindouf to **Trayning**

Tindouf Algeria **74** 27.42N 8.09W
Tindouf, Sebkha de *f.* Algeria **74** 27.45N 7.30W
Tineo Spain **26** 43.20N 6.25W
Tingha Australia **93** 29.58S151.16E
Tinglev Denmark **42** 54.56N 9.15E
Tingo María Peru **122** 9.09S 75.56W
Tingping China **55** 26.10N110.17E
Tingréla Ivory Coast **76** 10.26N 6.20W
Tingri China **63** 28.30N 86.34E
Tingsryd Sweden **43** 56.32N 14.59E
Tingstäde Sweden **43** 57.44N 18.36E
Tinguipaya Bolivia **124** 19.11S 65.51W
Tinkisso *r.* Guinea **76** 11.25N 9.05W
Tinnenburra Australia **93** 28.40S145.30E
Tinnoset Norway **42** 59.43N 9.02E
Tínos *i.* Greece **35** 37.38N 25.10E
Tínos *town* Greece **35** 37.32N 25.10E
Tinsukia India **61** 27.30N 95.22E
Tintinara Australia **92** 35.52S140.04E
Tinto *r.* Spain **27** 37.10N 6.54W
T'ī'o Ethiopia **72** 14.40N 40.15E
Tioga U.S.A. **114** 41.55N 77.08W
Tioman, Pulau *i.* Malaysia **58** 2.45N104.10E
Tionaga Canada **102** 48.05N 82.00W
Tione di Trento Italy **30** 46.02N 10.43E
Tionesta U.S.A. **114** 41.30N 79.27W
Tionesta Creek *r.* U.S.A. **114** 41.28N 79.22W
Tioughnioga *r.* U.S.A. **115** 42.14N 75.51W
Tipperary Rep. of Ire. **15** 52.29N 8.10W
Tipperary *d.* Rep. of Ire. **15** 52.37N 7.55W
Tīrān, Jazīrat Saudi Arabia **66** 27.56N 34.34E
Tiranë Albania **34** 41.20N 19.50E
Tiranë Durrës *d.* Albania **34** 41.19N 19.26E
Tirano Italy **30** 46.13N 10.11E
Tiraspol Moldavia **37** 46.50N 29.38E
Tirat Karmel Israel **67** 32.46N 34.58E
Tirat Yehuda Israel **67** 32.01N 34.57E
Tirat Zevi Israel **67** 32.25N 35.32E
Tirebolu Turkey **64** 41.02N 38.49E
Tiree *i.* U.K. **14** 56.30N 6.50W
Tîrgovişte Romania **37** 44.56N 25.27E
Tîrgu-Jiu Romania **37** 45.03N 23.17E
Tîrgu-Lăpuş Romania **37** 47.27N 23.52E
Tîrgu Mureş Romania **37** 46.33N 24.34E
Tîrgu-Neamţ Romania **37** 47.12N 26.22E
Tîrgu-Ocna Romania **37** 46.15N 26.37E
Tîrgu-Secuiesc Romania **37** 46.00N 26.08E
Tirins *site* Greece **35** 37.36N 22.48E
Tiris Zemmour *d.* Mauritania **74** 24.00N 9.00W
Tírnavos Greece **34** 39.45N 22.17E
Tirodi India **63** 21.41N 79.42E
Tirol *d.* Austria **39** 47.10N 11.00E
Tirón *r.* Spain **26** 41.23N 4.31W
Tir Pol Afghan. **65** 34.38N 61.19E
Tirschenreuth Germany **39** 49.53N 12.21E
Tirso *r.* Italy **32** 39.52N 8.33E
Tiruchchirāppalli India **61** 10.50N 78.43E
Tirunelveli India **60** 8.45N 77.43E
Tirupati India **61** 13.39N 79.25E
Tiruppur India **60** 11.05N 77.20E
Tisa *r.* Yugo. **31** 45.09N 20.16E
Tis'ah Egypt **66** 30.02N 32.35E
Tisdale Canada **101** 52.51N104.04W
Tisnaren *l.* Sweden **43** 58.57N 15.57E
Tisza *r.* Hungary *see* **Tisa** *r.* Yugo. **31**
Tit Algeria **75** 22.58N 5.11E
Titicaca, L. Bolivia / Peru **124** 16.00S 69.00W
Titikaveka Rarotonga Cook Is. **84** 21.16S159.45W
Titiwa Nigeria **77** 12.14N 12.53E
Titlagarh India **63** 20.18N 83.09E
Titova Korenica Croatia **31** 44.45N 15.43E
Titov Veles Macedonia **34** 41.46N 21.47E
Titov Vrh *mtn.* Macedonia **34** 42.00N 20.51E
Titran Norway **40** 63.42N 8.22E
Ti Tree Australia **90** 22.06S133.17E
Tittabawassee *r.* U.S.A. **104** 43.23N 83.59W
Tittmoning Germany **39** 48.04N 12.46E
Titule Zaïre **78** 3.17N 25.32E
Titusville Fla. U.S.A. **113** 28.37N 80.50W
Titusville Penn. U.S.A. **114** 41.38N 79.41W
Tiuni India **63** 30.57N 77.51E
Tivaouane Senegal **76** 14.57N 16.49W
Tiveden *hills* Sweden **43** 58.45N 14.40E
Tiverton U.K. **13** 50.54N 3.30W
Tiverton U.S.A. **115** 41.38N 71.12W
Tivoli Italy **32** 41.58N 12.48E
Tizimín Mexico **117** 21.10N 88.09W
Tizi Ouzou Algeria **75** 36.44N 4.05E
Tiznit Morocco **74** 29.43N 9.44W
Tjeuke Meer *l.* Neth. **16** 52.55N 5.51E
Tjöme *i.* Norway **42** 59.07N 10.24E
Tjörn *i.* Sweden **42** 58.00N 11.38E
Tlaxcala *d.* Mexico **116** 19.45N 98.20W
Tlemcen Algeria **74** 34.52N 1.19W
Tmassah Libya **75** 26.22N 15.48E
Tni Haïa *well* Algeria **74** 24.15N 2.45W
Toab U.K. **14** 59.53N 1.16W
Toamasina Madagascar **81** 18.10S 49.23E
Toano Italy **30** 44.23N 10.34E
Toanoano Tahiti **85** 17.52S149.12W
Toba Japan **57** 34.29N136.51E
Toba, Danau *l.* Indonesia **58** 2.45N 98.50E
Toba Kākar Range *mts.* Pakistan **62** 31.15N 68.00E
Tobar U.S.A. **108** 40.53N114.54W
Tobarra Spain **25** 38.35N 1.41W
Toba Tek Singh Pakistan **62** 30.58N 72.29E
Tobelo Indonesia **59** 1.45N127.59E
Tobermory Canada **104** 45.15N 81.39W
Tobermory U.K. **14** 56.37N 6.04W
Tobi *i.* Pacific Oc. **59** 3.01N131.10E
Tobin L. Canada **101** 53.40N103.35W
Tobi shima *i.* Japan **57** 39.12N139.32E
Toboali Indonesia **58** 3.00S106.30E
Tobol *r.* Russian Fed. **9** 58.15N 68.12E
Tobolsk Russian Fed. **9** 58.15N 68.12E
Tobruk *see* **Ţubruq** Libya **72**
Tobseda Russian Fed. **44** 68.34N 52.16E
Tocantinópolis Brazil **123** 6.20S 47.25W
Tocantins *d.* Brazil **123** 10.15S 48.30W
Tocantins *r.* Brazil **123** 1.50S 49.15W
Toccoa U.S.A. **113** 34.34N 83.21W
Töcksfors Sweden **42** 59.30N 11.50E
Tocopilla Chile **124** 22.05S 70.12W
Tocorpuri *mtn.* Bolivia / Chile **124** 22.26S 67.53W
Tocumwal Australia **93** 35.51S145.34E
Tocuyo *r.* Venezuela **122** 11.03N 68.23W
Todenyang Kenya **79** 4.34N 35.52E
Todi Italy **30** 42.47N 12.24E
Todos Santos Mexico **109** 23.27N110.13W
Todtnau Germany **39** 47.50N 7.56E
Tofte Norway **42** 59.33N 10.34E
Tofua *i.* Tonga **85** 19.45S175.05W
Togian, Kepulauan *is.* Indonesia **59** 0.20S122.00E
Togo Africa **76** 8.00N 1.00E
Tōhuku *d.* Japan **57** 35.00N137.00E
Toi Niue **84** 18.58S169.52W
Toijala Finland **41** 61.10N 23.52E
Toili Indonesia **59** 1.25S122.23E
Tojg Afghan. **62** 32.04N 61.48E
Tokaj Hungary **37** 48.08N 21.27E
Tokala *mtn.* Indonesia **59** 1.36S121.41E
Tokara kaikyō *str.* Japan **57** 30.10N130.10E
Tokat Turkey **64** 40.20N 36.35E
Tokelau Is. Pacific Oc. **84** 9.00S171.45W
Toki Japan **57** 35.21N137.11E
Toki *r.* Japan **57** 35.12N136.52E
Tokmak Kyrgyzstan **52** 42.49N 75.15E
Tokoname Japan **57** 34.53N136.51E
Tokoroa New Zealand **86** 38.13S175.53E
Tokuno shima *i.* Japan **53** 27.40N129.00E
Tokushima Japan **57** 34.03N134.34E
Tokuyama Japan **57** 34.04N131.48E
Tōkyō Japan **57** 35.42N139.46E
Tōkyō-wan *b.* Japan **57** 35.25N139.45E
Tolaga Bay *town* New Zealand **86** 38.22S178.18E
Toledo Spain **27** 39.52N 4.01W
Toledo *d.* Spain **27** 39.45N 4.10W
Toledo U.S.A. **112** 41.40N 83.35W
Toledo, Montes de *mts.* Spain **27** 39.33N 4.20W
Toledo Bend Resr. U.S.A. **111** 31.46N 93.25W
Tolentino Italy **30** 43.12N 13.17E
Toliara Madagascar **81** 23.21S 43.40E
Tolland U.S.A. **115** 41.52N 72.22W
Tollarp Sweden **43** 55.56N 13.59E
Tollense *r.* Germany **38** 53.54N 13.02E
Tolmezzo Italy **30** 46.24N 13.01E
Tolmin Slovenia **31** 46.11N 13.44E
Tolna Hungary **31** 46.26N 18.46E
Tolna *d.* Hungary **31** 46.35N 18.30E
Tolo, Teluk *g.* Indonesia **59** 2.00S122.30E
Tolosa Spain **26** 43.08N 2.04W
Tolstyy-Les Ukraine **37** 51.24N 29.48E
Tolti Jammu & Kashmir **62** 35.02N 76.06E
Toluca Mexico **116** 19.20N 99.40W
Toluca *mtn.* Mexico **116** 19.10N 99.40W
Tol'yatti Russian Fed. **44** 53.32N 49.24E
Tomah U.S.A. **110** 43.59N 90.30W
Tomakomai Japan **57** 42.39N141.33E
Tomar Portugal **27** 39.36N 8.25W
Tomás Gomensoro Uruguay **125** 30.26S 57.26W
Tomaszów Lubelski Poland **37** 50.28N 23.25E
Tomaszów Mazowiecki Poland **37** 51.32N 20.01E
Tombe Sudan **73** 5.49N 31.41E
Tombigbee *r.* U.S.A. **111** 31.04N 87.58W
Tombos Brazil **126** 20.53S 42.03W
Tombouctou Mali **76** 16.49N 2.59W
Tombouctou *d.* Mali **76** 19.35N 3.20W
Tombua Angola **78** 15.55S 11.51E
Tomé Chile **125** 36.37S 72.57W
Tomelilla Sweden **43** 55.33N 13.57E
Tomelloso Spain **27** 39.10N 3.01W
Tomiko Canada **104** 46.32N 79.49W
Tomingley Australia **93** 32.06S148.15E
Tomini Indonesia **59** 0.31N120.30E
Tomini, Teluk *g.* Indonesia **59** 0.30S120.45E
Tominian Mali **76** 13.17N 4.35W
Tomintoul U.K. **14** 57.15N 3.24W
Tomislavgrad Bosnia-Herzegovina **31** 43.43N 17.14E
Tomkinson Ranges *mts.* Australia **88** 26.11S129.05E
Tom Price Australia **88** 22.49S117.51E
Tomra China **63** 30.52N 87.30E
Tomra Norway **40** 62.34N 6.55E
Tomsk Russian Fed. **50** 56.30N 85.05E
Toms River *town* U.S.A. **115** 39.57N 74.07W
Tomtabacken *hill* Sweden **43** 57.30N 14.28E
Tonalá Mexico **116** 16.08N 93.41W
Tonalea U.S.A. **109** 36.20N110.58W
Tonasket U.S.A. **108** 48.42N119.26W
Tonawanda U.S.A. **114** 43.01N 78.53W
Tonbridge U.K. **13** 51.12N 0.16E
Tondano Indonesia **59** 1.19N124.56E
Tönder Denmark **42** 54.56N 8.54E
Tondibi Mali **76** 16.39N 0.14W
Tondoro Namibia **80** 17.45S 18.50E
Tone *r.* Japan **57** 35.44N140.51E
Tonga Pacific Oc. **85** 20.00S175.00W
Tonga Sudan **73** 9.28N 31.03E
Tongaat R.S.A. **80** 29.34S 31.07E
Tong'an China **55** 24.44N118.09E
Tongatapu *i.* Tonga **85** 21.10S175.10W
Tongatapu Group *is.* Tonga **85** 21.10S175.10W
Tonga Trench *f.* Pacific Oc. **84** 20.00S173.00W
Tongchuan China **54** 35.05N109.10E
Tongeren Belgium **16** 50.47N 5.28E
Tongguan Hunan China **55** 28.27N112.48E
Tongguan Shaanxi China **54** 34.32N110.26E
Tonghai China **61** 24.07N102.45E
Tonghua China **53** 41.40N126.52E
Tongking, G. of China / Vietnam **56** 20.00N108.00E
Tongliao China **54** 43.40N122.20E
Tongling China **55** 30.55N117.42E
Tonglu China **55** 29.49N119.40E
Tongnae S. Korea **57** 35.12N129.05E
Tongo Australia **92** 30.30S143.47E
Tongoa *i.* Vanuatu **84** 16.54S168.34E
Tongobory Madagascar **81** 23.32S 44.20E
Tongoy Chile **124** 30.15S 71.30W
Tongren China **55** 27.41N109.08E
Tongsa Dzong Bhutan **63** 27.31N 90.30E
Tongtianheyan China **63** 33.50N 92.19E
Tongue U.K. **14** 58.28N 4.25W
Tongue *r.* U.S.A. **108** 46.24N105.25W
Tongwei China **54** 35.18N105.10E
Tong Xian China **54** 39.52N116.45E
Tongxin China **54** 36.59N105.50E
Tongyu China **54** 44.48N123.06E
Tongzi China **55** 28.08N106.49E
Tonj Sudan **73** 7.17N 28.45E
Tonk India **62** 26.10N 75.47E
Tonkābon Iran **65** 36.49N 50.54E
Tônlé Sap *l.* Cambodia **56** 12.50N104.15E
Tonnay-Boutonne France **20** 45.58N 0.42W
Tonneins France **20** 44.23N 0.19E
Tonnerre France **19** 47.51N 3.58E
Tönning Germany **38** 54.19N 8.56E
Tonopah U.S.A. **108** 38.04N117.14W
Tonota Botswana **80** 21.28S 27.24E
Tons *r.* India **63** 25.17N 82.04E
Tönsberg Norway **42** 59.17N 10.25E
Tonstad Norway **42** 58.40N 6.43E
Tonto Basin *town* U.S.A. **109** 33.55N111.18W
Toobeah Australia **93** 28.22S149.50E
Toodyay Australia **89** 31.35S116.26E
Tooele U.S.A. **108** 40.32N112.18W
Toolondo Australia **92** 36.55S142.00E
Toowoomba Australia **91** 27.35S151.54E
Topeka U.S.A. **110** 39.03N 95.41W
Topko *mtn.* Russian Fed. **51** 57.20N138.10E
Topley Canada **100** 54.32N126.05W
Toplica *r.* Yugo. **34** 43.15N 21.30E
Topliţa Romania **37** 46.55N 25.21E
Topock U.S.A. **109** 34.44N114.27W
Topolovgrad Bulgaria **34** 42.05N 26.20E
Topozero, Ozero *l.* Russian Fed. **44** 65.45N 32.00E
Toppenish U.S.A. **108** 46.23N120.19W
Tor Ethiopia **73** 7.53N 33.40E
Tora-Khem Russian Fed. **51** 52.31N 96.13E
Torbat-e Ḩeydarīyeh Iran **65** 35.16N 59.13E
Torbat-e Jām Iran **65** 35.15N 60.37E
Tördal Norway **42** 59.16N 8.49E
Tordera *r.* Spain **25** 41.39N 2.47E
Tordesillas Spain **26** 41.30N 5.00W
Tordino Italy **31** 42.44N 13.59E
Töre Sweden **40** 65.54N 22.39E
Töreboda Sweden **43** 58.43N 14.08E
Torekov Sweden **43** 56.26N 12.37E
Toreno Spain **26** 42.42N 6.30W
Torgau Germany **38** 51.34N 13.00E
Torhamn Sweden **43** 56.05N 15.50E
Torhout Belgium **16** 51.04N 3.06E
Toride Japan **57** 35.53N140.04E
Torino Italy **30** 45.03N 7.40E
Torio *r.* Spain **26** 42.35N 5.34W
Torit Sudan **73** 4.24N 32.34E
Tormes *r.* Spain **26** 41.18N 6.29W
Torne *r.* Sweden *see* **Tornio** *r.* Finland **40**
Torneträsk Sweden **40** 68.15N 19.30E
Torneträsk *l.* Sweden **40** 68.20N 19.10E
Tornio Finland **40** 65.52N 24.10E
Tornio *r.* Finland **40** 65.53N 24.07E
Tornquist Argentina **125** 38.06S 62.14W
Toro Spain **26** 41.31N 5.24W
Toronaíos Kólpos *g.* Greece **34** 40.05N 23.30E
Toronto Canada **104** 43.39N 79.23W
Toropets Russian Fed. **44** 56.30N 31.40E
Tororo Uganda **79** 0.42N 34.13E
Toros Dağlari *mts.* Turkey **64** 37.15N 34.15E
Torquay Australia **92** 38.20S144.20E
Torquay U.K. **13** 50.27N 3.31W
Torquemada Spain **26** 42.02N 4.19W
Torrance U.S.A. **109** 33.50N118.19W
Torrão Portugal **27** 38.18N 8.13W
Torre Annunziata Italy **33** 40.45N 14.27E
Torre Baja Spain **25** 40.07N 1.15W
Torreblanca Spain **25** 40.13N 0.12E
Torrecilla *mtn.* Spain **27** 36.41N 4.59W
Torrecilla en Cameros Spain **26** 42.16N 2.37W
Torre del Campo Spain **27** 37.46N 3.53W
Torre de Moncorvo Portugal **26** 41.10N 7.03W
Torredonjimeno Spain **27** 37.46N 3.57W
Torrejón, Embalse de *resr.* Spain **27** 39.50N 5.50W
Torrejoncillo Spain **27** 39.54N 6.28W
Torrejón de Ardoz Spain **26** 40.27N 3.29W
Torrelaguna Spain **26** 40.50N 3.32W
Torrelavega Spain **26** 43.21N 4.03W
Torremaggiore Italy **33** 41.41N 15.17E
Torremolinos Spain **27** 36.37N 4.30W
Torrens, L. Australia **92** 31.00S137.50E
Torrens Creek *r.* Australia **90** 22.22S145.09E
Torrens Creek *town* Australia **90** 20.50S145.00E
Torrente Spain **25** 39.26N 0.28W
Torreón Mexico **111** 25.33N103.26W
Torre Pellice Italy **30** 44.49N 7.13E
Torreperogil Spain **26** 38.02N 3.17W
Torres Novas Portugal **27** 39.29N 8.32W
Torres Str. Australia **90** 10.00S142.20E
Torres Vedras Portugal **27** 39.06N 9.16W
Torrevieja Spain **25** 37.59N 0.41W
Torrey U.S.A. **108** 38.18N111.25W
Torridge *r.* U.K. **13** 51.01N 4.12W
Torridon U.K. **14** 57.23N 5.31W
Torridon, Loch U.K. **14** 57.35N 5.45W
Torriglia Italy **30** 44.31N 9.10E
Torrijos Spain **27** 39.59N 4.17W
Torrington Conn. U.S.A. **115** 41.48N 73.08W
Torrington Wyo. U.S.A. **108** 42.04N104.11W
Torrox Spain **27** 36.46N 3.58W
Torsås Sweden **43** 56.24N 16.00E
Torsby Sweden **43** 60.08N 13.00E
Torsö *i.* Sweden **43** 58.48N 13.50E
Tortola *i.* B.V.Is. **117** 18.28N 64.40W
Tortoli Italy **32** 39.55N 9.39E
Tortona Italy **30** 44.54N 8.52E
Tortorici Italy **33** 38.02N 14.39E
Tortosa Spain **25** 40.48N 0.31E
Tortosa, Cabo de *c.* Spain **25** 40.43N 0.55E
Tortue, Île de la *i.* Cuba **117** 20.05N 72.57W
Toruń Poland **37** 53.01N 18.35E
Torup Sweden **43** 56.58N 13.05E
Tory Hill *town* Canada **104** 44.58N 78.18W
Tory I. Rep. of Ire. **15** 55.16N 8.13W
Tory Sd. Rep. of Ire. **15** 55.14N 8.15W
Torzhok Russian Fed. **44** 57.02N 34.51E
Tosas, Puerto de *pass* Spain **25** 42.19N 2.01E
Tosa wan *b.* Japan **57** 33.10N133.40E
Toscana *d.* Italy **30** 43.35N 11.00E
Tosen Norway **40** 65.16N 12.50E
Toshkent *see* **Tashkent** Kyrgyzstan **9**
Tosno Russian Fed. **44** 59.38N 30.46E
Tostado Argentina **124** 29.15S 61.45W
Totak *l.* Norway **42** 59.42N 7.57E
Totana Spain **25** 37.46N 1.30W
Tôtes France **18** 49.41N 1.03E
Totma Russian Fed. **44** 59.59N 42.44E
Totora Bolivia **124** 17.42S 65.09W
Tottenham Australia **93** 32.14S147.24E
Tottenham Canada **104** 44.01N 79.49W
Tottori Japan **57** 35.32N134.12E
Touba Ivory Coast **76** 8.22N 7.42W
Toubkal *mtn.* Morocco **74** 31.03N 7.57W
Toucy France **19** 47.44N 3.18E
Tougan Burkina **76** 13.05N 3.04W
Touggourt Algeria **75** 33.06N 6.04E
Tougué Guinea **76** 11.25N 11.50W
Toul France **19** 48.41N 5.54E
Toulnustouc *r.* Canada **103** 49.35N 68.25W
Toulon France **21** 43.07N 5.56E
Toulon-sur-Arroux France **19** 46.42N 4.08E
Toulouse France **20** 43.36N 1.26E
Toummo Niger **75** 22.45N 14.08E
Tounassine, Hamada *des.* Algeria **74** 28.36N 5.00W
Toungoo Burma **56** 18.57N 96.26E
Touques *r.* France **18** 49.22N 0.06E
Touressine *well* Mauritania **74** 24.40N 11.20W
Tourcoing France **19** 50.43N 3.09E
Tourinan, Cabo *c.* Spain **26** 43.03N 9.18W
Tournai Belgium **16** 50.36N 3.23E
Tournon France **21** 45.04N 4.50E
Tournus France **19** 46.34N 4.54E
Tours France **18** 47.23N 0.41E
Toury France **19** 48.12N 1.56E
Toustain Algeria **32** 36.40N 8.15E
Touwsrivier *town* R.S.A. **80** 33.20S 20.02E
Toužim Czech Republic **39** 50.04N 13.00E
Tovdals *r.* Norway **42** 58.13N 8.08E
Towada ko *l.* Japan **57** 40.28N140.55E
Towanda U.S.A. **115** 41.46N 76.27W
Towcester U.K. **13** 52.07N 0.56W
Tower U.S.A. **110** 47.47N 92.19W
Towner U.S.A. **110** 48.21N100.25W
Townsend, Mt. Australia **93** 36.24S148.15E
Townshend I. Australia **90** 22.15S150.30E
Townsville Australia **90** 19.13S146.48E
Towrzī Afghan. **62** 30.11N 65.59E
Towson U.S.A. **115** 39.24N 76.36W
Towyn U.K. **13** 52.37N 4.08W
Toyah U.S.A. **111** 31.19N103.47W
Toyama Japan **57** 36.42N137.14E
Toyama wan *b.* Japan **57** 36.50N137.10E
Toyo *r.* Japan **57** 34.47N137.20E
Toyohashi Japan **57** 34.46N137.23E
Toyokawa Japan **57** 34.49N137.24E
Toyota Japan **57** 35.05N137.09E
Tozeur Tunisia **75** 33.55N 8.08E
Traben-Trarbach Germany **39** 49.57N 7.06E
Trabzon Turkey **64** 41.00N 39.43E
Tracadie Canada **103** 47.31N 64.54W
Tracy Canada **105** 46.01N 73.09W
Tracy U.S.A. **110** 44.14N 95.37W
Trade Town Liberia **76** 5.43N 9.56W
Trafalgar, Cabo *c.* Spain **27** 36.11N 6.02W
Tragacete Spain **25** 40.21N 1.51W
Traid Spain **25** 40.40N 1.49W
Traiguén Chile **125** 38.15S 72.41W
Trail Canada **100** 49.05N117.40W
Trajanova Vrata *pass* Bulgaria **34** 42.18N 23.58E
Trakt Russian Fed. **44** 62.40N 51.26E
Tralee Rep. of Ire. **15** 52.16N 9.42W
Tralee B. Rep. of Ire. **15** 52.18N 9.55W
Tranås Sweden **43** 58.03N 14.59E
Tranco, Embalse del *resr.* Spain **26** 38.10N 2.45W
Trancoso Portugal **26** 40.47N 7.21W
Tranebjerg Denmark **42** 50.50N 10.36E
Trang Thailand **56** 7.35N 99.35E
Trangan *i.* Indonesia **59** 6.30S134.15E
Trangie Australia **93** 32.03S148.01E
Trani Italy **33** 41.17N 16.26E
Tranoroa Madagascar **81** 24.42S 45.04E
Tranqueras Uruguay **125** 31.12S 55.45W
Transkei Africa **80** 31.30S 29.00E
Transkei *f.* R.S.A. **80** 32.12S 28.20E
Transvaal *d.* R.S.A. **80** 24.30S 29.30E
Transylvanian Alps *see* **Carpaţii Meridionali** *mts.* Romania **29**
Trapani Italy **32** 38.01N 12.31E
Traralgon Australia **93** 38.12S146.32E
Traryd Sweden **43** 56.35N 13.45E
Trarza *d.* Mauritania **74** 18.00N 14.50W
Trarza *f.* Mauritania **74** 18.00N 15.00W
Trasacco Italy **31** 41.57N 13.32E
Trasimeno, Lago *l.* Italy **30** 43.08N 12.06E
Träslövsläge Sweden **43** 57.04N 12.16E
Trat Thailand **56** 12.14N102.33E
Traun Austria **39** 48.13N 14.14E
Traunsee *l.* Austria **39** 47.51N 13.48E
Traunstein Germany **39** 47.52N 12.38E
Trave *r.* Germany **38** 53.54N 10.50E
Travellers L. Australia **92** 33.18S142.00E
Travers, Mt. New Zealand **86** 42.05S172.45E
Traverse City U.S.A. **112** 44.46N 85.38W
Travnik Bosnia-Herzegovina **31** 44.14N 17.40E
Trayning Australia **89** 31.09S117.46E

Trbovlje to Tzaneen

Trbovlje Slovenia **31** 46.10N 15.03E
Trebbia *r.* Italy **30** 45.04N 9.41E
Trebel *r.* Germany **38** 53.55N 13.01E
Třebíč Czech Republic **36** 49.13N 15.55E
Trebinje Bosnia-Herzegovina **31** 42.43N 18.20E
Trebisacce Italy **33** 39.52N 16.32E
Trebišov Slovakia **37** 48.40N 21.47E
Třeboň Czech Republic **36** 49.01N 14.50E
Trecate Italy **30** 45.26N 8.44E
Tredegar U.K. **13** 51.47N 3.16W
Treene *r.* Germany **38** 54.22N 9.05E
Tregaron U.K. **13** 52.14N 3.56W
Tregosse Islets and Reefs Australia **90** 17.41S150.43E
Tréguier France **18** 48.47N 3.14W
Treinta-y-Tres Uruguay **126** 33.16S 54.17W
Treis Germany **39** 50.10N 7.17E
Trélazé France **18** 47.27N 0.28W
Trelew Argentina **125** 43.15S 65.20W
Trelleborg Sweden **43** 55.22N 13.10E
Trélon France **19** 50.04N 4.06E
Tremadog B. U.K. **12** 52.52N 4.14W
Tremblant, Mont *mtn.* Canada **105** 46.16N 74.35W
Tremont U.S.A. **115** 40.38N 76.23W
Tremp Spain **25** 42.10N 0.54E
Trena Ethiopia **73** 10.45N 40.38E
Trenčín Slovakia **37** 48.54N 18.04E
Trenggalek Indonesia **59** 8.01S111.38E
Trenque Lauquen Argentina **125** 35.56S 62.43W
Trent *r.* Canada **105** 44.06N 77.34W
Trent *r.* U.K. **12** 53.41N 0.41W
Trente-et un Milles, Lac des *l.* Canada **105** 46.12N 75.49W
Trentino-Alto Adige *d.* Italy **30** 46.35N 11.20E
Trento Italy **30** 46.04N 11.08E
Trenton Canada **105** 44.06N 77.35W
Trenton Mich. U.S.A. **104** 42.09N 83.11W
Trenton Mo. U.S.A. **110** 40.05N 93.37W
Trenton Nebr. U.S.A. **110** 40.11N101.01W
Trenton N.J. U.S.A. **115** 40.13N 74.45W
Trepassey Canada **99** 46.44N 53.22W
Trepuzzi Italy **33** 40.24N 18.05E
Tres Árboles Uruguay **125** 32.24S 56.43W
Tres Arroyos Argentina **125** 38.26S 60.17W
Três Corações Brazil **126** 21.44S 45.15W
Três Lagoas Brazil **126** 20.46S 51.43W
Três Marias, Reprêsa *resr.* Brazil **126** 18.15S 45.15W
Três Pontas Brazil **126** 21.23S 45.29W
Três Rios Brazil **126** 22.07S 43.12W
Treuchtlingen Germany **39** 48.57N 10.54E
Treuenbrietzen Germany **38** 52.06N 12.52E
Treviglio Italy **30** 45.31N 9.35E
Treviño Spain **26** 42.44N 2.45W
Treviso Italy **30** 45.40N 12.15E
Trévoux France **21** 45.56N 4.46E
Trgovište Yugo. **34** 42.21N 22.05E
Triánda Greece **35** 36.25N 28.10E
Triberg Germany **39** 48.08N 8.13E
Tribsees Germany **38** 54.05N 12.45E
Tribulation, C. Australia **90** 16.03S145.30E
Tribune U.S.A. **110** 38.28N101.45W
Tricarico Italy **33** 40.37N 16.09E
Tricase Italy **33** 39.56N 18.22E
Trida Australia **93** 33.00S145.01E
Trier Germany **39** 49.45N 6.38E
Trieste Italy **31** 45.40N 13.46E
Trieux *r.* France **18** 48.47N 3.07W
Triglav *mtn.* Slovenia **31** 46.23N 13.50E
Trigno *r.* Italy **33** 42.04N 14.48E
Trigueros Spain **27** 37.23N 6.50W
Tríkala Greece **34** 39.34N 21.46E
Trikhonis, Límni *l.* Greece **35** 38.34N 21.28E
Tríkomon Cyprus **66** 35.17N 33.53E
Triman Pakistan **62** 29.38N 69.05E
Trincomalee Sri Lanka **61** 8.34N 81.13E
Trinidad Bolivia **124** 14.47S 64.47W
Trinidad Colombia **122** 5.25N 71.40W
Trinidad Cuba **117** 21.48N 80.00W
Trinidad Uruguay **125** 33.32S 56.54W
Trinidad U.S.A. **108** 37.10N104.31W
Trinidad & Tobago S. America **117** 10.30N 61.20W
Trinity *r.* U.S.A. **111** 29.55N 94.45W
Trinity B. Australia **90** 16.26S145.26E
Trinity B. Canada **103** 48.00N 53.40W
Trinity Range *mts.* U.S.A. **108** 40.13N119.12W
Trinkitat Sudan **72** 18.41N 37.43E
Trino Italy **30** 45.12N 8.18E
Tripoli *see* Ţarābulus Lebanon **66**
Tripoli *see* Ţarābulus Libya **75**
Trípolis Greece **35** 37.31N 22.21E
Tripolitania *f. see* Ţarābulus *f.* Libya **75**
Tripp U.S.A. **110** 43.13N 97.58W
Tripura *d.* India **63** 23.50N 92.00E
Tristan da Cunha *i.* Atlantic Oc. **127** 37.50S 12.30W
Triste Spain **25** 42.23N 0.43W
Trivandrum *see* Thiruvananthapuram India **60**
Trivento Italy **33** 41.47N 14.33E
Trnava Slovakia **37** 48.23N 17.35E
Troarn France **18** 49.11N 0.11W
Trobriand Is. P.N.G. **90** 8.35S151.05E
Trogir Croatia **31** 43.31N 16.15E
Troglav *mtn.* Croatia **31** 43.57N 16.36E
Troia Italy **33** 41.22N 15.18E
Troina Italy **33** 37.47N 14.37E
Troisdorf Germany **38** 50.49N 7.08E
Trois-Rivières *town* Canada **105** 46.21N 72.33W
Troitsk Russian Fed. **9** 54.08N 61.33E
Troitsko-Pechorsk Russian Fed. **44** 62.40N 56.08E
Troitskoye Russian Fed. **44** 52.18N 56.26E
Troitskoye Ukraine **37** 47.38N 30.19E
Trölladyngja *mtn.* Iceland **40** 64.54N 17.16W
Trollhättan Sweden **43** 58.16N 12.18E
Trollheimen *mts.* Norway **40** 62.50N 9.15E
Tromelin *i.* Indian Oc. **49** 15.52S 54.25E
Troms *d.* Norway **40** 69.20N 19.30E
Tromsö Norway **40** 69.42N 19.00E
Trondheim Norway **40** 63.36N 10.23E
Trondheimsfjorden *est.* Norway **40** 63.40N 10.30E
Troödos *mts.* Cyprus **66** 34.57N 32.50E
Troon U.K. **14** 55.33N 4.40W
Tropea Italy **33** 38.41N 15.54E
Tropic U.S.A. **108** 37.37N112.05W
Tropoja Albania **34** 42.23N 20.10E
Trosa Sweden **43** 58.54N 17.33E
Trosh Russian Fed. **44** 66.24N 56.08E
Trostan *mtn.* U.K. **15** 55.03N 6.10W
Trostyanets Ukraine **37** 48.35N 29.10E
Trout *r.* Canada **100** 61.19N119.51W
Trout Creek *town* Canada **104** 45.59N 79.22W
Trout L. N.W.T. Canada **100** 60.35N121.10W
Trout L. Ont. Canada **102** 51.13N 93.20W
Trout River *town* Canada **103** 49.29N 58.08W
Trout Run U.S.A. **114** 41.23N 77.03W
Trouville France **18** 49.22N 0.05E
Trowbridge U.K. **13** 51.18N 2.12W
Troy *site* Turkey **34** 39.57N 26.15E
Troy Ala. U.S.A. **113** 31.49N 86.00W
Troy Mo. U.S.A. **110** 38.59N 90.59W
Troy Mont. U.S.A. **108** 48.28N115.53W
Troy N.H. U.S.A. **115** 42.50N 72.11W
Troy N.Y. U.S.A. **115** 42.43N 73.40W
Troy Ohio U.S.A. **112** 40.02N 84.12W
Troy Penn. U.S.A. **114** 41.47N 76.47W
Troyan Bulgaria **34** 42.51N 24.43E
Troyes France **19** 48.18N 4.05E
Troy Peak *mtn.* U.S.A. **108** 38.19N115.30W
Trpanj Croatia **31** 43.00N 17.17E
Trstenik Yugo. **34** 43.37N 21.00E
Truchas Peak *mtn.* U.S.A. **109** 35.58N105.39W
Truckee U.S.A. **108** 39.20N120.11W
Trujillo Honduras **117** 15.55N 86.00W
Trujillo Peru **122** 8.06S 79.00W
Trujillo Spain **27** 39.28N 5.53W
Trujillo Venezuela **122** 9.20N 70.37W
Trumansburg U.S.A. **115** 42.33N 76.40W
Trŭn Bulgaria **34** 42.51N 22.38E
Trundle Australia **93** 32.54S147.35E
Trung-Luong Vietnam **56** 13.55N109.15E
Trunmore B. Canada **103** 53.48N 57.10W
Truro Australia **92** 34.23S139.09E
Truro Canada **103** 45.22N 63.16W
Truro U.K. **13** 50.17N 5.02W
Trŭstenik Bulgaria **34** 43.31N 24.28E
Trustrup Denmark **42** 56.21N 10.47E
Truth or Consequences U.S.A. **109** 33.08N107.15W
Truyère *r.* France **20** 44.39N 2.34E
Tryavna Bulgaria **34** 42.54N 25.25E
Trysil Norway **41** 61.19N 12.16E
Trysil *r.* Norway **41** 61.03N 12.30E
Trzemeszno Poland **37** 52.35N 17.50E
Tržič Slovenia **31** 46.22N 14.19E
Tsamandás Greece **34** 39.46N 20.21E
Tsaratanana Madagascar **81** 16.47S 47.39E
Tsaratanana, Massif de *mts.* Madagascar **81** 14.00S 49.00E
Tsaritsáni Greece **34** 39.53N 22.14E
Tsau Botswana **80** 20.10S 22.29E
Tsavo Nat. Park Kenya **79** 2.45S 38.45E
Tselinograd Kazakhstan **9** 51.10N 71.28E
Tsenovo Bulgaria **34** 43.32N 25.39E
Tses Namibia **80** 25.58S 18.08E
Tsévié Togo **77** 6.28N 1.15E
Tshabong Botswana **80** 26.03S 22.25E
Tshane Botswana **80** 24.02S 21.54E
Tshela Zaïre **78** 4.57S 12.57E
Tshesebe Botswana **80** 20.45S 27.31E
Tshikapa Zaïre **78** 6.28S 20.48E
Tshofa Zaïre **78** 5.13S 25.20E
Tshopo *r.* Zaïre **78** 0.30N 25.07E
Tshuapa *r.* Zaïre **78** 0.14S 20.45E
Tsihombé Madagascar **81** 25.18S 45.29E
Tsimlyansk Russian Fed. **45** 47.40N 42.06E
Tsimlyanskoye Vodokhranilishche *resr.* Russian Fed. **45** 48.00N 43.00E
Tsinan *see* Jinan China **54**
Tsínga *mtn.* Greece **34** 41.23N 24.44E
Tsingtao *see* Qingdao China **54**
Tsiribihina Madagascar **81** 19.42S 44.31E
Tsiroanomandidy Madagascar **81** 18.46S 46.02E
Tsivilsk Russian Fed. **44** 55.50N 47.28E
Tsivory Madagascar **81** 24.04S 46.05E
Tskhinvali Georgia **45** 42.14N 43.58E
Tsna Belorussia **37** 52.10N 27.03E
Tsna *r.* Russian Fed. **44** 54.45N 41.54E
Tsobis Namibia **80** 19.27S 17.30E
Tso Morïri *l.* Jammu & Kashmir **63** 32.54N 78.20E
Tsu Japan **57** 34.43N136.31E
Tsuchiura Japan **57** 36.05N140.12E
Tsudakhar Russian Fed. **45** 42.20N 47.11E
Tsugaru kaikyō *str.* Japan **57** 41.30N140.50E
Tsumeb Namibia **80** 19.12S 17.43E
Tsuru Japan **57** 35.30N138.56E
Tsuruga Japan **57** 35.40N136.05E
Tsuruoka Japan **57** 38.44N139.50E
Tsushima Japan **57** 35.10N136.43E
Tsushima *i.* Japan **57** 34.30N129.20E
Tsuyama Japan **57** 35.04N134.01E
Tua *r.* Portugal **26** 41.13N 7.26W
Tuam Rep. of Ire. **15** 53.32N 8.52W
Tuamotu, Îles *is.* Pacific Oc. **85** 17.00S142.00W
Tuapa Niue **84** 18.59S169.54W
Tuapse Russian Fed. **45** 44.06N 39.05E
Tuatapere New Zealand **86** 46.08S167.41E
Tubac U.S.A. **109** 31.37N111.03W
Tuba City U.S.A. **109** 36.08N111.14W
Tuban Indonesia **59** 6.55S112.01E
Tubarão Brazil **126** 28.30S 49.01W
Ţūbās Jordan **67** 32.19N 35.22E
Ţubayq, Jabal aţ *mts.* Saudi Arabia **66** 29.30N 37.15E
Tubbercurry Rep. of Ire. **15** 54.03N 8.45W
Tübingen Germany **39** 48.31N 9.03E
Ţubjah, Wādī *r.* Saudi Arabia **64** 25.35N 38.22E
Ţubruq Libya **72** 32.06N 23.58E
Tubuai *i.* Pacific Oc. **85** 23.23S149.27W
Tubuai Is. Pacific Oc. **85** 23.00S150.00W
Tucacas Venezuela **122** 10.48N 68.19W
Tuchola Poland **37** 53.35N 17.50E
Tuckerton U.S.A. **115** 39.36N 74.20W
Tucson U.S.A. **109** 32.13N110.58W
Tucumán *d.* Argentina **124** 26.30S 65.20W
Tucumcari U.S.A. **109** 35.10N103.44W
Tucupita Venezuela **122** 9.02N 62.04W
Tucuruí Brazil **123** 3.42S 49.44W
Tucuruí, Reprêsa de *resr.* Brazil **123** 4.35S 49.33W
Tudela Spain **25** 42.05N 1.36W
Tudela de Duero Spain **26** 41.35N 4.35W
Tuela *r.* Portugal **26** 41.30N 7.12W
Tufi P.N.G. **90** 9.05S149.20E
Tugela R.S.A. **80** 29.10S 31.25E
Tug Hill *mtn.* U.S.A. **115** 43.45N 75.39W
Tuguegarao Phil. **59** 17.36N121.44E
Tugur Russian Fed. **51** 53.44N136.45E
Tuineje Canary Is. **127** 28.18N 14.03W
Tukangbesi, Kepulauan *is.* Indonesia **59** 5.30S124.00E
Tukayyid *well* Iraq **65** 29.47N 45.36E
Ţūkh Egypt **66** 30.21N 31.12E
Tūkrah Libya **75** 32.32N 20.34E
Tuktoyaktuk Canada **98** 69.27N133.00W
Tukums Latvia **41** 57.00N 23.10E
Tukuyu Tanzania **79** 9.20S 33.37E
Tula Mexico **116** 23.00N 99.43W
Tula Russian Fed. **44** 54.11N 37.38E
Tūlāk Afghan. **62** 33.58N 63.44E
Tulare U.S.A. **109** 36.13N119.21W
Tulare L. *resr.* U.S.A. **109** 36.03N119.49W
Tularosa U.S.A. **109** 33.04N106.01W
Tulcan Ecuador **122** 0.50N 77.48W
Tulcea Romania **29** 45.10N 28.50E
Tulchin Ukraine **37** 48.40N 28.49E
Tulemalu L. Canada **101** 62.58N 99.25W
Tuli Zimbabwe **80** 21.50S 29.15E
Tuli *r.* Zimbabwe **80** 21.49S 29.00E
Tulia U.S.A. **111** 34.32N101.46W
Ţūlkarm Jordan **67** 32.19N 35.02E
Tullahoma U.S.A. **113** 35.21N 86.12W
Tullamore Australia **93** 32.39S147.39E
Tullamore Rep. of Ire. **15** 53.17N 7.31W
Tulle France **20** 45.16N 1.46E
Tullins France **21** 45.18N 5.29E
Tullow Rep. of Ire. **15** 52.49N 6.45W
Tully Australia **90** 17.55S145.59E
Tully U.S.A. **115** 42.48N 76.07W
Tuloma *r.* Russian Fed. **44** 68.56N 33.00E
Tulsa U.S.A. **111** 36.09N 95.58W
Tulsequah Canada **100** 58.39N133.35W
Tuluá Colombia **122** 4.05N 76.12W
Tulumbasy Russian Fed. **44** 57.27N 57.40E
Tulun Russian Fed. **51** 54.32N100.35E
Tulungagung Indonesia **59** 8.03S111.54E
Tulu Welel *mtn.* Ethiopia **73** 8.53N 34.47E
Tum Indonesia **59** 3.28S130.21E
Tumaco Colombia **122** 1.51N 78.46W
Tumba Sweden **43** 59.12N 17.49E
Tumba, L. Zaïre **78** 0.45S 18.00E
Tumbarumba Australia **93** 35.49S148.01E
Tumbes Peru **122** 3.37S 80.27W
Tumbler Ridge Canada **100** 55.20N120.49W
Tumby Bay *town* Australia **92** 34.20S136.05E
Tumd Youqi China **54** 40.33N110.30E
Tumd Zuoqi China **54** 40.42N111.08E
Tumeremo Venezuela **122** 7.18N 61.30W
Tummel, Loch U.K. **14** 56.43N 3.55W
Tump Pakistan **62** 26.07N 62.22E
Tumsar India **63** 21.23N 79.44E
Tumuc Humac Mts. S. America **123** 2.20N 54.50W
Tumut Australia **93** 35.20S148.14E
Tunari *mtn.* Bolivia **124** 17.18S 66.22W
Tūnat al Jabal Egypt **66** 27.46N 30.44E
Tunceli Turkey **64** 39.07N 39.34E
Tuncurry Australia **93** 32.17S152.29E
Tundubai *well* Sudan **72** 18.31N 28.33E
Tunduma Tanzania **79** 9.19S 32.47E
Tunduru Tanzania **79** 11.08S 37.21E
Tundzha *r.* Bulgaria **34** 42.00N 26.35E
Tungabhadra *r.* India **60** 16.00N 78.15E
Tungaru Sudan **73** 10.14N 30.42E
Tungchiang Taiwan **55** 22.28N120.26E
Tungsten Canada **100** 62.00N128.15W
Tungsten U.S.A. **108** 40.48N118.08W
Tunica U.S.A. **111** 34.41N 90.23W
Tunis Tunisia **32** 36.48N 10.11E
Tunis, Golfe de *g.* Tunisia **32** 37.00N 10.30E
Tunisia Africa **75** 34.00N 9.00E
Tunja Colombia **122** 5.33N 73.23W
Tunkhannock U.S.A. **115** 41.32N 75.57W
Tunnsjöen *l.* Norway **40** 64.45N 13.25E
Tunungayualok I. Canada **103** 56.05N 61.05W
Tunuyán *r.* Argentina **125** 33.33S 67.30W
Tunxi *see* Huangshan China **55**
Tuoy-Khaya Russian Fed. **51** 62.33N111.25E
Tupã Brazil **126** 21.57S 50.28W
Tupelo U.S.A. **111** 34.16N 88.43W
Tupinambaranas, Ilha *f.* Brazil **123** 3.00S 58.00W
Tupiza Bolivia **124** 21.27S 65.43W
Tupper Lake *town* U.S.A. **105** 44.13N 74.29W
Tuquan China **54** 45.22N121.41E
Túquerres Colombia **122** 1.06N 77.37W
Tura India **63** 25.31N 90.13E
Tura Russian Fed. **51** 64.05N100.00E
Tura Tanzania **79** 5.30S 33.50E
Turabah Saudi Arabia **72** 21.13N 41.39E
Turangi New Zealand **86** 38.59S175.48E
Turano *r.* Italy **30** 42.26N 12.47E
Turbaco Colombia **122** 10.20N 75.25W
Turbanovo Russian Fed. **44** 60.05N 50.46E
Turbat Pakistan **62** 25.59N 63.04E
Turbine Canada **104** 46.22N 81.31W
Turbo Colombia **122** 8.06N 76.44W
Turda Romania **37** 46.34N 23.47E
Turek Poland **37** 52.02N 18.30E
Turgay Kazakhstan **9** 49.38N 63.25E
Turgeon *r.* Canada **102** 50.00N 78.54W
Tŭrgovishte Bulgaria **34** 43.17N 26.38E
Turgutlu Turkey **29** 38.30N 27.43E
Turhal Turkey **64** 40.23N 36.05E
Türi Estonia **41** 58.48N 25.26E
Turia *r.* Spain **25** 39.27N 0.19W
Turiaçu Brazil **123** 1.41S 45.21W
Turiaçu *r.* Brazil **123** 1.36S 45.19W
Turin Canada **100** 49.59N112.35W
Turin *see* Torino Italy **30**
Turka Ukraine **37** 49.10N 23.02E
Turkana, L. Kenya **79** 4.00N 36.00E
Turkestan Kazakhstan **52** 43.17N 68.16E
Turkey Asia **64** 39.00N 35.00E
Turkey U.S.A. **111** 34.23N100.54W
Turkey Creek *town* Australia **88** 17.04S128.15E
Turkmenistan Asia **9** 40.00N 60.00E
Turks Is. Turks & Caicos Is. **117** 21.30N 71.10W
Turku Finland **41** 60.27N 22.17E
Turku-Pori *d.* Finland **41** 61.00N 22.35E
Turkwel *r.* Kenya **79** 3.08N 35.39E
Turnagain *r.* Canada **100** 59.06N127.35W
Turnberry Canada **101** 53.25N101.45W
Turneffe Is. Belize **117** 17.30N 87.45W
Turner U.S.A. **108** 48.51N108.24W
Turnhout Belgium **16** 51.19N 4.57E
Turnu Măgurele Romania **34** 43.45N 24.53E
Turnu Roşu, Pasul *pass* Romania **29** 45.37N 24.17E
Turnu-Severin Romania **29** 44.37N 22.39E
Turon *r.* Australia **93** 33.03S149.33E
Turon U.S.A. **111** 37.48N 98.26W
Turopolje *f.* Croatia **31** 45.40N 16.00E
Turov Belorussia **37** 52.04N 27.40E
Turpan China **52** 42.55N 89.06E
Turpan Pendi *f.* China **52** 43.40N 89.00E
Turquino *mtn.* Cuba **117** 20.05N 76.50W
Turriff U.K. **14** 57.32N 2.28W
Turtkul Uzbekistan **65** 41.30N 61.00E
Turtle Lake *town* N.Dak. U.S.A. **110** 47.31N100.53W
Turtle Lake *town* Wisc. U.S.A. **110** 45.23N 92.09W
Turtle Mtn. Canada / U.S.A. **101** 49.05N 99.45W
Turukhansk Russian Fed. **51** 65.21N 88.05E
Turya *r.* Ukraine **37** 51.48N 24.52E
Tuscaloosa U.S.A. **113** 33.12N 87.33W
Tuscany *see* Toscana *d.* Italy **30**
Tuscarawas *r.* U.S.A. **114** 40.17N 81.52W
Tuscarora U.S.A. **108** 41.19N116.14W
Tuscarora Mts. U.S.A. **114** 40.10N 77.45W
Tuscola Ill. U.S.A. **110** 39.48N 88.17W
Tuscola Tex. U.S.A. **111** 32.12N 99.48W
Tutera *see* Tudela Spain **25**
Tuticorin India **61** 8.48N 78.10E
Tutin Yugo. **34** 43.00N 20.20E
Tutóia Brazil **123** 2.45S 42.16W
Tutrakan Bulgaria **29** 44.02N 26.40E
Tuttle U.S.A. **110** 47.09N100.00W
Tuttlingen Germany **39** 47.59N 8.49E
Tutuala Indonesia **59** 8.24S127.15E
Tutubu Tanzania **79** 5.28S 32.43E
Tutuila *i.* Samoa **84** 14.18S170.42W
Ţuţūn Egypt **66** 29.09N 30.46E
Tutzing Germany **39** 47.54N 11.17E
Tuul Gol *r.* Mongolia **52** 48.53N104.35E
Tuvalu Pacific Oc. **84** 8.00S178.00E
Tuwayq, Jabal *mts.* Saudi Arabia **71** 23.30N 46.20E
Tuxpan Mexico **116** 21.00N 97.23W
Tuxtla Gutiérrez Mexico **116** 16.45N 93.09W
Túy Spain **26** 42.03N 8.38W
Tuyen Quang Vietnam **55** 21.48N105.21E
Tuz Gölü *l.* Turkey **64** 38.45N 33.24E
Ţūz Khurmātū Iraq **65** 34.53N 44.38E
Tuzla Bosnia-Herzegovina **31** 44.32N 18.41E
Tvaerå Faroe Is. **10** 61.34N 6.48W
Tvedestrand Norway **42** 58.37N 8.55E
Tveitsund Norway **42** 59.01N 8.32E
Tver' Russian Fed. **44** 56.47N 35.57E
Tvŭrditsa Bulgaria **34** 42.42N 25.52E
Tweed Canada **105** 44.29N 77.19W
Tweed *r.* U.K. **14** 55.46N 2.00W
Tweed Heads *town* Australia **93** 28.13S153.33E
Tweedsmuir Prov. Park Canada **100** 52.55N126.20W
Twentynine Palms U.S.A. **109** 34.08N116.03W
Twin Bridges *town* U.S.A. **108** 45.33N112.20W
Twin Falls *town* U.S.A. **108** 42.34N114.28W
Twining U.S.A. **104** 44.07N 83.48W
Twins Creek *r.* Australia **92** 29.10S139.27E
Twin Valley *town* U.S.A. **110** 47.16N 96.16W
Twizel New Zealand **86** 44.15S170.06E
Twofold B. Australia **93** 37.06S149.55E
Two Harbors *town* U.S.A. **110** 47.02N 91.40W
Twyford U.K. **13** 51.01N 1.19W
Tygart *r.* U.S.A. **114** 38.30N 80.03W
Tyler Minn. U.S.A. **110** 44.17N 96.08W
Tyler Tex. U.S.A. **111** 32.21N 95.18W
Tylösand Sweden **43** 56.39N 12.44E
Tylöskog *hills* Sweden **43** 58.45N 15.20E
Tyndinskiy Russian Fed. **51** 55.11N124.34E
Tyne *r.* U.K. **12** 55.00N 1.25W
Tyne and Wear *d.* U.K. **12** 54.57N 1.35W
Tynemouth U.K. **12** 55.01N 1.24W
Tynset Norway **41** 62.17N 10.47E
Tyre *see* Şūr Lebanon **67**
Tyrifjorden *l.* Norway **42** 60.02N 10.08E
Tyringe Sweden **43** 56.10N 13.35E
Tyron U.S.A. **113** 35.13N 82.14W
Tyrone *d.* U.K. **15** 54.35N 7.15W
Tyrone U.S.A. **114** 40.40N 78.14W
Tyrrel Canada **101** 54.35N 99.10W
Tyrrell *r.* Australia **92** 35.28S142.55E
Tyrrell, L. Australia **92** 35.22S142.50E
Tyrrhenian Sea Med. Sea **32** 40.00N 12.00E
Tysnesöy *i.* Norway **42** 60.00N 5.35E
Tyssedal Norway **42** 60.07N 6.34E
Tyumen Russian Fed. **9** 57.11N 65.29E
Tywi *r.* U.K. **13** 51.46N 4.22W
Tzaneen R.S.A. **80** 23.49S 30.10E

Ua Huka to **Val des Bois**

U

Ua Huka *i.* Is. Marquises **85** 8.55S139.32W
Ua Pu *i.* Is. Marquises **85** 9.25S140.00W
Uatumã *r.* Brazil **123** 2.30S 57.40W
Uaupés Brazil **122** 0.07S 67.05W
Uaupés *r.* Brazil **122** 0.00S 67.10W
Ubá Brazil **126** 21.08S 42.59W
Ubangi *r.* Congo / Zaïre **78** 0.25S 17.40E
Ubatuba Brazil **126** 23.26S 45.05W
Ubauro Pakistan **62** 28.10N 69.44E
Ubayyid, Wādī al *r.* Iraq **64** 32.04N 42.17E
Ube Japan **57** 34.00N131.16E
Ubeda Spain **26** 38.01N 3.22W
Uberaba Brazil **126** 19.47S 47.57W
Uberlândia Brazil **126** 18.57S 48.17W
Überlingen Germany **39** 47.46N 9.10E
Ubombo R.S.A. **81** 27.35S 32.05E
Ubort *r.* Belorussia **37** 52.06N 28.28E
Ubrique Spain **27** 36.41N 5.27W
Ubundu Zaïre **78** 0.24S 25.28E
Ucayali *r.* Peru **122** 4.40S 73.20W
Uch Pakistan **62** 29.14N 71.03E
Uchiura wan *b.* Japan **57** 42.20N140.40E
Uckermark *f.* Germany **38** 52.11N 13.50E
Udaipur India **62** 24.35N 73.41E
Udalguri India **63** 26.46N 92.08E
Udaquiola Argentina **125** 36.35S 58.30W
Udaypur Nepal **63** 26.54N 86.32E
Udbina Croatia **31** 44.32N 15.46E
Uddeholm Sweden **43** 60.01N 13.37E
Uddevalla Sweden **42** 58.21N 11.55E
Uddjaur *l.* Sweden **40** 65.55N 17.49E
Udhampur Jammu & Kashmir **62** 32.56N 75.08E
Udine Italy **30** 46.03N 13.14E
Udipi India **60** 13.21N 74.45E
údolní nádrž Lipno *l.* Czech Republic **39** 48.43N 14.04E
Udon Thani Thailand **56** 17.25N102.45E
Ueckermünde Germany **38** 53.44N 14.03E
Uele *r.* Zaïre **73** 4.09N 22.26E
Uelzen Germany **38** 52.58N 10.33E
Ueno Japan **57** 34.45N136.08E
Uere *r.* Zaïre **73** 3.42N 25.24E
Uetersen Germany **38** 53.41N 9.39E
Ufa Russian Fed. **44** 54.45N 55.58E
Ufa *r.* Russian Fed. **44** 54.45N 56.00E
Uffculme U.K. **13** 50.45N 3.19W
Uffenheim Germany **39** 49.32N 10.14E
Ugab *r.* Namibia **80** 21.12S 13.37E
Ugalla *r.* Tanzania **79** 5.43S 31.10E
Uganda Africa **79** 2.00N 33.00E
Ugep Nigeria **77** 5.48N 8.05E
Ughelli Nigeria **77** 5.33N 6.00E
Ugijar Spain **27** 36.57N 3.03W
Ugine France **21** 45.45N 6.25E
Uglegorsk Russian Fed. **51** 49.01N142.04E
Ugljan *i.* Croatia **31** 44.05N 15.10E
Uglovka Russian Fed. **44** 58.13N 33.30E
Ugoma *mtn.* Zaïre **79** 4.00S 28.45E
Ugra *r.* Russian Fed. **44** 54.30N 36.10E
Ugürchin Bulgaria **34** 43.06N 24.26E
Uherske Hradiště Czech Republic **37** 49.05N 17.28E
Uhrichsville U.S.A. **114** 40.24N 81.20W
Uig U.K. **14** 57.35N 6.22W
Uíge Angola **78** 7.40S 15.09E
Uíge *d.* Angola **78** 7.00S 15.30E
Uil Kazakhstan **45** 49.08N 54.43E
Uil *r.* Kazakhstan **45** 48.33N 52.25E
Uinta Mts. U.S.A. **108** 40.45N110.05W
Uitenhage R.S.A. **80** 33.46S 25.23E
Uithuizen Neth. **16** 53.24N 6.41E
Uivlleq *see* Nanortalik Greenland **99**
Ujhāni India **63** 28.01N 79.01E
Uji *r.* Japan **57** 34.53N135.48E
Ujiji Tanzania **79** 4.55S 29.39E
Ujjain India **62** 23.11N 75.46E
Ujpest Hungary **37** 47.33N 19.05E
Ujście Poland **36** 53.04N 16.43E
Ujung Pandang Indonesia **58** 5.09S119.28E
Uka Russian Fed. **51** 57.50N162.02E
Ukerewe I. Tanzania **79** 2.00S 33.00E
Ukhta Russian Fed. **44** 63.33N 53.44E
Ukiah U.S.A. **108** 39.09N123.13W
Ukmerge Lithuania **44** 55.14N 24.49E
Ukraine Europe **37** 49.45N 27.00E
Ukrina *r.* Bosnia-Herzegovina **31** 45.05N 17.56E
Uku Angola **78** 11.24S 14.15E
Ukwi Botswana **80** 23.22S 20.30E
Ulaanbaatar Mongolia **52** 47.54N106.52E
Ulaangom Mongolia **52** 49.59N 92.00E
Ulamba Zaïre **78** 9.07S 23.40E
Ulan Bator *see* Ulaanbaatar Mongolia **52**
Ulansuhai Nur *l.* China **54** 40.56N108.49E
Ulan-Ude Russian Fed. **52** 51.55N107.40E
Ulan Ul Hu *l.* China **61** 34.45N 90.25E
Ulcinj Yugo. **31** 41.55N 19.11E
Ulefoss Norway **42** 59.17N 9.16E
Ulenia, L. Australia **92** 29.57S142.24E
Ulfborg Denmark **42** 56.16N 8.20E
Ulhāsnagar India **62** 19.13N 73.07E
Uliastay Mongolia **52** 47.42N 96.52E
Ulindi *r.* Zaïre **78** 1.38S 25.55E
Ulla *r.* Spain **26** 42.40N 8.43W
Ulladulla Australia **93** 35.21S150.25E
Ullånger Sweden **40** 62.58N 18.16E
Ullapool U.K. **14** 57.54N 5.10W
Ullswater *l.* U.K. **12** 54.34N 2.52W
Ulm Germany **39** 48.24N 10.00E
Ulongwé Mozambique **79** 14.34S 34.21E
Ulricehamn Sweden **43** 57.47N 13.25E
Ulsan S. Korea **57** 35.34N129.19E
Ulsberg Norway **40** 62.45N 9.59E
Ulster U.S.A. **115** 41.51N 76.30W
Ultima Australia **92** 35.30S143.20E
Ulu Sudan **73** 10.43N 33.29E
Ulúa *r.* Honduras **117** 15.50N 87.38W
Uluguru Mts. Tanzania **79** 7.05S 37.40E
Uluru *mtn.* Australia **90** 25.20S131.01E
Ulverston U.K. **12** 54.13N 3.07W
Ulverstone Australia **91** 41.09S146.10E
Ul'yanovsk Russian Fed. **44** 54.19N 48.22E
Ulysses U.S.A. **111** 37.35N101.22W
Ulzë Albania **34** 41.41N 19.54E
Umag Croatia **31** 45.25N 13.32E
Umaisha Nigeria **77** 8.01N 7.12E
Umala Bolivia **124** 17.21S 68.00W
Uman Ukraine **37** 48.45N 30.10E
Umaria India **63** 23.32N 80.50E
Umarkot Pakistan **62** 25.22N 69.44E
Umbertide Italy **30** 43.18N 12.20E
Umbria *d.* Italy **30** 43.05N 12.30E
Ume *r.* Sweden **40** 63.47N 20.16E
Ume *r.* Zimbabwe **80** 17.00S 28.22E
Umeå Sweden **40** 63.45N 20.20E
Umfors Sweden **40** 65.56N 15.00E
Umfuli *r.* Zimbabwe **80** 17.32S 29.23E
Umiat U.S.A. **98** 69.25N152.20W
Umm-al-Qaywayn U.A.E. **65** 25.32N 55.34E
Umm Badr Sudan **72** 14.14N 27.57E
Umm Bel Sudan **73** 13.32N 28.04E
Umm Durmān Sudan **72** 15.37N 32.59E
Umm el Faḥm Israel **67** 32.31N 35.09E
Umm Kuwaykah Sudan **73** 12.49N 31.52E
Umm Lajj Saudi Arabia **64** 25.03N 37.17E
Umm Qays Jordan **67** 32.39N 35.41E
Umm Qurayn Sudan **73** 9.58N 28.55E
Umm Ruwābah Sudan **73** 12.54N 31.13E
Umm Shalīl Sudan **73** 10.51N 23.42E
Umm Shanqah Sudan **73** 13.14N 27.14E
Umniati Zimbabwe **80** 18.41S 29.45E
Umrer India **63** 20.51N 79.20E
Umreth India **62** 22.42N 73.07E
Umtata R.S.A. **80** 31.35S 28.47E
Umuahia Nigeria **77** 5.31N 7.26E
Umzimkulu R.S.A. **80** 30.15S 29.56E
Umzimvubu R.S.A. **80** 31.37S 29.32E
Una *r.* Bosnia-Herzegovina **31** 45.16N 16.55E
Una India **62** 20.49N 71.02E
Unac *r.* Bosnia-Herzegovina **31** 44.30N 16.09E
Unadilla *r.* U.S.A. **115** 42.20N 75.19W
Unalakleet U.S.A. **98** 63.53N160.47W
'Unayzah Jordan **66** 30.29N 35.48E
'Unayzah Saudi Arabia **65** 26.05N 43.57E
'Unayzah, Jabal *mtn.* Iraq **64** 32.15N 39.19E
Uncia Bolivia **124** 18.27S 66.37W
Uncompahgre Peak U.S.A. **108** 38.04N107.28W
Uncompahgre Plateau *f.* U.S.A. **108** 38.30N108.25W
Unden *l.* Sweden **43** 58.47N 14.26E
Underberg R.S.A. **80** 29.46S 29.26E
Underbool Australia **92** 35.10S141.50E
Undu, C. Fiji **84** 16.08S179.57W
Unecha Russian Fed. **37** 52.52N 32.42E
Ungarie Australia **93** 33.38S147.00E
Ungava, Péninsule d' *pen.* Canada **99** 60.00N 74.00W
Ungava B. Canada **99** 59.00N 67.30W
União Brazil **123** 4.35S 42.52W
União da Vitória Brazil **126** 26.13S 51.05W
Unije *i.* Croatia **31** 44.38N 14.15E
Unimak I. U.S.A. **98** 54.50N164.00W
Unini Peru **122** 10.41S 73.59W
Union Miss U.S.A. **111** 32.34N 89.14W
Union S.C. U.S.A. **113** 34.42N 81.37W
Union City Penn. U.S.A. **114** 41.54N 79.51W
Union City Tenn. U.S.A. **111** 36.26N 89.03W
Uniondale R.S.A. **80** 33.39S 23.07E
Union Gap U.S.A. **108** 46.34N120.34W
Union Springs *town* U.S.A. **113** 32.08N 85.44W
Uniontown U.S.A. **114** 39.54N 79.44W
Unionville U.S.A. **110** 40.29N 93.01W
United Arab Emirates Asia **65** 24.00N 54.00E
United Kingdom Europe **11** 55.00N 2.00W
United States of America N. America **106** 39.00N100.00W
Unity Canada **101** 52.27N109.10W
Universales, Montes *mts.* Spain **25** 40.20N 1.30W
University Park *town* U.S.A. **109** 32.17N106.45W
Unjha India **62** 23.48N 72.24E
Unna Germany **38** 51.32N 7.41E
Unnão India **63** 26.32N 80.30E
Unst *i.* U.K. **14** 60.45N 0.55W
Unstrut *r.* Germany **38** 51.10N 11.48E
Unterwalden *d.* Switz. **39** 46.55N 8.17E
Ünye Turkey **64** 41.09N 37.15E
Upata Venezuela **122** 8.02N 62.25W
Upemba, L. Zaïre **78** 8.35S 26.28E
Upemba Nat. Park Zaïre **78** 9.00S 26.30E
Upernavik Greenland **99** 72.50N 56.00W
Upington R.S.A. **80** 28.26S 21.12E
Upleta India **62** 21.44N 70.17E
Upolu *i.* W. Samoa **84** 13.55S171.45W
Upolu Pt. Hawaiian Is. **85** 20.16N155.51W
Upper Arrow L. Canada **100** 50.30N117.50W
Upper East *d.* Ghana **76** 10.40N 0.20W
Upper Egypt *see* Aş Şa'īd *f.* Egypt **64**
Upper Hutt New Zealand **86** 41.07S175.04E
Upper Klamath L. U.S.A. **108** 42.23N122.55W
Upper Laberge Canada **100** 60.54N135.12W
Upper Lough Erne U.K. **15** 54.13N 7.32W
Upper Pen. *f.* U.S.A. **104** 46.12N 84.32W
Upper Red L. U.S.A. **110** 48.05N 94.50W
Upper Tean U.K. **12** 52.57N 1.59W
Upper Volta *see* Burkina Africa **76**
Upper West *d.* Ghana **76** 10.25N 2.00W
Upper Yarra Resr. Australia **93** 37.43S145.56E
Uppland *f.* Sweden **43** 59.59N 17.48E
Upplands-Väsby Sweden **43** 59.31N 17.54E
Uppsala Sweden **43** 59.52N 17.38E
Uppsala *d.* Sweden **41** 60.10N 17.50E
Upshi Jammu & Kashmir **63** 33.50N 77.49E
Upton Canada **105** 45.39N 72.41W
Upton U.S.A. **108** 44.06N104.38W
Uqlat aş Şuqūr Saudi Arabia **64** 25.50N 42.12E
Ur *ruins* Iraq **65** 30.55N 46.07E
Uracoa Venezuela **122** 9.03N 62.27W
Uraga-suido *str.* Japan **57** 35.10N139.42E
Urahoro Japan **57** 42.48N143.39E
Urakawa Japan **57** 42.09N142.47E
Ural *r.* Kazakhstan **45** 47.00N 52.00E
Uralla Australia **93** 30.40S151.31E
Ural Mts. *see* Ural'skiye Gory *mts.* Russian Fed. **44**
Ural'sk Kazakhstan **45** 51.19N 51.20E
Ural'skiye Gory *mts.* Russian Fed. **44** 60.00N 59.00E
Urana Australia **93** 35.21S146.19E
Urana, L. Australia **93** 35.21S146.19E
Urandangi Australia **90** 21.36S138.18E
Uranium City Canada **101** 59.28N108.40W
Urapunga Australia **90** 14.41S134.34E
Uraricoera *r.* Brazil **122** 3.10N 60.30W
Urawa Japan **57** 35.51N139.39E
Uray Russian Fed. **50** 60.11N 65.00E
Urbana U.S.A. **110** 40.07N 88.12W
Urbania Italy **30** 43.40N 12.31E
Urbino Italy **30** 43.43N 12.38E
Urcos Peru **122** 13.40S 71.38W
Urda Kazakhstan **45** 48.44N 47.30E
Urdzhar Kazakhstan **50** 47.06N 81.33E
Ure *r.* U.K. **12** 54.05N 1.20W
Urechye Belorussia **37** 52.59N 27.50E
Uren Russian Fed. **44** 57.30N 45.50E
Urengoy Russian Fed. **50** 65.59N 78.30E
Ures Mexico **116** 29.26N110.24W
Ürgüp Turkey **64** 38.39N 34.55E
Uri *d.* Switz. **39** 46.45N 8.35E
Uribia Colombia **122** 11.43N 72.16W
Urim Israel **67** 31.18N 34.31E
Urisino Australia **92** 29.44S143.49E
Urjala Finland **41** 61.05N 23.32E
Urk Neth. **16** 52.40N 5.36E
Urlingford Rep. of Ire. **15** 52.44N 7.35W
Urmia, L. *see* Daryācheh-ye Orūmīyeh *l.* Iran **65**
Uroševac Yugo. **34** 42.22N 21.09E
Ursus Poland **37** 52.12N 20.53E
Uruaçu Brazil **123** 14.30S 49.10W
Uruapan Mexico **116** 19.26N102.04W
Urubamba Peru **122** 13.20S 72.07W
Urubamba *r.* Peru **122** 10.43S 73.55W
Urucará Brazil **123** 2.32S 57.45W
Uruçui Brazil **123** 7.14S 44.33W
Uruguaiana Brazil **125** 29.45S 57.05W
Uruguay *r.* Argentina / Uruguay **125** 34.00S 58.30W
Uruguay S. America **126** 33.15S 56.00W
Ürümqi China **52** 43.43N 87.38E
Urun P.N.G. **90** 8.36S147.15E
Urunga Australia **93** 30.30S152.28E
Urup *r.* Russian Fed. **45** 44.59N 41.12E
Uryu ko *l.* Japan **57** 44.22N142.15E
Urzhum Russian Fed. **44** 57.08N 50.00E
Urziceni Romania **29** 44.43N 26.38E
Usa *r.* Russian Fed. **44** 65.58N 56.35E
Uşak Turkey **64** 38.42N 29.25E
Usakos Namibia **80** 22.02S 15.35E
Usambara Mts. Tanzania **79** 4.45S 38.25E
Ušće Yugo. **34** 43.28N 20.37E
Usedom *i.* Germany **38** 54.00N 14.00E
Ushant *i.* *see* Ouessant, Île d' *i.* France **18**
Ush-Tobe Kazakhstan **52** 45.15N 77.59E
Ushuaia Argentina **125** 54.47S 68.20W
Ushumun Russian Fed. **51** 52.48N126.27E
Usisya Malaŵi **79** 11.10S 34.12E
Usk *r.* U.K. **13** 51.34N 2.59W
Uskedal Norway **42** 59.56N 5.52E
Üsküdar Turkey **29** 41.00N 29.03E
Uslar Germany **38** 51.39N 9.38E
Usman Russian Fed. **45** 52.02N 39.43E
Usovo Ukraine **37** 51.20N 28.01E
Uspenskiy Kazakhstan **50** 48.41N 72.43E
Ussel France **20** 45.33N 2.18E
Ussuriysk Russian Fed. **53** 43.48N131.59E
Ustaoset Norway **41** 60.30N 8.04E
Ustaritz France **20** 43.24N 1.27W
Ustica *i.* Italy **32** 38.42N 13.10E
Ust'-Ilga Russian Fed. **51** 54.59N105.00E
Ústí nad Labem Czech Republic **38** 50.40N 14.02E
Ust Ishim Russian Fed. **50** 57.45N 71.05E
Ustka Poland **36** 54.35N 16.50E
Ust'kamchatsk Russian Fed. **51** 56.14N162.28E
Ust-Kamenogorsk Kazakhstan **50** 50.00N 82.40E
Ust Kulom Russian Fed. **44** 61.34N 53.40E
Ust Kut Russian Fed. **51** 56.40N105.50E
Ust Lyzha Russian Fed. **44** 65.45N 56.38E
Ust'Maya Russian Fed. **51** 60.25N134.28E
Ust Nem Russian Fed. **44** 61.38N 54.50E
Ust Olenëk Russian Fed. **51** 72.59N120.00E
Ust-Omchug Russian Fed. **51** 61.08N149.38E
Ust Port Russian Fed. **50** 69.44N 84.23E
Ust Tapsuy Russian Fed. **44** 62.25N 61.42E
Ust'Tsilma Russian Fed. **44** 65.28N 53.09E
Ust-Tungir Russian Fed. **51** 55.25N120.15E
Ust Ura Russian Fed. **44** 63.06N 44.41E
Ust Vaga Russian Fed. **44** 62.42N 42.45E
Ust Vym Russian Fed. **44** 62.15N 50.25E
Ustyurt, Plato *f.* Kazakhstan **45** 43.30N 55.00E
Usu China **52** 44.27N 84.37E
Usumacinta *r.* Mexico **116** 18.22N 92.40W
U.S. Virgin Is. C. America **117** 18.30N 65.00W
Ut Belorussia **37** 52.18N 31.10E
Utah *d.* U.S.A. **108** 39.37N112.28W
Utah L. U.S.A. **108** 40.13N111.49W
'Uta Vava'u Tonga **85** 18.35S174.00W
'Utaybah, Buḥayrat al *l.* Syria **66** 33.31N 36.37E
Utembo *r.* Angola **78** 17.03S 22.00E
Utengule Tanzania **79** 8.55S 35.43E
Utersum Germany **38** 54.43N 8.24E
Utete Tanzania **79** 8.00S 38.49E
Uthal Pakistan **62** 25.48N 66.37E
Utiariti Brazil **122** 13.02S 58.17W
Utica Kans. U.S.A. **110** 38.39N100.10W
Utica Mich. U.S.A. **114** 42.38N 83.02W
Utica N.Y. U.S.A. **115** 43.05N 75.14W
Utica Ohio U.S.A. **114** 40.14N 82.27W
Utiel Spain **25** 39.34N 1.12W
Utikuma L. Canada **100** 55.50N115.30W
Utique Tunisia **32** 37.03N 10.03E
Utö *i.* Sweden **43** 58.56N 18.16E
Utopia Australia **90** 22.14S134.33E
Utraula India **63** 27.19N 82.25E
Utrecht Neth. **16** 52.04N 5.07E
Utrecht *d.* Neth. **16** 52.04N 5.10E
Utrecht R.S.A. **80** 27.38S 30.19E
Utrera Spain **27** 37.11N 5.47W
Utsira Norway **42** 59.18N 4.54E
Utsjoki Finland **40** 69.53N 27.00E
Utsunomiya Japan **57** 36.40N139.52E
Utta Russian Fed. **45** 46.24N 46.01E
Uttaradit Thailand **56** 17.38N100.05E
Uttarkāshi India **63** 30.44N 78.27E
Uttar Pradesh *d.* India **63** 26.30N 81.30E
Utterson Canada **104** 45.13N 79.20W
Uturoà Is. de la Société **85** 16.44S151.25W
Uummanarsuaq *see* Farvel, K. *c.* Greenland **99**
Uusikaupunki Finland **41** 60.48N 21.25E
Uusimaa *d.* Finland **41** 60.30N 25.00E
Uvalde U.S.A. **111** 29.13N 99.47W
Uvarovichi Belorussia **37** 52.35N 30.44E
Uvat Russian Fed. **50** 59.10N 68.49E
Uvdal Norway **42** 60.16N 8.44E
Uvéa, Île *i.* N. Cal. **84** 20.30S166.35E
Uvinza Tanzania **79** 5.08S 30.23E
Uvira Zaïre **79** 3.22S 29.06E
Uvs Nuur *l.* Mongolia **52** 50.30N 92.30E
Uwajima Japan **57** 33.13N132.32E
Uwayl Sudan **73** 8.46N 27.24E
'Uwaynāt, Jabal al *mtn.* Libya / Sudan **72** 21.54N 24.58E
Uxbridge Canada **104** 44.06N 79.07W
Uxin Qi China **54** 38.30N108.53E
Uyo Nigeria **77** 5.01N 7.56E
Uyuni Bolivia **124** 20.28S 66.50W
Uyuni, Salar de *f.* Bolivia **124** 20.20S 67.42W
Uzbekistan Asia **9** 42.00N 63.00E
Uzda Belorussia **37** 53.28N 27.11E
Uzerche France **20** 45.26N 1.34E
Uzès France **21** 44.01N 4.25E
Uzh *r.* Ukraine **37** 51.15N 30.12E
Uzhgorod Ukraine **37** 48.38N 22.15E
Užice Yugo. **31** 43.51N 19.51E
Uzunköpru Turkey **34** 41.16N 26.41E

V

Vä Sweden **43** 55.59N 14.05E
Vaagö *i.* Faroe Is. **10** 62.03N 7.14W
Vaal *r.* R.S.A. **80** 29.04S 23.37E
Vaala Finland **40** 64.26N 26.48E
Vaal Dam R.S.A. **80** 26.51S 28.08E
Vaasa Finland **40** 63.06N 21.36E
Vaasa *d.* Finland **40** 62.50N 22.50E
Vác Hungary **37** 47.49N 19.10E
Vaccarès, Étang de *b.* France **21** 43.32N 4.34E
Vadodara India **60** 22.19N 73.14E
Vado Ligure Italy **30** 44.17N 8.27E
Vadsö Norway **40** 70.05N 29.46E
Vadstena Sweden **43** 58.27N 14.54E
Vaduz Liech. **39** 47.09N 9.31E
Vaeröy *i.* Norway **40** 67.40N 12.40E
Vaga *r.* Russian Fed. **44** 62.45N 42.48E
Vågåmo Norway **41** 61.53N 9.06E
Vaganski Vrh *mtn.* Croatia **31** 44.22N 15.31E
Vaggeryd Sweden **43** 57.30N 14.07E
Váh *r.* Slovakia **37** 47.40N 17.50E
Vahsel B. Antarctica **128** 77.00S 38.00W
Vaiea Niue **84** 19.08S169.53W
Vaihu I. de Pascua **85** 27.10S109.22W
Vaijāpur India **62** 19.55N 74.44E
Vailly-sur-Aisne France **19** 49.25N 3.31E
Vairao Tahiti **85** 17.48S149.17W
Vaison-la-Romaine France **21** 44.14N 5.04E
Vaitupu *i.* Tuvalu **84** 7.28S178.41E
Vakaga C.A.R. **73** 9.50N 22.30E
Vakarai Sri Lanka **61** 8.08N 81.26E
Vålådalen Sweden **40** 63.09N 13.00E
Valais *d.* Switz. **39** 46.00N 7.20E
Valandovo Macedonia **34** 41.19N 22.34E
Valatie U.S.A. **115** 42.25N 73.41W
Valavsk Belorussia **37** 51.40N 28.38E
Val Barrette Canada **105** 46.31N 75.22W
Vålberg Sweden **43** 59.24N 13.12E
Valcartier Canada **105** 46.56N 71.27W
Valcheta Argentina **125** 40.40S 66.10W
Valdagno Italy **30** 45.39N 11.18E
Valdavia *r.* Spain **26** 42.24N 4.16W
Valday Russian Fed. **44** 57.59N 33.10E
Valdayskaya Vozvyshennost *mts.* Russian Fed. **44** 57.10N 33.00E
Valdecañas, Embalse de *resr.* Spain **27** 39.45N 5.30W
Valdemārpils Latvia **41** 57.22N 22.35E
Valdemarsvik Sweden **43** 58.12N 16.36E
Valdepeñas Spain **26** 38.46N 3.23W
Valderaduey *r.* Spain **26** 41.31N 5.42W
Valderas Spain **26** 42.05N 5.27W
Valderrobres Spain **25** 40.53N 0.09W
Valdés, Pen. Argentina **125** 42.30S 64.00W
Val des Bois Canada **105** 45.54N 75.35W

Vieux-Condé to **Wahai**

Vieux-Condé France **16** 50.29N 3.31E
Vif France **21** 45.03N 5.40E
Vigan France **20** 43.59N 3.35E
Vigan Phil. **59** 17.35N120.23E
Vigeland Norway **42** 58.05N 7.18E
Vigevano Italy **30** 45.19N 8.51E
Vignemale, Pic de *mtn.* France **20** 42.46N 0.08W
Vigneulles-lès-Hattonchâtel France **19** 48.59N 5.43E
Vigo Spain **26** 42.14N 8.43W
Vigo, Ría de *est.* Spain **26** 42.15N 8.45W
Vigrestad Norway **42** 58.34N 5.42E
Vihāri Pakistan **62** 30.02N 72.21E
Vihiers France **18** 47.09N 0.32W
Vihowa Pakistan **62** 31.08N 70.30E
Vijāpur India **62** 23.35N 72.45E
Vijayawāda India **61** 16.34N 80.40E
Vik Norway **40** 65.19N 12.10E
Vikajärvi Finland **40** 66.37N 26.12E
Vikeke Indonesia **59** 8.42S126.30E
Viken Sweden **43** 56.09N 12.34E
Viken *l.* Sweden **43** 58.39N 14.20E
Vikersund Norway **42** 59.59N 10.02E
Vikmanshyttan Sweden **43** 60.17N 15.49E
Vikna *i.* Norway **40** 64.52N 10.57E
Vikulovo Russian Fed. **50** 56.51N 70.30E
Vila Vanuatu **84** 17.44S168.19E
Vila da Maganja Mozambique **79** 17.25S 37.32E
Vila de Rei Portugal **27** 39.40N 8.09W
Vila do Bispo Portugal **27** 37.05N 8.55W
Vila do Conde Portugal **26** 41.21N 8.45W
Vila Flor Portugal **26** 41.18N 7.09W
Vila Franca Portugal **27** 38.57N 8.59W
Vilafranca del Penedès Spain **25** 41.21N 1.42E
Vilaine *r.* France **18** 47.30N 2.27W
Vilanculos Mozambique **81** 21.59S 35.16E
Vila Nova de Famalicão Portugal **26** 41.25N 8.32W
Vila Nova de Fozcoa Portugal **26** 41.05N 7.12W
Vila Nova de Gaia Portugal **26** 41.45N 8.34W
Vila Nova de Ourém Portugal **27** 39.39N 8.35W
Vilanova i La Geltrú *see* Villanueva y Geltrú Spain **25**
Vila Real Portugal **26** 41.18N 7.45W
Vila Real *d.* Portugal **26** 41.35N 7.35W
Vila Real de Santo António Portugal **27** 37.12N 7.25W
Vilar Formoso Portugal **26** 40.35N 6.53W
Vila Velha Brazil **126** 20.20S 40.17W
Vila Velha de Ródão Portugal **27** 39.38N 7.40W
Vila Verde Portugal **26** 41.39N 8.26W
Vila Verissimo Sarmento Angola **78** 8.08S 20.38E
Vila Viçosa Portugal **27** 38.47N 7.25W
Vildbjerg Denmark **42** 56.12N 8.46E
Vileyka Belorussia **37** 54.30N 26.50E
Vilhelmina Sweden **40** 64.37N 16.39E
Vilhena Brazil **122** 12.40S 60.08W
Viliga Kushka Russian Fed. **51** 61.35N156.55E
Viljandi Estonia **44** 58.22N 25.30E
Vilkavīškis Lithuania **37** 54.39N 23.02E
Vil'kitskogo, Proliv *str.* Russian Fed. **51** 77.57N102.30E
Vilkovo Ukraine **37** 45.28N 29.32E
Villa Adriana *site* Italy **30** 41.56N 12.45E
Villa Angela Argentina **124** 27.34S 60.45W
Villa Bella Bolivia **124** 10.23S 65.24W
Villablino Spain **26** 42.56N 6.19W
Villacañas Spain **27** 39.38N 3.20W
Villacarriedo Spain **26** 43.14N 3.48W
Villacarrillo Spain **26** 38.07N 3.05W
Villacastín Spain **26** 40.47N 4.25W
Villach Austria **31** 46.36N 13.50E
Villa Clara Argentina **125** 31.46S 58.50W
Villa Constitución Argentina **125** 33.14S 60.21W
Villada Spain **26** 42.15N 4.59W
Villa del Río Spain **27** 37.59N 4.17W
Villa de Santiago Mexico **111** 25.26N100.09W
Villadiego Spain **26** 42.31N 4.00W
Villa Dolores Argentina **124** 31.58S 65.12W
Villafranca del Bierzo Spain **26** 42.36N 6.48W
Villafranca de los Barros Spain **27** 38.34N 6.20W
Villafranca di Verona Italy **30** 45.21N 10.50E
Villagarcía Spain **26** 42.36N 8.45W
Villaguay Argentina **125** 31.55S 59.00W
Villahermosa Mexico **116** 18.00N 92.53W
Villa Hernandarias Argentina **125** 31.15S 59.58W
Villa Huidobro Argentina **125** 34.50S 64.34W
Villaines-la-Juhel France **18** 48.21N 0.17W
Villajoyosa Spain **25** 38.30N 0.14W
Villalba Spain **26** 43.18N 7.41W
Villalón de Campos Spain **26** 42.06N 5.02W
Villalpando Spain **26** 41.52N 5.24W
Villa María Argentina **124** 32.25S 63.15W
Villamartín Spain **27** 36.52N 5.38W
Villa Montes Bolivia **124** 21.15S 63.30W
Villandraut France **20** 44.28N 0.23W
Villanueva y Geltrú Spain **25** 41.14N 1.44E
Villanova Monteleone Italy **32** 40.30N 8.28E
Villanueva de Córdoba Spain **26** 38.20N 4.37W
Villanueva de la Serena Spain **26** 38.58N 5.48W
Villanueva de los Infantes Spain **27** 38.45N 3.01W
Villanueva del Río y Minas Spain **27** 37.39N 5.42W
Villaputzu Italy **32** 39.28N 9.33E
Villarcayo Spain **26** 42.56N 3.34W
Villard-de-Lans France **21** 45.04N 5.33E
Villardefrades Spain **26** 41.43N 5.15W
Villar del Arzobispo Spain **25** 39.44N 0.49W
Villarobledo Spain **27** 39.16N 2.36W
Villarreal Spain **25** 39.56N 0.06W
Villarrica Chile **125** 39.15S 72.15W
Villarrica Paraguay **126** 25.45S 56.28W
Villarrobledo Spain **24** 39.16N 2.36W
Villarrubia de los Ojos Spain **27** 39.13N 3.36W
Villa San Giovanni Italy **33** 38.13N 15.39E
Villa San José Argentina **125** 32.12S 58.15W
Villasayas Spain **26** 41.21N 2.37W
Villasimius Italy **32** 39.09N 9.31E
Villasor Italy **32** 39.22N 8.57E
Villavicencio Colombia **122** 4.09N 73.38W
Villaviciosa Spain **26** 43.29N 5.26W
Villaviciosa de Córdoba Spain **26** 38.05N 5.01W
Villazón Bolivia **124** 22.06S 65.36W
Villé France **19** 48.20N 7.18E
Villedieu France **18** 48.50N 1.13W
Villefort France **20** 44.26N 3.56E
Villefranche France **21** 45.59N 4.43E
Villefranche-de-Rouergue France **20** 44.21N 2.02E
Ville Marie Canada **104** 47.19N 79.26W
Villena Spain **25** 38.38N 0.51W
Villenauxe-la-Grande France **19** 48.35N 3.33E
Villeneuve France **20** 44.25N 0.42E
Villeneuve-d'Ascq France **19** 50.37N 3.10E
Villeneuve-d'Aveyron France **20** 44.26N 2.02E
Villeneuve-de-Berg France **21** 44.33N 4.30E
Villeneuve-St. Georges France **19** 48.44N 2.27E
Villeneuve-sur-Yonne France **19** 48.05N 3.18E
Villeroy Canada **105** 46.23N 71.53W
Villers Bocage France **18** 49.05N 0.39W
Villers-Cotterêts France **19** 49.15N 3.05E
Villersexel France **19** 47.33N 6.26E
Villers sur Mer France **18** 49.21N 0.02W
Villeurbanne France **21** 45.46N 4.53E
Villingen Germany **39** 48.03N 8.27E
Vilnius Lithuania **37** 54.40N 25.19E
Vils *r.* Germany **39** 48.39N 13.11E
Vilsbiburg Germany **39** 48.27N 12.12E
Vilshofen Germany **39** 48.39N 13.12E
Vilvoorde Belgium **16** 50.56N 4.25E
Vilyuy *r.* Russian Fed. **51** 64.20N126.55E
Vilyuysk Russian Fed. **51** 63.46N121.35E
Vimianzo Spain **26** 43.07N 9.02W
Vimmerby Sweden **43** 57.40N 15.51E
Vimoutiers France **18** 48.55N 0.12E
Vimperk Czech Republic **38** 49.03N 13.47E
Vina *r.* Chad **77** 7.43N 15.30E
Viña del Mar Chile **125** 33.02S 71.34W
Vinaroz Spain **25** 40.28N 0.29E
Vincennes France **19** 48.51N 2.26E
Vincennes U.S.A. **110** 38.41N 87.32W
Vincent U.S.A. **114** 39.23N 81.40W
Vindel *r.* Sweden **40** 63.54N 19.52E
Vindeln Sweden **40** 64.12N 19.44E
Vinderup Denmark **42** 56.29N 8.47E
Vindhya Range *mts.* India **62** 22.45N 75.30E
Vineland U.S.A. **115** 39.29N 75.02W
Vineyard Haven U.S.A. **115** 41.27N 70.36W
Vineyard Sd. U.S.A. **115** 41.25N 70.46W
Vingåker Sweden **43** 59.02N 15.52E
Vinh Vietnam **56** 18.42N105.41E
Vinhais Portugal **26** 41.50N 7.00W
Vinh Long Vietnam **56** 10.15N105.59E
Vinica Slovenia **31** 45.28N 15.15E
Vinita U.S.A. **111** 36.39N 95.09W
Vînju Mare Romania **37** 44.26N 22.52E
Vinkovci Croatia **31** 45.17N 18.49E
Vinnitsa Ukraine **37** 49.11N 28.30E
Vinson Massif Antarctica **128** 78.00S 85.00W
Vintar Phil. **55** 18.16N120.40E
Vinton U.S.A. **110** 42.10N 92.01W
Vioolsdrif R.S.A. **80** 28.45S 17.33E
Vipava Slovenia **31** 45.51N 13.58E
Vipiteno Italy **30** 46.54N 11.26E
Vir *i.* Croatia **31** 44.18N 15.04E
Virac Phil. **59** 13.35N124.15E
Viramgām India **62** 23.07N 72.02E
Viranşehir Turkey **64** 37.13N 39.45E
Virden Canada **101** 49.51N100.55W
Vire France **18** 48.50N 0.53W
Vire *r.* France **18** 49.20N 1.07W
Vírgenes, C. Argentina **125** 52.00S 68.50W
Virgin Gorda *i.* B.V.Is. **117** 18.30N 64.26W
Virginia U.S.A. **110** 47.31N 92.32W
Virginia *d.* U.S.A. **113** 37.30N 78.45W
Virginia Beach *town* U.S.A. **113** 36.51N 75.59W
Virginia City Mont. U.S.A. **108** 45.18N111.56W
Virginia City Nev. U.S.A. **108** 39.19N119.39W
Virieu-le-Grand France **21** 45.51N 5.39E
Virje Croatia **31** 46.04N 16.59E
Virovitica Croatia **31** 45.50N 17.23E
Virpazar Yugo. **31** 42.15N 19.05E
Virrat Finland **40** 62.14N 23.47E
Virserum Sweden **41** 57.19N 15.35E
Virton Belgium **16** 49.35N 5.32E
Virtsu Estonia **41** 58.34N 23.31E
Virunga Nat. Park Zaïre **79** 0.30S 29.15E
Vis Croatia **31** 43.03N 16.12E
Vis *i.* Croatia **31** 43.02N 16.11E
Visalia U.S.A. **109** 36.20N119.18W
Visayan Sea Phil. **59** 11.35N123.51E
Visby Sweden **43** 57.38N 18.18E
Visconde do Rio Branco Brazil **126** 21.00S 42.51W
Viscount Melville Sd. Canada **98** 74.30N104.00W
Visé Belgium **16** 50.44N 5.42E
Višegrad Bosnia-Herzegovina **31** 43.47N 19.17E
Viserum Sweden **43** 57.21N 15.34E
Viseu Brazil **123** 1.12S 46.07W
Viseu Portugal **26** 40.39N 7.55W
Viseu *d.* Portugal **26** 40.50N 7.55W
Viseu de Sus Romania **37** 47.44N 24.22E
Vishākhapatnam India **61** 17.42N 83.24E
Viskafors Sweden **43** 57.38N 12.50E
Viskan *r.* Sweden **43** 57.14N 12.12E
Visnagar India **62** 23.42N 72.33E
Viso, Monte *mtn.* Italy **30** 44.40N 7.07E
Visoko Bosnia-Herzegovina **31** 43.59N 18.11E
Visp Switz. **39** 46.18N 7.53E
Vissefjärda Sweden **43** 56.32N 15.35E
Visselhövede Germany **38** 52.59N 9.35E
Vista U.S.A. **109** 33.12N117.15W
Vistula *r. see* Wisła *r.* Poland **37**
Vit *r.* Bulgaria **34** 43.30N 24.30E
Vitanje Slovenia **31** 46.23N 15.18E
Vitarte Peru **122** 12.03S 76.51W
Vitebsk Belorussia **44** 55.10N 30.14E
Viterbo Italy **30** 42.25N 12.06E
Vitigudino Spain **26** 41.00N 6.26W
Viti Levu *i.* Fiji **84** 18.00S178.00E
Vitim Russian Fed. **51** 59.28N112.35E
Vitim *r.* Russian Fed. **51** 59.30N112.36E
Vitoria Spain **26** 42.51N 2.40W
Vitória Espírito Santo Brazil **126** 20.19S 40.21W
Vitré France **18** 48.08N 1.12W
Vitry-le-François France **19** 48.44N 4.35E
Vitteaux France **19** 47.24N 4.32E
Vittel France **19** 48.12N 5.57E
Vittoria Italy **33** 36.57N 14.32E
Vittorio Veneto Italy **32** 45.59N 12.18E
Vittsjö Sweden **43** 56.20N 13.40E
Viveiro *see* Vivero Spain **26**
Viver Spain **25** 39.55N 0.36W
Vivero Spain **26** 43.38N 7.35W
Viviers France **21** 44.29N 4.41E
Vivonne France **18** 46.26N 0.16E
Vivonne Bay *town* Australia **92** 35.58S137.10E
Vizcaíno, Desierto de *des.* Mexico **109** 27.40N114.40W
Vizcaíno, Sierra *mts.* Mexico **109** 27.20N114.30W
Vizcaya *d.* Spain **26** 43.25N 2.45W
Vizianagaram India **61** 18.07N 83.30E
Vizille France **21** 45.05N 5.46E
Vižinada Croatia **31** 45.20N 13.46E
Vizinga Russian Fed. **44** 61.06N 50.05E
Vizzini Italy **33** 37.09N 14.46E
Vjosë *r.* Albania **34** 40.37N 19.20E
Vlaardingen Neth. **16** 51.55N 4.20E
Vladičin Han Yugo. **34** 42.42N 22.04E
Vladikavkaz Russian Fed. **45** 43.02N 44.43E
Vladimir Russian Fed. **44** 56.08N 40.25E
Vladimirets Ukraine **37** 51.28N 26.03E
Vladimir Volynskiy Ukraine **37** 50.51N 24.19E
Vladivostok Russian Fed. **53** 43.09N131.53E
Vlasenica Bosnia-Herzegovina **31** 44.11N 18.56E
Vlieland *i.* Neth. **16** 53.15N 5.00E
Vlissingen Neth. **16** 51.27N 3.35E
Vlorë Albania **34** 40.27N 19.30E
Vlorë *d.* Albania **34** 40.29N 19.29E
Vltava *r.* Czech Republic **39** 50.21N 14.30E
Vočin Croatia **31** 45.37N 17.32E
Vöcklabruck Austria **39** 48.01N 13.39E
Vodňany Czech Republic **39** 49.09N 14.11E
Vodnjan Croatia **31** 44.57N 13.51E
Voerde Germany **16** 51.37N 6.39E
Vogelkop *f. see* Jazirah Doberai *f.* Indonesia **59**
Vogelsberg *mts.* Germany **38** 50.30N 9.15E
Voghera Italy **30** 44.59N 9.01E
Voh N. Cal. **84** 20.58S164.42E
Vohibinany Madagascar **81** 18.49S 49.04E
Vohimarina Madagascar **81** 13.21S 50.02E
Vohipeno Madagascar **81** 22.22S 47.51E
Voi Kenya **79** 3.23S 38.35E
Void France **19** 48.41N 5.37E
Voiron France **21** 45.22N 5.35E
Voitsberg Austria **31** 47.03N 15.10E
Vojens Denmark **42** 55.15N 9.19E
Vojnić Croatia **31** 45.19N 15.43E
Volary Czech Republic **38** 48.55N 13.54E
Volborg U.S.A. **108** 45.50N105.40W
Volcano Is. Japan **84** 25.00N141.00E
Volda Norway **41** 62.09N 6.06E
Volga *r.* Russian Fed. **45** 45.45N 47.50E
Volgograd Russian Fed. **45** 48.45N 44.30E
Volgogradskoye Vodokhranilishche *resr.* Russian Fed. **45** 51.00N 46.05E
Volissós Greece **35** 38.29N 25.58E
Volkach Germany **39** 49.52N 10.13E
Volkhov Russian Fed. **44** 59.54N 32.47E
Volkhov *r.* Russian Fed. **44** 60.15N 32.15E
Völklingen Germany **39** 49.15N 6.50E
Volkovysk Belorussia **37** 53.10N 24.28E
Vollenhove Neth. **16** 52.41N 5.59E
Volnovakha Ukraine **45** 47.36N 37.32E
Volochanka Russian Fed. **51** 70.59N 94.18E
Volochisk Ukraine **37** 49.34N 26.10E
Volodarsk Russian Fed. **44** 56.14N 43.10E
Vologda Russian Fed. **44** 59.10N 39.55E
Volokolamsk Russian Fed. **44** 56.02N 35.56E
Volonne France **21** 44.07N 6.01E
Vólos Greece **35** 39.21N 22.56E
Volovets Ukraine **37** 48.44N 23.14E
Volsk Russian Fed. **44** 52.04N 47.22E
Volta *d.* Ghana **76** 7.30N 0.25E
Volta *r.* Ghana **76** 5.50N 0.41E
Volta, L. Ghana **76** 7.00N 0.00
Volta-Noire *d.* Burkina **76** 12.30N 3.25W
Volta Redonda Brazil **126** 22.31S 44.05W
Volterra Italy **30** 43.24N 10.51E
Voltri Italy **30** 44.26N 8.45E
Volturno *r.* Italy **33** 41.01N 13.55E
Volvi, Límni *l.* Greece **34** 40.41N 23.23E
Volyně Czech Republic **38** 49.10N 13.53E
Volzhskiy Russian Fed. **45** 48.48N 44.45E
Vondrozo Madagascar **81** 22.49S 47.20E
Vónitsa Greece **35** 38.53N 20.58E
Voorburg Neth. **16** 52.05N 4.22E
Vopnafjördhur *est.* Iceland **40** 65.50N 14.30W
Vopnafjördhur *town* Iceland **40** 65.46N 14.50W
Vorarlberg *d.* Austria **39** 47.13N 9.55E
Vóras Óros *mts.* Greece **34** 40.57N 21.45E
Vorderrhein *r.* Switz. **39** 46.49N 9.25E
Vordingborg Denmark **42** 55.01N 11.55E
Voríai Sporádhes *is.* Greece **35** 39.17N 23.23E
Vórios-Evvoïkós Kólpos *b.* Greece **35** 38.45N 23.15E
Vorkuta Russian Fed. **44** 67.27N 64.00E
Vorma *r.* Norway **42** 60.09N 11.27E
Vormsi *i.* Estonia **41** 59.00N 23.20E
Voronezh Russian Fed. **45** 51.40N 39.13E
Voronovo Belorussia **37** 54.09N 25.19E
Vosges *d.* France **19** 48.10N 6.20E
Vosges *mts.* France **19** 48.30N 7.10E
Voss Norway **41** 60.39N 6.26E
Vostochno Sibirskoye More *sea* Russian Fed. **51** 73.00N160.00E
Vostochnyy Sayan *mts.* Russian Fed. **52** 51.30N102.00E
Vostok I. Kiribati **85** 10.05S152.23W
Votkinsk Russian Fed. **44** 57.02N 53.59E
Votkinskoye Vodokhranilishche *resr.* Russian Fed. **44** 57.00N 55.00E
Votuporanga Brazil **124** 20.26S 49.53W
Vouga *r.* Portugal **26** 40.41N 8.40W
Vouillé France **18** 46.39N 0.10E
Voulou C.A.R. **73** 8.33N 22.36E
Vouziers France **19** 49.24N 4.42E
Voves France **19** 48.16N 1.38E
Voxna Sweden **41** 61.20N 15.30E
Voxna *r.* Sweden **41** 61.17N 16.26E
Voyvozh Russian Fed. **44** 64.19N 55.12E
Vozhega Russian Fed. **44** 60.25N 40.11E
Voznesensk Ukraine **23** 47.34N 31.21E
Vrå Denmark **42** 57.21N 9.57E
Vrådal Norway **42** 59.20N 8.25E
Vrakhnéika Greece **35** 38.10N 21.40E
Vrangelya, Ostrov *i.* Russian Fed. **51** 71.00N180.00
Vranje Yugo. **34** 42.34N 21.54E
Vratsa Bulgaria **34** 43.13N 23.30E
Vrbas *r.* Bosnia-Herzegovina **31** 45.06N 17.31E
Vrbas Yugo. **31** 45.35N 19.39E
Vrbovec Croatia **31** 45.53N 16.25E
Vrbovsko Croatia **31** 45.23N 15.05E
Vrede R.S.A. **80** 27.24S 29.09E
Vredendal R.S.A. **80** 31.40S 18.28E
Vrena Sweden **43** 58.52N 16.41E
Vresse Belgium **16** 49.53N 4.57E
Vrgnmost Croatia **31** 45.21N 15.52E
Vrhnika Slovenia **31** 45.58N 14.18E
Vries Neth. **16** 53.06N 6.35E
Vrigstad Sweden **43** 57.21N 14.28E
Vrindāvan India **63** 27.35N 77.42E
Vrlika Croatia **31** 43.55N 16.24E
Vrnograč Bosnia-Herzegovina **31** 45.10N 15.57E
Vrondádhes Greece **35** 38.25N 26.08E
Vršac Yugo. **37** 45.08N 21.18E
Vryburg R.S.A. **80** 26.57S 24.42E
Vučitrn Yugo. **34** 42.49N 20.59E
Vught Neth. **16** 51.39N 5.18E
Vukovar Croatia **31** 45.21N 19.00E
Vulcano, Isola *i.* Italy **33** 38.27N 14.58E
Vülchedruma Bulgaria **34** 43.42N 23.16E
Vung Tau Vietnam **56** 10.21N107.04E
Vurshets Bulgaria **34** 43.12N 23.17E
Vyāra India **62** 21.07N 73.24E
Vyatka *r.* Russian Fed. **50** 55.40N 51.40E
Vyatskiye Polyany Russian Fed. **44** 56.14N 51.08E
Vyazma Russian Fed. **44** 55.12N 34.17E
Vyazniki Russian Fed. **44** 56.14N 42.08E
Vyborg Russian Fed. **44** 60.45N 28.41E
Vychegda *r.* Russian Fed. **44** 61.15N 46.28E
Vychodné Beskydy *mts.* Europe **37** 49.30N 22.00E
Vygozero, Ozero *l.* Russian Fed. **44** 63.30N 34.30E
Vyrnwy, L. U.K. **12** 52.46N 3.30W
Vyshka Turkmenistan **65** 39.19N 54.10E
Vyshniy-Volochek Russian Fed. **44** 57.34N 34.23E
Vyšší Brod Czech Republic **39** 48.37N 14.19E
Vytegra Russian Fed. **44** 61.04N 36.27E

W

Wa Ghana **76** 10.07N 2.28W
Waal *r.* Neth. **16** 51.45N 4.40E
Waalwijk Neth. **16** 51.42N 5.04E
Wabag P.N.G. **59** 5.28S143.40E
Wabasca *r.* Canada **100** 58.22N115.20W
Wabash U.S.A. **110** 40.47N 85.48W
Wabash *r.* U.S.A. **110** 37.46N 88.02W
Wabē Mena *r.* Ethiopia **73** 6.20N 40.41E
Wabeno U.S.A. **110** 45.27N 88.38W
Wabera Ethiopia **73** 6.25N 40.45E
Wabē Shebelē *r.* Ethopia *see* Shabeelle *r.* Somali Rep. **71**
Wabrzeźno Poland **37** 53.17N 18.57E
Wabush City Canada **103** 52.53N 66.50W
Waco U.S.A. **111** 31.55N 97.08W
Wacouno *r.* Canada **103** 50.50N 65.58W
Wad Pakistan **62** 27.21N 66.22E
Wad Bandah Sudan **73** 13.06N 27.57E
Waddān Libya **75** 29.10N 16.08E
Waddeneilanden *is.* Neth. **16** 53.20N 5.00E
Waddenzee *b.* Neth. **16** 53.15N 5.05E
Waddikee Australia **92** 33.18S136.12E
Waddington U.S.A. **105** 44.52N 75.12W
Waddington, Mt. Canada **100** 51.23N125.15W
Wadena U.S.A. **110** 46.26N 95.08W
Wädenswil Switz. **39** 47.14N 8.40E
Wad Ḥāmid Sudan **72** 16.30N 32.48E
Wadhurst U.K. **13** 51.03N 0.21E
Wādī as Sīr *town* Jordan **67** 31.57N 35.49E
Wādī Ḥalfā' Sudan **64** 21.56N 31.20E
Wādī Mūsā *town* Jordan **66** 30.19N 35.29E
Wad Madanī Sudan **72** 14.24N 33.32E
Wad Nimr Sudan **72** 14.32N 32.08E
Wadsworth U.S.A. **114** 41.02N 81.44W
Wafrah Kuwait **65** 28.39N 47.56E
Wageningen Neth. **16** 51.58N 5.39E
Wager B. Canada **99** 65.26N 88.40W
Wager Bay *town* Canada **99** 65.55N 90.40W
Wagga Wagga Australia **93** 35.07S147.24E
Wagin Australia **89** 33.18S117.21E
Wagon Mound *town* U.S.A. **109** 36.01N104.42W
Wagrien *f.* Germany **38** 54.15N 10.45E
Wāh Pakistan **62** 33.48N 72.42E
Wahai Indonesia **59** 2.48S129.30E

Wāḩat Salīmah to **Were Īlu**

Wāḩat Salīmah Sudan **72** 21.22N 29.19E
Wahiawa Hawaiian Is. **85** 21.30N158.01W
Wahiba Sands *des.* Oman **60** 21.56N 58.55E
Wahpeton U.S.A. **110** 46.16N 96.36W
Waiau New Zealand **86** 42.39S173.03E
Waiblingen Germany **39** 48.50N 9.19E
Waidhān India **63** 24.04N 82.20E
Waidhofen Austria **36** 47.58N 14.47E
Waigeo *i.* Indonesia **59** 0.05S130.30E
Waihi New Zealand **86** 37.24S175.50E
Waikato *d.* New Zealand **86** 38.15S175.10E
Waikato *r.* New Zealand **86** 37.19S174.50E
Waikerie Australia **92** 34.11S139.59E
Waikokopu New Zealand **86** 39.05S177.50E
Waikouaiti New Zealand **86** 45.36S170.41E
Wailuku Hawaiian Is. **85** 20.53N156.30W
Waimakariri *r.* New Zealand **86** 43.23S172.40E
Waimate New Zealand **86** 44.45S171.03E
Waimea Hawaiian Is. **85** 20.01N155.41W
Wainganga *r.* India **63** 18.50N 79.55E
Waingapu Indonesia **59** 9.30S120.10E
Wainwright Canada **101** 52.49N110.52W
Wainwright U.S.A. **98** 70.39N160.00W
Waiouru New Zealand **86** 39.39S175.40E
Waipara New Zealand **86** 43.03S172.45E
Waipawa New Zealand **86** 39.56S176.35E
Waipiro New Zealand **86** 38.02S178.21E
Waipu New Zealand **86** 35.59S174.26E
Waipukurau New Zealand **86** 40.00S176.33E
Wairau *r.* New Zealand **86** 41.32S174.08E
Wairoa New Zealand **86** 39.03S177.25E
Waitaki *r.* New Zealand **86** 44.56S171.10E
Waitara New Zealand **86** 38.59S174.13E
Waiuku New Zealand **86** 37.15S174.44E
Wajima Japan **57** 37.24N136.54E
Wajir Kenya **79** 1.46N 40.05E
Waka Ethiopia **73** 7.07N 37.26E
Waka Zaïre **78** 0.48S 20.10E
Wakasa wan *b.* Japan **57** 35.50N135.40E
Wakatipu, L. New Zealand **86** 45.10S168.30E
Wakayama Japan **57** 34.13N135.11E
Wakefield Canada **105** 45.38N 75.56W
Wakefield U.K. **12** 53.41N 1.31W
Wakefield U.S.A. **115** 41.26N 71.30W
Wake I. Pacific Oc. **84** 19.17N166.36E
Wakema Burma **56** 16.36N 95.11E
Wakkanai Japan **57** 45.26N141.43E
Wakonassin *r.* Canada **104** 46.28N 81.51W
Wakre Indonesia **59** 0.30S131.05E
Wakuach, L. Canada **103** 55.37N 67.40W
Walamba Zambia **79** 13.27S 28.44E
Wałbrzych Poland **36** 50.48N 16.19E
Walcha Australia **93** 31.00S151.36E
Walcheren *f.* Neth. **16** 51.32N 3.35E
Wałcz Poland **36** 53.17N 16.28E
Waldbröl Germany **16** 50.52N 7.34E
Waldeck Germany **38** 51.12N 9.04E
Walden U.S.A. **108** 40.34N106.11W
Waldkirch Germany **39** 48.05N 7.57E
Waldorf U.S.A. **114** 38.37N 76.54W
Waldport U.S.A. **108** 44.26N124.04W
Waldron U.S.A. **111** 34.54N 94.05W
Waldshut Germany **39** 47.37N 8.13E
Wales *d.* U.K. **13** 52.30N 3.45W
Wales U.S.A. **110** 47.13N 91.41W
Walgett Australia **93** 30.03S148.10E
Walhonding *r.* U.S.A. **114** 40.18N 81.53W
Walikale Zaïre **79** 1.29S 28.05E
Walker U.S.A. **110** 47.06N 94.35W
Walker L. U.S.A. **108** 38.44N118.43W
Walkerton Canada **104** 44.07N 81.09W
Wall U.S.A. **108** 43.59N102.14W
Wallace Canada **104** 45.23N 78.05W
Wallace Idaho U.S.A. **108** 47.28N115.55W
Wallace Nebr. U.S.A. **110** 40.50N101.10W
Wallaceburg Canada **104** 42.36N 82.23W
Wallachia *f.* Romania **37** 44.35N 25.00E
Wallambin, L. Australia **89** 30.58S117.30E
Wallangarra Australia **93** 28.51S151.52E
Wallaroo Australia **92** 33.57S137.36E
Walla Walla Australia **93** 35.48S146.52E
Walla Walla U.S.A. **108** 46.08N118.20W
Wallenpaupack, L. U.S.A. **115** 41.25N 75.12W
Wallingford U.S.A. **115** 41.27N 72.50W
Wallis, Îles *is.* Pacific Oc. **84** 13.16S176.15W
Wallkill *r.* U.S.A. **115** 41.51N 74.03W
Wallowa U.S.A. **108** 45.34N117.32W
Wallowa Mts. U.S.A. **108** 45.10N117.30W
Wallsend Australia **93** 32.55S151.40E
Walmsley L. Canada **101** 63.25N108.36W
Walpole Australia **89** 34.57S116.44E
Walsall U.K. **13** 52.36N 1.59W
Walsenburg U.S.A. **108** 37.37N104.47W
Walsrode Germany **38** 52.52N 9.35E
Walterboro U.S.A. **113** 32.54N 80.21W
Waltershausen Germany **38** 50.53N 10.33E
Waltham Canada **105** 45.55N 76.57W
Walton N.Y. U.S.A. **115** 42.10N 75.08W
Walton W.Va. U.S.A. **114** 38.40N 81.26W
Walton on the Naze U.K. **13** 51.52N 1.17E
Walton on the Wolds U.K. **12** 52.49N 0.49W
Walvis B. R.S.A. **80** 22.55S 14.30E
Walvisbaai R.S.A. **80** 22.57S 14.30E
Walvis Bay *town see* Walvisbaai R.S.A. **80**
Walvis Bay *d.* R.S.A. **80** 22.56S 14.35E
Walvis Ridge *f.* Atlantic Oc. **127** 28.00S 4.00E
Wamanfo Ghana **76** 7.16N 2.44W
Wamba Kenya **79** 0.58N 37.19E
Wamba Nigeria **77** 8.57N 8.42E
Wamba Zaïre **79** 2.10N 27.59E
Wamba *r.* Zaïre **78** 4.35S 17.15E
Wami *r.* Tanzania **79** 6.10S 38.50E
Wampsville U.S.A. **115** 43.05N 75.42W
Wamsasi Indonesia **59** 3.27S126.07E
Wan Indonesia **90** 8.23S137.55E
Wāna Pakistan **62** 32.17N 69.35E
Wanaaring Australia **92** 29.42S144.14E
Wanaka New Zealand **86** 44.42S169.08E
Wanaka, L. New Zealand **86** 44.30S169.10E
Wan'an China **55** 26.27N114.46E
Wanapiri Indonesia **59** 4.30S135.50E
Wanapitei *r.* Canada **104** 46.02N 80.51W
Wanapitei L. Canada **104** 46.45N 80.45W
Wanbi Australia **92** 34.46S140.19E
Wandana Australia **92** 32.04S133.45E
Wandoan Australia **90** 26.09S149.51E
Wanganella Australia **93** 35.13S144.53E
Wanganui New Zealand **86** 39.56S175.00E
Wangaratta Australia **93** 36.22S146.20E
Wangary Australia **92** 34.30S135.26E
Wangdu China **54** 38.43N115.09E
Wangdu Phodrang Bhutan **63** 27.29N 89.54E
Wangen Germany **39** 47.42N 9.50E
Wangerooge *i.* Germany **38** 53.46N 7.55E
Wanghai Shan *mtn.* China **54** 41.40N121.43E
Wangianna Australia **92** 29.42S137.32E
Wangjiang China **55** 30.07N116.41E
Wangpan Yang *b.* China **55** 30.30N121.30E
Wangqing China **57** 43.20N129.48E
Wangyuanqiao China **54** 38.24N106.16E
Wani India **63** 20.04N 78.57E
Wānkāner India **62** 22.37N 70.56E
Wanle Weyne Somali Rep. **71** 2.38N 44.55E
Wannian China **55** 28.42N117.03E
Wanning China **55** 18.48N110.22E
Wānow Afghan. **62** 32.38N 65.54E
Wantage U.K. **13** 51.35N 1.25W
Wanup Canada **104** 46.24N 80.49W
Wanxian China **55** 30.52N108.20E
Wanyang Shan *mts.* China **55** 26.01N113.48E
Wanyuan China **54** 32.04N108.02E
Wanzai China **55** 28.06N114.27E
Wanzleben Germany **38** 52.03N 11.26E
Wāpi India **62** 20.22N 72.54E
Wapiti *r.* Canada **100** 55.05N118.18W
Wappingers Falls U.S.A. **115** 41.36N 73.55W
Waqqāş Jordan **67** 32.33N 35.36E
Wārāh Pakistan **62** 27.27N 67.48E
Warangal India **61** 18.00N 79.35E
Waranga Resr. Australia **93** 36.32S145.04E
Wārāseoni India **63** 21.45N 80.02E
Waratah B. Australia **91** 38.55S146.04E
Warburg Germany **38** 51.29N 9.08E
Warburton *r.* Australia **91** 27.55S137.15E
Warburton Range *mts.* S.A. Australia **92** 30.30S134.32E
Warburton Range *mts.* W.A. Australia **88** 26.09S126.38E
Ward Rep. of Ire. **15** 53.26N 6.20W
Warden R.S.A. **80** 27.49S 28.57E
Wardenburg Germany **38** 53.04N 8.11E
Wardha India **63** 20.45N 78.37E
Wardha *r.* India **63** 19.38N 79.48E
Ward Hill U.K. **10** 58.54N 3.20W
Wardlow Canada **101** 50.54N111.33W
Ware U.S.A. **115** 42.16N 72.15W
Wareham U.S.A. **115** 41.46N 70.43W
Waren Germany **38** 53.31N 12.40E
Warendorf Germany **38** 51.57N 7.59E
Warfordsburg U.S.A. **114** 39.44N 78.15W
Warialda Australia **93** 29.33S150.36E
Wark Forest *hills* U.K. **12** 55.06N 2.24W
Warkopi Indonesia **59** 1.12S134.09E
Warkworth New Zealand **86** 36.24S174.40E
Warley U.K. **13** 52.29N 2.02W
Warmbad Namibia **80** 28.26S 18.41E
Warminster U.K. **13** 51.12N 2.11W
Warm Springs *town* U.S.A. **108** 39.39N114.49W
Warnemünde Germany **38** 54.10N 12.04E
Warner U.S.A. **115** 43.17N 71.49W
Warner Robins U.S.A. **113** 32.35N 83.37W
Warnow *r.* Germany **38** 54.06N 12.09E
Waroona Australia **89** 32.51S115.50E
Warracknabeal Australia **92** 36.15S142.28E
Warragul Australia **93** 38.11S145.55E
Warrakalanna, L. Australia **92** 28.13S139.23E
Warrambool *r.* Australia **93** 30.04S147.38E
Warrego *r.* Australia **93** 30.25S145.18E
Warrego Range *mts.* Australia **90** 24.55S146.20E
Warren Australia **93** 31.44S147.53E
Warren Ont. Canada **104** 46.27N 80.20W
Warren Ark. U.S.A. **111** 33.37N 92.04W
Warren Mich. U.S.A. **114** 42.28N 83.01W
Warren Minn. U.S.A. **110** 48.12N 96.46W
Warren N.H. U.S.A. **105** 43.56N 71.54W
Warren Ohio U.S.A. **114** 41.14N 80.52W
Warren Penn. U.S.A. **114** 41.51N 79.08W
Warren R.I. U.S.A. **115** 41.43N 71.17W
Warren Vt. U.S.A. **105** 44.06N 72.52W
Warrenpoint U.K. **15** 54.06N 6.15W
Warrensburg Mo. U.S.A. **110** 38.46N 93.44W
Warrensburg N.Y. U.S.A. **115** 43.30N 73.46W
Warrenton R.S.A. **80** 28.07S 24.49E
Warrenton U.S.A. **114** 38.43N 77.48W
Warri Nigeria **77** 5.36N 5.46E
Warrina Australia **92** 28.10S135.49E
Warriner Creek *r.* Australia **92** 29.15S137.03E
Warrington U.K. **12** 53.25N 2.38W
Warrington U.S.A. **111** 30.23N 87.16W
Warrnambool Australia **92** 38.23S142.03E
Warroad U.S.A. **110** 48.54N 95.19W
Warrumbungle Range *mts.* Australia **93** 31.20S149.00E
Warsaw *see* Warszawa Poland **37**
Warsaw Ind. U.S.A. **112** 41.13N 85.52W
Warsaw N.Y. U.S.A. **114** 42.44N 78.08W
Warsaw Ohio U.S.A. **114** 40.20N 82.00W
Warshiikh Somali Rep. **71** 2.19N 45.50E
Warszawa Poland **37** 52.15N 21.00E
Warta *r.* Poland **36** 52.45N 15.09E
Warud India **63** 21.28N 78.16E
Warwick Australia **93** 28.12S152.00E
Warwick Canada **105** 45.56N 71.59W
Warwick U.K. **13** 52.17N 1.36W
Warwick N.Y. U.S.A. **115** 41.16N 74.22W
Warwick R.I. U.S.A. **115** 41.43N 71.28W
Warwickshire *d.* U.K. **13** 52.13N 1.30W
Wasaga Beach Canada **104** 44.31N 80.01W
Wasatch Plateau *f.* U.S.A. **108** 39.20N111.30W
Wasco Calif. U.S.A. **109** 35.36N119.20W
Wasco Oreg. U.S.A. **108** 45.35N120.42W
Washago Canada **104** 44.45N 79.20W
Washburn N.Dak. U.S.A. **110** 47.17N101.02W
Washburn Wisc. U.S.A. **110** 46.41N 90.52W
Washburn L. Canada **98** 70.03N106.50W
Wāshim India **62** 20.06N 77.09E
Washington U.K. **12** 54.55N 1.30W
Washington *d.* U.S.A. **108** 47.43N120.00W
Washington D.C. U.S.A. **114** 38.55N 77.00W
Washington Ga. U.S.A. **113** 33.43N 82.46W
Washington Ind. U.S.A. **112** 38.40N 87.10W
Washington Iowa U.S.A. **110** 41.18N 91.42W
Washington N.C. U.S.A. **113** 35.33N 77.04W
Washington Penn. U.S.A. **114** 40.10N 80.15W
Washington Utah U.S.A. **108** 37.08N113.30W
Washington Va. U.S.A. **114** 38.43N 78.10W
Washington Crossing U.S.A. **115** 40.18N 74.52W
Wāshuk Pakistan **62** 27.44N 64.48E
Wasian Indonesia **59** 1.51S133.21E
Wasior Indonesia **59** 2.38S134.27E
Wasiri Indonesia **59** 7.30S126.30E
Waskaganish Canada **102** 51.29N 78.45W
Waskesiu L. Canada **101** 53.56N106.10W
Waskigomog L. Canada **104** 46.00N 78.59W
Wassen Switz. **39** 46.42N 8.36E
Wassenaar Neth. **16** 52.10N 4.26E
Wasseralfingen Germany **39** 48.52N 10.06E
Wasserburg Germany **39** 48.04N 12.13E
Wasserkuppe *mtn.* Germany **38** 50.30N 9.56E
Wassy France **19** 48.30N 4.57E
Waswanipi Lac *l.* Canada **102** 49.35N 76.40W
Watampone Indonesia **59** 4.33S120.20E
Watchet U.K. **13** 51.10N 3.20W
Waterbury U.S.A. **115** 41.33N 73.02W
Waterbury L. Canada **101** 58.16N105.00W
Waterford Canada **104** 42.56N 80.17W
Waterford Rep. of Ire. **15** 52.16N 7.08W
Waterford *d.* Rep. of Ire. **15** 52.10N 7.40W
Waterford U.S.A. **114** 41.57N 79.59W
Waterford Harbour *est.* Rep. of Ire. **15** 52.12N 6.56W
Waterloo Belgium **16** 50.44N 4.24E
Waterloo Ont. Canada **104** 43.28N 80.31W
Waterloo Que. Canada **105** 45.21N 72.31W
Waterloo Iowa U.S.A. **110** 42.30N 92.20W
Waterloo N.Y. U.S.A. **114** 42.54N 76.52W
Waterton Glacier International Peace Park U.S.A. / Canada **108** 48.47N113.45W
Watertown N.Y. U.S.A. **115** 43.59N 75.55W
Watertown S.Dak. U.S.A. **110** 44.54N 97.07W
Watervale Australia **92** 33.58S138.39E
Water Valley *town* U.S.A. **111** 34.09N 89.38W
Waterville Canada **105** 45.16N 71.54W
Waterville Rep. of Ire. **15** 51.50N 10.11W
Waterville Maine U.S.A. **112** 44.33N 69.38W
Waterville N.Y. U.S.A. **115** 42.56N 75.23W
Waterville Wash. U.S.A. **108** 47.39N120.04W
Watervliet U.S.A. **115** 42.44N 73.42W
Watford Canada **104** 42.57N 81.53W
Watford U.K. **13** 51.40N 0.25W
Watford City U.S.A. **110** 47.48N103.17W
Wa'th Sudan **73** 7.24N 28.58E
Wathaman L. Canada **101** 56.55N103.43W
Watkins Glen U.S.A. **114** 42.23N 76.52W
Watonga U.S.A. **111** 35.51N 98.25W
Watrous Canada **101** 51.40N105.28W
Watsa Zaïre **79** 3.03N 29.29E
Watson Canada **101** 52.07N104.31W
Watson Lake *town* Canada **100** 60.06N128.49W
Watsontown U.S.A. **114** 41.05N 76.52W
Watsonville U.S.A. **108** 36.55N121.45W
Wattiwarriganna Creek *r.* Australia **92** 28.57S136.10E
Wattwil Switz. **39** 47.18N 9.06E
Watzmann *mtn.* Germany **39** 47.33N 12.55E
Wau P.N.G. **59** 7.22S146.40E
Wauchope N.S.W. Australia **93** 31.27S152.43E
Wauchope N.T. Australia **90** 20.39S134.13E
Waukaringa Australia **92** 32.18S139.27E
Waukegan U.S.A. **110** 42.22N 87.50W
Waukesha U.S.A. **110** 43.01N 88.14W
Waukon U.S.A. **110** 43.16N 91.29W
Wauneta U.S.A. **110** 40.25N101.23W
Waurika U.S.A. **111** 34.10N 98.00W
Wausau U.S.A. **110** 44.58N 89.40W
Wautoma U.S.A. **110** 44.05N 89.17W
Wauwatosa U.S.A. **110** 43.04N 88.02W
Wave Hill *town* Australia **88** 17.29S130.57E
Waveney *r.* U.K. **13** 52.29N 1.46E
Waverly Ill. U.S.A. **110** 39.36N 89.57W
Waverly Iowa U.S.A. **110** 42.44N 92.29W
Waverly N.Y. U.S.A. **115** 42.00N 76.32W
Wavre Belgium **16** 50.43N 4.37E
Wāw Sudan **73** 7.42N 28.00E
Wāw al Kabīr Libya **75** 25.20N 16.43E
Waxahachie U.S.A. **111** 32.24N 96.51W
Waxweiler Germany **39** 50.05N 6.22E
Way, L. Australia **88** 26.47S120.21E
Waycross U.S.A. **113** 31.12N 82.22W
Wayland U.S.A. **114** 42.34N 77.35W
Wayne N.J. U.S.A. **115** 40.03N 75.23W
Wayne W.Va. U.S.A. **114** 38.13N 82.27W
Waynesboro Ga. U.S.A. **113** 33.04N 82.01W
Waynesboro Penn. U.S.A. **114** 39.45N 77.35W
Waynesboro Va. U.S.A. **113** 38.04N 78.53W
Waynesburg Ohio U.S.A. **114** 40.40N 81.16W
Waynesburg Penn. U.S.A. **114** 39.54N 80.11W
Waynesville U.S.A. **113** 35.30N 82.58W
Waynoka U.S.A. **111** 36.35N 98.53W
Wazay Afghan. **62** 33.22N 69.26E
Waziers France **19** 50.23N 3.07E
Wazīrābād Pakistan **62** 32.27N 74.07E
Wear *r.* U.K. **12** 54.55N 1.21W
Weatherford Okla. U.S.A. **111** 35.32N 98.42W
Weatherford Tex. U.S.A. **111** 32.46N 97.48W
Webbwood Canada **104** 46.16N 81.53W
Webster Mass. U.S.A. **115** 42.03N 71.53W
Webster N.Y. U.S.A. **114** 43.13N 77.26W
Webster Wisc. U.S.A. **110** 45.53N 92.22W
Webster City U.S.A. **110** 42.28N 93.49W
Webster Groves U.S.A. **110** 38.35N 90.21W
Webster Springs *town* U.S.A. **114** 38.29N 80.25W
Weda Indonesia **59** 0.30N127.52E
Weddell Sea Antarctica **128** 70.00S 40.00W
Wedderburn Australia **92** 36.26S143.39E
Wedgeport Canada **103** 43.44N 65.59W
Wedmore U.K. **13** 51.14N 2.50W
Wedza Zimbabwe **81** 18.37S 31.33E
Weedon Canada **105** 45.42N 71.28W
Weedsport U.S.A. **115** 43.03N 76.34W
Weeho *r.* Canada **100** 63.20N115.10W
Weelde Belgium **16** 51.25N 5.00E
Weemelah Australia **93** 29.02S149.15E
Weert Neth. **16** 51.14N 5.40E
Wee Waa Australia **93** 30.34S149.27E
Wegorzyno Poland **36** 53.32N 15.33E
Węgrów Poland **37** 52.25N 22.01E
Wegscheid Germany **39** 48.36N 13.48E
Weichang China **54** 41.56N117.34E
Weida Germany **38** 50.45N 12.04E
Weiden in der Oberpfalz Germany **39** 49.41N 12.10E
Weifang China **54** 36.40N119.10E
Weihai China **54** 37.28N122.05E
Wei He *r.* Shaanxi China **54** 34.27N109.30E
Wei He *r.* Shandong China **54** 36.47N115.42E
Weilburg Germany **38** 50.29N 8.15E
Weilheim Germany **39** 47.50N 11.08E
Weilmoringle Australia **93** 29.16S146.55E
Weimar Germany **38** 50.59N 11.19E
Weinan China **54** 34.25N109.30E
Weinheim Germany **39** 49.32N 8.39E
Weipa Australia **90** 12.41S141.52E
Weir *r.* Australia **93** 29.10S149.06E
Weirton U.S.A. **114** 40.25N 80.35W
Weiser U.S.A. **108** 44.37N116.58W
Weishan Hu *l.* China **54** 34.40N117.25E
Weishi China **54** 34.24N114.14E
Weisse Elster *r.* Germany **38** 51.26N 11.57E
Weissenburg in Bayern Germany **38** 49.01N 10.58E
Weissenfels Germany **38** 51.12N 11.58E
Weisswasser Germany **38** 51.30N 14.38E
Wei Xian China **54** 36.21N114.56E
Weixin China **55** 27.48N105.05E
Weiya China **52** 41.50N 94.24E
Weizhou *i.* China **55** 21.01N109.03E
Wejherowo Poland **37** 54.37N 18.15E
Wekusko Canada **101** 54.45N 99.45W
Weldiya Ethiopia **73** 11.50N 39.36E
Weldon U.S.A. **109** 35.40N118.20W
Welega *d.* Ethiopia **73** 9.40N 35.50E
Welkom R.S.A. **80** 27.59S 26.42E
Welland Canada **104** 42.59N 79.14W
Welland *r.* U.K. **12** 52.53N 0.00
Wellesley Is. Australia **90** 16.42S139.30E
Wellfleet U.S.A. **115** 41.56N 70.02W
Wellin Belgium **16** 50.05N 5.07E
Wellingborough U.K. **13** 52.18N 0.41W
Wellington N.S.W. Australia **93** 32.33S148.59E
Wellington S.A. Australia **92** 35.21S139.23E
Wellington Canada **105** 43.57N 77.21W
Wellington New Zealand **86** 41.17S174.47E
Wellington *d.* New Zealand **86** 40.00S175.30E
Wellington Shrops. U.K. **13** 52.42N 2.31W
Wellington Somerset U.K. **13** 50.58N 3.13W
Wellington Kans. U.S.A. **111** 37.16N 97.24W
Wellington Nev. U.S.A. **108** 38.45N119.22W
Wellington Ohio U.S.A. **114** 41.10N 82.13W
Wellington, Isla *i.* Chile **125** 49.30S 75.00W
Wells U.K. **13** 51.12N 2.39W
Wells Maine U.S.A. **115** 43.20N 70.35W
Wells Nev. U.S.A. **108** 41.07N114.58W
Wells N.Y. U.S.A. **115** 43.24N 74.17W
Wellsboro U.S.A. **114** 41.45N 77.18W
Wellsburg U.S.A. **114** 40.16N 80.37W
Wells Gray Prov. Park Canada **100** 52.30N120.15W
Wells L. Canada **101** 57.15N101.00W
Wells-next-the-Sea U.K. **12** 52.57N 0.51E
Wells River *town* U.S.A. **105** 44.09N 72.06W
Wellston U.S.A. **114** 39.07N 82.32W
Wellsville Mo. U.S.A. **110** 39.04N 91.34W
Wellsville N.Y. U.S.A. **114** 42.07N 77.57W
Wellton U.S.A. **109** 32.40N114.08W
Welmel *r.* Ethiopia **73** 6.00N 40.20E
Welo *d.* Ethiopia **73** 11.30N 40.00E
Wels Austria **39** 48.10N 14.02E
Welshpool U.K. **13** 52.40N 3.09W
Welwyn Garden City U.K. **13** 51.48N 0.13W
Wem U.K. **12** 52.52N 2.45W
Wembere *r.* Tanzania **79** 4.07S 34.15E
Wemindji Canada **102** 53.02N 78.55W
Wenatchee U.S.A. **108** 47.25N120.19W
Wenchang China **55** 19.37N110.43E
Wenchi Ghana **76** 7.40N 2.06W
Wendel U.S.A. **108** 40.20N120.14W
Wendo Ethiopia **73** 6.40N 38.27E
Wendover U.S.A. **108** 40.44N114.02W
Wenebegon L. Canada **102** 47.25N 83.05W
Wengfengzhen China **54** 34.56N104.38E
Wenlock *r.* Australia **90** 12.02S141.55E
Wenquan China **63** 33.13N 91.50E
Wenshan China **55** 23.20N104.11E
Wensleydale *f.* U.K. **12** 54.19N 2.04W
Wentworth Australia **92** 34.06S141.56E
Wen Xian China **54** 32.52N104.40E
Wenzhou China **53** 28.02N120.40E
Weott U.S.A. **108** 40.19N123.54W
Wepener R.S.A. **80** 29.43S 27.01E
Werda Botswana **80** 25.15S 23.16E
Werdau Germany **38** 50.44N 12.22E
Werdër *well* Ethiopia **71** 6.58N 45.21E
Werder Germany **38** 52.23N 12.56E
Werdohl Germany **38** 51.15N 7.45E
Were Īlu Ethiopia **73** 10.37N 39.28E

Weri to **Womelsdorf**

Weri Indonesia 59 3.10S132.30E
Werne Germany 16 51.39N 7.36E
Wernigerode Germany 38 51.50N 10.47E
Werra *r.* Germany 38 51.26N 9.39E
Werribee Australia 93 37.54S144.40E
Werris Creek *town* Australia 93 31.20S150.41E
Wertheim Germany 39 49.46N 9.31E
Wertingen Germany 39 48.34N 10.41E
Wesel Germany 38 51.40N 6.38E
Weser *r.* Germany 38 53.15N 8.34E
Weslaco U.S.A. 111 26.09N 97.59W
Weslemkoon L. Canada 105 45.02N 77.25W
Wesleyville Canada 103 49.09N 53.34W
Wesleyville U.S.A. 114 42.08N 80.01W
Wessel, C. Australia 90 10.59S136.46E
Wessel Is. Australia 90 11.30S136.25E
Wessington U.S.A. 110 44.27N 98.42W
Wessington Springs *town* U.S.A. 110 44.05N 98.34W
West U.S.A. 111 31.48N 97.06W
West *r.* U.S.A. 115 42.52N 72.33W
West Australian Basin *f.* Indian Oc. 49 15.00S100.00E
West B. U.S.A. 111 29.15N 94.57W
West Bank Jordan 67 32.00N 35.15E
West Bend U.S.A. 110 43.25N 88.11W
West Bengal *d.* India 63 23.00N 88.00E
West Branch U.S.A. 104 44.17N 84.14W
West Bromwich U.K. 13 52.32N 2.01W
Westbrook U.S.A. 112 43.41N 70.21W
West Burke U.S.A. 105 44.38N 71.59W
West Burra *i.* U.K. 10 60.05N 1.21W
West Canada Creek *r.* U.S.A. 115 43.01N 74.58W
West Caroline Basin Pacific Oc. 84 5.00N139.00E
West Chester U.S.A. 115 39.58N 75.36W
West Coast *d.* New Zealand 86 43.15S170.10E
West Des Moines U.S.A. 110 41.35N 93.43W
Westende Belgium 16 51.10N 2.46E
Westerland Germany 38 54.54N 8.18E
Westerly U.S.A. 115 41.22N 71.50W
Western *d.* Ghana 76 6.00N 2.40W
Western *d.* Kenya 79 0.30N 34.30E
Western *d.* Zambia 80 16.00S 23.45E
Western Australia *d.* Australia 88 24.20S122.30E
Western Duck I. Canada 104 45.45N 83.00W
Western Ghâts *mts.* India 60 15.30N 74.30E
Western Isles *d.* U.K. 14 57.40N 7.10W
Westernport U.S.A. 114 39.29N 79.03W
Western Sahara Africa 74 25.00N 13.30W
Western Samoa Pacific Oc. 84 13.55S172.00W
Westerschelde *est.* Neth. 16 51.25N 3.40E
Westerstede Germany 38 53.15N 7.55E
Westerville U.S.A. 114 40.08N 82.56W
Westerwald *f.* Germany 38 50.40N 7.45E
West Falkland *i.* Falkland Is. 125 51.40W 60.00W
West Felton U.K. 12 52.49N 2.58W
Westfield Mass. U.S.A. 115 42.08N 72.45W
Westfield N.J. U.S.A. 115 40.39N 74.21W
Westfield N.Y. U.S.A. 114 42.19N 79.35W
Westfield Penn. U.S.A. 114 41.55N 77.32W
Westfield *r.* U.S.A. 115 42.05N 72.35W
West Fork *r.* U.S.A. 114 39.28N 80.09W
West Frankfort U.S.A. 111 37.54N 88.55W
West Frisian Is. *see* Waddeneilanden Neth. 36
West Glamorgan *d.* U.K. 13 51.42N 3.47W
Westhampton U.S.A. 115 40.49N 72.39W
West Haven U.S.A. 115 41.16N 72.57W
Westhope U.S.A. 110 48.55N101.01W
West Indies *is.* C. America 127 21.00N 74.00W
West Lafayette U.S.A. 112 40.26N 86.56W
West Leyden U.S.A. 115 43.28N 75.28W
West Linton U.K. 14 55.45N 3.21W
Westlock Canada 100 54.09N113.55W
West Lorne Canada 104 42.36N 81.36W
Westmeath Canada 105 45.49N 76.54W
Westmeath *d.* Rep. of Ire. 15 53.30N 7.30W
West Memphis U.S.A. 111 35.08N 90.11W
West Middlesex U.S.A. 114 41.10N 80.27W
West Midlands *d.* U.K. 13 52.28N 1.50W
Westminster U.S.A. 114 39.35N 77.00W
Westmoreland Australia 90 17.18S138.12E
Westmoreland U.S.A. 115 42.59N 72.25W
West Nicholson Zimbabwe 80 21.06S 29.25E
Weston Malaysia 58 5.14N115.35E
Weston U.S.A. 114 39.02N 80.28W
Weston-Super-Mare U.K. 13 51.20N 2.59W
West Palm Beach *town* U.S.A. 113 26.42N 80.05W
West Plains *town* U.S.A. 111 36.44N 91.51W
West Point *town* U.S.A. 111 33.36N 88.39W
Westport Canada 105 44.41N 76.26W
Westport New Zealand 86 41.46S171.38E
Westport Rep. of Ire. 15 53.48N 9.32W
Westport Conn. U.S.A. 115 41.09N 73.22W
Westport N.Y. U.S.A. 105 44.13N 73.39W
Westport Wash. U.S.A. 108 46.53N124.06W
Westray Canada 101 53.36N101.24W
Westray *i.* U.K. 14 59.18N 2.58W
Westree Canada 104 47.26N 81.34W
West Road *r.* Canada 100 53.18N122.53W
West Siberian Plain *f.* *see* Zapadno-Sibirskaya Ravnina Russian Fed. 9
West Springfield U.S.A. 115 42.06N 72.38W
West Sussex *d.* U.K. 13 50.58N 0.30W
West Terschelling Neth. 16 53.22N 5.13E
West Union U.S.A. 114 39.18N 80.47W
West Virginia *d.* U.S.A. 114 38.45N 80.30W
West Vlaanderen *d.* Belgium 16 51.00N 3.00E
West Wyalong Australia 93 33.54S147.12E
West Yellowstone U.S.A. 108 44.30N111.05W
West York U.S.A. 114 39.57N 76.46W
West Yorkshire *d.* U.K. 12 53.45N 1.40W
Wetar *i.* Indonesia 59 7.45S126.00E
Wetaskiwin Canada 100 52.55N113.24W
Wetteren Belgium 16 51.00N 3.51E
Wetzlar Germany 38 50.33N 8.29E
Wewak P.N.G. 59 3.35S143.35E
Wewoka U.S.A. 111 35.09N 96.30W
Wexford Rep. of Ire. 15 52.20N 6.28W
Wexford *d.* Rep. of Ire. 15 52.20N 6.25W
Wexford B. Rep. of Ire. 15 52.27N 6.18W
Weyburn Canada 101 49.41N103.52W
Weyib *r.* Ethiopia 73 4.11N 42.09E
Weymouth U.K. 13 50.36N 2.28W
Weymouth, C. Australia 90 12.32S143.36E
Whakatane New Zealand 86 37.56S177.00E
Whalan *r.* Australia 93 29.10S148.42E
Whale Cove *town* Canada 101 62.11N 92.36W
Whalsay *i.* U.K. 14 60.22N 0.59W
Whangarei New Zealand 86 35.43S174.20E
Wharfe *r.* U.K. 12 53.50N 1.07W
Wharfedale *f.* U.K. 12 54.00N 1.55W
Wharton U.S.A. 111 29.19N 96.06W
Whataroa New Zealand 86 43.16S170.22E
Wheatland U.S.A. 108 42.03N104.57W
Wheatley Canada 104 42.06N 82.27W
Wheaton Md. U.S.A. 114 39.03N 77.03W
Wheaton Minn. U.S.A. 110 45.48N 96.30W
Wheeler *r.* Que. Canada 103 58.05N 67.12W
Wheeler *r.* Sask. Canada 101 57.25N105.30W
Wheeler Peak *mtn.* Nev. U.S.A. 108 38.59N114.19W
Wheeler Peak *mtn.* N.Mex. U.S.A. 108 36.34N105.25W
Wheeler Ridge *town* U.S.A. 109 35.06N119.01W
Wheeler Springs *town* U.S.A. 109 34.30N119.18W
Wheeling U.S.A. 114 40.05N 80.42W
Whernside *mtn.* U.K. 12 54.14N 2.25W
Whidbey Is. Australia 92 34.50S135.00E
Whiskey Gap *town* Canada 100 49.00N113.03W
Whitburn U.K. 14 55.52N 3.41W
Whitby Canada 104 43.52N 78.56W
Whitby U.K. 12 54.29N 0.37W
Whitchurch Shrops. U.K. 12 52.58N 2.42W
White *r.* Ark. U.S.A. 111 33.53N 91.10W
White *r.* Ind. U.S.A. 112 38.29N 87.45W
White *r.* S.Dak. U.S.A. 110 43.48N 99.22W
White *r.* Utah U.S.A. 106 40.04N109.41W
White *r.* Vt. U.S.A. 105 43.37N 72.20W
White, L. Australia 88 21.05S129.00E
White B. Canada 103 50.00N 56.30W
White Cliffs *town* Australia 92 30.51S143.05E
Whiteface, Mt. U.S.A. 105 44.22N 73.54W
Whitefield U.S.A. 105 44.22N 71.36W
Whitefish Canada 104 46.23N 81.20W
Whitefish U.S.A. 108 48.25N114.20W
Whitefish B. U.S.A. 104 46.40N 84.50W
Whitefish Falls *town* Canada 104 46.07N 81.44W
Whitefish L. Canada 101 62.41N106.48W
Whitefish Point *town* U.S.A. 104 46.45N 84.59W
Whitefish Pt. U.S.A. 104 46.45N 85.00W
Whitehall Mont. U.S.A. 108 45.52N112.06W
Whitehall N.Y. U.S.A. 115 43.33N 73.25W
Whitehall Ohio U.S.A. 114 39.58N 82.54W
Whitehall Wisc. U.S.A. 110 44.22N 91.19W
Whitehaven U.K. 12 54.33N 3.35W
White Haven U.S.A. 115 41.04N 75.47W
Whitehorse Canada 100 60.43N135.03W
White L. Canada 105 45.18N 76.31W
White L. U.S.A. 111 29.45N 92.30W
Whitemark Australia 91 40.07S148.00E
White Mountain Peak U.S.A. 108 37.38N118.15W
White Mts. Calif. U.S.A. 108 37.30N118.15W
White Mts. N.H. U.S.A. 105 44.10N 71.35W
Whitemud *r.* Canada 100 56.41N117.15W
White Nile *r.* *see* Abyaḍ, Al Baḩr al *r.* Sudan 72
White Otter L. Canada 102 49.09N 91.50W
White Plains *town* Liberia 76 6.28N 10.40W
White Plains *town* U.S.A. 115 41.02N 73.46W
Whitesand *r.* Canada 101 51.34N101.55W
Whitesboro U.S.A. 115 43.07N 75.18W
White Sea *see* Beloye More *sea* Russian Fed. 44
Whiteshell Prov. Park. Canada 101 50.00N 95.25W
Whitetail U.S.A. 108 48.54N105.10W
White Volta *r.* Ghana 76 9.13N 1.15W
Whitewater Baldy *mtn.* U.S.A. 109 33.20N108.39W
Whitfield Australia 93 36.49S146.22E
Whithorn U.K. 14 54.44N 4.25W
Whitianga New Zealand 86 36.50S175.42E
Whiting U.S.A. 115 39.57N 74.23W
Whitley Bay *town* U.K. 12 55.03N 1.25W
Whitney Canada 104 45.30N 78.14W
Whitney, Mt. U.S.A. 109 36.35N118.18W
Whitney Point *town* U.S.A. 115 42.20N 75.58W
Whitstable U.K. 13 51.21N 1.02E
Whitsunday I. Australia 90 20.17S148.59E
Whittemore U.S.A. 104 44.14N 83.48W
Whittier U.S.A. 98 60.46N148.41W
Whittlesea Australia 93 37.31S145.08E
Whitton U.K. 12 53.42N 0.39W
Wholdaia L. Canada 101 60.43N104.20W
Whyalla Australia 92 33.02S137.35E
Wiarton Canada 104 44.45N 81.09W
Wichita U.S.A. 111 37.41N 97.20W
Wichita Falls *town* U.S.A. 111 33.54N 98.30W
Wick U.K. 14 58.26N 3.06W
Wickenburg U.S.A. 109 33.58N112.44W
Wickepin Australia 89 32.45S117.31E
Wickliffe U.S.A. 114 41.36N 81.28W
Wicklow Rep. of Ire. 15 52.59N 6.03W
Wicklow *d.* Rep. of Ire. 15 52.59N 6.25W
Wicklow Head Rep. of Ire. 15 52.58N 6.00W
Wicklow Mts. Rep. of Ire. 15 53.06N 6.20W
Widdifield Canada 104 46.25N 79.20W
Widen U.S.A. 114 38.28N 80.52W
Widgiemooltha Australia 89 31.30S121.34E
Widnes U.K. 12 53.22N 2.44W
Wiehl Germany 38 50.57N 7.31E
Wiek Germany 38 54.37N 13.17E
Wieluń Poland 37 51.14N 18.34E
Wien Austria 36 48.13N 16.22E
Wiener Neustadt Austria 36 47.49N 16.15E
Wieprz *r.* Poland 37 51.34N 21.49E
Wiesbaden Germany 39 50.05N 8.14E
Wiesloch Germany 39 49.17N 8.42E
Wietze Germany 38 52.39N 9.50E
Wigan U.K. 12 53.33N 2.38W
Wight, Isle of U.K. 11 50.40N 1.17W
Wigton U.K. 12 54.50N 3.09W
Wigtown U.K. 14 54.47N 4.26W
Wigtown B. U.K. 14 54.47N 4.15W
Wikwemikong Canada 104 45.48N 81.44W
Wil Switz. 39 47.27N 9.03E
Wilber U.S.A. 110 40.29N 96.58W
Wilberforce Canada 104 45.03N 78.15W
Wilcannia Australia 92 31.33S143.24E
Wilcox U.S.A. 114 41.35N 78.41W
Wilderness U.S.A. 114 38.19N 77.48W
Wildhorn *mtn.* Switz. 38 46.22N 7.22E
Wildon Austria 31 46.53N 15.31E
Wildrose U.S.A. 110 48.38N103.11W
Wildspitze *mtn.* Austria 39 46.53N 10.52E
Wildwood U.S.A. 115 38.59N 74.49W
Wilgena Australia 92 30.46S134.44E
Wilhelm, Mt. P.N.G. 59 6.00S144.55E
Wilhelm II Land Antarctica 128 68.00S 89.00E
Wilhelm-Pieck-Stadt Guben Germany 38 51.57N 14.43E
Wilhelmshaven Germany 38 53.31N 8.08E
Wilkes-Barre U.S.A. 115 41.14N 75.53W
Wilkesboro U.S.A. 113 36.08N 81.09W
Wilkes Land *f.* Antarctica 128 69.00S120.00E
Wilkie Canada 101 52.25N108.43W
Wilkinsburg U.S.A. 114 40.27N 79.53W
Wilkinson Lakes Australia 91 29.40S132.39E
Willandra Billabong *r.* Australia 92 33.08S144.06E
Willard N.Mex. U.S.A. 109 34.36N106.02W
Willard Ohio U.S.A. 114 41.03N 82.44W
Willemstad Neth. Antilles 122 12.12N 68.56W
Willeroo Australia 88 15.17S131.35E
William, Mt. Australia 92 37.20S142.41E
William Creek *town* Australia 92 28.52S136.18E
Williams Australia 89 33.01S116.45E
Williams *r.* Australia 89 32.59S116.24E
Williamsburg U.S.A. 113 37.17N 76.43W
Williams Lake *town* Canada 100 52.08N122.10W
Williamson U.S.A. 113 37.42N 82.16W
Williamsport Md. U.S.A. 114 39.32N 77.50W
Williamsport Penn. U.S.A. 114 41.14N 77.00W
Williamston U.S.A. 113 35.53N 77.05W
Williamstown N.J. U.S.A. 115 39.41N 75.00W
Williamstown N.Y. U.S.A. 115 43.26N 75.55W
Williamstown W.Va. U.S.A. 114 39.24N 81.27W
Willimantic U.S.A. 115 41.43N 72.12W
Willis Group *is.* Australia 90 16.18S150.00E
Williston R.S.A. 80 31.21S 20.53E
Williston U.S.A. 110 48.09N103.37W
Williston L. Canada 100 55.40N123.40W
Willits U.S.A. 108 39.25N123.21W
Willmar U.S.A. 110 45.07N 95.03W
Willmore Wilderness Park Canada 100 53.45N119.00W
Willochra Australia 92 32.12S138.10E
Willochra *r.* Australia 92 31.57S137.52E
Willoughby U.S.A. 114 41.38N 81.25W
Willow U.S.A. 98 61.42N150.08W
Willow Grove U.S.A. 115 40.08N 75.06W
Willow Hill *town* U.S.A. 114 40.06N 77.48W
Willow L. Canada 100 62.10N119.08W
Willowmore R.S.A. 80 33.18S 23.28E
Willow Ranch U.S.A. 108 41.55N120.21W
Willow River *town* Canada 100 54.06N122.28W
Willsboro U.S.A. 105 44.22N 73.26W
Willunga Australia 92 35.18S138.33E
Wilmette U.S.A. 110 42.04N 87.43W
Wilmington Del. U.S.A. 115 39.44N 75.33W
Wilmington N.C. U.S.A. 113 34.14N 77.55W
Wilmington Vt. U.S.A. 115 42.52N 72.52W
Wilmslow U.K. 12 53.19N 2.14W
Wilpena *r.* Australia 92 31.13S139.25E
Wilson N.C. U.S.A. 113 35.43N 77.56W
Wilson N.Y. U.S.A. 114 43.19N 78.50W
Wilson's Promontory *c.* Australia 93 39.06S146.23E
Wilton *r.* Australia 90 14.45S134.33E
Wilton U.K. 13 51.05N 1.52W
Wilton N.Dak. U.S.A. 110 47.10N100.47W
Wilton N.H. U.S.A. 115 42.51N 71.44W
Wiltshire *d.* U.K. 13 51.20N 0.34W
Wiltz Lux. 16 49.59N 5.53E
Wiluna Australia 88 26.36S120.13E
Wimmera *r.* Australia 92 36.05S141.56E
Winam *b.* Kenya 79 0.15S 34.30E
Winburg R.S.A. 80 28.30S 27.01E
Wincanton U.K. 13 51.03N 2.24W
Winchendon U.S.A. 115 42.41N 72.03W
Winchester Canada 105 45.06N 75.21W
Winchester U.K. 13 51.04N 1.19W
Winchester Ky. U.S.A. 113 38.00N 84.10W
Winchester N.H. U.S.A. 115 42.46N 72.23W
Winchester Va. U.S.A. 114 39.11N 78.10W
Winchester Wyo. U.S.A. 108 43.51N108.10W
Windber U.S.A. 114 40.14N 78.50W
Windermere *l.* U.K. 12 54.20N 2.56W
Windfall Canada 100 54.12N116.13W
Windham U.S.A. 114 41.14N 81.03W
Windhoek Namibia 80 22.34S 17.06E
Windom U.S.A. 110 43.52N 95.07W
Windorah Australia 90 25.26S142.39E
Wind River Range *mts.* U.S.A. 108 43.05N109.25W
Windsor Australia 93 33.38S150.47E
Windsor Nfld. Canada 103 48.58N 55.40W
Windsor N.S. Canada 103 44.59N 64.08W
Windsor Ont. Canada 104 42.18N 83.01W
Windsor Que. Canada 105 45.34N 72.00W
Windsor U.K. 13 51.29N 0.38W
Windsor Conn. U.S.A. 115 41.51N 72.39W
Windsor N.Y. U.S.A. 115 42.05N 75.39W
Windsor Vt. U.S.A. 115 43.29N 72.23W
Windsor Locks U.S.A. 115 41.56N 72.38W
Windward Is. C. America 117 13.00N 60.00W
Windward Passage *str.* Carib. Sea 117 20.00N 74.00W
Winfield Kans. U.S.A. 111 37.15N 96.59W
Winfield W.Va. U.S.A. 114 38.32N 81.53W
Wingen Australia 93 31.43S150.54E
Wingham Australia 93 31.50S152.20E
Wingham Canada 104 43.53N 81.19W
Winifred U.S.A. 108 47.34N109.23W
Winisk Canada 102 55.20N 85.15W
Winisk *r.* Canada 102 55.00N 85.20W
Winisk L. Canada 102 53.00N 88.00W
Winkler Canada 101 49.11N 97.56W
Winklern Austria 39 46.52N 12.52E
Winneba Ghana 76 5.22N 0.38W
Winnebago, L. U.S.A. 110 44.00N 88.25W
Winnemucca U.S.A. 106 40.58N117.45W
Winnemucca L. U.S.A. 108 40.09N119.20W
Winner U.S.A. 110 43.22N 99.51W
Winnfield U.S.A. 111 31.55N 92.38W
Winnipeg Canada 101 49.53N 97.09W
Winnipeg *r.* Canada 101 50.38N 96.19W
Winnipeg, L. Canada 101 52.00N 97.00W
Winnipegosis, L. Canada 101 52.30N100.00W
Winnipesaukee, L. U.S.A. 115 43.35N 71.20W
Winnsboro La. U.S.A. 111 32.10N 91.43W
Winnsboro S.C. U.S.A. 113 34.22N 81.05W
Winona Kans. U.S.A. 110 39.04N101.15W
Winona Minn. U.S.A. 110 44.03N 91.39W
Winona Miss. U.S.A. 111 33.29N 89.44W
Winooski U.S.A. 105 44.29N 73.11W
Winooski *r.* U.S.A. 105 44.30N 73.15W
Winschoten Neth. 16 53.07N 7.02E
Winsen Germany 38 53.22N 10.12E
Winsford U.K. 12 53.12N 2.31W
Winslow Ariz. U.S.A. 109 35.01N110.42W
Winslow Maine U.S.A. 112 44.32N 69.38W
Winsted U.S.A. 115 41.55N 73.04W
Winston U.S.A. 108 46.28N111.38W
Winston-Salem U.S.A. 113 36.05N 80.18W
Winsum Neth. 16 53.20N 6.31E
Winter Haven U.S.A. 113 28.02N 81.46W
Winterset U.S.A. 110 41.20N 94.01W
Winterswijk Neth. 16 51.58N 6.44E
Winterthur Switz. 39 47.30N 8.43E
Winthrop Minn. U.S.A. 110 44.32N 94.22W
Winthrop Wash. U.S.A. 108 48.29N120.11W
Winton Australia 90 22.22S143.00E
Winton New Zealand 86 46.10S168.20E
Winton U.S.A. 108 41.45N109.10W
Wipper *r.* Germany 38 51.47N 11.42E
Wirrabara Australia 92 33.03S138.18E
Wirraminna Australia 92 31.11S136.04E
Wirrappa Australia 92 31.28S137.00E
Wirrega Australia 92 36.11S140.37E
Wirrida, L. Australia 92 29.45S134.39E
Wirulla Australia 92 32.24S134.33E
Wisbech U.K. 13 52.39N 0.10E
Wisconsin *d.* U.S.A. 110 44.30N 90.00W
Wisconsin *r.* U.S.A. 110 43.00N 91.15W
Wisconsin Dells U.S.A. 110 43.38N 89.46W
Wisconsin Rapids *town* U.S.A. 110 44.24N 89.50W
Wisdom U.S.A. 108 45.37N113.27W
Wisła *r.* Poland 37 54.23N 18.52E
Wismar Germany 38 53.53N 11.28E
Wisner U.S.A. 110 41.59N 96.55W
Wissembourg France 19 49.02N 7.57E
Wissen Germany 38 50.47N 7.43E
Wissmar Germany 38 50.38N 8.41E
Wisznice Poland 37 51.48N 23.12E
Witchekan L. Canada 101 53.25N107.35W
Witham *r.* U.K. 12 52.56N 0.04E
Witherbee U.S.A. 105 44.05N 73.32W
Withernsea U.K. 12 53.43N 0.02E
Witkowo Poland 37 52.27N 17.47E
Witney U.K. 13 51.47N 1.29W
Witsand R.S.A. 80 34.23S 20.49E
Witten Germany 16 51.26N 7.19E
Wittenberg Germany 38 51.53N 12.39E
Wittenberge Germany 38 53.00N 11.44E
Wittenburg Germany 38 53.31N 11.04E
Wittenoom Australia 88 22.19S118.21E
Wittingen Germany 38 52.43N 10.44E
Wittlich Germany 39 49.59N 6.53E
Wittstock Germany 38 53.10N 12.29E
Witu Kenya 79 2.22S 40.20E
Witvlei Namibia 80 22.25S 18.29E
Witzenhausen Germany 38 51.20N 9.51E
Wiveliscombe U.K. 13 51.02N 3.20W
Wkra *r.* Poland 37 52.27N 20.44E
Władysławowo Poland 37 54.49N 18.25E
Włocławek Poland 37 52.39N 19.01E
Włodawa Poland 37 51.33N 23.31E
Wodonga Australia 93 36.08S146.09E
Woerden Neth. 16 52.07N 4.55E
Wohutun China 54 43.40N123.30E
Wokam *i.* Indonesia 59 5.45S134.30E
Woking Canada 100 55.35N118.50W
Woking U.K. 13 51.20N 0.34W
Wolcott U.S.A. 114 43.13N 76.49W
Woleai *i.* Pacific Oc. 84 7.21N143.52E
Wolf *r.* U.S.A. 110 44.07N 88.43W
Wolfach Germany 39 48.17N 8.13E
Wolfboro U.S.A. 115 43.35N 71.12W
Wolf Creek *town* U.S.A. 108 46.50N112.20W
Wolfe Island *town* Canada 105 44.12N 76.26W
Wolfen Germany 38 51.40N 12.16E
Wolfenbüttel Germany 38 52.10N 10.32E
Wolfhagen Germany 38 51.19N 9.10E
Wolf Point *town* U.S.A. 108 48.05N105.39W
Wolfratshausen Germany 39 47.54N 11.25E
Wolfsberg Austria 31 46.51N 14.51E
Wolfsburg Germany 38 52.25N 10.47E
Wolgast Germany 38 54.03N 13.46E
Wolin Poland 36 53.51N 14.38E
Wollaston L. Canada 101 58.15N103.20W
Wollaston Pen. Canada 98 70.00N115.00W
Wollongong Australia 93 34.25S150.52E
Wolmaransstad R.S.A. 80 27.11S 25.58E
Wolomin Poland 37 52.21N 21.14E
Wolseley Australia 92 36.21S140.55E
Wolseley Bay *town* Canada 104 46.07N 80.22W
Wolvega Neth. 16 52.53N 6.00E
Wolverhampton U.K. 13 52.35N 2.06W
Wolverine U.S.A. 104 45.16N 84.36W
Womelsdorf U.S.A. 115 40.22N 76.11W

Wondai to **Yatakala**

Wondai Australia 90 26.19S151.52E
Wongan Hills *town* Australia 89 30.55S116.41E
Wonogiri Indonesia 59 7.48S110.52E
Wonosari Indonesia 59 7.55S110.39E
Wonosobo Indonesia 59 7.21S109.56E
Wŏnsan N. Korea 53 39.07N127.26E
Wonthaggi Australia 93 38.38S145.37E
Woocalla Australia 92 31.44S137.10E
Woodbine U.S.A. 115 39.14N 74.49W
Woodbridge U.K. 13 52.06N 1.19E
Woodbridge U.S.A. 114 38.39N 77.15W
Wood Buffalo Nat. Park Canada 100 59.00N113.41W
Woodburn Australia 93 29.04S153.21E
Woodbury U.S.A. 115 39.50N 75.10W
Wooded Bluff *f.* Australia 93 29.22S153.22E
Woodenbong Australia 93 28.28S152.35E
Woodgate U.S.A. 115 43.32N 75.12W
Woodland U.S.A. 108 38.41N121.46W
Woodlark I. P.N.G. 90 9.05S152.50E
Wood Mts. Canada 101 49.14N106.20W
Woodroffe, Mt. Australia 90 26.20S131.45E
Woods, L. Australia 90 17.50S133.30E
Woods, L. of the Canada/U.S.A. 102 49.15N 94.45W
Woodsfield U.S.A. 114 39.46N 81.07W
Woods Hole U.S.A. 115 41.31N 70.40W
Woodside Australia 93 38.31S146.52E
Woods L. Canada 103 54.40N 64.21W
Woodstock Canada 104 43.08N 80.45W
Woodstock U.K. 13 51.51N 1.20W
Woodstock U.S.A. 115 43.37N 72.31W
Woodstown U.S.A. 115 39.39N 75.20W
Woodsville U.S.A. 105 44.09N 72.02W
Woodville New Zealand 86 40.20S175.52E
Woodward U.S.A. 111 36.26N 99.24W
Wooler U.K. 12 55.33N 2.01W
Woolgoolga Australia 93 30.07S153.12E
Wooltana Australia 92 30.28S139.26E
Woomera Australia 92 31.11S136.54E
Woonsocket U.S.A. 115 42.00N 71.31W
Wooramel Australia 88 25.42S114.20E
Wooramel *r.* Australia 88 25.47S114.10E
Woorong, L. Australia 92 29.24S134.06E
Wooster U.S.A. 114 40.48N 81.56W
Worb Switz. 19 46.56N 7.34E
Worcester R.S.A. 80 33.39S 19.25E
Worcester U.K. 13 52.12N 2.12W
Worcester U.S.A. 115 42.16N 71.48W
Wörgl Austria 39 47.29N 12.04E
Workington U.K. 12 54.39N 3.34W
Worksop U.K. 12 53.19N 1.09W
Workum Neth. 16 53.00N 5.26E
Worland U.S.A. 108 44.01N107.57W
Worms Germany 39 49.38N 8.22E
Wörnitz *r.* Germany 39 48.42N 10.45E
Wörrstadt Germany 39 49.50N 8.07E
Wörther See *l.* Austria 31 46.37N 14.10E
Worthing U.K. 13 50.49N 0.21W
Worthington Minn. U.S.A. 110 43.37N 95.36W
Worthington Ohio U.S.A. 112 40.03N 83.03W
Worthville U.S.A. 112 38.38N 85.05W
Wosi Indonesia 59 0.15S128.00E
Wour Chad 77 21.21N 15.57E
Woutchaba Cameroon 77 5.13N 13.05E
Wowoni *i.* Indonesia 59 4.10S123.10E
Wragby U.K. 12 53.17N 0.18E
Wrangel I. *see* Vrangelya, Ostrov *i.* Russian Fed. 51
Wrangell U.S.A. 100 56.28N132.23W
Wrangell Mts. U.S.A. 98 62.00N143.00W
Wrangle U.K. 12 53.03N 0.09E
Wrath, C. U.K. 14 58.37N 5.01W
Wray U.S.A. 110 40.05N102.13W
Wrecks, B. of Kiribati 85 1.52N157.17W
Wrexham U.K. 12 53.05N 3.00W
Wrigley Canada 98 63.16N123.39W
Wrocław Poland 37 51.05N 17.00E
Wronki Poland 36 52.43N 16.23E
Wroxeter Canada 104 43.50N 81.07W
Września Poland 37 52.20N 17.34E
Wubin Australia 89 30.06S116.38E
Wuchang China 55 30.21N114.19E
Wucheng China 54 37.12N116.04E
Wuchuan Guangdong China 55 21.21N110.40E
Wuchuan Nei Monggol Zizhiqu China 54 41.08N111.24E
Wuda China 54 39.40N106.40E
Wuday'ah Saudi Arabia 71 16.05N 47.05E
Wudham 'Alwā' Oman 65 23.48N 57.33E
Wudinna Australia 92 33.03S135.28E
Wudu China 54 33.24N104.50E
Wufeng China 55 30.12N110.36E
Wugang China 55 26.42N110.31E
Wugong Shan *mts.* China 55 27.15N114.00E
Wuhai China 54 39.50N106.40E
Wuhan China 55 30.37N114.19E
Wuhu China 55 31.25N118.25E
Wūjang China 63 33.38N 79.55E
Wu Jiang *r.* China 55 29.41N107.24E
Wukari Nigeria 77 7.57N 9.42E
Wulian China 54 35.45N119.12E
Wuliang Shan *mts.* China 52 24.27N100.43E
Wum Cameroon 77 6.25N 10.03E
Wumbulgal Australia 93 34.25S146.16E
Wuming China 55 23.10N108.16E
Wuning China 55 29.17N115.05E
Wunnummin L. Canada 102 52.50N 89.20W
Wun Rog Sudan 73 9.00N 28.21E
Wunstorf Germany 38 52.25N 9.26E
Wuppertal Germany 38 51.16N 7.11E
Wuppertal R.S.A. 80 32.16S 19.12E
Wuqi China 54 37.03N108.14E
Wuqiao China 54 37.38N116.22E
Wuqing China 54 39.19N117.05E
Wurno Nigeria 77 13.20N 5.28E
Wurtsboro U.S.A. 115 41.35N 74.29W
Würzburg Germany 39 49.48N 9.56E
Wurzen Germany 38 51.22N 12.44E
Wusong China 55 31.20N121.30E
Wutach *r.* Germany 39 47.37N 8.15E
Wutongqiao China 55 29.20N103.48E
Wuwei China 54 38.00N102.59E
Wuxi Jiangsu China 55 31.34N120.20E
Wuxi Sichuan China 55 31.28N109.36E
Wuxing China 55 30.59N120.04E
Wuyi Shan *mts.* China 55 27.00N117.00E
Wuyuan China 54 41.06N108.16E
Wuzhan China 53 50.14N125.18E
Wuzhi Shan *mts.* China 55 18.50N109.30E
Wuzhou China 55 23.28N111.21E
Wyalkatchem Australia 89 31.21S117.22E
Wyalong Australia 93 33.55S147.17E
Wyandotte U.S.A. 114 42.12N 83.10W
Wyandra Australia 91 27.15S146.00E
Wyangala Resr. Australia 93 33.58S148.55E
Wyara, L. Australia 92 28.42S144.16E
Wycheproof Australia 92 36.04S143.14E
Wye U.K. 13 51.11N 0.56E
Wye *r.* U.K. 13 51.37N 2.40W
Wyk Germany 38 54.42N 8.34E
Wymondham U.K. 13 52.34N 1.07E
Wynbring Australia 91 30.33S133.32E
Wyndham Australia 88 15.29S128.05E
Wynne U.S.A. 111 35.14N 90.47W
Wyoming Canada 104 42.57N 82.07W
Wyoming *d.* U.S.A. 108 43.10N107.36W
Wyong Australia 93 33.17S151.25E
Wyszków Poland 37 52.36N 21.28E
Wytheville U.S.A. 113 36.57N 81.07W

X

Xa Cassau Angola 78 9.02S 20.17E
Xagquka China 63 31.50N 92.46E
Xainza China 63 30.56N 88.40E
Xaitongmoin China 63 29.22N 88.15E
Xai-Xai Mozambique 81 25.05S 33.38E
Xalin *well* Somali Rep. 71 9.08N 48.47E
Xam Nua Laos 56 20.25N 104.10E
Xangdoring China 63 32.06N 82.02E
Xangongo Angola 78 16.31S 15.00E
Xanten Germany 38 51.39N 6.26E
Xánthi Greece 34 41.08N 24.53E
Xarardheere Somali Rep. 71 4.32N 47.53E
Xar Hudag China 54 45.07N114.28E
Xar Moron He *r.* China 54 43.30N120.42E
Xarrama *r.* Portugal 27 38.14N 8.20W
Xassengue Angola 78 10.26S 18.32E
Xau, L. Botswana 80 21.15S 24.50E
Xebert China 54 44.02N122.00E
Xenia U.S.A. 112 39.41N 83.56W
Xequessa Angola 78 16.47S 19.05E
Xertigny France 19 48.03N 6.24E
Xhora R.S.A. 80 31.58S 28.40E
Xiachuan *i.* China 55 21.40N112.37E
Xiaguan *see* Dali China 52
Xiamen China 55 24.30N118.08E
Xi'an China 54 34.11N108.55E
Xianfeng China 55 29.41N109.02E
Xiangcheng China 54 33.50N113.29E
Xiangfan China 55 32.04N112.05E
Xiangfen China 54 35.52N111.24E
Xiang Jiang *r.* China 55 28.49N112.30E
Xiangkhoang Laos 56 19.21N103.23E
Xiangquan He *r.* China 63 31.45N 78.40E
Xiangshan China 55 29.29N121.51E
Xiangtan China 55 27.50N112.49E
Xiangtang China 55 28.26N115.58E
Xiangyin China 55 28.40N112.53E
Xiangyuan China 54 36.32N113.02E
Xiangzhou China 55 23.58N109.41E
Xianju China 55 28.51N120.44E
Xianning China 55 29.53N114.13E
Xian Xian China 54 38.12N116.07E
Xianyang China 54 34.20N108.40E
Xianyou China 55 25.28N118.50E
Xiao Hinggan Ling *mts.* China 53 48.40N128.30E
Xiaojiang China 55 27.34N120.27E
Xiaojiao China 54 38.24N113.42E
Xiaowutai Shan *mtn.* China 54 39.57N114.59E
Xiapu China 55 26.58N119.57E
Xiayang China 55 26.45N117.58E
Xichang China 52 27.53N102.18E
Xichou China 55 23.27N104.40E
Xichuan China 54 33.15N111.27E
Xifeng China 55 27.06N106.44E
Xigazê China 52 29.18N 88.50E
Xiheying China 54 39.53N114.42E
Xiji China 54 35.52N105.35E
Xi Jiang *r.* China 55 22.23N113.20E
Xiliao He *r.* China 54 43.48N123.00E
Xilin China 55 24.30N105.03E
Xilókastron Greece 35 38.04N 22.43E
Ximeng China 61 22.45N 99.29E
Xin'anjiang China 55 29.27N119.14E
Xin'anjiang Shuiku *resr.* China 55 29.32N119.00E
Xincheng Guang. Zhuang. China 55 24.04N108.40E
Xincheng Ningxia Huizu China 54 38.33N106.10E
Xincheng Shanxi China 54 37.57N112.35E
Xindu China 55 30.50N104.12E
Xinfeng Guangdong China 55 24.04N114.12E
Xinfeng Jiangxi China 55 25.27N114.58E
Xing'an China 55 25.35N110.32E
Xingcheng China 54 40.37N120.43E
Xinghua China 54 32.51N119.50E
Xingkai Hu *l. see* Khanka, Ozero Russian Fed./China 53
Xingren China 55 25.26N105.14E
Xingshan China 55 31.10N110.51E
Xingtai China 54 37.04N114.26E
Xingu *r.* Brazil 123 1.40S 52.15W
Xing Xian China 54 38.31N111.04E
Xingyi China 55 25.00N104.59E
Xinhe Hebei China 54 37.22N115.14E
Xinhe Xin. Uygur Zizhiqu China 52 41.34N 82.38E
Xinhua China 55 27.45N111.18E
Xining China 52 36.35N101.55E
Xinji China 54 35.17N115.35E
Xinjiang Uygur Zizhiqu *d.* China 52 41.15N 87.00E
Xinjie China 54 39.15N109.36E
Xinjin Liaoning China 54 39.27N121.48E
Xinjin Sichuan China 55 30.30N103.47E
Xinle China 54 38.15N114.40E
Xinlitun China 54 42.00N122.09E
Xinmin China 54 42.01N122.48E
Xinning China 55 26.31N110.48E
Xinshao China 55 27.20N111.26E
Xin Xian China 54 38.24N112.47E
Xinxiang China 54 35.12N113.57E
Xinyang China 54 32.08N114.04E
Xinyi Guangdong China 55 22.21N110.57E
Xinyi Jiangsu China 54 34.20N118.30E
Xinyu China 55 27.50N114.55E
Xinzheng China 54 34.25N113.46E
Xinzhu Taiwan 55 24.50N120.58E
Xiping Henan China 54 33.23N114.02E
Xiping Zhejiang China 55 28.27N119.29E
Xique Xique Brazil 123 10.47S 42.44W
Xi Ujimqin Qi China 54 44.32N117.40E
Xiuning China 55 29.48N118.20E
Xiushan China 55 28.27N108.59E
Xiushui China 55 29.01N114.37E
Xixabangma Feng *mtn.* China 63 28.21N 85.47E
Xixia China 54 33.30N111.30E
Xizang Zizhiqu *d.* China 63 31.45N 87.00E
Xorkol China 52 39.04N 91.05E
Xuancheng China 55 30.59N118.40E
Xuang *r.* Laos 56 19.59N102.20E
Xuanhan China 55 31.25N107.38E
Xuanhua China 54 40.30N115.00E
Xuanwei China 55 26.16N104.01E
Xuchang China 54 34.02N113.50E
Xuddur Somali Rep. 71 4.10N 43.53E
Xuefeng Shan *mts.* China 55 27.30N111.00E
Xueshuiwen China 53 49.15N129.39E
Xugou China 54 34.40N119.26E
Xunyang China 54 32.48N109.27E
Xupu China 55 27.54N110.35E
Xushui China 54 39.01N115.39E
Xuwen China 55 20.25N110.20E
Xuyong China 55 28.17N105.21E
Xuzhou China 54 34.14N117.20E

Y

Ya Gabon 78 1.17S 14.14E
Ya'an China 61 30.00N102.59E
Yaapeet Australia 92 35.48S142.07E
Ya'bad Jordan 67 32.27N 35.10E
Yabassi Cameroon 77 4.30N 9.55E
Yabēlo Ethiopia 73 4.54N 38.05E
Yābis, Wādī al Jordan 67 32.24N 35.35E
Yablonovyy Khrebet *mts.* Russian Fed. 51 53.20N115.00E
Yabrai Shan *mts.* China 54 39.50N103.30E
Yabrai Yanchang China 54 39.24N102.43E
Yabrūd Syria 66 33.58N 36.40E
Yacheng China 55 18.35N109.13E
Yacuiba Bolivia 124 22.00S 63.25W
Yādgīr India 60 16.46N 77.08E
Yadong China 63 27.29N 88.54E
Yagaba Ghana 76 10.13N 1.14W
Yagoua Cameroon 77 10.23N 15.13E
Yagra China 63 31.32N 82.27E
Yagur Israel 67 32.44N 35.04E
Yahagi *r.* Japan 57 34.50N136.59E
Yahisuli Zaïre 78 0.08S 24.04E
Yahuma Zaïre 78 1.06N 23.10E
Yaizu Japan 57 34.52N138.20E
Yajua Nigeria 77 11.27N 12.49E
Yakchāl Afghan. 62 31.47N 64.41E
Yakima U.S.A. 108 46.36N120.31W
Yakmach Pakistan 62 28.45N 63.51E
Yaksha Russian Fed. 44 61.51N 56.59E
Yaku shima *i.* Japan 57 30.20N130.40E
Yakutat U.S.A. 100 59.29N139.49W
Yakutat B. U.S.A. 100 59.29N139.49W
Yakutsk Russian Fed. 51 62.10N129.20E
Yala Thailand 56 6.32N101.19E
Yale U.S.A. 114 43.08N 82.48W
Yalgoo Australia 89 28.20S116.41E
Yalinga C.A.R. 73 6.31N 23.15E
Yallourn Australia 93 38.09S146.22E
Yalong Jiang *r.* China 52 26.35N101.44E
Yalta Ukraine 45 44.30N 34.09E
Yalu Jiang *r.* China 54 40.10N124.25E
Yalutorovsk Russian Fed. 50 56.41N 66.12E
Yamagata Japan 57 38.16N140.19E
Yamaguchi Japan 57 34.10N131.28E
Yamal, Poluostrov *pen.* Russian Fed. 50 70.20N 70.00E
Yamanashi Japan 57 35.40N138.40E
Yamanashi *d.* Japan 57 35.30N138.35E
Yamandjo Zaïre 78 1.38N 23.27E
Yamaska Canada 105 46.01N 72.55W
Yamaska *r.* Canada 105 46.06N 72.56W
Yamato Japan 57 35.29N139.29E
Yamato-takada Japan 57 34.31N135.45E
Yamba N.S.W. Australia 93 29.26S153.22E
Yamba S.A. Australia 92 34.15S140.54E
Yambéring Guinea 76 11.49N 12.18W
Yambio Sudan 73 4.34N 28.23E
Yambol Bulgaria 34 42.30N 26.30E
Yamdena *i.* Indonesia 59 7.30S131.00E
Yamenyingzi China 54 42.23N121.03E
Yamethin Burma 56 20.24N 96.08E
Yam HaMelaḥ *see* Dead Sea Jordan 67
Yam Kinneret *l.* Israel 67 32.49N 35.36E
Yamma Yamma, L. Australia 90 26.20S141.25E
Yamoussoukro Ivory Coast 76 6.51N 5.18W
Yampi Sound Australia 88 16.11S123.30E
Yampol Ukraine 37 48.13N 28.12E
Yamuna *r.* India 63 25.25N 81.50E
Yamzho Yumco *l.* China 63 29.00N 90.40E
Yan Nigeria 77 10.05N 12.11E
Yana *r.* Russian Fed. 51 71.30N135.00E
Yanac Australia 92 36.09S141.29E
Yan'an China 54 36.45N109.22E
Yanbu'al Baḥr Saudi Arabia 64 24.07N 38.04E
Yancannia Australia 92 30.16S142.50E
Yancheng China 54 33.22N120.05E
Yanchep Australia 89 31.32S115.33E
Yanchi China 54 37.47N107.24E
Yanchuan China 54 36.51N110.05E
Yanco Australia 93 34.36S146.25E
Yanco Glen *town* Australia 92 31.43S141.39E
Yanda *r.* Australia 93 30.22S145.38E
Yandong China 55 24.02N107.09E
Yandoon Burma 56 17.02N 95.39E
Yanfolila Mali 76 11.11N 8.09W
Yangarey Russian Fed. 44 68.46N 61.29E
Yangchun China 55 22.03N111.46E
Yangcun China 55 23.26N114.30E
Yangjiang China 55 21.50N111.54E
Yangmingshan Taiwan 55 25.18N121.35E
Yangon Burma 56 16.47N 96.10E
Yangon *see* Rangoon Burma 56
Yangqu China 54 38.03N112.36E
Yangquan China 54 37.49N113.28E
Yangshan Guangdong China 55 24.29N112.38E
Yangshan Liaoning China 54 41.15N120.18E
Yangshuo China 55 24.47N110.30E
Yangtze *r. see* Chang Jiang *r.* China 55
Yang Xian China 54 33.10N107.35E
Yangxin China 55 29.50N115.10E
Yangze China 55 26.59N118.19E
Yangzhou China 54 32.22N119.26E
Yanhuqu China 63 32.32N 82.44E
Yanji China 53 42.45N129.25E
Yanko Creek *r.* Australia 93 35.25S145.27E
Yankton U.S.A. 110 42.53N 97.23W
Yanqi China 52 42.00N 86.30E
Yanshan China 61 23.36N104.20E
Yanshiping China 63 33.35N 92.04E
Yanskiy Zaliv *g.* Russian Fed. 51 72.00N136.10E
Yantabulla Australia 93 29.13S145.01E
Yantai China 54 37.27N121.26E
Yantra *r.* Bulgaria 34 43.35N 25.37E
Yanxi China 55 28.11N110.58E
Yanzhou China 54 35.35N116.52E
Yao Chad 77 12.52N 17.34E
Yao Japan 57 34.37N135.36E
Yaopu China 55 26.05N105.42E
Yaoundé Cameroon 77 3.51N 11.31E
Yao Xian China 54 34.52N109.01E
Yap *i.* Federated States of Micronesia 59 9.30N138.09E
Yapehe Zaïre 78 0.10S 24.20E
Yapen *i.* Indonesia 59 1.45S136.10E
Yaqui *r.* Mexico 109 27.37N110.39W
Yar Russian Fed. 44 58.13N 52.08E
Yaraka Australia 90 24.53S144.04E
Yaransk Russian Fed. 44 57.22N 47.49E
Yardea Australia 92 32.23S135.32E
Yare *r.* U.K. 13 52.34N 1.45E
Yaremcha Ukraine 37 48.26N 24.29E
Yarensk Russian Fed. 44 62.10N 49.07E
Yargora Moldavia 37 46.25N 28.20E
Yariga take *mtn.* Japan 57 36.21N137.39E
Yārīn Lebanon 67 33.06N 35.14E
Yaritagua Venezuela 122 10.05N 69.07W
Yarkant He *r.* China 52 40.30N 80.55E
Yarker Canada 105 44.22N 76.46W
Yarlung Zangbo Jiang *r.* China *see* Brahmaputra *r.* Asia 63
Yarmouth Canada 103 43.50N 66.07W
Yarmūk *r.* Jordan/Syria 67 32.38N 35.34E
Yaroslavl Russian Fed. 44 57.34N 39.52E
Yarqon *r.* Israel 67 32.06N 34.47E
Yarra *r.* Australia 93 37.51S144.54E
Yarram Australia 93 38.30S146.41E
Yarrawonga Australia 93 36.02S145.59E
Yarrow *r.* U.K. 14 55.32N 2.51W
Yar Sale Russian Fed. 50 66.50N 70.48E
Yartsevo Russian Fed. 51 60.17N 90.02E
Yartsevo Russian Fed. 44 55.06N 32.43E
Yarumal Colombia 122 6.59N 75.25W
Yasanyama Zaïre 73 4.18N 21.11E
Yaselda *r.* Belorussia 37 52.07N 26.28E
Yasen Belorussia 37 53.10N 28.55E
Yashi Nigeria 77 12.23N 7.54E
Yashkul Russian Fed. 45 46.10N 45.20E
Yasinya Ukraine 37 48.12N 24.20E
Yasothon Thailand 56 15.46N104.12E
Yass Australia 93 34.51S148.55E
Yas'ur Israel 67 32.54N 35.10E
Yatakala Niger 76 14.52N 0.22E

Yaté to **Zhangpu**

Yaté N. Cal. **84** 22.09S166.57E
Yates Center U.S.A. **111** 37.53N 95.44W
Yathkyed L. Canada **101** 62.40N 98.00W
Yatsuo Japan **57** 36.35N137.10E
Yatsushiro Japan **57** 32.32N130.35E
Yaṭṭah Jordan **67** 31.27N 35.05E
Yāval India **62** 21.10N 75.42E
Yavatmāl India **63** 20.24N 78.08E
Yaví, Cerro *mtn.* Venezuela **122** 5.32N 65.59W
Yavne Israel **67** 31.53N 34.45E
Yavne'el Israel **67** 32.42N 35.30E
Yavorov Ukraine **37** 49.59N 23.20E
Yawng-hwe Burma **56** 20.35N 96.58E
Yaxi China **55** 27.35N106.40E
Ya Xian *see* Sanya China **55**
Yazd Iran **65** 31.54N 54.22E
Yazmān Pakistan **62** 29.08N 71.45E
Yazoo *r.* U.S.A. **111** 32.22N 91.00W
Yazoo City U.S.A. **111** 32.51N 90.28W
Ybbs Austria **36** 48.11N 15.05E
Yding Skovhöj *hill* Denmark **42** 56.00N 9.48E
Ydsteböhavn Norway **42** 59.08N 5.15E
Ye Burma **56** 15.15N 97.50E
Yea Australia **93** 37.12S145.25E
Yecla Spain **25** 38.37N 1.07W
Yedintsy Moldavia **45** 48.09N 27.18E
Yeeda Australia **88** 17.36S123.39E
Yefremov Russian Fed. **44** 53.08N 38.08E
Yegorlyk *r.* Russian Fed. **45** 46.30N 41.52E
Yegoryevsk Russian Fed. **44** 55.21N 39.01E
Yegros Paraguay **126** 26.24S 56.25W
Yei Sudan **73** 4.05N 30.40E
Yei *r.* Sudan **73** 7.20N 30.39E
Yeji China **55** 31.51N115.01E
Yekaterinburg Russian Fed. **44** 56.52N 60.35E
Yelets Russian Fed. **44** 52.36N 38.30E
Yeletskiy Russian Fed. **44** 67.04N 64.00E
Yélimané Mali **76** 15.08N 10.34W
Yell *i.* U.K. **14** 60.35N 1.05W
Yellowdine Australia **89** 31.19S119.36E
Yellowhead Pass Canada **100** 52.53N118.25W
Yellowknife Canada **100** 62.27N114.21W
Yellowknife *r.* Canada **100** 62.27N114.19W
Yellow Mt. Australia **93** 32.19S146.50E
Yellow Sea Asia **53** 35.00N123.00E
Yellowstone *r.* U.S.A. **106** 47.55N103.45W
Yellowstone L. U.S.A. **108** 44.25N110.38W
Yellowstone Nat. Park U.S.A. **108** 44.30N110.35W
Yell Sd. U.K. **14** 60.30N 1.11W
Yelma Australia **88** 26.30S121.40E
Yelsk Belorussia **37** 51.50N 29.10E
Yelwa Nigeria **77** 10.48N 4.42E
Yemen Asia **71** 14.00N 47.00E
Yemilchino Ukraine **37** 50.58N 27.40E
Yenagoa Nigeria **77** 4.59N 6.15E
Yenangyaung Burma **56** 20.28N 94.54E
Yen Bai Vietnam **56** 21.43N104.44E
Yenda Australia **93** 34.15S146.13E
Yendi Ghana **76** 9.29N 0.01W
Yengan Burma **56** 21.06N 96.30E
Yenisey *r.* Russian Fed. **51** 69.00N 86.00E
Yeniseysk Russian Fed. **51** 58.27N 92.13E
Yeniseyskiy Zaliv *g.* Russian Fed. **50** 73.00N 79.00E
Yenshui Taiwan **55** 23.20N120.16E
Yenyuka Russian Fed. **51** 57.57N121.15E
Yeo l. Canada **104** 45.24N 81.49W
Yeo L. Australia **89** 28.04S124.23E
Yeola India **62** 20.02N 74.29E
Yeoval Australia **93** 32.44S148.39E
Yeovil U.K. **13** 50.57N 2.38W
Yepáchic U.S.A. **109** 28.27N108.25W
Yeppoon Australia **90** 23.08S150.45E
Yeráki Greece **35** 37.00N 22.42E
Yerbent Turkmenistan **65** 39.23N 58.35E
Yercha Russian Fed. **51** 69.34N147.30E
Yerda Australia **92** 31.05S135.04E
Yerepol Russian Fed. **51** 65.15N168.43E
Yerevan Armenia **65** 40.10N 44.31E
Yerington U.S.A. **108** 38.59N119.10W
Yermak Kazakhstan **50** 52.03N 76.55E
Yermitsa Russian Fed. **44** 66.56N 52.20E
Yermo Mexico **111** 26.23N104.01W
Yermo U.S.A. **109** 34.54N116.50W
Yerolimín Greece **35** 36.28N 22.24E
Yershov Russian Fed. **45** 51.22N 48.16E
Yertom Russian Fed. **44** 63.31N 47.51E
Yerushalayim *d.* Israel **67** 31.45N 35.00E
Yerushalayim Israel / Jordan **67** 31.47N 35.13E
Yesa, Embalse de *resr.* Spain **25** 42.36N 1.09W
Yeşil *r.* Turkey **64** 41.22N 36.37E
Yeso U.S.A. **109** 34.26N104.37W
Yessey Russian Fed. **51** 68.29N102.15E
Yeste Spain **26** 38.22N 2.18W
Yetman Australia **93** 28.55S150.49E
Yeu Burma **56** 22.49N 95.26E
Yeu, Île d' *i.* France **18** 46.42N 2.20W
Yevpatoriya Ukraine **45** 45.12N 33.20E
Yevstratovskiy Russian Fed. **45** 50.07N 39.45E
Yew Mtn. U.S.A. **114** 38.05N 80.16W
Ye Xian China **54** 37.10N119.56E
Yeysk Russian Fed. **45** 46.43N 38.17E
Yi *r.* Uruguay **125** 33.17S 58.08W
Yiannitsá Greece **34** 40.46N 22.24E
Yiaros *i.* Greece **35** 37.36N 24.40E
Yibin China **55** 28.42N104.34E
Yibug Caka *l.* China **63** 33.50N 87.00E
Yichang China **55** 30.21N111.21E
Yichuan China **54** 34.25N112.26E
Yidu China **54** 36.45N118.24E
Yifag Ethiopia **73** 12.02N 37.44E
Yiftah Israel **67** 33.07N 35.33E
Yijun China **54** 35.23N109.07E
Yilan China **53** 46.22N129.31E
Yilehuli Shan *mts.* China **53** 51.20N124.20E
Yilliminning Australia **89** 32.54S117.22E
Yilong China **55** 31.34N106.24E
Yimen China **54** 34.21N107.07E
Yinan China **54** 35.33N118.27E
Yinchuan China **54** 38.27N106.18E
Yindarlgooda, L. Australia **89** 30.45S121.55E
Yingcheng China **55** 30.57N113.33E
Yingde China **55** 24.07N113.20E
Yinggehai China **55** 18.31N108.40E
Yingkou China **54** 40.39N122.18E
Yingshan China **55** 31.06N106.35E
Yingshang China **54** 32.42N116.20E
Yingtan China **55** 28.11N116.55E
Yinkanie Australia **92** 34.21S140.20E
Yinning China **52** 43.57N 81.23E
Yin Shan *mts.* China **54** 41.30N109.00E
Yirga' Alem Ethiopia **73** 6.52N 38.22E
Yirol Sudan **73** 6.33N 30.30E
Yirwa Sudan **73** 7.47N 27.15E
Yishan China **55** 24.37N108.32E
Yíthion Greece **35** 36.45N 22.34E
Yiwu China **55** 29.18N120.04E
Yi Xian China **54** 41.30N121.14E
Yiyang Henan China **54** 34.30N112.10E
Yiyang Hunan China **55** 28.20N112.30E
Yiyuan China **54** 36.12N118.08E
Yizhang China **55** 25.24N112.57E
Yizre'el Israel **67** 32.33N 35.20E
Ylitornio Finland **40** 66.19N 23.40E
Ylivieska Finland **40** 64.05N 24.33E
Yngaren *l.* Sweden **43** 58.52N 16.35E
Yoakum U.S.A. **111** 29.17N 97.09W
Yobe *d.* Nigeria **77** 12.30N 11.45E
Yodo *r.* Japan **57** 34.41N135.25E
Yogyakarta Indonesia **59** 7.48S110.24E
Yogyakarta *d.* Indonesia **59** 7.48S110.22E
Yokadouma Cameroon **77** 3.26N 15.06E
Yokkaichi Japan **57** 34.58N136.37E
Yoko Cameroon **77** 5.29N 12.19E
Yokohama Japan **57** 35.27N139.39E
Yokosuka Japan **57** 35.18N139.40E
Yola Nigeria **77** 9.14N 12.32E
Yom *r.* Thailand **56** 15.47N100.05E
Yona Guam **84** 13.25N144.47E
Yonago Japan **57** 35.27N133.20E
Yondok S. Korea **57** 36.26N129.23E
Yongcheng China **54** 33.56N116.22E
Yongchuan China **55** 29.19N105.55E
Yongchun China **55** 25.19N118.17E
Yongdeng China **54** 36.44N103.24E
Yonghe China **54** 36.44N110.39E
Yongnian China **54** 36.47N114.30E
Yongring China **55** 22.45N108.29E
Yongshou China **54** 34.40N108.04E
Yongxiu China **55** 28.58N115.43E
Yonkers U.S.A. **115** 40.56N 73.52W
Yonne *d.* France **19** 47.55N 3.45E
Yonne *r.* France **19** 48.23N 2.58E
York Australia **89** 31.55S116.45E
York Canada **104** 43.41N 79.29W
York U.K. **12** 53.58N 1.07W
York Nebr. U.S.A. **110** 40.52N 97.36W
York Penn. U.S.A. **114** 39.58N 76.44W
York *r.* U.S.A. **113** 37.15N 76.23W
York, C. Australia **90** 10.42S142.31E
Yorke Pen. Australia **92** 35.00S137.30E
Yorketown Australia **92** 35.02S137.35E
York Factory *town* Canada **101** 57.00N 92.18W
York Haven U.S.A. **114** 40.07N 76.43W
Yorkshire Wolds *hills* U.K. **12** 54.00N 0.39W
Yorkton Canada **101** 51.13N102.28W
York Village U.S.A. **115** 43.08N 70.38W
Yoro Honduras **117** 15.09N 87.07W
Yōrō Japan **57** 35.32N140.04E
Yosemite Nat. Park U.S.A. **108** 37.45N119.35W
Yoshino *r.* Japan **57** 34.22N135.40E
Yoshkar Ola Russian Fed. **44** 56.38N 47.52E
Yos Sudarsa, Pulau *i.* Indonesia **59** 8.00S138.30E
Yŏsu S. Korea **53** 34.46N127.45E
Youghal Rep. of Ire. **15** 51.58N 7.51W
You Jiang *r.* Guang. Zhuang. China **55** 23.28N111.18E
Youkou Ivory Coast **76** 5.16N 7.16W
Youkounkoun Guinea **76** 12.35N 13.11W
Young Australia **93** 34.19S148.20E
Young *r.* Australia **89** 33.45S121.12E
Young Uruguay **125** 32.41S 57.38W
Young U.S.A. **109** 34.06N110.57W
Younghusband, L. Australia **92** 30.51S136.05E
Younghusband Pen. Australia **92** 36.00S139.15E
Youngstown Canada **101** 51.32N111.13W
Youngstown U.S.A. **114** 41.06N 80.39W
Youngsville U.S.A. **114** 41.48N 74.54W
You Xian China **55** 26.59N113.12E
Youyang China **55** 28.52N108.45E
Youyu China **54** 39.59N112.27E
Yoxford U.K. **13** 52.16N 1.30E
Yozgat Turkey **64** 39.50N 34.48E
Ypsilanti U.S.A. **104** 42.15N 83.36W
Yreka U.S.A. **108** 41.44N122.38W
Yssingeaux France **21** 45.08N 4.07E
Ystad Sweden **43** 55.25N 13.49E
Ythan *r.* U.K. **14** 57.21N 2.01W
Ytterhogdal Sweden **41** 62.12N 14.51E
Yu'alliq, Jabal *mtn.* Egypt **66** 30.21N 33.31E
Yuanbaoshan China **54** 42.15N119.14E
Yuan Jiang *r.* Hunan China **55** 29.00N111.55E
Yuan Jiang *r.* Yunnan China *see* Hong Hâr. *r.* Vietnam **52**
Yuanling China **55** 28.28N110.15E
Yuanping China **54** 38.42N112.46E
Yuba City U.S.A. **108** 39.08N121.27W
Yūbari Japan **57** 43.04N141.59E
Yubdo Ethiopia **73** 9.00N 35.22E
Yucatán *d.* Mexico **117** 19.30N 89.00W
Yucatan Channel Carib. Sea **117** 21.30N 86.00W
Yucatan Pen. Mexico **116** 19.00N 90.00W
Yucca U.S.A. **109** 34.52N114.09W
Yuci China **54** 37.37N112.47E
Yudino Russian Fed. **50** 55.05N 67.55E
Yudu China **55** 25.57N115.16E
Yuendumu Australia **90** 22.14S131.47E
Yueqing China **55** 28.08N120.57E
Yuexi China **52** 28.36N102.35E
Yueyang China **55** 29.22N113.10E
Yugan China **55** 28.41N116.41E
Yugorskiy Poluostrov *pen.* Russian Fed. **44** 69.00N 62.30E
Yugoslavia Europe **29** 44.00N 20.00E
Yuhang China **55** 30.25N120.18E
Yuhebu China **54** 37.59N109.51E
Yukon *r.* U.S.A. **98** 62.35N164.20W
Yukon Territory *d.* Canada **98** 65.00N135.00W
Yulara Australia **90** 25.14S131.02E
Yule *r.* Australia **88** 20.19S118.08E
Yuleba Australia **90** 26.37S149.20E
Yulin Guang. Zhuang. China **55** 22.38N110.10E
Yulin Shaanxi China **54** 38.11N109.33E
Yuma Ariz. U.S.A. **109** 32.43N114.37W
Yuma Colo. U.S.A. **108** 40.08N102.43W
Yumen China **52** 40.19N 97.12E
Yunan China **55** 23.14N111.35E
Yuncheng China **54** 35.02N111.00E
Yungas *f.* Bolivia **124** 16.20S 65.00W
Yungera Australia **92** 34.48S143.10E
Yungxiao China **55** 23.59N117.27E
Yunkai Dashan *mts.* China **55** 22.30N111.05E
Yunnan *d.* China **52** 24.30N101.30E
Yunta Australia **92** 32.37S139.34E
Yunxi China **54** 33.00N110.22E
Yun Xian China **54** 32.48N110.50E
Yunyang China **55** 30.55N108.56E
Yuqing China **55** 27.12N107.56E
Yuribey Russian Fed. **50** 71.02N 77.02E
Yurimaguas Peru **122** 5.54S 76.07W
Yuryuzan Russian Fed. **44** 54.51N 58.25E
Yu Shan *mtn.* Taiwan **55** 23.20N121.03E
Yushkozero Russian Fed. **44** 64.45N 32.03E
Yushu China **52** 33.06N 96.48E
Yūtō Japan **57** 34.42N137.38E
Yu Xian China **54** 34.10N113.28E
Yuxikou China **55** 31.29N118.16E
Yuyao China **55** 30.03N120.11E
Yuzhno Sakhalinsk Russian Fed. **53** 46.58N142.45E
Yuzhnyy Bug *r.* Ukraine **37** 46.55N 31.59E
Yuzhong China **54** 35.52N104.02E
Yvelines *d.* France **19** 48.50N 1.50E
Yverdon Switz. **39** 46.47N 6.39E
Yvetot France **18** 49.37N 0.46E

Z

Zaandam Neth. **16** 52.27N 4.49E
Zabīd Yemen **72** 14.12N 43.19E
Žabljak Yugo. **31** 43.09N 19.07E
Zābol *d.* Afghan. **62** 32.00N 67.00E
Zābol Iran **65** 31.00N 61.32E
Zābolī Iran **65** 27.08N 61.36E
Zabqung China **63** 31.38N 87.20E
Zabrze Poland **37** 50.18N 18.47E
Zacapa Guatemala **117** 15.00N 89.30W
Zacatecas Mexico **116** 22.48N102.33W
Zacatecas *d.* Mexico **116** 24.00N103.00W
Zadar Croatia **31** 44.07N 15.14E
Zafra Spain **27** 38.25N 6.25W
Zafriyya Israel **67** 32.00N 34.51E
Zaglivérion Greece **34** 40.36N 23.15E
Zagorá Greece **34** 39.27N 23.06E
Zagreb Croatia **31** 45.48N 15.58E
Zāgros, Kūhhā-ye *mts.* Iran **65** 32.00N 51.00E
Zagros Mts. *see* Zāgros, Kūhhā-ye *mts.* Iran **65**
Zāhedān Iran **65** 29.32N 60.54E
Zaḥlah Lebanon **66** 33.50N 35.55E
Ẓahrān Saudi Arabia **71** 17.40N 43.30E
Zaindeh *r.* Iran **65** 32.40N 52.50E
Zaïre Africa **78** 2.00S 22.00E
Zaïre *d.* Angola **78** 6.30S 13.30E
Zaïre *r.* Zaïre **78** 6.00S 12.30E
Zaječar Yugo. **34** 43.53N 22.18E
Zákas Greece **34** 40.02N 21.16E
Zakataly Azerbaijan **65** 41.39N 46.40E
Zákinthos *i.* Greece **35** 37.52N 20.44E
Zákinthos *town* Greece **35** 37.47N 20.54E
Zakinthou, Porthmós *str.* Greece **35** 37.50N 21.00E
Zakopane Poland **37** 49.19N 19.57E
Zala *d.* Hungary **31** 46.35N 16.40E
Zalaegerszeg Hungary **31** 46.51N 16.51E
Zalalövö Hungary **31** 46.51N 16.35E
Zalamea de la Serena Spain **26** 38.39N 5.39W
Zalaszentgrót Hungary **31** 46.59N 17.02E
Zalău Romania **37** 47.11N 23.03E
Žalec Slovenia **31** 46.15N 15.10E
Zaleshchiki Ukraine **37** 48.39N 25.50E
Ẓalim Saudi Arabia **64** 22.43N 42.11E
Zalingei Sudan **73** 12.54N 23.29E
Zambezi *r.* Mozambique / Zambia **81** 18.15S 35.55E
Zambezi Zambia **78** 13.30S 23.12E
Zambezia *d.* Mozambique **81** 16.30S 37.30E
Zambia Africa **79** 14.00S 28.00E
Zamboanga Phil. **59** 6.55N122.05E
Zambrów Poland **37** 53.00N 22.15E
Zambue Mozambique **80** 15.09S 30.47E
Zamfara *r.* Nigeria **77** 12.04N 4.00E
Zamora Mexico **116** 20.00N102.18W
Zamora Spain **26** 41.30N 5.45W
Zamora *d.* Spain **26** 41.45N 6.00W
Zamość Poland **37** 50.43N 23.15E
Zamtang China **61** 32.26N101.06E
Zaña Peru **122** 7.00S 79.30W
Záncara *r.* Spain **27** 39.18N 3.18W
Zanda China **63** 31.29N 79.50E
Zanesville U.S.A. **114** 39.56N 82.01W
Zangoza *see* Sangüesa Spain **25**
Zanjān Iran **65** 36.40N 48.30E
Zanthus Australia **89** 31.02S123.34E
Zanzibar Tanzania **79** 6.10S 39.16E
Zanzibar I. Tanzania **79** 6.00S 39.20E
Zaouatallaz Algeria **75** 24.52N 8.26E
Zaouiet Azmour Tunisia **32** 36.55N 11.01E
Zaouiet el Mgaïz Tunisia **32** 36.56N 10.50E
Zaozhuang China **54** 34.48N117.50E
Zapadna Morava *r.* Yugo. **34** 43.50N 20.15E
Zapadni Rodopi *mts.* Bulgaria **34** 41.49N 23.58E
Zapadno-Sibirskaya Ravnina *f.* Russian Fed. **9** 60.00N 75.00E
Zapadnyy Sayan *mts.* Russian Fed. **51** 53.00N 92.00E
Západočeský *d.* Czech Republic **38** 49.40N 13.00E
Zapala Argentina **125** 38.55S 70.05W
Zapardiel *r.* Spain **26** 41.29N 5.02W
Zapata U.S.A. **111** 26.52N 99.19W
Zaporozhye Ukraine **45** 47.50N 35.10E
Zapug China **63** 33.17N 80.50E
Zara Turkey **64** 39.55N 37.44E
Zaragoza Spain **25** 41.38N 0.53W
Zaragoza *d.* Spain **25** 41.40N 1.10W
Zarand Iran **65** 30.50N 56.35E
Zaranj Afghan. **62** 31.06N 61.53E
Zárate Argentina **125** 34.05S 59.02W
Zarauz Spain **26** 43.17N 2.10W
Zaraza Venezuela **122** 9.23N 65.20W
Zard Kūh *mtn.* Iran **65** 32.21N 50.04E
Zarembo I. U.S.A. **100** 56.20N132.50W
Zarghūn Shahr Afghan. **60** 32.51N 68.25E
Zari Nigeria **77** 13.03N 12.46E
Zaria Nigeria **77** 11.01N 7.44E
Zárkon Greece **34** 39.37N 22.07E
Zaruma Ecuador **122** 3.40S 79.30W
Żary Poland **36** 51.40N 15.10E
Zarzal Colombia **122** 4.24N 76.01W
Zāskār *r.* Jammu & Kashmir **62** 34.10N 77.20E
Zāskār Mts. Jammu & Kashmir **63** 33.15N 78.00E
Zaslavl Belorussia **37** 54.00N 27.15E
Za'tarī, Wādī az Jordan **67** 32.09N 36.15E
Žatec Czech Republic **39** 50.18N 13.32E
Zatishye Ukraine **37** 47.20N 29.58E
Zave Zimbabwe **80** 17.14S 30.02E
Zavet Bulgaria **34** 43.46N 26.40E
Zavidovići Bosnia-Herzegovina **31** 44.27N 18.09E
Zavitinsk Russian Fed. **53** 50.08N129.24E
Zāwa Pakistan **62** 28.04N 66.23E
Zawīlah Libya **75** 26.10N 15.07E
Zāwiyat al Amwāt Egypt **66** 28.04N 30.50E
Zāwiyat al Mukhaylá Libya **72** 32.10N 22.17E
Zāyandeh *r.* Iran **65** 32.40N 52.50E
Zaydābād Afghan. **62** 34.17N 69.07E
Zaydī, Wādī az Syria **67** 32.45N 35.50E
Zaysan Kazakhstan **52** 47.30N 84.57E
Zaysan, Ozero *l.* Kazakhstan **52** 48.00N 83.30E
Zayzūn Syria **67** 32.43N 35.56E
Zbarazh Ukraine **37** 49.40N 25.49E
Zborov Ukraine **37** 49.40N 25.09E
Zbraslav Czech Republic **38** 49.59N 14.24E
Zdolbunov Ukraine **37** 50.30N 26.10E
Zduńska Wola Poland **37** 51.36N 18.57E
Zeballos Canada **100** 49.59N126.50W
Zebediela R.S.A. **80** 24.19S 29.17E
Zeebrugge Belgium **16** 51.20N 3.13E
Zeehan Australia **91** 41.55S145.21E
Zeeland *d.* Neth. **16** 51.30N 3.45E
Ze'elim Israel **67** 31.12N 34.32E
Zeerust R.S.A. **80** 25.32S 26.04E
Zefa' Israel **67** 31.07N 35.12E
Zefat Israel **67** 32.57N 35.27E
Zehdenick Germany **38** 52.59N 13.20E
Zeist Neth. **16** 52.03N 5.16E
Zeitz Germany **38** 51.03N 12.08E
Zelechów Poland **37** 51.49N 21.54E
Zelengora *mts.* Bosnia-Herzegovina **31** 43.20N 18.30E
Zelenodolsk Russian Fed. **44** 55.50N 48.30E
Zelenogorsk Russian Fed. **44** 60.15N 29.31E
Zelenokumsk Russian Fed. **45** 44.25N 43.54E
Zelentsovo Russian Fed. **44** 59.51N 44.59E
Zelina Croatia **31** 45.58N 16.15E
Zell Germany **39** 50.01N 7.10E
Zella-Mehlis Germany **38** 50.39N 10.39E
Zell am Ziller Austria **39** 47.14N 11.53E
Zelts Ukraine **37** 46.38N 30.00E
Zelzate Belgium **16** 51.12N 3.49E
Zembra, Île *i.* Tunisia **32** 37.08N 10.48E
Zemio C.A.R. **73** 5.02N 25.08E
Zemoul, Oued *wadi* Morocco **74** 29.12N 7.52W
Zemun Yugo. **29** 44.51N 20.23E
Zendeh Jān Afghan. **62** 34.21N 61.45E
Zenica Bosnia-Herzegovina **31** 44.12N 17.55E
Zenn *r.* Germany **39** 49.31N 10.58E
Zenne *r.* Belgium **16** 51.04N 4.25E
Zerbst Germany **38** 51.58N 12.04E
Zereh, Gowd-e *l.* Afghan. **62** 29.45N 61.50E
Zergan Albania **34** 41.30N 20.21E
Zetel Germany **38** 53.25N 7.58E
Zeulenroda Germany **38** 50.39N 11.58E
Zeven Germany **38** 53.18N 9.16E
Zevenaar Neth. **16** 51.57N 6.04E
Zevenbergen Neth. **16** 51.41N 4.42E
Zeya Russian Fed. **51** 53.48N127.14E
Zeya *r.* Russian Fed. **51** 50.20N127.30E
Zêzere *r.* Portugal **27** 39.28N 8.20W
Zgierz Poland **37** 51.52N 19.25E
Zgorzelec Poland **36** 51.12N 15.01E
Zhailma Kazakhstan **50** 51.37N 61.33E
Zhanatas Kazakhstan **52** 43.11N 69.35E
Zhangbei China **54** 41.08N114.44E
Zhanghua Taiwan **55** 24.05N120.30E
Zhangjiakou China **54** 40.47N114.56E
Zhangping China **55** 25.25N117.28E
Zhangpu China **55** 24.06N117.37E

Zhangwu China 54 42.22N122.31E
Zhang Xian China 54 34.48N104.27E
Zhangye China 52 38.56N100.27E
Zhangzhou China 55 24.57N118.32E
Zhanjiang China 55 21.08N110.22E
Zhanyu China 54 44.31N122.40E
Zhao'an China 55 23.45N117.14E
Zhaoping China 55 24.06N110.48E
Zhaoqing China 55 23.02N112.29E
Zhari Namco l. China 63 31.00N 85.30E
Zhashkov Ukraine 37 49.12N 30.05E
Zhashui China 54 33.41N109.06E
Zhaxi Co l. China 63 32.10N 85.00E
Zhaxigang China 63 32.31N 79.33E
Zhejiang d. China 55 29.00N120.00E
Zheleznodorozhnyy Russian Fed. 44 67.59N 64.47E
Zheleznodorozhnyy Russian Fed. 44 62.39N 50.59E
Zhen'an China 54 33.24N109.12E
Zhenba China 54 32.34N107.58E
Zheng'an China 55 28.30N107.30E
Zhenghe China 55 27.23N118.51E
Zhengyang China 54 32.36N114.23E
Zhengzhou China 54 34.40N113.38E
Zhenhai China 55 29.58N121.45E
Zhenjiang China 54 32.09N119.30E
Zhenxiong China 55 27.27N104.50E
Zhenyuan China 54 35.42N106.58E
Zherdnoye Belorussia 37 51.40N 30.11E
Zherong China 55 27.13N119.52E
Zhidachov Ukraine 37 49.20N 24.22E
Zhigansk Russian Fed. 51 66.48N123.27E
Zhijiang China 55 27.27N109.41E
Zhitkovichi Belorussia 37 52.12N 27.49E
Zhitomir Ukraine 37 50.18N 28.40E
Zhlobin Belorussia 37 52.50N 30.00E
Zhmerinka Ukraine 37 49.00N 28.02E
Zhob r. Pakistan 62 32.04N 69.50E
Zhongba China 63 29.40N 84.07E
Zhongdian China 61 28.00N 99.30E
Zhongli Taiwan 55 24.54N121.09E
Zhongning China 54 37.28N105.41E
Zhongshan Guangdong China 55 22.31N113.22E
Zhongtiao Shan China 54 36.00N113.30E
Zhongwei China 54 37.30N105.15E
Zhoucun China 54 36.49N117.49E
Zhoushan i. China 55 30.05N122.15E

Zhouzhi China 54 34.08N108.14E
Zhuanghe China 54 39.41N123.02E
Zhucheng China 54 36.00N119.24E
Zhugqu China 54 33.46N104.18E
Zhuji China 55 29.43N120.14E
Zhumadian China 54 32.58N114.02E
Zhuo Xian China 54 39.30N116.55E
Zhuozi China 54 40.52N112.33E
Zhuozi Shan mtn. China 54 39.36N107.00E
Zhupanovo Russian Fed. 51 53.40N159.52E
Zhuxi China 54 32.19N109.52E
Zhuzhou China 55 27.49N113.07E
Ziàrat Pakistan 62 30.23N 67.43E
Ziàrat-e Shàh Maqsûd Afghan. 62 31.59N 65.30E
Žiar nad Hronom Slovakia 37 48.36N 18.52E
Zibo China 54 36.50N118.00E
Zicavo France 21 41.54N 9.08E
Ziegenhain Germany 38 50.50N 9.07E
Ziel, Mt. Australia 88 23.24S132.23E
Zielona Góra Poland 36 51.57N 15.30E
Ziesar Germany 38 52.16N 12.17E
Ziftâ Egypt 66 30.43N 31.14E
Zigey Chad 77 14.43N 15.47E
Zigong China 55 29.18N104.45E
Zigui China 55 31.01N110.35E
Ziguinchor Senegal 76 12.35N 16.20W
Zikhron Ya'aqov Israel 67 32.34N 34.57E
Zile Turkey 64 40.18N 35.52E
Žilina Slovakia 37 49.14N 18.46E
Zillah Libya 75 28.33N 17.35E
Zillertaler Alpen mts. Austria/Italy 30 47.00N 11.55E
Zima Russian Fed. 51 53.58N102.02E
Zimatlán Mexico 116 16.52N 96.45W
Zimba Zambia 78 17.20S 26.25E
Zimbabwe Africa 80 18.55S 30.00E
Zimbor Romania 37 47.00N 23.16E
Zimi Sierra Leone 76 7.22N 11.21W
Zimnicea Romania 34 43.39N 25.21E
Zimniy Bereg f. Russian Fed. 44 65.50N 41.30E
Zinder Niger 77 13.46N 8.58E
Zinder d. Niger 77 14.20N 9.30E
Zinga Mtwara Tanzania 79 9.01S 38.47E
Ziniaré Burkina 76 12.34N 1.12W
Zinkgruvan Sweden 43 58.49N 15.05E
Zinnowitz Germany 38 54.04N 13.55E
Zion Grove U.S.A. 115 40.54N 76.13W

Zippori Israel 67 32.45N 35.17E
Žirje i. Croatia 31 43.40N 15.39E
Ziro India 61 27.38N 93.42E
Zi Shui r. China 55 28.38N112.30E
Zitong China 55 31.38N105.11E
Zítsa Greece 34 39.47N 20.40E
Zittau Germany 38 50.54N 14.47E
Zitundo Mozambique 81 26.45S 32.49E
Ziway Hâyk' l. Ethiopia 73 8.00N 38.50E
Zixi China 55 27.42N117.05E
Ziyang China 55 30.02N104.42E
Zizhong China 55 29.48N104.51E
Zlarin Croatia 31 43.42N 15.50E
Zlatar Croatia 31 46.06N 16.05E
Zlatograd Bulgaria 34 41.22N 25.07E
Zlatoust Russian Fed. 44 55.10N 59.38E
Zletovo Macedonia 34 41.59N 22.17E
Zlín Czech Republic 37 49.13N 17.41E
Zlîtan Libya 75 32.28N 14.34E
Zloczew Poland 37 51.25N 18.36E
Zlotów Poland 37 53.22N 17.02E
Žlutice Czech Republic 39 50.03N 13.10E
Zlynka Russian Fed. 37 52.24N 31.45E
Zmeinogorsk Russian Fed. 50 51.11N 82.14E
Žminj Croatia 31 45.09N 13.55E
Zmiyevka Russian Fed. 44 52.40N 36.22E
Znamenka Ukraine 45 48.42N 32.40E
Znin Poland 37 52.52N 17.43E
Znojmo Czech Republic 36 48.52N 16.05E
Zobia Zaïre 78 2.58N 25.56E
Zobue Mozambique 81 15.35S 34.26E
Zoétélé Cameroon 77 3.17N 11.54E
Zogno Italy 30 45.48N 9.40E
Zohreh r. Iran 65 30.04N 49.32E
Zolochev Ukraine 37 49.48N 24.51E
Zolotonosha Ukraine 45 49.39N 32.05E
Zomba Malawi 79 15.22S 35.22E
Zonguldak Turkey 64 41.26N 31.47E
Zong Xian China 55 30.16N108.01E
Zorita Spain 27 39.17N 5.42W
Zorzor Liberia 76 7.46N 9.28W
Zouar Chad 77 20.27N 16.32E
Zouîrât Mauritania 74 22.35N 12.20W
Zoutkamp Neth. 16 53.21N 6.18E
Zrenjanin Yugo. 29 45.22N 20.23E
Zrmanja r. Croatia 31 44.15N 15.32E

Zuckerhütl mtn. Austria 30 46.58N 11.09E
Zuénoula Ivory Coast 76 7.34N 6.03W
Zuera Spain 25 41.52N 0.47W
Zug Switz. 39 47.10N 8.31E
Zug d. Switz. 39 47.10N 8.40E
Zugspitze mtn. Germany 39 47.25N 10.59E
Zuid Beveland f. Neth. 16 51.30N 3.50E
Zuidelijk-Flevoland f. Neth. 16 52.22N 5.22E
Zuid Holland d. Neth. 16 52.00N 4.30E
Zuidhorn Neth. 16 53.16N 6.25E
Zújar r. Spain 26 39.01N 5.47W
Zújar, Embalse del resr. Spain 26 38.50N 5.20W
Zülpich Germany 38 50.41N 6.39E
Zululand see Kwa Zulu f. R.S.A. 80
Zumbo Mozambique 80 15.36S 30.24E
Zungeru Nigeria 77 9.48N 6.03E
Zunyi China 55 27.39N106.48E
Županja Croatia 31 45.04N 18.42E
Zurich Neth. 16 53.08N 5.25E
Zürich Switz. 39 47.23N 8.32E
Zürich d. Switz. 39 47.25N 8.45E
Zürichsee l. Switz. 39 47.13N 8.45E
Zuru Nigeria 77 11.26N 5.16E
Zushi Japan 57 35.18N139.35E
Žut i. Croatia 31 43.52N 15.19E
Zutphen Neth. 16 52.08N 6.12E
Zuwârah Libya 75 32.56N 12.06E
Zuwayzâ Jordan 67 31.42N 35.55E
Žužemberk Slovenia 31 45.50N 14.56E
Zvenigorodka Ukraine 37 49.05N 30.58E
Zverinogolovskoye Kazakhstan 50 54.23N 64.47E
Zvishavane Zimbabwe 80 20.20S 30.05E
Zvolen Slovakia 37 48.35N 19.08E
Zweibrücken Germany 39 49.15N 7.21E
Zweisimmen Switz. 39 46.33N 7.22E
Zwettl Austria 36 48.37N 15.10E
Zwickau Germany 38 50.44N 12.29E
Zwiesel Germany 39 49.01N 13.14E
Zwischenahn Germany 38 53.12N 8.00E
Zwoleń Poland 37 51.22N 21.35E
Zwolle Neth. 16 52.31N 6.06E
Zyryanovsk Kazakhstan 50 49.45N 84.16E
Żywiec Poland 37 49.41N 19.12E

OCEANIA
MAPS 82 – 93

NORTH AMERICA
MAPS 94 – 117

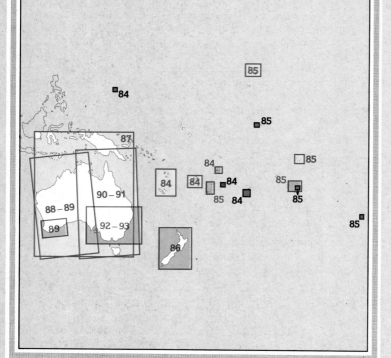

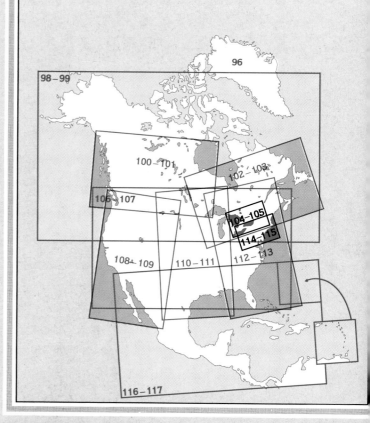

Continuation from Front Endpaper

SOUTH AMERICA
MAPS 118 – 126

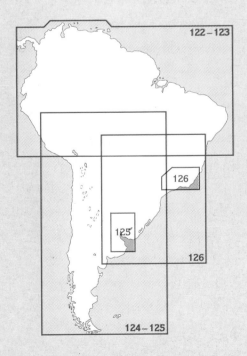

KEY TO MAPS

ATLANTIC & POLAR
MAPS 127 – 128

By reference to this Key to Maps, and its continuation on the front endpaper, the most suitable map of a required area can be found.

The map pages of the core World Atlas section are keyed according to their continental subsections and scale category. There are three scale categories, as indicated below. All scales are quoted as representative ratios expressed in millions (as denoted by the abbreviation M).

 Large scale: between 1:1M and 2½M

 Medium scale: between 1:2½M and 1:7½M

 Small scale: smaller than 1:7½M